W9-DBD-398

Encyclopedia *of*
Careers *and*
Vocational Guidance
Thirteenth Edition

Volume 2

Career Articles, A–C

Ferguson

An imprint of ☑®Facts On File

Encyclopedia of Careers and Vocational Guidance, Thirteenth Edition

Copyright © 2005 by Facts On File, Inc.

Ferguson
An imprint of Facts On File, Inc.
132 West 31st Street
New York NY 10001

Library of Congress Cataloging-in-Publication Data

Encyclopedia of careers and vocational guidance.— 13th ed.
   p. cm.
 Includes bibliographical references and index.
 ISBN 0-8160-6055-X (set)—ISBN 0-8160-6056-8 (vol. 1)—ISBN 0-8160-6057-6 (vol. 2)—ISBN 0-8160-6058-4 (vol. 3)—
 ISBN 0-8160-6059-2 (vol. 4)—ISBN 0-8160-6086-2 (vol. 5)
1. Vocational guidance—Handbooks, manuals, etc. 2. Occupations—Handbooks, manuals, etc. [1. Vocational guidance—
Encyclopedias. 2. Occupations—Encyclopedias.] I. J.G. Ferguson Publishing Company.
 HF5381.E52 2005
 331.702—dc22   2004022855

Ferguson books are available at special discounts when purchased in bulk quantities for businesses, associations, institutions, or sales promotions. Please call our Special Sales Department in New York at (212) 967-8800 or (800) 322-8755.

You can find Ferguson on the World Wide Web at http://www.fergpubco.com

Text design by David Strelecky
Cover design by Cathy Rincon

Printed in the United States of America

VB FOF 10 9 8 7 6 5 4 3 2 1

This book is printed on acid-free paper.

Contents

Volume 2: Career Articles A–C

Accountants and Auditors

■ OVERVIEW

Accountants compile, analyze, verify, and prepare financial records, including profit and loss statements, balance sheets, cost studies, and tax reports. Accountants may specialize in areas such as auditing, tax work, cost accounting, budgeting and control, or systems and procedures. Accountants also may specialize in a particular business or field; for example, *agricultural accountants* specialize in drawing up and analyzing financial statements for farmers and for farm equipment companies. *Auditors* examine and verify financial records to ensure that they are accurate, complete, and in compliance with federal laws. There are approximately 1.1 million accountants and auditors employed in the United States.

■ HISTORY

Accounting records and bookkeeping methods have been used from early history to the present. Records discovered in Babylonia (modern-day Iraq) date back to 3600 B.C., and accounts were similarly kept by the Egyptians, Greeks, and Romans.

Modern accounting began with the technique of double-entry bookkeeping, which was developed in the 15th and 16th centuries by Luca Pacioli, an Italian mathematician. After the Industrial Revolution, business grew more complex. As government and industrial institutions developed in the 19th and 20th centuries, accurate records and information were needed to assist in making decisions on economic and management policies.

The accounting profession in the United States dates back only to 1880, when English and Scottish investors began buying stock in American companies. To keep an eye on their investments, they sent over accountants who realized the great potential that existed in the accounting field and stayed on to establish their own businesses.

Federal legislation, such as the income tax in 1913 and the excess profits tax in 1917, helped cause an accounting boom that has made the profession instrumental to all business.

Accountants have long been considered "bean counters," and their work has been written off by outsiders as routine and boring. However, their image, once associated with death, taxes, and bad news, is making a turnaround. Accountants now do much more than prepare financial statements and record business transactions. Technology now counts the "beans," allowing accountants to analyze and interpret the results. Their work has expanded to encompass challenging and creative tasks such as computing costs and efficiency gains of new technologies, participating in strategies for mergers and acquisitions, supervising quality management, and designing and using information systems to track financial performance.

■ THE JOB

Accountants' duties depend on the size and nature of the company in which they are employed. The major fields of employment are public, private, and government accounting.

Public accountants work independently on a fee basis or as members of an accounting firm, and they perform a variety of tasks for businesses or individuals. These may include auditing accounts and records, preparing and certifying financial statements, conducting financial investigations and furnishing testimony in legal matters, and assisting in formulating budget policies and procedures.

Private accountants, sometimes called *industrial* or *management accountants,* handle financial records of the firms at which they are employed.

Government accountants work on the financial records of government agencies or, when necessary, they audit the records of private companies. In the federal government, many accountants are employed as *bank examiners* (See the article Bank Examiners), *Internal Revenue Service agents,* and *investigators,* as well as in regular accounting positions.

Within these fields, accountants can specialize in a variety of areas.

General accountants supervise, install, and devise general accounting, budget, and cost systems. They maintain records, balance books, and prepare and analyze statements on all financial aspects of business. Administrative officers use this information to make sound business decisions.

Budget accountants review expenditures of departments

QUICK FACTS

SCHOOL SUBJECTS
Business
Economics

PERSONAL SKILLS
Following instructions
Leadership/management

WORK ENVIRONMENT
Primarily indoors
One location with some travel

MINIMUM EDUCATION LEVEL
Bachelor's degree

SALARY RANGE
$30,320 to $61,630 to
$197,500+

CERTIFICATION OR LICENSING
Recommended

OUTLOOK
About as fast as the average

DOT
160

GOE
13.02.03

NOC
1111

O*NET-SOC
13-2011.00, 13-2011.01,
13-2011.02

This business owner is reviewing receipts and financial information with his accountant during tax season.

within a firm to make sure expenses allotted are not exceeded. They also aid in drafting budgets and may devise and install budget control systems.

Cost accountants determine unit costs of products or services by analyzing records and depreciation data. They classify and record all operating costs so that management can control expenditures.

Property accountants keep records of equipment, buildings, and other property owned or leased by a company. They prepare mortgage schedules and payments as well as appreciation or depreciation statements, which are used for income tax purposes.

Environmental accountants help utilities, manufacturers, and chemical companies set up preventive systems to ensure environmental compliance and provide assistance in the event that legal issues arise.

Systems accountants design and set up special accounting systems for organizations whose needs cannot be handled by standardized procedures. This may involve installing automated or computerized accounting processes and includes instructing personnel in the new methods.

Forensic accountants and auditors use accounting principles and theories to support or oppose claims being made in litigation. (See the article Forensic Accountants and Auditors.)

Tax accountants prepare federal, state, or local tax returns of an individual, business, or corporation according to prescribed rates, laws, and regulations. They also may conduct research on the effects of taxes on firm operations and recommend changes to reduce taxes. This is one of the most intricate fields of accounting, and many accountants therefore specialize in one particular phase such as corporate, individual income, or property tax.

Assurance accountants help improve the quality of information for clients in assurance services areas such as electronic commerce, risk assessment, and elder care. This information may be financial or non-financial in nature.

Auditors ensure that financial records are accurate, complete, and in compliance with federal laws. To do so they review items in original entry books, including purchase orders, tax returns, billing statements, and other important documents. Auditors may also prepare financial statements for clients and suggest ways to improve productivity and profits. *Internal auditors* conduct the same kind of examination and evaluation for one particular company. Because they are salaried employees of that company, their financial audits then must be certified by a qualified independent auditor. Internal auditors also review procedures and controls, appraise the efficiency and effectiveness of operations, and make sure their companies comply with corporate policies and government regulations.

Tax auditors review financial records and other information provided by taxpayers to determine the appropriate tax liability. State and federal tax auditors usually work in government offices, but they may perform a field audit in a taxpayer's home or office.

Revenue agents are employed by the federal government to examine selected income tax returns and, when necessary, conduct field audits and investigations to verify the information reported and adjust the tax liability accordingly.

Chief bank examiners enforce good banking practices throughout a state. They schedule bank examinations to ensure that financial institutions comply with state laws and, in certain cases, they take steps to protect a bank's solvency and the interests of its depositors and shareholders. (For more information, see the article Bank Examiners.)

■ REQUIREMENTS
High School

If you are interested in an accounting career, you must be very proficient in arithmetic and basic algebra. Familiarity with computers and their applications is equally important. Course work in English and communications will also be beneficial.

Postsecondary Training

Postsecondary training in accounting may be obtained in a wide variety of institutions such as private business schools, junior colleges, universities, and correspondence schools. A bachelor's degree with a major in accounting, or a related field such as economics, is highly recommended by professional associations for those entering the field and is required by all states before taking the licensing exam. It is possible, however, to become a successful accountant by completing a program at any of the above-mentioned institutions. A four-year college curriculum usually includes about two years of liberal arts courses, a year of general business subjects, and a year of specific accounting work. Better positions, particularly in public accounting, require a bachelor's degree with a major in accounting. Large public accounting firms often prefer people with a master's degree in accounting. For beginning positions in accounting, the federal government requires four years of college (including 24 semester hours in accounting or auditing) or an equivalent combination of education and experience.

Certification or Licensing

Certified public accountants (*CPA*s) must pass a qualifying examination and hold a certificate issued by the state in which they wish to practice. In most states, a college degree is required for admission to the CPA examinations; a few states allow candidates to substitute years of public accounting experience for the college degree requirement. Currently 43 states and jurisdictions require CPA candidates to have 150 hours of education, which is an additional 30 hours beyond the standard bachelor's degree. Five additional states plan to enact the 150-hour requirement in the future. These criteria can be met by combining an undergraduate accounting program with graduate study or participating in an integrated five-year professional accounting program. You can obtain information from a state board of accountancy or check out the website of the American Institute of Certified Public Accountants (AICPA) to read about new regulations and review last year's exam.

The Uniform CPA Examination administered by the AICPA is used by all states. Nearly all states require at least two years of public accounting experience or its equivalent before a CPA certificate can be earned.

Some accountants seek out other credentials. Those who have earned a bachelor's degree, pass a four-part examination, agree to meet continuing education requirements, and have at least two years of experience in management accounting may become a certified management accountant (CMA) through the Institute of Management Accounting.

The Accreditation Council for Accountancy and Taxation confers the following three designations: accredited business accountant or accredited business advisor (ABA), accredited tax preparer (ATP), and accredited tax advisor (ATA).

To become a certified internal auditor (CIA), college graduates with two years of experience in internal auditing must pass a four-part examination given by the Institute of Internal Auditors (IIA). The IIA also offers the following specialty certifications: certified financial services auditor and certified government auditing professional. Visit the IIA website for more information.

The designation certified information systems auditor (CISA) is conferred by the Information Systems Audit and Control Association to candidates who pass an examination and who have five years of experience auditing electronic data processing systems.

Other organizations, such as the Bank Administration Institute, confer specialized auditing designations.

Other Requirements

To be a successful accountant you will need strong mathematical, analytical, and problem-solving skills. You need to be able to think logically and to interpret facts and figures accurately. Effective oral and written communication are also essential in working with both clients and management.

Other important skills are attentiveness to detail, patience, and industriousness. Business acumen and the ability to generate clientele are crucial to service-oriented businesses, as are honesty, dedication, and a respect for the work of others.

■ EXPLORING

If you think a career as an accountant or auditor might be for you, try working in a retail business, either part time or during the summer. Working at the cash register or even pricing products as a stockperson is good introductory experience. You should also consider working as a treasurer for a student organization requiring financial planning and money management. It may be possible to gain some experience by volunteering with local groups such as churches and small businesses. You should also stay abreast of news in the field by reading trade magazines and checking out the industry websites of the AICPA and other accounting associations. The AICPA has numerous free educational publications available.

BECOMING A CERTIFIED PUBLIC ACCOUNTANT

How, exactly, does one become certified as a public accountant? Rules and regulations vary from state to state, but, in general, CPAs must have a certain amount of experience and pass a test. In New York, for instance, a potential CPA must be at least 21 years of age, of "good moral character" (i.e., not have been convicted of any crimes), and meet experience, education, and examination standards. The education requirements may be fulfilled by an accounting program registered by the New York State Department of Education or another program considered equivalent (such as a program in another state), or by 15 years of public accounting experience accepted by the State Board for Public Accountancy. The would-be CPA must also pass all four parts of the state-administered test (financial accounting and reporting, business law and professional responsibilities, accounting and reporting) within three years. Finally, they must also present evidence of at least two years' experience in the field, including having worked in all aspects of public accounting, and pay the licensing fee ($345, as of 2004).

■ EMPLOYERS

More than 1 million people are employed as accountants and auditors. Accountants and auditors work throughout private industry and government. About one-fifth work for accounting, auditing, and bookkeeping firms. Approximately 10 percent are self-employed. A large percentage of all accountants and auditors are certified.

■ STARTING OUT

Junior public accountants usually start in jobs with routine duties such as counting cash, verifying calculations, and other detailed numerical work. In private accounting, beginners are likely to start as cost accountants and junior internal auditors. They may also enter in clerical positions as cost clerks, ledger clerks, and timekeepers or as trainees in technical or junior executive positions. In the federal government, most beginners are hired as trainees at the GS-5 level after passing the civil service exam.

Some state CPA societies arrange internships for accounting majors, and some offer scholarships and loan programs.

You might also visit the Landing a Job section (http://www.aicpa.org/nolimits/job/index.htm) of the AICPA website. It has detailed information on accounting careers, hiring trends, job search strategies, resumes and cover letters, and job interviews. The section also has a list of internship opportunities for students.

■ ADVANCEMENT

Talented accountants and auditors can advance quickly. Junior public accountants usually advance to senior positions within several years and to managerial positions soon after. Those successful in dealing with top-level management may eventually become supervisors, managers, and partners in larger firms or go into independent practice. However, only 2 to 3 percent of new hires advance to audit manager, tax manager, or partner.

Private accountants in firms may become audit managers, tax managers, cost accounting managers, or controllers, depending on their specialty. Some become controllers, treasurers, or corporation presidents. Others on the finance side may rise to become managers of financial planning and analysis or treasurers.

Federal government trainees are usually promoted within a year or two. Advancement to controller and to higher administrative positions is ultimately possible.

Although advancement may be rapid for skilled accountants, especially in public accounting, those with inadequate academic or professional training are often assigned to routine jobs and find it difficult to obtain promotions. All accountants find it necessary to continue their study of accounting and related areas in their spare time. Even those who have already obtained college degrees, gained experience, and earned a CPA certificate may spend many hours studying to keep up with new industry developments. Thousands of practicing accountants enroll in formal courses offered by universities and professional associations to specialize in certain areas of accounting, broaden or update their professional skills, and become eligible for advancement and promotion.

■ EARNINGS

Beginning salaries for accountants with a bachelor's degree averaged $40,647 a year in 2003; those with a master's degree averaged $42,241 a year, according to the National Association of Colleges and Employers. Auditors with up to one year of experience earned between $29,500 and $40,500, according to a 2001 survey by Robert Half International. Some experienced auditors may earn between $47,500 and $197,500, depending on such factors as their education level, the size of the firm, and the firm's location.

Public and private accountants follow similar salary increases, and generally the larger the firm or corporation, the higher the salary. In public accounting, the bottom 10 percent of accountants and auditors earned $30,320 a year, according to the U.S. Department of Labor, and upper mid-level salaries range from $37,210 to $61,630, with those in the largest cities and employed by the Big Four firms earning the most. Departmental directors can earn between $66,750 and $197,500, depending on the size and location of the firm, while mid-level corporate accountants earn from $41,000 to $61,500, and managers bring in $47,500–$78,750.

Government accountants and auditors make substantially less, though they do receive more benefits. According to the U.S. Department of Labor, in 2003 starting salaries for accountants and auditors were approximately $23,442, though candidates with a master's degree could make as much as $35,519. The average annual salary for accountants and auditors employed by the federal government in nonsupervisory, supervisory, and managerial positions was $69,370, while auditors made, on average, $73,247. Accountants in large firms and with large corporations receive typical benefits including paid vacation and sick days, insurance, and savings and pension plans. Employees in smaller companies generally receive fewer fringe benefits.

■ WORK ENVIRONMENT

Accounting is known as a desk job, and a 40-hour (or longer) workweek can be expected in public and private accounting. Although computer work is replacing paperwork, the job can be routine and monotonous, and concentration and attention to detail are critical. Public accountants experience considerable pressure during the tax period, which runs from November to April, and they may have to work long hours. There is potential for stress aside from tax season, as accountants can be responsible for managing multimillion-dollar finances with no margin for error. Self-employed accountants and those working for a small firm can expect to work longer hours; 40 percent work more than 50 hours per week, compared to 20 percent of public and private accountants.

In smaller firms, most of the public accountant's work is performed in the client's office. A considerable amount of travel is often necessary to service a wide variety of businesses. In a larger firm, however, an accountant may have very little client contact, spending more time interacting with the accounting team.

■ OUTLOOK

In the wake of the massive changes and scandals that have swept through the industry in the last decade, and the increased demands for public accountability, the job outlook for accountants and auditors is good, with employ-ment expected to grow about as fast as the average through 2012, according to the U.S. Department of Labor.

Several factors will contribute to the expansion of the accounting industry: increasingly complex taxation, significant penalties for fraud, growth in both the size and the number of business corporations required to release financial reports to stockholders, a more general use of accounting in the management of business, and outsourcing of accounting services by small business firms.

As firms specialize their services, accountants will need to follow suit. Firms will seek out accountants with experience in marketing and proficiency in computer systems to build management consulting practices. As trade increases, so will the demand for CPAs with international specialties and foreign language skills. CPAs with an engineering degree would be well equipped to specialize in environmental accounting. Other accounting specialties that will enjoy good prospects include assurance, forensic, and tax accounting.

While the majority of jobs will be found in large cities with large businesses, smaller firms will start up, and smaller businesses will continue to seek outside accountants. Accountants without college degrees will find more paraprofessional accounting positions, similar to the work of paralegals, as the number of lower- and mid-level workers expands. Demand will also be high for specialized accounting temps; CPA firms have started to hire temps to smooth out their staffing through seasonal business cycles.

The role of public accountants will change as they perform less auditing and tax work and assume greater management and consulting responsibilities. Likewise, private accountants will focus more on analyzing operations rather than simply providing data and will develop sophisticated accounting systems.

Accounting jobs are more secure than most during economic downswings. Despite fluctuations in the nation's economy, there will always be a need to manage financial information, especially as the number, size, and complexity of business transactions increases. However, competition for jobs will remain, certification requirements will become more rigorous, and accountants and auditors with the highest degrees will be the most competitive.

■ FOR MORE INFORMATION

For information on accreditation and testing, contact

**Accreditation Council for Accountancy and
    Taxation**
1010 North Fairfax Street
Alexandria, VA 22314-1574
Tel: 888-289-7763

Email: info@acatcredentials.org
http://www.acatcredentials.org

For information on the Uniform CPA Examination and student membership, contact

American Institute of Certified Public Accountants
1211 Avenue of the Americas
New York, NY 10036-8775
Tel: 212-596-6200
http://www.aicpa.org

For information on accredited programs in accounting, contact

Association to Advance Collegiate Schools of Business
600 Emerson Road, Suite 300
St. Louis, MO 63141-6762
Tel: 314-872-8481
http://www.aacsb.edu

For information on certification for bank auditors, contact

Bank Administration Institute
One North Franklin, Suite 1000
Chicago, IL 60606-3421
Email: info@bai.org
http://www.bai.org

For more information on women in accounting, contact

Educational Foundation for Women in Accounting
PO Box 1925
Southeastern, PA 19399-1925
Tel: 610-407-9229
Email: info@efwa.org
http://www.efwa.org

For information on certification, contact

Information Systems Audit and Control Association and Foundation
3701 Algonquin Road, Suite 1010
Rolling Meadows, IL 60008
Tel: 847-253-1545
Email: certification@isaca.org
http://www.isaca.org

For information on internal auditing and certification, contact

Institute of Internal Auditors
247 Maitland Avenue
Altamonte Springs, FL 32701-4201
Tel: 407-937-1100
Email: iia@theiia.org
http://www.theiia.org

For information about management accounting and the CMA designation, as well as student membership, contact

Institute of Management Accountants
10 Paragon Drive
Montvale, NJ 07645-1718
Tel: 800-638-4427
Email: ima@imanet.org
http://www.imanet.org

Active and Contemplative Religious Sisters and Brothers

■ OVERVIEW

Within the Roman Catholic Church, the titles *sister* and *brother* are given to members of religious communities. Members take vows of poverty, chastity, and obedience and devote their lives to God. Sisters and brothers generally view their way of life not so much as a career but as a vocation—a calling. Another term for a sister or brother is a *religious*.

Active religious sisters and brothers divide their time between private prayer, communal worship, and service work. Each active religious community has a particular mission for which it was founded, ranging from educating children to caring for the sick to missionary work. *Contemplative religious sisters and brothers* devote themselves entirely to private prayer and the celebration of Mass. Through their hidden lives of contemplation, they praise God and intercede with him on behalf of the whole world. *Cloistered contemplative sisters and brothers* live apart from the rest of the world in monasteries and convents under papal enclosure, meaning that access to them is restricted. Contemplative brothers are often called *monks* (but are addressed as "brother"), while contemplative sisters are called *nuns* (but are addressed as "sister"). Active religious are usually just called brothers and sisters.

■ HISTORY

The history of contemplative religious sisters and brothers can be traced back to biblical times, when figures such as Elijah and John the Baptist sought intimate relationships with God in the solitude of the desert. Early Christian hermits who lived in the deserts of Egypt, Syria, and Palestine during the second and third centuries followed their examples. These men and women shunned the material and denied themselves all but the most basic possessions and links to the outside world, including family and sexual relations. In this isolation, they devoted their lives to prayer and to contemplation of spiritual matters.

The history of active religious sisters and brothers can be traced back to the original 12 disciples of Christ. They were the first missionaries, and among their followers were men and women who devoted themselves solely to serving God through the church, caring for the sick, helping the poor, and teaching the Gospel. By the fourth century, monasteries where monks lived together were established. St. Jerome was a prominent organizer of monasteries, setting up both male and female communities.

St. Benedict of Nursia, who lived during the fifth and sixth centuries, organized monastic communities that spread throughout Western Europe over the next few hundred years. Known as the Benedictines, these religious lived in a community, working together within the monastery while still maintaining a prayerful atmosphere. They were required to take solemn vows of obedience, permanence within the monastery, and adherence to poverty and chastity.

Other important male and female religious communities within the church followed the Benedictines. The 13th century saw the emergence of the mendicant orders of the Carmelites, Dominicans, and Franciscans. Unlike those in earlier communities, mendicants commonly traveled, sometimes great distances, to preach their Christian messages. Many were involved in the newly created universities of the Middle Ages.

The Jesuits, formally known as the Society of Jesus, were formed in the 16th century. St. Ignatius, their founder, introduced the practice of simple (as opposed to solemn) vows. Less stringent simple vows allowed for the ownership of personal property and made a more active mission possible. The Jesuits were especially important in the development of educational institutions and missionary work.

When female counterparts to these orders were initiated, they were usually of a cloistered contemplative nature. By the 17th century, groups of women religious, or sisters, also began to take simple vows, allowing them to forgo cloistered life if they so chose. Sisters increasingly devoted themselves to aiding the sick and poor and teaching children religion and basic educational skills. The Daughters of Charity, formed in France during the mid-

17th century, was one of the first active orders for women and became a model for later communities.

Contemplative religious life underwent an important renewal in the 16th century when St. Teresa of Avila and St. John of the Cross reformed the Carmelite order in Spain. They believed that both the male and female branches of the order had become too lax and were no longer true to the ideals of the desert fathers, so they formed the much stricter Discalced Carmelite order ("discalced" means barefoot, a reference to their commitment to poverty). This and other reforms, like the Colletine reform of the Poor Clares in the 15th century, have kept contemplative communities vital and faithful.

In the 20th century, the Second Vatican Council (1962–65), or Vatican II, unleashed far-reaching reforms for the religious communities, affecting such aspects of religious life as the wearing of habits and the selection process of new religious. Consequently, many brothers and sisters adopted a more comfortable, more publicly accessible lifestyle, while maintaining their vows and the missions of their orders. This was especially true of the active religious orders, who have since expanded their missions to include such modern concerns as caring for AIDS patients and those suffering from addictions. Cloistered contemplative orders are among the most traditional religious orders, but they have also made necessary changes after Vatican II.

■ THE JOB

Sisters and brothers form an important, though sometimes misunderstood, part of the Roman Catholic Church. Brothers, for example, are not priests, but lay people. Not all brothers can be properly called monks, a term usually reserved for contemplative brothers. The term "nun" properly refers to a female contemplative, though a nun is addressed as "sister."

In the United States there are more than 300 Roman Catholic orders and congregations, many

---

QUICK FACTS

SCHOOL SUBJECTS
English
Religion

PERSONAL SKILLS
Communication/ideas
Helping/teaching

WORK ENVIRONMENT
Primarily indoors
Primarily one location

MINIMUM EDUCATION LEVEL
High school diploma

SALARY RANGE
$0 to $15,000 to $30,000

CERTIFICATION OR LICENSING
None available

OUTLOOK
Much faster than the average

DOT
120

GOE
12.02.01

NOC
4217

O*NET-SOC
21-2011.00

CONTEMPLATIVE RELIGIOUS ONLINE

Many religious orders now have pages on the Internet—and more are going online all the time. Checking out an order on the Web when you're still really unsure about your vocation is a good idea; when you're ready to move on to contacting an order, all you have to do is email them from their site! These are the main sites for some contemplative religious orders; you may be able to link to individual communities from there:

- Benedictine Sisters of Perpetual Adoration [women]: http://www.benedictinesisters.org/
- Cistercians [men and women; includes Trappists]: http://www.pml.it/ocist/
- Discalced Carmelites [men and women]: http://www.ocd.pcn.net/
- Passionists [women are contemplative]: http://www.cptryon.org/passionist/links.html
- Poor Clares [women]: http://listserv.american.edu/catholic/franciscan/clares/index.html

of which have both male and female communities and some of which have both active and contemplative religious. In total, there are approximately 75,500 sisters and 5,700 brothers serving the country today.

Active religious brothers and sisters are primarily engaged in education, health care, social work, and spreading the Catholic faith, either as missionaries or through their daily work. Sisters and brothers who teach may work at the elementary, high school, or college level—usually, but not always, in Catholic-funded schools. Others may serve as librarians, counselors, or principals, or in other administrative positions. Those involved in health care work in hospitals owned by their religious order or by the local diocese, serving as nurses, physicians, pharmacists, medical technicians, administrators, physical therapists, or related positions.

In impoverished areas in the United States, such as inner cities, active religious may live among the people, teaching basic literacy and life skills such as sanitary procedures and rudimentary job skills. They may conduct programs to help the poor or homeless, or work in homes for disadvantaged children. Sisters and brothers who work as missionaries may work in countries plagued by famine, disease, war or civil strife, or places where the Catholic faith has not yet been established.

More and more active religious are working in parishes as pastoral associates or directors of religious education.

They may handle administrative duties, particularly if their parish does not have a priest of its own but shares one with another parish. Some serve as spiritual directors, counseling others on living the faith more deeply. Active sisters and brothers also work in communications, either on behalf of their order or their diocese. They might work in public relations or in the media, such as publishing books or producing video and audio recordings.

Contemplative sisters and brothers generally live their lives entirely within the bounds of the monastery or convent. They spend several hours a day in chapel for Mass and the Liturgy of the Hours. They may spend their private prayer time in the chapel, in their rooms, or outside in the monastery grounds. An hour or so is usually devoted to study, learning about church history, the lives of the saints, and other issues. Much of the rest of the day is spent on manual labor, tending to the needs of the community. Gardening, laundry, cooking, cleaning, and household repairs are some of the tasks to which brothers and sisters are assigned.

In many contemplative communities, particularly cloistered orders where there is little interaction with other people, an hour or two is set aside each day for recreation, when the religious can talk and relax in a less formal atmosphere. Meals are taken together, often in silence or while listening to a spiritual book on tape.

Cloistered contemplative communities enjoy papal enclosure, which restricts access to their monasteries or convents. This ensures that a quiet, reverent, prayerful atmosphere is maintained. To enter the enclosure, people must have special permission from the bishop or a superior within the order—except in case of emergency. To leave the enclosure, religious must also have this kind of special permission, although most have standing permission to visit doctors and dentists as needed.

Members of contemplative religious communities often perform additional work to raise money. Nuns, for example, traditionally earn funds by baking altar bread and sewing vestments. Cottage industries and small businesses such as crafts, a printing service, or wine and cheese production are now common.

■ REQUIREMENTS
High School

If you are interested in becoming a religious sister or brother, consider enrolling in a Catholic high school. However, this is by no means a requirement. Take as many religion courses as possible as well as courses in English and speech in order to promote communications skills. These are crucial to participation in the liturgy and the religious studies that contemplative sisters and brothers pursue.

Many active sisters and brothers are also skilled in secular professions. As a result, you should determine other career interests and take corresponding coursework to prepare for education in that field.

Postsecondary Training

Requirements for becoming a sister or brother vary by community. Many religious orders will accept candidates with only a high school diploma, but more and more are advising applicants to attend college first. Many communities want prospective members to have life experience before becoming a sister or brother, as the vocation requires a high level of dedication and maturity. Such life experience may include dating, pursuing another occupation, and extensive reflection on Christianity and life goals. Although candidates must be single, previously married men and women are not disqualified from consideration.

All sisters and brothers are trained for the religious life by the communities in which they take their vows. Training programs commonly last several years. In some orders, there are additional requirements. For active religious, additional education and training is necessary. Teaching communities, for example, may require that a candidate have a university degree, a teaching certificate, or both. Nursing communities generally require medical training. Some communities will assume all costs for obtaining a university degree or other education.

Contemplative sisters and brothers may spend up to eight or nine years learning about the religious life before committing to it with final vows. They may take formal classes for young religious inside their communities or attend informal discussion groups with experienced religious. Their superiors, especially their novice master or novice mistress, will offer personal guidance and recommend books to help them grow in the life.

Other Requirements

First and foremost, religious sisters and brothers must have a vocation to the religious life. They must believe that God is calling them to dedicate their lives to service of the church. Their religious communities must also feel certain that aspiring members are called.

All sisters and brothers must take the traditional vows of poverty, chastity, and obedience. In taking a vow of poverty, religious commit to living simply and to sharing all things with their community. Excessive accumulation of material possessions is not acceptable, even for active religious who earn outside income.

The vow of chastity requires that brothers and sisters not have sexual relations or marry. This requirement is not a condemnation of sexuality in general. It simply allows them to devote all their love to God. Prior sexual activity does not disqualify a candidate.

Obedience is understood as a listening vow. Sisters and brothers must listen to and faithfully serve the religious community, the church, and God. Each member is required to obey the superior (highest authority) of the community and follow the established rules of the order or congregation.

In addition to the above requirements, candidates must be in good physical and emotional health, have a sound character, and be free from monetary debt. Religious communities are not looking for people who are trying to escape from everyday problems or are afraid of marriage and intimate relationships. Good emotional health and maturity is absolutely essential to living the religious life.

■ EXPLORING

There are many ways to explore the religious life. The first step is to get in touch with a religious community that interests you, either directly or through your priest. Religious orders will be happy to provide you with plenty of information about their history and their way of life. Some offer special retreats or similar programs to help potential sisters and brothers discern their vocation. You may have the opportunity to participate in the work of

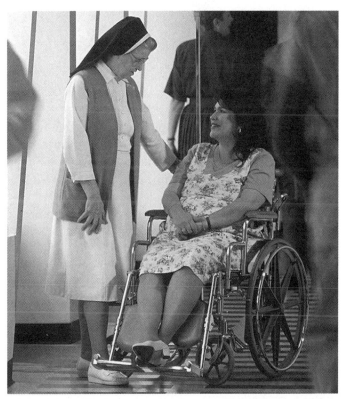

This nun is comforting a pregnant woman who is about to undergo a cesarean section.

FROM THE RULE OF ST. BENEDICT, C. 530

5. Concerning Obedience

The first grade of humility is obedience without delay. This becomes those who, on account of the holy service which they have professed, or on account of the fear of hell or the glory of eternal life, consider nothing dearer to them than Christ: so that, so soon as anything is commanded by their superior, they may not know how to suffer delay in doing it, even as if it were a divine command. Concerning whom the Lord said: "As soon as he heard of me he obeyed me."

7. Concerning Humility

. . . The sixth grade of humility is, that a monk be contented with all lowliness or extremity, and consider himself, with regard to everything which is enjoined on him, as a poor and unworthy workman; saying to himself with the prophet: "I was reduced to nothing and was ignorant; I was made as the cattle before thee, and I am always with thee." The seventh grade of humility is, not only that he, with his tongue, pronounce himself viler and more worthless than all; but that he also believe it in the inner-most workings of his heart; humbling himself and saying with the prophet, etc. The eighth degree of humility is that a monk do nothing except what the common rule of the monastery, or the example of his elders, urges him to do. The ninth degree of humility is that a monk restrain his tongue from speaking; and, keeping silence, do not speak until he is spoken to . .

(Source: Paul Halsall's Medieval Sourcebooks page http://www.fordham.edu/halsall/source/rul-benedict.html)

---

active religious orders, volunteering your time at their hospitals, religious education classes, or social services. Even if you are considering the contemplative life, it can be very rewarding to participate in the social work of active sisters and brothers.

In both exploring the religious life and preparing for it, you should be conscientious about living the Catholic faith as fully as you can; that is the essence of the contemplative life. Attend Mass and other services frequently; read about church history, doctrine, and current events; take part in parish activities. Finally, religious sisters and brothers will tell you that the key to preparing for a vocation and to discerning it is prayer.

■ EMPLOYERS

While the specific orders vary, all sisters and brothers ultimately serve the church. Active religious work in hospitals, colleges and universities, or grammar schools or high schools. Some work in parishes or church-run agencies. Other sisters and brothers work in foreign missions, urban slums, or rural areas. Essentially, members of active religious orders can be found virtually everywhere the church has a presence. As part of their vow of obedience, they may be required to serve wherever their community has made a commitment to minister. Contemplative religious are bound by their order's rule of life and the way their particular community applies that rule. The variations between communities are another good reason to take your time in finding the mode of religious life that best suits you.

■ STARTING OUT

Although the process of entering an order or congregation varies from community to community, in most cases there are four steps. First, an interested candidate contacts the religious community and begins a process of becoming acquainted with the life and mission of the members. Meetings with a brother or sister and periodic invitations to take part in prayer and community work may be arranged.

Second, the candidate is allowed to live within the community as a postulant but continues outside commitments, such as work or school. This allows the prospective member to more closely view the life of a religious and also gives the community a chance to evaluate the candidate. This step often takes one or two years.

Third, the person officially enters the community as a novice. During this period, lasting at least one year, final decisions are made on whether the candidate is suited to the religious life.

Fourth, the new member takes the vows of poverty, chastity, and obedience. These vows are at first temporary and may last for one, two, or three years. The length of the vow is decided by the brother or sister in consultation with his or her superior. Temporary vows are renewable up to nine years, after which the member must take final vows to remain in the community. Permanent vows can be made as early as three years after the first temporary vow.

■ ADVANCEMENT

The goal of a sister or brother is not the achievement of personal advancement but carrying out the mission of the community and serving the church and God. Even so, a religious may over time assume greater responsibility, such as filling a supervisory role. For example, an active sister may oversee the work of all nurses at a particular hospital, or an active brother may serve as his community's accountant. The highest authority of each community is the *superior,* a position of grave responsibility. Religious do not actively seek to become superiors; they are appointed by the community.

Both active and contemplative religious sisters and brothers can advance in the form of continuing education. They can also expect to grow spiritually through retreats and by working with their spiritual director, who may be their chaplain or confessor.

There is also the possibility of moving from the active religious life to contemplative religious life. However, moving between religious orders is a complicated process and must be approved by the Vatican.

■ EARNINGS

Salaries for active sisters and brothers are comparable to those of other people in their fields with similar education and skills. Contemplative religious sisters and brothers have no individual earnings. Income from their cottage industries and private donations belongs to the community as a whole. All of their needs, such as food, clothing, and medical insurance, are paid for out of community funds. They are supported by their community throughout their lives.

■ WORK ENVIRONMENT

The working conditions of religious depend on their community's location and mission. Most religious can count on a pretty conventional life in the settings they have chosen, such as the hustle and bustle of an urban mission, the steady work of a suburban parish or school, or the serenity of a monastery. Still, it is important for sisters and brothers to be ready and willing to serve wherever they are needed.

Religious tend to live in clean, sparsely furnished buildings, from convents and monasteries to large community houses, small homes, and apartments. The private room of a religious may consist of a simple bed, a desk, and a dresser. There is generally a common room for dining. They attend Mass with the rest of their community, usually in their own church or chapel, and they may also gather daily for recitation of the rosary or other common prayer.

Cloistered religious usually have "speak rooms" in their communities, where they meet with priests and other visitors who sit in the part of the room that is located outside the cloister boundary. It can be difficult to adapt to the physical restrictions of contemplative life (and cloistered life, in particular). Yet the life of obedience frees brothers and sisters from constant decision-making and anxiety over such mundane matters as when to eat, what to wear, and who is going to do the household chores.

Many active religious now have more contact with their family, friends, and other lay people. Manner of dress has also gained certain latitude since Vatican II. Many active and contemplative orders wear modified habits; for example, a sister might wear a plain suit with a simple veil and a crucifix. Other active sisters and brothers dress exactly like lay people. Religious sisters and brothers seek humility, trying not to set themselves above or apart from the rest of their communities; the uniform dress of the habit can help them do this. Most religious do not receive the habit until after they have completed their postulancy.

■ OUTLOOK

Opportunities for religious sisters and brothers are practically unlimited, for two major reasons. The first is that the Catholic Church wholeheartedly encourages those who have been called to live a life completely devoted to serving God. The second reason for the great opportunities in religious life is the decline in vocations over the past few decades. A majority of today's sisters and brothers are aged 50 or over. As long as they are certain of their calling and are deemed suitable for the religious life, young individuals will have plenty of opportunities to find a religious order to serve.

■ FOR MORE INFORMATION

The NRVC offers many resources for those considering a religious life.

National Religious Vocation Conference (NRVC)
5420 South Cornell Avenue, Suite 105
Chicago, IL 60615-5604
Tel: 773-363-5454
Email: NRVC@aol.com
http://www.nrvc.net

Vision magazine, published annually by the NRVC through Claretian Publications, provides information about sisters, brothers, and priests including brief vocation stories and reflections.

Vision
Claretian Publications
205 West Monroe
Chicago, IL 60606
Tel: 312-236-7782
Email: editor@visionguide.org
http://www.visionguide.org

Many religious orders now have pages on the Internet, and more are going online all the time. These are the main sites for some active religious orders; you may be able to link to individual communities from there.

Capuchin Franciscans of New York/New England
http://www.capuchin.net

Daughters of St. Paul
http://www.pauline.org

Order of Preachers (Dominicans)
http://www.op.org

School Sisters of Notre Dame
http://www.ssnd.org

Actors

■ OVERVIEW

Actors play parts or roles in dramatic productions on the stage, in motion pictures, or on television or radio. They impersonate, or portray, characters by speech, gesture, song, and dance. There are approximately 139,000 actors working in the United States.

■ HISTORY

Drama, which began as a component of religious festivals, was refined as an art form by the ancient Greeks, who used the stage as a forum for topical themes and stories. The role of actors became more important than in the past, and settings became more realistic with the use of scenery. Playgoing was often a great celebration, a tradition carried on by the Romans. The rise of the Christian church put an end to theater in the sixth century A.D., and for several centuries actors were ostracized from society, surviving as jugglers and jesters.

Drama was reintroduced during the Middle Ages but became more religious in focus. Plays during this period typically centered around biblical themes, and roles were played by craftspeople and other amateurs. This changed with the rediscovery of Greek and Roman plays in the Renaissance. Professional actors and acting troupes toured the countries of Europe, presenting ancient plays or improvising new dramas based on cultural issues and situations of the day. Actors began to take on more prominence in society. In England, actors such as Will Kemp and Richard Burbage became known for their roles in the plays of William Shakespeare. In France, Molière wrote and often acted in his own plays. Until the mid-17th century, however, women were banned from the stage, and the roles of women were played by young boys.

By the 18th century, actors could become quite prominent members of society, and plays were often written—or, in the case of Shakespeare's plays, rewritten—to suit a particular actor. Acting styles tended to be highly exaggerated, with elaborate gestures and artificial speech, until David Garrick introduced a more natural style to the stage in the mid-1700s. The first American acting company was established in Williamsburg, Virginia, in 1752, led by Lewis Hallan. In the next century, many actors became stars: famous actors of the time included Edwin Forrest, Fanny and Charles Kemble, Edmund Kean, William Charles Macready, and Joseph Jefferson, who was particularly well known for his comedic roles.

Until the late 19th century, stars dominated the stage. But in 1874, George II, Duke of Saxe-Meiningen, formed a theater troupe in which every actor was given equal prominence. This ensemble style influenced others, such as Andre Antoine of France, and gave rise to a new trend in theater called naturalism, which featured far more realistic characters in more realistic settings than before. This style of theater came to dominate the 20th century. It also called for new methods of acting. Konstantin Stanislavsky of the Moscow Art Theater, who developed an especially influential acting style that was later called method acting, influenced the Group Theater in the United States; one member, Lee Strasberg, founded the Actors Studio in New York, which would become an important training ground for many of the great American actors. In the early 20th century, vaudeville and burlesque shows were extremely popular and became the training ground for some of the great comic actors of the century.

By then, developments such as film, radio, and television offered many more acting opportunities than ever before. Many actors honed their skills on the stage and then entered one of these new media, where they could become known throughout the nation and often throughout the world. Both radio and television offered still more acting opportunities in advertisements. The development of sound in film caused many popular actors from the silent era to fade from view, while giving rise to many others. But almost from the beginning, film stars were known for their outrageous salaries and lavish style of living.

In the United States, New York gradually became the center of theater and remains so, although community

QUICK FACTS

SCHOOL SUBJECTS
English
Theater/dance

PERSONAL SKILLS
Artistic
Communication/ideas

WORK ENVIRONMENT
Indoors and outdoors
Primarily multiple locations

MINIMUM EDUCATION LEVEL
High school diploma

SALARY RANGE
$13,330 to $23,470 to $106,360+

CERTIFICATION OR LICENSING
None available

OUTLOOK
About as fast as the average

DOT
150

GOE
01.05.01

NOC
5135

O*NET-SOC
27-2011.00

theater companies abound throughout the country. Hollywood is the recognized center of the motion picture and television industries. Other major production centers are Miami, Chicago, San Francisco, and Austin.

■ THE JOB

The imitation or basic development of a character for presentation to an audience often seems like a glamorous and fairly easy job. In reality, it is demanding, tiring work requiring a special talent.

The actor must first find a part available in some upcoming production. This may be in a comedy, drama, musical, or opera. Then, having read and studied the part, the actor must audition before the director and other people who have control of the production. This requirement is often waived for established artists. In film and television, actors must also complete screen tests, which are scenes recorded on film, at times performed with other actors, which are later viewed by the director and producer of the film.

If selected for the part, the actor must spend hundreds of hours in rehearsal and must memorize many lines and cues. This is especially true in live theater; in film and television, actors may spend less time in rehearsal and sometimes improvise their lines before the camera, often performing several attempts, or "takes," before the director is satisfied. Television actors often take advantage of TelePrompTers, which scroll their lines on a screen in front of them while performing. Radio actors generally read from a script, and therefore rehearsal times are usually shorter.

In addition to such mechanical duties, the actor must determine the essence of the character being portrayed and the relation of that character to the overall scheme of the play. Radio actors must be especially skilled in expressing character and emotion through voice alone. In many film and theater roles, actors must also sing and dance and spend additional time rehearsing songs and perfecting the choreography. Some roles require actors to perform various stunts, which can be quite dangerous. Most often, these stunts are performed by specially trained *stunt performers*. Others work as *stand-ins* or *body doubles*. These actors are chosen for specific features and appear on film in place of the lead actor; this is often the case in films requiring nude or seminude scenes. Many television programs, such as game shows, also feature *models*, who generally assist the host of the program.

Actors in the theater may perform the same part many times a week for weeks, months, and sometimes years. This allows them to develop the role, but it can also become tedious. Actors in films may spend several weeks involved in a production, which often takes place on loca-

The final scene in an adaptation of the Christmas classic, It's a Wonderful Life

tion; that is, in different parts of the world. Television actors involved in a series, such as a soap opera or a situation comedy, also may play the same role for years, generally in 13-week cycles. For these actors, however, their lines change from week to week and even from day to day, and much time is spent rehearsing their new lines.

While studying and perfecting their craft, many actors work as *extras*, the nonspeaking characters who appear in the background on screen or stage. Many actors also continue their training. A great deal of an actor's time is spent attending auditions.

■ REQUIREMENTS
High School

There are no minimum educational requirements to become an actor. However, at least a high school diploma is recommended.

Postsecondary Training

As acting becomes more and more involved with the various facets of our society, a college degree will become more important to those who hope to have an acting career. It is assumed that the actor who has completed a liberal arts program is more capable of understanding the wide variety of roles that are available. Therefore, it is strongly recommended that aspiring actors complete at least a bachelor's degree program in theater or the dramatic arts. In addition, graduate degrees in the fine arts or in drama are nearly always required should the individual decide to teach dramatic arts.

College can also serve to provide acting experience for the hopeful actor. More than 500 colleges and universities throughout the country offer dramatic arts programs and present theatrical performances. Actors and directors recommend that those interested in acting gain as much experience as possible through acting in plays in high school and college or in those offered by community groups. Training beyond college is recommended, especially for actors interested in entering the theater. Joining acting workshops, such as the Actors Studio, can often be highly competitive.

Other Requirements

Prospective actors will be required not only to have a great talent for acting but also a great determination to succeed in the theater and motion pictures. They must be able to memorize hundreds of lines and should have a good speaking voice. The ability to sing and dance is important for increasing the opportunities for the young actor. Almost all actors, even the biggest stars, are required to audition for a part before they receive the role. In film and television, they will generally complete screen tests to see how they will appear on film. In all fields of acting, a love for acting is a must. It might take many years for an actor to achieve any success, if at all.

Performers on the Broadway stages must be members of the Actors' Equity Association before being cast. While union membership may not always be required, many actors find it advantageous to belong to a union that covers their particular field of performing arts. These organizations include the Actors' Equity Association (stage), Screen Actors Guild or Screen Extras Guild (motion pictures and television films), or American Federation of Television and Radio Artists (TV, recording, and radio). In addition, some actors may benefit from membership in the American Guild of Variety Artists (nightclubs, and so on), American Guild of Musical Artists (opera and ballet), or organizations such as the Hebrew Actors Union or Italian Actors Union for productions in those languages.

■ EXPLORING

The best way to explore this career is to participate in school or local theater productions. Even working on the props or lighting crew will provide insight into the field.

Also, attend as many dramatic productions as possible and try to talk with people who either are currently in the theater or have been at one time. They can offer advice to individuals interested in a career in the theater.

Many books, such as *Beginning* (New York: St. Martin's, 1989), by Kenneth Branagh, have been written about acting, not only concerning how to perform but also about the nature of the work, its offerings, advantages, and disadvantages.

■ EMPLOYERS

Motion pictures, television, and the stage are the largest fields of employment for actors, with television commercials representing as much as 60 percent of all acting jobs. Most of the opportunities for employment in these fields are either in Los Angeles or in New York. On stage, even the road shows often have their beginning in New York, with the selection of actors conducted there along with rehearsals. However, nearly every city and most communities present local and regional theater productions.

As cable television networks continue to produce more and more of their own programs and films, they will become a major provider of employment for actors. Home video will also continue to create new acting jobs, as will the music video business.

The lowest numbers of actors are employed for stage work. In addition to Broadway shows and regional theater, there are employment opportunities for stage actors in summer stock, at resorts, and on cruise ships.

■ STARTING OUT

Probably the best way to enter acting is to start with high school, local, or college productions and to gain as much experience as possible on that level. Very rarely is an inexperienced actor given an opportunity to perform on stage or in film in New York or Hollywood. The field is extremely difficult to enter; the more experience and ability beginners have, however, the greater the possibilities for entrance.

Those venturing to New York or Hollywood are encouraged first to have enough money to support themselves during the long waiting and searching period normally required before a job is found. Most will list themselves with a casting agency that will help them find a part as an extra or a bit player, either in theater or film. These agencies keep names on file along with photographs and a description of the individual's features and experience, and if a part comes along that may be suitable, they contact that person. Very often, however, names are added to their lists only when the number of people in a particular physical category is low. For instance, the agency may not have enough athletic young women on their roster, and if the applicant happens to fit this description, her name is added.

■ ADVANCEMENT

New actors will normally start in bit parts and will have only a few lines to speak, if any. The normal procession of advancement would then lead to larger supporting roles and then, in the case of theater, possibly to a role as *understudy* for one of the main actors. The understudy usually has an opportunity to fill in should the main actor be unable to give a performance. Many film and television actors get their start in commercials or by appearing in government and commercially sponsored public service announcements, films, and programs. Other actors join the afternoon soap operas and continue on to evening programs. Many actors have also gotten their start in on-camera roles such as presenting the weather segment of a local news program. Once an actor has gained experience, he or she may go on to play stronger supporting roles or even leading roles in stage, television, or film productions. From there, an actor may go on to stardom. Only a very small number of actors ever reach that pinnacle, however.

Some actors eventually go into other, related occupations and become drama coaches, drama teachers, producers, stage directors, motion picture directors, television directors, radio directors, stage managers, casting directors, or artist and repertoire managers. Others may combine one or more of these functions while continuing their career as an actor.

■ EARNINGS

The wage scale for actors is largely controlled through bargaining agreements reached by various unions in negotiations with producers. These agreements normally control the minimum salaries, hours of work permitted per week, and other conditions of employment. In addition, each artist enters into a separate contract that may provide for higher salaries.

In 2003, the minimum daily salary of any member of the Screen Actors Guild (SAG) in a speaking role was $678 or $2,352 for a five-day workweek. Motion picture actors may also receive additional payments known as residuals as part of their guaranteed salary. Many motion picture actors receive residuals whenever films, TV shows, and TV commercials in which they appear are rerun, sold for TV exhibition, or put on videocassette. Residuals often exceed the actors' original salary and account for about one-third of all actors' income.

A wide range of earnings can be seen when reviewing the Actors' Equity Association's *Annual Report 2003*, which includes a breakdown of average weekly salaries by contract type and location. According to the report, for example, those in "Off Broadway" productions earned an average weekly salary of $700 during the 2002–03 season.

SCREEN VERSUS STAGE ACTING

Screen acting differs from acting in a theater. The camera scrutinizes an actor the way a theater audience cannot, and performances must be subtle and lifelike. Exaggerated gestures and rhetorical speaking, often required on the stage, may appear comical on the screen.

Film actors must adjust themselves to waiting for scenes to be filmed, repeating the same scene over and over, playing scenes out of sequence, and doing only small segments of a scene at a time. As a result, the actor is unable to build up a continuity of emotions as the story progresses—an advantage enjoyed by stage actors. Another problem is that the screen actor does not see or hear the audience and therefore cannot judge how they are reacting. The actor must rely on the director to evaluate the proficiency of the performance.

Other average weekly earnings for the same period include: San Francisco Bay area theater, $318; New England area theater, $294; DisneyWorld in Orlando, Florida, $683; and Chicago area theater, $487. The report concludes that the median weekly salary for all contract areas is $487. Most actors do not work 52 weeks per year; in fact, the report notes that the 39,981 Equity members in good standing only worked an average 16.4 weeks during the 2002–03 season, with median earnings of $6,418.

According to the U.S. Department of Labor, the median yearly earnings of all actors was $23,470 in 2003. The department also reported the lowest paid 10 percent earned less than $13,330 annually, while the highest paid 10 percent made more than $106,360.

The annual earnings of persons in television and movies are affected by frequent periods of unemployment. Unions offer health, welfare, and pension funds for members working over a set number of weeks a year. Some actors are eligible for paid vacation and sick time, depending on the work contract.

In all fields, well-known actors have salary rates above the minimums, and the salaries of the few top stars are many times higher. Actors in television series may earn tens of thousands of dollars per week, while a few may earn as much as $1 million or more per week. Salaries for these actors vary considerably and are negotiated individually. In film, top stars may earn as much as $20 million per film, and, after receiving a percentage of the gross earned by the film, these stars can earn far, far more.

Until recent years, female film stars tended to earn lower salaries than their male counterparts; the emergence of stars such as Julia Roberts, Jodie Foster, Halle

LEARN MORE ABOUT IT

For over 50 years, The Actors Studio has taught the "method" style of acting to some of the greatest actors. Method acting, developed from the work of Konstantin Stanislavsky of Russia, and taught by Lee Strasberg, was made famous by Marlon Brando, Dustin Hoffman, Robert DeNiro, and many others.

A master of fine arts degree is now offered by The Actors Studio Drama School, a joint program of the New School University and The Actors Studio in New York. The three-year program was created by studio members James Lipton, Paul Newman, Ellen Burstyn, Arthur Penn, Norman Mailer, Carlin Glynn, Lee Grant, and Robert Wankel.

You can learn a great deal about the craft of acting by watching *Inside the Actors Studio*, a television series co-produced by Bravo and The Actors Studio. Taped before a live audience, the program features actors, directors, playwrights, and performers discussing their work, the acting process, and their individual experiences on the stage and in film. James Lipton, a lifetime member and vice president of The Actors Studio and dean of The Actors Studio Drama School, conducts the interviews. After the interview, the audience, including a master class of Actors Studio students, is permitted to ask questions. The Actors Studio Drama School website is http://www.newschool.edu/academic/drama.

Berry, and others has started to reverse that trend. The average annual earnings for all motion picture actors, however, are usually low for all but the best-known performers because of the periods of unemployment.

◼ WORK ENVIRONMENT

Actors work under varying conditions. Those employed in motion pictures may work in air-conditioned studios one week and be on location in a hot desert the next.

Those in stage productions perform under all types of conditions. The number of hours employed per day or week vary, as do the number of weeks employed per year. Stage actors normally perform eight shows per week with any additional performances paid for as overtime. The basic workweek after the show opens is about 36 hours unless major changes in the play are needed. The number of hours worked per week is considerably more before the opening, because of rehearsals. Evening work is a natural part of a stage actor's life. Rehearsals often are held at night and over holidays and weekends. If the play goes on the road, much traveling will be involved.

A number of actors cannot receive unemployment compensation when they are waiting for their next part, primarily because they have not worked enough to meet the minimum eligibility requirements for compensation. Sick leaves and paid vacations are not usually available to the actor. However, union actors who earn the minimum qualifications now receive full medical and health insurance under all the actors' unions. Those who earn health plan benefits for 10 years become eligible for a pension upon retirement. The acting field is very uncertain. Aspirants never know whether they will be able to get into the profession, and, once in, there are uncertainties as to whether the show will be well received and, if not, whether the actors' talent can survive a bad show.

◼ OUTLOOK

Employment in acting is expected to grow about as fast as average through 2012, according to the U.S. Department of Labor. There are a number of reasons for this. The growth of satellite and cable television in the past decade has created a demand for more actors, especially as the cable networks produce more and more of their own programs and films. The rise of home video has also created new acting jobs, as more and more films are made strictly for the home video market. Many resorts built in the 1980s and 1990s present their own theatrical productions, providing more job opportunities for actors. Jobs in theater, however, face pressure as the cost of mounting a production rises and as many nonprofit and smaller theaters lose their funding.

Despite the growth in opportunities, there are many more actors than there are roles, and this is likely to remain true for years to come. This is true in all areas of the arts, including radio, television, motion pictures, and theater, and even those who are employed are normally employed during only a small portion of the year. Many actors must supplement their income by working at other jobs, such as secretaries, waiters, or taxi drivers, for example. Almost all performers are members of more than one union in order to take advantage of various opportunities as they become available.

It should be recognized that of the 139,000 or so actors in the United States today, only a small percentage are working as actors at any one time. Of these, few are able to support themselves on their earnings from acting, and fewer still will ever achieve stardom. Most actors work for many years before becoming known, and most of these do not rise above supporting roles. The vast majority of actors, meanwhile, are still looking for the right break. There are many more applicants in all areas than there are positions. As with most careers in the arts, people enter this career out of a love and desire for acting.

■ FOR MORE INFORMATION

The following is a professional union for actors in theater and "live" industrial productions, stage managers, some directors, and choreographers.

Actors' Equity Association
165 West 46th Street
New York, NY 10036
Tel: 212-869-8530
Email: info@actorsequity.org
http://www.actorsequity.org

This union represents television and radio performers, including actors, announcers, dancers, disc jockeys, newspersons, singers, specialty acts, sportscasters, and stuntpersons.

American Federation of Television and Radio Artists
260 Madison Avenue
New York, NY 10016-2402
Tel: 212-532-0800
Email: aftra@aftra.com
http://www.aftra.com

A directory of theatrical programs may be purchased from NAST. For answers to a number of frequently asked questions concerning education, visit the NAST website.

National Association of Schools of Theater (NAST)
11250 Roger Bacon Drive, Suite 21
Reston, VA 20190
Tel: 703-437-0700
Email: info@arts-accredit.org
http://www.arts-accredit.org/nast

The following union provides general information on actors, directors, and producers. Visit the SAG website for more information.

Screen Actors Guild (SAG)
5757 Wilshire Boulevard
Los Angeles, CA 90036-3600
Tel: 323-954-1600
http://www.sag.com

For information about opportunities in not-for-profit theaters, contact

Theatre Communications Group
355 Lexington Avenue
New York, NY 10017
Tel: 212-697-5230
Email: tcg@tcg.org
http://www.tcg.org

This site has information for beginners on acting and the acting business.

Acting Workshop On-Line
http://www.redbirdstudio.com/AWOL/acting2.html

Actuaries

■ OVERVIEW

Actuaries use statistical formulas and techniques to calculate the probability of events such as death, disability, sickness, unemployment, retirement, and property loss. Actuaries develop formulas to predict how much money an insurance company will pay in claims, which determines the overall cost of insuring a group, business, or individual. Increase in risk raises potential cost to the company, which, in turn, raises its rates. Actuaries analyze risk to estimate the number and amount of claims an insurance company will have to pay. They assess the cost of running the business and incorporate the results into the design and evaluation of programs.

Casualty actuaries specialize in property and liability insurance, *life actuaries* in health and life insurance. In recent years, there has been an increase in the number of actuaries—called *pension actuaries*—who deal only with pension plans. The total number of actuaries employed in the United States is approximately 15,000.

■ HISTORY

The term actuary was used for the first time in 1762 in the charter for the Equitable Society of London, which was the first life insurance company to use scientific data in figuring premiums. The basis of actuarial work was laid in the early 17th century when Frenchmen Blaise Pascal and Pierre de Fermat derived an

QUICK FACTS

SCHOOL SUBJECTS
Business
Mathematics

PERSONAL SKILLS
Following instructions
Leadership/management

WORK ENVIRONMENT
Primarily indoors
One location with some travel

MINIMUM EDUCATION LEVEL
Bachelor's degree

SALARY RANGE
$39,700 to $69,970 to $137,650+

CERTIFICATION OR LICENSING
Required

OUTLOOK
About as fast as the average

DOT
020

GOE
02.06.02

NOC
2161

O*NET-SOC
15-2011.00

important method of calculating actuarial probabilities, resulting in what is now termed the science of probability.

The first mortality table was produced in the late 17th century, when Edmund Halley noticed the regularity of various social phenomena, including the excess of male over female births. Halley, an English astronomer for whom Halley's comet is named, is known as the father of life insurance. As more complex forms of insurance were developed in the 19th century, the need for actuaries grew.

In 1889, a small group of qualified actuaries formed the Actuarial Society of America. Two classes of members, fellows and associates, were created seven years later, and special examinations were developed to determine membership eligibility. Forms of these examinations are still used today. By 1909 the American Institute of Actuaries was created, and in 1949 these two groups consolidated into the present Society of Actuaries.

In 1911, the Casualty Actuary Society was formed in response to the development of workers' compensation laws. The compensation laws opened up many new fields of insurance, and the Casualty Actuarial Society has since moved into all aspects of property and liability insurance.

OASDI (Old Age, Survivors, and Disability Insurance), now known as Social Security, was created in 1935 and expanded the work of pension actuaries. The creation of this program greatly impacted the development, philosophy, and structure of private pension programs. The American Society of Pension Actuaries was formed in 1966; its members provide services to over 30 percent of the qualified retirement plans in the United States.

The first actuaries were concerned primarily with statistical, mathematical, and financial calculations needed in the rapidly growing field. Today they deal with problems of investment, selection of risk factors for insurance, agents' compensation, social insurance, taxation, development of policy forms, and many other aspects of insurance. Once considered mathematicians, actuaries are now referred to as "financial architects" and "social mathematicians" because they use their unique combination of numerical, analytical, and business skills to solve a variety of social and financial problems.

■ THE JOB

Should smokers pay more for their health insurance? Should younger drivers pay higher car insurance premiums? Actuaries answer questions like these to ensure that insurance and pension organizations can pay their claims and maintain a profitable business.

Using their knowledge of mathematics, probability, statistics, and principles of finance and business, actuaries determine premium rates and the various benefits of insurance plans. To accomplish this task, they first assemble and analyze statistics on birth, death, marriage, parenthood, employment, and other pertinent facts and figures. Based on this information, they are able to develop mathematical models of rates of death, accident, sickness, disability, or retirement and then construct tables regarding the probability of such things as property loss from fire, theft, accident, or natural disaster. After calculating all probabilities and the resulting costs to the company, the actuaries can determine the premium rates to allow insurance companies to cover predicted losses, turn a profit, and remain competitive with other businesses.

For example, based on analyses, actuaries are able to determine how many of each 1,000 people 21 years of age are expected to survive to age 65. They can calculate how many of them are expected to die this year or how many are expected to live until age 85. The probability that an insured person may die during the period before reaching 65 is a risk to the company. The actuaries must figure a price for the premium that will cover all claims and expenses as they occur and still earn a profit for the company assuming the risk. In the same way, actuaries calculate premium rates and determine policy provisions for every type of insurance coverage.

Employment opportunities span across the variety of different types of insurance companies, including life, health, accident, automobile, fire, or workers' compensation organizations. Most actuaries specialize either as casualty actuaries, dealing with property and liability insurance, or as life actuaries, working with life and health insurance. In addition, actuaries may concentrate on pension plan programs sponsored and administered by various levels of government, private business, or fraternal or benevolent associations.

Actuaries work in many departments in insurance companies, including underwriting, group insurance, investment, pension, sales, and service. In addition to their own company's business, they analyze characteristics of the insurance business as a whole. They study general economic and social trends as well as legislative, health, and other developments, all of which may affect insurance practices. With this broad knowledge, some actuaries reach executive positions, where they can influence and help determine company policy and develop new lines of business. *Actuary executives* may communicate with government officials, company executives, policyholders, or the public to explain complex technical matters. They may testify before public agencies regarding proposed legislation that has a bearing on the insurance business, for example, or they may explain proposed changes in premium rates or contract provisions.

Actuaries may also work with a consulting firm, providing advice to clients including insurance companies, corporations, hospitals, labor unions, and government agencies. They develop employee benefits, calculating future benefits and employer contributions, and set up pension and welfare plans. *Consulting actuaries* also advise health care and financial services firms, and they may work with small insurance companies lacking an actuarial department.

Since the government regulates the insurance industry and administers laws on pensions, it also requires the services of actuaries to determine whether companies are complying with the law. A small number of actuaries are employed by the federal government and deal with Social Security, Medicare, disability and life insurance, and pension plans for veterans, members of the armed forces, and federal employees. Those in state governments may supervise and regulate insurance companies, oversee the operations of state retirement or pension systems, and manage problems related to unemployment insurance and workers' compensation.

■ REQUIREMENTS
High School

If you are interested in this field, you should pursue a traditional college preparatory curriculum including mathematical and computer science classes and also take advantage of advanced courses such as calculus. Introductory business, economics, accounting, and finance courses are important, as is English to develop your oral and written skills.

Postsecondary Training

A bachelor's degree with a major in mathematics or statistics is highly recommended for entry into the industry, and course work in elementary and advanced algebra, differential and integral calculus, descriptive and analytical statistics, principles of mathematical statistics, probability, and numerical analysis are all important. Computer science is also a vital part of actuarial training. Degrees in actuarial science are offered by approximately 100 universities and colleges. Employers, however, are increasingly hiring graduates with majors in economics, business, and engineering who have a strong math background. College students should broaden their education to include business, economics, and finance as well as English and communications. Because actuarial work revolves around social and political issues, course work in the humanities and social sciences will also prove useful.

Certification or Licensing

Full professional status in an actuarial specialty is based on completing a series of 10 examinations. Success is based on both formal and on-the-job training. Actuaries can become Associate members of the Society of Actuaries after successfully completing seven of the 10 examinations for the life and health insurance, finance, and pension fields. Similarly, they can reach Associate status in the Casualty Actuarial Society after successfully completing seven out of 10 exams in the property and liability field. Most actuaries achieve Associateship in three to five years. Actuaries who successfully complete the entire series of exams for either organization are granted full membership and become Fellows.

The American Society of Pension Actuaries also offers several different designations (both actuarial and nonactuarial) to individuals who pass the required examinations in the pension field and have the appropriate work experience.

Consulting pension actuaries who service private pension plans must be enrolled and licensed by the Joint Board for the Enrollment of Actuaries (http://www.irs.gov/taxpros/actuaries), a U.S. government agency. Only these actuaries can work with pension plans set up under the Employee Retirement Income Security Act. To be accepted, applicants must meet certain professional and educational requirements stipulated by the Joint Board.

Completion of the entire series of exams may take from five to 10 years. Because the first exams offered by these various boards and societies cover core material (such as calculus, linear algebra, probability and statistics, risk theory, and actuarial math), students generally wait to commit to a specialty until they have taken the initial tests. Students pursuing a career as an actuary should complete the first two or three preliminary examinations while still in college, since these tests cover subjects usually taught in school; the more advanced examinations cover aspects of the profession itself.

Employers prefer to hire individuals who have already passed the first two exams. Once employed, companies generally give employees time during the workday to study. They may also pay exam fees, provide study materials, and award raises upon an employee's successful completion of an exam.

Other Requirements

An aptitude in mathematics, statistics, and computer science is a must to become a successful actuary, as are sound analytical and problem-solving skills. Solid oral and written communication skills are also required in order to be able to explain and interpret complex work to the client, as is skill with programming languages such as Visual Basic.

Prospective actuaries should also have an inquisitive mind with an interest in historical, social, and political issues and trends. You should have a general feel for the business world and be able to assimilate a wide range of complex information in order to see the "big picture" when planning policies. Actuaries like to solve problems; they are strategists who enjoy and excel at games such as chess. Actuaries need to be motivated and self-disciplined to concentrate on detailed work, especially under stress, and to undertake the rigorous study for licensing examinations.

■ EXPLORING

If you think you are interested in the actuarial field, try pursuing extracurricular opportunities that allow you to practice strategic thinking and problem-solving skills; these may include chess, math, or investment clubs at your school. Other activities that foster leadership and management, such as student council positions, will also be beneficial. Any kind of business or research-oriented summer or part-time experience will be valuable, especially with an accounting or law firm.

There are more than 45 local actuarial clubs and regional affiliates throughout the United States that offer opportunities for informal discussion and networking. Talk with people in the field to better understand the nature of the work, and use the association's resources to learn more about the field. The Society of Actuaries offers free educational publications.

College undergraduates can take advantage of summer internships and employment in insurance companies and consulting firms. Students will have the chance to rotate among jobs to learn various actuarial operations and different phases of insurance work.

■ EMPLOYERS

There are approximately 15,000 actuaries employed in the United States, and about half of them are employed in the insurance industry. Other actuaries work for financial service-providing firms including commercial banks, investment banks, and retirement funds. Others are employed by actuarial consulting services and in academia. Some actuaries are self-employed.

■ STARTING OUT

The best way to enter this field is by taking the necessary beginning examinations while still in college. Once students have graduated and passed these exams, they are in a very good position to apply for entry-level jobs in the field and can command higher starting salaries. Some college students organize interviews and find jobs through their college placement office, while others interview with firms recruiting on campus. Many firms offer summer and year-round actuarial training programs or internships that may result in a full-time job.

Beginning actuaries may prepare calculations for actuarial tables or work with policy settlements or funds. With experience, they may prepare correspondence, reports, and research. Beginners who have already passed the preliminary exams often start with more responsibility and higher pay.

■ ADVANCEMENT

Advancement within the profession to assistant, associate, or chief actuary greatly depends on the individual's on-the-job performance, competence on the actuarial examinations, and leadership capabilities.

Some actuaries qualify for administrative positions in underwriting, accounting, or investment because of their broad business knowledge and specific insurance experience. Because their judgment is so valuable, actuaries may advance to administrative or executive positions, such as head of a department, vice president or president of a company, manager of an insurance rating bureau, partner in a consulting firm, or, possibly, state insurance commissioner. Actuaries with management skills and a strong business background may move into other areas such as marketing, advertising, and planning.

■ EARNINGS

Starting salaries for actuaries with bachelor's degrees in actuarial science averaged $40,396 in 2003, according to a survey conducted by the National Association of Colleges and Employers. New college graduates who have not passed any actuarial examinations earn slightly less. Insurance companies and consulting firms offer merit increases or bonuses to those who pass examinations. According to a 2003 survey done by the Life Office Management Association, entry-level actuaries with the largest U.S. companies earned approximately $46,991. Associate actuaries with such companies earned approximately $91,000. Experienced actuaries in large companies earned approximately $104,235.

The U.S. Department of Labor reports that actuaries earned a median annual salary of $69,970 in 2002. Ten percent earned less than $39,700, while the top 10 percent earned more than $137,650. Actuaries working for insurance companies receive paid vacations, health and life insurance, pension plans, and other fringe benefits.

■ WORK ENVIRONMENT

Actuaries spend much of their 40-hour workweek behind a desk poring over facts and figures, although some travel to various units of the organization or to other businesses. This is especially true of the consulting actuary, who will most likely work longer hours and travel more. Consulting actuaries tend to have more diverse work and more personal interaction in working with a variety of clients. Though the work can be stressful and demands intense concentration and attention to detail, actuaries find their jobs to be rewarding and satisfying and feel that they make a direct and positive impact on people's lives.

■ OUTLOOK

The U.S. Department of Labor predicts about average growth for the actuary field through 2012. Growth of the insurance industry—traditionally the leading employer of actuaries—is expected to continue at a stable pace, with many new fields such as annuities and terrorism-related property-risk analysis, compensating for the shrinking life insurance industry. The field's stringent entrance requirements and competition for entry-level jobs will also continue to restrict the number of candidates for jobs.

Consulting actuaries should enjoy a stronger employment outlook than their counterparts in the insurance industry, as many large corporations increasingly rely on consultants to handle actuarial work that was formerly done in-house.

The insurance industry continues to evolve, and actuaries will be in demand to establish rates in several new areas of coverage, including prepaid legal, dental, and kidnapping insurance. In many cases, actuarial data that have been supplied by rating bureaus are now being developed in new actuarial departments created in companies affected by states' new competitive rating laws. Other new areas of insurance coverage that will involve actuaries include product and pollution liability insurance as well as greater workers' compensation and medical malpractice coverage. Insurers will call on actuaries to help them respond to new state and federal regulations while cutting costs, especially in the areas of pension reform and no-fault automobile insurance. In the future, actuaries will also be employed by non-insurance businesses or will work in business- and investment-related fields. Some are already working in banking and finance.

Actuaries will be needed to assess the financial impact of current issues such as AIDS, terrorism, and the changing health care system. As demographics change, people live and work longer, and as medicine advances, actuaries will need to reexamine the probabilities of death, sickness, and retirement.

Casualty actuaries will find more work as companies find themselves held responsible for product liability. In the wake of recent environmental disasters, there will also be a growing need to evaluate environmental risk.

As business goes global, it presents a whole new set of risks and problems as economies develop and new markets emerge. As private enterprise expands in the former Soviet Union, how does a company determine the risk of opening, say, a department store in Moscow?

Actuaries are no longer just mathematical experts. With their unique combination of analytical and business skills, their role is expanding as they become broad-based business professionals solving social as well as financial problems.

■ FOR MORE INFORMATION

For general information about actuary careers, contact

American Academy of Actuaries
1100 17th Street, NW, Seventh Floor
Washington, DC 20036
Tel: 202-223-8196
http://www.actuary.org

For information about continuing education and professional designations, contact

American Society of Pension Actuaries
4245 North Fairfax Drive, Suite 750
Arlington, VA 22203
Tel: 703-516-9300
Email: aspa@aspa.org
http://www.aspa.org

The Be An Actuary section of the CAS website offers comprehensive information on the career of actuary.

Casualty Actuarial Society (CAS)
1100 North Glebe Road, Suite 600
Arlington, VA 22201
Tel: 703-276-3100
Email: office@casact.org
http://www.casact.org

For information about continuing education and professional designations, contact

Society of Actuaries
475 North Martingale Road, Suite 600
Schaumburg, IL 60173
Tel: 847-706-3500
http://www.soa.org

Acupuncturists

■ OVERVIEW

Acupuncturists are health care professionals who practice the ancient East Asian healing art of acupuncture. Acupuncture is a complete medical system that helps to improve body functioning and promote natural healing.

It has been practiced in China for thousands of years to maintain health, prevent disease, treat illness, and alleviate pain. It has been proven to be effective in the treatment of emotional and psychological problems as well as physical ailments.

There are over 15,000 professional acupuncturists in the United States, 1,400 of whom are licensed medical doctors. Acupuncture is one of the fastest growing health care professions. Most acupuncturists work in private practice, although an increasing number work in clinics and hospitals.

■ HISTORY

Acupuncture has been practiced for thousands of years; in fact, the Chinese believe that acupuncture began during the Stone Age, when early people used sharp stone tools to puncture and drain boils. As time passed, primitive needles made of stone or pottery replaced the earlier tools. They, in turn, were replaced by metal needles, which evolved into the very thin needles acupuncturists use today.

Early metal needles had nine different shapes, and they were used for a variety of purposes. However, there were no specific points on the body where they were applied. Through centuries of experience and observation, the Chinese learned that the use of the needles on very specific points on the skin was effective in treating particular ailments. They later grouped specific acupuncture points into a system of channels, or *meridians*. Acupuncturists think that these channels run over and through the body, much like rivers and streams run over and through the earth. They teach that the body has a type of vital energy, called *qi* or *chi* (both are pronounced "chee"), and that this energy flows through the body. The acupuncture points along the channels are thought to influence the flow of the vital energy.

Acupuncture developed virtually uninterrupted over thousands of years until the Portuguese landed in China in 1504. Once China was opened to the rest of the world, Western medical concepts gradually began to influence the practice of medicine there. Over centuries, the practice of acupuncture declined, and in 1929, it was outlawed in China. Even so, it remained a part of folk medicine. When the Communist Party came to power in 1949, there were almost no medical services. The communists encouraged the use of traditional Chinese remedies, and acupuncture again began to grow.

Just as Western medicine filtered into China, the concept of acupuncture gradually traveled back to the West. It was probably known and used in Europe as early as the 17th century. The first recorded use was in 1810 at the Paris Medical School, where Dr. Louis Berlioz used it to treat abdominal pain. Acupuncture was also used in England in the early 1800s. Ear acupuncture, one of the newer forms of acupuncture, was largely developed outside of China. In the early 1950s, Dr. Paul Nogier of France developed the detailed map of the ear that most acupuncturists now use.

After President Nixon visited China in 1972, public awareness and use of acupuncture began to grow in North America. Today acupuncture is increasingly used in Europe, North America, and Russia. Over one-third of the world's population relies on acupuncture and Oriental medicine practitioners for prevention and treatment of disease, as well as for the enhancement of health. In the West, acupuncture is most well-known for pain relief, but a growing body of research shows that it is effective in health maintenance as well as the treatment of many diseases. In 1979, the World Health Organization, the medical branch of the United Nations, issued a list of more than 40 diseases and other health conditions that acupuncture helped alleviate.

During the last decade of the 20th century, major developments in the perception of health care in this country and throughout the world brought acupuncture and Oriental medicine to the forefront of health care. In 1996, the Food and Drug Administration reclassified acupuncture needles from "investigational" to "safe and effective" medical devices. This opened the door for acupuncture to be recognized by and covered under insurance programs. A 1997 report sponsored by the National Institutes of Health concluded that acupuncture should be integrated into standard medical practice and included in Medicare. These milestones have paved the way toward greater acceptance of acupuncture by the medical community and by the American public.

■ THE JOB

Acupuncture is the best-known component of a larger system of medicine encompassing a variety of healing

QUICK FACTS

SCHOOL SUBJECTS
Biology
Psychology

PERSONAL SKILLS
Helping/teaching
Technical/scientific

WORK ENVIRONMENT
Primarily indoors
Primarily one location

MINIMUM EDUCATION LEVEL
Associate's degree

SALARY RANGE
$22,000 to $45,000 to
$100,000+

CERTIFICATION OR LICENSING
Required by certain states

OUTLOOK
Faster than the average

DOT
N/A

GOE
N/A

NOC
3232

O*NET-SOC
N/A

modalities, including acupuncture, Chinese herbology, bodywork, dietary therapy, and exercise. A practitioner may practice them all or specialize in only one or two.

Acupuncturists treat symptoms and disorders by inserting very thin needles into precise acupuncture points on the skin. They believe that the body's *qi* (vital energy, also spelled *chi*) flows along specific channels in the body. Each channel is related to a particular physiological system and internal organ. Disease, pain, and other physical and emotional conditions result when the body's qi is unbalanced, or when the flow of qi along the channels is blocked or disrupted. Acupuncturists stimulate the acupuncture points to balance the circulation of this vital energy. The purpose of acupuncture and other forms of traditional Oriental medicine is to restore and maintain whole body balance.

Acupuncture has been used for centuries to maintain health and relieve a wide range of common ailments, including asthma, high blood pressure, headache, and back pain. A recent use of acupuncture is for treatment of substance abuse withdrawal. Some areas of medicine that use acupuncture include internal medicine, oncology, obstetrics and gynecology, pediatrics, urology, geriatrics, sports medicine, immunology, infectious diseases, and psychiatric disorders. In the United States, acupuncture is perhaps most frequently used for relief of pain.

Like many other health care professionals, acupuncturists take an initial health history when they receive a new patient. They need to know about the patient's past and present problems. They listen carefully and sensitively, and they incorporate the patient history into their plan of treatment.

Next, acupuncturists give a physical examination. During the examination, they try to determine if a patient's qi is unbalanced. If it is, they look for the location of the imbalance. They test the quality of the pulses in both of the patient's wrists. They examine the shape and color of the tongue, skin color, body language, and tone of voice. They also check the feel of diagnostic areas of the body, such as the back and the abdomen. Acupuncturists may test for weaknesses in the muscles or along the meridians.

Once acupuncturists identify the source of the qi imbalance, they choose the type of needle to be used. Traditionally, there are nine types of acupuncture needles, ranging in length from just over an inch to as long as seven inches. Each type of needle is used to treat certain conditions. Most acupuncturists in the United States and other Western countries use only three types of needles that range from one to three inches in length. After selecting the type of needle, acupuncturists determine where the needles will be inserted on the patient's

WORDS TO KNOW

Acupressure: A technique similar to acupuncture that uses finger pressure and hand strokes instead of needles.

Herbal medicine: A system of natural medicine that uses herbs in various combinations to treat symptoms and to promote health. It is often used as a supplement to acupuncture.

Oriental medicine: A larger system of medicine that incorporates acupuncture, herbal medicine, and other natural healing modalities. Sometimes called Chinese medicine or traditional Chinese medicine. In deference to the many contributions made to traditional Chinese practices by other East Asian countries, many professionals now prefer the term *Oriental medicine*.

Qi (or **chi**—both are pronounced "chee"): In Oriental medicine, qi is the vital energy that flows through the body. Western medical thought describes it as bio-electric energy. Oriental medicine is a science of understanding how qi works in the body. In Western terms, it is the science of understanding energetics in the body.

T'ai qi (or **t'ai chi**): A type of exercise based on a series of more than 100 postures, between which are slow, deliberate movements. T'ai qi is practiced both as a martial art and to achieve integration of mind and body.

Yoga: A system of exercise for achieving physical and mental control and well-being that originates from the Indian subcontinent.

body. There are thousands of possible insertion points on the body. Four to 12 needles are typically used in a treatment.

Acupuncture needles are flexible. They are about the diameter of a human hair—much thinner than injection-type needles. They are inserted to a depth of up to an inch. Insertion of the needles is generally painless, although sensitive individuals may feel fleeting discomfort. During treatment, acupuncturists may stimulate the needles to increase the effect. Stimulation is done by twirling the needles or by applying heat or a low electrical current to them.

The first visit usually lasts an hour or more because the history and physical require extra time. Follow-up visits are usually shorter—perhaps 15 to 45 minutes, although treatments sometimes last an hour or longer. Occasionally only one treatment is required. Other times, the patient may have to return for several sessions.

If acupuncturists incorporate other modalities of alternative medicine into their practices, they may supplement the acupuncture with the other treatments. They

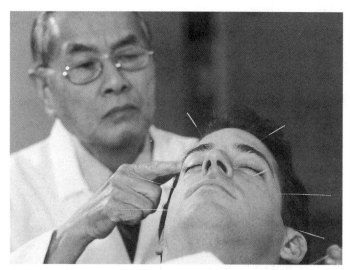

This acupuncturist inserts thin needles into his patient's face to alleviate pain.

might include herbal therapy, massage, exercise, or nutritional counseling.

In addition to treating patients, acupuncturists have a number of other duties. Most are self-employed, so they have to do their own paperwork. They write reports on their patients' treatments and progress. They bill insurance companies to make sure they get paid. They also have to market their services in order to build their clientele. It is important for them to maintain contacts with other professionals in the medical community, because other professionals may be good sources of referrals. Acupuncturists must also keep up with developments and changes in their profession through continuing education.

■ REQUIREMENTS
High School

If you are interested in a career in acupuncture, take courses that will give you an understanding of the human body. Courses in biology, physiology, and psychology will help you gain an understanding of the body and insight into the mind. Good communication skills are important in all professions, so take English, speech, drama, and debate classes to improve your communication skills.

You are likely to be self-employed if you become an acupuncturist, so math, business, and computer courses will also be helpful. A good, well-rounded education will help prepare you for any career you might choose.

Postsecondary Training

More than 50 schools in the United States are accredited by the Accreditation Commission for Acupuncture and Oriental Medicine (ACAOM). All of these programs offer master's degrees or master's level courses. To be admitted into a master's level program, virtually every school requires a minimum of two years of undergraduate study. Others require a bachelor's degree in a related field, such as science, nursing, or premed. Most acupuncture programs provide a thorough education in Western sciences, acupuncture techniques, and all aspects of traditional Oriental medical systems. See ACAOM's website (http://www.acaom.org) for names, addresses, and descriptions of the programs.

Choosing a school for acupuncture can be complex. One important decision is where you might like to live and practice. Eligibility requirements vary from state to state, so it is important to be sure the school you choose will prepare you to practice in the state in which you wish to live. In some states, only physicians can be licensed to practice acupuncture. In other states, there are no requirements for practicing acupuncture.

Another consideration in making a school choice is the tradition of acupuncture you want to study. There are a number of different types of acupuncture. You will need to find a school that offers the type that interests you. If you need financial assistance, it is important to choose a college that is accredited by ACAOM. These schools are recognized by the U.S. Department of Education and students may be eligible for federal student loans.

Certification or Licensing

For acupuncture, certification indicates that an individual meets the standards established by a nationally recognized commission. Licensing is a requirement established by a state's governmental body that grants individuals the right to practice within that state. Licensing requirements vary widely around the country and are changing rapidly.

Certification and licensing are usually achieved by meeting educational requirements and passing an examination. Thirty-seven states and the District of Columbia use National Certification Commission for Acupuncture and Oriental Medicine (NCCAOM) standards as an integral part of their licensing process. To become nationally board certified in acupuncture, NCCAOM requires applicants to have followed one of the following: a formal education route, apprenticeship route, professional acupuncture practice route, or combination of training and experience. All applicants are required to complete a Clean Needle Technique course and to pass the NCCAOM Acupuncture Examination, which consists of a written examination and the Point Location Examination.

Many states certify only licensed physicians to practice acupuncture, while some states extend this right to chiropractors. In certain states, an acupuncturist is granted the right to practice only after a ruling from the state's board of medical examiners. States that currently have no requirements for practicing acupuncture are considering legislation on the subject.

Other Requirements

Like other health care practitioners, acupuncturists frequently work with people who are in pain and who have been ill for a long time. Patients often come to acupuncturists after other medical treatments have failed. They may be especially pessimistic about finding relief or cures. Acupuncturists need to be good listeners, patient, and compassionate. Acupuncturists also need to have sensitive hands.

Claudette Baker, Lic. Ac. (licensed acupuncturist), has her office in Evanston, Illinois. She believes that people who become acupuncturists need to have a special perspective on health care. Baker says, "Those who consider a career in acupuncture should be interested in medicine and in healing, but they should also be aware that this profession requires a change in their perception of medicine. Oriental medicine is a science of understanding energetics in the body, and it is a healing art. Students should only consider acupuncture if they have an aptitude for understanding and learning this approach to medicine."

■ EXPLORING

If a career in acupuncture interests you, there are many ways to learn more about it. You will find many books at the library. Studying Oriental history, thought, and philosophy will help you learn to understand Oriental medicine's approach to healing.

Health food stores sometimes have books on acupuncture, and they are good places to learn about other alternative or complementary health modalities. Ask the staff if they know acupuncturists in your area. Talk with people who have experienced acupuncture. Find out what it was like and how they felt about it. Make an appointment for a health consultation with an acupuncturist. Find out if this approach to medicine works for you, and if you would like to use it to help others.

Read about or take courses in yoga or t'ai qi (t'ai chi). These are ancient methods for achieving control of the mind and body, and the principles on which they are based are similar to those of acupuncture.

You can also learn more about acupuncture by visiting the websites of the national and state professional associations. Some of them offer student memberships and many of them have excellent information online or for purchase.

You could also visit a college of acupuncture to sit in on classes and talk to the students. Ask them about their courseload and what they like and dislike about their programs.

■ EMPLOYERS

Most acupuncturists operate private practices. Some form or join partnerships with other acupuncturists or with people skilled in other areas of Oriental medicine. Professionals and clinics in other areas of health care, such as chiropractors, osteopaths, and medical doctors, increasingly include acupuncturists among them.

As acupuncture is finding more acceptance, there are growing opportunities for acupuncturists in hospitals and university medical schools. A few acupuncturists are engaged in medical research. They conduct studies on the effectiveness of acupuncture in treating various health conditions. There is a growing emphasis on research in acupuncture, and this area is likely to employ greater numbers in the future. A small number of acupuncturists work for government agencies, such as the National Institutes of Health.

■ STARTING OUT

To get started as an acupuncturist, one of the most important elements is being sure that you have the proper certification and licensing for your geographical area. This bears repeating, since the requirements for the profession, for each state, and for the nation are changing rapidly.

The placement office of your school may be able to help you find job opportunities. When starting out, some acupuncturists find jobs in clinics with doctors or chiropractors or in wellness centers. This gives them a chance to start practicing without having to equip an office. Some begin working with a more experienced acupuncturist and then later go into private practice. Acupuncturists frequently work in private practice. When starting a new practice, they often have full-time jobs and begin their practices part time.

Networking with professionals in local and national organizations is a good way to learn about job opportunities.

■ ADVANCEMENT

Acupuncturists advance in their careers by establishing their own practices and by building large bases of patients. Some start their own clinics. Because acupuncturists receive referrals from physicians and other health care practitioners, relationships with other members of the medical community can be very helpful in building a patient base.

Acupuncturists may eventually wish to teach acupuncture at a school of Oriental medicine. After much experience, an acupuncturist may achieve a supervisory

HOW DOES ACUPUNCTURE WORK?

Acupuncturists and other Oriental medicine practitioners believe that acupuncture works by balancing the flow of qi, the vital energy of the body. Although Western medicine is not yet able to explain in its own terms just how acupuncture works, there is growing research substantiating that it does work.

Some researchers believe that acupuncture works by increasing the release of endorphins—chemicals that the brain naturally produces in response to pain, stress, and physical exertion. There is also evidence that acupuncture may help regulate other chemicals in the body. Some researchers believe that acupuncture needles directly stimulate the nervous system. Still others think acupuncture may work by boosting the body's immune system.

Whichever point of view one uses to explain how it works, patients of acupuncture are determined in their affirmation that it does, in fact, work.

or directorship position in a school. The growing acceptance of acupuncture by the American public and the medical community will lead to an increasing need for research. Acupuncturists can build rewarding careers participating in this effort.

■ EARNINGS

Acupuncturists can expect starting earnings that range from $22,000 to $32,000. Experienced acupuncturists earn about $45,000 per year. Physicians who practice acupuncture as part of their medical practices have incomes that can be well over $100,000 per year. As with any other form of self-employment, income is directly related to the number of hours an acupuncturist works and the rates they can charge. Rates increase with experience. Like other self-employed individuals, acupuncturists must provide their own insurance, vacation, and retirement benefits.

■ WORK ENVIRONMENT

Acupuncturists usually work indoors in clean, quiet, comfortable offices. Since most are in solo practice, they can choose their surroundings. Private practitioners set their own hours, but many work some evenings and weekends to accommodate their patients' schedules. They usually work without supervision and must have a lot of self-discipline.

For acupuncturists who work in clinics, hospitals, and universities, the surroundings vary. They may work in large hospitals or small colleges. However, wherever they work, acupuncturists need clean, quiet offices. In these larger settings, acupuncturists need to be able to work well in a team environment. They may also need to be able to work well under supervision. Those who are employed in these organizations usually receive salaries and benefits. They may have to follow hours set by the employer.

■ OUTLOOK

Acupuncture is growing rapidly as a profession due to increasing public awareness and acceptance. There are more than 15,000 licensed acupuncturists in the United States. Some in the field estimate that figure will at least double by 2015. Each year more than 1,000 new acupuncturists become certified. The number of certified and licensed acupuncturists is expected to grow as additional states establish legal guidelines for acupuncturists to follow. The recent advances in research, changes in government policy, and interest from the mainstream medical community are strong indicators that the field will continue to expand. As insurance, HMOs (health maintenance organizations), and other third-party reimbursements increase, acupuncture is expected to grow even more rapidly.

The number of people who receive acupuncture treatments is growing annually. One of the areas of greatest growth is in the treatment of addictions. The United States has provided more than $1 million for research programs to investigate acupuncture's effect on cocaine addiction and alcoholism. Many hospitals and prisons now use acupuncture in their substance abuse programs. Besides the treatment of addictions, other areas of increase in acupuncture include the treatment of chronic pain, bronchial asthma, and premenstrual syndrome.

Despite these factors favoring job growth, much education and research still need to be done to integrate this system of natural healing into the conventional American health care system.

■ FOR MORE INFORMATION

For information for potential students, general information about acupuncture and Oriental medicine, and thorough information about national organizations, changes in legislation, and state standards, contact

Acupuncture and Oriental Medicine Alliance
6405 43rd Avenue, NW, Suite B
NW Gig Harbor, WA 98335
Tel: 253-851-6896
http://www.aomalliance.org

For general information, comprehensive information on the legal status of acupuncture and Oriental medicine in individual states, a list of schools, and a website with good links, contact

American Association of Oriental Medicine

5530 Wisconsin Avenue, Suite 1210

Chevy Chase, MD 20815

Tel: 888-500-7999

Email: info@aaom.org

http://www.aaom.org

For information on academic guidelines, contact

Council of Colleges of Acupuncture and Oriental
Medicine

7501 Greenway Center Drive, Suite 820

Greenbelt, MD 20770

Tel: 301-313-0868

http://www.ccaom.org

For information on certification, contact

National Certification Commission for
Acupuncture and Oriental Medicine

11 Canal Center Plaza, Suite 300

Alexandria, VA 22314

Tel: 703-548-9004

Email: info@nccaom.org

http://www.nccaom.org

For answers to frequently asked questions about acupuncture, contact

Acupuncture.com

http://www.acupuncture.com

Adult and Vocational Education Teachers

■ OVERVIEW

Adult and vocational education teachers teach basic academic subjects to adults who did not finish high school or who are new to speaking English, help prepare post-high school students and other adults for specific occupations, and provide personal enrichment. Adult education teachers offer basic education courses, such as reading and writing, or continuing education courses, such as literature and music. Vocational education teachers offer courses designed to prepare adults for specific occupations, such as data processor or automobile mechanic. Approximately 280,000 teachers of adult literacy, remedial, and self-enrichment education are employed in the United States.

■ HISTORY

In American colonial times, organized adult education was started to help people make up for schooling missed as children or to help people prepare for jobs. Apprenticeships were an early form of vocational education in the American colonies as individuals were taught a craft by working with a skilled person in a particular field. For example, a young boy might agree to work for a printer for five to ten years and at the end of that time be able to open up his own printing business. Training programs continued to develop as carpenters, bricklayers, and other craftspeople learned their skills through vocational training courses.

Peak periods in adult education typically occurred during times of large-scale immigration. Evening schools were filled with foreign-born persons eager to learn the language and culture of their new home and to prepare for the tests necessary for citizenship.

In 1911, Wisconsin established the first State Board of Vocational and Adult Education in the country, and in 1917 the federal government supported the continuing education movement by funding vocational training in public schools for individuals over the age of 14. Immediately after World War II, the federal government took another large stride in financial support of adult and vocational education by creating the G.I. Bill of Rights, which provided money for veterans to pursue further job training.

Today's colleges and universities, vocational high schools, private trade schools, private businesses, and other organizations offer adults the opportunity to prepare for a specific occupation or pursue personal enrichment. More than 20 million people in the United States take advantage of this opportunity each year, creating many jobs for teachers in this field.

■ THE JOB

Adult and vocational education courses take place in a variety of settings, such as high schools, universities, religious institutions, and businesses. The responsibilities of an adult or vocational education teacher are similar to those of a school teacher and include planning and conducting lectures, supervising the use of equipment, grading homework, evaluating students, writing and preparing reports, and counseling students.

Adult education is divided into two main areas: basic education and continuing education. Basic education includes reading, writing, and mathematics courses and is designed for adult students who have not finished high school. Many of these students are taking basic education courses to earn the equivalent of a high school diploma (the General Equivalency Diploma, or GED). Some high school graduates who received poor grades in high school also enroll in basic education classes before attending a four-year college. Recent immigrants may take basic education classes to learn to read, write, and do arithmetic in the language of their new country.

Unlike basic education, continuing education for adults is aimed at students who have finished high school or college and are taking courses for personal enrichment. Class topics might include creative writing, art appreciation, photography, history, and a host of other subjects. Often businesses will enroll employees in continuing education courses as part of job training to help them develop computer skills, learn to write grant proposals, or become convincing public speakers. Sometimes, businesses will hire an adult education teacher to come into the business to train employees on-site. These continuing education teachers are called *training representatives*.

Vocational education teachers prepare students for specific careers that do not require college degrees, such as cosmetologist, chef, or welder. They demonstrate techniques and then advise the students as they attempt these techniques. They also lecture on the class subject and direct discussion groups. Instruction by a vocational education teacher may lead to the student's certification, so teachers may follow a specific course plan approved by an accrediting association. They may also be involved in directing a student to an internship, and to local job opportunities.

Whether teaching in a basic education or continuing education classroom, adult and vocational education teachers work with small groups of students. In addition to giving lectures, they assign textbooks and homework assignments. They prepare and administer exams, and grade essays and presentations. Adult and vocational education teachers also meet with students individually to discuss class progress and grades. Some courses are conducted as part of a long-distance education program (tradi- tionally known as correspondence courses). For a distance education course, teachers prepare course materials, assignments, and work schedules to be sent to students, and then grade the work when it is turned in by the students.

■ REQUIREMENTS
High School

As an adult education teacher, you will likely focus on a particular area of study, so take the high school courses that best suit your interests. You'll also need to follow a college preparatory plan, taking courses in English, math, foreign language, history, and government. Speech and communications courses will help you prepare for speaking in front of groups of people. Writing skills are very important, no matter what subject you teach, because you'll be preparing reports, lesson plans, and grading essays.

Postsecondary Training

Before becoming an adult education teacher, you'll need to gain some professional experience in your area of teaching. A bachelor's degree is also usually required. Requirements vary according to the subject and level being taught, the organization or institution offering the course, and the state in which the instruction takes place. Specific skills, however, are often enough to secure a continuing education teaching position. For example, a person well trained in painting, with some professional success in the area, may be able to teach a course on painting even without a college degree or teaching certificate.

Certification or Licensing

There is no national certifying board for adult education teachers, but some states require their own teaching certification. Most community and junior colleges, however, require only a bachelor's degree of their teachers. Teachers in vocational education programs may have to be certified in their profession. If teaching English as a Second Language (ESL), you'll probably have to take some required workshops and seminars. For information on certification, contact local adult education programs and the department of education in the state in which you are interested in teaching.

Other Requirements

As a teacher, you should be able to deal with students at different skill levels, including some who might not have learned proper study habits or who have a different first language. This requires patience, as well as the ability to track the progress of each individual student. Good communication skills are essential, as you'll need to explain things clearly and to answer questions completely.

QUICK FACTS

SCHOOL SUBJECTS
English
Psychology
Speech

PERSONAL SKILLS
Communication/ideas
Helping/teaching

WORK ENVIRONMENT
Primarily indoors
Primarily one location

MINIMUM EDUCATION LEVEL
Bachelor's degree

SALARY RANGE
$20,970 to $41,470 to $71,350

CERTIFICATION OR LICENSING
Required by certain states

OUTLOOK
Faster than the average

DOT
N/A

GOE
12.03.02

NOC
4131

O*NET-SOC
25-3011.00, 25-3021.00

■ EXPLORING

Adult education classes are often held at high schools; if this is the case at your school, take the opportunity to discuss career questions with teachers before or after a class. You may also get the opportunity to observe one of these classes. Some of your high school teachers may be teaching adult or vocational education courses in the evenings; talk to them about the difference between teaching high school and teaching in an adult education program. Registering for a continuing education or vocational education course is another way of discovering the skills and disciplines needed to succeed in this field; if you have an interest in a particular subject not taught at your school, seek out classes at community colleges.

Your school may have a peer tutoring program that would introduce you to the requirements of teaching. You could also volunteer to assist in special educational activities at a nursing home, church, synagogue, mosque, or community center.

■ EMPLOYERS

There are approximately 280,000 adult literacy, remedial, and self-enrichment teachers employed in the United States. About one in five of these teachers is self-employed. Adult education teachers can find work in a variety of different schools and education programs. Community and junior colleges regularly have openings for teachers. Specially trained teachers can work for state-funded programs, such as literacy and ESL programs. Teachers are also hired for long-distance education programs and to lead continuing education courses for corporations and professional associations. Teachers are often needed in such institutions as prisons, hospitals, retirement communities, and group homes for disabled adults.

■ STARTING OUT

Most people entering this field have some professional experience in a particular area, a desire to share that knowledge with other adults, and a teaching certificate or academic degree. When pursuing work as an adult education teacher, you should contact colleges, private trade schools, vocational high schools, or other appropriate institutions to receive additional information about employment opportunities. Many colleges, technical schools, and state departments of education offer job lines or bulletin boards of job listings. You can also often find job openings in the classifieds of local newspapers.

■ ADVANCEMENT

A skilled adult or vocational education teacher may become a full-time teacher, school administrator, or director of a vocational guidance program. To be an

COMMUNITY COLLEGES

The American Association of Community Colleges and ACT Inc. surveyed 100,000 credit students at community colleges during the fall of 1999 and 2000.

Approximately 11 percent of respondents enrolled to upgrade occupational skills in order to advance in current positions. This group tended to be older than 25 and working full-time while enrolled in classes part-time.

Students preparing for future careers made up 29 percent of the respondents. Although most of these students were working while preparing for future careers, they did not list their current work needs as reasons for attending.

Life changers comprised 12 percent of the respondents. This group cited a recent major life change as the reason for attending community colleges, to acquire skills, enter the workforce, and find a new career.

Among all survey respondents, a common reason for attending community colleges was the desire for personal enrichment—to develop intellectual abilities, study new and different subjects, and meet new people.

administrator, a master's degree or a doctorate may be required. Advancement also may take the form of higher pay and additional teaching assignments. For example, a person may get a reputation as a skilled ceramics teacher and be hired by other adult education organizations as an instructor.

■ EARNINGS

Earnings vary widely according to the subject, the number of courses taught, the teacher's experience, and the geographic region where the institution is located. According to the U.S. Department of Labor's *2002 National Occupational Employment and Wage Estimates,* adult literacy and remedial education teachers earned an average salary of $41,470. The lowest paid 10 percent of these workers made $20,970 annually in 2002, while the highest paid 10 percent earned $71,350.

Because many adult and vocational education teachers are employed part time, they are often paid by the hour or by the course, with no health insurance or other benefits. Hourly rates range from $10 to more than $34.

■ WORK ENVIRONMENT

Working conditions vary according to the type of class being taught and the number of students participating. Courses are usually taught in a classroom setting but may also be in a technical shop, laboratory, art studio, music room, or other location depending on the subject

Smaller classes such as this allow for more individualized attention, but teachers must be capable of effectively teaching large groups as well.

matter. Of course, when teaching in such settings as prisons or hospitals, adult education teachers must travel to the students as opposed to the students traveling to the teacher's classroom. Average class size is usually between 10 and 30 students, but may vary, ranging from one-on-one instruction to large lectures attended by 60 or more students.

Some adult and vocational education teachers may only work nine or ten months a year, with summers off. About half of the adult and vocational education teachers work part time, averaging anywhere from two to 20 hours of work per week. For those employed full time, the average workweek is between 35 and 40 hours. Much of the work is in the evening or on weekends, as many adult students work on weekdays.

■ OUTLOOK

Employment opportunities in the field of adult education are expected to grow faster than the average through 2012, according to the U.S. Department of Labor. Adults recognize the importance of further education and training for succeeding in today's workplace. In fact, many courses are subsidized by companies that want their employees trained in the latest skills and technology of their field. The biggest growth areas are projected to be in computer technology, automotive mechanics, and medical technology. Many new teachers will also be needed, as current ones leave the occupation or retire. As demand for adult and vocational education teachers continues to grow, major employers will be vocational high schools, private trade schools, community colleges, and private adult education enterprises. Immigration also fuels a demand for adult-education and English teachers, espe-

cially in places such as New York, California, and Florida with high foreign-born populations.

Many "school-to-work" programs have evolved across the country as a result of the School-to-Work Opportunities Act of 1994. To prepare more graduating seniors for the high-wage jobs, "tech prep" programs offer course work in both academic and vocational subject matter. As more of these programs are developed, vocational education teachers will find many more opportunities to work in high schools and training schools. Finally, the recent economic downturn has led many workers to seek to upgrade their work skills in a more competitive environment.

■ FOR MORE INFORMATION

For information about conferences and publications, contact

American Association for Adult and Continuing Education
4380 Forbes Boulevard
Lanham, MD 20706
Tel: 301-918-1913
Email: aaace10@aol.com
http://www.aaace.org

For information about publications, current legislation, and school-to-work programs, contact

Association for Career and Technical Education
1410 King Street
Alexandria, VA 22314
Tel: 800-826-9972
Email: acte@acteonline.org
http://www.acteonline.org

For information about government programs, contact

U.S. Department of Education
400 Maryland Avenue, SW
Washington, DC 20202-0498
Tel: 800-872-5327
http://www.ed.gov

Adult Day Care Coordinators

■ OVERVIEW

Adult day care coordinators, also called *adult day services coordinators,* direct day service programs for adults who have physical or mental impairments or both. Clients of these programs are usually the elderly, although younger people with impairments, such as those recovering from strokes, may also participate in these programs. Coordinators oversee staff members who provide care, meals, and social activities to day care clients, and they serve as liaisons between their centers and their clients' families.

HISTORY

Adult day care had its beginnings in the 1940s in psychiatric hospitals. It started as an effort to help patients who had been released from mental institutions. Over the next 20 years the focus gradually shifted from psychiatric care to other kinds of health maintenance. The landmark publication, *Developing Day Care for Older People,* published by the National Council on the Aging (NCOA) in 1972, provided technical assistance for establishing adult day care, and by 1978 there were nearly 300 adult day care centers throughout the United States.

In the 1980s, the first Congressional hearing was held on adult day care programs and the Economic Recovery Act was passed, allowing a tax credit to families with elderly members in day care. NCOA established voluntary standards.

According to the National Adult Day Services Association, more than 3,500 adult day centers are currently operating in the United States. Approximately 78 percent operate on a nonprofit or public basis, and many are affiliated with larger organizations such as home care, skilled nursing facilities, medical centers, or multipurpose senior organizations.

THE JOB

Adult day care coordinators direct adult day care centers. Although specific duties vary depending on the size of the center and the services it offers, the general responsibility of coordinators is to ensure that their centers provide the necessary care for clients. Such care may include attention to personal hygiene and providing meals, medications, therapies, and social activities.

Although coordinators working in small day care centers may actually perform some services for clients, this is not the norm. Instead, coordinators usually oversee various staff members who provide the caregiving. A large center, for example, might have a nurse, physical therapist, social worker, cook, and several aides. Coordinators are responsible for staff hiring, training, and scheduling. They may meet with staff members either one-on-one or in group sessions to review and discuss plans for the clients.

Overseeing meal planning and preparation is also the responsibility of the adult day services coordinator. In most centers, clients are given a midday meal and usually juices and snacks in the morning and afternoon. Coordinators work with a cook or dietitian to develop well-rounded menus that take into account the nutritional needs of the clients, including any particular restrictions such as diabetic or low-sodium diets. The coordinator may also oversee purchasing and taking inventory of the center's food supply.

The coordinator schedules daily and weekly activities for the day care clients. Depending on the particular needs and abilities of the clients, a recreational schedule might include crafts, games, exercises, reading time, or movies. In some centers, clients are taken on outings to shopping centers, parks, or restaurants. The coordinator plans such outings, arranging for transportation and any reservations or special accommodations that may be necessary. Finally, the coordinator also organizes parties for special events, such as holidays and birthdays.

Finding new activities and visitors for the center is also part of the job. Coordinators might recruit volunteers to teach crafts or music to the clients. Often, church or civic groups come to such facilities to visit with clients. Some such groups institute buddy programs, in which each group member pairs with a day care client to develop an ongoing relationship. The day care coordinator must authorize and monitor any group visits, activities, or programs.

In addition to planning and overseeing the activities of the center and its clients, the adult day care coordinator also works closely with client family members to make sure that each individual is receiving care that best fits his or her needs. This relationship with the client's family usually begins before the client is placed in the day care center.

When a family is considering placing an elderly relative in day care, they often have many questions about the center and its activities. The coordinator meets with family members to show them the center and explain to them how it is run. The coordinator also gathers information about the potential client, including names and phone numbers of doctors and people to contact in

QUICK FACTS

SCHOOL SUBJECTS
Family and consumer science
Psychology
Sociology

PERSONAL SKILLS
Helping/teaching
Leadership/management

WORK ENVIRONMENT
Primarily indoors
Primarily one location

MINIMUM EDUCATION LEVEL
Associate's degree

SALARY RANGE
$18,000 to $31,000 to
$45,000

CERTIFICATION OR LICENSING
Required for certain positions

OUTLOOK
Much faster than the average

DOT
354

GOE
14.07.01

NOC
N/A

O*NET-SOC
N/A

FACTS ABOUT ADULT DAY CARE

A nationwide survey of adult day care centers conducted by the National Adult Day Services Association found the following:

- The average age of the adult day care consumer is 72.
- Two-thirds of all consumers are women.
- Average cost of care per day is $56 across the country.
- One-quarter of the participants live alone; three-quarters live with a spouse, adult children, or other family and friends.
- One-half of participants have some cognitive impairment, and one-third require nursing services at least weekly.
- Fifty-nine percent of the participants require assistance with two or more activities of daily living; eating, bathing, dressing, toileting, or transferring; 41 percent require assistance in three or more areas.

Source: National Adult Day Services Association

case of emergency, lists of medications taken with instructions on when and how they should be administered, and information on allergies, food choices, and daily habits and routines.

After the client is placed in the center, the coordinator may meet periodically with the client's family to update them on how the client is responding to the day care setting. If necessary, the coordinator may advise the family about social services, such as home health care, and refer them to other providers.

Adult day care coordinators may have other duties, depending on the center and how it is owned and operated. For example, they may be responsible for developing and adhering to a budget for the center. In centers licensed or certified by the state, coordinators may ensure that their centers remain in compliance with the regulations and necessary documentation. They may also be responsible for general bookkeeping, bill payment, and office management.

In addition to supervising centers, coordinators may also promote and advertise to the community. They may help with fund-raising, prepare press releases, and speak to various service clubs.

■ REQUIREMENTS
High School

Because this is a relatively new and growing field, there are no national standards to follow for becoming an adult day

care coordinator. Some people have learned their skills on the job; others have taken courses in home nursing or health care; still others have completed bachelor's degrees in areas such as health and human services. As the need for and popularity of day care services continue to grow, more employers will begin to expect coordinators to have at least some formal education. While you are in high school, therefore, you should take classes that prepare you for postsecondary training. These include mathematics, business, family and consumer science classes as well as science classes, such as biology. To improve your understanding of people, take history, psychology, and sociology classes. Because communication is an important skill, English and speech classes are also good choices.

Postsecondary Training

Many employers prefer to hire candidates who meet the standards set by the National Adult Day Services Association (NADSA). In order to meet these standards, a coordinator must have a bachelor's degree in health or social services or a related field, with one year's supervisory experience in a social or health services setting. In preparation for such a career, a college student might choose occupational, recreational, or rehabilitation therapy, or social work or human development. An increasingly popular major for potential adult day care coordinators is gerontology, or geriatrics.

The Association for Gerontology in Higher Education publishes the *Directory of Educational Programs in Gerontology and Geriatrics,* which contains information on more than 750 programs available from the associate's to the post-doctorate level. Although specific courses vary from school to school, most programs consist of classes in social gerontology, biology and physiology of aging, psychology of aging, and sociology of aging. In addition to these four core classes, most programs offer elective courses in such areas as social policy, community services, nutrition and exercise, diversity in aging, health issues, death and dying, and ethics and life extension.

A practicum or field placement is also a part of most gerontology programs. This allows students to obtain experience working with both well-functioning elderly people and those with age-related disabilities.

Certification or Licensing

According to NADSA, there are currently no national standards regarding the qualifications for adult day services workers. NADSA does offer voluntary certification to program assistants. The National Certification Council for Activity Professionals also offers certification to qualified adult day care coordinators. Those who meet the professional standards earn the designation certified activity professional (CAP). See the end of the article for contact information.

Regulations can vary by state. In some states, for example, the agency that a coordinator works for must be licensed or certified by the state health department. Any adult day care center that receives payment from Medicare or from other government agencies must be certified by the state department of health. In these cases, licensing requirements may include requirements for coordinators and other staff members. The trend is toward stricter standards.

Other Requirements

Regardless of what level of education a prospective coordinator has, there are certain personal characteristics that are necessary for success in this field. Compassion and an affinity for the elderly and disabled are vital, as are patience and the desire to help others. You should also be organized and able to manage other workers effectively. Communication skills are very important since you will be working with staff, clients, regulatory agencies, and clients' families.

■ EXPLORING

There are several ways you can learn more about the career of adult day care coordinator. The first and easiest way is to check your local library for books or articles on aging in order to learn more about the elderly, their issues, and the services available to them. Next, visit a nursing home or adult day care center in order to experience firsthand what it is like to spend time with and interact with elderly people. Arrange to talk with staff members and the center's coordinator to find out what their day-to-day jobs are like. Your high school guidance counselor may also be able to arrange for a coordinator to give a career talk at your school. Finally, get a volunteer position or part-time job in such a facility. This would allow you to gauge your aptitude for a career in adult day care work.

■ EMPLOYERS

Adult day care coordinators work at adult day care centers. These may be small or large. It is estimated that there are more than 3,500 adult day care centers currently operating in the United States. Most of them are operated on a nonprofit or public basis, and many are affiliated with large organizations such as nursing homes, hospitals, or multipurpose senior organizations. Standards and work environments vary.

■ STARTING OUT

In looking for a position as an adult day care coordinator, candidates should first locate and contact all such programs in the area. Checking the local Yellow Pages under Nursing Homes, Residential Care Facilities, Aging Services, or Senior Citizens Services should provide a list of leads. The job seeker might either send a resume and cover letter or call these potential employers directly. Prospective coordinators should also watch for job openings listed in area newspapers and on organizations' websites.

Another means of finding job leads is to become affiliated with a professional association, such as the American Geriatrics Society, the American Association of Homes and Services for the Aging, the Gerontological Society of America, or the National Council on the Aging. Many such organizations have monthly or quarterly newsletters that list job opportunities. Some may even have job banks or referral services.

Job seekers who have received associate's or bachelor's degrees should also check with the career placement offices at their colleges or universities.

■ ADVANCEMENT

Because the field of aging-related services continues to grow, the potential for advancement for adult day care coordinators is good. Some coordinators advance by transferring to a larger center that pays better wages. Others eventually start their own centers. Still others advance by moving into management positions in other, similar social service organizations, such as nursing homes, hospices, or government agencies on aging.

An adult day care coordinator might choose to return to school and complete a higher degree, often a master's degree in social work. For those who choose this option, there are many career opportunities in the field of social services. *Social workers*, for example, work with individuals and families dealing with AIDS, cancer, or other debilitating illnesses. They also work for agencies offering various types of counseling, rehabilitation, or crisis intervention.

■ EARNINGS

Starting salaries for this position depend partly on the experience and education of the coordinator and partly upon the size and location of the day care center. Larger centers located in metropolitan areas tend to offer the highest wages.

According to the Association for Gerontology in Higher Education, beginning annual salaries range from $18,000 to $31,000 for persons with a bachelor's degree and little experience. Generally, coordinators who do not have a bachelor's degree can expect to earn somewhat less. Experienced coordinators with a bachelor's degree employed in large, well-funded centers may earn from $20,000 to $45,000 annually.

In addition to salary, some coordinators are also offered a benefits package, which typically includes health insurance, paid vacation and sick days, and a retirement plan.

■ WORK ENVIRONMENT

Most adult day care centers have a schedule that corresponds to standard business hours. Most coordinators work a 40-hour week, Monday through Friday, with weekends off.

The coordinator's work environment will vary depending on the size and type of center he or she supervises. Some centers are fairly institutional, resembling children's day care centers or nursing homes. Others have a more residential feel, being carpeted and furnished like a private home. Regardless of the furnishings, the center is typically clean, well lit, and equipped with ramps, rails, and other devices that ensure the safety of clients.

Part of the coordinator's day may be spent in the center's common areas with clients and staff. He or she may also spend time working in an on-site office. If the staff members take clients on outings, the coordinator may accompany them.

Coordinators are on their feet much of the time, ensuring that meals and activities run smoothly and helping staff members when necessary. Attire for the job varies from center to center, ranging from very casual to standard office wear. Most coordinators, however, wear clothing that is comfortable and allows them freedom of movement.

Regardless of the size of the center, coordinators spend the majority of their time working with people, both staff members and day care clients. Working with clients is often very trying. Many of them may have had a stroke or have Alzheimer's disease, and they may be confused, uncooperative, or even hostile. The job may also be emotionally taxing for the coordinator who becomes attached to his or her clients. Most adults who use a day care center are elderly or permanently disabled; for this reason, day care staff must frequently deal with the decline and eventual death of their clients.

■ OUTLOOK

The career outlook for adult day care coordinators, as for all human services workers, is expected to be excellent through 2012. According to the U.S. Department of Labor, the number of human services workers is projected to grow tremendously between the years 2002 and 2012, with adult day care, specifically, being one of the fastest growing human services areas.

The main reason for this is that the senior citizen population is growing rapidly. According to the U.S. Census Bureau, approximately 35 million Americans were age 65 or older in 2001; the bureau projects this number to increase steadily, reaching approximately 82 million by 2050 as the "Baby Boomer" generation ages. This rapid growth has led to the development and increased popularity of aging-related services during the last several years. The increase in adult day care centers is one example of this trend. According to NADSA, there were only approximately 300 adult day care centers in existence by the late 1970s; today, there are more than 3,500. This growth should continue as Americans become increasingly aware of the diverse needs of the elderly and the various service options available to them. Adult day care is expected to be used more frequently as a cost-efficient and preferable alternative to nursing homes.

■ FOR MORE INFORMATION

For information on aging and services for the elderly, contact
American Association of Homes and Services for the Aging
2519 Connecticut Avenue, NW
Washington, DC 20008-1520
Tel: 202-783-2242
http://www.aahsa.org

AGHE, a section of the Gerontological Society of America, promotes education in the field of aging and offers a directory of gerontology and geriatrics programs. Visit the website http://www.careersinaging.com to read AGHE's Careers in Aging: Consider the Opportunities.
Association for Gerontology in Higher Education (AGHE)
1030 15th Street, NW, Suite 240
Washington, DC 20005-1503
Tel: 202-289-9806
Email: aghetemp@aghe.org
http://www.aghe.org

For career information and student resources, contact
Gerontological Society of America
1030 15th Street, NW, Suite 250
Washington, DC 20005
Tel: 202-842-1275
Email: geron@geron.org
http://www.geron.org

For information on the history of adult day service and day service facts, contact
National Adult Day Services Association
8201 Greensboro Drive, Suite 300
McLean, VA 22102

Tel: 866-890-7357
Email: info@nadsa.org
http://www.nadsa.org

This organization can provide information on services, including adult day care, available across the country.

National Association of Area Agencies on Aging
927 15th Street, NW, 6th Floor
Washington, DC 20005
Tel: 202-296-8130
http://www.n4a.org

For information on certification, contact

National Certification Council for Activity Professionals
PO Box 62589
Virginia Beach, VA 23466
Tel: 757-552-0653
Email: info@nccap.org
http://www.nccap.org

To learn about developments and current issues in the aging field, visit the following website:

National Council on the Aging
409 Third Street, SW, Suite 200
Washington, DC 20024
Tel: 202-479-1200
Email: info@ncoa.org
http://www.ncoa.org

Advanced Practice Nurses

■ OVERVIEW

Advanced practice nurses (APNs) are a broad category of registered nurses (RNs) who have completed advanced clinical nurses' educational practice requirements beyond the two to four years of basic nursing education required for all RNs. Under the advanced practice nursing designation fall four categories of nursing specialties: *clinical nurse specialists* (CNSs), *nurse practitioners* (NPs), *nurse-midwives* (NMs), and *nurse anesthetists* (NAs). (See the separate articles on each of these specialties.) According to the Health Resources and Service Administration, as of 2000 there were an estimated 196,279 advanced practice nurses employed in the United States.

■ THE JOB

Working in clinics, nursing homes, hospitals, and other health care settings, APNs are qualified to handle a wide range of basic health problems, usually in association with a physician, but in some cases working independently.

Specific duties of APNs are determined by their specialty, and to a certain extent their precise duties are prescribed by the state in which they practice. APNs are required to be certified in most states and can prescribe medications in 46 states.

Working within prescribed guidelines and instructions of the physician, the APN orders, interprets, and evaluates diagnostic tests to identify the patient's clinical problems and health care needs. Then based on their findings, he or she records patient data and develops a treatment plan aimed at restoring the patient to health. After discussing this plan with the physician and other health professionals, the APN submits the plan and goals for individual patients for periodic review and evaluation. When warranted, APNs may prescribe (in most states) drugs or other forms of treatment such as physical therapy, inhalation therapy, and related treatments. If warranted they may refer patients to the supervising physician for consultation and their special expertise in various areas of medical practice.

■ REQUIREMENTS

If you want to become an APN, you will first need to complete the high school and undergraduate education necessary to become a registered nurse. (See Registered Nurses.)

Postsecondary Training

A master's degree is usually necessary to prepare for a nursing specialty or to teach. For some specialties, such as nursing research, a Ph.D. is essential. After becoming a registered nurse, educational requirements for APNs vary depending on the category of APN under consideration.

QUICK FACTS

SCHOOL SUBJECTS
Biology
Chemistry
Mathematics

PERSONAL SKILLS
Helping/teaching
Technical/scientific

WORK ENVIRONMENT
Primarily indoors
Primarily multiple locations

MINIMUM EDUCATION LEVEL
Master's degree

SALARY RANGE
$40,000 to $60,000 to $80,000

CERTIFICATION OR LICENSING
Required by all states

OUTLOOK
Faster than the average

DOT
075

GOE
14.02.01

NOC
3152

O*NET-SOC
29-1111.00

CAREER PERSPECTIVES FOR NURSE-MIDWIVES

The 1980s and 1990s were boon years for nurse-midwives, boosted by immigration from Latin America (where the profession is common) and by women seeking alternatives to the institutional hospital births of the previous generation, where much of the control was in the hands of doctors, not the mother-to-be. According to the National Center for Health Statistics, certified nurse-midwives delivered only one percent of births in the United States in 1976; eleven years later, in 1987, they delivered more than three times as many. By 1994, one out of every 20 births was attended by a nurse-midwife. In the past few years, though, the number of such deliveries has slowed; the 2002 figure, 7.6 percent of all births, was the same as that in 2001.

One of the reasons for this has been a change in insurance provisions, and insurance companies' influence on health-care practice. Many HMOs and malpractice insurers stipulate that births must take place in a hospital, instead of at home or at a birthing center. Such companies also increase the operating costs, raising premiums until many nurse-midwives can no longer afford to pay them.

Certification or Licensing

Each of the four APN classifications has its own certification process. (See the separate articles on Nurse Practitioners, Nurse-Midwives, Nurse Anesthetists, and Clinical Nurse Specialists.)

■ EXPLORING

You can explore your interest in the nursing field in a number of ways. You can take a first aid class to help you learn the basics of treating sick or injured people. You can read books on careers in nursing, talk with your health teachers or school nurse about the career, or visit nursing association websites to learn more information. You might also consider visiting or volunteering at a hospital or clinic to observe the work of nurses and to talk with hospital personnel. Camp counseling jobs sometimes offer related experiences. Some schools offer participation in Future Nurses programs.

■ EMPLOYERS

Advanced practice nurses are employed by hospitals, managed-care facilities, long-term-care facilities, clinics, mental health facilities, nursing homes, home health care agencies, veterans affairs facilities, industrial organizations, nursing schools and other educational institutions, physicians' offices, and the military.

■ STARTING OUT

The only way to become a registered nurse is through completion of one of the three kinds of educational programs plus passing the licensing examination. Registered nurses may apply for employment directly to hospitals, nursing homes, companies, and government agencies that hire nurses. Jobs can also be obtained through school placement offices, by signing up with employment agencies specializing in placement of nursing personnel, or through the state employment office. Other sources of jobs include nurses' associations, professional journals, newspaper want ads, and the Internet.

■ ADVANCEMENT

Administrative and supervisory positions in the nursing field go to nurses who have earned at least the bachelor of science degree in nursing. Since advanced practice nurses must have master's degrees to enter the field, they often have a good chance to advance to supervisory or managerial positions.

■ EARNINGS

Average earnings for APNs range from $40,000 to $80,000 a year in 2000, the last year for which statistic were available. Certified registered nurse anesthetists (CRNAs) are at the top of the range, followed by CNSs. Salaries for certified nurse-midwives (CNMs) and NPs are comparable. Nurses employed in private clinics of government facilities as well as those employed in hospitals and short-term care facilities enjoy attractive benefits such as paid vacations, holidays, and sick days. They often are able to participate in pension and investment programs as well as receive health care coverage.

■ WORK ENVIRONMENT

Most hospital environments are clean and well lit. Inner-city hospitals may be in less than desirable locations, and safety may be an issue. Usually, nurses work eight-hour shifts. Those in hospitals generally work any of three shifts: 7:00 A.M. to 3:00 P.M.; 3:00 P.M. to 11:00 P.M.; or 11:00 P.M. to 7:00 A.M.

Nurses spend much of the day on their feet, either walking or standing. Handling patients who are ill or infirm can also be very exhausting. Nurses who come in contact with patients with infectious diseases must be especially careful about cleanliness and sterility. Although many nursing duties are routine, many responsibilities are unpredictable. Sick persons are often very demanding, or they may be depressed or irritable. Despite this, the nurse must retain her or his composure and should be cheerful to help the patient achieve emotional balance.

All nursing careers have some health and disease risks; however, adherence to health and safety guidelines greatly minimizes the chance of contracting infectious diseases such as hepatitis and AIDS. Medical knowledge and good safety measures are also needed to limit the nurse's exposure to toxic chemicals, radiation, and other hazards.

■ OUTLOOK

The U.S. Department of Labor predicts shortages of advanced practice nurses will continue over the next several years. APNs with the proper credentials and certification should have no trouble finding posts in a wide variety of health care facilities.

■ FOR MORE INFORMATION

For information on accredited training programs applying to various categories of advanced practice nurses, including curriculums, entrance requirements, financial assistance available, and so forth, contact the following organizations:

American Academy of Nurse Practitioners
PO Box 12846
Capitol Station, LBJ Building
Austin, TX 78711
Tel: 512-442-4262
Email: admin@aanp.org
http://www.aanp.org

American College of Nurse-Midwives
818 Connecticut Avenue, NW, Suite 900
Washington, DC 20006
Tel: 202-728-9860
http://www.midwife.org

National Association of Clinical Nurse Specialists
4700 West Lake Avenue
Glenview, IL 60025
Tel: 717-234-6799
http://www.nacns.org

American Association of Nurse Anesthetists
222 South Prospect Avenue
Park Ridge, IL 60068
Tel: 847-692-7050
http://www.aana.com

For information about state-approved programs and information on nursing, contact

National League for Nursing
61 Broadway
New York, NY 10006
Tel: 800-669-1656

Email: nlnweb@nln.org
http://www.nln.org

Discover Nursing, sponsored by Johnson & Johnson Health Care Systems, provides information on nursing careers, nursing schools, and scholarships.

Discover Nursing
http://www.discovernursing.com

Adventure Travel Specialists

■ OVERVIEW

Adventure travel specialists develop, plan, and lead people on tours of places and activities that are unfamiliar to them. Most adventure travel trips involve physical participation and/or a form of environmental education. A whitewater rafting trip, a mountain climbing expedition, or a safari are just some examples of adventure travel. Organized adventure travel has grown rapidly in popularity over the past few decades, and today it represents a segment of the travel industry generating more than $166 billion per year in the United States alone. In 1997, the Travel Industry Association of America estimated that of all adults in the United States, half, or approximately 98 million people, had taken some form of adventure trip in the past five years. Adventure travel tends to be most popular with the younger set, and slightly more popular with men.

■ HISTORY

Adventure travel as a formalized activity began developing in the late 20th century. As Americans enjoyed an increasingly high standard of living, as the advancement of technologies made everyday life easier (or "softer"), and as disposable incomes grew, some people began to see vacations as not simply a time for relaxation but for adventure. What distinguishes adventure travel from traditional activities such as camping in the great outdoors? Some experts maintain that those involved in adventure travel are deliberately seeking some type of risk in or an unknown outcome for the activity.

Mountain Travel, founded in 1969, and Sobek, founded in 1973, became two of the leading adventure travel companies in the United States, merging in 1991 as Mountain Travel Sobek. Today adventure travel is one of the fastest growing areas of specialization within the travel industry. Specialists escort paying customers to destinations all over the world—China, Nepal, Easter

Island, Alaska, to name a few—and organize activities such as mountain climbing, sea kayaking, and camelback desert crossings. The adventure travel industry looks to continue its growth in the 21st century. Some experts note that this is in part due to the computer and the Internet: as more and more people spend workdays sitting in cubicles facing computers, more and more feel distanced from fulfilling physical activities and real feelings of excitement. At the same time, the Internet, with its breadth of information, has made the world a smaller place and given people greater knowledge of travel destinations and possibilities.

■ THE JOB

Adventure travel specialists plan—and may lead—tours of unusual, exotic, remote, or wilderness locations. Almost all adventure travel involves some physical activity that takes place outdoors. Adventure travel is split into two categories: hard adventure and soft adventure. Hard adventure requires a fairly high degree of commitment from participants, as well as advanced skills. A high-adventure traveler might choose to climb Yosemite's El Capitan, raft the Talkeetna River in Alaska, or mountain-bike the logging trails in the Columbia River Gorge. Soft adventure travel, on the other hand, requires much less physical ability and is usually suitable for families. Examples of this kind of travel might be a guided horseback ride through the Rocky Mountains, a Costa Rican wildlife-viewing tour, or a hot air balloon ride over Napa Valley, California.

Steve Gilroy is a professional photographer who has turned his love of the Alaskan outdoors into a second career—that of "soft adventure" travel specialist and guide for photography tours. Each year, his company, Alaska Photo Tours, takes approximately 120 photography buffs on tours of the Alaskan countryside, allowing them to capture spectacular scenery and wildlife on film.

"We offer custom trips for small groups that put people into great photographic situations," he says. "It's for people who like taking pictures and who don't want to be caught in a huge tour group or be in the really touristy places." Gilroy's trips originate in either Anchorage or Juneau, Alaska, and last seven to 12 days. His tour groups are small, with no more than 11 travelers. He plans every detail of each of the company's 12 yearly trips, and he serves as a guide on about half of them.

Some adventure travel specialists work strictly in an office environment, planning trip itineraries, making reservations for transportation, activities, and lodging, and selling the tours to travelers. Others, typically called *outfitters,* work in the field, overseeing the travelers and guiding the tour activities. In some cases, such as Gilroy's, the adventure specialist both plans the logistics of the trip and guides it.

For every adventure tour that takes place, numerous plans must be made. Travelers who purchase a tour package expect to have every arrangement handled for them, from the time they arrive in the city where the trip begins. That means that ground transportation (such as vans, buses, or jeeps), accommodations (lodges, hotels, or camping sites), and dining (whether hiring cooks and arranging for food to be taken on the trip or finding appropriate restaurants) must all be planned and reserved, all depending upon the particular trip. Each day's activities must also be planned in advance, and arrangements must be made with adventure outfitters to supply equipment and guides.

Gilroy begins planning a trip more than 18 months in advance. With attention to every detail, he plans tours that will take travelers to the right places at the right times of the year for the best photographic opportunities. "We dictate the schedule around the wildlife and the scenery," he says. "I only travel at the best times." Long before the tour ever begins, he has reserved lodging, any in-state flights, natural history guides for certain locations, and even private rooms in restaurants.

Some companies serve as adventure travel brokers, selling both tours that they have developed and tours that have already been packaged by another company. Travel specialists working for brokers are responsible for marketing and selling these tours. They give potential customers information about the trips offered, usually over the phone. When a customer decides to purchase a tour package, the travel specialist takes the reservation and completes any necessary paperwork. Depending on their position in the company and their level of responsibility, adventure travel planners may decide where and how to advertise their tours.

Working as an adventure travel outfitter or guide is very different from working as an adventure travel plan-

QUICK FACTS

SCHOOL SUBJECTS
Business
Foreign language
Geography

PERSONAL SKILLS
Helping/teaching
Leadership/management

WORK ENVIRONMENT
Primarily outdoors
Primarily multiple locations

MINIMUM EDUCATION LEVEL
Some postsecondary training

SALARY RANGE
$6,600 to $26,630 to
$60,000+

CERTIFICATION OR LICENSING
Required for certain positions

OUTLOOK
About as fast as the average

DOT
353

GOE
11.02.01

NOC
N/A

O*NET-SOC
39-6021.00

ner or broker. The duties for these individuals vary enormously, depending upon the types of tours they lead. Adventure tours can take place on land, on water, or in the air. On a land adventure trip, guides may take their tour groups rock climbing, caving, mountain biking, wilderness hiking, horseback riding, or wildlife viewing. On a water trip, they may go snorkeling, scuba diving, surfing, kayaking, whitewater rafting, or canoeing. Air adventures include skydiving, parasailing, hang gliding, bungee jumping, and hot air ballooning.

Whatever the nature of the trip, guides are responsible for overseeing the group members' activities. For Gilroy, this starts at the beginning of a tour when he collects his travelers from the airport. He then conducts an orientation meeting and discusses the coming days' activities. "I give them a plan of attack and tell them what the next day's goals are," he says. "I'll say, 'We're hoping to see whales tomorrow . . . or we're going to see if we can get a bald eagle to swoop down by the boat.' I try to give them some expectation of what we might see."

Gilroy's tours usually consist of a segment in coastal Alaska, one near Mount McKinley, and one in his hometown of Talkeetna to give travelers a taste of life in rural Alaska. "Most visitors want a balanced trip," he says. "So this way, they get to see the glaciers, sea otters, whales, and puffins of coastal Alaska, plus the grandeur of Mount McKinley and the grizzlies, caribou, moose, wolves, and tundra." The tour group usually spends between three and five days in each location.

Tour guides are also responsible for demonstrating activities, helping with equipment, and assisting group members who are having difficulty. In many cases, where travelers are interested in the scenery, geography, wildlife, or the history of a location, guides serve as commentators, explaining the unique aspects of the region as the group travels.

As the tour guide, Gilroy's objective is to take his groups out into the Alaska landscape to look for photographic opportunities. When touring on land, they travel in a 15-passenger luxury van, which makes periodic stops at likely locations. "We take short hikes, with vehicle support," he says. "We'll stop, gather our equipment, and go for a short walk because I know of good photo opportunities in the area, or we've spotted an animal." During each of the visitors' hikes, Gilroy educates them on their surroundings. "As we walk, I give them background on the wildlife, what to look for, how to approach," he says. "It's important to me to share the whole Alaska experience . . . vegetation, wildlife, natural history."

Guides are also responsible for helping tour group members in the case of an emergency or unforeseen developments. Depending on the nature of their tour, they

A white water rapids trip is organized by an adventure travel specialist, seated in the back of the raft.

must be prepared to deal with injuries, dangerous situations, and unusual and unplanned happenings. In Gilroy's case, this means advising group members on how to stay safe in the unfamiliar territory. "I always tell them what to be careful of," he says. "I tell them about bear behaviors, how to walk on the lumpy tundra so that they don't twist an ankle, that sort of thing." All of the guides on Gilroy's tours are required to be trained in first aid and CPR.

Adventure tours are meant to be unique experiences. One way guides make their trips special is to provide their clients with unusual access to the environment or "up close and personal" experiences. Gilroy, for example, often contracts with a local flight service company to take his groups on aerial tours of Mount McKinley. Some tours also include short cruises off the coast in Zodiacs, on motorized rubber skiffs. "This allows us to go ashore, to walk a beach littered with car-sized icebergs, to go into a meadow where the wildflowers are gorgeous," Gilroy says. The goal is a photographic exploration of Alaska.

No matter what the theme of a trip is or its destination, it is the guide's responsibility to ensure that tour group members have a safe, memorable, and enjoyable time.

■ REQUIREMENTS
High School

If you are considering the business end of travel—working in a brokerage, planning tours, or eventually owning your own tour-packaging business—you should start

THE ECOTOURIST EXPOSED

An ecotourist's idea of a perfect vacation does not include time poolside sipping on cool margaritas. Such tourists, according to The International Ecotourism Society, look for "responsible travel to natural areas that conserves the environment and sustains the well-being of local people."

Here's a profile of the average Eco-Joe:

- Average age is between 35 and 54 years old.
- Even percentages of men and women enjoy ecotravel, although they often prefer different trip activities.
- 82 percent are college graduates.
- 60 percent prefer to travel as a couple, 15 percent with families, and 13 percent alone.
- 50 percent of those surveyed prefer trips lasting from eight to14 days.
- Experienced ecotourists don't pinch pennies—26 percent are willing to spend $1,000 to $1,500 per trip.
- What are the top three elements ecotourists want on their trips? Survey says: wilderness setting, wildlife viewing, and hiking or trekking.

Information from The International Ecotourism Society website, http://www.ecotourism.org.

taking business courses while still in high school. Accounting, computer science, mathematics, or any other business-related course will give you a good start. Classes in geography, geology, social studies, and history might also help you understand and discuss the locations you may be dealing with. It is important to take a foreign language, a study you will probably need to continue throughout your career. Finally, classes in English or speech are always good choices for helping you develop the ability and confidence to deal with people.

If you are more interested in the fieldwork aspect of adventure travel, you will need to take classes that help you understand how the earth's environment and ecosystem work. Because tour guides often explain the natural history of a location or educate tour groups on local wildlife and plant life, classes in earth science, biology, and geology are excellent choices. Classes that teach you about the social history of various places, such as social studies or anthropology, might also be beneficial.

Postsecondary Training

There are several different approaches you can take to prepare for a career in adventure travel. While it may not be necessary for all jobs, a college degree will likely give you a competitive edge in most employment situations. If you choose to obtain a college degree, some options for majors might be earth science, biology, geology, natural history, or environmental affairs. If you hope to become involved with an intensely physical form of adventure travel, a degree in health, physical education, or recreation may be a good choice.

If you are more interested in the planning and reservations end of adventure travel, a college degree in business is a good choice. Some adventure travel brokers suggest that attending one of the many travel agent schools also provides a good background for the administrative aspects of the business.

It may be possible to find a job in adventure travel without college training, if you happen to be very experienced and skilled in some form of adventure activity. If you choose this path, you should spend as much time as possible developing whatever skill interests you. There are classes, clubs, and groups that can teach you anything from beginning diving to advanced rock climbing.

Certification or Licensing

The Institute of Certified Travel Agents offers the designations certified travel associate (CTA) and certified travel counselor (CTC) to agents with the appropriate education and experience. While such certification is not required, it may be helpful to those running their own travel businesses.

Many employers do require employees to have certification in certain areas, such as CPR and first aid. Also, depending on the job, you may need special certification or licensing, such as scuba certification so that you can lead diving activities, or licensing as a commercial driver so that you can transport clients in a company van or other vehicle. If you plan to open your own adventure tour operation, you will need to apply for a business license. Check with your local government offices for details on how to obtain one.

Other Requirements

"People who enter this career are the kind of people who just naturally spend their free time outdoors," says Steve Gilroy. "So, they grew up hiking and fishing and camping . . . and that love of outdoors just carried them to the point where they decided to combine their love of nature with their career." Adventure travel tour guides need to have a passion for sharing their love of nature and their knowledge with others. Also, because of the nature of this job, you should be in good physical shape. Other important qualities to have are maturity, responsibility, and common sense, especially when leading groups of travelers into the relatively unknown. Some employers may have minimum age requirements for those in certain positions.

Adventure travel professionals who work in an office, developing and selling tours, need some different personal qualities than those who work in the field. Dave Wiggins, who owns one of the nation's oldest adventure travel brokerages, says that he looks for people with a good work ethic. "You can train someone to do everything else, but you can't teach the right attitude." Wiggins says that it's also important to be friendly and confident, and to have good phone skills. "We look for people with a good head on their shoulders who can speak intelligently about the different programs we sell," he says. While being an active, outdoorsy person may help you sell tours, it is not a requirement for working in this branch of adventure travel. Attention to detail and good organizational skills are more significant.

■ EXPLORING

Since much adventure travel involves physical activity, which may range from low to high impact, taking courses or becoming involved in activities that promote physical fitness is a good idea. If you already have an interest in a particular activity, you may be able to join clubs or take classes that help you develop your skills. For example, scuba diving, sailing, hiking, mountain biking, canoeing, and fishing are all activities found in adventure travel that you might be able to engage in while still in high school.

Another way to explore this field is to go on an adventure outing yourself. Outward Bound USA, for example, offers a wide variety of programs for teenagers, college students, and adults. And don't forget to check out summer camp options. YMCA camps, scouting camps, and others provide the opportunity to learn about the outdoors and improve your camping skills. Summer camps are also excellent places to gain hands-on experience as a worker, whether you are a counselor, a cook, or an activity instructor.

■ EMPLOYERS

Commercial adventure travel agencies, naturally, are employers of adventure travel specialists. In addition, a number of not-for-profit organizations, such as universities and environmental groups, are also offering nature and adventure programs.

■ STARTING OUT

Make a list of adventure groups and do some research. How long have they been in business? Do they specialize in soft or hard adventure travel? You can narrow your search to companies that specialize in the activity or activities with which you have experience. Use the Internet to help you do this; many companies have websites that advertise their specialties and list job openings. Other organizations, such as The International Ecotourism Society, also provide information on jobs and internships at their websites. Remember that for your best chance of finding a job in adventure travel, you may have to relocate, so your search should be geographically broad.

There are a number of magazines that may be helpful in compiling a list of companies involved in adventure travel. Some good publications to look into are *Outside* (http://www.outsidemag.com), *Backpacker* (http://www.backpacker.com), and *Bicycling* (http://www.bicycling.com). A final method of getting a list of travel wholesalers and outfitters is to contact one or all of the adventure travel organizations listed at the end of this article. These associations should be able to give you a list of their members.

To find not-for-profit organizations that hire adventure travel specialists, consider the National Audubon Society and the Sierra Club. Check with your local library for a complete listing of environmental groups. You might also contact universities to see if they have a

THE 10 COMMANDMENTS FOR ECOTOURISM

- Respect the frailty of the earth.
- Leave only footprints. Take only photographs. No graffiti! No litter!
- To make your travels more meaningful, educate yourself about the geography, customs, manners, and cultures of the region you visit.
- Respect the privacy and dignity of others. Ask first before snapping a picture.
- Do not buy products made from endangered plants or animals.
- Always follow designated trails.
- Learn about and support conservation-oriented programs.
- Whenever possible, walk or use environmentally sound methods of transportation.
- Patronize businesses that advance energy and environmental conservation.
- Encourage organizations to subscribe to environmental guidelines.

Source: American Society of Travel Agents

wilderness/adventure travel division in their schools of physical education or recreation.

You should also use any contacts you have—from clubs, organizations, previous travel experiences, or college classes—to find out about possible employment opportunities. If you belong to a diving or bicycling club, for example, be sure to ask other members or instructors if they are familiar with any outfitters you could contact. If you have dealt with outfitters in some of your adventure trips, you might contact them for potential job leads.

■ ADVANCEMENT

There is no clearly defined career path for adventure travel specialists. For those who work in an office environment, advancement will likely take the form of increased responsibility and higher pay. Assuming a managerial role or moving on to a larger company are other advancement possibilities.

For those who work in the field, advancement might mean taking more trips per year. Adventure travel in many locations is seasonal, and therefore, tour guides may not be able to do this sort of work year-round. It is not uncommon for an individual to guide tours only part time and have another job to fill in the slow times. For those who become experienced in two or more particular areas of travel and develop a reputation of expertise, however, there may be the opportunity to spend more, or even all, of the year doing adventure touring.

Another option for either the office worker or the guide would be to learn about the other side of the business. With experience in all aspects of developing, selling, and leading tours, ambitious travel specialists may be able to own their own company. "You could become your own tour operator in an area that you know and love," says Steve Gilroy, "which is what I've done."

■ EARNINGS

There is very little information available on what adventure travel specialists earn. Those who work in the field may find that they have peak and slack times of the year that correspond to destination weather conditions or vacation and travel seasons. Specialists, especially those just starting out in this line of work, may find they need to work two or three seasonal jobs in different locations and for different employers in order to have work throughout the year. As specialists gain experience, it may be possible for them to find year-round work with one employer, and, of course, many experienced travel specialists also have the goal of starting their own business and working for themselves. Experience, employer, and amount of work done are all factors that influence earnings per year.

A look at some specific figures gives an idea of the range of earnings in this field. A visit to Cool Works (http://www.coolworks.com), a website for outdoor jobs, provided the following information: One rafting company in Colorado offered summer positions for beginning rafting guides at $52 per day in 2001 and estimated that guides could expect summer earnings of between $1,800 to $2,000 plus $400 to $800 in tips their first summer (approximately four months of work). Twelve months of work at this pay rate makes a yearly income ranging between $6,600 and $8,400. A posting for a musher/dog sled tour guide in Wyoming advertised a salary of $1,500 per month plus tips. The job was for three and a half months in 2002. Someone working at this pay rate would make approximately $17,850 per year (excluding tips). A travel adventure company in Alaska offering positions such as sportfishing captain, sea kayaking guide, and river guide reported that the average income for their summer employees ranged from $7,000 to $10,000. At these pay rates, a person working 12 months would earn $21,000 to $30,000.

At the other end of the pay scale are adventure tour specialists who provide services only the very wealthy can afford. For example, a guided climb of Mount Everest can cost each tourist $60,000 or more. If the adventure specialist is leading three people on such a trip, he or she is being paid at least $180,000. Naturally, this is not all take-home pay. The guide will have expenses for equipment, food, lodging, and perhaps the employment of an assistant. However, an experienced, respected, highly qualified adventure travel specialist can make quite a healthy income.

Travel specialists who work strictly in an office environment may have earnings close to those of travel agents. According to the U.S. Department of Labor, travel agents had median yearly incomes of $26,630 in 2002. The lowest paid 10 percent made less than $16,530 per year, while the highest paid 10 percent earned more than $41,660.

Adventure travel specialists who work in the field generally receive free meals and accommodations while on tour, and they often receive a set amount of money per day to cover other expenses. Major tour packagers and outfitters may offer their employees a fringe benefits package, including sick pay, health insurance, and pension plans.

■ WORK ENVIRONMENT

Depending on where they work, an average day for adventure travel specialists might be anything from planning tours in the comfort of an air-conditioned office to leading a safari through southern Africa. Tour planners may do the majority of their work in comfortable offices. However, they need to spend some time in the field to better plan adventure tours. How can they recommend an activity without knowing the ins and outs?

For those who find cruising TV channels more appealing than rafting down the Colorado River or observing wildlife, this is definitely the wrong career choice. Adventure travel involves a great deal of physical activity. Tour guides are always on the go, whether guiding a group up and down a formation of rocks, or keeping an eye out for lichen-eating caribou.

Adventure specialists work with groups. In some cases, operators schedule up to 40 tourists per trip. Longer trips may require *step-on operators,* or *local specialized guides,* who give tours lasting one day or longer. In such cases, it helps to be able to work well with others. Communication is an important buzzword in this industry.

■ OUTLOOK

In 2002, there were approximately 703 million international travelers, according to the World Tourism Organization. Forty to 60 percent of all international tourists are nature tourists, while 20 to 40 percent are wildlife-related tourists. This indicates that the market for adventure travel is quite large.

Many trends in today's society indicate that this growth is likely to continue. One reason is that the public's awareness of and interest in physical health is growing; this leads more and more people to pursue physical activities as a form of recreation. Another reason is that as more people realize that a healthy environment means a better quality of life, there is an increased interest in wildlife and wilderness issues. Adventure travel often encompasses both physical activity and education on and preservation of natural areas, so it is a natural choice for many travelers.

Despite the general growth in the field, however, it should be noted that jobs as tour guides may not be easy to come by. Compared to the rest of the travel market, the adventure segment is still fairly small. Perhaps more significantly, tour guide positions are considered very desirable. According to Dave Wiggins, job openings for fieldwork in adventure travel are somewhat limited and highly sought-after. "There are outfitters out there who get maybe 500 applications a year," he says. "And they can hire maybe two new people."

While world events influence the number of people making trips and the travel industry as a whole, some experts believe the adventure travel industry is less likely to be affected by negative occurrences. For example, a survey done by *Outside* magazine found that the adventure travel sector was less affected by the terrorist attacks of September 2001 than the rest of the industry. While the American Society of Travel Agents reported cancellation rates as high as 50 percent, the cancellations in adventure travel were approximately 10 percent. One reason for this may be that those involved in adventure travel continue to want adventures. *Outside* predicts that the adventure travel business will continue to have the steady growth rate it has had for the past several years.

■ FOR MORE INFORMATION

For information on careers, training in niche travel, and travel news, contact
American Society of Travel Agents
1101 King Street, Suite 200
Alexandria, VA 22314
Tel: 703-739-2782
Email: askasta@astahq.com
http://www.astanet.com

For information on certification and continuing education for travel agents, contact
Institute of Certified Travel Agents
148 Linden Street
PO Box 812059
Wellesley, MA 02482
Tel: 800-542-4282
Email: info@icta.com
http://www.icta.com

For information on the ecotourism industry and related careers, contact
International Ecotourism Society
PO Box 668
Burlington, VT 05402
Tel: 802-651-9818
Email: ecomail@ecotourism.org
http://www.ecotourism.org

Visit the OIA website for the latest press releases and adventure travel news.
Outdoor Industry Association (OIA)
PO Box 1319
Boulder, CO 80306
Tel: 303-444-3353
Email: info@outdoorindustry.org
http://www.outdoorindustry.org

For statistical information and industry news, contact
World Tourism Organization (WTO)
Capitán Haya 42
28020 Madrid, Spain

Email: omt@world-tourism.org
http://www.world-tourism.org

Visit the Cool Works website for information on seasonal job opportunities in national parks, resorts, cruise ships, and more.

Cool Works
http://www.coolworks.com

Visit the Outward Bound USA website to learn more about its adventure activities.

Outward Bound USA
http://www.outwardbound.org

Advertising Account Executives

■ OVERVIEW

The *advertising account executive* coordinates and oversees everything related to a client's advertising account and acts as the primary liaison between the agency and the client. Account executives are also responsible for building and maintaining professional relationships among clients and coworkers to ensure the successful completion of major ad campaigns and the assurance of continued business with clients. Advertising account executives and related workers hold 700,000 jobs in the United States.

■ HISTORY

When the advertising industry formally developed in the late 1800s, advertisers themselves were usually the ones who handled the promotion of their products and services, placing ads in newspapers and magazines in order to reach their customers. As the number of newspapers increased and print advertising became more widespread, however, these advertisers called on specialists who knew how to create and coordinate effective advertisements. One such specialist, the advertising account executive, emerged to produce and handle the ad campaigns for businesses.

Advertising agencies were commonly used by companies by the 1920s, and account executives worked for such agencies. Together with a staff of creative professionals, the account executive was able to develop an advertising "package," including slogans, jingles, and images, as well as a general campaign strategy. In addition, account exec-

utives did basic market research, oversaw the elements that went into a campaign, and worked hand-in-hand with writers and artists to develop effective ads for their client companies.

Today, account executives handle all aspects of their clients' ad campaigns. As a result, they bring to the job a broad base of knowledge, including account management, marketing, sales promotion, merchandising, client accounting, print production, public relations, and the creative arts.

■ THE JOB

Account executives track the day-to-day progress of the overall advertising campaigns of their clients. Together with a staff commonly consisting of a creative director, an art director, a copywriter, researchers, and production specialists, the account executive monitors all client accounts from beginning to end.

Before an advertising campaign is actually launched, a lot of preparatory work is needed. Account executives must familiarize themselves with their clients' products and services, target markets, goals, competitors, and preferred media. Together with the agency team, the account executive conducts research and holds initial meetings with clients. Then the team, coordinated by the account executive, uses this information to analyze market potential and presents recommendations to the client.

After an advertising strategy has been determined and all terms have been agreed upon, the agency's creative staff goes to work, developing ideas and producing various ads to present to the client. During this time, the account executive works with *media buyers* (who purchase radio and television time and publication space for advertising) in order to develop a schedule for the project and make sure that the costs involved are within the client's budget.

When the ad campaign has been approved by the client, production can begin. In addition to supervising and coordinating the work of copywriters, editors, graphic artists, production specialists, and other employees on the agency team, the account executive must also write reports and draft business correspondence, follow up on all client meetings, interact with outside vendors, and ensure that all pieces of the advertising campaign clearly communicate the desired message. In sum, the account executive is responsible for making sure that the client is satisfied. This may require making modifications to the campaign, revising cost estimates and events schedules, and redirecting the efforts of the creative staff.

In addition to their daily responsibilities of tracking and handling clients' advertising campaigns, account executives must also develop and bring in new business, keep up to date on current advertising trends, evaluate the effectiveness of advertising programs, and track sales figures.

■ REQUIREMENTS
High School
You can prepare for a career as an advertising account executive by taking a variety of courses at the high school level. Basic courses in English, journalism, communication, economics, psychology, business, social science, and mathematics, are important for aspiring advertising account executives.

Postsecondary Training
Most advertising agencies hire college graduates whose degrees can vary widely, from English, journalism, or marketing to business administration, speech communications, or fine arts. Courses in psychology, sociology, business, economics, and any art medium are helpful. Some positions require a graduate degree in advertising, art, or marketing. Others may call for experience in a particular field, such as health care, insurance, or retail.

While most employers prefer a broad liberal arts background with courses in marketing, market research, sales, consumer behavior, communication, and technology, many also seek employees who already have some work experience. Those candidates who have completed on-the-job internships at agencies or have developed portfolios will have a competitive edge.

Other Requirements
While account executives do not need to have the same degree of artistic skill or knowledge as art directors or graphic designers, they must be imaginative and understand the communication of art and photography in order to direct the overall progress of an ad campaign. They should also be able to work under pressure, motivate employees, solve problems, and demonstrate flexibility, good judgment, decisiveness, and patience.

Account executives must be aware of trends and be interested in the business climate and the psychology of making purchases. In addition, they should be able to write clearly, make effective presentations, and communicate persuasively. It is also helpful to stay abreast of the various computer programs used in advertising design and management.

■ EXPLORING
Read publications like *Advertising Age* (http://www.adage.com), *Adweek* (http://www.adweek.com),

and *Brandweek* (http://www.brandweek.com) to become familiar with advertising issues, trends, successes, and failures. Visit the Clio Awards website (http://www.clioawards.com). Clios are given each year in the categories of TV, print, outdoor, radio, integrated media, design, Internet, and student work. The site also has information about advertising and art schools, trade associations, and links to some of the trade magazines of the industry.

To gain practical business experience, become involved with advertising or promotion activities at your school for social events, sports events, political issues, or fund-raising events. If your school newspaper or yearbook has paid advertising, offer to work in ad sales.

■ EMPLOYERS
More than 700,000 advertising, marketing, promotions, public relations, and sales managers work in the United States. Advertising agencies all across the country and abroad employ advertising account executives. According to the American Association of Advertising Agencies, there are more than 13,000 agencies in the United States; of these, the large firms located in New York, Chicago, and Los Angeles tend to dominate the industry. One in five firms and one in four people in the industry live in either California or New York. However, most organizations employ fewer than 10 people. These "small shops" offer employment opportunities for account executives with experience, talent, and flexibility.

■ STARTING OUT
Many people aspiring to the job of account executive participate in internships or begin as assistant executives, allowing them to work with clients, study the market, and follow up on client service. This work gives students a good sense of the rhythm of the job and the type of work required of account executives.

QUICK FACTS

SCHOOL SUBJECTS
Business
English
Speech

PERSONAL SKILLS
Communication/ideas
Helping/teaching

WORK ENVIRONMENT
Primarily indoors
Primarily one location

MINIMUM EDUCATION LEVEL
Bachelor's degree

SALARY RANGE
$30,310 to $57,130 to
$145,600+

CERTIFICATION OR LICENSING
None available

OUTLOOK
Faster than the average

DOT
164

GOE
10.01.01

NOC
1122

O*NET-SOC
11-2011.00

College graduates, with or without experience, can start their job search in the school placement office. Staff there can set up interviews and help polish resumes.

The advertising arena is rich with opportunities. When looking for employment, you don't have to target agencies. Instead, search for jobs with large businesses that may employ advertising staff. If you want to work at an agency, you'll find the competition intense for jobs there. Once hired, account executives often participate in special training programs that both initiate them and help them to succeed.

■ ADVANCEMENT

Since practical experience and a broad base of knowledge are often required of advertising account executives, many employees work their way up through the company, from assistant to account executive to account manager and finally to department head. In smaller agencies, where promotions depend on experience and leadership, advancement may occur slowly. In larger firms, management training programs are often required for advancement. Continuing education is occasionally offered to account executives in these firms, often through local colleges or special seminars provided by professional societies.

■ EARNINGS

According to the U.S. Department of Labor, advertising account executives earned between $30,310 and over $145,600 annually in 2002, with median annual earnings of approximately $57,130. In smaller agencies, the salary may be much lower ($20,000 or less), and in larger firms, it is often much higher (over $150,000). Salary bonuses are common for account executives. Benefits typically include vacation and sick leave, health and life insurance, and a retirement plan.

■ WORK ENVIRONMENT

It is not uncommon for advertising account executives to work long hours, including evenings and weekends. Informal meetings with clients, for example, frequently take place after normal business hours. In addition, some travel may be required when clients are based in other cities or states or when account executives must attend industry conferences.

Advertising agencies are usually highly charged with energy and are both physically and psychologically exciting places to work. The account executive works with others as a team in a creative environment where a lot of ideas are exchanged among colleagues.

As deadlines are critical in advertising, it is important that account executives possess the ability to handle pressure and stress effectively. Patience and flexibility are also essential, as are organization and time management skills.

■ OUTLOOK

The growth of the advertising industry depends on the health of the economy. In a thriving economy, advertising budgets are large, consumers tend to respond to advertising campaigns, and new products and services that require promotion are increasingly developed. Although the economy has been weaker as of late, the U.S. Department of Labor still predicts that employment for advertising account executives will grow faster than the average for all occupations through 2012.

Most opportunities for advertising account executives will be in larger cities, such as Chicago, New York, and Los Angeles, that enjoy a high concentration of business, as well as prestige. Competition for these jobs, however, will be intense. The successful candidate will be a college graduate with a lot of creativity, strong communications skills, and extensive experience in the advertising industry. Those able to speak another language will have an edge because of the increasing supply of products and services offered in foreign markets.

■ FOR MORE INFORMATION

The AAF combines the mutual interests of corporate advertisers, agencies, media companies, suppliers, and academia. Visit its website to learn more about internships, scholarships, and awards.

American Advertising Federation (AAF)
1101 Vermont Avenue, NW, Suite 500
Washington, DC 20005-6306
Tel: 202-898-0089
Email: aaf@aaf.org
http://www.aaf.org

For industry information, contact
**American Association of Advertising
   Agencies**
405 Lexington Avenue, 18th Floor
New York, NY 10174-1801
Tel: 212-682-2500
http://www.aaaa.org

For information on the practice, study, and teaching of marketing, contact
American Marketing Association
311 South Wacker Drive, Suite 5800
Chicago, IL 60606
Tel: 800-AMA-1150
http://www.marketingpower.com

Advertising and Marketing Managers

■ OVERVIEW

Advertising and marketing managers plan, organize, direct, and coordinate the operations of advertising and marketing firms. They may oversee an entire company, a geographical territory of a company's operations, or a specific department within a company. There are approximately 288,000 advertising and marketing managers employed in the United States.

■ HISTORY

The advertising industry formally emerged in the 1840s, when newspaper-advertising solicitors began representing groups of newspapers. In 1865, a new system was introduced: buying newspaper space and dividing and selling it to advertisers at higher prices. Other forms of advertising also came onto the scene. By the early 1900s, for example, outdoor posters developed into the billboard form, and the merchants who used them were the principal advertisers. In 1922, radio station WEAF in New York City offered program time to advertisers. The use of television advertising began just before the end of World War II. Today, the Internet is catapulting the world of advertising into a whole new realm, allowing vendors not only to target and reach customers but to interact with them as well.

The business discipline of marketing began to take shape as sellers realized that if a group of potential buyers could be found for a product, the product could be better designed to suit the needs of those buyers. Sellers also discovered the importance of identifying a group of buyers before starting an advertising campaign. By doing so, the producer could style the campaign to reach that specific group and would have a better chance of launching a successful product. Marketing, therefore, provided a service for both sides of the business world, the seller and the buyer.

As the need for advertising and marketing grew, companies specializing in product promotion and specialization were born. It is no surprise that the increasingly complex responsibilities involved in advertising and marketing products and services require managers to organize and run day-to-day office activities.

■ THE JOB

Advertising and marketing managers formulate policies and administer the advertising and marketing firm's operations. Managers may oversee the operations of an entire company, a geographical territory of a company's operations, or a specific department. Managers direct a company's or a department's daily activities within the context of the organization's overall plan. They implement organizational policies and goals. This may involve developing sales or promotional materials, analyzing the department's budgetary requirements, and hiring, training, and supervising staff. Advertising and marketing managers are often responsible for long-range planning for their company or department. This involves setting goals for the organization and developing a workable plan for meeting those goals.

Advertising and marketing managers work to coordinate their department's activities with other departments. If the firm is privately owned, the owner may be the manager. In a large corporation, however, there will be a management structure above the advertising and marketing manager.

In companies that have several different locations, advertising and marketing managers may be assigned to oversee specific geographic areas. For example, a large ad firm with facilities all across the nation is likely to have a number of managers in charge of various territories. There might be a Midwest manager, a Southwest manager, an Southeast manager, a Northeast manager, and a Northwest manager. These managers are often called *regional or area managers*. Some advertising and marketing firms break their management territories up into even smaller sections, such as a single state or a part of a state. Managers overseeing these smaller segments are often called *district managers* and typically report directly to an area or regional manager.

Advertising managers are responsible for coordinating the work of researchers, copywriters, artists, telemarketers, space buyers, time buyers, other specialists. One type of advertising manager is the *account manager*, who represents the agency to its clients. (See the article Advertising Account Executives for more information.)

Managers working at large advertising agencies usually handle a variety of accounts, while those working at smaller agencies usually only handle certain types of clients. For example, smaller firms may handle only financial accounts, hotels, book publishers, or industrial clients. Some managers work for agencies that are known for promoting package goods. Others work in retail and department store promotion.

In contrast, marketing managers work with their staff and other advertising professionals to determine how ads should look, where they should be placed, and when the advertising should begin. Managers must keep staff focused on a target audience when working on the promotion of a particular product or service. Managers must also carefully time the release of an ad. For example, launching an advertising campaign too early may create interest well before the product is available. In such cases, by the time the product is released, the public may no longer be interested.

The marketing manager must also oversee his or her department in developing a distribution plan for products. If a product is expected to sell well to a certain group, for example, then marketing professionals must decide how to deliver to members of that group based on when and where they shop.

Once markets are evaluated and merchandise is designed, the actual production begins. The job of the manager is not yet done, however. Along with the public relations department, marketing managers contact members of the press with the aim of getting product information out to the public.

Because research studies show how a product looks on the shelf can often affect sales, managers work with *designers* to explore new color combinations, more appealing shapes, interesting patterns, and new materials.

Marketing managers use a scientific and statistical approach in answering a client's questions about selling a product to the public. The advertising aspect of a marketing campaign must get attention, arouse interest, secure belief, create desire, and stir action. Beauty, comfort, convenience, and quality are the promises that sell all kinds of products, from consumables to cars.

■ REQUIREMENTS
High School

The educational background of advertising and marketing managers varies as widely as the nature of their diverse responsibilities. If you are interested in a managerial career, you should start preparing in high school by taking college preparatory classes. Because communication is important, take as many English classes as possible. Speech classes are another way to improve your communication skills. Courses in mathematics, business, economics, and computer science are also excellent choices to help you prepare for this career.

Postsecondary Training

Most advertising and marketing managers have a bachelor's degree in advertising, marketing, or business administration. However, degrees in English, journalism, speech communications, economics, or the fine arts are also applicable. Useful college classes include those in psychology, sociology, business, economics, and any art medium. Graduate and professional degrees are common at the managerial level.

Because managers coordinate the efforts of whole departments, most have worked in other lower level advertising and marketing jobs. Candidates for managerial positions who have extensive experience and developed portfolios will have a competitive edge.

Other Requirements

There are a number of personal characteristics that advertising and marketing managers need to succeed in their work. You will need good communication and interpersonal skills and the ability to delegate work to other members of your staff. Because advertising and marketing campaigns are often run under strict deadlines, the ability to think on your feet and work well under pressure is critical.

Other traits considered important for advertising and marketing managers are intelligence, decisiveness, intuition, creativity, honesty, loyalty, a sense of responsibility, and planning and abilities.

■ EXPLORING

To get experience in this line of work, try developing your own ad campaign. Take a product you enjoy, for example, a brand of soda you drink, and try to organize a written ad campaign. Consider the type of customers that you should target and what wording and images would work best to attract this audience.

You can also explore this career by developing your managerial skills in general. Whether you're involved in drama, sports, school publications, or a part-time job, there are managerial duties associated with any organized activity. These can involve planning, scheduling, managing other workers or volunteers, fund-raising, or budgeting.

■ EMPLOYERS

There are approximately 85,000 advertising and promotions managers and 203,000 marketing managers employed in the United States. Half of all advertising

QUICK FACTS

SCHOOL SUBJECTS
Business
Computer science

PERSONAL SKILLS
Helping/teaching
Leadership/management

WORK ENVIRONMENT
Primarily indoors
One location with some travel

MINIMUM EDUCATION LEVEL
Bachelor's degree

SALARY RANGE
$30,310 to $57,130 to $125,070 (advertising managers)
$39,730 to $78,250 to $145,600+ (marketing managers)

CERTIFICATION OR LICENSING
None available

OUTLOOK
Faster than the average

DOT
164

GOE
10.01.01, 13.01.01

NOC
0611

O*NET-SOC
11-2011.00, 11-2021.00

managers and nearly two-thirds of marketing managers work in the services and manufacturing industries.

Virtually every business in the United States has some form of advertising and marketing position. Obviously, the larger the company is, the more managerial positions it is likely to have. Another factor is the geographical territory covered by the business. It is safe to say that companies doing business in larger geographical territories are likely to have more managerial positions than those with smaller territories. For instance, computer software and hardware companies, which is an industry with global reach and where brand awareness is very important, tend to employ many people in marketing and promotions.

■ STARTING OUT

You will first need experience in lower-level advertising and marketing jobs before advancing to a managerial position. To break into an advertising or marketing firm, use your college placement office for assistance. In addition, a number of firms advertise job listings in newspapers and Internet job boards.

Your first few jobs in advertising and marketing should give you experience in working with clients, studying the market, and following up on client service. This work will give you a good sense of the rhythm of the job and the type of work required.

■ ADVANCEMENT

Most advertising and marketing management and top executive positions are filled by experienced lower-level workers who have displayed valuable skills, such as leadership, self-confidence, creativity, motivation, decisiveness, and flexibility. In smaller firms, advancement to a management position may come slowly, while promotions may occur more quickly in larger firms.

Advancement may be accelerated by participating in advanced training programs sponsored by industry and trade associations or by enrolling in continued education programs at local universities. These programs are sometimes paid for by the firm. Managers committed to improving their knowledge of the field and of related disciplines—especially computer information systems—will have the best opportunities for advancement.

■ EARNINGS

According to 2002 data from the U.S. Bureau of Labor Statistics, the median annual earnings for advertising managers was $57,130, and the median annual income for marketing managers was $78,250. The lowest 10 percent of advertising managers earned $30,310 or less, while the highest 10 percent earned $125,070 or more; the lowest paid 10 percent of marketing managers earned

Advertising and marketing managers discuss an ad campaign for a client.

$39,730, while the highest 10 percent earned more than $145,600. The median salary for marketing managers was $78,250; the median salary for advertising managers was $57,130.

Salary levels vary substantially, depending upon the level of responsibility, length of service, and type, size, and location of the advertising and marketing firm. Top-level managers in large firms can earn much more than their counterparts in small firms. Also, salaries in large metropolitan areas, such as New York City, are higher than those in smaller cities.

Benefit and compensation packages for managers are usually excellent, and may even include such things as bonuses, stock awards, and company-paid insurance premiums.

■ WORK ENVIRONMENT

Advertising and marketing managers are provided with comfortable offices near the departments they direct. Higher level managers may have spacious, lavish offices and may enjoy such privileges as executive dining rooms, company cars, country club memberships, and liberal expense accounts.

Managers often work long hours under intense pressure to meet advertising and marketing goals. Workweeks consisting of 55–60 hours at the office are not uncommon—in fact, some higher level managers spend up to 80 hours working each week. These long hours limit time available for family and leisure activities.

Advertising and marketing firms are usually highly charged with energy and are both physically and psychologically exciting places to work. Managers work with others as a team in a creative environment where a lot of ideas are exchanged among colleagues. As deadlines are critical in marketing and advertising campaigns, it is important that the manager possesses the ability to handle pressure and stress effectively. Patience and flexibility are also essential, as are organization and time management skills.

■ OUTLOOK

Overall, employment of advertising and marketing managers and executives is expected to grow faster than the average through 2012, according to the U.S. Bureau of Labor Statistics. Many job openings will be the result of managers being promoted to better positions, retiring, or leaving their positions to start their own businesses. Even so, the compensation and prestige of these positions make them highly sought-after, and competition to fill openings will be intense. College graduates with experience, a high level of creativity, and strong communication skills should have the best job opportunities.

The outlook for the advertising and marketing industries is closely tied to the overall economy. When the economy is good, business expands both in terms of the firm's output and the number of people it employs, which creates a need for more managers. In economic downturns, firms often lay off employees and cut back on production, which lessens the need for managers.

■ FOR MORE INFORMATION

The AAF combines the mutual interests of corporate advertisers, agencies, media companies, suppliers, and academia. Visit its website to learn more about internships, scholarships, student chapters, and awards.

American Advertising Federation (AAF)
1101 Vermont Avenue, NW, Suite 500
Washington, DC 20005-6306
Tel: 202-898-0089
Email: aaf@aaf.org
http://www.aaf.org

For industry information, contact
American Association of Advertising Agencies
405 Lexington Avenue, 18th Floor
New York, NY 10174-1801
Tel: 212-682-2500
http://www.aaaa.org

For information on the practice, study, and teaching of marketing, contact
American Marketing Association
311 South Wacker Drive, Suite 5800
Chicago, IL 60606
Tel: 800-AMA-1150
http://www.marketingpower.com

For a brochure on a career in management, contact
National Management Association
2210 Arbor Boulevard
Dayton, OH 45439
Tel: 937-294-0421
Email: nma@nma1.org
http://nma1.org

Advertising Workers

■ OVERVIEW

Advertising is defined as mass communication paid for by an advertiser to persuade a particular segment of the public to adopt ideas or take actions of benefit to the advertiser. *Advertising workers* perform the various creative and business activities needed to take an advertisement from the research stage, to creative concept, through production, and finally to its intended audience. There are 157,000 advertising sales agents and 85,000 advertising and promotions managers employed in the United States.

■ HISTORY

Advertising has been around as long as people have been exchanging goods and services. While a number of innovations spurred the development of advertising, it wasn't until the invention of the printing press in the 15th century that merchants began posting handbills in order to advertise their goods and services. By the 19th century, newspapers became an important means of advertising, followed by magazines in the late 1800s.

One of the problems confronting merchants in the early days of advertising was where to place their ads to generate the most business. In response, a number of people emerged who specialized in the area of advertising, accepting ads and posting them conspicuously. These agents were the first advertising workers. As competition among merchants increased, many of these agents offered to compose ads, as well as post them, for their clients.

Today, with intense competition among both new and existing businesses, advertising has become a necessity in the marketing of goods and services alike. At the same time, the advertising worker's job has grown more demanding and complex than ever. With a wide variety of media from which advertisers can choose—including newspapers, magazines, billboards, radio, television, film and video, the World Wide Web, and a variety of other new technologies—today's advertising worker must not only develop and create ads and campaigns but keep abreast of current and developing buying and technology trends as well.

◼ THE JOB

Approximately seven out of every 10 advertising organizations in the United States are full-service operations, offering their clients a broad range of services, including copywriting, graphics and other art-related work, production, media placement, and tracking and follow-up. These advertising agencies may have hundreds of people working in a dozen different departments, while smaller companies often employ just a handful of employees. Most agencies, however, have at least five departments: contact, research, media, creative, and production.

Contact department personnel are responsible for attracting new customers and maintaining relationships with existing ones. Heading the contact department, *advertising agency managers* are concerned with the overall activities of the company. They formulate plans to generate business, by either soliciting new accounts or getting additional business from established clients. In addition, they meet with department heads to coordinate their operations and to create policies and procedures.

Advertising account executives are the contact department employees responsible for maintaining good relations between their clients and the agency. Acting as liaisons, they represent the agency to its clients and must therefore be able to communicate clearly and effectively. After examining the advertising objectives of their clients, account executives develop campaigns or strategies and then work with others from the various agency departments to target specific audiences, create advertising communications, and execute the campaigns. Presenting concepts, as well as the ad campaign at various stages of completion, to clients for their feedback and approval, account executives must have some knowledge of overall marketing strategies and be able to sell ideas.

Working with account executives, employees in the research department gather, analyze, and interpret the information needed to make a client's advertising campaign successful. By determining who the potential buyers of a product or service will be, *research workers* predict which theme will have the most impact, what kind of packaging and price will have the most appeal, and which media will be the most effective.

Guided by a *research director,* research workers conduct local, regional, and national surveys in order to examine consumer preferences and then determine potential sales for the targeted product or service based on those preferences. Researchers also gather information about competitors' products, prices, sales, and advertising methods. To learn what the buying public prefers in a client's product over a competitor's, research workers often distribute samples and then ask the users of these samples for their opinions of the product. This information can then be used as testimonials about the product or as a means of identifying the most persuasive selling message in an ad.

Although research workers often recommend which media to use for an advertising campaign, *media planners* are the specialists who determine which print or broadcast media will be the most effective. Ultimately, they are responsible for choosing the combination of media that will reach the greatest number of potential buyers for the least amount of money, based on their clients' advertising strategies. Accordingly, planners must be familiar with the markets that each medium reaches, as well as the advantages and disadvantages of advertising in each.

Media buyers, often referred to as *space buyers* (for newspapers and magazines), or *time buyers* (for radio and television), do the actual purchasing of space and time according to a general plan formulated by the *media director.* In addition to ensuring that ads appear when and where they should, buyers negotiate costs for ad placement and maintain contact and extensive correspondence with clients and media representatives alike.

While the contact, research, and media departments handle the business side of a client's advertising campaign, the creative staff takes care of the artistic aspects. *Creative directors*

TECHNOLOGY FOR ADVERTISING

Considering a career in advertising? Becoming familiar with the appropriate software can give you an edge in the job market. Though the programs themselves can be rather expensive to buy on one's own, you can gain experience using them through college courses and adult-education programs.

- **Adobe Photoshop:** Ever wonder how so much of the eye-catching "trick photography" in today's ads is done? The answer is more than likely Adobe's Photoshop, the industry-standard photo-manipulation program. Using it, you can do everything from swapping one model's head to another's body to removing stray hairs from the pictures. More than just changing photos, though, Photo-Shop can also subtly change lighting, add shadows, brighten color, and quickly and easily do everything that you once needed a sophisticated darkroom to accomplish. Finally, Photoshop allows you to save pictures in formats that can be used on the World Wide Web or by other design programs.

- **Adobe Illustrator:** Another program from the Adobe Corporation, Illustrator allows designers to create logos, make background designs, and turn text into art. Illustrator files can easily be exported and used in other programs. Because of its versatility, Illustrator is an important design tool. However, to be most effective, it requires a great deal of expertise.

- **QuarkXPress:** A design and layout program, Quark is used to create everything from books and magazines to single-page ads. Text and pictures can be added and swapped around, so that the ad can be designed for the maximum possible impact. Finally, Quark allows work to be exported in formats that can easily be read and set into print.

oversee the activities of artists and writers and work with clients and account executives to determine the best advertising approaches, gain approval on concepts, and establish budgets and schedules.

Copywriters take the ideas submitted by creative directors and account executives and write descriptive text in the form of headlines, jingles, slogans, and other copy designed to attract the attention of potential buyers. In addition to being able to express themselves clearly and persuasively, copywriters must know what motivates people to buy. They must also be able to describe a product's features in a captivating and appealing way and be familiar with various advertising media. In large agencies, copywriters may be supervised by a *copy chief*.

Copywriters work closely with art directors to make sure that text and artwork create a unified, eye-catching arrangement. Planning the visual presentation of the client's message, from concept formulation to final artwork, the *art director* plays an important role in every stage of the creation of an advertising campaign. Art directors who work on filmed commercials and videos combine film techniques, music, and sound, as well as actors or animation, to communicate an advertiser's message. In publishing, art directors work with graphic designers, photographers, copywriters, and editors to develop brochures, catalogs, direct mail, and other printed pieces, all according to the advertising strategy.

Art directors must have a basic knowledge of graphics and design, computer software, printing, photography, and filmmaking. With the help of graphic artists, they decide where to place text and images, choose typefaces, and create storyboard ads and videos. Several layouts are usually submitted to the client, who chooses one or asks for revisions until a layout or conceptualization sketch meets with final approval. The art director then selects an illustrator, graphic artist, photographer, or TV or video producer, and the project moves on to the production department of the agency.

Production departments in large ad agencies may be divided into print production and broadcast production divisions, each with its own managers and staff. *Production managers* and their assistants convert and reproduce written copy and artwork into printed, filmed, or tape-recorded form so that they can be presented to the public. Production employees work closely with imaging, printing, engraving, and other art reproduction firms and must be familiar with various printing processes, papers, inks, typography, still and motion picture photography, digital imaging, and other processes and materials.

In addition to the principal employees in the five major departments, advertising organizations work with a variety of staff or freelance employees who have specialized knowledge, education, and skill, including photographers, photoengravers, typographers, printers, telemarketers, product and package designers, and producers of display materials. Finally, rounding out most advertising establishments are various support employees, such as production coordinators, video editors, word processors, statisticians, accountants, administrators, secretaries, and clerks.

The work of advertising employees is fast-paced, dynamic, and ever-changing, depending on each client's strategies and budgets and the creative ideas generated by agency workers. In addition to innovative techniques, methods, media, and materials used by agency workers, new and emerging technologies are impacting the work of everyone in the advertising arena, from marketing executives to graphic designers. The Internet is undoubtedly the most revolutionary medium to hit the advertising scene. Through this worldwide, computer-based network, researchers are able to precisely target markets and clearly identify consumer needs. In addition, the Internet's Web pages provide media specialists with a powerful vehicle for advertising their clients' products and services. New technology has also been playing an important role in the creative area. Most art directors, for example, use a variety of computer software programs, and many create and oversee websites for their clients. Other interactive materials and vehicles, such as CD catalogs, touch-screens, multidimensional visuals, and voice-mail shopping, are changing the way today's advertising workers are doing their jobs.

■ REQUIREMENTS
High School

You can prepare for a career as an advertising worker by taking a variety of courses at the high school level. General liberal arts courses, such as English, journalism, communications, economics, psychology, speech, business, social science, and mathematics, are important for aspiring advertising employees. In addition, those interested in the creative side of the field should take such classes as art, drawing, graphic design, illustration, and art history. Finally, since computers play a vital role in the advertising field, you should become familiar with word processing and layout programs, as well as the World Wide Web.

Postsecondary Training

The American Association of Advertising Agencies notes that most agencies employing entry-level personnel prefer college graduates. Copywriters are best prepared with a college degree in English, journalism, or communications; research workers need college training in statistics, market research, and social studies; and most account executives have business or related degrees. Media positions increasingly require a college degree in communications or a technology-related area. Media directors and research directors with a master's degree have a distinct advantage over those with only an undergraduate degree. Some research department heads even have doctorates.

While the requirements from agency to agency may vary somewhat, graduates of liberal arts colleges or those with majors in fields such as communications, journal-

ism, business administration, or marketing research are preferred. Good language skills, as well as a broad liberal arts background, are necessary for advertising workers. College students interested in the field should therefore take such courses as English, writing, art, philosophy, foreign languages, social studies, sociology, psychology, economics, mathematics, statistics, advertising, and marketing. Some 900 degree-granting institutions throughout the United States offer specialized majors in advertising as part of their curriculum.

Other Requirements

In addition to the variety of educational and work experiences necessary for those aspiring to advertising careers, many personal characteristics are also important. Although you will perform many tasks of your job independently as an advertising worker, you will also interact with others as part of a team. In addition to working with other staff members, you may be responsible for initiating and maintaining client contact. You must therefore be able to get along well with people and communicate clearly.

Advertising is not a job that involves routine, and you must be able to meet and adjust to the challenges presented by each new client and product or service. The ability to think clearly and logically is important, because commonsense approaches rather than gimmicks persuade people that something is worth buying. You must also be creative, flexible, and imaginative in order to anticipate consumer demand and trends, to develop effective concepts, and to sell the ideas, products, and services of your clients.

Finally, with technology evolving at breakneck speed, it's vital that you keep pace with technological advances and trends. In addition to being able to work with the most current software and hardware, you should be familiar with the Web, as well as with other technology that is impacting—and will continue to impact—the industry.

■ EXPLORING

If you aspire to a career in the advertising industry, you can gain valuable insight by taking writing and art courses offered either in school or by private organizations. In addition to the theoretical ideas and techniques that such classes provide, you can actually apply what you learn by working full or part time at local department stores or newspaper offices. Some advertising agencies or research firms also employ students to interview people or to conduct other market research. Work as an agency clerk or messenger may also be available. Participating in internships at an advertising or marketing organization is yet another way to explore the field, as well as to determine your aptitude for advertising work. You may find it helpful to read publications dedicated to this industry, such as *Advertising Age* (http://www.adage.com).

EMPLOYERS

Most advertising workers are employed by advertising agencies that plan and prepare advertising material for their clients on a commission or service fee basis. However, some large companies and nearly all department stores prefer to handle their own advertising. Advertising workers in such organizations prepare advertising materials for in-house clients, such as the marketing or catalog department. They also may be involved in the planning, preparation, and production of special promotional materials, such as sales brochures, articles describing the activities of the organization, or websites. Some advertising workers are employed by owners of various media, including newspapers, magazines, radio and television networks, and outdoor advertising. Workers employed in these media are mainly sales representatives who sell advertising space or broadcast time to advertising agencies or companies that maintain their own advertising departments.

In addition to agencies, large companies, and department stores, advertising services and supply houses employ such advertising specialists as photographers, photoengravers, typographers, printers, product and package designers, display producers, and others who assist in the production of various advertising materials.

According to the American Association of Advertising Agencies, there are more than 13,000 advertising agencies in the United States. Most of the large firms are located in Chicago, Los Angeles, and New York. Employment opportunities are also available, however, at a variety of "small shops," four out of five of which employ fewer than 10 workers each. In addition, a growing number of self-employment and home-based business opportunities are resulting in a variety of industry jobs located in outlying areas rather than in big cities.

STARTING OUT

Although competition for advertising jobs is fierce and getting your foot in the door can be difficult, there are a variety of ways to launch a career in the field. Some large advertising agencies recruit college graduates and place them in training programs designed to acquaint beginners with all aspects of advertising work, but these opportunities are limited and highly competitive.

Instead, many graduates simply send resumes to businesses that employ entry-level advertising workers. Newspapers, radio and television stations, printers, photographers, and advertising agencies are but a few of the businesses that will hire beginners. The *Standard Directory of Advertising Agencies* (New Providence, N.J.: National Register Publishing Company, 2003) lists the names and addresses of ad agencies all across the nation. You can find the directory in almost any public library.

Those who have had work experience in sales positions often enter the advertising field as account executives. High school graduates and other people without experience who want to work in advertising, however, may find it necessary to begin as clerks or assistants to research and production staff members or to copywriters.

ADVANCEMENT

The career path in an advertising agency generally leads from trainee to skilled worker to division head and then to department head. It may also take employees from department to department, allowing them to gain more responsibility with each move. Opportunities abound for those with talent, leadership capability, and ambition.

Management positions require experience in all aspects of advertising, including agency work, communication with advertisers, and knowledge of various advertising media. Copywriters, account executives, and other advertising agency workers who demonstrate outstanding ability to deal with clients and supervise co-workers usually have a good chance of advancing to management positions. Other workers, however, prefer to acquire specialized skills. For them, advancement may mean more responsibility, the opportunity to perform more specialized tasks, and increased pay.

Advertising workers at various department stores, mail order houses, and other large firms that have their own advertising departments can also earn promotions. Advancement in any phase of advertising work is usually dependent on the employee's experience, training, and demonstrated skills.

Some qualified copywriters, artists, and account executives establish their own agencies or become marketing consultants. For these entrepreneurs, advancement may take the form of an increasing number of accounts and/or more prestigious clients.

EARNINGS

Salaries of advertising workers vary depending on the type of work, the size of the agency, its geographic location, the kind of accounts handled, and the agency's gross earnings. Salaries are also determined by a worker's education, aptitude, and experience. The wide range of jobs in advertising makes it difficult to estimate average salaries for all positions.

According to a survey by the National Association of Colleges and Employers, marketing majors entering the job market in 2001 had average starting salaries of $35,000, while advertising majors averaged $29,700.

According to a 2002 salary survey by *Advertising Age*, creative directors at mid-sized advertising agencies (grossing $7.6 to $15 million) earned an average of $124,000 annually. Copywriters at these agencies earned $54,000, account executives earned $47,000, and media directors made $82,000 per year. CEOs at large agencies made more than $270,000 annually, while CEOs at smaller agencies reported yearly earnings of $123,000.

The U.S. Department of Labor's *Occupational Outlook Handbook* reports that the median annual earnings for advertising and promotions managers in 2002 were $57,130. For marketing managers the median was $78,250, sales managers earned $75,040, and public relations managers made $60,640 per year. The lowest paid 10 percent of advertising and promotions managers made less than $30,310, while the highest paid marketing and sales managers earned more than $145,600. The *2002 National Occupational Employment and Wage Estimates,* also published by the Department of Labor, reported that advertising sales agents earned an average of $37,670 per year; the lowest-paid earned less than $19,430 per year and the highest-paid earned more than $87,560 annually.

In advertising agencies, an executive vice president can earn from $113,000 to $500,000 a year or more. Account executives earned a median of $57,188, while senior account executives earned a median of $73,329. In the research and media departments, media directors earn a median of $102,455, and media planners and buyers between $40,000 and $45,000 per year. In the creative department, art directors earn a median of $60,000 or more annually. Salaries for relatively glamorous jobs at agencies can be low, due to high competition. In advertising departments at other businesses and industries, individual earnings vary widely. Salaries of advertising workers are generally higher, however, at consumer product firms than at industrial product organizations because of the competition among consumer product producers. The majority of companies offer insurance benefits, a retirement plan, and other incentives and bonuses.

■ WORK ENVIRONMENT

Conditions at most agencies are similar to those found in other offices throughout the country, except that employees must frequently work under great pressure to meet deadlines. While a traditional 40-hour workweek is the norm at some companies, almost half (44 percent) of advertising, marketing, promotions, public relations, and sales managers report that they work more hours per week, including evenings and weekends. Bonuses and time off during slow periods are sometimes provided as a means of compensation for unusual workloads and hours.

Although some advertising employees, such as researchers, work independently on a great many tasks, most must function as part of a team. With frequent meetings with coworkers, clients, and media representatives alike, the work environment is usually energized, with ideas being exchanged, contracts being negotiated, and schedules being modified.

Advertising work is fast-paced and exciting. As a result, many employees often feel stressed out as they are constantly challenged to take initiative and be creative. Nevertheless, advertising workers enjoy both professional and personal satisfaction in seeing the culmination of their work communicated to sometimes millions of people.

■ OUTLOOK

Employment opportunities in the advertising field are expected to increase about as fast as the average for all industries through 2012. Demand for advertising workers will grow as a result of increased production of goods and services, both in the United States and abroad. Network and cable television, radio, newspapers, the Web, and certain other media (particularly interactive vehicles) will offer advertising workers an increasing number of employment opportunities. Some media, such as magazines, direct mail, and event marketing, are expected to provide fewer job opportunities.

Advertising agencies will enjoy faster than average employment growth, as will industries that service ad agencies and other businesses in the advertising field, such as those that offer commercial photography, imaging, art, and graphics services.

At the two extremes, enormous "mega-agencies" and small shops employing up to only 10 workers each offer employment opportunities for people with experience, talent, flexibility, and drive. In addition, self-employment and home-based businesses are on the rise. Many nonindustrial companies, such as banks, schools, and hospitals, will also be creating advertising positions.

In general, openings will become available to replace workers who change positions, retire, or leave the field for other reasons. Competition for these jobs will be keen, however, because of the large number of qualified professionals in this traditionally desirable field. Opportunities will be best for the well-qualified and well-trained applicant. Employers favor college graduates with experience, a high level of creativity, and strong communications skills. People who are not well qualified or prepared for agency work will find the advertising field increasingly difficult to enter. The same is also true for those who seek work in companies that service ad agencies.

■ FOR MORE INFORMATION

For information on student chapters, scholarships, and internships, contact

American Advertising Federation
1101 Vermont Avenue, NW, Suite 500
Washington, DC 20005-6306
Tel: 202-898-0089
Email: aaf@aaf.org
http://www.aaf.org

For industry information, contact

American Association of Advertising Agencies
405 Lexington, 18th Floor
New York, NY 10174-1801
Tel: 212-682-2500
http://www.aaaa.org

For career and salary information, contact

American Marketing Association
311 South Wacker Drive, Suite 5800
Chicago, IL 60606
Tel: 800-AMA-1150
Email: info@ama.org
http://www.marketingpower.com

The Art Directors Club is an international, nonprofit organization for creatives in advertising, graphic design, interactive media, broadcast design, typography, packaging, environmental design, photography, illustration, and related disciplines.

Art Directors Club
106 West 29th Street
New York, NY 10001
Tel: 212-643-1440
Email: info@adcny.org
http://www.adcglobal.org

For information on student membership and careers, contact

Direct Marketing Educational Foundation
1120 Avenue of the Americas
New York, NY 10036-6700
Tel: 212-768-7277
http://www.the-dma.org

The Graphic Artists Guild promotes and protects the economic interests of the artist/designer and is committed to improving conditions for all creators of graphic art and raising standards for the entire industry.

Graphic Artists Guild
90 John Street, Suite 403
New York, NY 10038-3202

Tel: 212-791-3400
http://www.gag.org

Aerobics Instructors and Fitness Trainers

■ OVERVIEW

Aerobics instructors choreograph and teach aerobics classes of varying types. Classes are geared toward people with general good health as well as to specialized populations, including the elderly and those with specific health problems that affect their ability to exercise. Many people enjoy participating in the lively exercise routines set to music.

Depending on where they are employed, *fitness trainers* help devise health conditioning programs for clients, from professional athletes to average individuals looking for guidance. Fitness trainers motivate clients to follow prescribed exercise programs and monitor their progress. When injuries occur, either during training or sporting events, fitness trainers determine the extent of the injury and administer first aid for minor problems such as blisters, bruises, and scrapes. Following more serious injury, trainers may work with a physical therapist to help the athlete perform rehabilitative exercises.

There are approximately 185,000 aerobics instructors and fitness trainers employed in the United States.

■ HISTORY

Only recently has physical fitness become an organized industry. For many years, only professional athletes were trained by fitness trainers. However, as more people began to use exercise and weight training equipment, knowledgeable instructors were needed to teach beginners how to safely and effectively use the machines. Today, instructors' services usually are available to anyone who joins a health club.

Aerobics has also become much more widely respected by health professionals than when it first became popular in the late 1970s and early 1980s, mainly because the importance of aerobic activity is now universally recognized. In addition, aerobics itself has diversified to include many options and levels of difficulty. Although the element of dance is still evident in some aerobic moves, it has been de-emphasized in many classes, primarily to encourage those who are less coordinated to participate. Instead of focusing on coordinated dance steps or complicated routines that are difficult to memorize, aerobic workouts now are more focused on a series of movements that aim to elevate the heart rate and work various muscle groups. For example, a particular class may seek to shape and tone specific muscle groups, such as the abdominals or hamstrings. This past decade has seen the introduction of several new branches of aerobics, including water aerobics, step aerobics, interval training, and interval circuit training.

Water aerobics is a popular form of low-impact aerobics. Impact refers to the stress placed on joints and bones during exercise. Because the water supports the body and creates resistance, it is an ideal exercise medium. Provided participants wear the proper safety equipment and are in the presence of others, they don't necessarily need to know how to swim, because in most classes, all the movements are done standing upright or holding onto the side of the pool. Water aerobics is especially well suited to older individuals because the water can be therapeutic for aching joints and muscles.

Another popular fitness class is step aerobics. In 1986, an aerobics instructor and body builder named Gin Miller developed a formal step training program after using the technique to recover from a knee injury. Basically, step aerobics involves the use of a specially designed stool or bench that sits from four to 12 inches off the ground. Participants step up and down in different patterns, which provides an excellent cardiovascular workout.

Another exercise trend is called interval training. In the late 1980s, Arlette Perry, an exercise physiologist with the University of Miami's Human Performance Laboratory, determined that alternating intense exercise movements with slower-paced movements was better for aerobic fitness than a steady level of exercise, because it achieves higher heart rates. Interval classes today incorporate many different types of exercise to raise and maintain participants' heart rates, for example, blending high-impact aerobic moves with lower intensity exercises, such as marching in place or stretching.

Today, aerobics classes are often used in cross training, where amateur and professional athletes combine several different fitness activities to train for a certain sport. A popular workout is circuit training or interval circuit training, which combines aerobic exercise with weight lifting for a full body workout. In circuit training, the workout equipment is arranged to work one group of muscles at a time, alternating so that one set of muscles can rest while the next group is worked. As the athlete moves through each piece of equipment in the circuit, the heart rate remains elevated, without the participants tiring as quickly as they would if repeating the same exercise.

New trends in fitness include aerobics classes for the whole family, as well as the increased use of personal fitness trainers. In fact, the demand for qualified personal trainers has become so great that many organizations offer personal training certifications. Fitness trainer Brett Vicknair agrees: "Personal fitness training has become a fast-growing industry over the last five years and doesn't seem to be slowing down. One reason is that personal fitness trainers are not just for the rich and famous anymore."

As people have become more health conscious, they see a need for daily fitness activities. "People hire us for a number of reasons, such as motivation, knowledge, accountability, weight management, sports conditioning, special medical needs, and lifestyle management," Vicknair adds.

■ THE JOB

Three general levels of aerobics classes are recognized today: low impact, moderate, and high intensity. A typical class starts with warm-up exercises (slow stretching movements to loosen up muscles), followed by 35–40 minutes of nonstop activity to raise the heart rate, then ends with a cool-down period of stretching and slower movements. Instructors teach class members to monitor their heart rates and listen to their bodies for signs of personal progress.

Aerobics instructors prepare activities prior to their classes. They choose exercises to work different muscles and accompany these movements to music during each phase of the program. Generally, instructors use upbeat music for the more intense exercise portion and more soothing music for the cool-down period. Instructors demonstrate each step of a sequence until the class can follow along. Additional sequences are added continuously as the class progresses, making up a longer routine that is set to music. Most classes are structured so that new participants can start any given class. The instructor either faces the

QUICK FACTS

SCHOOL SUBJECTS
Health
Physical education
Theater/dance

PERSONAL SKILLS
Helping/teaching
Leadership/management

WORK ENVIRONMENT
Primarily indoors
Primarily one location

MINIMUM EDUCATION LEVEL
High school diploma

SALARY RANGE
$14,090 to $23,950 to
$54,540+

CERTIFICATION OR LICENSING
Required for certain positions

OUTLOOK
Faster than the average

DOT
153

GOE
01.10.01

NOC
5254

O*NET-SOC
39-9031.00

An aerobics instructor (far left) leads a class.

rest of the room or faces a mirror in order to observe class progress and ensure that participants do exercises correctly. Many aerobics instructors also lead toning and shaping classes. In these classes, the emphasis is not on aerobic activity but on working particular areas of the body. An instructor begins the class with a brief aerobic period followed by stretching and weight-bearing exercises that loosen and work major muscle groups.

In a health club, fitness trainers evaluate their clients' fitness level with physical examinations and fitness tests. Using various pieces of testing equipment, they determine such things as percentage of body fat and optimal heart and pulse rates. Clients fill out questionnaires about their medical background, general fitness level, and fitness goals. Fitness trainers use this information to design a customized workout plan using weights and other exercise options such as swimming and running to help clients meet these goals. Trainers also advise clients on weight control, diet, and general health. Some fitness trainers also work at the client's home or office. This convenient way of staying physically fit meets the needs of many busy, active adults today. Brett Vicknair owns an in-home personal training company that specializes in one-on-one personal training with their clients at home or the office.

To start a client's exercise program, the trainer often demonstrates the proper use of weight lifting equipment to reduce the chance of injury, especially if the client is a beginner. As the client uses the equipment, the trainer observes and corrects any problems before injury occurs. Preventing injury is extremely important, according to American Council Exercise Certified Personal Trainer (CPT) Nicole Gutter. "It is a good idea to carry your own

liability insurance. The bottom line is, know what you're doing because there is a huge risk of injury or even death for high-risk people," she says. "You should be insured in case anything beyond your control does happen."

Fitness trainers also use exercise tape to wrap weak or injured hands, feet, or other parts of the body. The heavy duty tape helps strengthen and position the joint to prevent further injury or strain. Fitness trainers also help athletes with therapy or rehabilitation, using special braces or other equipment to support or protect the injured part until it heals. Trainers ensure that the athlete does not overuse a weak joint or muscle, risking further damage.

■ REQUIREMENTS
High School

Aerobics instructors and fitness trainers should hold a high school diploma. If you are interested in a fitness career, take courses in physical education, biology, and anatomy. In addition, be involved in sports, weight lifting, or dance activities to stay fit and learn to appreciate the value of exercise.

Postsecondary Training

Although it isn't always necessary, a college degree will make you more marketable in the fitness field. Typically, aerobics instructors do not need a college education to qualify for jobs; however, some employers may be more interested in candidates with a balance of ability and education.

Fitness trainers are usually required to have a bachelor's degree from an accredited athletic training program or a related program in physical education or health. These programs often require extensive internships that can range from 500 to 1,800 hours of hands-on experience. Essential college-level courses include anatomy, biomechanics, chemistry, first aid, health, kinesiology, nutrition, physics, physiology, psychology, and safety.

Tony Hinsberger, owner of Summit Fitness Personal Training, highly recommends getting a college degree in physiology, kinesiology, exercise science, or athletic training. "As an owner of a small personal training firm, I hire trainers," he says. "If I had to make a choice between equally experienced and qualified candidates, I would pick the one with a degree."

Certification or Licensing

Most serious fitness trainers and aerobics instructors become certified. Certification is not required in most states, but most clients and fitness companies expect these professionals to have credentials to prove their worth.

As a current employer of fitness professionals, Hinsberger recommends certification. "I only hire certified trainers," he says. "Most facilities require certification and there are many, many certifying agencies. Certification is also required by most liability insurance plans."

Certifying agencies include the following: Aerobics and Fitness Association of America, American College of Sports Medicine, American Council on Exercise, and National Academy of Sports Medicine. Aerobics instructors should also be certified in cardiopulmonary resuscitation (CPR) before finding a job.

The National Athletic Trainers' Association and the American Athletic Trainers Association certify fitness trainers who have graduated from accredited college programs or have completed the necessary internship following a degree in a related field. Fitness trainers who seek certification generally also need Red Cross certification in CPR or as an emergency medical technician (EMT).

Whichever career path they follow, aerobics instructors and fitness trainers are expected to keep up to date with their fields, becoming thoroughly familiar with the latest knowledge and safety practices. They must take continuing education courses and participate in seminars to keep their certification current.

Other Requirements

Aerobics instructors and fitness trainers are expected to be physically fit, but are not expected to be specimens of human perfection. For example, members of an aerobics class geared to overweight people might feel more comfortable with a heavier instructor; a class geared towards the elderly may benefit from an older instructor.

■ EXPLORING

A visit to a health club, park district, or YMCA aerobics class is a good way to observe the work of fitness trainers and aerobics instructors. Part-time or summer jobs are sometimes available for high school students in these facilities. It may also be possible to volunteer in a senior citizen center where aerobics classes are offered.

"To explore this [career] path, I recommend working part-time in a gym or fitness facility," Tony Hinsberger suggests. "Some clubs have an orientation position. People in this job take new members on a tour of the facility and show new members how to use the equipment safely. It typically doesn't require a degree, only on-site training."

If possible, enroll in an aerobics class or train with a fitness trainer to experience firsthand what their jobs entail and to see what makes a good instructor. Brett Vicknair agrees: "I would encourage someone wanting to pursue a career as a personal trainer to get involved with working out first, maybe at a local fitness center, and take advantage of any help that is usually offered when someone first becomes a member."

Aerobics instructor workshops are taught to help prospective instructors gain experience. These are usually offered in adult education courses at such places as the YMCA. Unpaid apprenticeships are also a good way for future instructors to obtain supervised experience before teaching classes on their own. The facility may allow prospective aerobics instructors to take their training class for free if there is a possibility that they will work there in the future.

Opportunities for student fitness trainers are available in schools with fitness trainers on staff. This is an excellent way for students to observe and assist a professional fitness trainer on an ongoing basis.

■ EMPLOYERS

Most aerobics instructors work for fitness centers and gymnasiums. Most employers are for-profit businesses, but some are community-based, such as the YMCA or a family center. Other job possibilities can be found in corporate fitness centers, colleges, retirement centers, and resorts.

Some fitness trainers work in more than one facility. Others are self-employed and take clients on an appointment basis, working either in personal homes or in a public gym. Some fitness trainers will work with high-profile athletes on a one-on-one basis to meet specific fitness requirements.

"Trainers work in gyms or fitness centers, in private personal fitness centers where members are seen on an appointment basis only, and in country clubs, just to name some of the opportunities," Brett Vicknair says.

CLINICAL EXERCISE SPECIALISTS

One of the newest careers in the fitness field is that of clinical exercise specialist (CES). CESs do many of the same tasks as regular fitness trainers, but it's their specific clientele that make them specialized. They work exclusively with people who have had an injury or illness and have been given a physician's release to return to physical activity. The CES focuses on getting clients back to their normal quality of life through the resumption of physical exercise. With the popularity of exercise in our country today—and high rate of injury—CESs will be in high demand.

Most medium to large cities have one or more gyms or fitness centers; however, smaller towns may not have any such facilities. However, there may be limited openings at retirement homes, schools, and community centers in these small towns.

STARTING OUT

Students should use their schools' placement offices for information on available jobs. Often, facilities that provide training or internships will hire or provide job leads to individuals who have completed programs. Students can also find jobs through classified ads and by applying to health and fitness clubs, YMCAs, YWCAs, Jewish community centers, local schools, park districts, church groups, and other fitness organizations. Because exercise is understood to be a preventive measure for many health and medical problems, insurance companies often reward businesses that offer fitness facilities to their employees with lower insurance rates. As a result, students should consider nearby companies for prospective fitness instructor and trainer positions.

ADVANCEMENT

Experienced aerobics instructors can become instructor trainers, providing tips and insight on how to lead a class and what routines work well.

A bachelor's degree in either sports physiology or exercise physiology is especially beneficial for those who want to advance to the position of health club director or to teach corporate wellness programs.

Fitness trainers working at schools can advance from assistant positions to head athletic director, which may involve relocating to another school. Fitness trainers can advance to instruct new fitness trainers in college. They also can work in sports medicine facilities, usually in rehabilitation work. In health clubs, fitness trainers can advance to become health club directors or work in administration. Often, fitness trainers who build up a reputation and a clientele go into business for themselves as personal trainers.

EARNINGS

Aerobics instructors are usually paid by the class and generally start out at about $10 per class. Experienced aerobics instructors can earn up to $50 or $60 per class. The U.S. Department of Labor reports that aerobics instructors and fitness trainers earned median hourly earnings of $11.51 in 2002. A majority of these workers earned between $7.09 and $11.36. The top 10 percent of instructors and trainers earned $15.72 or more an hour.

Although a sports season lasts only about six months, athletes train year-round to remain in shape and require

trainers to guide them. Many personal trainers are paid on a client-by-client basis. Contracts are drawn up and the payment is agreed upon before the training starts. Some trainers get paid more or less depending on the results.

A compensation survey by health and fitness organization IDEA reports that many employers offer health insurance and paid sick and vacation time to full-time employees. They also may provide discounts on products sold in the club (such as shoes, clothes, and equipment) and free memberships to use the facility.

WORK ENVIRONMENT

Most weight training and aerobics classes are held indoors. Depending on the popularity of the class and/or instructor, aerobics classes can get crowded and hectic at times. Instructors need to keep a level head and keep a positive, outgoing personality in order to motivate people and keep them together. It is important that aerobics instructors make the class enjoyable yet challenging so that members will return class after class. They also need to be unaffected by complaints of class members, some of whom may find the routines too hard, too easy, or who may not like the music selections. Instructors need to realize that these complaints are not personal attacks.

Fitness trainers need to be able to work on a one-on-one basis with amateur and professional athletes and nonathletes. They may work with individuals who are in pain after an injury and must be able to coax them to use muscles they would probably rather not. Trainers must possess patience, especially for beginners or those who are not athletically inclined, and offer encouragement to help them along.

Most trainers find it rewarding to help others achieve fitness goals. "To truly be a great personal fitness trainer, first you must enjoy helping and being around people. I love being able to motivate and give my clients the knowledge to help them meet their fitness goals," Brett Vicknair says.

OUTLOOK

Because of the country's ever-expanding interest in health and fitness, the U.S. Department of Labor predicts that the job outlook for aerobics instructors should remain strong through 2012. As the population ages, more opportunities will arise to work with the elderly in retirement homes. Large companies and corporations are also interested in keeping insurance costs down by hiring aerobics instructors to hold classes for their employees. America's often touted "weight problem" will also have an effect on the popularity and demand for aerobics instructors. As communities, schools, and individuals attempt to shed the pounds, the need for fitness instructors and motivators will continue.

Fitness trainers are also in strong demand, especially at the high school level. Currently, some states require high schools to have a fitness trainer on staff. According to Brett Vicknair, home fitness trainers will remain in high demand. The convenience of being able to work out with a personal trainer before work, at lunch, early Saturday morning, or late Friday night make the use of a personal trainer a flexible option. With the hectic lifestyle of most people today, that aspect alone should keep personal training positions on the rise.

■ FOR MORE INFORMATION

For information on various certifications, contact the following organizations:

Aerobics and Fitness Association of America
15250 Ventura Boulevard, Suite 200
Sherman Oaks, CA 91403
Tel: 877-968-7263
Email: contactAFAA@afaa.com
http://www.afaa.com

National Athletic Trainers' Association
2952 Stemmons Freeway, Suite 200
Dallas, TX 75247-6916
Tel: 800-879-6282
http://www.nata.org

For free information and materials about sports medicine topics, contact
American College of Sports Medicine
PO Box 1440
Indianapolis, IN 46206-1440
Tel: 317-637-9200
http://www.acsm.org

For more information about certification and careers in fitness, contact ACE.
American Council on Exercise (ACE)
4851 Paramount Drive
San Diego, CA 92123
Tel: 800-825-3636
http://www.acefitness.org

For fitness facts and articles, visit IDEA's website.
IDEA: The Health and Fitness Association
6190 Cornerstone Court East, #204
San Diego, CA 92121-3773
Tel: 800-999-4332
Email: nonmemberquestions@ideafit.com
http://www.ideafit.com

Aeronautical and Aerospace Technicians

■ OVERVIEW

Aeronautical and aerospace technicians design, construct, test, operate, and maintain the basic structures of aircraft and spacecraft, as well as propulsion and control systems. They work with scientists and engineers. Many aeronautical and aerospace technicians assist engineers in preparing equipment drawings, diagrams, blueprints, and scale models. They collect information, make computations, and perform laboratory tests. Their work may include working on various projects involving aerodynamics, structural design, flight-test evaluation, or propulsion problems. Other technicians estimate the cost of materials and labor required to manufacture the product, serve as manufacturers' field service technicians, and write technical materials.

■ HISTORY

Both aeronautical engineering and the aerospace industry had their births in the early 20th century. The very earliest machine-powered and heavier-than-air aircraft, such as the first one flown by Wilbur and Orville Wright in 1903, were crudely constructed and often the result of costly and dangerous trial-and-error experimentation.

As government and industry took an interest in the possible applications of this new invention, however, our knowledge of aircraft and the entire industry became more sophisticated. By 1908, for instance, the Wright brothers had received their first government military contract, and by 1909, the industry had expanded to include additional airplane producers, such as Glenn Curtiss in the United States and several others in France.

Aeronautical engineering and the aerospace industry have been radically transformed since those early days, mostly because of the demands of two world wars and the tremendous increases in scientific knowledge that have taken place during this century. Aviation and aerospace developments continued after the end of World War II. The factories and workers that built planes to support the war were in place and the industry took off, with the jet engine, rocket propulsion, supersonic flight, and manned voyages outside the earth's atmosphere among the major developments. As the industry evolved, aeronautical and aerospace engineers found themselves taking on increasingly larger projects and were more in need of trained and knowledgeable assistants to help them. Throughout the years, these assistants have been known as engineering aides, as engineering associates, and, most recently, as aerospace technicians and technologists. Their main task today is to take on assignments that require technical skills but do not necessarily require the scientist's or engineer's special training and education.

■ THE JOB

There are no clear-cut definitions of "aeronautical technology" and "aerospace technology"; in fact, many employers use the terms interchangeably. This lack of a clear distinction also occurs in education, where many schools and institutes offer similar courses under a variety of titles: aeronautical, aviation, or aerospace technology. In general, however, the term "aerospace industry" refers to manufacturers of all kinds of flying vehicles: from piston and jet-powered aircraft that fly inside the earth's atmosphere, to rockets, missiles, satellites, probes, and all kinds of manned and unmanned spacecraft that operate outside the earth's atmosphere. The term "aeronautics" is often used within the aerospace industry to refer specifically to mechanical flight inside the earth's atmosphere, especially to the design and manufacture of commercial passenger and freight aircraft, private planes, and helicopters.

The difference between technicians and technologists generally refers to their level of education. Technicians generally hold associate's degrees, while technologists hold bachelor's degrees in aeronautical technology.

Whether they work for a private company working on commercial aircraft or for the federal government, aerospace technicians work side by side with engineers and scientists in all major phases of the design, production, and operation of aircraft and spacecraft technology. The aerospace technician position includes collecting and recording data; operating test equipment such as wind tunnels and flight simulators; devising tests to ensure qual-

ity control; modifying mathematical procedures to fit specific problems; laying out experimental circuits to test scientific theories; and evaluating experimental data for practical applications.

The following paragraphs describe jobs held by aerospace technicians; some may be used in other industries as well. Fuller descriptions of the work of some of these titles are provided in separate entries.

Aerospace physiological technicians operate devices used to train pilots and astronauts. These devices include pressure suits, pressure chambers, and ejection seats that simulate flying conditions. These technicians also operate other kinds of flight training equipment such as tow reels, radio equipment, and meteorological devices. They interview trainees about their medical histories, which helps detect evidence of conditions that would disqualify pilots or astronauts from further training.

Aircraft launch and recovery technicians work on aircraft carriers to operate, adjust, and repair launching and recovery equipment such as catapults, barricades, and arresting nets. They disassemble the launch and recovery equipment, replace defective parts, and keep track of all maintenance activities.

Avionics technicians repair, test, install, and maintain radar and radio equipment aboard aircraft and spacecraft.

Computer technicians assist mathematicians and subject specialists in checking and refining computations and systems, such as those required for predicting and determining orbits of spacecraft.

Drafting and design technicians convert the aeronautical engineer's specifications and rough sketches of aeronautical and aerospace equipment, such as electrical and mechanical devices, into accurate drawings that are used by skilled craft workers to make parts for aircraft and spacecraft.

Electronics technicians assist engineers in the design, development, and modification of electronic and electromechanical systems. They assist in the calibration and operation of radar and photographic equipment and also operate, install, troubleshoot, and repair electronic testing equipment.

Engineering technicians assist with review and analysis of postflight data, structural failure, and other factors that cause failure in flight vehicles.

Industrial engineering technicians assist engineers in preparing layouts of machinery and equipment, workflow plans, time-and-motion studies, and statistical studies and analyses of production costs to produce the most efficient use of personnel, materials, and machines.

Instrumentation technicians test, install, and maintain electronic, hydraulic, pneumatic, and optical instruments. These are used in aircraft systems and components in

QUICK FACTS

SCHOOL SUBJECTS
Mathematics
Physics
Technical/shop

PERSONAL SKILLS
Mechanical/manipulative
Technical/scientific

WORK ENVIRONMENT
Primarily indoors
Primarily one location

MINIMUM EDUCATION LEVEL
Associate's degree

SALARY RANGE
$27,370 to $51,650 to
$60,150

CERTIFICATION OR LICENSING
Recommended

OUTLOOK
About as fast as the average

DOT
002

GOE
02.08.04

NOC
N/A

O*NET-SOC
17-3021.00, 49-2091.00,
49-3011.00

manufacturing as well as research and development. One important responsibility is to maintain their assigned research instruments. As a part of this maintenance, they test the instruments, take readings and calibration curves, and calculate correction factors for the instruments.

Liaison technicians check on the production of aircraft and spacecraft as they are being built for conformance to specifications, keeping engineers informed as the manufacturing progresses, and they investigate any engineering production problems that arise.

Mathematical technicians assist mathematicians, engineers, and scientists by performing computations involving the use of advanced mathematics.

Mechanical technicians use metalworking machines to assist in the manufacture of one-of-a-kind parts. They also assist in rocket-fin alignment, payload mating, weight and center-of-gravity measurements, and launch-tower erection.

Target aircraft technicians repair and maintain pilotless target aircraft. They assemble, repair, or replace aircraft parts such as cowlings, wings, and propeller assemblies and test aircraft engine operation.

■ REQUIREMENTS
High School

A strong science and mathematics background is essential for entry into this field. High school courses that will be useful in preparing a student for college-level study include algebra, trigonometry, physics, and chemistry. In addition to math and science, courses in social studies, economics, history, blueprint reading, drafting, and industrial and machine shop practice will provide a valuable background for a career in aerospace technology. Computer experience is also important. English, speech, and courses in the preparation of test reports and technical writing are extremely helpful to develop communication ability.

Postsecondary Training

There are a variety of training possibilities for potential aerospace technicians: two-, three-, or four-year programs at colleges or universities, junior or community colleges, technical institutes, vocational-technical schools, industry on-the-job training, or work-study programs in the military. Graduates from a two- or three-year program usually earn an associate's degree in engineering or science. Graduates from a four-year program earn a bachelor's degree in engineering or science; in addition, several colleges offer four-year degree programs in aeronautical technology. There are also many technical training schools, particularly in areas where the aerospace industry is most active, that offer training in aeronautical technology. Aircraft mechanics, for instance, usually attend one of the

NOISE REDUCTION

In addition to learning new technology that will make the aircraft they work on safer, aerospace technicians face a different technological challenge in the coming years—quieter aircraft. Airlines are facing increasing regulatory constraints regarding the noise they make. Airports operate with strict noise budgets and curfews. Aerospace companies that can come up with the new designs and methods of reducing noise will have the upper hand in the competitive aerospace industry.

There are many sources of noise from current aircraft; among the sources the National Aeronautics and Space Administration is attempting to reduce are turbofan noise, jet exhaust noise, and fan noise. The turbofan is a part of the engine that sucks air into the front of the engine and pushes the same air out the back of the engine at a higher velocity. This provides thrust for the plane. Jet exhaust noise occurs when two different air flows (the fan stream and the core/combustion stream) mix with each other and create noise in the surrounding air. This noise is created after the exhaust leaves the engine. Reducing noise in the third area, fan noise, will be achieved by exploring concepts of basic geometry by making blades in different shapes and exploring fan speed, number of blades, and how air moves around the blades. Aerospace technicians will be involved in the actual testing of theories developed by engineers.

country's roughly 200 training schools. However, many employers require graduates of such programs to complete a period of on-the-job training before they are granted full technician status. When selecting a school to attend, check the listings of such agencies as the Accreditation Board for Engineering and Technology and the regional accrediting associations for engineering colleges. Most employers prefer graduates of an accredited school.

In general, post-high school programs strengthen the student's background in science and mathematics, including pretechnical training. Beyond that, an interdisciplinary curriculum is more helpful than one that specializes in a narrow field. Other courses, which are basic to the work of the aeronautical scientist and engineer, should be part of a balanced program. These include basic physics, nuclear theory, chemistry, mechanics, and computers, including data-processing equipment and procedures.

Certification or Licensing

Only a few aerospace technician positions require licensing or certification; however, certificates issued by professional organizations do enhance the status of qualified engineering technicians. Certification is usually required of those working with nuclear-powered engines or testing radioactive sources, for those working on aircraft in some test programs, and in some safety-related positions. Technicians and technologists working in areas related to national defense, and especially those employed by government agencies, are usually required to carry security clearances.

Other Requirements

Aeronautical and aerospace technicians must be able to learn basic engineering skills. They should enjoy and be proficient in mathematics and the physical sciences, able to visualize size, form, and function. The Aerospace Industries Association of America advises that today's aerospace production worker must be strong in the basics of manufacturing, have a knowledge of statistics and have the ability to work with computers.

■ EXPLORING

Visiting an aerospace research or manufacturing facility is one of the best ways to learn more about this field. Because there are so many such facilities connected with the aerospace industry throughout the United States, there is sure to be one in nearly every area. The reference department of a local library can help students locate the nearest facility.

Finding part-time or summer employment at such a facility is, of course, one of the best ways to gain experience or learn more about the field. Such jobs aren't available for all students interested in the field, but you can still find part-time work that will give you practical experience, such as in a local machine shop or factory.

Students should not overlook the educational benefits of visiting local museums of science and technology or aircraft museums or displays. The National Air and Space Museum at the Smithsonian Institution in Washington, D.C., is one of the most comprehensive museums dedicated to aerospace. Some Air Force bases or naval air stations also offer tours to groups of interested students. The tours may be arranged by teachers or career guidance counselors.

The Junior Engineering Technical Society (JETS) provides students a chance to explore career opportunities in engineering and technology, enter academic competitions, and design model structures. JETS administers a competition that allows students to use their technology skills. The Tests of Engineering, Aptitude, Mathematics, and Science is an open-book, open-discussion engineering problem competition. If your school doesn't have a JETS chapter, check with other schools in your area; sometimes smaller schools can form cooperatives to offer such programs.

■ EMPLOYERS

Aeronautical and aerospace technicians and technologists are principally employed by government agencies, commercial airlines, educational institutions, and aerospace manufacturing companies. Most technicians employed by manufacturing companies engage in research, development, and design; the remainder work in production, sales, engineering, installation and maintenance, and other related fields. Those employed by government and educational institutions are normally assigned to do research and specific problem-solving tasks. Airlines employ technicians to supervise maintenance operations and the development of procedures for new equipment; there were roughly 154,000 aircraft and avionics equipment mechanics and service technicians in 2002.

■ STARTING OUT

The best way for students to obtain an aeronautical or aerospace technician's job is through their college or university's job placement office. Many manufacturers maintain recruiting relationships with schools in their area. Jobs may also be obtained through state employment offices, newspaper advertisements, applications for government employment, and industry work-study programs offered by many aircraft companies.

■ ADVANCEMENT

Aeronautical and aerospace technicians continue to learn on the job. As they gain experience in the specialized areas, employers turn to them as experts who can solve problems, create new techniques, devise new designs, or develop practice from theory.

Most advancement involves taking on additional responsibilities. For example, with experience, a technician may take on supervisory responsibilities, overseeing several trainees, assistant technicians, or others. Such a technician may also be assigned independent responsibility especially on some tasks usually assigned to an engineer. Technicians with a good working knowledge of the company's equipment and who have good personalities may become company sales or technical representatives. Technicians seeking further advancement are advised to continue their education. With additional formal education, a technician may become an aeronautical or aerospace engineer.

■ EARNINGS

Aerospace technology is a broad field, so earnings vary depending on a technician's specialty, educational preparation, and work experience. In 2002, the median annual salary for all aerospace technicians was $51,650, according to the U.S. Department of Labor. Beyond that, salaries varied depending on specialty. For aircraft mechanics, including engine specialists, the annual mean wage was around $43,620 in 2002, with the lowest 10 percent earning $27,370 and more experienced mechanics earning more than $60,150. Avionics technicians earned salaries that ranged from $29,130 to $56,150 or more in 2002.

Benefits depend on employers but usually include paid vacations and holidays, sick pay, health insurance, and a retirement plan. Salary increases will likely be held to a minimum over the next few years as the industry struggles to achieve a new balance after years of cutbacks and difficult markets. Nearly all companies offer some form of tuition reimbursement for further education. Some offer cooperative programs with local schools, combining classroom training with practical paid experience.

■ WORK ENVIRONMENT

The aerospace industry, with its strong emphasis on quality and safety, is a very safe place to work. Special procedures and equipment make otherwise hazardous jobs extremely safe. The range of work covered means that the technicians can work in small teams in specialized research laboratories or in test areas that are large and hospital-clean.

Aerospace technicians are at the launch pad, involved in fueling and checkout procedures, and back in the blockhouse sitting at an electronic console. They work in large test facilities or in specialized shops, designing and fabricating equipment. They travel to test sites or tracking stations to construct facilities or troubleshoot systems. Working conditions vary with the assignment, but the work climate is always challenging, and co-workers are well-trained, competent people.

Aeronautical technicians may perform inside activities involving confined detail work, they may work outside, or they may combine both situations. Aeronautical and aerospace technicians work in many situations: alone, in small teams, or in large groups. Commonly, technicians participate in team projects, which are coordinated efforts of scientists, engineers, and technicians working on specific assignments. They concentrate on the practical aspects of the project and must get along well with and interact cooperatively with the scientists responsible for the theoretical aspects of the project.

Aerospace technicians must be able to perform under deadline pressure, meet strict requirements and rigid specifications, and deal with potentially hazardous situations. They must be willing and flexible enough to acquire new knowledge and techniques to adjust to the rapidly changing technology. In addition, technicians need persistence and tenacity, especially when engaged in experimental and research tasks. They must be responsible, reliable, and willing to accept greater responsibility.

Aerospace technology is never far from the public's attention, and aeronautical technicians have the additional satisfaction of knowing that they are viewed as being engaged in vital and fascinating work.

■ OUTLOOK

The U.S. Department of Labor predicts that the aerospace industry is likely to decline through 2012 due to foreign completion and the general slowdown in air travel. Furthermore, more efficient production methods and offshoring of industry means that any growth will not necessarily translate to new jobs. However, prospects for aircraft mechanics and avionics service technicians will remain good since, though industry conditions have created a large pool of un- or under-employed technicians, many will retire or seek employment in other industries. Many manufacturers in the aerospace industry have responded to the decline of the 1990s by broadening their production to include other areas of technology. The Aerospace Industries Association of America (AIA) predicts aerospace companies will be looking for qualified technicians in fields such as laser optics, mission operations, hazardous materials procedures, production planning, materials testing, computer-aided design, and robotic operations and programming.

■ FOR MORE INFORMATION

For a listing of accredited technology programs, check the website or contact

Accreditation Board for Engineering and Technology Inc.
111 Market Place, Suite 1050
Baltimore, MD 21202-4012
Tel: 410-347-7700
http://www.abet.org

Contact AIA for publications with information on aerospace technologies, careers, and space.

Aerospace Industries Association of America (AIA)
1000 Wilson Boulevard, Suite 1700
Arlington, VA 22209-3901
Tel: 703-358-1000
http://www.aia-aerospace.org

For career information and information on student branches of this organization, contact the AIAA.

American Institute of Aeronautics and Astronautics (AIAA)
1801 Alexander Bell Drive, Suite 500
Reston, VA 20191-4344

Tel: 800-639-2422

http://www.aiaa.org

This organization is dedicated to improving students' skills in math and science. For award and other information, contact

Aviation/Aerospace Education Foundation

PO Box 3015

Syracuse, NY 13220-3015

Tel: 315-233-4837

http://www.aaef.org

For career and scholarship information, contact

General Aviation Manufacturers Association

1400 K Street, NW, Suite 801

Washington, DC 20005

Tel: 202-393-1500

http://www.generalaviation.org

JETS has career information and offers high school students the opportunity to "try on" engineering through a number of programs and competitions. For more information, contact

Junior Engineering Technical Society

1420 King Street, Suite 405

Alexandria, VA 22314-2794

Tel: 703-548-5387

Email: jets@nae.edu

http://www.jets.org

SEDS is an international organization of high school and college students dedicated to promoting interest in space. The United States national headquarters are located at the Massachusetts Institute of Technology. Contact

Students for the Exploration and Development of Space (SEDS)

MIT Room W20-445

77 Massachusetts Avenue

Cambridge, MA 02139-4307

Email: mitseds-officers@mit

http://www.mit.edu/~mitseds

For more information on career choices and schools, contact

Aerospace Industries Association of Canada

60 Queen Street, Suite 1200

Ottawa, ON K1P 5Y7 Canada

Tel: 613-232-4297

Email: info@aiac.ca

http://www.aiac.ca

Aerospace Engineers

■ OVERVIEW

Aerospace engineering encompasses the fields of aeronautical (aircraft) and astronautical (spacecraft) engineering. *Aerospace engineers* work in teams to design, build, and test machines that fly within the earth's atmosphere and beyond. Although aerospace science is a very specialized discipline, it is also considered one of the most diverse. This field of engineering draws from such subjects as physics, mathematics, earth science, aerodynamics, and biology. Some aerospace engineers specialize in designing one complete machine, perhaps a commercial aircraft, whereas others focus on separate components such as for missile guidance systems. There are approximately 78,000 aerospace engineers working in the United States.

■ HISTORY

The roots of aerospace engineering can be traced as far back as when people first dreamed of being able to fly. Thousands of years ago, the Chinese developed kites and later experimented with gunpowder as a source of propulsion. In the 15th century, Renaissance artist Leonardo da Vinci created drawings of two devices that were designed to fly. One, the ornithopter, was supposed to fly the way birds do, by flapping its wings; the other was designed as a rotating screw, closer in form to today's helicopter.

In 1783, Joseph and Jacques Montgolfier of France designed the first hot-air balloon that could be used for manned flight. In 1799, an English baron, Sir George Cayley, designed an aircraft that was one of the first not to be considered "lighter than air," as balloons were. He developed a fixed-wing structure that led to his creation of the first glider in 1849. Much experimentation was performed in gliders and the science of aerodynamics through the late 1800s. In 1903, the first mechanically powered and controlled flight was completed in a craft designed by Orville and Wilbur Wright. The big boost in airplane development occurred during World War I. In the early years of the war, aeronautical engineering encompassed a variety of engineering skills applied toward the development of flying machines. Civil engineering principles were used in structural design, while early airplane engines were devised by automobile engineers. Aerodynamic design itself was primarily empirical, with many answers coming from liquid flow concepts established in marine engineering.

The evolution of the airplane continued during both world wars, with steady technological developments in materials science, propulsion, avionics, and stability and control. Airplanes became larger and faster. Airplanes are commonplace today, but commercial flight became a frequent mode of transportation only as recently as the 1960s and 1970s.

Robert Goddard developed and flew the first liquid-propelled rocket in 1926. The technology behind liquid propulsion continued to evolve, and the first U.S. liquid rocket engine was tested in 1938. More sophisticated rockets were eventually created to enable aircraft to be launched into space. The world's first artificial satellite, *Sputnik I*, was launched by the Soviets in 1957. In 1961, President John F. Kennedy urged the United States to be the first country to put a man on the moon; on July 20, 1969, astronauts Neil Armstrong and Edwin Aldrin Jr. accomplished that goal.

Today, aerospace engineers design spacecraft that explore beyond the earth's atmosphere, such as space shuttles and rockets. They create missiles and military aircraft of many types, such as fighters, bombers, observers, and transports. Today's engineers go beyond the dreams of merely learning to fly. For example, in 1998, the United States and 15 other countries began a series of joint missions into space to assemble a planned International Space Station. On the ground, space professionals, including aerospace engineers, will play a vital role in developing equipment that will be used on the station.

■ THE JOB

Although the creation of aircraft and spacecraft involve professionals from many branches of engineering (e.g., materials, electrical, and mechanical), aerospace engineers in particular are responsible for the total design of the craft, including its shape, performance, propulsion, and guidance control system. In the field of aerospace engineering, professional responsibilities vary widely depending on the specific job description. *Aeronautical engineers* work specifically with aircraft systems, and *astronautical engineers* specialize in spacecraft systems.

Throughout their education and training, aerospace engineers thoroughly learn the complexities involved in how materials and structures perform under tremendous stress. In general, they are called upon to apply their knowledge of the following subjects: propulsion, aerodynamics, thermodynamics, fluid mechanics, flight mechanics, and structural analysis. Less technically scientific issues must also often be dealt with, such as cost analysis, reliability studies, maintainability, operations research, marketing, and management.

There are many professional titles given to certain aerospace engineers. *Analytical engineers* use engineering and mathematical theory to solve questions that arise during the design phase. *Stress analysts* determine how the weight and loads of structures behave under a variety of conditions. This analysis is performed with computers and complex formulas.

Computational fluid dynamic (CFD) engineers use sophisticated high-speed computers to develop models used in the study of fluid dynamics. Using simulated systems, they determine how elements flow around objects; simulation saves time and money and eliminates risks involved with actual testing. As computers become more complex, so do the tasks of the CFD engineer.

Design aerospace engineers draw from the expertise of many other specialists. They devise the overall structure of components and entire crafts, meeting the specifications developed by those more specialized in aerodynamics, astrodynamics, and structural engineering. Design engineers use computer-aided design programs for many of their tasks. *Manufacturing aerospace engineers* develop the plans for producing the complex components that make up aircraft and spacecraft. They work with the designers to ensure that the plans are economically feasible and will produce efficient, effective components.

Materials aerospace engineers determine the suitability of the various materials that are used to produce aerospace vehicles. Aircraft and spacecraft require the appropriate tensile strength, density, and rigidity for the particular environments they are subjected to. Determining how materials such as steel, glass, and even chemical compounds react to temperature and stress is an important part of the materials engineer's responsibilities.

Quality control is a task that aerospace engineers perform throughout the development, design, and manufacturing processes. The finished product must be evaluated for its reliability, vulnerability, and how it is to be maintained and supported.

Marketing and sales aerospace engineers work with customers, usually industrial corporations and the government, informing them of product performance. They act as a liaison between the technical engineers and the clients to help ensure that the

QUICK FACTS

SCHOOL SUBJECTS
Mathematics
Physics

PERSONAL SKILLS
Mechanical/manipulative
Technical/scientific

WORK ENVIRONMENT
Primarily indoors
Primarily one location

MINIMUM EDUCATION LEVEL
Bachelor's degree

SALARY RANGE
$49,640 to $72,750 to
   $105,060+

CERTIFICATION OR LICENSING
Required by certain states

OUTLOOK
Decline

DOT
002

GOE
02.07.04

NOC
2146

O*NET-SOC
17-2011.00

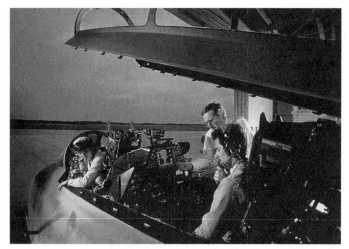

Aerospace engineers check the electronics in the cockpit of an F-14.

products delivered are performing as planned. Sales engineers also need to anticipate the needs of the customer, as far ahead as possible, to inform their companies of potential marketing opportunities. They also keep abreast of their competitors and need to understand how to structure contracts effectively.

■ REQUIREMENTS
High School

While in high school, follow a college preparatory program. Doing well in mathematics and science classes is vital if you want to pursue a career in any type of engineering field. The American Society for Engineering Education advises students to take calculus and trigonometry in high school, as well as laboratory science classes. Such courses provide the skills you'll need for problem solving, an essential skill in any type of engineering.

Postsecondary Training

Aerospace engineers need a bachelor's degree to enter the field. More advanced degrees are necessary for those interested in teaching or research and development positions.

While a major in aerospace engineering is the norm, other majors are acceptable. For example, the National Aeronautics and Space Administration recommends a degree in any of a variety of disciplines, including biomedical engineering, ceramics engineering, chemistry, industrial engineering, materials science, metallurgy, optical engineering, and oceanography. You should make sure the college you choose has an accredited engineering program. The Accreditation Board for Engineering and Technology (ABET) sets minimum education standards for programs in these fields. Graduation from an ABET-accredited school is a requirement for becoming licensed in many states, so it is important to select an

accredited school. Currently, approximately 250 colleges and universities offer ABET-accredited engineering programs. Visit ABET's website (http://www.abet.org) for a listing of accredited schools.

Some aerospace engineers complete master's degrees and even doctoral work before entering this field. Advanced degrees can significantly increase an engineer's earnings. Students continuing on to graduate school will study research and development, with a thesis required for a master's degree and a dissertation for a doctorate. About one-third of all aerospace engineers go on to graduate school to get a master's degree.

Certification or Licensing

Most states require engineers to be licensed. There are two levels of licensing for engineers. Professional Engineers (PEs) have graduated from an accredited engineering curriculum, have four years of engineering experience, and have passed a written exam. Engineering graduates need not wait until they have four years experience, however, to start the licensure process. Those who pass the Fundamentals of Engineering examination after graduating are called Engineers in Training (EITs) or Engineer Interns (EIs). The EIT certification usually is valid for 10 years. After acquiring suitable work experience, EITs can take the second examination, the Principles and Practice of Engineering exam, to gain full PE licensure.

In order to ensure that aerospace engineers are kept up to date on their quickly changing field, many states have imposed continuing education requirements for relicensure.

Other Requirements

Aerospace engineers should enjoy completing detailed work, problem solving, and participating in group efforts. Mathematical, science, and computer skills are a must. Equally important, however, are the abilities to communicate ideas, share in teamwork, and visualize the forms and functions of structures. Curiosity, inventiveness, and the willingness to continue learning from experiences are excellent qualities to have for this type of work.

■ EXPLORING

If you like to work on model airplanes and rockets, you may be good candidate for an aerospace engineering career. Consider working on special research assignments supervised by your science and math teachers for helpful experience. You may also want to try working on cars and boats, which provides a good opportunity to discover more about aerodynamics. A part-time job with a local manufacturer can give you some exposure to product engineering and development.

Exciting opportunities are often available at summer camps and academic programs throughout the country. For instance, the University of North Dakota (see address listed at the end of this article) presents an aerospace camp focusing on study and career exploration that includes instruction in model rocketry and flight. However, admission to the camp is competitive; the camp usually consists of two 10-day programs for 32 students each.

It is also a good idea to join a science club while in high school. For example, the Junior Engineering Technical Society provides members with opportunities to enter academic competitions, explore career opportunities, and design model structures. Contact information is available at the end of this article.

Aerospace America (http://www.aiaa.org/aerospace), published by the American Institute of Aeronautics and Astronautics, is a helpful magazine for exploring careers in aerospace. You should also check out *Engineering: Your Future* (http://www.asee.org/precollege) at the American Society for Engineering Education's website. It offers general information about careers in engineering, as well as answers to frequently asked questions about engineering.

■ EMPLOYERS

The U.S. Department of Labor reports that approximately 78,000 aerospace engineers are employed in the United States. Many aircraft-related engineering jobs are found in Alabama, California, and Florida, where large aerospace companies are located. Over 70 percent of all aerospace engineers work in products and parts. Government agencies, such as the Department of Defense and the National Aeronautics and Space Administration, employ approximately 12 percent of aerospace engineers. Other employers include engineering services, research and testing services, and electronics manufacturers.

■ STARTING OUT

Many students begin their careers while completing their studies through work-study arrangements that sometimes turn into full-time jobs. Most aerospace manufacturers actively recruit engineering students, conducting on-campus interviews and other activities to locate the best candidates. Students preparing to graduate can also send out resumes to companies active in the aerospace industry and arrange interviews. Many colleges and universities also staff job placement centers, which are often good places to find leads for new job openings.

Students can also apply directly to agencies of the federal government concerned with aerospace development and implementation. Applications can be made through the Office of Personnel Management or through an agency's own hiring department.

Professional associations, such as the National Society of Professional Engineers and the American Institute of Aeronautics and Astronautics, offer job placement services, including career advice, job listings, and training. Their Web addresses are listed at the end of this article.

■ ADVANCEMENT

As in most engineering fields, there tends to be a hierarchy of workers in the various divisions of aerospace engineering. This is true in research, design and development, production, and teaching. In an entry-level job, one is considered simply an engineer, perhaps a junior engineer. After a certain amount of experience is gained, depending on the position, one moves on to work as a project engineer, supervising others. Then, as a managing engineer, one has further responsibilities over a number of project engineers and their teams. At the top of the hierarchy is the position of chief engineer, which involves authority over managing engineers and additional decision-making responsibilities.

As engineers move up the career ladder, the type of responsibilities they have tend to change. Junior engineers are highly involved in technical matters and scientific problem solving. As managers and chiefs, engineers

---

EATING IN SPACE

Aerospace engineers don't just work on the nuts and bolts of spacecraft. Some are concerned with the more immediate needs of astronauts, such as developing special equipment to allow them to eat in space.

Behind each meal is hours of research and special processes such as irradiation, rehydration, and thermostabilization. Astronauts rehydrate foods (adding moisture to make food edible) at a hydration station on the shuttle. The station is an electronic dispensing system that moistens food and provides drinking water for the crew. Astronauts insert specially designed food packages into the station where a needle penetrates the rubber packaging and injects a specified amount of water into the food. After food is rehydrated, the package can be heated, if necessary.

Condiments available to astronauts include salt, pepper, taco sauce, hot pepper sauce, ketchup, mayonnaise, and mustard. The salt and pepper are liquids stored in small plastic squeeze bottles. The remaining condiments are packaged in individual pouches. Aerospace engineers help develop the equipment and packaging so scientists and others can ensure that the space diet provides the proper nutrients and calorie requirements (approximately 2,700 calories per day).

have the responsibilities of supervising, cost analyzing, and relating with clients.

All engineers must continue to learn and study technological progress throughout their careers. It is important to keep abreast of engineering advancements and trends by reading industry journals and taking courses. Such courses are offered by professional associations or colleges. In aerospace engineering especially, changes occur rapidly, and those who seek promotions must be prepared. Those who are employed by colleges and universities must continue teaching and conducting research if they want to have tenured (more guaranteed) faculty positions.

■ EARNINGS

In 2002, the median salary for all aerospace engineers was about $72,750 per year, according to the U.S. Department of Labor. The lowest paid 10 percent earned less than $49,640 per year, and the highest paid 10 percent earned more than $105,060 per year. Experienced engineers employed by the federal government tended to earn a little more, with a median salary of $81,580. Federal employees, however, enjoy greater job security and often more generous vacation and retirement benefits.

Aerospace engineers with bachelor's degrees earn average starting salaries of $48,028 per year, according to a 2003 salary survey conducted by the National Association of Colleges and Employers. With a master's degree, candidates were offered $61,162, and with a Ph.D., $68,406.

All engineers can expect to receive vacation and sick pay, paid holidays, health insurance, life insurance, and retirement programs.

■ WORK ENVIRONMENT

Aerospace engineers work in various settings depending on their job description. Those involved in research and design usually work in a traditional office setting. They spend considerable time at computers and drawing boards. Engineers involved with the testing of components and structures often work outside at test sites or in laboratories where controlled testing conditions can be created.

In the manufacturing area of the aerospace industry, engineers often work on the factory floor itself, assembling components and making sure that they conform to design specifications. This job requires much walking around large production facilities, such as aircraft factories or spacecraft assembly plants.

Engineers are sometimes required to travel to other locations to consult with companies that make materials and other needed components. Others travel to remote test sites to observe and participate in flight testing.

Aerospace engineers are also employed with the Federal Aviation Administration and commercial airline companies. These engineers perform a variety of duties, including performance analysis and crash investigations. Companies that are involved with satellite communications need the expertise of aerospace engineers to better interpret the many aspects of the space environment and the problems involved with getting a satellite launched into space.

■ OUTLOOK

The aerospace industry has gone through difficult times since the late 1980s, and more job losses are predicted for the immediate future. Shrinking space program budgets, the recession of the early 1990s, and the continuing wave of corporate downsizing have all combined to cut severely into the aerospace industry.

Nevertheless, the aerospace industry remains vital to the health of the national economy. Increasing airline traffic and the need to replace aging airplanes with quieter and more fuel-efficient aircraft will boost demand for aerospace engineers. The federal government has increased defense budgets in order to build up the armed forces. More aerospace engineers will be needed to repair and add to the current air fleet, as well as to improve defense technology. Engineers are also needed to help make commercial aircraft safer, designing and installing reinforced cockpit doors and onboard security screening equipment to protect pilots, crew, and commercial passengers.

Despite cutbacks in the space program, the development of new space technology and increasing commercial uses for that technology will continue to require qualified engineers. Facing reduced demand in the United States, aerospace companies are increasing their sales overseas, and depending on the world economy and foreign demand, this new market could create a demand for new workers in the industry.

Employment opportunities within aerospace will remain intensely competitive, however. Manufacturers and government agencies will seek only the top students to fill openings that result as engineers retire or switch to other areas of employment. These openings are expected to account for most of the new jobs in the industry, but job satisfaction and longevity are high, so turnover is usually low. Overall, employment in this field is expected to decline through 2012, according to the U.S. Department of Labor.

■ FOR MORE INFORMATION

For a list of accredited schools and colleges, contact

Accreditation Board for Engineering and
   Technology Inc.
111 Market Place, Suite 1050
Baltimore, MD 21202-4102
Tel: 410-347-7700
http://www.abet.org

For information about scholarships, colleges, and career opportunities, contact
   Aerospace Education Foundation
   1501 Lee Highway
   Arlington, VA 22209-1198
   Tel: 800-291-8480
   Email: aefstaff@aef.org
   http://www.aef.org

   American Institute of Aeronautics and Astronautics
   1801 Alexander Bell Drive, Suite 500
   Reston, VA 20191-4344
   Tel: 800-639-2422
   http://www.aiaa.org

   American Society for Engineering Education
   1818 N Street, NW
   Washington, DC 20036
   Tel: 202-331-3500
   http://www.asee.org

The following organizations offer information geared specifically toward students. Visit their websites or contact for information.
   Junior Engineering Technical Society
   1420 King Street, Suite 405
   Alexandria, VA 22314
   Tel: 703-548-5387
   Email: jetsinfo@jets.org
   http://www.jets.org

   National Society of Professional Engineers
   1420 King Street
   Alexandria, VA 22314-2794
   Tel: 703-684-2800
   http://www.nspe.org/students

For information on aerospace programs and summer camps, contact
   University of North Dakota
   John D. Odergard School of Aerospace Sciences
   PO Box 9007
   Grand Forks, ND 58202-9007
   Tel: 800-258-1525
   http://www.aero.und.edu

Agribusiness Technicians

OVERVIEW

Agribusiness technicians combine their agriculture and business backgrounds to manage or offer management consulting services to farms and agricultural businesses. Agribusiness technicians, also called *agricultural business technicians*, generally work as liaisons between farms and agricultural businesses, representing either the farm or the business.

HISTORY

The marketing of agricultural products first concerned farmers in the early 20th century. Cooperative organizations were formed in the 1920s, allowing farmers to control the marketing of their commodities, but farmers still struggled to make profits. It was about this time that the field of agricultural economics evolved; the International Association of Agricultural Economics was established in 1929.

The Dust Bowl of the 1930s complicated farm economics further, leading to New Deal legislation. Under the New Deal, which enacted the first effective farm legislation in the United States, the secretary of agriculture could control crop production. In the following years, agriculture expanded as a result of scientific advances and better methods of planting and harvesting. By the 1960s, marketing had become much more complicated for farmers, leading to the development of agribusiness as a major career field. Today, agribusiness is much larger than the farming industry; two-thirds of each dollar spent on food goes toward processing, packaging, marketing, and retailing, with only one-third going to the farm.

THE JOB

Agribusiness is as diverse a field as agriculture, and it involves professionals in economics, sales, marketing, commodities, science, and other areas. Technicians assist these professionals. They may work for a farm or for a business or organization that assists farmers. They may spend their workdays out in the field or behind a desk or a combination of these two. Their work may focus on such areas as grain, livestock, or dairy farm production.

Some agribusiness technicians choose to go into business management, working as part of a personnel-management office for a large corporate farm or dairy. In such a position, the technician manages staff, coordinates work plans with farm managers, and oversees the entire salary structure for farm or other production workers. Other agribusiness technicians work as *purchasing agents*, supervising all the buying for large commercial farms. Another option for the agribusiness technician is to work as a *farm sales representative*, finding the best markets for the produce of farms on a local, state, or national level. In this capacity, the technician travels a great deal and works closely with records technicians and other personnel of the farm or farms he or she represents.

Some agribusiness technicians assist farmers with record keeping. The records that farmers and other agricultural business people must keep are becoming more detailed and varied every year. Agribusiness technicians may set up complete record-keeping systems. They analyze records and help farmers make management decisions based on the accumulated facts. Computerized record keeping is common now, so there is a tremendous need for *agricultural records technicians* who can create tailor-made programs to help farmers get maximum benefit from their output. Furthermore, they analyze the output and make practical applications of the information.

In some positions, such as *agricultural quality control technician*, the technician works directly with farmers but is employed by another company. *Dairy production field-contact technicians*, for example, serve as contact people between dairy companies and the farms that produce the milk. They negotiate long- or short-term contracts to purchase milk and milk products according to agreed upon specifications; meet with farmers to test milk for butterfat content, sediment, and bacteria; and discuss ways to solve milk-production problems and improve production. They may suggest methods of feeding, housing, and milking to improve production or comply with sanitary regulations. They may set up truck routes to haul milk to the dairy; solicit membership in cooperative associations; or even sell items such as dairy-farm equipment, chemicals, and feed to the farmers they contact.

Poultry field-service technicians represent food-processing companies or cooperative associations. They inspect farms to ensure compliance with agreements involving facilities, equipment, sanitation, and efficiency. They also advise farmers on how to improve the quality of their products. Technicians may examine chickens for evidence of disease and growth rate to determine the effectiveness of medication and feeding programs. They may then recommend changes in equipment or procedures to improve production. They inform farmers of new techniques, government regulations, and company or association production standards so they can upgrade their farms to meet requirements. They may recommend laboratory testing of feeds, diseased chickens, and diet supplements. In these cases, they often gather samples and take them to a laboratory for analysis. They report their findings on farm conditions, laboratory tests, their own recommendations, and farmers' reactions to the company or association employing them.

Agribusiness technicians also work for credit institutions that solicit the business of farmers, make appraisals of real estate and personal property, organize and present loan requests, close loans, and service those loans with periodic reviews of the borrower's management performance and financial status. They also work as *farm representatives* for banks, cooperatives, or federal lending institutions. In this capacity they sell their organizations' services to farmers or agricultural business people, make appraisals, and do the paperwork involved with lending money.

■ REQUIREMENTS
High School

In high school, you should take social studies, laboratory science (biology, chemistry, or physics), mathematics, and, if possible, agriculture and business classes. English and composition will be particularly helpful, since oral and written communications are central to the work of the agribusiness technician. Also, take computer classes so that you are familiar with using this technology. Computers are often used in record keeping and production planning.

Postsecondary Training

After completing high school, it is necessary to train in a two-year agricultural or technical college. Many colleges offer associate's degrees in agribusiness or agricultural management. The programs concentrate on basic economic theory; training in management analysis and practical problem solving; and intensive communications training, such as public speaking and report writing.

Typical first-year courses in an agricultural or technical college include English, biology, health and physical

education, introductory animal husbandry, principles of accounting, agricultural economics, microbiology, botany, introductory data processing, soil science, and principles of business.

Typical second-year courses include marketing agricultural commodities, farm management, social science, agricultural finance, agricultural marketing institutions, forage and seed crops, personnel management, and agricultural records and taxation.

Other Requirements

You must be able to work well with other people, which includes being able to delegate responsibility and establish friendly relations with farmers, laborers, and company managers. You must be able to analyze management problems and make sound decisions based on your analysis. And you must have excellent oral and written communications skills: Technicians are expected to present written and oral reports, offer comments and advice clearly, and, when necessary, train other workers for a particular job.

■ EXPLORING

Try to get summer or part-time employment in your desired specialty—for example, a clerical job in a farm insurance agency or as a laborer in a feed and grain company. Because many technical colleges offer evening courses, it may be possible to obtain permission during your senior year to audit a course or even to take it for future college credit. Work experience on a farm will give you insight into the business concerns of farmers, as will industry periodicals such as *Farm Journal* (http://www. farmjournal.com) and *Grain Journal* (http://www.grainnet. com). Join your high school's chapter of the National FFA Organization (formerly known as Future Farmers of America) or a local 4-H group, where you may have the opportunity to work on farm-management projects.

■ EMPLOYERS

Many different agriculture-based businesses hire graduates of agribusiness programs. Employers include large commercial farms, grain elevators, credit unions, farm equipment dealerships, farm supply stores, fertilizer and processing plants, agricultural chemical companies, and local, state, and federal government agencies.

■ STARTING OUT

Your agribusiness program will likely require a semester or more of employment experience and will assist you in finding an internship or part-time job with agribusiness professionals. Many students are able to turn their internships into full-time work or make connections that lead to

LEARN MORE ABOUT IT

Baker, Gregory A., et al. *Introduction to Food and Agribusiness Management.* Upper Saddle River, N.J.: Prentice-Hall, 2001.

Beierlein, James G., et al. *Principles of Agribusiness Management.* 2nd ed. Prospect Heights, Ill.: Waveland Press, 1995.

Charles, Daniel. *Lords of the Harvest: Biotech, Big Money, and the Future of Food.* Cambridge, Mass.: Perseus Books, 2001.

Cramer, Gail L., et al. *Agricultural Economics and Agribusiness.* 8th ed. New York: John Wiley & Sons, 2000.

Martineau, Belinda. *First Fruit: The Creation of the Flavr Savr Tomato and the Birth of Biotech Foods.* New York: McGraw-Hill Professional Publishing, 2001.

Nelson, Gerald C., ed. *Genetically Modified Organisms in Agriculture: Economics and Politics.* Burlington, Mass.: Academic Press, 2001.

Ricketts, Cliff. *Introduction to Agribusiness.* Clifton Park, N.Y.: Thomson Learning, Delmar, 2001.

Schmitz, Andrew, et al. *Agricultural Policy, Agribusiness, and Rent-Seeking Behaviour.* Toronto, Ont.: University of Toronto Press, 2002.

Solbrig, Otto, and Dorothy Solbrig. *So Shall You Reap: Farming and Crops in Human Affairs.* Washington, D.C.: Island Press, 1996.

other job opportunities. Most agribusiness technician jobs are considered entry-level, or management trainee, positions and don't require a great deal of previous experience. These jobs are often advertised in the classifieds or posted with career placement centers at community colleges.

■ ADVANCEMENT

The ultimate aim of many technicians is to own a business. Technicians can start their own companies in any agricultural business area or act as *freelance agents* under contract to perform specific services for several firms. For example, an experienced agribusiness technician may purchase a computer and data-processing equipment, set up the necessary record-keeping programs, and act as a consulting firm for a host of farms and agricultural businesses.

There are many other positions an agribusiness technician may hold. *Farm managers* oversee all operations of a farm and work closely with owners and other management, customers, and all farm departments on larger farms. *Regional farm credit managers* supervise several of a bank's farm representatives. They may suggest training

BELIEVE IT OR NOT

You've heard of dairy, beef, and pork associations—but how about these other agricultural groups?

- American Alligator Council
- American Emu Association
- Great Plains Buffalo Association
- Mushroom Council
- National Christmas Tree Association
- National Hot Dog and Sausage Council
- Rocky Mountain Ostrich Association

programs for farm representatives, recommend changes in lending procedures, and conduct personal audits of randomly selected farm accounts. *Sales managers* act as liaisons between company sales representatives and individual dealers, distributors, or farmers.

■ EARNINGS

Salaries for agribusiness technicians range from between $19,180 and $67,810 or more annually. Those who provided management and technical consulting services, for instance, earned median annual salaries of $40,380 in 2002, according to the U.S. Department of Labor. Ten percent of all such farm and home advisors earned less than $19,180, and 10 percent earned $67,810 or more a year.

Fringe benefits vary widely, depending upon the employer. Some amount to as much as one-third of the base salary. More and more employers are providing such benefits as pension plans, paid vacations, insurance, and tuition reimbursement.

■ WORK ENVIRONMENT

Because the field is so large, working environments may be anywhere from a corporate office to a corn field. Those who work in sales are likely to travel a good deal, with a few nights spent on the road or even a few weeks spent out of the country. Technicians at banks or data-processing services usually work in clean, pleasant surroundings. The technician who goes into farm management or who owns a farm is likely to work outdoors in all kinds of weather.

Agribusiness technicians are often confronted with problems requiring careful thought and decision. They must be able to remain calm when things get hectic, to make sound decisions, and then to stand by their decisions in the face of possible disagreement. It is a profession that requires initiative, self-reliance, and the ability to accept responsibilities that may bring blame at times

of failure as well as substantial rewards for successful performance. For those technicians who possess the qualities of leadership and a strong interest in the agricultural business, it can be a challenging, exciting, and highly satisfying profession.

■ OUTLOOK

According to the U.S. Department of Labor, agribusiness provides employment to about 21 percent of the country's labor force. Despite the fluctuations in the agricultural industry, agribusiness professionals and technicians will continue to be in great demand in the marketing and production of food and other agricultural products.

Agribusiness technicians may find more opportunities to work abroad; agribusiness plays a large part in global trade issues and in the government's efforts to support farms and agricultural reforms in other countries, such as with the U.S. Department of Agriculture's program with the Russian Ministry of Agriculture and Food. Agribusiness construction is a subfield that is developing as a result of these reforms; technicians will be needed to assist in the planning and construction of farm-to-market roads in other countries, irrigation channels, bridges, grain silos, and other improvements.

■ FOR MORE INFORMATION

To learn about the roles economists play in agriculture, visit the AAEA website.

American Agricultural Economics Association (AAEA)
415 South Duff Avenue, Suite C
Ames, IA 50010-6600
Tel: 515-233-3202
http://www.aaea.org

For more information on opportunities in the agricultural field, schooling, and these organizations, contact

4-H
Families, 4-H & Nutrition
CSREES/USDA
1400 Independence Avenue, SW
Washington, DC 20250-2225
Tel: 202-720-2908
http://www.4h-usa.org

For information on careers and chapter membership, contact
National FFA Organization
National FFA Center
PO Box 68960
Indianapolis, IN 46268-0960
Tel: 317-802-6060
http://www.ffa.org

Agricultural Consultants

■ OVERVIEW

Agricultural consultants, sometimes known as *agricultural extension service workers*, live in rural communities and act as resources for farmers on a range of topics from agricultural technology to the issues facing the modern rural family. They are employed by either the U.S. Department of Agriculture (USDA) or by the Department of Agriculture and the agricultural colleges in that state. Agricultural consultants advise farmers on improved methods of agriculture and agricultural work such as farm management, crop rotation, soil conservation, livestock breeding and feeding, use of new machinery, and marketing. They assist individuals wishing to start their own farms, provide the most current agricultural advancements to the community, and speak to the community or local government groups on agricultural issues. They also supervise the work of family and community educators and young people's clubs such as 4-H. This government-sponsored program is called the Cooperative State Research, Education and Extension Service (CSREES).

■ HISTORY

In the late 18th century, President George Washington decided to establish an educational agency of the federal government dedicated to assisting the nation's farmers. Washington's proposal eventually developed into what is now known as the Department of Agriculture.

In 1862, President Abraham Lincoln promoted the Morrill Act, which established land grant colleges. Under this act, each state was given 30,000 acres of land for each senator and representative in Congress. The state was to sell the land and use the proceeds to build colleges that would specialize in education for agriculture and engineering.

Once established, the state agricultural colleges were faced with the task of compiling enough data to develop an agricultural curriculum that would be of use to the American farmer. Under the Hatch Act of 1887, experimental stations were created. These agricultural laboratory settings were devoted to gathering information regarding soils, crops, livestock, fruits, and machinery. They became sources of information for both agricultural colleges and farmers.

Land-grant colleges became important resources for agricultural data and education. However, it soon became clear that it would be more effective to send people into the field who were familiar with the farmers' work and who were educated in the agricultural sciences than to

expect farmers to leave their work or come from remote areas to attend college classes. Thus, the role of the agricultural consultant came into being.

The Cooperative Extension Service was developed and placed in operation in 1914 on a federal basis by the passage of the Smith-Lever Act. The service was opened to any state that wished to join the educational project on a cooperative basis, and most states accepted the opportunity. Because of this, every state agricultural college in the nation today has an extension service as one of its major departmental classifications.

In 1994, the U.S. Department of Agriculture Reorganization Act created the CSREES, which expands the research and higher education functions of the former cooperative State Research Service and the education and outreach functions of the former Extension Service.

■ THE JOB

Agricultural consultants teach agricultural subjects at places other than college campuses. The aim of these educational programs is to teach agricultural workers to analyze and solve agricultural problems. They cover such topics as soil and crop improvement, livestock, farm machinery, fertilizers, new methods of planting, and any other subject that may be of assistance to the farmer. Classroom settings are avoided. Rather, the consultants work on-site, possibly while the farmer is engaged in planting or harvesting, or in small evening meetings of five or six farmers. Occasionally, classes are offered in more formal settings during which the consultant speaks before larger groups and makes presentations.

County agricultural agents work closely with federal agricultural agents in gathering information to be presented to the farmers. Information on agronomy (the theory and practice of soil management and crop production), livestock, marketing, agricultural and home economics, horticulture, and entomology (the study of insects) may come either from the state agricultural

QUICK FACTS

SCHOOL SUBJECTS
Agriculture
Business
Economics

PERSONAL SKILLS
Helping/teaching
Leadership/management

WORK ENVIRONMENT
Indoors and outdoors
Primarily multiple locations

MINIMUM EDUCATION LEVEL
Bachelor's degree

SALARY RANGE
$24,075 to $35,519 to
$96,637

CERTIFICATION OR LICENSING
None available

OUTLOOK
Decline

DOT
096

GOE
12.03.02

NOC
2123

O*NET-SOC
25-9021.00

college or from the CSREES. The county agricultural worker's job is to review the new information, decide what is most pertinent to local operations, and then present it as effectively as possible to the farmers in that particular area. The county or federal extension service agent's work is primarily educational in nature and is aimed at increasing the efficiency of agricultural production and marketing and the development of new and different markets for agricultural products.

County agricultural agents also work closely with *family and community educators* (FCEs), who assist and instruct families on ways to improve their home life. This work ranges from offering advice and suggestions on preserving fruits and vegetables to improving health care and nutrition, assisting in balancing family budgets, and handling family stress. The FCE is responsible for keeping current in every area relating to the rural home and for sharing this information with families in a particular county or group of counties.

4-H Club agents organize and direct the educational projects and activities of the 4-H Club, the largest out-of-school youth program in the United States. Nearly seven million youths participate in 4-H Clubs in rural and urban settings. 4-H educational programs focus on building lifelong learning skills that develop youth potential. An extensive set of programs is designed to engage youth in healthy learning experiences, increasing self-esteem, and problem-solving skills. Programs address stress management, self-protection, parent-teen communication, personal development, careers, and global understanding. Youth are encouraged to explore science, technology, and citizenship. 4-H Club agents analyze the needs of individuals and the community, develop teaching materials, train volunteers, and organize exhibits at state and county fairs. They also introduce children and adolescents to techniques in raising animals and plants, including breeding, husbandry, and nutrition.

Due to technological advancements in electronic communication, there are interesting opportunities for careers in communications with the USDA Extension Service. There is a degree of specialization involved, especially at the federal level. Federal agricultural consultants often become program leaders who are responsible for developing and maintaining relationships with various land-grant colleges, universities, government agencies, and private agencies involved in agriculture. In some cases, they also become *educational research and training specialists* responsible for developing research programs in all phases of consulting work. The results of these programs are shared with the various state agencies.

Subject matter specialists develop programs through which new information can be presented to the farmers effectively. *Educational media specialists* condense information and distribute it as it becomes available to the states for use in their local extension programs. These consultants may be designated *extension service specialists.* An extension service worker who is in charge of programs for a group of counties is known as a *district extension service agent.*

■ REQUIREMENTS
High School
You should follow your high school's college preparatory program and take courses in English, government, foreign language, and history. Also, be sure to take courses in mathematics and the sciences, particularly biology and physics. Computer courses will also be beneficial. Take any economics courses available, along with accounting and business classes, as agricultural consultants are actively involved in farm management.

Postsecondary Training
To do this work, you'll need a bachelor's degree with a major in agriculture or economics. If you hope to join the on-campus staff at your state's agricultural college, you'll need at least a master's degree. College courses usually required for this work include English, history, chemistry, biology, economics, education, sociology, and speech, as well as animal science, crop production, horticulture, soils, and farm management. A number of colleges have developed regular agricultural extension curriculums to be followed by those hoping to enter the field.

After finishing college, county agents are kept up to date on the latest programs, policies, and teaching techniques through in-service training programs run by state agricultural colleges and the Department of Agriculture.

Other Requirements
You'll need a background of practical farming experience and a thorough knowledge of the types of problems confronting farmers, members of rural communities, and their families. Farmers naturally feel more comfortable seeking advice from people whom they feel have a complete understanding of their work.

You must be a good teacher and should enjoy working with people. You must also be assertive, yet diplomatic, and have a particular affinity for farmers and their problems. In addition, you will be expected to organize group projects, meetings, and broad educational programs that both adults and young people involved in agriculture will find stimulating and useful. You'll need the professional interest and enthusiasm that will enable you to keep up with the huge amount of new agricultural information constantly being released. You must be willing to learn and use the latest teaching techniques to disseminate current agricultural practices and knowledge to local residents.

EXPLORING

To get a sense of the job, you can read the pamphlets and occupational information brochures published by the USDA about this field, and you can request meetings with your local agricultural agent. Any of the state agricultural colleges will send materials or release the name of the local agent for interested students.

Another way to prepare to explore this field is to join groups such as 4-H, National FFA Organization (formerly Future Farmers of America), and the Boy or Girl Scouts. You may also volunteer to work at an extension office. It may be possible to visit with farmers or others engaged in agriculture to hear their impressions of the work carried on by the agricultural consultants in your particular county.

EMPLOYERS

Federal agricultural consultants are employed by the USDA to assist county extension officers and supervisors in planning, developing, and coordinating national, regional, and state extension programs. They're headquartered in Washington, D.C. County agricultural agents may be employed jointly by the Department of Agriculture and the agricultural college in each state.

County agents may also specialize, especially in those counties employing more than two or three agents. Many counties with diverse agricultural businesses and farms will often have five or more agents. A single county may employ specialists in fruit and grain production, dairy, poultry production, farm machinery, pest control, soils, nursery management, conservation, and livestock.

STARTING OUT

While your college's placement service may be of some help in finding a job, you will need to apply to the director of the extension service at the agricultural college in the state in which you hope to work. If a job vacancy is available, the director of the extension service will screen the qualifications of the various applicants and submit the names to a board or council responsible for making the final selection.

ADVANCEMENT

Competent consultants, as a rule, are promoted fairly rapidly and early in their careers. The promotions may be in the form of positions of higher responsibility within the same county, reassignment to a different county within the state, or an increase in salary. Many agents,

INSIDE THE USDA

Professionals and technicians with agricultural education and training can find work in a number of USDA programs, including:

- Agricultural Research Service (ARS) (http://www.ars.usda.gov): The principal in-house research agency of USDA.

- National Agricultural Library (http://www.nalusda.gov): Part of the ARS; a major international source for agriculture information; one of four national libraries in the country.

- Economic Research Service (http://www.ers.usda.gov): Provides information about agriculture and natural resources.

- National Agricultural Statistics Service (http://www.usda.gov/nass): Administers USDA's program for collecting and publishing timely national and state agricultural statistics.

after moving through a succession of more demanding extension jobs, join the staff at the state agricultural college. Many directors of extension services began their careers in this way.

It is also possible to branch out to other areas. Agricultural consultants often go into related jobs, especially those in industries that specialize in agricultural products. The training they have received and their background in agriculture makes them excellent candidates for many jobs in the agricultural industry.

EARNINGS

The earnings of agricultural consultants vary from state to state and from county to county. Most USDA professionals start out at the GS-5 level (government pay grade), which in 2004 ranged between $24,075 and $31,302 annually, depending on education and experience. Agricultural consultants then move up through the government pay grades, earning more. GS-9 level, for example, had a starting base pay of $35,519 in 2004. With some years of experience with the USDA, and with additional education, consultants can advance to GS-14, which in 2004 paid between $74,335 and $96,637 a year. Most consultants are eligible for other benefits such as paid vacations and sick days, health insurance, and pension plans.

WORK ENVIRONMENT

This work is often both mentally and physically taxing. Agricultural consultants will find themselves faced with numerous problems requiring their assistance in the field for long periods of time. They may be in their office handling routine matters every day for a month and then not work in the office for the next six weeks. (Consultants usually have a private office where they can speak in confidence with those who seek assistance.) As a rule, agricultural consultants spend about half of their time in the field working with farmers on specific problems, scheduling or conducting group meetings, or simply distributing new updated information. They usually drive from 500 to 1,500 miles per month while on the job. The work may be hard on the consultant's family, since evening meetings are required, and the agent is often invited to weekend events as well. For example, agents may conduct small informal meetings on Monday and Tuesday nights to discuss particular problems being faced by a small group of farmers in the county. They may be home on Wednesday, work with a students' 4-H Club on Thursday, conduct another meeting on Friday, and then judge a livestock show at the county fair on Saturday.

Hours for consultants are not regular, and the pay is not particularly high considering the number of hours agents are required to work. But this work can be very rewarding. There is great satisfaction to be found working with people who genuinely appreciate the time, advice, and assistance the agent brings.

■ OUTLOOK

The work of agricultural consultants is, naturally, heavily dependent on the employment of farmers and farm managers, and the U.S. Department of Labor predicts a decline in employment for these workers through 2012. As farms consolidate and there are fewer farm families, the need for agricultural consultants may also decline. However, consultants may find opportunities working with rural nonfarming families and various suburban residents who are interested in specialty areas such as urban horticulture and gardening.

As the farming industry is becoming more complex, those consultants with the most thorough education and training will have the best job prospects. The idea of agricultural consulting programs is spreading to many foreign countries. Job opportunities may come from a need for U.S. county and federal agents to assist their counterparts in other countries in setting up and operating agricultural consulting programs.

■ FOR MORE INFORMATION

To learn about CSREES and to access a list of land-grant universities, contact

U.S. Department of Agriculture
Cooperative State Research, Education, and Extension
   Service

1400 Independence Avenue, SW, Room 4008,
   Waterfront Centre
Washington, DC 20250-2216
Tel: 202-720-2047
http://www.reeusda.gov

For more information on opportunities and education in the agricultural field, contact the following organizations:

4-H
Families, 4-H, and Nutrition
CSREES/USDA
1400 Independence Avenue, SW
Washington DC 20250-2225
http://www.4h-usa.org

National FFA Organization
National FFA Center
PO Box 68960
Indianapolis, IN 46268-0960
Tel: 317-802-6060
http://www.ffa.org

Agricultural Equipment Technicians

■ OVERVIEW

Agricultural equipment technicians work with modern farm machinery. They assemble, adjust, operate, maintain, modify, test, and even help design it. This machinery includes automatic animal feeding systems; milking machine systems; and tilling, planting, harvesting, irrigating, drying, and handling equipment. Agricultural equipment technicians work on farms or for agricultural machinery manufacturers or dealerships. They often supervise skilled mechanics and other workers who keep machines and systems operating at maximum efficiency. Approximately 32,330 agricultural equipment technicians are employed in the United States.

■ HISTORY

The history of farming equipment stretches back to prehistoric times, when the first agricultural workers developed the sickle. In the Middle Ages, the horse-drawn plow greatly increased farm production, and in the early 1700s, Jethro Tull designed and built the first mechanical seed planter, further increasing production. The industrial revolution brought advances in the design and use of specialized machinery for strenuous and repetitive work. It had a great impact on the agricultural industry, beginning in 1831 with Cyrus McCormick's invention of the reaper.

In the first half of the 20th century, governmental experiment stations developed high-yielding, standardized varieties of farm crops. This, combined with the establishment of agricultural equipment-producing companies, caused a boom in the production of farm machinery. In the late 1930s, the abundance of inexpensive petroleum spurred the development of gasoline- and diesel-run farm machinery. During the early 1940s, the resulting explosion in complex and powerful farm machinery multiplied production and replaced most of the horses and mules used on farms in the United States.

Modern farming is heavily dependent on very complex and expensive machinery. Highly trained and skilled technicians and farm mechanics are therefore required to install, operate, maintain, and modify this machinery, thereby ensuring the nation's farm productivity. Recent developments in agricultural mechanization and automation make the career of agricultural equipment technicians both challenging and rewarding. Sophisticated machines are being used to plant, cultivate, harvest, and process food; to contour, drain, and renovate land; and to clear land and harvest forest products in the process. Qualified agricultural equipment technicians are needed not only to service and sell this equipment, but also to manage it on the farm.

Farming has increasingly become a highly competitive, big business. A successful farmer may have hundreds of thousands or even millions of dollars invested in land and machinery. For this investment to pay off, it is vital to keep the machinery in excellent operating condition. Prompt and reliable service from the farm equipment manufacturer and dealer is necessary for the success of both farmer and dealer. Interruptions or delays because of poor service are costly for everyone involved. To provide good service, manufacturers and dealers need technicians and specialists who possess agricultural and engineering knowledge in addition to technical skills.

■ THE JOB

Agricultural equipment technicians work in a wide variety of jobs both on and off the farm. In general, most agricultural equipment technicians find employment in one of three areas: equipment manufacturing, equipment sales and service, and on-farm equipment management.

Equipment manufacturing technicians are involved primarily with the design and testing of agricultural equipment such as farm machinery; irrigation, power, and electrification systems; soil and water conservation equipment; and agricultural harvesting and processing equipment. There are two kinds of technicians working in this field: agricultural engineering technicians and agricultural equipment test technicians.

Agricultural engineering technicians work under the supervision of design engineers. They prepare original layouts and complete detailed drawings of agricultural equipment. They also review plans, diagrams, and blueprints to ensure that new products comply with company standards and design specifications. In order to do this they must use their knowledge of biological, engineering, and design principles. They also must keep current on all of the new equipment and materials being developed for the industry to make sure the machines run at their highest capacity.

Agricultural equipment test technicians test and evaluate the performance of agricultural machinery and equipment. In particular, they make sure the equipment conforms with operating requirements, such as horsepower, resistance to vibration, and strength and hardness of parts. They test equipment under actual field conditions on company-operated research farms and under more controlled conditions. They work with test equipment and recording instruments such as bend-fatigue machines, dynamometers, strength testers, hardness meters, analytical balances, and electronic recorders.

Test technicians are also trained in methods of recording the data gathered during these tests. They compute values such as horsepower and tensile strength using algebraic formulas and report their findings using graphs, tables, and sketches.

After the design and testing phases are complete, other agricultural equipment technicians work with engineers to perform any necessary adjustments in the equipment design. By performing these functions under the general supervision of the design engineer, technicians do the engineers' "detective work" so the engineers can devote more time to research and development.

QUICK FACTS

SCHOOL SUBJECTS
Mathematics
Technical/shop

PERSONAL SKILLS
Mechanical/manipulative
Technical/scientific

WORK ENVIRONMENT
Indoors and outdoors
Primarily multiple locations

MINIMUM EDUCATION LEVEL
Some postsecondary training

SALARY RANGE
$18,150 to $27,950 to
$39,220+

CERTIFICATION OR LICENSING
None available

OUTLOOK
More slowly than the average

DOT
624

GOE
03.03.01

NOC
7316

O*NET-SOC
45-2091.00, 49-3041.00

Large agricultural machinery companies may employ agricultural equipment technicians to supervise production, assembly, and plant operations.

Most manufacturers market their products through regional sales organizations to individual dealers. Technicians may serve as *sales representatives* of regional sales offices, where they are assigned a number of dealers in a given territory and sell agricultural equipment directly to them. They may also conduct sales-training programs for the dealers to help them become more effective salespeople.

These technicians are also qualified to work in sales positions within dealerships, either as *equipment sales workers* or *parts clerks*. They are required to perform equipment demonstrations for customers. They also appraise the value of used equipment for trade-in allowances. Technicians in these positions may advance to sales or parts manager positions.

Some technicians involved in sales become *systems specialists*, who work for equipment dealerships, assisting farmers in the planning and installation of various kinds of mechanized systems, such as irrigation or materials-handling systems, grain bins, or drying systems.

In the service area, technicians may work as *field service representatives*, forming a liaison between the companies they represent and the dealers. They assist the dealers in product warranty work, diagnose service problems, and give seminars or workshops on new service information and techniques. These types of service technicians may begin their careers as specialists in certain kinds of repairs. *Hydraulic specialists*, for instance, maintain and repair the component parts of hydraulic systems in tractors and other agricultural machines. *Diesel specialists* rebuild, calibrate, and test diesel pumps, injectors, and other diesel engine components.

Many service technicians work as service managers or parts department managers. *Service managers* assign duties to the repair workers, diagnose machinery problems, estimate repair costs for customers, and manage the repair shop.

Parts department managers in equipment dealerships maintain inventories of all the parts that may be requested either by customers or by the service departments of the dealership. They deal directly with customers, parts suppliers, and dealership managers and must have good sales and purchasing skills. They also must be effective business managers.

Technicians working on the farm have various responsibilities, the most important of which is keeping machinery in top working condition during the growing season. During off-season periods they may overhaul or modify equipment or simply keep the machinery in good working order for the next season.

Some technicians find employment as *on-farm machinery managers*, usually working on large farms servicing or supervising the servicing of all automated equipment. They also monitor the field operation of all machines and keep complete records of costs, utilization, and repair procedures relating to the maintenance of each piece of mechanical equipment.

■ REQUIREMENTS
High School
You should take as many mathematics, technical/shop, and mechanical drawing classes as you can. Take science classes, including courses in earth science, to gain some insight into agriculture, soil conservation, and the environment. Look into adult education programs available to high school students; in such a program, you may be able to enroll in pre-engineering courses.

Postsecondary Training
A high school diploma is necessary, and some college and specialized experience is also important. A four-year education, along with some continuing education courses, can be very helpful in pursuing work, particularly if you're seeking jobs with the government.

Postsecondary education for the agricultural equipment technician should include courses in general agriculture, agricultural power and equipment, practical engineering, hydraulics, agricultural-equipment business methods, electrical equipment, engineering, social science, economics, and sales techniques. On-the-job experience during the summer is invaluable and frequently is included as part of the regular curriculum in these programs. Students are placed on farms, functioning as technicians-in-training. They also may work in farm equipment dealerships where their time is divided between the sales, parts, and service departments. Occupational experience, one of the most important phases of the postsecondary training program, gives students an opportunity to discover which field best suits them and which phase of the business they prefer. Upon completion of this program, most technical and community colleges award an associate's degree.

Other Requirements
The work of the agricultural equipment technician is similar to that of an engineer. You must have a knowledge of physical science and engineering principles and enough mathematical background to work with these principles. You must have a working knowledge of farm

crops, machinery, and all agricultural-related products. You should be detail-oriented. You should also have people skills, as you'll be working closely with professionals, other technicians, and farmers.

EXPLORING

If you live in a farming community, you've probably already had some experience with farming equipment. Vocational agriculture education programs in high schools can be found in most rural settings, many suburban settings, and even in some urban schools. The teaching staff and counselors in these schools can provide considerable information about this career.

Light industrial machinery is now used in almost every industry. It is always helpful to watch machinery being used and to talk with people who own, operate, and repair it.

Summer and part-time work on a farm, in an agricultural equipment manufacturing plant, or in an equipment sales and service business offers opportunities to work on or near agricultural and light industrial machinery. Such a job may provide you with a clearer idea about the various activities, challenges, rewards, and possible limitations of this career.

EMPLOYERS

Depending on their area of specialization, agricultural equipment technicians work for engineers, manufacturers, scientists, sales and services companies, and farmers. They can also find work with government agencies, such as the U.S. Department of Agriculture.

STARTING OUT

It is still possible to enter this career by starting as an inexperienced worker in a machinery manufacturer's plant or on a farm and learning machine technician skills on the job. However, this approach is becoming increasingly difficult due to the complexity of modern machinery. Because of this, some formal classroom training is usually necessary, and many people find it difficult to complete even part-time study of the field's theory and science while also working a full-time job.

Operators and managers of large, well-equipped farms and farm equipment companies in need of employees keep in touch with colleges offering agricultural equipment programs. Students who do well during their occupational experience period usually have an excellent chance of going to work for the same employer after graduation. Many colleges have an interview day on which personnel representatives of manufacturers, distributors, farm owners or managers, and dealers are invited to recruit students completing technician programs. In gen-

TILLERS INTERNATIONAL

While much of farm technology is devoted to new methods of crop production, Tillers International casts back to earlier days in its efforts to preserve historic equipment and farming methods. Through Tillers (http://www.wmich.edu/tillers), you can take classes in blacksmithing and woodworking, order videotapes on ox-driving, or get a rope-making kit.

eral, any student who does well in a training program can expect employment immediately upon graduation.

ADVANCEMENT

Opportunities for advancement and self-employment are excellent for those with the initiative to keep abreast of continuing developments in the farm equipment field. Technicians often attend company schools in sales and service or take advanced evening courses in colleges.

EARNINGS

Agricultural technicians working for the government may be able to enter a position at GS-5 (government wage scale), which was $24,075 in 2004. The U.S. Department of Labor reports that mean annual earnings for agricultural equipment mechanics was $27,950 in 2002. Hourly pay ranged from less than $8.73 to more than $18.86. Those working on farms often receive room and board as a supplement to their annual salary. The salary that technicians eventually receive depends—as do most salaries—on individual ability, initiative, and the supply of skilled technicians in the field of work or locality. There is opportunity to work overtime during planting and harvesting seasons.

In addition to their salaries, most technicians receive fringe benefits such as health and retirement packages, paid vacations, and other benefits similar to those received by engineering technicians. Technicians employed in sales are usually paid a commission in addition to their base salary.

WORK ENVIRONMENT

Working conditions vary according to the type of field chosen. Technicians who are employed by large farming operations will work indoors or outdoors depending on the season and the tasks that need to be done. Planning machine overhauls and the directing of such work usually are done in enclosed spaces equipped for it. As implied by its name, field servicing and repairs are done in the field.

This agricultural equipment technician tests the air pressure of a large tractor tire as part of a quality control procedure.

Some agricultural equipment sales representatives work in their own or nearby communities, while others must travel extensively.

Technicians in agricultural equipment research, development, and production usually work under typical factory conditions: some work in an office or laboratory; others work in a manufacturing plant; or, in some cases, field testing and demonstration are performed where the machinery will be used.

For technicians who assemble, adjust, modify, or test equipment and for those who provide customer service, application studies, and maintenance services, the surroundings may be similar to large automobile service centers.

In all cases, safety precautions must be a constant concern. Appropriate clothing, an acute awareness of one's environment, and careful lifting or hoisting of heavy machinery must be standard. While safety practices have improved greatly over the years, certain risks do exist. Heavy lifting may cause injury, and burns and cuts are always possible. The surroundings may be noisy and grimy. Some work is performed in cramped or awkward physical positions. Gasoline fumes and odors from oil products are a constant factor. Most technicians ordinarily work a 40-hour week, but emergency repairs may require overtime.

■ OUTLOOK

The *Occupational Outlook Handbook* reports that employment of agricultural equipment technicians is expected to grow more slowly than the average through 2012. However, agricultural equipment businesses now demand more expertise than ever before. A variety of complex specialized machines and mechanical devices are steadily being produced and modified to help farmers improve the quality and productivity of their labor. These machines require trained technicians to design, produce, test, sell, and service them. Trained workers also are needed to instruct the final owners in their proper repair, operation, and maintenance.

In addition, the agricultural industry is adopting advanced computer and electronic technology. Computer skills are becoming more and more useful in this field. Precision farming will also require specialized training as more agricultural equipment becomes hooked up to satellite systems.

As agriculture becomes more technical, the agricultural equipment technician will assume an increasingly vital role in helping farmers solve problems that interfere with efficient production. These opportunities exist not only in the United States, but also worldwide. As agricultural economies everywhere become mechanized, inventive technicians with training in modern business principles will find expanding employment opportunities abroad.

■ FOR MORE INFORMATION

To read equipment sales statistics, agricultural reports, and other news of interest to agricultural equipment technicians, visit the AEM website.

Association of Equipment Manufacturers (AEM)
10 South Riverside Plaza, Suite 1220
Chicago, IL 60606-3710
Tel: 312-321-1470
Email: info@aem.org
http://www.aem.org

At the FEMA website, you can learn about their publications and read industry news.

Farm Equipment Manufacturers Association (FEMA)
1000 Executive Parkway, Suite 100
St. Louis, MO 63141-6369
Tel: 314-878-2304
Email: info@farmequip.org
http://www.farmequip.org

Agricultural Pilots

◼ OVERVIEW

Agricultural pilots, also called *ag pilots* and *aerial applicators,* perform flying jobs related to the farming industry. They are skilled professionals who operate aircraft for such purposes as transporting cargo to market, aerial applications (also known as crop dusting), hauling feed, or planting seed. In addition to flying aircraft, agricultural pilots are responsible for performing a variety of safety-related tasks involving both the aircraft and the cargo. They may be self-employed or work for large pest control companies or government agencies.

◼ HISTORY

The history of agricultural aviation is, naturally, tied to that of modern aviation. This period is generally considered to have begun with the flight of Orville and Wilbur Wright's heavier-than-air machine on December 17, 1903. On that day, the Wright brothers flew their machine four times and became the first airplane pilots. In the early days of aviation, the pilot's job was quite different from that of the pilot of today. As he flew the plane, for example, Orville Wright was lying on his stomach in the middle of the bottom wing of the plane. There was a strap across his hips, and to turn the plane, he had to tilt his hips from side to side—hardly the way today's pilot makes a turn!

The aviation industry developed rapidly as designers raced to improve upon the Wright brothers' design. During the early years of flight, many aviators earned a living as "barnstormers," entertaining people with stunts and by taking passengers on short flights around the countryside. As airplanes became more dependable, they were adapted for a variety of purposes such as use in the military and for the United States government-run airmail service. According to the National Agricultural Aviation Association, the first time a plane was used to spread pesticide was in 1921. In an experiment conducted by the military, lead arsenate dust was spread by plane to stop a moth infestation in Ohio. By 1923 crop dusting was being done on a commercial basis.

Today planes used for agricultural aviation are specifically designed for that purpose. They can carry hundreds of gallons of pesticides and are equipped with the latest technology, such as Global Positioning Systems (GPS). Unlike the crop-dusting process of the past, which used dry chemicals, today's process typically involves liquid pesticides and other controlling products as well as fertilizer sprays. Advances in agricultural aviation have allowed U.S. farms to become increasingly productive.

◼ THE JOB

Agricultural pilots perform a number of duties that benefit the farming industry as well as the environment, assisting farmers in the prevention of crop damage and other duties performed. Some work for pest control companies while others are self-employed. In farm work, agricultural pilots spray chemicals over crops and orchards to fertilize them, control plant diseases or weeds, and control pests. They also drop seeds into fields to grow crops.

Before agricultural pilots begin the process of spraying farmland, they must survey the area for buildings, hills, power lines, and other obstacles and hazards. They must also notify residents and businesses in the general area where they will spray so that people and animals can be moved away from target areas.

Some agricultural pilots, particularly those who work for pest control companies, may mix their own chemicals, using their knowledge of what mixture may be best for certain types of plants, plant or soil conditions, or pest problems. Crop dusters fly small turboprop planes, which are slower compared to larger, transport craft, but which are good for flying close to the ground and for carrying heavy loads. They must fly close to the ground, often only a few feet above a crop, so that the chemicals will be spread only in designated areas.

Agricultural pilots can also help farmers by dropping food for livestock over pastures, photograph wildlife or count game animals for conservation programs, and fight forest fires by dumping water or fire-retardant materials over burning areas.

No matter what the job, pilots must determine weather and flight conditions, make sure that sufficient fuel is on board to complete the flight safely, and verify the maintenance status of the airplane before each flight. They perform system checks to test the proper functioning of instrumentation and electronic and mechanical systems on the plane.

QUICK FACTS

SCHOOL SUBJECTS
Mathematics
Physics

PERSONAL SKILLS
Leadership/management
Technical/scientific

WORK ENVIRONMENT
Indoors and outdoors
Primarily multiple locations

MINIMUM EDUCATION LEVEL
Some postsecondary training

SALARY RANGE
$26,100 to $49,970 to
$101,460+

CERTIFICATION OR LICENSING
Required by all states

OUTLOOK
Little change or more slowly
than the average

DOT
196

GOE
07.03.01

NOC
2271

O*NET-SOC
53-2011.00

RISKY BUT THRILLING

Agricultural aviation can be very exciting, but flying small aircraft at low levels is also quite dangerous. The optimal flight pattern for spraying a field may also be the most difficult, with hazards including cross-winds and being blinded by the sun. Besides avoiding hills, trees, and power lines, crop pilots have to avoid spraying livestock and neighboring houses—all while flying a straight line at over 100 miles per hour, with his landing gear mere feet above the field! Nor is crashing the only hazard inherent in the job: The pesticides used in crop dusting can also be very toxic.

Once all of these preflight duties are done, the pilot taxis the aircraft to the designated runway and prepares for takeoff. Takeoff speeds must be calculated based on the aircraft's weight, which is affected by the weight of the cargo being carried.

During flights, agricultural pilots must constantly be aware of their surroundings, since they fly so close to the ground and frequently near hazards such as power lines. They need good judgment to deal with any emergency situations that might arise. They monitor aircraft systems, keep an eye on the weather conditions, and perform the flight's assigned job, such as spraying fertilizer.

Once the pilot has landed and taxied to the appropriate area, he or she follows a "shutdown" checklist of procedures. Pilots also keep logs of their flight hours. Those who are self-employed or working for smaller companies are typically responsible for refueling the airplane, performing maintenance, and keeping business records.

■ REQUIREMENTS
High School

There are a number of classes you can take in high school to help prepare you for becoming a pilot. You should take science classes, such as chemistry and physics, as well as mathematics, such as algebra and geometry. Take computer classes to familiarize yourself with this tool. Since you will be responsible for the maintenance and care of a plane, you may also benefit from taking an electronics shop class or other shop class where you get to work on engines. Take English classes to improve your research and writing skills. Throughout your career you will need to study flying or repair manuals, file reports, and communicate with customers. Since you may be responsible for record keeping, take business or accounting classes. If your school offers agriculture classes, take any that will teach you about soils, crops, and growing methods.

Postsecondary Training

Many companies that employ pilots prefer to hire candidates with at least two years of college training. Courses in engineering, meteorology, physics, mathematics, and agriculture are helpful in preparing for this career. In addition to these courses, you will need training as a pilot. There are approximately 600 civilian flying schools certified by the Federal Aviation Administration (FAA), including some colleges and universities that offer degree credit for pilot training. A number of schools offer training specifically in agricultural aviation. Some people take up this career after leaving the military, where they trained as pilots.

Certification or Licensing

Agricultural pilots must hold a commercial pilot's license from the FAA. A fairly long and rigorous process is involved in obtaining a commercial license. The first step in this process is to receive flying instruction. Anyone who is 16 or over and can pass a rigid mandatory physical exam can apply for permission to take flying lessons. When you have finished this training, you can take a written exam. If you pass the exam and fulfill such requirements as being at least 17 years of age and have completed a solo flying requirement of 20 hours or more, you can apply for your private pilot's license. The next step in getting a commercial license is to continue to log flying time and increase your knowledge and skills. To receive your commercial license you must be at least 18 years of age, have 250 hours of flying time, and successfully complete a number of exams. These tests include a physical exam; a written test given by the FAA covering such topics as safe flight operations, navigation principles, and federal aviation regulations; and a practical test to demonstrate your flying skills. Pilots must also receive a rating for the kind of plane they can fly (such as single-engine or multi-engine). In addition, a commercial pilot needs an instrument rating by the FAA and a restricted radio telephone operator's permit by the Federal Communications Commission (FCC). In states where they spray restricted pesticides, agricultural pilots must be certified by the U.S. Department of Agriculture.

Other Requirements

All pilots must have sound physical and emotional health. They need excellent eyesight and eye-hand coordination as well as excellent hearing and normal heart rate and blood pressure. The successful agricultural pilot is also detail-oriented since much paperwork, planning, and following of regulations is involved in this job. Those who are self-employed or working for smaller companies may find that they have frequent contact with customers, and so they must be able to work well with others. Naturally, an agricultural pilot should have an interest in farming methods and the environment as well as a love of flying. Good judgment is essential for this work.

■ EXPLORING

You can explore this occupation through a number of activities. Join groups such as your high school aviation club and the National FFA Organization (formerly Future Farmers of America). These groups may give you the opportunity to meet with professionals in the field, learn about farm products and management, and find others with similar interests. Read publications related to these industries such as the magazines *AgAir Update* (http://www.agairupdate.com) and *Progressive Farmer* (http://progressivefarmer.com). If you have the financial resources, you can take flying lessons once you are 16 and have passed a physical exam. Also, consider learning how to operate a ham radio. This skill will help you when you apply for your restricted radio operator's permit, a requirement for commercial pilots.

■ EMPLOYERS

California and the southern states, where the crop growing season lasts longest, are where agricultural pilots find the most work. They also find some work with northern crops and in forests of the northeastern and western states. Federal and state government departments also employ agricultural pilots to assist with environmental, conservation, and preservation needs.

■ STARTING OUT

It is not unusual for people to enter this field after gaining experience in the agricultural industry itself, working on farms and learning about crop production while they also develop their flying skills. Others enter with flying as their first love and are drawn to the challenge of agricultural aviation. Once pilots have completed their training, they may find that contacts made through aviation schools lead to job openings. Those who have the financial means can begin by opening their own business. Equipment, however, is very expensive—a single plane appropriately outfitted can cost anywhere from $100,000 to $900,000. A number of people, therefore, begin by working for large aerial applications companies before they strike out on their own.

■ ADVANCEMENT

Agricultural pilots who work for a company can be promoted to manager. Self-employed agricultural pilots move up by charging more money for their services and increasing their client base. Another way to advance is to

An agricultural pilot applies a low-insecticide bait that is targeted against western corn rootworms.

work in other areas of commercial aviation. These pilots may fly cargo and people to remote locations or become aerial photographers.

■ EARNINGS

If they work throughout the entire year, agricultural pilots can make between $30,000 and $80,000 per year or more. Those who fly about half the year make near $25,000. Agricultural pilots who are employed by companies rarely get paid vacation and only a few companies offer health and accident insurance and profit-sharing and pension plans. (For commercial pilots in general, median annual earnings in 2002 were $47,970; the lowest 10 percent earned less than $26,100, while the highest 10 percent earned more than $101,460.)

■ WORK ENVIRONMENT

The vast majority of an agricultural pilot's job takes place outdoors, during the early morning and early evening hours. Their work is demanding and can be hazardous. When flying, agricultural pilots wear safety gear consisting of a helmet, safety belt, and shoulder harness, because they fly under such difficult conditions. They fly close to the ground in populated areas and must be cautious to avoid obstacles. They also face exposure to pesticides and other harsh substances. When mixing or loading chemicals onto the plane, they sometimes wear gloves or masks to prevent the inhaling of harmful vapors.

■ OUTLOOK

Employment opportunities for experienced agricultural pilots are expected to continue into the future. However, the demand for agricultural pilots depends largely on farmers' needs. For example, during times when insect and pest control becomes a problem, there is greater demand for agricultural pilots. There is also some concern within the industry that genetically engineered crops (resistant to certain diseases) may decrease the need for aerial applications and cause a loss of business for agricultural pilots. Finally, there has been an push from environmental groups for U.S. farmers to use less fertilizer and pesticide, as well as an increase in the use of organic farming techniques. Keeping these factors in mind, employment prospects will probably be best with larger farms and ranches and in states with long growing seasons.

■ FOR MORE INFORMATION

This organization has information on crop protection products and developments in the industry.

American Crop Protection Association
1156 Fifteenth Street, NW, Suite 400
Washington, DC 20005
Tel: 202-296-1585
http://www.acpa.org

This organization promotes high standards and continuing education in the field.

National Agricultural Aviation Association
1005 E Street, SE
Washington, DC 20003
Tel: 202-546-5722
Email: information@agaviation.org
http://www.agaviation.org

For information on opportunities in the agricultural field and local chapters, contact

National FFA Organization
National FFA Center
6060 FFA Drive
PO Box 68960
Indianapolis, IN 46268
Tel: 317-802-6060
http://www.ffa.org

These magazines, available in print, also have websites with feature articles and information related to their fields.

AgAir Update
PO Box 1548
Perry, GA 31069
Tel: 912-987-2250
http://www.agairupdate.com

Progressive Farmer
PO Box 830656
Birmingham, AL 35283

Tel: 800-292-2340
http://www.progressivefarmer.com

Agricultural Scientists

■ OVERVIEW

Agricultural scientists study all aspects of living organisms and the relationships of plants and animals to their environment. They conduct basic research in laboratories or in the field. They apply the results to such tasks as increasing crop yields and improving the environment. Some agricultural scientists plan and administer programs for testing foods, drugs, and other products. Others direct activities at public exhibits at such places as zoos and botanical gardens. Some agricultural scientists are professors at colleges and universities or work as consultants to business firms or the government. Others work in technical sales and service jobs for manufacturers of agricultural products. There are approximately 18,000 agricultural and food scientists in the United States; about 40 percent work for the federal, state, or local governments. Several thousand more are employed as university professors.

■ HISTORY

In 1840, Justius von Liebig of Germany published *Organic Chemistry in Its Applications to Agriculture and Physiology* and launched the systematic development of the agricultural sciences. A formal system of agricultural education soon followed in both Europe and the United States. Prior to the publication of this work, agricultural developments relied on the collective experience of farmers handed down over generations. Agricultural science has techniques in common with many other disciplines including biology, botany, genetics, nutrition, breeding, and engineering. Discoveries and improvements in these fields contributed to advances in agriculture. Some milestones include the discovery of the practice of crop rotation and the application of manure as fertilizer, which greatly increased farm yields in the 1700s. Farm mechanization was greatly advanced by the invention of the mechanical reaper in 1831 and the gasoline tractor in 1892. Chemical fertilizers were first used in the 19th century; pesticides and herbicides soon followed. In 1900, the research of an Austrian monk, Gregor Johann Mendel, was rediscovered. His theories of plant characteristics, based on studies using generations of garden peas, formed the foundation for the science of genetics.

In the 20th century, scientists and engineers were at the forefront of farm, crop, and food processing improvements. Conservationist Gifford Pinchot developed some of the first methods to prevent soil erosion in 1910, and Clarence Birdseye perfected a method of freezing food in the 1920s. Birdseye's discoveries allowed for new crops of produce previously too perishable for the marketplace. Engineers in the 1930s developed more powerful farm machinery and scientists developed hybrid corn. By the 1960s, high-powered machinery and better quality feed and pesticides were in common use. Today, advances in genetic engineering and biotechnology are leading to more efficient, economical methods of farming and new markets for crops.

■ THE JOB

The nature of the work of the agricultural scientist can be broken down into several areas of specialization. Within each specialization there are various careers.

The following are careers that fall under the areas of plant and soil science.

Agronomists investigate large-scale food-crop problems, conduct experiments, and develop new methods of growing crops to ensure more efficient production, higher yields, and improved quality. They use genetic engineering to develop crops that are resistant to pests, drought, and plant diseases.

Agronomists also engage in soil science. They analyze soils to find ways to increase production and reduce soil erosion. They study the responses of various soil types to fertilizers, tillage practices, and crop rotation. Since soil science is related to environmental science, agronomists may also use their expertise to consult with farmers and agricultural companies on environmental quality and effective land use.

Botanists are concerned with plants and their environment, structure, heredity, and economic value in such fields as agronomy, horticulture, and medicine.

Horticulturists study fruit and nut orchards as well as garden plants such as vegetables and flowers. They conduct experiments to develop new and improved varieties and to increase crop quality and yields. They also work to improve plant culture methods for the landscaping and beautification of communities, parks, and homes.

Plant breeders apply genetics and biotechnology to improve plants' yield, quality, and resistance to harsh weather, disease, and insects. They might work on developing strains of wild or cultivated plants that will have a larger yield and increase profits.

Plant pathologists research plant diseases and the decay of plant products to identify symptoms, determine causes, and develop control measures. They attempt to predict outbreaks by studying how different soils, climates, and geography affect the spread and intensity of plant disease.

Another area of specialization for agricultural scientists is animal science.

Animal scientists conduct research and develop improved methods for housing, breeding, feeding, and controlling diseases of domestic farm animals. They inspect and grade livestock food products, purchase livestock, or work in sales and marketing of livestock products. They often consult agricultural businesses on such areas as upgrading animal housing, lowering mortality rates, or increasing production of animal products such as milk and eggs.

Dairy scientists study the selection, breeding, feeding, and management of dairy cattle. For example, they research how various types of food and environmental conditions affect milk production and quality. They also develop new breeding programs to improve dairy herds.

Poultry scientists study the breeding, feeding, and management of poultry to improve the quantity and quality of eggs and other poultry products.

Animal breeders specialize in improving the quality of farm animals. They may work for a state agricultural department, agricultural extension station, or university. Some of their work is done in a laboratory, but much of it is done outdoors working directly on animals. Using their knowledge of genetics, animal breeders develop systems for animals to achieve desired characteristics such as strength, fast maturation, resistance to disease, and quality of meat.

Food science is a specialty closely related to animal science, but it focuses on meeting consumer demand for food products in ways that are healthy, safe, and convenient.

Food scientists use their backgrounds in chemistry, microbiology, and other sciences to develop new or better ways of preserving, packaging, processing, storing,

QUICK FACTS

SCHOOL SUBJECTS
Biology
Chemistry

PERSONAL SKILLS
Communication/ideas
Technical/scientific

WORK ENVIRONMENT
Indoors and outdoors
Primarily multiple locations

MINIMUM EDUCATION LEVEL
Bachelor's degree

SALARY RANGE
$28,750 to $48,670 to $85,460+

CERTIFICATION OR LICENSING
Voluntary (certification)
Required for certain positions (licensing)

OUTLOOK
Little change or more slowly than the average

DOT
040

GOE
02.03.03

NOC
2121

O*NET-SOC
17-2021.00, 19-1011.00, 19-1013.01

BEYOND THE LABORATORY

Agricultural science isn't limited to food, plant, soil, and animal science. Many scientists are also concerned with range lands and pastures, and grazing management. According to the USDA, one-half of the Earth's land surface is grazed. Fifty-five percent of U.S. land surface is made up of range lands, pastures, and hay lands. U.S. hay production amounts to $11 billion a year, and grazing lands support a livestock industry that contributes $78 billion a year in farm sales to the U.S. economy.

and delivering foods. *Food technologists* work in product development to discover new food sources and analyze food content to determine levels of vitamins, fat, sugar, and protein. Food technologists also work to enforce government regulations, inspecting food processing areas and ensuring that sanitation, safety, quality, and waste management standards are met.

Another field related to agricultural science is agricultural engineering.

Agricultural engineers apply engineering principles to work in the food and agriculture industries. They design or develop agricultural equipment and machines, supervise production, and conduct tests on new designs and machine parts. They develop plans and specifications for agricultural buildings and for drainage and irrigation systems. They work on flood control, soil erosion, and land reclamation projects. They design food processing systems and equipment to convert farm products to consumer foods. Agricultural engineers contribute to making farming easier and more profitable through the introduction of new farm machinery and through advancements in soil and water conservation. Agricultural engineers in industry engage in research or in the design, testing, or sales of equipment.

Much of the research conducted by agricultural scientists is done in laboratories and requires a familiarity with research techniques and the use of laboratory equipment and computers. Some research, however, is carried out wherever necessary. A botanist may have occasion to examine the plants that grow in the volcanic valleys of Alaska, or an animal breeder may study the behavior of animals on the plains of Africa.

■ REQUIREMENTS
High School
Follow your high school's college preparatory program, which will include courses in English, foreign language, mathematics, and government. Also take biology, chem-

istry, physics, and any other science courses available. You must also become familiar with basic computer skills, including programming. It may be possible for you to perform laboratory assistant duties for your science teachers. Visiting research laboratories and attending lectures by agricultural scientists can also be helpful.

Postsecondary Training
Educational requirements for agricultural scientists are very high. A doctorate is usually mandatory for careers as college or university professors, independent researchers, or field managers. A bachelor's degree may be acceptable for some entry-level jobs, such as testing or inspecting technicians, or as technical sales or service representatives. Promotions, however, are very limited for these employees unless they earn advanced degrees.

To become an agricultural scientist, you should pursue a degree related to agricultural and biological science. As an undergraduate, you should have a firm foundation in biology, with courses in chemistry, physics, mathematics, and English. Most colleges and universities have agricultural science curriculums, although liberal arts colleges may emphasize the biological sciences. State universities usually offer agricultural science programs, too.

While pursuing an advanced degree, you'll participate in research projects and write a dissertation on your specialized area of study. You'll also do fieldwork and laboratory research along with your classroom studies.

Certification or Licensing
A voluntary certification program is offered by the Federation of Certifying Boards in Agriculture, Biology, Earth and Environmental Sciences, which was originally known as American Registry of Certified Professionals in Agronomy, Crops and Soils (ARCPACS). The federation, however, still uses the acronym ARCPACS, and it is associated with the American Society of Argonomy. ARCPACS offers a number of certifications, such as certified professional agronomist (CPA) and certified professional plant pathologist (CPPP), to candidates based on their training and work. In general, requirements include meeting a minimum education level and having a certain amount of work experience (for example, a bachelor's degree and five years of work experience or a master's degree and three years of experience), passing an exam, and having appropriate references. Recertification requirements typically include the completion of a certain amount of continuing education credits every two years in addition to payment of dues and adherence to a code of ethics.

According to the American Society of Agricultural Engineers, agricultural engineers must hold an engineer's license.

Other Requirements

As a researcher, you should be self-motivated enough to work effectively alone, yet be able to function cooperatively as part of a team. You should have an inexhaustible curiosity about the nature of living things and their environments. You must be systematic in your work habits and in your approach to investigation and experimentation and must have the persistence to continue or start over when experiments are not immediately successful.

Work performed by agricultural scientists in offices and laboratories requires intense powers of concentration and the ability to communicate one's thoughts systematically. In addition to these skills, physical stamina is necessary for those scientists who do field research in remote areas of the world.

◼ EXPLORING

If you live in an agricultural community, you may be able to find part-time or summer work on a farm or ranch. Joining a chapter of the National FFA Organization (formerly Future Farmers of America) or a 4-H program will introduce you to the concerns of farmers and researchers and may involve you directly in science projects. Contact your county's extension office to learn about regional projects. You may also find part-time work in veterinarian's offices, florist shops, landscape nurseries, orchards, farms, zoos, aquariums, botanical gardens, or museums. Volunteer work is often available in zoos and animal shelters.

◼ EMPLOYERS

About 40 percent of all agricultural scientists work for federal, state, and local governments. They work within the U.S. Department of Agriculture and the Environmental Protection Agency and for regional extension agencies and soil conservation departments. Scientists with doctorates may work on the faculty of colleges and universities. Researchers work for chemical and pharmaceutical companies, and with agribusiness and consulting firms. Agricultural scientists also work in the food processing industry.

◼ STARTING OUT

Agricultural scientists often are recruited prior to graduation. College and university placement offices offer information about jobs, and students may arrange interviews with recruiters who visit the campus.

Direct application may be made to the personnel departments of colleges and universities, private industries, and nonprofit research foundations. People interested in positions with the federal government may contact the local offices of state employment services and

USDA RESEARCH

The Agricultural Research Service (ARS) of the USDA involves scientists in a number of projects aimed at improving farm production, global sales, and the environment. Among these projects:

National Program: Global Change. Because agriculture is vulnerable to the Earth's biological, geological, and atmospheric changes, ARS studies the effects of UV-B radiation, ozone, and elevated carbon dioxide levels on plants and animals.

National Program: Plant Biological and Molecular Processes. To improve production practices and timing of harvest, scientists are at work to identify and modify the genes that influence plant growth, quality, and resistance to pests and diseases.

the U.S. Office of Personnel Management or the Federal Job Information Centers, which are located in various large cities throughout the country. Private employment agencies are another method that might be considered. Large companies sometimes conduct job fairs in major cities and will advertise them in the business sections of the local newspapers.

◼ ADVANCEMENT

Advancement in this field depends on education, experience, and job performance. Agricultural scientists with advanced degrees generally start in teaching or research and advance to administrative and management positions, such as supervisor of a research program. The number of such jobs is limited, however, and often the route to advancement is through specialization. The narrower specialties are often the most valuable.

People who enter this field with only a bachelor's degree are much more restricted. After starting in testing and inspecting jobs or as technical sales and service representatives, they may progress to advanced technicians, particularly in medical research, or become high school biology teachers. In the latter case, they must have had courses in education and meet the state requirements for teaching credentials.

◼ EARNINGS

According to the U.S. Department of Labor, the median annual salary of agricultural and food scientists (from all specialty areas) was approximately $48,670 in 2002. The lowest paid 10 percent (which generally included those just starting out in the field) earned less than $28,750, while the highest paid 10 percent made approximately

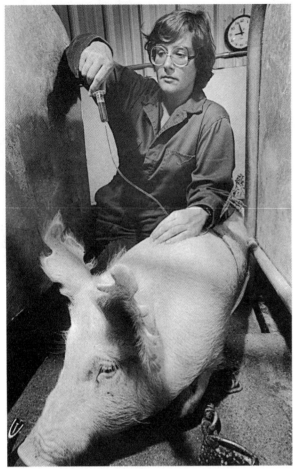

An agricultural scientist takes a blood sample from a pig for a study that will determine what effects modern methods of raising livestock have on farm animals.

$85,460 or more per year. In 2002, the U.S. Department of Labor also recorded a salary breakdown by specialty for those working for the federal government in nonsupervisory, supervisory, and managerial roles. The breakdown included the following: the average annual salary for those working in animal food manufacturing was $73,490; for those working in universities, $42,870; and for those employed by the federal government the average salary was $82,729 for those working in animal science and $68,846 for agronomists.

Unless hired for just a short-term project, agricultural scientists most likely receive health and retirement benefits in addition to their annual salary.

■ WORK ENVIRONMENT

Agricultural scientists work regular hours, although researchers often choose to work longer when their experiments have reached critical points. Competition in the research field may be stiff, causing a certain amount of stress.

Agricultural scientists generally work in offices, laboratories, or classrooms where the environment is clean, healthy, and safe. Some agricultural scientists, such as botanists, periodically take field trips where living facilities may be primitive and strenuous physical activity may be required.

■ OUTLOOK

According to the U.S. Department of Labor, employment for agricultural scientists is expected to grow more slowly than the average through 2012. This reflects a slowdown in government employment as well as in private industry, though the field as a whole is less vulnerable to recession than many other occupations. Despite slower growth, retirees and others who leave agricultural science will still need to be replaced.

The fields of biotechnology, genetics, and sustainable agriculture may hold the best opportunities for agricultural scientists. New developments, such as methods of processing corn for use in medicines, will alter the marketplace. Scientists will also be actively involved in improving both the environmental impact of farming and crop yields, as they focus on methods of decontaminating soil, protecting groundwater, crop rotation, and other efforts of conservation. Scientists will also have the challenge of promoting these new methods to farmers.

■ FOR MORE INFORMATION

To learn about opportunities for scientists in the dairy industry and for information on student divisions at the college level, contact

American Dairy Science Association
1111 North Dunlap Avenue
Savoy, IL 61874
Tel: 217-356-5146
Email: adsa@assochq.org
http://www.adsa.org

To learn about student competitions and scholarships, contact

American Society of Agricultural Engineers
2950 Niles Road
St. Joseph, MI 49085
Tel: 269-429-0300
http://www.asae.org

For the career resource guide Exploring Careers in Agronomy, Crops, Soils, and Environmental Sciences *and certification information, contact*

American Society of Agronomy
677 South Segoe Road
Madison, WI 53711

Tel: 608-273-8080
http://www.agronomy.org

For more information on agricultural careers and student programs, contact

National FFA Organization
PO Box 68960
6060 FFA Drive
Indianapolis, IN 46268
Tel: 317-802-6060
http://www.ffa.org

Visit the USDA website for more information on its agencies and programs as well as news releases.

United States Department of Agriculture (USDA)
http://www.usda.gov

Aircraft Mechanics

■ OVERVIEW

Aircraft mechanics examine, service, repair, and overhaul aircraft and aircraft engines. They also repair, replace, and assemble parts of the airframe (the structural parts of the plane other than the power plant or engine). There are about 154,000 aircraft mechanics working in the United States.

■ HISTORY

On December 17, 1903, Wilbur and Orville Wright made history's first successful powered flight. The Wright brothers—who originally built and repaired bicycles—designed, built, and repaired their airplane, including the engine, making them the first airplane mechanics as well. In the early years of aviation, most airplane designers filled a similar scope of functions, although many had people to assist them. As the aviation industry grew, the various tasks required to design, build, operate, and repair aircraft became more specialized. However, because of the instability of early planes and the uncertainty of the weather and other conditions, it was often necessary for pilots to have a strong working knowledge of how to repair and maintain their aircraft. In later years, one important route to becoming a pilot was to start as an aircraft mechanic.

As aircraft became capable of flying faster, for longer distances, and at higher altitudes, and especially after aircraft began to carry passengers, the role of the aircraft mechanic became vital to the safety of the aircraft and the growth of the aviation industry. New technologies have continually been introduced into the design of aircraft, and mechanics needed to be familiar with all the systems, from the airframe to the engine to the control systems. The complexity of airplane design increased to the point where the mechanics themselves began to specialize. Some mechanics had the skills to work on the entire aircraft. Others were able to work on the airframe, on the engines, or on the power plant. Some mechanics functioned as repairers, who completed minor repairs to the plane. Mechanics were assisted by technicians, who were often training to become fully qualified mechanics. With the introduction of electronics into aircraft, some mechanics specialized as avionics technicians.

The Air Commerce Act of 1926 imposed regulations on the commercial airlines and their fleets. The Federal Aviation Agency, later called the Federal Aviation Administration (FAA), also established training and licensing requirements for the mechanics servicing the airplanes. Mechanics were also an important part of the armed forces, especially as the world entered World War II, in which air power became a vital part of successful military operations.

The growth of the general aviation industry, which includes all flights operated outside of the airlines, provided still more demand for trained mechanics. The introduction of ultralight aircraft in the 1970s brought air flight back to its origins: these craft were often sold as kits that the purchasers had to build and repair themselves.

■ THE JOB

The work of aircraft mechanics employed by the commercial airlines may be classified into two categories, that of line maintenance mechanics and overhaul mechanics.

Line maintenance mechanics are all-around craft workers who make repairs on all parts of the plane. Working at the airport, they make emergency and other necessary repairs in the time between when aircraft land and when they take off again. They may be told by the pilot, flight

QUICK FACTS

SCHOOL SUBJECTS
Computer science
Technical/shop

PERSONAL SKILLS
Mechanical/manipulative
Technical/scientific

WORK ENVIRONMENT
Indoors and outdoors
One location with some travel

MINIMUM EDUCATION LEVEL
Some postsecondary training

SALARY RANGE
$27,370 to $43,070 to $60,150+

CERTIFICATION OR LICENSING
Recommended

OUTLOOK
About as fast as the average

DOT
621

GOE
05.03.01

NOC
2244, 7315

O*NET-SOC
49-3011.00, 49-3011.01, 49-3011.02, 49-3011.03

engineer, or head mechanic what repairs need to be made, or they may thoroughly inspect the plane themselves for oil leaks, cuts or dents in the surface and tires, or any malfunction in the radio, radar, and light equipment. In addition, their duties include changing oil, cleaning spark plugs, and replenishing the hydraulic and oxygen systems. They work as fast as safety permits so the aircraft can be put back into service quickly.

Overhaul mechanics keep the aircraft in top operating condition by performing scheduled maintenance, making repairs, and conducting inspections required by the FAA. Scheduled maintenance programs are based on the number of hours flown, calendar days, or a combination of these factors. Overhaul mechanics work at the airline's main overhaul base on either or both of the two major parts of the aircraft: the airframe, which includes wings, fuselage, tail assembly, landing gear, control cables, propeller assembly, and fuel and oil tanks; or the power plant, which may be a radial (internal combustion), turbojet, turboprop, or rocket engine.

Airframe mechanics work on parts of the aircraft other than the engine, inspecting the various components of the airframe for worn or defective parts. They check the sheet-metal surfaces, measure the tension of control cables, and check for rust, distortion, and cracks in the fuselage and wings. They consult manufacturers' manuals and the airline's maintenance manual for specifications and to determine whether repair or replacement is needed to correct defects or malfunctions. They also use specialized computer software to assist them in determining the need, extent, and nature of repairs. Airframe mechanics repair, replace, and assemble parts using a variety of tools, including power shears, sheet-metal breakers, arc and acetylene welding equipment, rivet guns, and air or electric drills.

Aircraft powerplant mechanics inspect, service, repair, and overhaul the engine of the aircraft. Looking through specially designed openings while working from ladders or scaffolds, they examine an engine's external appearance for such problems as cracked cylinders, oil leaks, or cracks or breaks in the turbine blades. They also listen to the engine in operation to detect sounds indicating malfunctioning components, such as sticking or burned valves. The test equipment used to check the engine's operation includes ignition analyzers, compression checkers, distributor timers, and ammeters. If necessary, the mechanics remove the engine from the aircraft, using a hoist or a forklift truck, and take the engine apart. They use sensitive instruments to measure parts for wear and use X-ray and magnetic inspection equipment to check for invisible cracks. Worn or damaged parts are replaced or repaired, then the mechanics reassemble and reinstall the engine.

Aircraft mechanics adjust and repair electrical wiring systems and aircraft accessories and instruments; inspect, service, and repair pneumatic and hydraulic systems; and handle various servicing tasks, such as flushing crankcases, cleaning screens, greasing moving parts, and checking brakes.

Mechanics may work on only one type of aircraft or on many different types, such as jets, propeller-driven planes, and helicopters. For greater efficiency, some specialize in one section, such as the electrical system, of a particular type of aircraft. Among the specialists, there are airplane electricians; pneumatic testers and pressure sealer-and-testers; aircraft body repairers and bonded structures repairers, such as burnishers and bumpers; and air conditioning mechanics, aircraft rigging and controls mechanics, plumbing and hydraulics mechanics, and experimental-aircraft testing mechanics. *Avionics technicians* are mechanics who specialize in the aircraft's electronic systems.

Mechanics who work for businesses that own their own aircraft usually handle all necessary repair and maintenance work. The planes, however, generally are small and the work is less complex than in repair shops.

In small, independent repair shops, mechanics must inspect and repair many different types of aircraft. The airplanes may include small commuter planes run by an aviation company, private company planes and jets, private individually owned aircraft, and planes used for flying instruction.

■ REQUIREMENTS
High School

The first requirement for prospective aircraft mechanics is a high school diploma. Courses in mathematics, physics, chemistry, and mechanical drawing are particularly helpful because they teach the principles involved in the operation of an aircraft, and this knowledge is often necessary to making the repairs. Machine shop, auto mechanics, or electrical shop are important courses for gaining many skills needed by aircraft mechanics.

Postsecondary Training

At one time, mechanics were able to acquire their skills through on-the-job training. This is rare today. Now most mechanics learn the job either in the armed forces or in trade schools approved by the FAA. The trade schools provide training with the necessary tools and equipment in programs that range in length from two years to 30 months. In considering applicants for certification, the FAA sometimes accepts successful completion of such schooling in place of work experience, but the schools do not guarantee an FAA certificate. There are about 200 such schools in the United States.

The experience acquired by aircraft mechanics in the armed forces sometimes satisfies the work requirements for FAA certification, and veterans may be able to pass the exam with a limited amount of additional study. But jobs in the military service are usually too specialized to satisfy the FAA requirement for broad work experience. In that case, veterans applying for FAA approval will have to complete a training program at a trade school. Schools occasionally give some credit for material learned in the service. However, on the plus side, airlines are especially eager to hire aircraft mechanics with both military experience and a trade school education.

Certification or Licensing

FAA certification is necessary for certain types of aircraft mechanics and is usually required to advance beyond entry-level positions. Most mechanics who work on civilian aircraft have FAA authorization as airframe mechanics, power plant mechanics, or avionics repair specialists. Airframe mechanics are qualified to work on the fuselage, wings, landing gear, and other structural parts of the aircraft; power plant mechanics are qualified for work on the engine. Mechanics may qualify for both airframe and power plant licensing, allowing them to work on any part of the plane. Combination airframe and power plant mechanics with an inspector's certificate are permitted to certify inspection work done by other mechanics. Mechanics without certification must be supervised by certified mechanics.

FAA certification is granted only to aircraft mechanics with previous work experience: a minimum of 18 months for an airframe or power plant certificate and at least 30 months working with both engines and airframes for a combination certificate. To qualify for an inspector's certificate, mechanics must have held a combined airframe and power plant certificate for at least three years. In addition, all applicants for certification must pass written and oral tests and demonstrate their ability to do the work authorized by the certificate.

Other Requirements

Aircraft mechanics must be able to work with precision and meet rigid standards. Their physical condition is also important. They need more than average strength for lifting heavy parts and tools, as well as agility for reaching and climbing. And they should not be afraid of heights, since they may work on top of the wings and fuselages of large jet planes.

In addition to education and certification, union membership may be a requirement for some jobs, particularly for mechanics employed by major airlines. The principal unions organizing aircraft mechanics are the

An aircraft mechanic rebuilds the engine of a small plane after engine problems grounded the craft.

International Association of Machinists and Aerospace Workers and the Transport Workers Union of America. In addition, some mechanics are represented by the International Brotherhood of Teamsters, Chauffeurs, Warehousemen and Helpers of America.

■ EXPLORING

Working with electronic kits, tinkering with automobile engines, and assembling model airplanes are good ways of gauging your ability to do the kinds of work performed by aircraft mechanics. A guided tour of an airfield can give you a brief overall view of this industry. Even better would be a part-time or summer job with an airline in an area such as the baggage department. Small airports may also offer job opportunities for part-time, summer, or replacement workers. You may also earn a Student Pilot (SP) license at the age of 16 and may gain more insight into the basic workings of an airplane that way. Kits for building ultralight craft are also available and may provide even more insight into the importance of proper maintenance and repair.

■ EMPLOYERS

Of the roughly 154,000 aircraft mechanics currently employed in the United States, about two-thirds work for airlines or airports, according to the U.S. Department of Labor. Each airline usually has one main overhaul base, where most of its mechanics are employed. These bases are found along the main airline routes or near large

TYPES OF AIRCRAFT ENGINES

Most people think that there are two basic types of aircraft engines: propellers and jets. The reality is a bit more complicated.

Propeller-driven aircraft were the first to be invented, and are still very common today. Commercial carriers use props on shorter flights, and they are also used by "bush pilots" in hard-to-reach areas. Propellers are driven by an internal-combustion engine, similar to a car's engine.

The first practical jets were built as warplanes during World War II. The first jetliner, the De Havilland Comet, entered commercial service in 1952. A jet engine combines fuel with air in an explosive mixture, but, rather than driving a piston, the force of the exhaust escapes from the rear of the engine, creating forward thrust.

Most jet aircraft today are actually *turbojets*. The turbojet engine was invented specifically for civilian air travel. It uses a turbine to drive a fan to more efficiently suck in air to power the fuel/air reaction. The reaction then both gives the plane is thrust and drives a compressor to runs the turbine. *Turboprops* are similar to turbojets, but, rather than driving a fan, the jet engine powers a conventional propeller.

More exotic types of engines also exist, such as rocket engines and scramjets, which can boost an aircraft to more than seven times the speed of sound. However, these types of engines are rarely seen outside of rare, highly experimental aircraft.

cities, including New York, Chicago, Los Angeles, Atlanta, San Francisco, and Miami.

About one out of eight aircraft mechanics works for the federal government. Many of these mechanics are civilians employed at military aviation installations, while others work for the FAA, mainly in its headquarters in Oklahoma City. About one out of 10 mechanics works for aircraft assembly firms. Most of the rest are general aviation mechanics employed by independent repair shops at airports around the country, by businesses that use their own planes for transporting employees or cargo, by certified supplemental airlines, or by crop-dusting and air-taxi firms.

■ STARTING OUT

High school graduates who wish to become aircraft mechanics may enter this field by enrolling in an FAA-approved trade school. (Note that there are schools offering this training that do not have FAA approval.) These schools generally have placement services available for their graduates.

Another method is to make direct application to the employment offices of companies providing air transportation and services or the local offices of the state employment service, although airlines prefer to employ people who have already completed training. Many airports are managed by private fixed-base operators, which also operate the airport's repair and maintenance facilities. The field may also be entered through enlistment in the armed forces.

■ ADVANCEMENT

Promotions depend in part on the size of the organization for which an aircraft mechanic works. The first promotion after beginning employment is usually based on merit and comes in the form of a salary increase. To advance further, many companies require the mechanic to have a combined airframe and power plant certificate, or perhaps an aircraft inspector's certificate.

Advancement could take the following route: journeyworker mechanic, head mechanic or crew chief, inspector, head inspector, and shop supervisor. With additional training, a mechanic may advance to engineering, administrative, or executive positions. In larger airlines, mechanics may advance to become flight engineers, then copilots and pilots. With business training, some mechanics open their own repair shops.

■ EARNINGS

Although some aircraft mechanics, especially at the entry level and at small businesses, earn little more than the minimum wage, the median annual income for aircraft mechanics was about $43,070 in 2002, according to the U.S. Department of Labor. The top 10 percent earned more than $60,150, while the bottom 10 percent earned $27,370 or less. Mechanics with airframe and power-plant certification earn more than those without it. Overtime, night shift, and holiday pay differentials are usually available and can greatly increase a mechanic's annual earnings.

Most major airlines are covered by union agreements. Their mechanics generally earn more than those working for other employers. Contracts usually include health insurance and often life insurance and retirement plans as well. An attractive fringe benefit for airline mechanics and their immediate families is free or reduced fares on their own and many other airlines. Mechanics working for the federal government also benefit from the greater job security of civil service and government jobs.

■ WORK ENVIRONMENT

Most aircraft mechanics work a five-day, 40-hour week. Their working hours, however, may be irregular and often include nights, weekends, and holidays, as airlines operate 24 hours a day, and extra work is required during holiday seasons.

When doing overhauling and major inspection work, aircraft mechanics generally work in hangars with adequate heat, ventilation, and lights. If the hangars are full, however, or if repairs must be made quickly, they may work outdoors, sometimes in unpleasant weather. Outdoor work is frequent for line maintenance mechanics, who work at airports, because they must make minor repairs and preflight checks at the terminal to save time. To maintain flight schedules, or to keep from inconveniencing customers in general aviation, the mechanics often have to work under time pressure.

The work is physically strenuous and demanding. Mechanics often have to lift or pull as much as 70 pounds of weight. They may stand, lie, or kneel in awkward positions, sometimes in precarious places such as on a scaffold or ladder.

Noise and vibration are common when testing engines. Regardless of the stresses and strains, aircraft mechanics are expected to work quickly and with great precision.

Although the power tools and test equipment are provided by the employer, mechanics may be expected to furnish their own hand tools.

■ OUTLOOK

Despite the post-September 11 falloff in air travel, the outlook for aircraft mechanics should remain steady over the course of the next decade. Employment opportunities will open up due to fewer young workers entering the labor force, fewer entrants from the military, and more retirees leaving positions. But the job prospects will vary according to the type of employer. Less competition for jobs is likely to be found at smaller commuter and regional airlines, FAA repair stations, and in general aviation. These employers pay lower wages and fewer applicants compete for their positions, while higher paying airline positions, which also include travel benefits, are more in demand among qualified applicants. Mechanics who keep up with technological advancements in electronics, composite materials, and other areas will be in greatest demand.

Employment of aircraft mechanics is likely to increase about as fast as the average through 2012, according to the U.S. Department of Labor. The demand for air travel and the numbers of aircraft created are expected to increase due to population growth and rising incomes. However, employment growth will be affected by the use of automated systems that make the aircraft mechanic's job more efficient.

■ FOR MORE INFORMATION

For career books and information about high school student membership, national forums, and job fairs, contact

Aviation Information Resources Inc.
3800 Camp Creek Parkway, Suite 18-100
Atlanta, GA 30331
Tel: 800-JET-JOBS
http://www.jet-jobs.com

Professional Aviation Maintenance Association
Ronald Reagan Washington National Airport
Washington, DC 20001
Tel: 703-417-8800
Email: hq@pama.org
http://www.pama.org

Airplane Dispatchers

■ OVERVIEW

Airplane dispatchers plan and direct commercial air flights according to government and airline company regulations. They read radio reports from airplane pilots during flights and study weather reports to determine any necessary change in flight direction or altitude. They send instructions by radio to the pilots in the case of heavy storms, fog, mechanical difficulties, or other emergencies. Airline dispatchers are sometimes called *flight superintendents*.

■ HISTORY

Commercial air service took off slowly in the United States. The first airmail flight occurred in 1911. The first passenger air service was organized in 1914, providing air transportation from Tampa to St. Petersburg, Florida, but this service lasted only six months. In 1917, however, the U.S. Post Office began its first airmail service. In 1925, the Kelly Air Mail Act turned over the airmail routes to 12 private contractors. This formed the basis of the commercial airline industry in the United States.

The airline industry developed rapidly in the years leading up to World War II. The Air Commerce Act of 1927 introduced licensing requirements for pilots and airlines and created a network of defined airways. Improvements in airplane design had brought larger, more comfortable airplanes, and the numbers of passengers reached into the millions. By 1933, the United States boasted the busiest airports in the world.

These developments created a need for people to organize and guide the increasing numbers of flights operated by the airlines. During the early days of aviation, the airplane dispatcher served in a number of capacities, including that of station manager, meteorologist, radio operator, and even mechanic. Often pilots were pressed into service as dispatchers because of their knowledge of weather and of the needs of flight crews. As the airline industry grew, these tasks became specialized. The first federal air traffic control center was opened in 1936. In 1938, federal licensing requirements were established for the airline's own dispatchers. Soon dispatchers were located all over the country.

Since that time, the work of dispatchers has become more involved and complicated, and the airline industry has relied on them extensively to make a major contribution to the safety of commercial air travel. Advancements in technology have eased parts of the airplane dispatcher's job and have also allowed the airlines to consolidate their remote dispatch offices to a smaller number of centrally located offices.

■ THE JOB

Airplane dispatchers are employed by commercial airlines, and they maintain a constant watch on factors affecting the movement of planes during flights. Dispatchers are responsible for the safety of flights and for making certain that they are operated on an efficient, profit-making basis. The work of dispatchers, however, is not the same as that of air traffic controllers, who are employees of the federal government.

Airplane dispatchers are responsible for giving the company's clearance for each flight that takes off during their shift. Their judgments are based on data received from a number of different sources. In their efforts to make certain that each flight will end successfully, they must take into consideration current weather conditions, weather fore-

casts, wind speed and direction, and other information. Before flights, they must decide whether the airplane crew should report to the field or whether the airline should begin notifying passengers that their flight has been delayed or canceled. Dispatchers may also have to determine whether an alternate route should be used, either to include another stop for passengers or to avoid certain weather conditions.

Upon reporting to the field before a flight, the pilot confers with the dispatcher and determines the best route to use, the amount of fuel to be placed aboard the aircraft, the altitude at which to fly, and the approximate flying time. The pilot and the dispatcher must agree on the conditions of the flight, and both have the option of delaying or canceling flights should conditions become too hazardous to ensure a safe trip.

Dispatchers may also be responsible for maintaining records and for determining the weight and balance of the aircraft after loading. They must be certain that all intended cargo is loaded aboard each of the appropriate flights. They must also be certain that all their decisions, such as those about the cargo, are in keeping with the safety regulations of the Federal Aviation Administration (FAA), as well as with the rules established by their own airline.

Once the planes are in the air, dispatchers keep in constant contact with the flight crews. A dispatcher may be responsible for communications with as many as 10 or 12 flights at any one time. Contact is maintained through a company-owned radio network that enables each company to keep track of all of its planes. Dispatchers keep the crews informed about the weather that they will encounter, and they record the positions and other information reported by the planes while they are en route. If an emergency occurs, dispatchers coordinate the actions taken in response to the emergency.

Following each flight, the pilot checks with the dispatcher for a debriefing. In the debriefing, the pilot brings the dispatcher up to date about the weather encountered in the air and other conditions related to the flight, so that the dispatcher will have this information available in scheduling subsequent flights.

Good judgment is an important tool of airplane dispatchers, for they must be able to make fast, workable, realistic decisions. Because of this, dispatchers often experience strains and tensions on the job, especially when many flights are in the air or when an emergency occurs.

In larger airlines, there is a certain degree of specialization among dispatchers. An assistant dispatcher may work with the chief dispatcher and have the major responsibility for just one phase of the dispatching activities, such as analyzing current weather information,

QUICK FACTS

SCHOOL SUBJECTS
Geography
Mathematics

PERSONAL SKILLS
Communication/ideas
Technical/scientific

WORK ENVIRONMENT
Primarily indoors
One location with some travel

MINIMUM EDUCATION LEVEL
Some postsecondary training

SALARY RANGE
$20,000 to $47,250 to
$100,000+

CERTIFICATION OR LICENSING
Required by all states

OUTLOOK
Little change or more slowly
than the average

DOT
912

GOE
07.02.01

NOC
2272

O*NET-SOC
43-5032.00

while a senior dispatcher may be designated to take care of another phase, such as monitoring the operating costs of each flight.

■ REQUIREMENTS
High School

Some college education is required to be an airplane dispatcher, so if you are interested in this career you should follow a college prep curriculum. Business administration and computer skills are vital to the job, so take any courses available in those subjects. While in high school, you can also pursue a student pilot's license, which is a great advantage, though not a requirement.

Postsecondary Training

Airplane dispatchers are required to have at least two years of college education with studies in meteorology or air transportation. Two years of work experience in air transportation may take the place of the college requirement. Airlines prefer college graduates who have studied mathematics, physics, or meteorology.

There are about 40 schools around the country licensed by the FAA that offer dispatcher training. For information on these courses, contact the Airline Dispatchers Federation or visit its website at http://www.flightdispatch.net.

Certification or Licensing

Airplane dispatchers must be licensed by the FAA. You may prepare for the FAA licensing examination in several different ways. You may work at least one year in a dispatching office under a licensed dispatcher, complete an FAA-approved airline dispatcher's course at a specialized school or training center, or show that you have spent two of the previous three years in air traffic control work or a related job.

Candidates who meet the preliminary requirements must also pass an examination covering such subjects as civil air regulations, radio procedures, airport and airway traffic procedures, weather analysis, and air-navigation facilities. In addition to a written test, you must also pass an oral examination covering the interpretation of weather information, landing and cruising speeds of various aircraft, airline routes, navigation facilities, and operational characteristics of different types of aircraft. You must not only demonstrate your knowledge of these areas to become a licensed dispatcher, but you are also expected to maintain these skills once licensed. Various training programs, some of which may be conducted by their employers, will assist you in staying current with new developments, which are frequent in this job.

Assistant dispatchers are not always required to be licensed. Thus, it may be possible to begin work in a dispatcher's office prior to earning the dispatcher's license.

Other Requirements

Airline dispatchers need to be able to work well either by themselves or with others and assume responsibility for their decisions. The job requires you to think and act quickly and sensibly under the most trying conditions. You may be responsible for hundreds of lives at any one time, and a poor decision could result in tragedy.

Airline dispatchers must be at least 23 years old and in good health. Your vision must be correctable to 20/20. A good memory, the ability to remain calm under great pressure and the ability to do many things at once, and to make decisions quickly are essential to a successful airplane dispatcher's career.

■ EXPLORING

Besides pursuing the course of study mentioned previously, there is little opportunity for an individual to explore the field of airplane dispatching directly. Part-time or summer jobs with airlines may provide interested students with a chance to observe some of the activities related to dispatching work. You can cultivate your interest in aircraft and aviation through reading and participating in flying clubs.

■ EMPLOYERS

Virtually all airplane dispatchers are employed by commercial airlines, both those that ship cargo and those that transport passengers.

■ STARTING OUT

The occupation is not easy to enter because of its relatively small size (there were only slightly over 1,000 air dispatchers in the United States as of 2002) and the special skills required. The nature of the training is such that it is not easily put to use outside of this specific area. Few people leave this career once they are in it, so only a few positions other than those caused by death or retirement become available.

People who are able to break into the field are often promoted to assistant dispatchers' jobs from related fields. They may come from among the airline's dispatch clerks, meteorologists, radio operators, or retired pilots. Obviously, airlines prefer those people who have had a long experience in ground-flight operations work. Thus, it is probably wise to plan on starting out in one of these related fields and eventually working into a position as airplane dispatcher.

ADVANCEMENT

The usual path of advancement is from dispatch clerk to assistant dispatcher to dispatcher and then, possibly, to chief flight dispatcher or flight dispatch manager or assistant manager. It is also possible to become a chief flight supervisor or superintendent of flight control.

The line of advancement varies depending on the airline, the size of the facility where the dispatcher is located, and the positions available. At smaller facilities, there may be only two or three different promotional levels available.

EARNINGS

Dispatcher salaries vary greatly among airlines. According to the Airline Dispatchers Federation, entry-level positions at smaller carriers pay about $20,000 a year. Senior dispatchers at major airlines earn more than $100,000 a year. A few dispatchers earn close to $150,000 including overtime pay. Licensed dispatchers earn an annual mean wage of about $47,250 per year, according to the Department of Labor. Flight superintendents make up to about $52,800 per year, and shift chiefs, $66,000.

Airline positions generally provide health insurance and other benefits. Beginning dispatchers usually work eight-hour shifts five days a week and receive two weeks paid vacation per year. Senior dispatchers usually work four 10-hour shifts a week and may receive as many as six weeks vacation each year. Most dispatchers and their families are also able to fly for free or at heavily discounted prices. Smaller airlines and air companies generally pay less, with some dispatchers earning as little as $8,000 per year.

WORK ENVIRONMENT

Airplane dispatchers are normally stationed at airports near a terminal or hangar, but in facilities away from the public. Some airlines use several dispatch installations, while others use a single office. Because dispatchers make decisions involving not only thousands of people but also a great deal of money, their offices are often located close to those of management, so that they can remain in close contact.

Frequently, the offices where airplane dispatchers work are full of noise and activity, with telephones ringing, computer printers chattering, and many people talking and moving about to consult charts and other sources of information. The offices usually operate 24 hours a day, with each dispatcher working eight-hour shifts, plus an additional half-hour used in briefing the relief person.

Many lives depend on airplane dispatchers every day. This means that there is often considerable stress in their jobs. Dispatchers must constantly make rapid decisions based on their evaluation of a great deal of information. Adding to the tension is the fact that they may work in noisy, hectic surroundings and must interact with many people throughout the day. However, dispatchers can feel deep satisfaction in knowing that their job is vital to the safety and success of airline operations.

OUTLOOK

In total, only about 1,000 dispatchers were employed in the United States as of 2002. Smaller airlines and some private firms also employ airplane dispatchers, but the number of dispatchers remains very small. The Airline Dispatchers Federation (ADF) says the job market for dispatchers is currently good, especially with smaller commuter airlines. An expected increase in air traffic in coming years may mean a slight increase in the number of airplane dispatchers needed. However, the centralization of dispatch offices using more advanced technology means that fewer dispatchers will be able to do more work. With improved communications equipment, a single dispatcher will be able to cover a larger area than is currently possible. Because of the relatively small size of this occupational field, its employment outlook is not particularly good.

Most major airlines consider dispatch positions as senior management level positions. Candidates are often selected from within the company after they have accumulated 15 to 20 years of experience in a variety of areas, including supervisory positions. Candidates selected from outside the company must have considerable experience with smaller carriers.

According to ADF, new graduates from dispatch schools should not expect to be hired by major airlines such as American or United. A better choice would be to seek a position with a smaller carrier and get at least five years' experience before attempting to apply for a position with a major airline.

FOR MORE INFORMATION

For career information, contact
Airline Dispatchers Federation
700 13th Street, NW, Suite 950
Washington, DC 20005
Tel: 800-676-2685
http://www.flightdispatch.net

For career books and information about high school student membership, national forums, and job fairs, contact
Aviation Information Resources Inc.
1001 Riverdale Court
Atlanta, GA 30337
Tel: 800-247-2777
http://www.airapps.com

Air Quality Engineers

■ OVERVIEW

Air quality engineers, or *air pollution control engineers,* are responsible for developing techniques to analyze and control air pollution by using sophisticated monitoring, chemical analysis, computer modeling, and statistical analysis. Some air quality engineers are involved in pollution-control equipment design or modification. Government-employed air quality experts keep track of a region's polluters, enforce federal regulations, and impose fines or take other action against those who do not comply with regulations. Privately employed engineers may monitor companies' emissions for certain targeted pollutants to ensure that they are within acceptable levels. Air quality engineers who work in research seek ways to combat or avoid air pollution.

■ HISTORY

The growth of cities and industry during the Industrial Revolution was a major contributor to the decline of air quality. Some contaminates (pollutants) have always been with us, for instance, particulate matter (tiny solid particles) from very large fires, volcanic eruption, or dust caused by wind. However, human populations were not really concentrated enough, nor did the technology exist, to produce conditions that are today considered hazardous until about 200 years ago. The industrialization of England in the 1750s, followed by that of France in the 1830s and Germany in the 1850s created high-density populations of millions of people who were drawn to cities to work in the smoke-belching factories, leading to huge increases in airborne pollutants. Work conditions in the factories were notoriously bad, and with no pollution-control or safety measures, living conditions in cities rapidly became equally bad. The severely polluted air was a major cause of respiratory and other diseases.

America's cities were slightly smaller and slower to industrialize, as well as more spread out than Old World capitals like London. Even so, levels of sulfur dioxide were so high in Pittsburgh in the early 1900s that ladies' stockings would disintegrate upon prolonged exposure to the air. The rapid growth of the American automobile industry in the first half of the 20th century contributed greatly to air pollution in two ways: initially, from the steel factories and production plants that made economic giants out of places like Pittsburgh and Detroit, and then from the cars themselves. This became an even greater problem as cars enabled people to move out from the fetid indus-trial city and commute to work from the suburbs. Mobility independent of public transportation greatly increased auto exhaust and created such modern nightmares as rush hour traffic.

The effects of air pollution were and are numerous. Particulate matter reacts chemically with heat to form ground-level ozone, or smog. Sulfur and nitrogen oxides form acid rain, which can cause extensive property damage over long periods. Carbon monoxide, the main automobile pollutant, is deadly at a relatively low level of exposure.

Air pollution affects the environment not only in well-publicized phenomena like acid rain and destroying the ozone layer, but in less obvious ways as well. For example, increased asthma rates in cities has often been statistically tied to the amount of pollution in the environment. Because pollution is so difficult to remove from the air, and because its effects are so difficult to alter, the problem tends to be cumulative and an increasingly critical public health issue.

Some private air pollution control was implemented in the 20th century, mainly to prevent factories from ruining their own works with corrosive and unhealthy emissions. The first attempt at governmental regulation was the Clean Air Act in 1955, but because environmental concerns were not considered viable economic or political issues, this act was not very effective. As environmentalists became increasingly visible and vigorous campaigners, the Air Quality Act was established in 1967. The Environmental Protection Agency (EPA) created National Ambient Air Quality Standards (NAAQS) in 1971, which set limits on ozone, carbon monoxide, sulfur dioxide, lead, nitrogen dioxide, and particulate levels in the emissions of certain industries and processes. States were supposed to design and implement plans to meet the NAAQS, but so few complied that Congress was forced to extend deadlines three times. Even now, many goals set

QUICK FACTS

SCHOOL SUBJECTS
Biology
Chemistry
Mathematics

PERSONAL SKILLS
Communication/ideas
Technical/scientific

WORK ENVIRONMENT
Primarily indoors
Primarily one location

MINIMUM EDUCATION LEVEL
Bachelor's degree

SALARY RANGE
$29,920 to $48,370 to
   $133,310+

CERTIFICATION OR LICENSING
Voluntary

OUTLOOK
Faster than the average

DOT
019

GOE
02.07.04

NOC
N/A

O*NET-SOC
N/A

by the first generation of air-quality regulations remain unmet, and new pollution issues demand attention. Airborne toxins, indoor air pollution, acid rain, carbon dioxide buildup (the greenhouse effect), and depletion of the ozone are now subjects of international controversy and concern.

■ THE JOB

The EPA has composed a list of more than 150 regions of the United States that are out of compliance with federal air quality regulations—some dramatically so—and provided deadlines within the next 20 years to bring these areas under control. The EPA regulations cover everything from car emissions to the greenhouse effect and have the weight of law behind them. There are few industries that will not be touched somehow by this legislation and few that will not require the services of an air quality engineer in the years to come.

Air quality engineers are the professionals who monitor targeted industries or sources to determine whether they are operating within acceptable emissions levels. These engineers suggest changes in the setup of specific companies, or even whole industries, to lessen their impact on the atmosphere. There will be ample opportunity in this field to combine interests, precisely because it is a new field with yet unestablished job paths. An air quality engineer with some background in meteorology, for example, might track the spread of airborne pollutants through various weather systems, using computer modeling techniques. Another air quality engineer might research indoor air pollution, discovering causes for the "sick building syndrome" and creating new architectural standards and building codes for safe ventilation and construction materials.

THE EPA AND SEPTEMBER 11

Following the terrorist attacks of September 11, 2001, many residents of New York City were concerned that the air was unsafe to breathe. Many were afraid that in the destruction of the World Trade Center, a cloud of dangerous substances, including asbestos and polyvinyl chloride, had spread over the city.

Officials from the Environmental Protection Agency (EPA) set up monitoring stations nearby, and quickly announced that the air in most of Manhattan was safe to breathe. However, it was later found that the EPA's report had been influenced by other branches of the federal government, which wanted Wall Street to re-open and the situation in Manhattan to return to normal as much as possible.

Air quality engineers work for the government, in private industry, as consultants, and in research and development. Government employees are responsible for monitoring a region, citing infractions, and otherwise enforcing government regulations. These workers may be called to give testimony in cases against noncompliant companies. They must deal with public concerns and opinions and are themselves regulated by government bureaucracy and regulations.

Air quality engineers in private industry work within industry or a large company to ensure that air quality regulations are being met. They might be responsible for developing instrumentation to continuously monitor emissions, for example, and using the data to formulate methods of control. They may interact with federal regulators or work independently. Engineers working in private industry also might be involved in what is known as "impact assessment with the goal of sustainable development." This means figuring out the most environmentally sound way to produce products—from raw material to disposal stages—while maintaining or, if possible, increasing the company's profits.

Engineers who work alone as consultants or for consulting firms do many of the same things as engineers in private industry, perhaps for smaller companies who do not need a full-time engineer but still need help meeting federal requirements. They, too, might suggest changes to be implemented by a company to reduce air pollution. Some consultants specialize in certain areas of pollution control. Many private consultants are responsible for selling, installing, and running a particular control system. The job requires some salesmanship and the motivation to maintain a variable clientele.

Finally, engineers committed to research and development may work in public or private research institutions and in academic environments. They may tackle significant problems that affect any number of industries and may improve air quality standards with the discovery of new contaminates that need regulation.

■ REQUIREMENTS

High School

High school students should develop their skills in chemistry, math, biology, and ecology.

Postsecondary Training

To break into this field, a bachelor's degree in civil, environmental, or chemical engineering is required. Advancement, specialization, or jobs in research may require a master's degree or Ph.D. Besides the regular environmental or chemical engineering curricula at the college level, future air quality engineers might engage in some mechanical or civil engineering if they are interested in product development. Modelers and planners should have a good knowledge of computer systems. Supporting course work in biology, toxicology, or meteorology can give the job seeker an edge for certain specialized positions even before gaining experience in the workforce.

Certification or Licensing

All engineers who do work that affects public health, safety, or property must register with the state. To obtain registration, engineers must have a degree from an accredited engineering program. Right before they get their degree (or soon after), they must pass an engineer-in-training (EIT) exam covering fundamentals of science and engineering. A few years into their careers, engineers also must pass an exam covering engineering practice.

Other Requirements

Prospective air quality engineers should be puzzle solvers. The ability to work with intangibles is a trait of successful air quality management. As in most fields, communications skills are vital. Engineers must be able to clearly communicate their ideas and findings, both orally and in writing, to a variety of people with different levels of technical understanding.

■ EXPLORING

Investigating air quality engineering can begin with reading environmental science and engineering periodicals, available in many large libraries. Familiarizing yourself with the current issues involving air pollution will give you a better idea of what problems will be facing this field in the near future.

The next step might be a call to a local branch of the EPA. In addition to providing information about local source problems, they can also provide a breakdown of air quality standards that must be met and who has to meet them.

To get a better idea about college-level course work and possible career directions, contact major universities, environmental associations, or even private environmental firms. Some private consulting firms will explain how specific areas of study combine to create their particular area of expertise.

■ EMPLOYERS

Most air quality engineers are privately employed in industries subject to emissions control, such as manufacturing. They may also work for the federal government, investigating and ensuring compliance with air quality regulations, as consultants to industry and large companies, and in research and development.

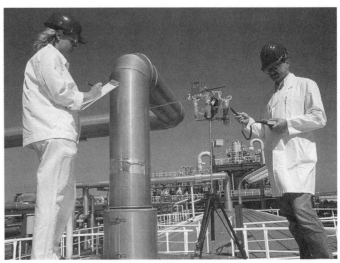

Air quality engineers check emissions from a factory exhaust outlet.

■ STARTING OUT

Summer positions as an air pollution technician provide valuable insight into the engineer's job as well as contacts and experience. Check with local and state EPA offices and larger consulting firms in your area for internship positions and their requirements. Environmentally oriented engineers may be able to volunteer for citizen watchdog group monitoring programs, patrolling regions for previously undiscovered or unregulated contaminates. Most air quality engineers can expect to get jobs in their field immediately after graduating with a bachelor's degree. Your school placement office can assist you in fine tuning your resume and setting up interviews with potential employers. Government positions are a common point of entry; high turnover rates open positions as experienced engineers leave for the more lucrative private sector, which accounts for four out of five jobs in air quality management. An entry-level job might focus on monitoring and analysis.

■ ADVANCEMENT

With experience and education, the engineer might develop a specialization within the field of air quality. Research grants are sometimes available to experienced engineers who wish to concentrate on specific problems or areas of study. Management is another avenue of advancement. The demand for technically oriented middle management in the private sector makes engineers with good interpersonal skills very valuable.

In many ways, advancement will be dictated by the increasing value of air quality engineers to business and industry in general. Successful development of air pollution control equipment or systems—perhaps that even cut costs as they reduce pollution—will make air quality engineers important players in companies' economic strategies. As regulations tighten and increasing emphasis is put on minimizing environmental impact, air quality engineers will be in the spotlight as both regulators and innovators. Advancement may come in the form of monetary incentives or bonuses or management positions over other parts of the organization or company.

EARNINGS

According to the Department of Labor, the lowest 10 percent of environmental scientists earned about $29,920 per year. The middle 50 percent earned between $48,370 and $102,120; the top 10 percent more than $133,310. The median government salary was $66,190; salaries in the private sector are higher. Other benefits may include tuition reimbursement programs, use of a company vehicle for fieldwork, full health coverage, and retirement plans.

WORK ENVIRONMENT

Working conditions differ depending on the employer, the specialization of the position, and the location of the job. An air quality engineer may be required to perform fieldwork, such as observing emission sources, but more often works in an office, determining the factors responsible for airborne pollutants and devising ways to prevent them. Coworkers may include other environmental engineers, lab technicians, and office personnel. An engineer may discuss specific problems with a company's economic planners and develop programs to make that company more competitive environmentally and economically. Those who monitor emissions have considerable responsibility and therefore considerable pressure to do their job well—failure to maintain industry standards could cost their employer government fines. Engineers in some consulting firms may be required to help sell the system they develop or work with.

Most engineers work a standard 40-hour week, putting in overtime to solve critical problems as quickly as possible. A large part of the job for most air quality engineers consists of keeping up to date with federal regulations, industry and regional standards, and developments in their area of expertise. Some employers require standard business attire, while some require more fieldwork from their engineers and may not enforce rigorous dress codes. Unlike water and soil pollution, air pollution can sometimes be difficult to measure quantitatively if the source is unknown. Major pollutants are generally easily identified (although not so easily eliminated), but traces of small "leaks" may literally change with the wind and make for time-consuming, deliberate, and frustrating work.

OUTLOOK

When the immediate scramble to modify and monitor equipment slackens as government regulations are met in the next 20 years, the focus in air quality engineering will shift from traditional "end of pipe" controls (e.g., modifying catalytic converters or gasoline to make cars burn gas more cleanly) to source control (developing alternative fuels and eliminating oil-based industrial emissions). As mentioned, impact assessment will play a large part on the corporate side of air quality management, as businesses strive to stay profitable in the wake of public health and safety regulations. Air pollution problems like greenhouse gas buildup and ozone pollution will not be disappearing in the near future and will be increasingly vital areas of research. International development will allow American pollution control engineers to offer their services in any part of the world that has growing industries or population. Pollution control in general has a big future: air pollution control is quickly taking up a major chunk of the expected expenditures and revenues in this category.

FOR MORE INFORMATION

For information on student chapters, scholarships, and a list of colleges and degrees offering environmental degrees, contact

Air and Waste Management Association
420 Fort Duquesne Boulevard
One Gateway Center, Third Floor
Pittsburgh, PA 15222
Tel: 412-232-3444
Email: info@awma.org
http://www.awma.org

The following are government pollution control boards:

State and Territorial Air Pollution Program
    Administrators /Association of Local Air
    Pollution Control Officials
444 North Capitol Street, NW, Suite 307
Washington, DC 20001
Tel: 202-624-7864
Email: 4clnair@sso.org
http://www.cleanairworld.org

For general information about air quality and other environmental issues, contact

U.S. Environmental Protection Agency
Ariel Rios Building
1200 Pennsylvania Avenue, NW
Washington, DC 20460
Tel: 202-260-2090
http://www.epa.gov

Air Traffic Controllers

■ OVERVIEW

Air traffic controllers monitor and direct the activities of aircraft into and out of airports and along specified flight routes. They radio pilots with approach, landing, taxiing, and takeoff instructions and advisories on weather and other conditions in order to maintain the safe and orderly flow of air traffic both in the air and on the ground. There are approximately 22,400 air traffic controllers employed in the United States. Most are employed by the federal government.

■ HISTORY

The goal of the first air traffic control efforts—beacon lights—was to guide airplanes along a specified airway. As airways and aircraft grew in number, radio communication and radio beacons were added to help planes navigate and to provide weather forecasts. In 1936, the federal government opened the first air traffic control center to regulate the increasing numbers of aircraft flying into and out of the country's growing airports. The Instrument Landing System, a method for signaling aircraft, was instituted in 1941. Airplanes were reaching higher speeds and altitudes, and the controllers' functions became more important to guard against collisions, to ensure safe landings, and to warn pilots of potential weather and geographic hazards in flights. Radar, developed during World War II, allowed air traffic controllers to track the movements of many aircraft and for longer distances. The air traffic control network was extended to include centers at airports, en route centers, and flight service stations, each of which performed specific tasks and controlled specific portions of the skies. After the war, more sophisticated communication systems were developed, including VOR (very high frequency omnidirectional range) transmission, which was used to signal flight path data directly to the plane. Computers were soon installed in order to provide still greater accuracy to the air traffic controller's instructions. Development of the Global Positioning System (GPS), however, has made it possible for airplanes to achieve greater control over their flight paths, so fewer air traffic controllers will be needed to protect the skies.

■ THE JOB

Air traffic controllers work in one of three areas: airport traffic control towers, en route air traffic control centers, or flight service stations. The Federal Aviation Adminis-

tration (FAA), which regulates all air traffic, employs almost every air traffic controller in the United States. Some private airports employ their own air traffic controllers; others are employed at military airports.

Terminal air traffic control specialists are stationed in airport control towers and are responsible for all air traffic entering, leaving, or passing through the airspace around the airport, as well as conducting airplane traffic on the ground. These controllers use radar and visual observation to maintain safe distances among aircraft, and they provide information on weather and other conditions to the pilots under their control. As an airplane prepares for departure, the *ground controller* issues taxiing instructions to bring it to the runway. A *local controller* contacts the pilot with weather, wind, speed, and visibility conditions and clears the pilot for takeoff. A *departure controller* monitors the aircraft on radar, maintains radio contact with the pilot until the aircraft has left the airport's airspace, and hands over control of the plane to an en route control center. A *radar controller* monitors the traffic above the airport and into the aircraft's flight route, communicating with the other controllers. Approaching aircraft are handled in a reverse procedure. When many aircraft are approaching the airport at the same time, the controllers arrange them in a holding pattern above the airport until they each can be cleared to land.

There are more than 440 air traffic control towers in airports across the country. At a small airport, an air traffic controller may be expected to perform all of these functions. Controllers at larger airports usually specialize in a single area. *Senior controllers* supervise the activities of the entire center. *Terminal air traffic controllers* may be responsible for all aircraft within as much as a 50-mile radius of their airport. Most controllers are responsible for many aircraft at once; they track their positions on the radar screen, receive instrument flight data such as an airplane's speed

An air traffic controller monitors the landing strip below and awaits the arrival of an inbound flight.

and altitude, coordinate the altitudes at which planes within the area will fly, keep track of weather conditions, and maintain constant communication with the pilots and with controllers at their and other control centers. An air traffic controller must be aware of all of the activities in the air traffic control center and around the airport. When an aircraft experiences an emergency, air traffic controllers must respond quickly, clearing a path for that aircraft through the traffic, alerting fire and rescue teams, and guiding the pilot to a safe landing.

En route air traffic control specialists work at one of 20 regional centers in the United States. They coordinate the movements of aircraft between airports but out of range of the airport traffic controllers. Because an en route center may be responsible for many thousands of square miles of airspace, these controllers generally work in teams of two or three, with each team assigned a particular section of the center's airspace. Each team consists of a radar controller, the senior member of the team, and radar associates. A center may employ as many as 700 controllers and have 150 or more on duty during peak flying hours. Within the center's airspace are designated routes that the aircraft fly. En route controllers monitor traffic along those air routes. They use radar and electronic equipment to track the flights within the center's airspace and to maintain contact with planes within their area, giving instructions, air traffic clearances, and advice about flight conditions. If flight plans for two airplanes conflict, the en route team will contact the team responsible for the preceding section in order to change one plane's flight path. The controllers will also coordinate changes in altitudes and speeds among pilots. En route controllers receive or transfer control of the aircraft to

controllers in adjacent centers or to an airport's approach controller as the craft enters that facility's airspace.

Flight service station air traffic control specialists make up the third group of controllers. They provide preflight or inflight assistance to pilots from more than 125 flight service stations linked by a broad communications system. These controllers give pilots information about the station's particular area, including terrain, weather, and anything else necessary to guarantee a safe flight. They may suggest alternate routes or different altitudes, alert pilots to military operations taking place along certain routes, inform them about landing at airports that have no towers, assist pilots in emergency situations, and participate in searches for missing or overdue aircraft.

■ REQUIREMENTS
High School
Because it is highly recommended for all air traffic controllers to have a college degree, high school students interested in the field will be best prepared by pursuing a college prep curriculum. Mathematics and science courses are especially useful courses to study because they are most directly related to air traffic control work.

Postsecondary Training
Trainees for air traffic control positions must have completed four years of college or have three years of work experience or a combination of both; entry to civil aviation is also possible through the military. Trainees are selected from applicants who receive a high score on the federal civil service examination. The written test measures aptitudes for arithmetic, abstract reasoning, three-dimensional spatial visualization, and other indicators of an ability to learn the controller's duties.

Following the civil service test, the highest scoring applicants are next subjected to an intensive one-week screening in an effort to determine if the candidates have the required alertness, decisiveness, motivation, poise, and ability to work under extreme pressure. This screening consists of an aptitude test, computer simulations, and physical and mental health examinations.

Those accepted into the training program receive seven months of intensive instruction at the FAA Academy in Oklahoma City. There they receive training in the fundamentals of the airway systems, civil air regulations, radar, and aircraft performance characteristics. They practice on machines designed to simulate emergency situations to determine their emotional stability under pressure. The standards for those who successfully complete this program are very high; about 50 percent of the trainees are dropped during this period. Those who complete the program are guaranteed jobs with the FAA.

Certification or Licensing

Training continues on the job, and new controllers also receive classroom instruction. Depending on the size and complexity of the facility, a new hire may require between 18 months and three years to become a fully certified air traffic controller. Controllers must be certified at each progressive level of air traffic control, usually within a certain period of time. Failure to be certified within the time limit is grounds for dismissal. Air traffic controllers are also required to pass annual physical exams and performance reviews.

Other Requirements

Applicants for airport tower or en route traffic control jobs must be under 31 years of age, pass physical and psychological examinations, and have vision that is or can be corrected to 20/20. Flight service stations will accept applicants age 31 and over. Those hoping to enter the field must be articulate, have a good memory, and show self-control. It is imperative that they be able to express themselves clearly, remember rapidly changing data that affect their decisions, and be able to operate calmly under very difficult situations involving a great deal of strain. They must also be able to make good, sound, and quickly derived decisions. A poor decision may mean the loss of a large number of lives.

■ EXPLORING

If you are interested in this career, you can begin exploring by arranging for a visit to an air traffic control center. Many centers welcome and encourage such visits. Talking with air traffic controllers and watching them work will provide you with a strong introduction to their day-to-day activities. Speaking with aircraft pilots may provide other insights into the role of the air traffic controller. Visits and interviews can be arranged through most airports, air traffic control centers, the Air Traffic Control Association, and many airlines. You should also be aware that every branch of the military services offers opportunities for experience in these and related jobs.

■ EMPLOYERS

Air traffic controllers are employed by the federal government. Most work for the FAA, although a small number work in such areas as the Department of Defense. Approximately 22,400 air traffic controllers work in the United States.

■ STARTING OUT

The first step in becoming an air traffic controller starts with the written civil service exam, followed by the one-week screening. Acceptance is on a highly competitive

basis. High grades in college or strong work experience is considered essential. Experience in related fields, including those of pilots, air dispatch operators, and other positions with either the civil airlines or the military service, will be important for those with and especially for those without a college degree. Actual air control experience gained in military service may be a plus. However, civil aviation rules are quite different from military aviation rules. Because the FAA provides complete training, applicants with strong skills and abilities in abstract reasoning, communication, and problem solving, as well as the ability to learn and to work independently, will have the best chance of entering this field.

■ ADVANCEMENT

After becoming a controller, those who do particularly well may reach the level of supervisor or manager. Many others advance to even more responsible positions in air control, and some might move into the top administrative jobs with the FAA. Competitive civil service status can be earned at the end of one year on the job, and career status after the satisfactory completion of three years of work in the area.

In the case of both airport control specialists and en route control specialists, the responsibilities become more complex with each successive promotion. Controllers generally begin at the GS-7 level and advance by completing certification requirements for the different air traffic control specialists. New hires at an airport control tower usually begin by communicating flight data and

---

TECHNOLOGY AND AIR TRAFFIC CONTROL

Technology is changing the way air traffic controllers do their jobs. More and more planes are being equipped with GPS technology. GPS allows planes to form a far more accurate picture of their position and the position of others in the sky. This allows planes to break away from the traditional air routes and essentially chart their own course, allowing for faster and more economical flights. Under pressure from the airlines, the FAA announced its intentions to adopt a "Free Flight" program, allowing the airlines to take advantage of their GPS equipment. This will mean a far more limited role for the air traffic controller, and especially en route controllers, who may see their functions reduced to monitoring aircraft and stepping in to assist in emergencies. Air traffic controllers will still be needed at the airports, although in fewer numbers. Openings in the field will come primarily from retiring controllers and others who leave the job.

airport conditions to pilots before progressing through the ranks of ground controller, local controller, departure controller, and, lastly, arrival controller. At an en route center, trainees begin by processing flight plans, then advance to become radar associate controllers, and, finally, radar controllers.

After becoming fully qualified, controllers who exhibit strong management, organizational, and job skills may advance to become area supervisors and managers and control tower or flight service station managers. Employees in the higher grades may be responsible for a number of different areas, including the coordination of the traffic control activities within the control area, the supervision and training of en route traffic controllers or airport traffic controllers in lower positions, and management in various aeronautical agencies. These positions generally become available after three to five years of fully qualified service.

EARNINGS

Air traffic control trainees start at the GS-7 level, which paid a minimum of $34,184 annually in 2004. According to the U.S. Department of Labor, in 2002 the average salary for air traffic controllers in nonsupervisory, supervisory, and managerial jobs was $95,700. The lowest paid 10 percent of controllers made less than $46,410. The highest paid controllers made $131,610 or more per year. The controller's experience, job responsibilities, and the complexity of the facility are also factors that influence the rate of pay. Controllers with a great deal of seniority and those at the nation's busiest airports earn the most. Controllers may also earn bonuses based on performance.

Because of the complexity of their job duties and the tension involved in their work, air traffic controllers are offered better benefits than other federal employees. Depending on their length of service, air traffic controllers receive 13 to 26 days of paid vacation and 13 days of paid sick leave per year, plus life insurance and health benefits. In addition, they are permitted to retire earlier and with fewer years of service than other federal employees. An air traffic controller with 20 years' experience may retire at the age of 50; those with 25 years' experience may retire at any age. Controllers who manage air traffic are required to retire at age 56.

WORK ENVIRONMENT

Air traffic controllers are required to remain constantly alert and focused while performing a large number of simultaneous duties. They must keep track of several aircraft approaching, departing, and passing through the airspace under their control, while receiving flight data from and giving instructions to several pilots at once. They must

remain alert to changes in weather and airport conditions, guide planes through intricate approach patterns, and maintain a safe separation of aircraft in the sky and on the ground. They must be able to interpret the symbols on the radar screen, form a clear image of what is happening in the sky above them, and react quickly and decisively to the activity of the aircraft. Controllers must also have strong communicative abilities and be able to give instructions to pilots in a firm and clear tone. The stress of the controller's job requires a great deal of emotional control, especially in times of potential danger and emergency. Traffic conditions change continuously throughout the controller's shift, and the controller must remain alert during times of light traffic as well as times of heavy traffic.

Terminal air traffic controllers work in towers as high as 200 feet off the ground; windows on all sides of the tower allow the pilot to see what is happening on the runways and in the sky around the airport. Radar control screens provide locations of all aircraft in the airport's airspace. Large air traffic control towers generally house the radar control center in a room below the observation tower. En route centers are usually housed in large, windowless buildings. These controllers monitor the sky entirely through radar and radio communication. Flight service stations are often located at airports in separate buildings from the control tower.

The numbers of air traffic controllers on duty varies from airport to airport and according to the number of scheduled flights expected in a center's airspace. At a small airport, a controller may work alone for an entire shift; larger airports may have up to 30 controllers on duty, while en route centers may have 150 to 700 controllers on duty during a shift. Air traffic controllers work a five-day, 40-hour week, usually on a rotating shift basis, which means they often work at night, during the weekends, and during holidays. Overtime is often available; during a shift, controllers are given breaks every two hours.

OUTLOOK

Employment for air traffic controllers should increase about as fast as the average 2012. Despite increasing air traffic, there is strong and continued competition for air traffic control positions, and the implementation of a new air traffic control system will reduce employment for workers in the field.

FOR MORE INFORMATION

Contact the following associations for additional information on air traffic control careers:

Air Traffic Control Association
2300 Clarendon Boulevard, Suite 711
Arlington, VA 22201-3367

Tel: 703-522-5717
Email: info@atca.org
http://www.atca.org

Federal Aviation Administration
800 Independence Avenue, SW, Room 810
Washington, DC 20591
Tel: 202-366-4000
http://www.faa.gov

National Association of Air Traffic Specialists
11303 Amherst Avenue, Suite 4
Wheaton, MD 20902
Tel: 301-933-6228
http://www.naats.org

For information on air traffic control careers in Canada, contact the following associations:

Canadian Air Traffic Control Association
162 Cleopatra Drive
Nepean, ON K2G 5X2 Canada
Tel: 613-225-3553
Email: catca@catca.ca
http://www.catca.ca

Nav Canada
PO Box 3411, Station D
Ottawa, ON K1P 5L6 Canada
Tel: 877-663-6656
http://www.navcanada.ca

Alcohol and Drug Abuse Counselors

■ OVERVIEW

Alcohol and drug abuse counselors (sometimes called *substance abuse counselors*) work with people who abuse or are addicted to drugs or alcohol. Through individual and group counseling sessions, they help their clients understand and change their destructive substance abuse behaviors. There are about 67,000 substance abuse counselors in the United States.

■ HISTORY

Throughout history people have used drugs for a variety of purposes—for healing, for religious ceremonies, to alter consciousness for self-understanding, to loosen inhibitions and have fun, or to dull the senses against emotional or physical pain. Alcohol and other substances were used in ancient Egypt, Greece, and India as offerings to spiritual beings, as well as to reach a higher consciousness. Many religions today, from Tibetan Buddhism and traditional Native American religions to Roman Catholicism, use alcohol and other consciousness-altering substances in traditional ceremonies.

Throughout the ages people have abused drugs and alcohol, too. No matter what the purpose for the initial drug use, it becomes for some people an obsession, and then an addiction. The history of treatment for substance abuse is much shorter. In the 1800s, alcoholics and morphine addicts were placed in asylums. Treatments sometimes included miracle medicines that were supposed to be quick "cures" for addicts. In the early 1900s doctors used electroshock therapies and psychosurgery to treat alcoholics.

In 1935, the Alcoholics Anonymous (AA) program was started by two men known as Bill and Dr. Bob. They helped each other achieve sobriety and continued to help others. This system of alcoholics helping other alcoholics grew into the AA movement, which is still strong today. AA's 12-step program has been adapted and used effectively to treat addictions of all kinds.

Today alcohol and a huge variety of dangerous drugs are readily available—marijuana, cocaine, LSD, heroin, inhalants, amphetamines, barbiturates, and more. Fortunately, treatment programs are also readily available for those who want them. Outpatient methadone programs give heroin addicts the medication methadone to reduce cravings for heroin and block its effects. Patients are also counseled, given vocational guidance and training, and taught how to find support services. Long-term residential programs last for several months to a year. Patients live in a drug-free environment with fellow recovering addicts and counselors. Outpatient drug-free programs use such therapies as problem-solving groups, insight-oriented

QUICK FACTS

SCHOOL SUBJECTS
Health
Psychology
Sociology

PERSONAL SKILLS
Communication/ideas
Helping/teaching

WORK ENVIRONMENT
Primarily indoors
Primarily one location

MINIMUM EDUCATION LEVEL
Associate's degree

SALARY RANGE
$19,540 to $31,860 to $45,570+

CERTIFICATION OR LICENSING
Required by certain states

OUTLOOK
Faster than the average

DOT
045

GOE
12.02.02

NOC
N/A

O*NET-SOC
21-1011.00

"Just Say No" versus Harm Reduction

Harm reduction is a drug and alcohol abuse-education philosophy. The most common response to the drug problem in the United States has been criminalization, with drug use seen as a moral deficiency best treated through the criminal justice system. A less common philosophy is for users to be treated as medically ill. Harm reduction, on the other hand, sees drug use as a common, if risky, human behavior that is often made even more dangerous by an uncontrolled market.

Harm-reduction organizations such as DanceSafe in the United States and Crew 2000 in Edinburgh, Scotland, try to realistically educate drug users about the perils of drug abuse and how to counter them. By winning users' trust and connecting to them as peers, not as authority figures, they can help stop the spread of dangerous drugs such as heroin and sometimes help connect users with such services as pill testing (to make sure they are free of dangerous contaminants) and needle exchanges, though they do not perform these services themselves. Harm-reduction organizations often provide safer-sex education. They are usually staffed by volunteers.

psychotherapy, cognitive-behavioral therapy, and 12-step programs. Short-term inpatient programs focus on stabilizing the patient, abstinence, and lifestyle changes.

■ THE JOB

The main goal of alcohol and drug abuse counselors is to help patients stop their destructive behaviors. Counselors may also work with the families of clients to give them support and guidance in dealing with the problem.

Counselors begin by trying to learn about a patient's general background and history of drug or alcohol use. They may review patient records, including police reports, employment records, medical records, or reports from other counselors.

Counselors also interview the patient to determine the nature and extent of substance abuse. During an interview, the counselor asks questions about what types of substances the patient uses, how often, and for how long. The counselor may also ask patients about previous attempts to stop using the substance and about how the problem has affected their lives in various respects.

Using the information they obtain from the patient and their knowledge of substance abuse patterns, coun-

selors formulate a program for treatment and rehabilitation. A substantial part of the rehabilitation process involves individual, group, or family counseling sessions. During individual sessions, counselors do a great deal of listening, perhaps asking appropriate questions to guide patients to insights about themselves. In group therapy sessions, counselors supervise groups of several patients, helping move their discussion in positive ways. In counseling sessions, counselors also teach patients methods of overcoming their dependencies. For example, they might help a patient develop a series of goals for behavioral change.

Counselors monitor and assess the progress of their patients. In most cases, counselors deal with several different patients in various stages of recovery—some may need help breaking the pattern of substance abuse; some may already have stopped using, but still need support; others may be recovered users who have suffered a relapse. Counselors maintain ongoing relationships with patients to help them adapt to the different recovery stages.

Working with families is another aspect of many alcohol and drug abuse counselors' jobs. They may ask a patient's family for insight into the patient's behavior. They may also teach the patient's family members how to deal with and support the patient through the recovery process.

Counselors may work with other health professionals and social agencies, including physicians, psychiatrists, psychologists, employment services, and court systems. In some cases, the counselor, with the patient's permission, may serve as a spokesperson for the patient, working with corrections officers, social workers, or employers. In other cases, a patient's needs might exceed the counselor's abilities; when this is the case, the counselor refers the patient to an appropriate medical expert, agency, or social program.

There is a substantial amount of paperwork involved in counseling alcohol and drug abusers. Detailed records must be kept on patients in order to follow their progress. For example, a report must be written after each counseling session. Counselors who work in residential treatment settings are required to participate in regular staff meetings to develop treatment plans and review patient progress. They may also meet periodically with family members or social service agency representatives to discuss patient progress and needs.

In some cases, alcohol and drug abuse counselors specialize in working with certain groups of people. Some work only with children or teenagers; others work with businesses to counsel employees who may have problems related to drugs and alcohol. In still other cases, counselors specialize in treating people who are addicted to specific drugs, such as cocaine, heroin, or alcohol. Counselors may need special training in order to work with specific groups.

REQUIREMENTS
High School
High school students who are considering a career in alcohol and drug abuse counseling should choose a curriculum that meets the requirements of the college or university they hope to attend. Typically, four years of English, history, mathematics, a foreign language, and social sciences are necessary. In addition, psychology, sociology, physiology, biology, and anatomy provide a good academic background for potential counselors.

The educational requirements for alcohol and drug abuse counselors vary greatly by state and employer. A high school education may be the minimum requirement for employers who provide on-the-job training, which ranges from six weeks to two years. These jobs, however, are becoming increasingly rare as more states are leaning toward stricter requirements for counselors.

Postsecondary Training
Some employers require an associate's degree in alcohol and drug technology. Most substance abuse counselors, however, have a bachelor's degree in counseling, psychology, health sociology, or social work. Many two- and four-year colleges now offer specific courses for students training to be substance abuse counselors.

Many counselors have a master's degree in counseling with a specialization in substance abuse counseling. Accredited graduate programs in substance abuse counseling are composed of a supervised internship as well as regular class work.

Certification or Licensing
Certification in this field, which is mandatory in some states, is available through state accreditation boards. Currently, 47 states and the District of Columbia have credentialing laws for alcohol and drug abuse counselors. These laws typically require that counselors have a minimum of a master's degree and two to three years of postacademic supervised counseling experience. Candidates must also have passed a written test.

The National Association of Alcoholism and Drug Abuse Counselors also offers a National Certified Addiction Counselor (NCAC) Certification.

Other Requirements
In order to be successful in this job, prospective counselors should enjoy working with people. They must have compassion, good communication and listening skills, and a desire to help others. They should also be emotionally stable and able to deal with the frustrations and failures that are often a part of the job.

EXPLORING
Students interested in this career can find a great deal of information on substance abuse and substance abuse counseling at any local library. In addition, by contacting a local hospital, mental health clinic, or treatment center, it might be possible to talk with a counselor about the details of his or her job.

Volunteer work or a part-time job at a residential facility, such as a hospital or treatment center, is another good way of gaining experience and exploring an aptitude for counseling work. Finally, the professional and government organizations listed at the end of this article can provide information on alcohol and drug abuse counseling.

EMPLOYERS
Counselors are hired by hospitals, private and public treatment centers, government agencies, prisons, public school systems, colleges and universities, health maintenance organizations (HMOs), crisis centers, and mental health centers. More and more frequently, large companies are hiring alcohol and drug abuse counselors as well, to deal with employee substance abuse problems.

SOBERING STATISTICS

- In 2000, an estimated 14 million Americans were current illicit drug users. This represents 6.3 percent of the population 12 years old and older.
- Approximately 2.1 million youths aged 12 to 17 had used inhalants at some time in their lives as of 2000. Of these youths, 3.9 percent had used glue, shoe polish, or Toluene, and 3.3 percent had used gasoline or lighter fluid.
- Almost half of Americans aged 12 and older reported being current drinkers of alcohol in 2000—a total of approximately 104 million people.
- Heavy drinking was reported by 5.6 percent of the population aged 12 and older, or 12.6 million people.

Source: The 2000 National Household Survey on Drug Abuse, a project of the Substance Abuse and Mental Health Services Administration

■ STARTING OUT

Counselors who have completed a two- or four-year college degree might start a job search by checking with the career placement office of their college or university. Those who plan to look for a position without first attending college might want to start by getting an entry-level or volunteer position in a treatment center or related agency. In this way, they can obtain practical experience and also make connections that might lead to full-time employment as a counselor.

Job seekers should also watch the classified advertisements in local newspapers. Job openings for counselors are often listed under "Alcohol and Drug Counselor," "Substance Abuse Counselor," or "Mental Health Counselor." Finally, one might consider applying directly to the personnel department of various facilities and agencies that treat alcohol and drug abusers.

■ ADVANCEMENT

Counselors in this field often advance initially by taking on more responsibilities and earning a higher wage. They may also better themselves by taking a similar position in a more prestigious facility, such as an upscale private treatment center.

As they obtain more experience and perhaps more education, counselors sometimes move into supervisory or administrative positions. They might become directors of substance abuse programs in mental health facilities or executive directors of agencies or clinics.

Career options are more diverse for those counselors who continue their education. They may move into research, consulting, or teaching at the college level.

■ EARNINGS

Salaries of alcohol and drug abuse counselors depend on education level, amount of experience, and place of employment. Generally, the more education and experience a counselor has, the higher his or her earnings will be. Counselors who work in private treatment centers also tend to earn more than their public sector counterparts.

Alcohol and drug abuse counselors earned a median annual salary of $31,860 in 2002, according to the *Occupational Outlook Handbook (OOH)*. The lowest 10 percent earned less than $19,540. The highest 10 percent earned $45,570 or more. The *OOH* reports the following median annual earnings for alcohol and drug abuse counselors by industry: local government, $35,400; hospitals, $36,240; outpatient care centers, $32,250; individual and family services, $29,130; and residential care in mental health facilities, $27,610. Directors of treatment programs or centers could earn considerably more.

Almost all treatment centers provide employee benefits to their full-time counselors. Benefits usually include paid vacations and sick days, insurance, and pension plans.

■ WORK ENVIRONMENT

The hours that an alcohol and drug abuse counselor works depends upon where he or she is employed. Many residential treatment facilities and mental health centers—and all crisis centers—have counselors on duty during evening and weekend hours. Other employers, such as government agencies and universities, are likely to have more conventional working hours.

Work settings for counselors also vary by employer. Counselors may work in private offices, in the rooms or homes of patients, in classrooms, or in meeting rooms. In some cases, they conduct support group sessions in churches, community centers, or schools. For the most part, however, counselors work at the same work site or sites on a daily basis.

The bulk of a counselor's day is spent dealing with various people—patients, families, social workers, and health care professionals. There may be very little time during a workday for quiet reflection or organization.

Working with alcohol and drug abusers can be an emotionally draining experience. Overcoming addiction is a very hard battle, and patients respond to it in various ways. They may be resentful, angry, discouraged, or profoundly depressed. They may talk candidly with their counselors about tragic and upsetting events in their lives. Counselors spend much of their time listening to and dealing with very strong, usually negative, emotions.

This work can also be discouraging, due to a high failure rate. Many alcoholics and drug addicts do not respond to treatment and return immediately to their addictions. Even after months and sometimes years of recovery, many substance abusers suffer relapses. The counselor must learn to cope with the frustration of having his or her patients fail, perhaps repeatedly.

There is a very positive side to drug and alcohol abuse counseling, however. When it is successful, counselors have the satisfaction of knowing that they had a positive effect on someone's life. They have the reward of seeing some patients return to happy family lives and productive careers.

■ OUTLOOK

Employment of alcohol and drug abuse counselors is projected to grow faster than the average for all occupations through 2012, according to the U.S. Department of Labor. There are more than 20 million alcoholics in the

United States and an equal, if not greater, number of drug abusers. Because no successful method to significantly reduce drug and alcohol abuse has emerged, these numbers are not likely to decrease. Overall population growth will also lead to a need for more substance abuse counselors. Finally, many states are shifting away from criminalizing drugs us, seeing it as a mental-health problem that should be treated through the medical system, not the criminal-justice system.

Another reason for the expected growth in counselors' jobs is that an increasing number of employers are offering employee assistance programs that provide counseling services for mental health and alcohol and drug abuse.

Finally, many job openings will arise as a result of job turnover. Because of the stress levels and the emotional demands involved in this career, there is a high burnout rate. As alcohol and drug abuse counselors leave the field, new counselors are needed to replace them.

■ FOR MORE INFORMATION
For more information on substance abuse and counseling careers, contact the following organizations:

American Counseling Association
5999 Stevenson Avenue
Alexandria, VA 22304-3300
Tel: 800-347-6647
http://www.counseling.org

**National Institute on Alcohol Abuse
    and Alcoholism**
National Institutes of Health
6000 Executive Boulevard
Willco Building
Bethesda, MD 20892-7003
http://www.niaaa.nih.gov

National Institute on Drug Abuse
National Institutes of Health
6001 Executive Boulevard, Room 5213
Bethesda, MD 20892-9561
Tel: 301-443-1124
http://www.nida.nih.gov

For information on certification, contact
**National Association of Alcoholism and Drug
    Abuse Counselors**
901 North Washington Street, Suite 600
Alexandria, VA 22314-1535
Tel: 800-548-0497
Email: naadac@naadac.org
http://www.naadac.org

For additional information, check out the following website run by the Substance Abuse and Mental Health Services Administration:
Prevline: Prevention Online
http://www.health.org

Allergists/ Immunologists

■ OVERVIEW
Allergists/immunologists are physicians that specialize in the treatment of allergic, asthmatic, and immunologic diseases. They treat patients with asthma, hay fever, food allergies, AIDS, rheumatoid arthritis, and other diseases. There are approximately 4,500 certified allergists/immunologists employed in the United States.

■ HISTORY
The first great physician was Hippocrates, a Greek who lived almost 2,500 years ago. He developed theories about the practice of medicine and the anatomy of the human body, but Hippocrates is remembered today for a set of medical ethics that continues to influence medical practice. The oath that he administered to his disciples is still administered to physicians about to start practice. His 87 treatises on medicine, known as the Hippocratic Collection, are believed to be the first authoritative record of early medical theory and practice. Hippocratic physicians believed in the theory that health was maintained by a proper balance of four "humors" in the body: blood, phlegm, black bile, and yellow bile.

Since the time of Ancient Greece, as you might imagine, there have been many advances in the medical field: the development of organized clinical

QUICK FACTS

SCHOOL SUBJECTS
Biology
Health

PERSONAL SKILLS
Helping/teaching
Technical/scientific

WORK ENVIRONMENT
Primarily indoors
Primarily multiple locations

MINIMUM EDUCATION LEVEL
Medical degree

SALARY RANGE
$39,809 to $59,978 to
$140,000+

CERTIFICATION OR LICENSING
Required by all states

OUTLOOK
About as fast as the average

DOT
070

GOE
14.02.01

NOC
3112

O*NET-SOC
29-1069.99

What Causes Allergies?

When you get sick, your body immediately mobilizes its defenses to fight the invading bacteria or virus. You may cough or sneeze, and your throat may get sore or tight. Your nose might run as your body produces more mucous, and you may also feel achy and tired and run a fever. Though these effects are not pleasant, they help you body rid itself of the invaders.

Allergies are when your body has an immune reaction to common, non-pathenogenic (disease-causing) substances. Common allergens, or allergy-causing substances, are mold, pollen, dust mites (tiny, invisible insects that live in our homes), certain types of food (such as peanuts), insect stings, or animal saliva or dander.

Allergic reactions vary in strength. Some peoples' eyes get itchy and watery, for instance, if they rub them after petting a dog or cat. Other people may break out in a rash or get hives, or have an asthma attack. Some allergic reactions may be so severe that a person's blood pressure drops drastically. There are even cases of people going into shock or suffering from laryngospasm (a swelling of the vocal cords) and even dying from these reactions, but, thankfully, this is very rare.

instruction, vaccinations, sterilization procedures, and instruments such as the stethoscope, to name a few. In addition to these advances, the medical profession also saw the development of specialists, doctors who concentrate their work in specific areas such as surgery, psychiatry, internal medicine, or allergies and immunology.

■ THE JOB

Over 20 percent of Americans suffer from some kind of allergy. Allergies to certain foods, plants, pollen, animal fur, air pollution, insects, colognes, chemicals, and cleansers may send sufferers to allergy and immunology specialists, doctors who specialize in the treatment of allergic, asthmatic, and immunologic diseases.

Allergists and immunologists also treat patients with hay fever, also called allergic rhinitis, which causes symptoms such as congestion, sneezing, and a scratchy throat caused by pollens or molds in the air. They treat asthma, a respiratory disease often triggered by an allergic reaction that causes restricted breathing, constricting the air flow to the lungs. Another serious allergic reaction is anaphylaxis. Triggered by a particular food or insect sting, anaphylaxis can quickly restrict breathing, swell the throat, and cause unconsciousness. Other allergies treated by an allergist include skin allergies, such as hives and eczema, and food and drug allergies.

Immunologic diseases are those that affect the immune system. Allergy and immunology specialists treat patients with conditions such as AIDS, rheumatoid arthritis, and lupus. An immunologist also treats patients who are receiving an organ or bone marrow transplant to help prevent the patient's body from rejecting the transplanted organ.

Allergists/immunologists first examine patients. They review medical histories and backgrounds and may also conduct skin tests and blood tests. Skin tests are often preferred because they are inexpensive and the results are available immediately. Skin tests are also better for identifying more subtle allergies.

Once the diagnosis is made, the doctor determines a treatment plan. In some cases, the solution may be as simple as avoiding the things that cause the allergic reaction. The allergist suggests ways to limit patients' exposure to the allergen. In other cases, a doctor prescribes medication such as antihistamines to relieve allergy symptoms such as nasal congestion, eye burning, and skin rashes.

Antihistamines can have side effects such as dizziness, headaches, and nausea. Should these side effects occur, the allergist may lower a dosage or prescribe a different medication. Sometimes a patient can build up a resistance to an antihistamine, and the doctor needs to prescribe a stronger variety.

Immunotherapy (a series of allergy shots) is another kind of treatment for asthma and for allergies to pollen, dust, bee venom, and a variety of other substances. Immunotherapy involves injecting the patient with a small amount of the substance that causes the allergic reaction. The immune system then becomes less sensitive to the substances and reduces the symptoms of allergy. An allergist will give weekly shots over an extended time, gradually increasing the dosage; eventually the shots are only necessary once a month.

■ REQUIREMENTS
High School

If you are interested in becoming an allergist/immunologist, start preparing for this career in high school by taking college preparatory classes. Science classes, including biology, chemistry, and physics, are especially important. Math and English classes will help you develop skills working with numbers and research. Social science classes can give you a better understanding of people and society.

Postsecondary Training

After earning an M.D. degree and becoming licensed to practice medicine (see Physicians), allergists/immunologists must complete a three-year residency in internal medicine or pediatrics, then a minimum of two years of training in an allergy and immunology fellowship. The American Academy of Allergy, Asthma, and Immunology publishes a training program directory, which lists accredited training programs and faculty and program information.

Certification or Licensing

Certification from the American Board of Allergy and Immunology requires a valid medical license, proof of residency completion, and written evaluation from the residency director. The evaluation reviews the candidate's clinical judgment, attitude, professional behavior, and other work skills and habits. The certification exam tests the candidate's knowledge of the immune system, human pathology, and the molecular basis of allergic and other immune reactions. The candidate must also show an understanding of diagnostic tests and therapy for immunologic diseases. There are about 4,500 certified allergists/immunologists in the United States.

Other Requirements

Allergists/immunologists should be compassionate and concerned for the well-being of their patients. They should also be careful listeners—a doctor must have a good understanding of a patient's background, environment, and emotional state to plan the best treatment. An allergist/immunologist must be prepared to deal with the stress of caring for sick patients; some of these patients may have life-threatening diseases such as AIDS, cancer, or severe asthma.

■ EXPLORING

To explore this career, expose yourself to the health care field early. Volunteer or look for a paid part-time job in any environment that allows you to be around patient care, such as hospitals or nursing homes. Such real-life experience will be looked on favorably in your applications for college admissions as well as give you a sense of what work in health care is like.

■ EARNINGS

Physicians are rewarded well for their years of intensive study, for their long hours, and for their level of responsibility. Physicians who are still in their residencies earn an average of between $39,809 to $57,978, according to the Association of Medical Colleges. The median income after expenses for all physicians in 2002 (the latest information available), according to the Department of Labor, was about $140,000 per year.

Though an allergist/immunologist can make a good living, a number of factors, such as geographical location, experience, and reputation of good work, can determine salary.

■ OUTLOOK

Employment of physicians will grow as fast as the average through 2012, according to the U.S. Department of Labor. Over 50 million Americans suffer from some kind of allergy, fueling the demand for allergists/immunologists. Though some doctors remain skeptical about the relationship between allergy and illness, allergy/immunology has become a respected field of medicine. As this field continues to grow, more doctors will refer their patients to these specialists.

■ FOR MORE INFORMATION

For career information and a list of accredited training programs, contact

**American Academy of Allergy, Asthma, and
   Immunology**
611 East Wells Street
Milwaukee, WI 53202
Tel: 414-272-6071
Email: info@aaaai.org
http://www.aaaai.org

For information on immunology, such as research, graduate programs, and fellowships, contact

American Association of Immunologists
9650 Rockville Pike
Bethesda, MD 20814
Tel: 301-530-7178
Email: infoaai@aai.faseb.org
http://www.aai.org

For information on certification, contact

American Board of Allergy and Immunology
510 Walnut Street, Suite 1701
Philadelphia, PA 19106-3699
Tel: 215-592-9466
Email: abai@abai.org
http://www.abai.org

For career information and a listing of medical schools, contact

Association of American Medical Colleges
2450 N Street, NW
Washington, DC 20037-1126
Tel: 202-828-0400
http://www.aamc.org

Ambassadors

■ OVERVIEW

Ambassadors manage the operations of the U.S. embassies in other countries. An embassy is the headquarters of a U.S. diplomatic mission established in the capital city of a foreign country. According to the *CIA World Factbook*, the United States maintains diplomatic relations with 185 of the other 188 U.N. members (plus the Vatican in Rome) and has an embassy in most foreign capitals. Each embassy is headed by only one ambassador. Charged with the responsibility of maintaining diplomatic relations, an ambassador represents the president in matters of foreign policy. Ambassadors help to promote peace, trade, and the exchange of information between the United States and foreign lands.

QUICK FACTS

SCHOOL SUBJECTS
Foreign language
Government

PERSONAL SKILLS
Communication/ideas
Leadership/management

WORK ENVIRONMENT
Primarily indoors
Primarily multiple locations

MINIMUM EDUCATION LEVEL
Bachelor's degree

SALARY RANGE
$100,000 to $118,000 to $125,000

CERTIFICATION OR LICENSING
None available

OUTLOOK
Little change or more slowly than the average

DOT
188

GOE
N/A

NOC
4168

O*NET-SOC
N/A

■ HISTORY

Even in the earliest years of the United States, diplomacy was recognized as an important element of a strong government. Men such as Benjamin Franklin, John Adams, John Jay, and Francis Dana were chosen for their intelligence, strength of character, and powers of persuasion to enlist the support of foreign countries for American independence. Benjamin Franklin was so successful in his commission to France, he inspired a pre-Disney marketing blitz—the French put his picture on watches, jewelry, and even snuffboxes. And the women of France had their hair done to resemble the fur caps Franklin wore. However, not all diplomats enjoyed such stardom; Francis Dana spent a cold, unproductive two years in Russia, unable to speak the language, and incapable of convincing Catherine II to support American independence.

Established in 1789, the State Department was placed under the direction of Thomas Jefferson, the first U.S. secretary of state and the senior member of President Washington's cabinet. It was his responsibility to initiate

foreign policy on behalf of the U.S. government, advise the president on matters related to foreign policy, and administer the foreign affairs of the United States with the help of employees both at home and abroad.

Before the invention of radio, telegraph, telephone, and email, the ambassador was entrusted to make final, binding decisions on behalf of the United States. More immediate means of communication narrowed the distances between embassies and their home countries; though today's ambassadors represent the president and actively contribute to international relations, they are more restricted in their powers.

■ THE JOB

Iceland. New Zealand. Venezuela. Sweden. Jordan. Egypt. Ambassadors to these or one of the other 185 countries that host U.S. embassies in their capital cities coordinate the operations of hundreds of government officers. An embassy serves as the headquarters for Foreign Service Officers (FSOs), and other personnel, all working together to maintain a positive, productive relationship between the host country and the United States. Though the work is important, the post of ambassador is sometimes largely ceremonial. The president offers an ambassadorship to someone who has a long, dignified history of political service or to a wealthy supporter of the president's political party. An ambassador will stay at a post for two to six years. *Career ambassadors* are those who are Foreign Service officers; *noncareer ambassadors* are those outside of the Foreign Service.

Ambassadors address many different concerns, such as security, trade, tourism, environmental protection, and health care. They are involved in establishing and maintaining international agreements, such as nuclear test bans and ozone layer protection. They help to promote peace and stability and open new markets. When negotiating treaties and introducing policies, they help the people of the host country understand the U.S. position, while also helping the United States understand the host country's position.

Ambassadors spend much of their time meeting with government officials and private citizens of the host country. Together they identify subjects of mutual interest, such as medical research and the development of new technologies. They meet with those involved in private industry in the country, including Americans doing business there. When a country is struggling due to natural disasters, epidemics of disease, and other problems, they may pursue aid from the United States.

Ambassadors' work isn't limited to the city in which the embassy is located. They travel across the country to learn about the other cities and regions and to meet the cities' representatives. Among the people of the country, ambassadors promote a good attitude toward the United States, as well as travel, business, and educational opportunities. When important U.S. visitors, such as the president, first lady, and Secretary of State, arrive in the country, the ambassador serves as host, introducing them to the country and its officials.

Of course, ambassadors for different countries must address very different issues, such as environmental concerns, the state of education and health care, political structure, the agriculture, and industry. For example, the United States has entered agreements with Budapest, Hungary; Bangkok, Thailand; and Gabarone, Botswana; to establish International Law Enforcement Academies. The academies, jointly financed, managed, and staffed by the cooperating nations, initially provide training to police and government officials.

In France, diplomatic relations have a long, successful history, beginning with Benjamin Franklin's arrival in 1776. Mutual interests between the United States and France have resulted in joint space and satellite programs, AIDS research, and nuclear nonproliferation policies. Tourism is also an important connection between the two countries; every year, over two million Americans vacation in France. A current issue of concern is biotechnology and how it affects agriculture and the environment.

▓ REQUIREMENTS
High School

In order to pursue any work that involves foreign government, you need a good, well-rounded education. Talk to your guidance counselor about the classes that will be most helpful in preparing for college. Courses in American history, western civilization, government, and world history are important, as well as classes in math and economics. English composition will help you develop writing and communication skills. Any foreign language course will give you a good foundation in language study—many ambassadors know more than two languages. Journalism courses develop writing and editing skills and keep you informed about current events.

Postsecondary Training

Many ambassadors and FSOs hold master's degrees and doctorates in international relations, political science, or economics. Many also hold law degrees. As an undergraduate, you should take general-requirement courses in English literature, foreign language, composition, geography, and statistics, along with courses for your particular major. There are many undergraduate majors relevant to foreign service, including foreign language, economics, political science, journalism, education, busi-

ness, and English. You may also want to consider programs designed specifically for foreign service and international relations. The Georgetown University School of Foreign Service (http://www.georgetown.edu/sfs) has undergraduate and graduate programs designed to prepare students for careers in international affairs. Many luminaries have graduated from the school, including Bill Clinton in 1968; former Secretary of State Madeleine Albright has served as a member of the school's faculty. Postgraduate programs, especially those in political science, are also very useful.

"Career Ambassador" is the highest rank for senior officers of the Foreign Service, but you don't have to be an FSO to be an ambassador. If you do choose to pursue work as an officer, the Foreign Service offers internship opportunities to college students in their junior and senior years and to graduate students. About half of these unpaid internships are based in Washington, D.C., while the other half are at U.S. embassies and consulates overseas. Interns may write reports, assist with trade negotiations, work with budget projects, or process visas or passports. The Foreign Service also offers a Foreign Affairs Fellowship Program, which provides funding to undergraduate and graduate students preparing academically to enter the Foreign Service.

Other Requirements

Ambassadors are usually already successful in their careers before being nominated for an ambassadorship. They also have some connection to top officials in the U.S. government. To achieve such success and good connections, you must be very intelligent and knowledgeable about government and politics. It is important to earn good grades, so as to earn admission to top schools, where such connections can be made. You should be comfortable in a leadership role and extremely ambitious and motivated—those who serve as ambassadors have often achieved success in a number of different areas and have held a variety of powerful positions. You should be flexible and adaptable to new cultures and traditions. You must be interested in the histories of foreign cultures and respectful of the practices of other nations. Good people skills are important for dealing diplomatically with officials from other countries.

▓ EXPLORING

As a member of a foreign language club at your school, you may have the opportunity to visit other countries. If such programs don't exist, check with your guidance counselor or school librarian about discounted foreign travel packages available to student groups. Also ask them about student exchange programs, if you're interested in spending several weeks in another country. There's also

ART IN EMBASSIES

The curator of the Art in Embassies Program works closely with ambassadors to select artwork that is representative of the cultural and artistic heritage of the United States. Museums, galleries, collectors, and artists loan their work for three-year exhibitions in the residences of U.S. ambassadors worldwide. Oil paintings, tapestries, sculptures, quilts, photographs, and other works are carefully crated and shipped by professional art handlers and are then analyzed by experts on arrival at the embassies. Works have included Native American pottery and baskets; paintings of American landscapes such as the Napa and Missouri Valleys; a series of photographs depicting sites along Route 66; and the works of famous artists Robert Rauschenberg, Maya Lin, Andy Warhol, Red Grooms, and Louise Nevelson.

a People to People Student Ambassador Program, which offers summer travel opportunities to students in grades six through 12. To learn about the expenses, destinations, and application process, visit the website (http:// www.studentambassadors.org). Visit the Department of State Web site (http://www.state.gov) to read the biographies of ambassadors around the world and for links to individual embassy Web sites.

The American Foreign Service Association (AFSA), a professional association serving FSOs, publishes the *Foreign Service Journal* (http://www.afsa.org/fsj), which features articles by FSOs and academics that can give you insight into the Foreign Service. AFSA offers a discount on student subscriptions.

■ EMPLOYERS

Ambassadors work for the U.S. State Department. They represent the interests of the president through the Secretary of State. Many ambassadors are FSOs who have worked up through the ranks of the Foreign Service.

■ STARTING OUT

Those who are appointed as ambassadors have already succeeded in their individual careers. While many ambassadors have worked in the Foreign Service in some capacity, many others have established themselves in other ways. They have worked as directors in other government agencies and as members of the U.S. Congress. They've served on the faculty of colleges and universities. They have directed philanthropic organizations and run large companies. Before getting an ambassadorship, ambassadors may have already had a great deal of experience with a particular country, possibly having served

as *Deputy Chief of Mission* (the second in command of an embassy). Or they may have been involved in negotiating international agreements or in establishing new markets for the country.

■ ADVANCEMENT

After being nominated for an ambassadorship by the president, nominees are then confirmed by the Senate. Positions with the Foreign Service are rotational, so the length of an ambassador's term varies. Most ambassadors only serve a few years with an embassy. After leaving a post, they may go on to serve as ambassador at a U.S. embassy in another country. Some career ambassadors spend several years moving from embassy to embassy. Many ambassadors have published books on foreign policy, international affairs, and world trade.

■ EARNINGS

Ambassadors earn salaries that range from $100,000 to $125,000, according to the State Department. FSOs receive health benefits, life insurance, and retirement benefits that include a pension plan.

■ WORK ENVIRONMENT

Ambassadors are highly respected. They may have the opportunity to live in comfortable quarters in glamorous cities; or they may be living in a struggling nation, wracked by poverty and political unrest. Regardless of the area of the world, ambassadors have the chance to learn about a culture from the inside. Working alongside a nation's government officials, they are exposed to the art, food, industry, politics, and language of another country, while meeting some of the country's most interesting and notable figures. They also have the opportunity to play host to visiting dignitaries from the United States.

Most embassy offices overseas are clean, pleasant, and well equipped, but ambassadors may occasionally travel into areas that present health hazards. Customs may differ considerably, medical care may be substandard or nonexistent, the climate may be extreme, or other hardships may exist. In some countries there is the danger of earthquakes, typhoons, or floods; in others, there is the danger of political upheaval.

Although embassy hours are normally the usual office hours of the host country, other tasks of the job may involve outside activities, such as attending or hosting dinners, lectures, public functions, and other necessary social engagements.

■ OUTLOOK

Since the end of the Cold War, diplomatic relations have changed. In the last decade, the U.S. international affairs budget has been drastically cut. Foreign aid funding has dropped from $20 billion in 1985 to $12.8 billion in 1999, though it increased again to $17 billion in 2004 (partially as a result of the war effort in Iraq and Afghanistan). Part of an ambassador's job is analyzing budgets to determine where cutbacks can be made. Experts worry that further cuts will not only hurt international trade but will result in disharmony among nations. Despite these budget cuts, the number of responsibilities of ambassadors and Foreign Service Officers has increased; war, drug trade, nuclear smuggling, and terrorism are some of the issues confronting embassies today. Those people interested in protecting diplomacy and the strength of the Foreign Service need to closely follow relevant legislation, as well as promote the importance of international affairs.

■ FOR MORE INFORMATION

This professional organization serving current and retired Foreign Service Officers has an informative website and publishes additional career information. To read selected publications online (including Inside a U.S. Embassy), or for additional information, contact

American Foreign Service Association
2101 E Street, NW
Washington, DC 20037
Tel: 800-704-2372
Email: member@afsa.org
http://www.afsa.org

The U.S. Department of State has a wealth of career information on its website, along with information about internships, the history of the Foreign Service, and current ambassadors and embassies. To request brochures, contact

U.S. Foreign Service
U.S. Department of State
2201 C Street, NW
Washington, DC 20520
Tel: 202-647-4000
http://careers.state.gov

Amusement Park Workers

■ OVERVIEW

Amusement park workers function in a variety of jobs. Some are employed to construct, maintain, and operate thrill rides; others, assigned to the front gate, issue tickets or passes; some work concession stands or manage park restaurants and gift shops; many are employed as entertainers. There are also numerous behind-the-scenes departments such as security, marketing, or personnel. Each particular department, regardless of the amount of customer contact, is necessary for the smooth and profitable operation of the park, as well as the enjoyment of the park patron. The *Occupational Outlook Handbook* lists the employment in the industry at 234,000 workers in 2002, though it is difficult to get an exact count since many people are employed on a seasonal basis.

■ HISTORY

Amusement parks, most often located at the end of a trolley line, were built as attractions to stimulate weekend ridership on trolley cars. The early amusement parks consisted of picnic grounds, dance halls, restaurants, and a few games and simple rides.

The World's Columbian Exposition held in Chicago, Illinois, in 1893, had a huge impact on the industry. The Expo featured the Ferris Wheel, a huge mechanical ride, that was the hit of the fair. The Ferris Wheel is still a staple in many parks today. One of the biggest innovations of the Expo was the introduction of the midway concept. By arranging gaming booths, concession stands, and rides on either side of a walkway, people had to pass every attraction to get from one end of the park to the other.

After enjoying success with his Water Chutes park in Chicago, Paul Boynton was inspired to establish another facility at the existing Coney Island resort in New York City in 1895. Many people came to visit the two-mile boardwalk and beach for the attractions, carnival games, and shows. For the next 30 years, Coney Island was a popular amusement park and served as a model for the many other parks opening throughout the United States. By 1919, there were over 1,500 amusement parks in operation. Coney Island remains a popular New York tourist attraction today.

In the 1930s and early 1940s, the Great Depression, and the onset of World War II, almost destroyed the industry. The poor economy and forced rationing of supplies closed many parks. Indeed, by 1939, only 400 amusement parks were still open. The industry received a boost with the post-war baby boom. Many parks, using a new concept, the Kiddieland, pulled in a new generation of park goers with family-oriented attractions and rides.

By far, the most successful pioneer of the amusement park industry was Walt Disney (1901–66). He opened Disneyland in 1955, using themes as the basis of the park layout and concept, instead of traditional rides and concessions. Disneyland offered the public, or "guests," five different theme lands and times, such as Tom Sawyer's Island, Futureland, and Cinderella's Castle, for a fixed price. Disneyland was, and still is, hugely successful, and it has become the springboard for future Disney parks—Disney World, Epcot Center, and Tokyo Disneyland.

Many companies have tried to duplicate Disney's achievements. One of the most successful has been the Six Flags company. Six Flags now has 29 theme parks throughout the United States, specializing in thrill rides, variety shows, and music concerts. Another popular park is Cedar Point, in Sandusky, Ohio.

A day at an amusement park remains a popular family activity. However, in order to keep fresh and attract repeat customers, parks are constantly adding new rides and more elaborate shows and parades, in essence reinventing themselves to suit the public's ever-changing tastes and attitudes.

■ THE JOB

Amusement parks employ a variety of workers to run their parks smoothly and efficiently. Of course, the number of employees depends on the size of the park, its attractions, and whether or not the park is open year-round.

Equipment maintenance and operation is one of the industry's largest departments. *Ride operators* work the control panel by monitoring the speed of the ride, accelerating or slowing down to load and unload passengers. Some operators are responsible for light maintenance of the rides—paint touch-ups, replacing light bulbs or other decorations, and refueling engines.

Ride attendants collect fares or tickets. They help passengers get on the rides and make sure they are safely fastened or locked in before the ride begins. Attendants are also responsible for lining up waiting groups of people in a quiet and orderly manner.

Some amusement parks have water-themed attractions such as the water logs or boat rides. Special attendants stationed at such rides make sure passengers load the water vehicles correctly and instruct them on certain rules for a safe and enjoyable trip.

QUICK FACTS

SCHOOL SUBJECTS
Business
Mathematics
Technical/shop

PERSONAL SKILLS
Following instructions
Mechanical/manipulative

WORK ENVIRONMENT
Indoors and outdoors
Primarily one location

MINIMUM EDUCATION LEVEL
High school diploma

SALARY RANGE
$12,200 to $14,920 to
$22,310

CERTIFICATION OR LICENSING
None available

OUTLOOK
Faster than the average

DOT
349

GOE
11.02.01

NOC
6671

O*NET-SOC
39-3091.00

Attendants may also be stationed at fun houses, haunted houses, or the hall of mirrors. Such attendants operate the special effects machinery and make sure patrons walk through the attraction in an orderly and timely manner.

Pony rides, petting zoos, and pig races are common attractions at amusement parks and carnivals. *Animal handlers* are needed to feed and care for the animals. They also help passengers mount the ponies, give children food to feed the animals, and match children who wish to ride with appropriately sized animals.

There are many kinds of concession stands at amusement parks, each one staffed by one or more attendants. Game booths are big draws at an amusement park. Games of chance using balls, milk jugs, water, rings, and bottles are just some examples of different booths. *Game attendants,* also called *concessionaires,* urge passersby to play, sell tickets, and maintain equipment needed to play. They also reward winners with prizes such as stuffed animals, candy, or small trinkets.

Some amusement parks sell ticket packages ranging from one to several days. The cost of the ticket covers all rides, shows, and attractions. *Ticket attendants* sell tickets at a booth or counter located at the entrance of the park. Their duties include calculating the amount of tickets sold, making change, and processing credit card transactions.

What's a day at the park without food and drink? Amusement parks offer a range of food—healthy and otherwise. *Food concession attendants* sell hot dogs, pizza, chips, popcorn, ice cream, cotton candy, lemonade, and beer, among other choices. The majority of these booths are located outside, though some attendants are stationed at indoor eateries. Food attendants are trained on the proper way to prepare and serve their snacks and make cash and credit card transactions as well.

Gift shop attendants work inside gift shops and also at outdoor souvenir booths. Besides making and completing cash and credit card sales, attendants are responsible for stocking and pricing items, helping customers with their purchases, and answering any questions regarding the merchandise. Attendants also make sure displays are clean and orderly.

The performance arts are favorite attractions at amusement parks. Many *singers, dancers, musicians,* and other *performers* are hired at the larger parks every year. Parades, comedy shows, and musical revues are just some examples of the entertainment provided at parks. Performers and *artists* are also needed to staff drawing and photo booths, fortune-telling tents, and other attractions.

The grounds crew is a important department no amusement park can do without. They are present throughout the day, though the bulk of their work takes place after hours. Maintenance and cleaning crews tidy the concession areas, ride platforms, and common walkways. They sanitize and re-supply bathrooms and picnic areas. *Security workers* roam the park during operating hours and are responsible for maintaining order. *Parking attendants* sell parking tickets and usher cars into the proper parking spaces. They are sometimes called to help families with many children, or patrons with special needs. Some of the larger parks offer transportation from the parking lot to the main park entrance. At such facilities, employees are hired to drive trolley cars, trams, or trains and give general assistance to passengers.

No park can survive without a strong business department. *General managers* oversee operations of all park departments and employees. *Department managers* are responsible for the activity of their division and the work of their employees. They make weekly work schedules, train new employees, and address any complaints of the department. *Public relations specialists* are responsible for sending press releases to newspapers and other media sources to advertise an upcoming concert, new attraction, or the reopening of the park after a seasonal closure. *Human resource consultants* manage park personnel, including such tasks as deciding on new hires and arranging an orientation program for these employees. The human resource department is also responsible for organizing and managing the internship program.

■ REQUIREMENTS
High School

Most larger amusement parks require their employees to be at least 16 years old. Many high school students work at amusement parks every summer as a way to supplement their income while in school. If you want to stand out from the other applicants, consider taking classes such as mathematics, if you want to work ticket booths, gift shops, or anyplace where calculating and giving correct change is important; mechanics or industrial arts, if you want to work and maintain thrill rides; or speech and theater, if you want to be a performer. Unless you bear an uncanny resemblance to Bugs Bunny or Goofy, then it will be helpful to know how to dance and sing!

Postsecondary Training

Training for entry-level jobs such as a ride operator, game booth attendant, or fast-food worker consists of on-the-job training lasting about a week or two. Most parks train their employees on the particulars of the job, park rules and regulations, and grooming and behavior guidelines.

Most companies prefer college-educated individuals for their management positions. Consider majors in recreation, business management, or marketing (or per-

---

THE FERRIS WHEEL

What amusement park is complete without the Ferris Wheel? The "wheel" was invented in 1893 by George Washington Gale Ferris for the World's Columbian Exposition held in Chicago, Illinois. It stood 264 feet high and had 36 pendulum cars that could hold 60 passengers each, for a total of 2,160 passengers. About one dozen steel companies were contracted to work on the wheel due to its immense size—1,200 tons. Though the wheel's price tag was steep, about $350,000 (in 1893), it was such a popular ride with the public that the manufacturing cost was recovered in a few weeks' time.

---

formance art, if you want to be involved with the entertainment side of the business).

Other Requirements

People go to amusement parks for fun and excitement. Employees, because they have such contact with the patrons, should always be courteous, enthusiastic, and friendly. When dealing with the public, patience is key. The ability to communicate well is important when explaining game rules or park regulations—over and over and over.

There are many employment opportunities available for workers with physical challenges. Some examples include traditional positions in the business office—accounting, personnel, and marketing. A ticket booth can be adapted to accommodate an employee that uses a wheelchair. It is best to contact each amusement park and check out their policies on such matters. Also, get in touch with your school counseling center, state office of vocational rehabilitation, or state department of labor for guidelines.

■ EXPLORING

Before you commit yourself to a lifelong career as an amusement park worker, why not spend some time exploring the field? Here are some suggestions:

Read up on the industry. An afternoon at the library or bookstore can educate you on the history, dynamics, and future of the amusement park industry.

Contact different amusement parks or their parent companies for research materials. Most public relations departments would be more than happy to send you press kits featuring park history, themes, and current attractions.

Spend some time at a local amusement park to get an idea of the different jobs available. (You'll have to convince your parents this is really for educational purposes!)

WORDS TO KNOW

Airtime: The exhilarating feeling of floating out of your seat while riding a roller coaster. (Or, when you've left your stomach back at the lift hill.)

Flat ride: A small spinning-type ride. Examples: Tilt-A-Whirls, Scramblers, Himalayas.

Hyper coaster: A roller coaster with at least one drop in excess of 200 feet.

Lift hill: The tallest part of a roller coaster, many times the first hill. It is the hill in which the train is hauled to the top and released.

Multi-looper: A roller coaster with several inversions.

Spin 'n' barf: Enthusiasts call them "flat rides."

Does your school have a job shadowing program? Why not arrange to spend a day tagging along with different amusement park workers? You'll not only see the ins and outs of the industry, but you'll experience how hard these employees work. If you don't have access to such a program, consult with your school counselors about starting one.

Good news! Amusement parks hire high school students, age 16 or older, for many of their entry-level jobs. What better way to get a feel for the industry than spending a summer ushering kids onto the carousel ride, cajoling people to play the ring toss, or twirling together the biggest cotton candy cone in the world?

Volunteer to be a bingo caller. This will help you hone skills needed to be a good game attendant or even a carnival barker. Some places to try would be a neighborhood senior center, park district, or your local church.

■ EMPLOYERS

Since amusement parks are located nationwide, jobs can be found in almost every state. Note that most jobs are seasonal—usually from April to October. The larger parks do maintain some employees year-round, mostly those working in the business departments. In fact, the winter months are usually the busiest time for amusement parks. Advertising, funding, recruiting, and company organization, new construction, and other prep work takes place during the off-season.

Only a few parks are open year-round, and these are located in warmer climates. Disneyland and Knotts Berry Farm, located in southern California, as well as Disney World and Busch Gardens, in Orlando, Florida, employ thousands of workers to run their parks.

Rarer still are indoor amusement parks. Some enclosed employment opportunities can be found at the Camp Snoopy amusement park located inside Minnesota's Mall of America.

■ STARTING OUT

Many amusement parks recruit at college campuses and job fairs; others visit local high schools. When attending such recruiting events, make sure your resume is up to date, and, if you're lucky, be ready for on-the-spot interviews. According to Scott Kirn, public relations specialist for Six Flags Great America in Gurnee, Illinois, the park hires about 3,000 full-time workers for the season, many of whom are high school and college students, as well as a growing number of senior citizens. Interns account for about 100 to 200 positions a year. "We look for people who are enthusiastic and entertaining, as well as hard working," Kirn says.

Technology plays a big part in today's job search process. The Walt Disney Company, for example, is increasing its reliance on online resume submissions. Its website (http://www.disney.com/DisneyCareers) offers a wealth of employment information such as job postings and their requirements, audition schedules, resume tips, and internship info. Any other questions? Click onto Disney's Q&A for answers to your job-related inquiries.

Whichever method you choose to apply for employment, it helps to be organized. First, contact your school placement center or the local library for a list of amusement parks in the area—or nationwide, if relocation is not a problem. Mail or electronically submit your resume/application to those that pique your interest. Follow up on your leads. Trade magazines such as *Amusement Business* (http://www.amusementbusiness.com), or organizations such as The International Association of Amusement Parks and Attractions (see For More Information), can be helpful in narrowing your job search. Some may even post employment or internship opportunities.

■ ADVANCEMENT

Advancement in this industry depends on the job. With work experience, a food and beverage cart attendant can be promoted to work at a park restaurant or snack shop and eventually become a restaurant manager. Employees with an interest in mechanics can start as an assistant in the mechanical department repairing and maintaining the rides and work their way to a supervisory position. A member of the chorus or dance troupe, after proper training and performing experience, can strive to be a principal dancer or one of Disney's character singers.

Interns stand an excellent opportunity for advancement. The time spent working on an internship brings valuable on-site work experience. Many companies may prefer to hire their former interns because they already know the company and the work involved. Knowledge and skills learned at amusement park jobs can easily be transferred to other fields such as hospitality or other areas of the entertainment industry.

Workers who aspire to work in a management position must understand that such jobs come with hard work and time served in the industry. College degree holders—in marketing, business management, hospitality, or related majors—will have the best chances at landing a management position.

■ EARNINGS

Though many entry-level amusement park employees earn minimum wage or slightly higher, weekly salaries will vary depending on the type and size of facility and its location. (Most amusement parks choose not to divulge salary information due to confidentiality reasons, though they do offer wages competitive with similar industries.) One amusement park located in the Wisconsin Dells offers internship positions paying from $5.75 to $6 an hour, including a year-end bonus of 75 cents for every hour worked during the season. A recent survey conducted by the International Association of Amusement Parks and Attractions reports that front-line managers earn from $10,000 to $50,000, middle managers average about $44,000, and general managers averaged about $64,000. The U.S. Department of Labor reports that amusement and recreation attendants earned a median hourly salary of $7.18 in 2002.

All employees, regardless of work status, are given free admission to their park, as well as discounts for food and merchandise. If a certain theme is needed for a ride or concession, parks usually will provide the proper uniform free of charge. Some facilities also reward employees with family tickets and employees-only nights at the park.

Full-time employees receive a standard benefits package consisting of paid vacation, sick time, and health insurance. Some parks may offer relocation assistance. Employees at the Tokyo Disneyland are offered airfare, accommodations, and a daily stipend in addition to their salary.

■ WORK ENVIRONMENT

Attendants who work for traveling carnivals must move from town to town, usually every week or two. Some employees are housed in trailers or in motels. Relocation is necessary, of course, when applying for employment, or an internship, at parks in other cities. One Chicago area amusement park houses seasonal help at a nearby college.

Attendants assigned to work a ride, game booth, or concession cart must work in all kinds of weather; most parks do not close for anything but the most severe of storms. Workers assigned to gift shops or restaurants usually have clean and comfortable indoor work spaces. Performers and entertainers work both indoors and out, depending on the stage they are assigned to. They must sometimes perform in heavy theatrical makeup and bulky costumes, which can be uncomfortable in hot summer weather. Most employees work alone; ride attendants may work in pairs or assigned to teams.

Most amusement park employees work about 40 hours a week. Amusement parks are open every day during the season, so be prepared to work weekends and holidays—traditionally the busiest and most crowded times of the year. Parks may be open as late as 10 o'clock in the evening.

■ OUTLOOK

According to the U.S. Department of Labor, employment of amusement park workers should continue to grow faster than the average through 2012. Most jobs will be for seasonal full-time work. Six Flags Great America, for example, hires over 3,000 employees during the spring and summer months, though only 100 employees work year-round. Most job opportunities will result from seasonal openings or current workers leaving the workforce. New construction of amusement parks is limited due to lack of funding, available land, and markets large enough to support such a project.

Though many people use their employment at amusement parks as a way to earn extra money during school, a number do take advantage of such jobs as a stepping stone to a full time career. If this appeals to you, consider a college degree in recreation, business management, or hospitality to help advance your goal. Do you have a knack for mechanics? Then look into work building, maintaining, and even designing roller coasters and other thrill rides. Many performers use their amusement park experience to build a career in the entertainment industry.

The ability to stay competitive and draw repeat customers with new attractions will greatly dictate a park's success. Amusement parks of the future will specialize in different themes or niches, to attract all interests, ages, and incomes, according to a recent article on the amusement industry in *Newsweek*. One remaining constant in this industry will be the thrill ride—roller coasters in particular. Watch for super effects, such as holography, heat blowers, and mind-boggling speed and drops, to enhance future coaster rides. Many countries abroad are now constructing amusement parks, so job opportunities will also exist outside of the United States.

■ **FOR MORE INFORMATION**

For information on the industry and job opportunities, contact

International Association of Amusement Parks and Attractions
1448 Duke Street
Alexandria, VA 22314
Tel: 703-836-4800
Email: iaapa@iaapa.org
http://www.iaapa.org

For information on the history of amusement parks and attractions, industry publications, conventions, and membership information, contact

National Amusement Park Historical Association
PO Box 83
Mt. Prospect, IL 60056
http://www.napha.org

For a list of amusement and theme parks in the United States, or for historical facts on the industry, contact

FunGuide
http://www.funguide.com

For information on career and internship opportunities, contact

Six Flags Theme Parks
http://www.sixflags.com/Jobs

For career information, employment opportunities, or audition schedules, or to submit a resume electronically, contact

The Walt Disney Company
http://www.disney.com/DisneyCareers

Anesthesiologists

■ **OVERVIEW**

Anesthesiologists are physicians who specialize in the planning, performance, and maintenance of a patient's anesthesia during surgical, obstetric, or other medical procedures. Using special equipment, monitors, and drugs, the anesthesiologist makes sure the patient feels no pain and remains uninjured during the procedure. There are approximately 24,780 anesthesiologists employed in the United States.

■ **HISTORY**

Before the mid-19th century, when modern anesthetics started to be developed, you would most likely live with your affliction or undergo surgery with little or no help for pain. Often patients would need to be restrained. An 18th-century French encyclopedia described how to perform bladder surgery by first restraining the patient in a special "surgical chair."

Efforts to manage pain have been a constant in human history. A variety of substances and techniques have been used, including opium, cannabis, alcohol, mandragora root, and hypnotism. None of these proved entirely reliable or completely effective.

Nitrous oxide, developed in the late 18th century, was the first gas recognized to have anesthetic properties. Its effects, which included giddiness, earned it the nickname of "laughing gas." Ether was developed shortly after nitrous oxide. Neither gas, however, was used to anesthetize humans at that time. In fact, nitrous oxide was often used for entertainment purposes at "laughing gas parties" or by sideshow entertainers.

The first successful use of ether as an anesthetic occurred in 1842 when Dr. Crawford W. Long used it when he removed a tumor from a friend's neck. Dr. Long, however, failed to publicize the event, and in 1846 a Boston dentist, Dr. William T. G. Morton, became credited with the discovery of general anesthesia when he successfully administered ether to anesthetize a patient while removing a tumor. As one would imagine, ether's reputation spread quickly. So did the reputation of chloroform, used successfully for the first time in 1847.

Anesthesiology continued to advance, and in 1875 intravenous administration of anesthetics was developed. Greater study of anesthesiology in the 20th century has led to many advances, and anesthesiology has become increasingly more sophisticated, revolutionizing the practice of surgery.

■ **THE JOB**

Anesthesiologists make sure that the patient's body is not overstimulated or injured by a medical procedure and that the patient feels no pain while undergoing the procedure. Traditionally, anesthesiologists deal mainly in the area of surgery. They do, however, also oversee the administration of anesthetics during other medical procedures, and if needed, during childbirth.

After reviewing a patient's medical history, the anesthesiologist will determine the best form of anesthesia for the patient. Different medical problems and various kinds of surgery require different kinds of anesthesia. These determinations are based on the anesthesiologist's broad background in medicine, which includes an understanding of surgical procedures, physiology, pharmacology, and critical care.

In the operating room, an anesthesiologist gives the patient an anesthetic, making the patient unconscious and numb to pain. This involves administering drugs to put the patient under and maintaining the anesthesia. In some cases, only a regional anesthesia is required—numbing only the part of the body on which the surgery is being performed. In more complex cases, anesthesiologists may need to prepare special equipment such as blood warming devices. Anesthesiologists use monitoring equipment and insert intravenous lines and breathing tubes. They make sure the mask is secure and allows for a proper airway. In an emergency situation, an anesthesiologist is also part of the cardiopulmonary resuscitation team.

An anesthesiologist pays close attention to the patient's well-being by monitoring blood pressure, breathing, heart rate, and body temperature throughout surgery. It is also the anesthesiologist's responsibility to position the patient properly, so that the doctor can perform the surgery and the patient remains uninjured. The anesthesiologist also controls the patient's temperature, cooling or heating different parts of the body during surgery.

Anesthesiologists are not limited to the operating room; they also spend time with patients before and after surgery. When meeting the patient beforehand, an anesthesiologist explains the kind of anesthesia to be used and answers any questions. This interaction helps put the patient at ease and allows the anesthesiologist to get to know the patient before surgery. Unlike other doctors, anesthesiologists do not have the opportunity to work closely for long periods of time with patients.

Anesthesiologists may specialize in different areas, such as pediatric anesthesia, respiratory therapy, critical care, and cardiovascular anesthesia. They often work in teams, consisting of anesthesiology residents, nurse anesthetists, and anesthesiology assistants. The anesthesiologist will delegate responsibilities to other members of the care team.

While emergency cases require anesthesiologists to make quick decisions and act without hesitation, in other cases they have time to carefully plan, to study a patient's medical history, to meet with the surgeons and the patients, and to work by a regular schedule. Most anesthesiologists work in hospitals, though they may actually be part of an individual or group practice. Others direct residents in teaching hospitals or teach at medical schools.

■ REQUIREMENTS
High School
If you are interested in becoming an anesthesiologist, focus your high school education on college preparatory courses. Mathematics classes and science classes, especially biology and chemistry, should be helpful. In addition, English classes will help you improve your communication and research skills. Also, consider taking a foreign language, since you may be required to show proficiency in another language later on in your schooling.

Postsecondary Training
You must first earn an M.D. degree and pass an examination to become licensed to practice medicine. (See Physicians.) Then you must complete a four-year residency. The first year is spent training in an area of clinical medicine other than anesthesia, such as internal or emergency medicine, pediatrics, surgery, obstetrics, or neurology. The final three years of study are then spent in an anesthesiology residency program accredited by the Accreditation Council for Graduate Medical Education. You can find these accredited residency programs listed in the *Directory of Graduate Medical Education Programs.*

Certification or Licensing
Anesthesiologists receive certification from the American Board of Anesthesiology. In addition to the license, the board requires applicants to have completed training in an accredited program and to pass an exam. Applicants must also have a Certificate of Clinical Competence (CCC). This certificate, filed by the residency training program, attests to the applicant's clinical competence.

Other Requirements
Every surgery requires anesthesiologists to pay careful attention and to remain alert. An anesthesiologist sometimes encounters emergency situations, requiring

QUICK FACTS

SCHOOL SUBJECTS
Biology
Chemistry
Psychology

PERSONAL SKILLS
Leadership/management
Technical/scientific

MINIMUM EDUCATION LEVEL
Medical degree

SALARY RANGE
$99,850 to $200,000 to $306,964+

OUTLOOK
About as fast as the average

DOT
070

GOE
14.02.01

NOC
3112

O*NET-SOC
29-1061.00

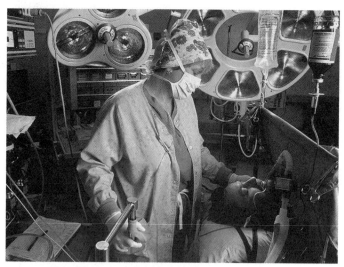
An anesthesiologist monitors a patient during surgery.

quick, clear-headed responses. The work, however, can also be slower paced and require patience to comfort people preparing for surgery. Not only must anesthesiologists be able to explain the surgery clearly to patients, but they must be able to direct other members of the anesthesia team.

■ EARNINGS

Salaries for anesthesiologists vary according to the kind of practice (whether the anesthesiologist works individually or as part of a group practice), the amount of overhead required to maintain the business, and geographic location. Though working fewer hours, an anesthesiologist can make as much as other doctors. The 2000 Economic Research Institute data, the average annual salary for a first-year anesthesiologist is $199,252. After five years, they average $232,623 a year, and after 10 years, they earn an average of $272,106 annually. According to the Department of Labor's 2002 estimates, the median yearly salary for an anesthesiologist is $306,964.

Fringe benefits for physicians typically include health and dental insurance, paid vacations, and retirement plans.

■ WORK ENVIRONMENT

Anesthesiologists typically work in well-equipped, well-lighted, well-ventilated hospitals. There are also opportunities at ambulatory care clinics and separate surgical centers, which also require a clean and well-lit environment. Since most surgeries are scheduled in advance, an anesthesiologist's work hours are fairly regular, especially compared to those of some other types of physicians. Anesthesiologists may work in an individual practice, in a group practice, or through affiliation with a medical center. In any of these situations, the anesthesiologist is part of a team and should enjoy working as part of a group.

■ OUTLOOK

According to the *Occupational Outlook Handbook*, the field of anesthesiology is expected to grow about as fast as the average through 2012. Attracted by the technological advancements, the regularity of the work, and the fewer hours, more people are entering the field. Most anesthesiologists find work immediately after finishing their residencies. As medical advances allow for different kinds of treatment facilities, anesthesiologists will find more work outside of a traditional hospital setting. The development of more outpatient clinics, freestanding surgical centers, and respiratory therapy clinics has opened up employment opportunities for anesthesiologists.

Managed care organizations have changed the way medicine is practiced and may continue to do so. Because anesthesiology is a hospital-based specialty, anesthesiologists must find ways to work within the guidelines of managed care, sometimes to the detriment of medical treatment. Anesthesiologists and other health care professionals will continue to challenge these organizations in order to practice medicine to the best of their abilities.

■ FOR MORE INFORMATION

Following are organizations that provide information about a career as an anesthesiologist:

American Board of Anesthesiology
4101 Lake Boone Trail, Suite 510
Raleigh, NC 27607-7506
Tel: 919-881-2570
http://www.abanes.org

American Society of Anesthesiologists
520 North Northwest Highway
Park Ridge, IL 60068-2573
Tel: 847-825-5586
Email: mail@asahq.org
http://www.asahq.org

Animal Breeders and Technicians

■ OVERVIEW

Animal breeders and technicians help breed, raise, and market a variety of animals: cattle, sheep, pigs, horses, mules, and poultry for livestock; pets such as canaries, parrots, dogs, and cats; and other more exotic animals such as ostriches, alligators, minks, and many zoo animals. Technicians who are primarily involved with the breeding and feeding of animals are sometimes referred to as *animal husbandry technicians.*

In general, animal breeders and technicians are concerned with the propagation, feeding, housing, health, production, and marketing of animals. These technicians work in many different settings and capacities. They may supervise unskilled farm workers; serve as field representatives assisting in the sales of animals to customers; work in kennels, stables, ranches, or zoos reproducing species and breeds for other clients or their own organization; or work on their own on a particular breed of interest. The diversity of employment available for well-trained and well-qualified animal breeders and technicians makes this career extremely flexible. As science progresses, opportunities for these technicians should broaden.

HISTORY

Breeding animals has been part of raising livestock since animals were first domesticated. With the discovery of genetics, the science behind the breeding selection became more exact. Great shifts can be made in a species with genetically selected breeding programs. All domesticated dogs extend from a precursor to the modern wolf. So even though miniature poodles and St. Bernards have extremely different appearances and are seemingly incompatible, they are actually so closely related genetically that they can reproduce with each other.

Farm animals have been bred to increase meat on the animal, increase production of eggs and milk, and increase resistance to disease. Both pets and farm animals have been bred for appearance, with show animals produced in almost every domesticated species.

As regions specialized in certain breeds, organizations developed to recognize and register them, eventually developing standards for accepted breeds. Organizations such as the American Kennel Club establish criteria by which species are judged, and the criteria can be quite specific. For example, dog breeds have specific ranges of height, shoulder width, fur color, arch of leg, and such, and any dog outside the variance cannot be shown in competition. This is partly to ensure that the species is bred by trained and informed individuals, and to keep the breed from inadvertently shifting over time. Breeds, however, can be intentionally shifted, and this is how new breeds begin.

Horse breeds may each have their own organization, such as the American Quarter Horse Association

(AQHA), established to maintain the breed. Some of these organizations, such as the Cria Caballar, which judges Andalusian horses, are not based in the United States; however, they may still certify American horses. Some breeds may also have multiple organizations, such as the rival Dutch and German registries for Friesian horses. Horse registries may also have wildly differing standards for what constitutes an acceptable example of the breed.

Until the end of the 20th century, breeding was controlled by reproduction through mating pairs, whether through natural or artificial insemination. Recently, however, there has been a radical breakthrough in cloning, where the gene pool of the offspring remains identical to the parent cloned. Although this work is extremely costly and experimental, it is expected to change the range of work that breeders can do in reproduction.

THE JOB

Most animal breeders and technicians work as *livestock production technicians* with cattle, sheep, swine, or horses; or as *poultry production technicians,* with chickens, turkeys, geese, or ducks. Other animal breeders work with domesticated animals kept as pets, such as song birds, parrots, and all dog and cat breeds. Even wildlife populations that are kept in reserves, ranches, zoos, or aquariums are bred with the guidance of a breeder or technician. Each category of animal (such as birds), family (parrot), species (African gray parrot), and even some individual breeds within a category have technicians working on their reproduction if they are bred for livestock or domestic use. Within each of these categories the jobs may be specialized for one aspect of the animal's reproductive cycle.

For example, technicians and breeders who work in food-source bird production can be divided into specific areas of concentration. In breeding-flock production, technicians may work as *farm managers,* directing the operation of one or more farms. They may be *flock supervisors*

QUICK FACTS

SCHOOL SUBJECTS
Biology
Business

PERSONAL SKILLS
Following instructions
Technical/scientific

WORK ENVIRONMENT
Indoors and outdoors
Primarily one location

MINIMUM EDUCATION LEVEL
High school diploma

SALARY RANGE
$15,630 to $29,340 to $49,810+

CERTIFICATION OR LICENSING
Voluntary

OUTLOOK
About as fast as the average

DOT
410

GOE
03.02.01

NOC
N/A

O*NET-SOC
45-2021.00

with five or six assistants working directly with farmers under contract to produce hatching eggs. On pedigree breeding farms, technicians may oversee all the people who transport, feed, and care for the poultry. Technicians in breeding-flock production seek ways to improve efficiency in the use of time, materials, and labor; they also strive to make maximum effective use of data-processing equipment.

Technicians in hatchery management operate and maintain the incubators and hatchers, where eggs develop as embryos. These technicians must be trained in incubation, sexing, grading, scheduling, and effectively using available technology. The egg processing phase begins when the eggs leave the farm. *Egg processing technicians*

Breeds of Horses

Some breeds of horses are uniquely American, while others are European imports esteemed for their beautiful looks and movement.

Thoroughbred: Best-known for their speed, Thoroughbreds were first developed as racehorses by English aristocrats in the 18th century. Because of the racing industry, breeding thoroughbreds is a large and a lucrative business in the United States. However, it is also brutal: In a few years, the horses' racing careers are over. Because Thoroughbreds can be "hot" and difficult to handle; only a lucky few are adopted into loving homes or kept for breeding, most are slaughtered.

Quarter Horse: The quintessential American workhorse, the Quarter Horse is a familiar sight at rodeos. Even-tempered and willing, a Quarter Horse can also be anything from an extremely athletic jumper to an ambling Western pleasure horse. The breed was named for their excellent performances in quarter-mile races; however, they also excel in barrel racing, roping, and most any equestrian sport.

Andalusian: The *pura raza Española,* Andalusians have been the favored mounts of kings and warriors since ancient times. Today, they excel at the beautiful movements of dressage, the "equestrian ballet" that developed from the military riding arts in the seventeenth and eighteenth centuries. The famous Lipizzaners of the Spanish Riding School in Vienna are closely related to the Andalusian.

Friesian: Large, jet-black horses with long manes feathered feet, Friesians are known both for their strength and their gentleness. Originating in Friesland in the northern Netherlands, Friesians are well suited to all sorts of disciplines, from dressage to jumping. They are also carriage horses, and a team of Friesians pulling an elegant coach is a striking sight.

handle egg pickup, trucking, delivery, and quality control. With experience, technicians in this area can work as supervisors and plant managers. These technicians need training in egg processing machinery and refrigeration equipment.

Technicians in poultry meat production oversee the production, management, and inspection of birds bred specifically for consumption as meat. Technicians may work directly with flocks or in supervisory positions.

Poultry husbandry technicians conduct research in breeding, feeding, and management of poultry. They examine selection and breeding practices in order to increase efficiency of production and to improve the quality of poultry products.

Egg candlers inspect eggs to determine quality and fitness for incubation according to prescribed standards. They check to see if eggs have been fertilized and if they are developing correctly.

Some poultry technicians also work as *field-contact technicians,* inspecting poultry farms for food-processing companies. They ensure that growers maintain contract standards for feeding and housing birds and controlling disease. They tour barns, incubation units, and related facilities to observe sanitation and weather protection provisions. Field-contact technicians ensure that specific grains are administered according to schedules, inspect birds for evidence of disease, and weigh them to determine growth rates.

For other livestock, the categories are similar, as are the range of jobs. For nonfarm animals, the average breeder works with several animals within a breed or species to produce offspring for sale. Although there are ranches that produce a large number of exotic animals and some stables and kennels that run full-staff breeding operations, most breeders for pets work out of their homes. There are also production shops, usually referred to as puppy mills, that produce pets for sale but do so without much regard to the quality or well-being of the animals they are producing. Dismissed as unprofessional by established breeders and usually challenged by local authorities for quality of care provided to the animals, these are commonly not reputable enterprises, although they may be profitable in the short term.

One area of animal production technology that merits special mention because of the increasing focus on its use in animal husbandry is that of artificial breeding. Three kinds of technicians working in this specialized area of animal production are *artificial-breeding technicians, artificial-breeding laboratory technicians,* and *artificial insemination technicians.*

Artificial breeding can be differentiated by the goal of the breeder: food (poultry and cattle), sport (horses and dogs), conservation (endangered species kept in captivity), and science (mice, rabbits, monkeys, and any other animals used for research). Breeders work to create better, stronger breeds of animals or to maintain good existing breeds.

Because of the increasing cost of shipping adult animals from location to location to keep the gene pool diverse in a species or breed, animal breeders have developed successful methods of shipping frozen semen to allow breeding across distances. For zoo animals such as the elephant, rhinoceros, and hippopotamus, this has allowed zoos to build their populations with good genetic diversity without the overwhelming difficulty of transporting a several-thousand-pound male over expressways to attempt breeding with a new female to which he may or may not be attracted. Because semen can be examined microscopically, the technician is able to eliminate problem samples before insemination occurs.

Artificial-breeding technicians collect and package semen for use in insemination. They examine the semen under a microscope to determine density and motility of sperm cells, and they dilute the semen according to standard formulas. They transfer the semen to shipping and storage containers with identifying data such as the source, date taken, and quality. They also keep records related to all of their activities. In some cases they may also be responsible for inseminating the females.

Artificial-breeding laboratory technicians handle the artificial insemination of all kinds of animals, but most often these technicians specialize in the laboratory aspects of the activity. They measure purity, potency, and density of animal semen and add extenders and antibiotics to it. They keep records, clean and sterilize laboratory equipment, and perform experimental tests to develop improved methods of processing and preserving semen.

Artificial insemination technicians do exactly what their name implies: they collect semen from the male species of an animal and artificially inseminate the female. Poultry inseminators collect semen from roosters and fertilize hens' eggs. They examine the roosters' semen for quality and density, measure specified amounts of semen for loading into inseminating guns, inject semen into hens, and keep accurate records of all aspects of the operation. This area of animal production is expected to grow as poultry production expands.

Whether the breeding is done artificially or naturally, the goals are the same. *Cattle breeders* mate males and females to produce animals with preferred traits such as leaner meat and less fat. It is desirable to produce cows who give birth easily and are less susceptible to illness than the average cow. In artificial insemination, cows are inseminated with a gun, much like hens, which allows for

many animals to be bred from the sperm of one male. By repeating the process of artificial breeding for many generations, a more perfect animal can be produced.

Horse and *dog breeders* strive to create more physically and physiologically desirable animals. They want horses and dogs who perform well, move fast, and look beautiful. Longer legs and high jumping are examples of desirable show traits for these animals. Temperament is another quality considered in reproduction and is one of the traits that a good breeder can work for, although it is not directly linked to a specific gene.

Some breeders produce many small animals such as mice, rabbits, dogs, and cats. These animals can be used in scientific research. For example, some laboratories raise thousands of mice to be used in experiments. These mice are shipped all over the world so that scientists can study them.

Animals raised for fur or skin also require extensive technological assistance. Mink farms, ostrich farms, and alligator farms are animal production industries that need husbandry, feeding, and health technicians. As the popularity of one species rises or falls, others replace it, and new animal specialists are needed.

For all breeders, it is essential that they keep track of the lineage of the animals they breed. The genetic history for at least three previous generations is usually considered the minimum background required to ensure no inbreeding. For animals sold as pedigreed, these records are certified by some overseeing organizations. For animals being bred from wildlife stock, purity of the genetic line within a breed or species is required before an animal is allowed to reproduce. Stud books list the lineage of all animals bred within a facility. Pedigree papers travel with an individual animal as a record of that animal's lineage. Both tools are essential to breeders to keep track of the breeding programs in operation.

There are several ways to decide which animals should be bred, and some or all of them weigh into the decisions that the animal breeders make. The physical appearance and the health of the animal usually come first; this is called mass selection—where the animal is selected of its own merits. If the animal has successfully reproduced before, this is called progeny selection. The animal can be bred again, knowing that the animal has produced desirable offspring previously. However, if that particular animal becomes genetically overrepresented in a generation, then the breeder runs the risk of inbreeding with the generations to follow. So the value of that animal's offspring has to be weighed against the need for diversity in parents. Family selection also determines the value of reproducing an animal. Some genetic diversity can come from breeding siblings of a good breeder, but it may not be enough diversity if the breeder is working with a limited stock of animals. Pedigree is the final determiner in evaluating a breeding animal.

REQUIREMENTS

High School

High school students seeking to enter this field will find that the more agriculture and science courses they select in high school, the better prepared they will be. In addition, courses in mathematics, business, communications, chemistry, and mechanics are valuable.

Postsecondary Training

Nine months to two years at a technical school or a college diploma are the usual minimum credentials for animal breeders and technicians. Many colleges now offer two- and four-year programs in animal science or animal husbandry where additional knowledge, skills, and specialized training may be acquired. Besides learning the scientific side of animal breeding, including instruction in genetics, animal physiology, and some veterinary science, students also take business classes that help them see the field from an economic point of view. With the increasing use of technology for breeding livestock and domesticated nonfarm animals, a bachelor's degree becomes more important for succeeding in the field. Master's and doctoral degrees are useful for the most specialized fields and the careers that require the most sophisticated genetic planning. Higher degrees are required for potential teachers in the field, and the current work being done in cloning is done exclusively by people with doctorates.

Whether trained by experience, at an academic institution, or both, all new hires at major breeding companies are usually put through some type of training program.

Certification or Licensing

Certification is not required, but nearly all major companies have certification programs that can enhance earnings and opportunities.

Other Requirements

Animal breeders and technicians should have great love, empathy, and respect for animals. You must be patient and compassionate in addition to being very knowledgeable about the needs and habits of all the animals in your care. You must also have interest in reproductive science, genetics and animal physiology. It is important to be able to communicate easily with agricultural scientists, farmers, and other animal owners and caretakers.

EXPLORING

Organizations such as 4-H Clubs (http://www.4-H.org) and the National FFA Organization (formerly known as Future Farmers of America) (http://www.ffa.org) offer good opportunities for hearing about, visiting, and participating in farm activities. Programs sponsored by 4-H allow students to learn firsthand about breeding small animals for show. Other organizations, such as the American Kennel Club, sponsor clubs dedicated to particular breeds, and these clubs usually provide educational programs on raising and breeding these animals.

Other opportunities might include volunteering at a breeding farm or ranch, kennel, or stable where animals are bred and sold. This will give you a chance to see the work required and begin to get experience in practical skills for the job.

For at-home experience, raising pets is a good introduction to the skills needed in basic animal maintenance. Learning how to care for, feed, and house a pet provides some basic knowledge of working with animals. In addition, you can learn more about this field by reading books on animals and their care. But unless you have background and experience in breeding, and a good mentor to work with, it is not recommended that you start breeding your pet. There are literally millions of unwanted dogs and cats that come from mixed breeds or unpedigreed purebreds, and many of these animals are destroyed because there are no homes for them.

Other opportunities that provide animal maintenance experience include volunteering to work at animal shelters, veterinary offices, and pet breeders' businesses.

EMPLOYERS

Animal breeders and technicians used to work for themselves, but today most are employed by corporate breeders. A few may still own their own livestock ranches, and some do it only as a sideline or hobby.

STARTING OUT

Many junior colleges participate in "learn-and-earn" programs, in which the college and prospective employer jointly provide the student's training, both in the classroom and through on-the-job work with livestock and other animals. Most technical programs offer placement services for graduates, and the demand for qualified people often exceeds the supply.

ADVANCEMENT

Even when a good training or technical program is completed, the graduate often must begin work at a low level before advancing to positions with more responsibility.

But the technical program graduate will advance much more rapidly to positions of major responsibility and greater financial reward than the untrained worker.

Those graduates willing to work hard and keep abreast of changes in their field may advance to livestock breeder, feedlot manager, supervisor, or artificial breeding distributor. If they have the necessary capital, they can own their own livestock ranches.

■ EARNINGS

Salaries vary widely depending on employer, the technicians' educational and agricultural background, the kind of animal the technicians work with, and the geographical areas in which they work. In general, the salaries of breeders tend to be higher in areas with a heavy concentration and in the breeding of certain specialty animals. Kentucky, for instance, leads the nation in the breeding of horses, and, unsurprisingly, that is where salaries are highest. The U.S. Department of Labor reports that animal breeders had mean annual wages of $29,340 in 2002. The top 10 percent made $49,810 or more, while the bottom 10 percent made only $15,630 or less. Fringe benefits vary according to employer but can include paid vacation time, health insurance, and pension benefits.

■ WORK ENVIRONMENT

Working conditions vary from operation to operation, but certain factors always exist. Much of the work is done inside in all types of facilities. Barns, pens, and stables are the most common facilities for farm animals; nonfarm animals may be bred in private homes or housing facilities. Both types of work often require long, irregular hours and work on Sundays and holidays. The work is also sometimes dangerous, especially when large animals such as stallions and bulls are involved. Salaries are usually commensurate with the hours worked, and there are usually slack seasons when time off is given to compensate any extra hours worked. But for people with a strong desire to work with animals, long working hours or other less desirable conditions are offset by the benefits of this career.

Animal breeders and technicians are often their own bosses and make their own decisions. While this can be an asset to those who value independence, prospective animal breeders and technicians must realize that self-discipline is the most valuable trait for success.

■ OUTLOOK

Continuing changes are expected in the next few years, in both the production and the marketing phases of the animal production industry. Because of the costs

A dairy artificial insemination technician prepares to store samples from a cow.

involved, it is almost impossible for a one-person operation to stay in business for farm animals. As a result, cooperatives of consultants and corporations will become more prevalent with greater emphasis placed on specialization. This, in turn, will increase the demand for technical program graduates. Other factors, such as small profit margins, the demand for more uniform products, and an increasing foreign market, will result in a need for more specially trained personnel. This is a new era of specialization in the animal production industry; graduates of animal production technology programs have an interesting and rewarding future ahead of them.

For domesticated nonfarm animals, breeders usually work with individual species and do so because they love the animals, not for a profit-bearing business. According to the American Kennel Club, the average dog breeder loses money on each successful litter.

■ FOR MORE INFORMATION

For more information on becoming an animal breeder, contact
American Kennel Club
260 Madison Avenue
New York, NY 10016
Tel: 212-696-8200
Email: info@akc.org
http://www.akc.org

For information on careers and graduate programs, contact
American Society of Animal Science
1111 North Dunlap Avenue
Savoy, IL 61874
Tel: 217-356-9050

Email: asas@assochq.org
http://www.asas.org

For industry information, contact
National Cattlemen's Beef Association
9110 East Nichols Avenue, #300
Centennial, CO 80112
Tel: 303-694-0305
http://www.beef.org

Animal Caretakers

■ OVERVIEW

Animal caretakers, as the name implies, take care of animals. The job ranges from the day-to-day normal activities for a healthy animal to caring for sick, injured, or aging animals. Daily animal routine usually involves feeding and providing drinking water for each animal, making sure that their enclosure is clean, safe, appropriately warm, and, if needed, stocked with materials to keep the animal active and engaged. Caretakers may be responsible for creating different enrichment materials so that the animal is challenged by new objects and activities. They may exercise or train the animals. They may assist veterinarians or other trained medical staff in working with animals that require treatment. Animal caretakers may also maintain the written records for each animal. These records can include weight, eating habits, behavior, medicines given, or treatment given. Animal caretakers and veterinary assistants hold about 151,000 jobs in the United States.

■ HISTORY

The concept of raising, caring for, and medically assisting nonfarm or nonworking animals is relatively new. The only animals, with few exceptions, that were kept by people were worked, such as plow-pulling oxen, or eaten, such as cattle, poultry, and pigs. The few examples of animals kept for pets are scattered accounts through history. The Egyptians kept cats as long ago as 3000 B.C.; cats were probably household pets, but perhaps they were also for religious purposes. Until immunizations and pest control became common, though, keeping animals in the house was unwise for health reasons.

Over the thousands of years that people have kept animals for use, they have learned how to care for animals in captivity. Successful early farmers understood that animals needed them to provide food, shelter, and a healthy environment in which to live. From these early efforts,

people have learned more specific methods of providing for animals' needs. But the idea to use these skills on animals which provide no labor or food was not accepted until nearly the 20th century.

The first institution that specifically focused on the humane treatment of animals was the Society for the Prevention of Cruelty to Animals, founded in England in 1824. In the United States, the American Humane Association was founded in 1916 to work with the animals used in the war effort. But these organizations focused on helping labor and food source animals. The first law protecting animals in the United States was passed in 1873. But changes in animal treatment and rights were gradual throughout the first part of the 20th century. During the boom of the ecology movement in the late 1960s and early 1970s, public attention became focused on the rights and the needs of wildlife and domestic animals.

Rachel Carson's *Silent Spring* brought attention to the plight of hunting birds, and their rapidly deteriorating numbers. Pesticides such as DDT were dramatically reducing the population in the wild. To save birds such as the bald eagle, massive ecological intervention was required to clean up the environment, but breeding programs, shelters, and rescue centers would need to save individual birds to keep the population high enough to allow recovery.

Animals used in medical and chemical experimentation were also gaining advocates who helped create laws to protect them and begin to develop standards by which animals could be used in labs. As the public saw films and still pictures of the substandard or even abusive treatment of animals, particularly primates, in labs, they began to review treatment of animals elsewhere. Zoos, circuses, parks, and other institutions were used to replacing their animals with ones pulled from the wild. These institutions were soon under criticism about their pillaging of wild populations for healthy animals that wouldn't survive long in their care.

The institutions responded by improving facilities, nutrition, breeding programs, vaccination programs, and other forms of assistance that kept their animals healthier longer. Part of that improvement was increased staff. Also, as public interest in wildlife increased, there was an increase in the pool of volunteers that these institutions could draw on for labor.

With the push to conserve and protect species and maintain the populations in captivity and in the wild, programs such as re-release programs for injured animals, rescue programs for threatened populations, zoo breeding programs, pet breeding and care programs, and sanctuary land for wild populations became much more prevalent. Many of these programs began and continue to be staffed by advocates, volunteers, and professionals who can all be called animal caretakers.

Finally, the horse industry provides a consistent source of work. In some areas, such as Kentucky, Oklahoma, and California, horses are a huge industry. Horses, though legally considered farm animals, occupy a strange middle ground between pets and livestock. Some, such as carriage horses or cow horses, are working animals. Others, such as dressage horses, polo ponies, and hunter/jumpers, are valued for their athletic potential, and can, at least in theory, be trained and then sold for a higher price, or bred and their offspring sold for a tidy profit. Yet others are strictly pleasure and companion animals.

■ THE JOB

Animal caretakers, also referred to by several other names depending on their specialty, perform the daily duties of animal care, which include feeding, grooming, cleaning, exercising, examining, and nurturing the individuals in their care. These caretakers have titles such as *animal shelter workers, grooms, veterinary assistants, wildlife assistants, animal shelter attendants, laboratory animal technicians, laboratory animal technologists,* and *kennel technicians.*

Animal caretakers are employed in kennels, stables, pet stores, boarding facilities, walking services, shelters, sanctuaries, rescue centers, zoos, aquariums, veterinary facilities, and animal experimentation labs. They may also be employed by the federal government, state or local parks that have educational centers with live animals, the Department of Agriculture in programs such as quarantine centers for animals coming into the United States, and the Centers for Disease Control laboratories.

Almost every one of these employers expects the animal caretaker to provide the daily maintenance routine for animals. The caretaker may be responsible for one animal or one species, or may be required to handle many animals and many species. A veterinary assistant is likely to encounter dogs and cats, with the occasional bird or reptile. A *wildlife shelter worker* works with the local wild population, so for much of the United States that means working with raccoons, skunks, porcupines, hunting birds, song birds, the occasional predator such as coyote or fox, and perhaps large animals such as bear, elk, moose, or deer.

Caretakers are responsible for some or all of the following tasks: selecting, mixing, and measuring out the appropriate food; providing water; cleaning the animal and the enclosure; changing bedding and groundcover if used; moving the animals from night facilities to day facilities or exercise spaces or different quarters; sterilizing facilities and equipment not in use; recording and filing statistics, medical reports, or lab reports on each animal; and providing general attention and affection to animals that need human contact.

The animal caretaker learns to recognize signs of illness such as lack of appetite, fatigue, skin sores, and changed behavior. They check the animals they can physically approach or handle for lumps, sores, fat, texture of the skin, fur, or feathers, and condition of the mouth. Since most animals do not exhibit signs of illness until they are very ill, it is important that the caretaker that sees the animal most regularly note any small change in the animal's physical or mental state.

The caretaker also maintains the animal's living quarters. For most animals in their care, this will be an enclosure of some type. The enclosure has to be safe and secure. The animal should not be able to injure itself within the enclosure, be able to escape, or have outside animals able to get into the enclosure. Small holes in an enclosure wall would not threaten a coyote, but small holes that a snake can pass through could threaten a rabbit. Horses can injure themselves in their stables, and in addition are vulnerable to a multitude of pasture injuries.

The quarters need to be the right size for the animal. If they are too large, the animal will feel threatened by the amount of open space, feeling it cannot protect the area adequately. Inappropriately small enclosures can be just as damaging. If the animal cannot get sufficient exercise within the enclosure, it will also suffer both psychologically and physically.

Caretakers set up and oversee enrichment activities that provide the animal with something to keep it engaged and occupied while in its home. For even the smallest rodent, enrichment activities are required. Most of us are familiar with enrichment toys for our pets. These are balls and squeaky toys for dogs and cats, bells and different foot surfaces for birds, and tunnels and rolling wheels for hamsters and gerbils. Wild animals require the same stimulation. Animal caretakers hide food in containers that require ingenuity and tools to

QUICK FACTS

SCHOOL SUBJECTS
Biology
Health

PERSONAL SKILLS
Following instructions
Helping/teaching

WORK ENVIRONMENT
Indoors and outdoors
One location with some travel

MINIMUM EDUCATION LEVEL
High school diploma

SALARY RANGE
$12,750 to $17,080 to $27,850+

CERTIFICATION OR LICENSING
None available

OUTLOOK
Faster than the average

DOT
410

GOE
03.02.01

NOC
6483

O*NET-SOC
39-2021.00

Rabies: The Facts

- Rabies is a deadly disease caused by a virus that attacks the nervous system. Most often the virus is transmitted by a bite from a rabid animal.

- Proper treatment, administered promptly after being bitten, can stop the infection.

- In the United States, the majority of cases of rabies have occurred in humans following close exposure to a bat—without any signs or recollection of a bite.

- Not all rabid animals foam at the mouth and appear mad; infected animals can appear tame and calm.

- Only mammals get rabies; birds, fish, reptiles, and amphibians do not.

- Cats are the most common domestic animal to become infected with rabies; this is attributed to the fact that many cats are not vaccinated but are exposed to rabid animals while outdoors.

- Most cases of rabies occur in wild animals, primarily bats, skunks, raccoons, and foxes.

open (ideal for a raccoon), or ropes and inner tubes for animals such as primates to swing on and play with.

Animals that can be exercised are taken to specially designed areas and worked. For hunting birds this may mean flying on a creance (tether); for dogs it may mean a game of fetch in the yard. Horses may be lunged (run around), or hacked (ridden); they may also simply be turned out in a field to exercise themselves, but some form of training is useful to keep them in optimal riding condition. Domestic animal shelters, vet offices, kennels, boarding facilities, and dog-walking services work predominantly with domesticated dogs and cats, and perhaps horses at boarding centers. Exercise often consists of walks or free runs within an enclosed space. The animal caretaker for these employers often works with a rotating population of animals, some of whom may be in their care only for a few hours or days, although some animals may be cared for over longer periods. Caretakers at sanctuaries, quarantines, laboratories, and such may care for the same animals for months or years.

It is also an unpleasant side of the job that in almost every facility, the caretaker will have to deal with the death of an animal in his or her care. For veterinary offices, shelters, and wildlife facilities of any type, animal deaths are a part of everyone's experience. Shelters may choose to euthanize (kill) animals that are beyond medical treatment, deemed unadoptable, or unmaintainable because of their condition or the facilities' inability to house them. But even for places without a euthanasia policy, any center working with older, injured, sick, or rescued animals is going to lose the battle to save some of them. For the animal caretaker, this may mean losing an animal that just came in that morning, or losing an animal that he or she fed nearly every day for years. It can be as painful as losing one's own pet.

As an animal caretaker gains experience working with the animals, the responsibilities may increase. Caretakers may begin to perform tasks that either senior caretakers were performing or medical specialists were doing. This can include administering drugs; clipping nails, beaks, and wing feathers; banding wild animals with identification tags; and training the animal.

There are numerous clerical tasks that may also be part of the animal caretakers' routine. Beyond the medical reports made on the animals, animal caretakers may be required to screen people looking to take an animal home and write status reports or care plans. The animal caretaker may be responsible for communicating to an animal's owner the status of the animal in his or her care. Other clerical and administrative tasks may be required, depending on the facilities, the specific job, and the employer. But for most animal caretakers, the day is usually spent looking after the well-being of the animals.

■ REQUIREMENTS
High School

Students preparing for animal caretaker careers need a high school diploma. While in high school, classes in anatomy and physiology, science, and health are recommended. Students can obtain valuable information by taking animal science classes, where available. Any knowledge about animal breeds, behavior, and health is helpful. The basics of human nutrition, disease, reproduction, and aging help to give a background for learning about these topics for different species. A basic grasp of business and computer skills will help with the clerical tasks.

Postsecondary Training

There are two-year college programs in animal health that lead to an associate's degree. This type of program offers courses in anatomy and physiology, chemistry, mathematics, clinical pharmacology, pathology, radiology, animal care and handling, infectious diseases, biology, and current veterinary treatment. Students graduating from these programs go on to work in veterinary practices, shelters, zoos and aquariums, pharmaceutical companies, and laboratory research facilities. Students should look for programs accredited by the American Veterinary Medical Association.

Apprenticing for the handling of wild hunting birds is required by most facilities. This can include having apprentices pursue a falconry license, which means apprenticing to a licensed falconer. Licenses for assistant laboratory animal technician, laboratory animal technician, and laboratory animal technologist are available through the American Association for Laboratory Animal Science and may be required by some employers.

A bachelor's degree is required for many jobs, particularly in zoos and aquariums. Degrees in wildlife management, biology, zoology, animal physiology, or other related fields are most useful.

Other Requirements

Animal caretakers should have great love, empathy, and respect for animals. They should have a strong interest in the environment. Patience, compassion, dependability, and the ability to work on repetitive, physically challenging, or unstimulating tasks without annoyance are essential characteristics for someone to be happy as an animal caretaker.

■ EXPLORING

Volunteering is the most effective method of experiencing the tasks of an animal caretaker. Most shelters, rescue centers, and sanctuaries, and some zoos, aquariums, and labs rely on volunteers to fill their staff. Opportunities as a volunteer may include the ability to work directly with animals in some or all of the capacities of a paid animal caretaker.

There is always a concern, sometimes justified, that an organization will never pay someone whose services they have gotten for free. You may not be able to get paid employment from the same organization for which you volunteered. But many organizations recognize the benefit of hiring prior volunteers: they get someone who already knows the institution, the system, and the preferred caretaking methods.

Volunteering also provides a line on your resume that demonstrates that you bring experience to your first paying job. It gives you references who can vouch for your skills with animals, your reliability, and your dedication to the field. Thus, you should treat any volunteer position with the same professionalism that you would a paid job.

Other avenues for exploration are interviewing people already in the position, or finding a paid position in a facility where animal caretakers work so you can see them in action. You may also begin by providing a pet walking or sitting service in your neighborhood, but be sure to only take on the number and kinds of animals you know you can handle successfully.

■ EMPLOYERS

There are many different types of facilities and businesses that employ animal caretakers, including veterinary offices, kennels, stables, breeding farms, boarding facilities, rescue centers, shelters, sanctuaries, zoos, aquariums, and pet stores. Other job opportunities for animal caretakers are provided by the government and state and local parks. This field is growing, and increasing job opportunities will be available all over the country for animal caretakers. Since pet ownership and interest in animals continues to increase, more and more jobs will become available with all kinds of employers, resulting in work in environments ranging from nonprofit organizations to retail stores to laboratories.

■ STARTING OUT

High school students who volunteer will be able to test the job before committing to it. They will also, as explained earlier, be able to get a job on their resume that demonstrates their experience in the field.

Two-year and four-year college programs offer some placement assistance, but familiarity with the regional market for organizations that use animal caretakers will assist you in selecting places to target with your resume. Many animal caretakers work in veterinary offices and boarding facilities or kennels, but animal research laboratories also hire many caretakers. Other employers include the federal government, state governments, pharmaceutical companies, teaching hospitals, and food production companies.

■ ADVANCEMENT

Advancement depends on the job setting. There may be promotion opportunities to senior technician, supervisor, assistant facilities manager, or facilities manager. Some animal caretakers may open their own facilities or services. Services such as dog walking require little in the way of offices or equipment, so these are easy ways for animal caretakers to start on their own, with an established clientele that they bring from a previous position.

Laboratory workers can move from assistant technician to technician to technologist with increased education and experience. But for most promotions, more education is usually required.

■ EARNINGS

Salaried animal caretakers had average annual earnings of $18,750 in 2002, according to the *Occupational Outlook Handbook*. Wages for the middle half of people employed in the field were about $17,080. The top 10 percent earned more than $27,850, but the bottom 10 percent earned less than $12,750 a year.

An animal caretaker at a llama farm grooms his charge's winter coat.

Self-employed animal caretakers who provide dog walking, kennel, sitting, or other cottage industry services do not have salaries that are readily available for review, but in large cities, boarding a dog overnight can cost $25 to $40, with a minimum of three dogs usually at one facility. Dog walkers charge between $5 and $12 a dog. There is little overhead for either service, beyond perhaps providing food.

■ WORK ENVIRONMENT

Animals may either be kept indoors or outdoors, in any type of weather. Eagles don't come in from the rain, so animal caretakers caring for eagles still have to traipse outside to feed them when it's raining. Horses are turned out in the middle of the winter, so horse grooms still have to carry bales of hay to the pasture in the middle of January snowdrifts. Though currying, saddling, exercising, medicating, and cleaning up after a horse—or horses—may seem like a dream job to some, it is considerably less romantic to clean a stable day in and day out, regardless of weather.

Depending on the facilities, heavy lifting may be part of the job. You may have to lift crates, animals, food, equipment, or other items big enough to accommodate a large animal. The work can sometimes be hard, repetitive, and dirty. Cleaning enclosures and disinfecting spaces can involve hot or cold water and chemicals.

The work can also be dangerous, depending on the animals you work with. Although animals that are han-

dled correctly and are treated with the proper respect and distance can be quite safe, situations can arise where the animal is unpredictable, or is frightened or cornered. Although this is more likely with animal caretakers working with wildlife populations, large dogs, horses, and cattle are quite capable of injuring and killing people. There is a certain physical risk involved in working with animals, which may be as minor as scratches from nails or bites, but can be as great as broken or crushed bones, or accidental death.

Many facilities require long workdays, long workweeks, odd hours, weekend work, holiday work, and intermittent schedules. Depending on the hours of the facility, the services provided, and the staffing, there may be several shifts, including a graveyard shift. Animal caretakers should be prepared to work a changing schedule. The needs of animals don't cease for weekends and holidays.

Also, for many facilities, animals that require round-the-clock care have to be taken home with an animal caretaker who is willing to provide whatever service the animal needs, including waking every two hours to bottlefeed a newborn chimp.

■ OUTLOOK

The animal care field is expected to grow faster than the average through 2012, according to the U.S. Department of Labor. More people have pets and are more concerned with their pets' care. Since most households have all the adults in full-time employment, animals are left home alone longer than in earlier times. Dog-walking services, pet sitting and in-house care, boarding facilities, kennels, and such that provide assistance with the daily care of an animal for the working or traveling owner are far more prevalent and successful than before.

Veterinary services are also on the rise, with the increased number of pets and the increased awareness on the part of owners that vet services are essential to an animal's well-being.

There is a high turnover in the profession. This is due in part to the seasonal nature of some of the jobs, the low pay, and the lack of advancement opportunities in the field. Wildlife sanctuaries, release and rescue programs, shelters, and zoos and aquariums are heavily dependent on charitable contributions and fundraising efforts. Staff employment can be tied to the rise and fall of donations. Many of these institutions rely heavily on volunteer labor. As such, the competitiveness for the paid jobs is quite high.

Positions as animal caretakers in zoos, aquariums, and rehabilitation and rescue centers are the most sought after, partly because of the ability to work with exotic and wild species. Aspiring animal caretakers will find few openings in these facilities.

Graduates of veterinary technician programs have the best employment prospects. Laboratory animal technicians and technologists also have good opportunities. Increasing concern for animal rights and welfare means that these facilities are staffing more professionals to operate their labs.

■ FOR MORE INFORMATION

For information about animal laboratory work and certification programs, contact

American Association for Laboratory Animal Science
9190 Crestwyn Hills Drive
Memphis, TN 38125
Tel: 901-754-8620
Email: info@aalas.org
http://www.aalas.org

For information on available training programs, such as the facility accreditation program, certification program for kennel operators, complete staff training program, and ethics program, contact

American Boarding Kennels Association
1702 East Pikes Peak Avenue
Colorado Springs, CO 80909
Tel: 719-667-1600
Email: info@abka.com
http://www.abka.com

For more information on careers, schools, and resources, contact AVMA.

American Veterinary Medical Association (AVMA)
1931 North Meacham Road, Suite 100
Schaumburg, IL 60173
Tel: 847-925-8070
Email: avmainfo@avma.org
http://www.avma.org

For information on the Student Career Experience Program, contact the U.S. Fish and Wildlife Service in your state or visit the following website:

U.S. Fish and Wildlife Service
http://www.fws.gov

Animal Handlers

■ OVERVIEW

Anybody who works directly with animals, from the caretaker of your local park's petting zoo, to the activist who reintroduces wild animals to national parks, is an *animal handler*. Animal handlers care for, train, and study animals in such places as zoos, parks, research laboratories, animal breeding facilities, rodeos, and museums. An animal handler's job involves feeding the animals, cleaning their living and sleeping areas, preparing medications, and other aspects of basic care. A handler may also be actively involved in an animal's training, and in presenting animals to the public in shows and parks.

■ HISTORY

From the old stable hand of the 19th-century Wild West to today's horse trainer for a movie western, animal handlers have long been in great demand. As long as animals have walked the earth alongside humans, society has invented ways to use animals for work, recreation, and research. Ancient Egyptian records of veterinary medicine date as far back as 2000 B.C. Animal medicine was considered as important as human medicine, because of the great importance animals played in transportation and production. But animals weren't just admired for their practicality; people have always held affection and fascination for animals. The domestication of animals began during the Stone Age, and zoo keeping can be traced back to the 12th century B.C. Egypt, Greece, and China all have early records of exotic animals kept in collections for admiration and competition. Though many of the earliest zoos were kept only for kings and queens, public zoos have been in existence for over two centuries. The French Revolution resulted in the Jardin de Plantes in Paris going public and becoming a model for all the zoos to follow as monarchies fell around the world.

With the development of engines and motors over the last century, the role of animals in society has changed. Though seeing-eye dogs, laboratory primates, police horses, and canine patrol dogs are still put to work to aid humans, animals today entertain

QUICK FACTS

SCHOOL SUBJECTS
Agriculture
Biology

PERSONAL SKILLS
Helping/teaching
Leadership/management

WORK ENVIRONMENT
Indoors and outdoors
Primarily one location

MINIMUM EDUCATION LEVEL
High school diploma

SALARY RANGE
$12,750 to $17,080 to $27,850

CERTIFICATION OR LICENSING
Voluntary

OUTLOOK
About as fast as the average

DOT
N/A

GOE
03.02.01

NOC
N/A

O*NET-SOC
39-2021.00

HOW MUCH DOES AN ELEPHANT EAT?

In the wild, of course, elephants graze on vegetation—about 500 pounds of it in a day. Elephants in zoos and circuses, however, have to be fed by their handlers. An elephant eats:

- About 6 and a half pounds of bran, mixed with water and minerals, for breakfast
- 55 pounds of hay
- 22 pounds of straw
- 30 pounds of turnips, carrots, or other vegetables
- 9 pounds of bread
- About 20 pounds of fruits and vegetables several times a week
- As many tree branches as he wants!

and fascinate more often than perform duties. Protecting animals has become an important aspect of every animal handler's job. For over 100 years, government agencies have been in place to ensure the humane treatment of animals. The first such agency in the United States was chartered in 1866; it was the still-active American Society for the Prevention of Cruelty to Animals (ASPCA).

■ THE JOB

Wrangling an iguana for a movie production; preparing the diet for a zoo's new albino alligator; comforting bison to keep them from committing "suicide"; training cats for an animal-assisted therapy program at a nursing home—all these responsibilities, strange as they may seem, actually exist for some animal trainers. Many western states have long telephone book listings of animal handlers who rent out trained iguanas, horses, cougars, cattle, and other animals for movie productions. Zoos and marine animal parks hire highly trained keepers to feed, shelter, and protect some of the most exotic animals in the world. Bison, if not properly prepared for transport, can easily be provoked to stampede, sometimes killing themselves. And even cats are therapists these days, as people introduce their pets to elderly and ill patients who respond well to interaction with animals.

Whether taking on jobs like those listed above or working for a small park or large zoo, all animal handlers are called upon for the daily care and safety of animals. They may have special training in a particular animal or breed or work with a variety of animals. Jennifer Gales works in the petting zoo of Knotts Berry Farm in California, caring for the goats, ponies, rabbits, tortoises, and other animals

visited every day. It is her responsibility to check the health of the animals, and to feed and water them. "You have to learn as much as you can about the animal's habits and personality," she says. "Every animal is different." With a wide knowledge of an animal's nutritional and exercise requirements, animal handlers make sure the animals in their care are well-fed, well-groomed, and healthy. They prepare food and formulas, which may include administering medications. Maintaining proper shelters for animals requires cleaning the area, ensuring good ventilation, and providing proper bedding. Animal handlers arrange for vaccinations, as well as look for diseases in their animals. They also prepare animals for transport, knowing how to use muzzles and kennels, and how to calm an animal. But an animal handler needs a rapport with the two-legged creatures as well; working with people is an important aspect of most animal care jobs, as many of these animals are kept for presentation and performance.

"Every day is different," Gales says, "because animals have good and bad days, just like people. There are days they just don't want to be touched at all, and they let you know it by their actions." The relationship between an animal and its handler can be very strong, particularly in training situations. Dogs trained for a police unit require specially certified trainers, and the dogs often both live and work alongside the officers to whom they are assigned. The same is true of handlers who train seeing-eye dogs or hearing-ear dogs; it is the handler's responsibility to train the animal to think of itself and its owner as one unit, thereby assuring it will watch out for both its own safety and that of its owner. Handlers who breed animals are often very devoted to the animals they place in other homes—they often interview prospective buyers, making sure the animal will have proper shelter, exercise, and feeding. Handlers who prepare animals for research in a lab must pay close attention to animal health, as well as their own; many states require health tests and immunizations of people who run the risk of catching diseases or illnesses from the animals they study.

■ REQUIREMENTS
High School

Take biology, chemistry, and other science courses offered by your high school. The study of science will be important to any student of animals, as will the study of psychology and sociology. Knowing about animal nutrition, health, behavior, and biology will help you to understand the animals you care for, and how to best provide for them. And if you do choose to go on to college, most animal-related courses of study are science based.

Some may think of animal handlers as people who spend all their time separate from the rest of the community, communicating only with animals and limiting interaction with humans. However, nothing could be further from the truth—most animal handlers work actively with the public; they present the animals in zoos and public programs, and may even perform with the animals. Join your speech and debate team, or your drama club, to prepare for speaking in front of groups of people.

Because so many animal programs, from petting zoos to animal-therapy programs, rely on community support, there are many volunteer opportunities for high school students looking to work with animals. Zoos, parks, and museums need volunteers, as do kennels, shelters, and local chapters of the Humane Society. These organizations may even offer students paid part-time positions. If few opportunities exist in your area, check with the nearest zoo about summer internship programs for high school students.

Postsecondary Training

Though Jennifer Gales doesn't have a college degree, some of her coworkers at the Knotts Berry Farm petting zoo are pursuing degrees in the veterinary sciences. The value of a college degree depends on the work you do. Many animal handlers do not have degrees, but zoos often prefer to hire people with a postsecondary education. A degree can often determine promotions and pay raises among the workers of a zoo. Many universities offer degrees in animal sciences, zoology, and zoological sciences. There are also graduate degrees in zoology, which may require courses in physiology, animal behavior, and oceanography. Courses for animal science programs generally focus on animal research, but some programs allow students to create their own course plans to involve hands-on experience as an animal handler. The Santa Fe Community College in Gainesville, Florida, offers a unique and popular zoo animal technology program; students work toward an associate's degree while gaining a great deal of first-hand zoo experience. The students run an 80-species zoo entirely on their own and, upon graduation, enter bachelor's programs or other animal care jobs.

Some consider a job as an animal handler an internship in and of itself; after gaining experience in a petting zoo or teaching zoo, or working with a breeder or stable hand, some animal handlers pursue careers as zookeepers, veterinarians, and animal researchers. Most college animal science and zoology programs offer some hands-on experience with animals; in the case of the Santa Fe Community College mentioned above, an internship with the school's zoo is required along with the academic classes.

Many unpaid internships are available for those willing to volunteer their time to researchers and other animal professionals. Check with your local university and zoo to find out about opportunities to study animals in the wild, or to reintroduce animals to their native habitats.

Certification or Licensing

Some animal handlers in very specialized situations, such as patrol dog trainers and lab animal technicians, are required to pursue certification. The American Association for Laboratory Animal Sciences offers certification for those working with lab animals. But for the majority of animal handlers, no certification program exists. Accreditation is generally only required of the institutions and programs that hire animal handlers. The American Zoo and Aquarium Association offers accreditation, as well as memberships to individuals. Though members are required to have a certain amount of experience, membership is not mandatory for those working with animals.

Other Requirements

"I have always had a love for animals," Gales says. "The only ones I don't like are snakes—I need legs on animals." It is important for animal handlers to love the animals they care for. What might not be as apparent, however, is the need for animal handlers to enjoy working with people as well. Animal handlers are often required to present the animals to park and zoo visitors, and to serve as tour guides; they also work as instructors in zoo and museum education programs. Some animal handlers even perform alongside their trained animals in theme parks and shows. Some shows, such as marine animal shows, can be particularly strenuous, calling for very athletic trainers.

Working with animals on a daily basis requires patience and calmness since animals faced with unfamiliar situations are easily frightened. Animal handlers must be very knowledgeable about the needs and habits of all the animals in their care. Handlers are often called upon to transport animals, and they must know ways to best comfort them. Impatience may result in serious injury to both the animal and the handler.

■ EXPLORING

If you grew up with a family pet or have spent time on a farm, you're probably already very familiar with how to care for animals. But if you want to gain experience handling a large group of animals, contact your local zoo about volunteer or part-time positions. Many zoos have programs in place to introduce young people to the duties and responsibilities of an animal handler. If your local zoo doesn't have such a program, try to create your own: contact zookeepers, express your interest in their work, and ask to "shadow" them for a few days.

Many part-time jobs are available to high school students interested in working with animals. Pet shops, petting zoos, stables, and kennels are likely to have a few after-school positions. In larger cities, you may be able to start your own animal care business as a dog walker or pet sitter. Or look under "animal handler" in the local telephone book. Some animal handlers work exclusively with movie production crews and other entertainment venues; you may be able to work as a temporary assistant on a production.

■ EMPLOYERS

Animal handlers are employed by zoos, aquariums, parks, animal shelters, movie studios, research laboratories, animal breeding facilities, rodeos, and museums. There are about 151,000 nonfarm animal care and service workers in the United States.

■ STARTING OUT

Jennifer Gales found it very easy to get her job with Knotts Berry Farm. "If you love animals," she said, "it just shows in what you say, and the way you talk about them. My interview was about an hour of me sitting there talking about animals." Depending on the area of animal care in which you want to work, you may be able to find many great opportunities. A high school job or internship is a good start; experience with animals is what is most important to employers hiring handlers. Any volunteering you've done will also look good to an employer because it shows that you have a personal dedication to the care of animals. Kennels, petting zoos, museums, and animal shelters often run classified ads in the newspaper; due to the lower pay and some of the hazards involved in handling animals, those positions are frequently available.

Jobs with zoos in major cities, or with animal shows, can be highly competitive. If you're hoping to work in a larger, more famous zoo, you should first pursue experience with a smaller zoo. Jobs working with marine mammals are also difficult to get; because there are few marine animal shows in the country (such as those performed at Sea World parks), you may first have to pursue experience with internships and college programs.

■ ADVANCEMENT

Most people who work with animals are not looking to climb any ladder of advancement. As a matter of fact, many people change from high-paying careers to lower paying animal care jobs just to do something they love. Much of the student body of the animal tech program at Santa Fe Community College is composed of people over thirty years old who have tried other careers. Some who have gained experience handling and training animals may start their own businesses, perhaps building their own stables of trained "actors" to hire out for area movie

shoots, stage shows, parades, and other performances. Some animal handlers may pursue higher education while working full or part time, taking courses toward veterinary sciences degrees, or degrees in biology. With a degree, an animal handler may have a better chance at the higher paying, supervisory zookeeper positions. After years with a particular zoo, an animal handler can take on more responsibility and make decisions that influence the direction of the zoo.

■ EARNINGS

The opportunity to work directly with a variety of different animals is often reward enough for animal handlers. Someone who owns a stable of well-trained animals used in performances may be able to negotiate for large contracts, or a successful dog breeder may make a comfortable living with an established business, but most animal handlers make do with small salaries and hourly wages. The Santa Fe Community College advises the graduates of their animal technology program to expect between $15,000 and $18,500 annually. This wage varies according to region—in the colder Midwestern and Northern states, and in California, animal handlers can make more than those living in the Southeast. An experienced animal handler may draw an hourly wage of $16 to $20. Many full-time, salaried zoo positions include health benefits. The U.S. Department of Labor estimates that nonfarm animal handlers earned a median salary of $17,080 in 2002, with 10 percent earning less than $12,750 and 10 percent more than $27,850.

■ WORK ENVIRONMENT

Depending on the lives of the animals for which they care, handlers usually work both indoors and outdoors. But the indoors is often nothing more than an animal shelter, and not much different from the pens outdoors. Be prepared for smelly, messy, and dusty environments; if you have allergies, they'll be under constant assault. It will be both to your benefit, and the animal's, to make sure you work in well-ventilated areas. Some institutions, particularly animal research labs, require handlers to have immunizations and physicals before working with the animals. In addition to allergies, there is some danger of diseases transferred from animals to humans. These risks can be lessened with protective clothing like lab coats, gloves, and ventilated hoods.

The temperament of your animals will also affect your work environment. Handlers must be prepared for occasional scratches, bites, and kicks from animals with even the best dispositions. Though some animals can be very noisy when disturbed, handlers attempt to keep their animals' surroundings quiet and calm.

■ OUTLOOK

With the popularity of cable channels such as the Discovery Channel and Animal Planet, as well as television specials and videos featuring animals, the public's interest in animals is only likely to increase. Zoos, parks, and museums will benefit a great deal from any increased exposure the public has to the animal kingdom. Zoos must also compete with television as family entertainment, and therefore are constantly striving to improve their facilities with more exotic animals, better shelters, and more programs to involve the public directly with animals.

Concerns about the treatment of animals will perhaps lead to more stringent laws and certification requirements. Some activists hope to end the capture of animals for display in zoos; some even object to filming animals in the wild. But zoos are likely to continue to operate and expand, with zoo professionals arguing that zoo animals are often safer and receive better care than they would in their natural habitats.

■ FOR MORE INFORMATION

For general information about zoos, aquariums, oceanariums, and wildlife parks, contact

American Zoo and Aquarium Association
8403 Colesville Road, Suite 710
Silver Spring, MD 20910-3314
Tel: 301-562-0777
http://www.aza.org

For information on their zoo animal technology program, and other career information, contact

Santa Fe Community College
3000 NW 83rd Street
Gainesville, FL 32606
Tel: 352-395-5604
http://inst.santafe.cc.fl.us/~zoo

Animal Trainers

■ OVERVIEW

Animal trainers teach animals to obey commands so the animals can be counted on to perform these tasks in given situations. The animals can be trained for up to several hundred commands, to compete in shows or races, to perform tricks to entertain audiences, to protect property, or to act as guides for the disabled. Animal trainers may work with several types of animals or specialize with one type. Approximately 30,200 animal trainers are employed in the United States.

■ HISTORY

Animals have been used for their skills for hundreds of years. The St. Bernard has assisted in search and rescue missions in the Swiss Alps for more than 300 years. The German shepherd was used in Germany after the First World War to guide blind veterans.

Dorothy Eustis, after visiting the program in Germany, founded the first American program for training guide dogs, called the Seeing Eye, in 1929. Basing the training program on the one that she visited in Potsdam, Eustis's program launched others that were modeled or developed from hers. The Seeing Eye still has only one facility in the United States, in Morristown, New Jersey, but dozens of programs now exist for the training of guide dogs for the blind.

Other programs began to utilize the guide dog training system to provide animal-based assistance to other disabled individuals. Most of these programs are less than 20 years old, and the majority of the programs were developed in the late 1980s and the 1990s. Programs now exist for a variety of animals over a range of disabilities for which an animal can be of assistance.

Programs to train search-and-rescue dogs in the United States are new, particularly compared to the programs in Europe. The Swiss program inspired search-and-rescue dog training programs in the United States in the 1970s. Various small programs were developed that relied on individuals with specific breeds of dogs to volunteer to train their pets for disaster or search operations. Programs such as the Black Paws for the Newfoundland breed offer certification that is accepted by law enforcement and search teams in selecting animals for search operations. After receiving state-recognized certification, dog and handler teams can choose to continue training for more intensive programs.

The Federal Emergency Management Agency (FEMA) established criteria and certification testing for disaster search dog

QUICK FACTS

SCHOOL SUBJECTS
Biology
Psychology

PERSONAL SKILLS
Following instructions
Helping/teaching

WORK ENVIRONMENT
Indoors and outdoors
One location with some travel

MINIMUM EDUCATION LEVEL
Some postsecondary training

SALARY RANGE
$14,290 to $22,950 to
$45,040+

CERTIFICATION OR LICENSING
Required by certain states

OUTLOOK
Faster than the average

DOT
N/A

GOE
03.02.01

NOC
N/A

O*NET-SOC
39-2011.00

and handler teams in 1991. They started with a few teams, funding established dog and dog-handler teams to undergo an intensive training program. FEMA-certified teams were used extensively in search-and-recovery operations in the aftermath of the September 11, 2001, terrorist attacks at the Pentagon and World Trade Center.

■ THE JOB

Many animals are capable of being trained. The techniques used to train them are basically the same, regardless of the type of animal. Animal trainers conduct programs consisting primarily of repetition and reward to teach animals to behave in a particular manner and to do it consistently.

First, trainers evaluate an animal's temperament, ability, and aptitude to determine its trainability. Animals vary in personality, just as people do. Some animals are more stubborn, willful, or easily distracted and would not do well with rigid training programs. All animals can be trained at some level, but certain animals are more receptive to training; these animals are chosen for programs that demand great skill.

One of the most familiar examples is the seeing-eye dog, now usually called a companion animal for the blind. These dogs are trained with several hundred verbal commands to assist their human and to recognize potentially dangerous situations. The dog must be able to, without any command, walk his companion around obstacles on the sidewalk. The companion dog must be able to read street lights and know to cross at the green, and only after traffic has cleared. The dog must also not be tempted to run to greet other dogs, grab food, or behave as most pet dogs do. Very few dogs make it

TRAINING HELPER DOGS

It takes about six months to train guide dogs for the blind. After mastering basic obedience and becoming accustomed to the shoulder harness that is the contact with their owners, the dogs learn to follow basic directions (forward, right, and left), to stop at curbs, to cross streets, and to lead their owners around hazards. The dog trainer also works with the new owners, usually for about a month. Together, they work with the dog and learn to master elevators, revolving doors, subway stations, and trains and buses.

Trainers may also train dogs to work with people who are hearing-impaired or physically disabled. Individualized training programs must be designed for the dogs in order to meet the specific needs of their new owners.

through the rigorous training program. The successful dogs have proved to be such aids to the visually impaired that similar programs have been developed to train dogs for people who are confined to a wheelchair, or are hearing impaired, or incapable of executing some aspect of a day-to-day routine where a dog can assist.

By painstakingly repeating routines many times and rewarding the animal when it does what is expected, animal trainers train an animal to obey or perform on command or, in certain situations, without command. In addition, animal trainers are responsible for the feeding, exercising, grooming, and general care of the animals, either handling the duties themselves or supervising other workers. In some training programs, trainers come in and work with the animals; in other programs, such as the companion animal program, the animal lives with the trainer for the duration of the program.

Trainers usually specialize in one type of animal and are identified by this type of animal. *Dog trainers*, for example, may work with police dogs, training them to search for drugs or missing people. The programs to train drug-detecting dogs use different detection responses, but each dog is trained in only one response system. Some dogs are trained to behave passively when the scent is detected, with a quiet signal given to the accompanying police officer that drugs have been detected. The signal can be sitting next to the scent, pointing, or following. Other dogs are trained to dig, tear, and destroy containers that have the drug in them. As one animal trainer from the U.S. Customs office pointed out, these dogs may be nightmare pets because they can destroy a couch in seconds, but they make great drug-detecting dogs. The common breeds for companion dogs and police dogs are German shepherds, rottweilers, and Labrador retrievers.

Some train guard dogs to protect private property; others train dogs for performance, where the dog may learn numerous stunts or movements with hand commands so that the dog can perform on a stage or in film without the audience hearing the commands spoken from offstage. Shepherding dogs are also trained with whistle or hand commands because commands may have to be given from some distance away from where the dog is working.

Dogs, partly because of the variety of breeds available and partly because of their nature to work for approval, have countless roles for which they are trained. Even pet dogs may be trained by animal trainers who work with owners to teach the dog routine commands that make walking the dog safer and easier, or break the dog of destructive or dangerous habits.

Horse trainers specialize in training horses for riding or for harness. They talk to and handle a horse gently to accustom it to human contact, then gradually get it to accept a harness, bridle, saddle, and other riding gear. Trainers teach horses to respond to commands that are either spoken or given by use of the reins and legs. Draft horses are conditioned to draw equipment either alone or as part of a team. Show horses are given special training to qualify them to perform in competitions. Horse trainers sometimes have to retrain animals that have developed bad habits, such as bucking or biting. Besides feeding, exercising, and grooming, these trainers may make arrangements for breeding the horses and help mares deliver their foals.

A highly specialized occupation in the horse-training field is that of *racehorse trainers*, who must create individualized training plans for every horse in their care. By studying the animal's performance record and becoming familiar with its behavior during workouts, trainers can adapt their training methods to take advantage of each animal's peculiarities. Like other animal trainers, racehorse trainers oversee the exercising, grooming, and feeding of their charges. They also clock the running time during workouts to determine when a horse is ready for competitive racing. Racehorse trainers coach jockeys on how best to handle a particular horse during a race and may give owners advice on purchasing horses.

Police horse trainers work with police horses to keep them from startling in crowds or responding to other animals in their presence. As with the police dogs, these animals require a very stable, calm personality that remains no matter what the situation the animal works in. Police officers who work with animals on a routine basis develop strong attachments to the animals.

Other animal trainers work with more exotic animals for performance or for health reasons. The dolphins and whales at the Shedd Aquarium in Chicago are trained to roll over, lift fins and tails, and open their mouths on command, so that much veterinary work can be done without anesthesia, which is always dangerous for animals. These skills are demonstrated for the public every day, so they function as a show for people, but the overriding reason for training the dolphins is to keep them healthy. Other training elements include teaching dolphins to retrieve items from the bottom of their pool, so that if any visitor throws or loses something in the pool, divers are not required to invade the dolphins' space.

Animal trainers work with hunting birds, training them to fly after an injury, or to hunt if the bird was found as a hatchling before a parent had trained it. Birds that are successfully trained to fly and hunt can be released into the wild; the others may remain in educational programs where they will perform for audiences. It is, however, illegal to keep any releasable hunting bird for more than one year in the United States.

An animal trainer rewards a dolphin for successfully completing a task.

Each species of animal is trained by using the instincts and reward systems that are appropriate to that species. Hunting birds are rewarded with food; they don't enjoy petting and do not respond warmly to human touch, unless they were hand-raised from hatchlings by humans. Dogs, on the other hand, respond immediately to petting and gentle handling, unless they were handled inappropriately or viciously by someone. Sea mammals respond to both food and physical contact.

Some animal species are generally difficult to train. Sea otters are extremely destructive naturally and do not train easily. African elephants are much more difficult to train than Asian elephants, and females are much more predictable and trainable than the larger males. Most circus elephants are Asian because they are much easier to handle. Captive elephants, though, kill more handlers and keepers than every other species combined.

■ REQUIREMENTS
High School

For high school students interested in becoming an animal trainer, courses in anatomy, physiology, biology, and psychology will be helpful. Understanding how the body and mind works helps a trainer understand the best methods for training. Knowledge of psychology will help the trainer recognize behaviors in the animals they train as well as in the people for whom the animals are helping.

Postsecondary Training

Although there are no formal education requirements to enter this field, some positions do have educational requirements that include a college degree. Animal trainers in circuses and the entertainment field may be required to have some education in animal psychology in addition to their caretaking experience. Zoo and aquarium animal trainers usually must have a bachelor's degree in a field related to animal management or animal physiology. Trainers of companion dogs prepare for their work in a three-year course of study at schools that train dogs and instruct the disabled owner-companion.

Most trainers begin their careers as keepers and gain on-the-job experience in evaluating the disposition, intelligence, and "trainability" of the animals they look after. At the same time, they learn to make friends with their charges, develop a rapport with them, and gain their confidence. The caretaking experience is an important building block in the education and success of an animal trainer. Although previous training experience may give job applicants an advantage in being hired, they still will be expected to spend time caring for the animals before advancing to a trainer position.

Establishments that hire trainers often require previous animal-keeping or equestrian experience, as proper care and feeding of animals is an essential part of a trainer's responsibilities. These positions serve as informal apprenticeships. The assistant may get to help an animal trainer on certain tasks but will be able to watch and learn from other tasks being performed around him or her. For example, racehorse trainers often begin as jockeys or grooms in training stables.

Certification or Licensing

Racehorse trainers must be licensed by the state in which they work. Otherwise, there are no special requirements for this occupation.

Other Requirements

Prospective animal trainers should like and respect animals and have a genuine interest in working with them. With most of the career options for an animal trainer, there is an underlying desire to help people as well. Most trained animals work with people to accomplish a goal, so the relationship between the animal, the trainer, and the owner or companion is an important one. It requires the trainer to be thoughtful, sensitive, and well-spoken. Also, the trainer should be prepared to work intensely with an animal and then have that animal go on to work somewhere else. The relationship with the trained animal may not be permanent, so separation is part of the trainer's job.

■ EXPLORING

Students wishing to enter this field would do well to learn as much as they can about animals, especially animal psychology, either through coursework or library study. Interviews with animal trainers and tours of their work-

places might be arranged to provide firsthand information about the practical aspects of this occupation.

Volunteering offers an opportunity to begin training with animals and learning firsthand about the tasks and routines involved in managing animals, as well as training them. Part-time or volunteer work in animal shelters, pet-training programs, rescue centers, pet shops, or veterinary offices gives potential trainers a chance to discover whether they have the aptitude for working with animals. Experience can be acquired, too, in summer jobs as animal caretakers at zoos, aquariums, museums that feature live animal shows, amusement parks, and for those with a special interest in horse racing, at stables.

■ EMPLOYERS

Animal trainers work for a wide variety of employers, including stables, dog-training and companion pet programs, zoos, aquariums and oceanariums, amusement parks, rescue centers, pet shops, and circuses. Many are self-employed, and a few very successful animal trainers work in the entertainment field, training animal "actors" or working with wild and/or dangerous animals. A number of these positions require a great deal of traveling and even relocating. Although some new zoos and aquariums may open and others may expand their facilities, the number of job opportunities for animal trainers at these facilities will remain relatively small. Companion programs that train animals to assist people who need help in daily living activities will employ an increasing number of trainers.

Tightened security measures around the globe have created demand for bomb-sniffing dogs and their trainers. An increasing number of animal trainers and handlers will be employed by government agencies such as the Federal Aviation Administration and U.S. Customs Service, Fortune 500 companies, amusement parks, and sports arenas.

■ STARTING OUT

People who wish to become animal trainers generally start out as animal keepers, stable workers, or caretakers and rise to the position of trainer only after acquiring experience within the ranks of an organization. You can enter the field by applying directly for a job as animal keeper, letting your employer or supervisor know of your ambition so you will eventually be considered for promotion. The same applies for volunteer positions. Learning as a volunteer is an excellent way to get hands-on experience, but you should be vocal in your interest in a paid position once you have gotten to know the staff and they have gotten to know you.

You should pay close attention to the training methods of any place at which you are considering working. No reputable organization, regardless of what it trains animals for, should use physical injury to train or discipline an animal. The techniques you learn at your first job determine the position you will qualify for after that. You want to be sure that you are witnessing and learning from an organization that has a sound philosophy and training method for working with animals.

The most coveted positions depend on the animals you want to work with. Sea mammals are a specialty of oceanariums and aquariums, and these positions are fiercely competitive. Dog-training programs are probably the most plentiful and offer the widest range of training philosophies and techniques. There are numerous books on dog training methods that you should consult to know what the differences are.

FEMA works only with established dog and handler teams, who usually work within the emergency systems for the regional or local authorities in some capacity. These teams choose to also be trained within the FEMA guidelines.

■ ADVANCEMENT

Most establishments have very small staffs of animal trainers, which means that the opportunities for advancement are limited. The progression is from animal keeper to animal trainer. A trainer who directs or supervises others may be designated *head animal trainer* or *senior animal trainer*.

Some animal trainers go into business for themselves and, if successful, hire other trainers to work for them. Others become agents for animal acts. But promotion may mean moving from one organization to another and may require relocating to another city, depending on what animal you specialize in.

■ EARNINGS

Salaries of animal trainers can vary widely according to specialty and place of employment. Salaries ranged from $14,290 to $45,040 a year or more in 2002, according to the U.S. Department of Labor. The median salary for animal trainers was $22,950. Those who earn higher salaries are in upper management and spend more time running the business than working with animals.

In the field of racehorse training, however, trainers are paid an average fee of $35 to $50 a day for each horse, plus 10 percent of any money their horses win in races. Depending on the horse and the races it runs, this can exceed the average high-end earnings for a trainer. Show horse trainers may earn as much as $30,000 to $35,000 a year. Trainers in business for themselves set their own fees for teaching both horses and owners.

■ WORK ENVIRONMENT

The working hours for animal trainers vary considerably, depending on the type of animal, performance schedule, and whether travel is involved. For some trainers, such as those who work with show horses, educational programs with hunting birds, or new animals being brought into zoos and aquariums, the hours can be long and quite irregular. Travel is common and will probably include responsibility for seeing to the animals' needs while on the road. This can include feeding, creative housing, and driving with the animal. For one program director of a rescue center that works with injured hawks, it means traveling frequently for educational shows with a suitcase full of frozen rats and chicks for food.

Much of the work is conducted outdoors. In winter, trainers may work indoors, but depending on the animal, they may continue outdoor training year-round. If the animal is expected to work or perform outdoors in winter, it has to be trained in winter as well. Companion animals have to cope with every type of weather, so the trainer is responsible for training and testing the animal accordingly.

Working with certain animals requires physical strength; for example, it takes arm strength to hold a falcon on your wrist for an hour, or to control an 80-pound dog who doesn't want to heel. Other aspects of the work may require lifting, bending, or extended periods of standing or swimming. Trainers of aquatic mammals, such as dolphins and seals, work in water and must feel comfortable in aquatic environments.

Patience is essential to the job as well. Just as people do, animals have bad days where they won't work well and respond to commands. So even the best trainer encounters days of frustration where nothing seems to go well. Trainers must spend long hours repeating routines and rewarding their pupils for performing well, while never getting angry with them or punishing them when they fail to do what is expected. Trainers must be able to exhibit the authority to keep animals under control without raising their voices or using physical force. Calmness under stress is particularly important when dealing with wild animals.

■ OUTLOOK

This field is expected to grow faster than the average through 2012, according to the U.S. Department of Labor. Although criticism of animals used for purely entertainment purposes has reduced the number used for shows and performances, programs have expanded for companion animals and animals used in work settings. Also, a growing number of animal owners are seeking training services for their pets.

An increased number of trainers will be needed to train the increasing number of search-and-rescue and bomb-sniffing dog teams. The latter will be in demand to ensure the safety of airports, government buildings, corporations, amusement parks, sports facilities, and public utilities.

In all fields, applicants must be well qualified to overcome the heavy competition for available jobs. Some openings may be created as zoos and aquariums expand or provide more animal shows in an effort to increase revenue.

FOR MORE INFORMATION

For information on careers, contact

American Zoo and Aquarium Association
8403 Colesville Road, Suite 710
Silver Spring, MD 20910-3314
Tel: 301-562-0777
http://www.aza.org

Canine Companions for Independence is a non-profit organization that assists people with disabilities by providing trained assistance dogs and ongoing support.

Canine Companions for Independence
PO Box 446
Santa Rosa, CA 95402-0446
Tel: 800-572-2275
http://www.caninecompanions.org

The Delta Society currently provides certification programs in animal evaluation and in training animal handlers for animal-assisted therapy and companion animal training.

Delta Society
580 Naches Avenue, SW, Suite 101
Renton, WA 98055-2297
Tel: 425-226-7357
Email: info@deltasociety.org
http://www.deltasociety.org

Anthropologists

OVERVIEW

Anthropologists study the origin and evolution of humans from a scientific point of view, focusing on the ways of life, physical characteristics, languages, values, customs,

and social patterns of people in various parts of the world. Social scientists, including anthropologists, held about 17,000 jobs in 2002.

HISTORY

Herodotus, a Greek historian, who wrote in the early 400s B.C. about the people of the Persian Empire, is generally considered the first anthropologist. His writings formed a foundation for centuries of studies to follow, as historians and other scholars researched the development of cultures and civilizations. The rise of imperialism paved the way for modern anthropology as Europeans took over foreign lands and were exposed to new cultures. In the early 19th century, amateur anthropologists formed their own societies. By the end of the 19th century, anthropologists began lecturing at colleges and universities.

Franz Boaz, through his teachings and research, helped to promote anthropology as a serious science in the 1920s. His students included Margaret Mead and Ruth Benedict, who later established their own anthropology departments. Mead conducted fieldwork, most notably among the Samoan people, that proved ground-breaking as well as controversial; for her research, she relied more on her interaction with individual groups of people than on statistics. Approaches and explanations expanded throughout the 20th century. Some, such as the Leakeys, expanded anthropology into scientifically researching human ancestors; this sort of anthropology overlaps greatly with archaeology. Today, anthropologists specialize in diverse areas, focusing on geographic areas and on such subjects as education, feminism, politics, and film and photography.

THE JOB

Anthropology is concerned with the study and comparison of people in all parts of the world, their physical characteristics, customs, languages, traditions, material possessions, and social and religious beliefs and practices. Anthropologists constitute the smallest group of social scientists, yet they cover the widest range of subject matter.

Anthropological data may be applied to solving problems in human relations in fields such as industrial relations, race and ethnic relations, social work, political administration, education, public health, and programs involving transcultural or foreign relations. Anthropology can be broken down into subsets: cultural anthropology, linguistic anthropology, and physical or biological anthropology.

Cultural anthropology, the area in which the greatest number of anthropologists specialize, deals with human behavior and studies aspects of both extinct and current societies, including religion, language, politics, social structure and traditions, mythology, art, and intellectual life. *Cultural anthropologists,* also called *ethnologists* or *social anthropologists,* classify and compare cultures according to general laws of historical, cultural, and social development. To do this effectively, they often work with smaller, perhaps less diverse societies. For example, a cultural anthropologist might decide to study Gypsies of eastern Europe, interviewing and observing Gypsies in Warsaw, Prague, and Bucharest. Or, a cultural anthropologist could choose to study Appalachian families of Tennessee and, in addition to library research, would talk to people in Appalachia to learn about family structure, traditions, morals, and values.

Carol Patterson Rudolph is a cultural anthropologist investigating Native American petroglyphs, focusing on the Southwest. "I study the culture associated with the petroglyphs," Rudolph says. "I study the myths of the cultures—the myths are the key factors in interpreting petroglyphs. The way hands, tails, body, and feet are positioned—all have meaning when matched up to myths." Her research has resulted in the books *On the Trail of Spider Woman: Petroglyphs, Pictographs, and Myths of the Southwest* (Santa Fe, N. Mex.: Ancient City, 1997) and *Petroglyphs and Pueblo Myths of the Rio Grande* (Albuquerque, N. Mex.: University of New Mexico Press, 1991). She also produced *Rock Markings,* a video on petroglyphs that aired on PBS.

"The two questions everyone wants to know," she says, "are 'How old is it?' and 'What does it mean?'" To find the answers, Rudolph works with Indian people who still know the sign language of petroglyphs, as well as other professionals. She's currently been working with an archeometrist who dates archeological material. Rudolph considers her work to be a bridge between the past and present. "Learning how people really thought comes from their original language—and that's translated on their rock."

Physical anthropologists, also called *biological anthropologists,* are concerned primarily with the biology of human groups. They study the differences between the members of past and present human societies and are particularly interested in the geographical distribution of human physical characteristics. They apply their intensive training in human anatomy to the study of human evolution and establish differences between races and groups of people. Physical anthropologists can apply their training to forensics or genetics, among other fields. Their work on the effect of heredity and environment on cultural attitudes toward health and nutrition enables medical anthropologists to help develop urban health programs.

One of the most significant contributions of physical anthropologists comes from their research on nonhuman primates. Knowledge about the social organization, dietary habits, and reproductive behaviors of chimpanzees, gorillas, baboons, and others helps explain a great deal about human behavior, motivation, and origins. People working in primate studies are increasingly interested in conservation issues because the places where primates live are threatened by development and the overharvesting of forest products. The work done by Jane Goodall is a good example of this type of anthropology.

Urban anthropologists study the behavior and customs of people who live in cities. They might concentrate on the growth and use of urban spaces and institutions, or on the behavior of a certain group or subculture. Many of these anthropologists are active in gender and lesbian, gay, bisexual, and transgender studies, as well.

■ REQUIREMENTS
High School
Follow your high school's college prep program to be prepared for undergraduate and graduate programs in anthropology. You should study English composition and literature to develop your writing and interpretation skills. Foreign language skills will also help you in later research and language study. Take classes in computers and classes in sketching, simple surveying, and photography to prepare for some of the demands of field work. Mathematics and science courses can help you develop the skills you'll need in analyzing information and statistics.

Postsecondary Training
You should be prepared for a long training period beyond high school. More anthropologists are finding jobs with only master's degrees, but most of the better positions in anthropology will require a doctorate, which entails about four to six years of work beyond the bachelor's degree. You'll need a doctorate in order to join the faculty of college and university anthropology programs. Before beginning graduate work,

QUICK FACTS

SCHOOL SUBJECTS
Geography
History

PERSONAL SKILLS
Communication/ideas
Helping/teaching

WORK ENVIRONMENT
Indoors and outdoors
One location with some travel

MINIMUM EDUCATION LEVEL
Doctorate degree

SALARY RANGE
$23,520 to $38,620 to $67,740+

CERTIFICATION OR LICENSING
None available

OUTLOOK
About as fast as the average

DOT
054

GOE
02.04.01

NOC
4169

O*NET-SOC
19-3091.00, 19-3091.01

Anthropologists excavate the remains of guerrilla fighters in Bolivia.

you will study such basic courses as psychology, sociology, history, geography, mathematics, logic, English composition, and literature, as well as modern and ancient languages. The final two years of the undergraduate program will provide an opportunity for specialization not only in anthropology but in some specific phase of the discipline.

Students planning to become physical anthropologists should concentrate on the biological sciences. A wide range of interdisciplinary study in languages, history, and the social sciences, as well as the humanities, is particularly important in cultural anthropology, including the areas of linguistics and ethnology. Independent field study also is done in these areas.

In starting graduate training, you should select an institution that has a good program in the area in which you hope to specialize. This is important, not only because the training should be of a high quality, but because most graduates in anthropology will receive their first jobs through their graduate universities.

Assistantships and temporary positions may be available to holders of bachelor's or master's degrees, but are usually available only to those working toward a doctorate.

Other Requirements

You should be able to work as part of a team, as well as conduct research entirely on your own. Because much of your career will involve study and research, you should have great curiosity and a desire for knowledge.

Carol Patterson Rudolph credits a passion and dedication to her work as key to her success. "I'm fascinated with other cultures," she says. "I'm against prejudice of any kind." This respect for other cultures is extremely important, as you'll be interacting closely with people with diverse backgrounds.

■ EXPLORING

Anthropology may be explored in a number of ways. For example, Boy Scout and Girl Scout troops participate in camping expeditions for exploration purposes. Local amateur anthropological societies may have weekly or monthly meetings and guest speakers, study developments in the field, and engage in exploration on the local level. You may begin to learn about other cultures on your own by attending local cultural festivals, music and dance performances, and cultural celebrations and religious ceremonies that are open to the public.

Trips to museums also will introduce you to the world of anthropology. Both high school and college students may work in museums on a part-time basis during the school year or during summer vacations. The Earthwatch Institute offers student expedition opportunities to a range of locations such as India, Greece, Guatemala, and England. For descriptions of programs and recent projects, see http://www.earthwatch.org.

■ EMPLOYERS

Accounts of how many working anthropologists there are vary widely: The U.S. Department of Labor reports there are about 4,400 working in the U.S., while the American Anthropological Association (AAA) reports that there are approximately 15,000 anthropologists active in the profession. Traditionally, most anthropologists have worked as professors for colleges, universities, and community colleges, or as curators for museums. But these numbers are changing. The AAA estimates that while about 70 percent of their professional members still work in academia, about 30 percent work in such diverse areas as social service programs, health organizations, city planning departments, and marketing departments of corporations. Others work for architectural and construction firms, to make sure that building sites are cleared of any material of archaeological interest, and others work for research institutions. Some also work as consultants or are "independent scholars" supporting themselves by working in other industries. For instance, Carol Patterson Rudolph works actively as an anthropologist but supports herself with her own graphic arts and advertising business.

■ STARTING OUT

The most promising way to gain entry into these occupations is through graduate school. Graduates in anthropology might be approached prior to graduation by prospective employers. Often, professors will provide you with introductions as well as recommendations. You may have an opportunity to work as a research assistant or a teaching fellow while in graduate school, and frequently this experience is of tremendous help in qualifying for a job in another institution.

You should also be involved in internships to gain experience. These internship opportunities may be available through your graduate program, or you may have to seek them out yourself. Many organizations can benefit from the help of an anthropology student; health centers, government agencies, and environmental groups all conduct research.

■ ADVANCEMENT

Because of the relatively small size of this field, advancement is not likely to be fast, and the opportunities for advancement may be somewhat limited. Most people beginning their teaching careers in colleges or universities will start as instructors and eventually advance to assistant professor, associate professor, and possibly full professor. Researchers on the college level have an opportunity to head research areas and to gain recognition among colleagues as an expert in many areas of study.

Anthropologists employed in museums also have an opportunity to advance within the institution in terms of raises in salary or increases in responsibility and job prominence. Those anthropologists working outside academia and museums will be promoted according to the standards of the individual companies and organizations for which they work.

■ EARNINGS

According to the Bureau of Labor Statistics (BLS), college and university professors of anthropology earned between $33,940 and $95,210 in 2002, depending on seniority and the type of institution. The median salary for these professors was $59,250. A 2001–02 survey by the American Association of University Professors reported that the average salary for professors at the bachelor's level was $67,000. At the doctoral level, anthropology professors earned an average of $94,788 a year. As faculty members, anthropologists benefit from standard academic vacation, sick leave, and retirement plans.

For those working outside of academia, the salaries vary widely. The BLS reports that the median annual salary for anthropologists and archeologists was $38,620 in 2002. Entry-level salaries were about $23,520, while the most experienced workers could make over $67,740. Salaries in urban areas are somewhat higher. Benefits vary, depending on employment and the company or organization for which one works.

DID YOU KNOW?

Picture writing is the earliest form of writing. Clay tablets found in Iraq and Iran date from around 3500 B.C., and seem to show the work of early accountants and business people—the tablets record land sales and tax payments.

■ WORK ENVIRONMENT

The majority of anthropologists are employed by colleges and universities and, as such, have good working conditions, although field work may require extensive travel and difficult living conditions. Educational facilities are normally clean, well lighted, and ventilated.

Anthropologists work about 40 hours a week, and the hours may be irregular. Physical strength and stamina is necessary for fieldwork of all types. Those working on excavations, for instance, may work during most of the daylight hours and spend the evening planning the next day's activities. Those engaged in teaching may spend many hours in laboratory research or in preparing lessons to be taught. The work is interesting, however, and those employed in the field are usually highly motivated and unconcerned about long, irregular hours or primitive living conditions.

Carol Patterson Rudolph appreciates the instant gratification of the work. "You're always working on the cutting edge," she says. "Nobody's done it before." But the constant struggle for funding can be frustrating.

■ OUTLOOK

Most new jobs arising in the near future will be non-teaching positions in consulting firms, research institutes, corporations, and federal, state, and local government agencies. Among the factors contributing to this growth is increased environmental, historic, and cultural preservation legislation. There is a particular demand for people with the ability to write environmental impact statements. Anthropologists will have to be creative in finding work outside of academia and convincing employers that their training in anthropology makes them uniquely qualified for the work. For these jobs, they will be competing with people from a variety of disciplines.

Although college and university teaching has been the largest area of employment for anthropologists, the demand is expected to decline in this area as a result of the steady decrease in student enrollment and the overall poor academic job market. Overall, the number of job applicants will be greater than the number of openings available. Competition will be great even for those with

LEARN MORE ABOUT IT

Barley, Nigel. *The Innocent Anthropologist: Notes from a Mud Hut.* Prospect Heights, Ill.: Waveland Press, 2000.

Behar, Ruth. *The Vulnerable Observer: Anthropology That Breaks Your Heart.* Boston, Mass.: Beacon, 1997.

Forsythe, Diana E. *Studying Those Who Study Us: An Anthropologist in the World of Artificial Intelligence.* Stanford, Calif.: Stanford University Press, 2001.

Gellner, David N., and Erich Hirsch, eds. *Inside Organizations: Anthropologists at Work.* New York: Berg Pub. Ltd., 2001.

Herzfeld, Michael, ed. *Anthropology: Theoretical Practice in Culture and Society.* Oxford, U.K.: Blackwell Publishing, 2001.

Howell, Carol L., and Omer Call Stewart. *Cannibalism Is an Acquired Taste, and Other Notes.* Boulder, Colo.: University Press of Colorado, 1998.

Kuper, Adam. *Culture: The Anthropologists' Account.* Cambridge, Mass.: Harvard University Press, 2000.

Moore, Henrietta, L., ed. *Anthropological Theory Today.* Oxford, U.K.: Blackwell Publishing, 2000.

doctorates who are seeking faculty positions, and many will find only temporary or nontenured jobs. Junior college and high school teaching jobs will be very limited, and those holding a bachelor's or master's degree will have few opportunities. Positions will be available in nonacademic areas, as well as a limited number in education. The U.S. Department of Labor predicts that employment for this career will growth about as fast as the average through 2012.

■ FOR MORE INFORMATION

The following organization offers valuable information about anthropological careers and student associations.

American Anthropological Association
2200 Wilson Boulevard, Suite 600
Arlington, VA 22201
Tel: 703-528-1902
http://www.aaanet.org

To learn more about the Student Challenge Awards and the other programs available, contact

Earthwatch Institute
3 Clock Tower Place, Suite 100
Box 75
Maynard, MA 01754
Tel: 800-776-0188
Email: info@earthwatch.org
http://www.earthwatch.org

The SFAA website has career listings and publications for those wanting to read more about current topics in the social sciences.

Society for Applied Anthropology (SFAA)
PO Box 2436
Oklahoma City, OK 73101-2436
Tel: 405-843-5113
Email: info@sfaa.net
http://www.sfaa.net

Antiques and Art Dealers

■ OVERVIEW

Antiques and art dealers make a living acquiring, displaying, and selling antiques and art. By strict definition, antiques are often defined as items more than 100 years old. However, over the last two decades, the term "antique" has been applied to furniture, jewelry, clothing, art, household goods, and many other collectibles, dating back to as recently as the 1970s. People collect a wide array of items, from traditional paintings and sculptures to unique period toys and cigar boxes. Many antiques and art dealers are self-employed and go into business after discovering an interest in collecting pieces themselves. The Antiques and Collectibles Dealer Association estimates there are approximately 200,000 to 250,000 antique dealers in the United States, based in antique shops, antique malls, and on the Internet.

■ HISTORY

Interest in collecting antiques and art can be traced back to the Renaissance, when people began to admire and prize Greek and Roman antiquities such as coins, manuscripts, sculptures, paintings, and pieces of architecture. In order to fulfill public interest and curiosity, as well as to supply the growing number of private and public collections, many pieces from Egypt, Italy, and Greece were looted and carried off to other countries.

The collectibles market, as it is known today, consists of everyday household objects, as well as furniture, clothing, art, and even automobiles, usually originating from another time period. After World War I, interest in collectibles grew. Many people began to purchase, preserve, and display pieces in their homes. As interest grew, so did the need for antiques and art businesses and dealers.

There are different categories of collectibles and different ways and reasons to acquire them. Some people choose to collect pieces from different time periods such as American Colonial or Victorian; others collect by the pattern or brand, such as Chippendale furniture or Coca-Cola memorabilia. Some people collect objects related to their career or business. For example, a physician may collect early surgical instruments, while a pharmacist may be interested in antique apothecary cabinets. A growing category in the collectibles industry is ephemera. Ephemera includes theater programs, postcards, cigarette cards, and food labels, among others. These items were produced without lasting value or survival in mind. Though many pieces of ephemera can be purchased inexpensively, others, especially items among the first of their kind or in excellent condition, are rare and considered very valuable.

Some larger antiques and art dealers specialize and deal only with items from a particular time period or design. Most, however, collect, buy, and sell most previously owned household items and decor. Such shops will carry items ranging from dining room furniture to jewelry to cooking molds.

The idea of what is worth collecting constantly changes with time and the public's tastes and interests. Art tastes range from traditional to contemporary, from Picasso to Warhol. Items representing the rock music industry of the 1960s and 1970s, as well as household items and furniture of the 1970s, are highly sought after today. Dealers not only stock their stores with items currently in demand but keep an eye on the collectibles of the future.

THE JOB

For Sandra Naujokas, proprietor of Favorite Things Antique Shop, in Orland Park, Illinois, the antiques business is never boring. Over 25 years ago, she started a collection of English-style china, and she's been hooked on antiques and collecting ever since. Naujokas spends her workday greeting customers and answering any questions they may have. When business slows down, she cleans the store and prices inventory. Sometimes people will bring in items for resale. It's up to Naujokas to carefully inspect each piece and settle on a price. She relies on pricing manuals such as *Kovels' Antiques & Collectibles Price List* and *Schroeder's Antiques Price Guide,* which give guidelines and a suggested price on a wide range of items.

Naujokas also goes on a number of shopping expeditions a year to restock her store. Besides rummage sales and auctions, she relies on buying trips to different parts of the country and abroad to find regional items. At times, she is invited to a person's home to view items for sale. "It's important to be open to all possibilities," Naujokas says.

She also participates in several shows a year, in order to reach customers that normally would not travel to the store's location. "You need to do a variety of things to advertise your wares," Naujokas advises.

She also promotes her business by advertising in her town's travel brochure, the local newspapers, and by direct mail campaigns. Her schedule is grueling, as the store is open seven days a week, but Naujokas enjoys the work and the challenge of being an antique dealer. Besides the social aspect—interacting with all sorts of people and situations—Naujokas loves having the first choice of items for her personal collections. Her advice for people interested in having their own antique store? "You have to really like the items you intend to sell."

REQUIREMENTS
High School

You can become an antique or art dealer with a high school diploma, though many successful dealers have become specialists in their field partly through further education. While in high school, concentrate on history and art classes to familiarize yourself with the particular significance and details of different periods in time and the corresponding art of the period. Consider studying home economics if you plan to specialize in household items. This knowledge can come in handy when distinguishing a wooden rolling pin from a wooden butter paddle, for example.

English and speech classes to improve communication skills are also helpful. Antiques and art dealing is a people-oriented business. For this reason, it's crucial to be able to deal efficiently with different types of people and situations. Operating your own small business will also require skills such as accounting, simple bookkeeping, and marketing, so business classes are recommended.

Postsecondary Training

While a college education is not required, a degree in fine arts, art history, or history will give you a working knowledge of the antiques you sell and the historical periods from which they

QUICK FACTS

SCHOOL SUBJECTS
Art
Art History
Business
Family and consumer science

PERSONAL SKILLS
Artistic
Leadership/management

WORK ENVIRONMENT
Primarily indoors
Primarily multiple locations

MINIMUM EDUCATION LEVEL
High school diploma

SALARY RANGE
$15,000 to $30,000 to $1,000,000+

CERTIFICATION OR LICENSING
None available

OUTLOOK
About as fast as the average

DOT
N/A

GOE
N/A

NOC
0621

O*NET-SOC
N/A

originated. Another option is obtaining a degree in business or entrepreneurship. Such knowledge will help you to run a successful business.

Certification or Licensing

Presently, there are no certification programs available for antique dealers. However, if you plan to open your own antique store, you will need a local business license or permit.

In addition, if you wish to conduct appraisals, it will be necessary to take appraisal courses that are appropriate for your interest or antique specialty. Certification is not required of those interested in working as an appraiser, but it is highly recommended, according to the International Society of Appraisers—which administers an accreditation and certification program to its members. Obtaining accreditation or certification will demonstrate your knowledge and expertise in appraisal and attract customers. To obtain accreditation, candidates must have three years of

experience in appraising, complete the ISA Core Course in Appraisal Studies, and pass an examination. In order to become certified, individuals must complete additional training in their specialty area, submit two appraisals for peer review, complete professional development study, and pass a comprehensive examination.

Other Requirements

To be an antique or art dealer, you'll need patience—and lots of it. Keeping your store well stocked with antiques, art, or other collectibles takes numerous buying trips to auctions, estate sales, flea markets, rummage sales, and even to foreign countries. Many times you'll have to sort through boxes of ordinary "stuff" before coming across a treasure. Unless you're lucky enough to have a large staff, you will have to make these outings by yourself. However, most dealers go into the profession because they enjoy the challenge of hunting for valuable pieces.

Tact is another must-have quality for success in this industry. Remember the old adage—one person's trash is another person's treasure.

Finally, with the growth of online auction sites such as eBay, computer skills have come to be an essential part of the antique or collectible dealer's toolkit.

◼ EXPLORING

If you want to explore this field further, you may want to start by visiting an antique store or art gallery. If you see valuable treasures as opposed to dull paintings, old furniture, outdated books, or dusty collectibles, then chances are this is the job for you.

You can also tune to an episode of public television's traveling antique show, *Antiques Roadshow*. The premise? Locals are encouraged to bring family treasures or rummage sale bargains for appraisal by antique industry experts.

◼ EMPLOYERS

Many antiques and art dealers and are self-employed, operating their own shops or renting space at a local mall. Others operate solely through traveling art shows or through mail-order catalogues. Some dealers prefer to work as employees of larger antique or art galleries. In general, the more well known the dealer, the more permanent and steady the business. Prestigious auction houses such as Christie's or Sotheby's are attractive places to work, but competition for such jobs is fierce.

◼ STARTING OUT

All dealers have a great interest in antiques or art and are collectors themselves. Often, their businesses result from an overabundance of their personal collections. There

---

WORDS TO KNOW

Auction house: A company that acts as a go-between for those who wish to sell (usually very expensive) antiques and those who wish to buy them. Perhaps the most famous is Sotheby's.

Baroque: An ornate style of European style of furniture, architecture, and art, dating from the 17th and 18th centuries. Authentic pieces from this period can sell for quite a lot of money.

Edwardian: The period between 1901 and 1919 (the death of Queen Victoria and the end of World War I, and the death of King Edward VII). The Edwardian style is less "overdone" than the Victorian but is still rather rich and ornate.

Ephemera: Objects that were not designed to last, such as programs, posters, and matchbooks. Often, these commemorate some important event, such as the World's Fair.

Regency: The period between 1811 and 1825. Regency-era style is somewhat simpler than the "busy" Baroque.

Restorer: Antiques are not always in the best condition; sometimes, they must be repaired before sale. Being able to fix a piece in the original style is a difficult skill. Interestingly, it is not always best to restore a piece to "new" condition—some items should show their age.

Victorian: The Victorian style marks the pinnacle of Western confidence and imperialism that coincided with the reign of Queen Victoria of England (1837–1901). Accordingly, "Victorian" furniture and art is very rich and ornate. It is also sometimes somewhat sentimental, and also often displays a romantic attachment to the past.

are many ways to build your collection and create inventory worthy of an antique business. Attending yard sales is an inexpensive way to build your inventory; you'll never know what kind of valuables you will come across. Flea markets, local art galleries, and antique malls will provide great purchasing opportunities and give you the chance to check out the competition. Sandra Naujokas finds that spring is an especially busy time for collecting. As people do their "spring cleaning," many decide to part with household items and décor they no longer want or need.

■ ADVANCEMENT

For those working out of their homes or renting showcase space at malls or larger shops, advancement in this field can mean opening your own antique shop or art gallery. Besides a business license, dealers that open their own stores need to apply for a seller's permit and a state tax identification number.

At this point, advancement is based on the success of the business. To ensure that their business thrives and expands, dealers need to develop advertising and marketing ideas to keep their business in the public's eye. Besides using the local library or Internet for ideas on opening their own businesses, newer dealers often turn to people who are already in the antiques and art business for valuable advice.

■ EARNINGS

It is difficult to gauge what antiques and art dealers earn because of the vastness of the industry. Some internationally known, high-end antique stores and art galleries dealing with many pieces of priceless furniture or works of art may make millions of dollars in yearly profits. This, however, is the exception. It is impossible to compare the high-end dealer with the lower end market. The majority of antiques and art dealers are comparatively small in size and type of inventory. Some dealers work only part time or rent showcase space from established shops.

According to a survey conducted by the Antiques and Collectibles Dealer Association, the average showcase dealer earns about $1,000 a month in gross profits. From there, each dealer earns a net profit as determined by the piece or pieces sold, after overhead and other business costs. Note that annual earnings vary greatly for antiques and art dealers due to factors such as size and specialization of the store, location, the market, and current trends and tastes of the public.

■ WORK ENVIRONMENT

Much of antiques and art dealers' time is spent indoors. Many smaller antique shops and art galleries do not operate with a large staff, so dealers must be prepared to work

An antiques dealer shows a customer the craftsman's identification on an antique vase.

alone at times. Also, there may be large gaps of time between customers. Most stores are open at least five days a week and operate during regular business hours, though some have extended shopping hours in the evening.

However, dealers are not always stuck in their store. Buying trips and shopping expeditions give them opportunities to restock their inventory, not to mention explore different regions of the country or world. Naujokas finds that spring is the busiest time for building her store's merchandise, while the holiday season is a busy selling time.

■ OUTLOOK

According to the Antiques and Collectibles Dealer Association (ACDA), the collectibles industry should enjoy moderate growth in future years. The Internet has quickly become a popular way to buy and sell antiques and art. Though this medium has introduced collecting to many people worldwide, it has also had an adverse affect on the industry, namely for dealers and businesses that sell antiques and art in more traditional settings such as a shop or mall, or at a trade show. However, Jim Tucker, co-founder and director of the ACDA, predicts that the popularity of Web sites devoted to selling collectibles will level off. There is a great social aspect to collecting art and antiques. Tucker feels that people want to see, feel, and touch the items they are interested in purchasing, which is obviously not possible to do while surfing the Web.

Though the number of authentic antique art and collectibles—items more than 100 years old—is limited, new items will be in vogue as collectibles. Also, people will be ready to sell old furniture and other belongings to make room for new, modern purchases. It is unlikely that there will ever be a shortage of inventory worthy of an antique shop or art gallery.

■ FOR MORE INFORMATION

For industry information, antique show schedules, and appraisal information, contact

Antique and Collectible Associations
PO Box 4389
Davidson, NC 28036
Tel: 800-287-7127
Email: info@antiqueandcollectible.com
http://www.antiqueandcollectible.com

For art resources and listings of galleries, contact

Art Dealers Association of America
575 Madison Avenue
New York, NY 10022
Tel: 212-940-8590
Email: adaa@artdealers.org
http://www.artdealers.org

For information about appraising and certification, contact

International Society of Appraisers
1131 Seventh Street, SW, Suite 105
Renton, WA 98055
Tel: 206-241-0359
Email: isahq@isa-appraisers.org
http://www.isa-appraisers.org

For programming schedules and tour information on the public television show that highlights unique and sometimes priceless antique finds, visit

Antiques Roadshow
http://www.pbs.org/wgbh/pages/roadshow

For information on collecting, art and antique shows, and collecting clubs, visit the following website:

Collectors.org
http://www.collectors.org

Apparel Industry Workers

■ OVERVIEW

Apparel industry workers produce, maintain, or repair clothing and other consumer products made from cloth, leather, or fur. The three basic processes of garment production are cutting, sewing, and pressing. According to the U.S. Department of Labor, there are approximately 1.3 million textile, apparel, and furnishings workers. Apparel industry employees work primarily in manufacturing firms, though some are employed in retail establishments or laundries and dry-cleaners. They may be involved in creating apparel, from working with the pattern to cutting or sewing together parts of a garment through the final stages of finishing or inspecting the item.

■ HISTORY

The first sewing machine was patented in Paris in 1830 by Barthelemy Thimonnier. But weavers and tailors, fearful of being driven out of business by the mass production machines, destroyed the factories where the work was taking place, causing instances of violence across Europe.

The history of apparel workers in the United States is intertwined with the history of the early American labor movement. In 1846 Elias Howe patented a sewing machine in the United States that used two threads in a lock stitch pattern, as sewing machines use today. However, the Howe sewing machine was no more accepted in the United States than Thimonnier's invention had been in Paris, and Howe sold part of the patent rights in England.

In 1851 Isaac Singer built a sewing machine that survived the objections of the tailors. The machine only made simple stitches, and tailors would still be needed for much of the work on clothing. The machine would speed production of the basic elements of garments. Workers were required to purchase their own sewing machines.

As the industrial revolution progressed, the sewing machine was joined in 1860 by a band-knife cutting machine, invented by John Barran of Leeds, England, that cut several layers of fabric. In the 1890s, the first spreading machine was put to use in garment making, as was the first buttonhole machine, invented in the United States at the Reece Machinery Company. Factories replaced craft shops.

In the early 20th century, New York City's East Side became the largest producer of clothing in the world. The small factories that sprang up during these early decades were poorly lit and ventilated, unsafe, and unsanitary. The rooms were packed with workers who labored 12 or 14 hours a day for meager wages. The term "sweatshop" came into being as a description of the apparel factories. On March 25, 1911, in New York City, a disastrous fire swept through the Triangle Shirtwaist Factory, killing 145 people, most of them young girls employed in the factory.

As a direct result of the tragedy, the city was forced to revise its building codes and labor laws, and membership in unions working in the apparel industry increased dramatically. The International Ladies' Garment Workers' Union, founded in 1900, developed enough support after the fire to lobby for labor laws to be enacted and enforced.

The Amalgamated Clothing Workers of America was established in 1914 and soon became one of the largest unions in the apparel industry.

In 1995 the International Ladies' Garment Workers' Union and the Amalgamated Clothing and Textiles Union combined to form UNITE (Union of Needle Trades Industrial and Textile Employees), located in New York City.

In early clothing factories each worker assembled and finished an entire garment. Since the 1940s, workers in the ready-to-wear apparel industry have operated in an assembly line fashion with strict divisions of labor among employees. However, apparel manufacturing firms are increasingly using modular manufacturing systems in which operators work together in a module or group.

The biggest change in the apparel industry in the last 50 years has been the migration of manufacturing jobs to Asia and other foreign markets. A substantial number of garments are made abroad because of the reduced cost of labor and taxes and technologically advanced, well-engineered factories. The quantity of clothing imported has increased by more than 300 percent in the late 20th and early 21st century. Employment in the apparel industry has risen slightly in the last few years but is expected to decline in the United States through 2012.

■ THE JOB

Apparel industry workers produce, maintain, or repair clothing and other consumer products made from cloth, leather, or fur. The three basic processes of garment production are cutting, sewing, and pressing.

Production of a garment begins after the designer's sample product has been shown to retail buyers and accepted by the merchandising department of the company. *Markers* make a paper pattern, usually with the aid of a computer. The pattern indicates cutting lines, buttonhole and pocket placement, pleats, darts, and other details. Computers also grade each pattern piece for several sizes. Then the pattern is ready for mass production. Small shops may combine two or more of the following operations into a single job.

Spreaders lay out bolts of cloth into exact lengths on the cutting table. Many layers of fabric are spread on the cutting table, depending on the quality and weight of the material and the number of products needed.

Cutters have a variety of responsibilities that may include spreading fabric, machine cutting, and hand cutting master patterns. A machine cutter follows the pattern outline on the cloth and cuts various garment pieces from layers of cloth. Using an electrical cutting machine, the cutter slices through all the layers at once. The cutting may be done by hand for expensive or delicate materials.

A cutting mistake can ruin yards of material; therefore, cutters must be extremely careful when cutting out the pattern. Newer technology has been developed, so that computer-controlled marker-makers and cutters are often used. Computers allow for more precise information to be programmed into set patterns and more uniform shapes to be cut.

The cut pieces of cloth are prepared for the sewing room by *assemblers* who bring together various pieces needed, including lining, interfacing, and trimmings, to make a complete garment. They match color, size, and fabric design and use chalk or thread to mark locations of pockets, buttonholes, buttons, and other trimmings. They identify each bundle with a ticket. (This ticket was also used to figure the earnings of workers who were paid according to the number of pieces they produced. Present technology uses bar codes and computers to calculate the worker's pay and track the bundles through the production line.) The bundles are then sent to the sewing room.

Sewers, who constitute 70 percent of all apparel workers, are responsible for attaching the cut pieces of fabric using sewing machines. These and other production workers must be careful to follow patterns supplied by the designers. *Sewing machine operators* usually perform specialized sewing operations, such as collars, hems, or bindings. Since a variety of sewing operations and machines are required for each product, workers are classified by the type of machine and specific product on which they work. Workers are categorized into those who produce clothing and those who produce such nongarment items as curtains, sheets, and towels.

Hand sewers are highly skilled workers who perform sewing operations on delicate or valuable materials. They may specialize in a particular operation, such as adding trim, lace, or sewing buttonholes. Some hand sewers also assist the designer in producing a sample product.

QUICK FACTS

SCHOOL SUBJECTS
Computer science
Technical/shop

PERSONAL SKILLS
Following instructions
Mechanical/manipulative

WORK ENVIRONMENT
Primarily indoors
Primarily one location

MINIMUM EDUCATION LEVEL
High school diploma

SALARY RANGE
$18,710 to $32,000 to $48,000

CERTIFICATION OR LICENSING
None available

OUTLOOK
Decline

DOT
786; 689

GOE
08.03.01, 08.03.02, 08.03.06

NOC
9216

O*NET-SOC
51-6021.03, 51-6031.00,
51-6031.01, 51-6031.02,
51-6051.00, 51-6092.00

An apparel industry worker cuts fabric at a factory.

After the sewing operations have been completed, workers remove loose threads, basting, stitching, and lint. The sewn product may be inspected at this time.

Pressers operate the automatic pressing machines. Some pressing is done as a garment is assembled; sometimes it is done at the completion of all sewing. Delicate garments must be pressed by hand. Pressers may specialize in a particular garment or final press finished garments before they are shipped to stores.

Apparel inspectors and *production control technicians* monitor all stages of the production process and keep materials flowing smoothly through the various departments. They may detect defects in uncut fabric so that the layout workers and markers can position the material to avoid the defects, or they may identify defects in semi-finished garments, which inspectors may mend themselves or send back to production for repair.

Inspected finished clothing is then sent to the shipping room. From there, the product is sent to the markets the manufacturer has created for the product.

Tailors make garments from start to finish and must be knowledgeable in all phases of clothing production. Custom tailors take measurements and assist the customer in selecting fabrics. Many tailors work in retail outlets where they make alterations and adjustments to ready-to-wear clothing.

Apparel manufacturers increasingly organize workers in groups or modules. Workers specialize in one operation but are cross-trained in the various operations performed within the module. This system allows operators to better communicate with other workers and take on responsibility for running the module, including scheduling, monitoring standards, and correcting problems. Production time is reduced, while product quality is increased.

Most manufacturers have small factories employing fewer than a hundred workers. Because many of these small firms lack the capital resources to invest in new, more efficient equipment, the nature of the work of many apparel workers has been relatively unaffected by increased use of technology. However, only 10 percent of all workers in the apparel and textile industries were self-employed. The relatively few companies employing more than 100 workers account for more than 60 percent of the work force. Some larger firms have modernized facilities with computerized operations and automated material handling systems.

■ REQUIREMENTS
High School

Few employers of apparel workers require a high school diploma or previous experience. However, high school courses in home economics, sewing, and vocational training on machinery are helpful. Since computers increasingly are being used in many types of production, a knowledge of them is advantageous.

A high school diploma is required for more technical positions involving computers. Mechanical drafting, design, and mathematics are excellent training, and communications classes may help you advance into supervisory or management positions.

Postsecondary Education

If you have secondary or postsecondary vocation training or work experience in apparel production, you usually have a better chance of getting a job and advancing to a supervisory position.

There are two-year associate's degrees offered at technical colleges and community colleges. Many of these degree programs offer internships or cooperative education sessions spent working as a paid employee of an apparel company. Some students attend school under the sponsorship of a clothing company and usually go to work for their sponsor after graduation. Some are cooperative students who attend school with the understanding that they will return to their sponsor company. Some employers, however, do not place any restriction on their co-op students and allow them to seek the best job they can find.

Apparel machinery operators usually are trained on the job by experienced employees or by machinery manufacturer's representatives. As apparel machinery becomes more complex, workers increasingly will require training in computers and electronics. The modular system's trend toward cross-training will increase operators' needs to learn different machines and increase their skills.

Other Requirements

A knowledge of fabrics and their characteristics as well as good eye-hand coordination and the ability to perform repetitive tasks is necessary for apparel workers. An interest in learning a variety of skills in the apparel trade provides a worker with more job options and security. You need to be able to work well with others and accept direction.

■ EXPLORING

High schools, vocational schools, or colleges may provide you with information about job opportunities in the apparel industry. Occupational information centers and catalogs of schools that offer programs for apparel technicians also are good sources of information. A visit to a clothing factory makes it possible to observe the machinery and activities and gives you an opportunity to talk to apparel workers and gain insight about the jobs. To test your aptitude for this work, you may also consider working on fabric projects yourself or joining an organization, such as 4-H, that offers such projects.

■ EMPLOYERS

Apparel industry workers are employed in many settings, from multinational corporations such as Levi Strauss to small companies with few employees. Production jobs are concentrated in California, New York, North Carolina, Pennsylvania, Tennessee, and Georgia, though small clothing manufacturers are located in many parts of the country. More than one-half of all pressers are employed in laundry and dry-cleaning businesses, which exist throughout the United States. This work does not require much prior training or experience. Only 7 percent of workers in this industry are self-employed; one-third of tailors, dressmakers, and sewers and more than one-quarter of upholsterers work for themselves. Custom tailors often work in retail clothing stores. Retailers prefer to hire custom tailors and sewers with previous experience in the apparel field. Hand sewers may find work adding trimming to a wide variety of apparel, from clothing to accessories.

■ STARTING OUT

If you are interested in working in the apparel industry, you may apply directly to apparel manufacturing firms. Jobs often are listed with state employment agencies, in newspaper classified ads, or in trade publications. Companies may also post openings on a sign outside the building. Local unions also may be good sources of job leads.

A small number of skilled workers such as tailors and patternmakers are trained in formal apprenticeship programs. Special courses in sewing, tailoring, and pattern-making are offered in apparel industry centers in New York City and parts of the South.

Many employers have a strong preference for graduates of a two-year program and give such graduates a short, intensive in-plant orientation and training program so they can be placed where their skills can be used immediately. Many graduate apparel technicians who have participated in a cooperative program are given responsible positions immediately upon graduation. Some in-plant training programs are designed to train new technicians to work as supervisors.

Custom tailors and sewers with experience in apparel manufacture are more likely to be hired by retailers. Knowledge of fabric design and construction is essential. Laundry and dry cleaning establishments often hire inexperienced workers. However, applicants with work experience are preferred.

■ ADVANCEMENT

Advancement for apparel workers is somewhat limited. Most apparel workers begin by performing simple tasks and are assigned more difficult operations as they gain

LEARN MORE ABOUT IT

Abernathy, Frederick H., et al. *A Stitch in Time: Lean Retailing and the Transformation of Manufacturing-Lessons from the Apparel and Textile Industries.* New York: Oxford University Press, 1999.

Dickerson, Kitty G., and Judith Hillman. *Textiles and Apparel in the Global Economy.* 3rd ed. Upper Saddle River, N.J.: Prentice Hall, 1998.

Gary, Sue P., and Connie Ulasewicz. *Made in America: The Business of Apparel and Sewn Products Manufacturing.* 2nd ed. Sebastopol, Calif.: Garmento Speak, 1998.

Hiba, Juan Carlos, ed. *Improving Working Conditions and Productivity in the Garment Industry: An Action Manual.* Geneva: International Labour Office, 1998.

Paleczny, Barbara. *Clothed in Integrity: Weaving Just Cultural Relations and the Garment Industry.* Waterloo, Ont.: Wilfrid Laurier University Press, 2000.

Shaeffer, Claire. *Sewing for the Apparel Industry.* Upper Saddle River, N.J.: Prentice Hall, 2000.

Tyler, Gus. *Look for the Union Label: A History of the International Ladies' Garment Workers' Union.* Armonk, N.Y.: M.E. Sharpe, 1995.

Wolensky, Kenneth C., et al. *Fighting for the Union Label: The Women's Garment Industry and the ILGWU in Pennsylvania.* University Park, Pa.: Pennsylvania State University Press, 2002.

experience. While most remain on the production line, some apparel production workers become first-line supervisors.

It doesn't take much time to acquire the skill of an experienced operator in most branches of the apparel industry. Though it takes many different operations to complete a garment, each individual step is relatively simple, and only a short training period is required for each one. In the men's clothing field and in the women's coat and suit field, however, more tailoring is necessary, and the learning period to become an experienced sewer or operator is longer.

To enter the cutting department, a person usually starts as a fabric spreader and then advances to machine cutting. After further experience is acquired, the worker may grade the master pattern for the sizes, lay out the patterns on the fabric or paper, and mark for the cutting of the fabric. These are skilled operations, and it takes some years to advance and become an experienced all-around cutter. However, the advantages of having acquired these skills are great, for a cutter can, without too much difficulty, transfer his or her cutting skill from one branch of the apparel industry to another. Cutters usually are the highest paid factory workers.

Patternmakers with design school training may become fashion designers.

Custom tailoring is a very competitive field. To be successful in their own shops, tailors need training and experience in small-business operations.

Opportunities for advancement are excellent for graduates of two-year apparel technician programs. They may become section supervisors, production superintendents, or plant managers. There are also opportunities to move into industrial engineering, quality control, production control, or specialized technical areas. Some technicians may become plant training specialists or plant safety experts and directors.

Graduates from regular engineering colleges or community colleges with applied engineering programs also have advantages in securing employment in the apparel industry. Such people may start their training as junior engineers or production assistants, but their advancement is usually rapid. Within a few years, they can achieve secure status in the industry and earn salaries at an executive level.

■ EARNINGS

The apparel industry is highly competitive, and low profits and wages are characteristic. According to the U.S. Department of Labor, sewing machine operators earned an average hourly wage of $8.99, or $18,710 a year, in 2002. Patternmakers and layout workers averaged $15.33 per hour; pressers, $8.54 an hour; and custom tailors,

$9.91 an hour. Many workers in the industry are paid according to the number of acceptable pieces they turn out; therefore, their total earnings also depend on their skill, accuracy, and speed.

Graduates of apparel manufacturing technician programs earn salaries ranging from $20,000 to $32,000. Georgia Institute of Technology's School of Textile and Fiber Engineering reports that its 2000–01 textile and fiber engineering graduates averaged beginning salaries of $47,600. According to North Carolina State College of Textiles, the average textile engineer in the class of 2001 earns about $48,000. The average student graduating with a degree in textile management or textile technology makes nearly $38,000 annually.

Due to the seasonal nature of the apparel industry, production workers may have periods of unemployment. However, during slack periods firms usually reduce the number of working hours for all workers rather than lay off some workers.

Large apparel employers usually include health and life insurance coverage, paid holidays and vacations, and often childcare. Small firms may offer only limited benefits. Unions also provide benefits to their members. Employees of some of the larger manufacturers who operate company stores may enjoy discounts of 10 to 30 percent on their purchases.

■ WORK ENVIRONMENT

Working conditions in apparel production vary by establishment and type of job. Older factories may be poorly lit and ventilated and may be congested. Modern facilities usually are more comfortable, better lit and ventilated, have more work space, and may even be carpeted. Patternmaking and spreading areas and retail stores are quiet, while sewing and pressing facilities often are noisy. Laundries and dry cleaning establishments frequently are hot and noisy.

Apparel workers generally work 35 to 40 hours, five days a week. Except for sewing, the apparel manufacturing industry traditionally has involved several shifts and therefore requires some employees to work evenings or weekends. Some companies have two sewing shifts to offset the cost of expensive machinery. Laundry and dry cleaning and retail workers may work evening and weekend hours.

Apparel production work can be monotonous, repetitive, and physically demanding. Workers may sit or stand many hours, leaning over tables or operating machinery. However, the physical demand on apparel workers has decreased as new machinery and production techniques, such as footpedal or computer-controlled pressing machines, have been implemented. While apparel workers face no serious health hazards or dangers, they need to be attentive while operating such equipment as automated cutters, sewing machines, or pressers. Some workers must wear gloves or other protective attire or devices.

Emphasis on teamwork and cooperation is increasing in those areas of apparel production that employ a modular system. As the module or team often must manage itself, groups and individual sewing machine operators may be under pressure to improve their performance while maintaining quality.

■ OUTLOOK

Employment of apparel workers is expected to decline through 2012, according to the U.S. Department of Labor. Increased imports, use of offshore assembly, and greater productivity through the introduction of labor-saving machinery will reduce the demand for these workers.

However, hand sewing is expected to decrease far less than other areas of apparel work due to the complexity of these tasks and difficulties in performing them by machine. Workers who have cross-trained and are capable of performing several different functions have a better chance at remaining in the field during periods of decline. Also, many pre-sewing functions are expected to be performed domestically, so workers in this area will not be as adversely affected. Also, the market for luxury hand-produced clothes is expected to remain steady.

The sewing process is expected to remain relatively nonautomated. Machine operators will continue to perform most sewing functions, and automated sewing will be limited to simple tasks. Better sewing machines will increase the productivity of operators and significantly decrease the amount of time needed to train them. Other functions such as training also will see productivity increases and further reduce the demand for production workers.

Because of the large size of this occupation, many thousands of job openings will arise each year to replace workers who retire, leave, or transfer to other fields.

Employment in the domestic apparel industry has declined in recent years as foreign companies have become able to produce goods less expensively than the United States. Imports now account for roughly half the domestic apparel consumption. Imports are expected to increase as the U.S. market opens further due to the North American Free Trade Agreement (NAFTA), the Agreement on Textiles and Clothing (ATC) of the World Trade Organization, and the Caribbean Basin Initiative (CBI). NAFTA and the CBI allow apparel produced in Mexico and Canada to be imported duty free to the United States. Some apparel companies are expected to move their production facilities to Mexico to reduce costs. In addition, the ATC will result in the elimination of quotas and a reduction in tariffs for many apparel products. As this agreement is phased in through 2005, domestic production will continue to move abroad and imports into the U.S. market will increase, causing further employment decline for apparel workers in the United States.

In those areas of apparel such as women's clothing, where market changes occur rapidly, domestic manufacturers can respond more quickly, giving them some advantage, especially in high-fashion items. Using computers and electronic data, manufacturers can keep retailers stocked with popular items and reduce production of those not selling well. However, the industry is changing in favor of large manufacturers who have more technology available than the smaller, less efficient companies. New technologies, such as computer-controlled processing and instrumentation, will require more technicians with computer skills.

As consumers increasingly prefer to buy new mass-produced apparel, the need for custom-made clothes, and thus for custom tailors and sewers, also will decline.

■ FOR MORE INFORMATION

For information on pop culture, latest fashion trends, and news in the industry, contact
American Apparel & Footwear Association
1601 North Kent Street, Suite 1200
Arlington, VA 22209
Tel: 800-520-2262
http://www.americanapparel.org

For industry information, employment data, and educational resources, contact
American Textile Manufacturers Institute
1130 Connecticut Avenue, NW, Suite 1200
Washington, DC 20036-3954
Tel: 202-862-0500
http://www.atmi.org

For career information, visit the following website:
Career Threads
http://careerthreads.com

Apparel Technicians

■ OVERVIEW

Apparel technicians work in specialized areas of clothing design and production. They are familiar with computer-controlled production, pattern analysis, machine evaluation, work measurement, heat setting, and warehouse and inventory control. They have expert knowledge of how fabrics must be laid out, marked, cut, sewn, formed, finished, inspected, packaged, stored, and shipped. Garment size grading, the way a garment is reproportioned during a size change, is a difficult and important part of their work.

■ HISTORY

The apparel industry began in New England, where waterpower and workers were abundant. In the past five decades, however, this industry has grown rapidly in the southern states and the West. Mississippi, North Carolina, California and the fashion industry in New York are all large employers. There are about 11,000 apparel technicians in the United States.

During the past decade or so, the U.S. apparel industry has been forced by intense foreign competition to improve its already highly developed technology and processing methods. Because the apparel market in this country is so large, it has attracted imports from Asian and other countries. In response to this competition, the industry has undergone the most revolutionary changes in its history.

The traditional art of marking a clothing pattern on fabric and cutting it to form the pieces of a garment has undergone technological change. A computerized marker-maker and cutting system has been developed that has brought the apparel industry into present day high technology.

To increase a company's efficiency, highly qualified technicians are needed to assist scientists and engineers and act as links with production workers.

■ THE JOB

Apparel technicians can work in three major areas: research and development, quality control and production, and customer service and sales.

Although technicians may devote some time to basic research

under the direction of scientists, engineers, and managers, they usually work to find new applications.

Technicians in quality control and production measure every major characteristic of the raw fiber material: fiber strength, elongation, chemical resistance, length and length distribution, diameter, condition, and character. Similarly, yarn properties such as evenness, elongation, and grade must be determined. Further, the finished fabrics must meet similar exacting standards of strength, weight, thickness, water and/or air permeability, color abrasion resistance, wrinkle resistance, and tear strength.

General laboratory technicians test cloth samples and chemically analyze fiber blends. *Evenness tester technicians* operate electronic testers, analyze the results, and report needed changes in machine settings to the appropriate department. This is a critical quality-control task requiring a high order of skill, intelligence, and reliability.

Dye-lab technicians use sample dyeing equipment to dye sample cloth according to dye formulas in order to verify that products meet company specifications. Dye-lab technicians calculate the amount of dye required for machines of different capacities, and they weigh and mix dyes and other chemicals, using scales, graduated cylinders, and titration cylinders.

Production control technicians gather data and make calculations necessary to keep materials flowing smoothly through the various production departments. *Job study technicians* conduct time and motion studies, establish job loads and piece rates, and make recommendations to management on work sequence, layout, cutting, and sewing.

In apparel manufacturing, *industrial engineers* seek the most effective ways to use the work force, materials, machines, space, and all other elements that go into making clothes. Industrial engineers are involved in everything from the layout of the factory to cost analysis to decisions that affect the entire company. In the case of an equipment failure or a last-minute order for clothing that needs to reach a department store within 10 days, the industrial engineer would be responsible for resolving the problem.

■ REQUIREMENTS
High School

A high school degree is necessary to prepare for the advanced training of apparel technicians. Courses in physics and chemistry that include laboratory work are important. Courses in computers and mechanical drafting and design are most valuable. Students who plan to enter a technical program in textiles should take four years of English and at least two years of mathematics, including algebra and geometry.

QUICK FACTS

SCHOOL SUBJECTS
Computer science
Mathematics
Technical/shop

PERSONAL SKILLS
Mechanical/manipulative
Technical/scientific

WORK ENVIRONMENT
Primarily indoors
Primarily one location

MINIMUM EDUCATION LEVEL
Some postsecondary training

SALARY RANGE
$15,900 to $26,360 to
$56,410

CERTIFICATION OR LICENSING
None available

OUTLOOK
More slowly than the average

DOT
689

GOE
08.03.01, 08.03.02, 08.03.06

NOC
9216

O*NET-SOC
51-6092.00

Postsecondary Training

Apparel technicians should have at least a two-year associate's degree from a technical institute, technical college, or community college.

In some programs, the summer between the first and second years is devoted to an internship or cooperative education session spent working as a paid employee of an apparel company.

Some students attend school under the sponsorship of a clothing company and usually go to work for their sponsor after graduation. Some are cooperative students who attend school with the understanding that they will return to their sponsor company. Some employers, however, do not place any restriction on their co-op students and allow them to seek the best job they can find.

Other Requirements

In addition to educational requirements, certain personal qualifications are needed to be successful, including the ability to work with others and to accept supervision; to work independently and accept responsibility for one's work; and to work accurately and carefully. Physical requirements for this career are not especially demanding. Average or better hand-eye coordination and manual dexterity are required.

■ EXPLORING

Interested students can obtain information from guidance centers in high schools, community colleges, or technical institutions. Occupational information centers and catalogs of schools that offer programs for apparel technicians also are good sources of information.

A visit to a clothing factory makes it possible to observe the machinery and work, and gives prospective technicians an opportunity to talk to workers and gain insight about the work. One of the best ways to gain experience is a summer job with an apparel company, preferably in some activity closely related to the tasks of apparel technicians.

■ EMPLOYERS

Apparel industry workers are employed in many settings, from multinational corporations such as Levi Strauss to small companies with few employees. Clothing manufacturers are concentrated in California, New York, North Carolina, Pennsylvania, Tennessee, and Georgia, though small manufacturers are located in many parts of the country.

■ STARTING OUT

Graduate apparel technicians often are hired by recruiters of major employers in the field. Recruiters regularly visit schools with apparel technician programs to interview graduating students through the school's placement center.

Many employers have a strong preference for graduates of a two-year program, and give such graduates a short, intensive in-plant orientation and training program so they can be placed where their skills can be used immediately. Many graduate technicians who have participated in a cooperative program are given responsible positions immediately upon graduation. Some in-plant training programs are designed to train new technicians to work as supervisors.

■ ADVANCEMENT

Opportunities for advancement are excellent for apparel technicians. They may become section supervisors, production superintendents, or plant managers. Not all technicians, however, are suited for the production floor. Those persons can advance to responsible positions in industrial engineering, quality control, production control, or specialized technical areas.

For factory management, training in industrial engineering is becoming increasingly important. Manufacturers with large factories are most interested in hiring people with engineering experience.

Graduates from regular engineering colleges or community colleges with applied engineering programs also have advantages in securing employment in the apparel industry. Such people may start their training as junior engineers or production assistants, but their advancement is usually rapid. Within a few years, they can achieve secure status in the industry and earn salaries at an executive level.

Outside technical engineering training is so valuable in factory management that people holding full-time employment in the apparel industry are advised, whenever possible, to supplement their practical experience by taking courses at night in appropriate schools or colleges. Familiarity with the theories in factory layout, time and motion study, and other related subjects can be of immeasurable aid to a person who desires to advance further than factory experience alone will allow.

Other advanced positions include quality-control analyst and technical service representative.

Some technicians may become plant training specialists or plant safety experts and directors. Safety training on the job is important in apparel manufacturing and for many it is an attractive and satisfying career.

■ EARNINGS

The U.S. Department of Labor reports that fabric and apparel patternmakers made median salaries of about

$26,360 in 2002. On average, graduates of apparel manufacturing technician programs generally earn salaries ranging from $20,000 to $32,000. Georgia Institute of Technology's School of Textile and Fiber Engineering reports that its 2000–01 textile and fiber engineering graduates averaged beginning salaries of $47,600. According to North Carolina State College of Textiles, the average textile engineer in the class of 2001 earns about $48,000. The average student graduating with a degree in textile management or textile technology makes nearly $38,000 annually.

Apparel technicians usually receive other benefits such as paid holidays, vacations, group insurance benefits, and employee retirement plans. In addition, they often have the benefit of company support for all or a part of educational programs. This is important because apparel technicians must study continually to keep up to date with technological changes in this rapidly developing field.

■ WORK ENVIRONMENT

The apparel industry of today is comparatively safe and grows more comfortable each year. Apparel plants have temperature and humidity controls that outdo those in most homes and apartments. The new plant is typically a one-story building and usually is clean, well-lighted, smaller than its counterpart of a few years ago, and far more efficient. The industry places great emphasis on safety, cleanliness, and orderliness.

Machines now handle most heavy lifting tasks. The work of apparel manufacturing technicians involves handling a succession of highly technical problems in a wide variety of situations. Technicians must define each problem, gather pertinent information, use the appropriate measurements and methods to obtain accurate data, analyze the facts, and arrive at a solution to the problem through logic and sound judgment. This process may involve consultation with scientists, engineers, or managers. All this requires patience, resourcefulness, and the ability to work calmly and systematically for extended periods of time. It also requires constant study of new developments in the field.

Apparel technicians can enjoy a deep sense of satisfaction as they solve problems in the production of garments that add immeasurably to the quality of our lives.

■ OUTLOOK

Faced with foreign competition, the outsourcing of labor overseas, and the increasing automation of tasks, employment in the textile and apparel industries is expected to decline. Furthermore, much clothing today is imported

from other countries. Therefore, the U.S. Department of Labor therefore expects job growth in this industry to be slower than the average.

■ FOR MORE INFORMATION

For a career booklet, contact

American Apparel Manufacturers Association
1601 North Kent Street, Suite 1200
Arlington, VA 22209
Tel: 800-520-2262
http://www.americanapparel.org

For brochures on the industry, contact

American Textile Manufacturers Institute
1130 Connecticut Avenue, NW, Suite 1200
Washington, DC 20036-3954
Tel: 202-862-0500
http://www.atmi.org

For an information packet on the school, contact

School of Textile and Fiber Engineering
Administrative Secretary
Georgia Institute of Technology
Atlanta, GA 30332-0295
Tel: 404-894-2430
http://www.tfe.gatech.edu/tfehome.html

Appliance Service Technicians

■ OVERVIEW

Appliance service technicians install and service many kinds of electrical and gas appliances, such as washing machines, dryers, refrigerators, ranges, and vacuum cleaners. Some repairers specialize in one type of appliance, such as air conditioners, while others work with a variety of appliances, both large and small, that are used in homes and business establishments. There are approximately 42,000 appliance technicians employed in the United States.

■ HISTORY

Although some small home appliances, including irons and coffee makers, were patented before the 20th century began, only a few types were in general use before the end of World War I. Around that time, however, more efficient and inexpensive electric motors were developed, which made appliances more affordable to the general public. In addition, electric and gas utility companies began extending their services into all parts of the nation. As a result, many new labor-saving appliances began to appear on the market. Eventually, consumers began to rely increasingly on a wide variety of machines to make everyday tasks easier and more pleasant, both at home and at work. Soon many kinds of equipment, such as washing machines and kitchen ranges, were considered an essential part of middle-class life.

Since the end of World War II, there has been a tremendous growth in the use and production of home appliances. The increasing use of appliances has created the need for qualified people to install, repair, and service them. Today's service technicians need a different mix of knowledge and skills than was needed by the appliance repairers of years ago, however, because today's appliances often involve complex electronic parts. The use of electronic components is advantageous to consumers because the electronic appliances are more reliable. However, the fact that modern appliances need fewer repairs means that the demand for appliance technicians is no longer growing as fast as the use of new appliances.

■ THE JOB

Appliance technicians use a variety of methods and test equipment to figure out what repairs are needed. They inspect machines for frayed electrical cords, cracked hoses, and broken connections; listen for loud vibrations or grinding noises; sniff for fumes or overheated materials; look for fluid leaks; and watch and feel other moving parts to determine if they are jammed or too tight. They may find the cause of trouble by using special test equipment made for particular appliances or standard testing devices such as voltmeters and ammeters. They must be able to combine all their observations into a diagnosis of the problem before they can repair the appliance.

Technicians often need to disassemble the appliance and examine its inner components. To do this, they often use ordinary hand tools like screwdrivers, wrenches, and pliers. They may need to follow instructions in service manuals and troubleshooting guides. To understand electrical circuitry, they may consult wiring diagrams or schematics.

After the problem has been determined, the technician must correct it. This may involve replacing or repairing defective parts, such as belts, switches, motors, circuit boards, or gears. The technician also cleans, lubricates, and adjusts the parts so that they function as well and as smoothly as possible.

Those who service gas appliances may replace pipes, valves, thermostats, and indicator devices. In installing gas appliances, they may need to measure, cut, and connect the pipes to gas feeder lines and to do simple carpentry work such as cutting holes in floors to allow pipes to pass through.

Technicians who make service calls to homes and businesses must often answer customers' questions and deal with their complaints. They may explain to customers how to use the appliance and advise them about proper care. These technicians are often responsible for ordering parts from catalogs and recording the time spent, the parts used, and whether a warranty applies to the repair job. They may need to estimate the cost of repairs, collect payment for their work, and sell new or used appliances. Many technicians who make service calls drive light trucks or automobiles equipped with two-way radios or cellular phones so that as soon as they finish one job, they can be dispatched to another.

Many appliance service technicians repair all different kinds of appliances; there are also those who specialize in one particular kind or one brand of appliances. *Window air-conditioning unit installers and technicians,* for example, work only with portable window units, while *domestic air-conditioning technicians* work with both window and central systems in homes.

Household appliance installers specialize in installing major household appliances, such as refrigerators, freezers, washing machines, clothes dryers, kitchen ranges, and ovens; *household appliance technicians* maintain and repair these units.

Small electrical appliance technicians repair portable household electrical appliances such as toasters, coffee makers, lamps, hair dryers, fans, food processors, dehumidifiers, and irons. Customers usually bring these types of appliances to service centers to have them repaired.

QUICK FACTS

SCHOOL SUBJECTS
Mathematics
Physics
Technical/shop

PERSONAL SKILLS
Mechanical/manipulative
Technical/scientific

WORK ENVIRONMENT
Primarily indoors
Primarily multiple locations

MINIMUM EDUCATION LEVEL
High school diploma

SALARY RANGE
$18,210 to $30,390 to $48,170+

CERTIFICATION OR LICENSING
Required by certain states

OUTLOOK
More slowly than the average

DOT
827

GOE
05.03.02

NOC
7332

O*NET-SOC
49-2092.00, 49-2092.01, 49-9031.00, 49-9031.01, 49-9031.02

THE LONELINESS OF THE LONG-DISTANCE WASHING MACHINE REPAIRMAN

The lonely Maytag man, staring forlornly at his phone (which never rings, since Maytag washers are so dependable), is one of the most recognizable commercial images in the history of television. The first to play the role was Tom Pedi, who played the morose mechanic in print ads until 1967 and later went on to make *The Taking of Pelham One Two Three*. From 1967 to 1988, the forlorn fixer was portrayed on television by Jesse White, who had had a long movie and television career. In 1988, Gordon Jump (formerly one of the stars of *WKRP in Cincinnati*) took over as the regretful, rotund repairman. Maytag added an eager young repairman named "The Apprentice" to the commercials in 2001. Jump retired in 2003, and today, the troubled technician, known as "Ol' Lonely," is played by actor Hardy Rawls.

Gas appliance technicians install, repair, and clean gas appliances such as ranges or stoves, heaters, and gas furnaces. They also advise customers on the safe, efficient, and economical use of gas.

■ REQUIREMENTS
High School

Appliance technicians usually must be high school graduates with some knowledge of electricity (especially wiring diagrams) and, if possible, electronics. If you are interested in this field you should take as many shop classes as possible to gain a familiarity with machines and tools. Electrical shop is particularly helpful because of the increasing use of electronic components in appliances. Mathematics and physics are good choices to build a knowledge of mechanical principles.

Postsecondary Training

Prospective technicians are sometimes hired as helpers and acquire most of their skills through on-the-job experience. Some employers assign such helpers to accompany experienced technicians when they are sent to do repairs in customers' homes and businesses. The trainees observe and assist in diagnosing and correcting problems with appliances. Other employers assign helpers to work in the company's service center where they learn how to rebuild used appliances and make simple repairs. At the end of six to 12 months, they usually know enough to make most repairs on their own, and they may be sent on unsupervised service calls.

An additional one to two years of experience is often required for trainees to become fully qualified. Trainees may attend service schools sponsored by appliance manufacturers and also study service manuals to familiarize themselves with appliances, particularly new models. Reading manuals and attending courses is a continuing part of any technician's job.

Many technicians train at public or private technical and vocational schools that provide formal classroom training and laboratory experience in the service and repair of appliances. The length of these programs varies, although most last between one and two years. Correspondence courses that teach basic appliance repair are also available. Although formal training in the skills needed for appliance repairing can be a great advantage for job applicants, newly graduated technicians should expect additional on-the-job training to acquaint them with the particular work done in their new employer's service center.

Certification or Licensing

In some states, appliance technicians may need to be licensed or registered. Licenses are granted to applicants who meet certain standards of education, training, and experience and who pass an examination. Since 1994, the Environmental Protection Agency has required certification for all technicians who work with appliances containing refrigerants known as chlorofluorocarbons. Since these refrigerants can be harmful to the environment, technicians must be educated and tested on their handling in order to achieve certification to work with them.

The National Appliance Service Technician Certification Program (NASTeC) offers certification on four levels: refrigeration and air conditioning; cooking; laundry, dishwashing, and food disposers; and universal technician (all three specialties). To earn NASTeC certification, candidates must pass a Basic Skills Exam and at least one of the three specialty exams. Technicians who pass all four exams are certified as NASTeC Universal Technicians. There are more than 400 test administrators who give the tests at locations such as local technician schools. Technicians should arrange for their test times.

The Professional Service Association (PSA) also offers certification to appliance repairers. PSA offers the following certifications to technicians who pass an examination: certified appliance professional (CAP), master certified appliance professional (MCAP), certified service manager (CSM), and certified consumer specialist (CCS). Certification is valid for four years, at which time technicians must apply for recertification and pass another examination. Certified technicians who complete at least 15 credit hours of continuing education annually during the four years do not need to retake the examination to gain recertification.

Other Requirements

Technicians must possess not only the skills and mechanical aptitude necessary to repair appliances but also skills in consumer relations. They must be able to deal courteously with all types of people and be able to convince their customers that the products they repair will continue to give satisfactory service for some time to come. Technicians must work effectively with little supervision, since they often spend their days alone, going from job to job. It is necessary that they be accurate and careful in their repair work since their customers rely on them to correct problems properly.

■ EXPLORING

You can explore the field by talking to employees of local appliance service centers and dealerships. These employees may know about part-time or summer jobs that will enable you to observe and assist with repair work. You can also judge interest and aptitude for this work by taking shop courses, especially electrical shop, and assembling electronic equipment from kits.

■ EMPLOYERS

Currently, there are about 42,000 appliance technicians employed throughout the United States in service centers, appliance manufacturers, retail dealerships, and utility companies. They may also be self-employed in independent repair shops or work at companies that service specific types of appliances, such as coin-operated laundry equipment and dry-cleaning machines.

■ STARTING OUT

One way of entering this occupation is to become a helper in a service center where the employer provides on-the-job training to qualified workers. To find a helper's job, prospective technicians should apply directly to local service centers or appliance dealerships. They also can watch area newspaper classified ads for entry-level jobs in appliance service and repair.

For those who have graduated from a technical or vocational program, their schools' placement offices may also prove helpful.

■ ADVANCEMENT

Advancement possibilities for appliance service technicians depend primarily on their place of employment. In a small service center of three to five people, advancement to a supervisory position will likely be slow, because the owner usually performs most of the supervisory and administrative tasks. However, pay incentives do exist in smaller service centers that encourage technicians to assume a greater share of the management load. Technicians working for large retailers, factory service centers, or gas or electric utility companies may be able to progress to supervisor, assistant service manager, or service manager.

Another advancement route leads to teaching at a factory service training school. A technician who knows the factory's product, works with proficiency, and speaks effectively to groups can conduct classes to train other technicians. Technical and vocational schools that offer courses in appliance repair work may also hire experienced repairers to teach classes.

Some service technicians aspire to opening an independent repair business or service center. This step usually requires a knowledge of business management and marketing and a significant investment in tools, parts, vehicles, and other equipment.

Some technicians who work for appliance manufacturers move into positions where they write service manuals, sell appliances, or act as manufacturers' service representatives to independent service centers.

■ EARNINGS

The earnings of appliance technicians vary widely according to geographic location, type of equipment serviced, workers' skills and experience, and other factors. In 2002, the U.S. Department of Labor reported that the median annual salary for home appliance technicians was about $30,390. At the low end of the salary scale, technicians earned approximately $18,210. Technicians at the high end of the pay scale earned $48,170 or more per year. Trainees are usually paid less than technicians who have completed their training period. Employees of gas utility companies and other large companies generally command higher hourly wages than those who work for service centers. Some service centers, however, offer incentives for technicians to increase their productivity. Some of these incentive plans are very lucrative and can allow a proficient worker to add considerably to his or her salary.

Opportunities for overtime pay are most favorable for repairers of major appliances, such as refrigerators, stoves, and washing machines. In addition to regular pay, many workers receive paid vacations and sick leave, health insurance, and other benefits such as employer contributions to retirement pension plans.

■ WORK ENVIRONMENT

Appliance technicians generally work a standard 40-hour week, although some work evenings and weekends.

An appliance service technician repairs a washing machine in a customer's home.

Repairers who work on cooling equipment, such as refrigerators and air conditioners, may need to put in extra hours during hot weather. In general, there is little seasonal fluctuation of employment in this occupation, since repairs on appliances are needed at all times of the year and the work is done indoors.

Technicians encounter a variety of working conditions depending on the kinds of appliances they install or repair. Those who fix small appliances work indoors at a bench and seldom have to handle heavy objects. Their workplaces are generally well lighted, properly ventilated, and equipped with the necessary tools.

Repairers who work on major appliances must deal with a variety of situations. They normally do their work on site, so they may spend several hours each day driving from one job to the next. To do repairs, they may have to work in small or dirty spaces or in other uncomfortable conditions. They may have to crawl, bend, stoop, crouch, or lie down to carry out some repairs, and they may have to move heavy items. Because they work in a variety of environments, they may encounter unpleasant situations, such as dirt, odors, or pest infestation.

In any appliance repair work, technicians must follow good safety procedures, especially when handling potentially dangerous tools, gas, and electric currents.

■ OUTLOOK

The U.S. Department of Labor reports that through 2012 the total number of repairers is expected to increase more slowly than the average. Although Americans will certainly continue buying and using more appliances, today's machines are often made with electronic components that require fewer repairs than their nonelectronic counterparts. Thus, the dependability of the technology

built into these new appliances will restrain growth in the repair field. Most openings that arise will be due to workers leaving their jobs who must be replaced. However, employment outlook will remain good, with job openings outnumbering job seekers, since relatively few people wish to enter this industry.

■ FOR MORE INFORMATION

For information on certification, contact

International Society of Certified Electronics Technicians
3608 Pershing Ave
For Worth, TX 76107
Tel: 800-946-0201
Email: info@iscet.org
http://www.iscet.org

For information on the Refrigerant Recovery Certification Test Program, contact

North American Retail Dealers Association
10 East 22nd Street, Suite 310
Lombard, IL 60148-6191
Tel: 800-621-0298
Email: nardahdq@narda.com
http://www.narda.com

For information on a career as an appliance service technician and certification, contact

Professional Service Association
71 Columbia Street
Cohoes, NY 12047
Tel: 888-777-8851
Email: psa@psaworld.com
http://www.psaworld.com

Aquaculturists

■ OVERVIEW

Aquaculturists, also known as *fish farmers, fish culturists,* or *mariculturists,* raise fish, shellfish, or other aquatic life (such as aquatic plants) under controlled conditions for profit and/or human consumption.

■ HISTORY

The roots of fish farming go far back in history. Fish culturing began in at least 1000 B.C., possibly even earlier in Egypt and China. Ancient China introduced ornamental-goldfish breeding to Japan, which in turn developed ornamental-carp breeding. Ancient Romans were the first mariculturists, creating ponds for fish breeding that let in ocean water. Brackish-water fish farms existed in Java by about 1400 A.D. However, historically, the vast majority of food-fish has come from capture, not farming. Capture fishery worldwide grew at rates of about 4 percent per year through most of the 20th century but increased by only 0.6 percent between 1986 and 1987 (to about 93 million metric tons). Since then, growth rates of less than 1 percent per year have been the norm. In a nutshell, the natural supply of fish is shrinking—natural waters are being "fished out"—while fish consumption is rising. Enter aquaculture.

U.S. aquaculture began in the 1920s and 1930s with some farming of minnows for bait and with growth of catfish, bass, and other food-fish farming in the 1950s, largely in the South. In 1975, U.S. aquaculture produced 130 million pounds of fish; by 1987, it produced more than 400 million pounds. Today, U.S. aquaculture produces catfish, crawfish, salmon, trout, oysters, and other products. U.S. restaurants offer a wide range of fish produced by aquaculture, including salmon, shrimp, catfish, crabs, clams, mussels, lobster, carp, sturgeon, cod, and mahi-mahi (dolphin). As capture yields have leveled off, aquaculture yields have grown at rates of 7 percent per year or more. Today, aquaculture is nearly a $1 billion industry in the United States.

Some hope aquaculture can help meet food needs in developing countries. Fish is a healthier source of protein than meat and requires less energy to produce (about two pounds of feed for one pound of catfish, versus eight pounds of feed for one pound of beef). Aquaculture can still be done simply and cheaply, such as in a pond, using farm waste as fertilizer. (Such setups, however, produce less desirable fish, like carp.)

■ THE JOB

The term *aquaculturist* typically is used to describe someone who raises fish for profit. This is not a conservation job; while aquaculturists may have a degree in fish biology or other fish science, just like some of the people working for the U.S. Fish and Wildlife Service, National Biological Service, other federal agencies, or for federal or state fish hatcheries, they do not share those agencies' goal of protecting rare and endangered species.

Technically speaking, aquaculture can be done in fresh water, brackish (salty or somewhat salty) water, seawater, flooded fields, rice paddies, and other waters. Practically speaking, limited areas in the United States are appropriate for aquaculture. Right now, U.S. aquaculture is focused in the South (catfish), the West (salmon), and a few other areas (like bait farms in Arkansas). There must be markets for the products, capital to develop the site,

appropriate water supplies, and proper structures for handling effluent. Conditions must be right; for example, catfish production in the South is successful because of the warmer waters, longer growing season, and other factors. Fish farms range in size from a few acres to 50 acres or more and typically focus on one type of fish (such as trout or catfish) or shellfish (such as clams, shrimp, or oysters). Rearing may be done in earth ponds, concrete ponds, or pens in seas, lakes, or ocean waters.

Fish farming differs significantly from regular farming. Raising fish is more complicated because of their environment—water. Also, intensely confined animals tend to be more susceptible to disease; many of these fish are in a confined space. Raising fish is more like a feedlot raising penned animals than a rancher raising cattle in open range lands. The raising of fish also requires closer monitoring than raising farm animals.

A primary goal of aquaculture is to increase fish production beyond what's possible in nature. In recent years, there's been a lot of research to determine which fish are most suited to fish farming, what to feed them and in what quantities, what conditions will optimize production and quality, and other areas. Biologists and other research scientists have experimented with things like crossbreeding for better genetics (such as for increased egg production). Commercial feeds and supplements have been developed to boost fish size. Aquaculturists also have been working on least-cost feeding formulas, or ratios of lowest-costing food to highest quantity and quality fish, for better profits. Experiments with the effects of light on growth, with limiting feeding, and other research studies also have been conducted. Since confined fish may be more susceptible to diseases, researchers also have developed drugs such as fluoroquinolone for FDA approval.

In fish farming, eggs are stripped from the female fish, fertilized by milt from the male fish, and placed in moist pans or hatchery trays. These are put in

QUICK FACTS

SCHOOL SUBJECTS
Biology
Business

PERSONAL SKILLS
Mechanical/manipulative
Technical/scientific

WORK ENVIRONMENT
Indoors and outdoors
Primarily one location

MINIMUM EDUCATION LEVEL
Bachelor's degree

SALARY RANGE
$16,640 to $28,000 to
$42,744+

CERTIFICATION OR LICENSING
Required by certain states

OUTLOOK
Faster than the average

DOT
446

GOE
03.01.01

NOC
N/A

O*NET-SOC
11-9011.03, 45-1011.06,
45-3011.00

incubators to spawn the eggs. Resulting fingerlings are put in the rearing ponds or other waters for further growth. They may be fed high-protein food or cereal with vitamins or minerals so they will achieve good size and quality. Aquaculturists also might monitor water quality, add drugs to fight disease, and otherwise optimize growing conditions. Once the right size is reached, which can take up to three years or more, the fish are removed from the water, counted, weighed, and loaded into a truck or dressed and packed in ice for shipment to the buyer.

In shellfish farming, clams, oysters, and other shellfish are cultivated in specially prepared beds near the shoreline and then harvested. Tide flats are laid out and dikes created to control water drainage at low tide. The spawn of oysters or other shellfish, known as spat, are sown in

GENETIC ENGINEERING AND AQUACULTURE: FRANKENFISH OR FOOD OF THE FUTURE?

One of the most exciting advances in aquaculture has been the use of genetic engineering to produce fish that grow bigger, mature quicker, and are less susceptible to disease. Inserting a gene from a sockeye salmon into a coho salmon, for instance, produces fish that grow four times faster than usual. Such fish are easier and quicker to raise, producing higher profits, and more useable protein, for aquaculturists. However, many environmental activists worry that if such "frankenfish" escape into nature—as has been known to happen—they will quickly outbreed "natural" fish and upset the delicate balance of the ecosystem. (Thus far, genetic engineers have been careful to supply experimental farms only with sterile fish.) Critics also point out that we do not yet know the health risks involved with eating modified fish.

the beds and may be covered with sand or broken shells. When the tide is up and the beds are covered with water, the beds may be dragged with nets to remove crabs, starfish, or other predators. Workers also might pour oil around the beds to discourage predators from getting the crop. At low tide, workers walk into the bed and collect full-grown shellfish for packing and sale.

Positions within the fish farm operation may include a *manager* or *superintendent, supervisors,* and workers. A manager or superintendent heads the operation, helping to establish policies and procedures and conferring with biologists or other scientists on optimal feeding and other conditions. They also may handle hiring, firing, payroll, and other personnel matters; monitor budgets and costs; and do other administrative work. Supervisors oversee the spawning, rearing, harvesting, and other day-to-day farming activities. They might train workers, prepare reports, and help monitor quality control. Workers may be called *assistants, attendants, bed workers,* or similar titles, and they do the labor-intensive parts of the fish farming operation.

Scientists working within the fish farming operation, or in research facilities supporting aquaculture, include *fisheries biologists* and *harvest management biologists.* They focus on fish living habits, relationships, growth, rearing, stocking, and the like.

Some aquaculturists work in universities trying to find ways to improve aquaculture production. For example, experiments done at Auburn University's aquaculture center have shown that limiting feed actually can increase fish weight and protein amount. Since aquaculture is still not that well developed in the United States, researchers and economists also have developed feasibility studies, focusing on the potential viability of different types of aquaculture for various regions. For example, a 1994 University of Florida study said tropical fish, aquatic plants, and bait-fish might be the future of aquaculture in that state, rather than catfish farming. Research goes on worldwide; for example, in 1995 the Institute of Aquaculture in Scotland studied the use of immune system stimulants to encourage macrophage growth in fish.

■ REQUIREMENTS
High School

Most jobs in aquaculture require a bachelor's degree, so follow a college preparatory plan of English, history, government, foreign language, and other courses recommended by your guidance counselor. Take science courses, particularly biology courses, to prepare for a marine science, aquaculture, or biology college program. Some management experience is also important, so take courses in business and accounting.

Postsecondary Training

A bachelor's degree is the minimum requirement for jobs in aquaculture beyond the laborer or assistant level. Researchers usually have an advanced degree in their specialty. Jobs in aquaculture tend to be more plentiful than jobs with fish and wildlife management agencies (which are very tough to get), but the educational requirements are basically the same. Without a bachelor's degree, it is very difficult to find work at the professional level. In part, fish farming is more complicated today, given new understanding of ecology (such as how one organism impacts another), fish genetics (such as how fish adapt themselves genetically to a natural environment), and other areas. A bachelor's degree in fish and wildlife biology is the primary path into this field. A minor in business or accounting may also be valuable to a prospective aquaculturist.

Certification or Licensing

The American Fisheries Society certifies associate fishery scientists, fishery scientists, fish pathologists (specialists in fish disease), and fish health specialists. A certain number of hours of experience plus a written test are necessary. Both private and government fish people obtain these certifications. In some areas, they are required for obtaining some positions and for receiving raises and promotions.

Other Requirements

You should be people-oriented because you'll often work with private market suppliers, the public, and politicians. Good writing skills will come in handy in some positions, as will business and administrative skills like budgeting. A knowledge of computer modeling and statistics can help in newer areas like harvest management and population dynamics.

■ EXPLORING

Contact the American Fisheries Society for information about careers in aquaculture. Also, read *Aquaculture Magazine* and visit its website (http://www.aquaculturemag.com) to learn more about the issues of the industry. Any hands-on experience you can get, even in high school, will be helpful in landing a job. Through a "shadowing" project, you may be able to spend some time in a local hatchery at the side of an aquaculturist. Volunteering at one of the approximately 75 federal fish hatcheries nationwide, or a state hatchery, is an option. Contact local hatcheries, go meet the people there, and find out about applying for a job. Experience at a pet shop that sells different varieties of salt-water fish, or at a state aquarium, can also give you insight into the industry.

Workers harvest catfish from a catfish farm in Mississippi.

■ EMPLOYERS

Aquaculturists can find work with commercial and private fish farms owned by corporations, states, or individuals. They may work with a small family-run operation or with a large operation employing hundreds of people. According to a recent survey by the U.S. Department of Agriculture (USDA), the top five producing states by value are Mississippi, Arkansas, Florida, Maine, and Alabama. The USDA also reports that 68 percent of the fish farms are located in the southern United States. Facilities, however, range across the country and include rainbow trout farms in Idaho, oyster farms in Washington state, and salmon farms in Maine. Some universities also hire aquaculturists, as do the U.S. Fish and Wildlife Service, and other national organizations.

■ STARTING OUT

Aquaculture work usually is easier to find than fishery or wildlife agency work, but it can't hurt to follow some of the same strategies used to land those jobs: namely, get experience. Become a student chapter member of the American Fisheries Society and explore this group's national job listings. Work with your university's placement department. A person looking for a job needs to be pretty flexible. Since U.S. aquaculture is more developed in some areas, such as the South and West, your first job may take you to a new region.

International opportunities are possible, too. Those who have considered the Peace Corps should know that some volunteers work in aquaculture. (Peace Corps volunteers are U.S. citizens, over 18 years old, with a college

WORDS TO KNOW

Aquaculture: The cultivation of the natural produce of water (fish, etc.).

Fingerling: A small fish, usually under one year old.

Hatchery: A place for hatching eggs (as of fish).

Macrophage: A tissue cell that functions in the body against infection and noxious substances.

Spat: A young bivalve (oyster, etc.).

Tide flats: A specially prepared stretch of land at the shore of a body of water.

education or at least three years' experience in their specialty.) Groups like UNICEF and USAID in Africa also use fish and wildlife specialists.

Beyond these types of organizations, other international job opportunities may be possible wherever aquaculture is practiced. Scandinavians raise a lot of coldwater fish; the Japanese raise shellfish, algae, and kelp. Of course, pollution has made some fresh waters in Europe, like the Thames in England, unsuitable for fish farming activities.

ADVANCEMENT

In fish farming, the professional typically enters as a fish biologist or other fish scientist and advances to some kind of manager or supervisor position. As noted earlier, state certification may help speed this process in some areas. Fish farming is a business; each operation is different, but further raises or promotions are likely to hinge on profits, customer satisfaction, development and sustaining of new markets, and similar business successes. On the research side, advancement will depend on the individual employer. With a young U.S. aquaculture industry clamoring for information, new research and development, and improved aquaculture technologies, it's possible for fish scientists in research to have a big impact with their studies and reap the financial benefits of doing so.

EARNINGS

Earnings in aquaculture can vary greatly. Aquaculture farms employ graduate students in assistantships, as well as experienced professionals with Ph.D.'s in genetics. Entry-level technicians may begin at $8 an hour; those with a great deal of experience and a degree may begin at a salary of $28,000 a year. The National Association of Colleges and Employers estimates that biologists with bachelor's degrees, working in private industry in 2000, had a starting wage of $29,235 a year; those with master's

degrees earned $35,667; and those with doctorates started at $42,744.

WORK ENVIRONMENT

A fish farm is not much different from a mink farm or other operation aimed at raising high volumes of animals. Those who don't like that idea should think twice about this career. On the other hand, fish farms and fish hatcheries give aquaculturists the opportunity to work outdoors, to apply scientific education in a concrete way, and to make a difference in a young and growing industry. Some fish farm operations are small, and some are large; trout farming, for example, is made up of both small and large operations. This variety allows workers in the field to find the size and style of operation that's right for them.

Fishery and wildlife careers sound romantic, and in some ways, they are; that's why they're so popular. Much of the work of an aquaculturist, however, is very pragmatic, including fighting fish diseases.

People drawn to fishery and wildlife management tend to like the outdoors. Keep in mind, however, that this work also involves frequent interaction with others, and the successful aquaculturist should have good people skills. Those who work in administrative positions are mainly business people and don't work directly with the fish.

OUTLOOK

The outlook for U.S. aquaculture is promising. A subcommittee of the U.S. Department of Commerce predicts there will be a 70 percent increase in world seafood demand by 2025. Commercial fisheries are over harvested, so much of this demand will be met by aquaculture. Aquaculture's ability to meet this demand, however, will depend on the growth and development of the industry. Many universities are currently benefiting from grants that allow them to explore better methods of growing and harvesting product and preventing disease. Advances in these areas will help to lower risk and increase profits, attracting more interest in the industry.

The business is regulated, but on the whole the government seems interested in helping to support and develop the industry. Federal assistance with development of needed aquaculture drugs and chemicals is one sign of this.

FOR MORE INFORMATION

For information about certification, educational programs, and the professional society serving fisheries scientists, contact
American Fisheries Society
5410 Grosvenor Lane
Bethesda, MD 20814-2199
Tel: 301-897-8616

Email: main@fisheries.org
http://www.fisheries.org

For information about industry journals, publications, membership, and job postings, contact

World Aquaculture Society (U.S. Branch)

143 J.M. Parker Coliseum
Louisiana State University
Baton Rouge, LA 70803
Tel: 225-578-3137
Email: wasmas@aol.com
http://www.was.org

This website provides information and links to state, national, and international associations, publications, and job services involved with aquaculture.

Aquaculture Network Information Center

http://aquanic.org

Aquarists

■ OVERVIEW

Aquarists (pronounced, like "aquarium," with the accent on the second syllable) work for aquariums, oceanariums, and marine research institutes. They are responsible for the maintenance of aquatic exhibits. Among other duties, they feed the fish, check water quality, clean the tanks, and collect and transport new specimens.

■ HISTORY

In 1853, the world's first public aquarium opened in Regents Park in London. Similar public aquariums opened throughout England, France, and Germany over the next 15 years. Many of the early aquariums closed because the fish could not survive in the conditions provided. By the early 1870s, knowledge of aeration, filtering, and water temperature had increased, and new aquariums opened.

In 1856, the U.S. government established what is today the Division of Fishes of the Smithsonian Institution's National Museum of Natural History. Over the next 50 years interest in fish and their environments grew rapidly. The Woods Hole Oceanographic Institute was established in 1885, and the Scripps Institution of Oceanography was established in 1903.

Today's notable aquariums include the John G. Shedd Aquarium, Chicago; the National Aquarium, Baltimore; the New York Aquarium, New York City; the Steinhart Aquarium, San Francisco; and the Aquarium of the Americas, New Orleans. Many aquariums recreate diverse aquatic environments, such as coral reefs, river bottoms, or various coastlines, in large tanks.

Some aquariums also have oceanariums—huge tanks that allow visitors to view marine animals from above as well as from the sides. Popular oceanariums include those at the Miami Seaquarium in Miami, Florida, and the Monterey Bay Aquarium in Monterey, California.

■ THE JOB

Aquarists are not animal trainers and do not work on marine shows. They do, however, support the staff who do. Their work is generally technical and requires a strong science background. With increased experience and education, aquarists may, in time, become involved in research efforts at their institution or become promoted to higher professional positions such as curator.

Aquarists' job duties are similar to those of zookeepers. Aquarists feed fish, maintain exhibits, and conduct research. They work on breeding, conservation, and educational programs.

Aquarists clean and take care of tanks every day. They make sure pumps are working, check water temperatures, clean glass, and sift sand. Some exhibits have to be scrubbed by hand. Aquarists also change the water and vacuum tanks routinely. They water plants in marsh or pond exhibits.

Food preparation and feeding are important tasks for aquarists. Some animals eat live food and others eat cut-up food mixtures. Some animals need special diets prepared and may have to be individually fed.

Aquarists carefully observe all the animals in their care. They must understand their normal habits (including mating, feeding, sleeping, and moving) in order to be able to judge when something is wrong. Aquarists write daily reports and keep detailed records of animal behavior.

Many aquarists are in charge of collecting and stocking plants and animals for exhibits. They may have to make several trips a year to gather live specimens.

QUICK FACTS

SCHOOL SUBJECTS
Biology
Earth science

PERSONAL SKILLS
Technical/scientific

WORK ENVIRONMENT
Indoors and outdoors
One location with some travel

MINIMUM EDUCATION LEVEL
Bachelor's degree

SALARY RANGE
$23,000 to $27,000 to $32,000

CERTIFICATION OR LICENSING
Required

OUTLOOK
Little change or more slowly than the average

DOT
N/A

GOE
03.02.01

NOC
6483

O*NET-SOC
39-2021.00

An aquarist feeds a moray eel in the Shedd Aquarium's (Chicago) Coral Reef Exhibit, a huge circular tank where different kinds of fish are displayed together as in a natural marine community.

■ REQUIREMENTS
High School

If you want to become an aquarist, get your start in high school. Take as many science classes as you can; biology and zoology are especially important. Learn to pay attention to detail; marine science involves a good deal of careful record keeping.

Postsecondary Training

Most aquariums, along with other institutions that hire aquarists, require that an applicant have a bachelor's degree in biological sciences, preferably with course work in such areas as parasitology, ichthyology, or other aquatic sciences. As the care of captive animals becomes a more complex discipline, it's no longer enough to apply without a four-year degree.

Certification or Licensing

Aquarists must be able to scuba dive, in both contained water, to feed fish and maintain tanks, and in open water, on trips to collect new specimens. You'll need to have scuba certification, with a rescue diver classification, for this job. Potential employers will expect you to be able to pass a diving physical examination before taking you on as an aquarist.

Other Requirements

As an aquarist, you may be required to travel at different times throughout the year, to participate in research expeditions and collecting trips. On a more basic level, aquarists need to be in good physical shape, with good hearing and visual acuity. Some employers also require a certain strength level—say, the ability to regularly exert 100 pounds of force—since equipment, feed, and the animals themselves can be heavy and often unwieldy.

■ EXPLORING

In addition to formal education, many aquariums, like other types of museums, look for a strong interest in the field before hiring an applicant. Most often, they look for a history of volunteering. That means you need to look for every avenue you can find to work around fish or other animals. Do as much as your schedule allows. Even working part-time or volunteering at a local pet store counts. Also, be sure to ask your career guidance counselor for information on marine science careers and opportunities for summer internships or college scholarships offered by larger institutes.

■ EMPLOYERS

Aquarists most often work in zoos, public aquariums, or in research jobs with marine science institutes.

■ STARTING OUT

Full-time jobs for aquarists can be scarce, especially for those just starting in the field. Part-time or volunteer positions with zoos, aquariums, science institutes, nature centers, or even pet stores could provide valuable preliminary experience that may eventually lead to a full-time position.

■ ADVANCEMENT

The usual career path for an aquarist progresses from intern/volunteer through part-time work to full-fledged aquarist, senior aquarist, supervisor, and finally, curator. Each step along the path requires additional experience and often additional education. Curators generally are expected to have a Ph.D. in a relevant marine science discipline, for example. The career path of an aquarist depends on how much hands-on work they like to do with animals. Other options are available for aquarists who are looking for a less "down and dirty" experience.

■ EARNINGS

Aquariums often are nonprofit institutions, limiting the earnings ability in this job somewhat. In general, aquarists make between $23,000 and $32,000 a year, or between about $11 and $15 per hour. Aquariums do offer fairly extensive benefits, however, including health insurance, 401(k) plans, continuing education opportunities, tuition reimbursement, and reciprocal benefits with many other cultural institutions.

WORK ENVIRONMENT

Aquarists may work indoors or outdoors, depending on the facility for which they work and the exhibit to which they're assigned. Aquarists spend a lot of time in the water. Their day will be filled with a variety of tasks, some repetitive, like feeding, others unusual, such as working with rescued marine mammals, perhaps. In the beginning, aquarists work under the supervision of a senior aquarist or supervisor and may work as part of a team. Aquarists also can expect to travel as part of the job.

OUTLOOK

There is, in general, little change in the availability of positions for aquarists. While terrestrial zoos have begun to add aquarium complexes to their campuses in growing numbers, an actual boom in the construction of new aquariums is unlikely at this time. Many aquarists do advance to other positions, however, so openings do become available.

FOR MORE INFORMATION

For information on careers in aquatic and marine science, including job listings, contact

American Zoo and Aquarium Association
8403 Colesville Road, Suite 710
Silver Spring, MD 20910-3314
Tel: 301-562-0777
Email: generalinquiry@aza.org
http://www.aza.org

For information on guided tours and other opportunities, contact

Columbus Zoo and Aquarium
9990 Riverside Drive
Powell, OH 43065
Tel: 614-645-3550
http://www.colszoo.org

For information on educational programs, summer internships, and courses, contact the following organizations:

Marine Science Center
Northeastern University
430 Nahant Road
Nahant, MA 01908
Tel: 781-581-7370
http://www.dac.neu.edu/msc

Marine Science Institute
500 Discovery Parkway
Redwood City, CA 94063-4715
Tel: 650-364-2760
Email: info@sfbaymsi.org
http://www.sfbaymsi.org

Marine Science Institute
University of Texas at Austin
750 Channel View Drive
Port Aransas, TX 78373-5015
Tel: 361-749-6711
http://www.utmsi.utexas.edu

Arborists

OVERVIEW

Arborists are professionals who practice arboriculture, which is the care of trees and shrubs, especially those found in urban areas. Arborists prune and fertilize trees and other woody plants as well as monitor them for insects and diseases. Arborists are often consulted for various tree-related issues.

HISTORY

Arboriculture developed as a branch of the plant science of horticulture. While related to the study of forestry, arborists view their specimens on an individual level; foresters manage trees as a group.

Trees are important to our environment. Besides releasing oxygen back to our atmosphere, trees enrich our soil with their fallen, decaying leaves, and their roots aid in the prevention of soil erosion. Trees provide shelter and a source of food for many different types of animals. People use trees as ornamentation. Trees are often planted to protect against the wind and glare of the sun, block offensive views, mark property lines, and provide privacy. Trees and shrubs often add considerably to a home's property value.

All trees need proper care and seasonal maintenance. The occupation of *tree surgeon,* as arborists were first known, came from the need for qualified individuals to care for trees and shrubs, as well as woody vines and ground-cover plants. Trees planted in busy city

QUICK FACTS

SCHOOL SUBJECTS
Biology
Earth science

PERSONAL SKILLS
Technical/scientific

WORK ENVIRONMENT
Primarily outdoors
Primarily multiple locations

MINIMUM EDUCATION LEVEL
Bachelor's degree

SALARY RANGE
$16,680 to $25,110 to $40,750+

CERTIFICATION OR LICENSING
Recommended

OUTLOOK
Faster than the average

DOT
408

GOE
03.01.02

NOC
2225

O*NET-SOC
37-3013.00

areas and in the suburbs face pollution, traffic, crowding, extreme temperatures, and other daily hazards. City trees often have a large percentage of their roots covered with concrete. Roots of larger trees sometimes interfere with plumbing pipes, sidewalks, and building foundations. Branches can interfere with buildings or power lines. Trees located along the sides of roads and highways must be maintained; branches are pruned, and fallen leaves and fruit are gathered. Proper intervention, if not prevention, of diseases is an important task of arborists.

THE JOB

Trees and shrubs need more than just sunlight and water. That's where arborists take over. Arborists perform many different tasks for trees and shrubs, some for the sake of maintenance and others for the tree's health and well-being.

Pruning. All trees need some amount of pruning to control their shape; sometimes limbs are trimmed if they interfere with power lines, if they cross property lines, or if they grow too close to houses and other buildings. Arborists may use tools such as pruning shears or hand and power saws to do the actual cutting. If the branches are especially large or cumbersome, arborists may rope them together before the sawing begins. After cutting, the branches can be safely lowered to the ground. Ladders, aerial lifts, and cranes may be used to reach extremely tall trees. Sometimes, arborists need to cable or brace tree limbs weakened by disease or old age or damaged by a storm.

Planting or transplanting. When cities or towns plan a new development, or wish to gentrify an existing one, they often consult with arborists to determine what types of trees to plant. Arborists can suggest trees that will thrive in a certain environment. Young plantings, or immature trees, are more cost effective and are often used, though sometimes, larger, more mature trees are transplanted to the desired location.

Diagnosis and treatment. A large part of keeping a tree healthy is the prevention of disease. There are a number of diseases that affect trees, among them anthracnose and Dutch elm disease. Insects pose a potential threat to trees, and have done considerable damage to certain species in the past, by boring into the trunk or spreading disease-causing organisms. Bacteria, fungi, viruses, and disease-causing organisms can also be fatal enemies of trees. Arborists are specially trained to identify the insect or the disease weakening the tree and apply the necessary remedy or medication. Common methods prescribed by arborists include chemical insecticides, or the use of natural insect predators to combat the problem. Arborists

closely monitor insect migrations or any other situations that may be harmful to a species of tree.

When a tree is too old or badly diseased, arborists may choose to cut it down. Arborists will carefully cut the tree into pieces to prevent injury to people or damage to surrounding property.

Prevention. Trees, especially young plantings, often need extra nourishment. Arborists are trained to apply fertilizers, both natural and chemical, in a safe and environmentally friendly manner. Arborists are also hired by golf courses and parks to install lightning protection systems for lone trees or mature, valuable trees.

REQUIREMENTS
High School

High school biology classes can provide you with a solid background to be a successful arborist. An interest in gardening, conservation, or the outdoors is also helpful.

Postsecondary Training

Take classes in botany, chemistry, horticulture, and plant pathology. Several colleges and universities offer programs in arboriculture and other related fields such as landscape design, nursery stock production, or grounds and turf maintenance. Entry-level positions such as assistants or climbers do not need a college degree for employment. Advanced education, however, is highly desired if you plan to make this field your career.

Certification or Licensing

The National Arborist Association (NAA) and the International Society of Arboriculture (ISA) both offer various home study courses and books on arboriculture. Most arborists are certified or licensed. Licensure ensures an arborist meets the state's regulations for working with pesticides and herbicides. Check with your local government—not all states require arborists to be licensed. Certification, given by the ISA after completion of required training and education, is considered by many as a measure of an arborist's skill and experience in the industry. Today's savvy consumers specifically look for certified arborists when it comes to caring for their trees and other precious landscaping plants. Arborists need to apply for recertification every three years and must complete 30 units of continuing education classes and seminars.

EXPLORING

Interested in this field? Surfing the Internet can provide a wealth of information for you to browse. Log onto the websites of the NAA or ISA for industry and career information. If you really want to test the waters, why not find summer work with an arborist? You'll earn extra spending money while at the same learning about the industry firsthand. Check with the NAA for a complete listing of certified arborists in your area.

■ EMPLOYERS

Landscaping companies and businesses that offer a host of expert tree services are common employers of arborists. Employment opportunities are also available with municipal governments, botanical gardens, and arboretums. For example, an arborist in the Chicago area may want to seek a position with the Chicago Botanic Gardens or the Morton Arboretum; both places are known for their lush gardens and wooded trails. According to the Department of Labor, there were about 59,000 arborists in the United States in 2002.

■ STARTING OUT

So you've decided to become an arborist—what's the next step? Start by compiling a list of tree care firms in your area, then send your resume or fill out an application to the companies that interest you. You should also consider employment with the highway or park department of your city or county—they often hire crews to maintain their trees.

Many colleges and universities offer job placement services, or they at least post employment opportunities in their office. Industry associations and trade magazines are often good sources of job openings.

Don't plan to climb to the top of an American elm your first day on the job. Expect to stay at ground level, at least for a few days. Trainees in this industry start as *helpers* or *ground workers,* who load and unload equipment from trucks, gather branches and other debris for disposal, handle ropes, and give assistance to climbers. They also operate the chipper—a machine that cuts large branches into small chips. After some time observing more experienced workers, trainees are allowed to climb smaller trees or the lower limbs of large trees. They are also taught the proper way to operate large machinery and climbing gear. Most companies provide on-the-job training that lasts from one to three months.

■ ADVANCEMENT

Experienced arborists can advance to supervisory positions such as crew manager or department supervisor. Another option is to become a consultant in the field and work for tree care firms, city or town boards, large nurseries, or gardening groups.

Arborists with a strong entrepreneurial nature can choose to open their own business, but aspiring entrepreneurs must make sure that their business skills are up to par. Even the most talented and hard-working arborists won't stand a chance if they can't balance their accounts or market their services properly.

Advancement to other industries related to arboriculture is another possibility. Some arborists choose to work in landscape design, forestry, or other fields of horticulture.

■ EARNINGS

The Department of Labor's *Occupational Outlook Handbook* lists the 2002 average yearly salary of arborists as $12.92 an hour, or $26,870 a year. The median salary was $25,110 a year, with the bottom 10 percent earning $16,680 a year or less, and 10 percent earning $40,750 a year or more.

According to Derick Vanice, ISA's director of education programs, entry-level positions, such as grounds workers or trainees, can earn between $7 to $10 an hour; supervisors, with three or more years of experience, earn from $20 to $30 an hour; private consultants with eight to 10 years of experience, or arborists in sales positions, can earn $50,000 to $60,000 or more annually. Salaries vary greatly depending on many factors, among them the size of the company, the region, and the experience of the arborist. Arborists servicing busy urban areas tend to earn more.

Full-time employees receive a benefits package including health insurance, life insurance, paid vacation and sick time, and paid holidays. Most tree companies supply necessary uniforms, tools, equipment, and training.

■ WORK ENVIRONMENT

Much of an arborist's work is physically demanding, and most of it is done outdoors. Arborists work throughout the year, though their busiest time is in the spring and summer. Tasks done at this time include fertilizing, pruning, and prevention spraying. During the winter months, arborists can expect to care for trees injured or damaged by excess snow, ice storms, or floods.

Equipment such as sharp saws, grinders, chippers, bulldozers, tractors, and other large machinery can be potentially dangerous for arborists. There is also the risk of falling from the top of a tall tree, many of which reach heights of 50 feet or more. Arborists rely on cleated shoes, security belts, and safety hoists to make their job easier as well as safer.

■ OUTLOOK

The future of arboriculture has never looked so promising. The public's increasing interest in the planning and the preservation of the environment has increased demand for qualified arborists. Many homeowners are willing to pay top dollar for professionally designed and maintained landscaping. According to Gallup's 1999 U.S. Homeowner Landscaping, Lawn Care, and Tree Care Survey, 24 million homeowners in the United States spent approximately $17.4 billion on professional landscape and care. Research from Clemson University found that homes with professional landscaping sell for 6 to 7 percent higher than homes with lesser quality landscaping.

Increased resistance to pesticides and new species of insects pose constant threats to all trees. While travel abroad is easier and, in a sense, has made our world smaller, it has also placed our environment at risk. For example, Asian long-horn beetles were unknowingly transported to the United States via packing material. By the time the insects were discovered, the beetles had irreversibly damaged hundreds of mature trees throughout New York, Chicago, and surrounding areas. Arborists, especially those trained to diagnose and treat such cases, will be in demand to work in urban areas.

■ FOR MORE INFORMATION

For industry and career information, or to receive a copy of Arborist News *or* Careers in Arboriculture, *contact*

International Society of Arboriculture
PO 3129
Champaign, IL 61826-3129
Tel: 217-355-9411
Email: isa@isa-arbor.com
http://www2.champaign.isa-arbor.com

For industry and career information, a listing of practicing arborists, or educational programs at the university level, or home study, contact

National Arborist Association Inc.
3 Perimeter Road, Unit 1
Manchester, NH 03103
Tel: 800-733-2622
Email: NAA@natlarb.com
http://www.natlarb.com

For industry information, membership requirements, contact

Society of Municipal Arborists
PO Box 641
Watkinsville, GA 30677
Tel: 706-769-7412
Email: urbanforestry@prodigy.net
http://www.urban-forestry.com

Archaeologists

■ OVERVIEW

Archaeologists study the origin and evolution of humans. They study the physical evidence of human culture, examining such items as tools, burial sites, buildings, religious icons, pottery, and clothing.

■ HISTORY

It wasn't until the 19th century that archaeology became an established discipline. The subjects of study in the field range from fossils of humans of 4.5 million years ago to the concerns of contemporary city-dwellers. The excavation of archaeological sites has provided information about the Ice Age, the development of agriculture, the civilizations of the ancient Egyptians and the Anasazi, and other historical cultures and events. In the 1870s, Heinrich Schliemann did some early work, excavating sites in Greece and Turkey that he believed to be the city of Troy described in Homer's *Iliad*. (It was later determined that the artifacts of the area were actually 1,000 years too old to have been part of Troy.) Arguably the most famous archeological excavation involved the tomb of the Egyptian pharaoh Tutankhamun, which was discovered by British archeologist Howard Carter in 1922.

These excavations, and others before the 1960s, were large in scale. Archaeologists preferred to clear as much land as possible, hoping to uncover more artifacts. But today's archaeologists understand that much can be lost in an excavation, and they limit their studies to smaller areas. With radar, sensors, and other technologies, archaeologists can discover a great deal about a site without any actual digging.

■ THE JOB

Archaeology is concerned with the study and comparison of people in all parts of the world, their physical characteristics, customs, languages, traditions, material possessions, and social and religious beliefs and practices. At most universities, archaeology is considered a branch of anthropology.

Archaeologists play an important role in the areas of anthropology, especially cultural anthropology. They apply specialized techniques to construct a record of past cultures by studying, classifying, and interpreting artifacts such as pottery, clothing, tools, weapons, and ornaments, to determine cultural identity. They obtain these artifacts through excavation of sites including buildings and cities, and they establish the chronological sequence of the development of each culture from simpler to more advanced levels. *Prehistoric archaeologists* study cultures that existed prior to the period of recorded history, while *historical archaeologists* study more recent societies. The historic period spans several thousand years in some parts of the world and sometimes only a few hundred years in others. *Classical archaeologists* concentrate on ancient Mediterranean and Middle Eastern cultures. Through the study of the history of specific groups of peoples whose societies may be extinct, archaeologists are able to reconstruct their cultures, including the pattern of daily life.

As faculty members of colleges and universities, archaeologists lecture on the subject, work with research assistants, and publish books and articles. Those who work outside of academia, such as for corporations and government agencies, have a variety of duties and responsibilities.

Though Thomas F. King, an archaeologist in Maryland, does travel across the country to teach and consult, most of his work is focused on cultural resource management. "The cultural resource laws of this and other nations," King says, "are designed to try to make sure that 'cultural resources' such as archeological sites, historic buildings, culturally valued landscapes, and culturally valued ways of life aren't thoughtlessly destroyed in the course of modern development." This involves prescribing various kinds of planning and review processes whenever a federal agency plans to do something that might harm a resource.

As a senior archaeologist in the field, King has published the book *Cultural Resource Laws and Practice: An Introductory Guide* (Lanham, Md.: AltaMira Press, 1998). "Most of my time is spent reading and writing documents, reviewing reports, meeting with people, etc.," he says.

He also works outside of cultural resource management as the chief archaeologist on The Amelia Earhart Project of The International Group for Historic Aircraft Recovery. King explains, "It's an interdisciplinary study of the fate of the lost aviatrix, whom we think ended up on a remote South Pacific island. In this effort, we do all kinds of historical, oral-historical, archaeological, and other kinds of research."

The research involves such unique tools as robotic submersibles, ultralight aircraft, and electromagnetic resistivity meters. "But fieldwork on that project, as opposed to other kinds of research, occurs only about every two years, as we raise the money. Fundraising goes on constantly," he says.

Archaeologists often must travel extensively to perform field work on the site where a culture once flourished. Site work is often slow and laborious. It may take years to uncover artifacts from an archaeological dig that produce valuable information. Another important aspect of archaeology is the cleaning, restoration, and preservation of artifacts. This work sometimes takes place on the site of discovery to minimize deterioration of textiles and mummified remains. Careful recording of the exact location and condition of artifacts is essential for further study.

■ REQUIREMENTS
High School

Follow your high school's college prep program to prepare for undergraduate and graduate programs in archaeology. You should study English composition and literature to develop your writing and interpretation skills. Foreign language skills will also help you in later research in other countries. Take classes in history and art to learn more about ancient and classical civilizations. Although it may seem that you'll be working mostly with fossils and ancient artifacts, you'll need computer skills to work with the many advanced technologies used in archaeological excavations. Mathematics and science courses can help you develop the skills you'll need in analyzing information and statistics.

Postsecondary Training

Most of the better positions in archaeology require a doctorate, which takes about four to six years of work beyond the bachelor's degree. Before beginning graduate work, however, you will study such basic courses as psychology, sociology, history, geography, mathematics, logic, English composition, and literature, as well as modern and ancient languages. Archaeology departments are typically part of anthropology departments; few separate archaeology departments exist in U.S. colleges and universities. As a student of archaeology, you'll follow a program that involves many disciplines, including art, architecture, classics, and history.

Because most archaeology graduates receive their first jobs through their graduate work, you should select a graduate school that has a good program in the area in which you hope to specialize.

THE AMELIA EARHART PROJECT

The International Group for Historic Aircraft Recovery (TIGHAR; pronounced "tiger") is behind The Earhart Project (mentioned in "The Job" section by Chief Anthropologist Thomas F. King). Over the years, members of TIGHAR have undertaken several expeditions to the island of Nikumaroro and the surrounding area, where it is believed Amelia Earhart crash-landed in her effort to circle the globe in 1937. The sudden disappearance of the world's most famous aviatrix, and the surrounding mysteries and myths, have haunted generations of archaeologists and historians. TIGHAR researchers have recovered various items from the area, including the remains of a shoe that appeared to be the same size and style worn by Earhart. Later analysis, however, led experts to conclude that "the shoe doesn't fit." In 2001, TIGHAR members led another expedition to the island and recovered glass and lightweight metal technology artifacts (small metal plates, a screw, and such). No human remains were found, but analysis of the newly recovered artifacts continues. To learn more about The Earhart Project and the other projects sponsored by TIGHAR, visit the website at http://www.tighar.org

Other Requirements

To succeed in archaeology, you need to be able to work well as part of a team and on your own. In order to be passionate about your study and research, you should be naturally curious and have a desire for knowledge. Communication skills are paramount, both for writing your reports and presenting your findings clearly and completely to professionals in the field.

■ EXPLORING

To explore your interest in archaeology, see if your local Boy Scout and Girl Scout group participate in camping or hiking expeditions. A trip to a museum also will introduce you to the world of archaeology. Better yet, see if your local museum offers part-time work or volunteer opportunities. You should also visit the website of the Earthwatch Institute (http://www.earthwatch.org) to learn more about its many exploration trips to locations as close as North America to as far as Africa or Asia.

■ EMPLOYERS

Archaeologists work for universities and community colleges. They also work for museums that may be independent or affiliated with universities. Government agencies, such as the National Park Service and state his-

toric preservation offices, employ archaeologists. More and more archaeologists are finding jobs in the private sector, for consulting firms, environmental companies, and other businesses.

■ STARTING OUT

You may have an opportunity to work as a research assistant or a teaching fellow while in graduate school, and frequently this experience is of tremendous help in qualifying for your first job. Your graduate school professors should be able to help you establish contacts in the field.

While in school, you should also be involved in internships to gain experience. Internship opportunities may be available through your graduate program, or you may have to seek them out yourself. You can check with your state's archaeological society or the National Forest Service to find out about volunteer opportunities.

■ ADVANCEMENT

Because of the relatively small size of this field, advancement opportunities can be scarce. Most archaeology teachers start as assistant professors, and move into associate professor, and possibly full professor positions. Archaeology researchers at the college level have the opportunity to head research areas and to gain recognition among colleagues as an expert in many areas of study.

Those working in museums also have an opportunity to advance within the institution in terms of higher pay or increased responsibility. Archaeologists working outside academia and museums will be promoted according to the standards of the individual companies and organizations for which they work.

■ EARNINGS

A large percentage of archaeologists work in academia. A 2002–03 survey by the American Association of University Professors reported that the average salary for full professors with Ph.D.'s was $97,910 a year.

For those working in the field, salaries ranged widely. The Bureau of Labor Statistics reports that the median annual salaries for archaeologists and anthropologists were $38,620 in 2002. The lowest 10 percent earned less than $23,520; the highest 10 percent earned more than $67,740.

■ WORK ENVIRONMENT

Archaeologists working in educational facilities have normally clean, well lighted, and ventilated environments. Those working in the field may work in a tougher environment, working in all types of weather and, depending on the area to which they are assigned, they may deal with potentially difficult living conditions.

Archaeologists work about 40 hours a week, and the hours may be irregular. Physical strength and stamina is necessary for field work of all types. Those working on excavations, for instance, may work during most of the daylight hours and spend the evening planning the next day's activities. Excavation work may be tough, but most find the work interesting and well worth the irregular hours or primitive living conditions.

"You can convince yourself that you're doing something good for the world, trying to get important stuff preserved," King says, citing the pros and cons of the work, "but it's possible to get pretty cynical about the whole business, since preserving stuff is, on balance, often a losing game."

■ OUTLOOK

"Recognize that the number of Indiana Jones jobs available are strictly limited," King advises. "On the other hand, there are lots more jobs than there used to be in 'applied' archaeology, in the context of cultural resource management. Think about being more than an archaeologist. If you can also do cultural anthropology, history, geomorphology, law, or politics, your career opportunities will expand exponentially."

The U.S. Department of Labor predicts that employment for archaeologists will grow about as fast as the average for all other occupations through 2012. Since the academic job market is poor, most new jobs in the near future will probably be nonteaching positions in consulting firms, research institutes, corporations, and federal, state, and local government agencies. Among the factors contributing to this growth is increased environmental, historic, and cultural preservation legislation. There is a particular demand for people with the ability to write environmental impact statements.

Overall, the number of job applicants for university faculty positions will be greater than the number of openings available. Competition will be great even for those with doctorates who are seeking faculty positions, and many will find only temporary or nontenured jobs.

■ FOR MORE INFORMATION

The following organization offers valuable information about anthropological careers and student associations.

American Anthropological Association
2200 Wilson Boulevard, Suite 600
Arlington, VA 22201
Tel: 703-528-1902
http://www.aaanet.org

Archaeologists often spend their summers on-site at digs. This one is the Koster Dig in southern Illinois.

To learn more about the Student Challenge Awards, and the other programs available, contact

Earthwatch Institute
3 Clock Tower Place, Suite 100
Box 75
Maynard, MA 01754
Tel: 800-776-0188
Email: info@earthwatch.org
http://www.earthwatch.org

To learn about field excavations and specific programs, contact

Archaeological Research Institute
PO Box 853
Bountiful, UT 84011-0853
Tel: 801-292-7061
http://www.ari-aerc.org

VISUAL ARCHAEOLOGY

Even artifacts of our own recent past can get easily lost in our rapidly paced society. With that in mind, Frank Jump has scaled walls and crawled over fences to photograph the old painted advertisements fading from the walls of the buildings of New York City. These images, which he considers "visual archaeology," feature ads for Fletcher's Castoria, Baby Ruth candy bars, bobby pins, and Seely shoulder shapes. Some ads have faded partially to reveal other ads, creating multiple images. The photos have been exhibited at the New York Historical Society, they are the subject of a photography book Jump is creating, and they are part of his efforts to preserve the ads.

For information on archaeological careers and job listings, contact

Society for American Archaeology
900 Second Street, NE, Suite 12
Washington, DC 20002-3557
Tel: 202-789-8200
Email: headquarters@saa.org
http://www.saa.org

For an overview of the career of archaeologist written by an associate professor of anthropology, visit

Frequently Asked Questions About a Career in Archaeology in the U.S.

http://www.museum.state.il.us/ismdepts/anthro/dlcfaq
.html

Architects

■ OVERVIEW

Architects plan, design, and observe construction of facilities used for human occupancy and of other structures. They consult with clients, plan layouts of buildings, prepare drawings of proposed buildings, write specifications, and prepare scale and full-sized drawings. Architects also may help clients to obtain bids, select a contractor, and negotiate the construction contract, and they also visit construction sites to ensure that the work is being completed according to specification. There are approximately 92,350 architects working in the United States.

■ HISTORY

Architecture began not with shelters for people to live in but with the building of religious structures—from Stonehenge in England and the pyramids in Egypt to pagodas in Japan and the Parthenon in Greece. It was the Romans who developed a new building method—concrete vaulting—that made possible large cities with permanent masonry buildings. As they extended the Roman Empire, they built for public and military purposes. They developed and built apartment buildings, law courts, public baths, theaters, and circuses. The industrial revolution with its demand for factories and mills developed iron and steel construction, which evolved into the steel and glass skyscraper of today.

Because the history of architecture follows that of human civilization, the architecture of any period reflects the culture of its people. Architecture of early periods has influenced that of later centuries, including the work of contemporary architects. The field continues to develop as new techniques and materials are discovered and as architects blend creativity with function.

■ THE JOB

The architect normally has two responsibilities: to design a building that will satisfy the client and to protect the public's health, safety, and welfare. This second responsibility requires architects to be licensed by the state in which they work. Meeting the first responsibility involves many steps. The job begins with learning what the client wants. The architect takes many factors into consideration, including local and state building and design regulations, climate, soil on which the building is to be constructed, zoning laws, fire regulations, and the client's financial limitations.

The architect then prepares a set of plans that, upon the client's approval, will be developed into final design and construction documents. The final design shows the exact dimensions of every portion of the building, including the location and size of columns and beams, electrical outlets and fixtures, plumbing, heating and air-conditioning facilities, windows, and doors. The architect works closely with consulting engineers on the specifics of the plumbing, heating, air conditioning, and electrical work to be done.

The architect then assists the client in getting bids from general contractors, one of whom will be selected to construct the building to the specifications. The architect helps the client through the completion of the construction and occupancy phases, making certain the correct materials are used and that the drawings and specifications are faithfully followed.

Throughout the process the architect works closely with a design or project team. This team is usually made up of the following: *designers,* who specialize in design development; a *structural designer,* who designs the frame of the building in accordance with the work of the architect; the *project manager* or *job superintendent,* who sees that the full detail drawings are completed to the satisfaction of the architect; and the *specification writer* and *estimator,* who prepare a project manual that describes in more detail the materials to be used in the building, their quality and method of installation, and all details related to the construction of the building.

The architect's job is very complex. He or she is expected to know construction methods, engineering principles and practices, and materials. Architects also must be up to date on new design and construction techniques and procedures. Although architects once spent most of their time designing buildings for the wealthy, they are now more often involved in the design of housing developments, individual dwellings, supermarkets, industrial plants, office buildings, shopping centers, air terminals, schools, banks, museums, churches, and dozens of other types of buildings.

Architects may specialize in any one of a number of fields, including building appraisal, city planning, teaching, architectural journalism, furniture design, lighting design, or government service. Regardless of the area of specialization, the architect's major task is that of understanding the client's needs and then reconciling them into a meaningful whole.

■ REQUIREMENTS
High School

To prepare for this career while in high school, take a college preparatory program that includes courses in English, mathematics, physics, art (especially freehand drawing), social studies, history, and foreign languages. Courses in business and computer science also will be useful.

Postsecondary Training

Because most state architecture registration boards require a professional degree, high school students are advised, early in their senior year, to apply for admission to a professional program that is accredited by the National Architectural Accrediting Board. Competition to enter these programs is high. Grades, class rank, and aptitude and achievement scores count heavily in determining who will be accepted.

Most schools of architecture offer degrees through either a five-year bachelor's program or a three- or four-year master's program. The majority of architecture students seek out the bachelor's degree in architecture, going from high school directly into a five-year program. Though this is the fastest route, you should be certain that you want to study architecture. Because the programs are so specialized, it is difficult to transfer to another field of study if you change your mind. The master's degree option allows for more flexibility but takes longer to complete. In this case, students first earn a liberal arts degree then continue their training by completing a master's program in architecture.

A typical college architecture program includes courses in architectural history and theory, the technical and legal aspects of building design, science, and liberal arts.

Certification or Licensing

All states and the District of Columbia require that individuals be licensed before contracting to provide architectural services in that particular state. Though many work in the field without licensure, only licensed architects are required to take legal responsibility for all work. Using a licensed architect for a project is, therefore, less risky than using an unlicensed one. Architects who are licensed usually take on projects with larger responsibilities and have greater chances to advance to managerial or executive positions.

The requirements for registration include graduation from an accredited school of architecture and three years of practical experience (called an internship) with a licensed architect. After these requirements are met, individuals can take the rigorous four-day Architect Registration Examination. Some states require architects to maintain their licensing through continued education. These individuals may complete a certain number of credits every year or two through seminars, workshops, university classes, self-study courses, or other sources.

In addition to becoming licensed, a growing number of architects choose to obtain certification by the National Council of Architecture Registration Boards. If an architect plans to work in more than one state, obtaining this certification can make it easier to become licensed in different states.

Other Requirements

If you are interested in architecture, you should be intelligent, observant, responsible, and self-disciplined. You should have a concern for detail and accuracy, be able to communicate effectively both orally and in writing, and be able to accept criticism constructively. Although great artistic ability is not necessary, you should be able to visualize spatial relationships and have the capacity to solve technical problems. Mathematical ability is also important. In addition, you should possess organizational skills and leadership qualities and be able to work well with others.

■ EXPLORING

Most architects will welcome the opportunity to talk with young people interested in entering architecture. You may be able to visit their offices to can gain a firsthand knowledge of the type of work done by architects. You can also visit a design studio of a

QUICK FACTS

SCHOOL SUBJECTS
Art
Mathematics

PERSONAL SKILLS
Artistic
Communication/ideas

WORK ENVIRONMENT
Primarily indoors
Primarily one location

MINIMUM EDUCATION LEVEL
Bachelor's degree

SALARY RANGE
$36,280 to $56,620 to $92,350 +

CERTIFICATION OR LICENSING
Required

OUTLOOK
About as fast as the average

DOT
001

GOE
02.07.03

NOC
2151

O*NET-SOC
17-1011.00

MIES VAN DER ROHE

A giant of 20th-century modern architecture was Ludwig Mies van der Rohe, who designed steel and glass structures in simple geometric forms. His sleek, modern office towers with steel bones and glass skins captured the spirit of the times and set the standard for American corporate architecture. "Architecture," Mies said, "is the will of an epoch translated into space—living, changing, new." The 21st century now challenges its new architects to define the new era.

school of architecture or work for an architect or building contractor during summer vacations. Also, many architecture schools offer summer programs for high school students. Books and magazines on architecture also can give you a broad understanding of the nature of the work and the values of the profession.

■ EMPLOYERS

Of the 92,350 architects working in the United States in 2002, most are employed by architectural firms or other firms related to the construction industry. About one in five architects, however, are self-employed—the ultimate dream of many people in the profession. A few develop graphic design, interior design, or product specialties. Still others put their training to work in the theater, film, or television fields, or in museums, display firms, and architectural product and materials manufacturing companies. A small number are employed in government agencies such as the Departments of Defense, Interior, and Housing and Urban Development and the General Services Administration.

■ STARTING OUT

Students entering architecture following graduation start as interns in an architectural office. As interns, they assist in preparing architectural construction documents. They also handle related details, such as administering contracts, coordinating the work of other professionals on the project, researching building codes and construction materials, and writing specifications. As an alternative to working for an architectural firm, some architecture graduates go into allied fields such as construction, engineering, interior design, landscape architecture, or real estate development.

■ ADVANCEMENT

Interns and architects alike are given progressively more complex jobs. Architects may advance to supervisory or

managerial positions. Some architects become partners in established firms, while others take steps to establish their own practice.

■ EARNINGS

Architects earned a median annual salary of $56,620 in 2002, according to the U.S. Department of Labor. The lowest paid 10 percent earned less than $36,280 annually, while the highest paid 10 percent earned $92,350 or more.

The American Institute of Architects (AIA) reports that the starting annual salary for graduates of schools of architecture working during their internship before licensing was approximately $30,000 in 2002.

Well-established architects who are partners in an architectural firm or who have their own businesses generally earn much more than salaried employees. According to the AIA, partners in very large firms can earn $132,000 or more a year. Most employers offer such fringe benefits as health insurance, sick and vacation pay, and retirement plans.

■ WORK ENVIRONMENT

Architects normally work a 40-hour week. There may be a number of times when they will have to work overtime, especially when under pressure to complete an assignment. Self-employed architects work less regular hours and often meet with clients in their homes or offices during the evening. Architects usually work in comfortable offices, but they may spend a considerable amount of time outside the office visiting clients or viewing the progress of a particular job in the field. Their routines usually vary considerably.

■ OUTLOOK

Employment in the field is expected to grow about as fast as the average through 2012, according to the U.S. Department of Labor. The number of architects needed will depend on the volume of construction. The construction industry is extremely sensitive to fluctuations in the overall economy, and a continued bad economic climate could result in layoffs. On the positive side, employment of architects is not likely to be affected by the growing use of computer technologies. Rather than replacing architects, computers are being used to enhance the architect's work.

Competition for employment will continue to be strong, particularly in prestigious architectural firms. Openings will not be newly created positions but will become available as the workload increases and established architects transfer to other occupations or leave the field.

INTERVIEW

Ryan Cain is a junior architect in the New York City area.

Q. How did you decide to become an architect?

A. When I was seven years old my older sister told me I would make a good architect because I was loud enough for people to hear me easily on a construction site. When I was 16 my high-school social studies teacher showed us a video on the Russian Revolution. During that time architecture was used to instill feelings of community, stability, and power into a very depressed country. That was the first time I became interested in architecture; my decision to become an architect came after another year of looking into the profession and schools.

Q. What are your main job responsibilities?

A. My job includes a very broad scope of activities: I design elevations and floor plans for office buildings; draw up details for just about every part of a building; draft floor plans and office layouts; and I even make blueprints of drawings and mail them to the clients. Architects do the jobs of many different professions: We are designers, plumbers, engineers, electricians, and graphic designers all wrapped into one. We do not have to be experts at each of these professions, but we need to have a good grasp on all of them.

Q. What type of training and education did you pursue to work in this field? Did you complete an internship?

A. This is what turns most people off to the field. To become an architect you need to complete a professional degree in the field—either a five-year professional degree or a four-year bachelor's degree followed by a two-year master's degree. After that you are required to complete an internship that supposedly only takes three years to complete, but which usually takes four or five years (due to the many hours of different kinds of work required). When you have finished and received highly documented proof of all of this, you must take a four-part test, each part taking eight to ten hours. After that you need to complete continuing-education credits: Basically you have to take a set number of classes per year to maintain your license.

Q. What would you say are the pros and cons of your job?

A. Pros: You get to design something that will be around for years after you are gone. It's always an interesting job, it changes every day with every project, and it is very rewarding. When the day is done you have something real to show for it.

Cons: You really don't get paid as well as you should for the amount of schooling you complete, the hours you put into it, and the stress involved. It's a lot of work, and it pays well, just not as well as most people think.

Q. What would you say are the most important skills and personal qualities for someone in your field?

A. There is a wide variety of skills invovled. Architect Le Corbusier was a painter; Santiago Calatrava is an engineer; many others are sculptors, musicians, and so forth. So I guess being artistic is a basic requirement. I excelled in math, science, and art, so I chose this profession because it combined those three interests.

As far as personal qualities go, being an honest, caring person is almost a requirement these days for becoming an architect. During your internship you have to complete a number of hours of community service or volunteer work to maintain professionalism. Ethics are also very important. For example, it is illegal for architects to advertise; also, if you are or ever were convicted of any level of felony, it is very possible that your license will be rejected, even if you have met all the other requirements to become an architect.

Q. How would someone starting out go about finding work in this field?

A. You can often find jobs through your school, which offers work-study programs and job fairs. But the number-one resource for job leads is your professors. Many times the connections you make with teachers enable you to get a foot in the door of many firms around the world. I chose a somewhat different path that allowed me to do things on my own. I moved to New York City and found a job using nothing but references from school. It was something I needed to do before going back to school for my master's. Once I receive my master's degree I will use the connections I have made either through work or school to start my career.

Q. What advice would you give to someone who is interested in pursuing this type of career?

A. Practice and try to excel at some type artwork, be it painting, drawing, dance, music, or fashion. What you learn there will prepare you for the lifelong journey of becoming an architect. Most architects don't make a name for themselves until they are 50. It takes a long time to learn everything there is to know about this profession, so start with art: It will give you an appreciation and an eye for the profession that will help you succeed. Also, don't enter the profession for the money, as you will be disappointed. The job itself should be reason enough to pursue it. You have to love being an architect, otherwise you will find yourself doing a lot of work with little reward.

Archivists

■ OVERVIEW

Archivists contribute to the study of the arts and sciences by analyzing, acquiring, and preserving historical documents, artwork, organizational and personal records, and information systems that are significant enough to be preserved for future generations. Archivists keep track of artifacts such as letters, contracts, photographs, filmstrips, blueprints, electronic information, and other items of potential historical significance.

■ HISTORY

For centuries, archives have served as repositories for the official records of governments, educational institutions, businesses, religious organizations, families, and countless other groups. From the first time information was recorded, a need for preserving those accounts has been necessary. The evolution of archiving information in a manner similar to what we know today can be traced back to the Middle Ages.

As the feudal system in Europe gave way to nations and a more systematic order of law, precise record keeping became increasingly important to keep track of land ownership and official policy. These records helped governments serve the needs of their nations and protected the rights of the common people in civil matters.

In America, early settlers maintained records using skills they brought from their European homelands. Families kept records of the journey to their new country and saved correspondence with family members still in Europe. Religious institutions kept records of the births, deaths, and marriages of their members. Settlers kept track of their business transactions, such as a land purchases, crop trades, and building constructions.

In the early 18th century, similar to what occurred in Europe in the Middle Ages, civic records in America became more prevalent as towns became incorporated. Leaders needed to maintain accurate records of property ownership and laws made by—and for—citizens.

Although archives have been incorporated in one form or another for centuries, archivists have established themselves as professionals only in the last hundred years or so. In the past, museums and societies accumulated records and objects rapidly and sometimes indiscriminately, accepting items regardless of their actual merit. Each archive had its own system of documenting, organizing, and storing materials. In 1884, the American Historical Association was formed to develop archival standards and help boost interaction among archivists.

An architect reviews blueprints at a construction site.

■ FOR MORE INFORMATION

For information on education, scholarships, and student membership opportunities, contact the following organizations:

American Institute of Architects

1735 New York Avenue, NW
Washington, DC 20006
Tel: 800-AIA-3837
Email: infocentral@aia.org
http://www.aia.org

American Institute of Architecture Students

1735 New York Avenue, NW
Washington, DC 20006
Tel: 202-626-7472
Email: mail@aiasnatl.org
http://www.aiasnatl.org

Association of Collegiate Schools of Architecture

1735 New York Avenue, NW
Washington, DC 20006
Tel: 202-785-2324
Email: vlove@acsa-arch.org
http://www.acsa-arch.org

Each year, as new scientific discoveries are made and new works are published, the need for sifting through and classifying items increases. More advanced computer systems will help archivists catalog archival materials as well as make archives more readily available to users. Advances in conservation techniques will help extend the life of fragile items, allowing them to be available to future generations.

■ THE JOB

Archivists analyze documents and materials such as government records, minutes of corporate board meetings, letters from famous people, charters of nonprofit foundations, historical photographs, maps, coins, works of art, and nearly anything else that may have historical significance. To determine which documents should be saved, they consider such factors as when the resource was written, who wrote it, and for whom it was written. In deciding on other items to archive, the archivist needs to consider the provenance, or history of creation and ownership, of the materials. They also take into account the physical capacity of their employer's archives. For instance, a repository with very little space for new materials may need to decline the gift of a large or bulky item, despite its potential value.

Archives are kept by various organizations, including government agencies, corporations, universities, and museums, and the value of documents is generally dictated by whichever group owns them. For example, the U.S. Army may not be interested in General Motors' corporate charter, and General Motors may not be interested in a Civil War battle plan. Archivists understand and serve the needs of their employers and collect items that are most relevant to their organizations.

Archivists may also be in charge of collecting items of historical significance to the institution for which they work. An archivist at a university, for instance, may collect new copies of the student newspaper to keep historical documentation of student activities and issues up to date. An archivist at a public library may prepare, present, and store annual reports of the branch libraries in order to keep an accurate record of library statistics.

After selecting appropriate materials, archivists help make them accessible to others by preparing reference aids such as indexes, guides, bibliographies, descriptions, and microfilmed copies of documents. These research aids may be printed up and kept in the organization's stack area, put online so off-site researchers have access to the information, or put on CD-ROM for distribution to other individuals or organizations. Archivists also file and cross-index archived items for easy retrieval when a user wishes to consult a collection.

Archivists may preserve and repair historical documents or send damaged items to a professional conservator. They may also appraise the items based on their knowledge of political, economic, military, and social history, as well as by the materials' physical condition, research potential, and rarity.

Archivists play an integral role in the exhibition programs of their organizations. A university library, for instance, may present an exhibit that honors former Nobel Prize-winning faculty members. Most accomplished faculty members leave their papers—notes, research, experiments, and articles—to their institution. An exhibition might display first drafts of articles, early versions of experiments, or letters between two distinguished scientists debating some aspect of a project's design. Exhibits allow members of the university and the community to learn about the history of an organization and how research has advanced the field. The archivist helps to sort through archival materials and decide what items would make for an interesting exhibition at the institution.

Many archivists conduct research using the archival materials at their disposal, and they may publish articles detailing their findings. They may advise government agencies, scholars, journalists, and others conducting research by supplying available materials and information. Archivists also act as reference contacts and teachers. An employee doing research at the company archives may have little knowledge of how and where to begin. The archivist may suggest the worker consult specific reference guides or browse through an online catalog. After the employee decides which materials will be of most use, the archivist may retrieve the archives from storage, circulate the collection to the user, and perhaps even instruct the user as to the proper handling of fragile or oversize materials.

Archivists may have assistants who help them with the sorting and indexing of archival collections. At a university library, undergraduate or graduate students usually act as archival assistants. Small community historical societies may rely on trained volunteers to assist the archivist.

Depending on the size of their employing organization, archivists may perform many or few administrative duties. Such duties may include preparing budgets, representing their institutions at scientific or association conferences, soliciting support for institutions, and interviewing and hiring personnel. Some help formulate and interpret institutional policy. In addition, archivists may plan or participate in special research projects and write articles for scientific journals.

■ REQUIREMENTS
High School

If you are interested in doing archival work, high school is not too early to begin your training. Since it is usually necessary to earn a master's degree to become an archivist, you should select a college preparatory curriculum in high school and plan on going to college. While in high school, you should pay special attention to learning library and research skills. Classes in English, history, science, and mathematics will provide you with basic skills and knowledge for university study. Journalism courses will hone your research skills, and political science courses will help you identify events of societal importance. You should also plan on learning at least one foreign language. If you are interested in doing archival work at a religious organization, Latin or Hebrew may be good language options. If you would like to work in a specialized archive, such as an art gallery or medical school archive, you should also focus on classes that will prepare you for that specialty.

Postsecondary Training

To prepare for archival work in college, you should get a degree in the liberal arts. You will probably want to study history, library science, or a related field, since there are currently no undergraduate or graduate programs that deal solely with the archival sciences. You should take any specific courses in archival methods that are available to you as an undergraduate. Since many employers prefer to hire archivists with a graduate degree, consider any course load that may help you gain entrance into a program to earn a master's degree in library and information science or history.

Graduate school will give you the opportunity to learn more specific details about archival work. Over 65 colleges and universities offer classes in the archival sciences as part of other degree programs. These courses will teach you how to do many aspects of archival work, from selecting items and organizing collections to preparing documentation and conserving materials. While in graduate school, you may be able to secure a part-time job or assistantship at your school's archives. Many university archives rely on their own students to provide valuable help maintaining collections, and students who work there gain firsthand knowledge and experience in the archival field.

Many positions require a second master's degree in a specific field or a doctorate degree. An archivist at a historical society may need a master's degree in history and another master's in library and information science. Candidates with bachelor's degrees may serve as assistants while they complete their formal training.

Certification or Licensing

Although not currently required by most employers, voluntary certification for archivists is available from the Academy of Certified Archivists. Certification is earned by gaining practical experience in archival work, taking requisite courses, and passing an examination on the history, theory, and practice of archival science. Archivists need to renew their certification status every five years, usually by examination. Certification can be especially useful to archivists wishing to work in the corporate world.

Other Requirements

Archivists need to have excellent research and organizational skills. They should be comfortable working with rare and fragile materials. They need to maintain archives with absolute discretion, especially in the case of closed archives or archives available only for specific users. Archivists also need to be able to communicate effectively with all types of people that may use the archives, since they will be explaining the research methods and the policies and procedures of their organization. Finally, archivists may be required to move heavy boxes and other awkward materials. An archivist should be comfortable lifting or carrying large objects, although requirements may be different for various organizations and arrangements can often be made for professionals with different abilities.

■ EXPLORING

If you are interested in archival work, a good way to learn about the field is by using archives for your own research. If you have a report due on Abraham Lincoln, for instance, you could visit an archive near your home that houses some of Lincoln's personal papers and letters. A visit to the archives of a candy manufacturer could help you with an assignment on the history of a specific type

QUICK FACTS

SCHOOL SUBJECTS
English
Foreign language
History

PERSONAL SKILLS
Communication/ideas
Leadership/management

WORK ENVIRONMENT
Primarily indoors
Primarily one location

MINIMUM EDUCATION LEVEL
Master's degree

SALARY RANGE
$20,010 to $35,270 to
$66,050+

CERTIFICATION OR LICENSING
Voluntary

OUTLOOK
About as fast as the average

DOT
101

GOE
12.03.04

NOC
5113

O*NET-SOC
25-4011.00

DIGITAL ARCHIVES

Archival work isn't just about sifting through moldy old papers. Many archivists are working to make archival collections available digitally so people can have quick and easy access to records from around the world. Below is a small sample of archival collections that are available, in whole or in part, on the Web.

Library of Congress
(http://lcweb.loc.gov/exhibits)
Past exhibits include:
- Sigmund Freud: Conflict and Culture
- American Treasures of the Library of Congress
- Religion and the Founding of the American Public
- For European Recovery: The Fiftieth Anniversary of the Marshall Plan
- Frank Lloyd Wright: Designs for an American Landscape, 1922–32
- Women Come to the Front: Journalists, Photographers, and Broadcasters During WWII
- Declaring Independence: Drafting the Documents
- Temple of Liberty: Building the Capitol for a New Nation
- In the Beginning Was the Word: The Russian Church and Native Alaskan Cultures
- The African-American Mosaic: African-American Culture and History
- The African-American Odyssey: A Quest for Full Citizenship

Glenbow Archives
(http://www.glenbow.org/archives.htm)
The digitized collections at these archives in Calgary (Alberta), Canada include:
- Alberta Between the Wars, 1919–39: The Photographs of William J. Oliver
- Magic Lantern Slide Show
- The "W" Files: Weird, Warped, and Wacky Offerings from Alberta's Archival Treasure Houses

Rowan Public Library
(http://www.lib.co.rowan.nc.us/HistoryRoom/digitalarchives)
This library in Salisbury, North Carolina, has digitized collections into a number of online collections, most dealing with local history. The Archibald Henderson Collection includes photographs of this university professor with one of his most famous biography subjects—Mark Twain. Digitized collections include:
- Asa Ribelin Papers
- Georgia Jordan Papers
- Mamie McCubbins Collection
- Archibald Henderson Collection
- Dr. McCorkle's Sermon
- Wiley Lash Interview

Berkeley Digital Library
(http://sunsite.berkeley.edu/Collections)
This site features the following collections online:
- Aerial Photography Online
- Anthropology Emeritus Lecture Series: UC Berkeley
- Days of Cal: A Virtual Tour Through the History of the University of California, Berkeley
- The Jack London Collection
- Nineteenth-Century Literature
- The Online Medieval and Classical Library: A Collection of Medieval and Classical texts
- Pictorial Highlights from UC Berkeley Archival Collections
- Tebtunis Papyri Collection

Paul Halsall's Internet History Sourcebooks
(http://www.fordham.edu/halsall/)
Paul Halsall, a history professor, has collected some key documents of world history online. The collection includes:
- Ancient History Sourcebook
- Medieval History Sourcebook
- African History Sourcebook
- East Asian History Sourcebook
- Global History Sourcebook
- Indian History Sourcebook
- Islamic History Sourcebook
- Lesbian/Gay History Sourcebook
- History of Science Sourcebook
- Women's History Sourcebook

of production method. Since institutions may limit access to their collections, be sure to contact the organization about your project before you make the trip.

Getting to know an archivist can give you a good perspective of the field and the specific duties of the professional archivist. You could also see if a professional archival or historical association offers special student memberships or mentoring opportunities.

You can also learn more about archival work by creating your own family archive consisting of letters, birth and marriage certificates, old photographs, special awards, and any other documents that would help someone understand your family's history.

Another way to gain practical experience is to obtain part-time or volunteer positions in archives, historical societies, or libraries. Many museums and cultural centers train volunteer guides (who are called docents) to give tours of their institutions. If you already volunteer for an organization in another capacity, ask to have a personal tour of the archives.

■ EMPLOYERS

Archivists can find employment in various fields. Nearly one-third of the nation's archivists are employed in government positions, working for the Department of Defense, the National Archives and Records Administration, and other local, state, and federal repositories. Approximately 18 percent of archivists work in academia, working in college and university libraries. Other archivists work in positions for museums, historical societies, and zoos, or for private, not-for-profit archives that serve special interests, such as the Lesbian Herstory Archives in New York.

Archivists are also on staff at corporations, religious institutions, and professional associations. Many of these organizations need archivists to manage massive amounts of records that will be kept for posterity, or to comply with state or federal regulations. Some private collectors may also employ an archivist to process, organize, and catalog their personal holdings.

■ STARTING OUT

There is no best way to become an archivist. Since there is no formal archivist degree, many people working in the field today have had to pave their own way. Daniel Meyer, associate curator of special collections and university archivist at the University of Chicago Library, began by earning a master's degree in history and then a Ph.D. In graduate school, he processed collections in his university's archives. By enhancing his educational credentials with practical experience in the field, he gradually moved on to positions with greater degrees of responsibility.

Another archivist may approach his or her career from another direction. For example, an archivist could start out with a master's degree in French and then earn a master's of library science (M.L.S.) degree, with a concentration in archival management. With a language background and the M.L.S., he or she could begin working in archival positions in colleges and universities.

Candidates for positions as archivists should apply to institutions for entry-level positions only after completing their undergraduate degrees—usually in history. An archivist going into a particular area of archival work, however, may wish to earn a degree in that field. If you are interested in working in a museum's archives, for instance, you may wish to pursue a degree in art or art history.

Many potential archivists choose to work part time as research assistants, interns, or volunteers in order to gain archival experience. School placement offices are good starting points to look for research assistantships and internships. Professional librarian and archivist associations often have job listings for those new to the field.

■ ADVANCEMENT

Archivists usually work in small sections, units, or departments, so internal promotion opportunities are often limited. Promising archivists advance by gaining more responsibility for the administration of the collections. They may begin to spend more time supervising the work of others. Archivists can also advance by transferring to larger repositories and taking more administration-based positions.

Because the best jobs as archivists are contingent upon education, the surest method of advancement is through pursuing advanced or specialized degrees. Ambitious archivists should also attend conferences and workshops to stay current with developments in their fields. Archivists can enhance their status by conducting independent research and publishing their findings. In a public or private library, an archivist may move on to a position such as curator, chief librarian, or library director.

Archivists may also move outside of the standard archival field entirely. With their background and skills, archivists may become teachers, university professors, or instructors at a library school. They may also set up shop for themselves as archival consultants to corporations or private collectors.

■ EARNINGS

Salaries for archivists vary considerably by institution and may depend on education and experience. People employed by the federal government or by prestigious museums generally earn more than those working for small organizations. The U.S. Department of Labor reported that the median annual salary for archivists working for the federal government was $42,230 in 2002. Those working in museums or historical sites earned a median salary of $38,910. The median salary for all archivists was $35,270. The lowest paid 10 percent earned $20,010 or less, while the highest paid 10 percent earned $66,050 or more.

Archivists who work for large corporations, institutions, or government agencies generally receive a full range of benefits, including health care coverage, vacation days, paid holidays, paid sick time, and retirement savings plans. Self-employed archival consultants usually have to provide their own benefits. All archivists have the added benefit of working with rare and unique materials. They have the opportunity to work with history and create documentation of the past.

■ WORK ENVIRONMENT

Because dirt, sunlight, and moisture can damage materials and documents, archivists generally work in clean, climate-controlled surroundings with artificial lighting rather than windows. Many archives are small offices, often employing the archivist alone, or with one or two part-time volunteers. Other archives are part of a larger department within an organization. The archives for DePaul University in Chicago, for instance, are part of the Special Collections department and are managed by the curator. With this type of arrangement, the archivist generally has a number of graduate assistants to help with the processing of materials and departmental support staff to assist with clerical tasks.

Archivists often have little opportunity for physical activity, save for the bending, lifting, and reaching they may need to do in order to arrange collections and make room for new materials. Also, some archival collections include not only paper records but some oversized items as well. The archives of an elite fraternal organization, for example, may house a collection of hats or uniforms that members wore throughout the years, each of which must be processed, cataloged, preserved, and stored.

Most archivists work 40 hours a week, usually during regular, weekday working hours. Depending on the needs of their department and the community they serve, an archive may be open some weekend hours, thus requiring the archivist to be on hand for users. Also, archivists spend some of their time traveling to the homes of donors to view materials that may complement an archival collection.

■ OUTLOOK

Job opportunities for archivists are expected to increase about as fast as the average through 2012, according to the U.S. Department of Labor. But since qualified job applicants outnumber the positions available, competition for jobs as archivists is keen. Candidates with specialized training, such as master's degrees in history and library science, will have better opportunities. A doctorate in history or a related field can also be a boon to job-seeking archivists. Graduates who have studied archival work or records management will be in higher demand than those without that background. Also, by gaining related work or volunteer experience, many potential archivists will be in a better position to find full-time employment. As archival work begins to reflect an increasingly digital society, an archivist with extensive knowledge of computers is likely to advance more quickly than an archivist with little desire to learn.

Jobs are expected to increase as more corporations and private organizations establish an archival history. Archivists will also be needed to fill positions left vacant by retirees and archivists who leave the occupation. On the other hand, budget cuts in educational institutions, museums, and cultural institutions often reduce demand for archivists. Overall, there will always be positions available for archivists, but the aspiring archivist may need to be creative, flexible, and determined in forging a career path.

■ FOR MORE INFORMATION

To find out about archival certification procedures, contact
Academy of Certified Archivists
48 Howard Street
Albany, NY 12207
Tel: 518-463-8644
Email: aca@caphill.com
http://www.certifiedarchivists.org

For information about archival programs, activities, and publications in North America, contact
American Institute for Conservation of Historic and Artistic Works
1717 K Street, NW, Suite 200
Washington, DC 20006
Tel: 202-452-9545
Email: info@aic-faic.org
http://aic.stanford.edu

If you are interested in working with the archives of film and television, contact
Association of Moving Image Archivists
1313 North Vine Street
Hollywood, CA 90028
Tel: 323-463-1500
Email: amia@amianet.org
http://amianet.org

For a list of educational programs and to read So You Want to Be an Archivist: An Overview of the Archival Profession, *visit the SAA's website.*

Society of American Archivists (SAA)
527 South Wells Street, Fifth Floor
Chicago, IL 60607
Tel: 312-922-0140
Email: info@archivists.org
http://www.archivists.org

For archival programs and activities in Canada, contact
Association of Canadian Archivists
PO Box 2596, Station D
Ottawa, ON K1P 5W6 Canada
Tel: 613-445-4564
Email: aca@magma.ca
http://archivists.ca

For information on archival work and publications in the United Kingdom, contact
Society of Archivists
Prioryfield House
20 Canon Street
Taunton, Somerset, TA1 1SW England
Email: offman@archives.org.uk
http://www.archives.org.uk

Aromatherapists

■ OVERVIEW

Aromatherapists are health care specialists who use essential plant oils to promote health in their clients. Essential oils are highly concentrated substances that give plants their fragrance. These substances are extracted from various parts of aromatic plants, such as roots, woods, seeds, fruits, leaves, and flowers. Only about 5 percent of all types of plants are used for their essential oils.

Since the early 20th century, the professions of cosmetology, medicine, and psychology have rediscovered the healing powers of essential oils that were known to earlier civilizations. Scientific studies show that inhaling the fragrance of certain essential oils has physiological and psychological effects on the brain. Aromatherapists study the oils and their effects on individuals. They use this knowledge to help improve their clients' quality of life.

Most aromatherapists are licensed in other areas of health care or body care, using aromatherapy as a supplementary tool in their licensed profession. Among these licensed professionals are beauticians, chiropractors, cos-

meticians, massage therapists, medical doctors, naturopathic doctors, nurse practitioners, and nurses. A few individuals who specialize in aromatherapy work as chemists, educators, or authors. A very few grow plants for the distillation of essential oils, become consultants, or start their own lines of aromatherapy products.

■ HISTORY

Humanity's use of fragrance probably began long before recorded history. Anthropologists think that primitive people burned gums and resin as incense. Throughout history, civilizations have used essential oils for many purposes—including healing. As an art and science, aromatherapy finds its roots in ancient cultures, dating back 4,000 to 5,000 years. Early Egyptians are often credited with being the first to make an art of the use of essential oils. They used myrrh and frankincense (fragrant resins from trees) in their daily rituals. However, other early cultures also used essential oils. In ancient Africa, people discovered that certain plants provided protection from the sun when they were rubbed on the skin. Chinese, Indian, Persian, and other African cultures used plant oils for incense burning, cooking, cosmetics, mummifying, bathing, perfumery, meditating, and healing.

In the spas of ancient Rome, oils were used in public baths and were applied during massages. The knowledge of oils went along with the spread of Roman culture. Europeans used oils during medieval times to fight disease. During the Middle Ages, the appearance of chemistry and the improvement of distillation helped simplify the process of extracting essential oils from plants. This opened the door to oil trading, which spread the new practices to more people and places.

Until the 19th century, when science began to introduce other medicines, Europeans used essential oils both as perfumes and for medicinal purposes. With the growth of newer medical practices, doctors began to choose modern medicine over the tradition of oils. It was not until the 20th century that several individuals "rediscovered" the healing power of essential oils. Once again the use of oils was integrated into Western culture.

In 1928, the French perfumer and chemist, René-Maurice Gattefossé, experienced the healing power of essential oils. When he severely burned his hand, he stuck it into the nearest liquid, which happened to be lavender oil. He was surprised how quickly the hand healed. His experience caused him to become interested in the therapeutic use of essential oils. It was Gattefossé who coined the term *aromatherapy.*

Dr. Jean Valnet, a French physician, was the first to reintegrate essential oils into Western medical practice. Dr. Valnet served as an army surgeon during World War

II. Inspired by the work of Gattefossé, he used essential oils to treat the soldiers' burns and wounds. He also successfully treated psychiatric problems with fragrances.

Marguerite Maury, an Austrian biochemist, was also influenced by the work of Gattefossé. She integrated the use of essential oils into cosmetics.

In 1977, Robert Tisserand, an expert in aromatherapy, wrote *The Art of Aromatherapy*. Tisserand was strongly influenced by the work of both Gattefossé and Valnet. His book caught the interest of the American public and made a major contribution to the growth of aromatherapy in this country.

The Western world has rediscovered the uses of essential oils and fragrances through the work of people like Valnet, Maury, and Tisserand. In France, aromatherapy is practiced by medical doctors. Conventional and alternative medicine practitioners in England, Australia, Sweden, Japan, the United States, and other parts of the world are recognizing and utilizing the healing power of essential oils. The world is reawakening to the healing and life-enhancing capabilities of aromatherapy.

■ THE JOB

Whether aromatherapists work primarily as beauticians, chiropractors, massage therapists, or doctors, they must possess a strong working knowledge of aromatherapy as a science and an art. They need to understand the components and healing benefits of many essential oils. The quality of essential oils varies greatly depending on the plant, where it is grown, the conditions under which it is grown, and other factors. As a result, aromatherapists must be very careful about choosing the sources from which their oils come. Pure, high-quality, therapeutic grade oils are essential to good aromatherapy. Aromatherapists must even know the differences between the oils of different species of the same plant. Essential oils are very powerful because of their high concentration. It may take well over 100 pounds of plant material to produce just one pound of essential oil.

Because of the powerful concentration of essential oils, aromatherapists use great care in diluting them and in adding them to what are called carrier oils. These are most often high-quality vegetable oils, such as almond, olive, or sesame. Unlike essential oils, carrier oils are fixed, rather than volatile. A small amount of an essential oil is blended into the carrier oil, which "carries" it across the body. Aromatherapists are especially careful when the oils are to be applied to a client's skin or put into a bath. In addition, aromatherapists must know how different essential oils work together because they are often combined to achieve certain results.

Aromatherapists need to know much more than what oils to use. They use the essential oils in three types of aro-

matherapy: cosmetic, massage, and olfactory. Aromatherapists have to know the differences among the types of therapy. They must decide which type or combination of types to use in a particular situation, and they must be skilled in each type.

Aromatherapists must know how the body, mind, and emotions work together. For example, a client who complains of muscle tension may need physical relief. A massage with relaxing oils that the skin soaks in will relax the client. However, aromatherapists are able to take this treatment a step further. They consider the underlying causes of the condition. Why is the client feeling tense? Is it stress? Anxiety? Strong emotion? Massage therapists who are trained in aromatherapy may inquire about the client's life in order to pinpoint the source of the tension. Once the source is identified, aromatherapists utilize specific oils to produce a certain emotional effect in the client. When the scents of these oils are inhaled, they create a response within the entire body. The oils may be added to a bath or a compress that is applied to the body. A compress is a towel soaked in water that has a bit of an essential oil added to it. An aroma may take the client back to happier times, as a reminder of warmth, comfort, and contentment.

An aromatherapist's client may have skin problems due to stress. The aromatherapist may use certain essential oils to help both the skin condition on the surface and the underlying emotional source of the problem. This might be accomplished through olfactory aromatherapy—the inhalation of the oil vapors.

In a hospital, nursing home, or hospice setting, an aromatherapist might choose essential oils that help relieve stress. In England, hospital nursing staffs utilize essential oil massage. This type of therapy has been shown to relieve pain and induce sleep. Essential oil massage has proven effective in relieving the stress that patients experience with general illness, surgery, terminal cancer, and AIDS. Aromatherapists emphasize

QUICK FACTS

SCHOOL SUBJECTS
Biology
Chemistry
English

PERSONAL SKILLS
Helping/teaching
Technical/scientific

WORK ENVIRONMENT
Primarily indoors
Primarily one location

MINIMUM EDUCATION LEVEL
Some postsecondary training

SALARY RANGE
$17,540 to $45,000 to
$70,000+

CERTIFICATION OR LICENSING
None available

OUTLOOK
Faster than the average

DOT
N/A

GOE
N/A

NOC
N/A

O*NET-SOC
N/A

THE THREE TYPES OF AROMATHERAPY

Cosmetic Aromatherapy: In cosmetic aromatherapy, essential oils are blended into skin and hair care products. The aromatherapist chooses oils that are appropriate for the client's skin and hair type. The products in which the oils are used have many purposes—cleansing or toning, drying or moisturizing.

Massage Aromatherapy: An aromatherapist chooses an essential oil especially to meet the needs of the individual. A small amount of the appropriate oil is blended with a pure vegetable carrier oil. When the blended oils are applied during a massage, the aroma of the essential oil enhances the massage both physiologically and psychologically.

Olfactory Aromatherapy: In olfactory aromatherapy, the aromatherapist carefully selects the essential oil that will produce the desired effect for the individual client. The oils are chosen for a specific purpose: perhaps to release stress, relax the mind, or enhance emotional wellness. The aroma of the oil may be inhaled directly or dispersed through a diffuser. When dispersed through a diffuser, essential oils may be used to improve respiratory conditions or to combat the transmission of airborne infections.

that these treatments are supplementary and enhancing to medical care—they do not replace medical treatment.

No two clients' problems are the same, and neither are the remedies for those problems. Each client must be treated as an individual. During the first visit, aromatherapists usually take a careful client history. Aromatherapists must listen carefully both for things their clients say and for things they don't say. Aromatherapists need to know if a client is taking any medicine or using any natural healing substances, such as herbs. They must understand the properties of the essential oils and how they might interact with any other treatment the client is using. Next, they use the information gathered from the client interview to determine the proper essential oils and the appropriate amounts to blend to serve the client's particular needs.

Aromatherapists are employed in a number of different work environments. Those connected to the beauty industry may work in salons, spas, or hotel resorts, incorporating aromatherapy into facial care, body care, and hair care. In the health care field, many professionals are turning to alternative approaches to care, and some conventional medical practitioners are beginning to implement more holistic approaches. As a result, a growing number of aromatherapists work in the offices of other health care specialists, where their aromatherapy treatments complement the other therapies used. Aromatherapists often give sem-

inars, teach, or serve as consultants. Some who become experts on essential oils buy farms to grow plants for the oils, create their own lines of aromatherapy products, or sell essential oils to other aromatherapists.

■ REQUIREMENTS
High School

If you are interested in working with aromatherapy, begin in high school by building up your knowledge of the human body's systems. Biology, anatomy, and physiology will help lay the foundation for a career in aromatherapy. Chemistry courses will familiarize you with laboratory procedures. Aromatherapists need to have an understanding of mixtures and the care involved in using powerful essential oils. Chemistry can help you gain the experience you need to handle delicate or volatile substances. It will also familiarize you with the properties of natural compounds.

Keep in mind that the majority of aromatherapists are self-employed. Math, business, and computer courses will help you develop the skills you need to be successful at running a business. Aromatherapists also need good communication and interpersonal skills to be sensitive to their clients. English, speech, and psychology classes can help you sharpen your ability to interact constructively with other people.

Eva-Marie Lind is an aromatherapist, author, and former Dean of the Aromatherapy Department of the Australasian College of Herbal Studies in Lake Oswego, Oregon. She has worked in the field of aromatherapy for over 15 years. According to Lind, "Education is the key to good aromatherapy. There is so much to learn, and it takes real dedication to study."

Postsecondary Training

In 1999, the National Association for Holistic Aromatherapy (NAHA) established criteria for aromatherapy education that have been voluntarily adopted by a number of schools and education programs. NAHA guidelines recommend that aromatherapy education include courses on topics such as the history of aromatherapy, physiology, production of essential oils, botany, chemistry, safety and methods of application, and business planning.

While NAHA provides a listing of schools complying with its guidelines, there are also other schools, seminars, and distance learning courses that offer training in aromatherapy. Be aware, however, that the quality of programs can vary. Take the time to call the schools or organizations that interest you. Ask how their programs are set up. For correspondence courses (or distance courses), ask if you will be able to talk to a teacher. How will you be evaluated? Are there tests? How are the tests taken and graded? Try to talk with current students. Ask how they are treated and what they learn. Ask what you receive when you graduate from the program. Will you receive help with job placement? Access to insurance programs? Other benefits? Depending on the program you pick, the length of study ranges from short workshops to four-year college courses. Vocational schools, major universities, and naturopathic colleges are increasingly offering training in aromatherapy.

Most aromatherapists are also professionals in other fields. Consider whether you would want to combine aromatherapy with a "base" profession, such as chiropractic, massage therapy, nursing, or some other field into which you might incorporate it. These base fields require additional education and certification as well as licensing. If you decide to add aromatherapy to another profession, learn the requirements for certification or licensing that apply to that profession. Adding aromatherapy to another profession requires a comprehensive understanding of both fields from a scientific standpoint.

Certification or Licensing

There are presently no certification or licensing requirements for aromatherapy in the United States. Aromatherapy is growing rapidly, and it is likely that these requirements will be established soon. Since aromatherapy is practiced by such a variety of professionals, developing standards is particularly complex. Nevertheless, professionals throughout the industry are working toward this goal. If you choose to study aromatherapy, you will need to keep up on these changes.

If you choose to combine aromatherapy with another profession, you must meet the national and local requirements for that field in addition to aromatherapy requirements.

Other Requirements

According to Eva-Marie Lind, "Aromatherapy demands love and passion at its roots. You need to honor, respect, and celebrate the beauty of this field."

You must also enjoy disseminating knowledge because clients often have many questions. More practically, it takes a good nose and a certain sensitivity to successfully treat clients through aromatherapy. It takes good listening skills and immense creativity to understand each client's personal issues and decide on the best means of administering a treatment. Which essential oils or combination of oils should you choose? Should you use a bath, a compress, a massage, or inhalation? What parts of the body are the best avenues for delivering the remedy?

Aromatherapists must be good self-teachers who are interested in continuing education. This is a relatively

HOW DOES AROMATHERAPY WORK?

Recent research shows that aromatic molecules given off by the essential oils transmit signals that the body modifies and passes on to the limbic system. The limbic system has been referred to as the "emotional switchboard" of the brain. Once in the limbic system, these modified signals are associated with memories and emotions.

The limbic system is connected to the areas of the brain that control many essential bodily functions, such as breathing, blood pressure, and memory. Due to this close connection, essential oils can have profound psychological and physiological effects on the individual.

new field that is developing and changing rapidly. To stay competitive and successful, you need to keep up with the changing trends, products, and technologies that affect the field. Like most healing professions, aromatherapy is a lifelong education process for the practitioner.

■ EXPLORING

There are many ways to explore the field of aromatherapy to see if it is for you. For one, there are many books and specialized periodicals available on the subject. Get a glimpse of the types of knowledge you need for the field. Find out whether it is too scientific or not scientific enough. Look in your local library for books and magazines that show you what a typical student of aromatherapy might be learning.

Visit health food stores. The staff members of health food stores are often very helpful. Most have books, magazines, and newspapers about many kinds of alternative health care, including aromatherapy. Ask about essential oils, and ask for the names of aromatherapists in the area. Find out if there are garden clubs that you can join—particularly ones that specialize in herbs. Consider taking up cooking. This could give you practice in selecting herbs and seasonings and blending them to create different aromas and flavors.

Contact local and national professional organizations. Some offer student memberships or free seminars. Check out their websites. They have a lot of valuable information and good links to other alternative health care sites. Join online forums and discussion groups where you can communicate with professionals from all over the country and the world. Some distance learning courses are open to students of all ages. Check into them.

If you find you have a real interest in aromatherapy, another way to explore the field is to seek a mentor, a professional in the field who is willing to help you learn. Tell everyone you know that you are interested in aromatherapy. Someone is bound to have a connection with someone you could call for an informational interview. Perhaps you could spend a day "shadowing" an aromatherapist to see what the work is like. If you are unable to find an aromatherapy specialist, you could call spas and salons in search of professionals who use aromatherapy in their work. Perhaps some would be willing to speak to you about their day-to-day work. Make an appointment and experience an aromatherapy treatment. Taking it a step further, you could explore the possibility of getting a part-time job at an establishment that employs aromatherapists.

■ EMPLOYERS

Most aromatherapists are self-employed. They run their own small businesses and build their own clientele. Some set up their own offices, but many build their businesses by working in the offices of other professionals and giving aromatherapy treatments as supplements to the treatments provided by the resident professionals. Many different kinds of employers are looking for skilled aromatherapists. In the cosmetic industry, beauticians, cosmeticians, and massage therapists employ aromatherapists to give treatments that complement their own. Spas, athletic clubs, resorts, and cruise ships may hire aromatherapists on a full-time basis. These types of employment may be temporary or seasonal.

In the health care industry, chiropractors, acupuncturists, and other alternative therapy practitioners and clinics may offer aromatherapy in addition to their basic services. Hospitals, nursing homes, hospice centers, and other medical establishments are beginning to recognize the physiological and psychological benefits of aromatherapy for their patients.

■ STARTING OUT

Because the practice of aromatherapy may be incorporated into numerous other professions, there are many ways to enter the field. How you enter depends on how you want to use aromatherapy. Is your interest in massage therapy, skin care, or hair care? Do you want to be a nurse, doctor, acupuncturist, or chiropractor? Are you interested in becoming an instructor or writer? Once you are certified in another area, you need to search for clinics, salons, spas, and other establishments that are looking for professionals who use aromatherapy in their treatments. School career services are also ways to find work. Classified ads in newspapers and trade magazines list positions in the related fields.

Networking can be an important source of job opportunities. Networking is simply getting to know others and exchanging ideas with them. Go to association meetings and conventions. Talk to people in the field. Job openings are often posted at such gatherings.

■ ADVANCEMENT

Aromatherapists can advance to many different levels, depending on their goals, ambitions, aspirations, and willingness to work. Those who are self-employed can increase their clientele and open their own offices or even a salon. Those who are employed at a spa or salon could become a department director or the director of the entire spa or salon. They might start a private practice or open a spa or salon.

As their skills and knowledge grow, aromatherapists may be sought after to teach and train other aromatherapists in seminars or at schools that offer aromatherapy programs or courses. Others become consultants or write books and articles. A few start their own aromatherapy product lines of esthetic or therapeutic products. Some may become involved in growing the plants that are the sources of essential oils. Still others work in distilling, analyzing, or blending the oils.

This is such a new field growing so rapidly that the potential for advancement is enormous. The field has so many facets that the directions for growth are as great as your imagination and determination. Geraldine Zelinsky, the public relations representative of the National Association for Holistic Aromatherapists, says, "If you are self-motivated, creative, and have a talent for any aspect of aromatherapy, the sky is the limit. It is what you make it."

■ EARNINGS

Since aromatherapists work in such a variety of settings, and aromatherapy is often a supplementary therapy added to other professional training, it is particularly difficult to make statements about average earnings in the field. Government agencies do not yet have wage statistics for the field. The national professional associations have not yet developed surveys of their members that give reliable information.

For those who are self-employed in any profession, earnings depend on the amount of time they work and the amount they charge per hour. Experienced professional aromatherapists estimate that hourly rates can range from $25 to $65 for beginning aromatherapists and instructors. Rates increase with experience to between $75 and $100 per hour. Based on those rates, a beginning aromatherapist who charged $25 an hour and averaged 10 appointments per week would earn around $13,000. According to the U.S. Department of Labor, in 2002 the median annual salary for people engaged in personal care and service occupations (the category aromatherapy would fall into) earned a median salary of $17,540, with the bottom 10 percent earning $13,000 per year and the top 10 percent $35,140 or more. Established aromatherapists who have a solid client base report earning $25,000 to $45,000.

The hourly rate an aromatherapist charges depends on his or her level of expertise, the type of clientele served, and even the area of the country. In many of the larger cities and much of the West Coast, people are already more aware and accepting of alternative health therapies. In those areas, higher hourly rates will be more accepted. Where such therapies are practically unknown, lower rates will apply. Another consideration for the self-employed is that they must provide their own insurance and retirement plans and pay for their supplies and other business expenses.

An aromatherapist with determination, creativity, and initiative can find jobs that pay well. Some who run exclusive spas or develop their own lines of aromatherapy products are reported to earn $70,000 to $80,000 or more.

Aromatherapists who are primarily employed in other professions, such as massage therapists, chiropractors, cosmetologists, and nurses, can expect to make the salaries that are average for their profession. Those professionals who use aromatherapy as a supportive therapy to their primary profession tend to have higher incomes than those who specialize in aromatherapy. The addition of aromatherapy to their profession will probably enhance their clients' and their own satisfaction, but it may not increase their income.

■ WORK ENVIRONMENT

Aromatherapists work in a service-oriented environment, in which the main duty involves understanding and helping their clients. The surroundings are usually clean, peaceful, and pleasant. They work with very potent substances (strong essential oils), but most aromatherapists love the scents and the experience of the oils. They often spend a great deal of time on their feet. They sometimes work long or inconsistent hours, such as weekends and evenings, to accommodate their clients' needs.

Aromatherapists are people-oriented. Those who are self-employed must be highly motivated and able to work alone. Aromatherapists who work in clinics, spas, hospitals, resorts, and other locations need to be able to work well with others.

■ OUTLOOK

Aromatherapy has been growing very rapidly and is gathering steam in the United States. Opportunities are increasing rapidly as public awareness of alternative therapies is increasing.

The status of aromatherapy in European and other countries may provide a glimpse of the future of the field in the United States. In Great Britain and France, for example, more doctors have embraced aromatherapy, and these services are covered by major health plans. If the United States follows this lead, new doors will open in this field. In general, the outlook is very good for aromatherapy because of an overwhelming increase in public awareness and interest.

■ FOR MORE INFORMATION

For information regarding state regulations for massage therapists and general information on therapeutic massage, contact

American Massage Therapy Association
820 Davis Street, Suite 100
Evanston, IL 60201-4444
Tel: 847-864-0123
http://www.amtamassage.org

The National Association for Holistic Aromatherapy has developed guidelines for aromatherapy training. See the website for a listing of schools in compliance with these guidelines.

National Association for Holistic Aromatherapy
4509 Interlake Avenue North, #233
Seattle, WA 98103-6773
Tel: 888-ASK-NAHA
Email: info@naha.org
http://www.naha.org

For general information about aromatherapy and education options, visit the following website:

AromaWeb
http://www.aromaweb.com

For comprehensive Internet information on alternative and conventional health care and extensive links, visit

HealthWorldOnline
http://www.healthy.net

Art Directors

■ OVERVIEW

Art directors play a key role in every stage of the creation of an advertisement or ad campaign, from formulating concepts to supervising production. Ultimately, they are responsible for planning and overseeing the presentation of their clients' messages in print or on screen—that is, in books, magazines, newspapers, television commercials, posters, and packaging, as well as in film and video and on the Internet.

In publishing, art directors work with artists, photographers, and text editors to develop visual images and generate copy, according to the marketing strategy. They are responsible for evaluating existing illustrations, determining presentation styles and techniques, hiring both staff and freelance talent, working with layouts, and preparing budgets.

In films, videos, and television commercials, art directors set the general look of the visual elements and approve the props, costumes, and models. In addition, they are involved in casting, editing, and selecting the music. In film (motion pictures) and video, the art director is usually an experienced animator or computer/graphic arts designer who supervises animators or other artistic staff.

In sum, art directors are charged with selling to, informing, and educating consumers. They supervise both in-house and off-site staff, handle executive issues, and oversee the entire artistic production process. There are more than 149,000 artists and art directors working in the United States.

■ HISTORY

Artists have always been an important part of the creative process throughout history. Medieval monks illuminated their manuscripts, painting with egg-white tempera on vellum. Each copy of each book had to be printed and illustrated individually.

Printed illustrations first appeared in books in 1461. Through the years, prints were made through woodblock, copperplate, lithography, and other means of duplicating images. Although making many copies of the same illustration was now possible, publishers still depended on individual artists to create the original works. Text editors usually decided what was to be illustrated and how, while artists commonly supervised the production of the artwork.

The first art directors were probably staff illustrators for book publishers. As the publishing industry grew more complex and incorporated new technologies such as photography and film, art direction evolved into a more supervisory position and became a full-time job. Publishers and advertisers began to need specialists who could acquire and use illustrations and photos. Women's magazines, such as *Vogue* (http://www.style.com/vogue) and *Harper's Bazaar* http://www.harpersbazaar.com), and photo magazines, such as *National Geographic* (http://www.nationalgeographic.com), relied so much on illustration and photography that the photo editor and art director began to carry as much power as the text editor.

With the creation of animation, art directors became more indispensable than ever. Animated short films, such as the early Mickey Mouse cartoons, were usually supervised by art directors. Walt Disney, himself, was the art director on many of his early pictures. And as full-length films have moved into animation, the sheer number of illustrations requires more than one art director to oversee the project.

Today's art directors supervise almost every type of visual project produced. Through a variety of methods and media, from television and film to magazines, comic books, and the Internet, art directors communicate ideas by selecting and supervising every element that goes into the finished product.

■ THE JOB

Art directors are responsible for all visual aspects of printed or on-screen projects. The art director oversees the process of developing visual solutions to a variety of communication problems. He or she helps to establish corporate identities; advertises products and services; enhances books, magazines, newsletters, and other publications; and creates television commercials, film and video productions, and websites. Some art directors with experience or knowledge in specific fields specialize in such areas as packaging, exhibitions and displays, or the Internet. But all directors, even those with specialized backgrounds, must be skilled in and knowledgeable about design, illustration, photography, computers, research, and writing in order to supervise the work of graphic artists, photographers, copywriters, text editors, and other employees.

In print advertising and publishing, art directors may begin with the client's concept or develop one in collaboration with the copywriter and account executive. Once the concept is established, the next step is to decide on the most effective way to communicate it. If there is text, for example, should the art director choose illustrations based on specific text references, or should the illustrations fill in the gaps in the copy? If a piece is being revised, existing illustrations must be reevaluated.

After deciding what needs to be illustrated, art directors must find sources that can create or provide the art. Photo agencies, for example, have photographs and illustrations on thousands of different subjects. If, however, the desired illustration does not exist, it may have to be commissioned or designed by one of the staff designers. Commissioning artwork means that the art director contacts a photographer or illustrator and explains what is needed. A price is negotiated, and the artist creates the image specifically for the art director.

Once the illustrations and other art elements have been secured, they must be presented in an appealing manner. The art director supervises (and may help in the production of) the layout of the piece and presents the final version to the client or creative director. *Layout* is the process of figuring out where every image, headline, and block of text will be placed on the page. The size, style, and method of reproduction must all be specifically indicated so that the image is recreated as the director intended it.

In broadcast advertising and film and video, the art director has a wide variety of responsibilities and often interacts with an enormous number of creative professionals. Working with directors and producers, art directors interpret scripts and create or select settings in order to visually convey the story or the message. The art director oversees and channels the talents of set decorators and designers, model makers, location managers, propmasters, construction coordinators, and special effects people. In addition, art directors work with writers, unit production managers, cinematographers, costume designers, and post-production staff, including editors and employees responsible for scoring and titles. The art director is ultimately responsible for all visual aspects of the finished product.

The process of producing a television commercial begins in much the same way that a printed advertising piece is created. The art director may start with the client's concept or create one in-house in collaboration with staff members. Once a concept has been created and the copywriter has generated the corresponding text, the art director sketches a rough storyboard based on the writer's ideas, and the plan is presented for review to the creative director. The next step is to develop a finished storyboard, with larger and more detailed frames (the individual scenes) in color. This storyboard is presented to the client for review and used as a guide for the film director as well.

Technology has been playing an increasingly important role in the art director's job. Most art directors, for example, use a variety of computer software programs, including Adobe PageMaker, FrameMaker, Illustrator, and Photoshop; Macromedia Dreamweaver; QuarkXPress; and CorelDRAW. Many others create and oversee websites for clients and work with other interactive media and materials, including CD-ROM, touch-screens, multidimensional visuals, and new animation programs.

Art directors usually work on more than one project at a time and must be able to keep numerous, unrelated details straight. They often work under pressure of a deadline and yet must remain calm and pleasant when dealing with clients and staff. Because they are supervisors, art directors are often called upon to resolve problems, not only with projects but with employees as well.

Art directors are not entry-level workers. They usually have years of experience working at lower-level jobs in the field before gaining the knowledge needed to supervise projects. Depending on whether they work primarily in publishing or film, art directors have to know how printing presses operate or how film is processed. They should also be familiar with a variety of production techniques in order to understand the wide range of ways that images can be manipulated to meet the needs of a project.

■ REQUIREMENTS
High School

A college degree is usually a requirement for art directors; however, in some instances, it is not absolutely necessary. A variety of high school courses will give you both a taste of college-level offerings and an idea of the skills necessary for art directors on the job. These courses include art, drawing, art history, graphic design, illustration, photography, advertising, and desktop publishing.

Math courses are also important. Most of the elements of sizing an image involve calculating percentage reduction or enlargement of the original picture. This must be done with a great degree of accuracy if the overall design is going to work. For example, type size may have to be figured within a thirty-second of an inch for a print project. Errors can be extremely costly and may make the project look sloppy.

Other useful courses that you should take in high school include business, computing, English, technical drawing, cultural studies, psychology, and social science.

Postsecondary Training

According to the American Institute of Graphic Arts, nine out of 10 artists have a college degree. Among them, six out of 10 have majored in graphic design, and two out of 10 have majored in fine arts. In addition, almost two out of 10 have a master's degree. Along with general two- and four-year colleges and universities, a number of professional art schools offer two-, three-, or four-year programs with such classes

QUICK FACTS

SCHOOL SUBJECTS
Art
Business
Computer science

PERSONAL SKILLS
Artistic
Communication/ideas

WORK ENVIRONMENT
Primarily indoors
Primarily one location

MINIMUM EDUCATION LEVEL
Bachelor's degree

SALARY RANGE
$32,410 to $61,850 to $115,570+

CERTIFICATION OR LICENSING
None available

OUTLOOK
About as fast as the average

DOT
164

GOE
01.01.01

NOC
5131

O*NET-SOC
27-1011.00

as figure drawing, painting, graphic design, and other art courses, as well as classes in art history, writing, business administration, communications, and foreign languages.

Courses in advertising, marketing, photography, filmmaking, set direction, layout, desktop publishing, and fashion are also important for those interested in becoming art directors. Specialized courses, sometimes offered only at professional art schools, may be particularly helpful for students who want to go into art direction. These include typography, animation, storyboard, website design, and portfolio development.

Because of the rapidly increasing use of computers in design work, it is essential to have a thorough understanding of how computer art and layout programs work. In smaller companies, the art director may be responsible for operating this equipment; in larger companies, a staff person, under the direction of the art director, may use these programs. In either case, the director must know what can be done with the available equipment.

In addition to course work at the college level, many universities and professional art schools offer graduates

JOIN THE CLUB

If you think that art direction may be the direction *you're* headed, a number of clubs—located all across the nation and abroad—can offer you a taste of the profession. Art directors clubs in Cincinnati, Denver, Portland (Maine), Indiana, Houston, New York, and other areas provide scholarships, volunteering opportunities, design contests, resources, events, job services, speakers, intern programs, and more, all intended for high school and college-level students.

The Art Directors Club of Metropolitan Washington (http://www.adcmw.org), for example, "seeks to ensure the quality of future professionals" by offering visual communications students the following:

- A series of walking tours of local art studios
- Career Day, which brings students and professionals together for one day for one-on-one critiques of students' portfolios and features presentations about the design profession by area designers and art directors
- The Real Show, an annual student competition in which students solve real-world design problems
- Brian Brown Scholarships—$2,000 in scholarships awarded on the merits of submitted student portfolio samples
- Student memberships to the club at the reduced rate of $25 per year

or students in their final year a variety of workshop projects, desktop publishing training opportunities, and internships. These programs provide students with opportunities to develop their personal design styles as well as their portfolios.

Other Requirements

The work of an art director requires creativity, imagination, curiosity, and a sense of adventure. Art directors must be able to work with all sorts of specialized equipment and computer software, such as graphic design programs, as well as make presentations on the ideas behind their work.

The ability to work well with different people and organizations is a must for art directors. They must always be up to date on new techniques, trends, and attitudes. And because deadlines are a constant part of the work, an ability to handle stress and pressure well is key.

Accuracy and attention to detail are important parts of the job. When art is done neatly and correctly, the public usually pays no notice. But when a project is done poorly or sloppily, people will notice, even if they have had no design training. Other requirements for art directors include time management skills and an interest in media and people's motivations and lifestyles.

■ EXPLORING

High school students can get an idea of what an art director does by working on the staff of the school newspaper, magazine, or yearbook, and developing their own websites or zines. It may also be possible to secure a part-time job assisting the advertising director of the local newspaper or to work at an advertising agency. Developing your own artistic talent is important, and this can be accomplished through self-training (reading books and practicing) or through courses in painting, drawing, or other creative arts. At the very least, you should develop your "creative eye," that is, your ability to develop ideas visually. One way to do this is by familiarizing yourself with great works, such as paintings or highly creative magazine ads, motion pictures, videos, or commercials.

Students can also become members of a variety of art or advertising clubs around the nation. If you have access to the Internet, check out Paleta: The Art Project (http://www.paletaworld.org) to join a free art club. In addition to keeping members up to date on industry trends, such clubs offer job information, resources, and a variety of other benefits.

■ EMPLOYERS

A variety of organizations in virtually all industries employ art directors. They might work at advertising agencies, publishing houses, museums, packaging firms, photography studios, marketing and public relations firms, desktop publishing outfits, digital pre-press houses, or printing companies. Art directors who oversee and produce on-screen products often work for film production houses, Web designers, multimedia developers, computer games developers, or television stations.

While companies of all sizes employ art directors, smaller organizations often combine the positions of graphic designer, illustrator, and art director. And although opportunities for art direction can be found all across the nation and abroad, many larger firms in such cities as Chicago, New York, and Los Angeles usually have more openings, as well as higher pay scales, than smaller companies.

■ STARTING OUT

Since an art director's job requires a great deal of experience, it is usually not considered an entry-level position. Typically, a person on a career track toward art director is hired as an assistant to an established director. Recent graduates wishing to enter advertising should have a portfolio of their work containing seven to 10 sample ads to demonstrate their understanding of both the business and the media in which they want to work.

Serving as an intern is a good way to get experience and develop skills. Graduates should also consider taking an entry-level job in a publisher's art department to gain initial experience. Either way, aspiring art directors must be willing to acquire their credentials by working on various projects. This may mean working in a variety of areas, such as advertising, marketing, editing, and design.

College publications offer students a chance to gain experience and develop portfolios. In addition, many students are able to do freelance work while still in school, allowing them to make important industry contacts and gain on-the-job experience at the same time.

■ ADVANCEMENT

While some may be content upon reaching the position of art director to remain there, many art directors take on even more responsibility within their organizations, become television directors, start their own advertising agencies, create their own websites, develop original multimedia programs, or launch their own magazines.

Many people who get to the position of art director do not advance beyond the title but move on to work at more prestigious firms. Competition for positions at companies that have national reputations continues to be keen because of the sheer number of talented people interested. At smaller publications or local companies, the

An art director at an advertising agency examines slides.

competition may be less intense, since candidates are competing primarily against others in the local market.

■ EARNINGS

The job title of art director can mean many different things, depending on the company at which the director is employed. According to the U.S. Department of Labor, a beginning art director or an art director working at a small firm can expect to make $32,410 or less per year in 2002, with experienced art directors working at larger companies earning more than $115,570. Median annual earnings for art directors employed in the advertising industry (the largest employer of salaried art directors) were $77,180 in 2002. The median annual earnings for art directors working in all industries were $61,850. (Again, it is important to note that these positions are not entry level; beginning art directors have probably already accumulated several years of experience in the field for which they were paid far less.)

According to the American Institute of Graphic Arts' Aquent Salary Survey 2003, the median salary for art directors was $60,000. Art directors in the 25th percentile earned $48,000 annually, while those in the 75th percentile made $75,000 per year.

Most companies employing art directors offer insurance benefits, a retirement plan, and other incentives and bonuses.

THE IMPACT OF TECHNOLOGY

New technologies are playing key roles in the art director's job. To prepare future professionals who will be using these emerging technologies, art and design schools across the country are offering a wide variety of related courses. Below are just some of the classes that students can take at the School of Visual Arts in New York:

- Basic 3D Graphic Design
- Computers in the Studio
- The Digital Image
- Advanced Digital Video
- Web Design
- Web Programming
- Internet Culture and Community
- Internet Studio
- 3D Animation Mechanics
- Telecommunications for Artists
- Music Composition and Sound Design
- Virtual Reality Seminar

■ WORK ENVIRONMENT

Art directors usually work in studios or office buildings. While their work areas are ordinarily comfortable, well lit, and ventilated, they often handle glue, paint, ink, and other materials that pose safety hazards, and they should, therefore, exercise caution.

Art directors at art and design studios and publishing firms usually work a standard 40-hour week. Many, however, work overtime during busy periods in order to meet deadlines. Similarly, directors at film and video operations and at television studios work as many hours as required—usually many more than 40 per week—in order to finish projects according to predetermined schedules.

While art directors work independently while reviewing artwork and reading copy, much of their time is spent collaborating with and supervising a team of employees, often consisting of copywriters, editors, photographers, graphic artists, and account executives.

■ OUTLOOK

The extent to which art director positions are in demand, like many other positions, depends on the economy in general; when times are tough, people and businesses spend less, and cutbacks are made. When the economy is

healthy, employment prospects for art directors will be favorable. The U.S. Department of Labor predicts that employment for art directors will grow about as fast as the average for all other occupations. One area that shows particularly good promise for growth is the retail industry, since more and more large retail establishments, especially catalog houses, will be employing in-house advertising art directors.

In addition, producers of all kinds of products continually need advertisers to reach their potential customers, and publishers always want some type of illustration to enhance their books and magazines. Creators of films and videos also need images in order to produce their programs, and people working with new media are increasingly looking for artists and directors to promote new and existing products and services, enhance their websites, develop new multimedia programs, and create multidimensional visuals. People who can quickly and creatively generate new concepts and ideas will be in high demand.

However, it is important to note that the supply of aspiring artists is expected to exceed the number of job openings. As a result, those wishing to enter the field will encounter keen competition for salaried, staff positions as well as for freelance work. And although the Internet is expected to provide many opportunities for artists and art directors, some firms are hiring employees without formal art or design training to operate computer-aided design systems and oversee work.

■ FOR MORE INFORMATION

The AAF is the professional advertising association that binds the mutual interests of corporate advertisers, agencies, media companies, suppliers, and academia. For more information, contact

American Advertising Federation (AAF)
1101 Vermont Avenue, NW, Suite 500
Washington, DC 20005-6306
Tel: 202-898-0089
Email: aaf@aaf.org
http://www.aaf.org

This management-oriented national trade organization represents the advertising agency business. For information, contact

American Association of Advertising Agencies
405 Lexington Avenue, 18th Floor
New York, NY 10174-1801
Tel: 212-682-2500
http://www.aaaa.org

For more information on design professionals, contact

American Institute of Graphic Arts
164 Fifth Avenue
New York, NY 10010
Tel: 212-807-1990
http://www.aiga.org

The Art Directors Club is an international, nonprofit organization of directors in advertising, graphic design, interactive media, broadcast design, typography, packaging, environmental design, photography, illustration, and related disciplines. For information, contact

Art Directors Club
106 West 29th Street
New York, NY 10001
Tel: 212-643-1440
Email: info@adcglobal.org
http://www.adcglobal.org

For information on the graphic arts, contact

Graphic Artists Guild
90 John Street, Suite 403
New York, NY 10038-3202
Tel: 212-791-3400
http://www.gag.org

Artist and Repertoire Workers

■ OVERVIEW

In the artist and repertoire (A&R) department of a record company, *A&R coordinators, executives,* and other workers locate new talent and convince the company to sign them to contracts. A&R workers are also involved in producing their artists' CDs, promoting them, arranging concert tours, and other details of management.

■ HISTORY

Talent scouts first became important to the recording industry in the 1950s, when pop and rock artists dominated the radio. For the first time in the country's history, teenagers were taken seriously as a consumer group, and their musical preferences made the small, independent companies that produced rock and roll records hugely successful. In the 1960s, record companies employed people who would match the professional musicians (artists) with songs (repertoire) written by professional com-

posers. After a period of poor sales in the 1970s, record companies bounced back in the 1980s with the advent of the music video. During this new era of big business, A&R executives became even more powerful in the entertainment industry. Record companies relied on A&R professionals to sign and promote artists who had potential for huge sales quickly. Though record companies increasingly rely on major, break-out performers to generate large profits, A&R workers are still needed to develop a diverse group of artists that can bring their companies stable long-term returns on their investment.

■ THE JOB

If you've ever been in a band, and you've tried to get some local, paying gigs, then you're familiar with how difficult it can be to get your music heard. You'll likely meet with even more frustration if you try to market your band nationally in an effort to get a record contract. A&R workers have firsthand knowledge of the number of artists hoping to sign with a record label—thousands of submissions cross their desks every year.

A&R workers review these submissions, looking and listening for talented musicians. They listen to demo tape after demo tape, and read through press clippings and artist biographies. They also keep track of the music scene by attending clubs and reading fanzines. A&R workers visit websites and download samples. Although they listen to a lot of music that doesn't interest them, occasionally they come across something that stands out. When they do, A&R workers set out to get to know the artist better. Just because A&R workers like an artist's demo tape, it doesn't mean they will automatically sign the artist to a contract. They first have to get a complete sense of the artist's talents. They may request additional recorded songs and go to live performances. Once they feel confident about the artist's talent, A&R workers attempt to get him or her a record deal. This

QUICK FACTS	
SCHOOL SUBJECTS	Business Music
PERSONAL SKILLS	Artistic Leadership/management
WORK ENVIRONMENT	Primarily indoors One location with some travel
MINIMUM EDUCATION LEVEL	Bachelor's degree
SALARY RANGE	$20,000 to $85,000 to $200,000+
CERTIFICATION OR LICENSING	None available
OUTLOOK	About as fast as the average
DOT	159
GOE	01.04.01
NOC	N/A
O*NET-SOC	N/A

LEARN MORE ABOUT IT

Many websites are devoted to music and the recording industry. Here are a few places to start:

- CMJ Online (http://www.cmj.com) features a great deal of information about new music and artists, including audio clips and artist interviews.
- R&R Online (http://www.rronline.com) is "The Radio & Record Industries Information Leader." There you'll find music news, lists of job opportunities across the country, music charts, and links to record labels and other industry sites.
- Billboard Online (http://www.billboard-online.com) lists top albums and features reviews, previews, classifieds, and a reader Q&A.

involves convincing executives at the record company that the artist is worth the risk. But an A&R worker may also work with an artist that is being pursued by A&R representatives from other companies. In such cases, the A&R worker has to convince the artist that he or she will receive the attention and care he or she needs.

The work of A&R representatives doesn't end when they've signed the talent to a contract. A&R workers become closely involved in the careers of their artists. They help match them with producers and assist in the mixing of the tracks. They also help promote the artists—from helping them select the right clothes to wear for the CD cover photograph, to arranging interviews, to deciding which singles should be played on the radio. In many cases, A&R representatives work with artists closely throughout their careers, helping them to stay successful as artists and business people.

■ REQUIREMENTS
High School

Most A&R workers have a college degree, so in high school you should pursue a college preparatory track. Classes in business, mathematics, speech, and English will be helpful. The most important thing you can do is to become involved in music, be it playing in a school band or with a group of friends, going to shows, or simply listening to a wide variety of music in your spare time.

Postsecondary Training

Executives in the music industry come from a variety of backgrounds. You'll likely need a college degree, but experience with a record company will be the most valuable training. An internship is highly recommended, and is

useful for making the right connections. Some A&R workers have degrees in communications, business, marketing, and music.

Other Requirements

Mainly, you'll need a love for music and an interest in the business end of the music industry. You should have a good sense of the history of popular music as well as the acts that are currently on the scene. You'll also need to be very organized; A&R workers for big companies generally must handle many different acts in different stages of production.

■ EXPLORING

Listen to a wide variety of music and follow the careers of your favorite recording artists by reading magazines and surfing the Internet. Listen especially to new talent as it emerges. There are certain radio stations that frequently feature new musicians. Visit clubs that regularly book live music.

Study music, including music performance and music history. If possible, join a group to learn about the challenges of performing with others, composing original music, booking gigs, and managing the business side of music.

■ EMPLOYERS

There are hundreds of record companies across the country, but many are small, independent labels staffed by very few people. Five corporations—Universal, Warner, Sony, BMG, and EMI—now control 80 percent of the recording industry in the United States and employ the majority of A&R workers. Major record labels include A&M, Geffen, MCA, Warner Bros., Atlantic, Columbia, Arista, Virgin, and Capitol. Most positions are located in Los Angeles, New York City, and Nashville.

■ STARTING OUT

Getting a job in A&R can be very difficult—such positions are highly sought after. Some major record companies offer internship opportunities; check with your college's internship office for information. After college, you can pursue an entry-level position with a record company. You should work in any department in which there's a job opening. Check the help wanted ads in such trade magazines as *Billboard* (http://www.billboard.com) and *Variety* (http://www.variety.com), or seek out temporary employment agencies that specialize in placing people in jobs in the entertainment industry.

■ ADVANCEMENT

Once A&R workers gain some experience in the music industry, whether within a company, or as a freelance producer or manager, they will be able to make connections with other, more experienced A&R professionals. An A&R worker may begin as an assistant, then work up into a position as a coordinator, and later as a vice-president or president of the department.

▨ EARNINGS

A&R workers in entry-level positions make around $20,000 a year. More senior positions can pay upwards of $85,000. Experienced executives with major record companies can make more than $200,000 a year. Full-time employment with a record company usually includes health and retirement benefits, as well as bonuses.

▨ WORK ENVIRONMENT

Work with a record company can be very exciting—A&R workers have the opportunity to make decisions about what music people will be listening to and which artists will get a shot at success. But the work can be very stressful and intense. A&R professionals work long hours, making phone calls, devising schedules, reviewing contracts, and handling many other details of management. They have to sort through a lot of bad music and insistent would-be stars to find the few artists that interest them. They also devote many evenings to scouting out new talent at clubs.

▨ OUTLOOK

The A&R worker will always be important to record companies, and positions within an A&R department will always be difficult to get. The work itself will be affected greatly by the Internet in the years to come. Already, A&R workers are surfing the Web for artists marketing themselves with their own websites. Technological advances have allowed for quick and easy downloading of music and other forms of media from the Internet, and some artists are now using the Web to bypass record companies entirely. So, in addition to competing with other record companies for talent, A&R workers may be competing with the artists themselves for the opportunity to distribute their music.

▨ FOR MORE INFORMATION

Visit the NARAS website to read about efforts to support the recording industry and to check out links to many music and recording-related sites:

National Academy of Recording Arts and Sciences (NARAS)
3402 Pico Boulevard
Santa Monica, CA 90405
Tel: 310-392-3777
http://grammy.com

For facts and statistics about the recording industry, contact
Recording Industry Association of America
1330 Connecticut Avenue, NW, Suite 300
Washington, DC 20036
Tel: 202-775-0101
http://www.riaa.com

For industry information, contact
The Society of Professional Audio Recording Services
PO Box 770845
Memphis, TN 38177-0845
Tel: 800-771-7727
Email: spars@spars.com
http://www.spars.com

Artists

▨ OVERVIEW

Visual artists convey thoughts, opinions, and ideas through their work, whether it is a realistic painting, a piece of pottery, or an abstract sculpture. They use one or more media, such as clay, paint, metal, or computer technology, to create two- or three-dimensional works. The field of visual arts is usually separated into three categories: commercial art, fine art, and craft. There are approximately 149,000 visual artists employed in the United States, and more than half of them are self-employed.

▨ HISTORY

The history of art is a huge topic that covers thousands of years of human history all over the world. Many people devote their entire careers to its study, and since art history is such a large topic, historians usually specialize, focusing on either a time period, such as the Renaissance or the early 20th century, or a particular area, such as Mexico or Southeast Asia.

Anthropologists and historians speculate that the earliest works of art were created for their function rather than for decorative or aesthetic value. The Venus of Willendorf, a figure carved from limestone around 21,000 to 25,000 B.C., might have been a part of fertility rites and rituals. The cave paintings of France and Spain, which date back to 15,000 B.C., were probably ceremonial, meant to bring good luck to the hunt.

Much of early visual art was religious, reflecting the beliefs and legends with which people tried to understand their place in the world and in life. Art was also political, used to glorify society or the leaders of society.

For example, the immense sculptures of Ramses II of ancient Egypt and the sculptures of Roman art depicted their rulers and their stature in society.

The art of Greece and Rome exerted a profound influence on much of the history of Western art. The sculptural ideals developed by the ancient Greeks, particularly with their perfection of anatomical forms, continued to dominate Western sculpture until well into the 19th century. In painting, artists sought methods to depict or suggest a greater realism, experimenting with techniques of lighting, shading, and perspective.

The rise of the Christian era brought a return to symbolism over realism. Illuminated manuscripts, which were written texts, usually religious in content, and decorated with designs and motifs meant to provide further understanding of the text, became the primary form of artistic expression for nearly a millennium. The artwork for these manuscripts often featured highly elaborate and detailed abstract designs. The human figure was absent in much of this work, reflecting religious prohibition of the creation of idols.

Artists returned to more naturalistic techniques during the 14th century with the rise of Gothic art forms. The human figure returned to art and artists began creating works not only for rulers and religious institutions, but also for a growing wealthy class. Portrait painting became an increasingly important source of work and income for artists. New materials, particularly oil glazes and paints, allowed artists to achieve more exact detailing and more subtle light, color, and shading effects.

During the Renaissance, artists rediscovered the art of ancient Greece and Rome. This brought new developments not only in artists' techniques but also in their stature in society. The development of perspective techniques in the 14th and 15th centuries revolutionized painting. Perspective allowed the artists to create the illusion of three dimensions, so that a spectator felt that he or she

looked not merely at a painting but into it. Advances in the study of anatomy enabled artists to create more dramatic and realistic figures, whether in painting or sculpture, providing the illusion of action and fluidity and heightening the naturalism of their work. Artists achieved higher status and were sought out by the wealthy, the church, and rulers for their talent and skill.

Renaissance artists became bolder and experimented with line, color, contour, shading, setting, and composition, presenting work of greater realism and at the same time of deeper emotional content. The style of an artist became more highly individualized, more a personal reflection of the artist's thoughts, beliefs, ideas, and feelings.

Artists continued to influence one another, but national and cultural differences began to appear in art as the Catholic Church lost its dominance and new religious movements took hold during the 16th and 17th centuries. Art academies, such as the Royal Academy of Painting and Sculpture in Paris, were established and sought to codify artistic ideals.

During the next two centuries there were profound changes in the nature of art, leading to the revolutionary work of the impressionists of the late 19th century and the dawn of the modern era in art. Sculpture, which had remained largely confined to the Greek and Roman ideals, found new directions. The individual sensibility of the artist took on a greater importance and led to a greater freedom of painting techniques. Many of the ideals of the French academy were challenged, leading to the avant-garde work of the early French impressionists. Artists began to take on a new role by presenting society with new concepts, ideas, and visions and radical departures in style. Artists no longer simply reflected prevailing culture but adopted leadership positions in creating culture, often rejecting entirely the artistic principles of the past.

The image of the artist as cultural outsider, societal misfit, or even tormented soul took hold. Artists working in the avant garde achieved notoriety, if not financial reward, and the "misunderstood" or "starving" artist became a popular 20th-century image.

The 20th century witnessed an explosion of artistic styles and techniques. Art, both in painting and sculpture, became increasingly abstracted from reality, and purely formal concerns developed. Impressionism and postimpressionism gave way to futurism, expressionism, fauvism, cubism, nonobjective art, surrealism, and other styles.

American art, which had largely followed the examples set by European artists, came into its own during the 1940s and 1950s, with the rise of abstract expressionism. During the 1950s, a new art form, pop art, reintroduced recognizable images and often mundane objects to satirize and otherwise comment on cultural and societal life.

QUICK FACTS

SCHOOL SUBJECTS
Art
History

PERSONAL SKILLS
Artistic
Communication/ideas

WORK ENVIRONMENT
Indoors and outdoors
One location with some travel

MINIMUM EDUCATION LEVEL
High school diploma

SALARY RANGE
$17,160 to $35,420 to
$114,390+

CERTIFICATION OR LICENSING
None available

OUTLOOK
About as fast as the average

DOT
144, 779

GOE
01.04.01, 01.06.01

NOC
5136, 5244

O*NET-SOC
27-1013.00, 27-1013.01,
27-1013.04, 51-9195.05

More recent trends in art have given the world the graffiti-inspired works of Keith Haring and the "non-art" sculpture of Jeff Koons, as well as the massive installations of Christo. Artists today work in a great variety of styles, forms, and media. Many artists combine elements of painting, sculpture, and other art forms, such as photography, music, and dance, into their work. The rise of video recording techniques and especially of three-dimensional computer animations has recently begun to challenge many traditional ideas of art.

This brief art history time line has covered only Western fine art, but different art trends and developments occurred around the world simultaneously. Europeans had acquired art objects from other parts of the world for centuries as curios, status symbols, and collectors' items, but the appreciation of these objects and paintings as works of art is relatively recent. Westerners now recognize paintings, sculpture, and functional objects from even the remotest parts of the world as having great artistic value and making significant contributions to the development of Western art.

The debate continues about whether some functional items, such as pottery, furniture, rugs, and jewelry, for example, can be considered works of art. The lines have become blurred between artistry and craftsmanship, since many objects created for a specific function are beautiful to look at, make social and cultural commentary, or push the limits of convention as much as any painting or sculpture. Many media forms traditionally considered craft media, such as woodworking, ceramics, silversmithing, and papier mâché, are used in sculpture and mixed-media works, further confusing the distinctions between art and craft.

Early commercial art may have its beginnings with signage, when symbols and pictures were used along with lettering to advertise places of business. Commercial art began to flourish with the advent of printing technology and the subsequent development of the publishing industry. Artists illustrated stories and advertisements and arranged type and artwork for books, magazines, and newspapers. The growth of the advertising industry throughout the 19th and 20th centuries fueled the growth of commercial art. Artists used black and white line art in the beginning, which gave way to color drawings, and then photography, and then computer-generated visuals. Today commercial artists work in all phases of publishing, including decorative and explanatory illustration, photography, layout, typography, and print production. Advertising art includes art direction, print advertising (magazines, newspapers, catalogs, and direct mail), package design, film production, and Web design.

A ceramic artist shapes a decorative vase.

■ THE JOB

Visual artists use their creative abilities to produce original works of art to express ideas; to provide social and cultural commentary; to communicate messages; to record events; to explore color, texture, line, and other visual elements; and for many other purposes. *Fine artists* usually create works for display in public areas or in private galleries. *Commercial artists* produce art that illustrates, explains, or draws attention to text, as in advertising and publishing. *Craft workers,* or *artisans,* create works that usually have a function.

Fine artists work for themselves. Their art comes from their own ideas and methods of working. They spend years developing their own style, focusing on a chosen subject, and refining their skills in a particular medium. Many artists work in only one technique or focus on one subject area throughout their lives, such as painting only large-scale oil portraits. Most artists change styles subtly as they gain experience in their art and in their lives, and some experiment with different media. For example, a sculptor who works in clay may switch to bronze casting later in his or her career. Many artists develop a particular style and apply that style across a broad range of techniques, from painting to etching to sculpture.

Painters use different media to paint a variety of subjects, such as landscapes, people, or objects. They work with oil paint, acrylic paint, tempera, watercolors, gouache, pen and ink, or pastels, but they may also incorporate such nontraditional media as clay, paper, cloth, and a variety of other material. They use brushes, palette knives, airbrushes, and other tools to apply color to canvas, paper, or other surfaces. Painters use line, texture, color, and other visual elements to produce the desired effect.

Sculptors create three-dimensional works of art. They may carve objects from stone, plaster, concrete, or wood.

They may use their fingers to model clay or wax into objects. Some sculptors create forms from metal or stone, using various masonry tools and equipment. Some sculptors form objects with clay or wax from which to make a mold, which is then cast in bronze or other metals, plastics, or other materials. Others create works from found objects, whether parts of a car, branches of a tree, or other objects. Like painters, sculptors may be identified with a particular technique or style. Their work can take monumental forms, or they may work on a very small scale.

Visual artists also include *printmakers,* who engrave, etch, or mask their designs on wood, stone, metal, or silk screen. These designs are then transferred, or printed, on paper. Printmakers can also create their art using computers. These artists use computer scanners to scan the prepared plates and then reproduce prints using high-quality color printers.

Mixed-media artists incorporate several techniques, such as painting, sculpture, collage, printing, and drawing, into one work of art.

Ceramic artists, also known as *potters, ceramists, sculptors,* and *clay artists,* work with clay to make both functional objects and sculpture. Their work often blurs the distinction between fine art and craft. They blend basic

elements (such as clay and water) and more specialized components (such as texture fillers, colorants, and talc) and form the mixture into shapes using either manual techniques or wheel-throwing techniques to create dinnerware, vases, beads, tiles, architectural installations, and sculptures. Some ceramic artists make molds from materials like plaster and use a casting method. The formed pieces, called greenware, are fired in kilns at very high temperatures. The artists apply glazes and other finishes and fire them again to set the pieces.

Other visual artists that blur the distinction between fine art and craft are *glass workers,* including *stained glass artists, glassblowers,* and *etchers.* Stained glass artists cut colored pieces of glass, arrange them in a design, and connect them with leading. The leading is then soldered to hold the glass pieces together. Glassblowers use a variety of instruments to blow molten glass into bottles, vases, and sculptures. Etchers use fine hand and power tools, and sometimes chemicals, to create a design in the surface of glass.

Fiber artists create wall hangings and sculpture from textiles, threads, and paper.

Visual artists are innovators and are not bound by tradition or convention. They respond to cultural and societal stimuli and incorporate them into works of art. In recent years, they have used copiers, laser beams, computers, and other technology not originally intended for art as alternative media.

Most fine artists work on their own. Once they create a body of work, they usually seek out a gallery to display and sell their work. The gallery owner and artist set the prices for pieces of art, and the gallery owner receives a commission on any work that sells. The relationship between the gallery owner and artist is often one of close cooperation. For example, a gallery owner may encourage artists to explore new techniques, styles, and ideas while helping to establish their reputation. As an artist becomes well known, selling his or her work often becomes easier, and many well-known artists receive commissions for their art. A sculptor, for example, might be commissioned to create a piece specifically for the lobby or outdoor plaza of a public building. A stained glass artist might be commissioned to make a window for a church.

Commercial artists include *graphic designers, illustrators, art directors,* and *photographers.* Their art differs from fine art in that it is usually created according to the wishes of a client or employer. Computers are now widely used to create illustrations, typography, and page layouts, but traditional methods are still being used for illustration. Original drawings, paintings, collage, and other two-dimensional pieces can be scanned and digitized and then the image can be manipulated using software programs.

PROFILE: JOSIAH WEDGWOOD (1730–95)

English potter Josiah Wedgwood is noted for the beauty and perfection of his ware and for his leadership in making pottery one of England's important industries. He introduced and frequently used the shade of blue named for him. Wedgwood ware is found in many private collections and in museums.

Wedgwood was born in Burslem, Staffordshire, of a family of potters. He opened his own factory in 1759, and in 1769, he founded Etruria, a colony in Staffordshire. The colony included a large factory and homes for its workers. Wedgwood applied scientific techniques to developing and perfecting his ware and mass production methods to its manufacture. He employed outstanding artists to design the many kinds of ornamental pieces and tableware for which his factories are famous. The Wedgwood potteries are still in operation.

Among Wedgwood's creations are queen's ware, a fine, cream-colored earthenware; basalt, a black stoneware (vitreous pottery); rosso antico, a red stoneware decorated with black figures in relief; and jasper, an unglazed porcelain in white or soft colors, decorated with cameolike designs in white. Jasper was Wedgwood's last and perhaps greatest creation and the most widely used and imitated of his wares.

Commercial artists work primarily in the advertising and publishing industries and for businesses that need advertising and publishing services, such as retail stores.

In most cases, commercial art is closely related to textual matter. For example, a medical illustrator might draw a series of pictures to demonstrate a surgical technique. Advertisements often show a product, or someone using a product, along with text that persuades viewers to buy that product. Photographs accompany feature articles in magazines and newspapers to show the people and places depicted in the story. Art is also included to draw the reader's attention to certain textual matter. Art directors and graphic designers commission, select, and arrange visuals and text on the page so it will be easy to read as well as attractive and pleasing to the reader.

Craft workers are artists who make decorative, usually three-dimensional items that are often functional. They make jewelry, furniture, dinnerware, musical instruments, pottery, and quilts, to name a few. They use many of the same techniques as fine artists, including painting, carving, casting, and modeling, and they use a variety of tools from needle and thread to chain saws.

Another specialized area of visual art is evaluation and restoration. Painting experts preserve and restore aged, faded, or damaged art. They also evaluate the age and authenticity of the work. Restoring art can be tedious and detailed work, requiring the precise and skillful application of solvents and cleaning agents to the work. *Art conservators* also repair damaged sculpture, pottery, jewelry, fabrics, and other items, depending on their area of expertise.

Visual art is an intensely personal endeavor. Most artists are people with a desire and need to explore visual representations of real and imagined worlds. Their work usually continues and develops throughout their lives. Creating art is rarely a career choice but rather a way of life.

■ REQUIREMENTS
High School
In the public school system, there is very little art instruction at the elementary level, so high school is your chance to take as many art courses as you can. Many schools offer general art instruction that exposes you to several techniques and principles. Some schools offer specialized art classes in painting, sculpture, design principles, graphic design, photography, and computer graphics. You may have to find other art instruction outside of your school if you are interested in ceramics, woodworking, stained glass, or another specialty. Check community centers, junior colleges, independent schools of art, or local galleries that might offer classes.

A wood sculptor at work in his studio

Postsecondary Training
There are no formal educational requirements for becoming a visual artist. However, most artists benefit from training, and many, about 90 percent, attend art schools or programs in colleges and universities. Twenty percent of all artists major in fine arts, according to the American Institute of Graphic Arts, and of those, 20 percent have at least a master's degree. Master's programs may offer majors in ceramic art, fiber art, art history, film and photography, sculpture, and a number of others.

Two-year or associate's degree programs are available in many art specialties, including computer graphics, advertising design, fashion design, illustration, and photography, among others.

Besides earning a degree, there are many workshops, private studios, and individuals that offer instruction, practice, and exposure to art and the works and ideas of other artists. It is wise to learn a variety of techniques, be exposed to as many media and styles as possible, and gain an understanding of the history and theory of art. By learning as much as possible, you will have more choices for your own artistic expression.

Some types of artists need training in an additional field. For example, medical illustrators are required to have training in biology and anatomy. Medical or scientific illustrators not only have a four-year degree in art with an emphasis in premedical courses, but most have a

WORDS TO KNOW

PAINTING

Broken color: Colors laid next to each other and blended by the eye of the viewer; thus instead of mixing red and blue on a palette to produce purple, red and blue are placed next to each other on the canvas.

Drybrush: A technique in which paint of a thick consistency is stroked lightly over a dry surface; it produces a broken or mottled effect.

Glaze: A film of transparent paint applied over a solid color, producing a luminous, rich effect.

Grisaille: A monochromatic painting, usually in shades of gray; it may be a finished painting or an underpainting.

Impasto: A thick application of paint to a canvas or panel; the marks of the brush or palette knife can be seen plainly.

Imprimatura: A toned ground created by a thin wash or glaze of transparent color.

Scumble: An application of opaque paint over a different color of paint; the original color is not covered entirely, giving an uneven effect.

Stippling: The technique of applying small dots of paint to a surface to build up tonal areas or textures.

Underpainting: A preliminary painting on the painting surface; using tones of one color, the artist makes an underpainting to establish the basic shapes, values, and overall composition of a painting.

Wash: A thin layer of paint spread evenly over a broad area.

Wet-in-wet: A technique in which fresh paint is applied on top of or into wet paint already on the support; used with watercolors and oils and can produce both distinctive contrasts of color and softly blended effects.

SCULPTURE

Bronzing: The process of coloring a plaster cast in imitation of bronze.

Cast: A work of sculpture that has been produced from a mold.

Cast stone: A mixture of cement or concrete and stone that is cast from a mold.

Dry lacquering: A technique in which a modeled clay form is covered with many layers of lacquer-soaked cloth; when the cloth is dry, the clay is removed, and the hollow form is finished with gesso (a fine plaster) and painted.

Mold: The shell-like impression into which a casting material is poured or pressed. A piece mold is made in several sections, or pieces; it can easily be pulled off the cast and used again. A waste mold has to be broken, or "wasted," to remove the cast.

Plastic: A sculpture that was produced by the modeling technique; it is the opposite of glyptic, a sculpture that was produced by carving. Any material that can be shaped by modeling is also referred to as plastic.

Repoussé: A term used in sculpture to describe a sculpture that has been hammered, or beaten, from a sheet of metal into the desired shape.

Stucco: A blend of gypsum or cement and pulverized marble used as a medium for relief sculpture.

master's degree in medical illustration. Only a few schools in the United States offer this specialized coursework.

Apprenticeships are sometimes available in certain art fields, such as glassmaking, ceramics, printmaking, woodworking, and papermaking. Apprenticeships allow young artists the opportunity for intensive training under master artists while actually producing art objects.

Other Requirements

While attending classes, earning a degree, or working under a master artist, it is important for fine artists and craft workers to build a body of work that shows a definite and unique style and a thematic progression. Gallery owners and sales representatives want to represent artists they can count on to keep producing work. They also like to see a certain amount of consistency of style to satisfy customer demand for a particular artist's work. Commercial artists need to build a portfolio of published work to show to potential clients and employers. A portfolio can be very specific—showing only portrait photography, for example—or it can be general, showing your ability to use a number of techniques for varied clients.

You need creativity and imagination to be a visual artist, but you also need patience, persistence, determination, independence, sensitivity, and confidence in your abilities.

Because earning a living as a fine artist or craft worker is very difficult, especially when you are starting out, you may have to work at another job. With the proper training and educational background, many fine artists are able to work in art-related positions, such as art teachers, art directors, or graphic designers, while pursuing their art activities independently.

■ EXPLORING

You need very little to begin to explore your interest in art. Crayons, pencil and paper, glue and found objects can get you started. Inexpensive paints, clays, markers, and other supplies are available at art supply stores and department stores.

Your school may have art-related clubs, such as poster clubs, drama clubs that allow you to design and construct sets and costumes, and publicity committees. School newspapers and magazines will give you exposure to commercial art, including illustration, photography, and page design.

Specialized art instruction may be available at community centers, art galleries, and private studios in your town.

Visit art galleries and museums often and begin to form opinions about what you like and don't like, both in terms of design and technique. Visit your library and look at art books and magazines that feature the art of particular periods or artists. There are also numerous resources that give step-by step instructions for art techniques.

The New York Foundation for the Arts hosts a valuable website (http://www.nyfa.org) that offers information on job leads, art events, and other concerns of visual artists.

■ EMPLOYERS

Fine artists are usually self-employed, and very few are able to support themselves completely by the sale of their art. They hold other jobs that allow them to pursue their artistic endeavors on a part-time basis, or they may work in art-related jobs, such as in teaching, commercial art, art therapy, or working in a gallery or art museum.

Most craft workers are also self-employed, although there are full-time positions in some fields. For example, a stained-glass artist might find a job with a small shop, or a ceramic artist might work for a pottery production factory.

Many commercial artists are self-employed, but they can more readily find full-time employment, primarily in the publishing and advertising industries. They also work in all kinds of businesses, including retail, public relations, fashion, and entertainment.

■ STARTING OUT

Visual artists interested in exhibiting or selling their products should first and foremost develop a portfolio, or a collection of work. The portfolio, which should be organized and showcase a wide variety of the artist's talent and capabilities, is an essential tool when looking for work.

To develop business opportunities, artists should investigate their potential markets. Reference books, such as *The Artist's & Graphic Designer's Market* (Cincinnati, Ohio: Writers Digest Books, 2003) may be helpful, as well as library books that offer information on business and tax law and related issues.

Local fairs and art shows often provide opportunities for new artists to display their work. Art councils are a good source of information on upcoming fairs. However, most successful artists are represented by a gallery or agent that displays their work and approaches potential buyers when new works are available. The gallery or agent gets a commission for each piece of artwork sold. Relationships between artists and gallery operators can be tricky, so legal advice is recommended, but such relationships can also be beneficial to both creator and seller. A good gallery operator encourages, supports, and believes in the artists he or she represents.

Many art schools and universities have placement services to help graduates find jobs. Although fine artists are generally self-employed, many need to work at another job, at least initially, to support themselves while they establish a reputation.

■ ADVANCEMENT

The channels of advancement for self-employed fine artists are not as well-defined as they would be for an artist employed at a company. An artist may become increasingly well known, both nationally and internationally, and may be able to command higher prices for his or her work. The success of a fine artist depends on a variety of factors, including talent, drive, and determination. However, luck often seems to play a role in many artists' successes, and some artists do not achieve recognition until late in life, if at all. Artists with business skills may open galleries to display their own and others' work. Those with the appropriate educational backgrounds may become art teachers, agents, or critics.

Commercial artists can start out in publishing or advertising as graphic designers and with experience become art directors or account executives.

■ EARNINGS

The amount of money earned by visual artists varies greatly. Because most work as freelancers, they can set their own prices.

According to the U.S. Department of Labor, the median annual earnings of salaried fine artists, including painters and sculptors, were $35,420 in 2003. Salaries ranged from less than $17,160 to more than $74,080.

The median salary for art directors was $62,260 in 2003. Salaries ranged from less than $34,160 to more than $114,390. Median annual earnings of salaried multimedia artists and animators were $45,920 in 2003.

Artists often work long hours and earn little, especially when they are first starting out. The price they charge is up to them, but much depends on the value the public places on their work. A particular item may sell for a few dollars or tens of thousands of dollars, or at any price in between. Often the value of a piece may increase considerably after it has been sold. Artwork that may have earned an artist only a few hundred dollars when it was first completed may earn many thousands of dollars the next time it is sold if the artist's work becomes well known and in demand.

Some artists obtain grants that allow them to pursue their art; others win prizes and awards in competitions. Most artists, however, have to work on their projects part time while holding a regular, full-time job. Many artists teach in art schools, high schools, or out of their studios. Artists who sell their products must pay social security and other taxes on any money they receive and provide their own benefits.

■ WORK ENVIRONMENT

Most painters and sculptors work out of their homes or in studios. Some work in small areas in their apartments; others work in large, well-ventilated lofts, garages, or warehouse space. An artist may choose complete solitude to work; others thrive on interaction with other artists and people. Occasionally, painters and sculptors work outside. Artists engaged in monumental work, particularly sculptors, often have helpers who assist in the creation of a piece of art, working under the artist's direction. They may contract with a foundry to cast a finished sculpture in bronze, iron, or another metal. In addition, artists often work at fairs, shops, museums, and other places where their work is being exhibited.

Artists often work long hours, and those who are self-employed do not have the security of a steady paycheck, paid vacations, insurance coverage, or any of the other benefits usually offered by a company or firm. However, artists are able to work at their own pace, set their own prices, and make their own decisions. The energy and creativity that go into an artist's work bring feelings of pride and satisfaction. Most artists genuinely love what they do.

■ OUTLOOK

Employment for visual artists is expected to grow as fast as the average through 2012, according to the U.S. Department of Labor. However, because they are usually self-employed, much of their success depends on the amount and type of work created, the drive and determination in selling the artwork, and the interest or readiness of the public to appreciate and purchase the work. Continued population growth, higher incomes, and increased appreciation for fine art will create a demand for visual artists.

Success for an artist, however, is difficult to quantify. Individual artists may consider themselves successful as their talent matures and they are better able to present their vision in their work. This type of success goes beyond financial considerations. Few artists enter this field for the money. Financial success depends on many factors, many of which have nothing to do with the artist or his or her work. Artists with good marketing skills or the ability to hire someone with marketing expertise will likely be the most successful in selling their work. Although artists should not let their style be dictated by market trends, those interested in financial success can attempt to determine what types of artwork the public wants.

It often takes several years for an artist's work and reputation to be established. Many artists have to support themselves through other employment. There are numerous employment opportunities for commercial artists in such fields as publishing, advertising, fashion and design, entertainment, and teaching, although there is strong competition from others who are attracted to these fields. Freelancers may have difficulty selling their work until they establish their artistic reputation. Artists skilled in computer techniques will have an edge.

This occupation may be affected by the amount of funding granted by the government. The National Endowment of the Arts, for example, awards grants and funding to help talented artists hone their craft.

■ FOR MORE INFORMATION

For general information on arts study, contact
National Art Education Association
1916 Association Drive
Reston, VA 20191-1590
Tel: 703-860-8000
Email: naea@dgs.dgsys.com
http://www.naea-reston.org

The following organization helps artists market and sell their art. It offers marketing tools, a newsletter, a directory of artists, and reference resources.
ArtNetwork
PO Box 1360
Nevada City, CA 95959
Tel: 800-383-0677
Email: info@artmarketing.com
http://www.artmarketing.com

For education information, contact

National Council on Education for the Ceramic Arts
77 Erie Village Square, Suite 280
Erie, CO 80516
Tel: 866-266-2322
Email: office@nceca.net
http://www.nceca.net

National Endowment for the Arts
1100 Pennsylvania Avenue, NW
Washington, DC 20506
Tel: 202-682-5400
Email: webmgr@arts.endow.gov
http://arts.endow.gov

The following organization provides an information exchange and sharing of professional opportunities.

Sculptors Guild
110 Greene Street, Suite 601
New York, NY 10012
Tel: 212-431-5669
http://www.sculptorsguild.org

Asbestos Abatement Technicians

■ OVERVIEW

Asbestos abatement technicians, also known as *asbestos removal technicians,* assist with the removal of asbestos-containing materials from buildings. Asbestos, now recognized as a hazardous material when released into the air, was once widely used in wall insulation, paint, pipes, ceiling tiles, and other building materials because of its fire-retardant properties. Many asbestos abatement technicians belong to the International Association of Heat and Frost Insulators and Asbestos Workers. Asbestos abatement technicians held about 2,300 jobs in the United States in 2002; all hazardous materials workers combined held about 38,000 jobs.

■ HISTORY

Asbestos is a tiny, fire-resistant fiber—a bundle of 600 equals the thickness of a human hair. It was used widely over the years on products and building materials to make them safer and stronger. Asbestos fibers were usu-

ally bundled together with other materials to keep them from being released into the air. Asbestos was used in insulation, carpet underlay, wall and ceiling panels, furnaces, and electrical wires, as well as hair dryers, toasters, and pot holders.

Asbestos fibers are considered safe when they stay bundled, but if a product is disturbed and the fibers are released, the asbestos can be seriously hazardous to your health. Breathing asbestos fibers can cause a scarring of the lungs, heart failure, and cancer. The Environmental Protection Agency (EPA) has been involved in banning asbestos since the 1970s, yet many buildings still contain asbestos, including schools and other public institutions. As a result, asbestos abatement services have evolved to remove or repair asbestos materials in buildings.

■ THE JOB

When materials such as ceiling tile or wall panels are determined to be undamaged, trained technicians coat them to seal them. Asbestos is removed only in cases of serious damage because it can cost a building owner a great deal of money and the process can be dangerous when not performed properly. If the materials are damaged, technicians install a covering to keep the fibers from being released into the air of the room.

Asbestos building inspectors collect samples and analyze them under a microscope in a laboratory. If a sample tests positive, the asbestos must be contained or removed in accordance with strict federal and state regulations.

Asbestos abatement technicians who have been trained in a state-approved program remove the asbestos with a variety of tools, procedures, and safety measures. They first prepare an area for work, which involves putting in a series of enclosures and possibly constructing scaffolds. In order to protect themselves and the areas outside of the enclosure, technicians wear disposable protective gear from head to toe and breathe through special masks. Using the

---

QUICK FACTS

SCHOOL SUBJECTS
Chemistry
Technical/shop

PERSONAL SKILLS
Following instructions
Mechanical/manipulative

WORK ENVIRONMENT
Primarily indoors
Primarily multiple locations

MINIMUM EDUCATIONAL LEVEL
Some postsecondary training

SALARY RANGE
$21,410 to $35,610 to $55,340

CERTIFICATION OR LICENSING
Required by all states

OUTLOOK
Much faster than the average

DOT
869

GOE
06.02.03

NOC
N/A

O*NET-SOC
47-4041.00

An asbestos abatement technician prepares to remove asbestos from a ceiling.

"wet method," technicians apply a mixture of water or other wetting agent to the asbestos to prevent the release of particles into the air. They use a variety of hand tools, such as scrapers and guns that spray chemicals, depending on the kind of material being removed. Mechanical tools are never used for fear of spreading fibers into the air. An air monitor continuously takes samples to ensure hazardous particles are few and are kept within the containment area.

Technicians then place the materials in plastic bags and prepare them for transport to a disposal site. Once the work has been completed, inspectors again survey and analyze the site to determine if it has been properly cleaned. If samples still show signs of asbestos, technicians must return to the site to remove any remaining asbestos-containing materials. If the work site is clear, the technicians then take down the enclosures and scaffolds, and the site is again open for use.

■ REQUIREMENTS
High School

You should take drafting courses, or any course that teaches you to read and create blueprints and detailed design plans. Basic arithmetic can help you with the design and construction of containment areas and will also help you with any monitoring. As a monitor or supervisor, you may also need to write reports. English

and composition courses can train you to communicate clearly with work teams, clients, and public officials.

Postsecondary Training

The employer usually pays for any necessary training for asbestos abatement workers. Many colleges and universities across the country offer EPA-accredited courses that instruct workers in safety regulations, protective equipment, confined-space-entry procedures, decontamination, technology, and other topics. The programs are typically 40 hours of instruction and take place over one week. Some programs include hands-on training in constructing a contamination unit, the use of protective clothing, and other relevant practices. The EPA requires asbestos abatement workers to also take refresher courses. Most states require an additional one-day course every year, along with a test.

Certification or Licensing

After completing the course work from an EPA-accredited program, workers receive the certification required of technicians. This certification must be updated, usually annually. Each individual state has its own regulations about the frequency of refresher courses and tests.

Other Requirements

This is physical work. Technicians must climb and balance on scaffolds in order to reach the materials. Also, because of the hazardous nature of the materials they handle, asbestos abatement workers must be aware of the health risks. Serious illness can result if skin, eyes, mouth, nose, or lungs are exposed to the loose fibers in the air. Technicians must work within all safety requirements and seek employment with reputable businesses that take all necessary precautions to keep workers healthy. Safety precautions cannot be taken lightly—excessive exposure to asbestos can increase your chance of lung cancer by 50 to 90 percent.

You must be able to keep focused on the work at hand; with so many safety concerns, you must follow the regulations and procedures closely. You work as part of a team, but you should also have the skills to work independently and follow the guidance of your supervisors. If you're a supervisor, you must be able to direct others and oversee their work as you fulfill your own responsibilities. You may also have to read plans and blueprints. When in charge, you may have to deal with emergency situations, in which case you need to remain calm and think clearly.

■ EXPLORING

Contact your local union representing this trade. It could offer a wealth of information regarding the job, including training programs and job openings. You may be able to speak with a journeyman and learn what it's really like to work in the field. You probably will not be allowed on a worksite, but you may be allowed to try on a respirator unit.

Visit your local library and read about asbestos, its history, use, benefits, and potential hazards. Visit the EPA website (http://www.epa.gov) to learn more about potential hazards in your environment and what you can do about them.

Is your school safe? Ask school officials or your school board if your facility has been tested and request the results from the test. If it hasn't been tested and the school was built before 1980, gather support from students, parents, and teachers to demand testing.

EMPLOYERS

Asbestos abatement contractors are located in most major cities in the country and frequently need technicians. To find area contractors, look in the yellow pages under "Asbestos abatement and removal service," "Asbestos consulting and testing," and "Hazardous material control and removal."

According to the U.S. Bureau of Labor Statistics, about 6 percent of hazardous materials removal workers are employed by special trade contractors. The next largest source of employment is sanitary services (treatment, storage, and disposal facilities).

STARTING OUT

Unionized asbestos abatement technicians start as apprentices. Apprentices work under the guidance of journeymen—skilled asbestos technicians—for a specific number of hours. Training is a combination of on-the-job work and classroom instruction. Once you fulfill the required training and certification, you are given journeyman status and benefits.

Non-union workers must complete a 32- to 40-hour training program before receiving a license. The employer provides additional technical training, most often on the job.

ADVANCEMENT

Because of the health risks involved with asbestos removal, technicians often move into related careers, such as construction. Some advancement opportunities exist, however, within the field. After a few years, experienced workers can move into supervisory positions in which they oversee day-to-day operations. With about four years of experience, technicians can become asbestos abatement contractors who oversee projects from beginning to end. Contractors are usually required to have detailed under-

standing of EPA regulations. They submit bids for projects, prepare reports, and speak to many different people, from workers to public authorities. Depending on the state's regulations, contractors may need a special license. With a contractor's license, you can also work as a project designer, which involves creating detailed plans for an asbestos removal project.

Experience as an asbestos abatement technician is necessary to move into a position as an asbestos building inspector. Inspectors inspect buildings to ensure that they meet federal and state regulations, and they usually need additional training.

EARNINGS

According to the *Occupational Outlook Handbook,* the median hourly wage for hazardous materials removal workers was $17.12 in 2002, or $35,610 annually. Those in the lowest 10 percent earned about $21,410 annually, and those in the highest 10 percent earned $55,340. With larger companies, full-time asbestos abatement technicians can expect some benefits, such as health and life insurance. Most employers also pay for initial training and annual refresher courses.

Many asbestos workers are represented by the International Association of Heat and Frost Insulators and

DID YOU KNOW?

Believe it or not, asbestos is a naturally occurring substance mined from the earth. Just as carbon can form a chunk of coal or a diamond, certain metamorphic minerals can likewise form fibrous structures. Asbestos has been valued for its flame-retardant qualities for centuries; Charlemagne supposedly had a tablecloth made of asbestos that he threw in the fire to clean, and in the 19th century, it was used for lamp wicks. In the 20th century, asbestos was used everywhere from buildings to hairdryers.

Asbestos comes in many forms, but two have been most common for industrial uses. One, amphibole, has straight, needlelike fibers, and is both very dusty and stays in the human body for a long time. It is easily breathed in, and can cause lung cancer and other health problems. However, chrysotile asbestos has a difference composition. It is silkier and has curlier fibers. It stays airborne for less time, and stays in the body for a shorter period, as well. Today, all asbestos used in industry is chrysotile asbestos.

For more information on asbestos, see the Asbestos Institute website at http://www.asbestos-institute.ca/main.html. Also see the "asbestos" Wikipedia article at http://en.wikipedia.org/wiki/Asbestos.

Asbestos Workers. The union has locals all across the country and assists members with job improvement. Union members often earn higher wages than other workers and receive union benefits, such as insurance, pension plans, and representation. Experienced workers with union membership may earn $25 or more per hour, or $52,000 a year. Apprentices earn about 50 percent of journeyman wages, including fringe benefits.

■ WORK ENVIRONMENT

Asbestos abatement technicians work indoors at various locations, most often office buildings and schools. They usually work a 40-hour week, although shift work is not uncommon, particularly if there is a deadline. For example, removal of asbestos from a school most likely will take place during the summer and have to be completed before school starts in the fall. An asbestos removal project may take several days or weeks.

This type of work is not for the claustrophobic. Technicians work in small, cramped enclosures, requiring them to stand, stoop, kneel, and climb on scaffolding. They wear protective suits that fully cover the body, including head, hands, and face. The protective clothing, which can be hot and uncomfortable, must be worn for several hours at a time. Working with hand tools and instruments while wearing gloves and face masks can be awkward, but technicians must do it with great care and attention to detail.

Asbestos abatement technicians work in a highly structured environment. There are strict regulations about asbestos removal, and workers follow specific steps in a carefully planned order to minimize risk to themselves and the environment. There are procedures not only for the actual asbestos removal, but also for dressing in protective clothing, entering and exiting work spaces, and removal and disposal of clothing at the end of a shift.

■ OUTLOOK

The U.S. Department of Labor expects overall employment of hazardous waste removal workers to grow much faster than the average for all occupations through 2012. Concerns about clean air and the environment continue to lead to more safety regulations and more strict requirements for building owners. Because asbestos-containing materials still fill many buildings built before 1982, contractors will need asbestos technicians to complete the many expected removal projects. Every year, the nation disposes of approximately 5.7 million cubic feet of regulated asbestos-containing material.

For federal and state studies, asbestos experts continue to study the best ways to treat or remove asbestos from buildings and to provide further protection for those who work closely with asbestos. Removal is often a last resort, and any errors in the process can create problems where they didn't exist before. For this reason, scientists hope to develop ways to eliminate hazards without actual asbestos removal.

■ FOR MORE INFORMATION

To learn about union membership, contact
International Association of Heat and Frost
Insulators and Asbestos Workers
1776 Massachusetts Avenue, NW, Suite 301
Washington, DC 20036-1989
Tel: 202-785-2388
http://www.insulators.org

For information about asbestos regulations and hazards, contact
U.S. Environmental Protection Agency
1200 Pennsylvania Avenue, NW
Washington, DC 20460
http://www.epa.gov

Assessors and Appraisers

■ OVERVIEW

Assessors and appraisers collect and interpret data to make judgments about the value, quality, and use of property. Assessors are government officials who evaluate property for the express purpose of determining how much the real estate owner should pay the city or county government in property taxes. Appraisers evaluate the market value of property to help people make decisions about purchases, sales, investments, mortgages, or loans. Rural districts or small towns may have only a few assessors, while large cities or urban counties may have several hundred. Appraisers are especially in demand in large cities but also work in smaller communities. There are over 57,100 real estate assessors and appraisers employed in the United States.

■ HISTORY

Until the 1930s, most assessors and appraisers were lay people using unscientific, informal methods to estimate the value of property. People who were not trained specifically in the field performed appraisals as a part-time adjunct to a general real estate business. As a result, the "boom" period of the 1920s saw many abuses of appraisals, such as approving loans in excess of the property's real value based on inaccurate estimates. The events of the Great Depression in the 1930s further highlighted the need for professionalism in appraising. Real estate owners defaulted on their mortgages, real estate bond issues stopped paying interest, and real estate corporations went into receivership.

In 1922 the National Association of Real Estate Boards (NAREB) defined specializations of its real estate functions to encourage professionalism in the industry. They did not organize an independent appraisal division, however, because there were few appraisers and the industry at large did not appreciate the importance of sound appraisals.

The NAREB recognized appraising as a significant branch of specialization in 1928 but did not formulate clearly defined appraisal standards and appraisal treatises until the 1930s.

Since then, appraising has emerged as a complex profession offering many responsibilities and opportunities. With the advent of computers, assessing and appraising have become more scientific. Today, assessments are based on a combination of economic and statistical analysis and common sense.

People need reliable appraisals when selling, mortgaging, taxing, insuring, or developing real estate. Buyers and sellers of property want to know the property's market value as a guide in their negotiations and may need economic feasibility studies or advice about other investment considerations for a proposed or existing development. Mortgage lenders require appraisals before issuing loans, and insurance companies often need an estimate of value before underwriting a property.

■ THE JOB

Property is divided into two distinct types: real property and personal property. Real property is land and the structures built upon the land, while personal property includes all other types of possessions. Appraisers determine the value, quality, and use of real property and personal property based on selective research into market areas, the application of analytical techniques, and professional judgment derived from experience. In evaluating real property, they analyze the supply and demand for different types of property, such as residential dwellings, office buildings, shopping centers, industrial sites, and farms, to estimate their values. Appraisers analyze construction, condition, and functional design. They review public records of sales, leases, previous assessments, and other transactions pertaining to land and buildings to determine the market values, rents, and construction costs of similar properties. Appraisers collect information about neighborhoods such as availability of gas, electricity, power lines, and transportation. They also may interview people familiar with the property, and they consider the cost of making improvements on the property.

Appraisers also must consider such factors as location and changes that might influence the future value of the property. A residence worth $300,000 in the suburbs may be worth only a fraction of that in the inner city or in a remote rural area. But that same suburban residence may depreciate in value if an airport will be built nearby. After conducting a thorough investigation, appraisers usually prepare a written report that documents their findings and conclusions.

Assessors perform the same duties as appraisers and then compute the amount of tax to be levied on property, using applicable tax tables. The primary responsibility of the assessor is to prepare an annual assessment roll, which lists all properties in a district and their assessed values.

To prepare the assessment roll, assessors and their staffs first must locate and identify all taxable property in the district. To do so, they prepare and maintain complete and accurate maps that show the size, shape, location, and legal description of each parcel of land. Next, they collect information about other features, such as zoning, soil characteristics, and availability of water, electricity, sewers, gas, and telephones. They describe each building and how land and buildings are used. This information is put in a parcel record.

Assessors also analyze relationships between property characteristics and sales prices, rents, and construction costs to produce valuation models or formulas. They use these formulas to estimate the value of every property as of the legally required assessment date. For example, assessors try to estimate the value of adding a bedroom to a residence or adding an acre to a farm, or how much

QUICK FACTS

SCHOOL SUBJECTS
Computer science
English
Mathematics

PERSONAL SKILLS
Communication/ideas
Mechanical/manipulative

WORK ENVIRONMENT
Indoors and outdoors
Primarily multiple locations

MINIMUM EDUCATION LEVEL
Some postsecondary training

SALARY RANGE
$21,500 to $41,760 to
$75,880

CERTIFICATION OR LICENSING
Recommended (certification)
Required for certain positions
(licensing)

OUTLOOK
About as fast as the average

DOT
191, 188

GOE
13.02.04

NOC
1235

O*NET-SOC
13-2021.00, 13.202.02

competition from a new shopping center detracts from the value of a downtown department store. Finally, assessors prepare and certify an assessment roll listing all properties, owners, and assessed values and notify owners of the assessed value of their properties. Because taxpayers have the right to contest their assessments, assessors must be prepared to defend their estimates and methods.

Most appraisers deal with land and buildings, but some evaluate other items of value. Specialized appraisers evaluate antiques, gems and jewelry, machinery, equipment, aircraft, boats, oil and gas reserves, and businesses. These appraisers obtain special training in their areas of expertise but generally perform the same functions as real property appraisers.

Art appraisers, for example, determine the authenticity and value of works of art, including paintings, sculptures, and antiques. They examine works for color values, brushstroke style, and other characteristics to establish the piece's age or to identify the artist. Art appraisers are well versed in art history, art materials, techniques of individual artists, and contemporary art markets, and they use that knowledge to assign values. Art appraisers may use complex methods such as X rays and chemical tests to detect frauds.

Personal property assessors help the government levy taxes by preparing lists of personal property owned by businesses and, in a few areas, householders. In addition to listing the number of items, these assessors also estimate the value of taxable items.

■ REQUIREMENTS
High School

If you are interested in the fields of assessing or appraising, there are a number of courses you can take in high school to help prepare you for this work. Take plenty of math classes, since you will need to be comfortable working with numbers and making calculations. Accounting classes will also be helpful for the same reasons. English courses will help you develop your researching and writing skills as well as verbal skills. Take computer classes in order to become accustomed to using this tool. Courses in civics or government may also be beneficial. Finally, if you know that a particular area interests you, take classes to enrich your background in that area. For example, if you are interested in art appraisal, take studio art classes as well as art history.

Postsecondary Training

Appraisers and assessors need a broad range of knowledge in such areas as equity and mortgage finance, architectural function, demographic statistics, and business trends. In addition, they must be competent writers and

able to communicate effectively with people. In the past, some people have been able to enter these fields with only a high school education and learn specialized skills on the job. Today, however, most appraisers and assessors have at least some college education. A number work in appropriate businesses, such as auction houses, while they earn their degrees. Some with several years of college experience are able to find employment and receive on-the-job training. Those wanting to receive professional designations and to have the best job opportunities, however, should complete a college degree.

A few colleges and universities, such as Lindenwood University (http://www.lindenwood.edu) in St. Charles, Missouri, now offer degrees in valuation sciences that will prepare you for this career. If you are unable to attend such a specialized program, though, there are numerous classes you can take at any college to prepare for this career. A liberal arts degree provides a solid background, as do courses in finance, statistics, mathematics, public administration and business administration, real estate and urban land economics, engineering, architecture, and computer science. Appraisers choosing to specialize in a particular area should have a solid background in that field. For example, art appraisers should hold at least a bachelor's degree in art history.

Courses in assessment and appraisal are offered by professional associations such as the American Society of Appraisers (ASA), the Appraisal Institute (AI), and the International Association of Assessing Officers.

Certification or Licensing

A number of professional organizations, such as the ASA and the AI, offer certification or designations in the field. It is highly recommended that you attain professional designation in order to enhance your standing in the field and demonstrate to consumers your level of expertise. To receive a designation, you will typically need to pass a written exam, demonstrate ethical behavior, and have completed a certain amount of education. To maintain your designation, you will also need to fulfill continuing education requirements.

Because all appraisals used for federally regulated real estate transactions must be conducted by licensed appraisers, most appraisers now obtain a state license. In addition, some states—known as "mandatory states"—require real estate appraisers to be licensed even if the appraisers do not deal with federally regulated transactions. You will need to check with your state's regulatory agency to learn more about the exact requirements for your state. In addition to a license, some states may require assessors who are government employees to pass civil service tests or other examinations before they can start work.

Other Requirements

Good appraisers are skilled investigators and must be proficient at gathering data. They must be familiar with sources of information on such diverse topics as public records, construction materials, building trends, economic trends, and governmental regulations affecting use of property. They should know how to read survey drawings and blueprints and be able to identify features of building construction.

■ EXPLORING

One simple way you can practice the methods used by appraisers is to write a detailed analysis of something you are considering investing in, such as a car, a computer, or even which college to attend. Your analysis should include both the benefits and the shortcomings of the investment as well as your final recommendation. Is the car over-priced? Does one particular school offer a better value for you? By doing this, you will begin to get a feel for the researching and writing done by an appraiser. Another way to explore this career is to look for part-time or summer work with an appraisal firm. Some firms also have jobs as appraiser assistants or trainees. Working at county assessors' or treasurers' offices, financial institutions, or real estate companies also might provide experience. If you are interested in working with real estate, you may want to learn the particulars of building construction by finding summer work with a construction company.

■ EMPLOYERS

Assessors are public servants who are either elected or appointed to office. The United States is divided into assessment districts, with population size affecting the number of assessors in a given area. Appraisers are employed by private businesses, such as accounting firms, real estate companies, and financial institutions, and by larger assessors' offices. Appraisers also work at auction houses, art galleries, and antique shops; some also work in government offices or for U.S. Customs. Assessors' offices might employ administrators, property appraisers, mappers, systems analysts, computer technicians, public relations specialists, word processors, and clerical workers. In small offices, one or two people might handle most tasks; in large offices, some with hundreds of employees, specialists are more common. Approximately 57,100 assessors and appraisers are employed in the United States in real estate alone.

■ STARTING OUT

After you have acquired the necessary technical and mathematical knowledge in the classroom, you should apply to area appraisal firms, local county assessors, real

DISCIPLINES IN APPRAISING

Appraising is a multifaceted career, with different appraisers specializaing in different types properties. Here are some of the various types of appraising:

- **Business appraisal:** On the surface, appraising a business might seem to be as easy as adding up such concrete items as money on hand, expected profits, physical plant, and intellectual property. However, there are also many intangibles, such as trademarks and customer goodwill, that it is difficult to put a dollar value to.

- **Gems and jewelry:** At once beautiful and signifiers of wealth and luxury, gems and jewelry are a traditional way of concentrating a lot of money in an easily portable investment. However, they are also easily lost, stolen, or damaged. Appraisers not only help determine the sale price of a piece, but how much it should be insured for.

- **Machinery and technical specialty assessors:** A business's machinery is its life, representing both a significant investment and a source of future profits. Accurately appraising such equipment, especially in today's high-tech world, is an important service.

- **Real property:** How much should a piece of land be sold for? How much tax should be assessed on a farm? How much should a house be insured for in case of a fire? All of these and more are the questions that real property assessors help to answer.

- **Personal property:** Covering everything from furniture to stamp collections, personal property assessors often have the most difficult jobs, assigning dollar values to the most diverse items imaginable.

- **Appraisal review and management:** Appraisers who specialize in review and management must have a broad general understanding of all sorts of appraisal. They must coordinate complex appraisals that involve more than one type of property, for instance, the valuation of a business that has various types of assets—land, machinery, and buildings.

estate brokers, or large accounting firms. Because assessing jobs are often civil service positions, they may be listed with government employment agencies. If you have graduated from a degree program in valuation sciences, your school's career guidance office should also be able to provide you with assistance in finding that first job.

■ ADVANCEMENT

Appraising is a dynamic field, affected yearly by new legislation and technology. To distinguish themselves in the business, top appraisers continue their education and pursue certification through the various national appraising organizations, such as the Appraisal Institute, the American Society of Appraisers, and the International Association of Assessing Officers. Certified appraisers are entrusted with the most prestigious projects and can command the highest fees. In addition to working on more and more prestigious projects, some appraisers advance by opening their own appraisal firms. Others may advance by moving to larger firms or agency offices, where they are more able to specialize.

■ EARNINGS

Income for assessors is influenced by their location and employer; their salaries generally increase as the population of their jurisdiction increases. For example, those working in large counties, such as Los Angeles County, may make up to $100,000 annually. Appraisers employed in the private sector tend to earn higher incomes than those in the public sector.

According to a recent survey by *Appraisal Today,* the average annual income of all appraisers is $58,132. Salaries range from $12,500 to $225,000.

Art appraisers usually charge fees that range from $125 to $1,250 or more per item, although fees can also be charged by the hour, by the day, or on another negotiated basis. Fees depend on the work being appraised and the time it takes to research and document the work.

The average fee for appraisal of a standard residential property is about $300, but fees can range from $75 for a re-inspection of new construction or repairs to $600 for inspection of a small residential income property.

According to the U.S. Department of Labor's *2002 National Occupational Employment and Wage Estimates,* real estate appraisers and assessors earned a median salary of $41,760. The lowest paid 10 percent earned $21,500 per year on average, while the highest paid earned $75,880 or more.

Earnings at any level are enhanced by higher education and professional designations. Fringe benefits for both public and private employees usually include paid vacations and health insurance.

■ WORK ENVIRONMENT

Appraisers and assessors have a variety of working conditions, from the comfortable offices where they write and edit appraisal reports to outdoor construction sites, which they visit in both the heat of summer and the bitter cold of winter. Many appraisers spend mornings at their desks and afternoons in the field. Experienced appraisers may need to travel out of state.

Appraisers and assessors who work for a government agency or financial institution usually work 40-hour weeks, with overtime when necessary. Independent appraisers often can set their own schedules.

Appraisal is a very people-oriented occupation. Appraisers must be unfailingly cordial, and they have to deal calmly and tactfully with people who challenge their decisions (and are usually angry). Appraising can be a high-stress occupation because a considerable amount of money and important personal decisions ride on appraisers' calculations.

■ OUTLOOK

The U.S. Department of Labor estimates that employment of assessors and appraisers will grow about as fast as the average for all occupations through 2012. In general, assessors work in a fairly secure field. As long as governments levy property taxes, assessors will be needed to provide them with information. The real estate industry, however, is influenced dramatically by the overall health of the economy, so appraisers in real estate can expect to benefit during periods of growth and experience slowdowns during recessions and depressions.

■ FOR MORE INFORMATION

For information on education and professional designations, contact

American Society of Appraisers
555 Herndon Parkway, Suite 125
Herndon, VA 20170
Tel: 703-478-2228
Email: asainfo@appraisers.org
http://www.appraisers.org

Visit this organization's website for a listing of state real estate appraiser regulatory boards.

Appraisal Foundation
1029 Vermont Avenue, NW, Suite 900
Washington, DC 20005-3517
Tel: 202-347-7722
Email: info@appraisalfoundation.org
http://www.appraisalfoundation.org

For information on professional designations, education, careers, and scholarships, contact

Appraisal Institute
550 West Van Buren Street, Suite 1000
Chicago, IL 60607
Tel: 312-335-4100
http://www.appraisalinstitute.org

For information on professional designations, education, and publications, contact

International Association of Assessing Officers
130 East Randolph, Suite 850
Chicago, IL 60601
Tel: 312-819-6100
http://www.iaao.org

Astronauts

■ OVERVIEW

Astronauts are the crews of America's manned space flights. They conduct experiments and gather information, pilot the spacecraft, and launch and repair satellites. They also conduct experiments with the spacecraft itself to develop new concepts in design, engineering, and the navigation of a vehicle outside the earth's atmosphere.

■ HISTORY

When the U.S. space program began in 1959, there were only seven astronauts in the entire country. There are 101 active astronauts and 43 management astronauts currently in the NASA astronaut corps, as well as 168 former astronauts (including those who have died). In total, 294 astronauts have been selected in the 18 groups from 1959 through 2000.

The first person to travel in space was a Russian, Yuri A. Gagarin, on April 12, 1961. The United States quickly followed suit, launching Alan Shepard, the first U.S. astronaut, into space on May 5, 1961. These men may have been the first to experience space, but the work of other pioneers made space travel possible. Robert H. Goddard of the United States and Hermann Oberth of Germany are recognized as the fathers of space flight. It was Goddard who designed and built a number of rocket motors and ground tested the liquid fuel rocket. Oberth published *The Rocket into Interplanetary Space* in 1923, which discussed technical problems of space and described what a spaceship would be like. Although there were few significant advances beyond this until after World War II, the Soviets and Germans did carry on experiments in the 1930s, and it was quite evident in the 1940s that space flights were to become a reality.

The U.S. space program began operations on October 1, 1958, when the National Aeronautics and Space Administration (NASA) was created. NASA was created largely in response to Soviet success at launching the world's first artificial satellite in 1957. The United States and Soviet Union continued space flights through the 1960s. Astronauts practiced maneuvering spacecraft and working in space on these missions. There were several firsts in this decade also: The Soviet Union placed the first spacecraft with more than one person into space in 1964; in 1965, Russian cosmonaut Alexei Leonov became the first person to step outside a spacecraft. NASA's first goal, to put a man on the moon by the end of the 1960s, was accomplished in 1969 when Neil Armstrong and Edwin Aldrin, Jr., were the first people to set foot on the moon. The triumph of this period was marred, however, by the loss of three astronauts in a launch pad test on January 27, 1967.

Both countries continued developing their programs throughout the 1970s, when astronauts carried out the first repair work in space. It was also during the 1970s when it became evident that a space station—a permanent orbiting laboratory in space in which astronauts could come and go and work from—could be a reality. The concept of a staffed outpost in Earth's orbit has been something people have imagined for years. In May 1973, the United States launched the *Skylab* space station. *Skylab* hosted crews for stays of 28, 56, and 84 days and proved that humans could live and work in space for extended periods. Crews conducted medical tests and made astronomical, solar, and Earth observations. However, *Skylab* was not designed for resupply or refueling and was allowed to disintegrate in the atmosphere in 1979.

In the 1980s, the United States began working with 15 other countries on planning on what became the International Space Station (see sidebar). The United States launched the first reusable manned spacecraft, the space shuttle *Columbia*. The Soviets also began using space shuttles during the 1980s and launched their version of a space station, *Mir*. Despite the progress of recent decades, however, both countries were still learning. On January 28, 1986, the U.S. space shuttle *Challenger* exploded shortly after takeoff, killing all seven crew members. On February 1, 2003, the *Columbia* disintegrated on re-entry over Texas, once again with the loss of seven crew members.

In late 1998, the Russian aerospace program delivered the first component of the International Space Station (ISS). An initial crew of three began living aboard the space station in late 2000. Despite setbacks and budget cuts, construction on the ISS is expected to continue through the decade.

■ THE JOB

The major role of astronauts is carrying out research; they conduct engineering, medical, and scientific experiments in space. Astronauts also operate and maintain the spacecraft that carries them and launch and recapture satellites. In the early days of space flight, spacecraft could contain only one or two astronauts. Today, a team of astronauts, each with their own specific duties for the flight, work aboard space shuttles and space stations.

Astronauts are part of a complex system. Throughout the flight, they remain in nearly constant contact with

A mission specialist works to install thermal blankets on mechanisms that rotate the International Space Station's main solar arrays.

Mission Control and various tracking stations around the globe. Space technology experts on the ground monitor each flight closely, even checking the crew members' health via electrodes fitted to their bodies. *Flight directors* provide important information to the astronauts and help them solve any problems that arise.

The basic crew of a space shuttle is made up of at least five people: the *commander,* the *pilot,* and three *mission specialists,* all of whom are NASA astronauts. Some flights also call for a payload specialist, who becomes the sixth member of the crew. From time to time, other experts will be on board. Depending on the purpose of the mission, they may be engineers, technicians, physicians, or scientists such as astronomers, meteorologists, or biologists. Now that the International Space Station (ISS) has become operable, crews may vary more, as astronauts who specialize in different areas come and go from the space station on space shuttles. Up to seven astronauts at a time will be able to live and work on the space station.

The commander and the pilot of a space shuttle are both pilot astronauts who know how to fly aircraft and spacecraft. Commanders are in charge of the overall mission. They maneuver the orbiter, supervise the crew and the operation of the vehicle, and are responsible for the success and safety of the flight. Pilots help the commanders control and operate the orbiter and may help manipulate satellites by using a remote control system. Like other crew members, they sometimes do work outside the craft or look after the payload.

Mission specialists are also trained astronauts. They work along with the commander and the pilot. Mission specialists work on specific experiments, perform tasks outside the orbiter, use remote manipulator systems to deploy payloads, and handle the many details necessary to carry out the mission. One or more *payload specialists* may be included on flights. A payload specialist may not be a NASA astronaut but is an expert on the cargo being carried into space.

Although much of their work is conducted in space, astronauts are involved in extensive groundwork before and during launchings. Just prior to lift-off, they go through checklists to be sure nothing has been forgotten. Computers on board the space shuttle perform the countdown automatically and send the vehicle into space. When the rocket boosters are used up and the external fuel tank becomes empty, they separate from the orbiter. Once in orbit, the astronauts take control of the craft and are able to change its position or course or to maneuver into position with other vehicles.

The research role of astronauts will expand with the operation of the ISS. The station will provide the only laboratory free of gravity where scientific research can be conducted. Such an environment unmasks the basic properties of materials, and astronauts will be conducting experiments that could lead to new manufacturing processes on Earth. Scientists have high expectations for medical research that astronauts will conduct aboard the space station. It is hoped research will help fight diseases such as influenza, diabetes, and AIDS. In conducting such tests, astronauts will operate a number of special cameras, sensors, meters, and other highly technical equipment.

Another important part of an astronaut's work is the deployment of satellites. Communications satellites transmit telephone calls, television programs, educational and medical information, and emergency instructions. Other satellites are used to observe and predict weather, to chart ocean currents and tides, to measure the earth's various surfaces and check its natural resources, and for defense-related purposes. Satellites released from a shuttle can be propelled into much higher orbits than the spacecraft itself is capable of reaching, thus permitting a much wider range of observation. While on their missions, astronauts may deploy and retrieve satellites or service them. Between flights, as part of their general duties, astronauts may travel to companies that manufacture and test spacecraft components, where they talk about the spacecraft and its mission.

Astronaut training includes instruction in all aspects of space flight and consists of classroom instruction in astronomy, astrophysics, meteorology, star navigation, communications, computer theory, rocket engines and fuels, orbital mechanics, heat transfer, and space medicine. Laboratory work will include work in space flight simulators during which many of the actual characteristics of space flight are simulated along with some of the emergencies that may occur in flight. To ensure their safety while in flight, astronauts also learn to adjust to changes in air pressure and extreme heat and observe their physical and psychological reactions to these changes. They need to be prepared to respond to a variety of possible circumstances.

■ REQUIREMENTS
High School

High school students interested in a career as an astronaut should follow a regular college preparatory curriculum in high school but should endeavor to take as much work as possible in mathematics and science. Preparing to get into a good college is important, because NASA takes into consideration the caliber of a college program when accepting astronaut candidates. Earning the best possible score on standardized test scores (ACT or SAT) will also help you get into a good college program. NASA contributes funds to 51 colleges and universities. By attend-

INTERNATIONAL SPACE STATION

The International Space Station (ISS) is the largest international scientific endeavor ever undertaken, both in scope and physical size. When it is completed, the international space station will be 356 feet across and 290 feet long. It will weigh about 1 million pounds.

There are 16 countries participating in the international space station project, with the United States and Russia leading the project. Other participants are Canada, Belgium, Denmark, France, Germany, Italy, Netherlands, Norway, Spain, Sweden, the United Kingdom, Japan, Brazil, and Switzerland. When completed, the space station will have capabilities for planned research in life, earth, space, and microgravity sciences, engineering research, and space product development. Seven astronauts (with different astronauts coming and going at different times) will continue to live and do research aboard the space station.

For more information on the ISS, visit http://spaceflight.nasa.gov/station.

ing these institutions, you are ensured that the curriculum for space programs offered will conform with NASA guidelines. To receive a list of the schools, write to: NASA Education Division, Mail Code FE, 300 E Street, SW, Washington, D.C. 20546-0001. You can also see the NASA crew-selection website at http://www.spaceflight.nasa.gov/outreach/jobsinfo/astronaut.html.

Postsecondary Training

Any adult man or woman in excellent physical condition who meets the basic qualifications can be selected to enter astronaut training, according to NASA. The basic requirements are U.S. citizenship and a minimum of a bachelor's degree in engineering, biological or physical science, or mathematics. There is no age limit, but all candidates must pass the NASA space flight physical. Beyond these basic requirements, there may be additional requirements, depending on the astronaut's role. NASA specifies further requirements for two other types of astronaut: the mission specialist and the pilot astronaut.

Mission specialists are required to have at least a bachelor's degree in one of the four areas of specialty (engineering, biological science, physical science, or mathematics), although graduate degrees are preferred. In addition, candidates must have at least three years of related work experience. Advanced degrees can take the place of part or all of the work experience requirements. Mission specialists must pass a NASA Class II physical, which includes the following standards: 20/200 or better

An astronaut maneuvers outside the space shuttle.

distance visual acuity, correctable to 20/20 in each eye, blood pressure no higher than 140/90, and height between 58.5 and 76 inches.

There are three major requirements for selection as a pilot astronaut candidate. A bachelor's degree in one of the four areas of specialty is required; an advanced degree is desirable. Candidates must also be jet pilots with at least 1,000 hours of pilot-in-command time in jet aircraft. Pilot astronauts must also pass a physical, with 20/70 or better distance visual acuity, correctable to 20/20 in each eye, blood pressure no higher than 140/90, and height between 64 and 76 inches. Because of the flight time requirement, it is rare for a pilot astronaut to come from outside the military.

Astronaut candidates undergo a year-long testing period. During this time, they are examined for how well they perform under zero-gravity conditions, in laboratory conditions, and as a member of a team with other candidates. If candidates are able to pass this first year, they are given astronaut status, and their training as astronauts begins.

Other Requirements

Astronauts must be highly trained, skilled professionals with a tremendous desire to learn about outer space and to participate in the highly dangerous exploration of it. They must have a deep curiosity with extremely fine and quick reactions. They may have to react in emergency conditions that may never before have been experienced, and to do so they must be able to remain calm and to think quickly and logically. As individuals they must be able to respond intelligently to strange and different conditions and circumstances.

◼ EXPLORING

Students who wish to become astronauts may find it helpful to write to various organizations concerned with space flights. There are lots of books available on space exploration, both in your school and city library.

The are also several excellent websites on space exploration. NASA's website is user-friendly, with biographies of actual astronauts, advice on becoming an astronaut, and news about current NASA projects. Other interesting sites include "Ask the Space Scientist," in which astronomer Dr. Sten Odenwald answers questions at http://image.gsfc.nasa.gov/poetry/ask/askmag.html, and space image libraries with images from the Hubble Space Telescope at http://www.okstate.edu/aesp/image.html.

The National Air and Space Museum (http://www.nasm.edu) at the Smithsonian Institution in Washington, DC, is an excellent way to learn about space exploration history. There are also several NASA-run space, research, and flight centers all over the country. Most have visitor centers and offer tours.

There are also space camps for high school students and older people all over the nation. These camps are not owned or operated by NASA, so the quality of their programs can vary greatly. Your high school counselor can help you find more information on space camps in your area.

◼ EMPLOYERS

All active astronauts are employed by NASA, although some payload specialists may also be employed elsewhere, such as at a university or private company. All are NASA-trained and paid. Within the NASA program, astronauts may be classified as civil service employees or military personnel, depending on their background. Astronauts who gain astronaut status through their military branch remain members of that military branch and maintain their rank. Astronauts who go to college and test into the program are civil service employees.

Inactive or retired astronauts may find employment opportunities outside NASA. Jobs might include teaching at a university, conducting research for other government agencies or private companies, working with manufacturers to develop space equipment, and educating the public on the space program.

◼ STARTING OUT

You can begin laying the groundwork toward making your astronaut application stand out from others when you are in college. Those who have been successful in becoming astronauts have distinguished themselves from the hundreds of other applicants by gaining practical experience. Internships and work/study positions in your chosen area of interest are a good way to gain vital experience. Your college placement office can help direct you to such opportunities. Working on campus as a teacher assistant or research assistant in a lab is another good way to make yourself more marketable later on.

Once other qualifications are met, a student applies to become an astronaut by requesting and filling out U.S. Government Application Form 171 from NASA, Johnson Space Center, ATTN: Astronaut Selection Office, Mail Code AHX, 2101 NASA Road 1, Houston, TX 77058. The form is reviewed at the Johnson Space Center, where all astronauts train. The application will be ranked according to height considerations, experience, and expertise. Active duty military applicants do not apply to NASA. Instead they submit applications to their respective military branch. Entrance into the profession is competitive. Aspiring astronauts compete with an average of 4,000 applicants for an average of 20 slots that open up every two years, according to NASA. From the pool of 4,000 applicants, an average of 118 are asked to come to the Johnson Space Center for a week of interviews and medical examinations and orientation. From there, the Astronaut Selection Board interviews applicants and assigns them a rating. Those ratings are passed on to a NASA administrator, who makes the final decision.

Entrance into the profession involves extensive piloting or scientific experience. Those hoping to qualify as pilot astronauts are encouraged to gain experience in all kinds of flying; they should consider military service and attempt to gain experience as a test pilot. People interested in becoming mission specialist astronauts should earn at least one advanced degree and gain experience in one or more of the accepted fields (engineering, biological or physical science, and mathematics).

■ ADVANCEMENT

Advancement is not a formal procedure. Astronauts who are members of the military generally rise in rank when they become astronauts and as they gain experience. Those employed by the civil service may rise from the GS-11 to the GS-13 rating. Those who gain experience as astronauts will likely work into positions of management as they retire from actual flight status. Some astronauts may direct future space programs or head space laboratories or factories. Some astronauts return to military service and may continue to rise in rank. As recognized public figures, astronauts can enter elected office and enjoy government and public speaking careers.

■ EARNINGS

For most, the attraction to being an astronaut is not the salary—and with good reason. The field is one of the most rewarding, but astronauts don't draw large salaries. Astronauts begin their salaries in accordance with the U.S. Government pay scale. Astronauts enter the field at a minimum classification of GS-11, which in 2004 paid a minimum of $44,136, according to the Office of Personnel Management General Schedule. As they gain experience, astronauts may advance up the classification chart to peak at GS-13, which pays between $64,035 and $83,243. Of course, there are opportunities outside NASA (although these don't involve space flight) that may pay higher salaries. Astronauts who go to work in the private sector can often find positions with universities or private space laboratories that pay six-figure salaries.

In addition, astronauts get the usual benefits, including vacations, sick leave, health insurance, retirement

LEARN MORE ABOUT IT

With America's fascination with human space travel, there has never been a shortage of books on space exploration. One title is *Apollo: An Eyewitness Account by Astronaut/ Explorer/Artist/Moonwalker*. This 176-page book, published in October 1998, was written by Alan Bean, *Apollo 12* and *Skylab II* astronaut. This book is unique because, in addition to Bean's personal accounts chronicling *Apollo's* missions to the moon and work aboard *Skylab,* it includes a collection of paintings by him of his experiences. Paintings include *Houston, We Have a Problem* from *Apollo 13,* Neil Armstrong's first step on the moon, and lunar landscapes of a place only 12 astronauts have ever visited.

Do Your Ears Pop in Space? And 500 Other Surprising Questions about Space Travel is a collection of interesting facts about space written in 1997 by Mike Mullane, a space shuttle astronaut. Mullane answers some of the most common questions about space in the 240-page paperback with 30 photos and 20 illustrations.

Space Shuttle: The First 20 Years—The Astronauts' Experiences in Their Own Words was written for the lay person by the curators Smithsonian Institution. Published in 2002, it chronicles the history of the shuttle program through 77 personal accounts by shuttle astronatus, complete with 300 photos and illustrations, in 320 hardcover pages.

Of course, the classic book on astronauts is *The Right Stuff*, by Tom Wolfe. Its 1979 publication established Wolfe as the chronicler of the courage of the men who blazed America's way into space—sometimes paying for it with their lives—and their wives, sick with worry, who had to remain stoic in front of the television cameras. Its 368 softcover pages are alternately exciting, spine-chilling, and heartwrenching—but never dull.

pensions, and bonuses for superior performance. Salaries for astronauts who are members of the armed forces consist of base pay, an allowance for housing and subsistence, and flight pay.

■ WORK ENVIRONMENT

Astronauts do work that is difficult, challenging, and potentially dangerous. They work closely as a team because their safety depends on their being able to rely on one another. They work a normal 40-hour week when preparing and testing for a space flight, but, as countdown approaches and activity is stepped up, they may work long hours, seven days a week. While on a mission, of course, they work as many hours as necessary to accomplish their objectives.

The training period is rigorous, and conditions in the simulators and trainers can be restrictive and uncomfortable. Exercises to produce the effect of weightlessness may cause air sickness in new trainees.

Astronauts on a space flight have to become accustomed to floating around in cramped quarters. Because of the absence of gravity, they must eat and drink either through a straw or very carefully with fork and spoon. Bathing is accomplished with a washcloth, as there are no showers in the spacecraft. Astronauts buckle and zip themselves into sleep bunks to keep from drifting around the cabin. Sleeping is generally done in shifts, which means that lights, noises, and activity are a constant factor.

During the launch and when working outside the spacecraft, astronauts wear specially designed spacesuits to protect them against the vacuum and radiation of space.

■ OUTLOOK

Only a very small number of people will ever be astronauts. NASA chooses its astronauts from an increasingly diverse pool of applicants. From thousands of applications all over the country, approximately 100 men and women are chosen for an intensive astronaut training program every two years. The small number of astronauts is not likely to change for the near future, and in fact, due to the *Columbia* disaster and budget cuts, is likely to decrease. Space exploration is an expensive venture for the governments that fund it, and often the program does well to maintain current funding levels. Great increases in funding, which would allow for more astronauts, is highly unlikely. While the ISS project has generated increased public interest and will likely continue to do so as discoveries are reported, the project still requires only a few astronauts at a time aboard the station.

Much of the demand will depend on the success of the space station and other programs and how quickly they develop. The satellite communications business is expected to grow as private industry becomes more involved in producing satellites for commercial use. But these projects are not likely to change significantly the employment picture for astronauts in the immediate future.

■ FOR MORE INFORMATION

For information on space launches, the International Space Station, and other educational resources, contact

Kennedy Space Center
Visitor Complex
Mail Code: DNPS
Kennedy Space Center, FL 32899
Tel: 321-452-2121
Email: kscinfo@dncinc.com
http://www.nasa.gov/centers/kennedy

For information on aeronautical careers, internships, and student projects, contact the information center or visit NASA's website.

National Aeronautics and Space Administration (NASA)
Headquarters Information Center
Washington, DC 20546-0001
Tel: 202-358-0000
Email: info-center@hq.nasa.gov
http://www.nasa.gov

Astronomers

■ OVERVIEW

Astronomers study the universe and its celestial bodies by collecting and analyzing data. They also compute positions of stars and planets and calculate orbits of comets, asteroids, and artificial satellites. Astronomers make statistical studies of stars and galaxies and prepare mathematical tables giving positions of the sun, moon, planets, and stars at a given time. They study the size and shape of the earth and the properties of its upper atmosphere through observation and through data collected by spacecraft and earth satellites. There are approximately 1,000 astronomers employed in the United States.

■ HISTORY

The term *astronomy* is derived from two Greek words: *astron*, meaning star, and *nemein*, meaning to arrange or distribute. It is one of the oldest sciences. The field has historically attracted people who have a natural fascination with our universe. Astronomers have traditionally been driven by a desire to learn; the pursuit of practical applications of astronomy has, for many, been secondary.

One of the earliest practical applications, the establishment of a calendar based on celestial movement, was pursued by many ancient civilizations, including the Babylonians, Chinese, Mayans, Europeans, and Egyptians. A chief aim of early astronomers was to study the motion of the bodies in the sky in order to create a calendar that could be used to predict certain celestial events and provide a more orderly structure to social life. The ancient Babylonians were among the first to construct a calendar based on the movement of the sun and the phases of the moon; their calendar has been found to have been accurate within minutes. In Europe, stone mounds constructed by ancient inhabitants also attest to astronomical work. Stonehenge is one of the largest and most famous of these mounds.

Ancient Greek astronomers introduced a new concept of astronomy by attempting to identify the physical structure of the universe, a branch of astronomy that has become known as *cosmology*. Astronomers such as Aristotle, Apollonius, Hipparchus, and Ptolemy succeeded in describing the universe in terms of circular movements. Their discoveries and theories were adopted by astronomers throughout much of the world. Modern astronomy was born with the theory of the sun-centered universe, first proposed by Nicolaus Copernicus in the 16th century. Copernicus's discovery revolutionized the field of astronomy and later would have a dramatic impact on many aspects of science.

After thousands of years, astronomers had succeeded in developing accurate predictions of celestial events. Next, they turned to newly evolving areas of astronomy, those of identifying the structure of the universe and of understanding the physical nature of the bodies they observed. Astronomers were aided by the invention of telescopes, and, as these increased in power, astronomers began to make new discoveries in the skies. For much of history, for example, it was believed that there were only five planets in the solar system. By the end of the 17th century, that number had increased to six, and, over the next two centuries, three more planets, Neptune, Uranus, and Pluto, were discovered.

Astronomers have always relied heavily on tools to bring faraway worlds close enough for study. As technology has evolved, so then has the field of astronomy. Spectroscopy, invented in the 19th century, allowed astronomers to identify the elements that make up the composition of the planets and other celestial bodies and gave rise to a new branch of astronomy, called *astrophysics*, which describes the components of the universe by measuring such information as temperature, chemical composition, pressure, and density. Later, photography, too,

became an important research aid. In the early years of the 20th century, new discoveries further revolutionized the field of astronomy, particularly with the discovery of other galaxies beyond our own. The understanding grew that the universe was constructed of many millions of galaxies, each an island in an infiniteness of space.

By the middle of the 20th century, scientists had learned how to send rockets, and later manned spacecraft, into space to gain a closer view of the universe surrounding us. Using satellites and unmanned space probes, astronomers have been able to travel far into the solar system, toward the most distant planets. A major event in astronomy occurred with the launching in 1990 of the powerful Hubble Space Telescope, which orbits Earth and continues to send back information and photographs of events and phenomena across the universe.

■ THE JOB

Astronomers study the universe and all of its celestial bodies. They collect and analyze information about the moon, planets, sun, and stars, which they use to predict their shapes, sizes, brightness, and motions.

They are interested in the orbits of comets, asteroids, and even artificial satellites. Information on the size and shape, the luminosity and position, the composition, characteristics, and structure as well as temperature, distance, motion, and orbit of all celestial bodies is of great relevance to their work.

Practical application of activity in space is used for a variety of purposes. The launching of space vehicles and satellites has increased the importance of the information astronomers gather. For example, the public couldn't enjoy the benefits of accurate weather prediction if satellites weren't keeping an eye on our atmosphere. Without astronomical data, satellite placement wouldn't be possible. Knowledge of the orbits of planets and their moons, as well as asteroid activity, is also vital to astronauts exploring space.

QUICK FACTS

SCHOOL SUBJECTS
Mathematics
Physics

PERSONAL SKILLS
Communication/ideas
Technical/scientific

WORK ENVIRONMENT
Primarily indoors
Primarily one location

MINIMUM EDUCATION LEVEL
Bachelor's degree

SALARY RANGE
$40,140 to $81,690 to $126,320

CERTIFICATION OR LICENSING
None available

OUTLOOK
More slowly than the average

DOT
021

GOE
02.02.01

NOC
2111

O*NET-SOC
19-2011.00

WILL ASTEROIDS STRIKE EARTH?

Earth and all the other planets and moons have been continuously pelted by asteroids and comets. Craters on the moon are evidence of such impacts. Hollywood and popular culture have picked up on this reality with speculation about the possibility of an asteroid or comet striking Earth with catastrophic effects. But how likely is this? Astronomers and other scientists say such an event is not very likely. The most dangerous asteroids, those capable of causing major regional or global disasters, are extremely rare, according to the National Aeronautics and Space Administration (NASA). These bodies impact Earth once every 100,000 years on average. The greatest risk is associated with objects larger than a half-mile to a mile, large enough to disturb Earth's climate by injecting large quantities of dust into the stratosphere. Such an event could depress temperatures and the amount of sunlight, possibly creating a loss of food crops. An ocean impact could trigger large ocean waves, or tsunamis. It is feasible, NASA says, that we could divert a large asteroid or comet that may collide with Earth. If astronomers can predict such an event early enough, then striking the body with conventional rockets and explosives to break it up would probably be adequate. Such a response would be coordinated in the United States by the departments of defense and energy.

Astronomers are usually expected to specialize in some particular branch of astronomy. The *astrophysicist* is concerned with applying the concepts of physics to stellar atmospheres and interiors. (For more information, see the article Astrophysicists.) *Radio astronomers* study the source and nature of celestial radio waves with extremely sensitive radio telescopes. The majority of astronomers either teach or do research or a combination of both. Astronomers in many universities are expected to teach such subjects as physics and mathematics in addition to astronomy. Other astronomers are engaged in such activities as the development of astronomical instruments, administration, technical writing, and consulting.

Astronomers who make observations may spend long periods of time in observatories. Astronomers who teach or work in laboratories may work eight-hour days. However, those who make observations, especially during celestial events or other peak viewing times, may spend long evening hours in observatories. Paperwork is a necessary part of the job. For teachers, it can include lesson planning and paper grading. Astronomers conducting research independently or for a university can expect to spend a considerable amount of time writing grant pro-

posals to secure funding for their work. For any scientist, sharing the knowledge acquired is a vital part of the work. Astronomers are expected to painstakingly document their observations and eventually combine them into a coherent report, often for peer review or publication.

Although the telescope is the major instrument used in observation, many other devices are also used by astronomers in carrying out these studies, including spectrometers for the measurement of wavelengths of radiant energy, photometers for the measurement of light intensity, balloons for carrying various measuring devices, and computers for processing and analyzing all the information gathered.

Astronomers use ground-based telescopes for night observation of the skies. The Hubble Space Telescope, which magnifies the stars at a much greater percentage than land-based capability allows, has become an important tool for the work of many astronomers.

■ REQUIREMENTS
High School

While in high school, prospective astronomers should take mathematics (including analytical geometry and trigonometry), science courses (including chemistry and physics), English, foreign languages, and courses in the humanities and social sciences. Students should also be well grounded in the use of computers and in computer programming.

Postsecondary Training

All astronomers are required to have some postsecondary training, with a doctoral degree being the usual educational requirement because most jobs are in research and development. A master's degree is sufficient for some jobs in applied research and development, and a bachelor's degree is adequate for some nonresearch jobs. Students should select a college program with wide offerings in physics, mathematics, and astronomy and take as many of these courses as possible. Graduate training will normally take at least three years beyond the bachelor's degree.

Bachelor's degrees in astronomy are offered by about 70 institutions in the United States, and 40 institutions offer master's degrees or doctorates in the field, often combined with physics departments. Some of the astronomy courses typically offered in graduate school are celestial mechanics, galactic structure, radio astronomy, stellar atmospheres and interiors, theoretical astrophysics, and binary and variable stars. Some graduate schools require that an applicant for a doctorate spend several months in residence at an observatory. In most institutions the student's graduate courses will reflect his or her chosen astronomical specialty or particular field of interest.

Other Requirements

The field of astronomy calls for people with a strong but controlled imagination. They must be able to see relationships between what may appear to be, on the surface, unrelated facts, and they must be able to form various hypotheses regarding these relationships. Astronomers must be able to concentrate over long periods of time. They should also express themselves well both in writing and verbally.

■ EXPLORING

A number of summer or part-time jobs are usually available in observatories. The latter may be either on a summer or year-round basis. These jobs not only offer experience in astronomy but often act as stepping stones to good jobs upon graduation. Students employed in observatories might work as guides or as assistants to astronomers.

Students can test their interest in this field by working part-time, either as an employee or as a volunteer, in planetariums or science museums. Many people enjoy astronomy as a hobby, and there are a number of amateur astronomy clubs and groups active throughout the country. Amateur astronomers have often made important contributions to the field of astronomy. In 1996, for example, a new comet was discovered by an amateur astronomer in Japan. Students may gain experience in studying the skies by purchasing, or even building, their own telescopes.

Reading or using the Internet to learn more on your own is also a good idea. What about astronomy interests you? You can find specific information in books or on the Internet. Check out NASA's website at http://www.nasa.gov. It contains useful information about careers in astronomy and aeronautics and information about current space exploration. When you hear in the news that a comet or meteor shower will be visible from Earth, be sure to set your alarm to get up and watch and learn. Science teachers will often discuss such events in class.

■ EMPLOYERS

Nearly one third of all physicists and astronomers worked for scientific research and development companies in 2002, according to the Department of Labor. Another 29 percent worked for the Federal government. Astronomers represented only a small portion of these—350 and 430 jobs, respectively. The federal government employs astronomers in agencies such as NASA, the U.S Naval Observatory, the Army Map Service, and the Naval Research Laboratory.

Astronomers more frequently find jobs as faculty members at colleges and universities or are affiliated with those institutions through observatories and laboratories. Other astronomers work in planetariums, in science museums, or in other public service positions involved in presenting astronomy to the general public; others teach physics or earth sciences in secondary schools or are science journalists and writers.

In the private sector, astronomers are hired by consulting firms that supply astronomical talent to the government for specific tasks. In addition, a number of companies in the aerospace industry hire astronomers to work in related areas in order to use their background and talents in instrumentation, remote sensing, spectral observations, and computer applications.

■ STARTING OUT

A chief method of entry for astronomers with a doctorate is to register with the college's placement bureau, which provides contacts with one of the agencies looking for astronomers. Astronomers can also apply directly to universities, colleges, planetariums, government agencies, aerospace industry manufacturers, and others who hire astronomers. Many positions are advertised in professional and scientific journals devoted to astronomy and astrophysics.

Graduates with bachelor's or master's degrees can normally obtain semiprofessional positions in observatories,

SEEING INTO SPACE

Astronomers make most of their observations using visible light in the form of radiation. There are several types of optical telescopes that allow astronomers to perform specialized, highly accurate observations from Earth. Photographic equipment supplements many optical telescopes. Time exposures taken on film make it possible for astronomers to detect very dim celestial objects. Some major optical telescopes obtain images with electronic devices instead of photography. One such device is called a CCD (charge-coupled device), which consists of an array of tiny, light-sensitive cells on a silicon chip. Photometers are devices that measure the intensity of light, and astronomers use this tool to compare the brightness of various stars. When a photometer is used with a series of filters, the intensity of light of each color that a star emits can be determined. Huge optical telescopes are housed at observatories, often found at major universities. The equipment is often housed in large domed facilities that allow free movement of the equipment to take in all areas of the sky. In many cases, the larger the equipment, the more powerful it is.

Using telescopes, astronomers can track the movements of stars, solar flares and storms, and comets, and search for new stars and galaxies hundreds of millions of miles away.

planetariums, or some of the larger colleges and universities offering training in astronomy. Their work assignments might be as research assistants, optical workers, observers, or technical assistants. Those employed by colleges or universities might well begin as instructors. Federal government positions in astronomy are usually earned on the basis of competitive examinations given periodically by the Board of United States Civil Service Examiners for Scientific and Technical Personnel. Jobs with some municipal organizations employing astronomers are often based on competitive examinations. The examinations are usually open to those with bachelor's degrees.

NASA offers internships for students with some postsecondary training. To find out more about NASA internships and other opportunities, explore the website at http://www.nasajobs.nasa.gov.

ADVANCEMENT

Because of the relatively small size of the field, advancement may be somewhat limited. A professional position in a large university or governmental agency is often considered the most desirable post available to an astronomer because of the opportunities it offers for additional study and research. Those employed in a colleges may well

advance from instructor to assistant professor to associate professor and then to professor. There is also the possibility of eventually becoming a department head.

Opportunities also exist for advancement in observatories or industries employing people in astronomy. In these situations, as in those in colleges and universities, advancement depends to a great extent on the astronomer's ability, education, and experience. Peer recognition, in particular for discoveries that broaden the understanding of the field, is often a determinant of advancement. Publishing articles in professional journals, such as *Scientific American* or the *American Journal of Astrophysics,* is a way for astronomers to become known and respected in the field. Advancement isn't usually speedy; an astronomer may spend years devoted to a specific research problem before being able to publish conclusions or discoveries in a scientific journal.

EARNINGS

According to the U.S. Department of Labor, astronomers had median annual earnings of $81,690 in 2002. The lowest paid 10 percent made less than $40,140 per year, and the highest paid 10 percent made more than $126,320. A 2001 survey conducted by the National Association of Colleges and Employers focuses on professionals who hold physics doctoral degrees, which covers many astronomers. According to the survey, the average starting salary offered to physics doctoral candidates was $68,273. The American Institute of Physics reported a median salary of $78,000 in 2000 for its members with doctorates; $63,800 for master's degree professionals; and $60,000 for those with bachelor's degrees. The average for space professionals employed by the federal government in 2001 was $89,734, according to the U.S. Department of Labor.

In educational institutions, salaries are normally regulated by the salary schedule prevailing in that particular institution. As the astronomer advances to higher-level teaching positions, his or her salary increases significantly.

Opportunities also exist in private industry for well-trained and experienced astronomers, who often find their services in demand as consultants. Fees for this type of work may run as high as $200 per day in some of the more specialized fields of astronomy.

WORK ENVIRONMENT

Astronomers' activities may center on the optical telescope. Most telescopes are located high on a hill or mountain and normally in a fairly remote area, where the air is clean and the view is not affected by lights from unrelated sources. There are approximately 300 of these observatories in the United States.

Astronomers working in these observatories usually are assigned to observation from three to six nights per month and spend the remainder of their time in an office or laboratory, where they study and analyze their data. They also must prepare reports. They may work with others on one segment of their research or writing and then work entirely alone on the next. Their work is normally carried on in clean, quiet, well-ventilated, and well-lighted facilities.

Those astronomers in administrative positions, such as director of an observatory or planetarium, will maintain fairly steady office hours but may also work during the evening and night. They usually are more involved in administrative details, however, spending less time in observation and research.

Those employed as teachers will usually have good facilities available to them, and their hours will vary according to class hours assigned. Work for those employed by colleges and universities may often be more than 40 hours per week.

■ OUTLOOK

The U.S. Department of Labor predicts employment to grow more slowly than the average for astronomers through 2012. Astronomy is one of the smallest science fields. Job openings result from the normal turnover when workers retire or leave the field for other reasons. Competition for these jobs, particularly among new people entering the profession, will continue to be strong. In recent years, the number of new openings in this field have not kept pace with the number of astronomers graduating from the universities, and this trend is likely to continue for the near future. Furthermore, there will likely be few new positions made, since funding in this area is hard to come by.

The federal government will continue to provide employment opportunities for astronomers. Defense expenditures are expected to increase over the next decade, and this should provide stronger employment opportunities for astronomers who work on defense-related research projects. However, government agencies, particularly NASA, may find their budgets reduced in the coming years, and the number of new positions created for astronomers will likely drop as well. Few new observatories will be constructed, and those currently in existence are not expected to greatly increase the size of their staffs.

The greatest growth in employment of astronomers is expected to occur in business and industry. Companies in the aerospace field will need more astronomers to do research to help them develop new equipment and technology.

■ FOR MORE INFORMATION

Visit the FAQ section at the following website to read the online article Career Profile: Astronomy.

American Association of Amateur Astronomers
PO Box 7981
Dallas, TX 75209-0981
Email: aaaa@corvus.com
http://www.corvus.com

For additional resources aimed at both professional and amateur astronomers, contact the following associations:

American Astronomical Society
2000 Florida Avenue, NW, Suite 400
Washington, DC 20009-1231
Tel: 202-328-2010
Email: aas@aas.org
http://www.aas.org

Astronomical Society of the Pacific
390 Ashton Avenue
San Francisco, CA 94112
Tel: 415-337-1100
http://www.astrosociety.org

This organization is a resource for professionals who work in many physics disciplines, including astronomy. For more information, contact

American Institute of Physics
1 Physics Ellipse
College Park, MD 20740-3843
Tel: 301-209-3100
Email: aipinfo@aip.org
http://www.aip.org

Astrophysicists

■ OVERVIEW

Astrophysics is a specialty that combines two fields of science: astronomy and physics. *Astrophysicists* use the principles of physics to study the solar system, stars, galaxies, and the universe. How did the universe begin? How is the universe changing? These are the types of questions astrophysicists try to answer through research and experimentation. Physicists may also be concerned with such issues, but they use physics to study broader areas, such as gravity, electromagnetism, and nuclear interactions.

■ HISTORY

Astrophysics began in the 1800s, when astronomers developed the spectroscope, which is used to determine the various properties of stars and planets. In spectroscopy, light is spread into a spectrum, and the resulting image can be used to determine a star's chemical composition, temperature, surface condition, and other properties. Astrophysicists knew that understanding the nature of stars would help them understand the larger question that all astrophysicists work toward answering: How did the universe begin?

A major advance in the field of astrophysics was the development of atomic theory. In 1803, a British chemist, John Dalton, proposed that each natural element consists of a particular kind of atom. In the early 1900s, scientists discovered that each atom has a nucleus, which contains protons, neutrons, and electrons that interact with each other.

Today, the atom is the basis of the study of physics. Physicists of all disciplines, from astrophysicists to nuclear physicists, use what we know about the atom and its parts to understand their respective fields.

In the case of astrophysicists, close examination of the parts of the atom will help to understand how matter and our universe formed. A widely held explanation today is the "Big Bang" theory, which hypothesizes that the universe was formed 15 to 20 billion years ago when a dense singular point of matter exploded and eventually formed stars and galaxies. Today, most astrophysicists believe the universe is still expanding from that initial explosion.

■ THE JOB

To do their work, astrophysicists need access to large, expensive equipment, such as radio telescopes, spectrometers, and specialized computers. Because this equipment is generally available only at universities with large astronomy departments and government observatories, most astrophysicists are employed by colleges or the government.

A primary duty of most astrophysicists is making and recording observations. What they observe and the questions they are trying to answer may vary, but the process is much the same across the profession. They work in observatories, using telescopes and other equipment to view celestial bodies. They record their observations on charts or, more often today, into computer programs that help them analyze the data.

Astrophysicists work to understand the beginning and end of the lives of stars. They use spectrometers, telescopes, and other instruments to measure infrared radiation, ultraviolet radiation, and radio waves. They study not only the formation of stars but also whether planets formed along with them. Understanding the lives of stars will help astrophysicists understand the origins and future of the universe. Their work is often tedious, requiring multiple measurements over time. The answer to one question, such as the age of a specific star, often leads to more questions about nearby planets and other formations. To address these larger questions, astrophysicists from all over the world must work together to come to agreements.

Most astrophysicists who work for universities also teach. Depending on their branch of research, teaching may be their primary duty. Astrophysicists share their findings with the scientific community. They often travel to conferences to speak about their findings and to listen to other scientists discuss techniques or research. Discoveries are also shared in professional journals, such as *The Astrophysical Journal*. Many scientists spend time compiling their data and writing articles for such journals.

■ REQUIREMENTS
High School

If you are interested in becoming an astrophysicist, concentrate on classes in mathematics and science. If they are available, take classes at an advanced level to better prepare yourself for challenging college courses. English skills are also important because astrophysicists must write up their results, communicate with other scientists, and lecture on their findings. Finally, make sure you are comfortable working with computers either by taking a computer science class or by exploring on your own.

Postsecondary Training

An advanced degree is highly desirable for a career in astrophysics. A few who have bachelor's degrees in physics, astronomy, or mathematics may work as research assistants in the field. To do your own research or teach, you should have at least a master's degree, with a Ph.D. preferred for full astrophysicists.

Other Requirements

Because astrophysicists deal with abstract concepts and faraway celestial bodies, an active imagination and the ability to draw logical conclusions from observational data are helpful traits. Some research can be tedious and take long periods of time; astrophysicists must be patient in their work and have the ability to remain focused and meet deadlines.

Astrophysicists who have a natural curiosity about why things occur no doubt enjoy their work most when research or experiments culminate in a discovery that will help them and others in the field gain a larger understanding of the universe.

■ EMPLOYERS

Because astrophysicists require such expensive equipment to do their job, their employers are generally limited to large colleges or government agencies. Some government agencies that employ astrophysicists include the National Aeronautics and Space Administration (NASA), the U.S. Naval Observatory, and Fermilab, a physics laboratory. Fermilab is the home of the world's most powerful particle accelerator, which scientists from various institutions use to conduct research to better understand energy and the atom.

According to the U.S. Department of Labor, there are approximately 12,400 physicists and astronomers working in the United States. Most work in colleges or universities, either as faculty members or in nonfaculty research positions. Approximately 30 percent work for the federal government, mostly with the Department of Defense and NASA. These scientists work all over the country, but most are employed in areas where large universities or research laboratories are located.

■ STARTING OUT

Many astrophysicists get their first paying job as graduate students who assist professors in astronomy, physics, or astrophysics. These assistant jobs are known in the field as postdoctoral positions. Students may help the professors grade undergraduate and graduate papers or assist them in recording and compiling astronomical data in the observatory. Beginning jobs in government may include internships or temporary positions with specific research projects. The job market for astrophysicists is very competitive; students and recent graduates often must volunteer their time at university or government observatories and work other jobs until they can find full-time, paid work.

■ ADVANCEMENT

Astrophysicists work with other highly educated people, including mathematicians, astronomers, and other scientists. Astrophysicists who work for large universities or the government should have a sense of the "department politics" that may go on at their university and be able to deal diplomatically with department heads and colleagues competing for resources such as grants and equipment.

At the beginning of their careers, astrophysicists may be assigned to work nights at the observatory. Hours can be long, and pay can be limited. After they have gained experience, astrophysicists can expect to be involved in the planning and development stages of research and may not be required to do as much observation and data recording. With further experience, astrophysicists can advance to become tenured professors, research institution leaders, or observatory managers.

■ EARNINGS

Salaries for astrophysicists tend to parallel those listed for astronomers and physicists because of their job similarities. According to the *Occupational Outlook Handbook,* the median annual salary of physicists was $85,020 in 2002. The lowest paid 10 percent earned less than $50,350, and the highest paid 10 percent earned over $129,250.

Salaries by education level also varied. The American Association of University Professors reports that members with doctoral degrees made over $100,000 per year, whereas those with master's degrees made just over $76,000. Doctorates are also usually requirements for tenure-track positions.

■ WORK ENVIRONMENT

Astrophysicists generally work regular hours in laboratories, observatories, or classrooms. However, some research may require them to work extended or irregular hours. A research deadline or a celestial event such as a meteor shower or asteroid may require extra hours or overnight observation. Some travel may be required and is generally paid for by the astrophysicist's employer, such as to an observatory with a needed piece of equipment or to a conference or training. Astrophysicists work with other highly educated professionals, such as mathematicians, astronomers, and other scientists. The work environment can be competitive and sometimes political because these professionals are often competing for the same limited resources.

■ OUTLOOK

The outlook for astrophysics, because it is so closely related to astronomy and physics, mirrors the outlook for those fields. According to the U.S. Department of Labor, employment in these fields will grow slower than the average for all other occupations through 2012. The need for scientists, especially those employed by the government, is affected by factors outside the field, such as budgetary cuts and political issues that draw attention (and funding) away from expensive research programs.

For many years, competition for jobs has been intense, as the number of doctorates awarded has exceeded the number of positions available for many science professions. This trend seems to be changing; the number of doctorate degrees has begun to drop. However, aspiring astrophysicists should still be prepared for a tight job market, especially in research positions. Within private industry, many companies are reducing their amount of basic research (which includes physics-related research) in favor of applied research and software development. Job openings for engineers and computer scientists will far outnumber those for physicists and astrophysicists.

■ FOR MORE INFORMATION

This is an organization for professionals who work in different areas of physics, including astrophysicists. For more information, contact

American Institute of Physics
1 Physics Ellipse
College Park, MD 20740-3843
Tel: 301-209-3100
Email: aipinfo@aip.org
http://www.aip.org

For additional information on the field of astronomy, contact

American Astronomical Society
2000 Florida Avenue, NW, Suite 400
Washington, DC 20009
Tel: 202-328-2010
Email: aas@aas.org
http://www.aas.org

To read past articles on astrophysics, check out the following website:

The Astrophysical Journal
http://www.journals.uchicago.edu/ApJ

Athletic Directors

■ OVERVIEW

Athletic directors coordinate and oversee athletic programs at public and private colleges and universities. They manage staff; calculate budgets; negotiate broadcasting and other business contracts; raise funds to meet budget short-

falls; ensure that their programs meet academic-, financial-, and gender-related compliance issues; and serve as the public faces of their institutions' athletic programs by talking with media and fans. Athletic directors may also be called *directors of athletics, athletic directors of intercollegiate athletics,* and *athletic administrators.*

■ HISTORY

The National Collegiate Athletic Association (NCAA) was formed in 1905 to address violence in intercollegiate football. Around this time, the position of athletic director was formally created by college administrators who saw the need for experienced professionals to run their institutions' athletic programs.

After World War II, the NCAA began to regulate and monitor recruiting and financial aid issues. With rule changes and NCAA regulation, college athletics blossomed in the second half of the 20th century. Athletic directors played an important role in the growth of collegiate athletics during this time, but it was not until the First and Second National Conferences on Athletic Administration in Colleges and Universities in 1959 and 1962, respectively, that these professionals began to take the first steps toward creating a professional organization.

At the third such conference in 1965, the National Association of Collegiate Directors of Athletics (NACDA) was founded to serve the needs of athletic directors at junior and four-year colleges. The association boasts a membership of over 6,000 athletic directors and associate and assistant athletic directors at NCAA, National Association of Intercollegiate Athletics (NAIA), and National Junior College Athletic Association (NJCAA) colleges throughout the United States.

In 1979, the Council of Collegiate Women Athletic Administrators was created to enhance opportunities for women in intercollegiate athletics. To better represent its members, the Council was renamed the National Association of Collegiate Women Athletic Administrators (NACWAA) in 1992. The NACWAA has nearly 1,200 members.

■ THE JOB

Athletic directors plan and implement athletic programs at colleges and universities. Athletic directors at large Division I schools oversee large budgets, supervise staffs that range from dozens to hundreds of employees, and make many important decisions daily. They are helped by assistant and associate athletic directors who specialize in financial, media relations, compliance, and other issues. Athletic directors at large schools spend much of their time raising money and marketing their programs to the public. At small colleges, athletic directors work alone or with very small staffs. In addition to their main duties, they might drive athletes to games, coach sports teams, write press releases or marketing copy, and teach classes. The work of athletic directors can be divided into the following general areas: staff management/administration, financial issues, compliance, and public relations.

Staff management/Administration. Athletic directors hire and supervise coaches and other department staff. They evaluate the performance of coaches and give them feedback. Athletic directors may have to fire coaches who fail to perform up to expectations.

Athletic directors have many administrative duties. They oversee coaches, athletic teams, and employees who assist with ticket sales, fund-raising, public relations, and other tasks. They make sure that stadiums, playing fields, and training, locker, and weight rooms are in good condition. Athletic directors meet with athletic directors from other schools and conference and association officials to coordinate athletic schedules and discuss rules and regulations. They meet with faculty representatives regarding academic issues relating to student-athletes.

Financial issues. Athletic directors create and manage the athletic budgets at their institutions. When creating budgets, they make sure that each sport is allotted enough money to operate effectively. Athletic directors must be aware of their institutions' spending rules, as well as the regulations established by the NCAA, the NAIA, and the NJCAA. They plan and oversee ticket sales and certify income reports from these sales. Athletic directors negotiate radio and television broadcasting contracts and other commercial contracts and agreements that earn revenue for their institutions. This revenue is used for scholarships, team equipment, travel expenses, coaching and administrative staff salaries, the design and printing of schedules and marketing materials, and other expenses. Revenue also comes from fans (known as *boosters*), who make donations to the program. Athletic directors must be expert fund-raisers to make up for any budget shortfalls.

Compliance. Navigating compliance issues relating to academic achievement, scholarships, gender issues, and other regulations established by their institutions; athletic conferences; the NCAA, NAIA, and NJCAA; and the federal government is one of the most critical tasks for athletic directors. They monitor the academic and graduation rates of student-athletes, and meet with student-athletes, parents, and faculty to resolve problems. If an athletic director's institution participates in federal student financial aid programs, they must prepare an annual Equity in Athletics Disclosure Act Report to account for scholarships. The director must also ensure that the institution is compliant with Title IX regulations, which guarantee the equal participation of women in collegiate sports.

Public relations. Athletic directors must be highly skilled at public relations. They need to develop strong relationships with donors and booster organizations that help raise much-needed revenue for their departments. They also speak at high schools, fan fests, and sports awards dinners. They oversee staff that produces and disseminates public relations material about the athletic program.

Athletic directors meet with newspaper, radio, and television reporters almost daily. They answer a variety of questions from these media professionals. They might be asked about the job security of the women's basketball coach, a generous gift to the athletic department by a donor, or the construction of the school's new multipurpose sports arena. Athletic directors speak at news conferences, on sports talk shows, and at other media events.

Athletic directors employed at small schools may only work part time. They spend the rest of their time teaching classes, chairing the physical education department, or coaching sports. All athletic directors, whether employed by a tiny sports program or a major, well-known program, must have a vision for the future of their programs. They must be able to explain this vision to administration officials, the media, and fans.

■ REQUIREMENTS
High School
A well-rounded education is important for anyone interested in becoming an athletic director. In high school, take accounting, mathematics, business, social studies, and other college preparatory classes. Since communication skills are of utmost importance to athletic directors, be sure to take English and speech courses as well.

Postsecondary Training
A bachelor's degree in sports administration, physical education, or a related field is the minimum educational requirement

QUICK FACTS

SCHOOL SUBJECTS
Business
Physical education
Speech

PERSONAL SKILLS
Communication/ideas
Leadership/management

WORK ENVIRONMENT
Primarily indoors
One location with some travel

MINIMUM EDUCATION LEVEL
Bachelor's degree

SALARY RANGE
$35,910 to $64,640 to $116,210+

CERTIFICATION OR LICENSING
None available

OUTLOOK
About as fast as the average

DOT
090

GOE
12.01.01

NOC
0513

O*NET-SOC
11-9033.00

TITLE IX

Title IX is part of the Educational Amendments of 1972, changes to federal law made by congress in response to activism from the women's movement. More generally, Title IX forbids discrimination in education, stating "No person in the U.S. shall, on the basis of sex be excluded from participation in, or denied the benefits of, or be subjected to discrimination under any educational program or activity receiving federal aid." Since most schools receive some sort of federal aid, this law has a great deal of influence over the nation's colleges an universities.

As it applies to athletics, Title IX has several applications. Most notably, financial and tuition assistance must be given equally to male and female athletes. Equal funds must also be allocated to men's and women's athletic programs for equipment, travel, and other expenses. Also, interests must be equally represented—there cannot be seven men's teams and only three women's teams.

Title IX has gone a long way towards remedying the problem of women being treated as second-class citizens in higher education, and has helped many women to succeed both in athletics and in life. However, what it has not changed is that high-profile, big-name men's teams, especially in basketball and football, continue to be both cash cows and the darlings of both athletic departments and wealthy alumni, and so are funded with disproportionate amounts of resources—drawing them away from other deserving athletes.

to become an athletic director. You will need a graduate degree to be hired by the best programs.

Ohio University in Athens, Ohio, has the oldest program in the country in sports administration. Administered by the School of Recreation and Sports Sciences within Ohio University's College of Health and Human Services, the program requires 55 credit hours (five of which are completed during an internship) and leads to a master of sports administration degree. The curriculum focuses on business administration, journalism, communications, management, marketing, sports administration, and facility management. The required internship lasts from three months to a year, and internship opportunities are provided by more than 400 different organizations worldwide.

Other Requirements

To be successful in this career, you need to have a love and knowledge of sports. Since athletic directors must juggle many different tasks at once, you need to be organized and able to delegate tasks. Developing strong people skills will help you work effectively with people from all types of backgrounds. You must be dedicated to academic excellence and have a high degree of integrity, as well as have strong management and leadership skills. Athletic directors are under constant pressure to create winning, financially sound programs. For this reason, you must be emotionally steady, a good judge of coaching ability, and expert at business and financial management.

■ EXPLORING

Reading industry publications is a good way to learn more about this career. The NACDA publishes *Athletics Administration,* a bimonthly journal that focuses on issues in collegiate athletics administration. The journal also has a Q&A Forum, where leading athletic directors are interviewed about current issues in the field. To learn more, visit the NACDA's website, http://www.nacda. com. The NACWAA publishes the *NACWAA Newsletter.* Recent issues featured articles on writing top-flight resumes and developing leadership skills. Visit http://www.nacwaa.org to read a sample issue of the newsletter.

If your high school has a large sports program, it might employ an athletic director. If so, talk with this person about his or her career. Good questions to ask include: What are your primary and secondary job duties? What type of training did you receive to qualify for this job? How did you get hired for this position? and How does working as a high school athletic director compare to working at the college level? If your school doesn't employ an athletic director, ask your guidance counselor or physical education teacher to set up an informational interview with one at a nearby college.

■ EMPLOYERS

Nearly every college and university in the United States employs athletic directors. Opportunities exist at private and public institutions, community colleges, and universities both large and small. At a smaller college, a coach, not a traditional administrator, may serve as the athletic director. High schools with large sports programs may also employ athletic directors.

■ STARTING OUT

Professional publications such as *The Chronicle of Higher Education* (http://www.chronicle.com) and *NCAA News* (http://www.ncaa.org/employment.html) have job listings for athletic directors. The human resources departments in most colleges and universities maintain listings of job openings at the institution and often advertise the positions nationally. The College and University Professional Association for Human Resources also has job listings at its website, http://www.cupahr.org.

Landing a job as an athletic director can be difficult; dozens of applicants may apply for a single position. For this reason, it is very important that you gain experience in the field and develop good networking skills. Work as a coach, assistant athletic director, or physical education instructor, or in another related position to get experience. Take advantage of any networking opportunities (league meetings, trade shows, association membership) to get to know others working in the field. Some of the best job leads in the industry come by word of mouth. The NACDA also offers internships for aspiring athletic administrators.

ADVANCEMENT

Athletic directors advance by taking positions at larger schools or at institutions that have better-known athletic programs. For example, an athletic director at a small Division II school might take a job at a larger, Division I institution. Or a director who is already at the top college level may take a position at a school that has a better-known athletic program. Some athletic directors become administrators in professional sports, commissioners of athletic conferences, or recreation administrators for cities or towns. Others choose to leave the profession entirely, working as deans or academic advisors at their universities.

EARNINGS

Salaries for college administrators vary widely among two-year and four-year colleges and among public and private institutions, but they are generally comparable to those of college faculty. According to the U.S. Department of Labor's *2001 National Occupational Employment and Wage Estimates,* the median salary for education administrators (which include athletic directors) was $64,640. The lowest paid 10 percent of administrators earned $35,910 or less per year, while the highest paid made $116,210 or more annually.

Most athletics directors receive benefits packages that include health insurance, paid vacation, and sick leave.

WORK ENVIRONMENT

Athletic directors work in a typical business office setting. Athletic directors at large schools have their own offices and large administrative staffs, while directors at small schools may have to share an office and do much of the work associated with this position themselves.

Athletic directors often work more than 40 hours a week, including evenings and weekends. They travel to professional conferences, to league meetings, and to other colleges for important games. They might be on the road an entire weekend for an important football game or a few weekdays for league or association meetings.

OUTLOOK

The U.S. Department of Labor predicts that overall employment for education administrators (which include athletic directors) will grow faster than the average through 2012. However, it is important to note how much of this will translate to athletic director's positions. While there will be an overall growth in higher education, the total number of athletic directors employed by colleges and universities remains fairly steady. Athletic directors also have little job security. They often lose their jobs if their athletic program fails to meet expectations. The total number of athletic directors employed by colleges and universities remains fairly steady. While many colleges and universities may cut athletic budgets, some new opportunities may become available as others add new programs. Competition for these positions, however, will be stiff.

FOR MORE INFORMATION

For information on internships, educational opportunities, job listings, and the journal Athletics Administration, *contact*

National Association of Collegiate Directors of Athletics
PO Box 16428
Cleveland, OH 44116
Tel: 440-892-4000
http://www.nacda.com

For information on student membership and the NACWAA Newsletter, *contact*

National Association of Collegiate Women Athletic Administrators (NACWAA)
4701 Wrightsville Avenue
Oak Park D-1
Wilmington, NC 28403
Tel: 910-793-8244
http://www.nacwaa.org

For information on the master of sports administration degree, contact

Sports Administration/Facility Management Program
Ohio University
School of Recreation and Sport Sciences
RTEC 218
Athens, OH 45701-2979
Tel: 740-593-4666
Email: sportsad@ohiou.edu
http://www.cats.ohiou.edu/sportadmin

Auctioneers

■ OVERVIEW

Auctioneers appraise, assemble, and advertise goods, which they subsequently sell to the highest bidder during an auction. They act as salespeople for the family, company, or agency selling the items to be auctioned. Depending on their area of expertise, they may auction off anything from a rare book to an entire office building.

■ HISTORY

In the United States many of the oldest auction firms are located in cities on the East Coast. For instance, Christie's in New York City is famous for auctioning luxury items such as fine art and celebrity memorabilia. Auctions have also long been popular in rural areas. Prior to the development of department stores, rural families had their own methods of dispensing with and acquiring the items and machinery they needed. For small or individual items, a barter or trade sometimes was made to exchange a needed tool or other possession. When many different items were being sold, however, a family would hold an auction, and an auctioneer would be hired to assist the family in disposing of the property. Families sometimes held auctions to raise cash or because they were moving and could not take along all their possessions.

Auctions are a popular way to buy farm equipment, real estate, artwork, livestock, or personal property from estates. An auction disposes of many varied items fairly quickly by selling one item to the highest bidder and then immediately moving through the rest of the collection. Auctions also are a popular way to raise money for charities and other groups. They are fun as well as functional and have become increasingly common in both rural areas and cities.

QUICK FACTS

SCHOOL SUBJECTS
Art
Mathematics
Speech

PERSONAL SKILLS
Helping/teaching
Leadership/management

WORK ENVIRONMENT
Indoors and outdoors
Primarily multiple locations

MINIMUM EDUCATION LEVEL
High school diploma

SALARY RANGE
$10,000 to $50,000 to
$100,000

CERTIFICATION OR LICENSING
Required by all states

OUTLOOK
About as fast as the average

DOT
294

GOE
N/A

NOC
6411

O*NET-SOC
N/A

■ THE JOB

An auctioneer's work has two main facets: the preliminary preparation and evaluation and the selling itself. The former takes more time and skill and is less familiar to most people. Prior to the auction itself, the auctioneer meets with the sellers to review the property to be sold. The auctioneer makes note of the lowest bid, called the "reserved bid," that the sellers will accept for each item. The auctioneer also advises clients when an item should be sold "absolute," or without a minimum bid. If there are legal issues to be discussed, an auctioneer confers with the sellers.

The most time-consuming activity often is the appraisal of the goods. The auctioneer determines the value of each item and compares it to the reserve bid established by the sellers. The auctioneer makes notes on the type of item being sold, its history, and any unique qualities the item may have. This background information can encourage higher bids and increase buyer interest.

Once the appraisal has taken place, an auctioneer must organize the items in the area where the auction is to be held. Sometimes the auctioneer issues a catalog or booklet describing the items for sale for that particular day. The catalog also may list the sequence in which the items will be sold so buyers know when the items they want will be up for sale. In addition to the catalog, auctioneers organize any advertising needed to promote the sale. Newspaper and magazine ads, flyers, signs, and broadcast announcements can reach people from many different areas and bring in a large crowd. Some rural areas hold auctions as special attractions for tourists around summer holidays or to commemorate town events and local celebrations.

Usually the auctioneer organizes and sets up the auction far enough in advance for people to come early, peruse the area, and see what is of interest to them. Antique furniture and clothing, farm equipment, and artwork are some of the things sold at auctions. Other auctions concentrate on large industrial machinery or cars, as well as livestock, stamps, coins, and books.

The auctioneer works to help both the buyer and the seller. An auctioneer is familiar enough with the potential value of the items to begin bids at a certain price. The encouragement and stimulation an auctioneer provides, however, often is matched by the excitement and competition among the buyers. Auctioneers must be quick-thinking and comfortable addressing crowds, not only offering them information about the items for sale but at times acting as entertainers to keep the crowd interested.

Auctioneers coordinate the pace of the auction and judge which items should be sold first. Sometimes to boost people's interest, an auctioneer saves the most popular items for last. At other times the best articles are sold first so that those who weren't able to purchase their first choice will feel free to bid on other items.

Auctioneers commonly enlist the help of assistants, who carry items to the auctioneer, ensuring a steady flow of goods. In addition, another assistant may be in charge of collecting money, issuing receipts, and keeping track of the purchaser of each item.

Most auctions follow a typical pattern. The items for sale are made available for inspection in a catalog or a display. In the case of real estate auctions, however, photographs may be circulated. In some instances, land that is miles away can be sold, though the auctioneer will describe some history and features of the area. Often these types of auctions take less time, but the preparation is more detailed. Auctioneers must know the dimensions of the buildings they are selling, boundary lines for lots and farms, and whether any money is owed or any environmental hazard exists on the property, as well as information about the terms of payment and zoning laws.

■ REQUIREMENTS
High School

A high school diploma generally is a basic requirement for auctioneers. Classes in sales, mathematics, speech, art, art history, and economics are useful.

Postsecondary Training

Training for auctioneers is available at many schools, such as the Missouri Auction School in Kansas City. More advanced training is provided by the National Auctioneers Association (NAA), which holds classes in numerous locations around the country. The Auction Marketing Institute (AMI), an organization affiliated with the NAA, offers the Certified Auctioneers Institute profession program, taught at Indiana University in Bloomington. One can also receive training in the Accredited Auctioneer Real Estate program, also sponsored by the AMI; classes for this program are held in various locations in the United States.

Auctioneer training can involve appraising and item presentation, as well as speech classes so that auctioneers do not strain their voices while working long hours. Auctioneers who plan to concentrate on specific areas may take classes to supplement their training. Livestock and real estate auctions require specialized knowledge. In addition, some auctioneers have backgrounds in art or antiques.

Auctioneers must be effective speakers. Their job is to command attention and interest in the items through the power of their voice and their personal manner and

WORDS TO KNOW

Absentee bid: A procedure that allows a bidder to participate in the bidding process without being physically present. The particular rules and procedures of absentee bids are unique to each auction company.

Absolute auction: An auction where the property is sold to the highest qualified bidder with no limiting conditions or amount; also known as an auction without reserve.

Appraisal: The process of estimating value.

Auction block: The podium where the auctioneer stands while conducting the auction.

Bid: A prospective buyer's indication or offer of a price he or she will pay to purchase property at auction. Bids are usually in standardized increments established by the auctioneer.

Caveat emptor: A Latin term meaning "Let the buyer beware"; a legal maxim stating that the buyer takes the risk regarding quality or condition of the property purchased, unless protected by warranty.

Collusion: The unlawful practice of two or more people agreeing not to bid against one another in order to deflate value; when the auctioneer accepts a fictitious bid on behalf of the seller so as to manipulate or inflate the price of the property.

Commission: The fee charged to the seller by the auctioneer for providing services, usually a percentage of the gross receipts.

Minimum opening bid: The lowest acceptable amount at which the bidding must commence.

Reserve auction: An auction in which the sellers or their agents reserve the right to accept or decline any and all bids, or to withdraw the property at any time prior to the announcement of the completion of the sale by the auctioneer.

Tie bid: Two or more bidders bid exactly the same amount at the same time and must be resolved by the auctioneer.

Source: National Auctioneers Association

good humor. Auctioneers should have a great deal of stamina, since auctions often take place outdoors in warm weather and can last for many hours at a stretch. Auctioneers must also be alert so they can keep track of the crowd activity, the progress of the assistants, and the selling of the goods.

Because of all the deliberation that goes into preparing an auction, an auctioneer should like working with people. A keen sense of evaluation and an honest nature also are useful attributes.

An auctioneer conducts an antiques auction at an estate sale in North Carolina.

Certification or Licensing

Because they handle large sums of money, most auctioneers are bonded; however, licensing for auctioneers varies from state to state. Approximately 27 states require auctioneers to be licensed. Licensing requirements vary, so be sure to contact the licensing board for the state in which you would like to work for more information.

The Auction Marketing Institute offers the following professional designation programs to practicing auctioneers who meet its experiential, educational, and ethical standards: Certified Auctioneers Institute (CAI), accredited auctioneer real estate (AARE), and graduate personal property appraiser (GPPA).

Other Requirements

Auctioneers who work in specialized areas, such as real estate and livestock, must conform to additional regulations. Those who sell land must be licensed real estate sales agents or brokers. Auctioneers should be familiar with laws and regulations in the states in which they practice.

■ EXPLORING

You can explore this field by attending an auction to see firsthand the responsibilities that are involved. Classes in speech, drama, and communications may be helpful because auctioneers rely heavily on their voices, not only for speaking and presentation but also to get the buyer's attention through style and performance.

More direct involvement is possible as well. Charities and other social organizations occasionally use nonprofessionals for fund-raising auctions, and established auctioneers often hire part-time assistants. It may also be useful to read periodicals, such as *Auctioneer* (published by the National Auctioneers Association), that publish articles about the field.

■ EMPLOYERS

Auctioneers often work as consultants on a freelance basis. They may be hired by private individuals or large companies anywhere that goods are offered for sale to the highest bidder. Others may work for private auction houses, which usually are located in large metropolitan areas such as New York, Los Angeles, and Chicago, as well as smaller cities. Those who wish to focus on specific areas such as real estate, art, or farm equipment should, of course, seek consulting assignments or permanent positions in locations and/or with companies where these items are sold; for example, farm equipment generally is auctioned in rural areas.

■ STARTING OUT

Beginning auctioneers may work as assistants, handling money and receipts or presenting the sale items to the experienced auctioneer. They also may begin by working local and county fairs or smaller auctions.

Professional trade schools may offer placement services or internships that link beginners with established practitioners. Beginners may have to work part-time until they gain experience and become better known. Auctioneers who work for large auction houses may receive more assignments as they become more experienced and complete training offered by the firm.

■ ADVANCEMENT

Professional auctioneers must have a reputation for skilled and honest performance. Since most auctioneers get paid by commission, they may decide to specialize in selling real estate, farm equipment, or artwork—areas that are likely to bring in more revenue for less preparation and shorter presentations.

Auctioneers who work with auction houses may move up the ranks and obtain more prestigious assignments. Auctioneers also advance as they develop their knowledge in specialized areas. Some people move into different lines of work but keep auctioning as a side job.

EARNINGS

Part-time auctioneers earn close to $10,000, while full-time auctioneers typically earn more than $20,000. The best-paid auctioneers earn $50,000 to $100,000 or more. On a daily basis, pay ranges between $100 and $2,000.

Auctioneers usually are paid on commission. Part-time auctioneers sometimes supplement their income by assisting more experienced workers, acting as cashiers, assisting with publicity, or helping to organize the items.

WORK ENVIRONMENT

Because auctioneers often travel to an assignment, they may encounter a wide range of working conditions. Auctions are held year-round. They take place in cities and small towns and occur in all types of weather. Auctioneers may work inside in a large hall or outside during a state fair. The type of goods being sold may also dictate their working conditions; for instance, farm equipment is commonly sold outdoors on the site of the owner's farm.

Auctioneers often are provided with a podium and a microphone, which are especially important at large auctions, which can draw more than 2,000 people. This allows the auctioneer to keep the crowd's attention when the noise and activity level become distracting or stressful.

OUTLOOK

The outlook for auctioneers is good, especially for those who have developed a specialty, such as real estate. Auctioneers with polished skills and a strong delivery usually have little trouble finding work. For an ambitious auctioneer who is willing to travel to various locations and invest time to gain experience, regular employment is possible, either as an independent auctioneer or as a staff member of an auction firm. However, this is tempered by the rise of Internet auction sites, such as eBay, which automate the process and make it easier for people to run their own sales.

Many auctioneers get assignments based on their reputation and notoriety within an area. Thus, auctioneers may find it difficult to reestablish themselves if they move to another area. Also, some types of auctions are found only in certain areas. Art auctions, for example, generally take place in cities, while livestock, farm equipment, and farm land most often are sold in rural areas.

FOR MORE INFORMATION

For information about the school, contact
Florida Auctioneer Academy
10376 East Colonial Drive
Orlando, FL 32817
Tel: 800-422-9155
http://f-a-a.com

For an information packet about the school, contact
Missouri Auction School
6329 Blue Ridge Boulevard
Raytown, MO 64133
Tel: 800-835-1955
http://www.auctionschool.com/

Contact the following organization for career and educational information:
National Auctioneers Association
8880 Ballentine
Overland Park, KS 66214
Tel: 913-541-8084
Email: hq@auctioneers.org
http://www.auctioneers.org

Audio Recording Engineers

OVERVIEW

Audio recording engineers oversee the technical end of recording. They operate the controls of the recording equipment—often under the direction of a music producer—during the production of music recordings; film, television, and radio productions; and other mediums that require sound recording. Recording engineers monitor and operate electronic and computer consoles to make necessary adjustments, and solve technical problems as they occur during a recording session. They assure that the equipment is in optimal working order and obtain any additional equipment necessary for the recording.

HISTORY

The job of the contemporary audio recording engineer as we know it began in the late 1940s with the development of magnetic tape as a recording medium. Tape provided a new and flexible method for recording engineers to influence the outcome of the recording session. Before tape, records were cut on warm wax blanks that allowed only minimal manipulation of sound quality. Generally, whatever the musicians produced in the recording studio is what came out on the record, and the degree of quality rested almost entirely in the hands of the studio engineer.

The innovation of tape and the introduction of long-playing (LP) records brought significant improvements to the recording industry. Since tape allowed recording on multiple tracks, recording engineers were now needed to edit and enhance tape quality and "mix" each track individually to produce a balanced sound on all tracks. Tape allowed recording engineers to perform patchwork corrections to a recording by replacing sections where musician errors or poor sound quality occurred.

By the 1950s recording engineers played a vital role in the record industry. The emergence of rock and roll brought an explosion of recordings in the industry, and each recording required a technically proficient, creative, and skilled audio recording engineer. Although engineers often had to produce sounds at the direction of the music producer, many worked at their own discretion and produced truly unique "sounds." Engineers also found employment for film productions in Hollywood and for radio station productions throughout the United States.

The development of music-related software for the computer has altered many aspects of music recording, particularly in the editing process. Many time-consuming tasks previously performed manually can now be done in half the time and less with new specially programmed software. More than ever before, today's audio recording engineer must be highly educated and up-to-date with the rapidly changing technology that ultimately affects the way he or she performs the job.

■ THE JOB

Audio recording engineers operate and maintain the equipment used in a sound recording studio. They record: music, live and in studios; speech, such as dramatic readings of novels or radio advertisements; and sound effects and dialogue used in television and film. They work in control rooms at master console boards often containing hundreds of dials, switches, meters, and lights, which the engineer reads and adjusts to achieve desired results during a recording. Today, the recording studio is often considered an extra instrument, and thus, the audio recording engineer becomes an extra musician

in his or her ability to dramatically alter the final sound of the recording.

As the owner of Watchmen Studios in Lockport, New York, Doug White offers audio recording services, digital audio mastering, audio duplication, and website construction. "I record a lot of hardcore and metal," he says. "It makes up about 60 percent of what we do here." His clients include Bughouse, Big Hair, Tugboat Annie, and Slugfest. Watchmen Studios features separate drum, vocal, and guitar booths, and offers 24-track, 16-track, and 8-track recording. The studio even offers spare guitars. "I try to keep it to a nine-hour day," White says. "Some studio engineers work up to 12 hours a day, but I feel my work suffers after too long."

As recording engineers prepare to record a session, they ask the musicians and producer what style of music they will be playing and what type of sound and emotion they want reflected in the final recording. Audio recording engineers must find out what types of instruments and orchestration will be recorded to determine how to manage the recording session and what additional equipment will be needed. For example, each instrument or vocalist may require a special microphone. The recording of dialogue will take considerably less preparation.

Before the recording session, audio recording engineers test all microphones, chords, recording equipment, and amplifiers to ensure everything is operating correctly. They load tape players and set recording levels. Microphones must be positioned in precise locations near the instrument or amplifier. They experiment with several different positions of the microphone and listen in the control room for the best sound. Depending on the size of the studio and the number of musicians or vocalists, audio recording engineers position musicians in various arrangements to obtain the best sound for the production. For smaller projects, such as three- to eight-piece bands, each instrument may be sectioned off in soundproof rooms to ensure the sounds of one instrument do not "bleed" into the recording of another instrument. For more complex recording of larger orchestration, specialized microphones must be placed in exact locations to record one or several instruments.

Once audio recording engineers have the musicians in place and the microphones set, they instruct musicians to play a sample of their music. At the main console, they read the gauges and set recording levels for each instrument. Recording engineers must listen for sound imperfections, such as hissing, popping, "mike bleeding," and any other extraneous noises, and pinpoint their source. They turn console dials to adjust recording level, volume, tone, and effects. Depending on the problem, they may have to reposition either the microphone or the musician.

QUICK FACTS

SCHOOL SUBJECTS
Computer science
Music

PERSONAL SKILLS
Mechanical/manipulative
Technical/scientific

WORK ENVIRONMENT
Primarily indoors
Primarily one location

MINIMUM EDUCATION LEVEL
Some postsecondary training

SALARY RANGE
$18,540 to $36,970 to
$82,510+

CERTIFICATION OR LICENSING
Recommended

OUTLOOK
About as fast as the average

DOT
194

GOE
01.08.01

NOC
5225

O*NET-SOC
27-4011.00, 27-4012.00,
27-4014.00

With the right sound and recording level of each microphone set, audio recording engineers prepare the recording equipment (either tape or digital). During the recording of a song or voice-over, they monitor the recording level of each microphone to ensure none of the tracks are too high, which results in distortion, or too low, which results in weak sound quality. Recording engineers usually record more than one "take" of a song. Before the mixing process, they listen to each take carefully and determine which one has the best sound. They often splice the best part of one take with the best part of another take.

In some recording sessions, two engineers work in the control room. One usually works with the recording equipment, and the other takes instruction from the producer. The engineers coordinate the ideas of the producer to create the desired sound. During each session, the volume, speed, intensity, and tone quality must be carefully monitored. Producers may delegate more responsibility to the recording engineer. Engineers often tell the musicians when to start and stop playing or when to redo a certain section. They may ask musicians or other studio technicians to move microphones or other equipment in the studio to improve sound quality.

After the recording is made, the individual tracks must be "mixed" to a master tape. When mixing, they balance each instrument in relation to the others. Together with the producer and the musicians, recording engineers listen to the song or piece several times with the instruments at different levels and decide on the best sound and consistency. At this stage, they also set equalization and manipulate sound, tone, intensity, effects, and speed of the recording. Mixing a record is often a tedious, time-consuming task that can take several weeks to complete, especially with some recordings that are 24 or more tracks. At a larger studio, this may be done exclusively by a *sound mixer*. Sound mixers exclusively study various mixing methodologies.

Audio recording engineers frequently perform maintenance and repair on their equipment. They must identify and solve common technical problems in the studio. They may have to rewire or move equipment when updating the studio with new equipment. They may write proposals for equipment purchases and studio design changes. Engineers are often assisted in many of the basic sound recording tasks by apprentices, who are also known as *studio technicians*.

Recording engineers at smaller studios may set studio times for musicians. They must keep a thorough account of the band or performer scheduled to play, the musical style of the band or performer, the specific equipment that will be needed, and any other special arrangements needed to make the session run smoothly. They make sure the studio is stocked with the right working acces-

An audio recording engineer works the mixing board at a sound studio.

sory equipment, including cords, cables, microphones, amplifiers, tapes, tuners, and effect pedals.

■ REQUIREMENTS
High School
You should take music courses to learn an instrument, study voice, or learn composition. High school orchestras and bands are an excellent source for both practicing and studying music performance. You should also take classes in computer science, mathematics, business, and, if offered, electronics. A drama or broadcast journalism class may allow you access to a sound booth, and the opportunity to assist with audio engineering for live theatrical productions and radio programs.

Postsecondary Training
More than ever before, postsecondary training is an essential step for becoming a successful recording engineer. This is when you will make your first contacts and be introduced to many of the highly technical (and continually changing) aspects of the field. To learn about educational opportunities in the United States and abroad, visit the websites of the Audio Engineering Society (http://www.aes.org) or *Mix* Magazine Online (http://mixonline.com).

Seminars and workshops offer the most basic level of education. This may be the best way to obtain an early, hands-on understanding of audio recording and prepare for entry-level apprentice positions. These programs are intended to introduce students to the equipment and technical aspects of the field, such as microphones, sound reinforcement, audio processing devices, tape and DAT machines, digital processing, and sound editing. Students will also become familiar with the newest technologies in the audio field, such as MIDI (musical instrument digital interface), synthesis, sampling, and current music software. A seminar can last from a couple of hours to several weeks. Many workshops are geared toward in-depth study of a certain aspect of recording such as mixing, editing, or music production.

Students looking for a more comprehensive course of study in specific areas of the recording industry can enroll in technical school or community college programs. Depending on the curriculum, these programs can take from several weeks to up to a year to complete. The most complete level of postsecondary education is a two- or four-year degree from a university. At many universities, students have access to state-of-the-art equipment and a teaching staff of knowledgeable professionals in the industry. Universities incorporate music, music technology, and music business in a comprehensive curriculum that prepare graduates to be highly competitive in the industry. Students can enroll in other non-audio courses, such as business, communications, marketing, and computers.

Certification or Licensing

In the broadcast industry, engineers can be certified by the Society of Broadcast Engineers (http://www.sbe.org). Certification is recommended because this step shows your dedication to the field and your level of competence. After completing technical training and meeting strict qualifications, you can also join the Society as a member or associate member. Membership gives you access to educational seminars, conferences, and a weekly job line.

Other Requirements

Being a recording engineer requires both technical skills and communication skills. You must be patient, capable of working well with a variety of people, and possess the confidence to function in a leadership position. Excellent troubleshooting skills are essential for an audio recording engineer.

"A very powerful, outgoing personality is the number one qualification," Doug White says. "You're dealing every day with picky musicians who never will be happy with their work, so they look to you for verification." White emphasizes that engineers need an even temperament and endless patience. "You have to be able to handle all types of personalities with kid gloves," he says.

■ EXPLORING

One way to learn more about this field is to read publications that focus on audio recording. *Mix* Magazine Online (http://mixonline.com) offers articles about education, technology, and production. Other publications that provide useful information on the industry and audio recording techniques include *Remix* (http://

www.remixmag.com), *Pro Sound News* (http://www.prosoundnews.com), and *Broadcast Engineering* (http://www.broadcastengineering.com).

Any experience you can get working in or around music will provide excellent background for this field. You could take up an instrument in the school band or orchestra, or perform with your own band. You might also have the opportunity to work behind the scenes with a music group, serving as a business manager, helping set up sound systems, or working as a technician in a school sound recording studio or radio station.

Write or call record companies or recording studios to get more information; local studios can usually be found in the classified telephone directory, and others can be located in the music trade magazines. The National Academy of Recording Arts and Sciences (the organization responsible for the Grammy Awards) is one source for information on the industry. Numerous books and music trade magazines that cover music production are available at bookstores or libraries.

Doug White recommends that prospective recording engineers make appointments to interview working sound professionals. "Even if you have to buy an hour of studio time to sit with them and talk," he says, "it's worth the cost. Ask as much about the personal/social side of working with artists. Don't be dazzled by the equipment. Believe me, it's a very small part of the job."

■ EMPLOYERS

Though most major recording studios are located in metropolitan areas such as New York and Los Angeles, many cities across the country have vibrant music scenes. Talented, skilled engineers will always be in demand, no matter the size of the recording studio. They may be employed by a studio, or they may be self-employed, either contracting with studios or operating their own recording business. Engineers also work for broadcast companies, engineering sound for radio and TV programs. Some recording engineers work for video production companies and corporate media libraries, helping to create in-house company presentations and films.

■ STARTING OUT

After high school, seek experience as an intern or apprentice or begin postsecondary training in audio at a university or college or trade school. Because most professional recording studios and broadcasters prefer to offer apprenticeship positions to students who have some previous experience in audio, those who have completed some trade school courses may have better chances at landing jobs. Most university and college programs offer semester internship programs at professional recording studios as a way of earning credit. Professional trade associations also support internships for their members by either matching students with employers or funding internship expenses. Universities and trade schools also have job placement services for their graduates.

Before going into the business, Doug White got an associate's degree from the Art Institute of Atlanta. "But in this business," he says, "your education doesn't get you very far. Reputation and experience are usually what open doors."

Internships and apprenticeships play an important role in helping students establish personal connections. Students are often hired by the studios or stations with which they've interned or their employer can make recommendations for other job openings at a different studio. Employers will often post entry-level openings at universities or trade schools, but very seldom will they advertise in a newspaper.

Most audio engineers begin their career in small studios as assistants, called studio technicians, and have varied responsibilities, which may entail anything from running out to pick up dinner for the musicians during a recording session, to helping the recording engineer in the mixing process. Positions in radio will also provide a good stepping-stone to a career in audio recording. Entry-level positions may be easier to come by at studios that specialize in educational recording and radio advertisements than at music recording studios.

■ ADVANCEMENT

Career advancement will depend upon an engineer's interests as well as on hard work and perseverance. They may advance to the higher paying, glamorous (yet high-pressure) position of music producer, either as an independent producer or working for a record label. Recording engineers may also advance to positions in the radio or television industries, which usually offer better pay than studio work. If engineers wish to stay in the field of audio recording, they can advance to managerial positions or choose to open their own recording studio.

The recording industry is continually changing in response to frequent technological breakthroughs. Recording engineers who adapt easily to such advances as digital recording and new computer software will have a better chance for success. Some recording engineers may team up with producers who work independently of the studio. They may form their own company, allowing for greater flexibility and higher salaries.

■ EARNINGS

According to the U.S. Department of Labor, the median income for sound engineering technicians was approximately $36,970 in 2002. At the low end of the scale, about

LEARN MORE ABOUT IT

Gibson, David. *The Art of Mixing: A Visual Guide to Recording, Engineering, and Production.* Emeryville, Calif.: Mix Books, 1997.

Massey, Howard. *Behind the Glass: Top Record Producers Tell How They Craft the Hits.* San Francisco, Calif.: Backbeat Books, 2000.

Owsinski, Bobby. *The Mastering Engineer's Handbook.* Milwaukee, Wisc.: Hal Leonard Publishing, 2001.

———. *The Mixing Engineer's Handbook.* Milwaukee, Wisc.: Hal Leonard Publishing, 1999.

Sokol, Mike. *The Acoustic Musician's Guide to Sound Reinforcement and Live Recording.* Upper Saddle River, N.J.: Prentice Hall, 1997.

Stark, Scott Hunter. *Live Sound Reinforcement: A Comprehensive Guide to P.A. and Music Reinforcement Systems and Technology.* 2nd ed. Emeryville, Calif.: Mix Books, 1996.

Talbot-Smith, Michael, ed. *Audio Engineer's Reference Book.* 2nd ed. Boston, Mass.: Focal Press, 2001.

White, Ira. *Audio Made Easy (Or How to Be a Sound Engineer Without Really Trying).* 2nd ed. Milwaukee, Wisc.: Hal Leonard Publishing, 1997.

Yakabuski, Jim. *Professional Sound Reinforcement Techniques: Tips and Tricks of a Concert Sound Engineer.* Milwaukee, Wisc.: Hal Leonard Publishing, 2001.

10 percent of these workers made less than $18,540. The highest paid 10 percent made $82,510 or more. Audio engineers in the broadcast industry often earn higher salaries than those in the music industry. Generally, those working at television stations earned more than those working at radio stations.

Benefits packages will vary from business to business. Audio recording engineers employed by a recording company or by a broadcast station receive health insurance and paid vacation. Other benefits may include dental and eye care, life and disability insurance, and a pension plan.

■ WORK ENVIRONMENT

Recording studios can be comfortable places to work. They are usually air conditioned because of the sensitivity of the equipment. They may be loud or cramped, however, especially during recording sessions where many people are working in a small space. The work is not particularly demanding physically (except when recording engineers must move equipment), but there may be related stress depending on the personalities of the producer and the performers. Audio recording engineers must be able to follow directions from producers and must often give directions. Their work must be quick and precise, and the engineer must be able to work as part of a team. Depending on the type of recording business, some engineers may be required to record off-site, at live concerts, for example, or other places where the recording is to take place. Engineers can usually come to work dressed however they wish.

Engineers must have patience when working with performers. For the engineer, there are often long periods of waiting while the musicians or performers work out problems and try to perfect parts of their songs. Engineers will frequently have to record the same song or spoken-word piece several times after mistakes have been made in the presentation. In addition, the mixing process itself can become tedious for many engineers—especially if they are not fond of the music. During the mix, engineers must listen to the same song over and over again to assure a proper balance of the musical tracks, and they often try various mixes.

Working hours depend on the job. Some studios are open at night or on the weekends to accommodate the schedules of musicians and performers. Other studios and recording companies only operate during normal business hours. Engineers work between 40 and 60 hours a week and may frequently put in 12-hour work days. Album or compact disc recordings typically take 300 to 500 hours each to record. In contrast, educational or language cassette recordings take only about 100 hours.

■ OUTLOOK

Employment in this field is expected to grow about as fast as the average through 2012, according to the U.S. Department of Labor. New computer technology (hardware and software) is rapidly changing the way many recording engineers perform their jobs, making the entire audio recording process easier. These technological advancements will negatively affect job prospects for entry-level studio technicians whose more mundane recording tasks will increasingly be performed by computers. However, technology will also have some beneficial impact. As American media expands through technology and markets such as digital cable open up, opportunities for audio recording engineers will likewise increase.

With computer technology making the recording process faster, easier, and ideally better, this will free up time in the studio—time that the studio managers can book with more recording sessions, which in turn may require a larger staff. As this technology becomes affordable, though, some performers, particularly rock or jazz groups, may choose to record themselves. With computers doing most of the grunt work and allowing complete control and manipulation of sound, some of these "home"

recordings (also called "low-fi" recordings) can sound just as good as a studio recording for certain music genres. However, to take full advantage of digital and multimedia technology, musicians will continue to seek out the expertise of studio professionals.

Competition for jobs will be steepest in high-paying urban areas. Audio recording engineers will find jobs more easily in small cities and towns.

■ FOR MORE INFORMATION

For information on graduate-level scholarships and audio recording schools and courses in the United States and abroad, contact

Audio Engineering Society
60 East 42nd Street, Room 2520
New York, NY 10165-2520
Tel: 212-661-8528
Email: HQ@aes.org
http://www.aes.org

For facts and statistics about the recording industry, contact
Recording Industry Association of America
1330 Connecticut Avenue, NW, Suite 300
Washington, DC 20036
Tel: 202-775-0101
http://www.riaa.com

For information on membership, contact
Society of Professional Audio Recording Services
PO Box 770845
Memphis, TN 38177-0845
Tel: 800-771-7727
Email: spars@spars.com
http://www.spars.com

Automatic Teller Machine Servicers

■ OVERVIEW

Automatic (or automated) *teller machine* (ATM) *servicers* maintain and repair the ATMs at banks, grocery stores, convenience stores, gas stations, and other locations. ATM servicers are also called *ATM network specialists, ATM field service technicians,* and *ATM technicians.*

■ HISTORY

Luther George Simjian (1905–97) invented the automatic teller machine (ATM) around 1960. ATMs are essentially computers that are connected to a central computer through a data network. ATMs enable people to make bank deposits and withdrawals electronically, sometimes in a location far away from their own banks. By mid-2004, there were some 1.4 million ATMs worldwide, according to the ATM Industry Association (ATMIA). As of 2002, computer, automated teller, and office machine repairers held about 156,000 jobs in the United States.

■ THE JOB

ATM servicers make sure that ATMs are in working order and available to the public often 24 hours a day, seven days a week. The service needed by any individual ATM may be as simple as clearing paper jams or situating cash properly, or it may be more complicated, requiring an understanding of electronics and computer programming.

The work of ATM servicers varies according to the position. *First line technicians* replenish the money, making sure it is positioned properly and that no sensors are blocked; replace receipt paper; remove any obstructions in the machine and perform other routine maintenance; balance the machine; and remove deposits and deliver them to a central office. When an ATM seems to be working improperly, technicians troubleshoot and try to define the problem. They may also check security equipment, such as cameras and VCRs, to ensure that it is working properly. Depending on the size of the city in which they work, ATM servicers may service 30 to 40 machines a day. These technicians are usually armed and drive armored trucks to and from the ATM locations. First line technicians are also stationed in the office to dispatch other technicians, count the money, and fill out forms for the banks. Processing deposits involves opening envelopes and documenting the contents. Supervisors train and oversee the work of technicians and assign them their routes. When understaffed, supervisors go out on runs. They also send out second line technicians when the first line technicians are unable to fix particular problems with the machines.

Second line technicians are typically on call and are paged when a repair is necessary. With an understanding of particular machines, networks, and electronic systems, they perform maintenance on the machines, replacing parts when necessary. They also perform preventive maintenance by testing machines. Technicians need to know how each network is balanced and what could go wrong. If the dispenser (the part of the machine that contains the money) needs to be serviced, first line technicians stand guard while the second line technicians make any necessary adjustments. A technician may be called in if a machine is unable to properly read bank cards because of worn magnetic heads or if it has a "fail" that prevents it

from dispensing the requested amount of cash. If a problem is too extensive to be corrected on-site, the technician may take the whole machine, or parts of it, to a *bench technician*, who works in a repair shop rather than in the field.

Some technicians are trained to install ATMs, which can involve securing the ATM at a particular site (indoors or outdoors) and programming the machine. Technicians put up signs and awnings over the machines, and they also remove or relocate machines.

Richard Wesley is a second line technician for an ATM overhaul and service company that contracts with an area bank. "I have to do whatever it takes to get the ATM back in service," he says. "ATMs can't stay down very long.

"When I get a call, I go to the branch or off-site, like a grocery store, that has the bank's ATMs." With his understanding of electronics, Wesley performs repairs on-site after speaking to the first line technician about the ATM's problems. "After each repair, I have to call the host, which electronically talks to the site and also to the bank via the ATM. I do that to close out the service call and to make sure that the ATM is working properly."

■ REQUIREMENTS
High School

To become an ATM servicer, you should take all available high school computer classes. Knowledge of and familiarity with computer languages will give you an edge as ATMs become more complex. Also take any electronics or mechanics courses your school offers, because ATM repair requires skills in both areas. By taking English courses, you'll develop communication skills that will prepare you to deal with ATM service clients as well as supervise other technicians.

Postsecondary Training

First line technicians typically get their training on the job, but second line technicians often must have electronics experience before being hired. Some positions require an associate's degree, or equivalent experience,

QUICK FACTS

SCHOOL SUBJECTS
Computer science
Mathematics
Technical/shop

PERSONAL SKILLS
Following instructions
Technical/scientific

WORK ENVIRONMENT
Indoors and outdoors
Primarily multiple locations

MINIMUM EDUCATION LEVEL
Some postsecondary training

SALARY RANGE
$20,770 to $33,250 to $52,130

CERTIFICATION OR LICENSING
Required by certain states

OUTLOOK
About as fast as the average

DOT
N/A

GOE
05.02.02

NOC
N/A

O*NET-SOC
49-2011.00

WORDS TO KNOW

Armored car: A truck with plates of armor and strong locks for transporting large sums of money.

Debit card: A plastic card with identification encoded into its electromagnetic strip; used in ATMs for bank service.

Dispenser: The compartment of the ATM that holds and distributes the cash.

Proprietary network: A network that is only accessible by one particular bank's customers.

Shared network: A network that links together a number of different banks and accounts.

in electronics or electronic equipment repair. Manufacturers of machines also provide training, and employers may require that technicians have an understanding of specific ATMs and data networks.

Electronics technology programs are available at community colleges and vocational schools and offer courses in such subjects as electrical circuits, technical mathematics, mechanics, electrical drafting, and industrial electronics.

Certification or Licensing

Various manufacturers, such as NCR, Triton Systems, and Diebold, offer certification in the use of their machines. This certification may be required by some employers. Some states also require that technicians driving armored trucks or carrying guns be licensed as security guards.

Other Requirements

Since ATM servicers handle other people's money, trustworthiness and responsibility are key qualities. Employers will check your credit, background, and driving records and conduct polygraph and drug tests.

You will often be on call to service machines at odd or irregular hours, so employers will expect you to be dependable. You must also be able to work without close supervision. Wesley says, "You have to have the desire to make sure the work is done right since no one is looking over your shoulder." The most successful technicians are those who can closely follow all the required steps.

Problem-solving skills are important, and if you supervise other technicians, you'll need people skills and the ability to coordinate the work of others. If you do second line service, you'll need some mechanical and computer skills. Finger dexterity and good vision are important too given that you will be working with various tools and often looking at small components.

■ EXPLORING

Read about what's happening in the industry by visiting ATMmarketplace.com online. To explore your interest and ability, you could observe and even help a family member or neighbor when they're doing some kind of computer repair work or you could pick up an electronics kit from a local hobby store or online. Join your school's computer club to learn more about computers. A part-time job at a local computer or electronics store could teach you about electronic equipment and repair. To hear firsthand what the job's like, request an information interview (in person, on the phone, or via e-mail) with someone who works as an ATM servicer. You should be able to find someone to talk to through an armored truck service or ATM supplier. Check your local phone book, conduct a Web search, or contact ATMIA (http://www.atmia.com/). Or someone at your bank might be able to provide you with a name.

■ EMPLOYERS

While banks and credit unions do hire technicians, the majority of work is available from businesses that contract with banks for the maintenance of ATMs. Armored truck services such as Brink's hire first and second line technicians, as do suppliers of ATMs and parts. Most technicians will find jobs with ATM installation and service companies that maintain the many ATMs in grocery and convenience stores, malls, department stores, and other citywide locations.

■ STARTING OUT

Jobs are frequently advertised in the newspaper, or you can check for area services in the yellow pages under "Automated Teller Machines." You can find installation companies that hire technicians nationwide by typing "ATM services" in an Internet search engine. ATMmarketplace.com offers free membership and allows you to search current job postings; it also links you to the sites of ATM manufacturers.

Wesley developed his electronics and supervisory skills before going to work as a second line technician. He found the job listing in the local newspaper. "I was hired because of my electronics training for work on the ATMs," he says, "and my supervisory skills to satisfy the banking personnel whenever the ATMs were down and customers got mad."

■ ADVANCEMENT

Within an installation and repair service, a technician may move on to become a bench technician who handles the more complex repairs that can't be made on-site.

Technicians may also go to work for manufacturers to assist engineers in designing equipment. Some technicians also start their own businesses, contracting with banks and credit unions to install and maintain their ATMs.

Advancement opportunities might also be found in areas indirectly related to ATM servicing. Software engineers create computer software programs tailored to the needs of specific businesses. Database administrators design, install, and update computer databases of business information. Sales managers oversee sales staff in direct interaction with customers. Computer and office machine service technicians install, calibrate, maintain, troubleshoot, and repair equipment such as computers and their peripherals, office equipment, and specialized electronic equipment used in factories, hospitals, airplanes, and numerous other businesses.

■ EARNINGS

According to the *Occupational Outlook Handbook*, computer, automated teller, and office machine repairers had median hourly wages of $15.98 in 2002. For full-time work, this comes to $33,250 annually. Those in the lowest 10 percent made less than $10.00 an hour or $20,770 a year, and those in the highest 10 percent made more than $25.00 or $52,130 a year. Technicians sometimes draw overtime and may also have benefits such as medical and dental insurance, paid vacation, and a 401(k). They may be allowed a company car or van for personal and work use.

■ WORK ENVIRONMENT

ATM servicers often work where the ATM is located, which could be either indoors or outdoors. Bench technicians work in repair shops. Sometimes work must be done in small, confined spaces where there is little room to move around. Since much work is conducted on-site where a machine is located, ATM servicers do some traveling. How much traveling they do depends on the area they service. In a week, Richard Wesley often drives between 400 and 1,200 miles, making about 40 stops per day. Even though Wesley does not enjoy all this driving, he does enjoy the benefits of working out of his home rather than at an office. "You're your own boss," he says. "As long as you do your job and keep the ATMs operational, the company doesn't interfere."

Because ATMs need servicing not only during the regular work day but also late at night, on weekends, and on holidays, both first line and second line technicians often work odd hours. Technicians may work day or night shifts, or they may be on call over long periods of time.

Wesley works a regular workweek, 8:00 A.M. to 5:00 P.M. Monday through Friday, and is also on call every other weekend and after 5:00 P.M. every other week. He is stationed at home and receives calls via cell phone and pager. Some days he doesn't have to answer a single call, while other days he may work for 12 hours straight.

■ OUTLOOK

The U.S. Department of Labor expects that employment of computer, automated teller, and office machine repairers will grow about as fast as the average through 2012. Workers who complete the most advanced training will be in high demand. According to a recent article at ATMmarketplace.com, some industry leaders don't believe there is much of a shortage of technicians because of the self-sufficiency of the machines themselves. ATMs are becoming more reliable and in less need of second line maintenance. The U.S. Department of Labor anticipates that employment opportunities will be available mostly to replace ATM servicers who retire rather than from growth in the industry. Others in the industry, however, believe the hardware is becoming more complex and computer-based, requiring more second line technicians with programming knowledge and more extensive training. Furthermore, the number of ATMs is increasing rapidly.

ATM manufacturers are constantly exploring new technology and developing ATMs that require less service while having more features. ATMs will soon be offering more than just money; additional dispensers will be added to offer stamps, phone cards, and even tickets for travel by bus, train, or plane. Some ATMs being developed have Web capabilities, allowing for more direct marketing. Although manufacturers promote these ATMs as requiring less maintenance, these machines may actually require the services of more extensively trained technicians to maintain all the various systems and hardware.

■ FOR MORE INFORMATION

To learn more about the ATM industry, contact
ATM Industry Association (ATMIA)
100 South Dakota Avenue, Suite 201
Sioux Falls, SD 57104
Tel: 888-208-1589
http://www.atmia.com

Read industry news, participate in discussion forums, and browse job listings at
ATMmarketplace.com
http://www.ATMmarketplace.com

Automobile Collision Repairers

■ OVERVIEW

Automobile collision repairers repair, replace, and repaint damaged body parts of automobiles, buses, and light trucks. They use hand tools and power tools to straighten bent frames and body sections, replace badly damaged parts, smooth out minor dents and creases, remove rust, fill small holes or dents, and repaint surfaces damaged by accident or wear. Some repairers also give repair estimates. There are approximately 175,370 automobile collision repairers working in the United States, plus 19,710 automotive glass specialists and 687,380 general auto mechanics.

■ HISTORY

The proliferation of the automobile in American society in the 1920s meant new opportunities for many who had not traveled far beyond their hometown. It also created something else by the thousands—jobs. One profession necessitated by America's new love for automobiles was that of the collision repairer. With ill-prepared roads suddenly overrun by inexperienced drivers, accidents and breakdowns became a common problem.

Automobiles were significantly simpler in the early years. Body repairs often could be performed by the owner or someone with general mechanical aptitude. Minor body dents, if they did not affect driving, were usually left alone. As cars became more complex and as society grew ever more fond of their automobiles, the need for qualified collision repairers grew. Automobiles suddenly became major status symbols, and people were no longer indifferent to minor dents and fender-benders. To many, dents were intolerable. New body styles and materials made body repairs

a difficult job. To meet this new demand, some automobile mechanics shifted their focus from repairs under the hood to repairs to the body of automobiles.

By the 1950s, automobile body repair garages were common in cities throughout the United States. More drivers carried vehicle insurance to protect against loss due to an accident. The insurance industry began to work more closely with automobile collision repairers. Since traffic control methods and driving rules and regulations were not very well established, frequent car accidents kept these repair garages busy year-round. Most collision repairers learned the trade through hands-on experience as an apprentice or on their own through trial and error. When automakers began packing their cars with new technology, involving complex electrical circuitry, computer controlled mechanisms, and new materials, as well as basic design changes, collision repairers found themselves in need of comprehensive training.

■ THE JOB

Automobile collision repairers repair the damage vehicles sustain in traffic accidents and through normal wear. Repairers straighten bent bodies, remove dents, and replace parts that are beyond repair. Just as a variety of skills are needed to build an automobile, so a range of skills is needed to repair body damage to vehicles. Some body repairers specialize in certain areas, such as painting, welding, glass replacement, or air bag replacement. All collision repairers should know how to perform common repairs, such as realigning vehicle frames, smoothing dents, and removing and replacing panels.

Vehicle bodies are made from a wide array of materials, including steel, aluminum, metal alloys, fiberglass, and plastic, with each material requiring a different repair technique. Most repairers can work with all of these materials, but as car manufacturers produce vehicles with an increasing proportion of lightweight fiberglass, aluminum, and plastic parts, more repairers specialize in repairing these specific materials.

Collision repairers frequently must remove car seats, accessories, electrical components, hydraulic windows, dashboards, and trim to get to the parts that need repair. If the frame or a body section of the vehicle has been bent or twisted, frame repairers and straighteners can sometimes restore it to its original alignment and shape. This is done by chaining or clamping it to an alignment machine, which uses hydraulic pressure to pull the damaged metal into position. Repairers use specialty measuring equipment to set all components, such as engine parts, wheels, headlights, and body parts, at manufacturer's specifications.

After the frame is straightened, the repairer can begin to work on the car body. Newer composite car bodies often have "panels" that can be individually replaced. Dents in a metal car body can be corrected in several different ways, depending on how deep they are. If any part is too badly damaged to repair, the collision repairers remove it with hand tools, a pneumatic metal-cutting gun, or acetylene torch, then weld on a replacement. Some dents can be pushed out with hydraulic jacks, pneumatic hammers, prying bars, and other hand tools. To smooth small dents and creases, collision repairers may position small anvils, called dolly blocks, against one side of the dented metal. They then hit the opposite side of the metal with various specially designed hammers. Tiny pits and dimples are removed with pick hammers and punches. Dents that cannot be corrected with this treatment may be filled with solder or a puttylike material that becomes hard like metal after it cures. When the filler has hardened, the collision repairers file, grind, and sand the surface smooth in the correct contour and prepare it for painting. In many shops the final sanding and painting are done by other specialists, who may be called *automotive painters*.

Since more than the body is usually damaged in a major automobile accident, repairers have other components to repair. Advanced vehicle systems on new cars such as anti-lock brakes, air bags, and other "passive restraint systems" require special training to repair. Steering and suspension, electrical components, and glass are often damaged and require repair, removal, or replacement.

Automotive painting is a highly skilled, labor-intensive job that requires a fine eye and attention to detail for the result to match the pre-accident condition. Some paint jobs require that less than the whole vehicle be painted. In this case, the painter must mix pigments to match the original color. This can be difficult if the original paint is faded, but computer technology is making paint matching easier.

A major part of the automobile collision repairer's job is assessing the damage and providing an estimate on the cost to repair it. Sometimes, the damage to a vehicle may cost more to repair than the vehicle is worth. When this happens, the vehicle is said to be "totaled," a term used by collision repairers as well as insurance companies. Many body repair shops offer towing services and will coordinate the transfer of a vehicle from the accident scene as well as the transfer of a totaled vehicle to a scrap dealer who will salvage the useable parts.

The shop supervisor or repair service estimator prepares the estimate. They inspect the extent of the damage to determine if the vehicle can be repaired or must be replaced. They note the year, model, and make of the car

An automobile collision repairer welds the frame of a van.

to determine type and availability of parts. Based on past experience with similar types of repair and general industry guidelines, estimates are calculated for parts and labor and then submitted to the customer's insurance company. One "walk around" a car will tell the collision repairer what needs to be investigated. Since a collision often involves "hidden" damage, supervisors write up repair orders with specific instructions so no work is missed or, in some cases, done unnecessarily. Repair orders often indicate only specific parts are to be repaired or replaced. Collision repairers generally work on a project by themselves with minimal supervision. In large, busy shops, repairers may be assisted by helpers or apprentices.

■ REQUIREMENTS
High School

Technology demands more from the collision repairer than it did 10 years ago. In addition to automotive and shop classes, high school students should take mathematics, English, and computer classes. Adjustments and repairs to many car components require numerous computations, for which good mathematics skills are essential. Reading comprehension skills will help a collision repairer understand complex repair manuals and trade journals that detail new technology. Oral communication skills are also important to help customers understand their options. In addition, computers are common in most collision repair shops. They keep track of customer histories and parts and often detail repair procedures. Use of computers in repair shops will only increase in the future, so students will benefit from a basic knowledge of them.

Postsecondary Training

A wide variety of training programs are offered at community colleges, vocational schools, independent organizations, and manufacturers. As automotive technology changes, the materials and methods involved in repair work change. With new high-strength steels, aluminum, and plastics becoming ever more common in newer vehicles and posing new challenges in vehicle repair, repairers will need special training to detect the many hidden problems that occur beyond the impact spot. Postsecondary training programs provide students with the necessary, up-to-date skills needed for repairing today's vehicles.

BUMPERS

The majority of vehicle collisions are low-speed "fender benders" that occur on busy urban streets or parking lots. Yet even these minor collisions can cause expensive damage. Part of the reason for high damage costs are the bumpers on newer vehicles, according to the Insurance Institute for Highway Safety (IIHS). According to IIHS, bumpers used to be stronger. Today, relaxed government standards for impact requirements translate into higher repair costs. Because more effective bumpers are heavier and reduce gas mileage, automakers pressured the government to ease standards and allow lighter-weight bumpers on vehicles. Bumpers on today's vehicles generally consist of a plastic cover and underneath, a reinforcement bar made of steel, aluminum, fiberglass composite, or plastic. Many bumpers also include materials to absorb crash energy, such as polypropylene foam or plastic honeycomb. These lighter materials and reduction in reinforcement mean higher repair costs. In IIHS tests of 12 small 1997–98 cars, damage repair costs from backing into a pole ranged from zero to $1,171. In the same test on six 1997 large luxury sedans, repair costs ranged from $1,118 to $6,046. Although automakers will likely continue their efforts to maintain current bumper standards, a 1990 survey by the Insurance Research Council indicated 70 percent of consumers want stronger bumpers. Collision repairers and insurance professionals will continue to follow this issue in the coming years as repair costs continue to climb.

Certification or Licensing

Entry-level technicians in the industry can demonstrate their qualifications through certification by the National Automotive Technicians Education Foundation (NATEF), an affiliate of the National Institute for Automotive Service Excellence (ASE). Certification is voluntary, but it assures students that the program they enroll in meets the standards employers expect from their entry-level employees. Many trade and vocational schools throughout the country have affiliation with NATEF. To remain certified, repairers must take the examination again within five years. Another industry-recognized standard of training is provided by the Inter-Industry Conference on Auto Collision Repair (I-CAR). I-CAR provides training for students and experienced technicians alike in the areas of advanced vehicle systems, aluminum repair and welding, complete collision repair, electronics for collision repair, finish matching, and other specialty fields.

Other Requirements

Automobile collision repairers are responsible for providing their own hand tools at an investment of approximately $6,000 to $20,000 or more, depending on the technician's specialty. It is the employer's responsibility to provide the larger power tools and other test equipment. Skill in handling both hand and power tools is essential for any repairer. Since each collision repair job is unique and presents a different challenge, repairers often must be resourceful in their method of repair.

While union membership is not a requirement for collision repairers, many belong to the International Association of Machinists and Aerospace Workers; the International Union, United Automobile, Aerospace and Agricultural Implement Workers of America; the Sheet Metal Workers International Association; or the International Brotherhood of Teamsters, Chauffeurs, Warehousemen and Helpers of America. Most collision repairers who are union members work for large automobile dealers, trucking companies, and bus lines.

■ EXPLORING

Many community colleges and park districts offer general auto maintenance, mechanics, and body repair workshops where students can get additional practice working on real cars and learn from experienced instructors. Trade magazines such as *Automotive Body Repair News* (http://www.abrn.com) are an excellent source for learning what's new in the industry. Such publications may be available at larger public libraries or vocational schools. Many journals also post current and archived articles on the Internet.

Working on cars as a hobby provides invaluable first-hand experience in repair work. A part-time job in a repair shop or dealership allows a feel for the general atmosphere and the kind of problems repairers face on the job as well as provide a chance to learn from those already in the business.

Some high school students may gain exposure to automotive repairs through participation in organizations, such as SkillsUSA-Vocational Industrial Clubs of America. VICA coordinates competitions in several vocational areas, including collision repair. The collision repair competition tests students' aptitudes in metal work, MIG welding, painting, alignment of body and frame, painting, estimation of damage to automobiles, and plastic identification and repair. VICA is represented in all 50 states. If your school does not have a VICA chapter, ask your guidance counselor about starting one or participating in a co-op arrangement with another school. (See sidebar on this page.)

■ EMPLOYERS

Automobile collision repairers hold about 175,370 jobs in the United States in 2002, not including 19,710 glass specialists and 687,380 general service technicians and mechanics. Most work for body shops specializing in body repairs and painting, including private shops and shops operated by automobile dealers. Others work for organizations that maintain their own vehicle fleets, such as trucking companies and automobile rental companies. About one of every six automobile collision repairers is self-employed, operating small shops in cities large and small.

■ STARTING OUT

The best way to start out in the field of automobile collision repair is, first, to attend one of the many postsecondary training programs available throughout the country and, second, to obtain certification. Trade and technical schools usually provide job placement assistance for their graduates. Schools often have contacts with local employers who seek highly skilled entry-level employees. Often, employers post job openings at nearby trade schools with accredited programs.

Although postsecondary training programs are considered the best way to enter the field, some repairers learn the trade on the job as apprentices. Their training consists of working for several years under the guidance of experienced repairers. Fewer employers today are willing to hire apprentices because of the time and cost it takes to train them, but since there currently is a shortage of high quality entry-level collision repair technicians, many employers will continue to hire apprentices

---

SKILLSUSA-VOCATIONAL INDUSTRIAL CLUBS OF AMERICA

Participation in skill training promoted by the SkillsUSA-Vocational Industrial Clubs of America (VICA) is one way students can prepare for a career as an automobile collision repairer. VICA is a professional society designed and run by students in the trade, industrial, technical, and health occupations. Rather than being an extracurricular activity, VICA's curriculum is integrated into classroom learning. Students work with an adviser or teacher who helps coordinate activities such as the Professional Development Program, which helps students meet national skill standards and develop job-seeking skills.

VICA's Skills USA Championships are competitions in which students use skills pertaining to their career field in competition with other students. Collision repair is one competition category, and includes hands-on tests in areas such as welding as well as written tests. If your school does not have a VICA chapter, ask a guidance counselor or vocational coordinator or teacher about starting one. For more information, contact SkillsUSA-VICA at PO Box 3000, Leesburg, VA 20177-0300, Telephone (703) 777-8810 or check their website at http://www.skillsusa.org.

---

who can demonstrate good mechanical aptitude and a willingness to learn. Those who do learn their skills on the job will inevitably require some formal training if they wish to advance and stay in step with the changing industry.

Internship programs sponsored by car manufacturers or independent organizations provide students with excellent opportunities to actually work with prospective employers. Internships can also provide students with valuable contacts who will be able to refer the student to future employers and provide a recommendation to potential employers once they have completed their training. Many students may even be hired by the company at which they interned.

■ ADVANCEMENT

Like NATEF training programs, currently employed collision repairers may be certified by ASE. Although certification is voluntary, it is a widely recognized standard of achievement for automobile collision repairers and the way many advance. Collision repairers who are certified are more valuable to their employers than those who are not and therefore stand a greater chance of advancement.

Certification is available in four specialty areas: structural analysis and damage repair, nonstructural analysis and damage repair, mechanical and electrical components, and painting and refinishing. Those who have passed all the exams are certified as master body/paint technicians. To maintain their certification, technicians must retake the examination for their specialties every five years. Many employers will hire only accredited technicians, basing salary on their level of accreditation.

With today's complex automobile components and new materials requiring hundreds of hours of study and practice to master, employers encourage their employees to advance in responsibility by learning new systems and repair procedures. A repair shop's reputation will only go as far as its employees are skilled. Those with good communications and planning skills may advance to shop supervisor or service manager at larger repair shops or dealerships. Those who have mastered collision repair may go on to teaching at postsecondary schools or work for certification agencies.

■ EARNINGS

Salary ranges of collision repairers vary depending on level of experience, type of shop, and geographic location. Most earned hourly salaries between $8.70 and $27.10, with a median hourly salary of $15.71 in 2002, according to the U.S. Department of Labor. At the lower end of the pay scale, collision repairers with less experience and repairers who were employed by smaller shops tended to earn less; experienced repairers with management positions earned more. The median annual wage in 2002 was $32,680, with the lowest 10 percent earning $18,090 or less, and the top 10 percent $56,360 or more. In many repair shops and dealerships, collision repairers can make more by working on commission, typically earning 40 to 50 percent of the labor costs charged to customers. Employers often guarantee a minimum level of pay in addition to commissions.

Benefits packages vary from business to business. Most repair technicians can expect health insurance and a paid vacation from employers. Other benefits may include dental and eye care, life and disability insurance, and a pension plan. Employers usually cover a technician's work clothes and may pay a percentage of the cost of hand tools they purchase. An increasing number of employers pay all or most of an employee's certification training, dependent on the employee passing the test. A technician's salary can increase through yearly bonuses or profit sharing if the business does well.

■ WORK ENVIRONMENT

Collision repair work is generally noisy, dusty, and dirty. In some cases, the noise and dirt levels have decreased as new technology such as computers and electrostatic paint guns are introduced. Automobile repair shops are usually well ventilated to reduce dust and dangerous fumes. Because repairers weld and handle hot or jagged pieces of metal and broken glass, they wear safety glasses, masks, and protective gloves. Minor hand and back injuries are the most common problems of technicians. When reaching in hard-to-get-at places or loosening tight bolts, collision repairers often bruise, cut, or burn their hands. With caution and experience, most learn to avoid hand injuries. Working for long periods in cramped or bent positions often results in a stiff back or neck. Collision repairers also lift many heavy objects that can cause injury if not handled carefully; however, this is less of a problem with new cars as automakers design smaller and lighter parts for better fuel economy. Automotive painters wear respirators and other protective gear, and they work in specially ventilated rooms to keep from being exposed to paint fumes and other hazardous chemicals. Painters may need to stand for hours at a time as they work.

By following safety procedures and learning how to avoid typical problems, repairers can minimize the risks involved in this job. Likewise, shops must comply with strict safety procedures to help employees avoid accident or injury. Collision repairers are often under pressure to complete the job quickly. Most repairers work a standard 40-hour week but may be required to work longer hours when the shop is busy or in emergencies.

■ OUTLOOK

Like many service industries, the collision repair industry is facing a labor shortage of skilled, entry-level workers in many areas of the country. Demand for collision repair services is expected to remain consistent, at the least, as the number of cars in the nation grows, and employment opportunities are expected to increase about as fast as the average through 2012. This demand, paired with technology that will require new skills, translates into a healthy job market for those willing to undergo the training needed. According to *Automotive Body Repair News,* as the need for skilled labor is rising, the number of people pursuing collision repair careers is declining. In many cases, vocational schools and employers are teaming up to recruit new workers.

Changing technology also plays a role in the industry's outlook. New automobile designs have body parts made of steel alloys, aluminum, and plastics—materials that are more time consuming to work with. In many cases, such materials are more prone to damage, increasing the need for body repairs.

The automobile collision repair business is not greatly affected by changes in economic conditions. Major body damage must be repaired to keep a vehicle in safe operating condition. During an economic downturn, however, people tend to postpone minor repairs until their budgets can accommodate the expense. Nevertheless, body repairers are seldom laid off. Instead, when business is bad, employers hire fewer new workers. During a recession, inexperienced workers face strong competition for entry-level jobs. People with formal training in repair work and automobile mechanics are likely to have the best job prospects in such times.

■ FOR MORE INFORMATION

For more information on careers, training, and accreditation, contact the following organizations:

Automotive Aftermarket Industry Association
4600 East-West Highway, Suite 300
Bethesda, MD 20814-3415
Tel: 301-654-6664
Email: aaia@aftermarket.org
http://www.aftermarket.org

Inter-Industry Conference on Auto Collision Repair
3701 Algonquin Road, Suite 400
Rolling Meadows, IL 60008
Tel: 800-422-7872
http://www.i-car.com

National Automotive Technicians Education Foundation
101 Blue Seal Drive, Suite 101
Leesburg, VA 20175
Tel: 703-669-6650
http://www.natef.org

National Institute for Automotive Service Excellence
101 Blue Seal Drive, SE, Suite 101
Leesburg, VA 20175
Tel: 877-273-8324
http://www.asecert.org

Automobile Sales Workers

■ OVERVIEW

Automobile sales workers inform customers about new or used automobiles, and they prepare payment, financing, and insurance papers for customers who have purchased a vehicle. It is their job to persuade the customer that the product they are selling is the best choice. They prospect new customers by mail, by telephone, or through personal contacts. To stay informed about their products, sales workers regularly attend training sessions about the vehicles they sell. There are more than 250,000 automobile sales workers employed in the United States.

■ HISTORY

By the 1920s, nearly 20,000 automobile dealerships dotted the American landscape as the "Big Three" automobile makers—Ford, General Motors, and Chrysler—increased production every year to meet the public's growing demand for automobiles. Automobile sales workers began to earn higher and higher wages. As automobiles became more popular, the need for an organization to represent the growing industry became evident. In 1917, the National Automobile Dealers Association (NADA) was founded to change the way Congress viewed automobiles. In the early years, NADA worked to convince Congress that cars weren't luxuries, as they had been classified, but vital to the economy. The group prevented the government from converting all automotive factories to wartime work during World War I and reduced a proposed luxury tax on automobiles from 5 percent to 3 percent.

During the lean years of the Depression in the early 1930s, automobile sales fell sharply until President Franklin Delano Roosevelt's New Deal helped jumpstart the industry. Roosevelt signed the Code of Fair Competition for the Motor Vehicle Retailing Trade, which established standards in the automotive manufacturing and sales industries. By 1942, the number of dealerships in the United States more than doubled to 44,000.

Automobile sales workers have suffered an image problem for much of the career's history. Customers sometimes felt that they were pressured to purchase new cars at unfair prices and that the dealer's profit was too large. The 1958 Price Labeling Law, which mandated cars display window stickers listing manufacturer

"CRAZY HENRY"

Many people played a role in developing the automobile as we know it today, but few have generated the historical interest that the unconventional Henry Ford did. As a young man, Ford was so obsessed with building a "horseless carriage" that people sometimes called him Crazy Henry. It was this drive that helped him build a wildly successful company. His $5-a-day wage made him a national figure overnight, and through the years his eccentricities and outspoken manner landed him frequently on the front pages of the national press. He felt America had no stake in World War I and launched a crusade to sway public opinion. He chartered a ship to send delegates of peace to Europe. The unsuccessful Peace Ship mission, which Ford himself went on, was ridiculed by Theodore Roosevelt and other politicians of the day. In the early years of World War II, Ford was sympathetic to Germany and again made known his view that the United States should not get involved in the European conflict. Those who worked for Ford were also familiar with his eccentricities. He was reported on several occasions to pick up tramps and hitchhikers and offer them jobs so that they could remake their lives. He was concerned that every man was saving his money and not living in sin. He authored the pamphlet *Rules of Living* that urged employees to use plenty of soap and water at home, not to spit on the ground, and to avoid debt by not purchasing anything on installment plans. There are many books on this enigmatic man that explore his place in history as well as his idiosyncrasies. *The Fords: An American Epic* (Encounter Books, 2002) by Peter Collier and David Horowitz, and *Wheels of Time: A Biography of Henry Ford* (Millbrook Press, 1997) by Catherine Gourley are two good examples.

suggested retail prices and other information, helped ease relations between sales workers and their customers. However, in the fiercely competitive automobile market, sales workers' selling methods and the thrifty customer remained at odds.

When it came to used vehicles, there was no way for customers to know whether they were getting a fair deal. Even in the automobile's early history, used vehicles have been popular. From 1919 through the 1950s, used car sales consistently exceeded new car sales. Despite the popularity of used vehicles, the automobile sales industry didn't quite know how to handle them. Some dealers lost money on trade-ins when they stayed on the lot too long. After debating for years how to handle trade-ins, dealers finally began today's common practice of applying their value toward down payments on new cars.

The industry suffered personnel shortages when the armed forces recruited mechanics during World War II. This affected the service departments of dealerships, which traditionally have generated the biggest profits, and many dealers had to be creative to stay in business. During these lean times, sales gimmicks, such as giveaways and contests, came into increased use. According to a history of NADA, one Indiana dealer bought radios, refrigerators, freezers, and furnaces to sell in his showroom and sold toys at Christmas to stay in business.

The energy crisis of the 1970s brought hard times to the entire automotive industry. Many dealerships were forced to close, and those that survived made little profit. In 1979 alone, 600 dealerships closed. As of 2003, according to NADA, there were 21,724 dealerships nationwide (down from 47,500 in 1951) accounting for about 20 percent of all retail sales and employing more than 1.1 million people. Most dealerships today sell more makes of cars than dealerships of the past. Still, they face competition from newer forms of automobile retailers, such as automotive superstores, the automotive equivalent to discount stores like Wal-Mart. Also, automotive information is becoming more widely available on the Internet, eroding the consumer's need for automobile sales workers as a source of information about automobiles.

■ THE JOB

The automobile sales worker's main task is to sell. Today, many dealerships try to soften the image of salesmen and women by emphasizing no pressure, even one-price shopping. But automobile dealers expect their employees to sell, and selling in most cases involves some degree of persuasion. The automobile sales worker informs customers of everything there is to know about a particular vehicle. A good sales worker finds out what the customer wants or needs and suggests automobiles that may fit that need—empowering the customer with choice and a feeling that he or she is getting a fair deal.

Since the sticker price on new cars is only a starting point to be bargained down, and since many customers come to dealerships already knowing which car they would like to buy, sales workers spend much of their time negotiating the final selling price.

Most dealerships have special sales forces for new cars, used cars, trucks, recreational vehicles, and leasing operations. In each specialty, sales workers learn all aspects of the product they must sell. They may attend information and training seminars sponsored by manufacturers. New car sales workers, especially, are constantly learning new car features. Sales workers inform customers about a car's performance, fuel economy, safety features, and luxuries or accessories. They are able to talk about innovations over previous models, engine and mechanical specifications, ease of handling, and ergonomic designs. Good sales workers also keep track of competing models' features.

In many ways, used car sales workers have a more daunting mass of information to keep track of. Whereas new car sales workers concentrate on the most current features of an automobile, used car sales workers must keep track of all features from several model years. Good used car dealers can look at a car and note immediately the make, model, and year of a car. Because of popular two- and three-year leasing options, the used car market has increased by nearly 50 percent in the last 10 years.

Successful sales workers are generally good readers of a person's character. They can determine exactly what it is a customer is looking for in a new car. They must be friendly and understanding of customers' needs in order to put them at ease (due to the amount of money involved, car buying is an unpleasant task for most people). They are careful not to oversell the car by providing the customers with information they may not care about or understand, thus confusing them. For example, if a customer only cares about style, sales workers will not impress upon him all of the wonderful intricacies of a new high-tech engine design.

Sales workers greet customers and ask if they have any questions about a particular model. It's very important for sales workers to have immediate and confident answers to all questions about the vehicles they're selling. When a sale is difficult, they occasionally use psychological methods, or subtle "prodding," to influence customers. Some sales workers use aggressive selling methods and pressure the customer to purchase the car. Although recent trends are turning away from the pressure-sell, competition will keep these types of selling methods prevalent in the industry, albeit at a slightly toned-down level.

Customers usually make more than one visit to a dealership before purchasing a new or used car. Because one sales worker "works" the customer on the first visit—forming an acquaintanceship and learning the customer's personality—he or she will usually stay with that customer until the sale is made or lost. The sales worker usually schedules times for the customer to come in and talk more about the car in order to stay with the customer through the process and not lose the sale to another sales worker. Sales workers may make follow-up phone calls to make special offers or remind customers of certain features that make a particular model better than the competition, or they may send mailings for the same purpose.

In addition to providing the customer with information about the car, sales workers discuss financing packages, leasing options, and warranty. When the sale is made, they go over the contract with the customer and obtain a signature. Frequently the exact model with all of the features the customer requested is not in the dealership, and the sales worker must place an order with the manufacturer or distributor. When purchasing a new or used vehicle, many customers trade in their old vehicle. Sales workers appraise the trade-in and offer a price.

At some dealerships sales workers also do public relations and marketing work. They establish promotions to get customers into their showrooms, print fliers to distribute in the local community, and make television advertisements. In order to keep their name in the back (or front) of the customer's mind, they may send past customers birthday and holiday cards or similar "courtesies." Most of the larger dealerships also have an auto maintenance and repair service department. Sales workers may help customers establish a periodic maintenance schedule or suggest repair work.

Computers are used at a growing number of dealerships. Customers use computers to answer questions they may have, consult price indexes, check on ready availability of parts, and even compare the car they're interested in with the competition's equivalent. Although computers can't replace human interaction and sell the car to customers who need reassurances, they do help the

This automobile sales worker discusses the pricing and payment options for this convertible.

customer feel more informed and more in control when buying a car.

■ REQUIREMENTS
High School
Because thorough knowledge of automobiles—from how they work to how they drive and how they are manufactured—is essential for a successful sales worker, automotive maintenance classes in high school are an excellent place to begin. Classes in English, speech, drama, and psychology will help you to achieve the excellent speaking skills you will need to make a good sale and gain customer confidence and respect. Classes in business and mathematics will teach you to manage and prioritize your work load, prepare goals, and work confidently with customer financing packages. As computers become increasingly prevalent in every aspect of the industry, you should take as many computer classes as you can. Speaking a second language will give you an advantage, especially in major cities with large minority populations.

Postsecondary Training
Those who seek management-level positions will have a distinct advantage if they possess a college degree, preferably in business or marketing, but other degrees, whether they be in English, economics, or psychology, are no less important, so long as applicants have good management skills and can sell cars. Many schools offer degrees in automotive marketing and automotive aftermarket management that prepare students to take high-level management positions. Even with a two- or four-year degree in hand, many dealerships may not begin new hires directly as managers, but first start them out as sales workers.

Certification or Licensing
By completing the certified automotive merchandiser (CAM) program offered by the NADA, students seeking entry-level positions gain a significant advantage. Certification assures employers that workers have the basic skills they require.

Other Requirements
In today's competitive job market you will need a high school diploma to land a job that offers growth possibilities, a good salary, and challenges; this includes jobs in the automobile sales industry. Employers prefer to hire entry-level employees who have had some previous experience in automotive services or in retail sales. They look for candidates who have good verbal, business, mathematics, electronics, and computer skills. A number of automotive sales and services courses and degrees are offered today at community colleges, vocational schools,

independent organizations, and manufacturers. Sales workers should possess a valid driver's license and have a good driving record.

Sales workers must be enthusiastic, well-organized self-starters who thrive in a competitive environment. They must show excitement and authority about each type of car they sell and convince customers, without being too pushy (though some pressure on the customer usually helps make the sale), that the car they're interested in is the "right" car, at the fairest price. Sales workers must be able to read a customer's personality and know when to be outgoing and when to pull back and be more reserved. A neat, professional appearance is also very important for sales workers.

■ EXPLORING
Automobile trade magazines and books, in addition to selling technique and business books, are excellent sources of information for someone considering a career in this field. Local and state automobile and truck dealer associations can also provide you with information on career possibilities in automobile and truck sales. Your local Yellow Pages has a listing under "associations" for dealer organizations in your area.

Students interested in automobile sales work might first stop by their local dealer and ask about training programs and job requirements there. On a busy day at any dealership there will be several sales workers on the floor selling cars. Students can witness the basic selling process by going to dealerships and unobtrusively watching and listening as sales workers talk with customers. Many dealerships hire students part time to wash and clean cars. This is a good way to see the types of challenges and pressures automobile sales workers experience every day. Although it may take a special kind of sales skill or a different approach to selling a $25,000 vehicle over $50 shoes, any type of retail sales job that requires frequent interaction with customers will prepare students for work as an automobile sales worker.

■ EMPLOYERS
Franchised automobile dealerships employ the majority of automobile sales workers in the United States. A franchised automobile dealer is a dealer that is formally recognized and authorized by the manufacturer to sell its vehicles. A small number of sales workers are employed by used car dealerships that are strictly independent and not recognized by any manufacturer. Automotive superstores need automobile sales workers as well, although some may argue that these workers aren't truly automobile sales specialists because they tend to have less training and experience in the automotive area.

STARTING OUT

Generally, those just out of high school are not going to land a job as an automobile sales worker; older customers do not feel comfortable making such a large investment through a teenager. Employers prefer to see some previous automotive service experience with certification, such as National Institute of Automotive Service Excellence certification, or postsecondary training in automotive selling, such as NADA's CAM program. Dealerships will hire those with proven sales skill in a different field for sales worker positions and give them on-the-job training.

Employers frequently post job openings at schools that provide postsecondary education in business administration or automotive marketing. Certified automotive technicians or body repairers who think they might eventually like to break into a sales job should look for employment at dealership service centers. They will have frequent contact with sales workers and make connections with dealership managers and owners, as well as become so familiar with one or more models of a manufacturer's cars that they will make well-informed, knowledgeable sales workers.

Some dealerships will hire young workers with little experience in automobile services but who can demonstrate proven skills in sales and a willingness to learn. These workers will learn on the job. They may first be given administrative tasks. Eventually they will accompany experienced sales workers on the showroom floor and learn "hands-on." After about a year, the workers will sell on their own, and managers will evaluate their selling skills in sales meetings and suggest ways they can improve their sales records.

ADVANCEMENT

The longer sales workers stay with a dealership, the larger their client base grows and the more cars are sold. Advancement for many sales workers comes in the form of increased earnings and customer loyalty. Other sales workers may be promoted through a combination of experience and further training or certification.

As positions open, sales workers with proven management skills go on to be assistant and general managers. Managers with excellent sales skills and a good client base may open a new franchise dealership or their own independent dealership.

The Society of Automotive Sales Professionals (SASP), a division of NADA, provides sales workers with advancement possibilities. Once sales workers have completed a certification process and have a minimum of six months' sales experience, they are eligible to participate in SASP seminars that stress improving the new car buying process by polishing a sales worker's professional image.

INTERNET CAR SHOPPING

The role the automobile sales worker plays in a consumer's car-buying decision is changing rapidly. Automotive superstores (warehouse-type discounters that sell late model used vehicles with no-haggle fixed prices and warranties) are a new option for consumers. The Internet is also changing the way Americans buy cars. According to a survey by J.D. Power and Associates, 21 percent of Americans shopping for a new car use some kind of shopping service to help them rather than going straight to the dealer. Consumers can use the Internet to research attributes of a specific model by searching the websites of manufacturers or consumer and automobile journals that review cars. Many also use auction websites or websites that serve as a go-between in the car-buying process. Consumers can describe the car they want, including make, model, year, mileage, and price, and the service links them with a dealer who can deliver what they're looking for. Here are some Internet sites for car shoppers:

- The Auto Channel: http://www.theautochannel.com
- Auto Connection: http://www.autoconnection.com
- DealerNet: http://www.dealernet.com
- eBay: http://www.ebay.com
- IntelliChoice Car Center: http://www.intellichoice.com
- Kelley Blue Book: http://www.kbb.com
- Yahoo! Autos: http://autos.yahoo.com

If you are considering a career in automotive sales, these services will be used by your customers. Becoming familiar with what they offer and how they work is one way you can be a valuable resource for your customers.

EARNINGS

Earnings for automobile sales workers vary depending on location, size, and method of salary. Previously, most dealerships paid their sales workers either straight commission or salary plus commission. This forced sales workers to become extremely aggressive in their selling strategy—and often too aggressive for many customers. With a new trend toward pressure-free selling, more sales workers are earning a straight salary. Many dealerships still offer incentives such as bonuses and profit sharing to encourage sales. The average hourly wage for automotive sales workers $18.25 in 2002, according to the U.S. Department of Labor. Those who work on a straight commission basis can earn considerably more; however, their earnings are minimal during slow periods. Sales workers who are just getting started in the field may earn lower annual salaries for a few years as they work to establish a client base. They may start in the low $20,000s. According to NADA, the average earnings for a new-car dealership employee is over $800 per week. Benefits vary by dealership but often include health insurance and a paid vacation. An increasing number of employers will pay all or most of an employee's certification training.

WORK ENVIRONMENT

Sales workers for new car dealerships work in pleasant indoor showrooms. Most used car dealerships keep the majority of their cars in outdoor lots where sales workers may spend much of their day. Upon final arrangements for a sale, they work in comfortable office spaces at a desk. Suits are the standard attire. During slow periods, when competition among dealers is fierce, sales workers often work under pressure. They must not allow "lost" sales to discourage their work. The typical workweek is between 40 and 50 hours, although if business is good, a sales worker will work more. Since most customers shop for cars on the weekends and in the evenings, work hours are irregular.

OUTLOOK

Automobile dealerships are one of the businesses most severely affected by economic recession. Conversely, when the economy is strong, the automobile sales industry tends to benefit. For the sales worker, growth, in any percentage, is good news, as they are the so-called front-line professionals in the industry who are responsible for representing the dealerships and manufacturers and for getting their cars out on the streets. In the late 1990s and early 2000s, automobile sales were especially strong in the United States; however, the economic recession has caused some setbacks. For instance, after a record-breaking year in 2001, sales dropped considerably in 2002. Also, incentives such as rebates and cut-rate financing were in part responsible for the industry's strong showing. These incentives, spurred by a competitive market, cost the industry money and ate into profits at every level.

The automobile sales worker faces many future challenges. A shift in customer buying preferences and experience is forcing sales workers to re-evaluate their selling methods. Information readily available on the Internet helps customers shop for the most competitive financing or leasing package and read reviews on car and truck models that interest them. Transactions are still brokered at the dealer, but once consumers become more familiar with the Internet, many will shop and buy exclusively from home.

Another trend threatening dealers is the automotive superstores, such as CarMax, AutoNation, and Car-Choice, where customers have a large inventory to select from at a base price and get information and ask questions about a car not from a sales worker, but from a computer. Sales workers are still needed to finalize the sale, but their traditional role at the dealership is lessened.

Nontheless, the number of cars and trucks on U.S. roads is expected to increase, and opportunities in this lucrative, but stressful, career should continue to increase about as fast as the average.

FOR MORE INFORMATION

For information on accreditation and testing, contact

National Automobile Dealers Association
8400 Westpark Drive
McLean, VA 22102
Tel: 800-252-6232
Email: nadainfo@nada.org
http://www.nada.org

For information on certification, contact

**National Institute for Automotive Service
  Excellence**
101 Blue Seal Drive, SE, Suite 101
Leesburg, VA 20175
Tel: 877-273-8324
http://www.asecert.org

Automobile Service Technicians

OVERVIEW

Automobile service technicians maintain and repair cars, vans, small trucks, and other vehicles. Using both hand tools and specialized diagnostic test equipment, they pinpoint problems and make the necessary repairs or adjustments. In addition to performing complex and difficult repairs, technicians perform a number of routine maintenance procedures, such as oil changes, tire rotation, and battery replacement. Technicians interact frequently with customers to explain repair procedures and discuss maintenance needs. Approximately 687,380 automotive service technicians work in the United States.

HISTORY

By the mid-1920s, the automobile industry began to change America. As automobiles changed through the years, mechanics—or automobile service technicians, as they are now called—have kept them running. The "Big Three" automobile makers—Ford, General Motors, and Chrysler—produced millions of cars for a public eager for the freedom and mobility the automobile promised. With the ill-prepared roads suddenly overrun by inexperienced drivers, accidents and breakdowns became common. People not only were unskilled in driving but also were ignorant of the basic maintenance and service the automobile required. It suddenly became apparent that a new profession was in the making.

Already in 1899 the American Motor Company opened a garage in New York and advertised "competent mechanics always on hand to make repairs when necessary." Gradually, other repair "garages" opened in larger cities, but they were few and far between. Automobiles were much simpler in the early years. Basic maintenance and minor repairs often could be performed by the owner or someone with general mechanical aptitude.

As cars became more complex, the need for qualified technicians grew. Dealerships began to hire mechanics to handle increasing customer concerns and complaints. Gas stations also began to offer repair and maintenance services. The profession of automobile mechanic was suddenly in big demand.

By the 1950s, automobile service and repair garages were common throughout the United States, in urban and rural areas alike. Most mechanics learned the trade through hands-on experience as an apprentice or on their own through trial and error. When automakers began packing their cars with new technology, involving complex electrical circuitry, and computer-controlled mechanisms as well as basic design changes, it became apparent that mechanics would need comprehensive training to learn new service and repair procedures. Until the 1970s, there was no standard by which automobile service technicians were trained. In 1972, the National Institute for Automotive Service Excellence (ASE) was established. It set national training standards for new technicians and provided continuing education and certification for existing technicians when new technology became widespread in the field.

Today, the demand for trained, highly skilled professionals in the service industry is more important than ever. To keep up with the technology that is continually incorporated in new vehicles, service technicians require more intensive training than in the past. Today, mechanics who have completed a high level of formal training are generally called automobile service technicians. They have studied the complexities of the latest automotive technology, from computerized mechanisms in the engine to specialized diagnostic testing equipment.

■ THE JOB

Many automobile service technicians feel that the most exciting part of their work is troubleshooting—locating the source of a problem and successfully fixing it. Diagnosing mechanical, electrical, and computer-related troubles requires a broad knowledge of how cars work, the ability to make accurate observations, and the patience to logically determine what went wrong. Technicians agree that it frequently is more difficult to find the problem than it is to fix it. With experience, knowing where to look for problems becomes second nature.

Generally, there are two types of automobile service technicians: *generalists* and *specialists*. Generalists work under a broad umbrella of repair and service duties. They have proficiency in several kinds of light repairs and maintenance of many different types of automobiles. Their work, for the most part, is routine and basic. Specialists concentrate in one or two areas and learn to master them for many different car makes and models. Today, in light of the sophisticated technology common in new cars, there is an increasing demand for specialists. Automotive systems are not as easy or as standard as they used to be, and they now require many hours of experience to master. To gain a broad knowledge in auto maintenance and repair, specialists usually begin as generalists.

When a car does not operate properly, the owner brings it to a service technician and describes the problem. At a dealership or larger shop, the customer may talk with a *repair service estimator,* who writes down the customer's description of the problem and relays it to the service technician. The technician may test-drive the car or use diagnostic equipment, such as motor analyzers, spark plug testers, or compression gauges, to determine the problem. If a customer explains that the car's automatic transmission does not shift gears at the right times, the technician must know how the functioning of the transmission depends on the engine vacuum, the throttle pressure, and—more common in newer cars—the onboard computer. Each factor must be thoroughly checked. With each test, clues help the technician pinpoint the cause

QUICK FACTS

SCHOOL SUBJECTS
Business
Technical/shop

PERSONAL SKILLS
Mechanical/manipulative
Technical/scientific

WORK ENVIRONMENT
Primarily indoors
Primarily one location

MINIMUM EDUCATION LEVEL
High school diploma

SALARY RANGE
$16,930 to $30,590 to
$52,430

CERTIFICATION OR LICENSING
Recommended

OUTLOOK
About as fast as the average

DOT
620

GOE
05.03.01

NOC
7321

O*NET-SOC
49-3023.00

of the malfunction. After successfully diagnosing the problem, the technician makes the necessary adjustments or repairs. If a part is too badly damaged or worn to be repaired, he or she replaces it after first consulting the car owner, explaining the problem, and estimating the cost.

Normal use of an automobile inevitably causes wear and deterioration of parts. Generalist automobile technicians handle many of the routine maintenance tasks to help keep a car in optimal operating condition. They change oil, lubricate parts, and adjust or replace components of any of the car's systems that might cause a malfunction, including belts, hoses, spark plugs, brakes, filters, and transmission and coolant fluids.

Technicians who specialize in the service of specific parts usually work in large shops with multiple departments, car diagnostic centers, franchised auto service shops, or small independent shops that concentrate on a particular type of repair work.

Tune-up technicians evaluate and correct engine performance and fuel economy. They use diagnostic equipment and other computerized devices to locate malfunctions in fuel, ignition, and emissions-control systems. They adjust ignition timing and valves and may replace spark plugs, points, triggering assemblies in electronic ignitions, and other components to ensure maximum engine efficiency.

Electrical-systems technicians have been in healthy demand in recent years. They service and repair the complex electrical and computer circuitry common in today's automobile. They use both sophisticated diagnostic equipment and simpler devices such as ammeters, ohmmeters, and voltmeters to locate system malfunctions. As well as possessing excellent electrical skills, electrical-systems technicians require basic mechanical aptitude to get at electrical and computer circuitry located throughout the automobile.

Front-end technicians are concerned with suspension and steering systems. They inspect, repair, and replace front-end parts such as springs, shock absorbers, and linkage parts such as tie rods and ball joints. They also align and balance wheels.

Brake repairers work on drum and disk braking systems, parking brakes, and their hydraulic systems. They inspect, adjust, remove, repair, and reinstall such items as brake shoes, disk pads, drums, rotors, wheel and master cylinders, and hydraulic fluid lines. Some specialize in both brake and front-end work.

Transmission technicians adjust, repair, and maintain gear trains, couplings, hydraulic pumps, valve bodies, clutch assemblies, and other parts of automatic transmission systems. Transmissions have become complex and highly sophisticated mechanisms in newer model automobiles. Technicians require special training to learn how they function.

Automobile-radiator mechanics clean radiators using caustic solutions. They locate and solder leaks and install new radiator cores. In addition, some radiator mechanics repair car heaters and air conditioners and solder leaks in gas tanks.

Alternative fuel technicians are relatively new additions to the field. This specialty has evolved with the nation's efforts to reduce its dependence on foreign oil by exploring alternative fuels, such as ethanol and electricity.

As more automobiles rely on a variety of electronic components, technicians have become more proficient in the basics of electronics, even if they are not electronics specialists. Electronic controls and instruments are located in nearly all the systems of today's cars. Many previously mechanical functions in automobiles are being replaced by electronics, significantly altering the way repairs are performed. Diagnosing and correcting problems with electronic components often involves the use of specialty tools and computers.

Automobile service technicians use an array of tools in their everyday work, ranging from simple hand tools to computerized diagnostic equipment. Technicians supply

ASE CREDENTIALS

Next time you are at a garage or service shop, you may notice that the automobile service technicians have more than their names embroidered on their shirts. Many also have a shoulder insignia with the letters ASE on it. The National Institute of Automotive Service Excellence can't guarantee the work of any automobile service technician, but it does certify that the technician has passed a competency exam. There are eight areas of ASE automobile/light truck certification: Engine Repair; Automatic Transmission/Transaxle; Manual Drive Train and Axles; Suspension and Steering; Brakes; Electrical Systems; Heating and Air Conditioning; and Engine Performance. Those who pass all eight exams are certified ASE Master Automobile Technicians. ASE conducts its tests twice a year, each May and November, at approximately 700 testing sites across the country. To earn certification in any area, the technician must have at least two years of hands-on work experience and pass the test. Tests for each area consist of 40 to 70 multiple-choice questions. Technicians must recertify every five years to keep current with changing technology. While certification is not required to be an automobile technician, you can see why consumers are likely to choose a certified technician over one who is not.

their own hand tools at an investment of $6,000 to $25,000 or more, depending on their specialty. It is usually the employer's responsibility to furnish the larger power tools, engine analyzers, and other test equipment.

To maintain and increase their skills and to keep up with new technology, automobile technicians must regularly read service and repair manuals, shop bulletins, and other publications. They must also be willing to take part in training programs given by manufacturers or at vocational schools. Those who have voluntary certification must periodically retake exams to keep their credentials.

■ REQUIREMENTS
High School
In today's competitive job market, aspiring automobile service technicians need a high school diploma to land a job that offers growth possibilities, a good salary, and challenges. There is a big demand in the automotive service industry to fill entry-level positions with well-trained, highly skilled persons. Technology demands more from the technician than it did 10 years ago.

In high school, you should take automotive and shop classes, mathematics, English, and computer classes. Adjustments and repairs to many car components require the technician to make numerous computations, for which good mathematical skills are essential. Good reading skills are also valuable, as a technician must do a lot of reading to stay competitive in today's job market. English classes will prepare you to handle the many volumes of repair manuals and trade journals you will need to remain informed. Computer skills are also vital, as computers are now common in most repair shops. They keep track of customers' histories and parts and often detail repair procedures. Use of computers in repair shops will only increase in the future.

Postsecondary Training
Employers today prefer to hire only those who have completed some kind of formal training program in automobile mechanics—usually a minimum of two years. A wide variety of such programs are offered at community colleges, vocational schools, independent organizations, and manufacturers. Many community colleges and vocational schools around the country offer accredited postsecondary education. Postsecondary training programs prepare students through a blend of classroom instruction and hands-on practical experience. They range in length from six months to two years or more, depending on the type of program. Shorter programs usually involve intensive study. Longer programs typically alternate classroom courses with periods of work experience. Some two-year programs include courses on applied mathe-

Part of an automobile service technician's job is to keep track of spare parts.

matics, reading and writing skills, and business practices and lead to an associate's degree.

Some programs are conducted in association with automobile manufacturers. Students combine work experience with hands-on classroom study of up-to-date equipment and new cars provided by manufacturers. In other programs, students alternate time in the classroom with internships in dealerships or service departments. These students may take up to four years to finish their training, but they become familiar with the latest technology and also earn a modest salary.

Certification or Licensing
One recognized indicator of quality for entry-level technicians is certification by the National Automotive Technicians Education Foundation (NATEF), an affiliate of ASE. NATEF's goals are to develop, encourage, and improve automotive technical education for students seeking entry-level positions as automobile service technicians. NATEF certifies many postsecondary programs for training throughout the country. Certification is

EMERGING TECHNOLOGIES

In the automotive industry, environmental friendliness is at the forefront of many of the developing technologies. Improvements in motor oil to work with more efficient, longer lasting engines is one such advancement. Today, motor oils are more refined (purified) and produce less pollution. Base oil, the primary ingredient in engine oil, is refined from crude oil through a series of separation and purification processes. Hydrocracking is a new method being applied in this process, used to make Pennzoil's "Pure Base" brand oil. Hydrocracking involves heating the crude oil to more than 700 degrees in the presence of hydrogen gas. The process removes sulfur and nitrogen and saturates the oil. The result is a base oil that is 97 percent pure. The oil is then combined with additives to make the finished product. Other advances in automotive maintenance involve ways to detect leaks in air conditioning systems, which are often difficult to locate. One successful method of detection involves the use of ultraviolet light. This method uses a black light lamp that detects an oil-based dye. This leak detection system is more expensive than others but provides the advantage of finding hard-to-find leaks. However, injecting the dye can be sloppy, and because the technology is so sensitive, it can create false leak impressions.

available in the areas of automatic transmission, brakes, electrical/electronic systems, engine performance, engine repair, heating and air conditioning, manual drive train and axles, and suspension and steering. Certification assures students that the program they enroll in meets the standards employers expect from their entry-level employees. ASE certification is not required, but job applicants who are certified have a competitive advantage over those who are not.

Other Requirements

To be a successful automobile service technician, you must be patient and thorough in your work; a shoddy repair job may put the driver's life at risk. You must have excellent troubleshooting skills and be able to logically deduce the cause of system malfunctions.

■ EXPLORING

Many community centers offer general auto maintenance and mechanics workshops where you can practice working on real cars and learn from instructors. Trade magazines are excellent sources for learning what's new in the industry and can be found at most public libraries or large bookstores. Many public television stations broadcast automobile maintenance and repair programs that can be of help to beginners to see how various types of cars differ.

Working on cars as a hobby provides valuable firsthand experience in the work of a technician. An afterschool or weekend part-time job in a repair shop or dealership can give you a feel for the general atmosphere and kinds of problems technicians face on the job. Oil and tire changes, battery and belt replacement, and even pumping gas may be some of the things you will be asked to do on the job; this work will give you valuable experience before you move on to more complex repairs. Experience with vehicle repair work in the armed forces is another way to pursue your interest in this field.

■ EMPLOYERS

Because the automotive industry is so vast, automobile service technicians have many choices concerning type of shop and geographic location. Automobile repairs are needed all over the country, in large cities as well as rural areas.

The majority of automobile service technicians work for automotive dealers and independent automotive repair shops and gasoline service stations. The field offers a variety of other employment options as well. The U.S. Department of Labor estimates that 18 percent of automobile service technicians are self-employed. Other employers include franchises such as PepBoys and Midas that offer routine repairs and maintenance, and automotive service departments of automotive and home supply stores. Some automobile service technicians maintain fleets for taxicab and automobile leasing companies or for government agencies with large automobile fleets.

Technicians with experience and/or ASE certification certainly have more career choices. Some master mechanics may go on to teach at technical and vocational schools or at community colleges. Others put in many years working for someone else and go into business for themselves after they have gained the experience to handle many types of repairs and oversee other technicians.

■ STARTING OUT

The best way to start out in this field is to attend one of the many postsecondary training programs available throughout the country and obtain accreditation. Trade and technical schools usually provide job placement assistance for their graduates. Schools often have contacts with local employers who need to hire well-trained people. Frequently, employers post job openings at nearby trade schools with accredited programs. Job openings are frequently listed on the Internet through regional and national automotive associations or career networks.

A decreasing number of technicians learn the trade on the job as apprentices. Their training consists of working for several years under the guidance of experienced mechanics. Fewer employers today are willing to hire apprentices due to the time and money it takes to train them. Those who do learn their skills on the job will inevitably require some formal training if they wish to advance and stay in step with the changing industry.

Intern programs sponsored by car manufacturers or independent organizations provide students with excellent opportunities to actually work with prospective employers. Internships can provide students with valuable contacts who will be able to recommend future employers once they have completed their training. Many students may even be hired by the shop at which they interned.

■ ADVANCEMENT

Currently employed technicians may be certified by ASE in eight different areas. Those who become certified in all eight areas are known as master mechanics. Although certification is voluntary, it is a widely recognized standard of achievement for automobile technicians and is highly valued by many employers. Certification also provides the means and opportunity to advance. To maintain their certification, technicians must retake the examination for their specialties every five years. Many employers only hire ASE-accredited technicians and base salaries on the level of the technicians' accreditation.

With today's complex automobile components requiring hundreds of hours of study and practice to master, more repair shops prefer to hire specialists. Generalist automobile technicians advance as they gain experience and become specialists. Other technicians advance to diesel repair, where the pay may be higher. Those with good communications and planning skills may advance to shop foreman or service manager at large repair shops or to sales workers at dealerships. Master mechanics with good business skills often go into business for themselves and open their own shops.

■ EARNINGS

Salary ranges of automobile service technicians vary depending on the level of experience, type of shop the technician works in, and geographic location. Generally, technicians who work in small-town, family-owned gas stations earn less than those who work at dealerships and franchises in metropolitan areas.

According to the U.S. Department of Labor, the lowest paid automobile service technicians earned about $8.14 per hour (or $16,930 annually) in 2002. The median hourly salary for automobile service technicians was $14.71 (or $30,590 annually), and top-paid technicians with experience and certification earned more than $25.21 per hour (or $52,430+ annually). Since most technicians work on an hourly basis and frequently work overtime, their salaries can vary significantly. In many repair shops and dealerships, technicians can earn higher incomes by working on commission. Master technicians who work on commission can earn more than $100,000 annually. Employers often guarantee a minimum level of pay in addition to commissions.

Benefit packages vary from business to business. Most technicians receive health insurance and paid vacation days. Additional benefits may include dental, life, and disability insurance and a pension plan. Employers usually pay for a technician's work clothes and may pay a percentage on hand tools purchased. An increasing number of employers pay for all or most of an employee's certification training, if he or she passes the test. A technician's salary can increase through yearly bonuses or profit sharing if the business does well.

■ WORK ENVIRONMENT

Depending on the size of the shop and whether it's an independent or franchised repair shop, dealership, or private business, automobile technicians work with anywhere from two to 20 other technicians. Most shops are well lighted and well ventilated. They can frequently be noisy with running cars and power tools. Minor hand and back injuries are the most common problems of technicians. When reaching in hard-to-get-at places or loosening tight bolts, technicians often bruise, cut, or burn their hands. With caution and experience most technicians learn to avoid hand injuries. Working for long periods of time in cramped or bent positions often results in a stiff back or neck. Technicians also lift many heavy objects that can cause injury if not handled carefully; however, this is becoming less of a problem with new cars, as automakers design smaller and lighter parts to improve fuel economy. Some technicians may experience allergic reactions to solvents and oils used in cleaning, maintenance, and repair. Shops must comply with strict safety procedures set by the Occupational Safety Hazard Administration and Environmental Protection Agency to help employees avoid accidents and injuries.

The U.S. Department of Labor reports that most technicians work a standard 40-hour week, but 30 percent of all technicians work more than 40 hours a week. Some technicians make emergency repairs to stranded automobiles on the roadside during odd hours.

■ OUTLOOK

With an estimated 221 million vehicles in operation today, automobile service technicians should feel confident that a good percentage will require servicing and repair. Skilled and highly trained technicians will be in particular demand. Less-skilled workers will face tough competition. The U.S. Department of Labor predicts that this field will grow as fast as the average through 2012, but in some areas, growth could be higher because of a tight labor market. According to ASE, even if school enrollments were at maximum capacity, the demand for automobile service technicians still would exceed the supply in the immediate future. As a result, many shops are beginning to recruit employees while they are still in vocational or even high school.

Another concern for the industry is the automobile industry's trend toward developing the "maintenance-free" car. Manufacturers are producing high-end cars that require no servicing for their first 100,000 miles. In addition, many new cars are equipped with on-board diagnostics that detect both wear and failure for many of the car's components, eliminating the need for technicians to perform extensive diagnostic tests. Also, parts that are replaced before they completely wear out prevent further damage from occurring to connected parts that are affected by a malfunction or breakdown. Although this will reduce troubleshooting time and the number of overall repairs, the components that need repair will be more costly and require a more experienced (and hence, more expensive) technician.

Most new jobs for technicians will be at independent service dealers, specialty shops, and franchised new car dealers. Because of the increase of specialty shops, fewer gasoline service stations will hire technicians, and many will eliminate repair services completely. Other opportunities will be available at companies or institutions with private fleets (e.g., cab, delivery, and rental companies, and government agencies and police departments).

■ FOR MORE INFORMATION

For more information on the automotive service industry, contact

Automotive Aftermarket Industry Association
4600 East-West Highway, Suite 300
Bethesda, MD 20814-3415
Tel: 301-654-6664
Email: aaia@aftermarket.org
http://www.aftermarket.org

For industry information and job listings, contact

Automotive Service Association
PO Box 929
Bedford, TX 76095-0929
Tel: 800-272-7467
Email: asainfo@asashop.org
http://www.asashop.org

For information and statistics on automotive dealers, contact

National Automobile Dealers Association
8400 Westpark Drive
McLean, VA 22102
Tel: 800-252-6232
Email: nadainfo@nada.org
http://www.nada.org

For information on certified educational programs, careers, and certification, contact

National Automotive Technicians Education Foundation
101 Blue Seal Drive, Suite 101
Leesburg, VA 20175
Tel: 703-669-6650
http://www.natef.org

For information on certification, contact

National Institute for Automotive Service Excellence
101 Blue Seal Drive, SE, Suite 101
Leesburg, VA 20175
Tel: 877-273-8324
http://www.asecert.org

Automotive Industry Workers

■ OVERVIEW

Automotive industry workers are the people who work in the parts production and assembly plants of automobile manufacturers. Their labor involves work from the smallest part to the completed automobiles. Automotive industry workers read specifications, design parts, build, maintain, and operate machinery and tools used to produce parts, and assemble the automobiles.

■ HISTORY

In our mobile society, it is difficult to imagine a time without automobiles. Yet just over 100 years ago, there were none. In the late 1800s, inventors were just beginning to tinker with the idea of a self-propelled vehicle. Early experiments used steam to power a vehicle's engine. Two German engineers developed the first internal combustion engine fueled by gasoline. Karl Benz finished the first model in 1885, and Gottlieb Daimler finished building a similar model in 1886. Others around the world had similar successes in the late 1800s and early 1900s. In these early days, no one imagined people would become so reliant on the automobile as a way of life. In 1898, there were 50 automobile manufacturing companies in the United States, a number that rose to 241 by 1908.

Early automobiles were expensive to make and keep in working order and could be used to travel only short distances; they were "toys" for those who had the time and money to tinker with them. One such person was Henry Ford. He differed from others who had succeeded in building automobiles in that he believed the automobile could appeal to the general public if the cost of producing them were reduced. The Model A was first produced by the Ford Motor Company in small quantities in 1903. Ford made improvements to the Model A, and in October 1908, he found success with the more practical Model T. The Model T was the vehicle that changed Ford's fortune and would eventually change the world. It was a powerful car with a possible speed of 45 miles per hour that could run 13 to 21 miles on a gallon of gasoline. Such improvements were made possible by the use of vanadium steel, a lighter and more durable steel than that previously used. Automobiles were beginning to draw interest from the general public as newspapers reported early successes, but they were still out of reach for most Americans. The automobile remained a curiosity to be read about in the newspapers until 1913. That's when Ford changed the way his workers produced automobiles in the factory. Before 1913, skilled craftsmen made automobiles in Ford's factory, but Ford's moving assembly line reduced the skill level needed and sped up production. The moving assembly line improved the speed of chassis assembly from 12 hours and 8 minutes to 1 hour and 33 minutes. Craftsmen were no longer needed to make the parts and assemble the automobiles. Anyone could be trained for most of the jobs required to build an automobile in one of Ford's factories, making it possible to hire unskilled workers at lower wages.

For many early automotive workers, Ford's mass production concept proved to be both a blessing and a curse. Demand was growing for the affordable automobile, even during the Depression years, bringing new jobs for people who desperately needed them. However, working on an assembly line could be tedious and stressful at the same time. Ford paid his workers well (he introduced the $5 day in 1914, a high wage for the time), but he demanded a lot of them. He sped up the assembly line on several occasions, and many workers performed the same task for hours at a frenzied pace, often without a break.

Such conditions led workers to organize unions and, through the years, workers have gained more control over the speed at which they work and pay rates. Many of today's automotive industry workers belong to unions such as the United Auto Workers (founded in 1936). The industry continued to evolve with automotive technology in the 1940s and 1950s. American automobiles were generally large and consumed a lot of gasoline, but a strong U.S. economy afforded many Americans the ability to buy and maintain such vehicles. In Europe and Japan, smaller, fuel-efficient cars were more popular. This allowed foreign automakers to cut deeply into the American automobile market during fuel shortages in the 1970s. Automotive workers suffered job cuts in the 1980s because of declining exports and domestic sales. Today, the industry has recovered from the losses of the 1980s largely by producing vehicles that can compete with fuel-efficient, foreign-made ones. Also, trade agreements have encouraged foreign automakers to build manufacturing plants in the United States, creating new jobs for U.S. workers. The United States currently has about one-quarter of the world's automobiles, some 128 million vehicles.

■ THE JOB

The term "automotive industry worker" covers the wide range of people who build the 5 million cars—about 14 percent of the world's total—produced in the United States each year. Automotive industry workers are employed in two types of plants: parts production plants and assembly plants. Similar jobs are also found with companies that manufacture farm and earth-moving equipment; their workers often belong to the same unions and undergo the same training. Major automobile manufacturers are generally organized so that automobiles are assembled at a few large plants that employ several thousand workers. Parts for the automobiles are made at smaller plants that may employ fewer than 100 workers. Some plants that produce parts are not owned by the automobile manufacturer but may be independent companies that specialize in making one important part. These independent manufacturers may supply parts to several different automobile makers.

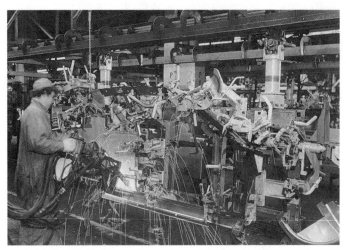

An assembly line worker at a General Motors auto plant

Whether they work in a parts plant or an assembly plant, automotive workers are generally people who work with their hands, spend a lot of time standing, bending, lifting, and do a lot of repetitive work. They often work in noisy areas and are required to wear protective equipment throughout their workday, such as safety glasses, earplugs, gloves, and masks. Because automotive industry workers often work in large plants that operate 24 hours a day, they usually work in shifts. Shift assignments are generally made on the basis of seniority.

Precision metalworker is one of the more highly skilled positions found in automotive production plants. Precision metalworkers create the metal tools, dies, and special guiding and holding devices that produce automotive parts—thus, they are sometimes called *tool and die makers.* They must be familiar with the entire manufacturing process and have knowledge of mathematics, blueprint reading, and the properties of metals, such as hardness and heat tolerance. Precision metalworkers may perform all or some of the steps needed to make machining tools, including reading blueprints, planning the sequence of operations, marking the materials, and cutting and assembling the materials into a tool. Precision metalworkers often work in quieter parts of the production plants.

Machinists make the precision metal parts needed for automobiles using tools such as lathes, drill presses, and milling machines. In automotive production plants, their work is repetitive as they generally produce large quantities of one part. Machinists may spend their entire shift machining the part. Some machinists also read blueprints or written specifications for a part. They calculate where to cut into the metal, how fast to feed the metal into the machine, or how much of the metal to remove. Machinists select tools and materials needed for the job and mark the metal stock for the cuts to be made. Increasingly, the machine tools used to make automotive parts are computerized. Computer numerically controlled machining is widespread in many manufacturing processes today. *Tool programmers* write the computer programs that direct the machine's operations, and machinists monitor the computer-controlled process.

Maintenance workers is a general category that refers to a number of jobs. Maintenance workers may repair or make new parts for existing machines. They also may set up new machines. They may work with sales representatives from the company that sold the automobile manufacturer the piece of equipment. Maintenance workers are responsible for the upkeep of machines and should be able to perform all of the machine's operations.

Welders use equipment that joins metal parts by melting and fusing them to form a permanent bond. There are different types of welds as well as equipment to make the welds. In manual welding, the work is controlled entirely by the welder. Other work is semi-automatic, in which machinery such as a wire feeder is used to help perform the weld. Much of the welding work in automotive plants is repetitive; in some of these cases, *welding machine operators* monitor machines as they perform the welding tasks. Because they work with fire, welders must wear safety gear, such as protective clothing, safety shoes, goggles, and hoods with protective lenses.

Inspectors check the manufacturing process at all stages to make sure products meet quality standards. Everything from raw materials to parts to the finished automobile is checked for dimensions, color, weight, texture, strength, and other physical characteristics, as well as proper operation. Inspectors identify and record any quality problems and may work with any of several departments to remedy the flaw. Jobs for inspectors are declining because inspection has become automated at many stages of production. Also, there is a move to have workers self-check their work on the production line.

Floor or line supervisors are responsible for a group of workers who produce one part or perform one step in a process. They may report to department heads or foremen who oversee several such departments. Many supervisors are production workers who have worked their way up the ranks; still others have a management background and, in many cases, a college degree in business or management.

■ REQUIREMENTS
High School

Many automotive industry jobs require mechanical skills, so you should take advantage of any shop programs your high school offers, such as auto mechanics, electronics, welding, drafting, and computer programming and design. In the core subject areas, mathematics, including algebra and geometry, is useful for reading blueprints and computer programs that direct machine functions. Chemistry is useful for workers who need to be familiar with the properties of metals. English classes are also important to help you communicate verbally with both supervisors and co-workers and to read and understand complex instructions.

Postsecondary Training

Many of the jobs in an automotive plant are classified as semiskilled or unskilled positions, and people with some mechanical aptitude, physical ability, and a high school diploma are qualified to do them. However, there is often stiff competition for jobs with large automakers like General Motors, Ford, and DaimlerChrysler because they offer good benefits and pay compared to jobs that require similar skill levels. Therefore, if you have some postsecondary training, certification, or experience, you stand a better chance of getting a job in the automotive industry than someone with only a high school diploma.

Formal training for machining, welding, and toolmaking is offered in vocational schools, vocational-technical institutes, community colleges, and private schools. Increasingly, such postsecondary training or certification is the route many workers take to getting an automotive industry job. In the past, apprenticeships and on-the-job training were the routes many workers took to get factory jobs, but these options are not as widely available today. Electricians, who generally must complete an apprenticeship, may find work in automotive plants as maintenance workers.

Certification or Licensing

Certification is available but not required for many of the positions in an automotive production plant. The American Welding Society offers the designations certified welding engineer (CWE) and certified welding inspector (CWI) to members who meet education and professional experience criteria as well as pass an examination. For precision metalworkers and machinists, the National Tooling and Machining Association operates training centers and apprentice programs and sets skill standards.

Other Requirements

Working in an automotive production plant can be physically challenging. For many jobs, you need the physical capability to stand for long periods, lift heavy objects, and maneuver hand tools and machinery. Of course, some jobs in an automotive production plant can be performed by a person with a physical disability. For example, a person who uses a wheelchair may work well on an assembly line job that requires only the use of his or her hands. Automotive workers should have hand and finger dexterity and the ability to do repetitive work accurately and safely.

■ EXPLORING

Do you enjoy working with your hands? Following complex instructions? Do you think you could do repetitive work on a daily basis? Are you a natural leader who would enjoy a supervisory position? Once you have an idea what area of the automotive industry you want to pursue, the best way to learn more is to find someone who does the job and ask him or her questions about the work. Assembly plants are generally located in or near large cities, but if you live in a rural area you can still probably find someone with a similar job at a parts plant or other manufacturer. Even small towns generally have machine shops or other types of manufacturing plants that employ machinists, tool and die makers, inspectors, and other production workers. Local machine shops or factories are a good place to get experience, perhaps through a summer or after-school job to see if you enjoy working in a production environment. Many high schools have cooperative programs that employ students who want to gain work experience.

■ EMPLOYERS

Automotive industry workers can find jobs with both domestic automakers, such as the Big Three, and with foreign automakers like Mitsubishi and Honda, which both have large assembly plants in the United States. Large assembly plants may employ several thousand workers.

LEARN MORE ABOUT IT

Aspatore Books Staff. *Inside the Minds: The Automotive Industry—Industry Leaders Share Their Knowledge on the Future of the Automotive World.* Boston: Aspatore Books, 2002.

Genat, Robert. *The American Car Dealership.* Osceola, Wisc.: MBI Publishing, 1999.

Ingrassia, Paul, and Joseph B. White. *Comeback: The Fall and Rise of the American Automobile Industry.* New York: Simon & Schuster, 1994.

Landmann, Ralf, et al., eds. *The Future of the Automotive Industry: Challenges and Concepts for the 21st Century.* Warrendale, Pa.: Society of Automotive Engineers, 2001.

Nelson, Dave, et al. *Powered by Honda: Developing Excellence in the Global Enterprise.* New York: John Wiley & Sons, 1998.

Walton, Mary. *Car: A Drama of the American Workplace.* New York: W. W. Norton & Company, 1999.

ELECTRIC CARS

Workers in the automotive industry are accustomed to changing technologies. Every year, many workers learn new processes to accommodate improvements in the way automobiles are manufactured. But the increasing popularity of alternative-fuel vehicles may someday radically change the way some workers produce automobiles. One such alternative fuel is electricity. Three manufacturers already sell electric-powered vehicles to consumers, and major automakers as well as small startup companies are working on electric automobiles. Currently, Ford, Honda, and General Motors offer electric vehicles to consumers. In many cases, people who buy such vehicles earn tax incentives and receive breaks on electricity rates for charging their electric vehicles. Ford offers an electricity-fueled truck, the Ranger EV. The truck seats two to three passengers and can travel 60 to 80 miles on a charge. Honda's EV+ seats four and can travel 100 to 120 miles. GM's EV1 seats two and can travel 60 to 80 miles on a charge. Today, electric vehicles are limited in their use by the distance they can travel on a charge. However, as they become more popular, the concept of charging stations instead of gas stations isn't out of the question. If these vehicles become more practical, as many predict they will, the automotive production industry and its workers could soon be mass producing electric vehicles.

Parts production plants may employ fewer workers, but there are more of these plants. Assembly plants are generally located in or near large cities, especially in the Northeast and Midwest where heavy manufacturing is concentrated. Parts production plants vary in size, from a few dozen workers to several hundred. Employees of these plants may all work on one small part or on several parts that make up one component of an automobile. Parts production plants are located in smaller towns as well as urban areas. The production processes in agricultural and earth-moving equipment factories are similar to those in the automotive industry, and workers trained in welding, toolmaking, machining, and maintenance may find jobs with companies like Caterpillar and John Deere.

The United Auto Workers Union, the largest union in the industry, currently reports 710,000 active members.

■ STARTING OUT

Hiring practices at large plants are usually very structured. Such large employers generally don't place "help wanted" ads. Rather, they accept applications year-round and keep them on file. Applicants generally complete an initial application and may be placed on a hiring list. Others get started by working as temporary or part-time workers at the plant and using their experience and contacts to obtain full-time, permanent positions. Some plants work with career placement offices of vocational schools and technical associations to find qualified workers. Others may recruit workers at job fairs. Also, as with many large factories, people who have a relative or know someone who works at the plant usually have a better chance of getting hired. Their contact may put in a good word with a supervisor or advise them when an opening occurs.

New hires are usually expected to join the UAW (United Auto Workers) or another union. Unions help negotiate with manufacturers and deal with the company on a worker's behalf; however, they are also very structured.

■ ADVANCEMENT

Automotive production plants are very structured in their paths of advancement. Large human resources departments oversee the personnel structures of all departments; each job has a specific description with specific qualifications. Union rules and contracts further structure advancement. Longevity is usually the key to advancement in an automotive plant. For many, advancement means staying in the same position and moving up on the salary scale. Others acquire experience and, often, further training to advance to a position with a higher skill level, more responsibility, and higher pay. For example, machinists may learn a lot about many different machines throughout their careers and may undergo training or be promoted to become precision metalworkers. Others with years of experience become supervisors of their departments.

■ EARNINGS

Salaries vary widely for automotive industry workers depending on their job and how long they've been with the company. Supervisors may earn $60,000 to $75,000 a year or more, depending on the number of people they supervise. Pay for semiskilled or unskilled workers, such as assemblers, is considerably lower, usually in the $27,000 range. Still, such production jobs are sought after because this pay is higher than such workers may find elsewhere based on their skill level. The *Occupational Outlook Handbook* reports the following 2002 median annual earnings for workers specializing in the production of motor vehicles and equipment: tool and die makers, $43,630; welders, $30,820; and first-line managers, $45,920. The median average salary for all machinists was $33,410 in 2002. Earnings are usually much higher for workers who are members of a union and employed by a Big Three automaker. Few of these workers earn less than $40,000 a year, and some earn as much as $100,000 a year because of mandatory overtime and six- or seven-day workweeks.

Workers employed by large, unionized companies such as Ford and DaimlerChrysler enjoy good benefits, including paid health insurance, paid holidays, sick days, and personal days. Large employers generally offer retirement plans and many match workers' contributions to retirement funds. Automotive industry workers who work for independent parts manufacturers may not enjoy the comprehensive benefit programs that employees of large companies do, but generally are offered health insurance and paid personal days.

■ WORK ENVIRONMENT

Working as a production worker in an automotive plant can be stressful, depending on the worker's personality, job duties, and management expectations. Assembly line workers have little control over the speed at which they must complete their work. They can generally take breaks only when scheduled. Norm Ritchie, a machine operator at a DaimlerChrysler parts plant in Perrysburg, Ohio, says the job can be stressful: "The pressure [of the assembly line] affects people in different ways. Sometimes people get pretty stressed out; other people can handle it." Ritchie, who works on steering shafts, also said that noise is a concern in his area of the plant. He estimated that the noise level is about 90 decibels all the time. Automotive production workers must follow several safety precautions every day, including wearing protective gear (such as earplugs) and undergoing safety training throughout their careers.

■ OUTLOOK

Job growth is not expected for the U.S. automotive industry for the next few years. The industry has recovered from the 1980s, which saw steep layoffs and job losses. Automotive industry employment is expected to remain steady at best. The industry reached its peak employment level in 1979 with 1.1 million workers. But fuel shortages in the late 1970s and early 1980s made the larger American-made cars less appealing than foreign cars, which for years had been made smaller and more fuel efficient. By 1982, the industry employed only 600,000 workers. In the 1990s, employment hovered around 700,000. As of 2000, approximately 1 million workers were employed in the industry, according to the U.S. Bureau of Labor Statistics.

Most industry analysts expect car sales to decline in the next several years. The slowing economy could cause production slowdowns and subsequent layoffs for auto industry workers, particularly those who work for American manufacturers. Many manufacturers have also found it more cost-effective to move operations overseas, where unions are weak and labor is cheaper. However, the decline in employment among American-owned automakers has been balanced by new foreign-owned manufacturing plants that have been built in the United States. Today, many U.S. automotive workers are employed by foreign-owned automakers such as Honda and Mitsubishi.

■ FOR MORE INFORMATION

These professional societies promote the skills of their trades and can provide career information.

American Welding Society
550 Lejeune Road, NW
Miami, FL 33126-5699
Tel: 800-443-9353
http://www.aws.org

National Tooling and Machining Association
9300 Livingston Road
Fort Washington, MD 20744
Tel: 800-248-6862
http://www.ntma.org

These are two of many unions that represent automotive production workers. They can provide information about training and education programs in your area.

International Association of Machinists and Aerospace Workers
9000 Machinists Place
Upper Marlboro, MD 20772-2687
Tel: 301-967-4500
http://www.iamaw.org

United Auto Workers
8000 East Jefferson Avenue
Detroit, MI 48214
Tel: 313-926-5000
http://www.uaw.org

Avionics Engineers and Technicians

■ OVERVIEW

Avionics (from the words *aviation* and *electronics*) is the application of electronics to the operation of aircraft, spacecraft, and missiles. *Avionics engineers* conduct research and solve developmental problems associated with aviation, such as instrument landing systems and other safety instruments. Avionics engineers hold about 14,700 jobs. *Avionics technicians* inspect, test, adjust, and repair the electronic components of aircraft communications, navigation, and flight-control systems and compile complete maintenance-and-overhaul records for the work they do. Avionics technicians also calibrate and adjust the frequencies of communications apparatus when it is installed and perform periodic checks on those frequency settings. Avionics technicians hold about 21,720 jobs.

■ HISTORY

The field of avionics grew out of World War II, when military aircraft were operated for the first time using electronic equipment. Rockets were also being developed during this time, and these devices required electronic systems to control their flight. As aircraft rapidly grew more complicated, the amount of electronic apparatus needed for navigation and for monitoring equipment performance greatly increased. The World War II B-29 bomber carried 2,000 to 3,000 avionic components; the B-52 of the Vietnam era carried 50,000; later, the B-58 supersonic bomber required more than 95,000. As the military grew increasingly reliant on electronic systems, specialists were required to build, install, operate, and repair them.

The development of large ballistic missiles during and after World War II and the rapid growth of the U.S. space program after 1958 increased development of avionics technology. Large missiles and spacecraft require many more electronic components than even the largest and most sophisticated aircraft. Computerized guidance systems became especially important with the advent of manned spaceflights. Avionics technology was also applied to civil aircraft. The race to be the first in space, and later, to be the first to land on the moon, stimulated the need for more and more trained specialists to work with newer and more complex electronic technology. The push for achieving military superiority during the Cold War era also created a demand for avionics specialists and technicians. From the 1950s to the present, the commercial airline industry grew rapidly; more and more planes were being built, and the drive to provide greater comfort and safety for passengers created still greater demand for avionics engineers and technicians.

Avionics continues to be an important branch of aeronautical and astronautical engineering. The aerospace industry places great emphasis on research and development, assigning a much higher percentage of its trained technical personnel to this effort than is usual in industry. In addition, stringent safety regulations require constant surveillance of in-service equipment. For these reasons there is a high demand for trained and experienced avionics engineers and technicians to help in the development of new satellites, spacecraft, aircraft, and their component electronic systems and to maintain those in service.

■ THE JOB

Avionics engineers develop new electronic systems and components for aerospace use. Avionics technicians assist engineers in these developments. They also adapt existing systems and components for application in new equipment. For the most part, however, they install, test, repair, and maintain navigation, communications, and control apparatus in existing aircraft and spacecraft.

Technicians use apparatus such as circuit analyzers and oscilloscopes to test and replace such sophisticated equipment as transceivers and Doppler radar systems, as well as microphones, headsets, and other standard electronic communications apparatus. New equipment, once installed, must be tested and calibrated to prescribed specifications. Technicians also adjust the frequencies of radio sets and other communications equipment by signaling ground stations and then adjusting set screws until the desired frequency has been achieved. Periodic maintenance checks and readjustments enable avionics technicians to keep equipment operating on proper frequencies. The technicians also complete and sign maintenance-and-overhaul documents recording the history of various equipment.

Avionics engineers and technicians involved in the design and testing of a new apparatus must take into account all operating conditions, determining weight limitations, resistance to physical shock, the atmospheric conditions the device will have to withstand, and other factors. For some sophisticated projects, technicians will have to design and make their tools first and then use them to construct and test new avionic components.

QUICK FACTS

SCHOOL SUBJECTS
Mathematics
Technical/shop

PERSONAL SKILLS
Mechanical/manipulative
Technical/scientific

WORK ENVIRONMENT
Primarily indoors
Primarily one location

MINIMUM EDUCATION LEVEL
Some postsecondary training

SALARY RANGE
$34,820 to $51,650 to $73,480 (engineers)
$29,130 to $42,030 to $56,150 (technicians)

CERTIFICATION OR LICENSING
Required by all states

OUTLOOK
About as fast as the average

DOT
823

GOE
02.07.04, 02.08.04

NOC
2244

O*NET-SOC
17-3021.00, 49-2091.00

The range of equipment in the avionics field is so broad that technicians usually specialize in one area, such as radio equipment, radar, computerized guidance, or flight-control systems. New specialty areas are constantly opening up as innovations occur in avionics. The development of these new specialty areas requires technicians to keep informed by reading technical articles and books and by attending seminars and courses about the new developments, which are often sponsored by manufacturers.

Avionics technicians usually work as part of a team, especially if involved in research, testing, and development of new products. They are often required to keep notes and records of their work and to write detailed reports.

■ REQUIREMENTS
High School

Persons interested in pursuing a career in avionics should take high school mathematics courses at least through solid geometry and preferably through calculus. They should take English, speech, and communications classes in order to read complex and detailed technical articles, books, and reports; to write technical reports; and to present those reports to groups of people when required. Many schools offer shop classes in electronics and in diagram and blueprint reading.

Postsecondary Training

Avionics engineers must have a bachelor's degree from an accredited college or university and may participate in a cooperative education program through their engineering school. Avionics technicians must have completed a course of training at a postsecondary technical institute or community college, of which there are some 200 in the United States. The training should include at least one year of electronics technician training. If not trained specifically in avionics, students should obtain a solid background in electronics theory and practice. Further specialized training will be done on the job, where technicians work with engineers and senior technicians until they are competent to work without direct supervision.

Larger corporations in the aerospace industry operate their own schools and training institutes. Such training rarely includes theoretical or general studies but concentrates on areas important to the company's functions. The U.S. armed forces also conduct excellent electronics and avionics training schools; their graduates are in high demand in the industry after they leave the service.

Certification or Licensing

Federal Communications Commission (FCC) regulations require that anyone who works with radio transmitting equipment have a restricted radiotelephone

THE X PRIZE

By far one the most interesting developments to happen in the aeronautics industry in the past few years is the X Prize, a $100 million award contributed by group of investors led by maverick millionaire Peter Diamandis. The goal: to build a spaceship that can carry three people into suborbital flight 100 kilometers (62.5 miles) above the Earth, and then repeat the feat within two weeks. Planned entries include traditional vertical-takeoff rockets, rocket/jet combinations, and even a rocket that launches from a balloon. Perhaps the most exciting is genius aircraft designer Burt Rutan's SpaceShipOne, a rocketplane that is given a lift by "piggybacking" on a jet aircraft, the White Knight. Some of the investors behind X Prize teams include Amazon.com's Jeff Bezos and Microsoft's Paul Allen, who not only hope to fulfill their boyhood dreams of space flight, but also to revolutionize the space industry, inexpensively launching satellites, opening up a whole world of "space tourism," and perhaps even building private space stations.

Source: *Wired* magazine 11.07

operator's license. Such a license is issued upon application to the FCC and is issued for life.

Other Requirements

Students who are thinking about this kind of work should have strong science and mathematics skills. In addition, they will need to have good manual dexterity and mechanical aptitude and the temperament for exacting work.

■ EXPLORING

Students interested in avionics should visit factories and test facilities where avionics technicians work as part of teams designing and testing new equipment. It is also possible to visit a large airfield's repair facilities where avionics technicians inspect, maintain, and calibrate communications and control apparatus. Students can also arrange to visit other types of electronics manufacturers.

Useful information about avionics training programs and career opportunities is available from the U.S. armed forces as well as from trade and technical schools and community colleges that offer such programs. These organizations are always pleased to answer inquiries from prospective students or service personnel.

■ EMPLOYERS

About a third of the 14,700 aerospace engineers employed in the United States work in the aircraft and parts and

An avionics technician prepares to calibrate the settings on a communications system in a small plane.

guided missile and space vehicle manufacturing industries. Many are employed in federal government agencies, primarily the Department of Defense and the National Aeronautics and Space Administration. Other employers include engineering and architectural services, research and testing services, and search and navigation equipment firms.

Most avionics technicians work for the federal government, or manufacturers and assembly firms. Other major employers include airports and flying fields and airlines.

■ STARTING OUT

Those entering the field of avionics must first obtain the necessary training in electronics. Following that training, the school's placement officer can help locate prospective employers, arrange interviews, and advise about an employment search. Other possibilities are to contact an employment agency or to approach a prospective employer directly. Service in the military is an excellent way to gain education, training, and experience in avionics; many companies are eager to hire technicians with a military background.

■ ADVANCEMENT

Avionics technicians usually begin their careers in trainee positions until they are thoroughly familiar with the requirements and routines of their work. Having completed their apprenticeships, they are usually assigned to

work independently, with only minimal supervision, doing testing and repair work. The most experienced and able technicians go on to install new equipment and to work in research and development operations. Many senior technicians move into training, supervisory, sales, and customer relations positions. Some choose to pursue additional training and become avionics engineers.

Avionics engineers are already at an advanced position but may move up to become engineering supervisors or managers.

■ EARNINGS

The U.S. Department of Labor reports that median annual earnings of avionics engineers were $51,650 in 2002. Salaries ranged from less than $34,820 to more than $73,480.

Median earnings of avionics technicians were $42,030 in 2002, according to the U.S. Department of Labor. The top 10 percent of technicians earned more than $56,150 a year. The lowest 10 percent earned less than $29,130 a year. Federal government employees (not including armed forces personnel) on the average earn slightly less than avionics technicians employed by private aerospace firms. Their jobs, however, are more secure.

■ WORK ENVIRONMENT

Avionics engineers and technicians work for aircraft and aerospace manufacturers, airlines, and NASA and other government agencies. Most avionics engineers and technicians specialize in a specific area of avionics; they are also responsible for keeping up with the latest technological and industry advances. Their work is usually performed in pleasant indoor surroundings. Because this work is very precise, successful engineers and technicians must have a personality suited to meeting exact standards and working within small tolerances. Technicians sometimes work in closely cooperating teams. This requires an ability to work with a team spirit of coordinated effort.

■ OUTLOOK

The U.S. Department of Labor predicts that employment for avionics engineers and technicians should grow as fast as the average for all other occupations through 2012.

Avionics is an important and constantly developing field for which more and more trained technicians will be required. Reliance on electronic technology has grown rapidly and in virtually every industry. Many defense contractors have begun to branch out into other products, especially in the areas of electronic and computer technology. Commercial applications of the space program, including the launching of privately owned satellites, are providing new opportunities in the aerospace industry.

However, the aerospace industry is closely tied to government spending and to political change, as well as to the economy, which also affects the aircraft and airline industries strongly. The cancellation of one spacecraft program or a fall in airline travel that leads to employee cutbacks may throw a large number of avionics engineers and technicians out of work, making competition for the remaining jobs very keen.

■ FOR MORE INFORMATION

Contact the following organization for information on avionics careers:

Aerospace Industries Association of America
1000 Wilson Boulevard, Suite 1700
Arlington, VA 22209-3901
Tel: 703-358-1000
http://www.aia-aerospace.org

General Aviation Manufacturers Association
1400 K Street, NW, Suite 801
Washington, DC 20005
Tel: 202-393-1500
http://www.gama.aero

For information on careers, lists of schools, and scholarships, contact

National Air Transportation Association
4226 King Street
Alexandria, VA 22302
Tel: 800-808-6282
Email: info@nata.aero
http://www.nata.aero

For career information, see AIAC's website.

Aerospace Industries Association of Canada (AIAC)
60 Queen Street, #1200
Ottawa, ON K1P 5Y7 Canada
Tel: 613-232-4297
Email: info@aiac.ca
http://www.aiac.ca

Ayurvedic Doctors and Practitioners

■ OVERVIEW

Ayurvedic doctors and practitioners use theories and techniques developed thousands of years ago in India to bring people into physical, mental, emotional, and spiritual balance, thereby maintaining health, curing diseases, and promoting happiness and fulfillment. In the West, where Ayurveda is not an officially accepted and licensed form of medicine, only licensed medical doctors who are also thoroughly trained in Ayurveda can legally practice Ayurvedic medicine. These individuals are referred to as Ayurvedic doctors.

Licensed practitioners of paramedical professions, such as nutritionists, psychologists, naturopaths, massage therapists, and acupuncturists, may, if they are also trained in Ayurveda and use Ayurvedic techniques in their professional work, be called Ayurvedic practitioners. Any non-M.D. who practices the full range of Ayurvedic medicine in the West, however, is seen as practicing medicine without a license, which is illegal.

■ HISTORY

The Vedas, which may be up to 5,000 years old, are the oldest and most important scriptures of Hinduism, which is the primary religion in India. The Sanskrit word *veda* means "knowledge," and the Vedas contain the knowledge and beliefs on which Hinduism is based. The Atharvaveda—the Veda that deals primarily with the practical aspects of life—contains chants, rites, and spells that are thought to enable believers to do such things as create love and goodwill among people, defeat enemies, and ensure success in agriculture. Most experts believe that the Atharvaveda is the basis of Ayurveda.

The word *Ayurveda* means "knowledge of life." The oldest of the specifically Ayurvedic texts, the *Charaka Samhita*, was written in approximately 1000 B.C. and deals with internal medicine. This and more recent texts, such as the *Astanga Hridayam*, a compilation of Ayurvedic knowledge written in approximately 1000 A.D., provide Ayurvedic practitioners with the knowledge they need to help their patients.

Ayurvedic medicine is officially accepted in India, where

QUICK FACTS

SCHOOL SUBJECTS
Biology
Chemistry
Health

PERSONAL SKILLS
Communication/ideas
Helping/teaching

WORK ENVIRONMENT
Primarily indoors
Primarily one location

MINIMUM EDUCATION LEVEL
High school diploma

SALARY RANGE
$20,000 to $60,000 to $150,000

CERTIFICATION OR LICENSING
Recommended

OUTLOOK
Faster than the average

DOT
N/A

GOE
N/A

NOC
N/A

O*NET-SOC
N/A

GLOSSARY OF AYURVEDIC TERMS

Ahamkara: The force that forms an individual person; an individual's "I."

Ama: Toxins created by improper digestion.

Aura: The energy field that surrounds the body.

Bhavana: A process in which a mortar and pestle are used to improve the quality of a substance such as an herb.

Dosha: Any of the three forces that allow the five elements to take form as flesh.

Laxation: The use of mild laxatives to decrease an overabundant dosha.

Prajnaparadha: A condition in which a person knowingly acts in a way that harms his or her health.

Prakriti or **prakruti:** A person's constitution.

Prana: Life force or energy; corresponds to the Chinese term *ch'i* and the Japanese term *ki.*

Purgation: The use of strong laxatives to decrease an overabundant dosha.

Sattva: Equilibrium, balance.

Shukra: Reproductive fluids.

Tantra: A set of practices that utilize energy for spiritual purposes.

Triphala: A compound used for purification and revitalization.

Virya: The energy contained in a substance.

Yukti: A process in which an effect is caused by making various factors unite at a particular place and time.

approximately 80 percent of those who seek medical help go to Ayurvedic doctors. In its country of origin, Ayurveda has been substantially modernized, and it now includes many techniques and medications that originated in the West. For example, in addition to ancient herbal formulas, Indian Ayurvedic doctors often prescribe antibiotics. Most Indian doctors have discarded the use of certain older practices that are described in early texts, such as the use of leeches for bloodletting.

■ THE JOB

Ayurveda is a way of life rather than simply a system of healing. It is a holistic system, which means that it views physical, mental, and spiritual health as intrinsically connected. An Ayurvedic doctor or practitioner treats the whole person, not simply the symptoms that a patient displays.

Ayurvedic doctors and practitioners base their treatments and recommendations on a complex body of beliefs. One of the most important beliefs holds that everything in the universe is composed of one or more of the five elements: air, fire, earth, water, and ether (space). These elements are concepts or qualities as much as they are actual entities. For example, anything that has the qualities that Ayurveda associates with fire is a manifestation of fire. A person's violent temper demonstrates the existence of fire within that person.

For the purposes of treating people, Ayurveda distills the concept of the five elements to three combinations of two elements. These are the *doshas,* which may be thought of as qualities or energies. The first dosha, Vata, is a combination of air and ether, with air predominating. The second dosha, Pitta, is a combination of fire and water, with fire predominating. The third dosha, Kapha, is a combination of water and earth, with water predominating. Every person is dominated by one or more doshas, although every person contains some element of all three. The unique combination of doshas that appears in a person is that person's *tridosha,* and that combination determines the person's constitution, or *prakriti.*

Because Ayurvedic theory holds that a person's nature and personality are based on his or her doshic makeup, or tridosha, the first thing that an Ayurvedic doctor or practitioner does when seeing a patient is to determine what that doshic makeup is. This is done by various means, including observation of physical qualities such as build, nails, lips, hair color, eye color, and skin type; taking the pulse in various locations; examination of the "nine doors," which are eyes, ears, nostrils, mouth, genitals, and anus; and questioning the patient about past history, present problems, goals, and so forth. After analyzing all this information, the practitioner determines which dosha or combination of doshas predominates in the patient's makeup.

Vata people tend to be extremely tall or extremely short and to have long fingers and toes. They are generally thin and have dark complexions and dry skin. The air element that predominates in their makeup makes them tend to be light, cold, and dry in various ways. They are often extremely creative, but their minds tend to flit from idea to idea, and they may be spacy and disorganized.

Pitta people, who are dominated by the fire element, are generally of medium build, and their fingers and toes are of medium length. They tend to be fair in complexion, with blond, light brown, or red hair. All redheads are said to have a significant amount of Pitta in their tridoshas. Pittas are quick to anger, can be forceful and domineering, and are highly organized. They make good engineers, accountants, and managers.

Kapha people, who are dominated by the water element, are generally large and well-built, with dark hair and oily skin. Their toes and fingers are short and thick. Kaphas may gain weight easily but have great physical stamina. They are usually calm people who avoid confrontation, but once they are angered, they hold a grudge. They like routine, tend not to be extremely creative, and are reliable.

Once the practitioner has determined the patient's tridosha and has ascertained what the patient's condition, problems, and desires are, the practitioner creates a program that will improve the patient's health and well-being. One of the most important methods that the practitioner will use is diet. If the patient's tridosha is out of balance, controlled to an extreme degree by one of the doshas, the practitioner may put together a diet that will decrease that dosha and/or increase the others, gradually and safely bringing the patient to a state of balance. Ayurvedic practitioners must therefore have a thorough knowledge of foods, traditional nutrition, and cooking.

Proper eating and good digestion are extremely important in Ayurveda, but Ayurvedic practitioners also use many other methods, among which are the techniques of *panchakarma*, which means "five actions." Panchakarma is a powerful set of cleansing practices that is ideally undertaken only under the guidance of an Ayurvedic doctor. The treatment varies by individual, but generally a patient must undergo one to seven days of preparation before the treatment begins. The preparation involves oil massage and steam baths, which sometimes include herbal treatments. After the body is sufficiently cleansed, the panchakarma may begin.

The first of the five practices is *vamana*, which involves removing excess Kapha from the stomach by inducing vomiting by gentle means. The second practice is *virechana*, which involves using laxatives to purge the body of excess Pitta. The third and fourth practices are both forms of *vasti*, or enema therapy, in which herbal preparations are used to remove Vata from the system. One form is relatively mild; the other is stronger. The fifth practice is *nasya*, which involves ingesting liquid or powdered substances through the nose. This practice is generally used to treat illnesses that affect the head and neck. It can take up to 30 days to complete the process of panchakarma.

There are many more aspects of Ayurvedic practice, and one of the most important things that doctors and practitioners do is advise patients regarding their lifestyle. They recommend various practices, such as cleaning the tongue daily, engaging in meditation, practicing yoga, and massaging the body with oils suitable for one's tridosha and the time of year. They may even advise patients regarding what kinds of clothes are best for them and where they will be most comfortable living.

■ REQUIREMENTS
High School

If Ayurvedic medicine interests you, learn as much as possible about health, medicine, science, and anatomy while in high school, just as you would to prepare for a career in Western medicine. Courses in biology and chemistry are important. It will also be important to study the Hindu tradition and become familiar with Sanskrit terms. Studying Sanskrit, the language of the Vedas and the Ayurvedic texts, is a good idea, although it is not absolutely essential. Although Sanskrit is not offered in high schools, correspondence courses are available, and students in large cities may find Sanskrit courses in universities or may find teachers in an Indian community.

Postsecondary Training

Postsecondary training depends on the path you want to take. To become a full-fledged Ayurvedic doctor in the West, you must be trained as a medical doctor as well as in Ayurveda, which means getting a bachelor's degree, going to medical school, and completing an internship.

LEARN MORE ABOUT IT

Atreya. Perfect Balance: *Ayurvedic Nutrition for Mind, Body, and Soul.* New York: Avery Penguin Putnam, 2001.

Chopra, Deepak, M.D. *Perfect Health: The Complete Mind Body Guide.* Rev. ed. New York: Three Rivers Press, 2000.

Davis, Roy Eugene. *An Easy Guide to Ayurveda: The Natural Way to Wholeness.* Hampton, Ga.: Alliance Book Company, 1999.

Frawley, David. *Ayurvedic Healing: A Comprehensive Guide.* 2nd Rev. ed. Twin Lakes, Wisc.: Lotus Press, 2000.

Frawley, David, and Subhash Ranade. *Ayurveda, Nature's Medicine.* Twin Lakes, Wisc.: Lotus Press, 2001.

Hope-Murray, Angela, and Tony Pickup. *Discover Ayurveda.* Berkeley, Calif.: Ulysses Press, 1998.

Joshi, Sunil V. *Ayurveda and Panchakarma: The Science of Healing and Rejuvenation.* Twin Lakes, Wisc.: Lotus Press, 1997.

Morrison, Judith H. *The Book of Ayurveda: A Holistic Approach to Health and Longevity.* New York: Fireside Press, 1995.

Ninivaggi, Frank John, M.D. *An Elementary Textbook of Ayurveda: A 6000 Year Old Healing Tradition.* Madison, Conn.: Psychosocial Press, 2001.

Tirtha, Swami Sada Shiva. *The Ayurveda Encyclopedia: Natural Secrets to Healing, Prevention, & Longevity.* Houston, Texas: Ayurveda Holistic Center Press, 1998.

According to Scott Gerson, M.D., a fully trained Ayurvedic doctor who runs the National Institute of Ayurvedic Medicine (NIAM), specializing in internal medicine or family practice is usually the best route for those who wish to become Ayurvedic doctors, although it is possible to combine other medical specialties with Ayurvedic practice in a beneficial way. Those who wish to combine Ayurveda with careers as nutritionists, psychologists, naturopaths, and so forth must complete the educational and training requirements for those specialties as well as study Ayurveda. It is not a good idea to go into business in a Western country simply as an expert in Ayurveda, since no licensing is available and doing so may leave you open to charges of practicing medicine without a license.

The single most important part of a doctor's or practitioner's Ayurvedic training is the completion of a rigorous course of study and practice. Naturally, a student who wishes to practice should select the most comprehensive course available. An excellent way to learn Ayurveda is to study at a good Indian institution and become a full-fledged Ayurvedic doctor in India. That kind of program typically takes five years to complete and also involves supervised practice afterward. Remember, though, that being licensed in India does not make it legal to practice as a doctor in the West. Alternatively, a student may study in the West, where various institutions offer Ayurvedic training. NIAM offers a three-year program in Ayurvedic medicine (see contact information at the end of this article).

Other Requirements

Ayurvedic practitioners and doctors work closely with their clients, so it is essential that they be able to gain their clients' or patients' trust, make them comfortable and relaxed, and communicate effectively enough with them to gather the information that they need in order to treat them effectively. It is unlikely that an uncommunicative person who is uncomfortable with people will be able to build a successful Ayurvedic practice. In addition, a practitioner must be comfortable making decisions and working alone.

Although some jobs are available in alternative health practices, most Ayurvedic doctors and practitioners have their own practices, and anyone who sets up shop will need to deal with the basic tasks and problems that all business owners face: advertising, accounting, taxes, legal requirements, and so forth. In addition, because Ayurveda is rooted in Hinduism, people whose religious beliefs are in conflict with Hinduism or who are uncomfortable with organized religion may be unwilling or unable to practice Ayurveda effectively.

EXPLORING

The best way to learn about Ayurveda is to speak with those who practice it. Call practitioners and ask to interview them. Find practitioners in your area if you can, but do not hesitate to contact people in other areas. There is no substitute for learning from those who actually do the work. Although many practitioners run one-person practices, it may be possible to find work of some kind with a successful practitioner or a clinic in your area, especially if you live in a large city.

You should also do as much reading as you can on the subject. Many books on Ayurveda are available. Also look for information on Ayurveda in magazines that deal with alternative medicine or Hinduism. You may also wish to read about traditional Oriental medicine, which is similar to Ayurveda in many ways.

EMPLOYERS

For the most part, Ayurvedic practitioners work for themselves, although some teach in institutions and others work for alternative clinics.

STARTING OUT

In addition to receiving training in medicine or in another professional field of your choice, you should begin by taking the best, most comprehensive Ayurvedic course of study you can find. After that, if you have not found an organization that you can work for, you should begin to practice on your own. You may rent an office or set up shop at home. Be sure to investigate the state and local laws that affect you.

A practitioner who runs his or her own business must be well versed in basic business skills. Take courses in business or get advice from the local office of the Small Business Administration. Seek advice from people you know who run their own businesses. Your financial survival will depend on your business skills, so be sure that you are as well prepared as possible.

ADVANCEMENT

Because most Ayurvedic doctors and practitioners work for themselves, advancement in the field is directly related to the quality of treatment they provide and their business skills. Ayurvedic practitioners can advance in their field by proving to the members of their community that they are skilled, honest, professional, and effective. Before they can be financially successful, there must be a strong demand for their services.

EARNINGS

Generally, Ayurvedic doctors earn what most doctors in their fields of specialty earn. The situation is the same for practitioners, who generally earn what other people in their fields earn. It is probably safe to say that Ayurvedic practitioners on the low end make $20,000 per year and up, practitioners in more lucrative fields make between $35,000 and $60,000. Ayurvedic doctors earn amounts up to—and in some cases even more than—$150,000.

WORK ENVIRONMENT

Ayurvedic practitioners usually work in their own homes or offices. Some practitioners may have office help, while others work alone. For this reason, they must be independent enough to work effectively on their own. Because they must make their clients comfortable in order to provide effective treatment, they generally try to make their workplaces as pleasant and relaxing as possible.

OUTLOOK

Although no official government analysis of the future of Ayurveda has yet been conducted, it seems safe to say that the field is expanding more rapidly than the average for all fields. Although science still views it with skepticism, Ayurveda has become relatively popular in a short period of time, largely because of the popularity of Deepak Chopra, an Ayurvedic expert who is also an M.D. It has certainly benefited from the popular acceptance of alternative medicine and therapies in recent years, particularly because it is a holistic practice that aims to treat the whole person rather than the symptoms of disease or discomfort. Because Western medicine is too often mechanical and dehumanizing, many people are looking for alternative forms of medicine.

FOR MORE INFORMATION

The AIVS provides on-site and correspondence training in Ayurveda, as well as courses in Sanskrit and other subjects that are of interest to Ayurvedic practitioners. It should be noted that correspondence courses do not qualify one as a practitioner, but they do prepare one for more in-depth training.

American Institute of Vedic Studies (AIVS)
PO Box 8357
Santa Fe, NM 87504-8357
Tel: 505-983-9385
Email: vedicinst@aol.com
http://www.vedanet.com

The Ayurvedic Institute offers both on-site and correspondence courses in Ayurveda. Some of the organization's resources are available only to those who pay a membership fee.

Ayurvedic Institute
11311 Menaul Boulevard, NE
Albuquerque, NM 87112
Tel: 505-291-9698
Email: info@ayurveda.com
http://www.ayurveda.com

Deepak Chopra's Center does not offer training for practitioners, but it does offer courses for those who are interested in using Ayurveda in their own lives.

Chopra Center at La Costa Resort and Spa
2013 Costa del Mar Road
Carlsbad, CA 92009
Tel: 888-424-6772
Email: info@chopra.com
http://www.chopra.com

The NIAM offers on-site training, sells correspondence courses, and sells Ayurvedic books and supplies. It offers a three-year training program in Ayurveda.

**National Institute of Ayurvedic Medicine
    (NIAM)**
584 Milltown Road
Brewster, NY 10509
Tel: 845-278-8700
Email: niam@niam.com
http://www.niam.com

Baggage Porters and Bellhops

■ OVERVIEW

Baggage porters and *bellhops,* known at some hotels as *uniformed service attendants, bell attendants,* or *guest services attendants,* are considered front-of-the-house jobs in the hotel industry. They are responsible for carrying guests' luggage to their room upon arrival and back to the lobby when they depart. At times they may be asked to run errands or deliver items for guests. Though bellhops work from the bellstand—a desk or podium located in the hotel lobby—their work takes them all over the hotel property. Bellhops are also employed at airports, bus terminals, train stations, and just about any place of travel.

There are about 57,650 baggage porters and bellhops employed in the United States.

■ HISTORY

Early in the hotel industry, the innkeepers—the hotel owners and their immediate families—were responsible for every aspect of running a hotel. Besides working the front desk, cleaning the rooms, and cooking the food, they also had to carry guests' trunks and bags. As the industry grew, innkeepers, many of whom had more than one hotel to manage, found themselves in need of reliable employees. The bellhop occupation grew from the idea of ultimate guest service. Many of the larger luxurious hotels have numerous bellhops in their bellstand department.

Bellhops and baggage porters are found in other areas of the travel and tourism industry as well. They work at transportation terminals such as airports, train stations, and cruise ships. In the late 1800s, the Pullman trains hired men, many of whom were African Americans, to work as porters for their first class sleeper cars. Referred to as Pullman porters, they were famous for the fine service and attention they gave to the first class passengers. The early Pullman porters had to abide by a strict behavior and work code and were highly respected members of the community. In time, Pullman porters became somewhat a symbol of black subservience, and the career became less popular.

■ THE JOB

Edward Wilson, a uniformed service attendant at the Hotel Intercontinental, Chicago, Illinois, starts his eight-hour shift at 7:00 A.M. There's no time for chatting or even a morning cup of coffee because a long morning of early checkouts and storage requests is about to begin. "We're really busy from about seven to nine in the morning," says Wilson. Guests who need to store their luggage until a flight later in the day can have the bellstand place their belongings in the storage area, more commonly known as the back closet. After guests are given claim tickets for each piece of luggage, the bags are stored according to size and weight. There is a late morning slow period before the crunch of the afternoon arrivals and check-ins.

All attendants are taught the proper way to carry a bag, especially the heavy ones, so as not to injure themselves. Many times guests will have questions about the room services, the hotel property, or the area surrounding the hotel. If Wilson or the other attendants cannot readily help, they direct the guests to the proper department. Sometimes Wilson is asked to deliver packages, mail, or faxes to guests or to run errands for them. If the hotel is particularly busy, he may help in other departments. Depending on the hotel, attendants may be asked to assist guests with disabilities, deliver ice or other supplies, provide directions to area attractions, or even drive the hotel van.

Tips are not mandatory, though hotel guests often give them in appreciation for good service. Attendants are allowed to keep the tips they receive, as compared to other industries where tips are pooled and divided equally among each employee. At the Hotel Intercontinental, Wilson and the other attendants are sent out in rotation. This method is fair and leaves working for big tippers to the "luck of the draw."

Much of Wilson's job relates to how well he deals with people—hotel guests and his co-workers. He views his fellow attendants as members of a team. "If I'm having a hard day at work," he says, "I can always count on the guys to crack a joke, cheer me up, and get me going again."

■ REQUIREMENTS
High School

There is no educational requirement for this position, though many hotels will insist that you have a high school diploma or a GED equivalent. Classes that will help pre-

QUICK FACTS

SCHOOL SUBJECTS
Physical education
Speech

PERSONAL SKILLS
Following instructions
Helping/teaching

WORK ENVIRONMENT
Primarily indoors
Primarily one location

MINIMUM EDUCATION LEVEL
High school diploma

SALARY RANGE
$6.10 per hour to $8.58 per hour to $20.29 per hour

CERTIFICATION OR LICENSING
Voluntary

OUTLOOK
About as fast as the average

DOT
324

GOE
11.03.01

NOC
6672

O*NET-SOC
39-6011.00

pare you for this work include any that will hone your people and communications skills as well as classes that will make you physically fit. Therefore, you should take English and speech classes, any business classes that focus on customer relations, and physical education classes. Edward Wilson credits his high school speech class in particular in helping him deal with the large and diverse groups of guests at the hotel. You may also benefit from taking basic math classes, local history courses, and geography. Bell attendants are often asked for information about the area or directions to special attractions, so you will do well to know as much as you can about the location surrounding the hotel where you work.

Certification or Licensing

Certification is not mandatory for this position. The most significant source of instruction for most bellhops is on-the-job training that may last up to one month. "At the Hotel Intercontinental, we had a week-long training program," says Wilson. "We were taught the correct way to handle bags and how to store them properly according to their weight class."

If certification does interest you, the Educational Institute of the American Hotel and Lodging Association offers training and certification classes for bellhops and baggage porters and other members of uniformed service. If you aspire to manage the bellstand someday or move to other departments in the hotel industry, you might want to consider certification.

Other Requirements

What makes a successful bellhop? Wilson says, "You should have good character and a friendly personality." Since bell attendants are often one of the first hotel employees with whom a guest interacts, it's important for them to make a good impression. This is a very people-oriented job. Even the most difficult guests must be served in an amiable and efficient manner. An outgoing personality and a desire to meet people from all over the country and world are good traits to have.

■ EMPLOYERS

Some of the smaller and simpler motels do not offer services such as those provided by bellhops. Most larger hotels, however, will often employ more than one bellhop per shift. This is especially true for large hotels located in busy urban areas, near airports, and hotels known for their luxury atmosphere. Other places of employment are Amtrak train stations, where porters, sometimes known as *red caps,* provide baggage help and airports, where those who help customers with bags may be known as *skycaps.*

A baggage porter takes a customer's luggage to the lobby.

■ STARTING OUT

Edward Wilson found his job through a church-sponsored job search program. He was looking to change careers when he came across a job description for the Hotel Intercontinental bellstand department. Other methods for finding similar jobs include job fairs, job placement centers, newspaper want ads, and the Internet. Large hotels with Web sites often include postings of job openings, and a number of job agencies deal specifically with placing those interested in hospitality jobs (for example, visit the Web site http://www.hospitalityonline.com). Don't forget the old-fashioned way of job hunting: Hit the pavement. Apply directly to the hotel's human resource department.

■ ADVANCEMENT

With enough work experience, go-getters can advance to the position of *bell captain.* Bell captains supervise the bellstand, give assignments to the bellhops, and take calls. Most hotels employ two bell captains, one each for the day and night shifts. Another position for advancement is that of *bellstand manager.* Considered the head of the department, bellstand managers are responsible for making work schedules, assigning extra staff when forecasts are heavy, and resolving any service problems.

■ EARNINGS

Most bell attendants are paid at an hourly rate, which may range from $6.10 per hour for the lowest 10 percent (making a yearly income of $12,690 for full-time work) to as high as $20.29 per hour for the highest 10 percent. The median salary is $8.58 an hour, or $17,860 per year. Bellhops are often paid the minimum wage, which varies by state, and in some cases is higher than the federal minimum of $5.15 per hour (or $10,712 annually for full-time work). For example, California has a minimum wage of $6.75 per hour (or $14,040 annually for full-time work). Some municipalities have even higher minimum wages; San Francisco's, for instance, is $8.50 per hour. Bell attendants' total earnings, however, are greatly supplemented with tips, which may add $100 a week or more to their income. A common rule for tipping bellhops is about $1 to $2 per piece of luggage. At some large, busy hotels bellhops may earn up to $100 a day in tips alone.

Full-time employees are offered health insurance, sick and vacation time, and employee discounts. Some hotels give discounted room rates for their employees.

■ WORK ENVIRONMENT

Their work takes bellhops all over the hotel property. They may be asked to unload luggage from a taxi and deliver it to a sleeping room, then be sent to a store to pick up a guest's special request. When the hotel is at full capacity, bellhops may be asked to help other departments, such as the concierge, mail department, or business center.

At larger hotels, there is usually more than one bellhop per shift. If checking in big groups or a guest with an extraordinarily large amount of luggage, attendants may be asked to work in pairs, so it helps to be a team player. Edward Wilson especially likes the camaraderie with the other attendants.

■ OUTLOOK

According to the U.S. Department of Labor, this field is expected to grow about as fast as the average through 2012. Employment in the hospitality industry, however, is greatly influenced by economic conditions, national events, and international events. During times of recession, fewer people spend money traveling for pleasure and businesses cut back on travel expenditures for employees. Additionally, events such as the terrorist attacks of September 11, 2001, have a powerful, adverse effect on this industry. And since future attacks are unpredictable, the threat of terrorism will remain a destabilizing factor for the employment outlook of those in the industry. In addition to these negative factors on employment for bell attendants, many motels and smaller hotels increasingly are offering discounted sleeping rooms but very little service. Guests are expected to locate their rooms and carry their luggage. Some travelers, especially those on limited budgets, prefer to stay at these types of establishments. If this trend continues, there will be fewer jobs available for bellhops.

Nevertheless, job openings will be created as workers leave due to retirement, job transfers, or for other reasons. Bellhops often have a high turnover rate. Large hotels and those focusing on customer comfort will always have a need for the bellstand department and bellhops. Part of a four-star hotel's appeal rests in the sense of luxury and guest service provided. Bellhops and baggage porters at such lodging establishments are as much an expectation as they are a necessity. Baggage porters will continue to work at other travel venues such as the train or bus depot. Baggage service at airports, also known as Skycap service, is also popular.

■ FOR MORE INFORMATION

For industry and career development information, contact
American Hotel and Lodging Association
1201 New York Avenue, NW, Suite 600
Washington, DC 20005-3931
Tel: 202-289-3100
Email: informationcenter@ahla.com
http://www.ahla.com

For information regarding training and certification, contact
American Hotel and Lodging Association
Educational Institute
800 North Magnolia Avenue, Suite 1800
Orlando, FL 32803
Tel: 800-752-4567
http://www.ei-ahla.org

Bail Bondsmen

■ OVERVIEW

When someone is arrested for a crime, a *bail bondsman* (also known as a *bail agent* or *bail bonding agent*) pays the bail so that person can go free until it is time for the trial. The bondsman charges a fee of 10 to 15 percent of the total cash bond assigned by the court. If the person doesn't appear for trial, the bondsman must either find the person or hire someone, known as a *bail enforcement agent, fugitive recovery agent,* or *bounty hunter,* to find the person and bring him or her back. Because the work bondsmen do relies on criminal activities, larger cities have the greatest need for bondsmen.

HISTORY

Bail bonding is a long-established tradition of the American legal system. Posting bail to temporarily free someone who is accused of a crime began in colonial times. Colonists lived under the English common law that they brought with them. People who were charged with crimes were released if someone in the community would vouch for them. At first, if the accused person didn't show up for the trial, the person who guaranteed the accused person's appearance had to face the punishment that would have been given to the accused person. Later, this practice changed so that property was used to guarantee the appearance of someone for trial. In that way, if the person failed to appear for trial, the person who promised that the accused would appear only lost property and did not have to face punishment. As crime increased and the need for making sure accused people showed up for court grew, the courts continued to allow the practice of posting bail. In fact, the Eighth Amendment to the U.S. Constitution states: "Excessive bail shall not be required, nor excessive fines imposed, nor cruel and unusual punishments inflicted." Bail bonding today allows jail space to be freed for serious criminals and helps to ensure that everyone is truly "innocent until proven guilty."

THE JOB

Bail bondsmen work to ensure that a person released from jail will appear again in court as ordered. A "typical" case (although, in reality, every case is unique) a bail bondsman handles may play out like this: It's late at night and the bondsman's office phone rings. A woman on the other end of the line says her son has been arrested and his court date for trial is four months down the road. The judge set her son's bail at $30,000, and she doesn't have that kind of money. She doesn't want her son to sit in jail for four months for something she's sure he didn't do. (The bondsman may have doubts about the arrested person's guilt or innocence, but that's not an issue for the bondsman to decide.) The mother wants the bondsman's help in getting her son out on bail. She offers to pay the bondsman's fee, which at 10 percent of the bail amount would be $3,000, in exchange for the bondsman covering the bail. At that point the bondsman must decide if the son is a good risk—if he doesn't show up for his court date, the bondsman loses the money posted for bail. Before deciding to take the case, the bondsman does research. Using the phone and computers, the bonding agent gathers more information, such as the type of crime the son allegedly committed, any past record he may have, if he works and what his employer says about him, and what other ties he has to the community. After this research, the bondsman may decide to post bond or reject the case. If the bondsman takes the case and posts bond, and the client shows up for his court date, the bondsman gets the posted money back. If the client fails to show up for court, either the bondsman himself goes after the client or the bondsman hires bounty hunters (also known as bail enforcement agents and fugitive recovery agents) to track down the son and bring him back. Depending on the state, the court gives the bondsman from 90 to 180 days to have the defendant back for trial before bail money is forfeited to the court system.

Like insurance agents, bail bondsmen are calculated risk takers. Every time they decide to post bail for someone, they are taking a financial risk. Most bondsmen have reliability standards that they use to determine whether someone is more likely to show up for court or to run and hide. The bondsman looks into the person's criminal record, employment history, living arrangements, family situation, and community ties. The type of alleged crime also affects whether a person will run. The arrestee's past criminal record and the state's case against him or her is looked into as well. Some bondsmen consider first time offenders bad risks because those people are often most terrified about going to jail. People who have a history of crime patterns, such as prostitutes and drug users, are also considered bad risks. On the other hand, drug dealers and professional criminals are good risks because these groups of people usually need to stay in the same area and they want to keep the trust of a bondsman so they can rely on him or her later.

To help cut down the risk of someone "jumping bail," the bondsman spends a lot of time monitoring the people for whom bail has been posted. Some even include a stipulation in the agreement for posting bail that the accused person must call in on a regular basis to verify his or her whereabouts. If the accused person isn't calling in on schedule, the bondsman can get a head start on tracking down the client.

QUICK FACTS

SCHOOL SUBJECTS
Business
Government
Mathematics

PERSONAL SKILLS
Communication/ideas
Leadership/management

WORK ENVIRONMENT
Indoors and outdoors
Primarily multiple locations

MINIMUM EDUCATION LEVEL
Some postsecondary training

SALARY RANGE
$21,730 to $40,750 to $101,460

CERTIFICATION OR LICENSING
Required by certain states

OUTLOOK
About as fast as the average

DOT
186

GOE
04.03.01

NOC
N/A

O*NET-SOC
N/A

For some bondsmen, tracking down bail jumpers is part of their job, and it takes up much of their time. Other bondsmen choose to hire bounty hunters, who capture and return the client to the bondsman for a fee. Sometimes the bondsman will pay the bounty hunter as much as 50 percent of the total bond if the accused person is returned. The bondsman pays this high amount because it's better to lose half the money that has been posted for bail than to lose all the money if the runaway isn't returned. For the bail bondsman who takes tracking into his or her own hands, the search can lead all over the country. The bondsmen call the accused's family, friends, employers, and anyone they can find to try and get a lead that will eventually take them to the bail jumper. They use computer databases to check into records showing credit activity, estates, and death certificates. When the person is located, the bondsman or bounty hunter confronts the individual and brings him or her back. For a potentially dangerous "skip," the bounty hunter and a backup team may have to break down a door with guns drawn, or opt to work with the local sheriff's department in the instance of known violent offenders.

Bail Me Out!

If you are arrested, you can't just flash a Get Out of Jail Free card and continue on your way. You do have four options; any or all of them may or may not be available to you depending on the court's decision.

- **Cash bail:** If you or someone on your behalf posts the full amount of the cash bail, you are free to go until your court date. If you show up for all proceedings, the money is returned to you. If you don't show up, the money is forfeited to the court.

- **Property bond:** Some states allow you or others on your behalf to put up property (like a house, boat, land) as a guarantee that you will return on the court date. The same consequences apply if you don't appear on the court date, the property is seized and later sold.

- **Personal recognizance:** This is the closest thing to a Get Out of Jail Free card—you are released and instructed to return for your court date. No money or property is put up to guarantee your return; the court is trusting in your character and conscience to bring you back. You're most likely to get this type of bail only if the crime is a minor one and you are well-known in the community.

- **Surety bail:** This is just another way of saying that a bail bondsman insures your return. You pay the bondsman a fee and the bondsman posts the bail with the court.

Some bondsmen use firearms to protect themselves from possible harm. However, the bail bondsman's job is mostly desk work, and often the reason a client misses a court date is because he or she has overslept, forgotten about it, or thought it was for a different day and time.

■ REQUIREMENTS

While the qualifications vary from state to state, the basic requirements for a bail bondsman are to be at least 18 or 21 years of age, have a high school diploma or GED, and have no felony police record.

High School

To prepare for a career as a bail bondsman, consider focusing on computers, accounting, mathematics, government, social studies, and geography. Accounting, computers, and mathematics will prepare you to handle bookkeeping, record keeping, and negotiations concerning bail money. Because you'll be using a computer for tracing bail jumpers, try to spend as much time as you can honing your computer skills.

Postsecondary Training

Some college-level course work in criminal justice and psychology and training in law enforcement techniques are helpful. Many of today's bail bondsmen have college degrees in criminal justice, although that is not a requirement. Depending on your state's regulations, you may need to complete a certain amount of specific pre-work and pre-licensing education. For example, one of Oklahoma's requirements for those wishing to work as bail bondsmen is to complete 16 hours of education sponsored by the Oklahoma Bondsman Association before they can sit for their licensing exam and begin working.

Certification or Licensing

Some states require would-be bail bondsmen to attain a property and casualty insurance license requiring several hours of class work under the jurisdiction of the State Director of Insurance or State Department of Professional Regulation. Wisconsin, Illinois, Oregon, and Kentucky ban for-profit bail bonding altogether. Other states require you to pass a bail-bond certification exam. Most states that require exams or licensing also require several hours of continuing education classes each year to keep the license current. You will need a gun license if you plan to use a firearm.

Other Requirements

Bail bondsmen need to have people skills that allow them to effectively communicate with the clients and law enforcement officers they contact daily. They must also be able to deal with high levels of stress and tense situations. Bail bondsmen who do not hire bounty hunters must be physically fit in order to be prepared for any violent or challenging situation.

■ EXPLORING

You can explore this career by becoming familiar with the justice system. For example, ask your high school guidance counselor or government teacher to help you arrange for a visit to the local police department. You can get a tour of the facilities, learn about arrest procedures, and hear from law enforcement professionals. In some cases, you may be able to arrange for a police ride-along to get a taste of what it takes to arrest or confront someone who does not want to cooperate. You can also familiarize yourself with the justice system by sitting in on open court proceedings. Another option is to give a bail bondsman a call and ask questions. Get on the Web and search under "bail bonding" to see just how many bail bondsmen are out there; check out their Web sites to learn what kinds of services are offered. Finally, try to get a part-time job that allows you to deal face-to-face with other people—anything from a crowd control team member at a concert to a security assistant at an amusement park. Working for a security office or for the local court system as a background checker is great experience as well.

■ EMPLOYERS

Bail bondsmen usually work for other bondsmen or own their own small businesses. Many bondsmen join together to form a partnership to share the workload and to pool their resources. Established bondsmen usually hire several young bondsmen to do the background checking and research. Although almost all towns and cities have bail bondsmen at work, most bondsmen are in large towns and cities. The larger the population, the greater the opportunity for crime and the greater the number of crimes committed, which means the greater the need for bail bonds to be posted.

■ STARTING OUT

You probably won't see as many ads in the newspaper for bondsmen as you do for say, administrative assistants, but keep an eye on the classifieds anyway—especially in the big city newspapers. If you want a more direct approach, try calling your local police for some recommendations of experienced bondsmen that you can contact to inquire about a job. Before becoming a bondsman, get your feet wet by doing background checks, chasing down leads, and handling paperwork. If work as a bondsman isn't immediately available, start out in related jobs, such as security positions. Quite a number of bail agents also

---

WHAT EVERY BONDSMAN SHOULD KNOW

Talk to anyone who is knowledgeable about bail bonding and bail bondsmen, and many of the following terms of the trade are sure to be heard.

Bail enforcement agent: Commonly known as a *bounty hunter,* the bail enforcement agent tracks down and arrests a bail skipper.

Collateral: Property that is sometimes given to the bail agent to guarantee payment.

Failure to appear: The defendant doesn't show up for the court date, and the bondsman begins the process for tracking the person down.

Premium: The bail bondsman's fee for posting bail for someone.

Skip: Not only does the defendant not show up, he or she runs and hides from law enforcement officials and the bondsman or the bondsman's bail enforcement agent. These bail "skippers" don't have the odds on their side.

---

start out in the insurance business, learning such things as risk assessment and how to underwrite bonds.

■ ADVANCEMENT

A bail bondsman can remain an independent agent, owning his or her own business, or can advance to managerial positions with a managing general agent. In a partnership, a bondsman can advance to become the *supervising bondsman,* assigning work to more inexperienced bondsmen. There are various jobs that relate to the work of bail bondsmen, such as property and casualty insurance agent, detective, and the court system jobs of pretrial release officer, release on recognizance worker, and probation officer.

■ EARNINGS

Because most bondsmen have their own businesses, earnings vary according to how much time and effort is invested in the job. Another important factor influencing the earnings of bail bondsmen is the number of their clients who show up for their court dates. According to the National Center for Policy Analysis in Dallas, 95 percent of a bondsman's clients must show up in court for the business to be successful. According to information from the *Occupational Outlook Quarterly,* a Bureau of Labor Statistics publication, bail bondsmen just starting out and working for a firm may have yearly earnings of approximately $25,000. The bails set for many common charges, such as driving under the influence (DUI) and drug possession, are often not extremely high, perhaps ranging from $500 or $600 to $3,000 or $4,000. In these cases a bondsman would earn $50 or $60 to $300 or $400, and because of these low amounts a bondsman must successfully handle quite a few cases a year to make a substantial living. While a specific annual salary range is difficult to determine, it may be helpful to consider earnings for insurance sales agents since bondsmen's work is similar to that of insurance agents and they are often regulated under state departments of insurance. According to the U.S. Department of Labor, the median yearly income for insurance sales agents in 2002 was $40,750. Fifty percent earned between $28,860 and $64,450 that same year, while the lowest 10 percent had earnings of $21,730 or less, and the highest 10 percent had earnings of over $101,460. Earnings also depend on where the bondsman conducts business. Larger cities offer the most opportunity to make money; however, a well-run business in a medium-sized city can also be highly profitable.

Bondsmen working for firms may receive typical benefits such as health insurance and vacation time. Those who run their own businesses must pay for such benefits themselves.

■ WORK ENVIRONMENT

Bondsmen work out of offices; some do the work from their homes. Usually the bondsman is located close to the courthouse so the accused can get immediate service. Bondsmen can work alone or as a team with other bondsmen and people who monitor clients and research background information. Bondsmen spend a lot of time doing paperwork; they must keep records detailing all of their actions and contracts with clients.

Bail bondsmen who choose to do their own tracking may also spend time traveling to find bail jumpers. Tracking bail jumpers and bringing them back to court can be dangerous because these people are obviously desperate to remain free.

Bail bonding is not a nine-to-five job. Because people get arrested at all hours, bondsmen are on call 24 hours a day. If a bail jumper needs to be rounded up, hours are spent in surveillance to determine just the right moment to move in.

Bondsmen are in contact with many different people during the course of a day. They interview friends and relatives of a bail jumper and work with court personnel. Bondsmen use beepers and cellular phones to remain available to clients who may need their services.

■ OUTLOOK

Opportunities for bail-bonding work are growing as people with criminal justice, law enforcement, and insurance training enter and gain success in the field, thus gaining the public's respect for the necessity of this work.

Professional Bail Agents of the United States says the bail bondsman career is a growing field, but the use of personal recognizance bail has had a negative impact on its growth. (When judges release an accused person on their own personal recognizance, there is no need for bail bond service; however, there is also no guarantee that the person will show up for court.)

Bail bonding is an industry under constant scrutiny by the justice system, primarily because of the authority of the bail bondsman to engage in activities that some law enforcers cannot perform (such as entering homes without a warrant in search of a bail jumper and crossing state lines to apprehend someone) and what is said to be a financial rather than moral interest in bringing criminals back to trial.

■ FOR MORE INFORMATION

Visit this coalition's website for information on bail laws and bounty hunter laws nationwide, state associations, and industry news.

American Bail Coalition
1725 Desales Street, NW, Suite 800
Washington, DC 20036
Tel: 800-375-8390
Email: dnabic@aol.com
http://www.americanbailcoalition.com

For general information about the field and for specific information about working in California, contact

California Bail Agents Association
1127 11th Street, Suite 331
Sacramento, CA 95814-3809
Tel: 916-446-3038
http://www.cbaa.com

For more information on the work of bail bondsmen and links of interest, visit the PBUS website.

Professional Bail Agents of the United States (PBUS)
444 North Capitol Street, NW, Suite 805
Washington, DC 20001
Tel: 800-883-7287
Email: info@pbus.com
http://www.pbus.com

Bailiffs

■ OVERVIEW

Bailiffs handle anything and everything that goes on in and is associated with a courtroom. From keeping the room secure to providing food and housing for sequestered juries, the bailiff is responsible for managing the court's business. Bailiffs also serve legal papers to individuals and businesses as ordered by the court. Although the majority of bailiffs work for the court system, some bailiffs are more like process servers because they work independently and own their own businesses. The Bureau of Labor Statistics reports there are approximately 14,390 bailiffs employed in the United States.

■ HISTORY

The first bailiffs date back to medieval England. Bailiffs in this time period were either in charge of managing a manor or managing a court. Bailiffs who worked for manors or estates had the responsibility of collecting fines and rent as well as supervising the activities on the grounds. Court bailiffs helped the judges during the two sessions of the Royal Court that were held every year. The early predecessor of the modern bailiff had police authority to protect the court and serve legal papers as well.

In America, the constable performed many of the duties that now fall on the bailiff's shoulders. Along with the more pressing duty of keeping the peace, the constable attended to the courts and was responsible for taking care of jury members.

Today, a bailiff is considered an officer of the court who has the authority to serve legal papers and confiscate property. Like the medieval bailiff and the American constable, modern bailiffs are responsible for attending to the needs of the court while it is in session and out of session.

■ THE JOB

The majority of bailiffs in the United States serve in the court or legal system; however, some bailiffs own their own service businesses. Most people are more familiar with the *courtroom bailiff* who instructs people in the court to rise and be seated when the judge does and who swears in witnesses. These tasks and many others make up the courtroom bailiff's main duty, which is to serve the judge and the courtroom to which he or she is assigned. Depending on the state in which the bailiff is employed and the judge, the duties vary, but all bailiffs in the court system have some common responsibilities. First, the bailiff must maintain order during trials. Security is an important part of the bailiff's job. Although the judge and the jury are the bailiff's first concern, every person in the courtroom is under the care of the bailiff as far as personal safety is concerned. If a bailiff is in tune with the goings-on in the court, potential problems can be avoided and trouble can be spotted before it erupts. Bailiffs are most respected if they run a safe and secure courtroom.

For Armando Suarez, a security transportation officer for the Juvenile Court in Allen County, Indiana, ensuring secure transportation and a safe environment at court are large parts of his job. "My primary responsibility is the transfer of juvenile inmates between the detention facility and our local courthouse. Once at the courthouse, my partner and I are responsible for maintaining security and safety in the juvenile courts division."

The bailiff is basically the judge's right hand. The bailiff swears in witnesses, handles articles of evidence, escorts prisoners to and from court, prepares reports, and does whatever else the judge may ask. Paperwork is also a segment of the bailiff's responsibilities, although the focus depends on the type of court in which the bailiff serves. "I am also responsible for processing all juvenile warrants by dispersing them to local law enforcement and issuing notices of cancellation when appropriate," Suarez adds. "Another part of my job entails collecting criminal records on those whom the court has ordered such information collected. This can be either on parents or guardians of juveniles in custody, persons applying for positions in the juvenile courts, or for purposes of determining court dispositions." Bailiffs must also remind people of courtroom rules and enforce those rules if necessary. For example, a bailiff may tell someone in the court that smoking is not allowed or that their conversation is interrupting court proceedings. If necessary, the bailiff may remove uncooperative persons from the courtroom.

Courtroom bailiffs are often also charged with taking care of the jury. When juries are sequestered, that is, not allowed to return to their homes during a trial, the bailiff must make arrangements for their food and lodging during the entire trial process. The bailiff usually accompanies jury members to any public places, such as restaurants, to make sure they do not have contact with the public. If a bailiff fails to keep the jury from seeing or hearing anything about

QUICK FACTS

SCHOOL SUBJECTS
English
Government

PERSONAL SKILLS
Communication/ideas
Following instructions

WORK ENVIRONMENT
Primarily indoors
Primarily one location

MINIMUM EDUCATION LEVEL
Some postsecondary training

SALARY RANGE
$16,870 to $32,710 to $55,270

CERTIFICATION OR LICENSING
Required by certain states

OUTLOOK
About as fast as the average

DOT
377

GOE
04.03.01

NOC
6461

O*NET-SOC
33-3011.00

the case at hand, the jury members may have to be replaced and the court proceedings brought to a grinding halt. The bailiff also serves as a guard wherever the jury is staying.

Outside the confines of the courtroom and the responsibilities of the jury, the bailiff also serves legal papers such as court summonses, restraining orders, and jury summonses. *Independent bailiffs* also serve this function. They act as process servers and track down individuals or companies to serve them legal documents. Independent bailiffs also collect money or property that has defaulted back under a lease, lien, or mortgage. A bailiff may get an assignment to repossess a vehicle, for instance, or to inform tenants that the landlord is throwing them out because they haven't paid the rent for six months. Independent bailiff work is usually done on an assignment or contract basis in which someone calls the bailiff and pays for a specific, one-time service.

■ REQUIREMENTS
High School

Do you find the idea of managing a courtroom intriguing? If you think a career as a bailiff might be right for you, start preparing for it while you're still in school. Take political science, communications, and law-related high school courses. If you have the opportunity to earn certificates in emergency skills, such as CPR or triage, take advantage of it as you prepare for a career that is centered on security and safety. Jim Marlow of Niagara Bailiff Ser-

---

BAILIFFS OF OLD

From medieval times in England to today, bailiffs have carried out various duties in service to individuals and courts. Although the term bailiff is used as a blanket term today, that is, it covers all services offered by bailiffs in the court process, in the past different kinds of bailiffs performed specific tasks. Consider the following titles and responsibilities for bailiffs in the past:

Bailiff-errant: A bailiff's deputy.

Bailiffs of franchises: In English law, these officers performed some of the duties of the sheriff's office.

Bedel: In English law, this court officer had the sole responsibility to summon men to appear in the court and make other public proclamations.

High bailiff: This bailiff worked expressly with the English county court.

Special bailiff: Specially appointed bailiff to serve papers or conduct some official proceeding for a one-time, specific case.

---

vices recommends computers and communication classes. "I believe this industry will rely more and more on technology in the future. Also, since this business has a lot of interaction between people, and sometimes these people are not happy to see us, I would recommend any course that would sharpen your 'people' skills."

Postsecondary Training

Many states require bailiffs to have training from police academies or from other programs approved by the local government's law enforcement training board. Smaller cities may substitute on-the-job training for police academy training. Since many courtroom bailiffs are assigned by sheriff's offices, the education requirements for bailiffs are generally the same as for other law enforcement officers. In fact, a good course of action is to contact your local sheriff's department and find out what deputy sheriff training programs are available. When you have completed the program and secured a position in the sheriff's department, you will have an inside edge for moving into a bailiff job. Training usually involves class work, meeting physical requirements, and getting supervised hands-on experience. Although college education is usually not required, many junior or community colleges offer classes related to public safety or protective services careers. Courses such as criminal law, report writing and communications, police functions, and ethics in the justice system can help you learn the courts and this type of work. The International Association of Court Officers & Services, Inc. (IACO&S), an affiliate of the National Sheriffs' Association (NSA), offers training, workshops, and seminars covering topics such as court security, transportation, and legal issues. IACO&S and NSA also sponsor a yearly court security conference. The NSA website (http://www.sheriffs.org) has more information on training and the IACO&S.

Certification or Licensing

Although most states do not require specific bailiff certification, certification as a peace officer or officer of the court is often required. States vary in their requirements; for example, requirements for bailiff certification in Missouri include completing a Peace Officer Standards and Training (POST) program, being at least 21 years of age, and having no criminal history. Candidates who fulfill such requirements and pass the Missouri Peace Officer Certification exam are then certified peace officers and can work as bailiffs. Other states may require bailiffs to be licensed law enforcement officers, such as police officers or sheriff's deputies. Some employers, such as sheriff's departments, may require bailiffs to have firearms certification. Other employers may require bailiffs to have valid driver's licenses for the state in which they work. Check with the law enforcement agency or your local courthouse to find out the specific requirements for your state.

Other Requirements

Bailiffs interact with many different kinds of people. From the judge, to the inmate, to the jury member, the bailiff must communicate effectively to ensure the organized flow of information in the courtroom. Bailiffs must be good listeners as well, because they must respond to requests for information and react to disturbances and problems. To be a successful bailiff, you must be able to speak clearly, respond quickly, concentrate on the task at hand, and be aware of potential trouble.

Also, because most bailiffs must be trained as law enforcement officers, you will need to pass physically demanding tests. Drug tests are also part of the requirements for becoming a peace officer.

■ EXPLORING

Do you like the sound of a career as a bailiff? If you'd like to know what it would really be like, take some steps on your own to explore the career and get some inside information. Any contact you can have with law enforcement officers will be a big plus. Contact your local police station and request a tour of the facilities. Explain that you are considering a law enforcement career and ask if anyone would be willing to talk to you about typical police work. Sit in on some hearings or trials at your local courthouse and pay close attention to every move the bailiff makes. Try to spot his or her main duties. Try to arrange an interview either at the courthouse or over the phone to ask the questions you'll no doubt have after seeing the bailiff in action. Talk to your guidance counselor or political science teacher about arranging a "Students in Court" day in which you and your friends play the role of different officers of the court in a mock trial. Do some research and interview a bailiff or two before the mock trial. Check into volunteer programs; many courts allow high school students to volunteer in various ways. If a program doesn't exist, suggest creating one to your school counselor or principal.

■ EMPLOYERS

Most bailiffs work for the state and local courts and are employed by sheriff departments. Some bailiffs are assigned to actual courtrooms and others are assigned to specific judges. Bailiffs work throughout the country, but more bailiff positions are usually found in larger cities as compared to the smaller ones. Independent bailiffs also work all across the country, although they too usually find more work in larger cities.

A bailiff hands court documents to the judge.

■ STARTING OUT

To get into the bailiff field, you must either be appointed by the sheriff's office or be hired after gaining experience as a peace officer. According to Armando Suarez, employment in the sheriff's office is the most common way to become a bailiff: "Most bailiffs are usually sheriffs' deputies or court officers assigned to work in the courts by the sheriff. If you are interested in this line of work, a career in law enforcement, specifically on a sheriff's department, would be the way to go." After you are working in the sheriff's department, making your desire to be a bailiff known is the best way to get an opportunity to move into that position when it becomes available.

■ ADVANCEMENT

Bailiffs can advance to many careers in the area of law enforcement. Because most bailiffs are appointed by the sheriff's office, they remain under the supervision of the sheriff. Bailiffs can often move into supervisory roles within the sheriff's department when they are prepared to end their work as bailiffs. Bailiffs can move laterally and become deputies focusing on something other than court security, or they can move up to become second-in-command or even sheriff. Additional training and experience are needed to move up to higher positions. Other possibilities include correctional officer and supervisory police officer. The many duties that a bailiff performs are an excellent preparation for most all other positions in law enforcement.

■ EARNINGS

Earnings for bailiffs are often subject to the budget amounts in the sheriff's department where the bailiff works. Bailiffs working for large, well-funded departments will have higher earnings than those at small departments with limited budgets. The Bureau of Labor Statistics estimates that bailiffs had a median yearly

IT'S NOT WHO YOU KNOW, IT'S WHAT YOU KNOW

Bailiffs are expected to know a lot about the courtroom process, but that's not all. To be a successful bailiff, you should be "in the know" about a lot of things. A well-rounded bailiff has knowledge in the following areas:

The Law: Makes sense, doesn't it? The bailiff needs to know the law of courtroom procedures, especially to ensure that all are abiding by them.

Security: You can't enforce security without some kind of force, so bailiffs must be knowledgeable about weapons, security operations and procedures, and prevention measures.

The Language: You knew those English term papers would come in handy some day! Bailiffs have to be able to speak so that others can understand. A solid command of our language is just as important as any other skill a bailiff possesses.

People: Bailiffs have to be ready for anything because they are working with defendants and inmates who may be dangerous or desperate. Learning how and why people behave the way they do can help the bailiff respond correctly. No, you don't have to get a degree in psychology, but learning how to manage people would be a great asset.

Source: Public Employment Service

income of $32,710 in 2002. In addition, the bureau estimates 10 percent of bailiffs earned less than $16,870 annually and 10 percent earned more than $55,270 annually during 2000.

Independent bailiffs are usually paid on a per-service contract, so income varies according to the prices set by the independent bailiff. Jim Marlow adds, "It is difficult to peg a salary for bailiffs, as most operate their own business. Bailiffs that work for another bailiff are usually paid a commission on the work completed."

Bailiffs usually receive comparable benefits to other sheriff's officers and deputies. Insurance, pension, vacation days, and other benefits are set by individual sheriff's departments.

■ WORK ENVIRONMENT

Most of a bailiff's workday is spent indoors in a courtroom or in an office building. The bailiff works with many different people, including all the courtroom personnel, not to mention other law enforcement officials, probation officers, court clerks, and so on. A bailiff is seldom alone and must interact with others all day long. Because of the nature of the work, bailiffs are often placed

in stressful situations and sometimes even dangerous ones. When not in the courtroom, a bailiff may transport prisoners or jury members to and from the courthouse. Bailiffs are also called on to leave the courtroom to serve papers or to conduct other official court business. Most of the bailiff's 40- to 45-hour workweek is spent inside the courtroom; the remaining hours are spent serving papers and performing other miscellaneous duties.

■ OUTLOOK

Although the U.S. Department of Labor does not give a specific employment outlook for bailiffs, the demand for these workers should remain steady. The bailiff career is a long-established one, and bailiffs are considered indispensable in courtroom settings. Because of this, bailiffs are needed and will continue to be a major part of the courtroom system. However, competition for positions in the entire law enforcement field is keen due to such factors as the challenges these jobs offer and the sense of purpose these job provide. In addition, the number of positions available may also be affected by local government funding.

Job opportunities should be best in urban areas with lowering paying positions and relatively high crime rates. Other job openings will result from turnover as officers retire, transfer to other positions, or leave the field. Because the number of positions available depends on the amount of turnover and budgetary constraints, the number of job opportunities varies from year to year and from place to place.

■ FOR MORE INFORMATION

The American Bar Association's Division for Public Education provides information to teachers, students, and the general public about law education projects at the state and national level, careers in law, a glossary of legal terms, and more on its website.

American Bar Association
Division for Public Education
541 North Fairbanks Court
Chicago, IL 60611
Tel: 312-988-5522
http://www.abanet.org/publiced

For more information on training opportunities and conferences, contact

National Sheriffs' Association
1450 Duke Street
Alexandria, VA 22314-3490
Tel: 703-836-7827
Email: nsamail@sheriffs.org
http://www.sheriffs.org

You will need to contact your local law enforcement office or state's commission on peace officer training to find out about opportunities in your area. However, to get a general idea of what this training involves, visit the informative California Commission on Peace Officer Standards and Training website.

California Commission on Peace Officer Standards and Training
http://www.post.ca.gov

Bakery Workers

■ OVERVIEW

Bakery workers are the many different professionals who work to produce bread, cakes, biscuits, pies, pastries, crackers, and other baked goods in commercial, institutional, and industrial bakeries. Approximately 48,300 people are employed in bakeries and manufacturing plants to tend equipment that mixes, blends, and cooks, and approximately 44,320 bakers are employed in such places as grocery stores. About 38,400 are employed in various sorts of restaurants.

■ HISTORY

Baking, the process of cooking food using dry heat, is one of the oldest methods of cooking. The ancient Egyptians are credited with building the first known ovens, which were shaped like beehives and made of clay from the banks of the Nile River. Later cultures introduced various technological improvements, including the Roman cylindrical oven. By the middle of the second century B.C., there were professional bakers in Rome, and ordinary people could buy bread instead of having to make it themselves. The first mechanical dough mixer, powered by a horse or donkey walking in circles, was built by the Romans. In European cities during the Middle Ages, bakers formed associations called guilds, which carefully regulated how bread was made and how bakers were trained. Outside of cities, however, most baking was done at home or in a single village oven.

Professional bakers were common in colonial America, but most settlers in small communities baked bread at home. The beginnings of an industrial society changed the American idea of self-sufficiency. Urban workers and apartment dwellers did not always have the time or facilities to make their own baked goods. Technology made possible huge ovens, mixers, and ways of controlling heat and measurements that enabled manufacturers to make mass quantities of good baked food at reasonable prices.

In recent years, the popularity of bread machines has led more and more people to bake their own bread. Most Americans, however, still buy bread and other baked goods at the grocery store or from retail bakeries. Manufactured cookies and crackers are found on the shelves of nearly every American kitchen. The freshness, taste, and consistency of these products are the responsibility of bakery workers.

■ THE JOB

Most bakery workers working for manufacturers (for example, a large company that produces hamburger buns or coffee cakes, which are eventually sold in the neighborhood grocery store) participate in only some of the stages involved in creating a baked item. These workers, or *food batchmakers*, are usually designated by the type of machine they operate or the stage of baking with which they are involved.

In preparing the dough or batter for goods baked in an industrial bakery, different workers make the different components. *Blenders* tend machines that blend flour. Skilled technicians known as *broth mixers* control flour sifters and various vats to measure and mix liquid solutions for fermenting, oxidizing, and shortening. These solutions consist of such ingredients as yeast, sugar, shortening, and enriching ingredients mixed with water or milk. The broth mixer must carefully control the temperature of the broth; if it is just a few degrees too hot or too cool, the dough or batter will not rise properly. The broth mixer runs these solutions through a heat regulator and into dough-mixing machines.

Batter mixers tend machines that mix ingredients for batters for cakes and other products. These workers must select and install mixing utensils in huge mixers, depending on the kind of batter to be mixed. They regulate the speed and time of mixing and check the consistency of the batter.

QUICK FACTS

SCHOOL SUBJECTS
Family and consumer science
Mathematics

PERSONAL SKILLS
Following instructions
Technical/scientific

WORK ENVIRONMENT
Primarily indoors
Primarily one location

MINIMUM EDUCATION LEVEL
High school diploma
Apprenticeship

SALARY RANGE
$14,100 to $20,580 to $33,470

CERTIFICATION OR LICENSING
Required by certain states

OUTLOOK
Little change or more slowly than the average

DOT
526

GOE
08.03.02, 11.05.01

NOC
6252

O*NET-SOC
51-3011.00

A bakery worker checks on racks of pastries baking in the oven.

Other kinds of mixers and shapers include *unleav-ened-dough mixers*, who use a five-position mixer to make matzo; *sweet-goods-machine operators*, who roll and cut sweet dough to make rolls and other sweet products; and *pretzel twisters*, who form pretzel shapes out of dough by hand or machine. *Cracker-and-cookie-machine operators* roll dough into sheets and form crackers or cookies before baking. They check the machine's work and remove any malformed items before baking. *Wafer-machine operators* perform similar tasks with wafer batter. *Batter scalers* operate machines that deposit measured amounts of batter on conveyors. *Doughnut makers* and *doughnut-machine operators* mix batter, shape, and fry doughnuts. Some workers operate machines that grease baking pans or that place pie-crusts and fillings into pie plates for baking.

Bakery helpers have general duties such as greasing pans, moving supplies, measuring dump materials, and cleaning equipment. Bakery helpers sit at benches or con-veyor belts, where they may fill, enrobe, slice, package, seal, stack, or count baked goods.

When baked goods are ready for delivery and sale, *bakery checkers* prorate and distribute baked goods to *route-sales drivers*, who deliver products to customers and try to drum up new business or increase business along their routes. Bakeries also employ *bakery-maintenance engineers*, also called *bakery-machine mechanics* or *plant mechanics*, to keep the many mixers, ovens, and other machines in good order.

Bakery supervisors, who work in industrial bakeries, are sometimes assisted by *bakers* or *all-around bakers* in overseeing production. Bakers and all-around bakers, however, most frequently work in small businesses, hotels, or restaurants where they develop recipes and mix, shape, bake, and finish baked goods.

Bread and pastry bakers, also known as *pastry chefs*, also work in restaurants, small businesses, such as the neigh-borhood bakery shop, and institutions, such as schools. Unlike bakery workers employed in industrial settings, these bakers and chefs often do much of their work by hand. They may have a fair amount of independence in deciding what items and how much of them to produce. Creativity is needed, especially when decorating an item made for a special occasion, such as a birthday cake for Billy or a wedding cake for John and Jane.

■ REQUIREMENTS
High School

Many bakers begin as bakery helpers. Most employers prefer to hire high school graduates. Classes that will help you in this field include family and consumer science, which should teach you about food preparation, health, to learn about nutrition, and math, such as algebra and geometry, so that you are comfortable using numbers and making calculations. You may also want to take sci-ence courses such as biology and chemistry to get an understanding of substances' properties and reactions. If you are interested in working as a bakery-maintenance engineer, take shop classes that will teach you to work with electricity and machinery.

Postsecondary Training

Some bakery workers acquire useful skills through educa-tion in technical schools or in the U.S. Armed Forces. How-ever, they usually complete their education on the job.

The skills that bakery helpers need to become bakers in wholesale baking plants can be learned in several ways. In some companies, bakery helpers can learn through formal apprenticeships. Apprenticeships consist of a blend of classroom and on-the-job instruction and take several years to complete.

After they have some experience, bakery workers who have proved they are good employees but want to upgrade their skills may attend training courses offered by the American Institute of Baking. Others take correspondence courses and seminars offered by the American Institute of Baking at various locations. Bakers who successfully complete this training receive specialty certification in bread, cake, or cracker production.

Some chef training schools have bakery programs for students interested in learning diverse baking skills, from basic bread to gourmet pastries.

Some companies provide apprenticeships for employees who are training to be bakery-maintenance engineers. Another option is to take classes, correspondence courses, and seminars offered by the American Institute of Baking.

Bakery workers may belong to the Bakery, Confectionery, and Tobacco Workers International Union. Route drivers may belong to the International Brotherhood of Teamsters, Chauffeurs, Warehousemen, and Helpers of America.

Certification or Licensing

As mentioned in the previous section, the American Institute of Baking offers courses leading to certification in a number of areas. Designations that bakery workers can earn include Certified Baker—Bread and Rolls, Certified Baker—Cookies and Crackers, and Certified Maintenance Technician. Some employers may require certification; in other cases, certification is recommended for those wanting to advance their careers. In addition, most states require bakery workers to pass a physical exam and have a health certificate stating that they are free from contagious diseases.

Other Requirements

Manual dexterity is important in many bakery jobs. Artistic ability is useful for those who enjoy decorating cakes, cookies, doughnuts, and other baked goods. Bakery workers must also be able to work well as part of a team, since they are all contributing something to create the finished products. Additionally, as with any professional working with food, they should have keen senses of smell and taste.

EXPLORING

While in high school, you may be able to get a part-time or summer job at a neighborhood bakery. Although you may only be responsible for taking customers' orders and ringing up sales, you will be able to experience working in this environment. In addition to school courses, take baking or cooking classes that are offered locally by community centers, grocery stores, or tech schools. Ask your guidance counselor to help you arrange for a tour of a local bakery and talk to workers about their jobs. If there is a cooking school in your area, visit it and meet with the teachers to discuss this line of work.

EMPLOYERS

Bakery workers can find jobs in a wide variety of settings, from small retail bakeries and bakery departments in supermarkets to multinational companies with huge manufacturing plants. They also may work in wholesale bakeries or distribution centers as well as in restaurants and hotels.

STARTING OUT

Aspiring bakers can apply to bakeries for jobs as helpers or apprentices. Students can often find jobs or apprenticeships through placement offices at baking schools. State employment offices and newspapers may provide leads. Local unions also have information about job openings.

ADVANCEMENT

Helpers who learn machine-operator skills may move into these positions, but usually only after years of experience. Because bakeries use many different kinds of

LEARN MORE ABOUT IT

Bathie, George. *Bakery for Profit: Starting a Small Bakery*. London: Intermediate Technology, 2001.

Calvel, Raymond. *The Taste of Bread*. Trans. Ronald L. Wirtz. New York: Aspen Publishers, Inc., 2001.

Gisslen, Wayne. *Professional Baking*. 3rd ed. Hoboken, N.J.: John Wiley & Sons, 2004.

Glezer, Maggie. *Artisan Baking Across America: The Breads, the Bakers, the Best Recipes*. Wedmore, U.K: Artisan Press, 2000.

Reinhart, Peter. *The Bread Baker's Apprentice: Mastering the Art of Extraordinary Bread*. Berkeley, Conn.: Ten Speed Press, 2001.

Schat, Zachary Y. *The Baker's Trade: A Recipe for Creating the Successful Small Bakery*. Ukiah, Calif.: Acton Circle Publishing Company, 1998.

Shapter, Jennie, and Christine Ingram. *Bread Bakers Bible*. London: Southwater Publishing, 2000.

Taber, Sara Mansfield. *Bread of Three Rivers: The Story of a French Loaf*. Boston, Mass.: Beacon Press, 2001.

Van Cleave, Jill. *The Neighborhood Bake Shop: Recipes and Reminiscences of America's Favorite Bakery Treats*. New York: William Morrow & Co., 1997.

machines and processes, versatile workers are the most likely to be promoted. Skilled machine operators can move into supervisory slots or become all-around bakers. These bakers may also move into work in hotels, restaurants, or retail bakeries. They may even open their own bakeries and bake their goods by hand.

Some experienced bakery workers can be promoted into management positions. The trend, however, is to fill management slots in bakeries with people who have college degrees in management or other business fields. Route-sales drivers may work into sales manager positions or become route supervisors.

■ EARNINGS

The salary range for bakers and food batchmakers is wide due to factors such as size and type of employer, the employee's experience, and job position. According to the U.S. Department of Labor, the median yearly earnings for all bakers were $20,580 in 2002. Median yearly earnings for bakers working in the bakery products industry, however, were $23,780; those in the grocery store industry, $21,740; and those in restaurants, $20,580. The highest paid 10 percent of all bakers, regardless of industry, made more than $33,470 in 2002, and the lowest paid 10 percent earned less than $14,100 annually.

Bakery workers who are members of a union generally earn more and have better job security than those who are not. Most bakery workers are eligible for overtime pay and premium pay for weekend work. Route drivers often work on commission, receiving base pay plus a percentage of their sales. Workers in apprentice positions are normally paid less than the full wages of experienced employees. In addition to regular pay, employees often receive benefits such as paid vacations and holidays, health insurance, and pension plans.

■ WORK ENVIRONMENT

Bakery workers usually work 40 hours a week, and some work night and evening shifts. Because baked goods can be frozen until they are needed, the number of plants operating around the clock is less than it used to be.

Some bakery plants are air-conditioned. All are clean, since bakeries must meet state and federal standards. Bakery employees wear uniforms and caps or hairnets for sanitary reasons. Machines can be noisy, and working near ovens can be hot. Some jobs are strenuous, requiring heavy lifting.

Those in a small bakery may find they must work early morning hours in order to have freshly baked goods ready for customers when the shop opens. They may spend much of their time on their feet and have a fair amount of interaction with the public.

■ OUTLOOK

The U.S. Department of Labor predicts that increasingly automated equipment and processes will result in an employment outlook of little change for food batchmakers and bakers in manufacturing. However, there may be a slight increase in the need for bakers at retail locations because of the growing number of traditional bakeries and specialty shops, such as cookie, muffin, and bagel shops. However, this will be offset by the emerging popularity of low-carbohydrate diets.

Overall, the Department of Labor predicts growth at a rate slower than the average through 2012 for all workers in this field. Many current positions will become available as workers retire or change jobs.

■ FOR MORE INFORMATION

For industry information, including salary surveys, contact
American Bakers Association
1350 I Street, NW, Suite 1290
Washington, DC 20005-3300
Tel: 202-789-0300
Email: info@americanbakers.org
http://www.americanbakers.org

For information on scholarships, online courses, and employment opportunities, contact
American Institute of Baking
1213 Bakers Way
PO Box 3999
Manhattan, KS 66505-3999
Tel: 800-633-5137
Email: info@aibonline.org
http://www.aibonline.org

This organization has industry information for the public and career information available to members.
American Society of Baking
1200 Central Avenue, Suite 360
Wilmette, IL 60091
Tel: 866-920-9885
http://www.asbe.org

Bank Examiners

■ OVERVIEW

Bank examiners investigate financial institutions to ensure their safety and soundness and to enforce federal and state laws. They arrange audits, review policies and procedures, study documents, and interview managers and employees. They prepare detailed reports that can be used to strengthen banks.

A bank examiner's fundamental duty is to make sure people do not lose the money they have entrusted to banks. Bank examiners protect account holders. They also protect the federal and state governments that are responsible for insuring financial institutions.

■ HISTORY

The First Bank of the United States, founded in Philadelphia in 1791, was an unqualified success. It acted as the federal government's banker and received private and business deposits. The bank issued banknotes that could be exchanged for gold and succeeded in creating a national currency. In 1811, the visionary experiment came to an untimely end; despite the bank's many successes, its charter was not renewed. In a time when states' rights were considered supreme, a national bank was an unpopular idea.

The second national bank fared just as well—and no better. Despite an impressive list of achievements, the bank failed when President Andrew Jackson (1767–1845) vetoed its charter renewal.

For the next several decades, the nation adhered to a system of "free banking," meaning that bank charters were readily granted to groups that met limited standards. The number of state banks multiplied rapidly. Each state bank issued its own banknotes, creating an untenable currency system.

In the 1860s, the U.S. Civil War destroyed the South's economy. Banks in the southern states did not have the resources to weather the difficulties. The only national financial organization, the Independent Treasury, was ill-equipped to meet the ensuing financial demands. The price of "free banking" became painfully clear.

In 1864, as the nation struggled to rebuild itself, the federal government passed the National Bank Act. Intended to bring about economic stability and prevent future bank failures, the act created the Office of the Comptroller of the Currency (OCC). The OCC initially had the power to charter national banks that could issue national banknotes. The OCC also was the first organization to conduct bank examinations.

Unfortunately, the National Bank Act of 1864 did not bring about the desired stability. Over the next several decades, the country experienced four bank panics, the worst of which occurred in 1907. Bank panics were characterized by "runs on the banks," during which people became fearful and tried to withdraw all their money, all at once. The banks often did not have enough cash in reserve and many failed. The Federal Reserve Act (1913) created a centralized reserve system that could lend banks money and prevent bank crises.

In its early form, the Federal Reserve System was unable to prevent the bank failures that led, in 1929, to the Great Depression. In 1933, in response to the Depression, the Federal Reserve's powers were extended. The Federal Reserve eventually would become a central bank that actively promoted monetary stability. Like the OCC, the Federal Reserve now regularly examines banks.

The Federal Deposit Insurance Corporation (FDIC) also was created in 1933. The FDIC pays depositors if an insured bank closes without the resources to repay people their money. The FDIC also is charged with the responsibility of preventing unsound banking practices within the banks it insures. The FDIC regularly examines all the banks it insures in order to ensure their safety and soundness. Since its creation, the FDIC has successfully prevented any widespread bank panics.

The years since 1933 have not been without challenges, however. In the mid-1980s, hundreds of savings and loan banks failed, reinforcing the need for the regular, thorough examination of banks by the OCC, the Federal Reserve, the FDIC, and a number of other federal and state agencies. Today, most banks are examined on an annual basis, often by more than one regulatory organization.

■ THE JOB

When most people think of bank examiners, they envision the examiner from *It's a Wonderful Life*—a humorless bureaucrat who threatens to destroy George Bailey. In reality, bank examiners are public servants. They work to ensure that our nation's banks remain strong and safe. Essentially, they protect our money and our nation's economy.

A bank examiner's primary responsibilities are to ensure the safety and soundness of the bank he or she examines and to enforce the rules and regulations of the state or federal organization he or she represents. To accomplish this, bank examiners travel to different banks throughout the year. In most small- to medium-sized banks, they set up temporary offices. In larger banks, they may

QUICK FACTS

SCHOOL SUBJECTS
English
Mathematics

PERSONAL SKILLS
Communication/ideas
Leadership/management

WORK ENVIRONMENT
Primarily indoors
One location with some travel

MINIMUM EDUCATION LEVEL
Bachelor's degree

SALARY RANGE
$31,090 to $56,220 to
$99,650

CERTIFICATION OR LICENSING
Required

OUTLOOK
Slower than the average

DOT
160

GOE
13.02.04

NOC
N/A

O*NET-SOC
13-2061.00

have permanent offices. The examination process can take anywhere from a few weeks to several months, depending on the size of the bank. A few extremely large banks are examined constantly throughout the year.

Bank examiners should not be confused with auditors or accountants. A bank examiner is as interested in a bank's operations as in the bank's financial records. Bank examiners conduct their examinations by reviewing a bank's policies to see, first of all, whether the policies are sound. They then review the bank's records to discover whether the bank is following its own policies. Bank examiners also observe the bank's day-to-day operations and interview managers and employees.

Ed Seifried, who served as a bank examiner within the OCC for more than 25 years, notes, "Bank examinations should involve dialogue and discussion. Banks may not like the process [of being examined], but they generally accept it if they feel that they are being assessed by people who treat them fairly and who understand banking."

Bank examiners usually work in teams under one bank-examiner-in-charge. Each member or group within a team studies a different area of the bank's operations. One person or group might study the bank's lending policies and procedures. Another might study the bank's asset management. Still others examine the bank's information technology or estate management. Different regulatory agencies examine different types of banks and different areas of operation. The *chief bank examiner* is responsible for assembling the team for each bank. The composition of these teams varies depending on the nature of each bank's business. Because banking practices today are so complex, many regulatory organizations design their examination strategy around a bank's greatest areas of risk. This so-called "supervision by risk" enables regulatory organizations to examine banks more frequently and with greater efficiency.

"Every examination is tailored to the individual bank," says Seifried. "The person in charge of the exam studies the bank in advance in order to develop an examination strategy."

Once a team of examiners has thoroughly reviewed different areas of a bank's operations, they analyze their findings, draw conclusions, and prepare a report. This report is forwarded to the regulatory agency for review. It is then returned to the bank's board of directors. These reports wield considerable power. A bank must act quickly to correct any problems identified in an examination. If a bank fails to do so, bank examiners have the authority to exact fines. In severe cases, a bank examiner can close banks or insist that they merge with other, more sound banks.

Because bank examiners must be able to exercise completely independent judgment about a bank's operations, their reports are strictly confidential. "The confidentiality is to ensure that there is no interference with the regulatory process," Seifried explains. "If bank examiners could be sued for rendering judgments, they might not be able to be as objective."

■ REQUIREMENTS
High School

If you are interested in entering this profession, you should begin laying a solid college prep foundation during high school. Take math courses, such as algebra and geometry, statistics, and business courses. Also, take as many computer courses as you can. You will be using computers throughout your career, and the more comfortable you are with this tool the better. You should also take English classes to develop good writing and communication skills. Researching, compiling reports, and presenting your findings will be a large part of your job as a bank examiner.

Postsecondary Training

After high school, the next step on your road to becoming a bank examiner is to get a college degree. Typical majors for this field include accounting, economics, business administration, commercial or banking law, or other business-related subjects. Once you have graduated from college, you may choose to work immediately for a regulatory agency or you may gain applied business experience by working, for example, for a financial institution. Either option is acceptable, though more and more regulatory agencies are actively recruiting candidates who have some business experience. Another possibility is to complete your education while working at the same time through such programs as the OCC's Bank Examiner Cooperative Education Program (see the website http://www.occ.treas.gov/jobs/coop.htm). Remember, though, that whatever route you pick, you won't become a full-fledged bank examiner overnight. Those who begin their careers working for a regulatory agency generally start as assistant or associate examiners. If you enter the field after gaining business experience, you may start at a higher-level position, but it will still take some time and training to become a bank examiner.

Regulatory agencies provide rigorous training for their bank examiners. Assistant bank examiners must take a series of courses and tests during their first several years as employees of a regulatory agency. They also gain on-the-job experience by working on examination teams. To become a bank examiner, you will need five or more years of experience in auditing or examining financial institutions. In addition, candidates with the best potential for advancement have experience with evaluating computer risk management in financial institutions. That is, they have a great deal of knowledge about assessing the security and flexibility of a financial institution's computer system.

Certification or Licensing

Some employers require their employees to have or give promotion preference to employees with industry certifications, such as certified financial analyst or certified information systems auditor. In addition, bank examiners must be commissioned (approved) to examine banks only by a state or federal regulator before they can function as full-fledged examiners. This process typically takes five years. The Bank Administration Institute (BAI), an organization for financial professionals, also offers a number of courses that can help individuals prepare for careers as examiners.

Other Requirements

Successful bank examiners are committed to lifelong learning. Even after you have reached the position of bank examiner, it will be important for you to stay on top of new computer developments, laws and regulations, and changes in the field. Also, you should be able to work well with others since you will be working with teams of examiners as well as interacting with professionals at the financial institutions being examined. Be prepared to travel as part of your job; often you will be sent from one financial institution to another to perform examinations. Finally, if you enjoy detailed and analytical work with numbers, this may be the field for you.

■ EXPLORING

A good way to learn more about this field is by conducting informational interviews with various banking professionals. You also should read all the literature banks produce in order to learn about different types of accounts and saving mechanisms.

College students should seek part-time jobs or internships within banks. Because bank examiners must be familiar with banking operations from the ground up, one of the best places for a college student to gain experience is by working as a teller in a bank.

■ EMPLOYERS

Almost all bank examiners are employees of federal or state governing agencies. They work for the Office of the Comptroller of the Currency (OCC), the Federal Reserve System, the Office of Thrift Supervision, the Federal

WHAT IS THE FEDERAL RESERVE?

One often hears about the Federal Reserve System in the news, and how it can have a great effect on the economy. How, exactly, this almost 100-year-old institution operates is somewhat of a mystery to most people.

The Federal Reserve, or "Fed," is a system of 12 privately owned, though publicly regulated, banks, overseen by a seven-person Board of Governors. As of 2004, the chairman of the Board of Governors was Dr. Alan Greenspan, a noted economist who has held the position since 1987. Though Governors are appointed by the president and confirmed by congress, the offices are generally held to be too important for political wrangling. It is a measure of the Reserve's importance, as well as his own expertise, that Greenspan has served through the Reagan, first Bush, Clinton, and second Bush presidencies.

The Fed's function is to attempt to regulate the economy. Naturally, in a free market, this can be extremely difficult. As a general rule, though, currency follows the laws of supply and demand: The more available money is, the greater inflation will be (as well as purchasing and investment); conversely, the less available money is, the slower inflation will be (and, of course, investment and buying will be less). Bearing this in mind, the Reserve has several tools it can use.

Firstly, the Fed can change the federal funds rate, or the percentage banks may charge one another for overnight loans. Since banks often do not have enough cash on hand to cover all their transactions (much of the money being tied up in investments, mortages, etc.), they must therefore dip into each others' reserves.

Secondly, the Fed can regulate the discount rate, or amount banks can borrow from the Reserve banks. This is closely tied to the federal funds rate.

Thirdly, the Fed can change the reserve requirements, or portion of all deposits that banks must have on hand. This is rarely changed, and usually remains about 10 percent.

By changing these rates, the Fed can indirectly influence the percentage banks charge for every sort of loan—mortgages, student loans, car loans, etc. Since our economy effectively functions on credit, this can, over time, have a tremendous ripple effect.

Deposit Insurance Corporation, and many other federal and state agencies.

■ STARTING OUT

College graduates can enter this field via a number of avenues. The Office of Personnel Management (OPM) is the federal government's human resources department. The OPM maintains a list of job listings and also can provide information about requirements, benefits, and salaries.

Someone interested in this work should also contact an agency, such as the OCC, directly and apply for openings. Most federal regulatory agencies, and many state agencies, maintain job hotlines and websites. (For examples on the Web, visit the Careers at the OCC page, http://www.occ.treas.gov/jobs/careers.htm and the Jobs@ FDIC page, http://www.fdic.gov/about/jobs/index.html.)

A number of private newsletters available in print or online, such as *Federal Career Opportunities* (http://www.fedjobs.com) and *Federal Jobs Digest* (http://www.jobsfed.com) also list federal job openings.

■ ADVANCEMENT

Individuals usually enter this field as assistant examiners and, over the course of four to five years, progress to *commissioned examiners*. Commissioned examiners might be given responsibility for several small banks. As the examiner gains experience and establishes a reputation for integrity, insight, and thoroughness, he or she may be given responsibility for larger banks and larger teams of examiners. Examiners who handle larger banks also tend to earn more money.

After many years, an examiner may be offered a supervisory position. *Supervisors* usually stay in one office and are responsible for managing a large number of examiners who are working in the field.

Examiners also advance by moving to agencies that offer higher salary scales. Still others leave the profession entirely and put their skills to work as *banking consultants*. Because examiners study so many different banks, of varying degrees of soundness and efficiency, they can become highly successful, sought-after consultants.

■ EARNINGS

Most federal jobs are ranked according to a General Schedule (GS) rating. This rating corresponds to a specific salary range. Positions that require a college education automatically start out at GS-5, which in 2004 corresponds to a range of $24,075 to $31,302. Each level includes ten steps. The amount of increase between each step is uniform. The amount of increase between each step within GS-5, for example is $803. With experience, examiners for federal agencies can rise quickly to higher GS levels.

Some regulatory organizations, such as the OCC and the Federal Reserve, have developed their own salary scales. Salaries vary depending on factors such as position, experience, and even location, with those living in large cities paid at a higher rate to compensate for cost of living. The OCC Web site, for example, listed a position for an assistant national bank examiner for its offices in the central United States with a beginning salary of $33,800 in the summer of 2000. A national bank examiner's position in the western United States was advertised with a beginning salary of $65,680 at that same time, and an examiner position in Washington, DC, was advertised with the top salary range of $108,138. The U.S. Department of Labor reports the median annual wage of bank examiners was $56,220, with 10 percent earning under $31,090 and 10 percent $99,650 or more. "Most experienced examiners earn about $60,000," notes Ed Seifried, "but it depends largely on where they want to end up. Supervisors can earn substantially more than that, but they also have additional responsibilities and pressures."

Most state and federal employees receive excellent benefits, such as health insurance, dental and vision coverage, life insurance, retirement packages, savings plans, sick leave, paid holidays, disability insurance, and child care allowance. The benefits for government employees tend to be extremely competitive and difficult to match in the private sector.

■ WORK ENVIRONMENT

A bank examiner is a nomadic creature, spending several weeks or months in each location before moving on. Bank examiners often work closely with teams of up to 30 or 40 other examiners who also are separated from their family and friends. Most examination teams develop a strong sense of camaraderie that sustains them during the weeks they must live out of hotels. To compensate for the travel, many regulatory agencies offer examiners an extra day off every other week. Examiners who work in these agencies work nine business days and take the 10th day off.

Bank examiners work in temporary offices, surrounded by professionals who may harbor ambiguous feelings about being examined. The work, however, can be interesting and rewarding.

"It can be a great job," says Ed Seifried. "I was with the OCC for more than 25 years and I spent 23 of those years in the field. I loved that part of it. When you're in the field, you are surrounded by knowledgeable people who have a strong interest in getting problems resolved. You also have a lot of interesting conversations."

■ OUTLOOK

The U.S. Department of Labor predicts job growth to be slower than average through 2012 for financial examiners. The banking industry is undergoing tremendous consolidation, and government regulations are changing. As more and more banks merge, fewer examiners may be needed at the state and federal levels. While there may be fewer new positions in this job, those who do enter the field can expect considerable job security. Employment in this field is usually not affected by general economic fluctuations. In addition, job openings will result from the need to replace those who retire or leave for other positions.

▓ FOR MORE INFORMATION

BAI is an organization for financial professionals offering such things as seminars, training courses, and Banking Strategies *magazine.*

Bank Administration Institute (BAI)
One North Franklin, Suite 1000
Chicago, IL 60606-3421
Tel: 800-224-9889
Email: info@bai.org
http://www.bai.org

The Federal Reserve System influences money and credit conditions in the United States, supervises and regulates banking, maintains the stability of the financial system, and provides certain financial services. For banking news, career opportunities, and publications, visit its website.

Board of Governors of the Federal Reserve System
20th Street and Constitution Avenue, NW
Washington, DC 20551
Tel: 202-452-3000
http://www.federalreserve.gov

The Federal Deposit Insurance Corporation (FDIC) is responsible for maintaining the public confidence in the nation's banking system. The FDIC provides deposit insurance for banks and savings associations. This resource can offer information about banking policies, regulations, and career opportunities.

Federal Deposit Insurance Corporation (FDIC)
550 17th Street, NW
Washington, DC 20429-9990
Tel: 877-275-3342
Email: publicinfo@fdic.gov
http://www.fdic.gov

The Federal Reserve Bank of Minneapolis is one of the 12 Federal Reserve Banks throughout the United States. This source can provide information about the economy, the history of banking in the United States, and career opportunities within the Federal Reserve.

Federal Reserve Bank of Minneapolis
90 Hennepin Avenue
PO Box 291
Minneapolis, MN 55401
Tel: 612-204-5000
http://woodrow.mpls.frb.fed.us

The Office of Personnel Management is the primary human resources center for the U.S. government. This resource can provide additional information about requirements, training, opportunities, and salaries.

Office of Personnel Management
1900 E Street, NW
Washington, DC 20415-0001
Email: eswebmaster@opm.gov
http://www.opm.gov

The Office of the Comptroller of the Currency supervises national banks to ensure a safe, sound, and competitive national banking system. This resource can offer information about the opportunities, training, requirements, and salary scale within the OCC.

Office of the Comptroller of the Currency
Independence Square
250 E Street, SW
Washington, DC 20219-0001
Tel: 202-874-5000
Email: careers@occ.treas.gov
http://www.occ.treas.gov

The Office of Thrift Supervision is the primary regulator of all federal and many state-chartered thrift institutions. This resource can offer information about the opportunities, training, requirements, and salary scale within the OTS.

Office of Thrift Supervision
1700 G Street, NW
Washington, DC 20552
Tel: 202-906-6000
Email: public.info@ots.treas.gov
http://www.ots.treas.gov

Barbers

▓ OVERVIEW

Barbers shampoo, cut, trim, and style hair and shave, trim, and shape beards. While barbers are formally trained to perform other services such as coloring and perming hair, most barbers in barbershops do not offer these services. Barbers may also call themselves *barberstylists,* and a few may even refer to themselves as *tonsorial artists,* an old-fashioned term which is derived from a Latin word meaning "to shear."

■ HISTORY

Barbering boasts a long and rich history. The word barber is derived from the Latin word "barba," meaning beard. Archaeologists tell us that the cave dwellers of 20,000 years ago scraped their whiskers with clam shells. There are several Biblical references that reflect the Egyptian preoccupation with facial hair and shaving. As early as 500 B.C., barbers began establishing themselves in Greece, and their sidewalk shops became gathering places for discussions of sports, philosophy, politics, and gossip. Of course, not everyone appreciated the talkative barber: When King Archelaus, who ruled Macedon from 413 to 399 B.C., was asked by his barber how he wanted his hair cut, he replied, "In silence." Greek barbers also served as dieticians, as well as setting broken bones, giving enemas, bloodletting, and performing minor surgeries.

During the Dark Ages, barbers began to be known as barber-surgeons. They performed medical procedures such as bloodletting, tooth-extraction, and minor surgeries. In England, during the reign of Henry VIII, from 1509 to 1547, the two professions were separated by an act forbidding barber-surgeons to perform any surgical procedures except tooth extractions and bloodletting. In 1745, the final split between barbers and surgeons occurred under an act of George II. Following this act, the barber profession gradually declined to the status of wig-makers, as wigs became the rage during the 18th century. By the end of the 1700s, nearly all barbers, except those in remote areas, had ceased practicing surgical or dental procedures. Bloodletting was not abandoned as a practice until the 19th century, long after George Washington's personal physician had literally bled him to death while attempting to cure a windpipe infection.

The period between the Civil War and World War II was truly the heyday of the American barbershop. The familiar red and white pole—symbolizing the bandages used on a bleeding patient—was a welcoming sight to a weary traveler. In a short time, the dirty, scruffy, smelly stranger would be transformed into a bathed, shaved, perfumed and shorn gentleman. His boots would be shined, his pants pressed, and he may even have been offered a cigar and a mug of beer. During his grooming session, he was sure to be informed of local employment opportunities and where he might find room and board. Many barbershops were open 12 hours a day and even early Sunday morning, when, for a few nickels, a man could get his face lathered and shaved before church. As in ancient Greece and Rome, barbershops were places of gossip, socializing, and often live music (the famous "barbershop quartet" style of singing in four-part harmony).

Today, barbershops—which once outnumbered saloons in many towns—are dwindling as beauty salons and spas flourish. With the gender line steadily eroding in matters of cosmetology, many men are turning to full-service shops for manicures and special hairstyles and procedures. However, most barbers have a loyal clientele, which steadily increases the longer a barber is in business. According to an executive of a national association for barbers, the average barber today has been on the job for 27.1 years.

Fashion and imitation have always played a significant role in the evolution of hairstyles. In earlier times, much like today, styles that met with disapproval among one generation became the accepted styles for the next. Barbers have observed various trends in business based upon the styles of the celebrities of the day. For example, many barbers saw business slow down gradually following the advent of Beatlemania. In the 1980s, the movie Top Gun spurred a renewed popularity of the short haircut. Today, celebrities such as Moby, Michael Stipe, and The Rock are credited by many for a surge in youngsters and men seeking very short haircuts that require frequent trimming.

■ THE JOB

Most barbers in barbershops focus primarily on the basics of men's grooming needs: hair cutting and trimming, shampooing, styling, and beard and mustache trimming and shaping. Many include a brief facial, scalp, and/or neck massage. While some barbers do perform other services, such as tinting or bleaching, most find that few of their customers seek such services, and those that do are more likely to head for a full-service salon. Shaving is far less common in barbershops today than it once was. The safety razor has made shaving at home a relatively quick and easy task, and the art of the straight-edge shave is little more than a relic of tonsorial history.

Most customers who frequent barbershops are men, but some women—particularly those with short hair—

<table>
<tr><td colspan="2">**QUICK FACTS**</td></tr>
<tr><td colspan="2">**SCHOOL SUBJECTS**
Business
Health</td></tr>
<tr><td colspan="2">**PERSONAL SKILLS**
Artistic
Mechanical/manipulative</td></tr>
<tr><td colspan="2">**WORK ENVIRONMENT**
Primarily indoors
Primarily one location</td></tr>
<tr><td colspan="2">**MINIMUM EDUCATION LEVEL**
Some postsecondary training</td></tr>
<tr><td colspan="2">**SALARY RANGE**
$12,720 to $19,550 to $37,370</td></tr>
<tr><td colspan="2">**CERTIFICATION OR LICENSING**
Required by all states</td></tr>
<tr><td colspan="2">**OUTLOOK**
About as fast as the average</td></tr>
<tr><td colspan="2">**DOT**
330</td></tr>
<tr><td colspan="2">**GOE**
11.04.01</td></tr>
<tr><td colspan="2">**NOC**
6271</td></tr>
<tr><td colspan="2">**O*NET-SOC**
39-5011.00</td></tr>
</table>

do patronize barbers. Likewise, most barbers are men, but the field includes some female barbers as well.

The equipment barbers utilize—clippers, razors, shears, combs, brushes, and so forth—must be kept in antiseptic condition. Often barbers must supply their own equipment. Barbers who operate their own shops must handle the details of answering phones and setting appointments, ordering supplies and paying bills, maintaining equipment, and keeping records. If they employ other barbers, they are responsible for the hiring and performance of their staff as well. Barbershops range from one-person operations to larger shops with many chairs and operators.

■ REQUIREMENTS
High School
Many states require that barbers be high school graduates, although a few states require only an eighth grade education. High school students considering a career as a barber might find it helpful to take courses in health and business. Involvement in theater can provide you with opportunities to practice working on hair and attempting to create different styles as well as give you the opportunity to develop "people skills" you will need later when dealing with the public.

Postsecondary Training
Generally, a barber must complete a certain number of hours of barber school (ranging from 1,000 to 2,000 hours, depending on the state). Most states offer programs that include classroom work, demonstrations, and hands-on work and can be completed in 10 to 24 months. The barber must then pass an examination that includes a written test (and sometimes an oral test) and a practical examination to demonstrate that skills are mastered. A health certificate must also be obtained. In selecting a barber school, a student should be sure the school meets (and preferably exceeds) the state's requirements for licensing. Some schools have waiting lists, so it may be prudent to apply early.

At one time, a one- to two-year apprenticeship was required in many states before a barber was "full-fledged"; this practice is becoming less common as formal training is increasingly emphasized. In a few rural states, an apprenticeship can take the place of formal education, but this is an uncommon and difficult way to acquire sufficient skill and knowledge.

Certification or Licensing
All barbers must be licensed to practice in the state in which they work, although the requirements vary from state to state. Some states have licensing reciprocity agreements that enable barbers to practice in another state

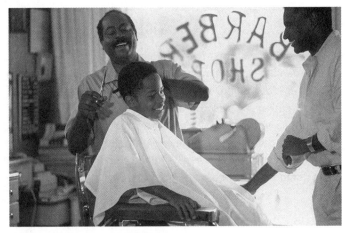
A barber cuts a young boy's hair.

without being retested. Some states require that barbers be at least 18 years old in order to be licensed.

Unions were once prevalent among barbers, but they are becoming less common, especially in rural areas. Today there are fewer barbers in the workforce than there were decades ago, and a large percentage of them are self-employed. The National Cosmetology Association lists the United Food and Commercial Workers International Union as the principal union that organizes barbers.

Other Requirements
Barbering requires good finger dexterity and stamina, since barbers are required to be on their feet most of the day (although work environments can often be adapted to accommodate workers with disabilities or special needs). Barbers should themselves be neat and well-groomed because they work in close proximity to their customers. Tact and patience are important characteristics, as is being a good listener. The ability to easily carry on light conversation is important, as well. Roy Bollhoffer, owner of Roy's Barbershop in Highland Park, Illinois, stresses the importance of being a "people-person." Says Bollhoffer about being a barber, "If you don't like people, you're in trouble." Bollhoffer has owned his barbershop for 34 years; he bought it from a barber who started his business just after World War I. Nearly all of Bollhoffer's customers have been with him for many years, and quite a few have patronized his shop for even longer than the 34 years Bollhoffer has been there. Like many barbers, Bollhoffer finds that once customers find a barber they like, they stick with him or her until the customers die or move, or until the barber retires.

To be successful, barbers must understand the importance their customers place on their appearances and seriously strive to provide a look that pleases their customers. An executive in a national association for barbers noted,

How Long Is Your Robe?

During the days of barber-surgeons (from the 12th to the 18th centuries), barbers performed many medical services, such as bloodletting, extracting teeth, cauterizing wounds, and treating disease. Barbers were distinguished from surgeons and physicians by their titles: Barbers trained through apprenticeship were referred to as doctors of the short robe, whereas university-trained doctors were known as doctors of the long robe.

"You're in the business of making people happy." Barbers should have a sense of form and style in order to determine what looks would be most flattering for individual customers. A barber must also recognize when a style desired by a customer isn't suited to the customer's features or hair type in order to avoid customer dissatisfaction. These situations require firmness and diplomacy.

■ EXPLORING

If you are interested in this career, try finding part-time employment in a barbershop or beauty salon to gain exposure to the nature of the work and the working conditions. Another avenue of exploration might be to call a barber school and ask for an opportunity to tour the facilities, observe classes, and question instructors. Of course, nothing compares to talking to someone with firsthand experience; a chat with a local barber is a sure and easy way to obtain helpful and informative feedback.

■ EMPLOYERS

A barber's domain is almost exclusively the barbershop. While some barbers may find work in a full-service styling salon, most of these businesses are seeking stylists with broader training and experience. Most barbers are self-employed, either owning their own shops or renting a chair at a barbershop. In the days before beauty salons were so prevalent—and before men frequented them—nearly all men had their hair cut by barbers. Today, these men still comprise a significant portion of barbershops' clienteles, so opportunities for barbers may be better in areas with a higher concentration of older men. Some barbers are employed as teachers/trainers at barber schools, and some may also serve as inspectors for the State Board of Barber Examiners.

■ STARTING OUT

In most states, the best way (and often the only way) to enter the field of barbering is to graduate from a barber school that meets the state's requirements for licensing and to pass the state's licensing examination. Nearly all barber schools assist graduates with the process of finding employment opportunities. As barbershops are few in many areas, calling or visiting a barbershop is an excellent way to find employment. In some areas, there may be barbering unions which may be helpful in one's job search. While a part-time job in a barbershop or beauty shop can be helpful in determining one's level of interest in the field, satisfying the graduation requirements of an accredited barber school and becoming licensed is usually the only way to enter this occupation.

■ ADVANCEMENT

The most common form of advancement in the barbering profession is owning one's own shop. This requires business experience and skill as well as proficiency in the barbering profession, and of course start-up requires capital outlay. Those who are successful as owners do reap higher earnings than barbers who rent a booth in a shop or are paid on a commission basis. Some even go on to own a chain of barbershops. In larger barbershops, there may be opportunities for management, but these are relatively rare. The longer a barber is on the job, though, the larger the clientele (and thus the security and income) becomes.

Barbers can increase their opportunities for advancement by becoming licensed as cosmetologists and working in larger beauty shops that provide more complicated, varied, and advanced services. Opportunities for management or specializing in certain services are increasingly plentiful in full-service salons. Many states require a separate license for cosmetology, but often barbering training can be applied toward a cosmetology license. In a few states, the two licenses are combined into one hair styling license.

Related career opportunities may exist if a barber wishes to become an instructor at a barber school or an inspector for the State Board of Barber Examiners.

■ EARNINGS

Incomes can vary widely depending on a barber's experience, the location of the shop, the number of hours worked, tipping habits of the clientele, and whether or not a barber owns the business. The personality and initiative of a barber also impacts the ability to draw a loyal following. The U.S. Department of Labor reports the median annual income for full-time, salaried barbers, including tips, as $19,550 in 2002. The highest paid 10 percent earned more than $37,370 per year, while the lowest paid 10 percent earned less than $12,720 annually.

Many established barbers and barber/owners earn incomes that well exceed the median.

One of the most frequently cited downsides to being a barber is a lack of benefits, particularly where there are no unions. Many barbers cannot get group insurance, and the cost of individual policies can be high. Also, since most barbers are either self-employed or working for small shops, benefits such as retirement plans, paid vacations, sick days, and so forth are often the exception to the rule.

■ WORK ENVIRONMENT

Barbers generally enjoy pleasant work surroundings. The barbershop environment is usually friendly, clean, and comfortable. Many barbers can set their own hours, and although many work Saturdays, they typically take Sundays and weeknights off. Of course, this depends largely on the schedules of their clientele; barbers whose clientele consists mostly of retirees rarely find the need to work evenings. Stress levels and job pressures are lower than is the case with most jobs. Established barbers enjoy a unique security in that their clients are usually very loyal and always need haircuts. Most barbers don't share the fears of lay-offs and other job insecurities common to other professions. Compared to their cosmetologist counterparts, barbers are exposed to fewer hair and nail chemicals, which also enhances the work environment. Most barbers have been on the job for many years, and there is clearly a great deal of pride and job enjoyment among barbers. This is a good profession for those who enjoy the company of other people.

■ OUTLOOK

Though as the beauty industry flourished, the number of old-fashioned barbershops has waned and more and more men turned to styling salons rather than barbershops to have their styling and grooming needs met, the trend is reversing. Short haircuts are coming back into style, and barbershops are reclaiming their place as neighborhood social centers. The U.S. Department of Labor predicts employment of barbers through 2012 should remain steady. Many job openings will also result from the need to replace retired workers, and since there are few qualified candidates, those entering the field may find good opportunities, depending on their location. Says Roy Bollhoffer, "I had another barber here with me for 27 years, but he retired. I'd love to find another barber to bring in, but there is a serious shortage of barbers now. And there will always be people who want to go to a barber. I've made a very nice living here." In all likelihood, the outlook for this profession will be different for various cities, states, and regions of the country.

■ FOR MORE INFORMATION

For information about the profession as well as a list of licensed training schools, contact

National Accrediting Commission of Cosmetology Arts & Sciences
4401 Ford Avenue, Suite 1300
Alexandria, VA 22302-1432
Tel: 703-600-7600
http://www.naccas.org

Bartenders

■ OVERVIEW

Bartenders mix and dispense alcoholic and nonalcoholic drinks in hotels, restaurants, cocktail lounges, and taverns. Besides mixing ingredients to prepare cocktails and other drinks, they serve wine and beer, collect payment from customers, order supplies, and arrange displays of bar stock and glassware. Bartenders, or their assistants, may also prepare fruit for garnishes, serve simple appetizers, replenish chips and pretzels, wash glasses, and clean the bar area. Approximately 453,390 bartenders work in the United States.

■ HISTORY

Tending bar was only one of the duties of the traditional innkeeper. When inns and small hotels were a family affair, and the drinks dispensed were no more complicated than a tankard of ale or a mug of mulled wine, bartending specialists were not required. Most recipes, such as rum punch, were commonly known; indeed alcoholic beverages were more commonly drunk more than nonalcoholic ones. However, beginning in the 19th century, the temperance movement helped to limit the acceptability of the widespread imbibing of distilled spirits. Drinking certain liquors in certain ways became a luxury and a fashionable statement, and the cocktail glass became the mark of the sophisticate. The trend towards increasing refinement of alcoholic beverages was only increased by the admittance of respectable women to bars, pubs, taverns, and saloons, and before long, everything from the absinthe frappe to the Manhattan had made its appearance. The number of recipes has only grown since; not even Prohibition could stop the emerging science of mixology, as the all too often foul taste of the bootleg "bathtub gin" of the 1920s was not uncommonly disguised by elaborate recipes. Today, even in the average neighborhood cocktail lounge or tavern, they may have to cope with requests for such exotic concoctions as Screaming Zombies, Harvey Wallbangers, Golden Cadillacs, Singapore Slings, and hundreds of new recipes for shot drinks, or "shooters," complicated by the multiplicity of brands and flavors of liquor, beer, and "alco-pops."

■ THE JOB

Bartenders take orders from waiters for customers seated in the restaurant or lounge; they also take orders from customers seated at the bar. They mix drinks by combining exactly the right proportion of liquor, wines, mixers, and other ingredients. In order to work efficiently, bartenders must know dozens of drink recipes off the top of their heads. They should also be able to measure accurately by sight in order to prepare drinks quickly, even during the busiest periods. They may be asked to mix drinks to suit a customer's taste, and they also serve beer, wine, and nonalcoholic beverages.

A well-stocked bar has dozens of types and brands of liquors and wines, as well as beer, soft drinks, soda and tonic water, fruits and fruit juices, and cream. Bartenders are responsible for maintaining this inventory and ordering supplies before they run out. They arrange bottles and glassware in attractive displays and often wash the glassware. In some of these duties they may be assisted by *bartender assistants,* also known as *bar backs.*

Bartenders are responsible for collecting payment on all drinks that are not served by the waiters of the establishment. This is done by either keeping a tab of the customers' drink orders and then totaling the bill before the customer leaves—the same way the wait staff does for food bills—or by charging for each drink served. In either case, the bartender must be able to calculate the bill quickly and accurately. Although many cash registers automatically total the bill, the bartender must also have a good idea of what customers have ordered to help ensure the cash register receipt is correct.

Bartenders who own their own businesses must also keep their own records, as well as hire, train, and direct their employees.

Today, special machines can automatically mix and dispense certain drinks. They are generally found in larger operations. But even if they became more widespread, they could not replace bartenders. Bartenders still have the knowledge and expertise needed to fill unusual orders or to dispense drinks manually in case the automatic equipment does not function properly.

In combination taverns and packaged-goods stores, bar attendants also sell unopened bottles of alcoholic and nonalcoholic beverages to be taken from the premises. Taproom attendants prepare and serve glasses or pitchers of draft beer.

One of the more important aspects of a bartender's job is making sure a customer does not drive a car after consuming too much alcohol. The bar and the bartender who sold a customer drinks can be held responsible if the customer is arrested or has an accident while driving under the influence of alcohol. It is no longer just an act of kindness to limit the number of drinks someone has, or to keep someone from driving under the influence; it's the law. The bartender must constantly evaluate the customers being served in the bar. It is the responsibility of the bartender to determine when a customer has had too much alcohol.

Bartenders should also have good listening skills, as the barstool often doubles as an informal confessional. Many people become talkative after a drink or two, and a friendly ear can increase the size of a bartender's tip significantly, and turn a customer into a "regular."

■ REQUIREMENTS
High School

Because bartenders must be good at calculating tabs, high school math classes are important to take. If you would like to own your own bar someday, consider taking business or accounting classes. You might also take home economics classes to gain exposure to food and beverage measurements and preparation. Communication is a key part of this job. The bartender who can chat with customers, making them feel at home and welcomed, and work well as part of a team will have the most success in this profession. To improve your communication abilities, therefore, take English, speech, and any other classes that offer you the opportunity to work on these skills.

Postsecondary Training

A wide variety of vocational and technical schools offer complete courses in bartending. The American Bartenders Association recommends the completion of formal training to prepare for this work. Such training will not only teach you about mixology (how to make mixed drinks) but also instruct you in areas such as business and marketing. It is important to note, though, that you must be old enough (usually at least 21) to serve alcohol in order to attend bartending school. Many bartenders also learn their trade on the job. They usually have had previous experience as bartender helpers, waiters' assistants, or waiters or waitresses.

Certification or Licensing

Bartenders must be familiar with state and local laws concerning the sale of alcoholic beverages. Although not required to by law, many restaurants and hotels hire bartenders who are certified in alcohol awareness. A bartender and an establishment that serves alcohol can be held liable in accidents or injuries caused by a customer who drinks too much. Most bartending courses include this certification in their training programs and some restaurants and hotels also offer alcohol awareness certification to all employees who serve alcohol.

Other Requirements

Generally, bartenders must be at least 21 years of age, although some employers prefer they be older than 25. Bartenders must be in good physical condition in order to stand comfortably for long periods of time and to lift heavy cases of beverages or kegs of beer. Because they deal with the public, they must have a pleasant personality and a clean, neat appearance. (Of course, for certain sorts of bars, a clean, neat appearance can be a detriment!) In some states, bartenders must have health certificates assuring that they are free of contagious diseases. Because of the large sums of money collected in some bars, bartenders must sometimes be bonded. Bartenders should also have good common sense, knowing when a customer has had too much to drink, and how to handle uncomfortable social situations. They should also be familiar with a variety of alcoholic beverages—a gin and tonic made with high-quality gin tastes markedly different from one made with ordinary liquor, and the proper technique for pouring a pint of heavy stout from a tap is an art form in itself.

■ EXPLORING

Because of the age requirement, students under the age of 21 will find it difficult to get actual bartending experience. Part-time or summer jobs as waiters' assistants or waiters, however, will allow you to watch a bartender at work and in that way learn how to mix drinks and perform other bartending tasks. Preparing drinks at home is good

STANDARD BAR MEASURES

1 dash (or splash)	$1/32$ oz.
1 teaspoon	$1/8$ oz.
1 tablespoon	$3/8$ oz.
1 pony	1 oz.
1 jigger	$1 1/2$ oz.
1 wineglass	4 oz.
1 split	6 oz.
1 cup	8 oz.

experience, although in itself it does not qualify you to become a bartender. Any part-time or summer job that involves serving food and beverages to the public will give you the opportunity to see if you have the right temperament for this occupation.

Further career exploration may include talking with school counselors, visiting vocational schools that offer bartending courses, interviewing bartenders, and reading bar guides and manuals.

■ EMPLOYERS

Bartenders may be employed in restaurants, bars, hotels, vacation resorts, social clubs, food service establishments, and anywhere alcohol is served to the public. Additionally, they can find work serving alcoholic drinks at private parties and residences. Catering services often hire bartenders to serve at special functions. Fewer than 10 percent are self-employed.

■ STARTING OUT

Those interested in becoming bartenders often begin by working as bartender helpers, waiters' assistants, or waiters. Small restaurants, neighborhood bars, and vacation resorts usually offer a beginner the best opportunity. Many people tend bar part-time while working at other jobs or attending college, often serving at banquets and private parties at restaurants, at hotels, or in private homes. Vocational schools offering bartending courses sometimes help their graduates find jobs.

Application may be made directly to hotels, restaurants, cocktail lounges, and other businesses that serve alcoholic beverages. Some employment agencies specialize in placing hotel and restaurant personnel. Information about job opportunities may also be obtained from the local offices of the state employment service. The Hotel Employees and Restaurant Employees International Union also offers information on bartender apprenticeship programs.

STANDARD BAR EQUIPMENT

Can and bottle openers

Corkscrew

Glass stirring rod or long spoon

Coil-rimmed bar strainer

Tall, heavy-duty mixing glass or shaker

Sharp stainless-steel paring knife for cutting fruit or peeling rind

Wooden muddler or the back of a large wooden spoon for mashing herbs, fruit, etc.

Large pitcher

Fruit juice extractor

Set of measuring spoons

Jigger measure with half- and quarter-ounce indications

Ice bucket and ice tongs

Blender for mixing frozen drinks

■ ADVANCEMENT

With experience, a bartender may find employment in a large restaurant or cocktail lounge where the pay is higher. Opportunities for advancement in this field, however, are limited. A few persons may earn promotions to head bartender, wine steward, or beverage manager. Some bartenders go on to open their own taverns or restaurants.

■ EARNINGS

Earnings for this occupation cover a broad range and are influenced by such factors as the bartender's experience, his or her ability to deal with the public, and even where he or she works. The U.S. Department of Labor reports that full-time bartenders had median hourly wages of $8.12 in 2002. A person working 40 hours a week at this pay rate would earn approximately $16,900 annually. The department also notes that the lowest paid 10 percent of full-time bartenders earned less than $5.76 per hour (or, less than approximately $11,970 annually), and the highest paid 10 percent made more than $11.96 per hour (more than approximately $24,870 annually). These earning figures do not include tips. With tips, bartenders' yearly incomes may increase by thousands of dollars, depending on factors such as the bartender's personality and service he or she gives, the establishment's location, and the size of the bar.

Besides wages and tips, bartenders may get free meals at work and may be furnished bar jackets or complete uniforms. Those who work full-time usually receive typical benefits, such as health insurance and vacation days.

■ WORK ENVIRONMENT

Many bartenders work more than 40 hours a week. They work nights, weekends, and holidays, and split shifts are common. They have to work quickly and under pressure during busy periods. Also, they need more strength than average to lift heavy cases of liquor and mixers.

Many bartenders feel the difficulties of the job are more than offset by the opportunity to talk to friendly customers, by the possibility of one day managing or owning a bar or restaurant, or by the need for good part-time work.

It is important that individuals entering this field like people, since they will be in constant contact with the public. Even when the work is hardest and the most hectic, bartenders are expected to be friendly and attentive to their customers. Patrons of a bar will often use the bartender as a sounding board or a confessor. All they really want is a sympathetic ear. Good bartenders will appear interested without getting personally involved in other people's problems.

The success of a restaurant or cocktail lounge depends on satisfied customers. For this reason, teamwork among the serving staff is crucial. Often working in cramped quarters, bartenders must cooperate quickly and willingly with other food and beverage service workers and make their workplace friendly and inviting to customers.

■ OUTLOOK

Employment for bartenders is expected to grow about as fast as the average through 2012, according to the U.S. Department of Labor. There is a high turnover rate in this profession because many students work as bartenders only for the duration of their education. Others view a bartending position as the first step on a career ladder that leads them to a career in restaurant or bar management. Because of turnover, bartending jobs should be readily available.

■ FOR MORE INFORMATION

This organization provides members with industry, education, and career news through its newsletter Mixin', *available on its website. The site also contains links to bartending schools.*

American Bartenders Association

PO Box D

Plant City, FL 33566

Tel: 800-935-3232

http://www.americanbartenders.org

This organization focuses on issues affecting those in hotel and restaurant management, foodservice management, and culinary arts. Among its publications are A Guide to College Programs in Hospitality and Tourism and Hosteur, a Webzine for high school and college students. For information about the broad field of hospitality, contact

International Council on Hotel, Restaurant & Institutional Education
3205 Skipwith Road
Richmond, VA 23294-4442
Tel: 804-747-4971
Email: info@chrie.org
http://chrie.org

This organization offers a training program in responsible alcoholic beverage service. For more information, contact

National Restaurant Association Educational Foundation
175 West Jackson Boulevard, Suite 1500
Chicago, IL 60604-2702
Tel: 800-765-2122
http://www.nraef.org

Bed and Breakfast Owners

■ OVERVIEW

A bed and breakfast is an inn, or small hotel, of about four to 20 rooms. *Bed and breakfast owners* either single-handedly, or with the help of spouse and family, provide guests with a comfortable, home-like environment. These workers, sometimes called *innkeepers* or abbreviated to *B & B owners*, clean rooms, assign rooms to guests, keep books and records, and provide some meals. They also actively interact with guests and provide information about tours, museums, restaurants, theaters, and recreational areas. According to a study conducted in 2000 by Professional Association of Innkeepers International (PAII), there are approximately 19,000 bed and breakfasts in the United States. Though a bed and breakfast may be located in the very heart of a large city, most are located in small towns, the country, and along oceans, lakes, or rivers.

■ HISTORY

"There was no room in the Inn"—it's a line that's been used for years in Christmas pageants, conjuring up the image of cranky innkeepers mean enough to turn away a pregnant woman in the dark of night. But Mary and Joseph didn't likely miss out on much by staying in a stable—the inns of their day were very primitive, stone structures that provided little more than a roof overhead.

So how did the lodging industry move from these stark offerings to the grand excess of something like Caesar's Palace in Las Vegas with its talking statues, moving sidewalks, and private Jacuzzis? And how do you explain the funky "motor hotels" of the 1950s—with cottages shaped like wigwams that contained vibrating beds? And where does the bed and breakfast fit in? Actually, the "B & B," as it's affectionately known, is an example of some of the most basic and traditional forms of lodging, along with some very comfortable and charming frills. Though initially considered nothing more than a bed for weary travelers, inns became, over the centuries, clean and comfortable establishments that provided good rest and good food and served as important community centers. Some of the first Elizabethan theaters were simply the courtyards of English lodges. The lodging houses of the first American colonies were styled after these English inns and were considered so necessary that a law in 18th-century Massachusetts required that towns provide roadside lodging.

These early examples of bed and breakfasts thrived for years, until the development of the railroad. Large luxury hotels popped up next to railroad stations and did a booming business. Some inns survived, but many became more like hotels in the process, adding rooms and giving less personal service. Other inns became boarding houses, renting rooms by the week and the month. When people took to the highways in automobiles, lodging changed once again, inspiring the development of motels and tourist camps. It has only been in the last 20 years or so that inns have become popular forms of lodging again, with bed and breakfasts opening up in historic houses and towns. In 1980, there were approximately 5,000 inns in the country; today, that number has almost quadrupled.

QUICK FACTS

SCHOOL SUBJECTS
Business
Family and consumer science

PERSONAL SKILLS
Communication/ideas
Leadership/management

WORK ENVIRONMENT
Primarily one location
Indoors and outdoors

MINIMUM EDUCATION LEVEL
High school diploma

SALARY RANGE
$7,000 to $58,000 to $168,000

CERTIFICATION OR LICENSING
Required by certain states

OUTLOOK
About as fast as the average

DOT
N/A

GOE
11.01.01

NOC
0632

O*NET-SOC
N/A

A bed and breakfast owner gets ready for breakfast.

■ THE JOB

Have you ever wanted to vacation with the FBI's Public Enemy #1? Probably not. But in Tucson, Arizona, you can sit in the Jacuzzi of the Dillinger House Bed and Breakfast and imagine yourself the pampered 1930s-era bank robber John Dillinger. Mark Muchmore now owns the house and grounds where Dillinger was captured. Though a house with such history may not seem a natural source for a bed and breakfast, the history actually gives the place a unique distinction in the area. Dillinger's respite in the desert town is part of local legend, and his capture is still celebrated with annual parties and dramatic re-creations in some of Tucson's bars. One of the great appeals of bed and breakfasts are the stories behind them. Though not every bed and breakfast has a history as colorful as that of the Dillinger House, many do have well-documented backgrounds. Bed and breakfast owners therefore become great sources of local history and valuable guides to area sites.

Most of the bed and breakfasts across the country are housed in historical structures: the Victorian houses of Cape May, New Jersey; Brooklyn brownstones; a house in Illinois designed by Frank Lloyd Wright. And many are furnished with antiques. Muchmore owned his house for some time before turning it into a bed and breakfast. A job change inspired him to start a new business, opening up his home to guests. "I had always wanted to do something like this," he says. "I already had the property, a large house, and two adjacent guest houses, so it seemed perfect."

As the name "bed and breakfast" suggests, a good home-made breakfast is an essential part of any inn stay. Muchmore's day starts much earlier than Dillinger's ever did and is likely much more serene; he's typically up at 5:00 A.M. grinding coffee beans, harvesting herbs, and preparing to bake. "I accommodate any and all dietary restrictions," Muchmore says, "and do it in such a way that my guests feel really paid attention to and respected." After serving his guests their breakfast and cleaning up, Muchmore sees to business concerns such as answering email messages, calling prospective guests, and taking reservations. Once the guests have left their rooms, Muchmore can clean the rooms and do some laundry. After grocery shopping, he returns to his office for book work and to prepare brochures for the mail.

Among all the daily tasks, Muchmore reserves time to get to know his guests and to make sure they're enjoying their stay. "I like interacting with my guests," he says. "I like hearing about their jobs, their lives, their likes and dislikes. I love to be able to give them sightseeing suggestions, restaurant tips, and from time to time, little extras like a bowl of fresh citrus from my trees." It is such close attention to detail that makes a bed and breakfast successful. The guests of bed and breakfasts are looking for more personal attention and warmer hospitality than they'd receive from a large hotel chain.

Though the owners of bed and breakfasts are giving up much of their privacy by allowing guests to stay in the rooms of their own homes, they do have their houses to themselves from time to time. Some bed and breakfasts are only open during peak tourist season, and some are only open on weekends. And even those open year-round may often be without guests. For some owners, inconsistency in the business is not a problem; many bed and breakfasts are owned by couples and serve as a second income. While one person works at another job, the other tends to the needs of the bed and breakfast.

The Professional Association of Innkeepers International (PAII), a professional association for the owners of bed and breakfasts and country inns, classifies the different kinds of bed and breakfasts. A host home is considered a very small business with only a few rooms for rent. Because of its small size, the owner of a host home may not be required by law to license the business or to have government inspections. Without advertising or signs, these homes are referred to guests primarily through reservation service organizations. A bed and breakfast and bed and breakfast inn are classified as having four to 20 rooms. They adhere to license, inspection, and zoning requirements and promote their businesses through brochures, print ads, and signs. A country inn is considered a bit larger, with six to 30 rooms, and it may serve one meal in addition to breakfast.

■ REQUIREMENTS
High School

Because you'll essentially be maintaining a home as a bed and breakfast owner, you should take home economics courses. These courses can prepare you for the requirements of shopping and cooking for a group of people, as well as budgeting household finances. But a bed and breakfast is also a business, so you need to further develop those budgeting skills in a business fundamentals class, accounting, and math. A shop class, or some other hands-on workshop, can be very valuable to you; take a class that will teach you about electrical wiring, woodworking, and other elements of home repair.

Postsecondary Training

As a bed and breakfast owner, you're in business for yourself, so there are no educational requirements for success. Also, no one specific degree program will better prepare you than any other. A degree in history or art may be as valuable as a degree in business management. Before taking over a bed and breakfast, though, you may consider enrolling in a hotel management or small business program at your local community college. Such programs can educate you in the practical aspects of running a bed and breakfast, from finances and loans to health and licensing regulations.

Opportunities for part-time jobs and internships with a bed and breakfast are few and far between. Bed and breakfast owners can usually use extra help during busy seasons, but can't always afford to hire a staff. But some do enough business that they can hire a housekeeper or a secretary, or they may have an extra room to provide for an apprentice willing to help with the business.

Certification or Licensing

Though bed and breakfast owners aren't generally certified or licensed as individuals, they do license their businesses, and seek accreditation for their inns from professional organizations such as PAII and the American Bed and Breakfast Association. With accreditation, the business can receive referrals from the associations and can be included in their directories. A house with only a room or two for rent may not be subject to any licensing

THE FIRST BED AND BREAKFAST

Le Grand Saint Bernard Hospice is considered the world's first inn. Established by monks in A.D. 961 in the Swiss Alps, it served as a resting spot for pilgrims on their way to Rome. The monks originated the practice of sending Saint Bernard dogs (which, in popular imagination, carried small barrels of brandy attached to their collars) out into the Alps to rescue lost travelers.

requirements, but most bed and breakfasts are state regulated. A bed and breakfast owner must follow zoning regulations, maintain a small business license, pass health inspections, and carry sufficient liability insurance.

Other Requirements

Bed and breakfast ownership calls upon diverse skills. You must have a head for business, but you have to be comfortable working among people, outside of an office. You must be creative in the way you maintain the house, paying attention to decor and gardening, but you should also have practical skills in plumbing and other household repair (or you should at least be capable of diagnosing any need for repair). A knowledge of the electrical wiring of your house and the phone lines is valuable. You'll also need an ability to cook well for groups both large and small.

"I'm easygoing," Mark Muchmore says in regard to how he makes his business a success, "and I know how to set, and follow through on, personal and professional goals. I'm also a natural organizer, and pay attention to details." Muchmore also enjoys meeting new people, which is very important. You'll be expected to be a gracious host to all your guests. But you'll also have to maintain rules and regulations; guests of bed and breakfasts expect a quiet environment, and smoking and drinking is often prohibited.

If turning your home into a bed and breakfast, you should learn about city planning and zoning restrictions, as well as inspection programs. Computer skills will help you to better organize reservations, registration histories, and tax records. You should have some knowledge of marketing in order to promote your business by ads, brochures, and on the Internet.

■ EXPLORING

PAII provides students with a free informational packet about innkeeping, and also puts together an "Aspiring Innkeepers Package" for those interested in the requirements of running a bed and breakfast. PAII publishes a newsletter and books on innkeeping, holds conferences,

WHAT TOWNS HAVE THE MOST B&Bs IN AMERICA?

Cape May, New Jersey, and Eureka Springs, Arkansas, are credited with having the most bed and breakfasts in the country—each town has over 70 bed and breakfasts, inns, and manors. Eureka Springs, in the mountains of Northwest Arkansas, has the largest historic district in the United States, as well as natural springs long considered to have healing properties. Cape May, which became the first seashore resort in America in 1761, boasts the largest number of authentic Victorian structures in the country.

and maintains a very informative website (http://www.paii.org). If there are inns in your town, interview the owners and spend a day or two with them as they perform their daily duties. The owner may even have part-time positions open for someone to assist with preparing breakfast or cleaning the rooms—employment of staff has increased in the last few years. Some bed and breakfast owners occasionally hire reliable "innsitters" to manage their inns when they're out of town.

Even a job as a motel housekeeper or desk clerk can give you experience with the responsibilities of innkeeping. Bed and breakfasts, hotels, and resorts across the country often advertise nationally for seasonal assistance. For years, high school and college students have made a little extra money working in exotic locales by dedicating their summers to full-time hotel or resort jobs. Wait staff, poolside assistants, kitchen staff, housekeepers, and spa assistants are needed in abundance during peak tourist seasons. In some cases, you can get a paid position, and in others you may be expected to work in exchange for room and board. Even if your summer job is at a large resort rather than a small bed and breakfast, you can still develop valuable people skills and learn a lot about the travel and tourism industry.

■ EMPLOYERS

Innkeepers work for themselves. The charm of bed and breakfasts is that they are owned and operated by individuals, or individual families, who live on the premises. Though bed and breakfast "chains" may be a thing of the future, they are not expected to greatly affect the business of the traditional "mom and pop" operations.

Most bed and breakfasts exist in rural areas and small towns where there are no large hotels. Though the number of inns in cities is increasing, only 19 percent of the inns in the United States are located in urban areas. According to PAII, the majority of inns (49 percent) are in small resort villages. Thirty-two percent of the inns are in rural areas.

An innkeeper's income is derived from room rental and fees for any "extras" such as additional meals and transportation. An inn's guests are often from outside of the local area, but an inn may also cater to many area residents. Most guests are screened by reservation service organizations or travel associations; this helps to protect both the guest and the owner. Bed and breakfasts must pass certain approval requirements, and guests must prove to be reliable, paying customers.

■ STARTING OUT

Probably all the bed and breakfast owners you speak to will have different stories about how they came to own their businesses. Some, like Mark Muchmore, convert their own homes into inns; others buy fully established businesses, complete with client lists, marketing plans, and furnishings. Others inherit their bed and breakfasts from family members. And still others lease a house from another owner. Usually, bed and breakfast ownership requires a large investment, both in time and money. Before starting your business, you must do a great deal of research. Make sure the local market can support an additional bed and breakfast and that your house and grounds will offer a unique and attractive alternative to the other lodging in the area. Research how much you can expect to make the first few years, and how much you can afford to lose. Muchmore suggests that you be sure to promote your business, but don't go overboard. "All advertising is not worth it," he says. "I have found that small ads in local publications, one listing in a nationally distributed magazine, a home or Web page, and word of mouth are more than enough."

Established bed and breakfasts for sale are advertised nationally, and by innkeeper associations. Prices range from under $100,000 to over $1,000,000. An established business is often completely restored and includes antique furniture and fixtures, as well as necessary equipment.

■ ADVANCEMENT

Mark Muchmore sees expansion in the future of the Dillinger House Bed and Breakfast. "I see buying another property in the neighborhood," he says, "and at that point operating as an inn/spa. This would enable me to hire a small staff and include some of the extras for my guests to make them feel even more pampered." With the free time that a staff would provide, Muchmore could dedicate more time to marketing and promotion.

In many cases, a married bed and breakfast owner may continue to work full-time outside of the home, while his or her spouse sees to the daily concerns of the inn. But once a business is well-established with a steady clientele, both spouses may be able to commit full-time to the bed and breakfast.

EARNINGS

Large, well-established bed and breakfasts can bring in tens of thousands of dollars every year, but most owners of average-sized inns must make do with much less. A survey by PAII provides a variety of income figures. A beginning bed and breakfast has an annual net operating income of $25,000, while one seven years or older has an average income of over $73,000. A small bed and breakfast with four rooms or fewer for rent has an annual net income of about $7,000; an inn of five to eight rooms has an income of $35,000; nine to 12 rooms, $80,000. An inn with 13 to 20 rooms has a net operating income of over $168,000. Fifty-five percent of bed and breakfast owners are dependent on outside income.

Bed and breakfasts in the western part of the United States make more money than those in other parts of the country. An average net income of $68,000 per year is figured for inns in the West, followed by $58,000 for those in the Northeast, $38,000 in the Southeast, and $33,000 in the Midwest. According to PAII, bed and breakfasts charge from $38 to $595 per day, depending on size of the room and whether it has a private bath, fireplace, and other amenities.

WORK ENVIRONMENT

Imagine yourself living in a beautiful, restored historical house among antiques and vacationers from all around the world. And you don't have to leave to go to work. Though it sounds like an ideal environment, and it may not seem like you're at work, bed and breakfast owners must perform many responsibilities to keep their property nice and pleasant. Their chores will mostly be domestic ones, keeping them close to the house with cooking, cleaning, gardening, and laundering. This makes for a very comfortable work environment over which they have a great deal of control. Though bed and breakfast owners work in their own home, they must sacrifice much of their privacy to operate their business. They must be available to their guests at all times to ensure that their stay is comfortable. However, even the most successful bed and breakfast isn't always full to capacity, and many are only open on weekends—this may result in a few long work days, then a few days of downtime. But to keep their business afloat, bed and breakfast owners will need to welcome as many guests as they can handle.

OUTLOOK

Some bed and breakfasts have been in business for decades, but it's only been in the last 20 years that inns have become popular vacation spots. PAII estimates the number of inns in the country to be approximately 19,000, up from a measly 5,000 in 1980. Tourists are seeking out inns as inexpensive and charming alternatives to the rising cost and sterile, cookie-cutter design of hotels and motels. People are even centering their vacation plans on bed and breakfasts, booking trips to historical towns for restful departures from cities. As long as bed and breakfasts can keep their rates lower than hotel chains, they are likely to flourish.

Recognizing the appeal of bed and breakfasts, some hotel chains are considering plans to capitalize on the trend with "inn-style" lodging. An inn-style hotel is even on its way to Disneyland! Smaller hotels composed of larger, suite-style rooms with more personalized service may threaten the business of some bed and breakfasts. But the charm and historic significance of an old house can't easily be reproduced, so bed and breakfasts are expected to maintain their niche in the tourism industry.

The Americans with Disabilities Act (ADA) will also have some effect on the future of bed and breakfasts. Inns with more than six rooms are required to comply with the ADA, making their rooms and grounds handicapped accessible. When purchasing a property for the purpose of a bed and breakfast, buyers must take into consideration the expense and impact of making such additions and changes. Though some businesses may have trouble complying, those that can will open up an area of tourism previously unavailable to people with disabilities.

FOR MORE INFORMATION

To explore the bed and breakfasts of New England, contact

New England Inns and Resorts Association
PO Box 1089
44 Lafayette Road, Unit 6
North Hampton, NH 03862-1089
Tel: 603-964-6689
Email: info@newenglandinns.com
http://www.newenglandinns.com

Contact PAII to request their free student packet, which includes information about innkeepers and their guests, seminars and consultants, and average operating expenses and revenues.

Professional Association of Innkeepers
 International
PO Box 90710
Santa Barbara, CA 93190
Tel: 805-569-1853
Email: info@paii.org
http://www.paii.org

Beekeepers

■ OVERVIEW

Beekeepers, also known as *apiarists,* care for and raise honeybees for commercial and agricultural purposes, such as honey production and crop pollination. Their duties might include assembling beehives and other equipment, buying and selling bees, establishing settlements close to pollination-dependent crops, transporting wild beehives to a central location, raising queen bees, and harvesting and selling honey. Beekeepers may work on farms or small plots of land to raise bees to assist in the production of grain and other agricultural crops. It is said that one-third of food production in the United States depends on bees. Beekeeping may be a full-time job, a "sideline" job, or a hobby. Beekeepers usually work alone or as a member of a small team.

■ HISTORY

Early rock paintings in Spain and Africa depict people gathering honey from trees or rock crevices while bees flew around them. Ancient Egyptian relics show the beekeeper taking honey from a hive while a helper drives the bees away with smoke. There is evidence that the Mayans kept a stingless, honey-storing bee. Relics from Belize and Mexico, including stone disks thought to have been the end stoppers on wooden log-shaped hives, represent the oldest artifacts related to beekeeping in the New World.

Early honey gatherers probably accidentally discovered that smoke calms bees when they used fire to drive off other animals. Beekeeping may have originally developed following the observation that swarms of bees will settle in any container with a dark, protected interior space. Pottery and natural containers, such as holes in trees or logs, provide shelter and protection for hive establishment. In some forested areas of Europe, hive clusters made from logs can still be found. Horizontal pottery hives are used along the Mediterranean, and straw hives, known as "skeps," are still used in Belgium and France.

The honeybee, which is not native to North America, was shipped to the colonies from England in the first half of the 17th century. For many years, straw skeps were used for hives, followed by log "gums." With these crude hives, it was difficult to know when the bees had problems with disease or starvation or if they were queenless; the beekeeper could not inspect the combs to determine what was wrong. By the same token, it was difficult to extract honey from these hives without damaging or destroying the bee colony. Typically, beekeepers had to kill their swarms each fall by burning sulphur at the entrance of the hive; then the honey and beeswax could be removed.

In the 17th and 18th centuries, beekeepers began to build movable-comb hives, which enabled them to inspect combs without damaging them. In 1789, Francis Huber invented the first movable-frame hive. The combs in this hive could be easily inspected like the pages of a book. In 1852, Lorenzo Langstroth, a minister from Pennsylvania, patented a hive with movable frames that hung from the top of the hive, leaving a 3/8-inch space between the frames and the hive body (the exact spacing at which bees will build comb they can move around, referred to today as "beespace"). By the turn of the 20th century, most beekeepers were using Langstroth's system. Langstroth is known as "the father of modern beekeeping."

Modern beekeeping methods evolved very rapidly following the invention of Langstroth's system. Wax-comb foundation, which made possible the consistent production of high-quality combs of worker cells, was invented in 1857. The centrifugal honey extractor was invented in 1865, enabling large-scale production of honey, and later in the century the radial extractor (where both sides of the frame are extracted at the same time) was invented. In 1889, G. M. Doolittle of New York developed the system for rearing queen bees that is still used today by all commercial queen-rearers. Bee smokers and veils evolved and improved. Also around this time, leaders in American beekeeping learned of the merits of the Italian honeybee, and they began to import these bees into the states. Today, the American version of the Italian honeybee is still widely used throughout the country.

Today the most significant advances in beekeeping are related to the areas of bee management and the extracting process. In general, the dimensions of hives and frames have become more standardized, drugs are available for disease control, artificial insemination of queen bees is being used commercially, and colony rental is being used increasingly for crop pollination.

QUICK FACTS

SCHOOL SUBJECTS
Agriculture
Biology
Earth science

PERSONAL SKILLS
Mechanical/manipulative
Technical/scientific

WORK ENVIRONMENT
Primarily outdoors
One location with some travel

MINIMUM EDUCATION LEVEL
Apprenticeship

SALARY RANGE
$0 to $10,000 to $20,000

CERTIFICATION OR LICENSING
Required by certain states

OUTLOOK
Decline

DOT
N/A

GOE
N/A

NOC
N/A

O*NET-SOC
N/A

■ THE JOB

In the spring, beekeepers set up new hives and repair old ones. A beginning beekeeper will have to purchase bees from a dealer. The beekeeper will set up the hive near an orchard or field where nectar will be available for the bees.

A beekeeper's primary task is the care and feeding of the bees. The hives must be inspected regularly for mite infestations and diseases. The bees must also occasionally be fed, especially during the winter months when forage is unavailable.

Beekeepers ensure that the bees and their surroundings are healthy and clean. They watch out for robber bees, who will try to rob food from other hives when they are unable to find enough nectar to make honey. Beekeepers make it easier for the bees to defend the hive by limiting the size of the entrance. Beekeepers must also watch for "swarming," a situation in which about half of the bees from a colony look for a new place to live because the hive has become too crowded or is no longer adequately ventilated. To prevent swarming, the entrance to the hive can be enlarged to improve air circulation, especially during the summer. The beekeeper might also clip the queen's wing to prevent her from leaving with the swarm or move half the bees to a new hive with another queen.

The queen bee also requires special attention. In a properly functioning hive the queen will be almost constantly laying eggs. If she becomes sick or old, the beekeeper will need to replace her.

Beekeepers must wear special equipment when working with bees. A veil and plastic helmet protect the beekeeper's head and neck from the stings of angry bees. Some beekeepers also wear thick clothing and gloves for protection, although many professionals feel that the thick clothes are too bulky and hot. Their choice is to risk the occasional sting to gain the benefit of wearing lighter clothing.

A beekeeper uses smoke to keep the bees from swarming in anger. An angry bee gives off a scent that alarms the rest of the hive. Smoke, produced in a special smoker device, masks the alarm scent, preventing the formation of an attack swarm.

Beekeepers must purchase or construct special enclosures to contain the beehives. The most popular model in the United States is the Langstroth hive, a rectangular wood and metal construction that sits upon a stand to keep it dry.

Harvesting honey is an important part of the beekeeper's job. When the honey is ready for harvesting, beekeepers seal the honeycomb with beeswax. They remove the frames of honeycombs and take them to the extractor, where the honey is spun out of the honeycomb. It is filtered and drained into a tank. The honey is stored in

Beekeepers need physical strength, endurance, and a love of the outdoors to be successful.

five-gallon buckets or in fifty-five gallon drums. This is a part of beekeeping where physical strength is important.

Beekeepers also spend time keeping data on their colonies. Their records track information regarding the queens, any extra food that may have been required, honey yields and dates, and so forth.

■ REQUIREMENTS
High School

If you're interested in beekeeping, you should take high school classes in business and mathematics to prepare you for the records-keeping aspect of this work. Science classes, such as natural sciences, biology, and earth science, will give you an understanding of the environment as well as processes such as pollination. If your high school offers agriculture classes, be sure to take those for added understanding of crop and animal production. Wood shop classes will also be useful if you intend to build your own hives.

Postsecondary Training

Many people learn to do this work by getting informal on-the-job training when working with an experienced beekeeper. Community or junior colleges that offer agriculture classes may also provide another avenue for learning about honey production and bee care. Finally, some states may offer apprenticeship programs in beekeeping. To find out what agency to contact in your state regarding apprenticeships, visit the Employment and Training Administration's website at http://www.doleta.gov.

Certification or Licensing

Beekeeping licenses are issued at the state level, and requirements vary from state to state. Some states do not require a license at all, although almost every state requires that the commercial beekeeper register every hive.

Other Requirements

While a love of nature and the ability and desire to work alone were once among the most important characteristics for a beekeeper, many beekeepers today feel that a shrewd business sense and marketing savvy are what's most necessary to survive. Most commercial beekeepers seem to agree that the key to success as a beekeeper lies less in working with the bees than in working in the commercial business marketplace. Therefore, a good understanding of economics and basic business accounting is essential to the practice of beekeeping.

Nevertheless, beekeepers still need physical strength, endurance, and a love of the outdoors to be successful. Of course, a beekeeper will also be working with large groups of insects, so this is not a job for people with aversions to insects or allergies to bee venom.

■ EXPLORING

If you are interested in beekeeping, you should contact a local beekeeping association for advice and guidance. You should find an experienced, successful beekeeper who is willing to share his or her knowledge. A part-time job with a beekeeper would be an ideal introduction to the trade, but the opportunity simply to observe a beekeeper and ask questions is also invaluable. Read as much as you can about beekeeping. Start by checking out your local library for books on the subject; look for books written specifically for your part of the country. You should also subscribe to a beekeeping magazine, such as *BeeCulture* (on the Web at http://beeculture.com) or *American Bee Journal* (http://www.dadant.com/abj.htm). Join a local chapter of 4-H or the National FFA (formerly Future Farmers of America). While you may not gain direct experience with beekeeping, you will be able to work on agricultural or other projects and gain management experience.

■ EMPLOYERS

Beekeeping is a small and specialized profession. Some in the field estimate that there are under 2,000 professional beekeepers in the United States. The vast majority of beekeepers today do not depend on beekeeping for their income; they're known in the trade as "sideliners" or hobbyists. Most beekeepers run their own independent business rather than work for a large commercial establishment.

■ STARTING OUT

Since most beekeepers work independently, the most likely route of entry is to learn the basics and invest in some starting equipment. You can contact your local beekeeping association for advice. Keep in mind that if you hope to raise bees for commercial profit, you will need a substantial amount of capital to get started, and you're likely to face several years without profits while you work to increase honey production. If you live in an area where bees are raised, you should contact local beekeepers who may hire you for part-time or seasonal work.

■ ADVANCEMENT

Advancement in this field most often comes as beekeepers increase the number of hives they own and increase their commercial sales. It isn't likely that new beekeepers

THE KILLER BEE THREAT

From time to time, one hears alarmist reports on the news about so-called "killer bees" making their way north. What is this threat?

In 1956, "Africanized," or crossbred strains of European and sub-Saharan African bees escaped from a lab in Brazil. The scientists at the lab had been trying to produce a hardier sort of bee that could improve honey production. Unfortunately, the new bees only produced one-fifth the honey, while they were much more defensive and prone to sting. While an Africanized bee's sting isn't any worse than a honeybee's, a number of bees will attack at one time, and they will pursue a victim up to a quarter-mile.

Africanized bees spread northwards through South and Central America, replacing honeybees. The first Africanized bee found in the United States was discovered in Texas in 1990. Many worry that Africanized bees will present a significant pest problem in the southern United States, where they can survive the milder winters. Currently, attempts to eradicate them include using pheromone-baited traps and crossbreeding the Africanized bees with milder European variants.

will be able to support themselves by beekeeping alone; most likely it will be a hobby or a sideline to supplement their living.

■ EARNINGS

Earnings for beekeepers vary greatly, even from year to year, as honey prices fluctuate and production from hives changes. Other variables that affect earnings include the number of hives a beekeeper has, the type of honey produced, and the season's weather conditions. Some beekeepers end up with no profits. Commercial beekeepers may only make in the $10,000 to $20,000 range. The National Agricultural Statistics Service reports the average price paid for the honey crop was approximately $.67 per pound in 2001, and colonies averaged a production of 74 pounds. This means that a beekeeper could potentially earn about $50 from every colony owned. Remember, however, expenses and taxes have not been subtracted from this amount. To make a profit, a beekeeper typically needs to have thousands of colonies producing well. Medium and small sized operations usually have a difficult time turning any profit.

Some beekeepers are able to earn income through raising hives to rent to crop growers. Rental fees vary, but it's not unusual for a beekeeper to get $40 to $50 per hive for a two- to three-week period. Some small-scale beekeepers are able to market and sell specialty items (for example, beeswax-based products) that can be profitable, but again, this is usually a hobby or sideline, not an exclusive source of income.

■ WORK ENVIRONMENT

Beekeepers work primarily outdoors. The "in-season" hours (mostly in the spring and summer) can be very long, and the work can be physically challenging. Those who enjoy nature might well be suited for beekeeping, but there are indoor components to the work as well, such as tending to business records, processing honey, and caring for equipment. This is a field that requires discipline and the ability to work without supervision. A beekeeper must spend many hours working alone in tasks that can be grueling. Many beekeepers work part-time at the trade while performing other agricultural duties. Those with a sensitivity to bee stings should certainly avoid this industry, as—despite protective gear—stings are an inevitable part of the job.

■ OUTLOOK

Since the 1980s, 90 percent of the nation's wild honeybees have been wiped out by tracheal and varroa mites. Many beekeepers find that their bee colonies dwindle by over half each year, while costs are up as much as 100 percent. With less than 2,000 commercial beekeepers currently in

*This beekeeper is examining the honeycomb from a honeybee (*Apis mellifera*) hive.*

operation in the United States and one third of our food supply dependent on honeybees for pollination, it might seem logical to assume that there will be increasing demand for their services in the future. However, since the North American Free Trade Agreement was passed, the need for orchard pollination services has shifted from the United States to Mexico. In addition, it is increasingly difficult for domestic producers to compete with the prices of imported honey. Foreign honey producers have fewer environmental regulations to abide by, lower wage rates to pay, and fewer worker benefits to provide. Thus, they are able to charge less for their product. Due to all of these factors, beekeepers in the United States are seeing demand for their services in decline. However, many continue to keep bees as a hobby or sideline business.

■ FOR MORE INFORMATION

The American Beekeeping Federation acts on behalf of the beekeeping industry on issues affecting the interests and the economic viability of the various sectors of the industry. The organization sponsors an essay contest in conjunction with 4-H and also has a Honey Queen and Honey Princess Program. For more information, contact

American Beekeeping Federation
PO Box 1337
Jesup, GA 31598-1038
Tel: 912-427-4233
Email: info@abfnet.org
http://www.abfnet.org

For information on the programs offered by these organizations and how to join, contact

National 4-H Headquarters
Families, 4-H & Nutrition
CSREES/USDA
1400 Independence Avenue, SW
Washington, DC 20250
http://www.reeusda.gov/4h/

National FFA Organization
6060 FFA Drive
PO Box 68960
Indianapolis, IN 46268
Tel: 317-802-6060
http://www.ffa.org

The National Honey Board serves the honey industry by increasing demand for honey and honey products. Check out the website for information on the industry.

National Honey Board
390 Lashley Street
Longmont, CO 80501-1421
Tel: 303-776-2337
http://www.nhb.org

The Back Yard Beekeepers Association is a national club that provides their membership with interesting and practical information about the "how-to's" of beekeeping. The club also provides the general public with educational programs about honeybees and the benefits of beekeeping in the community. Use the website to locate a club near you.

Back Yard Beekeepers Association
http://www.backyardbeekeepers.com

Beverage Industry Workers

■ OVERVIEW

Beverage industry workers are located throughout the United States, manufacturing and bottling (or otherwise packaging) soft drinks, including carbonated beverages, coffee, tea, juices, and more recently, mineral and spring waters, also called "designer waters."

In addition to major locations where manufacturing, research and development, and administrative work are performed, many companies have smaller sites for bottling and distribution. Thus there are a variety of sites for larger companies as well as small, local manufacturers.

■ HISTORY

According to the National Soft Drink Association in Washington, D.C., the manufacturing of soft drinks in America began in the 1830s. However, the evolution of soft drinks took place over a much longer time period. The forerunners of soft drinks began more than 2,000 years ago when Hippocrates, the "Father of Medicine," first suspected that mineral waters could be beneficial to our well-being.

In America, the transition resulted from the discovery of the natural springs in New York. Scientists began studying the tiny bubbles fizzing from these waters—carbon dioxide. They perfected a way to produce artificially carbonated water in the laboratory.

By the 1830s, pharmacists began to add ingredients from plants in an effort to improve the curative properties of soft drinks. Ginger ale, root beer, sarsaparilla, lemon, and strawberry were popular early flavors. The temperance movement, which tried to persuade people not to drink alcoholic beverages, helped create a market for these drinks.

For many years, soft drinks were mixed in local pharmacies, but demand grew for them to be consumed in the home. Methods of bottling carbonated drinks were developed and in 1892 the "crown cap" was invented. It revolutionized the soft drink industry by preventing the escape of carbon dioxide from bottled beverages. Retail outlets began carrying the bottled drinks and the invention of "Hom-Paks," the first six-pack carton, made it more convenient to carry products home.

■ THE JOB

The beverage industry provides jobs in many phases of manufacturing, from mixing syrups for soft drinks to working on assembly lines for bottling, sealing, shipping, distributing, and selling the products. Plant, distribution, and sales managers are a few of the administrative positions, while maintenance, shipping, and technical workers are employed by most companies. There are many small companies involved at the bottling and wholesale level, where workers process, sell, and distribute beverages.

Plants that process soft drinks require workers who control flows, pressures, temperatures, line speeds, carbonation, Brix (measurement of sugar solution), and in-line blending.

Workers may be employed in growing and harvesting of beverage industry products, such as coffee, tea, citrus, and other fruits, as well as the processing, packaging, shipping, distribution, and sales of these products.

Since many teas and coffees are imported from other countries, there are positions involving importing, processing, packaging, shipping, and distributing these products as well as in sales. There also are jobs in plants that create the sweeteners, syrups, bottles, cans labels, and other items that support the manufacturing and sale of beverages.

In all areas of the beverage industry, positions range from unskilled laborers to highly paid administrative and sales staff. There also are many technical and scientific positions, where people work to create new types of beverages, new flavors, and new packaging as well as in quality control. In 2001 the Food and Drug Administration announced a final rule on juice processors' need to comply with HACCP (Hazardous and Critical Control Point) principles to ensure safe production of juices. The purpose of the HACCP system is to eliminate illness-causing microbes and other hazards in the manufacturing process. To comply with the regulation, the industry began adding additional staff who have appropriate education and training in these areas. Still another area of employment related to the beverage industry is the recycling of cans and bottles.

■ REQUIREMENTS
High School

A high school degree is required for many positions in the beverage industry, but that is only the beginning of preparation for this work. Courses in family and consumer science, chemistry, shop, mathematics, and business will help prepare you for both the job itself and further training that is required in this complex and multilayered field. Although there are almost always some positions available for unskilled laborers, it is unlikely that any advancement or job security can be obtained without at least a high school diploma. Much training is provided by beverage companies, but basic education is necessary to qualify for more sophisticated training programs.

Postsecondary Training

Training as a laboratory technician can be advantageous in obtaining work in the beverage industry. An associate's degree also is helpful, but more education is required for many positions.

If you want to work in a management, supervisory, or quality control position, you will need at the minimum a college degree. Typical majors for those working in these areas include the sciences (biology and chemistry), engineering, or business. In addition, you will need to gain the applied skills and knowledge needed to manage a high-volume plant from in-house training, experience, and organizations, such as the International Society of Beverage Technologists (ISBT). ISBT, in conjunction with Florida International University, offers training workshops and seminars covering technical subjects related to the beverage industry. In addition, ISBT technical committees present papers or seminars on topics such as sanitation, packaging, and health and safety at the organization's annual meetings.

Other Requirements

The issue of water quality is increasingly critical in this field. The Environmental Protection Agency is decreasing the levels of lead it deems tolerable in beverages. The agency also is concerned about the by-products of disinfection: trihalomethanes and chloroforms.

Products that increase the biological oxygen demand stem primarily from the sweeteners and flavorings used in the industry, and several municipalities now demand pretreatment of such products. This means that more scientific education is required for some areas of the beverage industry. More issues involving quality control are likely to produce more jobs requiring technical skills. Additional business and management skills are needed for strategic planning to address these issues.

■ EXPLORING

If you are interested in a career in this field, begin exploring by doing some research. Read industry publications and visit their Web sites to learn about new trends, terminology, and important manufacturers. *Beverage World* magazine http://www.beverageworld.com), *Beverage Digest* newsletter (http://www.beverage-digest.com), and *Tea & Coffee Trade Journal* (http://www.teaandcoffee.net) are good publications to take a look at. If there is a manufacturing plant in your area, try to get a summer or part-time job there. No matter what position you get, you'll have an inside look at the beverage industry. If there isn't a plant in your area, look for work in any setting offering interaction with the beverage industry, such as grocery stores, juice bars, coffee shops, and delivery services. These should also provide you with valuable

QUICK FACTS

SCHOOL SUBJECTS
Chemistry
Family and consumer science

PERSONAL SKILLS
Following instructions
Technical/scientific

WORK ENVIRONMENT
Primarily indoors
Primarily one location

MINIMUM EDUCATION LEVEL
High school diploma

SALARY RANGE
$14,320 to $45,920 to $100,000+

CERTIFICATION OR LICENSING
None available

OUTLOOK
About as fast as the average

DOT
529

GOE
08.03.02

NOC
9213, 9461, 9465, 9617

O*NET-SOC
N/A

work experience and give you the opportunity to learn what consumers like, how supplies are ordered and delivered, and what new products are available.

EMPLOYERS

Employers in the beverage industry range from small bottling companies and importers of tea and coffee to international corporations such as Coca Cola, Pepsi Cola, Hills Brothers, Maxwell House, Nestle, and Lipton Tea. Positions in route sales, advertising, and distributing are available in most cities and many smaller communities.

STARTING OUT

Positions in the beverage industry may be advertised in the employment section of local newspapers. Some workers belong to unions, and information about employment is available through union offices. Some positions may be listed with employment agencies. Applying to the human resources department of a local plant or company is a good way to find out about available jobs. Talking to a route salesman who may be visiting a local supermarket is another method of gaining information about companies. Large plants may offer tours to students and other individuals who may be seeking employment or who want to learn about the industry.

ADVANCEMENT

With sufficient technical education and training, such as a degree in chemistry, workers can expect to advance to more technical positions in research and development or quality control. A college degree in business, management, or marketing as well as in-house training may lead to supervisory and management positions. Many years of experience in the industry may be necessary to reach higher administrative posts.

EARNINGS

Earnings for beverage industry workers vary based on their specific responsibilities, the size of their employer, the location, their union affiliation, their experience, and other such factors. Those in management, supervisory, research and development, or engineering positions naturally tend to have higher earnings. A sampling of job postings from Wade Palmer & Associates, a recruitment firm for food and beverage manufacturing professionals, provides some salary ranges for a variety of positions. For example, the firm's website (http://www.job-recruiters.com) advertised quality control/assurance supervisor positions from around the country with a general salary range of $35,000 to $50,000 in 2002. Maintenance team leaders, responsible for overseeing the maintenance and repair of processing and packaging machinery, had a range of $40,000 to $60,000. Warehouse/distribution team leaders had a general range of $42,000 to $55,000. These salary ranges did not include bonuses and earnings could be higher in individual cases. Of course, these earnings do not represent incomes for executives at the top of major corporations who may earn hundreds of thousands of dollars annually.

For workers on the production line, the U.S. Department of Labor provides earnings figures for a number of production occupations. The department reports, for example, that first-line supervisors/managers of production workers had mean annual earnings of $45,920 in 2002. Packaging and filling machine operators and tenders had a mean annual of $23,290, also in 2002. Ten percent of workers in this position made $14,320 or less annually, and 10 percent made $35,580 or more annually.

The National Soft Drink Association reports that the soft drink industry alone employs approximately 183,000 people across the country and creates a total of 1.6 million jobs and approximately $8 billion per year in salaries and wages.

Beverage industry workers generally have good benefits packages, including such things as health insurance, retirement plans or pensions, and paid vacation time.

WORDS TO KNOW

Concentrate or **beverage base:** Material manufactured from company-defined ingredients and sold to bottlers for use in the preparation of syrups through the addition of sweetener and/or water.

CSD: Carbonated soft drink.

Fountain: Beverage system used by retail outlets to dispense product into cups or glass for immediate consumption.

HFCS (High Fructose Corn Syrup): A common sweetener made from corn. High fructose corn syrup is less expensive than cane sugar.

PET (Polyethyene Terephthelate): Plastic used to make soft drink bottles.

Soft drink: Nonalcoholic carbonated beverage containing flavorings and sweeteners; excludes flavored waters and carbonated or noncarbonated teas, coffees, and sports drinks.

Syrup: Concentrate mixed with sweetener and water, sold to bottlers and customers who add carbonated water to produce finished soft drinks.

Unit case: Unit of measurement equal to 24 eight-ounce servings.

Source: National Soft Drink Association

■ WORK ENVIRONMENT

According to the National Soft Drink Association, the modern bottling plant is a highly automated, sanitary environment. Highly sophisticated equipment handles the entire process, from the delicate mixing procedure to bottling to packaging. Compliance with HACCP has resulted in stricter standards of sanitation in the beverage industry. As with any plant in which technical equipment is used, there are always some safety risks. Eye-hand coordination plays an important role in this area.

■ OUTLOOK

Beverage World Publications Group, publishers of *Beverage World* magazine, reports the global beverage marketplace is a $700 billion industry. The National Soft Drink association reported that in 2002, retail sales for domestic consumption alone was over $61 billion. Today, numerous mega-plants operate around the clock, seven days a week.

New drink products enter the market each year, and during the past decade, specialty companies, such as Starbucks Coffee and the many herbal tea manufacturers, have added millions of dollars and hundreds of jobs to the workplace. In addition to regular coffee, customers now can choose from espresso, café latte, hazelnut, mocha, and combinations of flavors. Energy drinks represent another growing area in the beverage industry. Figures from Beverage Marketing Corporation, a research group, revealed that dollar and volume growth in this segment was 110 percent during 2000 to 2001. In addition to growth from new products, carbonated soft drinks, the old stand-bys, continue to dominate the U.S. beverage industry. Despite rising concerns about obesity, the average American still drinks gallons and gallons of carbonated soft drinks every year. In fact, the National Soft Drink Association reported that in 2002 the average amount was just under 53 gallons for every American. As long as people are thirsty, there should be steady job opportunities in this field.

■ FOR MORE INFORMATION

To learn more about the bottled water industry, water facts, and read news releases, visit the International Bottled Water Association's website.

International Bottled Water Association
1700 Diagonal Road, Suite 650
Alexandria, VA 22314
Tel: 703-683-5213
http://www.bottledwater.org

For more information on education, the annual meeting, and links to related trade groups, visit the ISBT website.

SOFT DRINK FACTS

- The first cola-flavored beverage was produced in 1881.
- Approximately 450 different soft drinks are now available in the U.S. market.
- Of soft drinks consumed, approximately 77 percent are packaged and 23 percent dispensed from fountains.
- Approximately 500 bottlers operate in the United States.

Source: National Soft Drink Association

International Society of Beverage Technologists (ISBT)
8110 South Suncoast Boulevard
Homosassa, FL 34446
Tel: 352-382-2008
http://www.bevtech.org/homepage.html

For information on the soft drink market, contact
American Beverage Association
1101 16th Street, NW
Washington, DC 20036
Tel: 202-463-6732
http://www.nsda.org/

Bicycle Mechanics

■ OVERVIEW

Bicycle mechanics use hand and power tools to repair, service, and assemble all types of bicycles. They may do routine maintenance and tune-ups, or completely rebuild damaged or old bicycles. Bike manufacturers, dealers, retail bike and sporting goods stores, and general merchandise stores may employ bicycle mechanics. The popularity of bicycles and the fact that many riders lack the time to repair their bikes makes for a steady employment outlook for bicycle mechanics. Approximately 7,000 bicycle mechanics work in the United States.

■ HISTORY

Bicycles have been said to be the most efficient means ever devised to turn human energy into propulsion. The first successful bicycle was built in Scotland around 1839. It, like the bicycles built for many years afterward, had a large front wheel that was pedaled and steered, and a smaller wheel in back for balance. In time, advances in design and technology improved the ease with which riders could balance, steer, brake, and get on and off bicycles. The first modern-looking bicycle, with equal-sized front and rear wheels and a loop of chain on a sprocket drive, was built in 1874. By the early 1890s, pneumatic tires and the basic diamond-pattern frame made bicycles stable, efficient, and fairly inexpensive. Bicycle riding became a popular recreation, and, in some countries around the world, a major form of transportation. In the 20th century, bicycle performance was further improved by lightweight frames with new designs and improved gear mechanisms, tires, and other components.

After automobiles became the dominant vehicles on American roads, bicycles were usually considered children's toys in the United States. However, the environmental movement of the 1960s and 1970s, and the resulting concern with polluting fossil fuels, saw a resurgence in their popularity among adults that has continued to this day. With the increasing costs associated with cars and environmental concerns, more people are using bikes, not only for exercise, racing, or touring, but also for short trips to the store, to visit friends, or to go to work.

■ THE JOB

Repairing bicycles takes mechanical skill and careful attention to detail. Many repairs, such as replacing brake cables, are relatively simple, while others can be very complicated. Mechanics use a variety of tools, including wrenches, screwdrivers, drills, vises, and specialized tools to repair and maintain bikes. There are many different brands of bikes, both domestic and foreign, and each has its own unique characteristics and mechanical problems.

Bicycle mechanics work on both new and used bicycles. They may be required to do emergency repairs or routine tune-ups, or they may need to repair and recondition used bikes so they can be sold. Many new bikes come from the manufacturer unassembled, and mechanics working at a bicycle dealership or shop must assemble them and make adjustments so they operate properly. Many department stores and discount houses that sell bikes contract out this type of assembly work to dealerships or bike shops, and it can be very profitable.

Some of the basic repairs that bicycles need can easily be done by the owner, but many cyclists lack the tools, time, or initiative to learn how to service their bikes. They prefer to take most problems to professional bicycle mechanics. One type of repair is fixing a flat tire. Leaks in *clincher tires* (those with a separate inner tube) can be fixed at home, but many owners choose to take them to a bicycle mechanic. Repairing *sew-up tires* (which have no inner tube) is a more complicated process that generally requires a mechanic. Mechanics can also build wheels, replace and tighten spokes, and "true," or align the wheels. To build a wheel, the mechanic laces the spokes between the rim and the hub of the wheel and then tightens them individually with a special wrench until the wheel spins without wobbling. A truing machine is used to test the balance of the wheel as it spins.

The gear mechanism on multiple-speed bikes is another common concern for bicycle mechanics. On some bikes, gears are shifted by means of a derailleur, which is located on the back wheel hub or at the bottom bracket assembly where the pedals and chain meet. This derailleur frequently needs adjustment. The mechanic aligns the front and rear gears of the derailleur to reduce wear on both the chain and the gear teeth and adjusts the mechanism to keep constant pressure on the chain. Gear mechanisms vary greatly among different makes of bicycles so mechanics have to keep up with current models and trends.

Bicycle mechanics must be able to spot trouble in a bike and correct problems before they become serious. They may have to straighten a bent frame by using a special vise and a heavy steel rod. They may be asked to adjust or replace the braking mechanism so that the force on the brakes is spread evenly. They may need to take apart, clean, grease, and reassemble the headset, or front hub, and the bottom bracket that houses the axle of the pedal crank.

Mechanics who work in a bike shop sometimes work as salespeople, advising customers on their bike purchases or accessories, including helmets, clothing, mirrors, locks, racks, bags, and more. In some shops, especially those located in resort areas, bike mechanics may also work as bicycle-rental clerks. Where winters are cold and biking is seasonal, bike mechanics may work part of the year on other recreational equipment, such as fitness equipment, snowmobiles, or small engines.

QUICK FACTS

SCHOOL SUBJECTS
Physics
Technical/shop

PERSONAL SKILLS
Following instructions
Mechanical/manipulative

WORK ENVIRONMENT
Primarily indoors
Primarily one location

MINIMUM EDUCATION LEVEL
High school diploma

SALARY RANGE
$13,810 to $19,230 to
$27,750

CERTIFICATION OR LICENSING
Voluntary

OUTLOOK
About as fast as the average

DOT
639

GOE
05.03.02

NOC
7445

O*NET-SOC
49-3091.00

■ REQUIREMENTS
High School

Completion of high school or other formal education is not necessarily required for a job as a bicycle mechanic, although employers may prefer applicants who are high school graduates. If you are considering this kind of work, you will benefit from taking vocational-technical or shop classes in high school. Such classes will give you the opportunity to work with your hands, follow blueprints or other directions, and build equipment. Science classes, such as physics, will give you an understanding of the principles at work behind the design of equipment as well as helping you to understand how it functions. Since you will most likely be working in a retail environment, consider taking business, accounting, or computer classes that will give you business skills. Don't forget to take English or communication classes. These classes will help you develop your communication skills, an asset when dealing with customers, as well as your research and reading skills, an asset when your work includes reviewing maintenance and repair documentation for many different types of bikes.

Certification or Licensing

Bicycle maintenance courses are offered at some technical and vocational schools, and there are at least three privately operated training schools for mechanics. Bicycle manufacturers may also offer factory instruction to mechanics employed by the company's authorized dealers. Completion of many of the courses offered earns the mechanic certificates that may help when seeking a job or when seeking a promotion.

Other Requirements

For the most part, bike mechanics learn informally on the job. At least two years of hands-on training and experience is required to become a thoroughly skilled mechanic, but because new makes and models of bikes are constantly being introduced, there are always new things to learn that may require additional training. Many times a bicycle distributor visits bike mechanics at a shop to make sure the mechanic's work is competent before the shop is officially permitted to sell and service a new kind of bike. Because of this steady stream of new information, bicycle mechanics must have a desire to study and add to their knowledge.

Bicycle mechanics also need excellent hand-eye coordination and a certain degree of physical endurance. They may work with small tools to make fine adjustments. Often much of their work is performed while they stand, bend, or kneel. Mechanics must be independent decision makers, able to decide on proper repair strategies, but

---

STREET BIKES, MOUNTAIN BIKES, AND HYBRIDS

To most people, a bike is something that collects dust in the garage after you get your learner's permit, but to those lucky enough to live in a neighborhood or town where a bike path makes them a viable means of transportation, the choice of what to ride can make a big difference. *Mountain bikes* are what you see BMX (bicycle motor cross) riders use. They tend to be small, light, and rugged, and have smaller wheels and thicker tires that can grip the ground. Some are outfitted with accessories that allow the rider to do tricks, but their real advantage is that they can be even when the ground is muddy or snowy. Conversely, *road* or *touring* bikes are what you see Lance Armstrong riding on the Tour de France. They have thinner tires, turned-down handlebars, and larger wheels—all of which makes them very fast, but rather delicate and best used on pavement. There are also *hybrids* (or *trail bikes*), which are a compromise between the mountain bike and the street bike, and *comfort bikes*, which are designed for adults to ride with an upright posture and a more padded seat.

---

they should also be able to work comfortably with others. Frequently they will need to interact with customers and other workers.

■ EXPLORING

Many people become interested in bicycle repair because they own and maintain their own bikes. Taking general maintenance and tune-up classes that some bike shops offer for bicycle owners is a good way for you to explore your interest in working with bikes. Visit with the bicycle mechanics at these shops and ask them for their insights. How did they start in this line of work? What do they enjoy most about it? What is the most challenging aspect of the job? If a local shop does not offer classes, consider taking courses at a private school such as the United Bicycle Institute or the Barnett Bicycle Institute (contact information is at the end of this article).

Bike shops sometimes hire inexperienced students as assistants to work on a part-time basis or during the summer when their business is most brisk. Such a job is probably the best way to find out about this type of work.

There are various magazines available at larger newsstands, bookstores, or public libraries that are devoted to recreational cycling and serious bicycle racing. These magazines often include the technical aspects of how bicycles are constructed and operated, and they may provide

A bicycle mechanic tunes up a bicycle to get it ready for summer.

helpful information to anyone interested in bike repair. Bicycle associations can provide additional information regarding classes, industry news, and employment.

EMPLOYERS

There are approximately 7,000 bicycle mechanics working in the United States, and they are employed nationwide. They may work in local bicycle shops, for large sporting goods stores, or for bicycle manufacturers. Resorts and some retail stores also hire people with these skills. Bicycle mechanics may also be required to repair other types of equipment or serve as sales clerks.

STARTING OUT

If you are a beginner with no experience, start out by contacting local bike shops or bike manufacturers to find one that is willing to hire trainees. Check the Yellow Pages for a list of bicycle dealers in your area. Bike dealers may also be willing to provide on-the-job training. In addition, the want ads of your local newspaper are a source of information on job openings. Also, try joining a local bicycling club that will allow you to network with other enthusiasts who may know of open positions.

People who have learned bike repair and have accumulated the tools they need may be able to do repair work independently, perhaps using ads and referrals to gradually build a small business.

ADVANCEMENT

There are few opportunities for advancement for bicycle mechanics unless they combine their interest in bikes with another activity. For example, after a few years on the job, they may be able to start managing the bike shop where they work. Some mechanics move on to jobs with the bicycle department of a large department or sporting

goods store and from there move up to department manager or regional sales manager. Another possibility is to become a sales representative for a bicycle manufacturer or distributor.

Some bicycle mechanics are merely working their way through college. Others want to own and operate their own bike stores. If they gain enough experience and save or borrow enough money to cover start-up costs, they may be able to establish a successful new business. College courses in business, management, and accounting are recommended for aspiring shop owners. Bicycle businesses tend to do best in progressive communities where there are publicly-funded bike paths and people actively look for alternatives to America's automobile culture.

EARNINGS

Many bicycle mechanics work a standard 40-hour week. In some areas of the country, mechanics may find that their hours increase in the spring, when people bring their bikes out of storage, and decrease when the weather gets colder. Workers in this field are typically paid on an hourly basis, with salaries ranging from $6.64 per hour ($13,810 per year) for the lowest 10 percent, comprising trainees and inexperienced mechanics, to $13.34 an hour ($27,750 a year) for the top 10 percent. According to the Department of Labor, the median salary for bicycle repairers in 2002 was $9.25 an hour, or $19,230 a year.

Benefits vary depending on the shop or facility where employed and the number of hours worked. Some jobs may include standard benefits.

WORK ENVIRONMENT

Bicycle mechanics do much of their work indoors standing at a workbench. They work constantly with their hands and various tools to perform the prescribed tasks. It is a job that requires attention to detail and, in some cases, the ability to diagnose and troubleshoot problems. Because of the wide variety of bicycles on the market today, mechanics must be familiar with many different types of bicycles, and their problems and repair procedures. Although it is sometimes greasy and dirty work, it is, in general, not very strenuous. Most heavy work, such as painting, brazing, and frame straightening, is done in larger bike shops and specialty shops.

Once the job is mastered, workers may find it somewhat repetitious and not very challenging. It may also be frustrating in cases where bicycles are so old or in such bad shape that they are virtually irreparable. Most often, bicycle mechanics choose this profession because they are cycling enthusiasts themselves. If this is the case, it may be very enjoyable for them to be able to work with bicycles and interact with customers who are fellow cyclists.

Mechanics work by themselves or with a few co-workers as they service bikes, but in many shops they also deal with the public, working the register or helping customers select and purchase bicycles and accessories. The atmosphere around a bike shop can be hectic, especially during peak seasons in shops where mechanics must double as clerks. As is true in any retail situation, bicycle mechanics may sometimes have to deal with irate or rude customers.

◼ OUTLOOK

Cycling continues to gain in popularity. People are bicycling for fun, fitness, as a means of transportation, and for the thrill of racing. Bikes don't burn gas or pollute the atmosphere, and they are relatively cheap and versatile. With personal fitness and the preservation of the environment as two of the nation's biggest trends and concerns, the bicycling industry looks to a positive future. The U.S. Department of Labor predicts employment for bicycle mechanics to grow about as fast as the average through 2012.

Bicycle repair work is also relatively immune to fluctuations in the economy. In times of economic boom, people buy more new bikes and mechanics are kept busy assembling, selling, and servicing them. During economic recessions, people take their old bikes to mechanics for repair.

◼ FOR MORE INFORMATION

For biking news and to read online articles from the magazine Adventure Cyclist, *contact*

Adventure Cycling Association
150 East Pine Street
PO Box 8308
Missoula, MT 59807
Tel: 800-755-2453
Email: info@adventurecycling.org
http://www.adv-cycling.org

For information on courses in bicycle repair and mechanics, contact

Barnett Bicycle Institute
2755 Ore Mill Drive, Number 14
Colorado Springs, CO 80904
Tel: 719-632-5173
http://www.bbinstitute.com

For news and information about upcoming races and events, contact

League of American Bicyclists
1612 K Street, NW, Suite 800
Washington, DC 20006-2082
Tel: 202-822-1333

Email: bikeleague@bikeleague.org
http://www.bikeleague.org

For more information on the industry, contact

National Bicycle Dealers Association
777 West 19th Street, Suite O
Costa Mesa, CA 92627
Tel: 949-722-6909
Email: info@nbda.com
http://www.nbda.com

For information on beginning to advanced courses in repair, frame building, and mechanic certification, contact

United Bicycle Institute
401 Williamson Way
PO Box 128
401 Williamson Way
Ashland, OR 97520
Tel: 541-488-1121
Email: info@bikeschool.com
http://www.bikeschool.com

Billing Clerks

◼ OVERVIEW

Billing clerks produce and process bills and collect payments from customers. They enter transactions in business ledgers or spreadsheets, write and send invoices, and verify purchase orders. They are responsible for posting items in accounts payable or receivable, calculating customer charges, and verifying the company's rates for certain products and services. Billing clerks must make sure that all entries are accurate and up-to-date. At the end of the fiscal year, they may work with auditors to clarify billing procedures and answer questions about specific accounts. There are approximately 507,000 billing clerks employed in the United States.

◼ HISTORY

The need to record business transactions has existed ever since people began to engage in business and commerce. As far back as 3000 B.C., Sumerians in Mesopotamia recorded sales and bills for customers on clay tablets. Wealthy traders of early Egyptian and Babylonian civilizations often used slaves to make markings on clay tablets to keep track of purchases and sales.

With the rise of monarchies in Europe, billing clerks were needed to record the business transactions of kings, queens, and rich merchants and to monitor the status of the royal treasury. During the Middle Ages, monks carried out the tasks of billing clerks. As the industrial revolution spread across Europe, increasing commercial transactions, billing clerks became a necessary part of the workforce.

Computer technology has changed the way clerks record transactions today, allowing for billing information and financial transactions to be recorded electronically, eliminating the need for paperwork. But billing clerks continue to occupy a central role in the business world, managing the day-to-day inner workings of company finance.

■ THE JOB

Billing clerks are responsible for keeping records and up-to-date accounts of all business transactions. They type and send bills for services or products and update files to reflect payments. They also review incoming invoices to ensure that the requested products have been delivered and that the billing statements are accurate and paid on time.

Billing clerks set up shipping and receiving dates. They check customer orders before shipping to make sure they are complete and that all costs, shipping charges, taxes, and credits are included. Billing clerks are also troubleshooters. They contact suppliers or customers when payments are past due or incorrect and help solve the minor problems that invariably occur in the course of business transactions.

Billing clerks enter all transaction information onto the firm's account ledger. This ledger lists all the company's transactions such as items bought or sold as well as the credit terms and payment and receiving dates. As payments come in, the billing clerk applies credit to customer accounts and applies any applicable discounts. All correspondence is carefully filed for future reference. Nearly all of this work is currently done using spreadsheets and computer databases.

The specific duties of billing clerks vary according to the nature of the business in which they work. In an insurance company, the transaction sheet will reflect when and how much customers must pay on their insurance bills. Billing clerks in hospitals compile itemized charges, calculate insurance benefits, and process insurance claims. In accounting, law, and consulting firms, they calculate billable hours and work completed.

Billing clerks are also often responsible for preparing summary statements of financial status, profit-and-loss statements, and payroll lists and deductions. These reports are submitted periodically to company management, who can then gauge the company's financial performance. Clerks may also write company checks, compute federal tax reports, and tabulate personnel profit shares.

Billing clerks may have a specific role within a company. These areas of specialization include the following:

Invoice-control clerks post items in accounts payable or receivable ledgers and verify the accuracy of billing data.

Passenger rate clerks compute fare information for business trips and then provide this information to business personnel.

COD (cash-on-delivery) clerks calculate and record the amount of money collected on COD delivery routes.

Interline clerks compute and pay freight charges for airlines or other transportation agencies that carry freight or passengers as part of a business transaction.

Settlement clerks compute and pay shippers for materials forwarded to a company.

Billing-control clerks compute and pay utility companies for services provided.

Rate reviewers compile data relating to utility costs for management officials.

Services clerks compute and pay tariff charges for boats or ships used to transport materials.

Foreign clerks compute duties, tariffs, and price conversions of exported and imported products.

Billing-machine operators mechanically prepare bills and statements.

Deposit-refund clerks prepare bills for utility customers.

Raters calculate premiums to be paid by customers of insurance companies.

Telegraph-service raters compute costs for sending telegrams.

Billing clerks may work in one specific area or they may be responsible for several areas.

■ REQUIREMENTS
High School

A high school diploma is usually sufficient for a beginning billing clerk, although business courses in computer operations and bookkeeping are also helpful. In high school, take English, communications, and business writing courses. Computer science and mathematics courses will also be helpful. Training in spreadsheet programs such as Microsoft Excel will be invaluable. Some companies test their applicants on math, typing, and computer skills, and others offer on-the-job training.

Postsecondary Training

Community colleges, junior colleges, and vocational schools often offer business education courses that can provide you with additional training.

Other Requirements

If you hope to be a billing clerk, you should have excellent mathematical and organizational skills, be detail oriented, and be able to concentrate on repetitive tasks for long periods of time. In addition, you should be dependable, honest, and trustworthy in dealing with confidential financial matters.

■ EXPLORING

You can gain experience in this field by taking on clerical or bookkeeping responsibilities with a school club, student government, or other extracurricular activities. If you are interested in the field, you can work in retail operations, either part time or during the summer. Working at the cash register or even pricing products as a stockperson is a good introductory experience. It also may be possible to gain some experience by volunteering to help maintain the bookkeeping records for local groups, such as churches and small businesses.

■ EMPLOYERS

Employers of billing clerks include hospitals, insurance companies, banks, manufacturers, and utility companies. Of the approximately 507,000 billing clerks employed in the United States, roughly one-third work in the health care field.

■ STARTING OUT

Your high school job placement or guidance office can help you find employment opportunities or establish job contacts after you graduate. You may also find specific jobs through classified newspaper advertisements. Most companies provide on-the-job training for entry-level billing clerks in order to explain to them company procedures and policies and to teach them the basic tasks of the job. During the first month, billing clerks work with experienced personnel.

■ ADVANCEMENT

Billing clerks usually begin by handling routine tasks such as recording transactions. With experience, they may advance to more complex assignments—which entail computer training in databases and spreadsheets—and assume a greater responsibility for the work as a whole. With additional training and education, billing clerks can be promoted to positions as bookkeepers, accountants, or auditors. Billing clerks with strong leadership and management skills can advance to group manager or supervisor.

There is a high turnover rate in this field, which increases the chance of promotion for employees with ability and initiative.

■ EARNINGS

Salaries for billing clerks depend on the size and geographic location of the company and the employee's skills. Full-time billing and posting clerks earned a mean hourly wage of $13.04 in 2002, according to the U.S. Department of Labor (DOL). For full-time work at 40 hours per week, this hourly wage translates into an annual income of approximately $27,120. The DOL also reported that salaries for these workers ranged from less than $18,300 to more than $37,530. Earnings also vary by responsibilities; for example, the DOL reports that billing clerks working in the management offices of companies and enterprises earned a mean of $13.59 per hour in 2002. This hourly amount translates into a yearly salary of approximately $28,270 for full-time work. Billing clerks with high levels of expertise and management responsibilities may make more than this amount. Full-time workers also receive paid vacation, health insurance, and other benefits.

■ WORK ENVIRONMENT

Like most office workers, billing clerks usually work in modern office environments and average 37 to 40 hours of work per week. Billing clerks spend most of their time behind a desk, and their work can be routine and repetitive. Working long hours in front of a computer can often cause eyestrain, backaches, and headaches, although efforts are being made to reduce physical problems with ergonomically correct equipment. Billing clerks should enjoy systematic and orderly work and have a keen eye for numerical detail. While much of the work is solitary, billing clerks often interact with accountants and management and may work under close supervision.

■ OUTLOOK

The U.S. Department of Labor predicts that opportunities for billing clerks will grow more slowly than the average through 2012. A number of factors contribute to this slow growth rate. For example, technological advancements—computers, electronic billing, and automated payment methods—will streamline operations and result in the need for fewer workers. Additionally, the responsibilities of billing clerks may be combined with those of other positions. In smaller companies, for example, accounting clerks will make use of billing software, making billing clerks obsolete. Many job openings will result from the need to replace workers who have left for different jobs or other reasons. The health care sector should remain a large employer in this field.

■ FOR MORE INFORMATION

For additional career information, contact

Office & Professional Employees International Union
265 West 14th Street, 6th Floor
New York, NY 10011
Tel: 800-346-7348
Email: opeiu@opeiu.org
http://www.opeiu.org

Bindery Workers

■ OVERVIEW

Binding, or finishing, is the final step in the printing process. *Bindery workers* take the printed pages that go into books, magazines, pamphlets, catalogs, and other materials and fold, cut, sew, staple, stitch, and/or glue them together to produce the finished product.

Bindery workers typically work in commercial printing plants or specialized bindery shops. Some bindery workers perform highly specialized tasks that require a certain amount of training; other bindery workers perform simple, repetitive tasks that are easily mastered. Approximately 88,740 people are employed in bindery work in the United States.

■ HISTORY

Bookbinding is an ancient and honored craft. As early as the third century A.D., when books were still written on papyrus and animal skins, pages of parchment manuscripts were stored between two boards. During the Middle Ages, bookbinding was developed into a fine art by monks in monasteries who decorated the board covers of sacred books with elaborate bindings made of metal, jewels, ivory, and enamel.

Around the year 900, the English introduced the use of leather to cover the boards and soon became leaders in this field. English kings employed binders to decorate the books in the royal library. Nobles and other powerful fig-

ures followed their monarchs' lead and established their own libraries of luxuriously bound volumes. These fine bindings were usually decorated with coats of arms or family crests. In this way, the bookbinder became a highly regarded artist.

With the invention of the printing press in the 15th century, the demand for books grew among ordinary citizens, and the making and binding of books was transferred from monasteries and palaces to the shops of printers and binders.

Today, the art of hand bookbinding is increasingly rare. There are still shops where skilled workers bind rare and restored books, but most finishing is now highly automated both for books and for other printed pieces.

■ THE JOB

The average bindery worker today is a skilled machine operator. Collating, inserting, and other bindery tasks are periodically done by hand, but the bulk of binding processes are automated: cutting, folding, gathering, stitching, gluing, trimming, and wrapping. Finishing also might include embossing, die cutting, and foil stamping.

There are several different types of binderies: *edition binderies,* which specialize in large volumes of books and magazines; *pamphlet binderies,* which make pamphlets; *trade* or *job binderies,* which finish smaller quantities on a contract basis for printers and publishers; and *manifold* or *loose-leaf binderies,* which bind blank pages and forms into ledgers, notebooks, checkbooks, calendars, and notepads. *Hand bookbinders* work in small shops where they bind special-edition books or restore and rebind old books. Hand bookbinding offers a wide variety of projects.

Bindery work ranges from simple to complex. Some binding jobs, such as preparing leaflets or newspaper inserts, require only a single step—in this case folding. The most complicated binding work is edition binding, or the production of books from large printed sheets of paper. Book pages are usually not produced individually but are printed on a large sheet of paper, six or eight at a time. These large sheets are folded by a machine into units called signatures, and the signatures are joined together in the proper order to make a complete book. The signatures are then assembled by a gathering machine and sewed or glued together to make what is called a book block. The book blocks are compressed in a machine to ensure compactness and uniform thickness, trimmed to the proper size, and reinforced with fabric strips that are glued along the spine. The covers for the book are created separately and are pasted or glued to the book block by machine. Books may undergo a variety of finishing operations, such as gilding the edges of pages or wrapping with dust jackets, before they are inspected and packed for shipment. A

A woman at a print shop operates a binding machine.

similar procedure is used in the binding of magazines, catalogs, and directories.

In large binderies, the operations are usually done in an assembly-line fashion by workers who are trained in just one or two procedures. For example, a *stitcher operator* runs the machines that stitch printed matter along its spine or edge. Other workers might specialize in the cutting, folding, or gathering processes. Much of this work involves setting up equipment and adjusting it as needed during the binding process.

REQUIREMENTS
High School

People with some knowledge of printing and binding are likely to have an advantage when they apply for jobs in the field. High school students interested in bindery careers can gain some exposure to bindery work by taking shop courses or attending a vocational-technical high school.

Postsecondary Training

Occupational skill centers, often operated by unions, can also provide an introduction to the industry. Postsecondary training in graphic arts, often offered at community and junior colleges, is also useful. Local offices of printing industry associations offer individual courses related to the field.

Formal apprenticeships are becoming less common but are available for workers interested in acquiring highly specialized skills. A four-year apprenticeship is usually needed to learn how to restore and bind rare books.

Shorter apprenticeship programs combining on-the-job training with classroom instruction may be required for union shops. Four-year college programs in graphic arts are recommended for people who want to work in

bindery shop management. With today's fast-changing technology, all bindery workers are likely to need occasional retraining once employed in a job.

Other Requirements

Accuracy, neatness, patience, and good eyesight are among the qualities needed for bindery occupations. Careful attention to detail may be the most important requirement for a bindery worker. Errors made in this final stage of the printing process can be costly if it means reinvesting labor and materials to redo previous steps. Finger dexterity is essential for workers who count, insert, paste, and fold, while mechanical skill is required of those who operate automated equipment. Artistic ability and imagination are required for hand bookbinding. In general, employers look for individuals with good communication skills and strong mathematical and mechanical aptitude.

■ EXPLORING

You may be able to find out first-hand about bindery work through a summer job in a local bindery. By observing operations and talking with experienced employees, you can both learn and earn.

In addition, many trade and vocational schools offer courses that teach the basics of the trade. Some schools even have work-study arrangements with trade or job binderies that enable students to broaden their experience in the field. Contacts made during this training period may be useful in securing full-time employment after graduation.

Industry experts say that any exposure to the printing industry is valuable background for a job in the bindery field.

■ EMPLOYERS

Of the approximately 88,740 bindery workers in the United States, the majority are employed in commercial printing plants. In addition, a large number of bindery workers are employed at bindery trade shops. These shops provide binding services for

QUICK FACTS

SCHOOL SUBJECTS
Mathematics
Technical/shop

PERSONAL SKILLS
Mechanical/manipulative
Technical/scientific

WORK ENVIRONMENT
Primarily indoors
Primarily one location

MINIMUM EDUCATION LEVEL
High school diploma

SALARY RANGE
$14,460 to $23,970 to $37,330

CERTIFICATION OR LICENSING
None available

OUTLOOK
Decline

DOT
653

GOE
08.03.05

NOC
9473

O*NET-SOC
51-5011.02

THE TIES THAT BIND

You've seen one binding, you've seen them all, right? Wrong. Bindery work is highly specialized and involves a wide range of processes.

The average book is finished with a technique called **perfect binding,** in which the pages and the cover are held together with glue. Other common methods of binding:

Saddle stitching: Gathering and binding signatures of paper at the centerfold using wire stitches that looks like staples. As they move through the stitcher, the folded sheets rest on supports called saddles. This process is commonly used to bind booklets, brochures, and pamphlets.

Smyth sewing: Bookbinding by sewing thread through the backfold of a signature (group of pages) and from signature to signature. This holds the signatures together while allowing the book to lay flat.

Spiral binding: Binding loose sheets of paper together by threading a continuous wire coil through holes near the margin of the pages. This method is often used for notebooks and calendars.

Source: *Careers in Graphic Communications*, Graphic Arts Technical Foundation

printers without binderies or printers with too much binding work to complete on their own. Bindery work is done in printing plants, which may be located in out-of-the-way places where materials and labor are cheaper.

■ STARTING OUT

Information on apprenticeships and training opportunities is available through the state employment service, binderies, or local chapters of printing industry associations.

People who want to start working first and learn their skills on the job should contact potential employers directly, especially if they want to work in a small nonunion bindery. Openings for trainee positions may be listed in newspaper want ads or with the state employment service. Trade school graduates may find jobs through their school's placement office. And industry association offices often run job listing services.

■ ADVANCEMENT

Most bindery workers learn their craft through on-the-job training. Entry-level employees start by doing simple tasks, such as moving paper from cutting machines to folding machines. As workers gain experience, they advance to more difficult tasks and learn how to handle

one or more finishing processes. It generally takes one to three months to learn how to operate a new piece of equipment.

Skilled workers can advance to supervisory positions, but opportunities for this type of advancement are mostly limited to larger binderies. Advancement is likely to be faster for workers who have completed an apprenticeship program than for those who have learned skills solely through on-the-job training.

■ EARNINGS

Bindery workers' earnings vary according to the type of work they do, where they live, and if they are covered by union contracts. The U.S. Department of Labor reports that skilled bookbinders had median hourly wages of $11.53 in 2002. This wage translates in approximately $23,970 per year for full-time work. The lowest paid 10 percent earned less than $6.95 per hour (approximately $14,460 annually) that same year. At the top of the pay scale, the highest paid 10 percent made more than $17.95 per hour (approximately $37,330 per year).

Skilled bookbinders who finish books by hand tend to earn more money: a median salary of $14.27 per hour, or $29,680 per year. The lowest 10 percent of bookbinders made $7.84 per hour, or $16,310 per year, while the highly skilled bookbinders in the upper 10 percent made $21.90 per hour, or $45,550 per year.

Workers under union contracts usually have higher earnings. The average workweek for bindery workers is between 35 and 40 hours, although many work more than that. Generally, full-time employees are paid overtime wages if they work more than 40 hours. Benefits typically include health insurance, paid vacation time, and retirement plans.

■ WORK ENVIRONMENT

Modern binderies are usually well lighted and well ventilated, but they are often noisy. Certain jobs can be strenuous, requiring workers to stand for long periods of time and repeatedly reach, stoop, kneel, and lift and carry heavy items. Because many tasks are done in an assembly-line manner, bindery workers must be able to tolerate doing repetitive, monotonous tasks.

■ OUTLOOK

The U.S. Department of Labor predicts employment for bindery workers will decline through 2012. Because the binding process is becoming increasingly mechanized, the need for workers to do certain tasks is dwindling. New, automated equipment in binderies can perform a number of operations in sequence, beginning with raw stock at one end of the process and finishing with the final product. These machines shorten production time, increase plant productivity, and reduce overall labor requirements. Furthermore, the entire publishing industry is cutting back on expenses, looking to shave costs however possible. This tends to create a tight market environment for its manufacturing end.

Knowledgeable workers, however, are needed to oversee the use of new technologies. Those with up-to-date computer skills and mechanical aptitude will have the best opportunities in the field. "The pace of the industry has changed dramatically," says Bob Goodman of Zonne Bookbinders in Chicago, Illinois. "It used to be that a job was scheduled over three or four weeks. Now everything is needed 'by tomorrow.'" Because of this faster pace, Goodman says many binderies rely heavily on temporary workers to complete large jobs quickly.

Most full-time job opportunities will come from the need to replace workers who leave the field for different jobs, retirement, or other reasons.

■ FOR MORE INFORMATION

This trade association represents trade binders, loose-leaf manufacturers, and suppliers throughout the United States, Canada, and Europe. For industry news and other resources, contact

Binding Industries Association International
70 East Lake Street, #300
Chicago, IL 60601
Tel: 312-372-7606
http://www.bindingindustries.org

This coalition serves as a clearinghouse, resource center, and coordinator of programs promoting career awareness, training, and a positive industry image.

Graphic Communications Council
1899 Preston White Drive
Reston, VA 20191-4367
Tel: 703-264-7200
Email: npes@npes.org
http://www.npes.org

This union represents U.S. and Canadian workers in all craft and skill areas of the printing and publishing industries. For information on education and training programs available through local union schools, contact

Graphic Communications International Union
1900 L Street, NW
Washington, DC 20036
Tel: 202-462-1400
http://www.gciu.org

Biochemists

■ OVERVIEW

Biochemists explore the tiny world of the cell, study how illnesses develop, and search for ways to improve life on earth. Through studying the chemical makeup of living organisms, biochemists strive to understand the dynamics of life, from the secrets of cell-to-cell communication to the chemical changes in our brains that give us memories. Biochemists examine the chemical combinations and reactions involved in such functions as growth, metabolism, reproduction, and heredity. They also study the effect of environment on living tissue. If cancer is to be cured, the earth's pollution cleaned up, or the aging process slowed, it will be biochemists and molecular biologists who will lead the way.

■ HISTORY

Biochemistry is a fairly new science, even though the concept of biochemistry is said to have its roots in the discovery of the fermentation process thousands of years ago. In fact, the basic steps used to make wine from grapes were the same in ancient times as they are today. However, the rather unchanging methods used for alcohol fermentation do not nearly reflect the revolutionary changes that have occurred throughout recent history in our knowledge of cell composition, growth, and function.

Robert Hooke, an English scientist, first described and named cells in 1665, when he looked at a slice of bark from an oak tree under a microscope with a magnifying power of 30x. Hooke never realized the significance of his discovery, however, because he thought the tiny boxes or "cells" he saw were unique to the bark. Anton van Leeuwenhoek, a Dutchman who lived in Hooke's time, discovered the existence of single-celled organisms by observing them in pond water and in animal blood and sperm. He used

A biochemist investigates the effect of chemicals on plant growth.

grains of sand that he had polished into magnifying glasses as powerful as 300x to see this invisible world. In 1839, nearly two centuries after Hooke's and Leeuwenhoek's discoveries, two German biologists, Matthias Schleiden and Theodor Schwann, correctly concluded that all living things consisted of cells. This theory was later expanded to include the idea that all cells come from other cells, and that the ability of cells to divide to form new cells is the basis for all reproduction, growth, and repair of many-celled organisms, like humans.

Over the past 40 years, a powerful instrument called the electron microscope has revealed the complex structure of cells. Every cell, at some state in its life, contains DNA, the genetic material that directs the cell's many activities. Biochemists have widened their scope to include the study of protein molecules and chromosomes, the building blocks of life itself. Biology and chemistry have always been allied sciences, and the exploration of cells and their molecular components, carried out by biochemists and other biological scientists, has revealed much about life. Watson and Crick's breakthrough discovery of the structure of DNA in 1953 touched off a flurry of scientific activity that led to a better and better understanding of DNA chemistry and the genetic code. These discoveries eventually made it possible to manipulate DNA, enabling genetic engineers to transplant foreign genes into microorganisms to produce such valuable products as human insulin, which occurred in 1982.

Today, the field of biochemistry crosses over into many other sciences, as biochemists have become involved in genetics, nutrition, psychology, fertility, agriculture, and more. The new biotechnology is revolutionizing the pharmaceutical industry. Much of this work is done by biochemists and molecular biologists because this technology involves understanding the complex chemistry of life.

■ THE JOB

Depending on a biochemist's education level and area of specialty, this professional can do many types of work for a variety of employers. For instance, a biochemist could have a job doing basic research for a federal government agency or for individual states with laboratories that employ skilled persons to analyze food, drug, air, water, waste, or animal tissue samples. A biochemist might work for a drug company as part of a basic research team searching for the cause of diseases or conduct applied research to develop drugs to cure disease. A biochemist might work in a biotechnology company focusing on the environment, energy, human health care, agriculture, or animal health. There, he or she might do research or quality control, or work on manufacturing/production or information systems. Another possibility is for the biochemist to specialize in an additional area, such as law, business, or journalism, and use his or her biochemistry or molecular biology background for a career that combines science with regulatory affairs, management, writing, or teaching.

Ph.D. scientists who enter the highest levels of academic life combine teaching and research. In addition to teaching in university classrooms and laboratories, they also do basic research designed to increase biochemistry and molecular biology knowledge. As Ph.D. scientists, these professionals could also work for an industry or government laboratory doing basic research or research and development (R&D). The problems studied, research styles, and type of organization vary widely across different laboratories. The Ph.D. scientist may lead a research group or be part of a small team of Ph.D. researchers. Other Ph.D. scientists might opt for administrative positions. In government, for example, these scientists might lead programs concerned with the safety of new devices, food, drugs, or pesticides and other chemicals. Or they might influence which projects will get federal funding.

Generally, biochemists employed in the United States work in one of three major fields: medicine, nutrition, or agriculture. In medicine, biochemists mass-produce lifesaving chemicals usually found only in minuscule amounts in the body. Some of these chemicals have been helping diabetics and heart attack victims for years. Biochemists employed in the field of medicine might work to identify chemical changes in organs or cells that signal the development of such diseases as cancer, diabetes, or schizophrenia. Or they may look for chemical explanations for why certain people develop muscular dystrophy or become obese. While studying chemical makeup and changes in these situations, biochemists may work to discover a treatment or a prevention for a disease. For instance, biochemists discovering how certain diseases such as AIDS and cancer escape detection by the immune system are also devising ways to enhance immunity to fight these diseases. Biochemists are also finding out the chemical basis of fertility and how to improve the success of in vitro fertilization to help couples have children or to preserve endangered species.

Biochemists in the pharmaceutical industry design, develop, and evaluate drugs, antibiotics, diagnostic kits, and other medical devices. They may search out ways to produce antibiotics, hormones, enzymes, or other drug components, or they may do quality control on the way in which drugs and dosages are made and determined.

In the field of nutrition, biochemists examine the effects of food on the body. For example, they might study the relationship between diet and diabetes. Biochemists doing this study could look at the nutrition content of certain foods eaten by people with diabetes and study how these foods affect the functioning of the pancreas and other organs. Biochemists in the nutrition field also look at vitamin and mineral deficiencies and how they affect the human body. They examine these deficiencies in relation to body performance, and they may study anything from how the liver is affected by a lack of vitamin B to the effects of poor nutrition on the ability to learn.

Biochemists involved in agriculture undertake studies to discover more efficient methods of crop cultivation, storage, and pest control. For example, they might create genetically engineered crops that are more resistant to frost, drought, spoilage, disease, and pests. They might focus on helping to create fruit trees that produce more fruit by studying the biochemical composition of the plant and determining how to alter or select for this desirable trait. Biochemists may study the chemical composition of insects to determine better and more efficient methods of controlling the pest population and the damage they do to crops. Or they could work on programming bacteria to clean up the environment by "eating" toxic chemicals.

About seven out of 10 biochemists are engaged in basic research, often for a university medical school or nonprofit organization, such as a foundation or research institute. The remaining 30 percent do applied research, using the discoveries of basic research to solve practical problems or develop products. For example, a biochemist working in basic research may make a discovery about how a living organism forms hormones. This discovery will lead to a scientist doing applied research, making

hormones in the laboratory, and eventually to mass production. Discoveries made in DNA research have led to techniques for identifying criminals from a single strand of hair or a tiny blood stain left at the scene of a crime. The distinction between basic and applied research is one of degree, however; biochemists often engage in both types of work.

Biochemistry requires skillful use of a wide range of sophisticated analytical equipment and application of newly discovered techniques requiring special instruments or new chemical reagents. Sometimes, biochemists themselves must invent and test new instruments if existing methods and equipment do not meet their needs. Biochemists must also be patient, methodical, and careful in their laboratory procedures.

■ REQUIREMENTS

Although they usually specialize in one of many areas in the field, biochemists and molecular biologists should also be familiar with several scientific disciplines, including chemistry, physics, mathematics, and computer science. High school can provide the foundation for getting this knowledge, while four years of college expands it, and postgraduate work directs students to explore specific areas more deeply. The following describes possible strategies at each level and includes a community college option.

High School

If you have an interest in biochemistry as a high school student, you should take at least one year each of biology, chemistry, physics, algebra, geometry, and trigonometry. Introductory calculus is also a good idea. Because scientists must clearly and accurately communicate their results verbally and in writing, English courses that emphasize writing skills are strongly recommended. Many colleges and universities also require several years of a foreign language, a useful skill in this day and age, as scientists frequently exchange information with researchers from other countries.

Postsecondary Training

Some colleges have their own special requirements for admission, so you should do a little research and take any special courses you need for the college that interests you. Also, check the catalogs of colleges and universities to see if they offer a program in biochemistry or related sciences. Some schools award a bachelor's degree in biochemistry, and nearly all colleges and universities offer a major in biology or chemistry.

To best prepare yourself for a career in biochemistry or molecular biology, you should start by earning a bachelor's degree in either of these two areas. Even if your college does not offer a specific program in biochemistry or molecular biology, you can get comparable training by doing one of two things: (1) working toward a bachelor's degree in chemistry and taking courses in biology, molecular genetics, and biochemistry, including a biochemistry laboratory class, or (2) earning a bachelor's degree in biology, but taking more chemistry, mathematics, and physics courses than the biology major may require, and also choosing a biochemistry course that has lab work with it.

It really doesn't matter if you earn a bachelor of science (B.S.) or a bachelor of arts (B.A.) degree; some schools offer both. It is more important to choose your courses thoughtfully and to get advice in your freshman year from a faculty member who knows about the fields of biochemistry and molecular biology.

Many careers in biochemistry, especially those that involve teaching at a college or directing scientific research at a university, a government laboratory, or a commercial company, require at least a master's degree and prefer a doctorate or Ph.D. degree. Most students enter graduate programs with a bachelor's degree in biochemistry, or in chemistry or biology with supplementary courses. Because biochemistry and molecular biology are so broad-based, you can enter their graduate programs from such diverse fields as physics, psychology, nutrition, microbiology, or engineering. Graduate schools prefer students with laboratory or research experience.

However you get there, a graduate education program is intense. A master's degree requires about a year of course work and often a research project as well. For a Ph.D. degree, full-time course work can last up to two years, followed by one or more special test exams. But the most important part of Ph.D. training is the requirement for all students to conduct an extensive research project leading to significant new scientific findings. Most students work under a faculty member's direction. This training is vital, as it will help you develop the skills to frame scientific questions and discover ways to answer them. It will also teach you important laboratory skills useful in tackling other biochemical problems. Most students complete a Ph.D. program in four or five years.

Certification or Licensing

Biochemists who wish to work in a hospital may need certification by a national certifying board such as the American Board of Clinical Chemistry.

Other Requirements

A scientist never stops learning, even when formal education has ended. This is particularly true for biochemists and molecular biologists because constant breakthroughs

and technology advances make for a constantly changing work environment. That is why most Ph.D.'s go for more research experience (postdoctoral research) before they enter the workplace. As a "postdoc," you would not take course work, earn a degree, or teach; you would be likely to work full-time on a high-level research project in the laboratory of an established scientist. Typically, this postdoctoral period lasts two to three years, during which time you would get a salary or be supported by a fellowship. Though not essential for many industry research jobs, postdoctoral research is generally expected of those wishing to become professors. Also, because biochemistry and medicine are such allies, some Ph.D. recipients also earn their medical degrees, or M.D.'s, as a physician does. This is to get the broadest possible base for a career in medical research.

■ EXPLORING

The analytical, specialized nature of most biochemistry makes it unlikely that you will gain much exposure to it before college. Many high school chemistry and biology courses, however, allow students to work with laboratory tools and techniques that will give them a valuable background before college. In some cases, high school students can take advantage of opportunities to train as laboratory technicians by taking courses at a community college. You might also want to contact local colleges, universities, or laboratories to set up interviews with biochemists to learn as much as you can about the field. In addition, reading science and medical magazines will help you to stay current with recent breakthroughs in the biochemistry field.

■ EMPLOYERS

Government agencies at the federal, state, and local levels employ about four out of every 10 biological scientists. At such agencies these scientists may do basic research and analyze food, drug, air, water, waste, or animal tissue samples. Biochemists also work for university medical schools or nonprofit organizations, such as a foundation or research institute, doing basic research. Drug companies employ biochemists to search for the causes of diseases or develop drugs to cure them. Biochemists work in quality control, research, manufacturing/production, or information systems at biotechnology companies that concentrate on the environment, energy, human health care, agriculture, or animal health. Universities hire biochemists to teach in combination with doing research.

■ STARTING OUT

A bachelor's degree in biochemistry or molecular biology can help you get into medical, dental, veterinary, law, or business school. It can also be a stepping-stone to a career in many different but related fields: biotechnology, toxicology, biomedical engineering, clinical chemistry, plant pathology, animal science, or other fields. Biochemists fresh from a college undergraduate program can take advantage of opportunities to get valuable on-the-job experience in a biochemistry or molecular biology laboratory. The National Science Foundation and the National Institutes of Health, both federal government agencies, sponsor research programs for undergraduates. Groups who can particularly benefit from these programs include women, Hispanics, African Americans, Native Americans, Native Alaskans, and students with disabilities. Your college or university may also offer senior research projects that provide hands-on experience.

Another way to improve your chances of getting a job is to spend an additional year at a university with training programs for specialized laboratory techniques. Researchers and companies like these "certificate programs" because they teach valuable skills related to cell culture, genetic engineering, recombinant DNA technology, biotechnology, in vitro cell biology, protein engineering, or DNA sequencing and synthesis. In some universities, you can work toward a bachelor's degree and a certificate at the same time.

Biochemists with a bachelor's degree usually begin work in industry or government as research assistants doing testing and analysis. In the drug industry, for example, you might analyze the ingredients of a product to verify and maintain its quality. Biochemists with a master's degree may enter the field in management, marketing, or sales positions, whereas those with a doctorate usually go into basic or applied research. Many Ph.D. graduates work at colleges and universities where the emphasis is on teaching.

■ ADVANCEMENT

The more education you have, the greater your reward potential. Biochemists with a graduate degree have more opportunities for advancement than those with only an undergraduate degree. It is not uncommon for students to go back to graduate school after working for a while in a job that required a lesser degree. Some graduate students become research or teaching assistants in colleges and universities, qualifying for professorships when they receive their advanced degrees. Having a doctorate allows you to design research initiatives and direct others in carrying out experiments. Experienced biochemists with doctorates can move up to high-level administrative positions and supervise entire research programs. Other highly qualified biochemists who prefer to devote themselves to research often become leaders in a particular aspect of their profession.

■ EARNINGS

According to a report by the National Association of Colleges and Employers, beginning salaries in 2003 for graduates with bachelor's degrees in biological science ranged from $23,000 to $35,000.

The following mid-range earnings for R&D biochemists came from a report by Abbott, Langer and Associates: $52,000 for managers, $58,064 for R&D specialists, $83,500 for directors, and $90,479 for section heads. A report from the American Chemical Society gives the following industry earnings: $47,251 for biochemists with a bachelor's degree, $56,205 for those with a master's degree, and $79,176 for doctoral degree holders.

The U.S. Department of Labor reports that biochemists and biophysicists had average annual incomes of $65,620 in 2002. The mean annual earnings of such scientists not employed by the government were $75,120 in 2002. Additionally, the department reports that the median yearly income for agricultural scientists (which may include biochemists specializing in the field of agriculture) earned a median income of $48,670 annually in 2002. That same year the highest paid 10 percent of this group made more than $85,460.

Colleges and universities also employ many biochemists as professors and researchers. The American Association of University Professors reports that salaries for postsecondary teachers with Ph.D.'s range from $45,763 for a lecturer to $100,682 for a full tenured professor.

Biochemists who work for universities, the government, or industry all tend to receive good benefits packages, such as health and life insurance, pension plans, and paid vacation and sick leave. Those employed as university faculty operate on the academic calendar, which means that they can get summer and winter breaks from teaching classes.

■ WORK ENVIRONMENT

Biochemists generally work in clean, quiet, and well-lighted laboratories where physical labor is minimal. They must, however, take the proper precautions in handling chemicals and organic substances that could be dangerous or cause illness. They may work with plants and animals; their tissues, cells, and products; and with yeast and bacteria.

Biochemists in industry generally work a 40-hour week, although they, like their counterparts in research, often put in many extra hours. They must be ready to spend a considerable amount of time keeping up with current literature, for example. Many biochemists occasionally travel to attend meetings or conferences. Those in research write papers for presentation at meetings or for publication in scientific journals.

Individuals interested in biochemistry must have the patience to work for long periods of time on a project without necessarily getting the desired results. Biochemistry is often a team affair, requiring an ability to work well and cooperate with others. Successful biochemists are continually learning and increasing their skills.

■ OUTLOOK

Employment growth for biological scientists, including biochemists, is expected to be about as fast as the average through 2012, according to the U.S. Department of Labor, as the number of trained scientists has increased faster than available funding. Competition will be strong for basic research positions, and candidates with more education and the experience it brings will be more likely to find the positions they want. Employment is available in health-related fields, where the emphasis is on finding cures for such diseases as cancer, muscular dystrophy, AIDS, and Alzheimer's. Additional jobs will be created to produce genetically engineered drugs and other products in the new and rapidly expanding field of genetic engineering. In this area, the outlook is best for biochemists with advanced degrees who can conduct genetic and cellular research. A caveat exists, however. Employment growth may slow somewhat as the number of new biotechnology firms slows and existing firms merge. Biochemists with bachelor's degrees who have difficulty entering their chosen career field may find openings as technicians or technologists or may choose to transfer their skills to other biological science fields.

It is estimated that over the next decade, 68 percent of those entering the workforce will be women and members of other minority groups. The federal government, recognizing this situation, offers a variety of special programs (through the National Science Foundation and the National Institutes of Health) to bring women, minorities, and persons with disabilities into the field.

■ FOR MORE INFORMATION

For additional information about careers, education, and scholarships, contact the following organizations:

American Association for Clinical Chemistry
2101 L Street, NW, Suite 202
Washington, DC 20037-1558
Tel: 800-892-1400
Email: info@aacc.org
http://www.aacc.org

American Chemical Society
1155 16th Street, NW
Washington, DC 20036
Tel: 800-227-5558
http://www.chemistry.org

American Institute of Biological Sciences
1444 Eye Street, NW, Suite 200
Washington, DC 20005
Tel: 202-628-1500
Email: admin@aibs.org
http://www.aibs.org

American Society for Biochemistry and Molecular Biology
Education Information
9650 Rockville Pike
Bethesda, MD 20814-3996
Tel: 301-530-7145
Email: asbmb@asbmb.faseb.org
http://www.asbmb.org

American Society for Investigative Pathology
9650 Rockville Pike
Bethesda, MD 20814-3993
Tel: 301-634-7130
Email: asip@pathol.faseb.org
http://www.asip.org

Biofeedback Therapists

■ OVERVIEW

Biofeedback training is a process that helps patients gain control of their responses to stress, anxiety, physical strain, and emotional stimuli. Special instruments monitor a variety of physiological conditions, including heart rate, skin temperature, muscle tension, and blood pressure. *Biofeedback therapists* assist patients in interpreting the information gathered through monitoring. They help them learn to control individual body functions and reactions in ways that can decrease stress and alleviate the effects of a wide range of disorders, such as migraine headaches, gastrointestinal concerns, and epilepsy.

■ HISTORY

Biofeedback therapy has a relatively short history. The term itself did not come into widespread use until roughly 1969, when the results of four separate lines of research converged into a new approach to the treatment of a variety of medical and psychological conditions.

Until the early 1960s, psychologists generally accepted the premise that biological responses typically thought to be "involuntary," or under the control of the autonomic nervous system (such as heart rate, stomach acid secretion, blood pressure, or skin resistance) could not be modified or influenced using measurable instrumental means. Instead, this form of conditioned learning was thought possible only for responses that were under "voluntary" control, such as skeletal muscle responses. A definitive statement of this collective assumption appeared in a 1961 textbook, prompting a number of scientists to begin studies to refute it.

Four areas of study in particular yielded notable results. One approach employed a shock-avoidance paradigm in which subjects could avoid mild electrical shocks by making appropriate adjustments in heart rate. These studies demonstrated that statistically significant increases and decreases in heart rate could be obtained using instrument-based conditioning techniques. Other work achieved similar results using a positive reinforcement paradigm rather than shock avoidance.

About the same time, several other researchers showed that *galvanic skin response,* the ability of the body to conduct minute amounts of naturally occurring electrical current across the skin, could also be controlled by individuals.

As these reports surfaced, critics began to appear. They pointed to the fact that some voluntary responses can elicit a response that appears to be autonomic or involuntary. For instance, changes in heart rate can be initiated by altering respiration patterns or tensing certain muscle groups—both responses under voluntary control. If changes in heart rate, an autonomically mediated response, were "caused" by changes in responses under voluntary control, critics argued, such a demonstration would not prove that heart rate itself could be changed by voluntary control.

A third line of research sought to address this concern, removing the effect of voluntary responses from the equation. Laboratory rats were injected with curare, a drug that paralyzes all skeletal muscles (including those that enable the animals to breathe). They then were maintained on artificial respiration, which kept them alive and exactly regulated their breathing. Finally, an electrode was implanted in the hypothalamus, the part of the brain that regulates body temperature, certain metabolic processes, and other involuntary activities, so the researchers could control its actions. With this preparation, scientists showed that several involuntary responses could be spontaneously conditioned—not only heart rate, but blood pressure and urine formation, among others. This demonstration of large magnitude changes in the responses of the internal organs in animals encouraged researchers to speculate on the wide range of human psychosomatic disorders that might be treatable with biofeedback.

Eventually, a fourth avenue of research emerged in the field of electroencephalography (EEG), the study of electrical activity in the brain. Several scientists began to study whether subjects could "voluntarily" produce certain EEG patterns—particularly the *alpha rhythm,* a distinctive rhythm associated with deep relaxation. Because of the similarity in the subjective experience of a "high alpha state" with that reported for meditation, self-control of EEG patterns attracted much attention beyond the scientific community, helping the entire field to grow.

■ THE JOB

Biofeedback therapy is a treatment that over the last three decades has shown considerable promise for patients with a wide range of conditions and disorders. Because it can be adapted to so many uses, it has developed more as a complementary skill than as a separate career. Biofeedback therapists come from a variety of backgrounds—physicians, social workers, psychologists, physical therapists, chiropractors, speech pathologists, even dental hygienists, among others. These professionals incorporate biofeedback learning techniques into the more traditional treatments they regularly provide. While it is not impossible to have a career in biofeedback without underlying training in a different field, few people are trained only as biofeedback therapists. It is true, however, that many therapists with experience in other disciplines choose to focus their practices largely on biofeedback.

An understanding of the uses of biofeedback begins with an understanding of the effects of stress. Stress often arises from major life changes, such as divorce, the death of a loved one, a move to a new home, or even celebrating holidays with family. In such high-stress times, a person's body undergoes "fight-or-flight" reactions. The body reacts physiologically to a person's mental and emotional concerns.

The effects of a typical fight-or-flight situation, such as a mugging or assault, may be considerable. A

QUICK FACTS

SCHOOL SUBJECTS
Biology
Psychology

PERSONAL SKILLS
Helping/teaching
Technical/scientific

WORK ENVIRONMENT
Primarily indoors
Primarily one location

MINIMUM EDUCATION LEVEL
Bachelor's degree

SALARY RANGE
$30,000 to $50,000 to
$200,000

CERTIFICATION OR LICENSING
Recommended

OUTLOOK
Faster than the average

DOT
N/A

GOE
N/A

NOC
N/A

O*NET-SOC
N/A

person reacting to such a potentially life-threatening situation will experience physiological changes. But much smaller stresses to a person's system, such as anxiety the night before an important exam, can also have lingering negative effects. An exam is not a life-threatening situation, but if someone perceives it that way, these perceptions can cause the same types of physiological changes.

Some people are terrified to speak in front of a group. There is no physical danger, but the speaker feels threatened in nonphysical ways—he or she may trip, forget lines, mispronounce words, fail at getting a message across, or be ridiculed. The speaker becomes nervous and tense, activating the fight-or-flight response when there is no real reason to do so.

Scientists believe that if people can learn to make themselves ill in this way, by moving their body systems out of balance, they might very well be able to learn to reverse the process and make themselves well. Biofeedback training teaches patients to restore balance to their body systems by voluntarily controlling generally involuntary reactions to various forms of stress.

There are three primary forms of biofeedback therapy; they involve the measurement of skin temperature, muscle tension, and brain waves. Each form is useful in a different range of disorders and conditions, and the list continues to grow.

Skin temperature biofeedback is often used with a therapeutic technique called autogenic training. Skin temperature is affected by blood flow, which is affected by stress. When a person is tense, blood vessels narrow, limiting the flow of blood in the body and causing skin temperature to drop. Biofeedback therapists place sensors on the hands or feet to determine blood flow. *Autogenic training* involves mastering passive concentration, and when properly practiced, helps the patient relax deeply through a number of repeated formula phrases. ("My right arm is heavy. My right arm is heavy. My right arm is heavy. My left arm is heavy....") The relaxation improves blood flow and raises skin temperature. These techniques have been shown to aid patients suffering from severe migraine headaches, Raynaud's disease (a disorder of the blood vessels in the extremities characterized by extreme sensitivity to cold), and hypertension or high blood pressure, among other complaints.

Muscle tension biofeedback, or *electromyograph (EMG) biofeedback training,* involves using sensitive electrodes to detect the amount of electrical activity in muscles. Auditory and visual feedback helps patients learn to control the pace and intensity of this activity. Autogenic training may be used in these situations as well to encourage relaxation. Many disorders respond to EMG biofeedback therapy, including tension headaches, anxieties, phobias, and psychoses.

The last line of research is the study of brain waves using *electroencephalograph (EEG),* or *neurobiofeedback.* Brain waves display certain characteristic rhythmic patterns. *Beta rhythms* are fast and have small amplitude; they predominate when you are awake or mentally aroused. *Alpha rhythms,* the first to be identified in EEG biofeedback therapy, are extraordinarily symmetrical, have large amplitude, and increase in most patients when they close their eyes and relax their bodies. *Theta rhythms* continue the slide toward sleep and increase as a person becomes drowsy, corresponding to early dreaming states. *Delta rhythms* are irregular and occur in heavy, dreamless sleep. Biofeedback training that teaches patients to seek the alpha state has been shown to be helpful in the treatment of epilepsy, attention deficit disorder, autism, and obsessive-compulsive disorders, among other maladies. Scientists currently are exploring the use of EEG training in enhancing creativity and improving learning.

A biofeedback therapist's approach depends on his or her primary training. Physicians use biofeedback to complement medical remedies. Social workers use biofeedback to help patients cope with the social and emotional effects of chronic and sometimes debilitating problems. Music therapists use music and rhythm in conjunction with biofeedback to help patients understand and control physiological and emotional reactions. Other profes-

WHAT PROBLEMS CAN BIOFEEDBACK HELP?

According to the Association for Applied Psychophysiology and Biofeedback, this therapy can help in the treatment of the following:

- **Migraine and tension headaches.** Studies with follow-ups as long as 15 years show the treatment is effective.

- **Essential hypertension.** One study found 80 percent of individuals with this condition reduced their prescription medications or no longer needed them at all after biofeedback training.

- **Attention deficit disorder/attention deficit hyperactivity disorder (ADD/ADHD).** Practitioners report patients with these conditions who receive EEG biofeedback have 60 to 80 percent improvement and need less medication.

- **Panic and anxiety disorders.** Studies have shown people with these disorders who receive biofeedback training are much more able to control these states.

sionals who might use biofeedback therapy include nurses, psychiatrists, physical therapists, and anyone involved in health care or counseling work.

■ REQUIREMENTS
High School
To enter this range of careers you will need science courses, such as biology and anatomy. Physical education and health will give you some understanding of the physical aspects of biofeedback. Since counseling skills are also important, classes in psychology and sociology can be helpful.

Biofeedback currently is a rapidly expanding field. The marriages of art and biofeedback (as in an art therapy practice) or sports and biofeedback (as in the development of specialized training programs for top athletes) are just two of the many more unusual applications of this discipline.

Postsecondary Training
Most people who practice biofeedback therapy first become licensed in some other area of health care. Biofeedback then becomes an area of specialization within their practices. A biofeedback therapist may have a master's degree in social work, a Ph.D. in psychology, a nursing or medical degree, or some other professional designation. After receiving this professional degree (which may take 10 or more years, in the case of a medical degree), you then take courses in biofeedback from approved schools.

The Biofeedback Certification Institute of America (BCIA) provides a listing of approved schools and required course work on its website (http://www.bcia.org). Though many institutions offer workshops in biofeedback and may even offer biofeedback training programs and degrees, not all of them are approved by the certifying board. Some biofeedback therapists do practice without certification, but these uncertified therapists are not recognized by the professional organizations.

Certification or Licensing
The BCIA was created to establish and maintain standards for practitioners who use biofeedback and to certify practitioners who meet those standards. BCIA certification requires you to have a minimum of a bachelor's degree granted by a regionally accredited academic institution in one of the following approved health care fields: counseling, chiropractic, dental hygiene, dentistry, exercise physiology, medicine, nursing, occupational therapy, physical therapy, physician's assistant, psychology, recreational therapy, rehabilitation, respiratory therapy, social

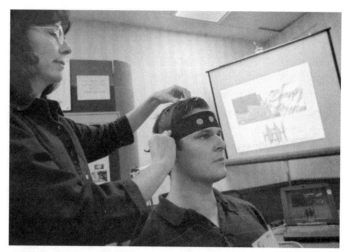

A biofeedback therapist fits sensors to a test subject at a biofeedback conference.

work, speech pathology, and sports medicine. Those who do not have a degree in one of these fields may be eligible for certification through a special review.

Candidates must complete 150 hours of training at an accredited biofeedback training program. This involves coursework as well as hands-on experience. Class work covers topics such as neuromuscular intervention, the autonomic nervous system, and professional conduct. The clinical training involves working directly with patients while under careful supervision and using a variety of biofeedback techniques. Candidates must also receive biofeedback, have supervised patient case conferences, and complete a comprehensive course in human anatomy, human biology, or human physiology. Once all of these requirements are fulfilled candidates are eligible to take the rigorous written certification exam.

At this time, BCIA certification is not mandatory, but is recommended. In addition to its general program, the BCIA offers a specialty certification in EEG biofeedback.

Other Requirements
The practice of biofeedback therapy involves a great deal of personal interaction. As a result, you must enjoy being around a variety of people. Biofeedback practitioners also need excellent communication skills and must be careful listeners, able to pay attention to details. A genuine empathy for patients is important as well. Because biofeedback is a growing but still fairly new field, business and management skills will be important. Therapists generally are responsible for building their own practices, and like most other health care professionals, typically spend many hours dealing with insurance, managed care, and financial issues.

BIOFEEDBACK AND MUSIC THERAPY

Audio feedback is a standard intervention which allows patients to hear physiological changes, and make adjustments to bring them further under control. But these tones needn't be limited to simple beeps any longer, and with the popularity of music therapy, many imaginative options are available.

Modern computerized biofeedback systems can assign live-sounding digital representations of musical instruments and sounds to muscle groups of choice—perhaps an orchestral string section to your bicep, a flute to your abs, or maybe a snare drum for your heart.

Music may also be used to assist patients in achieving a relaxed state. Spoken images of relaxation, light, and color, in conjunction with music, all are typical in guided imagery sessions and have been shown to be successful.

Other uses of music in biofeedback include music as a reward for appropriate behavior modification—for instance, the automatic playing of a favorite piece when the patient's heart rate has reached the desired point. Still other methods involve the patient more directly, such as vocal toning, chanting, or drumming.

■ EXPLORING

You can begin exploring this field by contacting and interviewing biofeedback therapists in your area to gain a more specific understanding of their day-to-day activities.

If your school participates in an annual science fair, consider using the opportunity to develop a presentation on biofeedback. Many simple experiments are possible and appropriate for this setting. (Consider a sophisticated take on mood rings, for instance.)

Outside school, you can practice a number of forms of noninstrumental biofeedback. Yoga and Zen meditation both will help you become more attuned to your own body and its rhythms—an important skill to have as a biofeedback therapist. Learning either of these disciplines will give you a taste of how body systems can be trained to respond to intention and outside control and will teach you how to recognize some of your own body's feedback patterns.

■ EMPLOYERS

Biofeedback therapy has been shown to be useful in the treatment of such a wide variety of conditions and disorders that therapists can be found in a number of background specialties, from medicine and psychology to occupational therapy and dentistry. This means that biofeedback therapists are employed by many different types of institutions. They often have private practices as well. If you can envision ways in which biofeedback can assist people in whatever career field you might find yourself, chances are you can build a practice around it, either alone, or working with a group or for an institutional employer. Medical centers are the most common place of employment for biofeedback therapists, but more and more corporations are finding applications for biofeedback in the workplace.

■ STARTING OUT

Most biofeedback therapists come to the discipline with established practices in other fields. Once you have received the minimum of a bachelor's degree in your primary field, you can begin to think about specific training in biofeedback therapy. (A master's or sometimes even a doctorate is preferred to a bachelor's, depending on your areas of study.)

BCIA certification may be the most appropriate first goal for beginning therapists as it will lend credibility to your training and help you build your practice. Therapist candidates can earn BCIA certification concurrently with training, and they offer the option of taking courses on a part-time basis.

■ ADVANCEMENT

Advancement opportunities are dependent on the main specialty a therapist has chosen and the environment in which he or she is working. Continuing education is important to any health care professional, so biofeedback therapists advance within their practices by developing their skills and learning about new methods of treatment. In some cases, such as academic medical centers, the addition of biofeedback therapy to a practice may assist the therapist in reaching promotion goals.

■ EARNINGS

Biofeedback therapists generally charge from $50 to $150 per session. Depending on the level of their experience, the size of their client base, and their level of training, biofeedback therapists can have substantial earnings. Because biofeedback therapists come from different professional backgrounds, however, it is difficult to give a salary range for them as a group. For example, a clinical psychologist with a Ph.D. is going to make more money practicing biofeedback than will a social worker with a master's degree. Therapists working in more urban areas generally make more money than those in smaller communities. A therapist just starting out may have annual earnings in the $30,000s. More established therapists, even in rural areas, may make around $50,000, while those working in larger communities, often handling many patients, may make up to $200,000 a year.

WORK ENVIRONMENT

Biofeedback therapists typically spend much of their time working one-on-one with patients. As with most health care practices, they may work in any number of environments, from solo private practices to larger medical centers or corporate complexes. Their responsibilities run the gamut from one-on-one patient visits to collaborative efforts with physicians and diagnosticians tackling difficult cases. Therapists primarily work in an office, although the increasing portability of computers means this may eventually change as well, allowing biofeedback practitioners even to consider house calls on a regular basis.

OUTLOOK

The employment outlook for biofeedback therapists is good. According to the U.S. Department of Labor, the overall rate of job growth in the health care field will be faster than the average through 2012. While the department does not provide specific projections for biofeedback therapists, it is logical to conclude they will be in demand for several reasons. One reason is the growing population of Americans aged 65 and over. People in this age group are more likely to need and seek out treatments for many different conditions. This will increase the demand for most health care industry workers, including biofeedback therapists. Also, because most individuals have some sort of medical insurance, the costs of care, including nontraditional courses of treatment such as biofeedback therapy, have become more affordable. According to EEG Spectrum International, many insurance plans cover biofeedback therapy for treatment of certain conditions. Government agencies are also beginning to recognize the benefits of biofeedback therapy. In 2000, the Centers for Medicare and Medicaid Services for example, mandated Medicare coverage for biofeedback training for patients with certain types of incontinence problems.

In many cases, patients seek the assistance of biofeedback therapists after more traditional medical treatment has failed. On the other hand, some people choose to look first to alternative forms of health care to avoid medications or invasive surgery.

In addition, continued research within the field of biofeedback should allow for the treatment of more disorders. Subspecialties like neurobiofeedback are increasing dramatically. The study of brain waves in cases involving alcoholism, attention deficit disorder, insomnia, epilepsy, and traumatic brain injury point to new biofeedback treatment methods.

Some conditions, such as chronic headaches, are often better treated through biofeedback therapy than through more invasive medical treatment.

FOR MORE INFORMATION

AAPB is dedicated to the promotion of biofeedback as a means of improving health. Their website is a good place to begin to gather more details about the field.

Association for Applied Psychophysiology and Biofeedback (AAPB)
10200 West 44th Avenue, Suite 304
Wheat Ridge, CO 80033-2840
Tel: 303-422-8436
Email: AAPB@resourcenter.com
http://www.aapb.org

For more information about biofeedback, certification, and approved programs, contact

Biofeedback Certification Institute of America
10200 West 44th Avenue, Suite 310
Wheat Ridge, CO 80033-2840
Tel: 303-420-2902
Email: bcia@resourcenter.com
http://www.bcia.org

For more on neurofeedback, including research, news, and practitioners, contact

EEG Spectrum International Inc.
21601 Vanowen Street, Suite 100
Canoga Park, CA 91303
Tel: 818-789-3456
http://www.eegspectrum.com

Biologists

OVERVIEW

Biologists study the origin, development, anatomy, function, distribution, and other basic principles of living organisms. They are concerned with the nature of life itself in humans, microorganisms, plants, and animals, and with the relationship of each organism to its environment. Biologists perform research in many specialties that advance the fields of medicine, agriculture, and industry. Approximately 75,000 biological scientists are employed in the United States.

HISTORY

The biological sciences developed slowly over the course of human history. Early humans practiced an inexact form of biology when they established agriculture. They observed the environment around them to determine what types of seeds yielded consumable food, when to plant, when to water, and when to harvest the seeds for planting in the next season. Early humans improved their way of life as a result of their primitive forays into science.

It wasn't until modern times that biology developed into an exact science. Our ancestors learned to differentiate between desirable and undesirable plants (taxonomy), to seek out and live in more habitable environments (ecology), to domesticate plants (agronomy and horticulture) and animals (animal husbandry), and to eat a suitable diet (nutrition). Eventually, plants and animals were classified; later they were studied to see how they functioned and how they related to other organisms around them. This was the beginning of zoology (animal science) and botany (plant science).

QUICK FACTS

SCHOOL SUBJECTS
Biology
Physiology

PERSONAL SKILLS
Mechanical/manipulative
Technical/scientific

WORK ENVIRONMENT
Indoors and outdoors
Primarily multiple locations

MINIMUM EDUCATION LEVEL
Bachelor's degree

SALARY RANGE
$33,930 to $60,390 to
$102,930

CERTIFICATION OR LICENSING
Required for certain positions

OUTLOOK
About as fast as the average

DOT
041

GOE
02.03.03

NOC
2121

O*NET-SOC
19-1020.01, 19-1021.00,
19-1022.00, 19-1023.00

The Greek philosopher Aristotle created one of the first documented taxonomic systems for animals. He divided animals into two types: blooded (mammals, birds, amphibians, reptiles, and fishes) and bloodless (insects, crustaceans, and other lower animals). He also studied reproduction and theorized, incorrectly, how embryos developed in animals.

From the second century to the 11th century, the Arabs made important advances in biological understanding. Unlike the Europeans, they continued to study from the base of knowledge established by the Greeks. Avicenna, a Persian philosopher and physician, wrote the *Canon of Medicine,* one of the most influential and important publications on medical knowledge in the world at its time—and for the next seven centuries.

The field of biology has expanded rapidly in the last two centuries. The French physician Louis Pasteur developed the field of immunology, and his studies of fermentation led to modern microbiology. Many other achievements became possible because of improvements in the microscope. Scientists could isolate much smaller structures than ever before possible. Matthias Schleiden and Theodor Schwann formulated the idea that the cell is the fundamental unit of all organisms. Gregor Mendel discovered the principles of heredity through crossbreeding pea plants.

While the 19th century can be considered the age of cellular biology, the 20th and early 21st has been dominated by studies and breakthroughs in biochemistry and molecular biology. The discovery of the atomic structure allowed the fundamental building blocks of nature to be studied. Living tissues were found to be composed of fats, sugars, and proteins. Proteins were found to be composed of amino acids. Discoveries in cell biology established the manner in which information was transmitted from one organism to its progeny. Chromosomes were recognized as the carriers of this information. In 1944, Oswald Avery and a team of scientists were able to isolate and identify DNA as the transmitter of genetic information. In 1953 James Watson and Francis Crick deciphered the complex structure of DNA and hypothesized that it carried the genetic code for all living matter.

Biological science is the foundation for most of the discoveries that affect people's everyday lives. Biologists break new ground to improve our health and quality of life and help us to better understand the world around us.

■ THE JOB

Biology can be divided into many specialties. The biologist, who studies a wide variety of living organisms, has interests that differ from those of the chemist, physicist, and geologist, who are concerned with nonliving matter. Biologists, or *life scientists*, may be identified by their specialties. Following is a breakdown of the many kinds of biologists and their specific fields of study:

Anatomists study animal bodies from basic cell structure to complex tissues and organs. They determine the ability of body parts to regenerate and investigate the possibility of transplanting organs and skin. Their research is applied to human medicine.

Aquatic biologists study animals and plants that live in water and how they are affected by their environmental conditions, such as the salt, acid, and oxygen content of the water and temperature, light, and other factors.

Biochemists study the chemical composition of living organisms. They attempt to understand the complex reactions involved in reproduction, growth, metabolism, and heredity.

Biophysicists apply physical principles to biological problems. They study the mechanics, heat, light, radiation, sound, electricity, and energetics of living cells and organisms and do research in the areas of vision, hearing, brain function, nerve conduction, muscle reflex, and damaged cells and tissues.

Biotechnicians, or *biological technicians*, assist the cornucopia of biological scientists in their endeavors.

Botanists study plant life. Some specialize in plant biochemistry, the structure and function of plant parts, and identification and classification, among other topics.

Cytologists, sometimes called *cell biologists*, examine the cells of plants and animals, including those cells involved in reproduction. They use microscopes and other instruments to observe the growth and division of cells and to study the influences of physical and chemical factors on both normal and malignant cells.

Ecologists examine such factors as pollutants, rainfall, altitude, temperature, and population size in order to study the distribution and abundance of organisms and their relation to their environment.

Entomologists study insects and their relationship to other life forms.

Geneticists study heredity in various forms of life. They are concerned with how biological traits such as color, size, and resistance to disease originate and are transmitted from one generation to another. They also try to develop ways to alter or produce new traits, using chemicals, heat, light, or other means.

Histopathologists investigate diseased tissue in humans and animals.

Immunologists study the manner in which the human body resists disease.

Limnologists study freshwater organisms and their environment.

Marine biologists specialize in the study of marine species and their environment. They gather specimens at different times, taking into account tidal cycles, seasons, and exposure to atmospheric elements, in order to answer questions concerning the overall health of sea organisms and their environment.

Microbiologists study bacteria, viruses, molds, algae, yeasts, and other organisms of microscopic or submicroscopic size. Some microorganisms are useful to humans; they are studied and used in the production of food, such as cheese, bread, and tofu. Other microorganisms have been used to preserve food and tenderize meat. Some microbiologists work with microorganisms that cause disease. They work to diagnose, treat, and prevent disease. Microbiologists have helped prevent typhoid fever, influenza, measles, polio, whooping cough, and smallpox. Today, they work on cures for AIDS, cancer, cystic fibrosis, and Alzheimer's disease, among others.

Molecular biologists apply their research on animal and bacterial systems toward the goal of improving and better understanding human health.

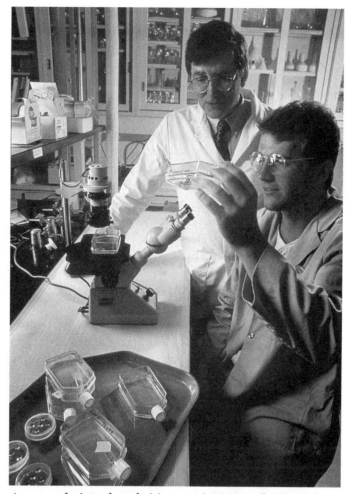

An entomologist and a technician examine insect cell cultures that will be used for metabolic studies.

Mycologists study edible, poisonous, and parasitic fungi, such as mushrooms, molds, yeasts, and mildews, to determine which are useful to medicine, agriculture, and industry. Their research has resulted in benefits such as the development of antibiotics, the propagation of mushrooms, and methods of retarding fabric deterioration.

Nematologists study nematodes (roundworms), which are parasitic in animals and plants. Nematodes transmit diseases, attack insects, or attack other nematodes that exist in soil or water. Nematologists investigate and develop methods of controlling these organisms.

Parasitologists study animal parasites and their effects on humans and other animals.

Pharmacologists may be employed as researchers by pharmaceutical companies. They often spend most of their time working in the laboratory, where they study the effects of various drugs and medical compounds on mice or rabbits. Working within controlled environments, pharmacologists precisely note the types, quantities, and timing of medicines administered as a part of their experiments. Periodically, they make blood smears or perform autopsies to study different reactions. They usually work with a team of researchers, headed by one with a doctorate and consisting of several biologists with master's and bachelor's degrees and some laboratory technicians.

Physiologists are biologists who specialize in studying all the life stages of plants or animals. Some specialize in a particular body system or a particular function, such as respiration.

Wildlife biologists study the habitats and the conditions necessary for the survival of birds and other wildlife. Their goal is to find ways to ensure the continuation of healthy wildlife populations, while lessening the impact and growth of civilization around them.

Zoologists study all types of animals to learn their origin, interrelationships, classifications, life histories, habits, diseases, relation to the environment, growth, genetics, and distribution. Zoologists are usually identified by the animals they study: *ichthyologists* (fish), *mammalogists* (mammals), *ornithologists* (birds), and *herpetologists* (reptiles and amphibians).

Biologists may also work for government agencies concerned with public health. *Toxicologists*, for example, study the effects of toxic substances on humans, animals, and plants. The data they gather are used in consumer protection and industrial safety programs to reduce the hazards of accidental exposure or ingestion. *Public-health microbiologists* conduct experiments on water, foods, and the general environment of a community to detect the presence of harmful bacteria so pollution and contagious diseases can be controlled or eliminated.

■ REQUIREMENTS
High School
High school students interested in a career in biology should take English, biology, physics, chemistry, Latin, geometry, and algebra.

Postsecondary Training
Prospective biologists should also obtain a broad undergraduate college training. In addition to courses in all phases of biology, useful related courses include organic and inorganic chemistry, physics, and mathematics. Modern languages, English, biometrics (the use of mathematics in biological measurements), and statistics are also useful. Courses in computers will be extremely beneficial. Students should take advantage of courses that require laboratory, field, or collecting work.

Nearly all institutions offer undergraduate training in one or more of the biological sciences. These vary from liberal arts schools that offer basic majors in botany and zoology to large universities that permit specialization in areas such as entomology, bacteriology, and physiology at the undergraduate level.

The best way to become a biologist is to earn a bachelor's degree in biology or one of its specialized fields, such as anatomy, bacteriology, botany, ecology, or microbiology. For the highest professional status, a doctorate is required. This is particularly true of top research positions and most higher-level college teaching openings. Many colleges and universities offer courses leading to a master's degree and a doctorate. A study made by the National Science Foundation showed that among a group of biologists listed on the National Scientific Manpower Register, 10 percent held a bachelor's degree, 33 percent held a master's or professional medical degree, and the remaining 57 percent had earned a doctorate.

Candidates for a doctorate specialize in one of the subdivisions of biology. A number of sources of financial assistance are available to finance graduate work. Most major universities have a highly developed fellowship (scholarship) or assistantship (part-time teaching or research) program.

Organizations, such as the U.S. Public Health Service and the National Science Foundation, make awards to support graduate students. In a recent year, for example, the Public Health Service made 8,000 fellowship and training grants. In addition, major universities often hold research contracts or have their own projects that provide part-time and summer employment for undergraduate and graduate students.

Certification or Licensing
A state license may be required for biologists who are employed as technicians in general service health organizations, such as hospitals or clinics. To qualify for this license, proof of suitable educational background is necessary.

Other Requirements
Biologists must be systematic in their approach to solving the problems that they face. They should have probing, inquisitive minds and an aptitude for biology, chemistry, and mathematics. Patience and imagination are also required since they may spend much time in observation and analysis. Biologists must also have good communication skills in order to effectively gather and exchange data and solve problems that arise in their work.

■ EXPLORING
Students can measure their aptitude and interest in the work of the biologist by taking courses in the field. Laboratory assignments, for example, provide information on techniques used by the working biologist. Many

schools hire students as laboratory assistants to work directly under a teacher and help administer the laboratory sections of courses.

School assemblies, field trips to federal and private laboratories and research centers, and career conferences provide additional insight into career opportunities. Advanced students often are able to attend professional meetings and seminars.

Part-time and summer positions in biology or related areas are particularly helpful. Students with some college courses in biology may find summer positions as laboratory assistants. Graduate students may find work on research projects conducted by their institutions. Beginning college and advanced high school students may find employment as laboratory aides or hospital orderlies or attendants. Despite the menial nature of these positions, they afford a useful insight into careers in biology. High school students often have the opportunity to join volunteer service groups at local hospitals. Student science training programs (SSTPs) allow qualified high school students to spend a summer doing research under the supervision of a scientist.

■ EMPLOYERS

Approximately half of all biological scientists work for the government at the federal, state, or local level. The majority of those who do not work for the government are involved in the drug industry, which includes pharmaceutical companies, hospitals, biotechnology companies, and laboratories. The area in which biologists work is influenced by their specialties. Marine biologists, for example, can find employment with the U.S. Department of Interior, the U.S. Fish and Wildlife Service, and the National Oceanic and Atmospheric Administration. They may also find employment in nongovernmental agencies, such as the Scripps Institution of Oceanography in California and the Marine Biological Laboratory in Massachusetts. Microbiologists can find employment with the U.S. Department of Health and Human Services, the Environmental Protection Agency, and the Department of Agriculture, among others. They may also work for pharmaceutical, food, agricultural, geological, environmental, and pollution control companies. Wildlife biologists can find employment for the U.S. Public Health Service, the U.S. Fish and Wildlife Service, and the Forest Service, among many others.

■ STARTING OUT

Biologists who are interested in becoming teachers should consult their college placement offices. Public and private high schools and an increasing number of colleges hire teachers through the colleges at which they studied. Private employment agencies also place a significant num-

PROFILE: CAROLUS LINNAEUS (1707–78)

Swedish naturalist Linnaeus developed systematic methods for classifying and naming plants and animals. He devised the classifications of class, order, genus, and species, and established as standard the binomial (two-name) system for giving scientific names to plants and animals. Linnaeus placed human beings in the order of primates, giving our species the scientific name *Homo sapiens.* Linnaeus classified thousands of plant species, assigning plants to 24 classes according to the number and position of their stamens and pistils. Although later botanical knowledge revealed that this system was inadequate, it did lay the foundation for the science of plant taxonomy, as well as for Darwin's theory of evolution.

Here, for instance, is the classification of the domestic dog, *Canis familiaris*:

Kingdom: *Animalia* (animals)
Phylum: *Chordata* (animals with a spinal cord)
Subphylum: *Vertebrata* (vertebrate)
Class: *Mammalia* (mammals)
Subclass: *Theria* (mammals that give birth to live young)
Order: *Carnivora* (carnivores)
Family: *Canidae* (related animals, such as coyotes, dogs, foxes, jackals, and wolves, some of which can cross-breed)
Genus: *Canis* (dog)
Species: *familiaris* (domesticated dog)

Classification of the cork oak tree, *Quercus suber:*
Kingdom: *Plantae* (plants)
Subkingdom: *Tracheophyta* (plants with a vascular system)
Division: *Anthophyta* (flowering plants)
Class: *Dicotyledonae* (seed plants that produce embryos with paired cotyledons and net-veined leaves)
Order: *Fagales* (a collection of similar families of trees)
Family: *Fagaceae* (beeches and other trees, chiefly having unisexual flowers)
Genus: *Quercus* (Latin for the oak tree)
Species: *suber* (Latin for "to be in season")

ber of teachers. Some teaching positions are filled through direct application.

Biologists interested in private industry and nonprofit organizations may also apply directly for employment. Major organizations that employ biologists often interview college seniors on campus. Private and public employment offices frequently have listings from these employers. Experienced biologists often change positions as a result of contacts made at professional seminars and national conventions.

Special application procedures are required for positions with government agencies. Civil service applications for federal, state, and municipal positions may be obtained by writing to the agency involved and from high school and college guidance and placement bureaus, public employment agencies, and post offices.

ADVANCEMENT

In a field as broad as biology, numerous opportunities for advancement exist. To a great extent, however, advancement depends on the individual's level of education. A doctorate is generally required for college teaching, independent research, and top-level administrative and management jobs. A master's degree is sufficient for some jobs in applied research, and a bachelor's degree may qualify for some entry-level jobs.

With the right qualifications, the biologist may advance to the position of project chief and direct a team of other biologists. Many use their knowledge and experience as background for administrative and management positions. Often, as they develop professional expertise, biologists move from strictly technical assignments into positions in which they interpret biological knowledge.

The usual path of advancement in biology, as in other sciences, comes from specialization and the development of the status of an expert in a given field. Biologists may work with professionals in other major fields to explore problems that require an interdisciplinary approach, such as biochemistry, biophysics, biostatistics (or biometrics). Biochemistry, for example, uses the methods of chemistry to study the composition of biological materials and the molecular mechanisms of biological processes.

EARNINGS

Earnings for biological scientists vary extensively based on the type and size of their employer, the individual's level of education and experience, and the area of biology in which the scientist specializes. The median salary for all biological scientists was $60,390 in 2002, as reported by the U.S. Department of Labor. In 2003 general biological scientists working for the federal government earned an average annual salary of $66,262. Those specializing in certain areas tended to have slightly higher annual incomes. Ecologists, for example, had an average salary of $65,207 per year; microbiologists reported an average of $73,513; geneticists averaged $78,652; and physiologists, $85,181.

According to the National Association of Colleges and Employers, those with bachelor's degrees in the biological sciences had beginning salaries averaging $23,000–$35,000 per year in 2003. In general, the highest salaries were earned by biologists in business and industry, followed by those self-employed, working for nonprofit organizations, in military service, and working for the U.S. Public Health Service or other positions in the federal government. The lowest salaries were earned by teachers and by those working for various state and local governments.

Biologists are usually eligible for health and dental insurance, paid vacations and sick days, and retirement plans. Some employers may offer reimbursement for continuing education, seminars, and travel.

WORK ENVIRONMENT

The biologist's work environment varies greatly depending upon the position and type of employer. One biologist may work outdoors or travel much of the time. Another wears a white smock and spends years working in a laboratory. Some work with toxic substances and disease cultures; strict safety measures must be observed.

Biologists frequently work under pressure. For example, those employed by pharmaceutical houses work in an atmosphere of keen competition for sales that encourages the development of new drug products, and, as they are identified, the rapid testing and early marketing of these products. The work is very exacting, however, and pharmaceutical biologists must exercise great care to ensure that adequate testing of products has been properly conducted.

Some biologists, including botanists, ecologists, and zoologists, may undertake strenuous, sometimes dangerous, fieldwork in primitive conditions. Marine biologists work in the field, on research ships or in laboratories, in tropical seas and ocean areas with considerably cooler climates. They will be required to perform some strenuous work, such as carrying a net, digging, chipping, or hauling equipment or specimens. Marine biologists who work underwater must be able to avoid hazards, such as razor-sharp coral reefs and other underwater dangers. Wildlife biologists work in all types of weather and in all types of terrain and ecosystems. They may work alone or with a group in inhospitable surroundings in order to gather information.

OUTLOOK

The U.S. Department of Labor predicts employment for biological scientists to be as fast as average through 2012, although competition will be stiff for some positions. For example, Ph.D.s looking for research positions will find strong competition for a limited number of openings. Government funding is currently plentiful (some 1 in 3 applications for research grants are approved), but a recession or shift in political power can cause the loss of funding for grants and the decline of research and development endeavors.

Private industry will need biologists to work in sales, marketing, and research management. Companies developing new drugs, modified crops, environmentally friendly products, and the like will need the expertise of biological scientists. The U.S. Department of Labor also predicts that even companies not solely involved in biotechnology will be increasingly using biotechnology developments and techniques in their businesses. This should cause more job opportunities for biological scientists in a variety of industries.

Biologists with advanced degrees will be best qualified for the most lucrative and challenging jobs, although this varies by specialty, with genetic, cellular, and biochemical research showing the most promise. Scientists with bachelor's degrees may find openings as science or engineering technicians or as health technologists and technicians. Many colleges and universities are cutting back on their faculties, but high schools and two-year colleges may have teaching positions available.

■ FOR MORE INFORMATION

For information on careers in biology, contact
American Institute of Biological Sciences
1444 Eye Street, NW, Suite 200
Washington, DC 20005
Tel: 202-628-1500
Email: admin@aibs.org
http://www.aibs.org

For a career brochure, career-related articles, and a list of institutions that award academic degrees with a major in physiology, contact
American Physiological Society
9650 Rockville Pike
Bethesda, MD 20814-3991
Tel: 301-634-7164
http://www.the-aps.org

For information on careers, educational resources, and fellowships, contact
American Society for Microbiology
1752 N Street, NW
Washington, DC 20036
Tel: 202-737-3600
http://www.asm.org

For career information, including articles and books, contact
Biotechnology Industry Organization
1225 Eye Street, NW, Suite 400
Washington, DC 20005
Tel: 202-962-9200
http://www.bio.org

For information on careers in the marine sciences, contact
National Aquarium in Baltimore
501 East Pratt Street, Pier 3
Baltimore, MD 21202-3194
Tel: 410-576-3800
http://www.aqua.org

For information on specific careers in biology, contact
National Institutes of Health
9000 Rockville Pike
Bethesda, MD 20892
Tel: 301-435-1908
Email: orsinfo@mail.nih.gov
http://www.nih.gov

For information on specific careers, contact the FDA's job hotline.
U.S. Food and Drug Administration (FDA)
5600 Fishers Lane
Rockville, MD 20857-0001
Tel: 888-463-6332
http://www.fda.gov

Biomedical Engineers

■ OVERVIEW

Biomedical engineers are highly trained scientists who use engineering and life science principles to research biological aspects of animal and human life. They develop new theories, and they modify, test, and prove existing theories on life systems. They design health care instruments and devices or apply engineering principles to the study of human systems. There are approximately 7,130 biomedical engineers employed in the United States.

■ HISTORY

Biomedical engineering is one of many new professions created by advancements in technology. It is an interdisciplinary field that brings together two respected professions: biology and engineering.

Biology, of course, is the study of life, and engineering, in broad terms, studies sources of energy in nature and the properties of matter in a way that is useful to humans, particularly in machines, products, and structures. A combination of the two fields, biomedical engineering developed primarily after 1945, as new technology allowed for the application of engineering principles to biology. The artificial heart is just one in a long list of the products of biomedical engineering. Other products include artificial organs, prosthetics, the use of lasers in surgery, cryosurgery, and ultrasonics, and the use of computers and thermography in diagnosis.

■ THE JOB

Using engineering principles to solve medical and health-related problems, the biomedical engineer works closely with life scientists, members of the medical profession, and chemists. Most of the work revolves around the laboratory. There are three interrelated work areas: research, design, and teaching.

Biomedical research is multifaceted and broad in scope. It calls upon engineers to apply their knowledge of mechanical, chemical, and electrical engineering as well as anatomy and physiology in the study of living systems. Using computers, biomedical engineers use their knowledge of graphic and related technologies to develop mathematical models that simulate physiological systems.

In biomedical engineering design, medical instruments and devices are developed. Engineers work on artificial organs, ultrasonic imagery devices, cardiac pacemakers, and surgical lasers, for example. They design and build systems that will update hospital, laboratory, and clinical procedures. They also train health care personnel in the proper use of this new equipment.

Biomedical engineering is taught on the university level. Teachers conduct classes, advise students, serve on academic committees, and supervise or conduct research.

Within biomedical engineering, an individual may concentrate on a particular specialty area. Some of the well-established specialties are *bioinstrumentation*, *biomechanics*, *biomaterials*, *systems physiology*, *clinical engineering*, and *rehabilitation engineering*. These specialty areas frequently depend on one another.

Biomechanics is mechanics applied to biological or medical problems. Examples include the artificial heart, the artificial kidney, and the artificial hip. *Biomaterials* is the study of the optimal materials with which to construct such devices, *bioinstrumentation* is the science of measuring physiological functions. *Systems physiology* uses engineering strategies, techniques, and tools to gain a comprehensive and integrated understanding of living organisms ranging from bacteria to humans. Biomedical engineers in this specialty examine such things as the biochemistry of metabolism and the control of limb movements.

Rehabilitation engineering is a new and growing specialty area of biomedical engineering. Its goal is to expand the capabilities and improve the quality of life for individuals with physical impairments. Rehabilitation engineers often work directly with the disabled person and modify equipment for individual use.

■ REQUIREMENTS
High School

You can best prepare for a career as a biomedical engineer by taking courses in biology, chemistry, physics, mathematics, drafting, and computers. Communication and problem-solving skills are necessary, so classes in English, writing, and logic are important. Participating in science clubs and competing in science fairs will give you the opportunity to design and invent systems and products.

Postsecondary Training

Most biomedical engineers have an undergraduate degree in biomedical engineering or a related field and a Ph.D. in some facet of biomedical engineering. Undergraduate study is roughly divided into halves. The first two years are devoted to theoretical subjects, such as abstract physics and differential equations in addition to the core curriculum most undergraduates take. The third and fourth years include more applied science. Worldwide, there are over 80 colleges and universities that offer programs in biomedical engineering.

During graduate programs, students work on research or product development projects headed by faculty.

Certification or Licensing

Engineers whose work may affect the life, health, or safety of the public must be registered according to regulations in all 50 states and the District of Columbia. Applicants for registration must have received a degree from an American Board for Engineering and Technology-accredited engineering program and have four years of experience. They must also pass a written examination administered by the state in which they wish to work.

QUICK FACTS

SCHOOL SUBJECTS
Biology
Chemistry

PERSONAL SKILLS
Helping/teaching
Technical/scientific

WORK ENVIRONMENT
Primarily indoors
Primarily one location

MINIMUM EDUCATION LEVEL
Bachelor's degree

SALARY RANGE
$38,250 to $60,410 to
$94,270

CERTIFICATION OR LICENSING
Voluntary

OUTLOOK
Faster than the average

DOT
019

GOE
02.07.04

NOC
2148

O*NET-SOC
17-2031.00

Biomedical engineers at a medical device design meeting

Other Requirements

You should have a strong commitment to learning if you plan on becoming a biomedical engineer. You should be scientifically inclined and be able to apply that knowledge in problem solving. Becoming a biomedical engineer requires long years of schooling because a biomedical engineer needs to be an expert in the fields of engineering and biology. Also, biomedical engineers have to be familiar with chemical, material, and electrical engineering as well as physiology and computers.

■ EXPLORING

Undergraduate courses offer a great deal of exposure to the field. Working in a hospital where biomedical engineers are employed can also provide you with insight into the field, as can interviews with practicing or retired biomedical engineers.

■ EMPLOYERS

There are approximately 7,130 biomedical engineers working in the United States. About 30 percent are employed by industry, mainly industry involving the manufacture of medical supplies and instruments. In addition, many biomedical engineers are employed in hospitals and medical institutions, and in research and

educational facilities. Employment opportunities also exist in government regulatory agencies.

■ STARTING OUT

A variety of routes may be taken to gain employment as a biomedical engineer. Recent graduates may use college placement services, or they may apply directly to employers, often to personnel offices in hospitals and industry. A job may be secured by answering an advertisement in the employment section of a newspaper. Information on job openings is also available at the local office of the U.S. Employment Service.

■ ADVANCEMENT

Advancement opportunities are tied directly to educational and research background. In a nonteaching capacity, a biomedical engineer with an advanced degree can rise to a supervisory position. In teaching, a doctorate is usually necessary to become a full professor. By demonstrating excellence in research, teaching, and departmental committee involvement, one can move from instructor to assistant professor and then to full professor, department chair, or even dean.

Qualifying for and receiving research grant funding can also be a means of advancing one's career in both the nonteaching and teaching sectors.

■ EARNINGS

The amount a biomedical engineer earns is dependent upon education, experience, and type of employer. According to the U.S. Department of Labor, biomedical engineers had a median yearly income of $60,410 in 2002. At the low end of the pay scale, 10 percent earned less than $38,250 per year, and at the high end, 10 percent earned more than $94,270 annually.

According to a 2003 survey by the National Association of Colleges and Employers, the average beginning

---

BIOMEDICAL INDUSTRY BREAKTHROUGHS

Artificial hearts and kidneys
Artificial joints
Automated medicine delivery systems
Blood oxygenators
Cardiac pacemakers
Defibrillators
Laser systems used in surgery
Medical imaging systems (MRIs, ultrasound, etc.)
Sensors that analyze blood chemistry

WORDS TO KNOW

Bioinstrumentation: Building machines for the diagnosis and treatment of disease.

Biomaterials: Anything that replaces natural tissue. These can be artificial materials or living tissues grown for implantation.

Biomechanics: Developing mechanical devices like the artificial hip, heart, and kidney.

Cellular, tissue, and genetic engineering: Application of engineering at the cellular and subcellular level to study diseases and design intervention techniques.

Clinical engineering: Application of engineering to health care through customizing and maintaining sophisticated medical equipment.

Systems physiology: Using engineering principles to understand how living systems operate.

salary for those with bachelor's degrees in biological sciences was between $23,000 and $35,000 per year.

The American Association of University Professors reports that assistant professors who teach in the top paying disciplines (which includes health professions and engineering) earned an average of $58,5766 for 2003. Those who were full professors earned an average of $100,682 during that same period.

Biomedical engineers can expect benefits from employers, including health insurance, paid vacation and sick days, and retirement plans.

■ WORK ENVIRONMENT

Biomedical engineers who teach in a university will have much student contact in the classroom, the laboratory, and the office. They also will be expected to serve on relevant committees while continuing their teaching, research, and writing responsibilities. As competition for teaching positions increases, the requirement that professors publish papers will increase. Professors usually are responsible for obtaining government or private research grants to support their work.

Those who work in industry and government have much contact with other professionals, including chemists, medical scientists, and doctors. They often work as part of a team, testing and developing new products. All biomedical engineers who do lab work are in clean, well-lighted environments, using sophisticated equipment.

■ OUTLOOK

It is expected that there will be a greater need for skilled biomedical engineers in the future. Prospects look particularly good in the health care industry, which will continue to grow rapidly, primarily because people are living longer. The U.S. Department of Labor predicts employment for biomedical engineers to increase faster than the average through 2012. New jobs will become available in biomedical research in prosthetics, artificial internal organs, computer applications, and instrumentation and other medical systems. In addition, a demand will exist for professors to train the biomedical engineers needed to fill these positions.

■ FOR MORE INFORMATION

For more information on careers in biomedical engineering, contact

American Society for Engineering Education
1818 N Street, NW, Suite 600
Washington, DC 20036
Tel: 202-331-3500
http://www.asee.org

For information on careers, student chapters, and to read the brochure Planning a Career in Biomedical Engineering, *contact or visit the following website:*

Biomedical Engineering Society
8401 Corporate Drive, Suite 225
Landover, MD 20785-2224
Tel: 301-459-1999
Email: info@bmes.org
http://www.bmes.org

For information on high school programs that provide opportunities to learn about engineering technology, contact JETS.

Junior Engineering Technical Society (JETS)
1420 King Street, Suite 405
Alexandria, VA 22314
Tel: 703-548-5387
Email: jetsinfo@jets.org
http://www.jets.org

For Canadian career information, contact

Canadian Medical and Biological Engineering Society
PO Box 51023
Orleans, ON K1E 3W4 Canada
Tel: 613-837-8649
Email: cmbes@magma.ca
http://www.cmbes.ca

Visit the following website for more information on educational programs, job listings, grants, and links to other biomedical engineering sites:

The Biomedical Engineering Network
http://www.bmenet.org

Biomedical Equipment Technicians

■ OVERVIEW

Biomedical equipment technicians handle the complex medical equipment and instruments found in hospitals, clinics, and research facilities. This equipment is used for medical therapy and diagnosis and includes heart-lung machines, artificial kidney machines, patient monitors, chemical analyzers, and other electrical, electronic, mechanical, or pneumatic devices.

Technicians' main duties are to inspect, maintain, repair, and install this equipment. They disassemble equipment to locate malfunctioning components, repair or replace defective parts, and reassemble the equipment, adjusting and calibrating it to ensure that it operates according to manufacturers' specifications. Other duties of biomedical equipment technicians include modifying equipment according to the directions of medical or supervisory personnel, arranging with equipment manufacturers for necessary equipment repair, and safety-testing equipment to ensure that patients, equipment operators, and other staff members are safe from electrical or mechanical hazards. Biomedical equipment technicians work with hand tools, power tools, measuring devices, and manufacturers' manuals.

Technicians may work for equipment manufacturers as salespeople or as service technicians, or for a health care facility specializing in the repair or maintenance of specific equipment, such as that used in radiology, nuclear medicine, or patient monitoring. In the United States, approximately 33,640 people work as biomedical equipment technicians.

■ HISTORY

Today's complex biomedical equipment is the result of advances in three different areas of engineering and scientific research. The first, of course, is our ever-increasing knowledge of the human body and of the disease processes that afflict it. Although the accumulation of medical knowledge has been going on for thousands of years, most of the discoveries leading to the development of medical technology have occurred during the last three hundred years. During the past one hundred years especially, we have learned a great deal about the chemical and electrical nature of the human body.

The second contribution to biomedical technology's development is the field of instrumentation—the design and building of precision measuring devices. Throughout the history of medicine, physicians and medical researchers have tried to learn about and to monitor the workings of the human body with whatever instruments were available to them. However, it was not until the industrial revolution of the 18th and 19th centuries that instruments were developed that could detect the human body's many subtle and rapid processes.

The third area is mechanization and automation. Biomedical equipment often relies on mechanisms, such as pumps, motors, bellows, control arms, etc. These kinds of equipment were initially developed and improved during the industrial revolution; however, it was not until the 1950s that the field of medical technology began incorporating the use of automation. During the 1950s, researchers developed machines for analyzing the various components of blood and for preparing tissue specimens for microscopic examination. Probably the most dramatic development of this period was the introduction of the heart-lung machine by John Haysham Gibbon of Philadelphia in 1953, a project he had been working on since 1937.

Since the 1950s, the growth of biomedical technology has been especially dramatic. Thirty years ago, even the most advanced hospitals had only a few pieces of electronic medical equipment; today such hospitals have thousands. And, to service this equipment, the biomedical equipment technician has become an important member of the health care delivery team.

In a sense, biomedical equipment technicians represent the newest stage in the history of technicians. The first technicians were skilled assistants who had learned a trade and gone to work for an engineer or scientist. The second generation learned a technology, such as electronics. The most recent generation of technicians needs integrated instruction and competence in at least two fields of science and technology. For the biomedical equipment technician, the fields may vary, but they will most often be electronics and human physiology.

QUICK FACTS

SCHOOL SUBJECTS
Biology
Technical/shop

PERSONAL SKILLS
Mechanical/manipulative
Technical/scientific

WORK ENVIRONMENT
Primarily indoors
Primarily one location

MINIMUM EDUCATION LEVEL
Associate's degree

SALARY RANGE
$21,410 to $36,380 to $58,050

CERTIFICATION OR LICENSING
Recommended

OUTLOOK
About as fast as the average

DOT
639

GOE
02.05.02

NOC
N/A

O*NET-SOC
49-9062.00, 51-9082.00

■ THE JOB

Biomedical equipment technicians are an important link between technology and medicine. They repair, calibrate, maintain, and operate biomedical equipment working under the supervision of researchers, biomedical engineers, physicians, surgeons, and other professional health care providers.

Biomedical equipment technicians may work with thousands of different kinds of equipment. Some of the most frequently encountered are the following: patient monitors; heart-lung machines; kidney machines; blood-gas analyzers; spectrophotometers; X-ray units; radiation monitors; defibrillators; anesthesia apparatus; pacemakers; blood pressure transducers; spirometers; sterilizers; diathermy equipment; patient-care computers; ultrasound machines; and diagnostic scanning machines, such as the CT (computed tomography) scan machine, PET (positron emission tomography) scanner, and MRI (magnetic resonance imaging) machines.

Repairing faulty instruments is one of the chief functions of biomedical equipment technicians. They investigate equipment problems, determine the extent of malfunctions, make repairs on instruments that have had minor breakdowns, and expedite the repair of instruments with major breakdowns, for instance, by writing an analysis of the problem for the factory. In doing this work, technicians rely on manufacturers' diagrams, maintenance manuals, and standard and specialized test instruments, such as oscilloscopes and pressure gauges.

Installing equipment is another important function of biomedical equipment technicians. They inspect and test new equipment to make sure it complies with performance and safety standards as described in the manufacturer's manuals and diagrams, and as noted on the purchase order. Technicians may also check on proper installation of the equipment, or, in some cases, install it themselves. To ensure safe operations, technicians need a thorough knowledge of the regulations related to the proper grounding of equipment, and they need to actively carry out all steps and procedures to ensure safety.

Maintenance is the third major area of responsibility for biomedical equipment technicians. In doing this work, technicians try to catch problems before they become more serious. To this end, they take apart and reassemble devices, test circuits, clean and oil moving parts, and replace worn parts. They also keep complete records of all machine repairs, maintenance checks, and expenses.

In all three of these areas, a large part of technicians' work consists of consulting with physicians, administrators, engineers, and other related professionals. For example, they may be called upon to assist hospital administrators as they make decisions about the repair, replacement, or purchase of new equipment. They consult with medical and research staffs to determine that equipment is functioning safely and properly. They also consult with medical and engineering staffs when called upon to modify or develop equipment. In all of these activities, they use their knowledge of electronics, medical terminology, human anatomy and physiology, chemistry, and physics.

In addition, biomedical equipment technicians are involved in a range of other related duties. Some biomedical equipment technicians maintain inventories of all instruments in the hospital, their condition, location, and operators. They reorder parts and components, assist in providing people with emergency instruments, restore unsafe or defective instruments to working order, and check for safety regulation compliance.

Other biomedical equipment technicians help physicians, surgeons, nurses, and researchers conduct procedures and experiments. In addition, they must be able to explain to staff members how to operate these machines, the conditions under which a certain apparatus may or may not be used, how to solve small operating problems, and how to monitor and maintain equipment.

In many hospitals, technicians are assigned to a particular service, such as pediatrics, surgery, or renal medicine. These technicians become specialists in certain types of equipment. However, unlike electrocardiograph technicians or dialysis technicians, who specialize in one kind of equipment, most biomedical equipment technicians must be thoroughly familiar with a large variety of

BEGINNINGS OF BIOMEDICAL TECHNOLOGY

Biomedical technology began in the 1970s, when consumer advocate Ralph Nader publicized a document that suggested that patients in hospitals were being killed by microshock, the leakage of an electrical current whose level is below the sensation of feel and is therefore almost impossible to detect. The leakage can be caused by improper grounding, a loose wire inside the instrument, or leaking components. According to the document, microshock was occasionally causing patients' hearts to fibrillate, which is similar to a heart attack.

The awareness of microshock and its potential hazards created a need for technicians who could test the electronic equipment to ensure proper grounding and minimal leakage of current. And this is where the biomedical technology industry began.

instruments. They might be called upon to prepare an artificial kidney or to work with a blood-gas analyzer. Biomedical equipment technicians also maintain pulmonary function machines. These machines are used in clinics for ambulatory patients, hospital laboratories, departments of medicine for diagnosis and treatment, and rehabilitation of cardiopulmonary patients.

While most biomedical equipment technicians are trained in electronics technology, there is also a need for technicians trained in plastics to work on the development of artificial organs and for people trained in glass blowing to help make the precision parts for specialized equipment.

Many biomedical equipment technicians work for medical instrument manufacturers. These technicians consult and assist in the construction of new machinery, helping to make decisions concerning materials and construction methods to be used in the manufacture of the equipment.

■ REQUIREMENTS
High School

There are a number of classes you can take in high school to help you prepare for this work. Science classes, such as chemistry, biology, and physics, will give you the science background you will need for working in a medical environment. Take shop classes that deal with electronics, drafting, or blueprint reading. These classes will give you experience working with your hands, following printed directions, using electricity, and working with machinery. Mathematics classes will help you become comfortable working with numbers and formulas. Don't neglect your English studies. English classes will help you develop your communication skills, which will be important to have when you deal with a variety of different people in your professional life.

Postsecondary Training

To become qualified for this work, you will need to complete postsecondary education that leads either to an associate's degree from a two-year institution or a bachelor's degree from a four-year college or university. Most biomedical equipment technicians choose to receive an associate's degree. Biomedical equipment technology is a relatively new program in some schools and may also be referred to as *medical electronics technology* or *biomedical engineering technology*. No matter what the name of the program, however, you should expect to receive instruction in such areas as anatomy, physiology, electrical and electronic fundamentals, chemistry, physics, and biomedical equipment construction and design. In addition, you will study safety methods in health care facilities and

This biomedical equipment technician is repairing blood pressure testing equipment.

medical equipment troubleshooting, as it will be your job to be the problem solver. You should also expect to continue taking communication or English classes since communications skills will be essential to your work. In addition to the classroom work, many programs often provide you with practical experience in repairing and servicing equipment in a clinical or laboratory setting under the supervision of an experienced equipment technician. In this way, you learn about electrical components and circuits, the design and construction of common pieces of machinery, and computer technology as it applies to biomedical equipment.

By studying various pieces of equipment, you learn a problem-solving technique that applies not only to the equipment studied, but also to equipment you have not yet seen, and even to equipment that has not yet been invented. Part of this problem-solving technique includes learning how and where to locate sources of information.

Some biomedical equipment technicians receive their training in the armed forces. During the course of an enlistment period of four years or less, military personnel can receive training that prepares them for entry-level or sometimes advanced-level positions in the civilian workforce.

Certification or Licensing

The Association for the Advancement of Medical Instrumentation (AAMI), affiliated with the International Certification Commission for Clinical Engineering and Biomedical Technology, issues a certificate for biomedical equipment technicians (called CBET) that is based on a written examination, work experience, and educational preparation. In some cases, the educational requirements for certification may be waived for technicians with appropriate employment experience. Although certification is not required for employment, it is highly recommended.

WORDS TO KNOW

Calibrate: To adjust or set a device so that it records and measures accurately

Defibrillator: An electronic device that creates an electric shock designed to restore the rhythm of a fibrillating heart

Fibrillation: Irregular, rapid contractions of the heart muscles that cause the heartbeat and pulse to fall out of synchronism

Heart-lung machine: A machine used to divert blood from the heart during heart surgery and to keep it oxygenated and in circulation

Metabolic imaging: Noninvasive methods of seeing inside the body, such as positron emission tomography (PET), magnetic resonance imaging (MRI), X-ray computed tomography (CT or CAT scan), and ultrasound

Pulmonary function machine: A machine that examines and measures a patient's breathing efficiency and analyzes the gases throughout the lungs

Technicians with certification have demonstrated that they have attained an overall knowledge of the field and are dedicated to their profession. Many employers prefer to hire technicians who have this certification.

Other Requirements

Biomedical equipment technicians need mechanical ability and should enjoy working with tools. Because this job demands quick decision-making and prompt repairs, technicians should work well under pressure. You should also be extremely precise and accurate in your work, have good communications skills, and enjoy helping others— an essential quality for anyone working in the health care industry.

■ EXPLORING

You will have difficulty gaining any direct experience in biomedical equipment technology until you are in a training program or working professionally. Your first hands-on opportunities generally come in the clinical and laboratory phases of your education. You can, however, visit school and community libraries to seek out books written about careers in medical technology. You can also join a hobby club devoted to chemistry, biology, radio equipment, or electronics.

Perhaps the best way to learn more about this job is to set up, with the help of teachers or guidance counselors, a visit to a local health care facility or to arrange for a biomedical technician to speak to interested students, either on site or at a career exploration seminar hosted by the

school. You may be able to ask the technician about his or her educational background, what a day on the job is like, and what new technologies are on the horizon. Try to visit a school offering a program in biomedical equipment technology and discuss your career plans with an admissions counselor there. The counselor may also be able to provide you with helpful insights about the career and your preparation for it.

Finally, because this work involves the health care field, consider getting a part-time job or volunteering at a local hospital. Naturally, you won't be asked to work with the biomedical equipment, but you will have the opportunity to see professionals on the job and experience being in the medical environment. Even if your duty is only to escort patients to their tests, you may gain a greater understanding of this work.

■ EMPLOYERS

Many schools place students in part-time hospital positions to help them gain practical experience. Students are often able to return to these hospitals for full-time employment after graduation. Other places of employment include research institutes and biomedical equipment manufacturers. Government hospitals and the military are also employers of biomedical equipment technicians.

■ STARTING OUT

Most schools offering programs in biomedical equipment technology work closely with local hospitals and industries, and school placement officers are usually informed about openings when they become available. In some cases, recruiters may visit a school periodically to conduct interviews. Also, many schools place students in part-time hospital jobs to help them gain practical experience. Students are often able to return to these hospitals for full-time employment after graduation.

Another effective method of finding employment is to write directly to hospitals, research institutes, or biomedical equipment manufacturers. Other good sources of leads for job openings include state employment offices and newspaper want ads.

■ ADVANCEMENT

With experience, biomedical equipment technicians can expect to work with less supervision, and in some cases they may find themselves supervising less-experienced technicians. They may advance to positions in which they serve as instructors, assist in research, or have administrative duties. Although many supervisory positions are open to biomedical equipment technicians, some positions are not available without additional education. In large metropolitan hospitals, for instance, the minimum educational requirement for biomedical engineers, who do much of the supervising of biomedical equipment technicians, is a bachelor's degree; many engineers have a master's degree as well.

EARNINGS

Salaries for biomedical equipment technicians vary in different institutions and localities and according to the experience, training, certification, and type of work done by the technician. According to the U.S. Department of Labor, the median hourly wage for medical equipment repairers was $17.49 in 2002. A technician earning this amount and working full-time would have a yearly salary of approximately $36,379. The Department of Labor lists the median annual salary of medical equipment repairers close to this, at $36,380. The top 10 percent in this profession made $58,050 a year, while the lowest 10 percent made $21,410 per year. In general, biomedical equipment technicians who work for manufacturers have higher earnings than those who work for hospitals. Naturally, those in supervisory or senior positions also command higher salaries. Benefits, such as health insurance and vacation days, vary with the employer.

WORK ENVIRONMENT

Working conditions for biomedical equipment technicians vary according to employer and type of work done. Hospital employees generally work a 40-hour week; their schedules sometimes include weekends and holidays, and some technicians may be on call for emergencies. Technicians working for equipment manufacturers may have to do extensive traveling to install or service equipment.

The physical surroundings in which biomedical equipment technicians work may vary from day to day. Technicians may work in a lab or treatment room with patients or consult with engineers, administrators, and other staff members. Other days, technicians may spend most of their time at a workbench repairing equipment.

OUTLOOK

Because of the expanding healthcare field and increasing use of electronic medical devices and other sophisticated biomedical equipment, there is a steady demand for skilled and trained biomedical equipment technicians. The U.S. Department of Labor predicts employment for this group to grow about as fast as the average through 2012.

In hospitals the need for more biomedical equipment technicians exists not only because of the increasing use of biomedical equipment but also because hospital administrators realize that these technicians can help

hold down costs. Biomedical equipment technicians do this through their preventive maintenance checks and by taking over some routine activities of engineers and administrators, thus releasing those professionals for activities that only they can perform. Through the coming decades, cost containment will remain a high priority for hospital administrators, and as long as biomedical equipment technicians can contribute to that effort, the demand for them should remain strong.

For the many biomedical equipment technicians who work for companies that build, sell, lease, or service biomedical equipment, job opportunities should also continue to grow.

The federal government employs biomedical equipment technicians in its hospitals, research institutes, and the military. Employment in these areas will depend largely on levels of government spending. In the research area, spending levels may vary; however, in health care delivery, spending should remain high for the near future.

FOR MORE INFORMATION

For information on student memberships, biomedical technology programs, and certification, contact

Association for the Advancement of Medical Instrumentation
1110 North Glebe Road, Suite 220
Arlington, VA 22201-4795
Tel: 800-332-2264
http://www.aami.org

Biotechnology Patent Lawyers

OVERVIEW

Biotechnology patent lawyers are lawyers who specialize in helping biotechnology researchers, scientists, and research corporations with all legal aspects of their biotechnology patents. They assist clients in applying for patents and enforcing those patents. Although some of their duties may be similar to those of intellectual property lawyers, these lawyers focus on work involving the biotechnology field.

HISTORY

Biotechnology patent law is a blending of two fields: science and law. The field of science dates back thousands of years. Ancient Egyptians, for example, organized knowledge about matter into systems, which was the beginning of chemistry. In the 4th century B.C., the field of biology advanced with the work of Greek philosopher Aristotle who created taxonomic (classification) systems for animals. The 11th-century A.D. Persian philosopher and physician Avicenna wrote the Canon of Medicine, a compendium of medical knowledge. In the 19th century, Louis Pasteur, Matthias Schleiden, and Theodor Schwann contributed to the growth of the field of microbiology; Gregor Mendel discovered the principles of genetics through his studies of peas. The modern history of genetics can be traced back to the early 1950s when James Watson and Francis Crick discovered the double helix structure of DNA, the genetic material that makes up the most basic component of living organisms. After that came the discovery of recombinant DNA techniques and finally the ability to genetically engineer cells and clone (make copies of) desired genes. These scientific advancements have resulted in such developments as nontoxic pesticides, longer lasting vegetables, advanced blood tests, and even Dolly, the cloned Scottish sheep.

The history of law also dates back thousands of years, although the area of patent law has been a relatively recent development. Dating back to the 1700s, people sought help from lawyers to protect their ideas and inventions from theft. Unfortunately, both lawyers and their clients were often frustrated in their attempts to gain support for patents and copyrights in court. By the 20th century, however, Congress and courts had begun to see innovative ideas and products as valuable to U.S. status in the global market. Today, scientists, researchers, and research companies involved with biotechnology rely on patent law to ensure that their discoveries and advancements are protected as their property. Biotechnology patent lawyers are the unique bridge between the scientific and legal worlds, making sure their clients receive the acknowledgements for and profits from their scientific work.

QUICK FACTS

SCHOOL SUBJECTS
Biology
Chemistry
English

PERSONAL SKILLS
Communication/ideas
Technical/scientific

WORK ENVIRONMENT
Primarily indoors
Primarily multiple locations

MINIMUM EDUCATION LEVEL
Doctorate

SALARY RANGE
$44,490 to $90,290 to
$145,600+

CERTIFICATION OR LICENSING
Required by all states

OUTLOOK
About as fast as the average

DOT
110

GOE
04.02.01

NOC
4112

O*NET-SOC
23-1011.00

■ THE JOB

The biotechnology patent lawyer's job actually begins only after researchers or scientists have done extensive work in their field. For example, researchers or scientists may draw on advances in molecular and cellular biology, genetics, and knowledge of the human immune system, to change and combine DNA in an effort to come up with a new vaccine. When they have developed this vaccine, they are ready to seek a patent for their invention from the Patent and Trademark Office. At this point, biotechnology patent lawyers join the process to help these researchers and research corporations with all legal aspects of their biotechnology patents. A patent gives the patent holder the right to exclude others from making, using, or selling an invention for a specific period of time.

Biotechnology patent lawyers have extensive scientific and legal knowledge. Like any other lawyer, they must be able to give clients legal advice and represent them in court when necessary. In addition, their scientific knowledge helps them prepare patent specifications for their clients' work.

For most biotechnology patent attorneys, the job falls into three major categories. First, they take their clients' patent claims before the Patent and Trademark Office and attempt to obtain patents for them. Second, they negotiate various kinds of business transactions that involve patents. For example, they might assist a client in licensing the rights to use or sell a certain patented technology. Third, biotechnology lawyers assist clients in the enforcement of patents, which might involve suing another party for patent infringement or defending a client from an infringement lawsuit. While some patent attorneys may find that most of their cases fall into one or the other of these categories, most patent attorneys take on cases in all three of these areas.

According to Lawrence Foster, a biotechnology patent attorney who practices on the East Coast, the best part of biotech practice is the chance to learn about the latest scientific discoveries and developments. "You can open a newspaper and see the first article will feature something you've known about for months," he remarks. "It's exciting to know that you're learning about these discoveries as they happen, long before most people have any idea." Although lawyers must keep these often thrilling developments quiet to protect their clients' confidentiality, they still have the satisfaction of knowing that they're party to the latest inventions in genetic and even cloning technology.

■ REQUIREMENTS
High School

To prepare for this field, take college preparatory classes in high school that include both the sciences, such as biology and chemistry, and government or law. In addition, take mathematics and economics classes, which will give you practice working with numbers and theories. Take history or social studies courses, which will provide you with an understanding of the development of societies, as well as the ability to turn research into a logical, progressive argument. Since much of your professional time will be spent researching documents, writing patent specifications, and presenting arguments, be sure to take English classes. These classes will help you develop your writing, speaking, and research skills. Finally, since many colleges have a foreign language requirement and biotechnology work takes place around the world, consider adding a language to your class schedule.

Postsecondary Training

Because this is a specialized field, you will need several years of postsecondary training that include undergraduate and graduate level work. Like any lawyer, you will need to get a college degree before attending law school. A liberal arts background is the most common to have. In addition to such courses as English, government, and economics, you will also want to load up on science courses and should consider majoring in one of the sciences. In fact, biotechnology patent lawyers in the greatest demand typically have Ph.D.s in a science field, such as genetic engineering, as well as their law degree. After college, a Ph.D. in one of the sciences may take between four and five years to complete. Law school typically lasts three years for full-time students. As part of their entrance requirements, most law schools require potential students to take the Law School Admission Test (LSAT), which measures critical thinking and reasoning abilities. In law school you will take such classes as legal writing and research, contracts, constitutional law, and property. You should also take courses in intellectual property law, which are necessary for any type of patent lawyer. You will graduate from law school with a juris doctor (J.D.) degree or a bachelor of laws (LL.B.) degree.

Certification or Licensing

To practice any type of law, you must pass the bar exam of the state where you intend to practice. To qualify for the bar exam in most states, you must usually have a college degree as well as a law degree from a law school accredited by the American Bar Association (ABA). Many find these requirements are tough enough, but would-be patent lawyers have a much longer and harder road to travel before they can practice. First, all patent attorneys must pass another bar exam specific to patent law and given by the Patent and Trademark Office. Patent attor-

---

CONTROVERSIES IN EMERGING BIOTECHNOLOGY

Genetic engineering has opened up enormous potential for ending hunger, healing the sick, and helping people live longer lives. However, there are a number of controversies that have arisen from the new technology. In addition to securing patents, biotechnology lawyers of the future will have to deal with many of these issues in the work—sometimes by dealing with established government bodies, sometimes by lobbying legislators to draft new laws, and sometimes in the courtroom.

According to law, it is possible to patent not just a DNA sequence that someone made in the lab, but one decoded from nature. Many people are disturbed by the fact that a corporation can "own" the sequence of nucleic acids that make them who they are. It also means that one company can control the snippet of genetic information that, say, causes Alzheimer's disease. Anyone who developed a therapy to prevent the disease would have to pay a royalty to the company, which can dramatically increase the price of treatment.

Another controversy concerns genetically modified organisms, or GMOs, used as food. Some worry that people who eat (for instance) corn that has a peanut gene inserted to make it more resistant to pests might have an allergic reaction to the peanut proteins. Others worry that hardier and stronger genetically engineered crops might spread into the wild, supplanting their natural kin and wreaking havoc on the ecosystem's delicate balance.

Cloning is another area of concern. Cloning, right now, is an imperfect science; cloned animals tend to age rapidly and be generally unwell. Should the desires of grieving parents who want an exact duplicate of their dead child be allowed to trump that child's quality of life? Who has a right to create a human being as a science experiment? And if a human baby is cloned with just enough of his or her genetic code modified, is the child patentable?

---

neys must then also prove that they have at least an undergraduate degree in one of the scientific fields that has been approved by the Patent and Trademark Office.

Other Requirements

While scientific aptitude and knowledge are clearly important for achieving success in this field, verbal skills tend to be at least as important as the more analytic, scientific ones. "When you're dealing with someone who has invented a specific technology," Lawrence Foster remarks, "you're dealing with probably one of the most knowledgeable people in this particular scientific area in the whole world." While just communicating with the inventor may take all your skill and scientific background, the even greater challenge often comes when you have to communicate that specialized and technical knowledge to a judge who may have no scientific training. "As a biotech patent attorney, your job often requires translating from the most specialized to the most general kinds of language," Foster sums up. "That takes just as much verbal skill as it does scientific knowledge."

EXPLORING

Since biotechnology patent law combines the areas of science and law, there are a number of ways you can explore this field. To investigate the law aspect of this career, try to get a part-time job or internship with a law office in your area. You will probably be doing tasks such as filing papers, photocopying, and answering phones, but this experience will give you an idea of what working in a law office is like. If you can't find such a job, try locating a lawyer in your area with whom you could do an informational interview. Even if the lawyer is not a biotechnology patent lawyer, he or she may be able to give you some insights into the practice of law and the experience of law school.

To explore the science aspects of this career, consider joining a science or engineering club at your school. Ask your science teacher about any contacts he or she might have with scientists at the university level. You may be able to set up an informational interview with a scientist working on or having completed a Ph.D. Find out what this person likes about the field and get any advice he or she may offer to a young scientist.

EMPLOYERS

Many biotechnology patent attorneys work for law firms that focus on biotechnology patent law or intellectual property law (see Intellectual Property Lawyers), although some practice at firms that offer a wider range of legal specialties. Other lawyers practice at larger biotechnology corporations that hire their own in-house counsels, or at the Patent and Trademark Office itself. For all biotechnology patent lawyers, however, the work environment tends to be formal and often intense, since the amount of money at issue in biotechnology patent suits is usually substantial. Biotechnology patent law tends to be most active in areas where the industry itself is strong; currently, these areas include Boston, San Francisco, San Diego, and Washington, D.C.

STARTING OUT

Internships and clerkships are often good ways to gain experience and enter the law field. Like other patent lawyers, you may want to apply for a clerkship in the U.S. Court of Appeals for the Federal Court in Washington, D.C. To gain a clerkship, you should write to the judge while you are still in law school. Another option is to get a job at the U.S. Patent and Trademark Office. Finally, many people are recruited by law firms right out of law school. Your law school should have a placement office as well as offer you professional contacts through alumni that help you find a position.

ADVANCEMENT

For biotechnology patent lawyers who excel at combining verbal and scientific skills, advancement can be rapid and exciting. It is not uncommon for lawyers with Ph.D.s in genetic engineering or related fields to find themselves flooded with clients. The most successful of these lawyers can hope to advance to partner positions at their firms or even to establish a sufficient client base with which to start their own firms.

EARNINGS

In the law field, salaries tend to increase in predictable increments as the lawyer gains in experience and seniority. According to the U.S. Department of Labor, the median annual income for all lawyers was $90,290 in 2002. The middle 50 percent earned salaries between $61,060 and $136,810. The highest paid 10 percent earned more than $145,600 annually, while the lowest paid 10 percent made less than $44,490. Higher salaries are generally found in major urban areas at large firms with 75 or more lawyers.

Because of the advanced training required and the high stakes of the biotech industry, biotechnology patent attorneys tend to earn about $10,000 to $20,000 more a year than their peers at each rung of this ladder. For example, while a starting attorney may earn about $70,000, a starting biotechnology patent attorney would make as much as $90,000. Other factors can also influence these numbers, however, including the degrees held by lawyers, the size of the firm, and the geographic location of the firm.

Most lawyers receive standard benefits from their employers, including health insurance and retirement plans.

WORK ENVIRONMENT

Generally, there is a heavy workload with this career, and stress is part of the job. Because there are still relatively few biotech patent lawyers, successful ones can find themselves in especially high demand, and keeping hours down to an even remotely reasonable number can be a challenge. However, even this negative aspect has its upside, since biotech patent lawyers entering the field in the next few years should find plenty of demand for their talents. Some travel may be involved in the work, and, of course, biotechnology patent lawyers must be able to work with a variety of people. In addition, these lawyers often have the benefit of having their intellectual curiosity satisfied by their work.

■ OUTLOOK

The U.S. Department of Labor predicts employment for all lawyers to grow about as fast as the average through 2012, although competition for the best jobs will be intense. Biotechnology patent attorneys should have a good future based on several factors. Because the legislation allowing for the patenting of biological organisms has only been in existence since the early 1980s, the pool of trained biotech patent attorneys is still relatively small. Currently, many of the practicing biotechnology patent attorneys came to the field as a second career once they had already obtained their scientific training. As Lawrence Foster points out, "It wasn't really until the mid-1990s that college students began to choose and pursue careers as biotechnology patent attorneys." In addition, the growing demand for sophisticated biotechnology tools has spurred growth in this industry. Protecting the rights of clients with new ideas and products and protecting the rights of clients who currently have patents should create many job opportunities for these specialty lawyers.

As with other law fields, the development of biotech patent law is closely tied to the development of the industry it supports. In recent years, many biotechnology corporations have begun merging with and buying out smaller companies, resulting in fewer and larger companies. If this development continues, more companies will be large enough to hire their own in-house counsels.

■ FOR MORE INFORMATION

For information on all areas of law, law schools, the bar exam, and career guidance, contact
American Bar Association
740 15th Street, NW
Washington, DC 20005-1019
Tel: 202-662-1000
Email: service@abanet.org
http://www.abanet.org

For more information on the specialty of intellectual property law, contact
American Intellectual Property Lawyers Association
2001 Jefferson Davis Highway, Suite 203
Arlington, VA 22202
Tel: 703-415-0780
Email: aipla@aipla.org
http://www.aipla.org

To learn more about the patents and trademarks, contact
U.S. Patent and Trademark Office
Crystal Plaza 3, Room 2C02
Washington, DC 20231
Tel: 800-786-9199
Email: usptoinfo@uspto.gov
http://www.uspto.gov

For information on the LSAT and law schools, contact
Law School Admission Council
Tel: 215-968-1001
Email: lsacinfo@lsac.org
http://www.lsac.org

For information on legal subjects, careers, and schools, visit the following website:
Find Law
http://www.findlaw.com

Bodyguards

■ OVERVIEW

Bodyguards, sometimes called *personal protection officers* or *personal security workers,* protect their clients from injury, kidnapping, harassment, or other types of harm. They may guard a politician during a political campaign, a business executive on a worldwide trip, a movie star going to the Academy Awards, or anyone else who wants personal protection. Bodyguards may be employed by a government agency, by a private security firm, or directly by an individual.

Bodyguards work in potentially dangerous situations and must be trained to anticipate and respond to emergencies. They may carry weapons. Bodyguards combine the ability to react quickly and expertly in a tense or dangerous situation with the ability to predict, prevent, or avoid many of these situations.

■ HISTORY

People, especially rich and powerful people, have always needed protection. Whether a CEO visiting an overseas plant or a Roman senator meeting with various plaintiffs in a legal case, people who made important decisions or controlled large sums of money always had guards whom they could trust by their side.

As security demands became more complex, the role of bodyguard evolved and expanded. No longer was it enough to simply know how to use a gun or to be particularly adept at martial arts. Bodyguards were expected to help devise strategies to avoid problem situations. They used new surveillance techniques, planning strategies, and other tactics to anticipate possible dangerous situations.

In recent times bodyguards have become involved in many different types of situations. Rock stars or movie stars hire bodyguards to protect themselves against being mobbed by overzealous fans. Executives of large corporations are also likely to enlist the aid of a bodyguard to protect against possible kidnapping or other types of harm. Bodyguards often accompany their clients overseas because police in other countries might not be able to provide the type of security the clients have come to expect. Bodyguards often drive their clients from place to place while on assignment.

■ THE JOB

Although a bodyguard's ultimate responsibility is relatively straightforward—to protect a client from danger—there are a wide variety of tasks involved in this assignment. Bodyguards are part personal aide and part police officer. As personal aides, bodyguards help plan and implement schedules; as police officers, they protect their clients at public or private events. They often act in their client's business and publicity interests, as well; stories of camera-snatching bodyguards have become common fodder for the gossip pages.

Bodyguards face possible danger whenever they are on duty. When there was an attempted assassination of President Ronald Reagan in March 1981, for example, his Secret Service bodyguards quickly shielded the president with their own bodies as gunshots were fired. Bodyguards may have to sacrifice their own security in defense of those they are hired to protect. Of course, bodyguards are not just sitting targets. They are trained to react appropriately in any situation, life-threatening or not. Skilled bodyguards do all they can to minimize danger to those they are protecting, as well as to themselves. As a result of their careful preparation, bodyguards carry out most assignments relatively uneventfully.

By keeping a watchful eye on their clients, bodyguards are able to avoid many possible problems. In many cases, people are not actually out to harm a client but are simply interested in meeting an important person. Bodyguards learn not to overreact to these encounters, and in most cases, a polite warning eliminates any potential problem.

When a client hires a bodyguard for a specific event, the bodyguard will determine how many additional people may be needed to provide adequate protection. The client's schedule and travel arrangements will be coordinated for maximum security and, if the client is appearing at a public event, the bodyguard will become familiar with the location, especially the exits and secured areas, in case the client needs sudden and immediate protection from danger.

Bodyguards often work in tandem with other security people as part of a large security operation. For example, bodyguards may help develop a plan to safeguard a major politician who is giving a speech, while *security guards* develop a plan to safeguard the building where the speech will take place. All security personnel meet to discuss overall arrangements to ensure that specific details are worked out. Typically, one person will coordinate the security operations.

Bodyguards are hired to protect their clients, and activities that infringe on this job must be avoided. At an awards ceremony, for example, a bodyguard must keep an eye on the client and not gawk at celebrities. Bodyguards should not confuse the glamour and excitement of an assignment with self-importance. Indeed, it is the person who can remain calm in the midst of an exciting event and can sense possible danger when all eyes are elsewhere who makes a skillful bodyguard.

■ REQUIREMENTS
High School

Since bodyguards must be prepared for any possibility, the more skilled and knowledgeable they are in a range of areas, the better the protection they can offer someone. If you are interested in becoming a bodyguard, in high school you should take courses in a variety of subjects, including psychology, English, and especially physical education.

Postsecondary Training

Bodyguards often begin their careers in civilian law enforcement or the military, where they learn the necessary skills of crowd control, use of weapons, and emergency response. Those wanting to become a security

QUICK FACTS

SCHOOL SUBJECTS
Physical education
Psychology

PERSONAL SKILLS
Following instructions
Helping/teaching

WORK ENVIRONMENT
Indoors and outdoors
Primarily multiple locations

MINIMUM EDUCATION LEVEL
Some postsecondary training

SALARY RANGE
$22,330 to $45,112 to
$70,000+

CERTIFICATION OR LICENSING
Recommended

OUTLOOK
About as fast as the average

DOT
372

GOE
04.03.03

NOC
6651

O*NET-SOC
33-9032.00

professional working for a government agency, such as the U.S. Department of State, will need to complete a bachelor's degree. Generally, bodyguards have some higher education, although a college degree is not always necessary. A well-educated person can often be the most responsive to rapidly changing situations, and, of course, work in crowd psychology, law, and criminal justice can help a bodyguard better understand the demands of the job. On-the-job experience with different types of people in stressful situations is an integral part of the training. Depending on the employer, new hires may also need to complete between several weeks to several months of training covering topics such as criminal law, use of firearms, personal protection techniques, and first aid.

Certification or Licensing

Certification, while not required, will enhance your professional image in the eyes of potential employers. The American Society for Industrial Security administers the certified protection professional program. Applicants must have a certain amount of professional experience and pass a multiple choice exam focusing on seven areas of security management: emergency management, investigations, legal aspects, personnel security, physical security, protection of sensitive information, and security management.

Other Requirements

Since many bodyguards are former police officers, bodyguards generally must be above the minimum age for police officers. This minimum age varies from 18 to 21, depending on the city or state. If a bodyguard comes from the police ranks, he or she must also have passed a thorough physical exam. Many bodyguards also begin their careers as security guards or as other types of security personnel, for which they receive special training. Other bodyguards come from a military background.

Excellent physical fitness is a requirement for a bodyguard. Despite a popular image of bodyguards as big and tough men, and despite the fact that larger men can serve as deterrents, extreme physical strength is not an absolute requirement and many women have made successful careers as bodyguards. It is much more important that a bodyguard combine intelligence, sensitivity, and bravery with the ability to act quickly and decisively. The ability to blend into a crowd is also helpful.

Many bodyguards receive training in martial arts, and increasingly they are incorporating the study of counter-intelligence operations, electronic security devices, and surveillance techniques. Bodyguards often have training in first aid. Many bodyguards are also trained in specialized defensive driving techniques that enable them to maintain better control of a vehicle in emergency situations. However, being a bodyguard is not carte blanche to engage in action-movie heroics. Bodyguards must understand the appropriate use of force, especially since they can be arrested—or sued—for going over the line.

Bodyguards who travel overseas must be well versed in the language and culture of the host country. Good verbal skills are vital, and a bodyguard must be able to communicate directions to people at all times. A bodyguard must also be aware of what to expect in any situation. That is why an understanding of the customs of a certain area can help the bodyguard perceive unusual events and be alert for possible problems. Similarly, the legal use, registration, and licensing of weapons differs from country to country, and the bodyguard who travels overseas needs to be familiar with the regulations governing weapons in the country in which he or she is working.

Since bodyguards often work with important people and around sensitive information, they may be required to take a lie detector test before they begin work. Background checks of their work and personal histories may also be required. Bodyguards who work as permanent employees of a client must also exercise discretion and maintain confidentiality. Bodyguards should have a keen eye for detail and be able to spot trouble long before it happens. This ability to anticipate problems is crucial. A good bodyguard should rarely have to stop a kidnapping attempt as it occurs, for example, but should rather prevent the attempt from happening, through a combination of careful planning and skilled observation. If action is needed, however, the response must be swift and effective.

◾ EXPLORING

Because bodyguards must be mature and highly skilled, it is difficult to obtain real opportunities to explore this career while still in high school. Nevertheless, there are chances to take classes and talk to people to get a feel for the demands of the profession. Classes in criminal justice should give an indication of the challenges involved in protecting people. Talking to a police officer who works part-time as a bodyguard is another good way of learning about opportunities in this field. Many police departments hire high school students as police trainees or interns, providing an excellent introduction to careers in security and law enforcement.

Without the requisite skills and experience, it is difficult to get summer work as a bodyguard. It may be possible, however, to work in some other capacity at a security firm that hires bodyguards and in this way interact with bodyguards and learn more about the day-to-day rewards and challenges of the profession.

■ EMPLOYERS

Bodyguards can find work with private security firms and government agencies. They are also employed by politicians, rock stars, and other individuals in the public eye who need personal protection.

■ STARTING OUT

Many people begin a career as a bodyguard on a part-time basis; for example, police officers often take on assignments while off-duty from police work. The reason that most of them start on a part-time basis is that the police training they receive is ideal preparation for work as a bodyguard. In addition to the excellent training a police officer receives, the officer is often in a good spot to receive job offers. Someone looking for a bodyguard may call the local police station and ask if there are officers willing to take on an assignment. Then, as a person acquires greater experience in being a bodyguard and more and more people know of the person's skills and availability, additional work becomes available. That person may then work full-time as a bodyguard or continue on a part-time basis.

Military service may also provide the background and skills for entry into this field. Many bodyguards enter this career after service in one of the Special Forces, such as the Green Berets or the Navy SEALs, or after experience in the Military Police. Other bodyguards enter this field through a career with private security companies and often begin training while employed as security guards. Careers with the Secret Service, the Federal Bureau of Investigation, or other government police and intelligence agencies may also provide the necessary background for a career as a bodyguard. In fact, a successful history with one of these respected agencies is one of the most attractive factors for potential employers.

■ ADVANCEMENT

Those who enter the field as part-time bodyguards may soon find full-time work. As bodyguards develop their skills and reputation, they may be hired by private security firms or government agencies. They may be given additional training in intelligence operations, surveillance techniques, and the use of sophisticated firearms.

Some bodyguards find opportunities as *personal protection and security consultants*. These consultants work for private companies, evaluating personal security operations and recommending changes. They may begin their own security services companies or advance to supervisory and director's positions within an existing company.

■ EARNINGS

Many bodyguards begin their careers on a part-time basis and earn between $25 and $50 per hour for routine assignments. These assignments might last several hours. Earnings for full-time bodyguards vary enormously, depending on factors such as the guard's experience, the notoriety or prestige of the client, the type of assignment, and whether the bodyguard is employed directly by the client or through a security agency. Highly dangerous, sensitive, or classified assignments generally pay more highly than do more routine protective assignments. Training in special skills, such as electronic surveillance also brings higher wages. According to findings by the Economic Research Institute, bodyguards just starting out in the field average a salary of approximately $22,330. Those with five years of experience average approximately $27,570 annually, and those with 10 years of experience average approximately $31,400. Depending on who the bodyguard works for, earnings may be higher than these. For example, in 2002 Distinguished Domestic Services, a placement agency for domestic professionals, reported on its Web site (http://distinguisheddomestics.com) that personal protection officers can expect a salary range of $40,000 to $70,000 annually. The agency also notes that these security personnel have usually had some type of government training. On its website, the Bureau of Diplomatic Security of the U.S. Department of State (http://ds.state.gov/employment/spagent.htm) reported a starting salary range for its special agents in security of $32,590 to $45,112 in 2002.

Bodyguards employed by private security firms may receive health and life insurance benefits and other benefits. Benefits vary for those employed by private clients. Bodyguards who work as part of a government agency receive health and life insurance, vacation, holiday, and sick leave pay, and a pension plan. Self-employed bodyguards must provide their own insurance.

■ WORK ENVIRONMENT

A bodyguard goes wherever the client goes. This means that the job can be physically demanding. Bodyguards must also have the strength and coordination to take actions to protect the client if the situation warrants it. A bodyguard must be able to act swiftly and decisively to thwart any attempt to harm a client.

Bodyguards must be willing to risk their own safety to protect their clients. They should be comfortable handling firearms and using physical means of restraining people.

Since bodyguards must accompany their clients at all times, there is no set work schedule. Bodyguards often work highly irregular hours, such as late evenings followed by morning assignments. It is also not unusual to work weekends, since this is when many high-profile clients make public appearances. Travel is a frequent component of the job.

OUTLOOK

Opportunities for bodyguards are likely to be strong as more and more people look for protection from an increasing number of threats such as stalkers, terrorists, and violent demonstrators. In addition, the threat of kidnapping and terrorism is always present for politicians, celebrities, business leaders, and others who enjoy wide recognition, and these individuals will take steps to safeguard themselves and their families by hiring bodyguards. As more and more companies enter the global economy, their business will take their executives to more areas of social and political unrest, and companies will need to increase their efforts for protecting their employees.

Government agencies will continue to hire bodyguards, but much of the growth in employment will take place in the private sector. Many bodyguards will find work with private security companies. Some estimates suggest that employment in private security may nearly double over the next decade.

Those with the most skill and experience will enjoy the best employment prospects. While the majority of bodyguards continue to be men, the increasing use of advanced security technologies will open up more and more opportunities for women.

FOR MORE INFORMATION

For information on security careers and the certified protection professional designation, contact

American Society for Industrial Security
1625 Prince Street
Alexandria, VA 22314-2818
Tel: 703-519-6200
Email: asis@asisonline.org
http://www.asisonline.org

For more information on the Bureau of Diplomatic Security and the U.S. Department of State, visit this agency's website.

Bureau of Diplomatic Security
U.S. Department of State
2201 C Street, NW
Washington, DC 20520
Tel: 202-647-4000
http://www.state.gov/m/ds

Your local Secret Service field office or headquarters office can provide more information on becoming a special agent. To learn more about secret service work, find career fairs, and get contact information for field offices, visit the agency's website.

U.S. Secret Service
950 H Street, NW, Suite 8400
Washington, DC 20223
Tel: 202-406-5708
http://www.treas.gov/usss

Boilermakers and Mechanics

OVERVIEW

Boilermakers and *boilermaker mechanics* construct, assemble, and repair boilers, vats, tanks, and other large metal vessels that are designed to hold liquids and gases. Following blueprints, they lay out, cut, fit, bolt, weld, and rivet together heavy metal plates, boiler tubes, and castings. Boilermaker mechanics maintain and repair boilers and other vessels made by boilermakers. There are approximately 24,560 boilermakers working in the United States.

HISTORY

Boilers first became important during the Industrial Revolution, when steam power emerged as a practical way to drive various kinds of machinery. A *boiler* is an apparatus that heats a liquid, usually water, and converts it to vapor. Boilers were first made and used in England in the beginning of the 18th century. Manufacturers first used iron and then began using steel in boilers because steel could withstand more heat and pressure in use. During the 19th and 20th centuries, a series of design changes and improved alloys made boilers useful in a wide variety of industrial applications.

Because boilers are often operated at extremely high pressures, faulty construction, bad repairs, or improper operation can be very dangerous. Explosions were not uncommon. During the late 19th century, regulations were put in place in some localities to prevent accidents caused by careless construction. Workers in the industry began organizing in the 1880s. By 1893, the two unions representing workers in boiler and similar trades met in Chicago to unite into what was then called the International Brotherhood of Boiler Makers, Iron Ship Builders, Blacksmiths, Forgers, and Helpers.

It was not until 1908, however, that rules and regulations were developed to apply to any sizable area. Massachusetts created a Board of Boiler Rules in that year, and Ohio followed with its own set of rules in 1911. By 1934, 19 states and 15 cities had such codes. Today, as a result of the combined efforts of industry, labor unions, and government, safety codes are practically universal. The American Society of Mechanical Engineers and the International Brotherhood of Boilermakers have been leaders in the promotion and enforcement of the codes of safe manufacture and maintenance.

■ THE JOB

Some boilermakers and mechanics work at or near the site where the boiler, tank, or vat is installed. Such sites include petroleum refineries, schools and other institutions with large heating plants, factories where boilers are used to generate power to run machines, factories that make and store products, such as chemicals or beer in large tanks, and atomic energy plants. Others work in shops or factories where boilers and other large vessels are manufactured.

Boilermakers who do layout work usually work in a shop or factory. These workers follow drawings, blueprints, and patterns to mark pieces of metal plate and tubing to indicate how the metal will be cut and shaped by other workers into the sections of vessels. Once the sections are fabricated, other workers at the shop, called *fitters*, temporarily put together the plates and the framework of the vessels. They check the drawings and other specifications and bolt or tack-weld pieces together to be sure that the parts fit properly.

In doing the final assembly at the site, boilermakers first refer to blueprints and mark off dimensions on the base that has been prepared for the finished vessel. They use measuring devices, straightedges, and transits. They attach rigging equipment, such as hoists, jacks, and rollers, to any prefabricated sections of the vessel that are so large they must be lifted into place with cranes. After crane operators move the sections to the correct positions, the boilermakers fine-tune the alignment of the parts. They use levels and check plumb lines and then secure the sections in place with wedges and turnbuckles. With cutting torches, files, and grinders, they remove irregularities and precisely adjust the fit and finally weld and rivet the sections together. They may also attach other tubing, valves, gauges, or other parts to the vessel and then test the container for leaks and defects.

Boilermakers also work in shipbuilding and in repairing the hulls, bulkheads, and decks of iron ships. In a typical repair, boilermakers first remove damaged metal plates by drilling out rivets and cutting off rivet heads with a chipping hammer. Then they take measurements of the damaged plates or make wooden patterns of them so that new plates can be made. They install the new plates, reaming and aligning rivet holes, then fastening on the plates by driving in rivets. Sometimes similar work is done on ships' boilers, condensers, evaporators, loaders, gratings, and stacks.

Field construction boilermakers work outdoors and move from one geographic location to another. They join construction teams in erecting and repairing pressure vessels, air pollution equipment, blast furnaces, water treatment plants, storage tanks, and stacks and liners. They can be involved in the erection of a 750,000-gallon water storage tank, the placement of a nuclear power plant reactor dome, or the construction of components on a hydroelectric power station.

Boilermaker mechanics maintain and repair boilers and other vessels. They routinely clean or direct others to clean boilers, and they inspect fittings, valves, tubes, controls, and other parts. When necessary, they check the vessels to identify specific weaknesses or sources of trouble. They update components, such as burners and boiler tubes, to make them as efficient as possible. They dismantle the units to replace worn or defective parts, using hand and power tools, gas torches, and welding equipment. Sometimes repairs require that they use metalworking machinery, such as power shears and presses to cut and shape parts to specification. They strengthen joints and supports, and they put patches on weak areas of metal plates. Like fabrication and installation work, all repairs must be done in compliance with state and local safety codes.

■ REQUIREMENTS
High School

A high school diploma is required for applicants to the boilermaking trade. In the past, people have become boil-

QUICK FACTS

SCHOOL SUBJECTS
Mathematics
Technical/shop

PERSONAL SKILLS
Mechanical/manipulative
Technical/scientific

WORK ENVIRONMENT
Indoors and outdoors
Primarily multiple locations

MINIMUM EDUCATION LEVEL
Apprenticeship

SALARY RANGE
$25,450 to $41,960 to
$60,240

CERTIFICATION OR LICENSING
None available

OUTLOOK
Little change or more slowly
than the average

DOT
805

GOE
06.02.02

NOC
7262

O*NET-SOC
47-2011.00

ermakers through on-the-job training, but apprenticeships are now strongly recommended. To gain an apprenticeship, an applicant must score well on an aptitude test. You can prepare yourself for this test and the career by taking math classes and shop classes throughout high school. Courses that give you the opportunity to learn blueprint reading, welding, and metalworking are especially helpful.

Postsecondary Training

Formal apprenticeships usually last four years. An apprentice receives practical training while working as a helper under the supervision of an experienced boilermaker. In addition to working, trainees attend classes in the technical aspects of the trade. Apprentices study subjects, such as blueprint reading, layout, welding techniques, mechanical drawing, the physics and chemistry of various metals, and applied mathematics. While on the job, apprentices practice the knowledge they have acquired in the classroom. They develop such skills as using rigging and hoisting equipment, welding, riveting, and installing auxiliary devices and tubes onto vessels.

Other Requirements

Mechanical aptitude and manual dexterity are important characteristics for prospective boilermakers. Because the work can be very strenuous, stamina is needed for jobs that require a great deal of bending, stooping, squatting, or reaching. Before they begin work, boilermakers may need to pass a physical examination showing that they are in good enough health to do the work safely. On the job, they must be able to work well despite noisy surroundings, odors, working at heights or in small, enclosed spaces, and other discomforts and dangers. It is also important that they be cautious and careful in their work and that they closely follow safety rules.

■ EXPLORING

You may be able to observe boilermakers or workers who use similar skills as they work on construction projects or repair and maintenance jobs. For example, welders and equipment operators lifting heavy objects with elaborate rigging can sometimes be seen working at sites where large buildings are being erected. High school shop courses, such as blueprint reading and metalworking, can give you an idea of some of the activities of boilermakers. With the help of shop teachers or guidance counselors, you may be able to arrange to talk with people working in the trade. Information may also be obtained by contacting the local union-management committee in charge of apprenticeships for boilermakers.

A fitter at a boilermaking plant welds together metal sections.

■ EMPLOYERS

Approximately 24,560 boilermakers work in the United States. Of that number, slightly more than half work in the construction industry. Others work in manufacturing, employed primarily in boiler manufacturing shops, iron and steel plants, petroleum refineries, chemical plants, and shipyards. Still others work for boiler repair firms, for railroads, and in Navy shipyards and federal power facilities.

■ STARTING OUT

There are a limited number of apprenticeships available in boilermaking; only the best applicants are accepted, and there may be a waiting period before the apprenticeship starts. Sometimes workers begin as helpers in repair shops and enter formal apprenticeships later. These helper jobs are often advertised in newspapers. Vocational and technical schools and sometimes high schools with metal shop courses may also help their graduates locate such positions. Other good approaches are to apply directly to employers and to contact the local office of the state employment service.

IS BOILERMAKING FOR YOU?

Working as a field construction boilermaker is challenging though lucrative. Take a minute to answer these questions from the Boilermakers Apprenticeship Program; your responses will help you decide.

Are you willing to do demanding and strenuous physical work?

Are you willing to work at heights of 200 to 1,000 feet above the ground?

Are you willing to travel and live away from home for long periods of time to maintain employment?

Are you willing to work in all types of adverse conditions?

Are you willing to make a commitment to four years of on-the-job training?

Are you willing to complete the self-study lessons and on-the-job modules?

Do you understand that, based on employment conditions, you may be unemployed from time to time?

Are you dedicated to performing a job to the best of your ability and in compliance with employer standards?

Are you willing to attend classroom instructions, when available, in addition to your regular working hours?

Are you willing to be drug tested and remain drug free?

■ ADVANCEMENT

Upon completing their training programs, apprentices qualify as journeymen boilermakers. With experience and the right kind of leadership abilities, boilermakers may be able to advance to supervisory positions. In fabrication shops, layout workers and fitters who start as helpers can learn the skills they need in about two years. In time, they may move up to become shop supervisors, or they may decide to become boilermakers who work on-site to assemble vessels.

■ EARNINGS

According to the U.S. Department of Labor, the median hourly wage for boilermakers in 2002 was $20.17. For full-time work at 40 hours per week, this wage translates into a median annual income of $41,960. The department also reported that the lowest paid 10 percent earned less than $12.24 per hour, or less than approximately $25,450 per year for full-time work. At the other end of the pay scale, the highest paid 10 percent made more than $28.96 per hour (approximately $60,240 annually).

According to the International Brotherhood of Boilermakers, annual earnings vary greatly because of the temporary, cyclical nature of the work. Apprentices start at about 60 percent of journeyman wages. Earnings also vary according to the part of the country where boilermakers work, the industry that employs them, and their level of skill and experience. Pay rates are usually highest for boilermakers doing installation work in the construction industry and lower for those in manufacturing industries, although workers in construction may not be employed as steadily. Workers in the Northeast, the Great Lakes area, and cities in the far West tend to earn the highest wages.

Boilermakers tend to make more than boilermaker mechanics. Among employees in boiler-fabrication shops, layout workers generally earn more while fitters earn less. Both layout workers and fitters normally work indoors; therefore, their earnings are not limited by seasonal variations in weather.

Most boilermakers are members of unions, and union contracts set their wages and benefits. The largest union is the International Brotherhood of Boilermakers, Iron Ship Builders, Blacksmiths, Forgers, and Helpers. Other boilermakers are members of the Industrial Union of Marine and Shipbuilding Workers of America; the Oil, Chemical, and Atomic Workers International Union; the United Steelworkers of America; the International Association of Machinists and Aerospace Workers; and the United Automobile, Aerospace, and Agricultural Implement Workers of America. Among the fringe benefits established under union contracts are health insurance, pension plans, and paid vacation time.

■ WORK ENVIRONMENT

Boilermaking tends to be more hazardous than many other occupations. Boilermakers often work with dangerous tools and equipment; they must manage heavy materials; and they may climb to heights to do installation or repair work. Despite great progress in preventing accidents, the rate of on-the-job injuries for boilermakers remains higher than the average for all manufacturing industries. Employer and union safety programs and standards set by the federal government's Occupational Safety and Health Administration (OSHA) are helping to control dangerous conditions and reduce accidents.

The work often requires physical exertion and may be carried on in extremely hot, poorly ventilated, noisy, and damp places. At times it is necessary to work in cramped quarters inside boilers, vats, or tanks. At other times, workers must handle materials and equipment several stories above ground level. Sometimes installation workers work on jobs that require them to remain away from home for considerable periods of time.

To protect against injury, boilermakers and mechanics use a variety of special clothing and equipment, such as hard hats, safety glasses and shoes, harnesses, and respirators. A 40-hour week is average, but in some jobs, deadlines may require overtime.

■ OUTLOOK

The U.S. Department of Labor projects little or no change in the employment rate of boilermakers through 2012. One reason for this is the current trend of repairing and retrofitting, rather than replacing, boilers. In addition, the smaller boilers currently being used require less on-site assembly. Finally, the automation of production technologies and the increasing use of imported boilers will cut down on the need for boilermakers.

During economic downturns, boilermakers, including layout workers and fitters, may be laid off because many industries stop expanding their operations and install very few new boilers. On the other hand, boilermaker mechanics are less affected by downturns because they work more on maintaining and repairing existing equipment, which requires their services regardless of economic conditions.

Despite little projected growth, there will be openings for boilermakers every year as experienced workers leave the field. Workers who have completed apprenticeships will have the best opportunities for good jobs.

■ FOR MORE INFORMATION

For information about boilermaker apprenticeships, contact

Boilermakers National Apprenticeship
Program
1017 North 9th Street
Kansas City, KS 66101
Tel: 913-342-2100
Email: info@bnap.com
http://www.bnap.com

For additional career information, contact

International Brotherhood of Boilermakers,
Iron Ship Builders, Blacksmiths, Forgers
and Helpers, AFL-CIO
753 State Avenue
Kansas City, KS 66102
Tel: 913-371-2640
http://www.boilermakers.org

Book Conservators

■ OVERVIEW

Book conservators treat the bindings and pages of books and nonbook items to help preserve original materials for future use. Their work often includes removing a book block from its binding, sewing, measuring, gluing, rebinding, and using special chemical treatments to maintain the integrity of the item. Most conservators work in libraries, in museums, or for special conservation centers.

■ HISTORY

In order to understand the history of book conservation as a field, it is important to learn something about the evolution of books and bookbinding. Early books were not bound, but rather rolled, such as ancient Egyptian papyrus rolls and early Christian parchment rolls. Eventually the rolls were cut into a number of flat panels sewn together along one edge, thus allowing for a book that was more convenient, portable, and enduring. Early Latin codex manuscripts were made up of folded sheets gathered into signatures, or groups of folded pages, and sewn together. Wooden boards were then placed on either side of the sewn signatures. In time, the entire volume was covered with leather or other animal skins to hide the sewing cords and provide protection to the pages. The basic constructional elements of bookbinding have changed little in the past 1,800 years, but the materials and methods used have matured considerably.

Before the invention of the printing press, religious orders were often charged with copying texts by hand. These same monastic groups also assumed the roles of bookbinder and conservator. One of the main goals in creating books is the conservation and dissemination of knowledge.

In order to pass that knowledge on to future generations,

QUICK FACTS

SCHOOL SUBJECTS
Art
History

PERSONAL SKILLS
Artistic
Mechanical/manipulative

WORK ENVIRONMENT
Primarily indoors
Primarily one location

MINIMUM EDUCATION LEVEL
Bachelor's degree

SALARY RANGE
$20,010 to $35,270 to
$66,050

CERTIFICATION OR LICENSING
Voluntary

OUTLOOK
About as fast as the average

DOT
102

GOE
01.06.01

NOC
5112

O*NET-SOC
25-4013.00

many early bookbinders began the legacy of conservation by using high quality materials and excellent craftsmanship. A book that is well-crafted in the first place will need less invasive conservation as the material ages. Historically, then, the people who created the books had the specialized knowledge to conserve them.

Conservators today are often from the same mold as early bookbinders. They have the specialized knowledge of how books have traditionally been crafted, and they use technologically advanced adhesives, papers, and binding techniques to ensure that materials created centuries ago will be around for years to come.

The establishment of book conservation as a career field apart from bookbinding probably began when the first courses in conservation and preservation were taught at a library school, or when a professional library association first addressed the topic. Thus, although early bookbinders dealt with issues of material longevity, conservation as a field has only been around for 100 years or so.

■ THE JOB

Book conservators work to slow down or stabilize the deterioration of books and other print-based materials. They repair books that have been damaged by misuse, accident, pests, or normal wear and tear; treat items that may have been produced or repaired with inferior materials or methods; and work to ensure that the books will be around for the future.

Before beginning any conservation efforts, book conservators must examine the item to be restored, determine the extent and cause of the deterioration, evaluate their own conservation skills, and decide on a proper course of action. In deciding how to treat an item, the book conservator must first consider the history of the item. When was it made? Book conservators must have a good knowledge of the history of bookmaking in order to serve the needs of the item. A book bound by hand in Italy in 1600 will have different needs than a volume bound by machine in 1980.

The book conservator also needs to consider what other repairs have been made to the book over the years. Sometimes a shoddy repair job in the past can create more work for today's conservator. For example, someone 30 years ago may have taped a torn page to keep it from ripping out entirely. Unfortunately, this hasty action, coupled with tape that will not stand the test of time, could lead to cracked, yellowing tape and stained book pages. When repairing a ripped sheet, book conservators use a pH-neutral (acid-free) adhesive, such as wheat paste, and Japanese paper, or a special acid-free book tape. Since high levels of acidity in papers and materials increase the rate of deterioration, all materials that conservators use must be acid-free and of archival quality.

Book conservators also think about the current and future use of the book. For a common, high-use volume that will be checked out of the library frequently, they may repair the book with cheaper, lower-quality materials that will survive being tossed into a backpack and repeated trips through the return chute. For a textbook that is reprinted each year, for example, a thick piece of tape may be an adequate conservation method. If such a book is falling out of its cover, the conservator may need to remove the bookblock entirely, repair or replace the end sheets and headbands, and re-glue the bookblock back into the cover. If the cover of the book is broken, the conservator may need to fit the text block into a new cover. This involves measuring out the binder's board and book cloth, cutting the materials to size, gluing the cloth onto the board, sizing in the bookblock, then finally gluing and setting the book. After the glue is dry, the conservator will inspect the item to ensure that all materials were fitted in properly, and that all problems were corrected.

Rare books that are handled less frequently or only by specially trained and careful users can have less invasive repairs in order to maintain the integrity of the original item. For instance, a conservator may choose to make a box to house a book rather than repair a broken spine. If the conservation work would lessen the value of the book, sometimes it's better to simply stop the deterioration rather than repair the damage.

The historical and monetary value of a book is a key factor in deciding upon treatment. As with any antique, often less restoration is more. On a recent antiques television program, an owner refinished an antique table and thereby reduced its resale value by thousands of dollars. The same can be said for books. Many old and rare books have great value because of the historical materials and methods in evidence.

Sometimes pests are encountered in conservation work. Beetle larvae and other insects may feast upon crumbs left in books, the pulp of the paper, or the adhesive, and make holes in the text. The conservator will assess the extent of the damage and prescribe a treatment. For critter damage to books, the most important thing is to ensure that any infestation is under control. The conservator needs to make sure that all bugs in a book are dead; if not, the items may need to be taken to a professional for fumigation. Once that is complete, the conservator can look at possible repair options. If the damage is under control, the conservator will probably opt for further damage prevention in lieu of repair.

Often conservators treat books for only part of their day. They might also spend much time working on ways to minimize the need for conservation and repair work in the first place. Book conservators who work as part of a large department have other duties, such as dealing with patrons, reference work, security, training assistants, fielding calls from the public, giving seminars, and teaching. Conservators may also serve on groups and committees devoted to preservation, conservation, and the administration of a conservation lab or department.

REQUIREMENTS
High School
You should plan on taking a college preparatory course load while in high school. Classes, such as history, literature, art, foreign languages, chemistry, and mathematics will all help you build a strong background for book conservation. By studying history, you can learn the social and historical contexts of books and knowledge. Understanding the history of an item can give you a better perspective on approaching the material as a conservator. Strong knowledge of literature can help you appraise the potential value of a book. A comprehension of foreign languages allows you to deal with a wider variety of books from around the globe. Chemistry and math will begin to teach you about the composition and measurement of the materials you will be using. Art will teach you how to use your hands to create beautiful works that last.

Postsecondary Training
In the past, book conservators gained their training by participating in an apprenticeship or internship. Today, graduate programs in book conservation have become the primary method of training to enter this field, although some students still enter this field after earning a bachelor's degree and completing an apprenticeship or internship to round out their training. A bachelor's degree in art, art history, or one of the fine arts may help you gain entry into a book conservation apprenticeship or internship program. Your school may offer courses, or even an undergraduate degree, in the book or paper arts, which often include classes in preservation and conservation. You will also need to take courses that help you learn how to select items for conservation, how to purchase and best utilize your conservation materials, and how to prepare documentation on your conservation methods and treatments.

Upon earning a bachelor's degree, you should attend a graduate school that offers training in book conservation. These programs are commonly offered by the art conservation departments of academic institutions. Some students may wish to attend library school to earn a master's degree in library science with a concentration in book and document conservation. Again, advanced

BE A BOOK CONSERVATOR NOW
Although in-depth conservation is best left to the professionals, there are many ways you can begin your career as a conservator today. The key to conservation is to avoid the need for conservation. You can help in these efforts by doing the following:
- Keep books out of the sun; ultraviolet rays can discolor materials and increase deterioration.
- Don't throw materials around; treat them with respect.
- Never bend pages to mark your place; use a bookmark.
- Keep food and drinks away from the materials you are using; crumbs left in books can be an invitation to pests.
- Don't hold books open face down on a surface; this can break the binding.
- Don't use books as coasters; find something else to hold your drink!
- Use quality materials for basic repairs.
- If you accidentally damage a library book, bring it to the attention of the librarian when you return it so it can be repaired before further damage occurs.

degrees may not be necessary for some positions, but they can always help you gain more prominent positions—particularly in administration—and perhaps command a higher salary. Additionally, any special skills you gain through advanced education will make you more attractive to potential employers and private clients.

Certification or Licensing
Some book conservators gain certification from their library school or from professional organizations such as the Academy of Certified Archivists. The certification process generally requires a mix of formal study of theory and practice, as well as a certain amount of actual experience in the field. Certification is not officially required by any federal, state, or local agencies, but some employers may request, or require, a certified book conservationist for particular positions or projects. Also, certifying organizations compile a list of all their certified conservators. If someone contacts an organization looking for a conservator, the agency will refer the client to member book conservators in the area.

Other Requirements
Book conservators need be able to think creatively. Conservation projects require the conservator to visualize the end product before beginning work. Conservators should

This book conservator hand-repairs rare library books.

Contact the conservation or preservation department at your local library. The department may offer tours of its facilities or workshops on the proper care of books. Contact professional librarian associations; they may have divisions devoted to conservation. Community colleges and art museums often have weekend or evening classes in the conservation and book arts.

Finally, you might try contacting your local park district or community center to suggest sessions about book conservation. Many such groups offer summer day camps or after-school programs and look for input from participants about what types of activities are of interest. Plus, if you have had some conservation experience of your own, you could offer to teach younger students about how they can begin conserving books by taking good care of their own materials and the books they check out of the library.

enjoy problem solving and be able to decide the best way to conserve the materials. Having a knack for hands-on work is key as well, since book conservators spend a majority of their time inspecting materials and making repairs by hand.

Since book conservators routinely work with musty, moldy, and mildewed books, they should not be overly sensitive to odors. They also deal with sharp instruments, such as awls, knives, and paper cutters, so for safety reasons they should have a certain amount of facility with their hands. Book conservators also work with adhesives and chemicals, so they must take care not to spill materials.

Although much of their day is spent working with the materials, many conservators deal with the public as well. Book conservators, therefore, should be able to communicate well, and with a certain measure of tact, with many types of people. They should be able to explain conservation options to clients and to best determine what procedures will meet the needs of the material and the owner.

■ EXPLORING

If you are interested in becoming a book conservator, you should start out by learning all you can about how books are made. Study the history of books and of binding. Purchase an inexpensive, hardcover book at a used bookstore and take it apart to see how the bookblock is sewn together and how it is connected to the cover. Then try to put the book back together. There are many "how to" bookbinding guides to help you. Check out *Hand Bookbinding: A Manual of Instruction* by Aldren A. Watson (New York: Dover Publications, 1996) or *ABC of Bookbinding: A Unique Glossary With Over 700 Illustrations for Collectors & Librarians* by Jane Greenfield (New Castle, Del.: Oak Knoll Books, 1998) for the history of different styles of bookbinding and definitions of terms used in the field.

■ EMPLOYERS

College and university libraries, public libraries, institutional libraries, and special libraries all employ book conservators. These organizations may have an entire department devoted to the conservation and preservation of materials, or the tasks of conservation may be bestowed upon another division, such as an archival or rare book collection. Museums sometimes have a specific book conservator post, or they may offer such duties to an interested art conservationist. Book conservators also work for companies devoted to material conservation. Binderies may hire a conservationist as a quality control consultant.

A number of book conservators are self-employed, working on a freelance or part-time basis for organizations and private citizens. They may be part of a nationwide network of certified book conservators. Often, potential clients contact book conservators through membership in professional organizations.

■ STARTING OUT

Book conservation is a field that relies heavily on skill, reputation, and word-of-mouth communication. While earning your bachelor's or master's degree, you should try to get an internship, apprenticeship, or assistantship in conservation or a related field. Take all the courses you can that will help you gain conservation skills.

You may also be able to get a part-time or summer job in your school library's preservation or conservation department. Many part time positions or internships can turn into full-time jobs after the incumbent has proven his or her skills or completed specific educational requirements.

Once you complete a training period, you might consider becoming certified. Certification can be a deciding factor in gaining employment, since certain companies and organizations may require book conservators to have official affirmation of their qualifications from an outside agency.

You should also join a conservator's organization in order to get to know professionals in the field. Since many conservator positions are in libraries, you may wish to join a professional library association as well. Professional organizations often have job listings available to members. They also publish journals and newsletters to keep members up-to-date on new developments in the field.

If you are looking to be a self-employed conservator, you may wish to volunteer your services until you have established yourself. Volunteering to assist nonprofit organizations with their conservation needs will give you good exposure to help you learn more about the book conservator world and the skills that potential clients are seeking.

■ ADVANCEMENT

Book conservators who demonstrate a high level of skill in their craft can move on to positions with more responsibility. They may be called upon to train assistants in book conservation or to teach conservation techniques at a library school, certification program, or conservation lab.

They may also transfer their skill in dealing with rare and fine materials and work more in the art community as art conservators, appraisers, or artists. With more experience and education, a book conservator can become an archivist, curator, or librarian. Many book conservators prefer to move away from full-time conservation and work on freelance projects instead.

With advanced computer knowledge, book conservators can help bring rare and fragile materials into the digital age. They may learn how to make materials available on the Internet and become virtual curators. They may also move on to actual exhibition work. Knowing how to preserve materials gives them the advantage in knowing how to exhibit them safely.

As book conservators gain more prominent positions, the trend is away from materials and toward administration. Beginning conservators will often spend most of their day dealing directly with the materials to be conserved. Conservators who move on to more advanced positions generally spend more time training others; evaluating materials and methods; dealing with outside suppliers, customers, and associations; attending meetings; and planning for the future of the department and the field.

■ EARNINGS

It is difficult to say how much the average book conservator makes, since many conservators work part time, are self-employed, or have positions that encompass other duties as well. In general, the salary range for book conservators may fall within the range the U.S. Department of Labor reports for all conservators, archivists, and other museum workers. In 2002, this group of professionals had a median annual income of $35,270. The lowest paid 10 percent earned less than $20,010 yearly, and the highest paid 10 percent made more than $66,050 per year. Often the size of the employer affects how much a conservator earns, with larger employers able to pay more. In addition, book conservators in major metropolitan areas generally earn more than those in small cities, and those with greater skills also command higher salaries.

Conservators who work for libraries, conservation organizations, large corporations, institutions, or government agencies generally receive a full range of benefits, including health care coverage, vacation days, paid holidays, paid sick time, and retirement savings plans. Self-employed book conservators usually have to provide their own benefits. All conservators have the added benefit of working with rare and unique materials. They have the opportunity to work with history and preserve an artifact for the future.

■ WORK ENVIRONMENT

Because of the damage that dirt, humidity, and the sun can cause to books, most conservators work in clean, climate-controlled areas away from direct sunlight. Many conservation labs are small offices, which often employ the conservator alone or perhaps with one or two part-time assistants. Other labs are part of a larger department within an organization; the University of Chicago's Regenstein Library, for instance, has a conservation lab within the Special Collections department. With this type of arrangement, the book conservator generally has a few student and nonstudent assistants who work part-time to help with some of the conservation duties.

Book conservators are always on the move. They use their hands constantly to measure, cut, and paste materials. They also bend, lift, and twist in order to reach items they work on and make room for new materials. Also, books are not always an easy size or weight to handle. Some oversized items need to be transported on a book truck from the stack area to the conservation area for treatment.

Most book conservators work 40 hours a week, usually during regular, weekday working hours. Depending on the needs of their department and the clientele they serve, book conservators may need to be available some weekend hours. Also, some book conservators may agree to travel to the homes of clients to view materials that may require conservation.

■ OUTLOOK

The future of book conservation as a profession will most likely grow about as fast as the average through 2012. The U.S. Department of Labor notes that while the outlook for conservators in general is favorable, there is strong competition for jobs. Book conservators who are graduates of conservation programs and are willing to relocate should have the best opportunities for employment. Those who can use their conservation skills in tandem with other abilities may also find more job openings. Book conservators with an artistic bent, for instance, could bring their conservation skills to an exhibition program at an art museum. Conservators who enjoy public contact could use their practical experience to teach classes in conservation techniques.

Some people are concerned that our increasingly digital society will create fewer opportunities for book conservators. They claim that new technologies, such as television, computers, telephones, and the Internet have changed communication styles so drastically that printed books will eventually become obsolete. While it is true that more advanced technology will bring new challenges to conservation, these advances should also increase opportunities for conservators who can blend these developments with traditional conservation efforts. For example, a book conservator with excellent computer skills and Web-authoring knowledge can work on a project to digitize rare book collections and make them available to people all over the world.

■ FOR MORE INFORMATION

For certification information, contact

Academy of Certified Archivists
48 Howard Street
Albany, NY 12207
Tel: 518-463-8644
Email: aca@caphill.com
http://www.certifiedarchivists.org

For information about how to become a conservator, contact

American Institute for Conservation of Historic and Artistic Works
1717 K Street, NW, Suite 200
Washington, DC 20006
Tel: 202-452-9545
Email: info@aic-faic.org
http://aic.stanford.edu

For information about preservation methods, services, and opportunities, contact the following association:

Library of Congress Preservation Directorate
101 Independence Avenue, SE
Washington, DC 20540-4500

Tel: 202-707-5213
http://lcweb.loc.gov/preserv

For a wealth of information about conservation topics, check out this project of the Preservation Department of Stanford University Libraries:

Conservation OnLine
http://palimpsest.stanford.edu

Book Editors

■ OVERVIEW

Book editors acquire and prepare written material for publication in book form. Such formats include trade books (fiction and nonfiction), textbooks, and technical and professional books (which include reference books, such as this one). A book editor's duties may include contracting for and evaluating a manuscript, accepting or rejecting it, rewriting, correcting spelling and grammar, researching, and fact checking. Book editors may also work directly with printers in arranging for proofs and with artists and designers in arranging for illustration matter and determining the physical specifications of the book.

Approximately 106,520 editors work for newspapers, magazines, and book publishers in the United States. Book editors are employed at small and large publishing houses, book packagers (companies that subcontract book production for larger publishing houses), associations, and government agencies.

■ HISTORY

The origins of the publishing industry probably began soon after people developed written language, perhaps in Sumer in approximately 4000 B.C. After it became possible to record information in writing, somebody had to decide which information was worth recording. Technically speaking, the first record-keepers were the first publishers and editors. Some of the first things deemed suitable for publication were accounting records, genealogies, laws, and religious rituals and beliefs.

For thousands of years, European books were produced by the laborious process of hand copying—first by the slave-secretaries of ancient Greece and Rome, and then by the monks of the medieval world, whose busy quills preserved both sacred and secular texts. Editors ensured that errors did not creep into the manuscripts—a critical task, when the words on the page were those originally written by the fathers of the Church, or handed down by God himself. The works that were published were intended for the small, elite group of educated people who could read and who could afford to buy books. For the most part, these people were clergymen and members of the upper class who had intellectual interests. Books of that era generally were written and edited in Latin, the common languages of the educated classes in Europe.

The first printed books in the West were produced in the Rhine Valley by Johannes Gutenberg in about 1440. Gutenberg's press, adapted from the wine press, began the first revolution in information technology. Over time literacy spread and newly affordable books on all sorts of subjects began to be written in the languages of the countries in which they were published. In addition to setting the author's words in type, printers also often performed what we would now call editorial tasks. Having a book printed was often a risky business venture, often financed by the author himself.

Beginning in the 19th century, the various tasks performed by publishing concerns became more specialized. Whereas in early publishing a single person would often perform various functions, in later publishing, employees performed a narrow range of tasks. Instead of having a single editor, a publication would have an editorial staff. One person would be responsible for acquisitions, another would copyedit, another would be responsible for editorial tasks that related to production, and so forth.

Editing has also been powerfully affected by technology. Printing came into existence only after Gutenberg had adapted the necessary technology, and it has changed in various ways as technology has developed. The most important recent developments have been those that have made it possible to transfer and edit information rapidly and efficiently. The development of the computer has revolutionized editing, making it possible to write and rewrite texts electronically and transmit corrected stories almost instantaneously from one part of the world to another. This article, for instance, was written on one computer, e-mailed to the publisher, sent out to a copyeditor, and then uploaded back to the publisher, and then sent with others to the designer for electronic typesetting.

■ THE JOB

The editorial department is generally the main core of any publishing house. Procedures and terminology may vary from one type of publishing house to another, but there is some general agreement among the essentials. Publishers of trade books, textbooks, and reference books all have somewhat different needs for which they have developed different editorial practices.

The editor responsible for seeing a book through to publication may hold any of several titles. The highest-level editorial executive in a publishing house is usually the *editor in chief* or *editorial director*. The person holding either of these titles directs the overall operation of the editorial department. Sometimes an executive editor occupies the highest position in an editorial department. The next level of editor is often the *managing editor*, who keeps track of schedules and deadlines and must know where all manuscripts are at any given time. Other editors who handle copy include the *senior editors, associate editors, assistant editors, editorial assistants*, and *copy editors*.

In a trade-book house, the editor, usually at the senior or associate position, works with manuscripts that he or she has solicited from authors or that have been submitted by known authors or their agents. Editors who seek out authors to write manuscripts or conceptualize other projects are also known as *acquisitions editors*.

In technical/professional book houses, editors commonly do more researching, revising, and rewriting than trade-book editors do. These editors are often required to be skilled in certain subjects. Editors must be sure that the subject is comprehensively covered and organized according to an agreed-upon outline. Editors contract for virtually all of the material that comes into technical/professional book houses. The authors they solicit are often scholars.

The editor has the principal responsibility in evaluating the manuscript. Editors who edit heavily or ask an author to revise extensively must learn to be highly diplomatic; the art of author-editor relations is a critical aspect of the editor's job.

When the editor is satisfied with the manuscript, it goes to the copy editor. The copy editor usually does the final editing of the manuscript before it goes to the typesetter. On almost any type of manuscript, the copy editor is responsible for correcting errors of spelling, punctuation, grammar, and usage. It is important for a copy editor to be aware of the house style and procedures for the publishing house for

QUICK FACTS

SCHOOL SUBJECTS
Computer science
English
Journalism

PERSONAL SKILLS
Artistic
Communication/ideas

WORK ENVIRONMENT
Primarily indoors
Primarily one location

MINIMUM EDUCATION LEVEL
Bachelor's degree

SALARY RANGE
$24,010 to $41,170 to $76,620

CERTIFICATION OR LICENSING
None available

OUTLOOK
About as fast as the average

DOT
132

GOE
01.02.01

NOC
5122

O*NET-SOC
27-3041.00

This book editor is proofreading pages.

which he or she works. Consistency is the mark of a professional copy editor.

The copy editor marks up the manuscript to indicate where different kinds of typefaces are used and where charts, illustrations, and photos may be inserted. It is important for the copy editor to discover any inconsistencies in the text and to query the author about them. The copy editor then usually acts as a liaison between the typesetter, the editor, and the author as the manuscript is typeset into galley proofs and then page proofs.

In a small house, one editor might do the work of all of the editors described here. There can also be separate fact checkers, proofreaders, style editors (also called line editors), and indexers. An assistant editor could be assigned to do many of the kinds of jobs handled by the senior or associate editors. *Editorial assistants* provide support for the other editors and may be required to proofread and handle some administrative duties. They also often read through a trade book house's "slush pile" of submissions.

Finally, and most importantly, there is the paperwork. Though working with words is the main attraction of a career in publishing, all editors must keep careful records. Changes must be recorded, manuscripts must be tracked, and authors and copy editors must be paid on time.

■ REQUIREMENTS
High School

If you have an interest in a career as an editor, the most obvious classes that will prepare you include English, literature, and composition classes. You should also become familiar and comfortable working with word processing

programs, either through taking a computer science class or through your own schoolwork. Taking journalism classes will give you the opportunity to practice different writing styles, including short feature pieces and long investigative stories. Art classes can also be useful to learn basics of photography and illustration, and to learn about elements of design and page appearance. Take advantage of any clubs or extracurricular activities that will give you a chance to write or edit. Joining the school newspaper staff is a great way to explore different tasks in publishing, such as writing, editing, layout, and printing.

Postsecondary Training

A college degree is a requirement for entry into the field of book editing. For general editing, a degree in English or journalism is particularly valuable, although most degrees in the liberal arts are acceptable. Degrees in other fields, such as the arts, history, sciences, psychology, or mathematics can be useful in publishing houses that produce books related to those fields. Textbook and technical/professional book houses in particular seek out editors with strengths in certain subject areas.

Other Requirements

Book editors should have a sharp eye for detail and a compulsion for accuracy (of both grammar and content). Intellectual curiosity, self-motivation, and a respect for deadlines are important characteristics for book editors to have. Knowledge of word processing and desktop publishing programs is necessary as well.

It goes without saying that if you are seeking a career in book editing, you should not only love to read, but love books for their own sake as well. If you are not an avid reader, you are not likely to go far as a book editor. The craft and history of bookmaking itself is also something in which a young book editor should be interested. A keen interest in any subject, be it a sport, a hobby, or an avocation, can lead you into special areas of book publishing.

■ EXPLORING

As previously mentioned, joining your school's newspaper staff is a great way to explore editing and writing while in high school. Even if your duties are not strictly editorial, gaining experience by writing, doing layout work, or even securing advertisements will help you to understand how the editing stage relates to the entire field of publishing. Joining your school's yearbook staff or starting your own literary magazine are other ways to gain valuable experience.

You might be able to find a part-time job with a local book publisher or newspaper. You could also try to publish your own magazine or newsletter. Combine one of your other interests with your desire to edit. For example, if you are interested in sports, you could try writing and editing your own sports report to distribute to family and friends.

Since editing and writing are inextricably linked, be sure to keep your writing skills sharp. Outside of any class assignments, try keeping a journal. Try to write something every day and gain practice at reworking your writing until it is as good as you can make it. Explore different kinds of writing, such as short stories, poetry, fiction, essays, comedic prose, and plays.

If you are interested in becoming a book editor, you might consider joining a book club. Other interesting book websites, such as http://www.literarymarketplace.com or http://www.mediabistro.com, may be of interest if you'd like to learn more about publishing companies.

■ EMPLOYERS

Book editors may find employment with small publishing houses, large publishing houses, the federal government, or book packagers, or they may be self-employed as freelancers. The major book publishers are located in larger cities, such as New York, Chicago, Los Angeles, Boston, Philadelphia, San Francisco, and Washington, DC. Publishers of professional, religious, business, and technical books are dispersed throughout the country. There are approximately 106,520 editors employed in the United States (including book editors and all other editors).

■ STARTING OUT

New graduates can find editing positions through their local newspaper or through contacts made in college. College career counselors may be able to assist in finding book publishers to apply for jobs. Another option is to simply look them up in the Yellow Pages or Internet and apply for positions directly. Many publishers will advertise job openings on their corporate websites. However, by far the most helpful thing a would-be editor can do is to gain experience and contacts through internships and volunteer work. Starting positions are generally at the assistant level and can include administrative duties in addition to basic editing tasks.

■ ADVANCEMENT

An editor's career path is dependent on the size and structure of the book publisher. Those who start as editorial assistants or proofreaders generally become copy editors. The next step may be a position as a senior copy editor, which involves overseeing the work of junior copy editors, or as a *project editor*. The project editor performs a

TYPES OF PUBLISHERS

The publishing industry is very diverse, and not all publishing houses are alike. Different companies have different specialties. Here's a brief look at some of the types of publishing houses where an editor might be employed.

Trade publishing is what most people think about when they think of book publishing. Most of the fiction and non-fiction books you find at your local bookstore fit into the trade category. However, not every editor at a trade house gets to work with the next bestseller! There are many niches, such as how-to, fine art books, romance novels, and science fiction.

Academic publishers produce books for a scholarly audience. They tend to have a smaller audience, less distribution, and pay less in royalties than other publishing houses, but are extremely important to academic disciplines.

Reference publishers publish encyclopedias, dictionaries, and directories. Putting these complicated works together can be somewhat hectic, but working for a reference publisher can be very interesting, since you will get to help develop and edit a variety of materials.

Small presses, or *independent publishers,* tend to have less scope, distribution, and resources than larger publishers, but they are nonetheless important, since they can take risks or appeal to niche markets that would not be worthwhile to larger companies. They might have a very focused audience, they may publish books that are controversial or carry a heavy political slant, or they may publish works by up-and-coming authors who do not yet have enough of a following to be on the larger presses' radar screens.

Vanity presses, also sometimes called *subsidy presses*, work on a "pay-to-be-published system," relying on funding from their authors, rather than the sales of the books they publish, to make a profit. (The usual system is that an author will receive a *royalty*, or percentage on sales of their book, and an *advance* against the royalties up front.) Many vanity presses are of somewhat dubious quality, and have the reputation of being more concerned with the author's money than for the success of their book.

There are also other sorts of publishers for every market, such as those who produce calendars and novelty books—each of which has its own sorts of demands. It is important to know that these categories of publishers are neither exhaustive nor mutually exclusive. For example, one publishing house might publish both trade and reference titles, and perhaps even journals.

wide variety of tasks, including copyediting, coordinating the work of in-house and freelance copy editors, and managing the schedule of a particular project. From this position, an editor may move up to become first assistant editor, then managing editor, then editor in chief. As editors advance, they are usually involved in more management work and decision-making. The editor in chief works with the publisher to ensure that a suitable editorial policy is being followed, while the managing editor is responsible for all aspects of the editorial department. Head editors employed by a publisher may choose to start their own editing business, freelancing full time.

■ WORK ENVIRONMENT

Book editors do most of their work on a computer, either in an office setting or at home. When working alone, the environment is generally quiet to allow the editor to concentrate on the work at hand. Editors also work in teams, allowing for an exchange of ideas and collaboration. They typically work a normal workweek schedule of 40 hours per week, though if a book is near a deadline, they may work longer hours to get assignments done on schedule.

■ EARNINGS

Earnings for book editors vary based on the size of the employer and the types of books it publishes, geographic location, and experience of the editor. The U.S. Department of Labor reports the median yearly salary for book editors was $46,410 in 2002. For all editors in 2002, the salaries ranged from a low of less than $24,010 to a high of more than $76,620 annually. The median salary for all editors in 2002 was $41,170. In general, editors are paid higher salaries at large companies, in major cities, and on the East and West Coasts.

Publishers usually offer employee benefits that are about average for U.S. industry. There are other benefits, however. Most editors enjoy working with people who like books, and the atmosphere of an editorial department is generally intellectual and stimulating. Some book editors have the opportunity to travel in order to attend meetings, to meet with authors, or to do research.

■ OUTLOOK

According to the U.S. Department of Labor, employment for writers and editors should grow about as fast as the average through 2012, although competition for positions will be strong. The growth of online publishing will increase the need for editors who are Web experts. Other areas where editors may find work include advertising, public relations, and businesses with their own publica-

tions, such as company newsletters. Turnover is relatively high in publishing—editors often advance by moving to another firm or by establishing a freelance business. There are many publishers and organizations that operate with a minimal salaried staff and hire freelance editors for everything from project management to proofreading and production.

■ FOR MORE INFORMATION

The following organization's website is an excellent source of information about careers in editing. The ACES organizes educational seminars and maintains lists of internships.

American Copyeditors Society (ACES)
3 Healy Street
Huntington, NY 11743
http://www.copydesk.org

For additional information about careers in publishing, contact the following:

Association of American Publishers
71 Fifth Avenue
New York, NY 10003-3004
Tel: 212-255-0200
http://www.publishers.org

Publishers Marketing Association
627 Aviation Way
Manhattan Beach, CA 90266
Tel: 310-372-2732
Email: info@pma-online.org
http://www.pma-online.org

Small Publishers Association of North America
PO Box 1306
425 Cedar Street
Buena Vista, CO 81211
Tel: 719-395-4790
Email: span@spannet.org
http://www.spannet.org

Literary Market Place, published annually by R. R. Bowker, lists the names of publishing companies in the United States and Canada as well as their specialties and the names of their key personnel.

Literary Market Place
http://www.literarymarketplace.com

Mediabistro is an online community and networking center for media professionals.

Mediabistro
http://www.mediabistro.com

Bookkeeping and Accounting Clerks

OVERVIEW

Bookkeeping and accounting clerks record financial transactions for government, business, and other organizations. They compute, classify, record, and verify numerical data in order to develop and maintain accurate financial records. There are approximately 1.7 million bookkeeping, accounting, and auditing clerks employed in the United States.

HISTORY

The history of bookkeeping developed along with the growth of business and industrial enterprise. The first known records of bookkeeping date back to 2600 B.C., when the Babylonians used pointed sticks to mark accounts on clay slabs. By 3000 B.C., Middle Eastern and Egyptian cultures employed a system of numbers to record merchants' transactions of the grain and farm products that were distributed from storage warehouses. The growth of intricate trade systems brought about the necessity for bookkeeping systems.

Sometime after the start of the 13th century, the decimal numeration system was introduced in Europe, simplifying bookkeeping record systems. The merchants of Venice—one of the busiest trading centers in the world at that time—are credited with the invention of the double entry bookkeeping method that is widely used today.

As industry in the United States expands and grows more complex, simpler and quicker bookkeeping methods and procedures have evolved. Technological developments include bookkeeping machines, computer hardware and software, and electronic data processing.

THE JOB

Bookkeeping workers keep systematic records and current accounts of financial transactions for businesses, institutions, industries, charities, and other organizations. The bookkeeping records of a firm or business are a vital part of its operational procedures because these records reflect the assets and the liabilities, as well as the profits and losses, of the operation.

Bookkeepers record these business transactions daily in spreadsheets on computer databases, and accounting clerks often input the information. The practice of posting accounting records directly onto ledger sheets, in journals, or on other types of written accounting forms is decreasing as computerized record keeping becomes

more widespread. In small businesses, bookkeepers sort and record all the sales slips, bills, check stubs, inventory lists, and requisition lists. They compile figures for cash receipts, accounts payable and receivable, and profits and losses.

Accounting clerks handle the clerical accounting work; they enter and verify transaction data and compute and record various charges. They may also monitor loans and accounts payable and receivable. More advanced clerks may reconcile billing vouchers, while senior workers review invoices and statements.

Accountants set up bookkeeping systems and use bookkeepers' balance sheets to prepare periodic summary statements of financial transactions. Management relies heavily on these bookkeeping records to interpret the organization's overall performance and uses them to make important business decisions. The records are also necessary to file income tax reports and prepare quarterly reports for stockholders.

Bookkeeping and accounting clerks work in retail and wholesale businesses, manufacturing firms, hospitals, schools, charities, and other types of institutional agencies. Many clerks are classified as financial institution bookkeeping and accounting clerks, insurance firm bookkeeping and accounting clerks, hotel bookkeeping and accounting clerks, and railroad bookkeeping and accounting clerks.

General bookkeepers and *general-ledger bookkeepers* are usually employed in smaller business operations. They may perform all the analysis, maintain the financial records, and complete any other tasks that are involved in keeping a full set of bookkeeping records. These employees may have other general office duties, such as mailing statements, answering telephone calls, and filing materials. *Audit clerks* verify figures and may be responsible for sending them on to an audit clerk supervisor.

QUICK FACTS

SCHOOL SUBJECTS
Business
Computer science
Mathematics

PERSONAL SKILLS
Following instructions
Technical/scientific

WORK ENVIRONMENT
Primarily indoors
Primarily one location

MINIMUM EDUCATION LEVEL
High school diploma

SALARY RANGE
$17,670 to $27,380 to
$41,870

CERTIFICATION OR LICENSING
None available

OUTLOOK
Little change or more slowly
than the average

DOT
216

GOE
09.03.01

NOC
1431

O*NET-SOC
43-3031.00

In large companies, an accountant may supervise a department of bookkeepers who perform more specialized work. *Billing and rate clerks* and *fixed capital clerks* may post items in accounts payable or receivable ledgers, make out bills and invoices, or verify the company's rates for certain products and services. *Account information clerks* prepare reports, compile payroll lists and deductions, write company checks, and compute federal tax reports or personnel profit shares. Large companies may employ workers to organize, record, and compute many other types of financial information.

In large business organizations, bookkeepers and accountants may be classified by grades, such as Bookkeeper I or II. The job classification determines their responsibilities.

■ REQUIREMENTS
High School
In order to be a bookkeeper, you will need at least a high school diploma. It will be helpful to have a background in business mathematics, business writing, typing, and computer training. Pay particular attention to developing sound English and communication skills along with mathematical abilities.

Postsecondary Training
Some employers prefer people who have completed a junior college curriculum or those who have attended a post-high school business training program. In many instances, employers offer on-the-job training for various types of entry-level positions. In some areas, work-study programs are available in which schools, in cooperation with businesses, offer part-time, practical on-the-job training combined with academic study. These programs often help students find immediate employment in similar work after graduation. Local business schools may also offer evening courses.

Other Requirements
Bookkeepers need strong mathematical skills and organizational abilities, and they have to be able to concentrate on detailed work. The work is quite sedentary and often tedious, and you should not mind long hours behind a desk. You should be methodical, accurate, and orderly and enjoy working on detailed tasks. Employers look for honest, discreet, and trustworthy individuals when placing their business in someone else's hands.

Once you are employed as a bookkeeping and accounting clerk, some places of business may require you to have union membership. Larger unions include the Office and Professional Employees International Union; the International Union of Electronics, Electrical, Salaried, Machine, and Furniture Workers; and the American Federation of State, County, and Municipal Employees. Also, depending on the business, clerks may be represented by the same union as other manufacturing employees.

■ EXPLORING
You can gain experience in bookkeeping by participating in work-study programs or by obtaining part-time or summer work in beginning bookkeeping jobs or related office work. Any retail experience dealing with cash management, pricing, or customer service is also valuable.

You can also volunteer to manage the books for extracurricular student groups. Managing income or cash flow for a club or acting as treasurer for student government are excellent ways to gain experience in maintaining financial records.

Other options are visiting local small businesses to observe their work and talking to representatives of schools that offer business training courses.

■ EMPLOYERS
Of the approximately 1.7 million bookkeeping, auditing, and accounting clerks, many work for personnel supplying companies; that is, those companies that provide part-time or temporary office workers. Approximately 25 percent of bookkeeping and accounting clerks work part time, according to the U.S. Department of Labor. Many others are employed by government agencies and organizations that provide educational, health, business, and social services.

■ STARTING OUT
You may find jobs or establish contacts with businesses that are interested in interviewing graduates through your guidance or placement offices. A work-study program or internship may result in a full-time job offer. Business schools and junior colleges generally provide assistance to their graduates in locating employment.

You may locate job opportunities by applying directly to firms or responding to ads in newspaper classified sections. State employment agencies and private employment bureaus can also assist in the job search process.

■ ADVANCEMENT
Bookkeeping workers generally begin their employment by performing routine tasks, such as the simple recording of transactions. Beginners may start as entry-level clerks, cashiers, bookkeeping machine operators, office assistants, or typists. With experience, they may advance to more complex assignments that include computer training in databases and spreadsheets and assume a greater responsibility for the work as a whole.

With experience and education, clerks become department heads or office managers. Further advancement to positions, such as office or division manager, department head, accountant, or auditor, is possible with a college degree and years of experience. There is a high turnover rate in this field, which increases the promotion opportunities for employees with ability and initiative.

■ EARNINGS

According to the U.S. Department of Labor, bookkeepers and accounting clerks earned a median income of $27,380 a year in 2002. Earnings are also influenced by such factors as the size of the city where they work and the size and type of business for which they are employed. Clerks just starting out earn approximately $17,670. Those with one or two years of college generally earn higher starting wages. Top-paying jobs average about $41,870 a year.

Employees usually receive six to eight paid holidays yearly and one week of paid vacation after six to 12 months of service. Paid vacations may increase to four weeks or more, depending on length of service and place of employment. Fringe benefits may include health and life insurance, sick leave, and retirement plans.

■ WORK ENVIRONMENT

The majority of office workers, including bookkeeping workers, usually work a 40-hour week, although some employees may work a 35- to 37-hour week. Bookkeeping and accounting clerks usually work in typical office settings. They are more likely to have a cubicle than an office. While the work pace is steady, it can also be routine and repetitive, especially in large companies where the employee is often assigned only one or two specialized job duties.

Attention to numerical details can be physically demanding, and the work can produce eyestrain and nervousness. While bookkeepers usually work with other people and sometimes under close supervision, they can expect to spend most of their day behind a desk; this may seem confining to people who need more variety and stimulation in their work. In addition, the constant attention to detail and the need for accuracy can place considerable responsibility on the worker and cause much stress.

■ OUTLOOK

Although the growing economy produces a demand for increased accounting services, the automation of office functions will continue to improve overall worker productivity. Fewer people will be needed to do the work, and employment of bookkeeping and accounting clerks is expected to grow more slowly than the average through

2012, according to the U.S. Department of Labor. Excellent computer skills will be vital to securing a job.

Despite lack of growth, there will be numerous replacement job openings, since the turnover rate in this occupation is high. Offices are centralizing their operations, setting up one center to manage all accounting needs in a single location. As more companies trim back their workforces, opportunities for temporary work should continue to grow.

■ FOR MORE INFORMATION

For information on accredited educational programs, contact
Association to Advance Collegiate Schools of Business
600 Emerson Road, Suite 300
St. Louis, MO 63141-6762
Tel: 314-872-8481
http://www.aacsb.edu

For more information on women in accounting, contact
Educational Foundation for Women in Accounting
PO Box 1925
Southeastern, PA 19399-1925
Tel: 610-407-9229
Email: info@efwa.org
http://www.efwa.org

Border Patrol Officers

■ OVERVIEW

Border patrol officers patrol more than 8,000 miles of border between the United States and Canada and between the United States and Mexico, as well as the coastal areas of the Gulf of Mexico and Florida. It is their duty to enforce laws regulating the entry of aliens and products into the United States. They are employed by the U.S. Citizenship and Immigration Service (USCIS) of the Department of Homeland Security.

■ HISTORY

As long as civilizations have created borders for their countries, people have guarded those borders and fought over them. All over the world, societies have created rules and regulations for entry into their communities. Some welcome strangers from other lands, but other societies only allow foreigners to live among them briefly before requiring them to leave. The borders between the United

States and its northern and southern neighbors have been peacefully maintained almost continuously since the founding of the countries.

However, federal immigration laws make it necessary for border patrol officers to protect the citizens of the United States by patrolling its borders. Their job is to prevent illegal entry at all of the borders and to arrest or deport those who attempt to enter illegally. In recent years, an increase in narcotics trafficking has made the job of the border patrol officer even more challenging. In addition to preventing the entry of aliens, border patrol officers also prevent the entry of illegal substances.

■ THE JOB

Border patrol officers are federal law enforcement officers. The laws that they are hired to enforce deal with immigration and customs. U.S. immigration law states that people wishing to enter the United States must apply to the government for permission to do so. Those who want to work, study, or vacation in the United States must have appropriate visas. Those who want to move here and stay must apply for citizenship. Customs laws regulate materials, crops, and goods entering the United States. To ensure that foreigners follow these rules, border patrol officers are stationed at every border entry point of the United States.

Members of the border patrol cover the border on foot, on horseback, in cars or jeeps, in motor boats, in airplanes, and, most recently, on mountain-bikes. They track people near the borders to detect those who attempt to enter the country illegally. They may question people who live or work near the border to help identify illegal aliens. When border patrol officers find violators of U.S. immigration laws, they are authorized to apprehend and detain the violators. They may deport, or return, illegal aliens to their country, or arrest anyone who is assisting foreigners to enter the country illegally.

Border patrol officers work with local and state law enforcement agencies in discharging their duties. Although the uniformed patrol is directed from Washington, D.C., the patrol must have a good working relationship with officials in all of the border states. Local and state agencies can be very helpful to border patrol officers, primarily because these agencies are aware of the peculiarities of the terrain in their area, and they are familiar with the operating procedures of potential aliens or drug smugglers.

Border patrol officers work 24 hours a day along the borders with Mexico and Canada. During this time they may be called upon to do "just about anything you can imagine," according to Paul Nordstrom, a GS-7 border patrol agent at Truth or Consequences, New Mexico. "I've worked with snow rescues of illegal aliens, catching attempted murderers, apprehending stolen vehicles," he says. He has escaped gunfire more than once. At night, border patrol officers may use night-vision goggles to spot trespassers. In rugged areas that are difficult to patrol on foot or on horseback, helicopters are used for greater coverage. At regular border crossing points, officers check all incoming vehicles for people or materials hidden in car trunks or truck compartments.

The prevention of drug smuggling has become a major part of the border patrol officer's work. The increase in drug traffic from Central and South America has led to increased efforts by the USCIS to control the border with Mexico. Drug-sniffing dogs have been added to the patrol's arsenal. Work for border patrol officers has become more dangerous in recent years, and all officers are specially trained in the use of firearms.

Some employees of the USCIS may specialize in areas of immigration or customs. Immigration inspectors enforce laws pertaining to border crossing. They work at airports, seaports, and border crossing points and may question people arriving in the United States by boats, trains, or airplanes. They arrest violators of entry or immigration laws.

Customs officers work to prevent the import of contraband, or illegal merchandise. Most of their work is involved with illegal narcotics. Customs officers search the cargo of ships and airplanes; baggage in cars, trucks, trains, or buses; and mail. They work with travelers as well as with the crews of ships or airplanes. If they discover evidence of drug smuggling or other customs violations, they are responsible for apprehending the offenders.

Occasionally, border patrol officers may also be called upon to help local law enforcement groups in their work. This may involve searching for lost hikers or travelers in rugged wilderness areas of the northern or southern United States.

QUICK FACTS

SCHOOL SUBJECTS
Foreign language
Geography
Government

PERSONAL SKILLS
Following instructions
Leadership/management

WORK ENVIRONMENT
Indoors and outdoors
Primarily multiple locations

MINIMUM EDUCATION LEVEL
High school diploma

SALARY RANGE
$24,075 to $36,478 to
$57,375

CERTIFICATION OR LICENSING
None available

OUTLOOK
Faster than the average

DOT
375

GOE
04.03.01

NOC
N/A

O*NET-SOC
N/A

■ REQUIREMENTS
High School

The minimum educational requirement for anyone wishing to train as a border patrol officer is a high school diploma, although a bachelor's degree is preferred. If you are still in high school, take geography, social studies, and government courses. This will help give you a general background for the field. Take a foreign language class, specifically, Spanish; fluency in this language will give you an advantage over other job applicants.

Postsecondary Training

College majors in criminal justice, law, and sociology are highly regarded as preparation for this field, as is previous military training or law enforcement experience. Knowledge of Spanish and other languages is also helpful.

Other Requirements

Border patrol officers must be U.S. citizens. Test scores on an entrance exam admit potential patrol officers to the training program. Successful completion of post-academy courses during the one-year probation period following training, as well as acceptable scores on two mandatory tests in Spanish and law, is required before placement. Good character references are important, and civil service tests are also sometimes required.

■ EXPLORING

Because of the nature of border patrol work, you will not be able to receive direct experience. Courses in immigration law, Spanish, and criminal justice are helpful, however, as is a good sense of direction, geography, and experience hiking in and knowledge of wilderness areas. Also, since the job can be very demanding physically, you should build your stamina and strength by exercising regularly. School and local libraries may have books containing information on criminal justice and law enforcement.

■ EMPLOYERS

Border patrol officers are employed by the federal government. After training and completion of the one-year probation period, a border patrol officer may be appointed to one of four states: California, Texas, Arizona, or New Mexico. These Southwest border states are the largest employers with nearly 150 stations throughout the United States and Puerto Rico. While employment at these sites tends to fluctuate depending on the employers' perception of need for a given area each year, the larger sites employ anywhere from 100 to 1,000 officers, and recent improvements in funding have guaranteed a steady increase for both officers and support staff nationwide.

A U.S. border patrol agent frisks an illegal alien caught in Texas.

An officer's placement is determined at the time of graduation. An individual may request relocation at this time, but at the risk of termination. Though not all states are equipped with border patrol stations, all are required to have at least two immigration stations. Upon promotion, supervisory or investigative positions with the USCIS may be available in these areas.

■ STARTING OUT

Prospective border patrol officers must pass an entrance exam before being accepted into a 16-week training course at one of three Border Patrol Academies: the Federal Law Enforcement Training Center in Glynco, Georgia; the Advanced Training Facility in Artesia, New Mexico; or the Satellite Training Facility in Charleston, South Carolina. The course teaches the basics of the immigration laws the officers will uphold. They undergo physical training and instruction in law enforcement and the safe use of firearms. Border patrol officer trainees are also taught Spanish as part of their training.

After graduation from the Border Patrol Academy, agents return to their duty stations for a one-year probation period, where they will continue their academic and

INTERVIEW

William Botts has spent practically his whole life with the INS/USCIS and the border patrol. After all, his father, Gene Botts, is a 33-year veteran of the Immigration and Naturalization Service who spent 10 years with the border patrol and wrote a book, The Border Game, *on the challenges confronting today's USCIS officers and investigators. Botts is a GS-13-level assistant border patrol agent-in-charge at the Nogales station. His station is one of eight on the Arizona/Mexico border that comprise the Tucson sector, which is currently the number-one sector for total alien arrests and the number-two sector for narcotics seizures.*

Q. Why did you decide to pursue the border patrol?

A. I was looking for something that was not behind the desk. Unfortunately, in my present position, I still spend more time behind the desk. But I was looking for something outdoors. My father is a 33-year veteran of the INS, a retired investigator, so I had a pretty good idea of the nature of the job. It sounded interesting.

Q. What part of the job do you find most challenging?

A. The smuggling operations. Smuggling organizations, in particular, have grown more sophisticated with the aid of cellular phones and other means. And narcotics, for the obvious reasons.

Q. Can you recall the first time you were confronted with a dangerous situation?

A. An alien smuggler tried to run me over. This was probably one to one-and-a-half years after I started duty. Now, in particular it's very dangerous with the increase in narcotics smuggling. There are a lot more aliens, and a lot more guns. We had an agent, assigned to this station, who was killed in the line of duty three days before I arrived at this duty station.

Q. What do you most like about the border patrol?

A. The outdoors. I particularly like this part of the country. And the periodic moments of excitement.

Q. What might others find most challenging about the job?

A. You see a lot of poor people, desperate people. You can certainly understand why they're coming to this country, but our job is to send them back to theirs. It's more than aliens from Mexico. We see Romanians, Bulgarians, aliens from Guatemala, El Salvador, and, more recently, Hondurans and Nicaraguans. You see some really heartbreaking situations.

Q. What is the biggest misconception about the border patrol?

A. The most common misconception is that we have a high degree of dislike for people from Mexico and other aliens, that we treat them poorly. That's just not true. Quite often we are saving the lives of the people we are arresting. We commonly administer first-aid to aliens. We carry water and bandages. And we quite frequently feed the people we arrest before we send them back to their country.

Q. What activities can prepare those who wish to enter the border patrol?

A. Physical fitness is chief. A working knowledge of Spanish is also helpful, but not required.

Q. What advice would you give to those wishing to become a border patrol agent?

A. Try to research the job. Contact the border patrol stations. You can ask to speak to an agent or supervisor, or quite often you will be put in contact with a public information officer who can provide you with information. If you live in proximity to a station, just stop by. Also, understand that if you are hired by the border patrol, there is a 99.9 percent chance you will be stationed at the southern border.

---

field training under the supervision of a sector training officer. Two mandatory tests in Spanish and law are administered at six and 10 months. All agents must pass these mandatory exams or they will be refused admittance into the border patrol.

Once they complete the course, they will be stationed along the Mexican border. Border patrol officers take orders from their sector chiefs. Border patrol officers generally enter at the GS-5 or GS-7 levels, depending on the level of their education. Entry at the GS-7 level is generally restricted as part of the Outstanding Scholars' Program, which requires a grade-point average of 3.5 or higher during specified periods of an applicant's college career.

■ ADVANCEMENT

After their first year, all border patrol officers advance to the GS-9 journeyman level. From there, they may compete for positions at the GS-11 level. With experience and training, border patrol officers can advance to other positions. They may become immigration inspectors or examiners, deportation officers, or special agents. Some border patrol officers concentrate on the prevention of drug smuggling. They may advance to become *plainclothes investigators* who spend months or even years cracking a smuggling ring. They may lead criminal investigations into an alien's background, especially if there is suspicion of drug involvement. Others may prefer the immigration area and work checking passports and visas at border crossings. Border patrol officers may also advance to supervisory positions.

With experience, some border patrol officers leave the front lines and work in the service areas of the USCIS. They may interview people who wish to become naturalized citizens or administer examinations or interviews. Many of the higher echelon jobs for border patrol officers require fluency in Spanish. Advancement within the border patrol comes with satisfactory work. To rise to supervisory positions, however, border patrol officers must be able to work competitively. These positions are earned based on the agency's needs as well as on merit.

■ EARNINGS

Border patrol officers begin at either the GS-5 or GS-7 grade, depending on their level of education. In 2004 these grades paid $24,075 to $31,302 and $29,821 to $38,767 per year, respectively. GS-9 or journeyman salaries paid $36,478 to $47,422 per year. The highest nonsupervisory grade for a border patrol officer is GS-11, which paid between $44,136 and $57,375 in 2004. Officers in certain cities, such as New York, Los Angeles, Boston, San Francisco, Chicago, Washington, D.C., and others are entitled to receive additional locality pay, which adds roughly 16 percent to the base salary. Law enforcement officials employed by the federal government are also entitled to additional pay of 25 percent of their base salary. Overtime and pay differentials for night, weekend, and holiday work can also greatly increase an officer's salary.

As federal workers, border patrol officers enjoy generous benefits, including health and life insurance, pension plans, and paid holidays, sick leave, and vacations.

■ WORK ENVIRONMENT

The work of a border patrol officer can be tiring and stressful. Because officers must cover the borders continuously, hours are irregular and shifts tend to vary. "Balancing shift work and having to adjust to that in your family is difficult," says border patrol agent Paul Nordstrom. Most officers spend more time outdoors in jeeps, cars, helicopters, or on horseback than they do in offices. Still, there is a great deal of paperwork to process on each person detained; that usually requires several hours. The work may be dangerous, and many decisions must be made quickly. Border patrol officers must confront many people throughout their shift, and they must remain alert for potential illegal entry into the United States. Many people who attempt to enter the United States illegally have undergone extreme risk and hardship. Border patrol officers encounter emotionally intense situations just as frequently as hostile, violent ones. For example, illegal

LEARN MORE ABOUT IT

Andreas, Peter. *Border Games: Policing the U.S.—Mexico Divide.* Ithaca, N.Y.: Cornell University Press, 2000.

Botts, Gene. *The Border Game: Enforcing America's Immigration Laws.* Phoenix, Ariz.: Quest Publishing Group, 1997.

Byrd, Bobby, and Susannah Mississippi Byrd, eds. *The Late Great Mexican Border: Reports from a Disappearing Line.* El Paso, Tex.: Cinco Puntos Press, 1996.

Demmer, Byron, et al. Border Patrol Exam. 2nd ed. Albany, N.Y.: LearningExpress, 2001.

Hart, John M. *Border Crossing: Mexican and Mexican-American Workers.* Wilmington, Del.: Scholarly Resources, 1998.

Lorey, David E. *The U.S.-Mexican Border in the Twentieth Century: A History of Economic and Social Transformation.* Wilmington, Del.: Scholarly Resources, 1998.

Moore, Alvin E. *Border Patrol.* Santa Fe, N. Mex.: Sunstone Press, 1988.

Urrea, Luis Alberto. *By the Lake of Sleeping Children: The Secret Life of the Mexican Border.* New York: Anchor Books, 1996.

Vila, Pablo. *Crossing Borders, Reinforcing Borders: Social Categories, Metaphors and Narrative Identities on the U.S.-Mexico Frontier.* Austin, Tex.: University of Texas Press, 2000.

aliens suffer extremes of heat and discomfort of crowding into the back of a hot, stuffy truck in order to enter the United States; returning to their country is oftentimes as uncomfortable. Border patrol officers must be able to cope with the stress and trauma of such situations. Finally, most of those who attempt to enter the country illegally will do so again and again. Even as agents prevent one group from entering the country, elsewhere several other groups of illegal aliens may be successfully crossing the border. Border patrol officers must be able to work at what may, at times, seem a futile and frustrating task.

Despite the difficulty of the job, work as a border patrol officer can be very rewarding. Border patrol officers perform a necessary function and know they are contributing to the safety of our society.

■ OUTLOOK

The U.S. Department of Labor projects employment for all police officers and detectives (including border patrol officers) to increase faster than average through 2012. There has been growing public support of drug prevention activities, including the prevention of drug smuggling. Public support of the war on drugs has enabled the INS to continue to increase its surveillance of U.S. borders.

After the terrorist attacks in 2001, growing concerns over the level of illegal immigration have created an urgent need for more border patrol officers. According to the INS, the 2003 budget included approximately $711.7 million and 1,790 new positions to increase security at U.S. borders. This includes $105.9 million allocated for emergency counter-terrorism actions. For 2004, INS and the Department of Homeland Security has requested even more money over this.

■ FOR MORE INFORMATION

For information about employment opportunities, frequently asked questions, and links to other government sites, check out the USCIS website or contact

U.S. Citizenship and Immigration Service
425 I Street, NW
Washington, DC 20536
Tel: 800-375-5283
http://www.uscis.gov

Information about entrance requirements, training, and career opportunities for all government jobs can be obtained from the U.S. Office of Personnel Management. For more information about publications, job listings, or qualifying screening exams, contact

U.S. Office of Personnel Management
1900 E Street, NW
Washington, DC 20415-0001
Tel: 202-606-1800
http://www.opm.gov

For current information on employment procedures, compensation, benefits, and requirements, as well as links to helpful books and other sources of information, check out the following website:

United States Border Patrol Unofficial Web Site
http://honorfirst.com

Botanists

■ OVERVIEW

Botanists study all different aspects of plant life, from cell structure to reproduction, to how plants are distributed, to how rainfall or other conditions affect them, and more. Botany is an integral part of modern science and industry, with diverse applications in agriculture, agronomy

(soil and crop science), conservation, manufacturing, forestry, horticulture, and other areas. Botanists work for the government, in research and teaching institutions, and for private industry. The primary task of botanists is research and applied research. Nonresearch jobs in testing and inspection, or as lab technicians/technical assistants, also are available. Botany is an extremely diverse field with many specialties.

■ HISTORY

Plant science is hundreds of years old. The invention of microscopes in the 1600s was very important to the development of modern botany. Microscopes allowed minute study of plant anatomy and cells and led to considerable research in the field. It was in the 1600s that people started using words like *botanographist* or *botanologist,* for one who describes plants.

In the 1700s, Carolus Linnaeus, a Swedish botanist and *taxonomist* (one who identifies, names, and classifies plants) was an important figure. He came up with the two-name (genus and species) system for describing plants that is still used today. In all, Linnaeus wrote more than 180 works on plants, plant diseases, and related subjects.

In Austria during the 19th century, the first experiments in hybridization were done by a monk, Gregor Johann Mendel. He experimented on garden peas and other plants to figure out why organisms inherit the traits they do. His work is the basis for 20th and 21st century work in plant and animal genetics. As interest in botany grew, botanical gardens became popular in Europe and North America.

Botany is a major branch of biology; the other is zoology. Today, studies in botany reach into many areas of biology, including genetics, biophysics, and other specialized studies. It has taken on particular urgency as a potential source of help for creating new drugs to fight disease, meeting food needs of developing countries, and battling environmental problems.

■ THE JOB

Research and applied research are the primary tasks of botanists. Literally every aspect of plant life is studied: cell structure, anatomy, heredity, reproduction, and growth; how plants are distributed on the earth; how rainfall, climate, soil, elevation, and other conditions affect plants; and how humans can put plants to better use. In most cases, botanists work at a specific problem or set of problems in their research. For example, they may develop new varieties of crops that will better resist disease. Some botanists focus on a specific type of plant species, such as fungi (mycology), or plants that are native to a specific area, such as a forest or prairie. A botanist working in private industry, for example, for a food or drug company, may focus on new-product development, testing and inspection, regulatory compliance, or other areas.

Research takes place in laboratories, experiment stations (research sites found at many universities), botanical gardens, and other facilities. Powerful microscopes and special mounting, staining, and preserving techniques may be used in the research.

Some botanists, particularly those working in conservation or ecological areas, also go out into the field. They inventory species, help recreate lost or damaged ecosystems, or direct pollution cleanup efforts.

Nonresearch jobs in testing and inspection or as lab technicians/technical assistants for universities, museums, government agencies, parks, manufacturing companies, botanical gardens, and other facilities also are available.

Botany is an extremely diverse field with many specialties. *Ethnobotanists* study the use of plant life by a particular culture, people, or ethnic group to find medicinal uses of certain plants. Study of traditional Native American medicinal uses of plants is an example. (For more information, see the article Ethnoscientists.)

Forest ecologists focus on forest species and their habitats, such as forest wetlands. Related studies include forest genetics and forest economics. Jobs in forestry include work in managing, maintaining, and improving forest species and environments.

Mycologists study fungi and apply their findings in agriculture, medicine, and industry for development of drugs, medicines, molds, and yeasts. They may specialize in research and development in a field such as antibiotics.

Toxicologists study the effect of toxic substances on organisms, including plants. Results of their work may be used in regulatory action, product labeling, and other areas. (For more information, see Toxicologists.)

Other botanical specialists include *pteridologists*, who study ferns and other related plants, *bryologists*, who study mosses and similar plants, and *lichenologists*, who study lichens, which are dual organisms made of both alga and fungus.

■ REQUIREMENTS
High School
To prepare for a career in botany, high school students can explore their interests by taking biology, doing science projects involving plants, and working during summers or school holidays for a nursery, park, or similar operation. College prep courses in chemistry, physics, biology, mathematics, English, and foreign language are a good idea because educational requirements for professional botanists are high. Nonresearch jobs (test and inspection

professionals, lab technicians, technical assistants) require at least a bachelor's degree in a biological science or botany; research and teaching positions usually require at least a master's or even a doctorate.

Postsecondary Training
At the undergraduate level, there are numerous programs for degrees in botany or biology (which includes studies in both botany and zoology). The master's level and above usually involves a specialized degree. One newer degree is conservation biology, which focuses on the conservation of specific plant and animal communities. The University of Wisconsin has one of the biggest programs in this area. Another key school is Yale's forestry school, which offers degrees in areas such as natural resource management.

Other Requirements
Botanists become botanists because of their love for plants, gardening, and nature. They need patience, an exploring spirit, the ability to work well alone or with other people, good writing and other communication skills, and tenacity.

■ EXPLORING
The Botanical Society of America (BSA) suggests high school students take part in science fairs and clubs and get summer jobs with parks, nurseries, farms, experiment stations, labs, camps, florists, or landscape architects. Hobbies like camping, photography, and computers are useful, too, says BSA. Tour a botanical garden in your area and talk to staff. You can also get information by contacting national associations. For example, write to the Botanical Society of America for a booklet on careers in botany.

■ EMPLOYERS
Botanists find employment in the government, in research and teaching institutions, and in private industry. Local, state, and federal agencies, including the Department of Agriculture,

QUICK FACTS

SCHOOL SUBJECTS
Agriculture
Biology

PERSONAL SKILLS
Helping/teaching
Technical/scientific

WORK ENVIRONMENT
Indoors and outdoors
Primarily one location

MINIMUM EDUCATION LEVEL
Bachelor's degree

SALARY RANGE
$29,256 to $61,000 to $90,000+

CERTIFICATION OR LICENSING
None available

OUTLOOK
About as fast as the average

DOT
041

GOE
02.03.02

NOC
2121

O*NET-SOC
19-1020.01

PROFILE: JOHN BARTRAM (1699–1777)

John Bartram was the first native-born American botanist. Born at Marple, near Philadelphia, he became interested in botany as a child and studied the subject on his own. In 1728 he founded the first botanical gardens in North America at Kingsessing. The 27-acre tract is now a part of the Philadelphia park system.

Bartram was the first American botanist to experiment with breeding and improving plants. In search of new plants, he explored the Allegheny and Catskill mountains and made trips to Florida and the Carolinas. Famous in Europe as well as in America, he was appointed botanist to King George III of England in 1765. Bartram exchanged plants with many European botanists. The Swedish botanist Carolus Linnaeus called him the "greatest natural botanist" of his time.

Environmental Protection Agency, Public Health Service, National Biological Service, and the National Aeronautics and Space Administration (NASA) employ botanists. Countless colleges and universities have botany departments and conduct botanical research. In private industry, botanists work for agribusiness, biotechnology, biological supply, chemical, environmental, food, lumber and paper, pharmaceutical, and petrochemical companies. Botanists also work for greenhouses, arboretums, herbariums, seed and nursery companies, and fruit growers.

■ STARTING OUT

With a bachelor's degree, a botanist's first job may be as a technical assistant or technician for a lab. Those with a master's degree might get work on a university research project. Someone with a doctorate might get into research and development with a drug, pharmaceutical, or other manufacturer.

For some positions, contract work might be necessary before the botanist gains a full-time position. Contract work is work done on a per-project, or freelance, basis: You sign on for that one project, and then you move on. Conservation groups like The Nature Conservancy (TNC) hire hundreds of contract workers, including ecologists and botanists, each year to do certain work. Contract workers are especially in demand in the summer when there's a lot of biology inventory work to be done.

Opportunities for internships are available with local chapters of TNC. It's also possible to volunteer. Contact the Student Conservation Association for volunteer opportunities. (Contact information can be found at the end of this article.) Land trusts are also good places to check for volunteer work.

■ ADVANCEMENT

Federal employees generally move up the ranks after gaining a certain number of hours of experience and obtaining advanced degrees. The Botanical Society of America, whose membership primarily comes from universities, says keys for advancing in university positions include producing quality research, publishing a lot, and obtaining advanced degrees. Advancing in the private sector depends on the individual employer. Whatever the botanist can do to contribute to the bottom line, such as making breakthroughs in new product development, improving growing methods, and creating better test and inspection methods, will probably help the botanist advance in the company.

■ EARNINGS

The U.S. Department of Labor reports that biological scientists made median annual salaries of about $61,000 a year. According to the National Association of Colleges and Employers, in 2003 graduates with a bachelor's degree in biological sciences received average starting salary offers of $29,256 a year; those with master's degrees received offers of $33,600, and those with Ph.D.'s received offers of $42,244. Biological scientists working for the federal government earned average salaries of $66,200 a year in 2003, with some making more than $90,000.

At times, research botanists deeply involved with a project put in a lot of overtime. In exchange, they may be able to work fewer hours other weeks, depending on the specific employer. Botanists performing fieldwork also might have some flexibility of hours. In private industry, the workweek is likely to be a standard 35 to 40 hours. Benefits vary but usually include paid holidays and vacations, and health insurance.

■ WORK ENVIRONMENT

Botanists work in a wide variety of settings, some of them very pleasant: greenhouses, botanical gardens, and herbariums, for example. A botanist working for an environmental consultant or conservation organization may spend a lot of time outdoors, rain or shine. Some botanists interact with the public, such as in a public park or greenhouse, sharing their enthusiasm for the field. Other botanists spend their days in a lab, poring over specimens and writing up the results of their research.

As scientists, botanists need to be focused, patient, and determined. Some research spans many hours and even years of work. A botanist needs to believe in what he or she is doing and keep at a project until it's completed

The mite species Aceria anthocoptes *may prove useful as a control agent for weeds. From left to right, Chris Frye, botanist with the Maryland Department of Natural Resources, ARS acarologist Ron Ochoa, and ARS plant physiologist John Lydon identify a thistle species as* Cirsium horridulum *and note where the highest mite population is most likely to be.*

satisfactorily. The ability to work on one's own is important, but few scientists work in a vacuum. They cooperate with others, share the results of their work orally and in writing, and, particularly in private industry, may need to explain what they're doing in layman's terms.

Because educational requirements for botanists are high, and because so much of the work involves research, it is important to be a good scholar and enjoy digging for answers.

■ OUTLOOK

Employment growth at a rate about as fast as the average for all biological scientists, including botanists, is expected through 2012, according to the U.S. Department of Labor. Botanists will be needed to help meet growing environmental, conservation, pharmaceutical, and similar demands. However, budget cuts and a large number of graduates have made competition for jobs strong. Government employment opportunities should stay strong, but will depend in part on the continued health of the national economy. Federal budget cuts may jeopardize some projects and positions. Experts say the outlook is best for those with an advanced degree.

■ FOR MORE INFORMATION

For the booklets Careers in Botany *and* Botany for the Next Millennium, *contact*

Botanical Society of America
PO Box 299
St. Louis, MO 63166-0299
Tel: 314-577-9566
Email: bsa-manager@botany.org
http://www.botany.org

For information on school and internship programs, news on endangered species, and membership information, contact

National Wildlife Federation
11100 Wildlife Center Drive
Reston, VA 20190-5362
Tel: 800-822-9919
http://www.nwf.org

For information about internships with state chapters or at TNC headquarters, contact

The Nature Conservancy (TNC)
4245 North Fairfax Drive, Suite 100
Arlington, VA 22203-1606

Tel: 800-628-6860

Email: comment@tnc.org

http://nature.org

To learn about volunteer positions in natural resource management, contact

Student Conservation Association

689 River Road

PO Box 550

Charlestown, NH 03603

Tel: 603-543-1700

Email: ask-us@sca-inc.org

http://www.sca-inc.org

This government agency manages more than 450 national wildlife refuges. The service's website has information on volunteer opportunities, careers, and answers to many frequently asked questions.

U.S. Fish & Wildlife Service

U.S. Department of the Interior

1849 C Street, NW

Washington, DC 20240

Email: contact@fws.gov

http://www.fws.gov

Bounty Hunters

■ OVERVIEW

Bounty hunters, also known as *bail enforcement agents* or *fugitive recovery agents,* track down and return individuals who are fugitives from justice. People who get arrested are often given the opportunity to post bail money so they can go free while waiting for a hearing or trial. When these people post the bail money, they are promising that they will return on the assigned court date. If they don't return on that date, they lose their bail money (or the bail bondsman loses his) and become fugitives from justice. Bounty hunters spend time researching and interviewing to get leads on the person they are tracking. Bounty hunters working in the United States account for thousands of arrests annually.

■ HISTORY

The history of the bail process dates back to English common law. People who were charged with crimes against the king were allowed to go free if someone else guaranteed that the individual would return. If that didn't happen, the person who guaranteed the return of the individual often had to pay the price instead. In America,

this process continued but gave birth to the modern bail bondsman and bounty hunter, who worked together to ensure that accused people appeared for hearings, trials, and sentences. Specifically, bounty hunting grew as a profession during the westward expansion of the United States. Because fugitives would often run as far west as possible to get away from local law enforcement, bounty hunters were often found tracking lawbreakers in the Old West. Though in many states fugitive-recovery activities have come to be performed by marshals, sheriffs, and detectives, the bail-bond system ensures that bounty hunters still flourish in our country.

■ THE JOB

Bounty hunters work in conjunction with bail bondsmen and the court system. The scenario plays out as follows: An individual is arrested for breaking a law. The individual is given the chance to be freed from jail if he or she guarantees to be at court on a certain date by posting a large amount of money. Most people who are arrested don't have these large sums of money on hand, so they enlist the services of a bail bondsman who provides the money to the court. The individual must pay the bondsman a fee—usually 10 percent of the actual posted bond. If the individual does not show up on the court date, the bondsman can either try to bring the person in or hire a bounty hunter to track the person down. The bounty hunter is paid only if the fugitive is returned to court.

After the bounty hunter is on the case, the main goal is to locate the fugitive as quickly and as safely as possible. Although the time frame varies from state to state and court to court, bail enforcement agents usually have 90 days at the most to bring back the fugitive. Locating a fugitive requires research, detection, and law enforcement skills. "Most of the time it takes time and patience," explains bail enforcement agent John Norman. "Many days are spent interviewing people, tracing paper trails, sitting in vehicles for countless hours of surveillance, just to await that moment to re-arrest this individual." Bounty hunters can use almost any means possible to re-arrest a fugitive. In most states they can enter the homes of fugitives if they believe, beyond a reasonable doubt, that the fugitive is inside. Sometimes the bounty hunter will interview family members or check the trash at the fugitive's home to find a clue as to where he or she has gone. Most bounty hunters use weapons to persuade a fugitive to return peacefully and to protect themselves. "The field can also be very dangerous," Norman cautions. "Getting shot at, knifed, and even fought is not uncommon." After the fugitive is found, the bounty hunter makes a private arrest of the individual and takes the fugitive back to jail to await trial. "This process of retrieval can be easy sometimes and hard others," Norman adds. Although most bounty hunters re-arrest the fugitive themselves, some locate the fugitive and then alert the local law officials to make the actual arrest.

Bounty hunting is not all tracking people and bringing them back alive, however. Bounty hunting is a business, and like any other business, it must be run efficiently. In order to get work, bail enforcement agents must be able to advertise their services to become part of as many bail bondsmen "networks" as possible. Some bondsmen work with just a select few bounty hunters, while others send out their fugitive recovery requests to large networks of bounty hunters who compete against each other to bring back the fugitive. Because bounty hunters only get paid if they bring the person back, care must be taken to use resources wisely. Someone who spends $1,000 to find a fugitive who's only worth $750 won't be in business long. Besides monetary resources, many bail enforcement agents have research assistants who work for them. Enforcement agents must be able to manage their employees in these situations. Bounty hunters also often work under contracts with law enforcement or bail bondsmen. They must be able to draw up contracts and be well-informed of all the legal aspects of those contracts.

■ REQUIREMENTS
High School

Although you won't find a class at school called Bounty Hunting 101, there are some courses that can help you prepare for a job in this field while you're still in high school. Classes in government, political science, communication, and business will help you prepare for the legal and business side of bounty hunting. If you have the opportunity to take self-defense or martial arts courses, they can give you skills sometimes necessary in the actual apprehension of the fugitive. Foreign languages may come in handy as well, depending on the area of the country where you may be working.

Postsecondary Training

You are not required to have any college training to be a bounty hunter. However, training is important for success and safety as a bail enforcement agent. "One way or another, you should have at least some sort of training in law enforcement and criminal justice," John Norman recommends. If a college degree or vocational school is in your future, aim for criminal justice studies or police academy training. If you want to focus immediately on bail enforcement, some training opportunities are available. The National Institute of Bail Enforcement in Arizona and the National Association of Bail Enforcement

Agents, for example, provide training seminars. (For contact information on these programs see the list at the end of this article.)

Certification or Licensing

Regulations covering bounty hunters' activities vary by state. It is, therefore, very important that you check with your state's attorney general's office, department of public safety, or professional licensing board to determine the rules for your area. In addition, it is important to be aware of other state's regulations in case your work takes you there. For example, some states, such as Illinois, prohibit bounty hunting. Some states, such as North Carolina, have as part of their requirements that "bail runners" work for only one bail bondsman or bail bond agency. Other states, such as Mississippi and Connecticut, have licensing requirements for bail enforcement agents; however, the licensing requirements themselves vary from state to state. And finally, some states, such as Georgia, have requirements such as registration with a sheriff's department or other agency. Generally, licensing involves passing a written test, passing a drug test and background check, being at least a certain age, being a U.S. citizen, and having completed some type of approved training. Anyone using a gun must, of course, have a license to do so.

Other Requirements

Bounty hunters must be able to handle high-stress situations that are often dangerous. Because of the nature of the work, the bounty hunter should be trained in the use of firearms and other weapons. Bounty hunters must be physically fit and able to defend themselves in dangerous situations.

■ EXPLORING

Bounty hunting can be dangerous, so you may be wondering how you can explore the field without getting hurt. That's a good question, but there are ways you can get an idea about

QUICK FACTS

SCHOOL SUBJECTS
English
Government

PERSONAL SKILLS
Communication/ideas
Following instructions

WORK ENVIRONMENT
Indoors and outdoors
Primarily multiple locations

MINIMUM EDUCATION LEVEL
Some postsecondary training

SALARY RANGE
$20,000 to $40,000 to
$60,000+

CERTIFICATION OR LICENSING
Required by certain states

OUTLOOK
About as fast as the average

DOT
N/A

GOE
N/A

NOC
N/A

O*NET-SOC
N/A

BOUNTY HUNTERS ON TV

The Lone Ranger began airing in 1949 and portrayed a ranger and his sidekick Tonto cleaning up the Old West. It helped popularize the Western as a television genre. *Wanted: Dead or Alive*, starring Steve McQueen, aired from 1958 to 1961 and showed bounty hunting as a respectable career. *Gunsmoke* (1955–75) depicted the bounty hunter as lawless instead, and often showed the main character, Matt Dillon (played by James Arness), going up against ruthless bounty hunters. More recently, the cameras of *American Bounty Hunter* (1996) and *U.S. Bounty Hunter* (2003) have followed real bounty hunters as they tracked down fugitives. Then, of course, there are always science-fiction treatments of the subject, like the famous 1998 Japanese anime series *Cowboy Bebop*, which follows the misadventures of a group of wisecracking intergalactic bounty hunters.

the situations you would be encountering without being thrown into the thick of a fight. First, do some research. Contact your local and state authorities and ask for information about current laws and how they affect bounty hunters. Now that you have that information under your belt, you can contact your local police and ask to go on a ride-along with the specific focus on the times officers assist bounty hunters. (This "assistance" is usually just sitting in the patrol car to further persuade the fugitive that this is the real thing.) You may get the chance, from a safe distance, to watch the bounty hunter in action. Some cities and counties also conduct "citizen police academies" that train the public on many police situations and safety issues. Enroll in any programs you can find that provide this kind of information and training. Contact a bail bondsman (you'll find many listed in the phone book) and find out if they are also bounty hunters. Ask any questions you may have. Try to interview several bondsmen to get a more balanced view of what it's like to work in the bail bonding and fugitive recovery business. As stated earlier, much of the bounty hunter's time is spent running the business. Join any clubs at school that focus on business, such as Junior Achievement.

■ EMPLOYERS

Most bounty hunters work independently. Many run their own businesses and contract their services to bail bondsmen and other individuals. Some bounty hunters are also bondsmen, and they combine the services into one business. These bounty hunters are part-timers, because most of their time is spent on bail bonding or investigating. "Some [bail enforcement agents] such as

myself have their own companies," explains John Norman. "However, a lot of agents work directly under the bondsman. The bondsman is our main source of work in either case." Bondsmen either hire bounty hunters on a case-by-case basis or they hire them as full- or part-time employees. Some bounty hunters are also hired by private individuals for other services, such as recovering missing persons, finding persons who are not paying child support, and uncovering insurance fraud.

■ STARTING OUT

Although most bail enforcement agents own their own businesses, the majority start out working and learning the business from bail bondsmen or other bail enforcement agents. The best, most direct way to get started in the fugitive recovery field is to approach several bondsmen or bail enforcement agencies in your area. Most bounty hunters start out as research assistants or *skip tracers*. Skip tracers do the background and frontline interviewing to try to find the general location of the fugitive. The more training you have, the better chance you'll have at landing that first job. You may have to start off in some form of law enforcement before you will be considered experienced or skilled enough to go into bounty hunting for a bondsman. Some starting points include jobs such as security guards, campus police, and researchers for private investigators.

■ ADVANCEMENT

Because most bail enforcement agents own their own agencies, they are at the top of their business with no higher position to be had. However, because of the competition within the fugitive recovery field, there is a drive to be the "best of the best" and have the highest fugitive recovery rate. Bail enforcement agents want to be able to maintain and advertise a very high rate of return, and the best and highest paid in the field produce over 90 percent of the fugitives they track. Many bail enforcement agents chase the goal of perfection as strongly as they chase each fugitive.

Bounty hunters who work for other bail enforcement agents or bondsmen can work toward owning their own agency. Usually success in tracking down fugitives is the path toward the recognition and marketability necessary to start a new fugitive recovery business.

■ EARNINGS

The bounty hunting business, like any other, takes time to develop, and bounty hunters who start their own agencies have many out-of-pocket expenses for items such as handcuffs and advertising. Some may end up losing money or only earning enough to break even. For those who manage to build up a business, however, earnings can be quite good. The National Center for Policy Analysis' 2000 report *Privatizing Probation and Parole* states that bounty hunters generally earn between $20,000 and $30,000 for part-time work. A 2001 article on the CNN-Money Web site (http://money.cnn.com/smbusiness) notes that while most bonds are fairly small (meaning that a bounty hunter doesn't earn much from one recovery), annual incomes can be good because there are plenty of fugitives on the run and lots of work is available. According to CNNMoney, bounty hunters generally earn between $40,000 and $60,000 per year. It's important to note, however, that in this business earnings can vary greatly from month to month, depending on how many fugitives the bounty hunter is able to bring in, the bail bond for these fugitives, and expenses incurred in the process. Well-established bail enforcement agents with excellent reputations often get the highest paying cases, such as for a fugitive who has run on a $100,000 bail, and may find their yearly earnings approaching the hundred thousand dollar mark.

Because they own their own businesses, most bail enforcement agents do not receive medical benefits. A few who work for well-established agencies may receive some types of benefits, but it is not the norm for the field. "In this business, sometimes it is slow or there is no business and there are lengthy times between paychecks. There are also no benefits like pensions, insurance, or things of that nature in most cases," says John Norman.

■ WORK ENVIRONMENT

Bounty hunters spend much of their time traveling in search of a fugitive or waiting for hours for a fugitive to appear. Because apprehending a fugitive is easiest in the middle of the night or early morning, the bounty hunter keeps odd hours and may work especially long hours when close to capturing a fugitive. A bail enforcement agent works on an as-needed basis, so there may be stretches of inactivity depending on the bondsman's needs for service. The number of hours worked varies with the number of fugitives being sought at any one time and the amount of time remaining to bring the fugitive in. Bounty hunters are often in perilous situations where injury or even death is a possibility. John Norman describes bail enforcement as a "painstaking, unforgiving business."

■ OUTLOOK

Employment for bounty hunters is increasing about as fast as the average for all other occupations, although this field has a narrow niche in the bail bonding business. Competition among bail enforcement agents continues to propel the field as a profession and as an asset to our legal system.

Because bail bond agents and bail enforcement agents are working in private business, there is no cost to the taxpayer for the apprehension of these fugitives (as there would be if, for example, police officers worked exclusively on these cases). Another benefit of the private bail enforcement agent system is its high success rate (some professionals estimate it at 85 percent) for recovery of fugitives. Given the large percentage of recoveries and the lack of cost to local government, the future looks good for this profession. The ability of bail enforcement agents to work successfully within the parameters of the law should keep this field growing steadily in the future.

■ FOR MORE INFORMATION

Visit the Bail Bond Recovery Resource Center of The National Association of Investigative Specialists, Inc., website. The resource center has information on the work of bounty hunters, laws affecting bounty hunting, and training materials.

Bail Bond Recovery Resource Center
The National Association of Investigative Specialists, Inc.
PO Box 33244
Austin, TX 78764
Tel: 512-719-3595
http://www.pimall.com/nais/bailr.html

For training information and to read sections from the newsletter Hunters Net, visit the NABEA website.

National Association of Bail Enforcement Agents (NABEA)
PO Box 129
Falls Church, VA 22040
Tel: 703-534-4211
http://www.nabea.org

For information about fugitive recovery seminars, contact

National Institute of Bail Enforcement
PO Box 32230
Tucson, AZ 85751
Tel: 520-290-8051
Email: nibe@bounty-hunter.net
http://www.bounty-hunter.net

Brewers

■ OVERVIEW

Brewers oversee the production of many different styles of beer. They develop recipes that consist of various types and blends of the four basic ingredients: barley malt, hops, yeast, and water (and occasionally fruits, wheat, rice, and corn). Brewers add these ingredients into brewing vessels in accordance with the style of beer they are brewing and their own recipe. Brewers also tend to the brewing equipment. They monitor gauges and meters, as well as turn valves, open hatches, and occasionally stir.

■ HISTORY

The brewing of beer predates recorded history. Fermented drinks were a necessity, as early civilizations often could not help polluting their water supplies. Various beer-like drinks were discovered by many ancient civilizations including the Babylonians, Egyptians, Chinese, and Incas. Beer became especially prevalent in regions unsuitable for growing wine grapes. In the ninth century, Charlemagne (742–814) declared brewmasters among the artisans and laborers necessary for the prosperity of his kingdom. By the 11th century, modern beer, as we know it, was produced in the great breweries of Germany, and its commercial success grew significantly for the next several hundred years.

In 1609, American colonists placed want ads in a London newspaper asking for brewers to come to America. Many prominent Americans were concerned with the brewing of beer, including Samuel Adams (1722–1803), Thomas Jefferson (1743–1826), and George Washington (1732–99), who employed brewers at his Mount Vernon estate. The great American brewing dynasties began with the German immigrants who arrived in the mid-1800s and settled in the Midwest. By the late 1800s there were more than 2,200 commercial breweries in the United States, the largest of them being Anheuser-Busch, Pabst, Miller, Stroh, and Schlitz.

The basic methods of brewing quality beers haven't changed much in the last 500 years. Although mass-market beers common in America today may skip steps, hasten others, or substitute ingredients for cost-cutting measures, the true science and art of craftbrewing has endured and resurged in the 1990s to produce fine American beers comparable (or, arguably, superior) to the best of the European market. Today's serious American brewer who is concerned with producing quality beers in the European or early American tradition is typically called a *craftbrewer*. Craftbrewers work at microbreweries, brewpubs, and contract brewers, known in the industry as third-tier brewers.

■ THE JOB

Brewers are concerned with all aspects of beer production, from selecting the exact blend and kind of flavoring hops, to the number of minutes the *wort* (liquid formed by soaking mash in hot water and fermenting it) boils. Beer styles and flavors are as multifarious as wine, and the craftbrewer can produce any number of beers for any occasion. Like great chefs, craftbrewers take particular pride in their recipes and enjoy presenting their "masterpieces" to others.

There are certain guidelines for each style of beer, but within those guidelines the brewer may experiment to create a truly unique flavor of a particular style. For example, a brewer who is making a pilsner must use bottom-fermenting lager yeasts (as opposed to top-fermenting ale yeasts), a light, dry barley malt (as opposed to a darker, roasted barley malt), and a specific few types of hops (most notably saaz, spalt, tettnanger, and hallertauer). With these basic guidelines observed, the brewer can experiment with such things as blending malts and hops, adding other flavors (such as honey, fruit, herbs, and spices), and varying boiling and lagering times.

The first step in brewing a batch of beer is for the brewer to decide what style he or she wants to brew. There are more than 50 styles of beer, many cousins of each other. Others are completely original and in their own class. All beers fall in one of two categories: ales or lagers. Among the more common styles many American craftbrewers are brewing today are ales (including pale ales, brown ales, and Scotch ales), pilsners, bocks, and double bocks, stouts, porters, and wheat beers (commonly know by their German name Weiss- or Weizenbier). With a particular beer style in mind, the brewer will seek the best ingredients to brew it.

The four basic ingredients of beer are malted barley, hops, yeast, and water. Some smaller breweries may use a malt extract. Some beers may call for wheat, rice, or corn in addition to barley. *Malted barley* not only contributes to the flavor and color of the beer, but more important, it provides food (fermentable sugars) for the yeast to produce alcohol. Brewers have a host of different types of yeast to choose from depending on the particular flavor

QUICK FACTS

SCHOOL SUBJECTS
Biology
Chemistry

PERSONAL SKILLS
Following instructions
Technical/scientific

WORK ENVIRONMENT
Primarily indoors
Primarily one location

MINIMUM EDUCATION LEVEL
Some postsecondary training

SALARY RANGE
$28,750 to $48,670 to $85,460

CERTIFICATION OR LICENSING
Required for certain positions

OUTLOOK
About as fast as the average

DOT
183

GOE
08.03.02

NOC
9213, 9465

O*NET-SOC
N/A

they seek. There are two main varieties, top-fermenting ale yeasts and bottom-fermenting lager yeasts, and within each of these two varieties there are hundreds of strains, each imparting a different flavor to the beer. *Hops* come from a flower added to provide a contrasting bitterness and flavor to the sweet malt (called boiling hops), and to add a very important bouquet to the beer (called finishing, or aroma hops). Because beer is about 90 percent water, all serious brewers take the purity of their water very seriously. Water that has been treated with chlorine or that is rich in other minerals can impart unwanted flavors into a beer.

Malted barley must go through a mashing stage in the brewing process. Brewers grind the malted barley in specialized machines so that its husk is removed and the kernel broken. Next they add a precise amount of water and raise the temperature to between 150 and 160 degrees Fahrenheit to dissolve the natural sugars, starches, and enzymes of the barley. Brewers may vary the temperature and time of the mashing process to achieve a desired color or flavor. To complete the mashing process, the brewer strains out the barley grains. The remaining sweetened liquid, called malt extract, is now ready to become the wort.

Initially, wort is concentrated, unhopped beer. The brewer transfers the wort from the mashing vessel to a brewing kettle where boiling hops are added. This is usually just a matter of turning valves. Depending on the style of beer, the brewer will have selected a particular style or blend of hops. Some brewers use the actual hop leaf, others use a pelletized version. The hopped wort is boiled for an hour and a half to two and a half hours according to brewer preferences. After the wort has cooled to 50–60 degrees Fahrenheit for lagers and 60–70 degrees Fahrenheit for ales, the hop leaves or pellet residue are removed in a process called *sparging,* and the wort is now ready for its most vital ingredient, yeast.

To ensure quality and consistency, many brewers culture their own yeast, but some smaller brewpubs or microbreweries use prepackaged yeast. Once the wort is cooled, the brewer transfers it to a starting tank where the yeast is added and the fermentation process begins. Depending on the style of beer and the desired results, the brewer will choose either an open or closed fermentation. Open fermentation is less common because it leaves the beer susceptible to airborne bacteria. However, some styles of beer require it.

Most beers go through two basic fermentations; some beers require more. The initial contact of the wort and yeast spurs a fervent fermentation that produces alcohol and a foamy head called *kraeusen.* The brewer decides how long he or she wants this fermentation to last, gen-

This brewer monitors the pH levels of the beer he is brewing.

erally between five and 14 days. After the desired time for the primary fermentation, the brewer transfers the beer to a lagering kettle (also called a conditioning kettle) where the beer is allowed to age. The fermentation continues but at a slower pace. The brewer must strictly regulate the temperature during the lagering time: 60–70 degrees Fahrenheit for ales, and 35–50 degrees Fahrenheit for lagers. After the desired aging or maturation of the beer, anywhere from two weeks to several months, the beer is again transferred to a storage tank where it is ready to be bottled. This step is necessary to leave any yeast or hops sediment behind so it is not present in the bottle or keg.

Brewers add carbonation to their beers either by injecting carbon dioxide into the storage tank just before it is to be bottled or kegged (this is typical of mass-produced beers) or, more common among craftbrewers, by adding a priming sugar, usually dry malt extract or corn sugar diluted in boiled water. If the brewer uses priming sugars, the beer must sit again for one to four weeks before it is ready to be served.

Brewing is both a creative and highly methodical craft requiring precise attention to detail. Brewers must monitor pH (acidity and alkalinity) levels in water and test water purity. They frequently use calculations to predict yields, efficiencies of processes, yeast maturation cycles, alcohol volume, bittering units, and many other factors. They study yeast physiology, metabolism, the biochemistry of fermentation and maturation, and the effects alternative brewing methods as well as bacteria, protozoa, and mold have on beer flavor and color. They constantly study methods of quality control and brewing efficiency.

Some craftbrewers at microbreweries may also help in bottling their beer. Workers at a brewpub (an establishment that is a combination brewery and restaurant) may stand behind the bar to pour drafts as well as work as waitstaff. At small breweries, brewers frequently sterilize their tanks, kettles, hoses, and other brewing equipment. Brewers who have the right resources and live in the right environment may grow, harvest, and store their own hops. Many craftbrewers are responsible for marketing their beer or designing logos. Some comanage the brewpub or microbrewery. But a brewer's primary duty is always to brew beer, to experiment and come up with new recipes, and to seek out the right ingredients for the particular style of beer that is being brewed.

■ REQUIREMENTS
High School

In today's competitive job market, aspiring brewers will need a high school degree to land a job that offers growth possibilities, a good salary, and challenges, including positions in the craftbrewing industry.

High school classes in biology, chemistry, and mathematics will be particularly useful if you are interested in becoming a brewer. Classes in biochemistry and microbiology will prepare you for the more specialized aspects of brewing that serious craftbrewers must master. A background in science and mathematics is needed for brewers to perform basic brewing and engineering calculations and to follow technical discussions on brewing topics. Classes in home economics or family and consumer science can teach you basic kitchen skills, common units of cooking measurement, and the organizational skills you need to prepare and complete complex recipes. If you are interested in running your own microbrewery, be sure to take business, accounting, and computer science classes to help you prepare for managing a business.

Postsecondary Training

Employers today prefer to hire only brewers who have completed some kind of formal training program in brewing sciences, or who have had extensive apprenticeship training at another brewery. The following three institutions are the most prominent U.S. schools offering programs on brewing sciences and the business of brewing. The Siebel Institute of Technology & World Brewing Academy is located in Chicago, Illinois, with a partner campus in Munich, Germany. The Siebel Institute offers courses on specific topics, such as brewing microbiology, and the World Brewing Academy offers a diploma program that lasts 12 weeks and involves work done in Chicago and Munich. The American Brewers Guild is located in Woodland, California. The Craft Brewers Apprenticeship Program of the American Brewers Guild lasts 27 weeks and combines classroom work with hands-on experience. Graduates receive a diploma and job placement assistance. The University Extension, University of California, Davis, Professional Brewing Programs offers certificate options as well as a master brewers program. Although a college degree is not required for admission to the professional brewing programs, you will need to have completed college coursework in the following areas: biological sciences (biology, biochemistry, microbiology), chemistry, physics, mathematics (pre-calculus), and engineering.

It is highly recommended that you complete an organized course of study through one of these programs. Students who learn at a brewing sciences school will have a particular advantage in landing a job as a brewer because employers know graduates have received training in the many highly technical aspects of brewing. Topics covered usually include brewing raw materials, brewhouse theory and practice, fermentation, storage and finishing, packaging and engineering topics, quality control, microbiology laboratory, and sensory evaluation.

Certification or Licensing

Breweries of any size must be licensed both by the state in which they are located and the Bureau of Alcohol, Tobacco, and Firearms, which is part of the U.S. Treasury Department. Owners of breweries are responsible for obtaining and maintaining these licenses.

Other Requirements

Brewers must have an avid appreciation for beer and an excellent sense of taste. They must be able to detect all of a particular beer's subtleties and nuances through taste and aroma. They should also be able to distinguish between styles of beer.

Brewers need good organizational and problem-solving skills as well as creativity. If a batch of beer turns out bad, the brewer must be able, through tests or experience, to pinpoint what went wrong and why. Beer takes time to brew. While the process can be hastened, craftbrewers should have the patience to allow beer to brew in its natural time. Brewers must be able to follow recipes and procedures closely, but they must also know when and how to go beyond a recipe's direction, or when to vary a procedure to achieve a desired result. Since they must be able to legally sample their wares, brewers must be 21 or older.

■ EXPLORING

Most breweries, whether a microbrewery, a brewpub, or one of the major mass-production breweries, offer tours of their facilities. This is an excellent opportunity to learn what actually goes on in a brewery, to see the brewing equipment and the raw ingredients, and to ask questions. Those 21 and older will be able to sample the various styles of beer at the brewery and ask questions of the masterbrewer.

Homebrewing is a popular trend that has been growing rapidly for the past decade. Those 21 and over can learn firsthand how to brew small batches of beer at home. The equipment and ingredients needed to begin brewing can be found at some larger liquor stores or through mail order.

There are numerous books and magazines available on the subject. *Zymurgy,* the American Homebrewers Association's magazine, focuses on homebrewing issues, and *The New Brewer,* the Institute for Brewing Studies' magazine, covers topics of interest to micro- and pub-brewers. Sample articles as well as information on other publications can be found at the Association of Brewers' website, http://www.beertown.org. Most brewers began their experience with brewing by brewing first at home. So you're not of legal drinking age yet? Don't worry, you can still learn some of the basic skills of a brewer by making nonalcoholic carbonated drinks, such as sodas. Articles on this topic are frequently found in beer magazines because so much of the same equipment is used to make each.

Some breweries have part-time jobs available to students. They usually entail sanitizing the brewing equipment after a batch has been made or transporting heavy bags of ingredients. This is an excellent opportunity to learn how the brewing machines work, to get to know the various types of ingredients, and to see the types of challenges and pressures brewers face.

■ STARTING OUT

The best career path for an aspiring craftbrewer is to begin as a homebrewer, learning the basic methods and science of brewing and possibly developing a personal style. Until recently, many brewers still learned the trade through hands-on experience as an apprentice at a microbrewery or brewpub. Although this is still an option, an increasing number of brewers are completing formal postsecondary training, making the market more competitive. Due to the recent renaissance in American brewing, employers are looking to hire highly qualified

LEARN MORE ABOUT IT

Fix, George J. *Principles of Brewing Science: A Study of Serious Brewing Issues.* 2nd ed. Boulder, Colo.: Brewers Publications, 2000.

Foster, Terry. *Pale Ale: History, Brewing Techniques, Recipes.* 2nd ed. Boulder, Colo.: Brewers Publications, 1999.

Gold, Elizabeth, and Kim Adams, eds. *Brewery Planner: A Guide to Opening and Running Your Own Small Brewery.* 2nd ed. Boulder, Colo.: Brewers Publications, 1997.

Goldhammer, Ted. *The Brewers' Handbook.* Mt. Shasta, Calif.: KVP Publishers, 2000.

Leventhal, Josh. *Beer Lover's Companion: A Guide to Producing, Brewing, Tasting, Rating and Drinking Around the World.* New York: Blackdog & Leventhal Publishing, 1999.

Lewis, Michael J., and Tom W. Young. *Brewing.* New York: Kluwer Academic/Plenum Publishers, 2000.

Nachel, Marty. *Regional Guide to Brewpubs and Microbreweries.* Pownal, Vt.: Storey Books, 1995.

brewers who will not require years of on-the-job-training but can immediately begin producing quality beers. An added benefit of getting postsecondary training is the job placement assistance any respected school provides to its graduates.

Currently, however, there are not enough trained craftbrewers to fill the demand, so many breweries still employ apprentices who have some experience in brewing—generally as homebrewers. Apprentices may spend several years learning the craft from a masterbrewer. They usually begin by sanitizing brewing vessels, preparing ingredients for the masterbrewer, and doing some administrative work, all the while taking notes and observing brewing techniques.

Breweries looking for trained craftbrewers often post job openings at brewing schools or advertise in trade magazines or local papers. There are many beer festivals and homebrewing contests where breweries—particularly new breweries—seek out the brewers of winning beers and offer them work.

■ ADVANCEMENT

Brewers advance as the popularity of their beer increases and continual sales are made. Most microbreweries and brewpubs are led by the so-called *masterbrewer* (often the one who developed the recipe), and depending on the size of the brewery, there may be *general brewers* who help in the brewing process. After demonstrating resourcefulness in technique, or after developing a successful beer recipe on their own, these general brewers may advance to masterbrewer at the brewery where they work, or they may transfer to become masterbrewer at a different brewery. Their work will still be the same, but as masterbrewer, they will be able to relegate work to others and earn a larger salary. After an approximate two-year period of learning the brewing process, an apprentice will advance to become a general brewer or even masterbrewer.

Most brewers are content to remain masterbrewer of a microbrewery or brewpub, but some may advance to management positions if the opportunity arises. *Brewery managers* are responsible for the day-to-day operations of a brewery, including managing finances, marketing, and hiring employees. Many microbreweries are operated by a small staff, and advancement for brewers may simply mean increasing brewery output and doing good business.

■ EARNINGS

Salaries for those in the brewing business vary considerably based on several factors, including the exact position a person holds, the size of the brewery, its location, the popularity of its beer, and the length of time the brewery has been in business. Brewers running their own microbreweries or brewpubs, like any small business owner, may have very low take-home wages for several years as the business becomes established. An article appearing on November 11, 2000, in *Creative Loafing Atlanta,* a newsweekly, reports masterbrewers at microbreweries may expect earnings in the $35,000 to $45,000 range. According to the Economic Research Institute, masterbrewers with five years of experience average $46,170, with top earnings at $57,250 per year. The institute also reports that those with 10 years of experience average $53,098 annually, and top earnings were $65,000. This is consistent with the U.S. Department of Labor's figures, which state that in 2002, food scientists (which is, essentially, what a brewer is) earned a median of $48,670, with the lowest 10 percent earning less than $28,750, and the highest 10 percent earning more than $85,460.

Benefits packages vary from business to business. Brewers running their own businesses must pay for benefits (health insurance, retirement plans, etc.) themselves. Brewers employed by breweries can generally expect health insurance and paid vacation time. Other benefits may include dental and eye care, life and disability insurance, and a pension plan. Many employers will pay for all or part of a brewer's training. A brewer's salary can increase by yearly bonuses or profit sharing if the brewery does well in the course of a year. Most brewers confess that the greatest benefit of their job is free beer.

■ WORK ENVIRONMENT

Brewers perform a variety of tasks requiring different skills. Most of their time is spent in the brewery preparing the next batch of beer. At many small microbreweries and brewpubs, brewers are responsible for all of the brewery operations. Before preparing a batch of beer, they use hoses and brushes with a sanitizing solution and clean all of the kettles. Since sanitization is a crucial part of brewing, this job must be a very thoroughly and is, therefore, often strenuous. Temperatures in breweries are strictly controlled, in some cases to as low as 40 degrees Fahrenheit.

On brewing days, the brewer weighs and measures ingredients. He or she inspects the brewing equipment to ensure it is both properly sanitized and in working order. Frequently a brewer watches over several different batches of beer all at different stages of production. The most stressful part of a brewer's job is waiting for the beer to be completed and wondering if anything went wrong. Throughout various stages of the brewing process, brewers sample the beer to make certain everything is as it should be. Brewers generally produce the same one to four beer recipes each time they brew. With standardization of the brewing process, most errors can be eliminated. The size of the brewery dictates a craftbrewer's working hours. A small brewery can only produce a limited amount of beer at one time. Brewers may have days when they are not brewing at all. Instead they may perform maintenance on equipment, prepare yeast cultures, or even grow and harvest hops. Many brewers experiment with new styles of beer by brewing small five-gallon batches. Brewers spend a lot of time tasting many different styles and brands of beers to determine what qualities make the beer good and what qualities make it bad, so that they can improve their own beer. Brewers, especially those at small breweries, may work odd hours (until very late at night or very early in the morning) in order to move the brew from one stage in the brewing process to another. Brewers usually work about 40 hours a week. Those who own breweries or brewpubs, however, often work much longer hours than this to complete all the management tasks required of a business.

■ OUTLOOK

America is currently in the midst of a beer renaissance. An increasing number of people have discovered that beer can be as complex as wine and equally enjoyable. Clearly, taste preferences have changed for a large segment of the beer-drinking population from the bland, almost watery styles of the major beer manufacturers to a more complex, hearty style of the craftbeer producers. Even the major brewers like Miller, Anheuser Busch, and Coors have acknowledged the craftbrewing trend by introducing their own premium-style beers—and to great success.

Although craftbrewing accounts for only a small percentage (about 3 percent) of the U.S. beer market, it is a growing segment of the beer industry. According to the Institute for Brewing Studies, there are now more than 1,450 microbreweries, brewpubs, and regional specialty breweries operating across the country. The craftbrewing industry's annual dollar volume was approximately $3.2 billion in 2000. As people have become accustomed to the availability of unique tasting beers, they have created a growing market for these products.

Like any small business, just-opened brewpubs and microbreweries will succeed or fail on an individual basis. The craftbrewing industry itself, however, is here to stay. A strong demand for excellent brewers exists, and those with training should have the best opportunities.

■ FOR MORE INFORMATION

ABG prepares people to work in the craftbrewing field and offers its Craftbrewers Apprenticeship Program both at the school and through distance education. For more information, contact

American Brewers Guild (ABG)
908 Ross Drive
Woodland, CA 95776
Tel: 800-636-1331
Email: abg@abgbrew.com
http://www.abgbrew.com

Visit the website of the Association of Brewers for industry statistics, information on professional brewing and homebrewing, and related publications. Information and links are also available to the American Homebrewers Association and the Institute for Brewing Studies, which are divisions of the Association of Brewers.

Association of Brewers
736 Pearl Street
Boulder, CO 80302
Tel: 303-447-0816
http://www.beertown.org

For information on courses and the diploma in brewing technology, contact

Siebel Institute of Technology & World Brewing Academy
1777 North Clybourn Street
Suite 2F
Chicago, IL. 60614
Tel: 312-255-0705
Email: info@siebelinstitute.com
http://www.siebelinstitute.com

For more information about the Professional Brewing Programs offered through the University Extension, University of California, Davis, contact

University Extension
1333 Research Park Drive
Davis, CA 95616
Tel: 800-752-0881
http://universityextension.ucdavis.edu/brewing

Bricklayers and Stonemasons

■ OVERVIEW

Bricklayers are skilled workers who construct and repair walls, partitions, floors, arches, fireplaces, chimneys, and other structures from brick, concrete block, gypsum block, and precast panels made of terra cotta, structural tile, and other masonry materials. *Stonemasons* build stone walls, floors, piers, and other structures, and they set the decorative stone exteriors of structures, such as churches, hotels, and public buildings. Approximately 165,000 bricklayers and stonemasons work in the United States.

■ HISTORY

Sun-baked clay bricks were used in constructing buildings more than 6,000 years ago in Mesopotamia. Along with brick, stone was used in ancient Egypt in many structures. The Romans introduced masonry construction to the rest of Europe and made innovations in bricklaying, including the use of mortar and different types of bonds, or patterns. As the Roman Empire declined, so did the art of bricklaying. During the most intense period of cathedral building in Europe, from about the tenth century to the 17th century, stonemasons formed guilds in various cities and towns. These guilds functioned much as today's unions do. They had the same categories of workers: apprentices, journeymen, and masters. Not until the great fire of London in 1666 did the English start to use brick again in building. The Chinese also were experts in bricklaying and stonemasonry, the best example of their work being the Great Wall of China. High in the Andes of South America, Incan stoneworkers had perfected their art by the 12th century.

Although some brick houses made of imported bricks were built in Florida by the Spanish, the first bricks made by Europeans in North America were manufactured in Virginia in 1612. These bricks were handmade from clay, just as they were in ancient times. Machines were not used in the manufacturing of bricks until the mid-18th century. Changes in the content of bricks came shortly afterwards. Concrete and cinder blocks were developed at this time, as was structural clay tile.

Today, attractive kinds of brick, called face brick, can be used in places where appearance is especially important. The use of face brick has helped to popularize brick in modern construction. Various colors of brick can be made by using iron oxides, iron sulfides, and other materials. By varying the bond and hue of brick, many interesting artistic effects can be achieved.

Stone is a durable, adaptable material for building purposes, although one of its drawbacks is that it may be much more difficult to cut and transport than alternative materials. Today it remains popular, particularly as a material for enhancing the appearance of important structures like hotels, public buildings, and churches. In modern construction, a covering of stone veneer about two inches thick is applied in various patterns to exterior surfaces of buildings; the veneer is anchored and supported on a steel frame.

■ THE JOB

When bricklayers and stonemasons begin work on a job, they usually first examine a blueprint or drawing to determine the designer's specifications. Then they measure the work area to fix reference points and guidelines in accordance with the blueprint.

If they are building a wall, bricklayers traditionally start with the corners, or leads, which must be precisely established if the finished structure is to be sound and straight. The corners may be established by more experienced bricklayers, with the task of filling in between the corners left to less experienced workers. Corner posts, or masonry guides, may be used to define the line of the wall, speeding the building process. A first, dry course may be put down without mortar so that the alignment and positioning of the brick can be checked.

In laying brick, bricklayers use a metal trowel to spread a bed or layer of soft mortar on a prepared base. Then they set the brick into the mortar, tapping and working each brick into the correct position. Excess mortar is cut off, and the mortar joints are smoothed with special tools that give a neat, uniform look to the wall. In walls, each layer, or course, is set so that vertical joints do not line up one on top of another but instead form a pleasing, regular pattern. The work must be continually checked for horizontal and vertical straightness with mason's levels, gauge strips, plumb lines, and other equipment. Sometimes it is necessary to cut and fit brick to size using a power saw or hammer and chisel. Around doors and windows, bricklayers generally use extra steel supports in the wall.

Bricklayers must know how to mix mortar, which is made of cement, sand, and water, and how to spread it so that the joints throughout the structure will be evenly spaced, with a neat appearance. They may have helpers who mix the mortar as well as move materials and scaffolding around the work site as needed.

Some bricklayers specialize in working with one type of masonry material only, such as gypsum block, concrete block, hollow tile used in partitions, or terra-cotta products. Other bricklayers, called *refractory masons,* work in the steel and glass manufacturing industries and specialize in installing firebrick and refractory tile linings of furnaces, kilns, boilers, cupolas, and other high-temperature equipment. Still others are employed to construct manholes and catch basins in sewers.

Stonemasons work with two types of stone: natural cut stone, such as marble, granite, limestone, or sandstone; and artificial stone, which is made to order from concrete, marble chips, or other masonry materials. They set the stone in many kinds of structures, including piers, walls, walks, arches, floors, and curbstones. On some projects, the drawings that stonemasons work from specify where to set certain stones that have been previously identified by number. In such cases, helpers may locate the stones and bring them to the masons. Large stones may have to be hoisted into place with derricks.

In building stone walls, masons begin by setting a first course of stones in a bed of mortar, then build upward by alternating layers of mortar and stone courses. At every stage, they may use leveling devices and plumb lines, correcting the alignment of each stone. They often insert wedges and tap the stones into place with rubber mallets. Once a stone is in good position, they remove the wedges, fill the gaps with mortar, and smooth the area using a metal tool called a tuck pointer. Large stones may need to be anchored in place with metal brackets that are welded or bolted to the wall.

QUICK FACTS

SCHOOL SUBJECTS
Mathematics
Technical/shop

PERSONAL SKILLS
Mechanical/manipulative
Technical/scientific

WORK ENVIRONMENT
Primarily outdoors
Primarily multiple locations

MINIMUM EDUCATION LEVEL
High school diploma
Apprenticeship

SALARY RANGE
$24,030 to $42,600 to
    $63,770 (bricklayers)
$19,610 to $35,530 to
    $55,310 (stonemasons)

CERTIFICATION OR LICENSING
None available

OUTLOOK
Faster than the average

DOT
861

GOE
06.02.01

NOC
7281

O*NET-SOC
47-2021.00, 47-2022.00

Similarly, when masons construct stone floors, they begin by spreading mortar. They place stones, adjusting their positions using mallets and crowbars and periodically checking the levelness of the surface. They may cut some stones into smaller pieces to fit, using hammer and chisel or a power saw with a diamond blade. After all the stones are placed, the masons fill the joints between the stones with mortar and wash off the surface.

Some stonemasons specialize in setting marble. Others work exclusively on setting alberene, which is an acid-resistant soapstone used in industrial settings on floors and for lining vats and tanks. Other specialized stone workers include composition stone applicators, monument setters, patchers, and chimney repairers. *Stone repairers* mend broken slabs made of marble and similar stone.

Bricklayers and stonemasons sometimes use power tools, such as saws and drills, but for the most part they use hand tools, including trowels, jointers, hammers, rulers, chisels, squares, gauge lines, mallets, brushes, and mason's levels.

■ REQUIREMENTS
High School

As with many jobs, employers of bricklayers and stonemasons will often prefer that you have a high school education or at least a GED. Take as many courses as possible in shop, basic mathematics, blueprint reading, and mechanical drawing. Take college prep courses in engineering if your school offers them. It may also help you on the job if you have taken core courses like English and general science and have a driver's license.

Another piece of good advice is to join or help form a student chapter of an organization like the National Association of Home Builders. You will get benefits like issues of various journals in the building industry, low-cost admission to the International Builders' Show, and opportunities to take part in exciting activities like visiting construction sites, sponsoring restoration projects at your school, and helping repair homes for the elderly and underprivileged. Check such websites as http://www.hbi.org.

Postsecondary Training

The best way for you to become a bricklayer or stonemason is to complete an apprenticeship. Vocational schools also provide training in these fields. However, many people learn their skills informally on the job simply by observing and helping experienced workers. The disadvantage of this approach is that informal training is likely to be less thorough, and it may take workers much longer to learn the full range of skills necessary for the trade.

A stonemason begins at a corner of a new site to lay the first of many tiers of stone.

Apprenticeship programs are sponsored by contractors or jointly by contractors and unions. Nonunion-sponsored programs are also available. Applicants for apprenticeships need to be at least 17 years old and in good physical condition. As an apprentice, you would spend about three years learning as you work under the supervision of experienced bricklayers or stonemasons. In addition, you would get at least 144 hours of classroom instruction in related subjects, such as blueprint reading, applied mathematics, and layout work. In the work portion of your apprenticeship, you would begin with simple jobs, like carrying materials and building scaffolds. After becoming familiar with initial tasks, you would eventually take part in a broad range of activities. In the course of an apprenticeship, you can become qualified to work with more than one kind of masonry material.

Other Requirements

In bricklaying and stone masonry, you often have to carry materials and sometimes relatively heavy equipment, such as scaffold parts and rows of brick. Since you'll be mixing mortar and laying brick and stone, you must not mind getting dirty and being on your hands and knees.

HOW DO YOU BEGIN TO BUILD A BUILDING?

In the United States, the construction of any building often can't proceed without the input of a diverse group of subindustries, with many individuals and organizations involved at many stages, from the making of necessary components to the final touch-up work. As a general rule, the laws in each state require a registered architect or engineer (or both) to first execute the design of the structure and to make sure that it complies with public health, zoning, and building code requirements; it must also conform to the requirements of the owner. The architect or engineer then converts these requirements into a set of drawings and written specifications that usually are sent to interested general contractors for bids (a bid is like an estimate, or quote, of the work to be performed and of the cost of the work).

The contractors who make the most acceptable bids then give work out to other contractors, called the subcontractors, who will do such work as the plumbing, painting, electrical wiring, and structural frame construction and erection. Contractors usually work under the observation of an architect or engineer, who acts as an agent of the owner of the building being built. State and local inspectors review the work for general compliance with the local building codes. The responsibilities of the contractor, architect, and engineer usually end when the local authorities approve the building for occupancy and the owner accepts the building.

Source: *Funk & Wagnalls New Encyclopedia*, 1995

You should enjoy doing demanding work and be disciplined and motivated enough to do your job without close and constant supervision. Sometimes, you might be presented with building challenges that require either mental or physical aptitude. The ability to get along with co-workers is also important as many bricklayers and masons work in teams.

■ EXPLORING

Opportunities are sometimes limited for high school students to directly experience work in the field of bricklaying and stonemasonry. It is fortunate, however, that student groups exist that provide opportunities for experience and exploration. One such group is the National Association of Home Builders Student Chapters Program, which has chapters in high schools and vocational and technical schools. By becoming a member, you get to experience the "real world" of construction, including bricklaying and stone masonry. Some groups visit construction sites; others participate in repairing homes; others help organize repairs on their own school buildings.

Hands-on experience is one of the best ways to explore the building trades. If you are too young to get such experience, at least contact others who have already started their careers. For example, try to contact participants from the International Masonry Institute's Masonry Camp. In 1998, participants were expected to develop a ferry terminal/visitors' center on Swan's Island, Maine. One camper from Hawaii had this to say: "I learned a great deal more about masonry in the 10 days I was at camp than the six years I was in architecture school. That's something worth shouting from the top of the volcanoes here!" (For more information, visit the IMI's website at http://www.imiweb.org.)

■ EMPLOYERS

Bricklayers and stonemasons are employed in the building industry for such companies as general contractors or specific building contractors, both large and small. Jobs are available across the country but are concentrated in city areas. Those who are skilled in business matters can start their own companies or be contractors; more than 1 in 4 of the approximately 165,000 bricklayers and stonemasons in the United States are self-employed.

■ STARTING OUT

The two main ways that people start out in these fields are through formal apprenticeship programs and as helpers or laborers who gradually learn their skills on the job. Helper jobs can be found through newspaper want ads and from the local office of the state. If you want to apply for an apprenticeship, you can get more information from local contractors, the state employment service, and the local office of the International Union of Bricklayers and Allied Craftworkers. The Home Builders Institute can also be of help.

Another option may be to enter a bricklaying program at a vocational school. Such a program combines classroom instruction with work experience. If you've taken classes at a vocational school, the placement office there may be able to help you find a job.

■ ADVANCEMENT

Bricklayers and stonemasons with enough skill and experience may advance to supervisory positions. Some union contracts require a supervisor if three or more workers are employed on a job.

Supervisors sometimes become superintendents at large construction sites. With additional technical training, bricklayers and stonemasons may become cost estimators. *Cost estimators* look at building plans, obtain quotations on masonry material, and prepare and submit bids on the costs of doing the proposed job. Another possible advancement is to become a city or county inspector who checks to see if the work done by contractors meets local building code regulations. Some bricklayers and stonemasons go into business for themselves as contractors.

■ EARNINGS

According to the U.S. Department of Labor, the median hourly pay of bricklayers was $20.48 in 2002. A person working full-time at this pay rate would have annual earnings of approximately $42,600. Earnings for bricklayers ranged from a low of less than $11.55 per hour (approximately $24,030 annually) to a high of more than $30.66 per hour (about $63,770 yearly) during that same time period.

The U.S. Department of Labor reports the median hourly wage for stonemasons as $17.08 in 2002. This wage translates into annual earnings of approximately $35,530 for full-time work. The lowest paid 10 percent of stonemasons earned less than $9.43 per hour (approximately $19,610 yearly), and the highest paid 10 percent made more than $26.59 hourly (about $55,310 annually).

Of course, earnings for those who work outside can be affected by bad weather, and earnings are lower for workers in areas where the local economy is in a slump. The pay also varies according to geographic region.

The beginning hourly rate for apprentices is about half the rate for experienced workers. In addition to regular pay, various fringe benefits, such as health and life insurance, pensions, and paid vacations, are available to many workers in this field.

■ WORK ENVIRONMENT

Most bricklayers and stonemasons have a 40-hour workweek. They are usually paid time and a half for overtime and double time for work on Saturdays, Sundays, and holidays.

Most of the work is done outdoors, where conditions may be dusty, hot, cold, or damp. Often workers must stand on scaffolds that are high off the ground. They may need to bend or stoop constantly to pick up materials. They may be on their feet most of the working day, or they may kneel for long periods.

Some of the hazards in this work include falling off a scaffold, being hit by falling material, and getting injuries common to lifting and handling heavy material. Whereas poor weather conditions used to affect work schedules and job site conditions, protective sheeting is now used to enclose work areas. This sheeting makes it possible to work through most inclement weather.

Apprentices and experienced workers must furnish their own hand tools and measuring devices. Contractors supply the materials for making mortar, scaffolding, lifts, ladders, and other large equipment used in the construction process.

Well-qualified bricklayers and stonemasons can often find work at wages higher than those of most other construction workers. But because the work is seasonal, bricklayers and stonemasons must plan carefully to make it through any periods of unemployment.

■ OUTLOOK

Employment for bricklayers and stonemasons is predicted to be excellent through 2012, according to the U.S. Department of Labor. Many workers leave the field each year for less strenuous work, retirement, or other reasons. In addition, the U.S. is experiencing a building boom, and population and business growth will always

CYCLOPEAN MASONRY

If you were an ancient Egyptian stonemason, you probably would have worked on some of the most dramatic structures in history: the pyramids. Unlike today's masonry, which generally involves using mortar to join stones, in ancient Egypt stonework was generally squared and fitted without mortar. This type of building using huge irregular blocks of stone without mortar is called Cyclopean masonry, and examples of this style have been found throughout Europe, in China, and in Central and South America.

The Great Pyramid was built as the tomb of the Pharaoh Khufu and is one of the Seven Wonders of the Ancient World. When it was built, it measured 481 feet high, with a square base measuring 756 feet on each side. The remains of about 70 pyramids can still be seen in Egypt and Sudan.

The pyramids in the Americas are arranged around ceremonial plazas. The earliest complex, built around 1200 B.C., is at the Olmec site of La Venta in southeastern Mexico. Other ceremonial centers in central Mexico, the Mayan region of the Yucatan Peninsula, Guatemala, Honduras, and the Andean region of Peru may have been based on the Olmec plan. The largest mounds in the New World include the Pyramid of Quetzalcoatl at Cholula outside Puebla, Mexico; the Pyramid of the Sun in Teotihuacan, near Mexico City; and the Huaca del Sol in Moche, Peru.

Source: *Funk & Wagnalls New Encyclopedia*, 1995

create the need for new facilities (such as homes, hospitals, long-term care facilities, and offices) and result in a demand for these skilled workers.

During economic downturns, bricklayers and stonemasons, like other workers in construction-related jobs, can expect to have fewer job opportunities and perhaps be laid off.

■ FOR MORE INFORMATION

This labor union promotes quality construction and builds markets for general contractors. For more information on apprenticeships and training through its National Center for Construction Education and Research, contact

Associated General Contractors of America

333 John Carlyle Street, Suite 200

Alexandria, VA 22314

Tel: 703-548-3118

Email: info@agc.org

http://www.agc.org

The HBI is the educational arm of the National Association of Home Builders. For more information on education and training programs, contact

Home Builders Institute (HBI)

1201 15th Street NW, Sixth Floor

Washington, DC 20005

Tel: 202-371-0600

http://www.hbi.org

For information on design and technical assistance as well its annual masonry camp for chosen apprentices, contact

International Masonry Institute

The James Brice House

42 East Street

Annapolis, MD 21401

Tel: 410-280-1305

http://imiweb.org

For information on available publications, contact

International Union of Bricklayers and Allied Craftworkers

1776 Eye Street, NW

Washington, DC 20006

Tel: 202-783-3788

Email: askbac@bacweb.org

http://www.bacweb.org

For information on specialized education and research programs and apprenticeship opportunities, contact

Mason Contractors Association of America

33 S. Roselle Rd.

Schaumburg, IL 60193

Tel: 847-301-0001

Email: info@masoncontractors.org

http://www.masoncontractors.org

Broadcast Engineers

■ OVERVIEW

Broadcast engineers, also referred to as *broadcast technicians,* or *broadcast operators,* operate and maintain the electronic equipment used to record and transmit the audio for radio signals and the audio and visual images for television signals to the public. They may work in a broadcasting station or assist in broadcasting directly from an outside site as a *field technician.* Approximately 35,000 broadcast engineers work in the United States.

■ HISTORY

At the end of the 19th century, Guglielmo Marconi (1874–1937), an Italian engineer, successfully sent radio waves across a room in his home and helped launch the 20th-century age of mass communication. Marconi quickly realized the potential for his experiments with radio waves. By 1901 he had established the Marconi Wireless Company in England and the United States and soon after successfully transmitted radio signals across the Atlantic Ocean for the first time.

At first, radio signals were used to transmit information and for communication between two points, but eventually the idea was developed that radio could be used for entertainment, and in 1919, the Radio Corporation of America, or RCA, was founded. Families everywhere gathered around their radios to listen to music, drama, comedy, and news programs. Radio became a commercial success, and radio technology advanced, creating the need for skilled engineers to operate the complicated electronic equipment.

In 1933, frequency modulation, or FM, was introduced; originally there had been only amplitude modulation, or AM. This vastly improved the quality of radio broadcasting. At the same time, experimentation was occurring with higher frequency radio waves, and in 1939 at the World's Fair in New York City, RCA demonstrated television.

The effect television had on changing mass communication was as dramatic as the advent of the radio. Technology continued to advance with the introduction of color imaging, which became widely available in 1953.

The number of VHF and UHF channels continued to increase; in the 1970s cable television and subscription television became available, further increasing the amount and variety of programming. Continuing advances in broadcast technology ensure the need for trained engineers who understand and can maintain the highly technical equipment used in television and radio stations.

One of the recent changes in technology that affects broadcast engineers is the switch from analog to digital signals. These changes provide ongoing challenges for television stations.

■ THE JOB

Broadcast engineers are responsible for the transmission of radio and television programming, including live and recorded broadcasts. Broadcasts are usually transmitted directly from the station; however, engineers are capable of transmitting signals on location from specially designed, mobile equipment. The specific tasks of the broadcast engineer depend on the size of the television or radio station. In small stations, engineers have a wide variety of responsibilities. Larger stations are able to hire a greater number of engineers and specifically delegate responsibilities to each engineer. In both small and large stations, however, engineers are responsible for the operation, installation, and repair of the equipment.

The *chief engineer* in both radio and television is the head of the entire technical operation and must orchestrate the activities of all the technicians to ensure smooth programming. He or she is also responsible for the budget and must keep abreast of new broadcast communications technology.

Larger stations also have an *assistant chief engineer* who manages the daily activities of the technical crew, controls the maintenance of the electronic equipment, and ensures the performance standards of the station.

Maintenance technicians are directly responsible for the installation, adjustment, and repair of the electronic equipment.

Video technicians usually work in television stations to ensure the quality, brightness, and content of the visual images being recorded and broadcast. They are involved in several different aspects of broadcasting and videotaping television programs. Technicians who are mostly involved with broadcasting programs are often called *video-control technicians*. In live broadcasts using more than one camera, they operate electronic equipment that selects which picture goes to the transmitter for broadcast. They also monitor on-air programs to ensure good picture quality. Technicians mainly involved with taping programs are often called *videotape-recording technicians*. They record performances on videotape using video cameras and tape-recording equipment, then splice together separate scenes into a finished program; they can create special effects by manipulating recording and re-recording equipment. The introduction of robotic cameras, six-foot-tall cameras that stand on two legs, created a need for a new kind of technician called a *video-robo technician*. Video-robo technicians operate the cameras from a control room computer, using joysticks and a video panel to tilt and focus each camera. With the help of new technology, one person can now effectively perform the work of two or three camera operators. Engineers may work with producers, directors, and reporters to put together videotaped material from various sources. These include networks, mobile camera units, and studio productions. Depending on their employer, engineers may be involved in any number of activities related to editing videotapes into a complete program.

■ REQUIREMENTS
High School

Take as many classes as you can in mathematics, science, computers, and shop, especially electronics. Speech classes will help you hone your abilities to effectively communicate ideas to others.

Postsecondary Training

Positions that are more advanced require a bachelor's degree in broadcast communications or a related field. To become a chief engineer, you should aim for a bachelor's degree in electronics or electrical engineering. Because field technicians also act as announcers on occasion, speech courses and experience as an announcer in a school radio station can be helpful. Seeking education beyond a bachelor's degree will further the possibilities for advancement, although it is not required.

Certification or Licensing

The Federal Communications Commission licenses and permits are no longer required of broadcast engineers. However, certification from the Society of Broadcast Engineers (SBE) is

QUICK FACTS

SCHOOL SUBJECTS
Computer science
Mathematics

PERSONAL SKILLS
Mechanical/manipulative
Technical/scientific

WORK ENVIRONMENT
Indoors and outdoors
Primarily multiple locations

MINIMUM EDUCATION LEVEL
Some postsecondary training

SALARY RANGE
$14,600 to $27,760 to
$65,970

CERTIFICATION OR LICENSING
Recommended

OUTLOOK
About as fast as the average

DOT
194

GOE
08.01.01

NOC
5224

O*NET-SOC
27-4011.00, 27-4012.00,
27-4014.00

desirable, and certified engineers consistently earn higher salaries than uncertified engineers. The SBE offers an education scholarship and accepts student members; members receive a newsletter and have access to their job line.

Other Requirements

Broadcast engineers must have both an aptitude for working with highly technical electronic and computer equipment and minute attention to detail to be successful in the field. You should enjoy both the technical and artistic aspects of working in the radio or television industry. You should also be able to communicate with a wide range of people with various levels of technical expertise.

■ EXPLORING

Reading association publications is an excellent way to learn more about broadcast engineering. Many of the associations listed at the end of this article offer newsletters and other publications to members—some even post back issues or selected articles on their Web sites. You might also consider reading *Broadcast Engineering*

Words to Know

Amplifier: A device used to boost the strength of an electronic signal.

Analog: A form of transmitting information.

Bandwidth: A measure of spectrum (frequency) use or capacity.

Bit: A single digital unit of information.

Broadcasting: Process of transmitting radio or television signals via an antenna to multiple receivers.

Broadcast quality: May refer to both technical specifications and artistic quality.

Channel: A frequency band in which a broadcast signal is transmitted.

Circuit: The connection of facilities that provides telecommunications service.

Digital: Conversion of information into bits of data for transmission; allows simultaneous transmission of voice, data, or video.

Encryption: To code or "scramble."

HDTV: High-definition television with a higher resolution and sound quality than NTSC.

MPEG-2: The name given to new international video compression standards.

NTSC: Refers to current analog television standards.

Transmitter: An electric device consisting of circuits that produce a radio or television electromagnetic wave signal.

(http://www.broadcastengineering.com), a trade publication for broadcast engineers and technicians.

Experience is necessary to begin a career as a broadcast engineer, and volunteering at a local broadcasting station is an excellent way to gain experience. Many schools have clubs for persons interested in broadcasting. Such clubs sponsor trips to broadcasting facilities, schedule lectures, and provide a place where students can meet others with similar interests. Local television station technicians are usually willing to share their experiences with interested young people. They can be a helpful source of informal career guidance. Visits or tours can be arranged by school officials. Tours will allow you to see engineers involved in their work. Most colleges and universities also have radio and television stations where students can gain experience with broadcasting equipment.

Exposure to broadcasting technology also may be obtained through building and operating an amateur, or ham, radio and experimenting with electronic kits. Dexterity and an understanding of home-operated broadcasting equipment will aid in promoting success in education and work experience within the field of broadcasting.

■ EMPLOYERS

According to the Federal Communications Commission, there were 10,945 radio stations and 1,220 television stations in the United States in 2003. These stations might be independently operated or owned and operated by a network. Smaller stations in smaller cities are good starting places, but it is at the larger networks and stations in major cities where the higher salaries are found. Some broadcast engineers work outside of the radio and television industries, producing, for example, corporate employee training and sales programs.

■ STARTING OUT

In many towns and cities there are public-access cable television stations and public radio stations where high school students interested in broadcasting and broadcast technology can obtain an internship. An entry-level technician should be flexible about job location; most begin their careers at small stations and with experience may advance to larger-market stations.

■ ADVANCEMENT

Entry-level engineers deal exclusively with the operation and maintenance of their assigned equipment; in contrast, a more advanced broadcast engineer directs the activities of entry-level engineers and makes judgments on the quality, strength, and subject of the material being broadcast.

After several years of experience, a broadcast engineer may advance to assistant chief engineer. In this capacity, he or she may direct the daily activities of all of the broadcasting engineers in the station as well as the field engineers broadcasting on location. Advancement to chief engineer usually requires at least a college degree in engineering and many years of experience. A firm grasp of management skills, budget planning, and a thorough knowledge of all aspects of broadcast technology are necessary to become the chief engineer of a radio or television station.

■ EARNINGS

Larger stations usually pay higher wages than smaller stations, and television stations tend to pay more than radio stations. Also, commercial stations generally pay more than public broadcasting stations. The median annual earnings for broadcast technicians were $27,760 in 2002, according to the U.S. Department of Labor. The department also reported that the lowest-paid 10 percent earned less than $14,600 and the highest-paid 10 percent earned more than $65,970 during that same period. Experience, job location, and educational background are all factors that influence a person's pay.

■ WORK ENVIRONMENT

Most engineers work in a broadcasting station that is modern and comfortable. The hours can vary; because most broadcasting stations operate 24 hours a day, seven days a week, there are engineers who must work at night, on weekends, and on holidays. Transmitter technicians usually work behind the scenes with little public contact. They work closely with their equipment and as members of a small crew of experts whose closely coordinated efforts produce smooth-running programs. Constant attention to detail and having to make split-second decisions can cause tension. Since broadcasts also occur outside of the broadcasting station on location sites, field technicians may work anywhere and in all kinds of weather.

■ OUTLOOK

According to the U.S. Department of Labor, the overall employment of broadcast technicians is expected to grow about as fast as the average through 2012. There will be strong competition for jobs in metropolitan areas. In addition, the Department of Labor predicts that a slow growth in the number of new radio and television stations may mean few new job opportunities in the field. Technicians trained in the installation of transmitters should have better work prospects as television stations switch from their old analog transmitters to digital transmitters. Job openings will also result from the need to replace existing engineers who often leave the industry for other jobs in electronics.

Two broadcast engineers run a news program from the central control room at a television station.

■ FOR MORE INFORMATION

Visit the BEA website for useful information about broadcast education and the broadcasting industry.

Broadcast Education Association (BEA)
1771 N Street, NW
Washington, DC 20036-2891
Tel: 888-380-7222
Email: beainfo@beaweb.org
http://www.beaweb.org

For broadcast education, support, and scholarship information, contact

National Association of Broadcasters
1771 N Street, NW
Washington, DC 20036-2891
Tel: 202-429-5300
Email: nab@nab.org
http://www.nab.org

For information on union membership, contact

National Association of Broadcast Employees and Technicians
Email: nabet@nabetcwa.org
http://nabetcwa.org

For information on student membership, scholarships, and farm broadcasting, contact

National Association of Farm Broadcasters
PO Box 500
Platte City, MO 64079
Tel: 816-431-4032
Email: nafboffice@aol.com
http://nafb.com

For information on careers in the cable industry, visit the NCTA website.

National Cable & Telecommunications Association (NCTA)
1724 Massachusetts Avenue, NW
Washington, DC 20036
Tel: 202-775-3550
http://www.ncta.com

For scholarship and internship information, contact

Radio-Television News Directors Association & Foundation
1600 K Street, NW, Suite 700
Washington, DC 20006-2838
Tel: 202-659-6510
Email: rtnda@rtnda.org
http://www.rtnda.org

For information on membership, scholarships, and certification, contact

Society of Broadcast Engineers
9247 North Meridian Street, Suite 305
Indianapolis, IN 46260
Tel: 317-846-9000
http://www.sbe.org

Business Managers

■ OVERVIEW

Business managers plan, organize, direct, and coordinate the operations of firms in business and industry. They may oversee an entire company, a geographical territory of a company's operations, or a specific department within a company. There are approximately 7 million managerial jobs in the United States.

■ HISTORY

Everyone has some experience in management. For example, if you schedule your day so that you can get up, get to school on time, go to soccer practice after school, have the time to do your homework, and get to bed at a reasonable hour, you are practicing management skills. Running a household, paying bills, balancing a checkbook, and keeping track of appointments, meetings, and social activities are also examples of managerial activities. Essentially, the term "manage" means to handle, direct, or control.

Management is a necessary part of any enterprise in which a person or group of people are trying to accomplish a specific goal. In fact, civilization could not have grown to its present level of complexity without the planning and organizing involved in effective management. Some of the earliest examples of written documents had to do with the management of business and commerce. As societies and individuals accumulated property and wealth, they needed effective record keeping of taxes, trade agreements, laws, and rights of ownership.

The technological advances of the industrial revolution brought about the need for a distinct class of managers. As complex factory systems developed, skilled and trained managers were required to organize and operate them. Workers became specialized in a limited number of tasks, which required managers to coordinate and oversee production.

As businesses began to diversify their production, industries became so complex that their management had to be divided among several different managers, as opposed to one central, authoritarian manager. With the expanded scope of managers and the trend toward decentralized management, the transition to the professional manager took place. In the 1920s, large corporations began to organize with decentralized administration and centralized policy control.

Managers provided a forum for the exchange and evaluation of creative ideas and technical innovations. Eventually these management concepts spread from manufacturing and production to office, personnel, marketing, and financial functions. Today, management is more concerned with results than activities, taking into account individual differences in styles of working.

■ THE JOB

Management is found in every industry, including food, clothing, banking, education, health care, and business services. All types of businesses have managers to formulate policies and administer the firm's operations. Managers may oversee the operations of an entire company, a geographical territory of a company's operations, or a specific department, such as sales and marketing.

Business managers direct a company's or a department's daily activities within the context of the organization's overall plan. They implement organizational policies and goals. This may involve developing sales or promotional materials, analyzing the department's budgetary requirements, and hiring, training, and supervising staff. Business managers are often responsible for long-range planning for their company or department. This involves setting goals for the organization and developing a workable plan for meeting those goals.

A manager responsible for a single department might work to coordinate his or her department's activities with other departments. A manager responsible for an entire company or organization might work with the managers of various departments or locations to oversee and coordinate the activities of all departments. If the business is privately owned, the owner may be the manager. In a large corporation, however, there will be a management structure above the business manager.

Jeff Bowe is the Midwest General Manager for Disc Graphics, a large printing company headquartered in New York. Bowe oversees all aspects of the company's Indianapolis plant, which employs about 50 people. When asked what he is responsible for, Bowe answers, "Everything that happens in this facility." Specifically, that includes sales, production, customer service, capital expenditure planning, hiring and training employees, firing or downsizing, and personnel management.

The hierarchy of managers includes top executives, such as the *president,* who establishes an organization's goals and policies along with others, such as the chief executive officer, chief financial officer, chief information officer, executive vice president, and the board of directors. Top executives plan business objectives and develop policies to coordinate operations between divisions and departments and establish procedures for attaining objectives. Activity reports and financial statements are reviewed to determine progress and revise operations as needed. The president also directs and formulates funding for new and existing programs within the organization. Public relations plays a big part in the lives of executives as they deal with executives and leaders from other countries or organizations, and with customers, employees, and various special interest groups.

The top-level managers for Bowe's company are located in the company's New York headquarters. Bowe is responsible for reporting certain information about the Indianapolis facility to them. He may also have to work collaboratively with them on certain projects or plans. "I have a conversation with people at headquarters about every two to three days." he says. "I get corporate input on very large projects. I would also work closely with them if we had some type of corporate-wide program we were working on—something where I would be the contact person for this facility."

Although the president or chief executive officer retains ultimate authority and responsibility, Bowe is responsible for overseeing the day-to-day operations of the Indianapolis location. A manager in this position is sometimes called a *chief operating officer* or *COO.* Other duties of a COO may include serving as chairman of committees, such as management, executive, engineering, or sales.

Some companies have an *executive vice president,* who directs and coordinates the activities of one or more departments, depending on the size of the organization.

In very large organizations, the duties of executive vice presidents may be highly specialized. For example, they may oversee the activities of business managers of marketing, sales promotion, purchasing, finance, personnel training, industrial relations, administrative services, data processing, property management, transportation, or legal services. In smaller organizations, an executive vice president might be responsible for a number of these departments. Executive vice presidents also assist the chief executive officer in formulating and administering the organization's policies and developing its long-range goals. Executive vice presidents may serve as members of management committees on special studies.

Companies may also have a *chief financial officer* or *CFO.* In small firms, the CFO is usually responsible for all financial management tasks, such as budgeting, capital expenditure planning, cash flow, and various financial reviews and reports. In larger companies, the CFO may oversee financial management departments, to help other managers develop financial and economic policy and oversee the implementation of these policies.

Chief information officers, or *CIOs,* are responsible for all aspects of their company's information technology. They use their knowledge of technology and business to determine how information technology can best be used to meet company goals. This may include researching, purchasing, and overseeing the set up and use of technology systems, such as Intranet, Internet, and computer networks. These managers sometimes take a role in implementing a company's Web site. For more information on this career, see the article Chief Information Officers.

In companies that have several different locations, managers may be assigned to oversee specific geographic areas. For example, a large retailer with facilities all across the nation is likely to have a number of managers in charge of various territories. There might be a Midwest manager, a Southwest

QUICK FACTS

SCHOOL SUBJECTS
Business
Computer science
Economics

PERSONAL SKILLS
Helping/teaching
Leadership/management

WORK ENVIRONMENT
Primarily indoors
One location with some travel

MINIMUM EDUCATION LEVEL
Bachelor's degree

SALARY RANGE
$31,850 to $67,120 to $144,620+

CERTIFICATION OR LICENSING
None available

OUTLOOK
About as fast as the average

DOT
189

GOE
13.01.01

NOC
0611

O*NET-SOC
11-1011.00, 11-1011.02, 11-1021.00, 11-3031.01

MAGS FOR MANAGERS

Most successful business managers try to keep up to date with current happenings in the business world by reading daily newspapers and business-related magazines. To get a taste of what managers read, browse through some of the following periodicals:

Business Week (http://www.businessweek.com)

CIO (http://www.cio.com)

Chief Executive (http://www.chiefexecutive.net)

The Economist (http://www.economist.com)

Fast Company (http://www.fastcompany.com)

Fortune (http://www.fortune.com)

Forbes (http://www.forbes.com)

Inc. (http://www.inc.com)

Industry Week (http://www.iwgc.com)

Newsweek (http://www.newsweek.com)

U.S. News and World Report (http://www.usnews.com)

Wall Street Journal (http://www.wsj.com)

manager, an Southeast manager, a Northeast manager, and a Northwest manager. These managers are often called *regional* or *area managers*. Some companies break their management territories up into even smaller sections, such as a single state or a part of a state. Managers overseeing these smaller segments are often called *district managers,* and typically report directly to an area or regional manager.

■ REQUIREMENTS
High School

The educational background of business managers varies as widely as the nature of their diverse responsibilities. Many have a bachelor's degree in liberal arts or business administration. If you are interested in a business managerial career, you should start preparing in high school by taking college preparatory classes. According to Jeff Bowe, your best bet academically is to get a well-rounded education. Because communication is important, take as many English classes as possible. Speech classes are another way to improve your communication skills. Courses in mathematics, business, and computer science are also excellent choices to help you prepare for this career. Finally, Bowe recommends taking a foreign language. "Today speaking a foreign language is more and more important," he says. "Which language is not so important. Any of the global languages are something you could very well use, depending upon where you end up."

Postsecondary Training

Business managers often have a college degree in a subject that pertains to the department they direct or the organization they administer; for example, accounting or economics for a business manager of finance, computer science for a business manager of data processing, engineering or science for a director of research and development. As computer usage grows, many managers are expected to have experience with the information technology that applies to their field.

Graduate and professional degrees are common. Bowe, along with many managers in administrative, marketing, financial, and manufacturing activities, has a master's degree in business administration. Managers in highly technical manufacturing and research activities often have a master's degree or doctorate in a technical or scientific discipline. A law degree is mandatory for business managers of corporate legal departments, and hospital managers generally have a master's degree in health services administration or business administration. In some industries, such as retail trade or the food and beverage industry, competent individuals without a college degree may become business managers.

Other Requirements

There are a number of personal characteristics that help one be a successful business manager, depending upon the specific responsibilities of the position. A manager who oversees other employees should have good communication and interpersonal skills. The ability to delegate work is another important personality trait of a good manager. The ability to think on your feet is often key in business management, according to Bowe. "You have to be able to think extremely quickly and not in a reactionary manner," he says. Bowe also says that a certain degree of organization is important, since managers are often managing several different things simultaneously. Other traits considered important for top executives are intelligence, decisiveness, intuition, creativity, honesty, loyalty, a sense of responsibility, and planning and abilities. Finally, the successful manager should be flexible and interested in staying abreast of new developments in his or her industry. "In general, you need to be open to change because your customers change, your market changes, your technology changes," he says. "If you won't try something new, you really have no business being in management."

■ EXPLORING

To get experience as a manager, start with your own interests. Whether you're involved in drama, sports, school publications, or a part-time job, there are managerial duties associated with any organized activity. These can involve planning, scheduling, managing other workers or volunteers, fund-raising, or budgeting. Local businesses also have job opportunities through which you can get firsthand knowledge and experience of management structure. If you can't get an actual job, at least try to schedule a meeting with a business manager to talk with him or her about the career. Some schools or community organizations arrange job-shadowing, where you can spend part of a day "shadowing" a selected employee to see what his or her job is like. Joining Junior Achievement is another excellent way to get involved with local businesses and learn about how they work. Finally, take every opportunity to work with computers, since computer skills are vital to today's business world.

EMPLOYERS

There are approximately 7 million general managers and executives employed in the United States. These jobs are found in every industry, and virtually every business in the United States has some form of managerial positions. Obviously, the larger the company is, the more managerial positions it is likely to have. Another factor is the geographical territory covered by the business. It is safe to say that companies doing business in larger geographical territories are likely to have more managerial positions than those with smaller territories.

STARTING OUT

Generally you will need a college degree, although many retail stores, grocery stores, and restaurants hire promising applicants who have only a high school diploma. Job seekers usually apply directly to the manager of such places. Your college placement office is often the best place to start looking for these positions. A number of listings can also be found in newspaper help wanted ads.

Many organizations have management trainee programs that college graduates can enter. Such programs are advertised at college career fairs or through college job placement services. Often, however, these management trainee positions in business and government are filled by employees who are already working for the organization and who demonstrate management potential. Jeff Bowe suggests researching the industry you are interested in to find out what might be the best point of entry for that field. "I came into the printing company through customer service, which is a good point of entry because it's one of the easiest things to learn," he says. "Although it requires more technical know-how now than it did then, customer service is still not a bad entry point for this industry."

ADVANCEMENT

Most business management and top executive positions are filled by experienced lower-level managers and executives who display valuable managerial traits, such as leadership, self-confidence, creativity, motivation, decisiveness, and flexibility. In small firms advancement to a higher management position may come slowly, while promotions may occur more quickly in larger firms.

Advancement may be accelerated by participating in different kinds of educational programs available for managers. These are often paid for by the organization. Company training programs broaden knowledge of company policy and operations. Training programs sponsored by industry and trade associations and continuing education courses in colleges and universities can familiarize managers with the latest developments in management techniques. In recent years, large numbers of middle managers were laid off as companies streamlined operations. Competition for jobs is keen, and business managers committed to improving their knowledge of the field and of related disciplines—especially computer information systems—will have the best opportunities for advancement.

Business managers may advance to executive or administrative vice president. Vice presidents may advance to peak corporate positions—president or chief executive officer. Presidents and chief executive officers, upon retirement, may become members of the board of directors of one or more firms. Sometimes business managers establish their own firms.

EARNINGS

Salary levels for business managers vary substantially, depending upon the level of responsibility, length of service, and type, size, and location of the organization. Top-level managers in large firms can earn much more than their counterparts in small firms. Also, salaries in large metropolitan areas, such as New York City, are higher than those in smaller cities. According to the U.S. Department of Labor, all managers had a median yearly income of $67,120 in 2002. To show the range of earnings for general managers, however, the Department notes that those in the computer and data processing industry had an annual median of $85,240; those in public relations, $60,640; and those at eating and drinking establishments, $35,790.

Again, salaries varied by industry. For example, the median yearly salary for those in engineering was $90,930, while those in financial services earned a median of $73,340. A survey by Abbott, Langer, & Associates found that chief executives working for nonprofits had a

LEARN MORE ABOUT IT

Ash, Mary Kay. *Mary Kay: You Can Have It All: Lifetime Wisdom from America's Foremost Woman Entrepreneur.* Rocklin, Calif.: Prima Publishing, 1995.

Belker, Loren B. *The First-Time Manager.* 4th ed. New York: AMACOM, 1997.

Bell, Chip R. *Managers as Mentors: Building Partnerships for Learning.* 2nd ed. San Francisco: Berrett-Koehler, 2002.

Bibb, Peter. *Ted Turner: It Ain't as Easy as It Looks: A Biography.* Boulder, Colo: Johnson Books, 1997.

Buckingham, Marcus, and Curt Coffman. *First, Break All the Rules: What the World's Greatest Managers Do Differently.* New York: Simon & Schuster, 1999.

Erickson, Gregory. *What's Luck Got to Do with It: Twelve Entrepreneurs Reveal the Secrets Behind Their Success.* New York: John Wiley & Sons, 1997.

Gross, Daniel, et al. *Forbes Greatest Business Stories of All Time.* New York: John Wiley & Sons, 1997.

Heller, Robert, and Tim Hindle. *Essential Manager's Manual.* New York: DK Publishing, 1998.

Jeffrey, Laura. *Great American Businesswomen.* Springfield, N.J.: Enslow Publishers, Inc., 1996.

Miles, Robert P. *The Warren Buffett CEO: Secrets of the Berkshire Hathaway Managers.* New York: John Wiley & Sons, 2002.

Ortega, Bob. *In Sam We Trust: The Untold Story of Sam Walton and Wal-Mart, the World's Most Powerful Retailer.* New York: Times Books, 2000.

Welch, Jack. *Jack: Straight from the Gut.* New York: Warner Books, 2000.

median yearly salary of $75,000 in 2000. According to the Department of Labor, chief executives officially earned a median of $134,960 annually in 2002. Most executives, however, earn hundreds of thousands—or millions—of dollars more than this annually in benefits and stock options. According to the *New York Times*, the CEO of a major company received $9.2 million in total compensation in 2003.

Benefit and compensation packages for business managers are usually excellent, and may even include such things as bonuses, stock awards, company-paid insurance premiums, use of company cars and aircraft, paid country club memberships, expense accounts, and generous retirement benefits.

■ WORK ENVIRONMENT

Business managers are provided with comfortable offices near the departments they direct. Top executives may have spacious, lavish offices and may enjoy such privileges as executive dining rooms, company cars, country club memberships, and liberal expense accounts.

Managers often travel between national, regional, and local offices. Top executives may travel to meet with executives in other corporations, both within the United States and abroad. Meetings and conferences sponsored by industries and associations occur regularly and provide invaluable opportunities to meet with peers and keep up with the latest developments. In large corporations, job transfers between the parent company and its local offices or subsidiaries are common.

Business managers often work long hours under intense pressure to meet, for example, production and marketing goals. Jeff Bowe's average workweek consists of 55 to 60 hours at the office. This is not uncommon—in fact, some executive spend up to 80 hours working each week. These long hours limit time available for family and leisure activities.

■ OUTLOOK

Overall, employment of business managers and executives is expected to grow about as fast as the average through 2012, according to the U.S. Bureau of Labor Statistics. Many job openings will be the result of managers being promoted to better positions, retiring, or leaving their positions to start their own businesses. Even so, the compensation and prestige of these positions make them highly sought-after, and competition to fill openings will be intense.

Projected employment growth varies by industry. For example, employment in the service industry, particularly business services, should increase faster than the average, while employment in some manufacturing industries is expected to decline.

The outlook for business managers is closely tied to the overall economy. When the economy is good, businesses expand both in terms of their output and the number of people they employ, which creates a need for more managers. In economic downturns, businesses often lay off employees and cut back on production, which lessens the need for managers.

■ FOR MORE INFORMATION

For news about management trends, resources on career information and finding a job, and an online job bank, contact

American Management Association
1601 Broadway
New York, NY 10019-7420
Tel: 800-262-9699
http://www.amanet.org

For brochures on careers in management for women, contact

Association for Women in Management
927 15th Street, NW, Suite 1000
Washington, DC 20005
Tel: 202-659-6364
Email: awm@benefits.net
http://www.womens.org

For information about programs for students in kindergarten through high school, and information on local chapters, contact

Junior Achievement
One Education Way
Colorado Springs, CO 80906
Tel: 719-540-8000
Email: newmedia@ja.org
http://www.ja.org

For a brochure on management as a career, contact

National Management Association
2210 Arbor Boulevard
Dayton, OH 45439
Tel: 937-294-0421
Email: nma@nma1.org
http://nma1.org

Buyers

■ OVERVIEW

There are two main types of *buyers. Wholesale buyers* purchase merchandise directly from manufacturers and resell it to retail firms, commercial establishments, and other institutions. *Retail buyers* purchase goods from wholesalers (and occasionally from manufacturers) for resale to the general public. In either case, buyers must understand their customers' needs and be able to purchase goods at an appropriate price and in sufficient quantity. Sometimes a buyer is referred to by the type of merchandise purchased—for example, jewelry buyer or toy buyer. *Government buyers* have similar responsibilities but need to be especially sensitive to concerns of fairness and ethics since they use public money to make their purchases. There are approximately 527,000 buyers and related workers currently working in the United States.

■ HISTORY

The job of the buyer has been influenced by a variety of historical changes, including the growth of large retail stores in the 20th century. In the past, store owners typically performed almost all of the business activities, including the purchase of merchandise. Large stores, in contrast, had immensely more complicated operations, requiring large numbers of specialized workers, such as sales clerks, receiving and shipping clerks, advertising managers, personnel officers, and buyers. The introduction of mass production systems at factories required more complicated planning, ordering, and scheduling of purchases. A wider range of available merchandise also called for more astute selection and purchasing techniques.

■ THE JOB

Wholesale and retail buyers are part of a complex system of production, distribution, and merchandising. Both are concerned with recognizing and satisfying the huge variety of consumer needs and desires. Most specialize in acquiring one or two lines of merchandise.

Retail buyers work for retail stores. They generally can be divided into two types: The first, working directly under a merchandise manager, not only purchases goods but directly supervises salespeople. When a new product appears on the shelves, for example, buyers may work with salespeople to point out its distinctive features. This type of retail buyer thus takes responsibility for the products' marketing. The second type of retail buyer is concerned only with purchasing and has no supervisory responsibilities. These buyers cooperate with the sales staff to promote maximum sales.

All retail buyers must understand the basic merchandising policies of their stores. Purchases are affected by the size of the buyer's annual budget, the kind of merchandise needed in each buying season, and trends in the market. Success in buying is directly related to the profit or loss shown by particular departments. Buyers often work with *assistant buyers,* who spend much of their time maintaining sales and inventory records.

All buyers must be experts in the merchandise that they purchase.

QUICK FACTS

SCHOOL SUBJECTS
Business
Economics
Mathematics

PERSONAL SKILLS
Helping/teaching
Leadership/management

WORK ENVIRONMENT
Primarily indoors
One location with some travel

MINIMUM EDUCATION LEVEL
High school diploma

SALARY RANGE
$23,270 to $40,780 to $76,070

CERTIFICATION OR LICENSING
Voluntary

OUTLOOK
Slower than the average

DOT
162

GOE
13.02.02

NOC
6233

O*NET-SOC
11-3061.00, 13-1021.00, 13-1022.00

They order goods months ahead of their expected sale, and they must be able to predetermine marketability based upon cost, style, and competitive items. Buyers must also be well acquainted with the best sources of supply for each product they purchase.

Depending upon the location, size, and type of store, a retail buyer may deal directly with traveling salespeople (ordering from samples or catalogs), order by mail or by telephone directly from the manufacturer or wholesaler, or travel to key cities to visit merchandise showrooms and manufacturing establishments. Most use a combination of these approaches.

Buying trips to such cities as New York, Chicago, and San Francisco are an important part of the work for buyers at a larger store. For specialized products, such as glassware, china, liquors, and gloves, some buyers make yearly trips to major European production centers. Sometimes manufacturers of similar items organize trade shows to attract a number of buyers. Buying trips are difficult; a buyer may visit six to eight suppliers in a single day. The buyer must make decisions on the spot about the opportunity for profitable sale of merchandise. The important element is not how much the buyer personally likes the merchandise but about customers' taste. Most buyers operate under an annual purchasing budget for the departments they represent.

Mergers between stores and expansion of individual department stores into chains of stores have created central buying positions. *Central buyers* order in unusually large quantities. As a result, they have the power to develop their own set of specifications for a particular item and ask manufacturers to bid on the right to provide it. Goods purchased by central buyers may be marketed under the manufacturer's label (as is normally done) or ordered with the store's label or a chain brand name.

To meet this competition, independent stores often work with *resident buyers,* who purchase merchandise for a large number of stores. By purchasing large quantities of the same product, resident buyers can obtain the same types of discounts enjoyed by large chain stores and then pass along the savings to their customers.

Because they work with public funds and must avoid any appearance of favoritism or corruption, *government buyers* sometimes purchase merchandise through open bids. The buyer may establish a set of specifications for a product and invite private firms to bid on the job. Some government buyers are required to accept the lowest bid. Each purchase must be well documented for public scrutiny. Like other types of buyers, government buyers must be well acquainted with the products they purchase, and they must try to find the best quality products for the lowest price.

■ REQUIREMENTS
High School

A high school diploma generally is required for entering the field of buying. Useful high school courses include mathematics, business, English, and economics.

Postsecondary Training

A college degree may not be a requirement for becoming a buyer, but it is becoming increasingly important, especially for advancement. A majority of buyers have attended college, many majoring in business, engineering, or economics. Some colleges and universities also offer majors in purchasing or materials management. Regardless of the major, useful courses in preparation for a career in buying include accounting, economics, commercial law, finance, marketing, and various business classes, such as business communications, business organization and management, and computer applications in business.

Retailing experience is helpful to gain a sense of customer tastes and witness the supply and demand process. Additional training is available through trade associations, such as the National Association of Purchasing Management, which sponsors conferences, seminars, and workshops.

Certification or Licensing

Certification, although not required, is becoming increasingly important. Various levels of certification are available through the American Purchasing Society, the National Association of Purchasing Management, and the National Institute of Government Purchasing. To earn most certifications you must have work experience, meet education requirements, and pass written and oral exams.

Other Requirements

If you are interested in becoming a buyer, you should be organized and have excellent decision-making skills. Predicting consumer tastes and keeping stores and wholesalers appropriately stocked requires resourcefulness, good judgment, and confidence. You should also have skills in marketing to identify and promote products that will sell. Finally, leadership skills are needed to supervise assistant buyers and deal with manufacturers' representatives and store executives.

■ EXPLORING

One way to explore the retailing field is through part-time or summer employment in a store. A good time to look for such work is during the Christmas holiday season. Door-to-door selling is another way to gain business retailing experience. Occasionally, experience in a retail store can be found through special high school programs.

■ EMPLOYERS

Buyers work for a wide variety of businesses, both wholesale and retail, as well as for government agencies. Employers range from small stores, where buying may be only one function of a manager's job, to multinational corporations, where a buyer may specialize in one type of item and buy in enormous quantity.

Of the approximately 527,000 purchasing managers, buyers, and purchasing agents employed throughout the country, about 42 percent work in wholesale trade and manufacturing, 15,600 work in management and 16,570 in farm products. Approximately 7,900 work in retail trade, such as for grocery stores and department stores. Others work in businesses that provide services and in government agencies.

■ STARTING OUT

Most buyers find their first job by applying to the personnel office of a retail establishment or wholesaler. Because knowledge of retailing is important, buyers may be required to have work experience in a store.

Most buyers begin their careers as retail sales workers. The next step may be *head of stock.* The head of stock maintains stock inventory records and keeps the merchandise in a neat and well-organized fashion both to protect its value and to permit easy access. He or she usually supervises the work of several employees. This person also works in an intermediate position between the salespeople on the floor and the buyer who provides the merchandise. The next step to becoming a buyer may be assistant buyer. For many department stores, promotion to full buyer requires this background.

Large department stores or chains operate executive training programs for college graduates who seek buying and other retail executive positions. A typical program consists of 16 successive weeks of work in a variety of departments. This on-the-job experience is supplemented by formal classroom work that most often is conducted by senior executives and training department personnel. Following this orientation, trainees are placed in junior management positions for an additional period of supervised experience and training.

■ ADVANCEMENT

Buyers are key employees of the stores or companies that employ them. One way they advance is through increased responsibility, such as more authority to make commitments for merchandise and more complicated buying assignments.

Buyers are sometimes promoted to *merchandise manager,* which requires them to supervise other buyers, help develop the store's merchandising policies, and coordi-

LEARN MORE ABOUT IT

Cash, R. Patrick. *Management of Retail Buying.* 3rd ed. New York: John Wiley & Sons, 1995.

Donellan, John. *Merchandise Buying and Management.* New York: Fairchild Publications, 1996.

Field, Shelly. *Career Opportunities in the Retail and Wholesale Industry.* New York: Facts on File, 2001.

Tepper, Bette K. *Mathematics for Retail Buying.* 5th ed. New York: Fairchild Publications, 2000.

Varley, Rosemary. *Retail Product Management: Buying and Merchandising.* New York: Routledge, 2001.

nate buying and selling activities with related departments. Other buyers may become vice presidents in charge of merchandising or even store presidents. Because buyers learn much about retailing in their job, they are in a position to advance to top executive positions. Some buyers use their knowledge of retailing and the contacts they have developed with suppliers to set up their own businesses.

■ EARNINGS

How much a buyer earns depends on various factors, including the employer's sales volume. Mass merchandisers, such as discount or chain department stores, pay among the highest salaries.

The U.S. Department of Labor reports the median annual income for nonagricultural wholesale and retail buyers was $40,780 in 2002. The lowest paid 10 percent of these buyers made less than $23,270 yearly, and at the other end of the pay range, the highest paid 10 percent earned more than $76,070 annually. The Department also reports that buyers working for the federal government had mean annual earnings of $70,780 in 2002.

Most buyers receive the usual benefits, such as vacation, sick leave, life and health insurance, and pension plans. Retail buyers may receive cash bonuses for their work and may also receive discounts on merchandise they purchase from their employer.

■ WORK ENVIRONMENT

Buyers work in a dynamic and sometimes stressful atmosphere. They must make important decisions on an hourly basis. The results of their work, both successes and failures, show up quickly on the profit and loss statement.

Buyers frequently work long or irregular hours. Evening and weekend hours are common, especially during the holiday season, when the retail field is at its busiest. Extra hours may be required to bring records up to date, for example, or to review stock and to become familiar with the store's overall marketing design for the coming season. Travel may also be a regular part of a buyer's job, possibly requiring several days away from home each month.

Although buyers must sometimes work under pressure, they usually work in pleasant, well-lit environments. They also benefit from having a diverse set of responsibilities.

■ OUTLOOK

According to the U.S. Department of Labor, employment of wholesale and retail buyers is projected to grow slower than the average through 2012. Reasons for this decrease include the large number of business mergers and acquisitions, which results in the blending of buying departments and the elimination of redundant jobs. In addition, the use of computers, which increases efficiency, and the trend of some large retail companies to centralize their operations will both contribute to fewer new jobs for buyers. Some job openings will result from the need to hire replacement workers for those who leave the field. On the other hand, companies in the service sector are beginning to realize the advantages of having professional buyers.

■ FOR MORE INFORMATION

For career information and job listings, contact
American Purchasing Society
8 East Galena Boulevard, Suite 203
Aurora, IL 60506
Tel: 630-859-0250
http://www.american-purchasing.com

For information on the magazine, Your Future Purchasing Career, *lists of colleges with purchasing programs, and interviews with people in the field, contact the ISM:*
Institute for Supply Management (ISM)
PO Box 22160
Tempe, AZ 85285-2160
Tel: 800-888-6276
http://www.napm.org

For information on purchasing careers in the government and certification, contact
National Institute of Government Purchasing
151 Spring Street
Herndon, VA 20170-5223
Tel: 800-367-6447
http://www.nigp.org

For materials on educational programs in the retail industry, contact
National Retail Federation
325 7th Street, NW, Suite 1100
Washington, DC 20004
Tel: 800-673-4692
http://www.nrf.com

Cable Television Technicians

■ OVERVIEW

Cable television technicians install, inspect, maintain, and repair antennas, cables, and amplifying equipment used in cable television transmission. There are approximately 156,160 people working in the installation, maintenance, and repair sector of the cable and other pay television services industry.

■ HISTORY

The growth of cable television transmission systems greatly affected the broadcast industry. The birth of cable television can be traced to the development of coaxial cable (copper wire inside an aluminum tube, both with the same axis), which was invented in the 1930s in the Bell Telephone Laboratories, primarily to improve telephone transmission. It was soon found that a coaxial cable could also carry television transmissions very efficiently. One coaxial cable can carry up to 500 television signals, enabling a cable system to offer a wide variety of programming and still reserve channels for public-service use.

No one knows for sure when or where the first cable television system was installed, but by 1950, early cable television systems were in use. The first cable television systems used a central receiving antenna to pick up programs from broadcast stations and were used to carry television signals to areas where conventional transmission could not reach: valleys, extremely hilly regions, and large cities where buildings interfered with radio waves. Cable systems were then built in areas with good reception as a way of offering subscribers an increased number of channels.

In the 1950s and 1960s, cable television operators began using microwave radio relays for signals. This allowed the Federal Communications Commission (FCC) to establish its authority over cable television, as the FCC regulates any use of microwave transmission systems.

Channel converters were introduced in the 1960s, allowing cable television systems to deliver a greater number of channels, and thus, a wider choice of programs. When cable television operators offered pay-TV to the public in the 1960s, there was much public outcry. The public was so accustomed to being offered TV programming at no charge that they could not accept what seemed to be an outrageous concept. California, in fact, passed a state referendum that actually outlawed pay-TV. The referendum was later overruled by the state supreme court as being unconstitutional.

The broadcast industry also opposed cable television, fearing competition in its markets. In 1968, the FCC actually forbade new cable construction in some areas. Though it later lifted this ban, it continued to restrict what cable television companies could offer the public.

In 1972, pay-TV, or pay-cable, was reintroduced by Home Box Office (HBO), which offered special programs to subscribers who paid a fee in addition to its charge for basic cable service. At first, HBO distributed its programs through a tape distribution system, then a microwave distribution network. Three years later, HBO began distributing pay-cable by satellite, which led to the rapid expansion of cable television as we know it today.

Satellites supply programming to cable television systems by relaying signals from one point on earth to another. To receive signals from a communications satellite, an earth station, or satellite receiving dish, is used. The signals are then transmitted across coaxial lines or hybrid fiber/coaxial cables to the subscriber's television.

Today, 68 percent of households with televisions subscribe to a pay service, and for the majority of these households the service is cable television. Other pay television services, such as satellite subscriptions, are also becoming popular. Cable operators are currently upgrading their systems to offer even more services, such as digital and high-definition television (HDTV) programming and high-speed Internet access. According to the *Chicago Tribune*, approximately 12 million cable subscribers receive digital TV. The FCC has also been involved in introducing digital television transmission. The FCC required major network affiliates in the top 10 markets to build digital transmitting facilities in 1999. All other commercial stations in all markets are required to construct digital broadcast facilities by 2006.

■ THE JOB

Cable television technicians perform a wide range of duties in a variety of settings. Television cables usually follow the routes

A cable television technician tightens connectors at a junction box.

of telephone cables, running along poles in rural and suburban areas and through tunnels in cities. Working in tunnels and underground cable passageways, cable television technicians inspect cables for evidence of damage and corrosion. Using diagrams and blueprints, they trace cables to locate sites of signal breakdown. Technicians may also work at pole-mounted amplifiers, where they analyze the strength of incoming television signals, using field-strength meters and miniature television receivers to evaluate reception. At customers' homes, technicians service the terminal boxes, explain the workings of the cable system, answer questions, and respond to complaints that may indicate cable or equipment problems. When major problems arise, they repair or replace damaged or faulty cable systems.

John Manaro works as a technician for Comcast Cablevision in Santa Ana, California. He's had years of experience as both a maintenance technician and a construction technician. As a construction technician, his work has involved expanding underground service by the trenching and boring of grass, dirt, asphalt, and concrete as well as the coordination of city and county projects. As a maintenance technician, John maintained a cable television plant in three cities within a seven-city system. "I was required to maintain a level of performance and picture quality," he says, "set by system, industry, and FCC proof of performance specifications standards." To do so, Manaro followed a routine of preventive maintenance procedures. "This included the sweep and balance of all receivers and amplifiers in the system and operational checks and periodic tests of all power supply units. Also, I was required by the FCC to furnish documentation of all signal leakage detected in my area including corrective actions taken and dates of

occurrence and correction." He was also required to perform "on-call" duties once a month for seven days. "This required response, within 30 minutes, to any outage consisting of five or more subscribers at any time, 24 hours a day."

Cable television technicians use various electrical measuring instruments (voltmeters, field-strength meters) to diagnose causes of transmission problems. They also use electricians' hand tools (including screwdrivers, pliers, etc.) to dismantle, repair, or replace faulty sections of cable or disabled equipment, such as amplifying equipment used to boost the signal at intervals along the cable system.

Some cable television technicians may perform a specific type of work, rather than a full range of tasks. Following are some of the specialized positions held by cable television technicians.

Trunk technicians, or *line technicians,* perform routine maintenance and fix electronic problems on the trunk line, which connects the feeder lines in the street to the headend. They also fix electronic failures in the feeder amplifiers. Amplifiers increase the strength of the electronic signal for clear reception and are spaced throughout the cable system. Some trunk technicians install both underground and aboveground cables. Using a sweep analyzer, they check signals in all parts of the cable television system to make sure all parts are operating correctly.

Headend technicians and *microwave technicians* check that the equipment providing input to the cable television system is working properly. The *headend,* or control center of a cable television system, is where incoming signals are amplified, converted, processed, and combined into a common cable. Headend technicians check antennas, preamplifiers, frequency converters, processors, demodulators, modulators, and other related equipment using power meters, frequency counters, and waveform monitors. In some companies, the headend technician works with satellite receiving stations and related equipment. This person may be the *chief technician* in some companies. Many electronics technicians work as headend technicians and microwave technicians.

Service technicians respond to problems with subscribers' cable reception. They work on amplifiers, poles, and lines, in addition to making calls to subscribers' homes. They check the lines and connections that go into a home and those inside it, troubleshoot problems, and repair faulty equipment.

Bench technicians work in a cable television system's repair facility. They examine malfunctioning equipment that is brought into the shop, diagnose the problem, and repair it. They may also repair and calibrate test equipment. Some bench technicians are electronics technicians.

Technical supervisors oversee the technicians who work in the field and provide on-the-job training to technicians. Duties vary but can include dealing with contractors and coordinating with outside agencies such as utilities companies, municipalities, and large customers.

Chief technicians and *lead technicians* are among the most highly skilled of the technical staff. Many chief technicians do not work in the field except in emergency situations or complex situations requiring their special expertise. Chief technicians provide technical information to technicians in the field and may supervise the technical staff. They may work with satellite receiving equipment. These positions are usually held by senior staff personnel and require a strong background in electronics.

An important aspect of the work of cable television technicians involves implementing regular programs of preventive maintenance on the cable system. Technicians inspect connections, insulation, and the performance of amplifying equipment, using measuring instruments and viewing the transmitted signals on television monitors.

■ REQUIREMENTS
High School
You should take high school mathematics courses at least through plane geometry and have a solid knowledge of shop mathematics. You should also take English classes to develop the language skills needed to read technical manuals and instructions and to follow detailed maintenance procedures.

Postsecondary Training
Although training beyond high school is not required, many employers prefer to hire applicants with an electronics background or people who have had some technical training. Technical training in electronics technology or communications technology is available through both one- and two-year programs at community colleges, trade schools, and technical institutes. Two-year programs provide hands-on training and include courses that cover the basics of electrical wiring and electronics, broadcasting theory and practice, blueprint and schematic diagram reading, and physics. The National Cable Television Institute offers distance-learning courses for technicians.

Certification or Licensing
Certification in special skills can be obtained through one-year certification programs at community colleges. Certification classes in specialized technology, such as digital technology, digital compression, and fiber optics, prepare students to work with the more advanced technologies commonly used in many cable television sys-

tems. Because cable technology is evolving so rapidly, students who learn new technology have better chances at employment, and once hired, they have better chances for advancement. All workers are encouraged to continue training throughout their careers to learn new technology, new equipment, and new methods.

Professional associations, such as the Society of Cable Telecommunications Engineers (SCTE), also offer training programs and certification in areas, such as broadband communications technology. Examinations for certification are offered in different areas of cable technology including video and audio signals and systems, signal processing centers, terminal devices, and data networking and architecture.

Other Requirements
You'll need mechanical aptitude, physical agility, the ability to work at heights or in confined spaces, and the capacity to work as part of a team. Acute vision, with no color-perception deficiency, is needed, as it is essential for analyzing cable reception. In addition, it is helpful to feel at ease in using electrical equipment and electricians' tools. "I have a desire for knowledge," John Manaro says about the personal qualities that make him good at his work, "and a dedication to perfection. And I'm detail oriented."

You'll have much public contact, so you'll need good people skills. You must be helpful and courteous. You may need to explain cable system operations and costs to customers, answer questions, and analyze customer descriptions of problems so repairs and other work can be done. The ability to communicate well with others is essential.

HDTV Facts

- HDTV uses a 16:9 aspect ratio that gives five times the resolution of an analog television picture, which uses a 4:3 aspect ratio.

- An HDTV signal is made of up to 2 million pixels, compared to conventional TV's 224,000 pixels.

- Digital TV has 5.1 channel CD-quality Dolby Digital (AC-3) surround sound.

- HDTV has the ability to send data directly to a screen or to a personal computer as a download. The actual HDTV transmission is based on a 19.3-Mbps digital data stream.

Source: *USA Today* and National Association of Broadcasters

MORE HDTV FACTS

- The first HDTV station was WRAL-HD in Raleigh, N.C.

- Local television stations are spending between $2 million and $10 million to convert to digital television. This includes costs for new cameras, titling and editing equipment, tape machines, rigs for their news vans, and transmission equipment.

- More than 1216 stations are now broadcasting a digital signal.

- Prices for digital TV sets have decreased by 50 percent in the past several years, and they are now available for under $2,000 (for an average of $1,700). However, only 4 percent of homes still have them.

Source: *USA Today* and National Association of Broadcasters

■ EXPLORING

Because of the special training required, rarely are any part-time or summer technician jobs available for high school students. However, educational seminars are offered by local cable television personnel across the country; these are available to interested student groups and can be arranged through a school guidance counselor or teacher. These presentations provide valuable career information and an opportunity to speak with cable technicians and their employers about the field. For more information about these seminars, contact the SCTE for the name and address of the nearest local chapter.

Those interested in this career can explore electronics or related activities such as building a shortwave radio set or repairing radios and televisions, and participate in science clubs that emphasize electronics.

■ EMPLOYERS

Cable television technicians work for cable-TV companies in large cities and small towns. Some smaller towns may have only one cable provider, while there may be more than one in large cities. Technicians may work for a locally owned company or for the local office of a large, national corporation, such as Cox Communications. The company may offer services in addition to cable television, such as Internet access and local telephone service.

■ STARTING OUT

Two ways to enter this field are to enter as an unskilled installer and move up after receiving on-the-job training or to complete an electronics or telecommunications program in a technical school or through the SCTE and start work as an electronics technician or cable television technician. Many times, recruiters from various companies visit technical schools or hold job fairs in which they interview students for positions that begin immediately after training has been completed. Students can also check with their schools' job placement services for postings by employers or to get leads on companies that are hiring.

State employment offices and classified ads are other good sources of job leads. Interested persons also can apply directly to a cable television company or contractor.

■ ADVANCEMENT

Most companies provide on-the-job training, including classes in basic technical and troubleshooting skills, basic electronics, and electronics in reference to the cable television business, parts of the cable television system, installation, and safety practices. Students who have already received technical training usually are able to advance into more highly skilled positions more quickly than those who require extensive training. Many cable television technicians start out as installers or repairers and then move into technical positions, such as line technician, service technician, and bench technician. Workers with a strong industrial background, advanced training in electronics, and several years of experience can advance to supervisory and administrative positions, such as technical supervisor, headend technician, chief technician, lead technician, and plant manager.

Workers also can advance to the position of *chief engineer* with additional training. Chief engineers are responsible for cable systems design, equipment planning, specification of standards for equipment and material, layout for cable communications networks, and technical advice to technicians and system operating managers. A degree in electrical engineering or a related field is required to be a chief engineer.

"I hope to remain a field-oriented person," John Manaro says, "in either the cable or telecommunications industry. More and more, I see that this is the area where you can never become obsolete."

■ EARNINGS

According to the U.S. Department of Labor, the average annual pay for nonsupervisory cable and other pay television installers and repairers was $39,640 in 2002 for full-time work. Salaries, however, vary based on the type of job done, an employee's experience and education, and the company's location. At the low end of the pay scale, 10 percent of line installers and repairers had annual earnings of less than $21,440 annually, while at the high, end, 10 percent earned greater than $57,620.

Cable television technicians may receive a variety of benefits, depending on their employer. The benefits can include any of the following: paid holidays, vacations, and sick days; personal days; medical, dental, and life insurance; profit-sharing plans; 401(k) plans; retirement and pension plans; and educational assistance programs.

■ WORK ENVIRONMENT

The work is moderately heavy, involving occasional lifting of up to 50 pounds. A large part of the cable television technician's time is spent on ladders and poles or in confined or underground spaces. These activities require care and precision. As with all maintenance work around conductors, there is some danger of electrical shock. The coaxial cables used to transmit television signals are from one-half inch to over one inch in diameter. Cables have to be manipulated into position for splicing, which involves medium to heavy physical work.

Normal working hours are a five-day, 40-hour week, although technicians may often need to work evenings or weekends to make necessary repairs. Some technicians work in shifts, working four 10-hour days a week. Many technicians, especially line technicians, are on call 24 hours a day and carry pagers. They may be called in for special repairs or in emergency situations.

Technicians working in the field work in all kinds of weather. Their work involves extensive driving. Most companies provide a company vehicle, tools, equipment, and sometimes uniforms. "A job in the field is very demanding," John Manaro says. "Not just physically, but intellectually and emotionally. It can be very stressful. Maintaining a system requires real dedication and perseverance and can consume a great deal of time and energy."

■ OUTLOOK

Employment in the cable and other pay television services industry is expected to grow rapidly through 2012, according to the U.S. Department of Labor. There are several reasons for this projected growth. High-speed Internet access through cable lines, digital television programming, the addition of telephone services, and increased customer demand for more and improved services should all contribute to strong employment in this field. Cable companies will need technicians to install additional fiber optic cables, work with new technologies that increase cable line capacities and capabilities, and maintain the systems. In addition, installation of systems may become more time consuming as customers personalize their selection of services for their various needs.

This will also create a demand for more technicians. Those with strong technical skills should have good employment opportunities.

■ FOR MORE INFORMATION

For information on careers and the cable industry, contact

**National Cable & Telecommunications
    Association**
1724 Massachusetts Avenue, NW
Washington, DC 20036
Tel: 202-775-3550
http://www.ncta.com

For technician training course information and to receive a informational kit, contact

National Cable Television Institute
8022 Southpark Circle Suite 100
Littleton, CO 80120-5658
Tel: 303-797-9393
Email: info@ncti.com
http://www.ncti.com

For information on careers, educational programs, educational seminars, distance learning, and certification, contact

Society of Cable Telecommunications Engineers
140 Philips Road
Exton, PA 19341-1318
Tel: 800-542-5040
Email: scte@scte.org
http://www.scte.org

For information about conferences, special programs, careers, and membership, contact

Women in Cable & Telecommunications
14555 Avion Parkway, Suite 150
Chantilly, VA 20151
Tel: 703-234-9810
http://www.wict.org

Camera Operators

■ OVERVIEW

Camera operators use motion picture cameras and equipment to photograph subjects or material for movies, television programs, or commercials. They usually use 35-millimeter or 16-millimeter cameras or camcorders and a variety of films, lenses, tripods, and filters in their work. Their instructions usually come from cinematographers or directors of photography. Approximately 21,370 camera operators work in the United States.

HISTORY

Motion pictures were made as early as 1877, using a series of still photographs to create the illusion of motion. But it was Thomas Edison who, in 1889, produced the first single-unit motion picture camera that set the standard for today.

The motion picture industry blossomed in the United States during the 20th century. With the growth of the television industry and the addition of commercial advertising to television, camera operators became indispensable members of the production crew. Motion picture directors and producers rely on camera operators to create the images on film that the directors and producers envision in their minds. As camera equipment becomes more complex and sophisticated, the camera operator will need to be more proficient at his or her craft.

THE JOB

Motion picture camera operators may work on feature films in Hollywood or on location elsewhere. Many work on educational films, documentaries, or television programs. The nature of the camera operator's work depends largely on the size of the production crew. If the film is a documentary or short news segment, the camera operator may be responsible for setting up the camera and lighting equipment as well as for supervising the actors during filming. Equipment that camera operators typically use include cranes, dollies, mounting heads, and different types of lenses and accessories. Often the camera operator is also responsible for maintenance and repair of all of this equipment.

With a larger crew, the camera operator is responsible only for the actual filming. The camera operator may even have a support team of assistants. The *first assistant camera operator* will typically focus on the cameras, mak-

ing sure cameras are loaded and operating correctly and conferring with lighting specialists. In larger productions, there are also backup cameras and accessories for use if one should malfunction during filming. *Second assistant camera operators* help the first assistant set up scenes to be filmed and assist in the maintenance of the equipment.

Sometimes camera operators must use shoulder-held cameras. This often occurs during the filming of action scenes for television or motion pictures. *Special effects camera operators* photograph the optical effects segments for motion pictures and television. They create visual illusions that can add mood and tone to the motion picture. They usually add fades, dissolves, superimpositions, and other effects to their films at the request of the *director of photography*, also known as the *director of cinematography* or the *cinematographer*.

Brian Fass is a cinematographer/camera assistant in New York City. On a project, he works closely with the other professionals to help establish a visual style for the film. "During the project," he says, "I work on setting up the camera in various positions for coverage of scenes and then lighting each chosen angle." Fass has worked as a camera assistant for the Woody Allen films *Everyone Says I Love You* and *Deconstructing Harry*, as well as the Sidney Lumet film *Gloria*.

REQUIREMENTS
High School

Take classes that will prepare you for the technical aspect of the work—courses in photography, journalism, and media arts should give you some hands-on experience with a camera. Mathematics and science can help you in understanding cameras and filters. You should also take art and art history classes and other courses that will help you develop appreciation of visual styles.

Postsecondary Training

A college degree is not necessary to get a position as a motion picture camera operator, but a film school can help you expand your network of connections. A bachelor's degree in liberal arts or film studies provides a good background for work in the film industry, but practical experience and industry connections will provide the best opportunities for work. Upon completing an undergraduate program, you may wish to enroll in a master's program at a film school. Schools offering well-established programs include the School of Visual Arts in New York, New York University, and the University of Southern California. These schools have film professionals on their faculties and provide a very visible stage for student talent, being located in the two film business hot spots-New York and California. Film school offers overall formal training, providing an education in fundamental skills by working with student productions. Such education is rigorous, but in addition to teaching skills it provides you with peer groups and a network of contacts with students, faculty, and guest speakers that can be of help after graduation.

Other Requirements

You must be able to work closely with other members of a film crew and to carefully follow the instructions of the cinematographer and other camera operators. Since lighting is an integral part of filmmaking, you should have a thorough understanding of lighting equipment in order to work quickly and efficiently. In addition to the technical aspects of filmmaking, you should also understand the artistic nature of setting up shots. "I'm dyslexic and have always gravitated toward the visual mediums," Brian Fass says. "I feel that this impairment, along with my love of movies, made me turn toward cinematography."

■ EXPLORING

You should join a photography or camera club, or become involved with the media department of your school. You may have the opportunity then to videotape sports events, concerts, and school plays. You can also learn about photography by working in a camera shop. A part-time job in a camera shop will give you a basic understanding of photographic equipment. Some school districts have television stations where students can learn the basics of camera operation. This kind of hands-on experience is invaluable when it comes time to find work in the field. You can also learn about the film industry by reading such publications as *American Cinematographer* (http://www.theasc.com/magazine) and *Cinefex* (http://www.cinefex.com).

■ EMPLOYERS

There are approximately 21,370 television, video, and movie camera operators working in the United States. About 1 in 5 of these operators are self-employed. The majority of camera operators who are salaried employees work for the film and television industry at TV stations or film studios. Most jobs are found in large, urban areas.

■ STARTING OUT

Most entry-level jobs require little formal preparation in photography or camera operation. A college degree is not required by most film or television studios, but you may have to belong to the International Alliance of Theatrical Stage Employees (IATSE) Local 600, the national union for camera operators. An entry-level job as a camera assistant usually begins with assignments such as set-

LEARN MORE ABOUT IT

Carlson, Sylvia. *The Professional Cameraman's Handbook.* 4th ed. Boston: Focal Press, 1994.
Elkins, David E. *The Camera Assistant's Manual.* Boston: Focal Press, 2000.
Fauer, Jon. *Arriflex 35 Book.* 3rd ed. Boston: Focal Press, 1999.
———. *Arriflex 16SR Book.* 3rd ed. Boston: Focal Press, 1999.
Hart, Douglas C. *The Camera Assistant: A Complete Professional Handbook.* Boston: Focal Press, 1995.
Ward, Peter. *Multi-Camera Camerawork.* Boston: Focal Press, 1998.

ting up or loading film into cameras and adjusting or checking lighting. With experience, the assistant may participate in decisions about what to photograph or how to film a particular scene.

Before you receive any paying jobs, you may have to work for awhile as a volunteer or intern on a film project. You can surf the Internet for postings of openings on film productions, or contact your state's film commission.

■ ADVANCEMENT

It usually takes two to four years for a motion picture camera operator to learn the techniques necessary for the job. Those who become proficient in their field, after several years of training, may be able to work on film projects as a cinematographer or director of photography (DP). The DP supervises other camera operators and works more closely with the directors, producers, and actors in the creation of the film. Some camera operators study cinematography part time while keeping their jobs as camera operators. They may later move to larger studios or command higher salaries.

"I work as an assistant for the money," Brian Fass says, "but hope to jump into work as a DP full time if the jobs come along. I also own my own Aaton XTR camera package, which makes me more marketable for DP jobs."

■ EARNINGS

Self-employed camera operators typically work on a project-by-project basis and may have periods of unemployment between jobs. Those working on movies may be paid per-day, and their role in the creation of the movie may last anywhere from several weeks to several months. Camera operators who are salaried employees of, for example, a television network have steady, year-round employment. Because of these factors and others, such as

Camera operators usually stand so that they can move the camera quickly from side to side and up and down to catch all the action.

area of the country in which the operator works and the size of the employer, salaries vary widely for these professionals. The U.S. Department of Labor reports the median annual earnings of all television, video, and movie camera operators as $32,720 in 2002. The department also reports that the lowest paid 10 percent of operators earned less than $14,710 per year, but at the top end of the pay scale, the highest earning 10 percent made more than $65,070 annually.

Salaried employees usually receive benefits such as health insurance, retirement plans, and vacation days. Those who are self-employed must pay for such extras themselves.

■ WORK ENVIRONMENT

Motion picture camera operators work indoors and outdoors. Most work for motion picture studios or in television broadcasting. During filming, a camera operator may spend several weeks or months on location in another city or country. Most often the camera operator lives and works in their home city and works during reg-

ular business hours. Hours can be erratic, however, if the film includes scenes that must be shot at night, or if a deadline must be met by after-hours filming.

Much of the work of a camera operator becomes routine after a few years of experience. Camera operators get used to loading and unloading film, carrying cameras and equipment from trucks or workshops into studios or sets, and filming segments over and over again. The glamour of working on motion pictures or television programs may be diminished by the physically demanding work. Also, the actors, directors, and producers are the individuals in the limelight. They often receive credit for the work the camera operators have done.

Many camera operators must be available to work on short notice. Since motion picture camera operators are generally hired to work on one film at a time, there may be long periods during which a camera operator is not working. Few can make a living as self-employed camera operators.

Motion picture camera operators working on documentary or news productions may work in dangerous places. Sometimes they must work in uncomfortable positions or make adjustments for imperfect lighting conditions. They usually operate their cameras while standing hours at a time. Deadline pressure is also a constant in the camera operator's work. Working for directors or producers who are on tight budgets or strict schedules may be very stressful.

■ OUTLOOK

Employment for camera operators is expected to increase about as fast as the average for all occupations through 2012, according to the U.S. Department of Labor. The use of visual images continues to grow in areas such as communication, education, entertainment, marketing, and research and development. More businesses will make use of video training films and public relations projects that use film. The entertainment industries are also expanding. However, competition for positions is very fierce. Camera operators work in what is considered a desirable and exciting field, and they must work hard and be aggressive to get good jobs, especially in Los Angeles and New York.

■ FOR MORE INFORMATION

For lists of tricks of the trade and favorite films of famous cinematographers, visit the ASC's website.

American Society of Cinematographers (ASC)
PO Box 2230
Hollywood, CA 90078
Tel: 800-448-0145
Email: info@theasc.com
http://www.theasc.com

For information on membership benefits, contact this branch of the International Alliance of Theatrical Stage Employees (IATSE):

International Cinematographers Guild (IATSE Local 600)

National Office/Western Region

7715 Sunset Boulevard, Suite 300

Hollywood, CA 90046

Tel: 323-876-0160

http://www.cameraguild.com

To learn about student chapters sponsored by the SMPTE, contact

Society of Motion Picture and Television Engineers (SMPTE)

595 West Hartsdale Avenue

White Plains, NY 10607

Tel: 914-761-1100

Email: smpte@smpte.org

http://www.smpte.org

Visit this website organized by the ASC for a list of film schools and to learn about the career of cinematographer—the next step on the career ladder for camera operators.

Cinematographer.com

http://www.cinematographer.com

Campaign Workers

■ OVERVIEW

Campaign workers help candidates for government offices get elected. By calling voters, sending out fliers, and advertising on TV, radio, and the Internet, they educate the public about a candidate's strengths and concerns. Candidates for mayor, governor, Congress, president, and other local, state, and federal offices must use campaign workers and managers to handle many of the details of an election, such as budgets and expenses, fund-raising, and press relations. Campaign workers are needed all across the country, in cities large and small, to assist with primaries and elections.

■ HISTORY

"Tippecanoe and Tyler Too"—you may have heard of this song, an old tune from way back in 1840. It's not a folk ditty, but rather part of the presidential campaign of William Henry Harrison (known as "Old Tippecanoe"). Harrison, whose running mate was John Tyler, capitalized on his victory in the Battle of Tippecanoe. The tune, and the image of Harrison as a military hero, caught on, and it expanded the methods of campaigning to include slogans, press promotions, and "whistle-stop" tours (speeches at the railroad stations all along the campaign trail). Along with these new campaign methods, politicians also bought votes when they could, which led to campaign restrictions being passed in 1890. Variations on these concerns remain today, as government officials push for campaign reform that would limit the methods and sources of campaign funding.

■ THE JOB

If you've ever run for student council or for an office with an organization, you've already walked on the campaign trail. Maybe you've even volunteered at the campaign headquarters of a candidate for government office. If so, then you've seen that a good campaign requires much more than a good candidate—it must also have devoted volunteers and an organized manager. Colorful buttons with catchy slogans, brochures outlining the candidate's strengths, posters on walls, and signs in yards—all these things contribute to drawing the voter's attention to your candidate.

Campaign workers help develop campaign tactics, prepare speeches and press releases, and arrange for the candidate to shake hands, kiss babies, and generally connect with the public. Depending on the importance of the office their candidate is pursuing and whether it's on the local, state, or national level, the campaign is composed of workers taking on different responsibilities. Every campaign should have a manager who will organize the talents of all those working on a campaign: volunteers, media and political consultants, pollsters, and others. "The candidate hadn't put much of an organization into place," says Claudia Lindley about her experiences managing a congressional campaign. "I set up the office, arranged for a phone account, fax machine, computer. I hired a staff

QUICK FACTS

SCHOOL SUBJECTS
Business
Government

PERSONAL SKILLS
Communication/ideas
Leadership/management

WORK ENVIRONMENT
Indoors and outdoors
Primarily multiple locations

MINIMUM EDUCATION LEVEL
High school diploma

SALARY RANGE
$3,000/month to
$20,000/year to
$100,000+/year

CERTIFICATION OR LICENSING
None available

OUTLOOK
About as fast as the average

DOT
N/A

GOE
N/A

NOC
N/A

O*NET-SOC
N/A

A campaign worker hands out campaign materials to other volunteers who will walk through precincts.

and developed a strategy for asking for money." She also worked with a volunteer coordinator and the media people who created the radio and TV spots.

Campaign managers oversee fund-raising efforts, budgets, and expenses. Together with the consultants, they determine the public's interests and needs by analyzing public opinion polls and demographics. Then they produce ads and Web pages and arrange for media coverage that will allow their candidate to speak to those needs. Campaign managers also direct volunteers in putting together mailers, making phone calls, and distributing signs and fliers.

■ REQUIREMENTS
High School

During high school, you should take government, history, math, computer science, and business classes. English, speech, and foreign language classes will help you hone your oral and written communication skills.

Postsecondary Training

You can volunteer on a campaign, or even manage one, without any college education. Because the level of work consists of making calls and stuffing envelopes, you won't need much training outside of the specifics of how to use the campaign office machines. But to manage a large campaign, and to work as a campaign director for such organizations as the Democratic or Republican National Committees, you'll need a good, four-year education. You should major in political science, journalism, economics, history, or some other undergraduate program that includes course work in English composition, government, and math. The school you attend is important, as well—politics is all about connections.

Other Requirements

Claudia Lindley emphasizes the importance of self-confidence and energy when working as a campaign manager. People skills are important in organizing a campaign and in reaching the public. "You should be extremely assertive," she says, "without being abrasive." You should also have some sense of the industry and issues of the region in which you're working. You'll need the ability to analyze situations and statistics and to reach decisions quickly.

■ EXPLORING

There are many ways to gain experience as a campaign worker. You might help one of your friends run for student council, or even run for office yourself. You might also consider volunteering at the campaign office of a candidate who is running for local, state, or national office. Good workers are always needed to answer phones, prepare mailings, or perform general clerical duties. You may consider joining the local youth chapters of the political party of your choice. Contact the Democratic or Republican National Committees for more information. You might also consider learning more about the Green Party, a grass roots party that is organized in 33 states. Its platform focuses on environmentalism, non-violence, and social justice.

■ EMPLOYERS

From campaigns for the smallest local office to that of the president of the United States, workers are needed. However, once the campaign is over, campaign workers usually lose their jobs. Campaign workers find more steady employment working for political consultant firms or assisting pollsters and other political researchers. They might also find work organizing the fund-raising campaigns of nonprofit groups, colleges, and other organizations.

■ STARTING OUT

Volunteer for local political campaigns and advocate for public policy issues of interest to you. You can even participate in national elections by volunteering at your local Democratic, Republican, or Green Party headquarters. Claudia Lindley first became involved in campaigning when the state was considering putting a low-level radioactive waste compound near her farm. "I got very involved, very quickly," she says. "I got in touch with people around the country." The skills she developed in the process made her valuable to candidates needing campaign workers.

■ ADVANCEMENT

After a successful campaign, campaign workers may move on to manage other campaigns, or they may go to work on the staff of the official they helped get elected. They may become political consultants, contracting with candidates in a variety of different races across the country and around the world. They could also advance into a position with the Democratic or Republican National Committees or become political director for an organization or association.

■ EARNINGS

Campaign workers who answer phones, prepare mailings, and post fliers are generally unpaid. Managers, however, can make around $3,000 a month for their work, or much more when working on a large campaign. A manager overseeing a budget of millions of dollars is paid well, as are consultants. Political consultants can make well over $100,000 a year. These earnings are paid for by the candidate or by donations from campaign supporters. Unless they work full-time for an organization, campaign workers usually do not receive benefits.

■ WORK ENVIRONMENT

The work can be very stressful and require long days and weekends during a campaign. A manager must be available to the candidate at all times. Campaign workers may work in an active, energetic office, sharing in the excitement of a candidate's pursuit of office. But they may also be discouraged by the apathy of the general public in regard to government and politics.

The work can be tedious and exhausting, but those dedicated to a campaign usually receive recognition from the candidate. "You can distinguish yourself easily by actually doing the grunt work," Claudia Lindley says. "There are a lot of groupies who don't offer much to a campaign."

■ OUTLOOK

The media has become even more important in a political campaign. Campaign workers in the coming years will have to possess a good understanding of the use of TV and radio in gathering voter support. Campaign managers are also just learning how to best use the Internet. Maintaining a Web page has proven a popular way of educating the public about a candidate, while mass emails often provoke hostility among Internet users. Campaign workers will be involved in devising new methods of emailing voters and attracting more people to campaign websites.

■ FOR MORE INFORMATION

For information about political parties, election results, and campaign efforts, contact the following organizations:

Democratic National Committee
430 South Capitol Street, SE
Washington, DC 20003

Tel: 202-863-8000
http://www.democrats.org

Republican National Committee
310 First Street, SE
Washington, DC 20003
Tel: 202-863-8500
Email: info@rnc.org
http://www.rnc.org

Canning and Preserving Industry Workers

■ OVERVIEW

Canning and preserving industry workers monitor equipment and perform routine tasks in food-processing plants that can, preserve, and quick-freeze such foods as vegetables, fruits, frozen dinners, jams, jellies, preserves, pickles, and soups. They also process and preserve seafood, including shrimp, oysters, crabs, clams, and fish.

■ HISTORY

As soon as people learned to grow and harvest food, they faced the problem of keeping that food from spoiling so that it could last until the next harvest. Centuries ago, people discovered that salting, drying, and pickling could preserve many meats, fruits, and vegetables. In colonial America, most of this preserving was done in the home. Families grew their own fruits and vegetables and preserved them to make them last through the winter months.

In 1795, the French government sought better ways to feed its army, especially ways to keep foods from spoiling, and it offered a prize to anyone who could develop a method of keeping foods edible and portable for a long period of time. Nicolas Appert, a chef in Paris, took up the challenge and developed the first canning process. In 1810, Appert developed a system of bottling foods, corking the bottles and holding the corks in place with wire, and then heating the bottles. At the same time in England, the first tin-coated metal cans were developed, and these were soon applied to food preservation using Appert's method. Appert's process became known as *canning*.

Since the Industrial Revolution, and especially in the 20th century, advances in refrigeration and sanitation and new applications of many industrial processes of food preparation have almost completely transferred the business of preserving food to large factories. Freezing was applied to food preservation in the 1920s, and ways were sought to freeze foods as quickly as possible, thereby preserving not only their flavor but also their nutritional value. Scientists also discovered that certain chemicals could preserve food by killing off microorganisms or preventing them from reproducing. Later, irradiation became another, albeit controversial, method of food preservation.

Very few Americans today grow and preserve large quantities of their own food, and factory-preserved fruits, fish, soup, and vegetables are found in almost every refrigerator and kitchen cupboard in the nation. Canning and preservation techniques have made it possible for people to enjoy foods from all over the world, and at all times of the year.

For much of the past century, canning and preserving were labor-intensive; that is, they required many people to manually perform the various steps of processing, preserving, and packaging foods. In recent years, automated machinery and equipment, which are often computer-controlled, have greatly increased the quantity of foods that can be processed and have made it possible for many foods to be processed, canned, and preserved without ever being touched by human hands.

■ THE JOB

In order to operate successfully, a food-processing plant must have plenty of the foodstuff it processes. Therefore, many workers in the canning and preserving industry work outside processing plants arranging for this supply of raw materials. *Field contractors* negotiate with farmers to grow certain kinds of food crops for processing. They work with farmers to decide what to plant, how to grow the crop, and when to harvest it. They reach agreements concerning price, the quantity that will be delivered, and the quality standards that the crop

must meet. *Purchasing agents* purchase raw materials and other goods for processing.

When unprocessed food arrives at the factory, *graders,* including *fruit-buying graders,* examine produce and record its quality, or grade, and mark it for separation by class, size, color, and condition.

Wharf laborers unload catches of fish for processing from the wharf and transport the fish to the processing plant's storage area. *Fish-bin tenders* sort fish according to species and size.

At the plant, the *plant superintendent* coordinates processing activities to coincide with crop harvesting. The *plant manager* hires workers, contacts buyers, and coordinates maintenance and operation of plant machinery.

Most processing of food is done with automatic machines. *Dumping-machine operators* run machines that grip, tilt, and dump boxes of produce onto conveyor belts leading to washing vats. Workers then wash food and inspect the produce, removing damaged or spoiled items before they can be processed. *Sieve-grader tenders* and *sorting-machine operators* tend machines that sort vegetables, shrimp, and pickles according to size.

Many foods are bathed in brine, a concentrated solution of salt in water that acts as a preservative. *Brine makers* measure ingredients for the solution and boil it in a steam cooker for a specified amount of time. They test the solution's salinity with a hydrometer and pump it to a processing vat. They may also operate the vats and empty and clean them when necessary.

Plants that process fish and shellfish may kill, shell, and clean the fish before processing. *Crab butchers* butcher live crabs before canning. *Fish cleaners* and *fish-cleaning-machine operators* scale, slice open, and eviscerate fish. Using a shucking knife, *shellfish shuckers* pry open oyster, clam, and scallop shells and remove the meat. Shrimp are often shelled by machines that are operated by workers who must make adjustments according to the size of the shrimp. Later *separator operators* remove any sand or remaining shell particles from shellfish meats using water or air-agitating machines. Alternatively, bone pickers look for shell particles by placing shellfish meats under ultraviolet light and picking shell bits out by hand. Other workers operate machines that wash, steam, brine, and peel shellfish.

Often only one part of a fruit or vegetable is wanted for processing. Many workers operate machines that peel or extract the desired parts from produce. *Finisher operators* run machines that remove the skin and seeds from tomatoes, leaving pulp that is used in sauces and catsup. *Lye-peel operators* run machines that use lye and water to remove skins of fruits and vegetables. *Fruit-press opera-*

QUICK FACTS

SCHOOL SUBJECTS
Agriculture
Chemistry

PERSONAL SKILLS
Following instructions
Technical/scientific

WORK ENVIRONMENT
Primarily indoors
Primarily one location

MINIMUM EDUCATION LEVEL
High school diploma

SALARY RANGE
$13,930 to $21,920 to
$35,110

CERTIFICATION OR LICENSING
Required for certain positions

OUTLOOK
Decline

DOT
529

GOE
08.03.02

NOC
9461

O*NET-SOC
N/A

tors run power presses to extract juice from fruit for flavorings and syrup, and *extractor-machine operators* extract juice from citrus fruits.

Food must often be cut into pieces of the proper size and shape for preserving. *Meat blenders* grind meat for use in baby food. Many workers operate machines that cut or chop produce, and *fish butchers* and *fish choppers* cut fish into pieces and lengths for freezing or canning.

Next, foods are cooked. Some are cooked before and others after they are sealed in packages. Many vegetables are blanched (scalded with hot water or steam) before packaging, by *blanching-machine operators. Kettle cooks* and *kettle cook helpers* cook other fish, fruits, and vegetables in large kettles before packaging. These workers must measure and load water and uncooked food into the kettles; stir, monitor, and test foods as they cook; and remove cooked food from the kettles. Other workers cook fish, meat, and vegetables by deep-frying before freezing. *Vacuum-kettle cooks* vacuum-cook fruits and berries for jam and jelly.

Other foods, including many vegetables, are processed after they have been sealed in cans. *Packers* fill cans or jars with food to specified volume and weight. Other workers operate closing machines to put an airtight seal on the containers. Containers are then taken to retort chambers. *Retorts* are like huge steam pressure cookers, and they can heat food containers to temperatures between 240 degrees Fahrenheit and 260 degrees Fahrenheit. *Retort operators* load, start, and stop these machines according to specifications. Food must then be quickly cooled to stop cooking. *Pasteurizers* kill bacteria in bottles, canned foods, and beverages using a hot water spray or steam.

Some food is preserved using brine. *Picklers* mix ingredients for pickling vegetables, fruits, fish, and meat and soak these foods for a specified period of time. *Briners* immerse fresh fish fillets in brine to condition them for freezing.

Some food is prepared for canning by removing moisture, and some fish is smoked to preserve it. *Fish smokers* put salt-cured fish on racks in a smoke chamber and turn a valve to admit smoke into the chamber.

Many foods are frozen fresh or after blanching. *Freezing-room workers* move racks of packaged food in and out of freezing rooms. They keep track of the amount of time food has been in the freezing room and remove the food when it is sufficiently frozen to transport to a warehouse or onto delivery trucks. *Freezer-tunnel operators* quick-freeze foods.

Other foods, especially fruits, are preserved by drying. *Dehydrator tenders* bleach and dehydrate fruit, while other workers dry eggs, milk, and potatoes.

Cans are filled by a filling machine (left), then they pass through a closing machine (right). The filled cans are then weighed, cooked, labeled, and cased.

Once food has been canned, it is labeled, tested, and inspected. *Vacuum testers* tap can lids to make sure they are vacuum sealed. *Can inspectors* check seams of closed food and beverage cans by cutting and taking measurements of seams of sample cans. *X-ray inspectors* x-ray jars of baby food to ensure they contain no foreign materials.

Other workers clean cooking kettles and other equipment. *Production helpers* perform a variety of unskilled tasks in canning and preserving plants. Workers may also be designated according to the food they prepare: steak sauce makers, mincemeat makers, relish blenders, and horseradish makers, for example.

Cook room supervisors and *preparation supervisors* monitor and coordinate the activities of workers in preparing and canning foods. *Fish-processing supervisors* train new workers and inspect fish.

In large plants, each worker may perform one specific task. In smaller plants, one worker may perform many of the tasks necessary to preserve the food.

■ REQUIREMENTS
High School

There are no minimum educational requirements for many food-processing jobs, although most employers

CLARENCE BIRDSEYE AND FROZEN FOODS

Born in Brooklyn in 1886, Clarence Birdseye had to drop out of college and enter the business world due to his lack of funds. He spent the next five years as a fur trader in Labrador, Canada. While there, Birdseye observed that food preserved by the native technique of quickly freezing it in the dead of winter in barrels of seawater preserved its flavor and freshness, even when thawed and cooked months later.

Returning to the United States, by 1923 Birdseye had invented a machine for quick-freezing food under high pressure, then packing it into waxed cardboard boxes. His investment of $7 for ice, a fan, and barrels of brine netted him $22 million when the Goldman-Sachs Trading Corporation and the Postum Company (which later became known as General Foods) bought his patents and trademarks in 1929. By 1930, the general public could buy Birds Eye Frosted Foods-brand vegetables, seafood, and meat. Birdseye later went on to invent an infrared heat lamp, store-window spotlight, and a harpoon used for marking whales.

Source: http://inventors.about.com/library/inventors/blfrfood.htm

prefer to hire high school graduates; a high school diploma is essential for those seeking advancement. Beginners seldom need previous experience, and usually they can learn their jobs quickly. Generally there is up to one month of on-the-job training.

Postsecondary Training

Many plants provide orientation sessions for new workers and programs on safety and sanitation. For those who aspire to management positions, a college degree is recommended, with studies in accounting, management, and other business courses as well as chemistry.

Certification or Licensing

Some skilled and technical staff in plants in some states must be licensed. Retort room supervisors are required by the Food and Drug Administration to attend an instructional program in retort operation.

Other Requirements

Manual dexterity is a useful characteristic for many workers in the canning and preserving industry, as are reliability and willingness to learn.

■ EXPLORING

Students may arrange to tour a food-processing plant in their area. Such a visit can be a good way to get a general overview of the jobs in the plant. Talking to people employed in different jobs in canning or preserving plants is another good way to learn something about the field. Because some food-processing work is seasonal, part-time job opportunities for students may be limited. However, temporary employment, such as during summer harvest season, may be possible.

■ EMPLOYERS

Canning and preserving work is available in a variety of manufacturing plants. The types of products to be canned or preserved depend in part on what grows, grazes, or swims in a particular area. Coastal areas may have fish-processing plants (Alaska is famous for its salmon canneries), while the Midwest has more meat products. Farm regions may have plants that process products grown nearby. However, because of refrigeration and other technology, other factors, such as shipping routes and access to workers, may determine where plants are located. Manufacturers may be small companies or multinational organizations.

■ STARTING OUT

Applying to canneries, freezing plants, and other food-processing plants is the most direct method of finding work in this area. Employers may advertise openings in newspaper want ads or with the state employment service. Those interested in processing fish and seafood may find year-round work in canneries and processing ships in Alaska or follow the fishing seasons along the west and east coasts.

■ ADVANCEMENT

Workers with a high school education start out as sorters or helpers or in similar unskilled positions. Advancement opportunities from these positions are limited. In time, some workers can move into field contractor positions. For those interested in more advanced positions, such as food technologists and food scientists, a college degree in a related course of study is required.

■ EARNINGS

Although some products can be processed at any time during the year, the level of activity in many food-processing plants varies with the season, and earnings of workers vary accordingly. Larger plants overcome the seasonality of their food products by maintaining large inventories of raw foodstuffs, and workers for these plants generally work full time throughout the year. Earnings for workers in the canning and preserving industry vary widely. Many positions, especially at the entry level, pay little more than the minimum wage. The following averages show the variety of earnings possible in this industry. According to the U.S. Department of Labor, those processing workers working in preserving fruits and vegetables earned an average of $11.78 per hour in 2002. For full-time work, this wage translates into a yearly income of approximately $24,490. Packaging and filling machine operators and tenders earned an average of $11.07 per hour (approximately $23,005 annually) in 2002. Slaughterers and meat packers made $9.80 an hour, or $20,384 per year. Those in supervisory positions, such as plant managers, have higher earnings. According to the U.S. Department of Labor, supervisors made an average of $18.78 an hour, or $39,062 per year. Industry-wide, the Department of Labor reported that the lowest 10 percent of food batchmakers (the category that best describes canning and preserving workers) made $13,930 per year, and the top 10 percent made $35,110 per year, with a median of $21,920.

Generally, seasonal workers earn an hourly wage; some, particularly those working on processing ships or for canneries in Alaska, also receive board and lodging. Benefits vary from company to company.

WORK ENVIRONMENT

Canning and preserving plants are located in many parts of the country. Most plants are located close to the supply source and are staffed by local people who sometimes hold other jobs as well. During harvest season, plants may operate 24 hours a day, with three work shifts.

In plants where food is frozen, some workers spend considerable time in temperatures that are well below freezing. These workers wear special clothing and take periodic warm-up breaks during the day. Canneries, on the other hand, may be damp, noisy, and odorous. In some jobs, workers need to be on their feet for long periods, and often the tasks are very repetitive. Injuries, whether from accidents or repetitive stress, are common.

OUTLOOK

The use of automated equipment and computer technology throughout the food-processing industry means that fewer people will be needed to process, preserve, and can foods. Wherever it is efficient and economical, machines will take over the tasks that people have been doing. Therefore, the U.S. Department of Labor predicts a decline in overall employment in the industry through 2012. Researchers and technical workers with specialized expertise and college-level training will have the best employment opportunities. Furthermore, jobs will be difficult to get, as many companies will prefer to employ migrant

workers and undocumented immigrants, who can be paid lesser wages and do not demand worker's compensation or benefits.

In some kinds of food processing, such as the fish canneries in Alaska, employment levels are related to weather and other natural factors that vary from year to year.

■ FOR MORE INFORMATION

For information on the frozen food industry, contact
American Frozen Food Institute
2000 Corporate Ridge, Suite 1000
McLean, VA 22102
Tel: 703-821-0770
Email: info@affi.com
http://www.affi.com

For information on careers, education, scholarships, and student memberships, contact
Institute of Food Technologists
525 West Van Buren, Suite 1000
Chicago, IL 60607
Tel: 800-438-3663
http://www.ift.org

For information on the industry and safety issues, contact
National Food Processors Association
1350 I Street, NW, Suite 300
Washington, DC 20005
Tel: 202-639-5900
http://www.nfpa-food.org

Cardiologists

■ OVERVIEW

Cardiologists are physicians who practice in the subspecialty of internal medicine that concentrates on the diagnosis and treatment of heart disease. In most instances, cardiologists treat patients on a consultative basis to determine if the symptoms the patients are exhibiting are signs of heart disease.

■ HISTORY

In 1749, cardiology became a medical specialty when Jean Baptiste Senac published a comprehensive study of the heart. The development of modern cardiology heightened in 1816 when Rene Laennec invented the stethoscope. By the middle of the 19th century, the stethoscope was refined and routinely used as a diagnostic tool for the heart. Further developments, such as Carlo Matteucci's illustrated discovery of the heart's electrical charge in 1838 and Willem Einthoven's modification of the string galvanometer used to record the electrical impulses of the heart in 1903, led to the beginning stages of electrocardiography. Einthoven later refined his device and invented the electrocardiograph, an achievement that won him the Nobel Prize in 1924. Werner Forssman, Dickinson Richards, and Andre F. Cournand also won the Nobel Prize in 1956 for their use of the catheter to study the circulatory system and the heart. This achievement was made possible because of Forssman's earlier invention of the cardiac catheterization technique.

During the latter half of the 20th century, cardiology was marked by advancements in heart surgery. The first heart transplant was performed by Christiaan Barnard in 1967, while the first artificial heart was used in 1982 by a team at the University of Utah. In July 2001, a man received the first completely implanted, battery-operated artificial heart in an experimental procedure at the University of Louisville.

■ THE JOB

During their initial interview, cardiologists review the patient's medical history. After taking the medical history, cardiologists then perform a physical examination. This is their first opportunity to listen to the patient's heart. Often, a cardiologist can tell if there is a cardiac problem by listening to the rhythm of the heartbeat. For example, when examining a patient for a heart murmur (an abnormal sound), cardiologists will be able to tell if it is an innocent murmur, or whether it could cause problems.

There are several tests cardiologists use to aid in patient evaluation and diagnosis. The most common test is the *electrocardiogram* (ECG or EKG). An ECG measures the electrical activity produced by heart contractions and outputs a graph illustrating this. Many problems can be detected through ECGs.

Cardiac catheterization is another type of test. A small tube is inserted through a blood vessel into or near the heart. This procedure is used to take pictures of the heart, which cardiologists can use for diagnosis as well as to evaluate the body's electrical system and in some cases, to remove obstructions.

Another test is the *echocardiogram*. During this procedure, high-pitched sounds, inaudible to the human ear, are sent into the body. Their echoes are plotted by a transducer to create a picture of the heart. A stress echocardiogram evaluates the heart to measure the supply of blood going to the muscles before and after exercise.

After a diagnosis is made, cardiologists prescribe treatment, which may include drugs, such as blood pressure medications or blood thinners, or lifestyle changes, such as diet and exercise. If surgery is required cardiologists refer patients to thoracic surgeons. Even though cardiologists do not perform surgery, many surgeons request cardiologists to consult in the pre-operative phase of treatment.

A patient may not necessarily have symptoms of heart disease but may have risk factors. These might include a family history of heart problems, history of smoking or obesity, or presence of diseases like diabetes. In such cases, cardiologists often provide information and advice to their patients regarding the prevention of cardiac disease.

■ REQUIREMENTS
Postsecondary Training

Once you receive your M.D. degree and become licensed to practice medicine (see Physicians), you must take seven to eight more years of additional training. This includes an internship that may last from one to two years and a six-year residency program. Cardiologists spend three years in a residency program in internal medicine and another three years in a residency program in the subspecialty of cardiology.

Certification or Licensing

Cardiologists should be board certified by the American Board of Internal Medicine (ABIM) in both internal medicine and then in the cardiology subspecialty. To be certified in internal medicine, you need to have completed medical school and at least three years of additional training as well as pass a comprehensive exam. Certification in cardiology requires at least three more years of accredited training (in cardiology), proven clinical competence, and passing another comprehensive exam. In 1990, the ABIM began issuing certificates that carried time limitations. This was done to ensure that all certified doctors maintain a high level of competency. For continuing medical education, cardiologists can attend conferences, lectures, or specialized readings.

QUICK FACTS

SCHOOL SUBJECTS
Biology
Health

PERSONAL SKILLS
Helping/teaching
Technical/scientific

WORK ENVIRONMENT
Primarily indoors
Primarily multiple locations

MINIMUM EDUCATION LEVEL
Medical degree

SALARY RANGE
$47,710 to $111,740 to $385,000+

CERTIFICATION OR LICENSING
Required by all states

OUTLOOK
About as fast as the average

DOT
070

GOE
02.03.01

NOC
3112

O*NET-SOC
29-1069.99

Other Requirements

Many cardiologists choose to become members of the American College of Cardiology. Membership is a sign of a high level of professionalism and competence. To be considered for various levels of membership, the college takes into account the physician's length of service, board certifications, and scientific accomplishments. The highest level, Fellow, allows the use of the initials F.A.C.C. (Fellow of the American College of Cardiology).

Cardiologists need a nurturing personality. The needs of the patient must always come before their own needs. Cardiologists must be willing to put aside their own concerns while they are responsible for the care of a patient.

■ EARNINGS

Earnings for cardiologists vary due to factors such as the number of years the cardiologist has been in practice, the size and type of practice (private practice, large group practice, hospital, etc.), and the geographic location. Interns may only make only about $47,710 per year. More experienced cardiologists make significantly more money. According to a 2002 Medical Group Management Association report, physicians specializing in invasive cardiology reported average earnings of $385,000; those in noninvasive cardiology $307,618 per year. American Medical Group Association reported average earnings of $307,497. Even though these figures were about 6 percent below 2001 earnings, cardiologists remain some of the best-compensated of all doctors.

Benefits will depend on the employer, but usually include such things as health insurance and retirement plans.

■ OUTLOOK

The influence of managed care is being felt in the field of cardiology. The usual inpatient time for someone who has suffered a heart attack has been greatly reduced. Years ago it was common for heart attack patients to remain in the hospital for a month. However, inpatient hospital time has been steadily decreasing. Today it is not uncommon for a patient to stay in the hospital only five days, and sometimes just two.

Another effect of managed care is that before its introduction, it was not unusual for a patient with chest pain to automatically have an angiogram. Angiograms are very expensive, however, and doctors do not prescribe them as quickly as before.

Another influence on cardiology is the constant research that is being performed in the field. With the influx of new information, treatment processes are continually evolving. According to the U.S. Department of Labor, the employment of physicians in general is expected to increase about as fast as the average for all occupations through 2012. Due to the aging population, cardiologists should continue to see a strong outlook.

■ FOR MORE INFORMATION

Following are organizations that provide information on the field of cardiology and possible sources of certification information.

American Board of Internal Medicine
510 Walnut Street, Suite 1700
Philadelphia, PA 19106-3699
Tel: 800-441-2246
Email: request@abim.org
http://www.abim.org

American College of Cardiology
9111 Old Georgetown Road
Bethesda, MD 20814-1699
Tel: 800-253-4636 ext. 694
http://www.acc.org

THE ARTIFICIAL HEART

Sometimes called the "Holy Grail" of modern medicine, the artificial heart remains an elusive goal of twenty-first century science. The human heart may seem to be a simple pump, but its intricacies—and its ability to pump thousands upon thousands of times a day—defy even advanced engineering. Added to this is the need for an external power source and massive foreign-body rejection problems.

In late 1982, Barney Clark, a retired dentist, became the first human subject to receive an artificial heart. The device, Dr. Robert Jarvik's Jarvik-7, was an unwieldy apparatus; its need for a power supply outside the body left the patient open to the possibility of infection. Nonetheless, Clark survived 112 days with the device.

In the two decades since Barney Clark, bioengineering technology has advanced greatly. In 2001, a man named Robert Tools was implanted with the first fully self-contained, internal artificial heart, the AbioCor Implantable Replacement Heart, at Jewish Hospital in Louisville, Kentucky. By 2004, six other patients had also been fitted with the device.

The teams of scientists, engineers, and doctors working on developing the artificial heart is making great progress, but the device is still considered experimental. It is for this reason that implantation is limited to those with a high probability of dying within 30 days without the device, and who are not candidates for heart transplants or other treatments.

Source: http://wikipedia.org and http://www.heartpioneers.com

Cardiovascular Technologists

■ OVERVIEW

Cardiovascular technologists assist physicians in diagnosing and treating heart and blood vessel ailments. Depending on their specialties, they operate electrocardiograph machines, perform Holter monitor and stress testing, and assist in cardiac catheterization procedures and ultrasound testing. These tasks help the physicians diagnose heart disease and monitor progress during treatment. Cardiovascular technologists hold approximately 42,870 jobs in the United States.

■ HISTORY

Electrocardiography can be traced back 300 years to the work of the Dutch anatomist and physiologist Jan Swammerdam, who in 1678 demonstrated that a frog's leg will contract when stimulated with an electrical current. It was not until 1856, however, that two German anatomists, Albert von Kolliker and Heinrich M. Mueller, showed that when a frog's heart contracted, it produced a small electrical current. In succeeding years, the electrical behavior of beating hearts was extensively studied, but always with the chest open and the heart exposed.

In 1887, Augustus Desire Waller discovered that the electrical current of the human heart could be measured with the chest closed. He was able to do this by placing one electrode on a person's chest and another on the person's back and connecting them to a monitoring device. In 1903, a Dutch professor of physiology, Willem Einthoven, perfected the monitoring device so that even the faintest currents from the heart could be detected and recorded graphically.

Throughout the rest of the 20th century, medical researchers made further advancements and refinements on this machine. By the 1940s, for instance, portable electrocardiographs were in use, allowing electrocardiograms to be made in a physician's office or at a patient's bedside. During the 1960s, computerized electrocardiographs were developed to aid physicians in the interpretation of test results. Today, electrocardiographs are widely used in routine physicals, in presurgical physicals, in diagnosing disease, and in monitoring the effects of prescribed therapy. The wide use of these devices ensures a continuing need for trained personnel to operate them.

■ THE JOB

Technologists who assist physicians in the diagnosis and treatment of heart disease are known as cardiovascular technologists. (*Cardio* means heart; *vascular* refers to the blood vessel/circulatory system.) Increasingly, hospitals are centralizing cardiovascular services under one full cardiovascular "service line" overseen by the same administrator. In addition to cardiovascular technologists, the cardiovascular team at a hospital may include radiology (X-ray) technologists, nuclear medicine technologists, nurses, physician assistants, respiratory technicians, and respiratory therapists. For their part, the cardiovascular technologists contribute by performing one or more of a wide range of procedures in cardiovascular medicine, including invasive (enters a body cavity or interrupts normal body functions), noninvasive, peripheral vascular, or echocardiography (ultrasound) procedures. In most facilities, technologists use equipment that is among the most advanced in the medical field; drug therapies also may be used as part of the diagnostic imaging procedures or in addition to them. Technologists' services may be required when the patient's condition is first being explored, before surgery, during surgery (cardiology technologists primarily), or during rehabilitation of the patient. Some of the work is performed on an outpatient basis.

Depending on their specific areas of skill, some cardiovascular technologists are employed in nonhospital health care facilities. For example, they may work for clinics, mobile medical services, or private doctors' offices. Much of their equipment can go just about anywhere.

Some of the specific duties of cardiovascular technologists are described in the following paragraphs. Exact titles of these technologists often vary from medical facility to medical facility because there is no standardized naming system. *Electrocardiograph technologists,* or *EKG technologists,* use an electrocardiograph machine to detect the electronic impulses that come from a patient's heart. The EKG machine records these signals on a paper graph called an *electrocardiogram.* The electronic impulses recorded by the EKG machine can tell the physician about the action of the heart during and between the individual heartbeats. This in turn reveals important information about the condition of the heart, including irregular heartbeats or the presence of blocked arteries, which the physician can use to diagnose heart disease, monitor progress during treatment, or check the patient's condition after recovery.

To use an EKG machine, the technologist attaches electrodes (small, disklike devices about the size of a silver dollar) to the patient's chest. Wires attached to the electrodes lead to the EKG machine. Twelve or more leads may be attached. To get a better reading from the electrodes, the technologist may first apply an adhesive gel to the patient's skin that helps to conduct the electrical impulses. The technologist then operates controls on the

EKG machine or (more commonly) enters commands for the machine into a computer. The electrodes pick up the electronic signals from the heart and transmit them to the EKG machine. The machine registers and makes a printout of the signals, with a stylus (pen) recording their pattern on a long roll of graph paper.

During the test, the technologist may move the electrodes in order to get readings of electrical activity in different parts of the heart muscle. Since EKG equipment can be sensitive to electrical impulses from other sources, such as other parts of the patient's body or equipment in the room where the EKG test is being done, the technologist must watch for false readings.

After the test, the EKG technologist takes the electrocardiogram off the machine, edits it or makes notes on it, and sends it to the physician (usually a cardiologist, or heart specialist). Physicians may have computer assistance to help them use and interpret the electrocardiogram; special software is available to assist them with their diagnoses.

EKG technologists do not have to repair EKG machines, but they do have to keep an eye on them and know when they are malfunctioning so they can call someone for repairs. They also may keep the machines stocked with paper. Of all the cardiovascular technical positions, EKG technologist positions are the most numerous.

Holter monitoring and stress testing may be performed by *Holter monitor technologists* or *stress test technologists*, respectively, or they may be additional duties of some EKG technologists. In *Holter monitoring*, electrodes are fastened to the patient's chest, and a small, portable monitor is strapped to the patient's body, often at the waist. The small monitor contains a magnetic tape or cassette that records the action of the heart during activity—as the patient moves, sits, stands, sleeps, etc. The patient is required to wear the Holter monitor for 24 to 48 hours while he or she goes about normal daily activities. When the patient returns to the hospital, the technologist removes the magnetic tape or cassette from the monitor and puts it in a scanner to produce audio and visual representations of heart activity. (Hearing how the heart sounds during activity helps physicians diagnose a possible heart condition.) The technologist reviews and analyzes the information revealed in the tape. Finally, the technologist may print out the parts of the tape that show abnormal heart patterns or make a full tape for the physician.

Stress tests record the heart's performance during physical activity. In one type of stress test, the technologist connects the patient to the EKG machine, attaching electrodes to the patient's arms, legs, and chest, and obtains a reading of the patient's resting heart activity and blood pressure. Then, the patient is asked to walk on a treadmill for a designated period of time while the technologist and the physician monitor the heart. The treadmill speed is increased so that the technologist and physician can see what happens when the heart is put under higher levels of exertion.

Cardiology technologists specialize in providing support for *cardiac catheterization* (tubing) procedures. These procedures are classified as invasive because they require the physician and attending technologists to enter a body cavity or interrupt normal body functions. In one cardiac catheterization procedure—an *angiogram*—a catheter (tube) is inserted into the heart (usually by way of a blood vessel in the leg) in order to see the condition of the heart blood vessels, whether there is a blockage. In another procedure, known as *angioplasty*, a catheter with a balloon at the end is inserted into an artery to widen it. According to the American Heart Association's 2004 Heart and Stroke Statistical Update, 1,051,000 angioplasties were done in the United States in 2001. Of these, 571,000 were percutaneous transluminal coronary angioplasties. Cardiology technologists also perform a variety of other procedures.

Unlike some of the other cardiovascular technologists, cardiology technologists actually assist in surgical procedures. They may help secure the patient to the table, set up a 35mm video camera or other imaging device under the instructions of the physician (to produce images that assist the physician in guiding the catheter through the cardiovascular system), enter information about the surgical procedure (as it is taking place) into a computer, and provide other support. After the procedure, the technologist may process the angiographic film for use by the physician. Cardiology technologists may also assist during open-heart surgery by preparing and monitoring the patient and placing or monitoring pacemakers.

Vascular technologists and *echocardiographers* are specialists

QUICK FACTS

SCHOOL SUBJECTS
Biology
Health

PERSONAL SKILLS
Communication/ideas
Technical/scientific

WORK ENVIRONMENT
Primarily indoors
Primarily one location

MINIMUM EDUCATION LEVEL
Some postsecondary training

SALARY RANGE
$20,920 to $36,430 to $56,080

CERTIFICATION OR LICENSING
Voluntary

OUTLOOK
Faster than the average

DOT
078

GOE
14.05.01

NOC
3217

O*NET-SOC
29-2031.00

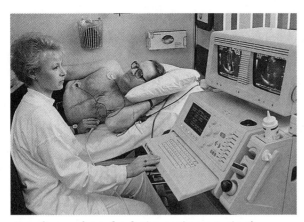

A cardiovascular technologist monitors a patient's heart rate.

in noninvasive cardiovascular procedures and use ultrasound equipment to obtain and record information about the condition of the heart. Ultrasound equipment is used to send out sound waves to the area of the body being studied; when the sound waves hit the part being studied, they send echoes to the ultrasound machine. The echoes are "read" by the machine, which creates an image on a monitor, permitting the technologist to get an instant "image" of the part of the body and its condition. Vascular technologists are specialists in the use of ultrasound equipment to study blood flow and circulation problems. Echocardiographers are specialists in the use of ultrasound equipment to evaluate the heart and its structures, such as the valves.

Cardiac monitor technicians are similar to and sometimes perform some of the same duties as EKG technologists. Usually working in the intensive care unit or cardio-care unit of the hospital, cardiac monitor technicians keep watch over the patient, monitoring screens to detect any sign that a patient's heart is not beating as it should. Cardiac monitor technicians begin their shift by reviewing the patient's records to familiarize themselves with what the patient's normal heart rhythms should be, what the current pattern is, and what types of problems have been observed. Throughout the shift, cardiac monitor technicians watch for heart rhythm irregularities that need prompt medical attention. Should there be any, they notify a nurse or doctor immediately so that appropriate care can be given.

In addition to these positions, other cardiovascular technologists specialize in a particular aspect of health care. For example, *cardiopulmonary technologists* specialize in procedures for diagnosing problems with the heart and lungs. They may conduct electrocardiograph, phonocardiograph (sound recordings of the heart's valves and of the blood passing through them), echocardiograph, stress testing, and respiratory test procedures.

Cardiopulmonary technologists also may assist on cardiac catheterization procedures, measuring and recording information about the patient's cardiovascular and pulmonary systems during the procedure and alerting the cardiac catheterization team to any problems.

■ REQUIREMENTS
High School

At a minimum, cardiovascular technologists need a high school diploma or equivalent to enter the field. Although no specific high school classes will directly prepare you to be a technologist, learning how to learn and getting a good grounding in basic high school subjects are important to all technologist positions.

During high school, you should take English, health, biology, and typing. You also might consider courses in social sciences to help you understand the social and psychological needs of patients.

Postsecondary Training

In the past, many EKG operators were trained on the job by an EKG supervisor. This still may be true for some EKG technician positions. Increasingly, however, EKG technologists get postsecondary schooling before they are hired. Holter monitoring and stress testing may be part of your EKG schooling, or they may be learned through additional training. Ultrasound and cardiology technologists tend to have the most postsecondary schooling (up to a four-year bachelor's degree) and have the most extensive academic/experience requirements for credentialing purposes.

You can enter these positions without having had previous health care experience. However, some previous exposure to the business side of health care or even training in related areas is helpful. With academic training or professional experience in nursing, radiology science, or respiratory science, for example, you may be able to move into cardiology technology.

As a rule of thumb, medical employers value postsecondary schooling that gives you actual hands-on experience with patients in addition to classroom training. At many of the schools that train cardiovascular technologists, you work with patients in a variety of health care settings and train on more than one brand of equipment.

Some employers still have a physician or EKG department manager train EKG technicians on the job. Training generally lasts from one to six months. Trainees learn how to operate the EKG machine, how to produce and edit the electrocardiogram, and other related tasks.

Some vocational, technical, and junior colleges have one- or two-year training programs in EKG technology, Holter monitoring, stress testing, or all three; otherwise,

EKG technologists may obtain training in Holter and stress procedures after they've already started working, either on the job or through an additional six months or more of schooling. Formal academic programs give technologists more preparation in the subject than is available with most on-the-job training and allow them to earn a certificate (one-year programs) or associate's degree (two-year programs). The American Medical Association (AMA)'s *Allied Health Directory* has listings of accredited EKG programs.

Ultrasound technologists usually need a high school diploma or equivalent plus one, two, or four years of postsecondary schooling in a trade school, technical school, or community college. Vascular technologists also may be trained on the job. Again, a list of accredited programs can be found in the AMA's *Allied Health Directory;* also, a directory of training opportunities in sonography is available from the Society of Diagnostic Medical Sonography.

Cardiology technologists tend to have the highest academic requirements of all; for example, a four-year bachelor of science degree, a two-year associate's degree, or a certificate of completion from a hospital, trade, or technical cardiovascular program. A two-year program at a junior or community college might include one year of core classes (e.g., mathematics, biology, chemistry, and anatomy) and one year of specialized classes in cardiology procedures.

Cardiac monitor technicians need a high school diploma or equivalent, with additional educational requirements similar to those of EKG technicians.

Certification or Licensing

Right now, certification or licensing for cardiovascular technologists is voluntary, but the move to state licensing is expected in the near future. Many credentialing bodies for cardiovascular and pulmonary positions exist, including American Registry of Diagnostic Medical Sonographers (ARDMS), Cardiovascular Credentialing International (CCI), and others, and there are more than a dozen possible credentials for cardiovascular technologists. For example, sonographers can take an exam from ARDMS to receive credentialing in sonography. Their credentials may be as registered diagnostic medical sonographer, registered diagnostic cardiac sonographer, or registered vascular technologist. Credentialing requirements for cardiology technologists or ultrasound technologists may include a test plus formal academic and on-the-job requirements. Professional experience or academic training in a related field, such as nursing, radiology science, and respiratory science, may be acceptable as part of these formal academic and professional require-

ments. As with continuing education, certification is a sign of interest and dedication to the field and is generally favorably regarded by potential employers.

Cardiology is a cutting-edge area of medicine, with constant advancements, and medical equipment relating to the heart is continually updated. Therefore, keeping up with new developments is vital. In addition, technologists who add to their qualifications through taking part in

WORDS TO KNOW

Angioplasty: Procedure involving insertion into the heart of a catheter (tube) with a balloon at one end to widen a blocked blood vessel.

Cardiologist: Physician who specializes in the heart; the prefix "cardio" means "heart."

Cardiology: Of or relating to the heart.

Cardiopulmonary: Of or relating to the heart or lungs.

Cardiovascular: Having to do with the heart ("cardio") and the vessels around it ("vascular").

Catheter: Small tube.

Catheterization: Procedure involving insertion of a catheter (tube).

Congenital: Condition or opportunity for condition that has existed since birth.

Diagnostic: Disease- or condition-identifying (such as "diagnostic tests").

Echocardiography: Procedure for studying the structure and motion of the heart using ultrasound technology.

Electrocardiogram: The paper printout showing the results of the EKG test.

Electrocardiograph (EKG) machine: Detects the electronic impulses that come from a patient's heart during or between heartbeats, which may reveal heart abnormalities, and records that information in the form of a paper graph called an electrocardiogram.

Electrode: Device that conducts electricity.

Holter monitor: Cardiac-function monitoring device.

Invasive: A medical procedure that penetrates into a body cavity or interrupts normal body functions; examples in cardiology include cardiac catheterization procedures.

Noninvasive: A medical procedure that does not penetrate into a body cavity or interrupt body functions; examples in cardiology include ultrasound tests.

Phonocardiograph: Sound recordings of the heart's valves and of the blood passing through them.

Radiographs: X rays.

Vascular: Relating to the blood vessels; vascular technologists are concerned about the blood vessels around the heart.

Did You Know?

Were you surprised to read that heart disease is the leading killer of both American men and women? You're not alone. The perception is that heart disease primarily haunts men; everyone thinks of the middle-aged, overweight Type A business executive as being the most likely to have a heart attack. But the truth is that women have about half of the cases of heart disease in this country and suffer from half of the heart attacks (which kill six times more women than breast cancer every year).

Men tend to have heart attacks beginning around age 40, while women are more likely to have one after age 60. Physicians think this may be due to the loss of estrogen in women after menopause. The last several years have seen the medical profession begin to make a stronger effort to include female subjects in their heart disease studies and otherwise recognize that heart disease is an equal-opportunity killer.

continuing education tend to earn more money and have more employment opportunities. Major professional societies encourage and provide the opportunities for professionals to continue their education.

Other Requirements

Technicians must be able to put patients at ease about the procedure they are to undergo. Therefore, you should be pleasant, patient, alert, and able to understand and sympathize with the feelings of others. When explaining a procedure to patients, cardiovascular technicians should be able to do so in a calm, reassuring, and confident manner.

■ EXPLORING

Prospective cardiovascular technologists will find it difficult to gain any direct experience on a part-time basis in electrocardiography. The first experience with the work generally comes during on-the-job training sessions. You may, however, be able to gain some exposure to patient-care activities in general by signing up for volunteer work at a local hospital. In addition, you can arrange to visit a hospital, clinic, or physician's office where electrocardiographs are taken. In this way, you may be able to watch a technician at work or at least talk to a technician about what the work is like.

■ EMPLOYERS

There are approximately 42,870 cardiovascular technologists employed in the United States. Most work in hos-

pitals, but employment can be found in physicians' offices, clinics, rehab centers, or anyplace electrocardiographs are taken.

■ STARTING OUT

Because most cardiovascular technologists receive their initial training on their first job, great care should be taken in finding this first employer. Pay close attention not only to the pay and working conditions, but also to the kind of on-the-job training that is provided for each prospective position. High school vocational counselors may be able to tell you which hospitals have good reputations for EKG training programs. Applying directly to hospitals is a common way of entering the field. Information also can be gained by reading the classified ads in the newspaper and from talking with friends and relatives who work in hospitals.

For students who graduate from one- to two-year training programs, finding a first job should be easier. First, employers are always eager to hire people who are already trained. Second, these graduates can be less concerned about the training programs offered by their employers. Third, they should find that their teachers and guidance counselors can be excellent sources of information about job possibilities in the area. If the training program includes practical experience, graduates may find that the hospital in which they trained or worked before graduation would be willing to hire them after graduation.

■ ADVANCEMENT

Opportunities for advancement are best for cardiovascular technologists who learn to do or assist with more complex procedures, such as stress testing, Holter monitoring, echocardiography, and cardiac catheterization. With proper training and experience, these technicians may eventually become cardiovascular technologists, echocardiography technologists, cardiopulmonary technicians, cardiology technologists, or other specialty technicians or technologists.

In addition to these kinds of specialty positions, experienced technicians may also be able to advance to various supervisory and training posts.

■ EARNINGS

The median salary for cardiovascular technologists was $36,430 in 2002, according to the U.S. Department of Labor. The lowest paid 10 percent earned less than $20,920, and the highest paid 10 percent earned more than $56,080 annually. Earnings can vary by size and type of employer. For example, technologists working in doctors' offices had the mean annual income $53,030, while those in hospitals had the median $36,780. Those with formal training earn more than those who trained on the job, and those who are able to perform more sophisticated tests, such as Holter monitoring and stress testing, are paid more than those who perform only the basic electrocardiograph tests.

Technologists working in hospitals receive the same fringe benefits as other hospital workers, including medical insurance, paid vacations, and sick leave. In some cases, benefits also include educational assistance, retirement plans, and uniform allowances.

WORK ENVIRONMENT

Cardiovascular technologists usually work in clean, quiet, well-lighted surroundings. They generally work five-day, 40-hour weeks, although technicians working in small hospitals may be on 24-hour call for emergencies, and all technicians in hospitals, large or small, can expect to do occasional evening or weekend work. With the growing emphasis in health care on cost containment, more jobs are likely to develop in outpatient settings, so in the future it is likely that cardiovascular technologists will work more often in clinics, health maintenance organizations, and other nonhospital locations.

Cardiovascular technologists generally work with patients who are ill or who have reason to fear they might be ill. With this in mind, there are opportunities for the technicians to do these people some good, but there is also a chance of causing some unintentional harm as well: A well-conducted test can reduce anxieties or make a physician's job easier; a misplaced electrode or an error in recordkeeping could cause an incorrect diagnosis. Technicians need to be able to cope with these responsibilities and consistently conduct their work in the best interests of their patients.

Part of the technician's job includes putting patients at ease about the procedure they are to undergo. Toward that end, technicians should be pleasant, patient, alert, and able to understand and sympathize with the feelings of others. In explaining the nature of the procedure to patients, cardiovascular technicians should be able to do so in a calm, reassuring, and confident manner.

Inevitably, some patients will try to get information about their medical situation from the technician. In such cases, technicians need to be both tactful and firm in explaining that they are only taking the electrocardiogram; the interpretation is for the physician to make.

Another large part of a technician's job involves getting along well with other members of the hospital staff. This task is sometimes made more difficult by the fact that in most hospitals there is a formal, often rigid, status structure, and cardiovascular technologists may find themselves in a relatively low position in that structure. In emergency situations or at other moments of frustration, cardiovascular technologists may find themselves dealt with brusquely or angrily. Technicians should not take outbursts or rude treatment personally, but instead should respond with stability and maturity.

OUTLOOK

The overall employment of cardiovascular technologists and technicians should grow faster than the average through 2012, according to the U.S. Department of Labor. Growth will be primarily due to the increasing numbers of older people who have a higher incidence of heart problems. The labor department, however, projects employment for EKG technicians to decline during this same period as hospitals train other health care personnel to perform basic EKG procedures.

FOR MORE INFORMATION

For information on careers, contact
Alliance of Cardiovascular Professionals
Thalia Landing Offices, Bldg. 2
4356 Bonney Road, #103
Virginia Beach, VA 23452-1200
Tel: 757-497-1225
http://www.acp-online.org

For information on the medical field, including listings of accredited medical programs, contact
American Medical Association
515 North State Street
Chicago, IL 60610
Tel: 312-464-5000
http://www.ama-assn.org

For information on certification or licensing, contact
**American Registry of Diagnostic Medical
   Sonographers**
51 Monroe Street
Plaza East One
Rockville, MD 20850-2400
Tel: 800-541-9754
http://www.ardms.org

For information on credentials, contact
Cardiovascular Credentialing International
1500 Sunday Drive, Suite 102
Raleigh, NC 27607
Tel: 800-326-0268
http://cci-online.org

Career and Employment Counselors and Technicians

■ OVERVIEW

Career and employment counselors and technicians, who are also known as *vocational counselors*, provide advice to individuals or groups about occupations, careers, career decision making, career planning, and other career development-related questions or conflicts. *Career guidance technicians* collect pertinent information to support both the counselor and applicant during the job search.

■ HISTORY

The first funded employment office in the United States was established in San Francisco in 1886. However, it wasn't until the turn of the century that public interest in improving educational conditions began to develop. The Civic Service House in Boston began the United States' first program of vocational guidance, and the Vocational Bureau was established in 1908 to help young people choose, train, and enter appropriate careers.

The idea of vocational counseling became so appealing that by 1910 a national conference on vocational guidance was held in Boston. The federal government gave support to vocational counseling by initiating a program to assist veterans of World War I in readjusting to civilian life. During the Depression years, agencies such as the Civilian Conservation Corps and the National Youth Administration made attempts at vocational counseling.

On June 6, 1933, the Wagner-Pyser Act established the United States Employment Service. States came into the Service one by one, with each state developing its own plan under the prescribed limits of the Act. By the end of World War II, the Veterans Administration was counseling more than 50,000 veterans each month. Other state and federal government agencies now involved with vocational guidance services include the Bureau of Indian Affairs, the Bureau of Apprenticeship and Training, the Office of Manpower Development, and the Department of Education. In 1980, the National Career Development Association (NCDA), founded in 1913, established a committee for the pre-service and in-service training of vocational guidance personnel. The NCDA established a national credentialing process in 1984.

The profession of employment counseling has become important to the welfare of society as well as to the individuals within it. Each year thousands of people need help in acquiring the kinds of information that make it possible for them to take advantage of today's career opportunities.

■ THE JOB

Certified career counselors help people make decisions and plan life and career directions. They tailor strategies and techniques to the specific needs of the person seeking help. Counselors conduct individual and group counseling sessions to help identify life and career goals. They administer and interpret tests and inventories to assess abilities and interests and identify career options. They may use career planning and occupational information to help individuals better understand the work world. They assist in developing individualized career plans, teach job-hunting strategies and skills, and help develop resumes. Sometimes this involves resolving personal conflicts on the job. They also provide support for people experiencing job stress, job loss, and career transition.

Vocational-rehabilitation counselors work with disabled individuals to help the counselees understand what skills they have to offer to an employer. A good counselor knows the working world and how to obtain detailed information about specific jobs. To assist with career decisions, counselors must know about the availability of jobs, the probable future of certain jobs, the education or training necessary to enter them, the kinds of salary or other benefits that certain jobs offer, the conditions that certain jobs impose on employees (night work, travel, work outdoors), and the satisfaction that certain jobs provide their employees. *Professional career counselors* work in both private and public settings and are certified by the National Board for Certified Counselors (NBCC).

College career planning and placement counselors work exclusively with the students of their universities or colleges. They may specialize in some specific area appropriate to the students and graduates of the school, such as law and education, as well as in part-time and summer work, internships, and field placements. In a liberal arts college, the students may need more assistance in identifying an appropriate career. To do this, the counselor administers interest and aptitude tests and interviews students to determine their career goals.

The counselor may work with currently enrolled students who are seeking internships and other work programs while still at school. Alumni who wish to make a career change also seek the services of the career counseling and placement office at their former schools.

College placement counselors also gather complete job information from prospective employers and make the information available to interested students and alumni.

Just as counselors try to find applicants for particular job listings, they also must seek out jobs for specific applicants. To do this, they will call potential employers to encourage them to consider a qualified individual.

College and career planning and placement counselors are responsible for the arrangements and details of on-campus interviews by large corporations. They also maintain an up-to-date library of vocational guidance material and recruitment literature.

Counselors also give assistance in preparing the actual job search by helping the applicant to write resumes and letters of application, as well as by practicing interview skills through role playing and other techniques. They also provide information on business procedures and personnel requirements in the applicant's chosen field. University-based counselors will set up online accounts on career websites for students, giving them access to information regarding potential employers.

Some career planning and placement counselors work with secondary school authorities, advising them on the needs of local industries and specific preparation requirements for both employment and further education. In two-year colleges the counselor may participate in the planning of course content, and in some smaller schools the counselor may be required to teach as well.

The principal duty of career guidance technicians is to help order, catalog, and file materials relating to job opportunities, careers, technical schools, scholarships, careers in the armed forces, and other programs. Guidance technicians also help students and teachers find materials relating to a student's interests and aptitudes. These various materials may be in the form of books, pamphlets, magazine articles, microfiche, videos, computer software, or other media.

Often, career guidance technicians help students take and score self-administered tests that determine their aptitude and interest in different careers or job-related activities. If the career guidance center has audiovisual equipment, such as VCRs or film or slide projectors, career guidance technicians are usually responsible for the equipment.

■ REQUIREMENTS
High School

In order to work in the career and employment counseling field, you must have at least a high school diploma. For most jobs in the field, however, higher education is required. In high school, in addition to studying a core curriculum, with courses in English, history, mathematics, and biology, you should take courses in psychology and sociology. You will also find it helpful to take business and computer science classes.

Postsecondary Training

When hiring a career guidance technician, most employers look for applicants who have completed two years of training beyond high school, usually at a junior, community, or technical college. These two-year programs, which usually lead to an associate's degree, may combine classroom instruction with practical or sometimes even on-the-job experience.

In some states, the minimum educational requirement in career and vocational counseling is a graduate degree in counseling or a related field from a regionally accredited higher education institution, and a completed supervised counseling experience, which includes career counseling. A growing number of institutions offer post-master's degrees with training in career development and career counseling. Such programs are highly recommended if you wish to specialize in vocational and career counseling. These programs are frequently called Advanced Graduate Specialist (AGS) programs or Certificates of Advanced Study (CAS) programs.

For a career as a college career planning and placement counselor, the minimum educational requirement is commonly a master's degree in guidance and counseling, education, college student personnel work, behavioral science, or a related field. Graduate work includes courses in vocational and aptitude testing, counseling techniques, personnel management and occupational research, industrial relations, and group dynamics and organizational behavior.

As in any profession, there is usually an initial period of training for newly hired counselors and counselor trainees. Some of the skills you will need as an employment counselor, such as testing-procedures skills and interviewing skills, can be acquired only through on-the-job training.

Certification or Licensing

The NBCC offers the national certified counselor (NCC) designation as well as the national

QUICK FACTS

SCHOOL SUBJECTS
Business
Psychology
Sociology

PERSONAL SKILLS
Communication/ideas
Helping/teaching

WORK ENVIRONMENT
Primarily indoors
Primarily one location

MINIMUM EDUCATION LEVEL
High school diploma

SALARY RANGE
$24,930 to $44,100 to $70,320

CERTIFICATION OR LICENSING
Required by certain states

OUTLOOK
Faster than the average

DOT
094

GOE
12.03.01

NOC
4143, 4213

O*NET-SOC
13-1071.00, 13-1071.01, 21-1012.00

certified school counselor (NCSC) designation. In order to apply for the NCC, you must have earned a master's degree with a major study in counseling and you must pass the National Counselor Examination. NCCs are certified for a period of five years. In order to be recertified, they must complete 100 contact clock hours of continuing education or pass the examination again. In order to receive the NCSC credential, you must complete the above requirements, plus gain field experience in school counseling as a graduate student and then complete two years of post-masters supervised school counseling. Many states require some type of credentialing or certification for counselors, and all states require those who work in school settings to be certified.

Other Requirements

In order to succeed as a career counselor, you must have a good background in education, training, employment trends, the current labor market, and career resources. You should be able to provide your clients with information about job tasks, functions, salaries, requirements, and the future outlook of broad occupational fields.

Knowledge of testing techniques and measures of aptitude, achievement, interests, values, and personality is required. The ability to evaluate job performance and individual effectiveness is helpful. You must also have management and administrative skills.

■ EXPLORING

Summer work in an employment agency is a good way to explore the field of employment counseling. Interviewing the director of a public or private agency might give you a better understanding of what the work involves and the qualifications such an organization requires of its counselors.

If you enjoy working with others, you will find helpful experiences working in the dean's or counselor's office. Many schools offer opportunities in peer tutoring, both in academics and in career guidance-related duties. (If your school does not have such a program in place, consider putting together a proposal to institute one. Your guidance counselor should be able to help you with this.) Your own experience in seeking summer and part-time work is also valuable in learning what job seekers must confront in business or industry. You could write a feature story for your school newspaper on your and others' experiences in the working world.

If you are interested in becoming a career counselor, you should seek out professional career counselors and discuss the field with them. Most people are happy to talk about what they do.

While in high school, consider working part time or as a volunteer in a library. Such work can provide you with some of the basic skills for learning about information resources, cataloging, and filing. In addition, assisting schools or clubs with any media presentations, such as video or slide shows, will help you become familiar with the equipment used by counselors. You may also find it helpful to read publications relating to this field, such as *The National Certified Counselor* newsletter (http://www.nbcc.org/users/productseekers.htm).

■ EMPLOYERS

There are approximately 228,000 educational, vocational, and school counselors employed in the United States. Career and employment counselors work in guidance offices of high schools, colleges, and universities. They are also employed by state, federal, and other bureaus of employment, and by social service agencies.

■ STARTING OUT

Journals specializing in information for career counselors frequently have job listings or information on job hotlines and services. School placement centers also are a good source of information, both because of their standard practice of listing job openings from participating firms and because schools are a likely source of jobs for you as a career counselor. Placement officers will be aware of which schools are looking for applicants.

To enter the field of college career planning and placement, you might consider working for your alma mater as an assistant in the college or university placement office. Other occupational areas that provide an excellent background for college placement work include teaching, business, public relations, previous placement training, positions in employment agencies, and experience in psychological counseling.

Career guidance technicians should receive some form of career placement from schools offering training in that area. Newspapers may list entry-level jobs. One of the best methods, however, is to contact libraries and education centers directly to inquire about their needs for assistance in developing or staffing their career guidance centers.

■ ADVANCEMENT

Employment counselors in federal or state employment services or in other vocational counseling agencies are usually considered trainees for the first six months of their employment. During this time, they learn the specific skills that will be expected of them during their careers with these agencies. The first year of a new counselor's employment is probationary.

Positions of further responsibility include supervisory or administrative work, which may be attained by counselors after several years of experience on the job. Advancement to administrative positions often means giving up the actual counseling work, which is not an advantage to those who enjoy working with people in need of counseling.

Opportunity for advancement for college counselors—to assistant and associate placement director, director of student personnel services, or similar administrative positions—depends largely on the type of college or university and the size of the staff. In general, a doctorate is preferred and may be necessary for advancement.

New employees in agencies are frequently considered trainees for the first six months to a year of their employment. During the training period, they acquire the specific skills that will be required of them during their tenure with the agency. Frequently, the first year of employment is probationary. After several years' experience on the job, counselors may reach supervisory or administrative positions.

EARNINGS

Salaries vary greatly within the career and vocational counseling field. The U.S. Department of Labor places career counselors within the category of educational, vocational, and school counselors. The median yearly earnings for this group were $44,100 in 2002, according to the Department's National Occupational Employment and Wage Estimates. The lowest paid 10 percent of these workers earned $24,930 per year, and the highest paid 10 percent made $70,320 annually. The department further broke down salaries by type of employer: Those working for state governments had median annual incomes of $45,480 in 2002; for colleges and universities, $36,990; and for junior colleges, $43,250. Annual earnings of career counselors vary greatly among educational institutions, with larger institutions offering the highest salaries. Counselors in business or industry tend to earn higher salaries.

In private practice, the salary range is even wider. Some practitioners earn as little as $20,000 per year, and others, such as elite "headhunters" who recruit corporate executives and other high-salaried positions, earn in excess of $100,000 per year.

Salaries for career guidance technicians vary according to education and experience and the geographic location of the job. In general, career guidance technicians who are graduates of two-year post high school training programs can expect to receive starting salaries averaging $15,000 to $20,000 a year.

Benefits depend on the employer, but they usually include paid holidays and vacation time, retirement plans, and, for those at some educational institutions, reduced tuition.

WORK ENVIRONMENT

Employment counselors usually work about 40 hours a week, but some agencies are more flexible. Counseling is done in offices designed to be free from noise and distractions, to allow confidential discussions with clients.

College career planning and placement counselors also normally work a 40-hour week, although irregular hours and overtime are frequently required during the peak recruiting period. They generally work on a 12-month basis.

Career guidance technicians work in very pleasant surroundings, usually in the career guidance office of a college or vocational school. They will interact with a great number of students, some of whom are eagerly looking for work, and others who are more tense and anxious. The technician must remain unruffled in order to ease any tension and provide a quiet atmosphere.

OUTLOOK

Growth in the field of employment counseling should be faster than the average through 2011, according to the U.S. Department of Labor. One reason for this growth is increased school enrollments, even at the college level, which means more students needing the services of career counselors. Another reason is that there are more counselor jobs than graduates of counseling programs. Opportunities should also be available in government agencies as many states institute welfare-to-work programs or simply cut welfare benefits. And finally, in this age of outsourcing and lack of employment security, "downsized" workers, those re-entering the workforce, and those looking for second careers all create a need for the skills of career and employment counselors.

FOR MORE INFORMATION

For a variety of career resources for career seekers and career counseling professionals, contact the following organizations:

American Counseling Association
5999 Stevenson Avenue
Alexandria, VA 22304-3300
Tel: 800-347-6647
http://www.counseling.org

Career Planning & Adult Development Network
PO Box 1484
Pacifica, CA 94044
Tel: 650-359-6911
Email: network@psctr.com
http://www.careernetwork.org

For resume and interview tips, general career information, and advice from the experts, contact or visit the following website:

National Association of Colleges and Employers (NACE)
62 Highland Avenue
Bethlehem, PA 18017-9085
Tel: 800-544-5272
http://www.naceweb.org

For information on certification, contact
National Board for Certified Counselors
PO Box 651051
Charlotte, NC 28265-1051
Tel: 336-547-0607
Email: nbcc@nbcc.org
http://www.nbcc.org

For more information on career counselors, contact
National Career Development Association
10820 East 45th Street, Suite 210
Tulsa, OK 74146
Tel: 918-663-7060
http://ncda.org

Carpenters

■ OVERVIEW

Carpenters cut, shape, level, and fasten together pieces of wood and other construction materials, such as wallboard, plywood, and insulation. Many carpenters work on constructing, remodeling, or repairing houses and other kinds of buildings. Other carpenters work at construction sites where roads, bridges, docks, boats, mining tunnels, and wooden vats are built. They may specialize in building the rough framing of a structure, and thus be considered *rough carpenters,* or they may specialize in the finishing details of a structure, such as the trim around doors and windows, and be *finish carpenters.* Approximately 1.2 million carpenters work in the United States.

■ HISTORY

Wood has been used as a building material since the dawn of civilization. Tools that resembled modern hand tools first began to be made around 1500 B.C. By the Middle Ages, many of the basic techniques and the essential tools of carpentry were perfected, largely by monks in the early monasteries.

Over time, as local societies advanced, many specialties developed in the field of carpentry. The primary work came from building construction. Buildings were mostly built with braced-frame construction, which made use of large, heavy timbers held together with mortised joints and diagonal bracing. In this kind of construction, carpenters were often the principal workers on a house or other building.

Carpenters also were responsible for many of the necessities that kept their towns running from day to day. Pit sawyers milled lumber from trees. Carts and wagons called for wheelwrights, who fabricated wheels and axles, and then, as transportation became more sophisticated, coach- and wagonmakers appeared. The increased use of brass and iron led to work for patternmakers, who created the wooden forms that were the first step in casting. On the domestic front, cabinetmakers and joiners were skilled in building furniture or creating interior trimwork.

It's no surprise that the role of carpenters has continued to change, largely due to the rise of machine technology. Since the mid-19th century, balloon-frame construction, which makes use of smaller and lighter pieces of wood, has simplified the construction process, and concrete and steel have replaced wood for many purposes, especially in floors and roofs. Power tools have replaced hand tools in many instances. But as some carpentry tasks in building construction have become easier, other new jobs, such as making forms for poured concrete, have added to the importance of carpenters at construction sites. Carpentry continues to be an important and necessary trade.

■ THE JOB

Carpenters remain the largest group of workers in the building trades—there are more than 1.2 million carpenters in the United States today. The vast majority of them work for contractors involved in building, repairing, and remodeling buildings and other structures. Manufacturing firms, schools, stores, and government bodies employ most other carpenters.

Carpenters do two basic kinds of work: rough carpentry and finish carpentry. Rough carpenters construct and install temporary structures and supports and wooden structures used in industrial settings, as well as parts of buildings that are usually covered up when the rooms are finished. Among the structures built by such carpenters are scaffolds for other workers to stand on, chutes used as channels for wet concrete, forms for concrete foundations, and timber structures that support machinery. In buildings, they may put up the frame and install rafters, joists, subflooring, wall sheathing, prefabricated wall panels and windows, and many other components.

Finish carpenters install hardwood flooring, staircases, shelves, cabinets, trim on windows and doors, and other woodwork and hardware that make the building look complete, inside and outside. Finish carpentry requires especially careful, precise workmanship, since the result must have a good appearance in addition to being sturdy. Many carpenters who are employed by building contractors do both rough and finish work on buildings.

Although they do many different tasks in different settings, carpenters generally follow the same basic steps. First, they review blueprints or plans (or they obtain instructions from a supervisor) to determine the dimensions of the structure to be built and the types of materials to be used. Sometimes local building codes mandate how a structure should be built, so carpenters need to know about such regulations.

Using rulers, framing squares, chalk lines, and other measuring and marking equipment, carpenters lay out how the work will be done. Using hand and power tools, they cut and shape the wood, plywood, fiberglass, plastic, or other materials. Then they nail, screw, glue, or staple the pieces together. Finally, they use levels, plumb bobs, rulers, and squares to check their work, and they make any necessary adjustments. Sometimes carpenters work with prefabricated units for components such as wall panels or stairs. Installing these is, in many ways, a much less complicated task, because much less layout, cutting, and assembly work is needed.

Carpenters who work outside of the building construction field may do a variety of installation and maintenance jobs, such as repairing furniture and installing ceiling tiles or exterior siding on buildings. Other carpenters specialize in building, repairing, or modifying ships, wooden boats, wooden railroad trestles, timber framing in mine shafts, woodwork inside railcars, storage tanks and vats, or stage sets in theaters.

■ REQUIREMENTS
High School

A high school education is not mandatory for a good job as a carpenter, but most contractors and developers prefer applicants with a diploma or a GED. A good high school background for prospective carpenters would include carpentry and woodworking courses as well as other shop classes; applied mathematics; mechanical drawing; and blueprint reading.

Postsecondary Training

As an aspiring carpenter, you can acquire the skills of your trade in various ways, through formal training programs and through informal on-the-job training. Of the differ-

ent ways to learn, an apprenticeship is considered the best, as it provides a more thorough and complete foundation for a career as a carpenter than do other kinds of training. However, the limited number of available apprenticeships means that not all carpenters can learn the trade this way.

You can pick up skills informally on the job while you work as a carpenter's helper—and many carpenters enter the field this way. You'll begin with little or no training and gradually learn as you work under the supervision of experienced carpenters. The skills that you'll develop as a helper will depend on the jobs that your employers contract to do. Working for a small contracting company, a beginner may learn about relatively few kinds of carpentry tasks. On the other hand, a large contracting company may offer a wider variety of learning opportunities. Becoming a skilled carpenter by this method can take much longer than an apprenticeship, and the completeness of the training varies. Some individuals who are waiting for an apprenticeship to become available work as helpers to gain experience in the field.

Some people first learn about carpentry while serving in the military. Others learn skills in vocational educational programs offered in trade schools and through correspondence courses. Vocational programs can be very good, especially as a supplement to other practical training. But without additional hands-on instruction, vocational school graduates may not be adequately prepared to get many jobs in the field because some programs do not provide sufficient opportunity for students to practice and perfect their carpentry skills.

Apprenticeships, which will provide you with the most comprehensive training available, usually last four years. They are administered by employer groups and by local chapters of labor unions that organize carpenters. Applicants must meet the specific requirements of local apprenticeship committees. Typically, you must be at least 17 years old, have

A carpenter works on the roof of a new home.

a high school diploma, and be able to show that you have some aptitude for carpentry.

Apprenticeships combine on-the-job work experience with classroom instruction in a planned, systematic program. Initially, you will work at such simple tasks as building concrete forms, doing rough framing, and nailing subflooring. Toward the end of your training, you may work on finishing trimwork, fitting hardware, hanging doors, and building stairs. In the course of this experience, you'll become familiar with the tools, materials, techniques, and equipment of the trade, and you'll learn how to do layout, framing, finishing, and other basic carpentry jobs.

The work experience segment of an apprenticeship is supplemented by about 144 hours of classroom instruction per year. Some of this instruction concerns the correct use and maintenance of tools, safety practices, first aid, building code requirements, and the properties of different construction materials. Other subjects you'll study include the principles of layout, blueprint reading, shop mathematics, and sketching. Both on the job and in the classroom, you'll learn how to work effectively with members of other skilled building trades.

Certification or Licensing

The United Brotherhood of Carpenters and Joiners of America (UBCJA), the national union for the industry, offers certification courses in a variety of specialty skills. These courses teach the ins and outs of advanced skills— like scaffold construction—that help to ensure worker safety, while at the same time giving workers ways to enhance their abilities and so qualify for better jobs. Some job sites require all workers to undergo training in safety techniques and guidelines specified by the Occupational

Safety and Health Administration. Workers who have not passed these courses are considered ineligible for jobs at these sites.

Other Requirements

In general, as a carpenter, you'll need to have manual dexterity, good hand-eye coordination, and a good sense of balance. You'll need to be in good physical condition, as the work involves a great deal of physical activity. Stamina is much more important than physical strength. On the job, you may have to climb, stoop, kneel, crouch, and reach as well as deal with the challenges of weather.

■ EXPLORING

Beyond classes such as woodshop or mechanical drawing, there are a number of real-world ways to begin exploring a career in carpentry and the construction trades. Contact trade organizations like the National Association of Home Builders or the Associated General Contractors of America; both sponsor student chapters around the country. Consider volunteering for an organization like Habitat for Humanity; their Youth Programs accept volunteers between the ages of five and 25, and their group building projects provide hands-on experience. If your school has a drama department, look into it—building sets can be a fun way to learn simple carpentry skills. In addition, your local home improvement store is likely to sponsor classes that teach a variety of skills useful around the house; some of these will focus on carpentry.

A less direct but equally useful method to explore carpentry is via television. PBS and some cable stations show how-to programs—such as *This Old House* and *New Yankee Workshop*—that feature the work of carpenters.

■ EMPLOYERS

Carpenters account for a large group of workers in the building trades, holding approximately 1.2 million jobs. About one third of carpenters work for general-building contractors, and one fifth work for specialty contractors. About 30 percent are self-employed.

Some carpenters work for manufacturing firms, government agencies, retail and wholesale establishments, or schools. Others work in the shipbuilding, aircraft, or railroad industries. Still others work in the arts, for theaters and movie and television production companies as set builders, or for museums or art galleries, building exhibits.

■ STARTING OUT

Information about available apprenticeships can be obtained by contacting the local office of the state employment service, area contractors that hire carpenters, or the local offices of the United Brotherhood of Carpenters, which cooperates in sponsoring apprenticeship programs. Helper jobs that can be filled by beginners without special training in carpentry may be advertised in newspaper classified ads or with the state employment service. You also might consider contacting potential employers directly.

■ ADVANCEMENT

Once an applicant has completed and met all the requirements of apprenticeship training, he or she will be considered a journeyman carpenter. With sufficient experience, journeymen may be promoted to positions responsible for supervising the work of other carpenters. If a carpenter's background includes exposure to a broad range of construction activities, he or she may eventually advance to a position as a general construction supervisor. A carpenter who is skillful at mathematical computations and has a good knowledge of the construction business, may become an estimator. An experienced carpenter might one day go into business for himself or herself, doing repair or construction work as an independent contractor.

■ EARNINGS

According to the U.S. Bureau of Labor Statistics, carpenters had median hourly earnings of $16.44 in 2002. Someone making this wage and working full time for the year would have an income of approximately $34,190. The lowest paid 10 percent of carpenters earned less than $9.95 per hour (or approximately $20,700 per year), and the highest paid 10 percent made more than $27.97 hourly (approximately $58,170 annually). It is important to note, however, that these annual salaries are for full-time work. Many carpenters, like others in the building trades, have periods of unemployment during the year, and their incomes may not match these.

Starting pay for apprentices is approximately 40 percent of the experienced worker's median, or roughly $13,700. The wage is increased periodically so that by the fourth year of training apprentice pay is 80 percent of the journeyman carpenter's rate.

Fringe benefits, such as health insurance, pension funds, and paid vacations, are available to most workers in this field and vary with local union contracts. In general, benefits are more likely to be offered on jobs staffed by union workers.

■ WORK ENVIRONMENT

Carpenters may work either indoors or outdoors. If they do rough carpentry, they will probably do most of their work outdoors. Carpenters may have to work on high

scaffolding, or in a basement making cement forms. A construction site can be noisy, dusty, hot, cold, or muddy. Carpenters can expect to be physically active throughout the day, constantly standing, stooping, climbing, and reaching. Some of the possible hazards of the job include being hit by falling objects, falling off scaffolding or a ladder, straining muscles, and getting cuts and scrapes on fingers and hands. Carpenters who follow recommended safety practices and procedures minimize these hazards.

Work in the construction industry involves changing from one job location to another, and from time to time being laid off because of poor weather, shortages of materials, or simply lack of jobs. Carpenters must be able to arrange their finances so that they can make it through sometimes long periods of unemployment.

Though it is not required, many carpenters are members of a union such as the UBCJA. Among many other

SPECIAL TRAINING PROGRAMS

The Craft Skills Department of the Home Builders Institute (HBI) has developed a number of innovative and comprehensive trades training programs designed to help workers interested in a career in carpentry and construction gain entry into the field.

CRAFT: Community, Restitution, Apprenticeship Focused Training is a national training program for high-risk and adjudicated youth. Working with state juvenile justice systems, nonprofits, and other youth service agencies, CRAFT can fit prevention, day-treatment, facility-based, community-based, or after-care needs. Participants, age 17 or older, receive 21 weeks of training that includes extensive hands-on work in community service projects. Through HBI's certificate initiative (PACT: Pre-Apprenticeship Certificate Training), students learn the basics of carpentry, building maintenance, or other trades. Equipped with a certificate and tools, graduates are placed in related employment and/or apprenticeships. HBI project coordinators assist graduates with community transition and other support services for six months.

Other HBI projects include TRADE: Training, Restitution, Apprenticeship, Development and Education, which offers pre-apprenticeship training to adult offenders in state or local correctional institutions; and HEART: Homeless Employment and Related Training, a program working to assist homeless men and women in their efforts to gain reasonable employment and safe housing. For more information on any of these programs, contact the Home Builders Institute (http://www.hbi.org/).

BEING GREEN . . .

Being "green," or environmentally friendly, is easier for today's carpenter than you might think. Across the construction industry, the spotlight is turning to issues of resource efficiency, sustainable design practices, and building with an eco-friendly approach.

The construction industry got into the act with the first national Green Building Conference in April 1999, sponsored by the National Association of Home Builders (NAHB), the NAHB Research Center, and Professional Builder magazine. The annual conference features speakers and presentations targeted to builders, sharing ways to design, develop, build, market, and finance environmentally sensible homes.

For more information about eco-oriented building practices and the burgeoning movement, contact the NAHB (http://www.nahbrc.org). Here are some additional resources:

- *Environmental Design + Construction* is a magazine exclusively covering the rapidly growing green building industry. Topics include resource and energy efficiency, alternative and renewable energy sources, indoor air quality, and life cycle assessment. (http://www.edcmag.com)

- The Sustainable Architecture Building & Culture website has links to environmentally inspired building techniques, technologies, architecture, and engineering. (http://www.sustainableabc.com)

- Building Green is a company that publishes the periodical, *Environmental Building News* and offers a variety of information resources including a green building product directory, *GreenSpec,* and a software green design tool, *The Green Building Advisor.* (http://www.buildinggreen.com)

services, such as the certification courses mentioned previously, the union works with employers, seeking to ensure that members receive equitable pay and work in safe conditions.

OUTLOOK

Although the U.S. Department of Labor predicts employment growth for carpenters to increase about as fast as the average through 2012, job opportunities for carpenters are expected to be very strong. This is because replacement carpenters are needed for the large number of experienced carpenters who leave the field every year for work that is less strenuous. Replacement workers are also needed for the fair amount of workers just starting out in the field who decide to move on to more comfortable occupations. And, of course, replacements are needed for

those who retire. Increased home-building, home modifications for the growing elderly population, two-income couples' desire for larger homes, and the growing population of all ages should contribute to the demand for carpenters.

Factors that will hold down employment growth in the field include the use of more prefabricated building parts and improved tools that make construction easier and faster. In addition, a weak economy has a major impact on the building industry, causing companies and individuals to put off expensive building projects until better times. Carpenters with good all-around skills, such as those who have completed apprenticeships, will have the best job opportunities even in difficult times.

FOR MORE INFORMATION

For information on activities and student chapters, contact
Associated General Contractors of America
333 John Carlyle Street, Suite 200
Alexandria, VA 22314
Tel: 703-548-3118
Email: info@agc.org
http://www.agc.org

Habitat for Humanity is an internationally recognized non-profit organization dedicated to the elimination of poverty housing. For information on programs and local chapters found all over the United States, contact
Habitat for Humanity International
121 Habitat Street
Americus, GA 31709
Tel: 229-924-6935, ext. 2551
Email: publicinfo@hfhi.org
http://www.habitat.org

For information on apprenticeships, training programs, and general information about trends in the industry, contact
Home Builders Institute
1201 15th Street, NW, Sixth Floor
Washington, DC 20005
Tel: 202-371-0600
Email: postmaster@hbi.org
http://www.hbi.org

For information about careers in the construction trades and student chapters, contact
National Association of Home Builders
1201 15th Street, NW
Washington, DC 20005
Tel: 800-368-5242
Email: info@nahb.com
http://www.nahb.com

Cartographers

■ OVERVIEW

Cartographers prepare maps, charts, and drawings from aerial photographs and survey data. They also conduct map research, investigating topics such as how people use maps.

■ HISTORY

Explorers, warriors, and traders have all used maps as a way of navigating around the world or establishing property rights. Early civilizations, such as the Egyptians and the Greeks, used maps drawn on papyrus to show a specific trade route or to trace the conquests of an army. Advances such as the establishment of a system of measuring longitude and latitude helped create more uniform and accurate mapping procedures.

In the 15th and 16th centuries, mapmaking, or cartography, began to change because of the impact of world travel. Explorers such as Christopher Columbus observed and collected geographic information from around the world and used this information to make maps.

Mapmaking continued to develop as surveying and other means of mathematical measurements evolved. Today, the most sophisticated technology is used in compiling geographic information and planning and drafting maps. Such advances have significantly changed the cartographer's job. Computer and satellite technology have been applied to mapmaking with great success. For example, video signals from a satellite detector are digitized and transmitted to Earth, where a computer process is used to read the data and create a map with enhanced geographic patterns that can show variations in types of vegetation or soils as well as spatial relationships. With the addition of computer-mapping software and data-merging software, mapping exercises can be done in a fraction of the time that it once took.

■ THE JOB

Cartographers use manual and computerized drafting instruments, standard mathematical formulas, photogrammetric techniques, and precision stereoplotting apparatuses throughout the mapmaking process. They work with other mapping scientists to plan and draft maps and charts. For example, cartographers may work with land surveyors to interpret geographic information and transfer that information into a series of symbols that are plotted onto a map. They must also be able to plot the names and exact locations of places onto overlays from which a final map is made. Cartographers often work with old maps, using updated information to keep the maps current. Research also may be a part of their job.

Several specializations exist within the field of cartography. *Cartography supervisors* design maps and coordinate and oversee the activities of all those involved in the mapmaking process. Supervisors are most often employed in larger mapmaking operations.

Mosaicists lay out photographic prints on tables, according to the sequence in which the photographs were taken, to form a visual composite of the geographic area. These mosaics are subsequently used in photogrammetric activities such as topographic mapping. Mosaicists examine aerial photographs in order to verify the location of established landmarks.

Stereoplotter operators also prepare maps from aerial photographs, using instruments that produce simultaneous projections of two photographs taken of the same area.

New technology has made cartography work much more accurate and efficient. Cartographers now use Geographic Information Systems (GIS), which is a computer system that can store, manipulate, and display geographically referenced information. Data is organized by location, stored in map form, and analyzed as a map rather than as a list of numbers. Cartographers use another advanced technology called Global Positioning Systems (GPS) to gather the spatial data used by GIS.

■ REQUIREMENTS
High School

To prepare for a career in cartography, high school students should study mathematics, geography, mechanical drawing, and computer science. English classes will help hone research and communication skills that students will need later in this career. Foreign languages may be helpful in working on maps of other countries.

Postsecondary Training

Mapmaking companies and government agencies prefer that their cartographers hold at least a bachelor's degree. Frequently cartographers have degrees in

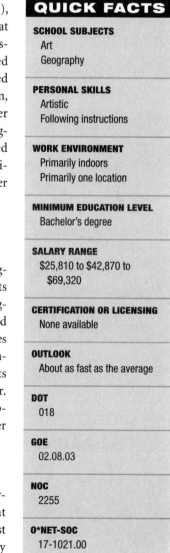

QUICK FACTS

SCHOOL SUBJECTS
Art
Geography

PERSONAL SKILLS
Artistic
Following instructions

WORK ENVIRONMENT
Primarily indoors
Primarily one location

MINIMUM EDUCATION LEVEL
Bachelor's degree

SALARY RANGE
$25,810 to $42,870 to $69,320

CERTIFICATION OR LICENSING
None available

OUTLOOK
About as fast as the average

DOT
018

GOE
02.08.03

NOC
2255

O*NET-SOC
17-1021.00

This cartographer from the CIA is creating a digital map of Russia for an agency publication.

geography, civil engineering, forestry, or another branch of the physical sciences. In addition, some cartographers have master's degrees in fields such as geography, cartography, and civil engineering.

Other Requirements

Attention to detail is an obvious personal requirement for those working in the field of cartography. Patience and painstaking effort are further requirements. In addition, cartographers should be adept at visualizing objects and distances. These professionals should also be comfortable with computers and with learning new software programs.

■ EXPLORING

One of the best opportunities for experience is a summer job or internship with a construction firm or other company that prepares maps. The federal government also may have some part-time opportunities for cartographic assistants. While in high school, you can get accustomed to map reading, perhaps through a scouting organization.

■ EMPLOYERS

Mapmaking companies are, of course, the primary employers of cartographers. Government agencies, at the federal and the state level, also employ cartographers, as does the military, which has a need for highly specialized maps.

■ STARTING OUT

Most cartographers are hired upon completion of a bachelor's degree in engineering or geography. A person who is interested in becoming a cartographic technician instead of a full-fledged cartographer may be able to secure an entry-level position after completing a specialized training program. A portfolio of completed maps may be required by a prospective employer during the interviewing process.

■ ADVANCEMENT

A cartographer who proves adept at drafting and designing maps and understands the other steps in mapmaking stands a good chance of becoming a supervisor. However, cartographers should expect to work directly on maps throughout their careers, even when holding supervisory positions.

■ EARNINGS

According to the U.S. Department of Labor, the median yearly income for cartographers and photogrammetrists was $42,870 in 2002. The lowest paid 10 percent of this group earned less than $25,810 during that same time. The highest paid 10 percent, on the other hand, earned more than $69,320. The Cartography and Geographic Information Society (CaGIS) reports that cartographers employed by the federal government typically have starting salaries that range from the GS-5 to GS-11 pay levels, depending on such factors as education and experience. In 2002, the GS-5 salary started at $22,737, and the GS-11 salary started at $41,684. The U.S. Department of Labor reports the average salary for cartographers working for the federal government in supervisory, non-supervisory, and managerial positions was $62,369 in 2001. According to the CaGIS, those who work for state governments tend to earn less than federal employees.

■ WORK ENVIRONMENT

Cartographers work in office settings with drafting tables and computer-mapping systems. Most cartographers never visit the locations that they are mapping. The average workweek is 35 to 40 hours, although longer hours are occasionally required if a mapping project is on a deadline.

Many cartographers are freelancers who are hired by companies for a specific project. For large map-producing companies, project cartographers may be brought in to help during heavy deadline work. Because of the cost of mapping, most small companies buy rights to maps produced by large firms.

■ OUTLOOK

Through 2012, employment for cartographers and other mapping scientists is expected to grow about as fast as the average. Opportunities will be best for those with excellent technical skills who are able to work with increasingly sophisticated technologies such as GIS and GPS.

■ FOR MORE INFORMATION

For information on scholarships and colleges and universities offering surveying/geomorphics programs, contact

American Congress on Surveying and Mapping
6 Montgomery Village Avenue, Suite 403
Gaithersburg, MD 20879
Tel : 240-632-9716
Email: info@acsm.net
http://www.acsm.net

For information on photogrammetry and careers in the field, contact

American Society for Photogrammetry and Remote Sensing
5410 Grosvenor Lane, Suite 210
Bethesda, MD 20814-2160
Tel: 301-493-0290
Email: asprs@asprs.org
http://www.asprs.org

The Cartography and Geographic Information Society (CaGIS) is a member organization of the American Congress on Surveying and Mapping. For membership information and the booklet Careers in Cartography and GIS, *contact*

Cartography and Geographic Information Society (CaGIS)
6 Montgomery Village Avenue, Suite 403
Gaithersburg, MD 20879
Tel: 240-632-9716
Email: info@acsm.net
http://www.acsm.net/cagis

FLAT OR ROUND?

The art of cartography dates back to prehistoric times when hunting and fishing territories were marked off in cave drawings. The ancient Babylonians mapped the world as a flattened disk. Ptolemy in the second century first drew maps showing the earth as a sphere. It was not until the 14th century that seaman's charts for navigation were developed with some accuracy, although blank spaces were marked with the warning "Here be dragons." The discoveries of America, Australia, and other New World lands demanded new techniques, such as a way to depict on a flat surface the features of a curved surface. The development of the Mercator projection, which treats the earth as a cylinder divided by horizontal and vertical lines, allowed navigators for the first time to plot bearings as a straight line.

You can also obtain information on cartography from

North American Cartographic Information Society
AGS Collection
PO Box 399
Milwaukee, WI 53201
Tel: 414-229-6282
Email: nacis@nacis.org
http://www.nacis.org

Cartoonists and Animators

■ OVERVIEW

Cartoonists and *animators* are artists who draw either still or moving pictures and cartoons to amuse, entertain, educate, and persuade people. Computers have become increasingly important to the field of animation over the past decade.

■ THE JOB

Cartoonists and animators draw and animate illustrations for newspapers, books, magazines, publishers, greeting cards, movies, television shows, civic organizations, and private businesses. Cartoons are most often associated with newspaper comics, children's television, and the World Wide Web, but they are also used to highlight and interpret information in publications as well as in advertising.

Whatever their individual specialty, cartoonists and animators translate ideas onto paper or film in order to communicate these ideas to an audience. Sometimes the ideas are original; at other times they are directly related to the news of the day, to the content of a magazine article, or to a new product. After cartoonists come up with ideas, they discuss them with their employers, who include editors, producers, and creative directors at advertising agencies. Next, cartoonists sketch drawings and submit these for approval. Employers may suggest changes, which the cartoonists then make. Cartoonists use a variety of art materials, including pens, pencils, markers, crayons, paints, transparent washes, and shading sheets. They may draw on paper, acetate, or bristol board.

Animators are relying increasingly on computers in various areas of production. Computers are used to color animation art, whereas formerly, every frame was painted by hand. Computers also help animators create special effects or even entire films. (One program, Macromedia's Flash, has given rise to an entire Internet cartoon subculture.)

Comic strip artists tell jokes or short stories with a series of pictures. Each picture is called a frame or a panel, and each frame usually includes words as well as drawings. *Comic book artists* also tell stories with their drawings, but their stories are longer, and they are not necessarily meant to be funny. In fact, "graphic novels" such as Art Spiegelman's *Maus* and Frank Miller's *The Dark Knight Returns* have blurred the line between comics and serious literature.

Animators, or *motion cartoonists,* also draw individual pictures, but they must draw many more for a moving cartoon. Each picture varies only slightly from the ones before and after it in a series. When these drawings are photographed in sequence to make a film and then the film is projected at high speed, the cartoon images appear to be moving. (One can achieve a similar effect by drawing stick figures on the pages of a notepad and then flipping through the pages very quickly.) Animators today also work a great deal with computers.

Other people who work in animation are *prop designers,* who create objects used in animated films, and *layout artists,* who visualize and create the world that cartoon characters inhabit.

Editorial cartoonists comment on society by drawing pictures with messages that are usually funny, but which often have a satirical edge. Their drawings often depict famous politicians. *Portraitists* are cartoonists who specialize in drawing caricatures. Caricatures are pictures that exaggerate someone's prominent features, such as a large nose, to make them recognizable to the public. Most editorial cartoonists are also talented portraitists.

Storyboard artists work in film and television production as well as at advertising agencies. They draw cartoons or sketches that give a client an idea of what a scene or television commercial will look like before it is produced. If the director or advertising client likes the idea, the actions represented by cartoons in the storyboard will be reproduced by actors on film.

■ REQUIREMENTS
High School

If you are interested in becoming a cartoonist or animator, you should, of course, study art in high school in addition to following a well-rounded course of study. To comment insightfully on contemporary life, it is useful to study political science, history, and social studies. English and communications classes will also help you to become a better communicator.

Postsecondary Training

Cartoonists and animators need not have a college degree, but some art training is usually expected by employers. Animators must attend art school to learn specific technical skills. Training in computers in addition to art can be especially valuable.

Other Requirements

Cartoonists and animators must be creative. In addition to having artistic talent, they must generate ideas, although it is not unusual for cartoonists to collaborate with writers for ideas. Whether they create cartoon strips or advertising campaigns, they must be able to come up with concepts and images to which the public will respond. They must have a good sense of humor (or a good dramatic sense) and an observant eye to detect peo-

QUICK FACTS

SCHOOL SUBJECTS
Art
Computer science
History

PERSONAL SKILLS
Artistic
Communication/ideas

WORK ENVIRONMENT
Primarily indoors
Primarily one location

MINIMUM EDUCATION LEVEL
High school diploma

SALARY RANGE
$16,900 to $35,250 to $73,560 (cartoonists)
$25,830 to $43,980 to $85,160 (animators)

CERTIFICATION OR LICENSING
None available

OUTLOOK
About as fast as the average

DOT
141

GOE
01.04.01, 01.04.02

NOC
5241

O*NET-SOC
27-1013.03, 27-1014.00

ple's distinguishing characteristics and society's interesting attributes or incongruities.

Cartoonists and animators need to be flexible. Because their art is commercial, they must be willing to accommodate their employers' desires if they are to build a broad clientele and earn a decent living. They must be able to take suggestions and rejections gracefully.

■ EXPLORING

If you are interested in becoming a cartoonist or an animator, you should submit your drawings to your school paper. You also might want to draw posters to publicize activities, such as sporting events, dances, and meetings.

Scholarship assistance for art students is available from some sources. For example, the Society of Illustrators awards some 125 scholarships annually to student artists from any field. Students do not apply directly; rather, they are selected and given application materials by their instructors. The International Animated Film Society offers scholarships to high school seniors.

■ EMPLOYERS

Employers of cartoonists and animators include editors, producers, creative directors at advertising agencies, comics syndicates, newspapers, movie studios, and television networks. In addition, a number of these artists are self-employed, working on a freelance basis. Some do animation on the Web as a part-time business or a hobby.

■ STARTING OUT

A few places, such as the Walt Disney studios, offer apprenticeships. To enter these programs, applicants must have attended an accredited art school for two or three years.

Formal entry-level positions for cartoonists and animators are rare, but there are several ways for artists to enter the cartooning field. Most cartoonists and animators begin by working piecemeal, selling cartoons to small publications, such as community newspapers, that buy freelance cartoons. Others assemble a portfolio of their best work and apply to publishers or the art departments of advertising agencies. In order to become established, cartoonists and animators should be willing to work for what equals less than minimum wage.

One new way up-and-coming animators have made themselves known to the animating community is by attracting an audience on the World Wide Web. A portfolio of well-executed Web 'toons can help an animator build his reputation and get jobs. Some animators, such as the Brothers Chaps (creators of homestarrunner.com), have even been able to turn their website into a profitable business.

Many cartoonists and animators use computers to create their work, but drawing skills are still necessary for quick sketches.

■ ADVANCEMENT

Cartoonists' success, like that of other artists, depends on how much the public likes their work. Very successful cartoonists and animators work for prestigious clients at the best wages; some become well known to the public.

■ EARNINGS

Freelance cartoonists may earn anywhere from $100 to $1,200 or more per drawing, but top dollar generally goes only for big, full-color projects such as magazine cover illustrations. Although the Department of Labor does not give specific information regarding cartoonists' earnings, it does note that the median annual earnings for salaried fine artists was $35,250 in 2002, with 10 percent earning $16,900 or less and 10 percent earning $73,560 and on up, although syndicated cartoonists on commission can earn much more. Salaries depend on the work performed. Cel painters, as listed in a salary survey conducted by *Animation World,* start at about $750 a week; animation checkers, $930 a week; story sketchers, $1,500 weekly. According to the Department of Labor, multimedia artists and animators earned an annual median of $43,980 in 2002, with the lowest 10 percent earning $25,830 or less and the top 10 percent $85,160 or more. Comic strip artists are usually paid according to the number of publications that carry their strip.

Self-employed artists do not receive fringe benefits such as paid vacations, sick leave, health insurance, or pension benefits. Those who are salaried employees of companies, agencies, newspapers, and the like do typically receive these fringe benefits.

■ WORK ENVIRONMENT

Most cartoonists and animators work in big cities where employers such as television studios, magazine publishers, and advertising agencies are located. They generally work in comfortable environments, at drafting tables or drawing boards with good light. Staff cartoonists work a regular 40-hour workweek but may occasionally be expected to work evenings and weekends to meet deadlines. Freelance cartoonists have erratic schedules, and the number of hours they work may depend on how much money they want to earn or how much work they can find. They often work evenings and weekends but are not required to be at work during regular office hours.

Cartoonists and animators can be frustrated by employers who curtail their creativity, asking them to follow instructions that are contrary to what they would most like to do. Many freelance cartoonists spend a lot of time working alone at home, but cartoonists have more opportunities to interact with other people than do most working artists.

■ OUTLOOK

Employment for artists and related workers is expected to grow at a rate about as fast as the average through 2012, according to the U.S. Department of Labor. The growing trend of sophisticated special effects in motion pictures should create opportunities at industry effects houses such as Sony Pictures Imageworks, DreamQuest Software, Industrial Light & Magic, and DreamWorks SKG. Furthermore, growing processor and Internet connection speeds are creating a Web animation renaissance. Because so many creative and talented people are drawn to this field, however, competition for jobs will be strong.

Cartoons are not just for children anymore. Much of the animation today is geared for an adult audience. Interactive games, animated films, network and cable television, and the Internet are among the many employment sources for talented cartoonists and animators. More than half of all visual artists are self-employed, but freelance work can be hard to come by, and many freelancers earn little until they acquire experience and establish a good reputation. Competition for work will be keen; those with an undergraduate or advanced degree in art or film will be in demand. Experience in action drawing and computers is a must.

■ FOR MORE INFORMATION

For membership and scholarship information, contact
International Animated Film Society
721 South Victory Boulevard
Burbank, CA 91502
Tel: 818-842-8330
Email: info@asifa-hollywood.org
http://www.asifa-hollywood.org

For an art school directory, a scholarship guide, or general information, contact
National Art Education Association
1916 Association Drive
Reston, VA 20191-1590
Tel: 703-860-8000
Email: naea@dgs.dgsys.com
http://www.naea-reston.org

For education and career information, contact
National Cartoonists Society
PO Box 713
Suffield, CT 06078
http://www.reuben.org

For scholarship information for qualified students in art school, have your instructor contact
Society of Illustrators
Museum of American Illustration
128 East 63rd Street
New York, NY 10021-7303
Tel: 212-838-2560
http://www.societyillustrators.org

MOST NEW JOBS

Cashiers

■ OVERVIEW

Cashiers are employed in many different businesses, including supermarkets, department stores, restaurants, and movie theaters. In general, they are responsible for handling money received from customers.

One of the principal tasks of a cashier is operating a cash register. The cash register records all the monetary transactions going into or out of the cashier's workstation. These transactions might involve cash, credit card charges, personal checks, refunds, and exchanges. To assist in inventory control, the cash register often tallies the specific products that are sold. Approximately 3.4 million cashiers are employed in the United States.

HISTORY

In earlier times, when most stores were small and independently owned, merchants were usually able to take care of most aspects of their businesses, including receiving money from customers. The demand for cashiers increased as large department stores, supermarkets, and self-service stores became more common. Cashiers were hired to receive customers' money, make change, provide customer receipts, and wrap merchandise. Cashiers, who dealt with customers one-on-one, also became the primary representatives of these businesses.

THE JOB

Although cashiers are employed in many different types of businesses and establishments, most handle the following tasks: receiving money from customers, making change, and providing customers with a payment receipt. The type of business dictates other duties. In supermarkets, for example, they might be required to bag groceries. Typically, cashiers in drug or department stores also package or bag merchandise for customers. In currency exchanges, they cash checks, receive utility bill payments, and sell various licenses and permits.

At some businesses, cashiers handle tasks not directly related to customers. Some cashiers, for example, prepare bank deposits for the management. In large businesses, where cashiers are often given a lot of responsibility, they may receive and record cash payments made to the firm and handle payment of the firm's bills. Cashiers might even prepare sales tax reports, compute income tax deductions for employees' pay rates, and prepare paychecks and payroll envelopes.

Cashiers usually operate some type of cash register or other business machine. These machines might print out the amount of each purchase, automatically add the total amount, provide a paper receipt for the customer, and open the cash drawer for the cashier. Other, more complex machines, such as those used in hotels, large department stores, and supermarkets, might print out an itemized bill of the customer's purchases. In some cases, cashiers use electronic devices called *optical scanners*, which read the prices of goods from bar codes printed on the merchandise. As the cashier passes the product over the scanner, the scanner reads the code on the product and transmits the code to the cashier's terminal. The price of the item is then automatically displayed at the terminal and added to the customer's bill. Cashiers generally have their own drawer of money, known as a *bank*, which fits into the cash register or terminal. They must keep an

accurate record of the amount of money in the drawer. Other machines that are used by cashiers include adding machines and change-dispensing machines.

Job titles vary depending on where the cashier is employed. In supermarkets, cashiers might be known as *check-out clerks* or *grocery checkers;* in utility companies they are typically called *bill clerks* or *tellers;* in theaters they are often referred to as *ticket sellers* or *box office cashiers;* and in cafeterias they are frequently called *cashier-checkers, food checkers,* or *food tabulators.* In large businesses, cashiers might be given special job titles such as *disbursement clerk, credit cashier,* or *cash accounting clerk.*

In addition to handling money, theater box office cashiers might answer telephone inquiries and operate machines that dispense tickets and change. Restaurant cashiers might receive telephone calls for meal reservations and for special parties, keep the reservation book current, type the menu, stock the sales counter with candies and smoking supplies, and seat customers.

Department store or *supermarket cashiers* typically bag or wrap purchases. During slack periods they might price the merchandise, restock shelves, make out order forms, and perform other duties similar to those of food and beverage order clerks. Those employed as hotel cashiers usually keep accurate records of telephone charges and room-service bills to go on the customer's account. They might also be in charge of overseeing customers' safe-deposit boxes, handling credit card billing, and notifying room clerks of customer checkouts.

Cashier supervisors, money-room supervisors, and *money counters* might act as cashiers for other cashiers—receiving and recording cash and sales slips from them and making sure their cash registers contain enough money to make change for customers. Other cashier positions include *gambling cashiers,* who buy and sell chips for cash; *parimutuel ticket cashiers and sellers,* who buy and sell betting tickets at

QUICK FACTS

SCHOOL SUBJECTS
Business
Mathematics

PERSONAL SKILLS
Following instructions
Helping/teaching

WORK ENVIRONMENT
Primarily indoors
Primarily one location

MINIMUM EDUCATION LEVEL
High school diploma

SALARY RANGE
$12,200 to $15,420 to $22,810

CERTIFICATION OR LICENSING
None available

OUTLOOK
About as fast as the average

DOT
211

GOE
09.05.01

NOC
6611

O*NET-SOC
41-2011.00

racetracks; *paymasters of purses,* who are responsible for collecting money for and paying money to racehorse owners; and *auction clerks,* who are responsible for collecting money from winning bidders at auctions.

■ REQUIREMENTS

Some employers require that cashiers be at least 18 years old and have graduated from high school. Employers might also prefer applicants with previous job experience, the ability to type, or knowledge of elementary accounting. Cashiers typically receive on-the-job training from experienced employees. In addition, some businesses have special training programs, providing information on the store's history, for example, as well as instruction on store procedures, security measures, and the use of equipment.

High School

High school courses useful to cashiers include bookkeeping, typing, business machine operation, and business arithmetic.

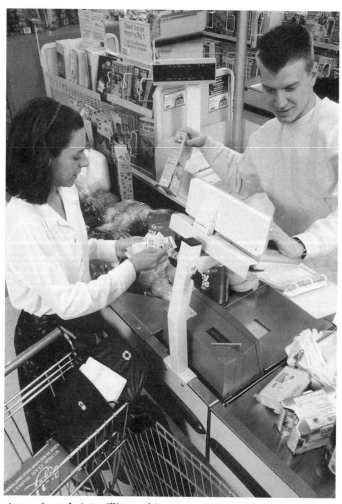

Approximately 3.4 million cashiers are employed in the United States.

Postsecondary Training

For some kinds of more complicated cashier jobs, employers might prefer applicants who are graduates of a two-year community college or business school. Businesses often fill cashier positions by promoting existing employees, such as clerk-typists, baggers, and ushers.

Other Requirements

Most cashiers have constant personal contact with the public. A pleasant disposition and a desire to serve the public are thus important qualities. Cashiers must also be proficient with numbers and have good hand-eye coordination and finger dexterity. Accuracy is especially important.

Because they handle large sums of money, some cashiers must be able to meet the standards of bonding companies. Bonding companies evaluate applicants for risks and frequently fingerprint applicants for registration and background checks. Not all cashiers are required to be bonded, however.

In some areas, cashiers are required to join a union, but fewer than 20 percent of cashiers are union members. Most union cashiers work in grocery stores and supermarkets and belong to the United Food and Commercial Workers International Union.

■ EXPLORING

You can try to find part-time employment as a cashier. This will enable you to explore your interest and aptitude for this type of work. You can sometimes obtain related job experience by working in the school bookstore or cafeteria or by participating in community activities, such as raffles and sales drives that require the handling of money. It can also be useful to talk with persons already employed as cashiers.

■ EMPLOYERS

Of the approximately 3.4 million cashiers working in the country, about 33 percent work in supermarkets and grocery stores. Large numbers are also employed in restaurants, department stores, drug stores, and other retail stores, and many work in hotels, theaters, and casinos.

■ STARTING OUT

People generally enter this field by applying directly to the personnel directors of large businesses or to the managers or owners of small businesses. Applicants may learn of job openings through newspaper help wanted ads, through friends and business associates, or through school placement agencies. Private or state employment agencies can also help. Employers sometimes require that applicants provide personal references from schools or former employers attesting to their character and personal qualifications.

■ ADVANCEMENT

Opportunities for advancement vary depending on the size and type of business, personal initiative, experience, and special training and skills. Cashier positions, for example, can provide people with the business skills to move into other types of clerical jobs or managerial positions. Opportunities for promotion are greater within larger firms than in small businesses or stores. Cashiers sometimes advance to cashier supervisors, shift leaders, division managers, or store managers. In hotels, they might be able to advance to room clerks or related positions.

For most people, cashiering is a temporary job. The Department of Labor noted in 2002 that half of all cashiers were twenty-four years of age or under.

■ EARNINGS

New cashiers with no experience are generally paid the minimum wage. Employers can pay workers younger than 20 a lower training wage for up to six months.

The median hourly earnings for cashiers, excluding those in the gaming industry, were $7.41 in 2002, according to the U.S. Department of Labor. A cashier working full time at this rate of pay would have a yearly income of approximately $15,420. The department also reports that the lowest paid 10 percent earned less than $5.86 per hour (about $12,200 annually), and the highest paid 10 percent made more than $10.97 hourly (about $22,810 per year). Wages are generally higher for union workers; union workers in service occupations who were paid about 6 percent more than nonunion, and experienced, full-time cashiers belonging to the United Food and Commercial Workers International Union averaged about $27,900 a year in 2000; beginners make much less, averaging about $5.90 per hour. Cashiers employed in restaurants generally earn less than those in other businesses do.

Some cashiers, especially those working for large companies, receive health and life insurance as well as paid vacations and sick days. Some are also offered employee retirement plans or stock option plans. Cashiers are sometimes given merchandise discounts. Benefits are usually available only to full-time employees. Many employers try to save money by hiring part-time cashiers and not paying them benefits.

■ WORK ENVIRONMENT

Cashiers sometimes work evenings, weekends, and holidays, when many people shop and go out for entertainment. The work of the cashier is usually not too strenuous, but employees often need to stand during most of their working hours. Cashiers must be able to work rapidly and under pressure during rush hours. Handling many items very quickly and dealing with irate customers can be very stressful. Many cashiers complain about repetitive-stress injuries.

Most cashiers work indoors and in rooms that are well ventilated and well lighted. The work area itself, however, can be rather small and confining; cashiers typically work behind counters, in cages or booths, or in other small spaces. Workspaces for cashiers are frequently located near entrances and exits, so cashiers may be exposed to drafts.

■ OUTLOOK

Employment for cashiers is expected to grow about as fast as the average through 2012, according to the U.S. Department of Labor. Not only are we experiencing a changeover to a more and more service-based economy, but the growth of huge retail shopping chains has helped fuel a constant need for cashiers, who are, unfortunately, considered low-paid and disposable workers. Moreover, due to a high turnover rate among cashiers, many jobs will become available as workers leaving the field are replaced. Each year almost one-third of all cashiers leave their jobs for various reasons.

Factors that could limit job growth include the increased use of automatic change-making machines, vending machines, and e-commerce, which could decrease the number of cashiers needed in some business operations. Future job opportunities will be available to those experienced in bookkeeping, typing, business machine operation, and general office skills. Many part-time jobs should also be available. Although the majority of cashiers employed are 24 years of age or younger, many businesses have started diversifying their workforce by hiring older persons and those with disabilities to fill some job openings.

LEARN MORE ABOUT IT

Brown, Stephen A. *Revolution at the Checkout Counter: The Explosion of the Bar Code.* Cambridge, Mass.: Harvard University Press, 1997.

Kahn, Barbara E. *Grocery Revolution: The New Focus on the Consumer Today!* Boston, Mass.: Addison-Wesley Publishing, 1997.

Segel, Rick. *Retail Business Kit for Dummies.* New York: Wiley, 2001.

Seth, Geoffrey Randall. *The Grocers: The Rise and Rise of the Supermarket Chains.* Dover, N.H.: Kogan Page Ltd., 2000.

■ FOR MORE INFORMATION

For information about educational programs in the retail industry, contact

National Retail Federation
325 Seventh Street, NW, Suite 1100
Washington, DC 20004
Tel: 800-NRF-HOW2
http://www.nrf.com

The UFCW represents workers in retail food, meatpacking, poultry, and other food processing industries. For more information, contact

**United Food and Commercial Workers
International Union (UFCW)**
1775 K Street, NW
Washington, DC 20006
Tel: 202-223-3111
http://www.ufcw.org

Caterers

■ OVERVIEW

Caterers plan, coordinate, and supervise food service at parties and at other social functions. Working with their clients, they purchase appropriate supplies, plan menus, supervise food preparation, direct serving of food and refreshments, and ensure the overall smooth functioning of the event. As entrepreneurs, they are also responsible for budgeting, bookkeeping, and other administrative tasks.

■ HISTORY

Catering is part of the food service industry and has been around for as long as there have been restaurants. Once viewed as a service available only to the very wealthy, catering today is used by many people for various types of gatherings.

■ THE JOB

A caterer is a chef, purchasing agent, personnel director, and accountant. Often a caterer will also play the role of host, allowing clients to enjoy their own party. A caterer's responsibilities vary, depending on the size of the catering firm and the specific needs of individual clients. While preparing quality food is a concern no matter what the size of the party, larger events require far more planning and coordination. For example, a large catering firm may organize and plan a formal event for 1,000 people, including planning and preparing a seven-course meal, decorating the hall with flowers and wall hangings, employing 20 or more wait staff to serve food, and arranging the entertainment. The catering firm will also set up the tables and chairs and provide the necessary linen, silverware, and dishes. A catering company may organize 50 or so such events a month or only several a year. A smaller catering organization may concentrate on simpler events, such as preparing food for an informal buffet for 15 people.

Caterers service not only individual clients but also industrial clients. A caterer may supervise a company cafeteria or plan food service for an airline or cruise ship. Such caterers often take over full-time supervision of food operations, including ordering food and other supplies, supervising personnel and food preparation, and overseeing the maintenance of equipment.

Caterers need to be flexible in their approach to food preparation, that is, able to prepare food both on- and off-premises, as required by logistical considerations and the wishes of the client. For example, if the caterer is handling a large banquet in a hotel or other location, he or she will usually prepare the food on-premises, using kitchen and storage facilities as needed. The caterer might also work in a client's kitchen for an event in a private home. In both cases, the caterer must visit the site of the function well before the actual event to determine how and where the food will be prepared. Caterers may also prepare food off-premises, working either in their own kitchens or in a mobile kitchen.

Working with the client is obviously a very important aspect of the caterer's job. Clients always want their affairs to be extra special, and the caterer's ability to present such items as a uniquely shaped wedding cake or to provide beautiful decorations will enhance the ambiance and contribute to customer satisfaction. The caterer and the client work together to establish a budget, develop a menu, and determine the desired atmosphere. Many caterers have their own special recipes, and they are always on the lookout for quality fruits, vegetables, and meats. Caterers should have an eye for detail and be able to make fancy hors d'oeuvres and eye-catching fruit and vegetable displays.

Although caterers can usually prepare a variety of dishes, they may have a specialty, such as Cajun or Italian cuisine. Caterers may also have a special serving style (for example, serving food in Renaissance period dress) that sets them apart from other caterers. Developing a reputation by specializing in a certain area is an especially effective marketing technique.

The caterer is a coordinator who works with suppliers, food servers, and the client to ensure that an event comes off as planned. The caterer must be in frequent contact with all parties involved in the affair, making sure, for example, that the food is delivered on time, the flowers are fresh, and the entertainment shows up and performs as promised.

Good management skills are extremely important. The caterer must know how much food and other supplies to order, what equipment will be needed, how many staff to hire, and how to coordinate various activities to ensure a smooth-running event. Purchasing the proper supplies entails knowledge of a variety of food products, their suppliers, and the contacts needed to get the right product at the best possible price.

Caterers working in a large operation may appoint a manager to oversee an event. The manager will take care of the ordering, planning, and supervising responsibilities and may even work with the client.

As entrepreneurs, caterers have many important day-to-day administrative responsibilities, such as overseeing the budgeting and bookkeeping of the operation. They must make sure that the business continues to make a profit while keeping its prices competitive. Additionally, caterers must know how to figure costs and other budgetary considerations, plan inventories, buy food, and ensure compliance with health regulations.

Caterer helpers may prepare and serve hors d'oeuvres and other food and refreshments at social functions under the supervision of the head caterer. They also help arrange tables and decorations and then assist in the cleanup.

■ REQUIREMENTS
High School

Does working as a caterer sound interesting to you? If so, you should take home economics or family and consumer science classes in high school. Any class that will teach you about food preparation, presentation, and nutrition will be valuable. Since caterers run their own businesses, you should also take math, accounting and bookkeeping, and business classes to prepare for dealing with budgets, record keeping, and management. Like so many small business owners today, most caterers will use computers for such things as planning schedules, keeping addresses, and updating accounts, so be sure to take computer classes. English classes will help you to hone your communication skills, which will be essential when you deal with customers. Finally, round out your education by taking health and science classes, which will give you an added understanding of nutrition, how the body works, and how to prevent food contamination.

Postsecondary Training

The best way to enter the catering industry is through a formal training program. One way of obtaining this edu-

cation is to attend a vocational or community college with an appropriate program. Many of these schools and colleges offer professional training in food science, food preparation, and catering. Often these programs will provide opportunities for students to work in apprentice positions to gain hands-on experience.

As the catering field has grown more competitive, many successful caterers are now choosing to get a college degree in business administration, family and consumer science (home economics), nutrition, or a related field. If you decide to get a four-year college degree, make sure your course work includes subjects in nutrition, health, and business management, regardless of your major. A number of colleges and universities also offer assistance to their students in finding apprenticeships. The Foundation of the National Association of Catering Executives (NACE) provides information on universities and colleges offering programs relevant to those interested in the catering profession.

Certification or Licensing

As a measure of professional status, many caterers become certified through the NACE. To qualify for this certification, called the certified professional catering executive (CPCE), caterers must meet certain educational and professional requirements as well as pass a written examination. To keep their certification current, caterers must also fulfill requirements such as completing continuing education courses and attending professional conferences. The International Food Service Executives Association also offers the certified food executive (CFE) and the certified food manager (CFM) designations. Applications are available online; see the website listed at the end of the article for more information.

Most states require caterers to be licensed, and inspectors may make periodic visits to catering operations to ensure that local health and safety regulations are being maintained in food preparation, handling, and storage.

Caterers must be organized and diplomatic when planning an event for a client.

Other Requirements

The professional caterer should have a commitment to learning. Foods go in and out of fashion, new techniques develop, and our understanding of nutrition and health is always growing. The successful caterer will want to keep up with these new developments in the field. Because caterers run their own businesses, they should be organized, able to work on tight schedules, and conscientious about keeping accurate records. The successful caterer enjoys working with people and also has an artistic eye, with the ability to arrange food and settings in an appealing manner.

■ EXPLORING

One relatively simple way for you to begin exploring your interest in catering is to do some cooking at home. Make dinner for your family once a week, try out a new recipe for muffins, or bake cookies for your friends. If people enjoy your creations, you may be able to offer catering services to them when they have parties.

If your high school has a club for those interested in home economics, join it. You'll meet other people with similar interests and may find others to cook with. Some

organizations, such as 4-H, offer programs about food preparation and careers in food service. Find out if there is such a group in your area and join it as well.

Another great way to explore food service is through service work. Volunteering in the kitchen of a local homeless shelter where you can help prepare meals for large numbers of people can provide a great experience, both for your professional ambitions and for humanitarian reasons.

Finally, get part-time or summer work at a local restaurant. Even if you end up working at an ice cream parlor when what you really want to do is cater eight-course meals, you'll still gain valuable experience working with food, money, and customers.

■ EMPLOYERS

Most caterers own their own businesses and are, therefore, self-employed. Caterers, however, do have many different types of clients. Individuals may need catering services for a party or special family celebration. Industrial clients, such as company cafeterias, airlines, country clubs, schools, banquet halls, cruise ships, and hotels, may require catering services on a large scale or at regular intervals.

■ STARTING OUT

Some caterers enter the profession as a matter of chance after helping a friend or relative prepare a large banquet or volunteering to coordinate a group function. Most caterers, however, begin their careers after graduating from college with a degree in a program such as home economics or finishing a culinary training program at a vocational school or community college.

Qualified individuals can begin working as a manager for a large catering firm or as a manager for a hotel or country club or banquet service. Those most likely to start a catering business will have extensive experience and sufficient finances to purchase equipment and cover other start-up costs.

■ ADVANCEMENT

As with most service-oriented businesses, the success of a caterer depends on the quality of work and a good reputation. Well-known caterers can expand their businesses, often growing from a small business to a larger operation. This may mean hiring assistants and buying more equipment in order to be able to serve a larger variety of clientele. Caterers who initially worked out of their own home kitchens may get an office or relocate to another area in order to take advantage of better catering opportunities. Sometimes successful caterers use their skills and reputations to secure full-time positions in large hotels or restaurants as banquet coordinators and planners. Independent caterers may also secure contracts with industrial clients, such as airlines, hospitals, schools, and corporations, to staff their cafeterias or supply food and beverages. They may also be employed by such companies to manage their food operations.

■ EARNINGS

Earnings vary widely, depending on the size and location of the catering operation and the skill and motivation of the individual entrepreneur. Many caterers charge according to the number of guests attending a function. In many cases, the larger the event, the larger the profit. Earnings are also influenced by whether a caterer works full-time or only part time. Even very successful caterers often work part time, working another job either because they enjoy it or to protect themselves against a possible downturn in the economy.

Full time caterers can earn between $15,000 and $60,000 per year, depending on skill, reputation, and experience. An extremely successful caterer can easily earn more than $75,000 annually. A part-time caterer may earn $7,000 to $15,000 per year, subject to the same variables as the full-time caterer. Because most caterers are self-employed, vacations and other benefits are usually not part of the wage structure.

According to the U.S. Department of Labor, a caterer who is employed as a manager for a company cafeteria or other industrial client may earn a median of $24,390 per year with the lowest 10 percent making $15,790 annually and the highest 10 percent making $40,490, with vacation, health insurance, and other benefits usually included.

■ WORK ENVIRONMENT

A caterer often works long hours planning and preparing for an event, and the day of the event might easily be a 14-hour workday, from setup to cleanup. Caterers often spend long hours on their feet, and although the work can be physically and mentally demanding, they usually enjoy a great deal of work flexibility. As entrepreneurs, they can usually take time off when necessary. Caterers often work more than 60 hours a week during busy seasons, with most of the work on weekends and evenings, when events tend to be scheduled.

There is a lot of variety in the type of work a caterer does. The caterer must work closely with a variety of clients and be able to adapt to last-minute changes. Caterers must be able to plan ahead and work gracefully under pressure. Attention to detail is critical, as is the ability to work long hours under demanding situations. They must

be able to direct a large staff of kitchen workers and waitpersons and be able to interact well with clients, guests, and employees.

■ OUTLOOK

The U.S. Department of Labor projects that employment opportunities in food service should continue to grow at an average rate through 2012. Opportunities will be good for individuals who handle special events, such as weddings, bar and bat mitzvahs, and other festive occasions less affected by downswings in the economy. On the other hand, events such as business functions may offer less catering opportunities during times of recession and cutbacks.

Competition is keen as many hotels and restaurants branch out to offer catering services. However, despite competition and fluctuating economic conditions, highly skilled and motivated caterers should be in demand throughout the country, especially in and around large metropolitan areas.

■ FOR MORE INFORMATION

For information on scholarships, student branches, certification, and industry news, contact

International Food Service Executives Association
836 San Bruno Avenue
Henderson, NV 89015-9006
Tel: 888-234-3732
http://www.ifsea.org

For information on certification programs and catering publications, contact

National Association of Catering Executives
9881 Broken Land Parkway, Suite 101
Columbia, MD 21046
Tel: 410-997-9055
http://www.nace.net

For more information on programs and chapters, contact

National 4-H Council
7100 Connecticut Avenue
Chevy Chase, MD 20815
Tel: 301-961-2800
Email: info@fourhcouncil.edu
http://www.fourhcouncil.edu

For education information, visit the following website:

Foundation of the National Association of Catering Executives
http://www.nacefoundation.org

Cement Masons

■ OVERVIEW

Cement masons, who usually work for contractors in the building and construction industries, apply the concrete surfaces in many different kinds of construction projects, ranging from small patios and sidewalks to highways, dams, and airport runways. Cement masons' responsibilities include building forms for holding the concrete, determining the correct mixture of ingredients, and making sure the structure is suitable to the environment. Roughly 178,000 cement masons and concrete finishers are employed in the United States.

■ HISTORY

Cement has been used for thousands of years as a hard building material. It is made by mixing such elements as powdered alumina, silica, and limestone with water to make a solid mass. One could say that the ancient Egyptians and the Greeks were cement masons—both groups made cements. The most effective masons were perhaps the Romans, for they developed a kind of cement made from slaked lime and volcanic ash and used it throughout Europe in building roads, aqueducts, bridges, and other structures. After the collapse of the Roman Empire, however, the art of making cement practically disappeared.

In the 18th century, an English engineer named John Smeaton developed a cement that set even under water. Smeaton successfully used this cement in building the famous Eddystone Lighthouse in Devon, England. Later it was used in some parts of the Erie Canal, the waterway built to connect the Great Lakes and New York City.

Joseph Aspdin, an English stonemason, developed the first portland cement mixture in 1824 by burning and grinding together limestone and clay. He called his product "portland" cement because it resembled the limestone quarried on the Isle of Portland. It soon became the most widely used cement because of its strength and resistance to water. The first American portland cement plant was built in 1871. Cement manufactured today is essentially made of the same material as Aspdin's portland cement.

Masons seldom use cement by itself in large quantities. More often, they mix it with another material, like sand, to form a mortar to be used in structures such as brick walls and buildings. When they mix it with gravel or crushed rock, it forms concrete, a cheap, versatile, durable structural material. Today concrete is one of the most widely used building materials in the world. With the development of ways to reinforce concrete with metal and the appropriate machinery for handling it, concrete has become useful in building many structures, including fence posts, swimming pools, sculptures, roofs, bridges, highways, dams, helicopter pads, and missile launching sites.

■ THE JOB

The principal work of cement masons, also known as *concrete masons,* is to put into place and then smooth and finish concrete surfaces in a variety of different construction projects. Sometimes they add colors to the concrete to change its appearance or chemicals to speed up or slow down the amount of time that the concrete takes to harden. They use various tools to create specified surface textures on fresh concrete before it sets. They may also fabricate beams, columns, or panels of concrete.

Cement masons must know their materials well. They must be able to judge how long different concrete mixtures will take to set and how factors such as temperature and wind will affect the curing, or hardening, of the cement. They need to be able to recognize these effects by examining and touching the concrete. They need to know about the strengths of different kinds of concrete and how different surface appearances are produced.

In addition to understanding the materials they work with, cement masons must also be familiar with blueprint reading, applied mathematics, building code regulations, and the procedures involved in estimating the costs and quantities of materials.

On a construction job, the preparation of the site where the concrete will be poured is important. Cement masons begin by setting up the forms that will hold the wet concrete until it hardens into the desired shape. The forms must be properly aligned and allow for the correct dimensions, as specified in the original design. In some structures, reinforcing steel rods or mesh are set into place after the forms are put in position. The cement masons then pour or direct the pouring of the concrete into the forms so that it flows smoothly. The cement masons or their helpers spread and tamp the fresh concrete into place. Then they level the surface by moving a straightedge back and forth across the top of the forms.

Using a large wooden trowel called a bull float, cement masons begin the smoothing operation. This process covers up the larger particles in the wet concrete and brings to the surface the fine cement paste in the mixture. On projects where curved edges are desired, cement masons may use an edger or radius tool, guiding it around the edge between the form and the concrete. They may make grooves or joints at intervals in the surface to help control cracking.

The process continues with more finishing work, done either by hand with a small metal trowel or with a power trowel. This smoothing gets out most remaining irregularities on the surface. To obtain a nonslip texture on driveways, sidewalks, and similar projects, cement masons may pass a brush or broom across or embed pebbles in the surface. Afterward, the concrete must cure to reach its proper strength, a process that can take up to a week.

On structures such as walls and columns with exposed surfaces, cement masons must leave a smooth and uniform finish after the forms are removed. To achieve this, they may rub down high spots with an abrasive material, chip out rough or defective spots with a chisel and hammer, and fill low areas with cement paste. They may finish off the exposed surface with a coating of a cement mixture to create an even, attractive appearance.

Cement masons use a variety of hand and power tools, ranging from simple chisels, hammers, trowels, edgers, and leveling devices to pneumatic chisels, concrete mixers, and troweling machines. Smaller projects, such as sidewalks and patios, may be done by hand, but on large-scale projects, such as highways, power-operated floats and finishing equipment are necessary. Although power equipment can speed up many tasks, most projects have corners or other inaccessible areas that require hand work.

Various cement specialists have jobs that involve covering, leveling, and smoothing cement and concrete surfaces. Among them are *concrete-stone finishers,* who work with ornamental stone and concrete surfaces; *concrete rubbers,* who polish concrete surfaces; and *nozzle cement sprayers,* who use spray equipment to apply cement mixtures to surfaces.

Poured concrete wall technicians make up another occupational group whose activities are related to those of cement masons. These workers use surveying instruments to mark construction sites for excavation and to set up and true (that is, align correctly) concrete forms. They direct the pouring of concrete to form walls of buildings, and, after removing the forms, they may waterproof lower walls and lay drainage tile to promote drainage away from the building. Unlike cement masons, however, poured concrete wall technicians generally get at least two years of technical training in such subjects as surveying and construction methods.

■ REQUIREMENTS
High School

As with many jobs, if you want to work as a cement mason you will have an advantage if you have been to high school or have a GED. Take mathematics courses, and choose shop classes like mechanical drawing and blueprint reading if your school offers these; if it does not offer these specifically, ask your teachers which classes are similar to them. It may also help you on the job if you have taken core courses like English and general science and have a driver's license.

Sometimes, a high school diploma may not be required, but you should have at least taken some kind of vocational-technical classes. If you have no special skills or experience, you might find work as a helper and gradually learn the trade informally over an unspecified number of years by working with experienced masons. In considering applicants for helper jobs, most employers prefer to hire people who are at least 18 and in good physical condition.

Postsecondary Training

It is recommended that you first work as an apprentice to acquire the necessary skills for being a cement mason because apprenticeships provide balanced, in-depth training. Such full-time programs often last two to three years, and they are usually jointly sponsored by local contractors and unions. If you want to apply for an apprenticeship program, you might need to be approved by the local joint labor-management apprenticeship committee. You also might have to take a written test and pass a physical examination.

Training consists of a combination of planned work experience and classroom instruction. On the job as an apprentice, you would learn about the tools and materials of the trade, layout work and finishing techniques, grinding and paving, and job safety. Further classroom instruction involves around 144 hours each year in such related subjects as mathematics, blueprint reading, architectural drawing, procedures for estimating materials and costs, and local building regulations.

Other Requirements

As a cement mason, you will be involved in a great amount of physical, often strenuous, work. You may be required to show your physical fitness by, for

QUICK FACTS

SCHOOL SUBJECTS
Chemistry
Mathematics
Technical/shop

PERSONAL SKILLS
Mechanical/manipulative
Technical/scientific

WORK ENVIRONMENT
Primarily outdoors
Primarily multiple locations

MINIMUM EDUCATION LEVEL
Apprenticeship

SALARY RANGE
$19,350 to $30,660 to
$54,120

CERTIFICATION OR LICENSING
None available

OUTLOOK
Faster than the average

DOT
844

GOE
06.02.01

NOC
7282

O*NET-SOC
47-2051.00

Cement masons put the finishing touches on the foundation for a new home.

example, lifting a 100-pound sack of sand to your shoulder and carrying it 50 feet.

You should enjoy doing demanding work and be disciplined and motivated enough to do your job without close and constant supervision. The ability to get along with co-workers is important, as most cement masons work in teams. Also, as mentioned, you should have a valid driver's license.

■ EXPLORING

Since this job involves using your hands to build surfaces and forms, you might like working as a cement mason if you enjoy building things like sculptures or even sandcastles at the beach. But you also have to use your head—you can learn more about your mental aptitude for this kind of work by taking courses like general mathematics, drafting, and various shop classes. In addition, try to find a summer job on a local construction crew to gain valuable firsthand experience. Some people are introduced to the building construction trades, including the work of cement masons, while they are serving in the military, especially with the Army Engineering Corps.

Why not help build or repair a walkway where you live? Or ask your local Parks Department if you can help or at least watch workers making playground areas and skateboard hills. Keep your eyes open for construction work going on in your neighborhood, and ask if you can watch—maybe you'll even be given a hard hat to wear!

■ EMPLOYERS

Most cement masons are employed by concrete contractors or general contractors in the building and construction industries to help build roads, shopping malls,

factories, and many other structures. Some cement masons work for large contractors for such big operations as utility companies and public works departments; others work for small contractors to construct buildings such as apartment complexes, shopping malls, and schools. Cement masons who are disciplined and skilled enough in the trade and in business may have the goal of one day starting their own companies, perhaps specializing in walkways, swimming pools, or building foundations.

■ STARTING OUT

You don't have to attend college to become a cement mason. After graduating from high school or getting a GED, you can either go through a formal apprenticeship training program or get work that offers the opportunity for on-the-job training. For information about becoming an apprentice cement mason, contact local cement contractors, the offices of your state's employment service, or the area headquarters of one of the unions that organize cement masons. Many cement masons are members of either the Operative Plasterers and Cement Masons International Association of the United States and Canada or the International Union of Bricklayers and Allied Craftsmen. Also, don't forget that the Internet is a valuable resource; search for websites in the construction and trades industries. For example, the Oregon Building Congress has a site (http://www.obcweb.com) that gives information on career descriptions and wages and applying for its apprenticeships.

If you want a job as a trainee, get in touch with contractors in your area who may be hiring helpers. Follow up on job leads from the state employment service and newspaper classified ads.

■ ADVANCEMENT

Once a beginning cement mason has gained some skills and become efficient in the trade, he or she can specialize in a certain phase of the work. A cement mason may become, for example, a lip-curb finisher, an expansion joint finisher, or a concrete paving-finishing machine operator.

An experienced mason—with good judgment, planning skills, and the ability to deal with people—can try advancing to a supervisory position. Supervisors with a broad understanding of other construction trades may eventually become *job superintendents*, who are in charge of the whole range of activities at the job site. A cement mason may also become an *estimator* for concrete contractors, calculating materials requirements and labor costs. A self-disciplined and highly motivated cement mason can eventually go into business on his or her own by opening a company to do small projects like sidewalks and patios.

EARNINGS

The earnings of cement masons vary widely according to factors such as geographic location, whether they do much overtime work, and how much bad weather or local economic conditions reduce the number of hours worked. Nonunion workers generally have lower wage rates than union workers. The U.S. Department of Labor reports that in 2002 cement masons earned a median wage of $14.74 per hour. A mason doing steady, full-time work at this wage would earn $30,660 annually. The department also reports that at the low end of the pay scale 10 percent of masons earned less than $9.31 per hour (or less than approximately $19,350 annually). While at the high end, 10 percent earned more than $26.02 hourly (more than approximately $54,120 yearly). Since the amount of time spent working is limited by weather conditions, many workers' earnings vary from these figures. Apprentices start at wages that are approximately 50 to 60 percent of a fully qualified mason's wage. They receive periodic raises, so in the last phase of training, their wage is between 90 and 95 percent of the experienced worker's pay.

Benefits for cement masons typically include overtime pay, health insurance, and a pension plan.

WORK ENVIRONMENT

Cement masons do strenuous work, and they need to have good stamina. Many work outdoors and with other workers. Although cement masons might not work much in rainy and snowy conditions because cement cannot be poured in such weather, they might frequently work overtime because, once the cement has been poured, the finishing operations must be completed quickly. Temporary heated shelters are sometimes used to extend the time when work can be done.

Masons work in a variety of locations—sometimes on the ground, sometimes on ladders and scaffolds. Cement masons may need to lift or push weights, and they often are kneeling, bending, and stooping. To protect their knees, they routinely wear kneepads; they might also need to wear water-repellent boots and protective clothing.

Common hazards on the job include falling off ladders, being hit by falling objects, having muscle strains, and getting rough hands from contact with wet concrete. By exercising caution and following established job safety practices, masons minimize their exposure to hazardous conditions.

Although most contractors hire workers for 40-hour weeks, many jobs are limited by weather conditions. Masons sometimes have unexpected days off because of rain or snow. Then employers may expect masons to help catch up by working longer than eight hours on days when the weather permits.

OUTLOOK

According to the U.S. Department of Labor, job growth for cement masons should be faster than the average through 2012. The number of trained workers is relatively small, and cement masons often leave the profession for less strenuous lines of work. In addition, construction activity is expected to expand during this period, and concrete will be an important building material, especially in nonresidential building and construction.

A WORLD WITHOUT CEMENT?

Today our sidewalks, swimming pools, building foundations, roads, and many other structures are made with cement. Yet there was a period in history—hundreds of years, in fact—when cement was not used at all.

After the fall of the Roman Empire (in the fifth century A.D.), during which time cement was used extensively for building roads, aqueducts, and other infrastructure, the use of cement in building virtually disappeared. Thirteen centuries passed before John Smeaton, an English engineer, experimented with cement mixtures to develop one that could harden even under water. He used his cement to build the famous Eddystone Lighthouse, in Devon, England. The Eddystone Rocks are a group of rocks in the English Channel that have caused many shipwrecks. Lighthouses were built at this spot to warn sailors of the danger of hitting the rocks. The first lighthouse was destroyed by a storm in 1699; the second, made of oak, was destroyed by fire in 1755. Smeaton's Tower was built with stone, using a cement to bind the stones together. This lighthouse was perhaps the first structure made with cement since the fall of the Roman Empire. (The stones and cement began crumbling in the 19th century, after which bronze bolts were used for reinforcement.)

Can you imagine a world without cement? Do some research and try to find out why cement was not used for so many centuries. Were other materials more popular? Was it too difficult to find the raw materials needed for making cement? Was there just no need for cement structures? Use your imagination and research skills to think of some concrete possibilities.

Cement masons will be in demand to help build roads, bridges, buildings, subways, shopping malls, and many other structures. Although the productivity of masons will be improved by the introduction of better tools and materials (resulting in the need for fewer workers), cement masons will be needed to replace those who leave the field for retirement or other occupations.

In areas where the local economy is thriving and there are plenty of building projects, there may be occasional shortages of cement masons. At other times, even skilled masons may experience periods of unemployment because of downturns in the economy and declining levels of construction activity.

■ FOR MORE INFORMATION

For information on apprenticeship and training programs, contact

Associated General Contractors of America
333 John Carlyle Street, Suite 200
Alexandria, VA 22314
Tel: 703-548-3118
Email: info@agc.org
http://www.agc.org

For information on an annual masonry camp for chosen apprentices, contact

International Masonry Institute
The James Brice House
42 East Street
Annapolis, MD 21401
Tel: 410-280-1305
http://imiweb.org

For information on available references and publications, contact

International Union of Bricklayers and Allied Craftworkers
1776 Eye Street, NW
Washington, DC 20006
Tel: 202-783-3788
Email: askbac@bacweb.org
http://www.bacweb.org

For information on education and research programs and apprenticeships, contact

Mason Contractors Association of America
33 South Roselle Road
Schaumburg, IL 60193
Tel: 800-536-2225
Email: totoole@masoncontactors.org
http://www.masoncontactors.org

For information on apprenticeship and training programs, contact

Operative Plasterers' and Cement Masons' International Association
14405 Laurel Place, Suite 300
Laurel, MD 20707
Tel: 301-470-4200
Email:opcmiaintl@opcmia.org
http://www.opcmia.org

Ceramics Engineers

■ OVERVIEW

Ceramics engineers work with nonmetallic elements such as clay and inorganic elements such as zirconia. They are part of the ceramics and glass industry, which manufactures such common items as tableware and such highly technical items as ceramic tiles for the space shuttle. These engineers perform research, design machinery and processing methods, and develop new ceramic materials and products. They work at engineering consulting firms, manufacturing plants, and commercial support facilities. There are approximately 23,000 materials engineers in the United States; ceramics engineers belong to this group.

■ HISTORY

When we refer to ceramics we often think only of objects made of clay, like cups and saucers. Thousands of years ago, ceramics makers were limited by a dependence on this one raw material. Originally, clay was probably merely dried in the sun to harden before use. By 7,000 years ago it was being fired to make it more durable, but not many further advancements were made in its development and use for thousands of years. Ceramics makers produced things made of clay to fulfill the basic household need of storing and serving food and liquids. Based on research, it is believed that making pottery was exclusively the work of women. Throughout the world and over the centuries, changes made by workers were relatively minor when considering the many uses of ceramics today; they changed basic forms and glazings, their artistic impressions developed and spread, and they used higher-temperature materials.

Not until the scientific and industrial revolutions of the 19th century did people begin to use ceramics in complex scientific and industrial processes. Individuals skilled with ceramic materials began to develop new, manmade materials to be used in high-technology applications. New uses were also developed for naturally occurring materials, which made possible the development of new products that were stronger, more transparent, or more magnetic. The earliest ceramics engineers used porcelains for high-voltage electrical insulation. Ceramics engineers benefited other industries as well, developing, for example, material for spark plugs (automotive and aerospace industries) and magnetic and semiconductor materials (electronics industry).

Today, basic ceramic materials such as clay and sand are being used not only by artists and craftspeople but also by engineers to create a variety of products—memory storage, optical communications, and electronics. Ceramics engineers are working with more advanced materials as well (many produced by chemical processes), including high-strength silicon carbides, nitrides, and fracture-resistant zirconias.

THE JOB

Like other materials engineers, ceramics engineers work toward the development of new products. They also use their scientific knowledge to anticipate new applications for existing products.

Ceramics research engineers conduct experiments and perform other research. They study the chemical properties (such as sodium content) and physical properties (such as strength) of materials as they develop the ideal mix of elements for each product's application. Many research engineers are fascinated by the chemical, optical, and thermal interactions of the oxides that make up many ceramic materials.

Ceramics design engineers take the information culled by the researchers and further develop actual products to be manufactured. In addition to working on the new products, these engineers may need to design new equipment or processes in order to produce the products. Examples of such equipment include grinders, milling machines, sieves, presses, and drying machines.

Ceramics test engineers test materials that have been chosen by the researchers to be used as sample products, or they might be involved in ordering raw materials and making sure the quality meets the ceramics industry standards. Other ceramics engineers are involved in more hands-on work, such as grinding raw materials and firing products. Maintaining proper color, surface finish, texture, strength, and uniformity are further tasks that are the responsibility of the ceramics engineer.

Beyond research, design, testing, and manufacturing, there are the *ceramics product sales engineers*. The industry depends on these people to anticipate customers'

needs and report back to researchers and test engineers on new applications.

Ceramics engineers often specialize in an area that is associated with selected products. For example, a ceramics engineer working in the area of glass may be involved in the production of sheet or window glass, bottles, fiberglass, tableware, fiber optics, or electronic equipment parts. Another engineer may specialize in whitewares, which involves production of pottery, china, wall tile, plumbing fixtures, electrical insulators, and spark plugs.

Other segments of the industry—advanced, or technical, ceramic—employ a great number of specialized engineers. Workers may focus on engineered ceramics (for things such as engine components, cutting tools, and military armor), bioceramics (for things such as artificial teeth, bones, and joints), and electronic and magnetic ceramics (for products such as computer chips and memory disks).

REQUIREMENTS
High School

If you are interested in this field, no doubt you like to ask questions about how materials work and how elements react to each other. What makes concrete crackable? What makes fiber optics carry messages over space? Ceramics engineers have inquiring minds, often analyzing and trying to figure things out.

Ceramics engineering involves learning a lot of scientific material. In high school, science classes are the key—physics and chemistry in particular. However, all other basic courses need to be concentrated on as well: English, math, history, and social science.

High school will not be your last stop for education. You will need at least a bachelor's degree to get a job in ceramics engineering.

Postsecondary Training

Your first college courses will initially be geared toward getting you to think logically and analytically. Thus, the first two years of engineering programs typically

QUICK FACTS

SCHOOL SUBJECTS
Chemistry
Physics

PERSONAL SKILLS
Mechanical/manipulative
Technical/scientific

WORK ENVIRONMENT
Primarily indoors
Primarily one location

MINIMUM EDUCATION LEVEL
Bachelor's degree

SALARY RANGE
$39,360 to $62,590 to $92,690

CERTIFICATION OR LICENSING
Recommended

OUTLOOK
More slowly than the average

DOT
006

GOE
02.07.03

NOC
2142

O*NET-SOC
17-2131.00, 19-2032.00

CERAMICS IN SPACE

Your bathroom is not the only place where ceramic tiles are found. Would you believe that ceramic tiles are also found in space, with the space shuttle?

When spacecraft are in the final phase of their journey, they are involved in intense aerodynamic action. Reentry is the term applied to the problem of slowing down a returning spacecraft so that it lands on earth without being destroyed by aerodynamic heating. In the past, all American manned spacecraft would land in the ocean when they returned to Earth so that the water would cushion the impact of landing. The astronauts and capsules would be retrieved quickly afterward by helicopter and taken aboard waiting naval vessels.

For the manned spaceflights of the U.S. Mercury, Gemini, and Apollo programs, a specially developed heat shield was produced that would overcome the problem of reentry by protecting the leading surface of the returning capsule from the intense temperature. The heat shield was made of metals, plastics, and ceramic materials that would melt and vaporize during reentry, thereby carrying off the heat without damaging the capsule and its astronauts. The space shuttle program was likewise designed with ceramic tiles individually cemented to the ship's hull.

The U.S. space programs are not the only ones to have benefited from ceramics engineering. Soviet cosmonauts also landed on solid ground in various sites in Siberia.

center on math, physics, chemistry, and computer courses. You should be inspired and challenged to approach problems first theoretically and then practically. For instance, after you are presented with a problem, you will first think about how it would be solved, then formulate a step-by-step method by which to solve it, and then actually tackle the problem according to that method. This thinking process should be nurtured throughout your core college courses geared toward ceramics engineering, for engineers are expected to have such an aptitude for problem solving.

In your junior and senior years, you will focus particularly on your chosen area of specialization. If you major in ceramics engineering, classes and problems will be concentrated on issues in the research, development, and manufacturing ceramics engineering discipline. During these last two years of undergraduate work, it is important to consider and evaluate your goals in the field and to determine whether you prefer research, development/design, production, sales, or management. Focusing on this objective makes it easier for you to plan your job search.

Certification or Licensing

According to the National Institute of Ceramic Engineers (NICE), licensing is not required for most ceramics engineering professions. However, licensing is recommended to enhance your credentials and make yourself open to more job opportunities. The NICE oversees the licensing of ceramics engineers; see end of article for contact information. According to the U.S. Department of Labor, license requirements for engineers usually include the following: a degree from an engineering program that is approved by the Accreditation Board for Engineering and Technology (ABET), four years of work experience, and successful completion of a state exam.

Other Requirements

As mentioned earlier, you should be an inquisitive person with somewhat of an analytical mind. Since you might be doing testing and recording of process results, you'll need to be relatively comfortable working with details. You should enjoy doing intellectually demanding work and be disciplined and motivated enough to do your job without close and constant supervision, paying close attention to what you are doing. It's also important that you be able to communicate well and get along with your co-workers because engineers often work together.

■ EXPLORING

If you're interested in ceramics engineering, it's a good idea to take on special research assignments from teachers who can provide guidance on topics and methods. There are also summer academic programs where students with similar interests can spend a week or more in a special environment. The NICE notes, for example, that Alfred University and Rutgers University offer summer programs that allow you to explore both engineering in general and the work of a ceramics engineer in particular. It's also a good idea to join a national science club, such as the Junior Engineering Technical Society. In this organization, member students have the opportunity to compete in academic events, take career exploration tests, and enter design contests where they build models of such things as spacecraft and other structures based on their own designs.

For hands-on experience with materials, take pottery or sculpture classes; this will allow you to become familiar with materials such as clay and glass. You can learn how the materials are obtained and how to shape and fire them. This will give you an opportunity to learn firsthand about stress and strain, tension and compression, heat resistance, and ideal production equipment. In pottery classes, you can also learn about glazes and how various chemicals affect different materials.

FROM BUTTONS TO WATCHES

Many objects in our everyday lives are made of ceramics, things you may never have guessed. The International Museum of Ceramic Art at the New York State College of Ceramics at Alfred University recently had an exhibit called "Conspicuous Applications of Advanced Ceramics," featuring items like these:

- Coors Ceramic Company makes a ceramic hammer. The museum says, "While a ceramic hammer may not seem that practical to use in the home or shop, pounding in a few nails with a ceramic hammer certainly makes a point."

- Kyocera Industrial Ceramics Corporation makes engine parts from ceramics. The material used, silicon nitride, is an excellent material for engine components because it is extremely hard and wear resistant; it has high stiffness with low density and can withstand extremely high temperatures and harsh chemical environments.

- Police officers and soldiers appreciate this one: a bulletproof vest. The vest is made by Ceradyne from boron carbide ceramic backed by reinforced plastic laminate. When a bullet hits the armor, it is fractured by the ceramic. A major portion of the kinetic energy is absorbed by the ceramic, and residual energy is absorbed by the backing.

- Knives and scissors made by Kyocera of the ceramic materials zirconia (white) and zirconium carbide (black) are ultrasharp and stay sharp much longer than steel because of the extreme hardness of the ceramic materials.

They are also resistant to corrosion and staining, are easy to clean, and don't give food a metallic taste.

- The material used in K2 Four and Merlin Smart Skis is of the same technology first developed to dampen vibrations in optical components of antimissile weapons systems. The ceramic materials are piezoelectric: If they are deformed, they generate an electric field, and, conversely, if they are subjected to an electric field, they deform. The piezoelectric devices in these skis do both—they detect vibrations and then act to cancel them out, so the skier has better control on the slopes.

- Some cosmetics made by Elizabeth Arden contain boron nitride, a raw ingredient used in the ceramic industry. The material is of "cosmetic grade," meaning that the impurities have been removed. According to the Arden company, the cosmetic has a "positive effect" on application to the skin.

- The Rado Watch Company makes some of its watches using high-tech ceramics. Apparently the materials have the qualities of being scratchproof, durable, brilliant in appearance, and "skin friendly."

- The buttons on some of Nordstrom's shirts will outlast the shirts themselves because the buttons are made of zircon, a ceramic material that is very strong and resistant to chemicals. The buttons hold up extremely well to commercial laundering.

Source: International Museum of Ceramic Art

EMPLOYERS

Many different kinds of employers hire ceramics engineers for the variety of positions they can fill. They are involved at research, development, and manufacturing companies, electronics industries, and research and testing organizations. They work in industries that produce and process metal; machinery; electrical equipment; aircraft; and stone, clay, and glass products. They work in chemical industries that make and use ceramic products, as well as in computer and semiconductor industries. They also work in federal government agencies, and some work at engineering consulting companies.

STARTING OUT

As a high school senior, you might want to inquire with established manufacturing companies about internships and summer employment opportunities. College placement centers can also help you find employers that participate in cooperative education programs, where high school students work at materials engineering jobs in exchange for course credits.

Companies looking for engineers often send recruiters to colleges to talk with students, so when you are a senior in college you should register with your school's placement office. You must have at least a bachelor's degree to get an entry-level job in ceramics engineering. In your first job you will often be working as part of a team supervised by experienced engineers. Many companies provide newly hired engineers with a series of training courses to assist them in starting their ceramics engineering career.

ADVANCEMENT

As these engineers continue to gain research experience, they can apply for higher-level jobs in production and marketing. After becoming familiar with the materials and products at their company or organization, they may move into management or supervisory positions.

Opportunities for advancement are available especially for those who continue their education throughout their work years. Technology is always advancing, and new products and applications continue to be developed, so if a ceramics engineer keeps up to date on issues in materials science he or she is more likely to succeed. Some engineers leave the field after many years to take top-level management positions in other industries. Education beyond the bachelor's degree level is available at a number of schools across the country. Those who want to pursue a career in college-level teaching and research need to have graduate degrees, usually a Ph.D.

EARNINGS

According to the U.S. Department of Labor, earnings for ceramics engineers are quite good. The department reports a median annual income for all materials engineers (a category including ceramics engineers) of $62,590 in 2002. At the low end of the scale, 10 percent of materials engineers earned less than $39,360 annually. The highest paid 10 percent had annual incomes of more than $92,690 during this same time period. Starting salaries for those with bachelor's degrees in materials engineering averaged approximately $44,680 in 2003, according to a survey by the National Association of Colleges and Employers. Salaries for government workers are generally less than those who work for private companies.

The fringe benefits that most ceramics engineers earn are similar to those in many other industries: health insurance, sick leave, paid holidays, pension plans, and paid vacations.

WORK ENVIRONMENT

Working conditions in ceramics engineering positions vary depending on the specific field and department in which one works. Hands-on engineers work in plants and factories. Researchers work mainly in laboratories, research institutes, and universities. Those in management positions work mostly in offices; and teachers, of course, work in school environments.

Whatever the job description, a ceramics engineer typically works a standard eight-hour day, five days a week. These engineers work indoors, in either an office, a research lab, a classroom, or a manufacturing plant. A ceramic research engineer, for example, might be in a lab conducting studies on the properties of ceramics and how processing affects them. Production engineers develop the processes needed by a manufacturing plant for making products that include some type of ceramic. Other ceramics engineers work to design such things as medical instruments or artificial body parts. In any case, an engineer's scientific knowledge and analytical capabilities will continue to be challenged.

OUTLOOK

Overall employment growth for all materials engineers is predicted by the U.S. Department of Labor to grow more slowly than the average through 2012. In certain areas, however, job opportunities should be good; for example, those involved in research and testing, health, and electronic products will be in demand. In addition, the NICE reports that several high-growth industries, such as those involved in producing optical fiber and photonics, need the expertise of ceramics engineers to develop, manufacture, and market their products. Ceramics engineers will also be needed, of course, to replace those who leave the field for retirement or other work.

FOR MORE INFORMATION

The following international association provides the latest technical, scientific, and educational information to its members and others in the ceramics and related materials field.

American Ceramic Society
PO Box 6136
Westerville, OH 43086-6136
Tel: 614-890-4700
Email: info@acers.org
http://www.ceramics.org

The JETS provides activities, events, competitions, programs, and materials that allow high school students to "try on" engineering. Visit the JETS homepage for a complete list of programs, including a broad range of guidance materials about the various engineering disciplines.

Junior Engineering Technical Society (JETS)
1420 King Street, Suite 405
Alexandria, VA 22314
Tel: 703-548-5387
Email: jets@nae.edu
http://www.jets.org

For licensing and educational information, contact

National Institute of Ceramic Engineers
c/o American Ceramic Society
PO Box 6136
Westerville, OH 43086-6136
Tel: 614-890-4700
http://www.ceramics.org

The TMS is a society committed to promoting the global science and engineering professions concerned with minerals, metals, and materials.

The Minerals, Metals & Materials Society (TMS)
184 Thorn Hill Road
Warrendale, PA 15086-7514
Tel: 724-776-9000
Email: tmsgeneral@tms.org
http://www.tms.org

Frontiers, a program for high school students who have completed their junior year, covers science material not traditionally offered in high school. For information, contact

Worcester Polytechnic Institute
Frontiers
100 Institute Road
Worcester, MA 01609-2280
Tel: 508-831-5796
Email: frontiers@wpi.edu
http://www.wpi.edu/Admin/AO/Frontiers

Chemical Engineers

■ OVERVIEW

Chemical engineers take chemistry out of the laboratory and into the real world. They are involved in evaluating methods and equipment for the mass production of chemicals and other materials requiring chemical processing. They also develop products from these materials, such as plastics, metals, gasoline, detergents, pharmaceuticals, and foodstuffs. They develop or improve safe, environmentally sound processes, determine the least costly production method, and formulate the material for easy use and safe, economic transportation. Approximately 33,000 chemical engineers work in the United States.

■ HISTORY

Chemical engineering, defined in its most general sense as applied chemistry, existed even in early civilizations. Ancient Greeks, for example, distilled alcoholic beverages, as did the Chinese, who by 800 B.C. had learned to distill alcohol from the fermentation of rice. Aristotle, a fourth-century B.C. Greek philosopher, wrote about a process for obtaining fresh water by evaporating and condensing water from the sea.

The foundations of modern chemical engineering were laid out during the Renaissance, when experimentation and the questioning of accepted scientific theories became widespread. This period saw the development of many new chemical processes, such as those for producing sulfuric acid (for fertilizers and textile treatment) and alkalies (for soap). The atomic theories of John Dalton and Amedeo Avogadro, developed in the 1800s, supplied the theoretical underpinning for modern chemistry and chemical engineering.

With the advent of large-scale manufacturing in the mid-19th century, modern chemical engineering began to take shape. Chemical manufacturers were soon required to seek out chemists familiar with manufacturing processes. These early chemical engineers were called chemical technicians or industrial chemists. The first course in chemical engineering was taught in 1888 at the Massachusetts Institute of Technology, and by 1900, "chemical engineer" had become a widely used job title.

Chemical engineers are employed in increasing numbers to design new and more efficient ways to produce chemicals and chemical by-products. In the United States, they have been especially important in the development of petroleum-based fuels for internal combustion engine-powered vehicles. Their achievements range from the large-scale production of plastics, antibiotics, and synthetic rubbers to the development of high-octane gasoline.

■ THE JOB

Chemical engineering is one of the four major engineering disciplines (the others are electrical, mechanical, and civil). Because chemical engineers are rigorously trained not only in chemistry but also in physics, mathematics,

QUICK FACTS

SCHOOL SUBJECTS
Chemistry
Physics

PERSONAL SKILLS
Communication/ideas
Technical/scientific

WORK ENVIRONMENT
Primarily indoors
Primarily one location

MINIMUM EDUCATION LEVEL
Bachelor's degree

SALARY RANGE
$48,450 to $72,490 to $107,520

CERTIFICATION OR LICENSING
Required for certain positions

OUTLOOK
Little or no growth

DOT
008

GOE
02.07.01

NOC
2134

O*NET-SOC
17-2041.00

Chemical engineers must spend time making on-site inspections of plants in order to anticipate potential problems or correct existing ones.

and other sciences such as biology or geology, they are among the most versatile of all engineers, with many specialties, and they are employed in many industries. Chemical industries, which transform raw materials into desired products, employ the largest number of chemical engineers.

Research engineers work with chemists to develop new processes and products, or they may develop better methods to make existing products. Product ideas may originate with the company's marketing department; with a chemist, chemical engineer, or other specialist; or with a customer. The basic chemical process for the product is then developed in a laboratory, where various experiments are conducted to determine the process's viability. Some projects die here.

Others go on to be developed and refined at pilot plants, which are small-scale versions of commercial plants. Chemical engineers in these plants run tests on the processes and make any necessary modifications. They strive to improve the process, reduce safety hazards and waste, and cut production time and costs. Throughout the development stage, engineers keep detailed records of

the proceedings, and they may abandon projects that aren't viable.

When a new process is judged to be viable, *process design engineers* determine how the product can most efficiently be produced on a large scale while still guaranteeing a consistently high-quality result. These engineers consider process requirements and cost, convenience and safety for the operators, waste minimization, legal regulations, and preservation of the environment. Besides working on the steps of the process, they also work on the design of the equipment to be used in the process. These chemical engineers are often assisted in plant and equipment design by mechanical, electrical, and civil engineers.

Project engineers oversee the construction of new plants and installation of new equipment. In construction, chemical engineers may work as *field engineers,* who are involved in the testing and initial operation of the equipment and assist in plant start-up and operator training. Once a process is fully implemented at a manufacturing plant, *production engineers* supervise the day-to-day operations. They are responsible for the rate of production, scheduling, worker safety, quality control, and other important operational concerns.

Chemical engineers working in environmental control are involved in waste management, recycling, and control of air and water pollution. They work with the engineers in research and development, process design, equipment and plant construction, and production to incorporate environmental protection measures into all stages of the chemical engineering process.

As *technical sales engineers,* chemical engineers may work with customers of manufactured products to determine what best fits their needs. They answer questions such as "Could our products be used more economically than those now in use? Why does this paint peel?" etc. Others work as managers, making policy and business decisions and overseeing the training of new personnel. Still others may act as *biomedical engineers,* who work with physicians to develop systems to track critical chemical processes in the body or look for the best method of administering a particular drug to a patient. The variety of job descriptions is almost limitless because of chemical engineers' versatility and adaptability.

■ REQUIREMENTS
High School

High school students interested in chemical engineering should take all the mathematics and science courses their schools offer. These should include algebra, geometry, calculus, trigonometry, chemistry, physics, and biology. Computer science courses are also highly recommended.

In addition, students should take four years of English, and a foreign language is valuable. To enhance their desirability, students should participate in high school science and engineering clubs and other extracurricular activities.

Postsecondary Training

A bachelor's degree in chemical engineering is the minimum educational requirement for entering the field. For some positions, an M.S., an M.B.A., or a Ph.D. may be required. A Ph.D. may be essential for advancement in research, teaching, and administration.

For their college studies, students need a chemical engineering program approved by the Accreditation Board for Engineering and Technology and the American Institute of Chemical Engineers (AIChE). There are about 145 accredited undergraduate programs in chemical engineering in the United States offering bachelor's degrees. Some engineering programs last five or six years; these often include work experience in industry.

As career plans develop, students should consult with advisors about special career paths in which they are interested. Those who want to teach or conduct research will need a graduate degree. There are approximately 140 accredited chemical engineering graduate programs in the United States. A master's degree generally takes two years of study beyond undergraduate school, while a Ph.D. program requires four to six years.

In graduate school, students specialize in one aspect of chemical engineering, such as chemical kinetics or biotechnology. Graduate education also helps to obtain promotions, and some companies offer tuition reimbursement to encourage employees to take graduate courses. For engineers who would like to become managers, a master's degree in business administration may be helpful. Chemical engineers must be prepared for a lifetime of education to keep up with the rapid advances in technology.

Certification or Licensing

Chemical engineers must be licensed as professional engineers if their work involves providing services directly to the public. All 50 states and the District of Columbia have specific licensing requirements, which include graduation from an accredited engineering school, passing a written exam, and having at least four years of engineering experience. About one-third of all chemical engineers are licensed; they are called *registered engineers.*

Other Requirements

Important personal qualities are honesty, accuracy, objectivity, and perseverance. In addition, chemical engineers must be inquisitive, open-minded, creative, and flexible.

Problem-solving ability is essential. To remain competitive in the job market, they should display initiative and leadership skills, exhibit the ability to work well in teams and collaborate across disciplines, and be able to work with people of different linguistic and cultural backgrounds.

■ EXPLORING

High school students should join science clubs and take part in other extracurricular activities and join such organizations as the Junior Engineering Technical Society (JETS). JETS participants have opportunities to enter engineering design and problem-solving contests and to learn team development skills. Science contests are also a good way to apply principles learned in classes to a special project. Students can also subscribe to the American Chemical Society's *Chem Matters,* a quarterly magazine for high school chemistry students.

College students can join professional associations, such as the American Chemical Society (ACS), AIChE, and the Society of Manufacturing Engineers (composed of individual associations with specific fields of interest), as student affiliates. Membership benefits include subscription to magazines—some of them geared specifically toward students—that provide the latest industry

WONDER DRUGS

The era of modern medicine began in 1929 when Sir Arthur Fleming discovered penicillin. Shortly thereafter, in the 1930s, sulfa drugs were discovered. However, little was done with them until the United States entered World War II. The U.S. Armed Forces realized that the only medications available to treat wounded and sick servicemen were those used in the previous war—and that these were woefully inadequate. The pharmaceutical companies initiated an all-out effort, aided by chemical engineers, to produce the new antibiotic and sulfa drugs for our servicemen. The results were astounding. As a result, our troops suffered the lowest casualty rates in the history of warfare. After the war, these products were prescribed by physicians to their civilian patients, again with astonishing results. People were cured from potentially fatal bouts of pneumonia, tuberculosis, and a large variety of bacterial infections. Many chemical engineers are involved in the pharmaceutical industry and continue to make amazing progress in the development of new medical products. They will continue to be needed, as overuse of antibiotics has led to the evolution of antibiotic-resistant bacteria. More and different types of powerful drugs will be needed to combat this threat.

CHEMICAL ENGINEERS AND THE BATTLE OF BRITAIN

In August of 1940, the critical Battle of Britain began when Germany pitted its awesome Luftwaffe against Great Britain's modest Royal Air Force (RAF) to prepare for a ground attack. By October of that year, however, the Luftwaffe had lost the battle and Great Britain had escaped Nazi invasion. This stunning British victory was made possible by the use of a vastly superior aircraft fuel that was created by the Universal Oil Products Research Laboratories at the very beginning of World War II.

Chemical engineers set up the manufacturing processes in record time to produce this aviation fuel for the RAF. The fuel enabled RAF pilots to outfly, outmaneuver, and outfight their Luftwaffe counterparts. With this fuel in the gas tanks of its Spitfires and Hurricanes, the RAF was able to maintain air superiority over Great Britain's skies and thus prevent Germany from winning World War II outright. At that time, Great Britain was Germany's only remaining combatant—until Russia and America entered the fight in 1941.

information. College students can also contact ACS or AIChE local sections to arrange to talk with some chemical engineers about what they do. These associations can also help them find summer or co-op work experiences.

In addition, the Society of Women Engineers (SWE) has a mentor program in which high school and college women are matched with an SWE member in their area. This member is available to answer questions and provide a firsthand introduction to a career in engineering.

■ EMPLOYERS

There are approximately 33,000 chemical engineers working in the United States. While the majority of chemical engineers (about 55 percent) work in manufacturing industries, others are employed by the federal and state governments, colleges and universities, and research and testing services. The list of individual employers, if cited, would take many pages. However, the following industry classifications indicate where most chemical engineers are employed: fuels, electronics, food and consumer products, design and construction, materials, aerospace, biotechnology, pharmaceuticals, environmental control, pulp and paper, public utilities, and consultation firms. Because of the nature of their training and background, chemical engineers can easily obtain employment with another company in a completely different field if necessary or desired.

■ STARTING OUT

Most chemical engineers obtain their first position through company recruiters sent to college campuses. Others may find employment with companies with whom they have had summer or work-study arrangements. Many respond to advertisements in professional journals or newspapers. The Internet now offers multiple opportunities to job seekers, and many libraries have programs that offer assistance in making use of the available job listings. Chemical engineers may also contact colleges and universities regarding positions as part-time teaching or laboratory assistants if they wish to continue study for a graduate degree. Student members of professional societies often use the employment services of these organizations, including resume data banks, online job listings, national employment clearinghouses, and employers' mailing lists.

Typically, new recruits begin as trainees or process engineers. They often begin work under the supervision of seasoned engineers. Many participate in special training programs designed to orient them to company processes, procedures, policies, and products. This allows the company to determine where the new personnel may best fulfill their needs. After this training period, new employees often rotate positions to get an all-around experience in working for the company.

■ ADVANCEMENT

Entry-level personnel usually advance to project or production engineers after learning the ropes in product manufacturing. They may then be assigned to sales and marketing. A large percentage of engineers no longer do engineering work by the tenth year of their employment. At that point, they often advance to supervisory or management positions. An M.B.A. enhances their opportunities for promotion. A doctoral degree is essential for university teaching or supervisory research positions. Some engineers may decide at this point that they prefer to start their own consulting firms. Continued advancement, raises, and increased responsibility are not automatic but depend on sustained demonstration of leadership skills.

■ EARNINGS

Though starting salaries have dipped somewhat in recent years, chemical engineering is still one of the highest paid scientific professions. Salaries vary with education, experience, industry, and employer. The U.S. Department of Labor reports that the median annual salary for chemical engineers was $72,490 in 2002. The lowest paid 10 percent earned less than $48,450; the highest paid 10 percent earned more than $107,520 annually. The ACS conducted a salary survey of recent graduates for 2002–03. Their findings reveal that those with bachelor's degrees had median earnings of $32,000; those with master's degrees, $44,500; and those with doctorates, $63,300. According to a 2002 salary survey by the National Association of Colleges and Employers, starting annual salaries for those with bachelor's degrees in chemical engineering averaged $51,254. Chemical engineers with doctoral degrees and many years of experience in supervisory and management positions may have salaries exceeding $100,000 annually.

Benefits offered depend on the employer; however, chemical engineers typically receive such things as paid vacation and sick days, health insurance, and retirement plans.

◼ WORK ENVIRONMENT

Because the industries in which chemical engineers work are so varied—from academia to waste treatment and disposal—the working conditions also vary. Most chemical engineers work in clean, well-maintained offices, laboratories, or plants, although some occasionally work outdoors, particularly construction engineers. Travel to new or existing plants may be required. Some chemical engineers work with dangerous chemicals, but the adoption of safe working practices has greatly reduced potential health hazards. Chemical engineers at institutions of higher learning spend their time in classrooms or research laboratories.

The workweek for a chemical engineer in manufacturing is usually 40 hours, although many work longer hours. Because plants often operate around the clock, they may work different shifts or have irregular hours.

◼ OUTLOOK

The U.S. Department of Labor projects employment for chemical engineers to experience little or no growth through 2012. Most openings will be due to personnel retiring or otherwise leaving the profession and needing to be replaced. Certain areas of the field, should offer more job opportunities than others. Chemical companies, for example, will need engineers in research and development to work on new chemicals and more efficient processes. Areas in manufacturing that should be promising include pharmaceuticals, biotechnology, and electronics. Additionally, growth will come in service industries, such as companies providing research and testing services.

◼ FOR MORE INFORMATION

For information on undergraduate internships, summer jobs, and co-op programs, contact

American Chemical Society
1155 16th Street, NW
Washington, DC 20036
Tel: 800-227-5558
Email: help@acs.org
http://www.chemistry.org

For information on awards, student chapters, and career opportunities, contact

American Institute of Chemical Engineers
3 Park Avenue
New York, NY 10016-5991
Tel: 800-242-4363
Email: xpress@aiche.org
http://www.aiche.org

For information about programs, products, and a chemical engineering career brochure, contact

Junior Engineering Technical Society
1420 King Street, Suite 405
Alexandria, VA 22314
Tel: 703-548-5387
Email: jetsinfo@jets.org
http://www.jets.org

For information on National Engineers Week Programs held in many U.S. locations, contact

National Engineers Week Headquarters
1420 King Street
Alexandria, VA 22314
Tel: 703-684-2852
Email: eweek@nspe.org
http://www.eweek.org

For information on training programs, seminars, and how to become a student member, contact

Society of Manufacturing Engineers
One SME Drive
Dearborn, MI 48121
Tel: 800-733-4763
Email: careermentor@sme.org
http://www.sme.org

For information on career guidance literature, scholarships, and mentor programs, contact

Society of Women Engineers
230 East Ohio Street, Suite 400
Chicago, IL 60611-3265
Tel: 312-596-5223
Email: hq@swe.org
http://www.swe.org

Chemical Technicians

■ OVERVIEW

Chemical technicians assist chemists and chemical engineers in the research, development, testing, and manufacturing of chemicals and chemical-based products. Approximately 67,230 chemical technicians work in the United States.

■ HISTORY

The practice of modern chemistry goes back thousands of years to the earliest days when humans extracted medicinal substances from plants and shaped metals into tools and utensils for daily life. In the late 18th century, chemistry became established as a science when Antoine Lavoisier formulated the law of the conservation of matter. From that time until the present, the number and types of products attributed to the development and expansion of chemistry are almost incalculable.

The period following World War I was a time of enormous expansion of chemical technology and its application to the production of goods and consumer products such as high octane gasoline, antifreeze, pesticides, pharmaceuticals, plastics, and artificial fibers and fabrics. This rapid expansion increased the need for professionally trained chemists and technicians. The technicians, with their basic chemical knowledge and manual skills, were able to handle the tasks that did not require the specialized education of their bosses. These nonprofessionals sometimes had the title of *junior chemist.*

During the last 30 years, however, there has been a radical change in the status of the chemical technician from a "mere" assistant to a core professional. Automation and computerization have increased laboratory efficiency, and corporate downsizing has eliminated many layers of intermediate hierarchy. The result has been to increase the level of responsibility and independence, meaning greater recognition of the importance of today's highly skilled and trained chemical technicians.

■ THE JOB

Most chemical technicians who work in the chemical industry are involved in the development, testing, and manufacturing of plastics, paints, detergents, synthetic fibers, industrial chemicals, and pharmaceuticals. Others work in the petroleum, aerospace, metals, electronics, automotive, and construction industries. Some chemical technicians work in universities and government laboratories.

They may work in any of the fields of chemistry, such as analytical, biochemistry, inorganic, organic, physical, or any of the many sub-branches of chemistry. Chemical engineering, which is a combination of chemistry and engineering, develops or improves manufacturing processes for making commercial amounts of chemicals, many of which were previously produced only in small quantities in laboratory glassware or a pilot plant.

Within these subfields, chemical technicians work in research and development, design and production, and quality control. In research and development, chemical laboratory technicians often work with Ph.D. chemists and chemical engineers to set up and monitor laboratory equipment and instruments, prepare laboratory setups, and record data.

Technicians often determine the chemical composition, concentration, stability, and level of purity on a wide range of materials. These may include ores, minerals, pollutants, foods, drugs, plastics, dyes, paints, detergents, chemicals, paper, and petroleum products. Although chemists or chemical engineers may design an experiment, technicians help them create process designs, develop written procedures, or devise computer simulations. They also select all necessary glassware, reagents, chemicals, and equipment. Technicians also perform analyses and report test results.

In the design and production area, chemical technicians work closely with chemical engineers to monitor the large-scale production of compounds and to help develop and improve the processes and equipment used. They prepare tables, charts, sketches, diagrams, and flowcharts that record and summarize the collected data.

They work with pipelines, valves, pumps, and metal and glass tanks. Chemical technicians often use their input to answer manufacturing questions, such as how to transfer materials from one point to another, and to build, install, modify, and maintain processing equipment. They also train and supervise production operators. They may operate small-scale equipment for determining process parameters.

Fuel technicians determine viscosities of oils and fuels, measure flash points (the temperature at which fuels catch fire), pour points (the coldest temperature at which the fuel can flow), and the heat output of fuels.

Pilot plant operators make erosion and corrosion tests on new construction materials to determine their suitability. They prepare chemicals for field testing and report on the effectiveness of new design concepts.

Applied research technicians help design new manufacturing or research equipment.

■ REQUIREMENTS
High School
You should take several years of science and mathematics in high school, and computer training is also important. While a minority of employers still hire high school graduates and place them into their own training programs, the majority prefer to hire graduates of community colleges who have completed two-year chemical technician programs or even bachelor degree recipients. If you plan on attending a four-year college, take as much as three years of high school mathematics, including algebra, geometry, and trigonometry; three years of physical sciences, including chemistry; and four years of English.

Postsecondary Training
Graduates of community college programs are productive much sooner than untrained individuals because they have the technical knowledge, laboratory experience, and skills for the job. Computer courses are necessary, as computers and computer-interfaced equipment are routinely used in the field. Realizing that many students become aware of technical career possibilities too late to satisfy college requirements, many community and technical colleges that offer chemical technician programs may also have noncredit courses that allow students to meet college entrance requirements.

Approximately 40 two-year colleges in the United States have chemical technology programs. Once enrolled in a two-year college program designed for chemical technicians, students should expect to take a number of chemistry courses with strong emphasis on laboratory work and the presentation of data. These courses include basic concepts of modern chemistry, such as atomic structure, descriptive chemistry of both organic and inorganic substances, analytical methods including quantitative and instrumental analysis, and physical properties of substances. Other courses include communications,

physics, mathematics, industrial safety, and organic laboratory equipment and procedures.

Other Requirements
Besides the educational requirements, certain personal characteristics are necessary for successful chemical technicians. You must have both the ability and the desire to use mental and manual skills. You should also have a good supply of patience because experiments must frequently be repeated several times. You should be precise and like doing detailed work. Mechanical aptitude and good powers of observation are also needed. You should be able to follow directions closely and enjoy solving problems. Chemical technicians also need excellent organizational and communication skills. Other important qualities are a desire to learn new skills and a willingness to accept responsibility. In addition, you should have good eyesight, color perception, and hand-eye coordination.

■ EXPLORING
You can explore this field by joining high school science clubs or organizations and taking part in extracurricular activities such as the Junior Engineering Technical Society (JETS). Science contests are a good way to apply principles learned in classes to a special project. You can also subscribe to the American Chemical Society (ACS's) *ChemMatters,* a quarterly magazine for students taking chemistry in high school. Examples of topics covered in the magazine include the chemistry of lipstick, suntan products, contact lenses, and carbon-14 dating. Also, qualifying students can participate in Project SEED (Summer Education Experience for the Disadvantaged), a summer program designed to provide high school students from economically disadvantaged homes with the opportunity to experience science research in a laboratory environment.

Once you are in college, you can join the student affiliates of professional associations such as the ACS and the American Institute of Chemical Engineers (AIChE). Membership allows students to experience the professionalism of a career in chemistry. You can also contact ACS or AIChE local sections to talk with chemists and chemical engineers about what they do. These associations may also help students find summer or co-op work experiences.

■ EMPLOYERS
Almost all chemical laboratories, no matter their size or function, employ chemical technicians to assist their chemists or chemical engineers with research as well as routine laboratory work. Therefore, chemical technicians can find employment wherever chemistry is involved: in

KILOTON ENERGY FROM MICROGRAM QUANTITIES

We stand in awe of the stupendous energies released when an atomic bomb explodes. Many people think that the amount of material involved must be massive. Actually the amount of matter that is converted into energy is astonishingly small. The total amount of radioactive material that the chemists, chemical engineers, physicists, and their assistants had available to work out the intricate chemical processes for obtaining enough uranium 235 and plutonium to make the original atomic bombs was actually less than a gram.

Lisa Meitner, a Jewish refugee chemist from Germany, demonstrated to Albert Einstein the first atomic bomb reaction ever run in the USA. Meitner used only a few atoms of uranium 235. She also revealed that this reaction was already known to Nazi scientists. Based on this demonstration, Einstein wrote to President Franklin Delano Roosevelt for an audience and the president immediately responded. This led to the formation of the agency that created the atomic bombs that ended World War II.

industrial laboratories, in government agencies such as the Departments of Health and Agriculture, and at colleges and universities. They can work in almost any field of chemical activity, such as industrial manufacturing of all kinds, pharmaceuticals, food, and production of chemicals. There are approximately 67,230 chemical technicians currently employed in the United States.

■ STARTING OUT

Graduates of chemical technology programs often find jobs during the last term of their two-year programs. Some companies work with local community colleges and technical schools to maintain a supply of trained chemical technicians. Recruiters regularly visit most colleges where chemical technology programs are offered. Most employers recruit locally or regionally. Because companies hire locally and work closely with technical schools, placement offices are usually successful in finding jobs for their graduates.

Some recruiters also go to four-year colleges and look for chemists with bachelor's degrees. Whether a company hires bachelor's-level chemists or two-year chemical technology graduates depends on both the outlook of the company and the local supply of graduates.

Internships and co-op work are highly regarded by employers, and participation in such programs is a good way to get your foot in the door. Many two- and four-year schools have co-op programs in which full-time students work approximately 20 hours a week for a local company. Such programs may be available to high school seniors as well. Students in these programs develop a good knowledge of the employment possibilities and frequently stay with their co-op employers.

More and more companies are using contract workers to perform technicians' jobs, and this is another way to enter the field. There are local agencies that place technicians with companies for special projects or temporary assignments that last anywhere from a month to a year or more. Many of these contract workers are later hired on a full-time basis.

■ ADVANCEMENT

Competent chemical technicians can expect to have long-term career paths. Top research and development positions are open to technically trained people, whether they start out with an associate's degree in chemical technology, a bachelor's degree in chemistry, or just a lot of valuable experience with no degree. There are also opportunities for advancement in the areas of technology development and technology management, providing comparable pay for these separate but equal paths. Some companies have the same career path for all technicians, regardless of education level. Other companies have different career ladders for technicians and chemists but will promote qualified technicians to chemists and move them up that path.

Some companies may require additional formal schooling for promotion, and the associate's degree can be a stepping-stone toward a bachelor's degree in chemistry. Many companies encourage their technicians to continue their education, and most reimburse tuition costs. Continuing education in the form of seminars, workshops, and in-company presentations is also important for advancement. Chemical technicians who want to advance must keep up with current developments in the field by reading trade and technical journals and publications.

■ EARNINGS

Earnings for chemical technicians vary based on their education, experience, employer, and location. The U.S. Department of Labor reports the median hourly wage for chemical technicians as $18.00 in 2002. A technician making this wage and working full-time would earn a yearly salary of approximately $37,430. The top 10 percent earned $27.54 per hour (or $57,280 annually) or more in 2002. The department also reports that science technicians (a category including chemical technicians) working for the federal government had average salaries ranging from $30,440 to $52,585 in 2003. Salaries tend to be highest in private industry and lowest in colleges and universities.

If a technician belongs to a union, his or her wages and benefits depend on the union agreement. However, the percentage of technicians who belong to a union is very small. Benefits depend on the employer, but they usually include paid vacations and holidays, insurance, and tuition refund plans. Technicians normally work a five-day, 40-hour week. Occasional overtime may be necessary.

WORK ENVIRONMENT

The chemical industry is one of the safest industries in which to work. Laboratories and plants normally have safety committees and safety engineers who closely monitor equipment and practices to minimize hazards. Chemical technicians usually receive safety training both in school and at work to recognize potential hazards and to take appropriate measures.

Most chemical laboratories are clean and well lighted. Technicians often work at tables and benches while operating laboratory equipment and are usually provided office or desk space to record data and prepare reports. The work can sometimes be monotonous and repetitive, as when making samples or doing repetitive testing. Chemical plants are usually clean, and the number of operating personnel for the space involved is often very low.

OUTLOOK

The U.S. Department of Labor expects employment for all science technicians to grow about as fast as the average for all occupations through 2012. Chemical technicians will be in demand as the chemical and drug industries work to improve and produce new medicines and personal care products. Chemical technicians will also be needed by businesses that provide environmental services and "earth-friendly" products, analytical development and services, custom or niche products and services, and quality control. Growth, however, will be somewhat offset by a general slowdown in overall employment in the chemical industry.

Graduates of chemical technology programs will continue to face competition from bachelor's level chemists. The chemical and chemical-related industries will continue to become increasingly sophisticated in both their products and their manufacturing techniques. Technicians trained to deal with automation and complex production methods will have the best employment opportunities.

FOR MORE INFORMATION

For general career information, as well as listings of chemical technology programs, internships, and summer job opportunities, contact

American Chemical Society
1155 16th Street, NW
Washington, DC 20036
Tel: 800-227-5558
Email: help@acs.org
http://www.chemistry.org

For information on awards, student chapters, and career opportunities, contact

American Institute of Chemical Engineers
3 Park Avenue
New York, NY 10016-5991
Tel: 800-242-4363
Email: xpress@aiche.org
http://www.aiche.org

For information about programs, products, and a chemical engineering career brochure, contact

Junior Engineering Technical Society
1420 King Street, Suite 405
Alexandria, VA 22314-2794
Tel: 703-548-5387
Email: jetsinfo@jets.org
http://www.jets.org

For fun and educational information on the field of chemistry, check out the following website:

Rader's Chem 4 Kids
http://www.chem4kids.com

Chemists

OVERVIEW

Chemists are scientists who study the composition, changes, reactions, and transformations of matter. They may specialize in analytical, biological, inorganic, organic, or physical chemistry. They may work in laboratories, hospitals, private companies, government agencies, or colleges and universities. Approximately 91,000 chemists are employed in the United States.

HISTORY

The ancient Egyptians began gathering knowledge about matter and organizing it into systems, developing what is now known as alchemy, which mixed science with metaphysics. This was the beginning of chemistry. Alchemists concentrated their efforts on trying to convert lead and other common metals into gold. Alchemy dominated the European chemical scene until modern chemistry started to replace it in the 18th century.

In the late 1700s, Antoine Lavoisier discovered that the weight of the products of a chemical reaction always equaled the combined weight of the original reactants. This discovery became known as the law of the conservation of matter. In the 1800s, the work of scientists such as John Dalton, Humphrey Davy, Michael Faraday, Amadeo Avogadro, Dmitri Mendeleyev, and Julius Meyer laid the foundations for modern chemistry. The latter two men independently established the periodic law and periodic table of elements, making chemistry a rational, predictable science. The technological advances of the Industrial Revolution provided both the necessity and the incentive to get rid of alchemy and make chemistry the science it is today.

QUICK FACTS

SCHOOL SUBJECTS
Chemistry
Mathematics

PERSONAL SKILLS
Communication/ideas
Technical/scientific

WORK ENVIRONMENT
Primarily indoors
Primarily one location

MINIMUM EDUCATION LEVEL
Bachelor's degree

SALARY RANGE
$30,980 to $52,890 to
$92,170

CERTIFICATION OR LICENSING
None available

OUTLOOK
About as fast as the average

DOT
022

GOE
02.02.01

NOC
2112

O*NET-SOC
19-2031.00

■ THE JOB

Many chemists work in research and development laboratories. However, some chemists spend most of their time in offices or libraries, where they do academic research on new developments or write reports on research results. Often these chemists determine the need for certain products and tell the researchers what experiments or studies to pursue in the laboratory.

Chemists who work in research are usually focused on either basic or applied research. Basic research entails searching for new knowledge about chemicals and chemical properties. This helps scientists broaden their understanding of the chemical world, and often these new discoveries appear later as applied research. Chemists who do applied research use the knowledge obtained from basic research to create new and/or better products that may be used by consumers or in manufacturing processes, such as the development of new pharmaceuticals for the treatment of a specific disease or superior plastics for space travel. In addition, they may hold marketing or sales positions, advising customers about how to use certain products. These jobs are especially important in the field of agriculture, where customers need to know the safe and effective doses of pesticides to use to protect workers, consumers, and the environment. Chemists who work in marketing and sales must understand the scientific terminology involved so they can translate it into nontechnical terms for the customer.

Some chemists work in quality control and production in manufacturing plants. They work with plant engineers to establish manufacturing processes for specific products and to ensure that the chemicals are safely and effectively handled within the plant.

Chemists also work as instructors in high schools, colleges, and universities. Many at the university level are also involved in basic or applied research. In fact, most of America's basic research is conducted in a university setting.

There are many branches of chemistry, each with a different set of requirements. A chemist may go into basic or applied research, marketing, teaching, or a variety of other related positions. *Analytical chemists* study the composition and nature of rocks, soils, and other substances and develop procedures for analyzing them. They also identify the presence of pollutants in soil, water, and air. *Biological chemists*, also known as *biochemists*, study the composition and actions of complex chemicals in living organisms. They identify and analyze the chemical processes related to biological functions, such as metabolism or reproduction, and they are often involved directly in genetics studies. They are also employed in the pharmaceutical and food industries.

The distinction between organic and inorganic chemistry is based on carbon-hydrogen compounds. Ninety-nine percent of all chemicals that occur naturally contain carbon. *Organic chemists* study the chemical compounds that contain carbon and hydrogen, while *inorganic chemists* study all other substances. *Physical chemists* study the physical characteristics of atoms and molecules. A physical chemist working in a nuclear power plant, for example, may study the properties of the radioactive materials involved in the production of electricity derived from nuclear fission reactions.

Because chemistry is such a diverse field, central to every reaction and the transformation of all matter, it is necessary for chemists to specialize in specific areas. Still, each field covers a wide range of work and presents almost limitless possibilities for experimentation and study. Often, chemists will team up with colleagues in other specialties to seek solutions to their common problems.

■ REQUIREMENTS
High School

If you are interested in a chemistry career, begin preparing yourself in high school by taking advanced-level courses in the physical sciences, mathematics, and English. A year each of physics, chemistry, and biology is essential, as are the abilities to read graphs and charts, perform difficult mathematical calculations, and write scientific reports. Computer science courses are also important to take, since much of your documentation and other work will involve using computers.

Postsecondary Training

The minimum educational requirement for a chemist is a bachelor's degree in science. However, in the upper levels of basic and applied research, and especially in a university setting, most positions are filled by people with doctoral degrees.

Over 600 bachelor's degree programs are accredited by the American Chemical Society (ACS). Many colleges and universities also offer advanced degree programs in chemistry. Upon entering college, students majoring in chemistry must expect to take classes in several branches of the field, such as organic, inorganic, analytical, physical chemistry, and biochemistry. Chemistry majors must advance their skills in mathematics, physics, and biology and be proficient with computers.

Other Requirements

Chemists must be detail-oriented, precise workers. They often work with minute quantities, taking minute measurements. They must record all details and reaction changes that may seem insignificant and unimportant to the untrained observer. They must keep careful records of their work and have the patience to repeat experiments over and over again, perhaps varying the conditions in only a small way each time. They should be inquisitive and have an interest in what makes things work and how things fit together. Chemists may work alone or in groups. A successful chemist is not only self-motivated but should be a team player and have good written and oral communication skills.

■ EXPLORING

The best means of exploring a career in chemistry while still in high school is to pay attention and work hard in chemistry class. This will give you the opportunity to learn the scientific method, perform chemical experiments, and become familiar with chemical terminology. Advanced placement (AP) courses will also help. Contact the department of chemistry at a local college or university to discuss the field and arrange tours of their lab-

NYLON

Dr. Wallace Carothers, a research chemist in the employ of the DuPont Chemical Company, was assigned the task of investigating the synthesis of thermoplastic polymers and their potential uses. (A thermoplastic material is one that softens and loses strength as it is heated.) His investigations started in the late 1920s and culminated in the commercial development of nylon just before the start of World War II. At the time these studies began, there were only a few polymers in use. Among these were Bakelite for heat and electrical insulators, Cellophane for wrappings, and Celluloid for detachable shirt collars and cuffs and billiard balls. There was a very limited market for synthetic polymers.

Nylon is in a class of polymers known as polyamides and is related chemically to proteins. During the course of the research studies, a chemist working on the synthesis of polyamides prepared a small sample in a test tube. After he put the hot test tube into a test tube rack, he pulled out the stirring rod. As he did, a long fiber of hot product came out. The more he pulled, the longer, stronger, and thinner the fiber thread became. In addition, the fiber thread was pliable and flexible. Dr. Carothers realized at once that this fiber, when woven into a fabric, would rival and perhaps supplant imported silk. This is exactly what happened. Likewise, nylon rope replaced hemp rope—aided by legislation making the growing of hemp illegal.

oratories or classrooms. Due to the extensive training involved, it is very unlikely that a high school student will be able to get a summer job or internship working in a laboratory. However, you may want to contact local manufacturers or research institutions to explore the possibility.

■ EMPLOYERS

About 44 percent of the approximately 91,000 chemists employed in the United States work for manufacturing companies. Most of these companies are involved in chemical manufacturing, producing such products as plastics, soaps, paints, drugs, and synthetic materials. Chemists are also needed in industrial manufacturing and pilot plant locations. Examples of large companies that employ many chemists are Dow Chemical, DuPont, Monsanto, Standard Oil, and Campbell Soup.

Chemists also work for government agencies, such as the Departments of Health and Agriculture, the Bureau of Standards, and the Bureau of Mines. Chemists may find positions in laboratories at institutions of higher learning that are devoted to research. In addition, some chemists work in full-time teaching positions in high schools and universities.

STARTING OUT

Once you have a degree in chemistry, job opportunities will begin to open up. Summer jobs may become available after your sophomore or junior year of college. You can attend chemical trade fairs and science and engineering fairs to meet and perhaps interview prospective employers. Professors or faculty advisors may know of job openings, and you can begin breaking into the field by using these connections.

If you are a senior and are interested in pursuing an academic career at a college or university, you should apply to graduate schools. You will want to begin focusing even more on the specific type of chemistry you wish to practice and teach (for example, inorganic chemistry or analytical chemistry). Look for universities that have strong programs and eminent professors in your intended field of specialty. By getting involved with the basic research of a specific branch of chemistry while in graduate school, you can become a highly employable expert in your field.

ADVANCEMENT

In nonacademic careers, advancement usually takes the form of increased job responsibilities accompanied by

A chemistry professor and her graduate student helper work on a research project at a university laboratory.

salary increases. For example, a chemist may rise from doing basic research in a laboratory to being a group leader, overseeing and directing the work of others. Some chemists eventually leave the laboratory and set up their own consulting businesses, serving the needs of private manufacturing companies or government agencies. Others may accept university faculty positions.

Chemists who work in a university setting follow the advancement procedures for that institution. Typically, a chemist in academia with a doctoral degree will go from instructor to assistant professor to associate professor and finally to full professor. In order to advance through these ranks, faculty members at most colleges and universities are expected to perform original research and publish their papers in scientific journals of chemistry and/or other sciences. As the rank of faculty members increases, so do their duties, salaries, responsibilities, and reputations.

EARNINGS

Salary levels for chemists vary based on education, experience, and the area in which they work. According to the U.S. Department of Labor, median annual earnings for all chemists in 2002 were $52,890. The lowest paid 10 percent earned less than $30,980 at that time, and the highest paid 10 percent made more than $92,170 annually. The department also notes that chemists working for the federal government had average incomes of $76,857 in 2003.

According to the ACS's salary survey of 2003, the median starting salary of its members with Ph.D.'s was $63,300; those with master's degrees, a median of $44,500, and those with bachelor's degrees, a median of $32,000. Salaries tend to be highest on the East Coast and West Coast. In addition, those working in industry usually

---

PIERRE AND MARIE CURIE

Serendipity (the ability to recognize the importance of an accidental occurrence) is a valuable asset for a scientist. In the summer of 1896, in the laboratories of Dr. Henri Becquerel, radioactivity was accidentally discovered. One of Dr. Becquerel's assistants placed an unexposed photographic plate on a lab desk for him to use. Another assistant put his laboratory key on top of the photographic plate. Finally, a third person placed a piece of uranium ore on top of the key. After Dr. Becquerel used the plate, he discovered that it had been exposed and that there was an image of a key on the film. He then assigned the task of finding out the source of this unusual phenomenon to one of his graduate students, Marie Curie. After several years of tedious, laborious work, she isolated a tiny amount of two naturally occurring radioactive elements, radium and polonium, from tons of uranium ore. In this work, she was assisted by her husband, Dr. Pierre Curie. In 1903, they and Dr. Becquerel received the Nobel Prize for the discovery of radioactivity. In 1911, Madam Curie received another Nobel Prize for the isolation of radium and polonium.

have the highest earnings, while those in academia have the lowest.

As highly trained, full-time professionals, most chemists receive health insurance, paid vacations, and sick leave. The specifics of these benefits vary from employer to employer. Chemists who teach at the college or university level usually work on an academic calendar, which means they get extensive breaks from teaching classes during summer and winter recesses.

■ WORK ENVIRONMENT

Most chemists work in clean, well-lighted laboratories that are well organized and neatly kept. They may have their own offices and share laboratory space with other chemists. Some chemists work at such locations as oil wells or refineries, where their working conditions may be uncomfortable. Occasionally, chemical reactions or substances being tested may have strong odors. Other chemicals may be extremely dangerous to the touch, and chemists will have to wear protective devices such as goggles, gloves, and protective clothing and work in special, well-ventilated hoods.

■ OUTLOOK

The U.S. Department of Labor predicts the employment of chemists to grow about as fast as the average rate through 2012. The outlook is expected to be particularly good for researchers interested in working in pharmaceutical firms, biotechnology firms, and firms producing specialty chemicals. In addition, chemists working for research and testing firms and those involved in environmental research should enjoy a strong demand for their expertise. Aspiring chemists will do well to get doctoral degrees to maximize their opportunities for employment and advancement. The ACS reports that 37 percent of 2002–03 chemistry Ph.D. graduates found full-time permanent jobs

Those wishing to teach full time at the university or college level should find opportunities but also stiff competition. Many of these institutions are choosing to hire people for adjunct faculty positions (part-time positions without benefits) instead of for full-time, tenure-track positions. Nevertheless, a well-trained chemist should have little trouble finding some type of employment.

■ FOR MORE INFORMATION

For a copy of Partnerships in Health Care, *a brochure discussing clinical laboratory careers, and other information, contact*

American Association for Clinical Chemistry
2101 L Street, NW, Suite 202
Washington, DC 20037-1558

Tel: 800-892-1400
Email: info@aacc.org
http://www.aacc.org

For general information about chemistry careers and approved education programs, contact

American Chemical Society
1155 16th Street, NW
Washington, DC 20036
Tel: 800-227-5558
Email: help@acs.org
http://www.chemistry.org

Chief Information Officers

■ OVERVIEW

Chief information officers (CIOs), also known as *information systems directors,* are responsible for all aspects of their company's information technology. They use their knowledge of technology and business to determine how information technology can best be used to meet company goals. This may include researching, purchasing, and overseeing set-up and use of technology systems, such as intranet, Internet, and computer networks. These managers sometimes take a role in implementing a company's website. CIOs work for a variety of employers, including businesses, government agencies, libraries, and colleges and universities.

■ HISTORY

Over the past few decades, the importance of computer technology and the Internet has increased rapidly. The Internet, which did not exist in its current form until 1983, is now an integral part of nearly all business. It allows companies to conduct transactions in a matter of seconds, and people all over the world now rely on the World Wide Web as a quick resource on everything from education and current events to shopping and the stock market.

Because of this boom in the use and importance of computers and the Internet, workers must constantly be updated about changes in technology. It is the job of the chief information officer to make sure that all technology runs smoothly in an office, and that no workers are in the dark when it comes to the company's computer systems. The position of chief information officer, though a relatively new job title, has quickly risen in importance and prestige and is firmly established among the top executive positions available in the business world.

■ THE JOB

Anyone who has read Scott Adams' comic strip *Dilbert* knows something about the imaginary wall between business executives and technology experts in the corporate world. On one side of the wall (so the Dilbert story goes), there are the folks who wear business suits and who don't know a laptop from an Etch-A-Sketch. On the other side of the wall, there are the geeks in tennis shoes who hang out in *X-Files* chat rooms and couldn't care less about the company's mission statement. If popular lore is to be believed, confusion, hostility, and poor business practices abound whenever these two groups try to join forces.

It's the job of the CIO to enter this ongoing battle and find a way to straddle the wall between business and technology. Although they're up to date on cutting-edge information technology, today's CIOs must know their way around the company's business as well as any other high-level manager. That means they attend strategy sessions and management meetings, in addition to meeting with computer professionals and other members of the technical staff. Using their combined business and technical know-how, CIOs usually oversee the selection and implementation of their company's information systems—from email programs to corporation-wide intranets.

Making these decisions requires enough technical savvy to choose appropriate technology systems from an array of complex options. Decisions like these, though, also require a sophisticated sense of how information in a company circulates and how that information relates to business practices. Does the company's customer database need to connect to the World Wide Web? What security issues are created if that connection is established? Who needs to be able to access the most sensitive information, and who needs to be locked out?

Answering these sorts of questions can take all of a CIO's mix of executive knowledge and technical expertise.

For Chuck Cooper, the director of information systems at a major public library, making these sorts of decisions also requires a good understanding of the financial situation of his organization. He must select systems for his library staff that fit their needs and the library's often-limited budget. At the same time, he must consider what the library may need five and even 10 years down the road, since a lack of vision now can mean more money and time spent later. After systems have been selected, Cooper must establish and oversee vendor relationships (contractual agreements between the library and companies that supply technical equipment). Evaluating potential vendor relationships for financial and technological advantages takes up a large part of the CIO's working hours.

For most CIOs, though, actually choosing and implementing technology systems is just the beginning. For example, Cooper spends much of his time getting employees enthusiastic and informing them about new computer technology. "I spend a lot of my time trying to convince people of the utility of new systems," he explains. "Library people are reality-oriented. They have to kick the tires." For Cooper, giving his employees a chance to "kick the tires" of new systems means organizing targeted, hands-on demonstration sessions. Once they have a chance to test-drive new programs themselves, employees often become excited about the new services they'll be able to provide to library patrons.

■ REQUIREMENTS
High School

If you are interested in this career, you should start preparing in high school by taking college preparatory classes. Take as many computer science, mathematics, business, and English classes as possible. Speech classes are another way to improve your communication skills.

Postsecondary Training

Becoming a CIO requires a solid technology background and solid business understanding. In general, companies require their executives to have at least a bachelor of arts or bachelor of science degree, and often a master's in business administration as well.

If you're interested in becoming a CIO, you should be sure that your college degree provides you with both business and computer skills. Some programs devoted to providing this sort of background have begun to spring up, such as the School of Information Management and Systems (SIMS) at the University of California at Berkeley. The SIMS offers a master's and Ph.D. in information management and systems.

QUICK FACTS

SCHOOL SUBJECTS
Business
Computer science
English

PERSONAL SKILLS
Helping/teaching
Leadership/management

WORK ENVIRONMENT
Primarily indoors
One location with some travel

MINIMUM EDUCATION LEVEL
Bachelor's degree

SALARY RANGE
$51,650 to $126,260 to $450,000+

CERTIFICATION OR LICENSING
None available

OUTLOOK
About as fast as the average

DOT
189

GOE
13.01.01

NOC
0611

O*NET-SOC
11-1011.00

INTERNET TIME LINE

1958 The USSR launches Sputnik, the first artificial satellite. Fearing a disadvantage in the Cold War arms race, the U.S. created ARPA, the Advanced Research projects Administration.

1961 Leonard Kleinrock of MIT publishes the first paper on packet-switching technology, which allows information to be broken down into "packets," which are then sent individually to their destination and reassembled. This is followed by MIT's J. C. R. Licklider and W. Clark's 1962 paper on distributed social networks and Paul Baran of the RAND corporation's 1964 paper on distributed computing networks.

1965 ARPA sponsors a study on a "cooperative network of time-sharing computers."

1966–67 ARPA computer scientists discuss creating such a network of computers.

1969 The Department of Defense begins construction of ARPANET, a four-node system connecting UCLA, Stanford, the University of California Santa Barbara, and the University of Utah.

1970 ARPANET interface protocols begin to be codified.

1971 First email program is written by Ray Tomlinson. He modifies it for use on ARPANET in 1972. ARPANET has 23 nodes on 15 hosts.

1973 ARPANET expands to Europe when University College of London is added. Research on constructing an Internet begins. Number of ARPANET users is estimated as 2,000.

1974 First commercial version of ARPANET established.

1975 ARPANET communications are now taking place by packet radio and satellite. Other packet-switching networks, such as BITNET, a cooperative venture between the City University of New York and Yale University (established in 1981), begin to propagate, bringing connected computing to a far greater number of people.

1979 USENET established.

1983 *Wargames*, the first "hacker movie," released. Local bulletin board systems begin to sprout up.

1984 Number of hosts exceeds 1,000.

1986 Internet Engineering Task Force established.

1987 Number of hosts reaches 10,000.

1989 Number of hosts exceeds 100,000.

1990 ARPANET taken offline, replaced entirely by the nascent Internet.

1991 CERN, the European research consortium, releases the World Wide Web.

1992 The Internet Society is chartered. Number of hosts breaks 1 million. The Internet is now common in colleges, even amongst non-computer scientists.

1993 InterNIC created to provide domain registration services. The U.S. White House comes online. Businesses begin to come online and commercial ISPs begin to grow. Mosaic, the first Web browser, is released.

1995 Netscape's IPO starts the Internet boom. Scott Heiferman founds i-traffic, the first Internet ad agency.

Source: Hobbe's Internet Timeline, http://www. zakon.org/robert/internet/timeline/

Other Requirements

Equally important to training, though, are the communication skills you'll need to sell your co-workers and staff on the information strategies that you build. "Writing and especially speaking are crucial in this business," Chuck Cooper points out. "You are constantly presenting yourself and your work to others, and you need to be able to communicate well in order to succeed." English, writing, and speech classes should help you hone your verbal communication skills.

■ EXPLORING

The best way to explore this field while you are still in high school is by joining computer clubs at school and community centers and learning all you can about the Internet, networks, and computer security. You might also get a part-time job that includes computer work. This can help you get exposure to computer systems and how they are used in a business.

To get management experience, start with your own interests. There are managerial duties associated with almost every organized activity, from the drama club or theatrical productions to sports or school publications.

■ EMPLOYERS

Until fairly recently, CIOs were found primarily at large corporations that could afford another high-level executive salary. According to *Inc.* magazine, though, smaller companies are now beginning to see the value of having a dedicated information director. "At smaller companies, technology has often been placed too low in the organization," Chuck Cooper points out. Without executive decision-making power, technology professionals often found their recommendations given insufficient weight. While this sort of strategy might save money in the short-term, small companies have gradually discovered that they pay later when outdated systems must be upgraded or altered. In fact, even nonprofits and other less mainstream small businesses have begun to hire CIOs.

■ STARTING OUT

Since CIOs are high-level executives, people usually spend several years working in business administration or information management before they apply for jobs at the CIO level. Lower- and mid-level information management jobs usually involve specialization in a certain area. For example, middle-level systems management professionals in Chuck Cooper's department may run technology training programs, design and implement help desks, or oversee small database systems.

■ ADVANCEMENT

After they've proven themselves at lower-level information management jobs, these employees begin to manage larger units, such as the user support program or the larger library database system. Eventually, some of these employees may have the business experience and broad technical background required to apply for jobs at the CIO level.

Other CIOs may find work at the executive level after making what's known as a lateral move—a move from a position in one department to a position at the same level in another department. For example, successful business administration professionals might be able to move into an information systems department as a manager rather than an entry-level database administrator. But they would still need to prove they had managed to gain the technical know-how required to do the job.

■ EARNINGS

Earnings among CIOs vary substantially based on the type of business, the size of the employer, the executive's experience, and other such factors. According to the U.S. Department of Labor, the median annual income for all top executives, which includes CIOs, was $126,260 in 2002. Fields in which executives had higher median salaries included Internet publishing and broadcasting, with a median of $185,140, securities and commodity exchanges, with a median of $181,100 annually, and ISPs (Internet Service Providers) and Web search portals, with a median of $181,430 for 2002. A survey by Abbott, Langer, & Associates shows that executives working in the nonprofit sector had yearly median incomes of over $72,000 in 2003. Even those working for nonprofits, however, can command extremely high salaries. Some of the highest paid earned more than $450,000 annually.

The SIMS at the University of California, Berkeley, reports that the 2003 starting salary for its graduates who supplied income information averaged $67,400 with bonuses. Graduates reported incomes ranging from $58,000 to $75,000 per year.

Benefits for CIOs depend on the employer but generally include health insurance, retirement plans, and paid vacation and sick days. Bonuses and stock options may also be offered.

■ WORK ENVIRONMENT

The best part of being a CIO for Chuck Cooper comes when new technology is actually put in place. "When you see the effect of probably a year of planning, and it has a positive impact on the way the public uses the library, that's a nice feeling," he remarks. Especially because CIOs often spend time thinking about changes several years down the road, having a program actually "hit the streets," as Cooper puts it, is gratifying, especially when it allows library patrons and staff to access information in a way they never could before.

Although the payoff can be gratifying, the planning may not be, Cooper admits. "There's a lot of frustration caused by dead ends," he explains. "There are often projects that you try to get started that are dependent on other people, and you may have to wait or start over." The interdependence between technology and other library areas means that Cooper often spends years revising plans before they can get the go-ahead. The need to take strategies back to the drawing board can be the worst part of Cooper's work.

■ OUTLOOK

According to the U.S. Department of Labor, top executives, including CIOs, should experience employment growth at a rate about as fast as the average through 2012. As consumers and industries are increasingly reliant on computers and information technology, the expertise of CIOs will be in continuous demand. As computer technology becomes more sophisticated and more complex, corporations will increasingly require Information Science professionals capable of choosing among the ever-growing array of information technology options. Additionally, as small organizations begin to prioritize information management, more jobs should be available for CIOs outside of large corporations. Because some of these jobs are likely to be at nonprofit and educational institutions, IS professionals may have wider options when choosing an employer. Although salaries can be expected to be lower at these sorts of organizations, they may provide interested employees with a less formal and more service-oriented atmosphere.

■ FOR MORE INFORMATION

For information on careers, contact

Information Technology Association of America
1401 Wilson Boulevard, Suite 1100
Arlington, VA 22209
Tel: 703-522-5055
http://www.itaa.org

For information on training, contact

School of Information Management and Systems
University of California at Berkeley
102 South Hall
Berkeley, CA 94720-4600
Tel: 510-642-1464
Email: info@sims.berkeley.edu
http://info.berkeley.edu

Child Care Service Owners

■ OVERVIEW

Child care service owners provide care for infants, toddlers, and pre-school aged children. While the parents and guardians are at work, child care providers watch the children and help them develop skills through games and activities. The child care service may be part of the owner's home, or it may be a separate center composed of classrooms, play areas, and areas for infant care. The service owner must hire, train, and schedule child care workers, or teachers, to assist with large numbers of children. The owner must also manage the center's finances, assure that the center meets legal requirements and accreditation standards, and meet with prospective clients. Child care centers are in demand all across the country, as the majority of parents of young children have jobs outside the home. There are approximately 456,000 child care workers in the United States. According to the National Child Care Association, there are currently about 113,000 licensed child care centers in the United States.

■ HISTORY

Most people probably think daytime child care is a fairly modern idea. It's true that only 17 percent of the mothers of one-year-olds were part of the labor force in 1965. That number seems small when compared to statistics from the U.S. Department of Labor—today, approximately 65 percent of mothers of children under age six are working outside the home. But child care centers were needed as far back as the 18th century. In England, factories opened nurseries to care for the workers' children, a trend that carried over to the United States in the 19th century. Of course, working conditions in factories were often terrible before the 1900s, and the children were put to work at very young ages. So the child care service as we know it today didn't really begin to evolve until World War II, when women joined the workforce while the men were off fighting. Though many of these women quit their jobs when the men returned from the war, roles for women began to change. The last half of the 20th century saw more opportunities for women in the

QUICK FACTS

SCHOOL SUBJECTS
Business
Family and consumer science

PERSONAL SKILLS
Helping/teaching
Leadership/management

WORK ENVIRONMENT
Primarily indoors
Primarily one location

MINIMUM EDUCATION LEVEL
Some postsecondary training

SALARY RANGE
$12,300 to $37,570 to $60,000

CERTIFICATION OR LICENSING
Required by certain states

OUTLOOK
Faster than the average

DOT
N/A

GOE
12.03.03

NOC
N/A

O*NET-SOC
39-9011.00

workplace and, for many families, two incomes became necessary to meet the rising costs of living. Findings by the U.S. Census Bureau indicate that today only about 15 percent of married couples with young children have one parent working and one parent staying at home. Some 65 percent of women with children under the age of six are in the labor force. This has put dependable, safe child care services in high demand.

■ THE JOB

Child care workers are responsible for taking care of several children of various ages every single workday, and owners of child care services must make sure that the care the children receive is of the highest possible quality. Parents expect those working at care centers to help their children learn basic skills, such as using a spoon and playing together, and to prepare them for their first years of school by, for example, teaching colors and letters. Service owners come up with activities that build on children's abilities and curiosity. Attention to the individual needs of each child is important, so that activities can be adapted to specific needs. For example, a three-year-old child has different motor skills and reasoning abilities than a child of five years of age, and the younger child will need more help completing the same project. Child care centers typically provide care for babies, toddlers, and children of pre-kindergarten age, and because of this, they offer many different kinds of instruction. Some kids will just be learning how to tie their shoes and button their coats, while others will have begun to develop reading and computer skills. And, of course, the infants require much individual attention for things such as feedings, diaper changings, and being held when awake. Owners of small facilities are typically the primary care givers and do the majority of these activities in addition to the administrative activities involved in running a business—ordering supplies, paying the bills, keeping records, making sure the center meets licensing requirements, and so forth. Owners of large facilities hire aides, teachers, and assistant directors to help provide care.

Nancy Moretti owns a child care center in Smithfield, Rhode Island, called Just For Kids. The center is licensed to care for 54 children and is composed of five classrooms—each room for a different age group. She has a staff of 18 who work with kids from six weeks to five years old. "Everyone here loves children," Moretti says. "We're an extended family; we all look out for each other." Moretti's day starts with a walk through the classrooms to make sure everything is in order and to make sure all the staff members and children are there. Much of Moretti's work consists of attending to staff concerns, such as payment and scheduling. When hiring teachers for her center, she looks for people with some background in child development, such as a college degree or some years of practical experience.

A background in child development gives owners and teachers the knowledge of how to create a flexible and age-appropriate schedule that allows time for music, art, playtime, academics, rest, and other activities. Owners and child care staff work with the youngest children to teach them the days of the week and to recognize colors, seasons, and animal names and characteristics; older children are taught number and letter recognition and simple writing skills. Self-confidence and the development of communications skills are encouraged in day care centers. For example, children may be given simple art projects, such as finger painting, and after the paintings are completed everyone takes a turn showing and explaining the finished projects to the rest of the class. Show and tell gives students opportunities to speak and listen to others. Other skills children are taught may include picking up their toys after play time and washing their hands before snack time.

Owners of both small and large facilities have many other responsibilities aside from lessons and instruction. They may need to spend a large portion of a day comforting a child, helping him or her to adjust to being away from home, and finding ways to include the child in group activities. Children who become frightened or homesick need reassurance. Children also need help with tasks, such as putting on and taking off their coats and boots in the winter. If a child becomes sick, the owner must decide how to handle the situation and may contact the child's parents, a doctor, or even a hospital. Owners also order supplies for activities and supervise events, such as snack time, during which they teach children how to eat properly and clean up after themselves.

Child care center owners also work with the parents of each child. It is not unusual for parents to come to preschool and observe a child or go on a field trip with the class, and child care workers often take these opportunities to discuss the progress of each child as well as any specific problems or concerns. Scheduled meetings are available for parents who cannot visit the school during the day. Moretti makes it a point to be frequently available for the parents when they're dropping off and picking up the children. "Parents need to know that I'm here," she says. "For the owner to be involved is important to the parents."

■ REQUIREMENTS
High School

You should take courses in early childhood development when available. Many home economics courses include units in parenting and child care. English courses will help you to develop communication skills important in dealing with children, their parents, and a child care staff. In teaching children, you should be able to draw from a wide base of education and interests, so take courses in art, music, science, and physical education. Math and accounting courses will prepare you for the bookkeeping and management requirements of running your own business.

Postsecondary Training

A college degree isn't required for you to open a day care center, but it can serve you in a variety of ways. A child development program will give you the background needed for classroom instruction, as well as for understanding the basics of child care and psychology. A college degree will also demonstrate to your clients that you have the background necessary for good child care. A college degree program should include course work in a variety of liberal arts subjects, including English, history, and science, as well as nutrition, child development, psychology of the young child, and sociology.

Certification or Licensing

Requirements for the licensing or registering of child care workers vary from state to state. You can visit the website of the National Child Care Information Center (http://nccic.org), part of the Administration for Children and Families, to find out about your state's regulatory bodies and contact information. Requirements for a child care administrator, director, or owner may include having a certain amount of child care experience or education, completing a certain amount of continuing education per year, being at least 21 years of age, and having a high school diploma. Cardiopulmonary resuscitation training is also often required. National certification may not be required of child care service owners and workers in every state, but some organizations do offer it. The Council for Professional Recognition offers the Child Development Associate (CDA) National Credentialing Program. To become a CDA, you must meet competency standards and have experience in child care. There are over 100,000 CDAs across the country. The National Child Care Association offers the National Administrator Credential (NAC). To receive this credential, you must complete a special five-day training course. (Contact information for these organizations is at the end of this article.)

Other Requirements

Obviously, a love for children and a concern for their care and safety are most important. Child care comes naturally to most of those who run child care services. "I can't see myself doing anything but this," Nancy Moretti says. You should be very patient and capable of teaching children in many different stages of development. Because young children look up to adults and learn through example, it is important that a child care worker be a good role model—you should treat the children with respect and kindness, while also maintaining order and control. You must also be good at communicating with the parents, capable of addressing their concerns, and keeping them informed as to their children's progress.

■ EXPLORING

You can gain experience in this field by volunteering at a child care center or other preschool facility. Some high schools provide internships with local preschools for students interested in working as teacher's aides. Your guidance counselor can provide information on these opportunities. Summer day camps or Bible schools with preschool classes also hire high school students as counselors or counselors-in-training. Take tours of child care centers of various sizes, and talk to the owners about how they started their businesses.

■ EMPLOYERS

According to data from the National Child Care Association, there are approximately 113,000 licensed child care centers in the United States. Child care centers are located all across the country. Those who buy an established day care facility often find that most of the clients will come along with it. For those who start their own centers, word-of-mouth, a variety of offerings, and a good reputation will draw clients. Franchising is a viable option in this industry. Child care franchising operations are among the fastest growing centers. Primrose School Franchising Company and Kids 'R' Kids International are two of the child care companies offering franchises.

In some cases, people work from their homes, watching only their own children and some of the children from their neighborhoods; this is usually referred to as "family child care." Quality child care is a concern of most parents, regardless of economic standing. Single working mothers are often the hardest hit with child care expenses, and federal mandates requiring states to find work for welfare recipients means even more children need daytime care outside the home. Government programs and subsidies help to provide child care services for lower-income families.

■ STARTING OUT

At your first opportunity, you should take part-time work at a child care center to gain firsthand experience. Contact child care centers, nursery schools, Head Start programs, and other preschool facilities to learn about job opportunities. Often there are many jobs for child care workers listed in the classified sections of newspapers. The turnover rate for child care workers is high because of the low wages and long hours. "You need to make sure child care is something you want to do," Nancy Moretti says, "before starting your own center." Some owners of child care centers are not actively involved with the day-to-day running of the business; parents, however, prefer to leave their children at a center where the owner takes an active interest in each child's well-being. Moretti purchased a day care center that had been in operation for nearly 10 years, and she had worked as a teacher and director at that center for eight of them. Knowing all the parents already helped her ease into ownership without losing a single client. For those considering buying an established daycare center, Moretti recommends that they spend a few months getting to know the parents first.

■ ADVANCEMENT

As an owner's child care center becomes better known in the community, and as it gains a reputation for providing quality child care, owners may advance by expanding their businesses. With enough income, owners can hire staff members to help with child care, instruction, and administrative requirements. Nancy Moretti is currently in the process of expanding Just For Kids in a variety of ways. She'll be putting an addition onto the building to allow for a number of new services: a full-day kindergarten, a before- and after-school program, and a summer day camp. Moretti also recently sent surveys out to the parents to determine whether Saturday child care is needed.

In addition to expanding offerings at one child care center, some owners choose to open more centers. Primrose School Franchising Company, for example, notes that 61 percent of its franchisees own two or more Primrose Schools.

■ EARNINGS

It is difficult to determine exact salaries for child care service owners since revenue for child care centers varies according to the number of children cared for, whether the center is owned or rented, number of staff, and other factors. A center in a city with a higher cost of living and more staffing and licensing requirements will charge more than a center in a smaller town. No matter where it is located, however, a large percentage of a child care center's earnings goes to paying the staff. In 2001, Amercians spent $31 billion on licensed child care. A 2000 report by the Children's Defense Fund found that parents paid an annual average of between $4,000 and $6,000 nationwide for the care of a four-year-old at a child care center. Some centers charged even more, in the range of $10,000. If a center cared for 54 children (like Nancy Moretti's) and charged $4,000 per child, the center's annual budget would be $216,000. Although this sounds like a fair amount of money, keep in mind that staff salaries must come out of this amount, and these usually account for 60 percent to 70 percent of expenses. Sixty percent of $216,000 is $129,600, which leaves the owner with $86,400 to pay for all other expenses, such as any rent or mortgage on the center, any maintenance expenses, any food served, liability insurance premiums, and other equipment or items that are needed, such as playground equipment, paper cups, or books. After all such expenses are paid, owners can then draw their salaries.

According to the Center for the Child Care Workforce, a study of child care centers in California found the average annual income for center directors was approximately $37,570 in 2000. The U.S. Department of Labor reports the median earnings for all child care workers were $8.32 per hour in 2002. Someone working at this rate for 40 hours a week year-round would have an annual income of approximately $16,350. The department also reports the lowest paid 10 percent of child care workers earned less than $5.91 per hour (approximately $12,300 annually), and the highest paid 10 percent earned more than $11.46 per hour (approximately $23,840 annually). A child care center owner just starting out in the business and working as the only employee may have earnings comparable to that of the average child care worker. An experienced child care service owner running a large and well-established center, on the other hand, may have annual earnings in the $60,000s.

Since they run their own businesses, owners must pay for their own benefits, such as health insurance and retirement plans.

■ WORK ENVIRONMENT

Center owners spend a lot of time on their feet, helping staff, directing children, and checking on classrooms. Most child care centers have play areas both inside and outside. In the spring and summer months, owners—especially those with a small staff or none at all—may spend some time outside with the kids, leading them in playground exercises and games. The colder winter months will keep the kids confined mostly indoors. Though child care workers can control the noise somewhat, the work conditions are rarely quiet. An owner's work is divided between child care and administrative responsibilities, but the size of the center often determines how much time is spent on each. For example, the owner of a small service with one part-time employee will spend most of the day with the children, directing activities, serving snacks, settling arguments over toys, and talking with parents as they drop off or pick up their children. For the most part, this owner will do administrative work—record keeping of attendance, billing for services, paying the center's bills, filing tax forms—during short periods of free time in the day and during the evenings and on weekends when the center is closed. Owners of large centers with several staff members often have more time during the day to attend to administrative duties. Even these owners, however, often work on business matters after hours. Nancy Moretti's center is open Monday through Friday, 6:30 A.M. to 6:00 P.M., but she also works weekends. "It's fun most of the time," she says, despite 70 to 80 hour workweeks.

■ OUTLOOK

The U.S. Department of Labor projects overall employment in the field of child care services to grow faster than the average through 2012. More women than ever are part of the workforce; of those who have children, many take only an abbreviated maternity leave. The Children's Defense Fund reports that every day more than 13 million preschool-aged children in the United States are in some type of child care. By 2010, the nation will have another 1.2 million children aged four and under. Corporations have tried to open their own day care centers for the children of employees but haven't always had much success. Often these corporations turn to outside sources and contract with independent care centers to meet these child care needs.

Staffing problems in general plague the child care industry, as centers struggle to find reliable, long-term employees. Other concerns of child care centers include providing better child care for low-income families; making child care more inclusive for children with disabilities; and possible competition from state funded pre-kindergarten programs.

On the bright side, though, licensed child care centers continue to open and provide opportunities for those wanting to run their own businesses. According to Wilson Marketing Group, which specializes in child care information, approximately 3,000 new licensed centers opened every year from 1996 to 2001, meaning growth went up by 43 percent. Those centers that offer a number of services, such as after-school programs for older children and computer instruction for children at a variety of age levels, should have the most success and continue to draw new clients.

■ FOR MORE INFORMATION

For information about the CDA credential, contact
Council for Professional Recognition
2460 16th Street, NW
Washington, DC 20009
Tel: 800-424-4310
http://www.cdacouncil.org

Visit the NAEYC website to read relevant articles concerning issues of child care and to learn about membership and accreditation for programs.
National Association for the Education of Young Children (NAEYC)
1509 16th Street, NW
Washington, DC 20036
Tel: 800-424-2460
http://www.naeyc.org

For information about student memberships and training opportunities, contact
National Association of Child Care Professionals
PO Box 90723
Austin, TX 78709-0723
Tel: 800-537-1118
http://www.naccp.org

For information about the NAC credential and to learn about the issues affecting child care, visit the NCCA webpage or contact
National Child Care Association (NCCA)
1016 Rosser Street
Conyers, GA 30012
Tel: 800-543-7161
http://www.nccanet.org

Child Care Workers

■ OVERVIEW

Child care workers are employed by day care centers, preschools, and other child care facilities and work with infants, toddlers, and preschool-aged children. While parents and guardians are at work, child care providers watch the children and help them develop skills through games and activities. Today there are approximately 456,000 child care workers, outside of preschool teachers and teacher-assistants, in the United States. According to the National Child Care Association, there are currently about 113,000 licensed child care centers in the United States.

■ HISTORY

You probably think daytime child care is a fairly modern idea. It's true that only 17 percent of the mothers of one-year-olds were part of the labor force in 1965. That number seems small when you look at statistics from the U.S. Census Bureau—today, approximately 55 percent of mothers with infants (children under the age of one) are in the workforce. Additionally, most preschool-aged children are cared for in child care centers, according to findings by the Center for Women in the Economy. But child care centers were needed as far back as the 18th century. In England, factories employed child care workers to run nurseries for the factory workers' children, a trend that carried over to the United States in the 19th century. Of course, working conditions in factories were often terrible before the 1900s, and the children were put to work at very young ages. So the child care service as we know it today didn't really begin to evolve until World War II, when women joined the workforce while the men were away fighting. Though many of these women quit their jobs when the men returned from the war, roles for women began to change. In the last half of the 20th century there were more opportunities for women in the workplace, and for many families, two incomes became necessary to meet the rising costs of living. Daytime child care consequently became necessary. The U.S. Census Bureau reports that by the end of the 20th century, in close to 70 percent of married couples with children under age 18, both the husband and wife held paying jobs. Since the bureau projects the number of children under 18 to increase from approximately 70 million in 1999 to about 77 million in 2020, we can logically assume that dependable, safe, and caring child care services will continue to be in high demand.

■ THE JOB

Anyone who has ever baby-sat or worked with a group of kids in a summer camp knows something about the demands of child care. Professional child care workers take on the responsibility of providing quality care to young children. But the parents don't just expect these workers to simply keep an eye on the kids while they're at work—they also expect child care workers to help the children learn basic skills and to prepare them for their first years of school. Child care workers assist teachers and center directors in coming up with activities that build on children's abilities and curiosity. Child care workers must also pay attention to the individual needs of each child so that they can adapt activities to these specific needs. For example, a worker should plan activities based on the understanding that a three-year-old child has different motor skills and reasoning abilities than a child five years of age. Because child care workers care for babies, toddlers, and kids of pre-kindergarten age, these workers need to provide many different kinds of instruction. Some kids will just be learning how to tie their shoes and button their coats, while others will have begun to develop reading and computer skills. And, of course, the infants require less teaching and more individual attention from the child care workers—they ensure that the babies are fed, diapered, and held when awake.

When working with children, child care workers rely on a background in child development to create a flexible schedule allowing time for music, art, play time, academics, rest, and other activities. Depending on the size and structure of the center, workers may be assigned to deal with a particular age group, or they may work with many age groups. Liz Rahl, who holds a bachelor's degree in human development, works as an assistant director for the Discovery Academy, a child care center in Omaha, Nebraska. Her mornings begin with caring for the infants—feeding and diapering them. "My job is to provide comfort," she says. "And hopefully some stimulus." She then works with the preschoolers for most of the morning, returning to the infant room to feed them lunch and put them down for their naps, before returning to the preschoolers to assist them with their lunch. When working with the preschoolers, Rahl helps them to develop skills for kindergarten. "They need to know their numbers, one through 15, and to have alphabet recognition. They need to know how to spell their names and to know their addresses and phone numbers. And their social skills have to be on track for kindergarten. They need to know to share and to take turns and to not talk back." Rahl also works with the children on rhyming and other word skills. "And they need to understand pattern schemes, such as triangle, circle, triangle. Or red, red, blue." To help direct the children, the center organizes a different "theme" every few weeks. The theme may center around a holiday or a season, or a specific letter or number that

QUICK FACTS

SCHOOL SUBJECTS
Art
Family and consumer science

PERSONAL SKILLS
Communication/ideas
Helping/teaching

WORK ENVIRONMENT
Primarily indoors
Primarily one location

MINIMUM EDUCATION LEVEL
High school diploma

SALARY RANGE
$12,300 to $16,350 to $23,840

CERTIFICATION OR LICENSING
Recommended (certification)
Required by certain states (licensing)

OUTLOOK
About as fast as the average

DOT
359

GOE
12.03.03

NOC
6474

O*NET-SOC
39-9011.00

the children should learn. A nursery rhyme or fairy tale may also be part of the theme.

Workers at a child care center have many responsibilities in addition to giving lessons and instruction. Anyone who has worked with children at all knows they need a lot of assistance in a variety of ways. A major portion of a child care worker's day is spent helping children adjust to being away from home and encouraging them to play together. Children who become frightened or homesick need gentle reassurance. Child care workers often help kids with their coats and boots in the winter and also deal with the sniffles, colds, and generally cranky behavior that can occur in young children. These workers supervise snack time, teaching children how to eat properly and clean up after themselves.

Child care workers also work with the parents of each child. It is not unusual for parents to come to a center and observe a child or go on a field trip with the class, and child care workers often take these opportunities to discuss the progress of each child as well as any specific problems or concerns. Rahl makes sure the parents of the children she cares for are aware of the child's progress. "I send home sheets," she says, "listing any problems along with the good things the kids are doing."

■ REQUIREMENTS
High School
You should take courses in early childhood development when available. Many home economics courses include units in parenting and child care. English courses will help you to develop communication skills important in dealing with children and their parents. In teaching children, you should be able to draw from a wide base of education and interests, so take courses in art, music, science, and physical education.

Postsecondary Training
A high school diploma and some child care experience is usually all that's required to get a job as a child care worker, but requirements vary among employers. Some employers prefer to hire workers who have taken college courses or hold bachelor's degrees; they may also pay better wages to those with some college education. A college program should include course work in a variety of liberal arts subjects, including English, history, and science, as well as nutrition, child development, psychology of the young child, and sociology. Some employers also offer on-the-job training.

Certification or Licensing
Requirements for child care workers vary from state to state. Each state sets its own licensing requirements for

A child care worker plays with children at a day care facility.

child care workers. Some states require that you complete a certain number of continuing education hours every year; these hours may include college courses or research into the subject of child care. CPR training is also often required. National certification isn't required of child care workers, but some organizations do offer it. The Council for Professional Recognition offers the Child Development Associate (CDA) National Credentialing Program. To complete the program and receive the CDA credential, you must do a certain amount of field and course work, and pass a final evaluation. According to the council, there are now more than 100,000 CDAs. The National Child Care Association offers the Certified Childcare Professional (CCP) credential. To receive this credential, you must have extensive child care experience, along with special training.

Other Requirements
You should have love and respect for children and a genuine interest in their well-being. You'll also need a great deal of patience and the ability to understand the needs of preschool-aged children in all stages of development. "You need to be able to be on the child's level," Liz Rahl says. "You need to be able to talk directly to them, not down to them." She also emphasizes the importance of a sense of humor. "You need to be laid back, but you can't let them run all over you."

■ EXPLORING
Talk to neighbors, relatives, and others with small children about baby-sitting some evenings and weekends. Preschools, day care centers, and other child care programs often hire high school students for part-time positions as aides. There are also many volunteer opportunities for working with kids—check with your library or local literacy program about tutoring children and reading to

IT TAKES ALL KINDS

The National Association of Child Care Resource and Referral Agencies lists the following types of child care providers available to parents:

Family Child Care: A service in which a child care worker cares for unrelated children in his or her own home. The average family child care service cares for six children.

For-Profit Chain Center: A closely held corporation; may operate only a few centers in a single community, or more than 1,000 across the country; cares for an average of 125 children.

Independent For-Profit Center: A center individually owned and operated; cares for an average of 70 children.

Independent Nonprofit Center: A small community center focused primarily on serving poor families; cares for an average of 70 children.

Church-Housed Center: A center based in a church, offering services to the community at large; cares for an average of 65 children.

Head Start Center: Funded by the federal government; serves three- and four-year-olds on a part time basis; cares for an average of 55 children.

preschoolers. Summer day camps, Bible schools, children's theaters, museums, and other organizations with children's programs also hire high school students as assistants or have need of volunteers.

■ EMPLOYERS

Both the government and the private sector are working to provide for the enormous need for quality child care. Child care workers should find many job opportunities in private and public preschools, day care centers, government-funded learning programs, religious centers, and Montessori schools. Work is available in small centers or at large centers with many children. Franchisers, like Primrose Schools and Kids 'R' Kids International, are also providing more employment opportunities. Approximately four out of 10 child care workers are self-employed.

■ STARTING OUT

At your first opportunity, you should take part-time work at a child care center to gain firsthand experience. Contact child care centers, nursery schools, Head Start programs, and other preschool facilities to identify job opportunities. The Child Care Bureau estimates that one-third of all child care teachers leave their centers each year. Check the classified section of local newspapers, and you are likely to see many job openings for child care workers. Liz Rahl advises that you get a degree in early

child development, so you can advance into a director position if you choose. "And be careful when you choose a child care center," she says. "Make sure you're comfortable with their policies and approaches to child care."

■ ADVANCEMENT

As child care workers gain experience, they receive salary increases and promotions to such positions as assistant director or preschool teacher. With additional experience and education, they may be able to advance into an administrative position, such as director of a center. Some experienced child care workers with advanced degrees become directors of Head Start programs and other government programs. If a child care worker has a head for business, he or she may choose to open a child care facility. Some child care workers also decide to pursue a degree in education and become certified to teach kindergarten or elementary school.

■ EARNINGS

Earnings for child care workers depend on their education level, the type of employer, the number of children being cared for, and other such variables. According to the U.S. Department of Labor, the median annual earnings for child care workers in 2002 were $16,350 for full-time work. The department also reports that 10 percent of child care workers earned less than $5.91 per hour (approximately $12,300 annually based on a 40-hour workweek). At the high end of the pay scale, 10 percent of child care workers made more than $11.46 per hour (approximately $23,840 annually based on a 40-hour workweek). Few child care workers receive full benefits from their employers. Some large day care centers and preschools, however, do offer limited health care coverage and vacation pay.

■ WORK ENVIRONMENT

Child care workers spend much of their work day on their feet in a classroom or on a playground. Facilities vary from a single room to large buildings. Class sizes also vary; some child care centers serve only a handful of children, while others serve several hundred. Classrooms may be crowded and noisy, but those who love children enjoy all the activity.

Part-time employees generally work between 18 and 30 hours a week, while full-time employees work 35 to 40 hours a week. Part-time work gives the employee flexibility, and for many, this is one of the advantages of the job. "It's a great starter job," Liz Rahl says. The job also allows workers to play with the children and to direct them in games and other activities. "Most adults don't get to have fun at work," she says. She also enjoys watching the children go through all the different stages of development, from infant to preschooler. "It's very rewarding when a preschooler comes in unable to even write a letter," she says, "then soon they're writing their names." Among the children she cares for is her daughter Christa. "The job allows me to be with my child," she says, "so I know what her day's like."

OUTLOOK

Employment is projected to increase about as fast as the average through 2012, according to the U.S. Department of Labor. Job opportunities, however, should be good because there is high turnover in this field, resulting in the need for many replacement workers. One reason for this turnover rate is the low pay; in order to keep quality employees, center owners may have to charge clients more so that they may better compensate staff members. Jobs will also be available as more child care centers, both nonprofit and for-profit, open to meet the increased demand for child care as more mothers take jobs outside the home. There will be more franchises and national chains offering job opportunities to child care workers, as well as centers that cater exclusively to corporate employees. Child care workers may be working with older children, as more day care centers expand to include elementary school services. Bilingual child care workers will find more job opportunities and better salaries.

FOR MORE INFORMATION

For information about certification, contact

Council for Professional Recognition
2460 16th Street, NW
Washington, DC 20009-3575
Tel: 800-424-4310
http://www.cdacouncil.org

For information about student memberships and training opportunities, contact

National Association of Child Care Professionals
PO Box 90723
Austin, TX 78709-0723
Tel: 800-537-1118
Email: admin@naccp.org
http://www.naccp.org

For information about certification and to learn about the issues affecting child care, visit the NCCA website, or contact

National Child Care Association (NCCA)
1016 Rosser Street
Conyers, GA 30012
Tel: 800-543-7161
http://www.nccanet.org

Child Life Specialists

OVERVIEW

Child life specialists work in health care settings to help infants, children, adolescents, and their families through illness or injury. One of the primary roles of the child life specialist is to ease the anxiety and stress that often accompany hospitalization, injury, or routine medical care. Child life specialists help children, adolescents, and their families maintain living patterns that are as close to normal as possible, and they try to minimize the potential trauma of hospitalization. Child life specialists do this by providing opportunities for play and relaxation, interaction with other children, and personalized attention. They also encourage family involvement, which can play a major role in helping children and adolescents cope with difficult situations. Child life specialists may help children and their families to develop coping skills and educate them about the experience that they are going through.

Some hospitals refer to their child life specialists as *play therapists, patient activity therapists, activity therapists,* or *therapeutic recreation specialists.*

HISTORY

At one time physicians and nurses were the only adults responsible for the care of children in hospitals. Parents left their children in hospitals, frequently for long periods of time, for treatment of their illnesses. But many parents felt that their children's emotional needs were not being met. Children were often not told about what tests, treatments, or procedures they were to undergo, and as a result their hospital experience was frequently traumatic. In addition, social workers who were part of the health care team sometimes were not specially trained to work with children and could not provide them with support.

QUICK FACTS

SCHOOL SUBJECTS
Health
Psychology

PERSONAL SKILLS
Communication/ideas
Helping/teaching

WORK ENVIRONMENT
Primarily indoors
Primarily one location

MINIMUM EDUCATION LEVEL
Bachelor's degree

SALARY RANGE
$21,870 to $33,810 to $56,120

CERTIFICATION OR LICENSING
Recommended

OUTLOOK
About as fast as the average

DOT
195

GOE
12.02.02

NOC
N/A

O*NET-SOC
21-1021.00

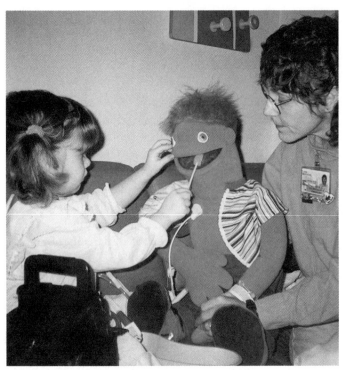

A child life specialist encourages a young patient to "prep" a puppet patient for surgery. This will make the child comfortable with what she will experience in preparation for her own upcoming surgery.

During the early 20th century attempts were made to improve health care workers' understanding of children's needs and to make hospital stays less emotionally difficult for children. C. S. Mott Hospital in Ann Arbor, Michigan, for example, created the nation's first child life department, focusing on child development, in 1922. Gradually, during the 1940s and 1950s, "play programs" were developed at various care facilities across the country. In these settings children were allowed to relax, play, and feel safe. As professional interest in and understanding of child development grew, the play programs began to be seen not only as a play time but also as a therapeutic part of children's care during hospital stays. During the 1960s and 1970s the field of child life grew dramatically as it gained increasing acceptance.

The profession of child life specialists was formally recognized in 1974, when the Association for the Care of Children's Health formed a committee for child life and activity specialists. The committee, which became the independent organization Child Life Council (CLC) in 1982, had as its goals to promote the profession of child life specialist as well as to strengthen these specialists' professional identity. The committee's members recognized that the interruption of a hospitalization or even an ambulatory procedure can have negative consequences for children's growth and development. Today, child life specialists are recognized as an integral part of a child's health care team.

■ THE JOB

When children are hospitalized, the experience can be frightening. Child life specialists need to be tuned into the child's or adolescent's concerns. For some children, separation from their families and the familiarity of home can be traumatic. For others, repeated blood tests, needles, or painful procedures can cause fears or nightmares. Emotional damage can be a danger even for adolescents. No matter how short or long the hospital stay and no matter how serious the illness or injury, children can experience anxiety or other emotional effects.

Child life specialists try to ease the possible trauma of being in the hospital. They play an important role in educating and comforting both the patients and their families. They become familiar and trusted adults, and they are usually the only professionals who do not perform tests on the children.

Child life specialists may use dolls and medical instruments to show children what the doctor will be doing. They may help children act out their concerns by having them give a doll a shot if they receive one. The child life specialist may use recreational activities, art projects, cooking, music, and outdoor play in their work. Programs are tailored to meet the needs of individual patients. Some children are unable to express their fears and concerns and may need the child life specialist to draw them out. Some children rely on the child life specialist to help them understand what is happening to them. Still others need the child life specialist to explain children's emotional outbursts or withdrawal to their families.

When children are hospitalized for a long period of time, child life specialists may accompany them to procedures, celebrate successful treatment, or plan a holiday celebration. Child life specialists may also take children on preadmission orientation and hospital tours. They serve as advocates for children's issues by promoting rooming-in or unrestricted parental or sibling visits. Many child life specialists work in conjunction with local school districts to help children keep up with school while they are in the hospital.

Child life administrators supervise the staffs of child life personnel. In larger hospitals, the administrators work with other hospital administrators to run the child life programs smoothly within the hospital setting.

Child life specialists can turn their patients' hospital stays into a time of growth. Children are very resilient, and with proper care by their entire health team, they can emerge from hospital stays with a sense of accomplishment and heightened self-esteem.

REQUIREMENTS

High School

If you are interested in becoming a child life specialist, you will need to plan on going to college after high school. Therefore, you should take a college preparatory curriculum. As a child life specialist you will need to understand family dynamics, child development, educational play, and basic medical terminology. To help you prepare for this specialty, take psychology and sociology courses and, if available, child development classes. In addition, be sure that your class schedule includes science courses, including health and biology. Because communication is such an important aspect of this work, take English, communication, and speech classes. You may also want to take art, physical education, and drama classes to develop skills that you can use in a variety of therapies, such as play, art, and recreation therapy.

Postsecondary Training

Some colleges or universities offer specific programs in child life, and quite a number of schools offer course work in areas related to child life. Those who attend colleges or universities that do not have specific child life programs should major in another appropriate field, such as child development, psychology, and social work. Do some research before you select a school to attend. The CLC advises those considering this career to look for a school program that has sufficient faculty, a variety of field opportunities, and positive student evaluations. The CLC offers the *Directory of Child Life Programs,* which has information on both undergraduate and graduate programs. Typical classes to take include child psychology, child growth and development, family dynamics, and theories of play. Select a program that offers internships. An internship will give you supervised experience in the field as well as prepare you for future employment.

A child life administrator is usually required to have a master's degree in child development, behavioral psychology, education, or a related field. Graduate-level course work typically includes the areas of administration, research, and advanced clinical issues. Those who wish to be considered for positions as child life administrators must also have work experience supervising staff members, managing budgets, and preparing educational materials.

Certification or Licensing

Certification as a certified child life specialist (CCLS) is available through the CLC's Child Life Certifying Committee. Certification criteria include passing an examination and fulfilling education requirements. Although certification is voluntary, it is highly recommended. Some health care centers will not hire a child life specialist who is not certified.

Other Requirements

To be a successful child life specialist you should enjoy working with people, especially children. You will be part of a health care team, so you must be able to communicate effectively with medical professionals as well as able to communicate with children and their families. You must be creative in order to come up with different ways to explain complicated events, such as a surgery, to a child without frightening him or her. You will also need maturity and emotional stability to deal with situations that may otherwise upset you, such as seeing chronically ill or severely injured children. Those who enjoy this work are able to focus on its positive aspects—helping children and their families through difficult times.

EXPLORING

An excellent way to explore your interest in and aptitude for this work is to volunteer. For volunteer opportunities in medical settings, find out what local hospitals, outpatient clinics, or nursing homes have to offer. Opportunities to work with children are also available through organizations such as Easter Seals, Boy Scouts and Girl Scouts, and Big Brothers/Big Sisters of America. In addition, volunteer or paid positions are available at many summer camps. Baby-sitting, of course, is another way to work with children as well as earn extra money. And a good baby-sitter is always in demand, no matter where you live.

Once you are in college you can join the CLC as a student member. Membership includes a subscription to the council's newsletter, which can give you a better understanding of the work of a child life specialist.

EMPLOYERS

Child life specialists work as members of the health care team typically in hospitals. Increasingly, though, specialists are finding employment outside of hospitals at such places as rehabilitation centers, hospices, and ambulatory care facilities. Most child life programs in hospitals are autonomous and report to hospital administrations as other departments and programs do.

Child life programs often work with school programs within hospitals. Specialists may work with teachers to coordinate the curriculum with recreational activities. They also may encourage hospital administrations to provide adequate classroom facilities and highly qualified teachers.

STARTING OUT

Your internship may provide you with valuable contacts that can give you information on job leads. In addition, the career center or placement office of your college or university should be able to help you locate your first job. The CLC offers its members use of a job bank that lists openings at hospitals and clinics. You may also contact hospitals' placement offices directly for information on available positions.

■ ADVANCEMENT

Becoming certified and keeping up with new developments through continuing education workshops and seminars are the first two steps anyone must take in order to advance in this field. The next step is to get a graduate degree. Advancement possibilities include the positions of child life administrator, assistant director, or director of a child life program. Advanced positions involve management responsibilities, including the overseeing of a staff and coordinating a program's activities. Those in advanced positions must also keep their knowledge up to date by completing continuing education, attending professional conferences, and reading professional journals.

■ EARNINGS

Salaries for child life specialists vary greatly depending on such factors as the region of the country a specialist works in, education level, certification, and the size of the employer. For example, salaries tend to be higher in large metropolitan teaching hospitals than in small community hospitals. In 2000, the Department of Human Development and Family Studies of the University of Alabama, Tuscaloosa, conducted a salary survey of child life professionals to determine national salary trends for the field. According to this survey, those just starting out in the field had annual salaries ranging from a low of $12,500 to a high of approximately $55,540. The mean income for this group was approximately $28,560. Those with three to five years of work experience had mean annual earnings of $31,585. Child life specialists with more than 10 years of experience reported salaries ranging from $30,000 to $70,000 annually, with a mean income of approximately $40,920. Those with the highest earnings are usually child life administrators or directors. In addition, those with certification tend to earn more than their noncertified counterparts.

Child life specialists' salaries may be compared to those of social workers. According to the Department of Labor, in 2003, such workers made a median of $33,810 per year, with the bottom 10 percent making $21,870 or less and the top 10 percent making $56,120 or more.

Benefits vary by employer, but they usually include such items as paid vacation and sick days, medical insurance, and retirement plans.

■ WORK ENVIRONMENT

Child life specialists are members of the health care team in a variety of settings, including hospitals, clinics, and hospice facilities. In most hospitals, the child life specialist works in a special playroom. Sometimes the specialist may go to the child's hospital room. In outpatient facilities, the specialist may work in a waiting room or a designated playroom. According to the American Academy of Pediatrics (AAP), the ratio of child life specialists to children that works well is about one to 15. Child life specialists must be comfortable in hospital settings. They need to adjust easily to being around children who are sick. Since the children and their families need so much support, child life specialists need to be emotionally stable. Their own support network of family and friends should be strong, so that the specialist can get through difficult times at work. Child life specialists may have patients who die, and this can be difficult.

Most child life personnel work during regular business hours, although specialists are occasionally needed on evenings, holidays, or weekends to work with the children. It is important for child life personnel to have hobbies or outside interests to avoid becoming too emotionally drained from the work. The rewards of a child life specialist career are great. Many child life specialists see the direct effects of their work on their patients and on their patients' families. They see anxiety and fear being eased, and they see their patients come through treatments and hospitalizations with a renewed pride.

■ OUTLOOK

The employment outlook for child life specialists is good. The AAP reports that most hospitals specializing in pediatric care have child life programs. In addition, the number of these programs has doubled since 1965. And although managed-care providers encourage short hospital stays that may result in a reduced need for staffing in hospitals, opportunities for child life specialists are increasing outside of the hospital setting. The possible employers of today and tomorrow include outpatient clinics, rehabilitation centers, hospice programs, and other facilities that may treat children, such as sexual assault centers and centers for abused women and children.

■ FOR MORE INFORMATION

For current news on issues affecting children's health, visit the AAP's website.

American Academy of Pediatrics (AAP)
141 Northwest Point Boulevard
Elk Grove Village, IL 60007-1098
Tel: 847-434-4000
Email: pedscareer@aap.org
http://www.aap.org

For education, career, and certification information as well as professional publications, contact

Child Life Council
11820 Parklawn Drive, Suite 202
Rockville, MD 20852-2529
Tel: 301-881-7090
Email: clcstaff@childlife.org
http://www.childlife.org

For information on children's health issues and pediatric care, contact

**National Association of Children's Hospitals and
    Related Institutions**
401 Wythe Street
Alexandria, VA 22314
Tel: 703-684-1355
Email: mbrsvcs@nachri.org
http://www.childrenshospitals.net

Chimney Sweeps

■ OVERVIEW

Chimney sweeps, also known as *sweeps* and *chimney technicians,* inspect—or evaluate, as it is known in the industry—chimneys, fireplaces, stoves, and vents according to safety codes. They clean, or sweep, the chimneys and make repairs, which may involve masonry work and relining. They also educate homeowners and building maintenance crews in how to properly care for their stoves and fireplaces, as well as train apprentice chimney sweeps. In the United States and Canada, there are between 6,000 and 6,500 chimney sweeps.

■ HISTORY

The traditional image of the soot-faced chimney sweep in top hat and tails, carrying a long brush, is still very much a part of the chimney sweep industry. Many chimney sweep businesses and organizations use the image in advertising and logos, including the National Chimney Sweep Guild (NCSG). The sweep of popular imagination originated in the city of pre-industrial London, with its tight rows of brick houses. Before the introduction of central heating, chimney sweeps thrived. The sweep took on an almost mythical quality, leaping from roof to roof, chimney pot to chimney pot. Unfortunately, the industry didn't have the safety codes, equipment, and technology of today, which resulted in health hazards. Cancer and other illnesses particularly affected the small boys and girls who, long before child labor laws, were cruelly sent

into the chimneys to do the work a brush couldn't. Today's chimney sweep, however, working under the strict codes of the National Fire Protection Association (NFPA), is more closely associated with health—their evaluations and repairs save lives and homes from destruction by fire.

Though chimney sweeping has a long tradition, only in the last 30 years has it developed as a modern career choice. The energy crisis of the early 1970s resulted in many homeowners converting from central heat to fireplaces and stoves. The popularity of wood-burning stoves has waned somewhat since then because of fears of fire and carbon monoxide poisoning, but the chimney sweep industry is hard at work to educate the public about advances in the technology and equipment that keeps fireplaces and chimneys perfectly safe.

■ THE JOB

The Chimney Safety Institute of America (CSIA) estimates that in 1992, a particularly devastating year for house fires, 39,200 residential fires originated in chimneys, fireplaces, and solid fuel appliances. These fires resulted in 290 injuries, 90 deaths, and $206 million in property damage. It's no wonder, then, that many chimney sweeps have worked as firefighters. With an understanding of the damage a chimney fire can do to a home, sweeps not only keep chimneys safer, they also serve as advocates for fire prevention.

The NFPA recommends that homeowners have their chimneys, fireplaces, and vents evaluated at least once a year. Just as a dentist will send out annual reminder cards, so does John Pilger, the owner and operator of Chief Chimney Services, Inc. Pilger sweeps, restores, relines, and waterproofs the chimneys of Brentwood, New York, and surrounding areas. "The work used to be seasonal," Pilger says, "but more people are recognizing the need for chimney upkeep, so I work year-round."

Sweeps clean flues and remove creosote. Creosote is a residue

---

QUICK FACTS

SCHOOL SUBJECTS
Business
Technical/shop

PERSONAL SKILLS
Mechanical/manipulative
Technical/scientific

WORK ENVIRONMENT
Indoors and outdoors
Primarily multiple locations

MINIMUM EDUCATION LEVEL
Apprenticeship

SALARY RANGE
$25,000 to $50,000 to
$80,000+

CERTIFICATION OR LICENSING
Recommended

OUTLOOK
About as fast as the average

DOT
891

GOE
11.07.01

NOC
6662

O*NET-SOC
N/A

TO SWEEP OR NOT TO SWEEP THE SWIFTS

The chimney swift, or chimney swallow, is a bird with long wings and cigar-shaped body. It gets its name from its home: The chimney swift builds its nest inside unused chimneys. Despite sharp claws perfect for clinging to the bricks of chimney walls, swifts are unable to perch and therefore spend most of their time in flight. But the tiny, nesting baby birds have stirred up big controversy in the industry. The chirping of the baby birds after the heating season is enough to send homeowners seeking the aid of a chimney sweep. Some sweeps will oblige homeowners and knock the nests from the chimneys; others sweeps refuse, citing a law of 1918 that forbids interfering with the nesting practices of migratory birds.

that develops from wood and smoke and glazes the bricks of the insides of chimneys; sometimes chemicals are required to break down creosote. Sweeps also install stoves and perform a number of different repairs. People contact chimney sweeps with specific problems, such as too much smoking from the fireplace, or rain and snow getting in through the chimney. A sweep will attach a "cap" at the chimney top to prevent moisture, animals, and debris from entering the chimney. Crown repair also may be needed to keep the rain out.

Carbon monoxide poisoning is another concern of homeowners. Sweeps reline deteriorating chimneys to keep carbon monoxide from seeping through into the home. With their masonry skills, chimney sweeps perform much brick repair and replacement. But sweeps don't just keep the home fires burning safely; they also attend to the chimneys and stoves of commercial businesses and industrial buildings. Some sweeps even specialize in the maintenance of the large smokestacks of electric and gas companies, which often involves traveling to multiple cities all across the country.

Pilger makes four to seven stops in a workday. He usually makes it to his first customer's house between 8:30 and 9 A.M. Once there, he'll spend from one to one-and-a-half hours sweeping the customer's oil or gas chimney, examining and sweeping the fireplace, and checking brickwork inside and out. He also does a video scan of the chimney, using equipment composed of a camera at the end of a pole. Despite such state-of-the-art equipment, Pilger says, "We haven't even touched the future of chimney technology."

The tools of the trade have advanced a great deal since the days of the 18th century, when white geese were sent through chimneys; sweeps would determine how much

creosote was inside the chimney from how darkly the geese's feathers were soiled. These days, in addition to the brushes, poles, and ladders that have long been necessary for cleaning, sweeps rely on a number of power tools. "From a demolition jackhammer to a cordless drill," Pilger says. Pilger owns special vacuums, hand grinders, and circular saws with diamond-tipped blades. "The blades are expensive and may only last three to four months," Pilger says. But most of the tools, if treated well, can last a long time. Pilger once had two trucks and four employees, but he decided he preferred to do the work himself. "It drove me crazy to get complaints," he says. So Pilger and his wife, Diane, also a certified chimney sweep, now operate the business entirely themselves.

Some chimney sweeps sell a number of products. They sell wood and gas stoves, cook stoves, and gas barbecues. They sell fireplace inserts, fireplace glass doors, and gas logs. As with any small business, chimney sweeping involves a fair amount of office work. Detailed billing and client records must be kept, and customer phone calls must be answered and returned. Sweeps must also market their services. Many sweeps work to educate their communities on fire safety by distributing brochures and speaking at public events. Pilger is a past president of the New York State Chimney Sweeps Guild, and he sits on the boards of directors of the NCSG and the CSIA.

■ REQUIREMENTS
High School

To understand the damage done to chimneys by smoke, fire, and creosote, take science courses—particularly chemistry classes. In chemistry class, you'll learn more about the chemical reactions from fireplaces, such as carbon monoxide, that can cause illness and death if not contained. You may also be working with some chemicals to break down creosote glaze. With a clear understanding of the chemistry involved, you can easily explain problems to customers and stress the importance of chimney sweeping and repair.

In business courses, you can learn about marketing, budgeting, tax requirements, insurance, and other details of small business management. A computer course will give you some experience with databases, spread sheets, and other programs that assist in record keeping and billing.

Postsecondary Training

The CSIA, the educational branch of the NCSG, actively trains sweeps and venting specialists and provides information to the general public about chimney safety. The CSIA Technology Center, a training facility, that was opened in Plainfield, Indiana, in 2002 to satisfy the educational needs of chimney sweeps. CSIA also offers a number of workshops and seminars across the country, which introduce new sweeps to the business and provide continuing education to established sweeps. Training in such subjects as safety codes, environmental protection requirements, chimney construction, and technique helps sweeps prepare for the difficult CSIA certification exam.

No college degree is required, but community college courses in small business management or tech school training in brickwork can help you prepare for ownership of your own chimney sweep service. Some experienced sweeps may even take you on as an apprentice; though the opportunity may not pay anything, it will provide you with valuable experience and education, and help you in your pursuit of certification. Many chimney sweeps have worked as firefighters or in other aspects of fire control and prevention. You may consider applying to the state fire academy for their extensive training. With experience in fire fighting, you'll learn to recognize fire hazards, which is important knowledge for sweeps.

Certification or Licensing

Certification isn't required to work as a chimney sweep but is highly recommended by professionals in the industry. In its education of the public regarding chimney safety, the CSIA strongly advises homeowners to use only the services of certified sweeps. An unskilled sweep may be unable to recognize the potential for fire and health hazards in a deteriorating chimney and may even do more damage in the sweeping and repairing process. The CSIA certification exam is a difficult, 100-question test and requires complete knowledge of safety codes.

With certification, you can offer your clients additional security, and you can also receive referrals from the NCSG. Certification is valid for three years, after which you can re-test or attend CSIA-approved continuing education programs. Currently, the state of Vermont requires that only certified sweeps work with commercial and apartment buildings. Five other states are planning to follow suit.

Liability insurance is also important for chimney sweeps. Some sweeps have been named in lawsuits following fires in homes they serviced. Even if a sweep alerts a homeowner to potential hazards and the homeowner chooses not to have the work done, the sweep may be held liable if he or she didn't document the warning.

Other Requirements

You should have good technical and mechanical skills, as you'll be working with power tools and construction. Patience is important because replacing linings and tiles and removing hard, glazed creosote can be time con-

suming and tedious. Communication skills are also valuable, as you'll need to clearly explain to your clients the repairs needed and how to maintain a safe hearth. "Good customer service is very important," John Pilger emphasizes. His outgoing personality and background in customer relations helps him to attract clients and to keep them. He also once worked as a fire chief, and this background in dealing with fire hazards and educating the public about fire safety has served him well.

■ EXPLORING

Contact the NCSG for the names of chimney sweeps in your area, and look in the yellow pages of your phone book. A local sweep may allow you to follow him or her around for a day or two. Because of a shortage of chimney sweeps in the country, many sweeps and sweep organizations are anxious to recruit young people into the business. Speak to a guild representative about apprenticeship opportunities, or find one on your own by speaking to the sweeps in your town. The CSIA can also direct you to nearby educational seminars and conferences. By attending a conference, you'll get inside information about the business and also get to talk with experienced chimney sweeps. There are a few publications devoted to chimney sweeping: *Sweeping,* the technical publication of the NCSG, *SNEWS—The Chimney Sweep News* (http://hometown.aol.com/snewsmail/index.html), and *Chimney Topics.*

■ EMPLOYERS

According to the NCSG, there are 6,000 to 6,500 chimney sweeps working in the United States and Canada. Ninety-five percent of the chimney sweep services are made up of three or fewer people. Many of them are literally "mom and pop" businesses, with pop tending to the chimney sweeping, and mom managing the office and telephone. Sweeps are in business in every region of the country but fare the best in larger cities, or areas with an affluent

---

THE HEART OF THE HEARTH

Whether your fireplace is masonry (made of bricks and mortar, and weighing up to seven tons) or factory-built with a metal chimney, it is composed of many pieces beyond the mantel. The *lintel* is the piece above the opening of the fireplace, supporting the mantel. The *damper* is the movable plate at the throat of the fireplace, that regulates the draft. The *smoke chamber* is the enlarged area between the throat of the fireplace and the chimney flue. And the *flue* is the duct that carries the smoke up through the top of the chimney.

suburban or rural area. Some sweeps work only within a specific area, while others may travel to smaller towns and into the country, where no other services may be available.

STARTING OUT

Having developed experience as a fire chief, John Pilger bought a few chimney service companies and went into business. "The business can be as big or as small as you want it to be," Pilger says. Though he has had a few employees in the past, he prefers to keep all the work for himself and his wife, therefore maintaining a smaller, more manageable business.

The equipment you need, which includes a truck, power tools, and other special equipment as well as protective gear, will be costly at first. You may have to work for a few years with another business, saving up money and building a list of reliable, paying customers. Once you've gained experience with chimney sweeping and have taken certification courses, you may be able to hire on with a large sweep service or go into business with another sweep. Large businesses that sell and install wood and gas stoves will probably hire assistants, as will masonry businesses. Some of these businesses will advertise jobs in the classifieds, but your best bet would be to contact them directly. The CSIA seminars and conferences can help you get to know other chimney sweeps, both new and established, who could prove to be valuable contacts.

ADVANCEMENT

Once you've established your own chimney sweep service, you can advance by making more connections in the community and expanding your client base. If the amount of work warrants it, you may choose to hire assistants and office staff. With a successful business, you can also afford the best equipment and the newest tools. You should attend the seminars and conferences offered by the CSIA to learn about the advances in technology for the industry. You can also advance your business by expanding the services offered. Some sweeps move into

other areas of home repair, or they offer chimney and fireplace products for sale.

EARNINGS

The NCSG says salaries for chimney sweeps are too variable to estimate. Charges for services are also difficult to gauge. Sweeps working in larger cities and affluent neighborhoods can make much more for their services than those working in less populated areas. Sweeps charge anywhere from $50 to $100 for an annual cleaning and $50 to $100 for a chimney cap. In areas where many people use stoves and fireplaces to heat their homes, such as in the New England states or the Northwest, a sweep may have four or more cleanings scheduled for every workday. In other parts of the country, the work may be seasonal, the bulk of servicing done in the months following the heating season. In addition to service fees, some sweeps also make money from the sales of stoves and fireplace products. According to an old article in *Mother Earth News,* sweeps can make from $25,000 to $50,000 to $80,000 per year—a number that has surely increased since the time of that publication.

WORK ENVIRONMENT

Chimney sweeps work both indoors and out. Some deskwork is required to manage scheduling and finances, but sweeps spend most of their time climbing and bending, working in and around the homes of their customers. They climb ladders to the roofs of the homes to sweep and evaluate, and they spend some time down at the hearth within the home. This work can be noisy, due to the power tools and vacuums chimney sweeps use, and it can be dirty and messy as well. Chimney sweeps need to wear protective gear to prevent health problems. They will also carry their equipment from their truck to their home.

Though some established sweeps can afford to set their own schedules, working whatever hours they choose, others must be flexible to best accommodate their customers. A sweep may work an average 40-hour workweek, with a 24-hour phone number for emergency situations. Chimney sweeps do much of their work by themselves, but some sweeps work as members of small teams.

OUTLOOK

The United States is likely to follow the advances made by European countries in environmental testing and protection. The NCSG closely follows these advanced practices and actively promotes new standards to the NFPA and other agencies. In Germany, for example, homeowners are required by law to keep their chimneys within code. It may not come to that here, with organizations such as the CSIA and the Hearth Education Foundation working hard to increase awareness of the many dangers of faulty chimneys.

With more rigid emissions testing expected in the United States, more home and business owners will call upon sweeps for chimney evaluations. Some states are beginning to require that chimney sweeps be CSIA-certified before working on commercial and apartment buildings. This will result in more sweeps becoming certified and better regulation of the industry. Along with new emissions standards, the industry will also benefit from technology in such areas as gas usage, more efficient appliances, and better water repellents.

■ FOR MORE INFORMATION

For career materials and information on certification and training, contact

Chimney Safety Institute of America
2155 Commercial Drive
Plainfield, IN 46168
Tel: 317-837-5362
Email: office@csia.org
http://www.csia.org

To learn about the industry and educational conferences and seminars in your area, contact

National Chimney Sweep Guild
2155 Commercial Drive
Plainfield, IN 46168
Email: office@ncsg.org
http://www.ncsg.org

For information on fire protection careers, contact

National Fire Protection Association
1 Batterymarch Park
PO Box 9101
Quincy, MA 02269-9101
Tel: 617-770-3000
Email: public_affairs@nfpa.org
http://www.nfpa.org

Chiropractors

■ OVERVIEW

Chiropractors, or *doctors of chiropractic,* are health care professionals who emphasize health maintenance and disease prevention through proper nutrition, exercise, posture, stress management, and care of the spine and the nervous system. Approximately 20,210 chiropractors practice in the United States. Most work in solo practice;

other work settings include group practices, health care clinics, and teaching institutions.

Because of its emphasis on health maintenance, the whole person, and natural healing, chiropractic is considered an alternative health care approach. At the same time, chiropractic has more of the advantages enjoyed by the medical profession than does any other alternative health care field: Chiropractic has licensure requirements, accredited training institutions, a growing scientific research base, and insurance reimbursement.

■ HISTORY

Although chiropractic as we know it is just over 100 years old, spinal manipulation dates back to ancient civilizations. Reports of manipulative therapy were recorded in China as early as 2700 B.C. Hippocrates, the "father of medicine," used spinal manipulation around the fourth century B.C. to reposition vertebrae and to heal other ailments. Galen, a renowned Greek physician who practiced in Rome during the second century A.D., used spinal manipulation. Ambroise Paré, who is sometimes called the "father of surgery," used it in France in the 16th century. These "bone-setting" techniques were passed down through the centuries through family tradition. They can be found in the folk medicine of many countries. In 1843, Dr. J. Evans Riadore, a physician, studied the irritation of spinal nerves and recommended spinal manipulation as a treatment.

Daniel D. Palmer, an American, founded the system of chiropractic in 1895. He also coined the term *chiropractic.* Palmer believed that deviations of the spinal column, or subluxations, were the cause of practically all disease and that chiropractic adjustment was the cure. Like many others who have tried to change the practice of medicine, Dr. Palmer encountered strong opposition from the medical establishment. He and other early chiropractors were imprisoned for practicing medicine without a

QUICK FACTS

SCHOOL SUBJECTS
Biology
Chemistry

PERSONAL SKILLS
Mechanical/manipulative
Technical/scientific

WORK ENVIRONMENT
Primarily indoors
Primarily one location

MINIMUM EDUCATION LEVEL
Medical degree

SALARY RANGE
$32,100 to $65,990 to $145,600+

CERTIFICATION OR LICENSING
Required

OUTLOOK
Faster than the average

DOT
079

GOE
14.04.01

NOC
3122

O*NET-SOC
29-1011.00

license. In spite of the hardships, he and his followers persevered because of the success of their treatments in alleviating pain and promoting health. Their treatments at times had exceptionally positive results.

In spite of their successful work and a growing number of supporters, chiropractors were attacked by the medical establishment because they had little scientific research to support their claims. In the 1970s, Dr. Chang Ha Suh, Ph.D., a Korean immigrant who was working at the University of Colorado, had the courage to conduct studies that provided extensive scientific research related to chiropractic. Since then, numerous important studies have added to the research and to the credibility of chiropractic.

Today, chiropractic is the third largest primary health care profession in the United States. Many quality schools of chiropractic exist, and doctors of chiropractic are licensed in all 50 states and the District of Columbia. Chiropractic is one of the fastest growing health care professions in the country.

■ THE JOB

Chiropractors are trained primary health care providers, much like medical physicians. Chiropractors focus on the maintenance of health and disease prevention. In addition to symptoms, they consider each patient's nutrition, work, stress levels, exercise habits, posture, and so on. Chiropractors treat people of all ages—from children to senior citizens. They see both women and men. Doctors of chiropractic most frequently treat conditions such as backache, disk problems, sciatica, and whiplash. They also care for people with headaches, respiratory disorders, allergies, digestive disturbances, elevated blood pressure, and many other common ailments. Some specialize in areas such as sports medicine or nutrition. Chiropractors do not use drugs or surgery. If they determine that drugs or surgery are needed, they refer the individual to another professional who can meet those needs.

Doctors of chiropractic look for causes of disorders of the spine. They consider the spine and the nervous system to be vitally important to the health of the individual. Chiropractic teaches that problems in the spinal column (backbone) affect the nervous system and the body's natural defense mechanisms and are the underlying causes of many diseases. Chiropractors use a special procedure called a "spinal adjustment" to try to restore the spine to its natural healthy state. They believe this will also have an effect on the individual's total health and well-being.

On the initial visit, doctors of chiropractic meet with the patient and take a complete medical history before beginning treatment. They ask questions about all aspects of the person's life to help determine the nature of the illness. Events in the individual's past that may seem unrelated or unimportant may be significant to the chiropractor.

After the consultation and the case history, chiropractors perform a careful physical examination, sometimes including laboratory tests. When necessary, they use X rays to help locate the source of patients' difficulties. Doctors of chiropractic study the X rays for more than just bone fractures or signs of disease. X rays are the only means of seeing the outline of the spinal column. Chiropractors are trained to observe whether the structural alignment of the spinal column is normal or abnormal.

Once they have made a diagnosis, chiropractic physicians use a variety of natural approaches to help restore the individual to health. The spinal adjustment is the treatment for which chiropractic is most known. During this procedure, patients usually lie on a specially designed adjusting table. Chiropractic physicians generally use their hands to manipulate the spine. They apply pressure and use specialized techniques of manipulation that are designed to help the affected areas of the spine. Doctors of chiropractic must know many sophisticated techniques of manipulation, and they spend countless hours learning to properly administer spinal adjustments. Chiropractic treatments must often be repeated over the course of several visits. The number of treatments needed varies greatly.

In addition to the spinal adjustment, chiropractic physicians may use "physiologic therapeutics" to relieve symptoms. These are drugless natural therapies, such as light, water, electrical stimulation, massage, heat, ultrasound, and biofeedback. Chiropractors also make suggestions about diet, rest, exercise, and support of the afflicted body part. They may recommend routines for the patient to do at home to maintain and improve the results of the manipulation.

Chiropractors pay special attention to lifestyle factors, such as nutrition and exercise. They believe the body has an innate ability to remain healthy if it has the proper ingredients. Doctors of chiropractic propose that the essential ingredients include clean air, water, proper nutrition, rest, and a properly functioning nervous system. Their goal is to maintain the health and well being of the whole person. In this respect they have been practicing for many years what has recently become known as "health maintenance."

Chiropractors who are in private practice and some who work as group practitioners also have responsibility for running their businesses. They must promote their practices and develop their patient base. They are responsible for keeping records on their patients and for general bookkeeping. Sometimes they hire and train employees.

In larger practices or clinics, chiropractic assistants or office managers usually perform these duties.

■ REQUIREMENTS
High School

To become a doctor of chiropractic (DC), you will have to study a minimum of six to seven years after high school. Preparing for this profession is just as demanding as preparing to be a medical doctor, and the types of courses you will need are also similar. Science classes, such as biology, chemistry, physics, and psychology, will prepare you for medical courses in college. English, speech, drama, and debate can sharpen the communication skills that are essential for this profession. Math, business, and computer classes can help you get ready to run a private practice.

Postsecondary Training

Most chiropractic colleges require at least two years of undergraduate study before you can enroll. Some require a bachelor's degree. Currently, 18 institutions in the United States have chiropractic programs that are accredited by the Council on Chiropractic Education (CCE). Find out which chiropractic colleges interest you and learn about their requirements. Selecting chiropractic schools well in advance will allow you to structure your undergraduate study to meet the requirements of the schools of your choice. Some chiropractic colleges provide opportunities for prechiropractic study and bachelor's degree programs. In general, you need course work in biology, communications, English, chemistry, physics, psychology, and social sciences or humanities. Contact the national professional associations listed at the end of this article for information about schools and their requirements.

Upon completing the required undergraduate work and enrolling in a chiropractic college, you can expect to take an array of science and medical courses, such as anatomy, pathology, and microbiology. During the first two years of most chiropractic programs you will spend a majority of your time in the classroom or the laboratory. The last two years generally focus on courses in spinal adjustments. During this time, potential chiropractors also train in outpatient clinics affiliated with the college. Upon successful completion of the six- or seven-year professional degree program, you will receive the DC degree.

Certification or Licensing

All 50 states and the District of Columbia require that chiropractors pass a state board examination to obtain a license to practice. Educational requirements and types of practice for which a chiropractor may be licensed vary from state to state. Most state boards recognize academic

CHIROPRACTIC AND HEALTH MAINTENANCE

With the increasing focus on health care in the United States, there has recently been much talk about health maintenance. For more than 100 years, doctors of chiropractic have promoted the importance of maintaining health, rather than simply treating symptoms of disease.

A basic principle of chiropractic is that the human body can naturally maintain health if it has certain basic "raw materials." Chiropractors include among the essential components clean air, water, food, rest, exercise, and a properly functioning nervous system. Assisting patients in incorporating these elements of wellness into their lives is central to the chiropractic approach to health care.

training only in chiropractic colleges accredited by the CCE. Most states will accept all or part of the National Board of Chiropractic Examiners' test given to fourth-year chiropractic students in place of a state exam. Most states require that chiropractors take continuing education courses each year to keep their licenses.

Other Requirements

Perhaps the most important personal requirement for any health care professional is the desire to help people and to promote wholeness and health. To be a successful chiropractor, you need good listening skills, empathy, and understanding. As a doctor of chiropractic, you will also need a good business sense and the ability to work independently. Especially sharp observational skills are essential in order for you to recognize physical abnormalities. Good hand dexterity is necessary to perform the spinal adjustments and other manipulations. However, you do not need unusual strength.

■ EXPLORING

If you are interested in becoming a chiropractor, there are many ways to start preparing right now. Join all the science clubs you can, design projects, and participate in science fairs. To develop interviewing and communication skills, you might join the school newspaper staff and ask for interview assignments. Learn to play chess, take up fencing, or study art history to increase your powers of observation. Take up an instrument, such as the piano, guitar, or violin, to improve your manual dexterity. Learning to give massages is another way to increase manual dexterity and learn the human body. Be sure to stay in shape and maintain your own health, and learn all you can about homeopathy, yoga, the Alexander technique, Rolfing, and other systems of mind/body wholeness.

rienced chiropractor. Other salaried positions can be found in traditional hospitals, in hospitals that specialize in chiropractic treatment, or in alternative health care centers and clinics. More than 50 percent of the doctors of chiropractic in the United States are in private practice. Most maintain offices in a professional building with other specialists or at their own clinics.

Chiropractors practice throughout the United States. Jobs in clinics, hospitals, and alternative health care centers may be easier to find in larger cities that have the population to support them. However, most doctors of chiropractic choose to work in small communities. Chiropractors tend to remain near chiropractic institutions, and this has resulted in higher concentrations of chiropractic practices in those geographical areas.

■ STARTING OUT

Placement offices of chiropractic colleges have information about job openings, and they may be able to help with job placement. As a newly licensed chiropractor, you might begin working in a clinic or in an established practice with another chiropractor on a salary or income-sharing basis. This would give you a chance to start practicing without the major financial investment of equipping an office. It is sometimes possible to purchase the practice of a chiropractor who is retiring or moving. This is usually easier than starting a new solo practice because the purchased practice will already have patients. However, some newly licensed practitioners do go straight into private practice.

National chiropractic associations and professional publications may also list job openings. Attend an association meeting to get to know professionals in the field. Networking is an important way to learn about job openings.

■ ADVANCEMENT

As with many other professions, advancement in chiropractic usually means building a larger practice. A chiropractor who starts out as a salaried employee in a large practice may eventually become a partner in the practice. Chiropractors also advance their careers by building their clientele and setting up their own group practices. They sometimes buy the practices of retiring practitioners to add to their own practices.

Another avenue for advancement is specialization. Chiropractors specialize in areas such as neurology, sports medicine, or diagnostic imaging (X-ray). As the demand for chiropractors is growing, more are advancing their careers through teaching at chiropractic institutions or conducting research. A few doctors of chiropractic become executives with state or national organizations.

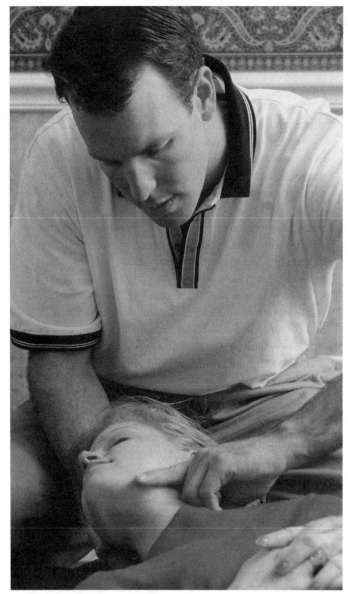

A chiropractor adjusts a patient's neck.

Contact the chiropractic professional associations and ask about their student programs. Check the Internet for bulletin boards or forums related to chiropractic and other areas of health care. Volunteer at a hospital or nursing home to gain experience working with those in need of medical care.

If there is a doctor of chiropractic or a clinic in your area, ask to visit and talk to a chiropractor. Make an appointment for a chiropractic examination so you can experience what it is like. You may even find a part-time or summer job in a chiropractic office.

■ EMPLOYERS

A newly licensed doctor of chiropractic might find a salaried position in a chiropractic clinic or with an expe-

■ EARNINGS

Self-employed chiropractors usually earn more than salaried chiropractors, such as those working as an associate with another chiropractor or doctor. Chiropractors running their own office, however, must pay such expenses as equipment costs, staff salaries, and health insurance.

According to the Bureau of Labor Statistics, the median annual income for chiropractors working on a salary basis was $65,990 in 2003. The middle 50 percent earned between $45,600 and $97,160 that same year, while the top 10 percent earned over $145,600 per year. The American Chiropractic Association reports the average income for all chiropractors, including those who were self-employed, was $81,500 in 2002.

Self-employed chiropractors must provide for their own benefits. Chiropractors who are salaried employees, such as those working on the staff of another doctor or those working for health clinics, usually receive benefits including health insurance and retirement plans.

■ WORK ENVIRONMENT

Chiropractic physicians work in clean, quiet, comfortable offices. Most solo practitioners and group practices have an office suite. The suite generally has a reception area. In clinics, several professionals may share this area. The suite also contains examining rooms and treatment rooms. In a clinic where several professionals work, there are sometimes separate offices for the individual professionals. Most chiropractors have chiropractic assistants and a secretary or office manager. Those who are in private practice or partnerships need to have good business skills and self-discipline to be successful.

Doctors of chiropractic who work in clinics, hospitals, universities, or professional associations need to work well in a group environment. They will frequently work under supervision or in a team with other professionals. Chiropractors may have offices of their own, or they may share offices with team members, depending on their work and the facility. In these organizations, the physical work environment varies, but it will generally be clean and comfortable. Because they are larger, these settings may be noisier than the smaller practices.

Most chiropractors work about 42 hours per week, although many put in longer hours. Larger organizations may determine the hours of work, but chiropractors in private practice can set their own. Evening and weekend hours are often scheduled to accommodate patients' needs.

■ OUTLOOK

Employment for doctors of chiropractic is expected to grow faster than the average through 2012, according to the U.S. Department of Labor. Many areas have a shortage of chiropractors. Public interest in alternative health care is growing. Many health-conscious individuals are attracted to chiropractic because it is natural, drugless, and surgery-free. Because of their holistic, personal approach to health care, chiropractors are increasingly seen as primary physicians, especially in rural areas. The average life span is increasing, and so are the numbers of older people in this country. The elderly frequently have more structural and mechanical difficulties, and the growth of this segment of the population will increase the demand for doctors of chiropractic.

More insurance policies and health maintenance organizations (HMOs) now cover chiropractic services, but this still varies according to the insurer. As a result of these developments in HMO and insurance coverage, chiropractors receive more referrals for treatment of injuries that result from accidents.

While the demand for chiropractic is increasing, college enrollments are also growing. New chiropractors may find increasing competition in geographic areas where other practitioners are already located. Because of the high cost of equipment such as X-ray and other diagnostic tools, group practices with other chiropractors or related health care professionals are likely to provide more opportunity for employment or for purchasing a share of a practice.

■ FOR MORE INFORMATION

For general information, and a career kit, contact
American Chiropractic Association
1701 Clarendon Boulevard
Arlington, VA 22209
Tel: 800-986-4636
http://www.amerchiro.org

For information on educational requirements and accredited colleges, contact
Council on Chiropractic Education
8049 North 85th Way
Scottsdale, AZ 85258-4321
Tel: 480-443-8877
Email: cce@cce-usa.org
http://www.cce-usa.org

For information on student membership and member chiropractors in your area, contact
International Chiropractors Association
1110 North Glebe Road, Suite 1000
Arlington, VA 22201
Tel: 800-423-4690
http://www.chiropractic.org

For information on licensure, contact
National Board of Chiropractic Examiners
901 54th Avenue
Greeley, CO 80634
Tel: 970-356-9100
Email: nbce@nbce.org
http://www.nbce.org

Cinematographers and Directors of Photography

■ OVERVIEW

The cinematographer, also known as the *director of photography* or *DP*, is instrumental in establishing the mood of a film by putting the narrative aspects of a script into visual form. The cinematographer is responsible for every shot's framing, lighting, color level, and exposure—elements that set the artistic tone of the film.

■ HISTORY

Motion picture cameras were invented in the late 1800s. In 1903, Edwin Porter made *The Great Train Robbery,* the first motion picture that used modern filmmaking techniques to tell a story. Porter filmed the scenes out of sequence, then edited and spliced them together to make the film, as is done today.

In the early years of film, the director handled the camera and made the artistic decisions that today are the job of the director of photography. The technical sophistication and artistic choices that are part of today's filming process had not yet emerged; instead, directors merely filmed narratives without moving the camera. Lighting was more for functional purposes of illumination than for artistic effect. Soon, however, directors began to experiment. They moved the camera to shoot from different angles and established a variety of editing techniques.

In the 1950s, the dominance of major studios in film production was curbed by an antitrust court decision, and more independent films were made. Changes in the U.S. tax code made independent producing more profitable. New genres and trends challenged the director and artistic staff of a production. Science fiction, adventure, mystery, and romance films grew in popularity. By the late 1960s, university film schools were established, training students in directing and cinematography as well as in other areas.

New developments in technologies and equipment have continued to influence both how films are made and how they look. The end of the 20th century and the beginning of the 21st saw the production of movies incorporating such elements as computer graphics, digital imaging, and digital color. Films such as *Titanic, Gladiator, Lord of the Rings,* and new "prequel" episodes of *Star Wars,* with their amount and complexity of their special effects, presented new visual challenges to filmmakers. Other films, such as the *Toy Story* movies, *Shrek* and its sequel, and *Finding Nemo,* are made entirely digitally. DPs lead the way in understanding and using new technologies to push the art of filmmaking into a new, digital era.

■ THE JOB

Cinematographers consider how the "look" of a film helps to tell its story. How can the look enhance the action, the emotions expressed, or the characters' personalities? Should the scene be filmed from across the room or up close to the actors? Should the lighting be stark or muted? How does the angle of the camera contribute to the scene? These are just some of the questions DPs must answer when composing a shot. Because DPs have both artistic and technical knowledge, they are integral members of the production team. They work in both film and television, helping directors to interpret a script and bring it to life.

At the beginning of a project, the DP reads the script and talks to the director about how to film each scene. Together they determine how to achieve the desired effects by deciding on camera angles and movement, lighting, framing, and which filters to use. By manipulating effects, DPs help determine the mood of a scene. For example, to raise the level of tension and discomfort in an argument, the DP can tell a camera operator to film at an unusual angle or move around the actors as they speak. The director may choose to film a scene in more than one way and then decide which best suits the project. With good collaboration between the director and the DP, decisions will be made quickly and successfully.

DPs are responsible for assembling the camera crew and telling crew members how to film each scene. They must be knowledgeable about all aspects of camera operation, lighting, filters, and types of film. There are multiple ways an effect can be approached, and DPs must be aware of them in order to make suggestions to the director and to capture the mood desired.

For small, low-budget films, some of the crew's roles may be combined. For example, the DP may operate a camera in addition to overseeing the crew. In a large production, the crew's roles will be more specialized. The *camera operator* either operates the camera physically or controls it remotely, using a control panel. The *first assis-*

tant camera operator helps with focus, changes lenses and filters, sets the stop for film exposure, and makes sure the camera is working properly. Camera focus is extremely important and is not judged simply by how the shot looks to the eye. Instead, the first assistant carries a measuring tape and measures all the key positions of the actors and makes calculations to ensure correct focus. The *second assistant camera operator,* also called the *loader,* loads film magazines, keeps track of how much film stock is left, and keeps camera reports. Camera reports record which shots the director likes and wants to have printed. A *gaffer* leads the electrical crew, and the *grips* handle the dollies and cranes to move the cameras.

When shooting begins, cinematographers take a series of test shots of film locations to determine the lighting, lenses, and film stock that will work best. Once filming starts, they make adjustments as necessary. They may also film screen tests of actors so the director can be sure they are right for their parts.

Richard Shore, A.S.C., has had a career that extends over 40 years, 20 countries, and 200 films. His feature work includes *Bang the Drum Slowly,* a film that Robert DeNiro credits as starting his career. Currently, Shore is a lecturer at the New York Film Academy, where he teaches basic and advanced courses in filmmaking and works one-on-one with students. He teaches classes in cinematography, lighting, scripts, and other aspects of filmmaking.

One of Shore's early filmmaking jobs was making training films for the U.S. Army during the Korean War. "After the war," he says, "I got work making travel films, documentaries, industrial films. I also made TV commercials." This eventually led to a career filled with awards, including two Oscar awards, three Emmy awards, and induction into the American Society of Cinematographers.

Different projects have different demands—for one of the films for which he won an Oscar, a short film about poet Robert Frost, Shore was involved in many aspects of the filmmaking process beyond the duties of DP. For one of the Emmy-winning projects, Shore worked as a director. While working on a documentary about French president Francois Mitterand, Shore traveled extensively, spending two months with Mitterand in Paris, then flying with him to Washington, DC, to meet with President Reagan. "In the film industry," Shore says, "you have experiences you can't get anywhere else."

■ REQUIREMENTS
High School
You should take courses that will prepare you for college, such as math, English, government, and foreign language. Courses in English composition and literature will give you a background in narrative development, and art and photography courses can help you understand the basics of lighting and composition. A broadcast journalism or media course may give you some hands-on experience in camera operation and video production.

Postsecondary Training
A bachelor's degree in liberal arts or film studies provides a good background for work in the film industry, but practical experience and industry connections will provide the best job opportunities. Upon completing an undergraduate program, you may wish to enroll in a master's program or master's of fine arts program at a film school. Schools offering well-established programs include the School of Visual Arts in New York, New York University, and the University of Southern California. These schools have film professionals on their faculties and provide a very visible stage for student talent. In addition to classroom time, film school offers students the opportunity to work on their own productions. Such education is rigorous, but in addition to teaching skills it provides you with peer groups and a network of contacts with students, faculty, and guest speakers that can be of help after graduation.

An alternative to film school is the New York Film Academy (NYFA). NYFA gives students an idea of the demands of filmmaking careers by immersing them in an intensive six-week course. During this time, students have access to cameras and editing tables and are required to make three short films of their own. (Contact information for all schools is listed at the end of this article.)

"A lot of people want to make films," Richard Shore says, "but there is really no direct route to entering the film industry. All production companies care about is what you can show them that you've done. You need to make a short film and submit it to a festival. If it's shown and gets recognition, that's your entrée."

Other Requirements
You'll need to keep abreast of technological innovations while

QUICK FACTS

SCHOOL SUBJECTS
Art
English

PERSONAL SKILLS
Artistic
Technical/scientific

WORK ENVIRONMENT
Indoors and outdoors
Primarily multiple locations

MINIMUM EDUCATION LEVEL
Bachelor's degree

SALARY RANGE
$15,000 to $34,330 to
$66,700

CERTIFICATION OR LICENSING
None available

OUTLOOK
Faster than the average

DOT
143

GOE
01.08.01

NOC
5131

O*NET-SOC
27-4031.00

HISTORICAL MOMENTS IN THE ACADEMY AWARDS

- The first Oscar winners in the category of cinematography were Charles Rosher and Karl Struss for *Sunrise* (1927–28).

- In 1939, the Academy began to give separate awards for achievement in black-and-white and color cinematography. That year, Gregg Toland won in the black-and-white category for *Wuthering Heights,* and Ernest Haller and Ray Rennahan won in the color category for *Gone with the Wind.*

- The last award for black-and-white cinematography was awarded to Haskell Wexler for *Who's Afraid of Virginia Woolf?* in 1966.

- A few cinematographers, such as Vittorio Storraro and Winton Hoch, have won three Oscars, but only one cinematographer has won four Oscars: Leon Shamroy for *The Black Swan* (1942), *Wilson* (1944), *Leave Her to Heaven* (1945), and *Cleopatra* (1963). All Shamroy's wins were in the color category.

working in the industry. You must be comfortable with the technical as well as artistic aspects of the profession. You also must be a good leader to make decisions and direct your crew effectively.

"You really have to want it," Shore says about the work of a DP. "It's almost like a calling. You can't go into it halfway." Shore says it's also helpful to have your own original story ideas when embarking on a film career. "Film is a storytelling art, a narrative art. Someone with the ideal background is someone interested in literature, particularly the novel."

■ EXPLORING

With cable television, videos, and DVDs, it is much easier to study films today than it was 25 years ago. It's likely to become even easier as the Internet might someday allow you to download any film you choose. You should take full advantage of the availability of great films and study them closely for different filmmaking styles. The documentary *Visions of Light: The Art of Cinematography,* directed by Arnold Glassman, Todd McCarthy, and Stuart Samuels, is a good introduction to some of the finest cinematography in the history of film. You can also experiment with composition and lighting if you have access to a 16-millimeter camera, a camcorder, or a digital camera. Check with your school's media center or journalism department about recording school events. Your school's

drama club can also introduce you to the elements of comedy and drama and may involve you with writing and staging your own productions.

You should subscribe to *American Cinematographer* magazine or read selected articles at the magazine's website (http://www.theasc.com/magazine). Other industry magazines such as *Daily Variety* (http://www.variety.com), *Hollywood Reporter* (http://www.hollywoodreporter.com), and *Cinefex* (http://www.cinefex.com) can also give you insight into filmmaking.

■ EMPLOYERS

Motion picture studios, production companies, independent producers, and documentary filmmakers all employ DPs, either as salaried employees or as freelancers. The U.S. Department of Labor reports that 20 percent of all camera operators work on a freelance basis. Most freelancers are responsible for finding their own projects to work on, but a few are represented by agents who solicit work for them.

■ STARTING OUT

Internships are a very good way to gain experience and help you to become a marketable job candidate. Since local television stations and lower-budget film productions operate with limited funds, they may offer internships for course credit or experience instead of a salary. You should check with your state's film commission to learn of productions in your area and volunteer to work in whatever capacity needed. Many production opportunities are also posted on the Web. By working on productions, you'll develop relationships with crew members and production assistants, and you'll be able to build a network of industry connections.

Before working as a DP, you'll likely work as a camera assistant or production assistant. To prepare yourself for this work, try to gain some experience in camera work with a college broadcasting station, a local TV crew, or advertising agency.

Camera operators may choose to join a union because some film studios will hire only union members. The principal union for this field is the International Alliance of Theatrical Stage Employees, Moving Picture Technicians, Artists, and Allied Crafts of the United States and Canada (IATSE). Union members work under a union contract that determines their work rules, pay, and benefits.

■ ADVANCEMENT

The position of cinematographer is in itself an advanced position. Richard Shore says securing a job as a DP "takes years and years of training. You must work your way up from first assistant, to camera operator, to DP. It's not a union thing, it's a way of learning. You learn from watching cinematographers work."

Those wanting to be DPs must get a foot in the door by making short films and getting them seen by producers. "Not only do you need skills, but you must make connections with people," Shore explains.

Camera operators may have opportunities to work as cinematographers on some projects. As they continue to develop relationships with filmmakers and producers, their DP work may increase, leading to better-paying, high-profile film projects. Once a DP has begun working in the industry, advancement may come as the DP develops a reputation for excellent, innovative work. Directors and producers may then request to work with that particular DP, which can also lead to higher pay.

■ EARNINGS

Many DPs do freelance work or have jobs under union contracts. They may work for a variety of employers ranging from major studios producing films with multimillion-dollar budgets to small, independent producers who are financing a film with their credit cards. As a result, their earnings vary widely.

When starting out as a camera operator, an individual may volunteer for a job, without pay, simply to get experience. At the other end of the earnings scale, a well-established DP working on big-budget productions can make well over a million dollars a year. The IATSE establishes minimum wage scales for DPs who are union members, based on the nature of a film shoot. In 2003, for feature film studio shoots, a cinematographer was paid about $520 a day. For location shoots, the wage was about $670 a day. Special provisions for holiday and overtime work are also made.

For an idea of what the average cinematographer may make in a year, consider government findings. The U.S. Department of Labor, which categorizes DPs with all camera operators, reports the median annual earnings for those working in motion picture production were $34,330 in 2003. The lowest paid 10 percent of camera operators, including those working in television and video, made less than $15,000. At the high end, 10 percent earned more than $66,700.

Freelancers must pay for their own benefits, such as health insurance, and they usually must buy their own equipment, which can be quite expensive.

■ WORK ENVIRONMENT

Conditions of work will vary depending on the size and nature of the production. In television production and in movies, DPs may work both indoors and outdoors. Indoors, conditions can be cramped, while outdoors there may be heat, cold, rain, or snow. DPs may need to travel for weeks at a time while a project is being shot on location, and some locations, such as the middle of a desert, may mean staying miles from civilization. Hours can be long and the shooting schedule rigorous, especially when a film is going over budget. DPs work as members of a team, instructing assistants while also taking instruction from directors and producers. Those making a film with a small budget may be required to oversee many different aspects of the production.

Filming challenges, such as how to shoot effectively underwater, in the dark, or in public areas, are a normal part of the job. DPs need patience in setting up cameras and preparing the lighting, as well as in dealing with the variety of professionals with whom they work.

"If you can get into film," Richard Shore says, "it's a wonderful career." One reason DPs enjoy their work so much is that they work with talented, artistic, and skillful professionals. "There's a camaraderie among film crew members," Shore says.

■ OUTLOOK

The U.S. Department of Labor predicts employment for camera operators to grow faster than the average through 2012. More opportunities, though, will be available for those willing to work outside of the film industry at, for example, advertising agencies and TV broadcasting companies. The department anticipates that other types of

---

AND THE OSCAR GOES TO . . .

Want to see the work of some Academy Award winning cinematographers? Check out these films:

- Boris Kaufman's *On the Waterfront* (1954)
- Freddie Young's *Doctor Zhivago* (1965)
- Geoffrey Unsworth's *Cabaret* (1972)
- Vittorio Storaro's *The Last Emperor* (1987)
- Janusz Kaminski's *Schindler's List* (1993)
- Peter Pau's *Crouching Tiger, Hidden Dragon* (2000)
- Russell Boy's *Master and Commander: The Far Side of the World* (2003)

For more films by Academy Award winning cinematographers, visit http://www.oscars.org/awardsdatabase

programming, such as Internet broadcasts of music videos, sports, and general information shows, will provide job openings in this field.

However, competition for work will be fierce because so many people are attracted to this business. "There are so many more qualified people than there are jobs," Richard Shore says. "It's impossible to guarantee success." Nevertheless, those with the right connections, strong samples of their work, and some luck are likely to find opportunities.

DPs of the future will be working more closely with special effects houses, even on films other than science fiction, horror, and other genres typically associated with special effects. Digital technology is used to create crowd scenes, underwater images, and other effects more efficiently and economically. DPs will have to approach a film with an understanding of which shots can be produced digitally and which will require traditional methods of filmmaking.

■ FOR MORE INFORMATION

For information about education and training workshops for television and film production and to read about events in the industry, visit the AFI website.

American Film Institute (AFI)
2021 North Western Avenue
Los Angeles, CA 90027
Tel: 323-856-7600
http://www.afi.com

This website has information on the ASC, articles from American Cinematographer *magazine, industry news, and a students' section with grants and fellowship information. The ASC online store sells many helpful publications covering aspects of film production.*

American Society of Cinematographers (ASC)
PO Box 2230
Hollywood, CA 90036
Tel: 800-448-0145
Email: info@theasc.com
http://theasc.com

For information on membership benefits, contact this branch of the International Alliance of Theatrical Stage Employees (IATSE).

International Cinematographers Guild
 (IATSE Local 600)
National Office/Western Region
7755 Sunset Boulevard
Hollywood, CA 90046
Tel: 323-876-0160
http://www.cameraguild.com

To read about film programs at several schools, visit the following websites:

New York Film Academy
http://www.nyfa.com

New York University
http://www.nyu.edu

School of Visual Arts
http://schoolofvisualarts.edu

University of Southern California
http://www.usc.edu

Circus Performers

■ OVERVIEW

Circus performers entertain with a wide variety of unusual acts that terrify, amuse, and amaze their audiences. Circus artists appear to defy death as they swing from a trapeze or walk a tightwire high above the ground. Some perform gymnastic feats on the ground, and clowns entertain with their absurd antics. Others train and perform with animals, such as elephants and tigers. Most circus performers are able to perform a variety of circus skills. Though "running away to join the circus" may seem like a fun way to earn a living, in reality, it is grueling, hard work.

■ HISTORY

The first circus in the United States was established by John Bill Ricketts in Philadelphia in 1793. Ricketts' circus featured equestrian acts, as well as a tightrope walker, a clown, and an acrobatic act. Performances were given inside a ring, which was surrounded by a low fence. Ricketts' troupe toured through most of the northeastern United States until 1800, when Ricketts went to England. By then, the tradition of the circus parade had already been established by a competing circus organized by Philip Lailson. Toward the middle of the 19th century, colorful circus wagons were also included in circus parades. Other traveling circuses toured the United States, although they were not formally called circuses until 1824. These early circuses usually featured equestrian showmanship, and their proprietors were also featured performers.

A new type of circus originated in 1825, when J. Purdy Brown introduced the "big top." Instead of constructing a wooden building in which to perform, Brown erected a large tent or pavilion. The big top could be set up and taken down more easily and moved from location to location every day. In this way, a circus could reach a wider audience. In the 1830s, circuses also added menageries, which featured wild and exotic animals; soon, performers risked their lives by going into the cages of the most ferocious animals.

Circuses grew larger and more varied through the 19th century. More and more circuses were being run by people who did not perform. Noted proprietors in the mid-19th century were Aaron Turner, Rufus Welch, James Raymond, and Gilbert Spalding. Some performers became well-known figures for their acts, such as John Glenroy, who could turn a backwards somersault while riding bareback. Traveling circuses usually spent their winters on the East Coast. This meant that as they traveled they often reached no further than the midwestern territories before being forced to turn back for the winter. In 1847, the Mabie Brothers circus established its winter headquarters in Delavan, Wisconsin. Many other circuses followed this idea, and over the years more than 100 circuses have been founded or have wintered in Wisconsin.

Perhaps the most famous of all circus proprietors entered the scene in 1871. Phineas Taylor Barnum, known as P. T. Barnum, was born in 1810 in Connecticut. For most of his career, Barnum was a showman, featuring acts such as the 161-year-old nurse of George Washington, the "Feejee Mermaid" (which was, in fact, the upper half of a monkey that had been attached to the lower half of a fish), the famous midget Tom Thumb, and others. Barnum, known for the slogan "There's a sucker born every minute," was famous for his elaborate publicity campaigns. From 1848 to 1868, Barnum ran the American Museum in New York City, which specialized in curiosities, wild animals, and "freaks" and was one of the most popular attractions in the country, selling over 40 million tickets.

In 1870, Barnum was approached by circus proprietors William C. Coup and Dan Castello, and the three formed a partnership, renaming the circus the P. T. Barnum Circus. In 1872, Barnum suggested that the circus travel by train, stopping only at the bigger cities, where the audiences were largest. In addition to the big top, Barnum's circus featured a sideshow and museum and was advertised heavily before every performance. By the end of the 1870s, there were 25 traveling circuses, the largest traveling by train; by 1905, more than 100 circuses toured the United States. The circus had become the most popular form of entertainment.

A large circus could fill 60 railroad cars and had big top tents more than 500 feet long, capable of seating as many as 10,000 people. Until 1872, circuses still featured a single performance area, or ring; two-ring circuses appeared in the 1870s, and the three-ring circus appeared in 1882. Performances grew more and more spectacular, with the flying trapeze, aerial gymnastics, human cannonball acts, and other death-defying feats. In 1891, wild animal acts moved under the big top, presented by Miss Carlotta and Colonel Boone of the Adam Forepaugh Circus.

James A. Bailey was another renowned circus owner. In 1880, the first live birth of an elephant in captivity occurred at Bailey's Great London Circus, and the baby elephant became a huge attraction. Bailey and P. T. Barnum soon became partners. They brought over an African elephant named "Jumbo," which was billed as the largest animal on Earth and became the biggest circus attraction of the day. Another elephant, the so-called "white elephant," was so widely publicized that the term has entered our vocabulary.

The five Ringling Brothers from Baraboo, Wisconsin, organized their first circus in 1884. By 1890, their circus had grown large enough to become a railroad show, and by the end of the century, the Ringling Brothers' Circus was one of the largest in the United States. In 1888, P. T. Barnum took the Barnum & Bailey Circus and its *Greatest Show on Earth* to England, where people went as much to see P. T. Barnum himself as they did to see the circus.

After Barnum's death in 1891, and Bailey's death in 1903, the Ringling Brothers bought the Barnum & Bailey Circus in 1907. For the next 10 years, the two circuses operated separately. But in 1919, the shows were merged into the most well-known circus of all, Ringling Brothers and Barnum & Bailey Circus, which featured a wide array of performances, from bareback riding to the flying trapeze to feats of strength, and included the famous Flying Wallendas.

While the largest circuses traveled by railroad, there were many smaller circuses still performing in the smaller cities and towns. The development of the automobile

Although riding gracefully atop an elephant may look easy, this circus performer has spent hours practicing.

and a paved road system soon allowed these circuses to travel more quickly and to more places than ever before, and by the 1920s, the first successful truck circuses were traveling the country. By the 1950s, most circuses, especially the tented circuses such as the Clyde Beatty Circus, traveled by truck. Others, including the Ringling Brothers and Barnum & Bailey Circus, no longer used a tent at all, but performed instead inside the largest arenas and auditoriums.

Modern circuses are more varied than ever before. Circus performers often become famous celebrities, such as Dolly Jacobs, who amazed audiences by performing somersaults on the Roman Rings; Miguel Vasquez, the originator of the quadruple somersault on the flying trapeze; and Gunther Gebel-Williams, whose world-famous animal act included tigers, leopards, elephants, and horses.

Today there are some 40 traveling circuses in the United States and many more throughout the world. In the 1980s, Cirque du Soleil of Canada created a new type of circus, featuring elaborately choreographed dance, music, lighting, and costumes to augment its stage performances. Vaudeville, sideshows, and burlesque have

also seen a revival, with Coney Island, in Brooklyn, New York, emerging as one of the centers.

■ THE JOB

Circus historian George Chindahl has identified as many as 200 different circus acts, and new ones are being created every day. Some circus performers work alone, although most work as part of a troupe. Every performer, whether solo or a group, develops a unique act. The aim is to amaze, entertain, and thrill the audience with their performances, which often feature risky, even death-defying, stunts. A great deal of a performance is the suspense created until the performer is once again safe on the ground. When not performing, the performers and their apprentices and other helpers maintain their equipment, oversee the set-up of the equipment, maintain their costumes and other props used during performances, and train and rehearse their routines.

At the beginning of the circus show, all the performers join in the circus parade around the arena. Performers wait backstage during the show until it is time for them to perform. They usually wait near the entrances, so that they are ready to go on as soon as they are called. Circus shows may feature 20 or more separate acts, and each performance and the entire show are precisely timed.

Aerialists perform vaulting, leaping, and flying acts, such as trapeze, rings, and cloud swings. Balancing acts include *wire walkers* and *acrobats*. *Jugglers* handle a variety of objects, such as clubs, balls, or hoops, and they perform on the ground or on a high wire. *Aquatic performers* perform water stunts, usually only in very large circuses. *Animal trainers* work with lions, tigers, bears, elephants, or horses. These performers almost always own and care for the animals they work with. *Clowns* dress in outlandish costumes, paint their faces, and use a variety of performance skills to entertain audiences. *Circus musicians* and *conductors* play in bands, called windjammers, which provide dramatic and comedic accompaniment for all acts. Each act has its own music, and the windjammers cue each act as it begins its music. Other common circus entertainers are daredevil performers and trick bicyclists.

Almost all circus performers combine several skills and may participate in more than one act during a show. All circus acts are physically demanding, requiring strength, endurance, and flexibility.

Circus work is seasonal. Performers work during the spring, summer, and fall, giving perhaps two or three shows a day on weekends and holidays. Some circuses, such as Ringling Brothers, perform from February to November. During the winter months, they train, improve their acts, or work in sponsored indoor circuses.

Circus performers sometimes take jobs on stage while not in season. Many circus performers develop variety acts that they can perform in places like Las Vegas or on cruise ships.

Circus performers can spend up to 10 years in training. Once they have developed their act, they may join a circus for one or several seasons, or they may travel from circus to circus as independent acts. In either case, there is a great deal of travel involved.

■ REQUIREMENTS
High School

There are no educational requirements for circus performers. Those who have a high school or college education, however, will have an advantage because they will be better able to manage their business affairs and communicate with others. Knowledge of foreign languages will be helpful for performers hoping to travel overseas.

Athletic training that develops coordination, strength, and balance is necessary for almost all circus performers and should be developed at a young age. Other training includes acting, music, dance, and for those interested in animals, veterinary care. Animal trainers usually must complete a long apprenticeship.

Postsecondary Training

Most circus performers learn their skills as apprentices to well-established acts. There are a few skills that can be learned on your own in a few weeks or months, such as juggling, unicycling, and puppetry, but most circus skills take many years to learn and perfect. Most circus performers develop skills in two or more areas, which makes them more attractive to employers.

Depending on your interests, you can receive some formal training in a number of areas. The San Francisco School of Circus Arts (http:// www.circuscenter.org/), for example, is open to the public and offers classes in juggling, flying trapeze, and contortion, among other activities. The Dell'Arte International School of Physical Theatre (http://www.dellarte.com), in Blue Lake, California, while not a circus arts school, does offer classes in physical theater useful for anyone interested in clowning, miming, and relating to audiences through performance. If you would like to combine a college education with circus experience, consider attending Florida State University (FSU), home of the FSU Flying High Circus (http://www.fsu.edu/~circus). This circus is an extracurricular activity open to Florida State students in good standing and provides the opportunity to work in any area of the circus that interests you. The majority of circus performers begin their careers as children, as members of performing families.

Other Requirements

Circus performers must be physically fit and must be able to withstand the rigors of their act as well as the hardships of constant travel. Some acts require unusual strength, flexibility, or balance.

■ EXPLORING

If circus performance interests you, see a circus. Go to every circus that comes to your area. Talk to the performers about their work. Ask outright if there are jobs available, or write to circuses to express your interest in finding circus work.

Gymnastics teams, drama clubs, and dance troupes provide performance experience and may help you decide if you have talent for this type of work. Those interested in animal training should volunteer at nearby zoos or stables. Ballet and mime are also valuable sources of insight into this field.

You may wish to join an association of jugglers, unicyclists, or another specialty. They often hold festivals, events, and seminars where you can train, get to know other circus performers, and perhaps find a mentor who can help you get into the field.

Attending a circus camp is also an excellent way to learn skills and find out about this career. Camps, such as Circus Camp (http://www.circuscamp.org) in Georgia, and Circus Smirkus (http://www.circussmirkus.org) in Vermont, are available across the country, and you can find out about them by searching the Web with the words "circus camp." In addition to being a camper, you may be able to find summer work as a counselor or instructor at such a camp once you have some experience.

■ EMPLOYERS

While it goes without saying that circus performers are largely employed by traveling circuses, they are being used in a variety of other venues, including stage shows, nightclubs, casinos, on Broadway, and on television. As with many other performing arts professions, more opportunities of this type are available in larger cities, especially those that appeal to tourists, such as New York, Los Angeles, and Las Vegas.

■ STARTING OUT

Circus performers usually enter the field through one of four methods. First, they may join a circus in a relatively low position and work their way up through the ranks. One option for someone joining the circus this way is to look at the websites of larger circuses, such as Big Apple Circus (http:// www.bigapplecircus.org/), for job openings. Those who enter the circus profession this way, known as "walk-ons," may start as part of a set-up or clean-up crew, or they may care for animals. Then, as they get to know performers, they become apprentices. After learning the necessary skills, they gradually work their way into the act.

The second way is to purchase an existing act. Beginners do not usually start with this method. The buyer often receives training, costumes, and equipment as a condition of purchase.

The third method is to enter a preprofessional program that offers a placement service once training is completed. There are very few of these programs in the United States.

The fourth method is to be raised in a circus performing family. Most circus performers enter the field by this method. From 75 to 90 percent of all circus performers come from circus performing families. Obviously, joining the circus this way is more a matter of luck than choice—but perhaps you can be "adopted" into such a family.

Most circus performers develop their acts and then hire an agent who finds work for them. There are only a few agents in the United States who specialize in circus acts. Performers have to audition for potential employers the agent finds.

Circus performers counsel that it is wise to get as much work in as many different places as you can and to not limit your skills. Develop a specialty or gimmick, but learn several skills. Most circus owners look for performers who can perform a variety of acts during a single show.

ADVANCEMENT

It helps if an aspiring circus performer is born into a circus family and can begin training as soon as he or she is able to walk. Later, the performer will be incorporated into the family's act and over time, he or she will take a more and more prominent position. But many successful circus performers started at the bottom as laborers and learned their skills by watching. Once performers have developed skill in a variety of areas, they gain journeyman status and may set out on their own, acquire their act from the performer who trained them, join an established act, or form a new act with others. Those with the

most unusual and unique acts and skills may find themselves in great demand and can sign long-term contracts with a circus.

Some circus performers become quite famous and can command large sums of money. Some circus performers enter other performing areas, such as the stage, Broadway, Las Vegas variety shows, and television programs and commercials.

EARNINGS

Earnings for circus performers vary so widely that it is difficult to determine the average salaries. It is clear, however, that people entering this field do so out of love and not for the money.

According to the Circus World Museum, those just starting out usually do not earn much more than the minimum wage, and sometimes even lower, perhaps $200 to $400 per week. Generally, however, they are provided with food and lodging while they complete their training, which may last 10 years or more. Those on the lower level of performing, such as showgirls and clowns, may jump to $600 to $700 per week, while those whose acts involve animals may earn from several thousand per week up to $100,000 or more for the circus season. The amount performers earn depends on a number of factors, but especially the degree of fame or recognition they achieve. Performers who develop highly unusual and distinctive acts stand the best chance of higher earnings. A few star performers may sign multi-year contracts for many millions of dollars.

Salaries also range widely among the different circuses. Some circuses, like Cirque du Soleil, pay their performers quite well. Performers at Ringling Brothers, on the other hand, may accept lower pay because the Ringling Brothers' fame more than compensates for the lower salaries, and gaining experience at Ringling Brothers means that they can later command higher salaries elsewhere.

Circus performers often pay for their own transportation and manage their own business affairs. Rarely do they get a paid vacation.

WORK ENVIRONMENT

Circus performers work long hours performing and even longer hours preparing their acts. The learning and relearning periods are intense and physically demanding. Heavy travel is involved, and most acts require expensive equipment, props, and costumes.

Circus performers enjoy being able to choose their engagements and be their own bosses. They have the freedom to create their own art form that showcases their particular talent. They face the continual challenge of creating new routines never done before.

OUTLOOK

P. T. Barnum once said, "As long as there are children, there will always be circuses." Circuses will continue, though their formats change with the times.

Traditional circuses are changing. Tents are seldom used because they are costly and impractical. It's often more convenient to perform in an arena. Also, many animal acts are being eliminated because of the large costs involved in maintaining and transporting them, as well as complaints from animal-rights activists. There is less emphasis on props and equipment, to make travel easier and cheaper. Circus acts are more flexible: They are able to perform in either a three-ring format or on a proscenium stage. Circuses are becoming more theatrical, using professional designers, lighting, and musicians. They often have a special theme. Specialty circuses are expanding, such as Cirque du Soleil, Big Apple Circus, and Circus Flora.

Those who work in a resident company of a circus can become well known and have greater job security. There are more opportunities for circus performers outside the circus, and there is always an interest for new, unusual, never-been-seen acts. The private party business is growing, and circus performers may be used in television and music videos. Even with the changes, the popularity of circuses has remained steady and should remain so for the next 10 years.

The number of circus performers far outnumbers job openings. More and more circus acts from overseas, especially from Eastern Europe, Russia, and China, are competing for openings in American circuses. In addition, the rise of animal activism has made the development of acts involving animals more challenging. So while opportunities remain good for highly skilled performers, they are marginal for those at the entry level.

FOR MORE INFORMATION

This circus travels across the country providing education programs to schools, businesses, and other groups. Visit its website to find out where the troupe is now and the programs offered.

Circus of the Kids
926 Waverly Road
Tallahassee, FL 32312-2813
Tel: 866-247-2875
http://www.circusofthekids.com

To learn more about circuses of the past as well as the present, visit Circus World Museum. If you can't make it in person, check out its website.

Circus World Museum
550 Water Street
Baraboo, WI 53913

Tel: 866-693-1500
Email: ringmaster@circusworldmuseum.com
http://www.circusworldmuseum.com

This website offers facts and information about Ringling Brothers and Barnum & Bailey Circus, including news, games, animals, history and tradition, performers, and show dates.

Ringling Brothers and Barnum & Bailey
8607 Westwood Center Drive
Vienna, VA 22182
Tel: 703-448-4000
http://www.ringling.com

This website includes information on treatment of circus animals, membership, and links to circus-related sites.

Circus Fans Association of America
http://www.circusfans.org

City Managers

OVERVIEW

A *city manager* is an administrator who coordinates the day-to-day running of a local government. Usually an appointed position, the manager directs the administration of city or county government in accordance with the policies determined by the city council or other elected authority.

HISTORY

There have been all sorts of governments and political theories in our world's history, and much of the structure of U.S. government is based on the theories and practices of other nations. The "council-manager" form of government, however, is truly American in origin. With government reforms of the early 1900s came government managers. Before the reform, cities were run by city councils or boards of aldermen. Because of rigged elections and other corruption by aldermen, a mayoral form of government was brought into practice. The council-manager form of government also evolved. Though a mayor is elected and holds political power, the city manager is appointed by the council. When the elected officials develop policies, the city managers use their administrative and management skills to put these policies into action. Some Southern towns began to develop council-manager forms of government as early as 1908; Dayton, Ohio, became the first large city to put the council-manager form into place in 1913. According to the

International City/County Management Association (ICMA), 3,400 cities and 371 counties operate in the council-manager form today. More than 89 million people live in these communities.

■ THE JOB

Have more bus routes been added to provide transportation to a new shopping area? Has the small park near the lake been cleaned up so children can play safely there? Will a new performing arts center be built downtown? These are some of the kinds of questions a city manager faces on the job. Even the smallest community has hundreds of concerns, from quality day care options for its citizens to proper housing for the elderly, from maintaining strong law enforcement in the city to preserving the surrounding environment. Every day, local newspapers feature all the changes underway in their communities. The mayor introduces these developments, speaking to reporters and appearing on the TV news and at city meetings. But, it's the city manager who works behind the scenes to put these changes into effect. A city manager uses managerial experience and skills to determine what programs are needed in the community, to design the programs, and to implement them. The council-manager form of government is somewhat like a smooth-running business—the executives make the decisions about a company, while the managers see that these decisions are put into practice efficiently and effectively.

A city has many different departments in place to collect and disburse taxes, enforce laws, maintain public health and a ready fire department, construct public works such as parks and other recreational facilities, and purchase supplies and equipment. The city manager prepares budgets of the costs of these services and submits estimates to the elected officials for approval. The manager is also responsible for providing reports of ongoing and completed work and projects to the representatives of the residents. The city manager keeps in touch with the community in order to understand what is most important to the people of the city. A city manager also needs to stay several steps ahead, in order to plan for growth, population expansion, and public services. To oversee planning for population growth, crime prevention, street repairs, law enforcement, and pollution and traffic management problems, the manager prepares proposals and recommends zoning regulations. The manager then presents these proposals at meetings of the elected authorities as well as at public meetings of citizens.

In addition to developing plans and budgets, city managers meet with private groups and individuals who represent special interests. Managers explain programs, policies, and projects. They may also seek to enlist the aid of citizen groups in a variety of projects that help the public as a whole. They work closely with urban planners to coordinate new and existing programs. In smaller cities that have no planning staff, this work may be done entirely by the manager. Additional staff may be provided for the city manager of a large city, including an assistant city manager, department head assistants, administrative assistants, and management analysts.

The staff of a city manager have a variety of titles and responsibilities. Changes in administration are studied and recommended by *management analysts*. Administrative and staff work, such as compiling statistics and planning work procedures, is done by *administrative assistants*, also called *executive assistants*. Department head assistants may work in several areas, such as law enforcement, finance, or law, but they are generally responsible for just one area. *Assistant city managers* are responsible for specific projects, such as developing the annual budget, as well as organizing and coordinating programs. They may supervise city employees and perform other administrative tasks, such as answering correspondence, receiving visitors, preparing reports, and monitoring programs.

■ REQUIREMENTS
High School

Take courses in government and social studies to learn about the nature of cities and counties. Math and business courses are important because you'll be working with budgets and statistics and preparing financial reports. English and composition courses, and speech and debate teams are also very important, as you'll need good communication skills for presenting your thoughts and ideas to policy makers, special interest groups, and the community. Computer science is an important tool in any administrative profession. Take journalism courses and report for your school newspaper to learn about research and conducting polls and surveys.

QUICK FACTS

SCHOOL SUBJECTS
Business
Government
Mathematics

PERSONAL SKILLS
Communication/ideas
Leadership/management

WORK ENVIRONMENT
Primarily indoors
Primarily multiple locations

MINIMUM EDUCATION LEVEL
Bachelor's degree

SALARY RANGE
$28,489 to $48,772 to $137,887

CERTIFICATION OR LICENSING
None available

OUTLOOK
Little change or more slowly than the average

DOT
188

GOE
13.01.01

NOC
0414

O*NET-SOC
11-1011.01

Postsecondary Training

You'll need at least a bachelor's degree to work as a city manager. As an undergraduate, you'll major in such programs as public administration, political science, sociology, or business. The ICMA notes that an increasing number of local governments are requiring job candidates for manager positions to have master's degrees in public administration or business. Programs resulting in a master's in public administration (M.P.A) are available all across the country; some schools offer dual degrees, allowing you to also pursue a master's of business administration or master's of social work along with the M.P.A. The National Association of Schools of Public Affairs and Administration (NASPAA) offers voluntary accreditation to schools with degree programs in public affairs and administration. The association has a membership of approximately 250 schools, of which slightly more than half are accredited. The NASPAA website (http://www.naspaa.org) provides a roster of accredited programs, which is updated annually.

Course work in public administration programs covers topics such as finance, budgeting, municipal law, legal issues, personnel management, and the political aspects of urban problems. Degree requirements in some schools also include completion of an internship program in a city manager's office that may last from six months to a year, during which time the degree candidate observes local government operations and does research under the direct supervision of the city manager.

People planning to enter city management positions frequently must pass civil service examinations. This is one way to become eligible for appointments to local government. Other requirements will vary from place to place. Most positions require knowledge of computerized tax and utility billing, electronic traffic control, and applications of systems analysis to urban problems.

Other Requirements

"You have to have the will, desire, and strength to want to lead an organization," says Michael Roberto, former city manager of Clearwater, Florida. He emphasizes that, as manager, you're the person held primarily responsible for the administration of the city. You should have a thick skin: "You'll be yelled at a lot," he says. In addition to handling the complaints, you must be able to handle the stress of the job and the long and frequently unpredictable hours that are required. "But you're only limited by your dreams in what you can create," Roberto says.

You'll need to be decisive, confident, and staunch in making managerial decisions. You need to be skilled at solving problems, while flexible enough to consider the ideas of others. Managers must also have a knack for

City managers work in all aspects of management, from urban planning to public health to law enforcement. Here, a city manager reviews site plans for a new park.

working with people, have the ability to negotiate and tactfully debate with co-workers and other officials, and be able to listen to the opinions and concerns of the people they represent.

■ EXPLORING

You can learn about public administration by becoming involved in student government or by serving as an officer for a school club, such as a business or Internet club. A summer job in a local government office can give you a lot of insight into the workings of a city. Work for the school newspaper and you'll learn about budgets, projects, and school administrators. An internship with a local newspaper or radio or TV station may give you the opportunity to interview the mayor, council members, and the city manager about city administration.

■ EMPLOYERS

Cities large and small have council-manager forms of government and require city managers for the administration of policies and programs. Counties and suburbs also have managers. The ICMA reports that out of the 237 American cities with more than 100,000 residents, 141 use a council-manager form of government. Those with a master's degree in public administration may find work as a city planner. Other employment possibilities include working as an administrator of a hospital or an association, or in private industry. Some professionals with this background work as instructors for undergraduate public administration programs at universities or community colleges.

STARTING OUT

In addition to college internships with local public administrators, you can apply to the ICMA internship programs. There is heavy competition for these internship positions because they often lead to full-time work. The ICMA also publishes a newsletter announcing job vacancies. Nearly all city managers begin as management assistants. As a new graduate, you'll work as a management analyst or administrative assistant to city managers for several years to gain experience in solving urban problems, coordinating public services, and applying management techniques. Or you may work in a specific department such as finance, public works, civil engineering, or planning. You'll acquire supervisory skills and also work as an assistant city manager or department head assistant. After a few years of competent service, you may be hired to manage a community.

Other avenues of potential employment include listings in the job sections of newspapers and professional journals. There are also private firms that specialize in filling government job openings. Those willing to relocate to smaller cities at lower salaries should have better job opportunities.

ADVANCEMENT

An assistant to a city manager is gradually given more responsibilities and assignments as he or she gains experience. At least five years of experience are generally necessary to compete for the position of city manager. City managers are often employed in small cities at first, and during their careers they may seek and obtain appointments in growing cities. Experienced managers may become heads of regional government councils; others may serve several small jurisdictions at one time. Those city managers with a master's degree in business management, political science, urban planning, or law stand the best chance for employment.

EARNINGS

City managers' earnings vary according to such factors as the size of the city, the city's geographical location, and the manager's education and experience. The ICMA reports that in 2004, the mean annual income for city managers ranged from an average of $48,772 per year (in the east-south central region) to $91,552 (on the Pacific coast). Overall salaries ranged from a low of approximately $28,489 annually to a high of approximately $137,887 during that same period.

Salaries are set by the city council, and good city managers are sometimes given higher than average pay as an incentive to keep them from seeking more lucrative opportunities. Benefits for city managers include paid vacations, health insurance, sick leave, and retirement plans. Cities may also pay travel and moving expenses and provide a city car or a car allowance.

WORK ENVIRONMENT

Typically a city manager has an office and possibly a trained staff to assist him or her. But a city manager also spends many hours attending meetings. To provide information to citizens on current government operations or to advocate certain programs, the manager frequently appears at public meetings and other civic functions and often visits government departments and inspects work sites. A city manager often works overtime at night and on weekends reading and writing reports or finishing paperwork. The manager also needs to attend dinners and evening events and go out of town for conferences. Any extra days worked on weekends are usually compensated for in vacation time or additional pay. "The long hours," Michael Roberto says, "can be tough on your home life, tough on your family." A city manager can be called at any hour of the day or night in times of crisis. Managers must be prepared for sometimes stressful interaction with co-workers and constituents, as well as the acclaim that comes to them for completing a job successfully or solving a particularly complex problem. "You're scrutinized by the press," Roberto says, and he emphasizes that a manager shouldn't be too affected by the coverage, whether negative or positive.

OUTLOOK

Although city management is a growing profession, the field is still relatively small. The U.S. Department of Labor predicts that employment at the local government level will increase by approximately 10 percent through 2012, which is at a rate somewhat slower than the average for all occupations. One reason for this is that few new governments are likely to form and, therefore, there will be few new job openings. Applicants with only a bachelor's degree will have the most difficulty finding employment. Even an entry-level job often requires an advanced degree. The ICMA provides funds to those cities wanting to establish the county-manager form of government, as well as to cities where the form is threatened.

City managers are finding that they are sharing more and more of their authority with many different groups, such as unions and special interest groups. "This dilutes the system," Michael Roberto says, "and makes it harder to manage."

The issues that affect a city are constantly changing. Future city managers will need to focus on clean air regulations, promoting diversity, providing affordable housing, creating new policing methods, and revitalizing old downtown areas.

■ FOR MORE INFORMATION

For statistics and internship opportunities, contact

International City/County Management Association
777 North Capitol Street, NE, Suite 500
Washington, DC 20002-4201
Tel: 202-289-4262
http://www.icma.org

For more information on finding a school, the M.P.A. degree, and public affairs work, contact

National Association of Schools of Public Affairs and Administration
1120 G Street, NW, Suite 730
Washington, DC 20005
Tel: 202-628-8965
Email: naspaa@naspaa.org
http://www.naspaa.org

For information on policy and legislative issues, membership, and conferences, contact

National League of Cities
1301 Pennsylvania Avenue, NW, Suite 550
Washington, DC 20004
Tel: 202-626-3000
http://www.nlc.org

Civil Engineering Technicians

■ OVERVIEW

Civil engineering technicians help civil engineers design, plan, and build public as well as private works to meet the community's needs. They are employed in a wide range of projects, such as highways, drainage systems, water and sewage facilities, railroads, subways, airports, dams, bridges, and tunnels.

■ HISTORY

Engineering, both military and civil, is one of the world's oldest professions. The pyramids of ancient Egypt and the bridges, roads, and aqueducts of the Roman Empire (some of which are still in use) are examples of ancient engineering feats. It was not until the 18th century in France and England that civil engineers began to organize themselves into professional societies to exchange information or plan projects. At that time, most civil engineers were still self-taught, skilled craft workers. Thomas Telford, for instance, Britain's leading road builder and first president of the Institution of Civil Engineers, started his career as a stonemason. And John Rennie, the builder of the new London Bridge, began as a millwright's apprentice.

The first major educational programs intended for civil engineers were offered by the École Polytechnique, founded in Paris in 1794. Similar courses at the Bauakadamie, founded in Berlin in 1799, and at University College London, founded in 1826, soon followed. In the United States, the first courses in civil engineering were taught at Rensselaer Polytechnic Institute, founded in 1824.

From the beginning, civil engineers have required the help of skilled assistants to handle the many details that are part of all phases of civil engineering. Traditionally, these assistants have possessed a combination of basic knowledge and good manual skills. As construction techniques have become more sophisticated, however, there is an increased need for assistants to be technically trained in specialized fields relevant to civil engineering.

These technically trained assistants are today's civil engineering technicians. Just as separate educational programs and professional identity developed for the civil engineer in the 18th and 19th centuries, so they have developed for civil engineering technicians in this century. The civil engineering technician is a distinguished member of the civil engineering team.

QUICK FACTS

SCHOOL SUBJECTS
Mathematics
Physics

PERSONAL SKILLS
Following instructions
Technical/scientific

WORK ENVIRONMENT
Indoors and outdoors
Primarily multiple locations

MINIMUM EDUCATION LEVEL
Associate's degree

SALARY RANGE
$23,330 to $38,050 to $57,190

CERTIFICATION OR LICENSING
Recommended

OUTLOOK
About as fast as the average

DOT
005

GOE
02.08.04

NOC
2231

O*NET-SOC
17-3022.00

■ THE JOB

Civil engineering technicians work in many areas. State highway departments, for example, use their services to collect data, to design and draw plans, and to supervise the construction and maintenance of roadways. Railroad and airport facilities require similar services. Cities and counties need to have transportation systems, drainage systems, and water and sewage facilities planned, built, and maintained with the help of civil engineering technicians.

Civil engineering technicians participate in all stages of the construction process. During the planning stages, they help engineers prepare lists of materials needed and estimate project costs. One of the most important technician positions at this stage is the structural engineering technician. *Structural engineering technicians* help engineers calculate the size, number, and composition of beams and columns and investigate allowable soil pressures that develop from the weight of these structures. If the pressure will cause excessive settling or some other failure, they may help design special piers, rafts, pilings, or footings to prevent structural problems.

During the planning stages, civil engineering technicians help engineers prepare drawings, maps, and charts; during the actual construction phase, construction technicians assist building contractors and site supervisors in preparing work schedules and cost estimates and in performing work inspections. One of their most important duties is to ensure that each step of construction is completed before workers arrive to begin the next stage.

Some technicians specialize in certain types of construction projects. *Highway technicians,* for example, perform surveys and cost estimates as well as plan and supervise highway construction and maintenance. *Rail and waterway technicians* survey, make specifications and cost estimates, and help plan and construct railway and waterway facilities. *Assistant city engineers* coordinate the planning and construction of city streets, sewers, drainage systems, refuse facilities, and other major civil projects.

Other technicians specialize in certain phases of the construction process. For example, *construction materials testing technicians* sample and run tests on rock, soil, cement, asphalt, wood, steel, concrete, and other materials. *Photogrammetric technicians* use aerial photographs to prepare maps, plans, and profiles. *Party chiefs* work for licensed land surveyors, survey land for boundary-line locations, and plan subdivisions and other large-area land developments.

There are other specialized positions for civil engineering technicians: *research engineering technicians* test and develop new products and equipment; *sales engineering technicians* sell building materials, construction equipment, and engineering services; and *water resources technicians* gather data, make computations and drawings for water projects, and prepare economic studies.

■ REQUIREMENTS
High School

While in high school, you should follow the course for admission into an institution offering either a two- or four-year degree in civil engineering technology. Helpful classes include mathematics, physics, and chemistry. Because the ability to read and interpret material is very important, four years of English and language skills courses are basic requirements. Reports and letters are an essential part of the technician's work, so a firm grasp of English grammar is important. Other useful courses include mechanical drawing and shop; civil engineering technicians often make use of mechanical drawings to convey their ideas to others, and neat, well-executed drawings are important to convey a sense of accuracy and competence.

Postsecondary Training

Once you have graduated, you should choose a school that offers an accredited program in civil engineering technology. In such programs, more mathematics and science subjects, including physics, will be studied to prepare the student for later specialty courses, such as surveying, materials, hydraulics, highway and bridge construction and design, structures, railway and water systems, heavy construction, soils, steel and concrete construction, cost and estimates, and management and construction technology. You should also take courses in computer programming and photogrammetry.

Certification or Licensing

To advance in professional standing, civil engineering technicians should try to become Certified Engineering Technicians (CETs). The National Institute for Certification in Engineering Technologies is one organization that offers certification for technicians. To achieve certification, typically a candidate must graduate from an accredited program, pass a written exam, and have some work experience.

Other Requirements

Civil engineering projects are often complex and long-term, requiring a variety of specialized skills. Civil engineering technicians need the ability to think and plan ahead, as well as the patience to work through all the necessary details. "The devil is in the details" could be the motto for the engineering technicians whose job it is to see that each part of the whole project is correct.

EXPLORING

One of the best ways to acquire firsthand experience in this field is through part-time or summer work with a construction company. Even if the job is menial, you can still observe surveying teams, site supervisors, building inspectors, skilled craft workers, and civil engineering technicians at work. If such work is not possible, students can organize field trips to various construction sites or to facilities where building materials are manufactured.

EMPLOYERS

Civil engineers work for various construction companies and, very frequently, for the government. Some choose to go into business for themselves after acquiring a great deal of experience working for others.

STARTING OUT

Most schools maintain placement offices, which many prospective employers contact when they have job openings. The placement offices, in turn, help the student or graduate prepare a resume of relevant school and work experiences, and they usually arrange personal interviews with prospective employers. Many schools also have cooperative work-study programs with particular companies and government agencies. With such a program, the company or government agency often becomes the new technician's place of full-time employment after graduation.

ADVANCEMENT

Civil engineering technicians must study and learn throughout their careers. They must learn new techniques, master the operation of new equipment, and gain greater depth of knowledge in their chosen fields to keep themselves abreast of the latest developments. Some technicians move on to supervisory positions, while others pursue additional education to become civil engineers.

EARNINGS

The U.S. Department of Labor reports that the median annual salary for civil engineering technicians was $38,050 in 2003. That same year, the highest paid 10 percent of civil engineering technicians earned more than $57,190, while the lowest paid 10 percent earned less than $23,330. The department also reports the annual median incomes for civil engineering technicians by leading employers: those working for local governments earned a median of $42,980; for engineering and architectural services, $39,010; and for state governments, $36,240. Naturally, higher paying jobs go to those with advanced education and experience. The incomes of many civil engineering technicians who operate their own construction, surveying, or equipment businesses are excellent. Some of these companies can earn millions of dollars each year.

Paid vacations, pension plans, and insurance are normal parts of the benefits paid to civil engineering technicians. Many companies pay a bonus if a job is completed ahead of schedule or if the job is completed for less than the estimated cost. These bonuses sometimes amount to more than the employee's regular annual salary.

WORK ENVIRONMENT

Technicians usually work 40 hours a week with extra pay for overtime. Working conditions vary from job to job: Technicians who enjoy being outdoors may choose a job in construction or surveying; those who prefer working indoors may work in a consulting engineer's office on computations, drafting, or design. In either case, the work done by civil engineering technicians is usually cleaner than the work done by most other construction trades workers.

Civil engineering technicians feel the pride that comes from being a member of a team that constructs major buildings, bridges, or dams. In a way, such projects become monuments to the efforts of each member of the team. And there is the accompanying satisfaction that the project has improved, if only in a modest way, the quality of life in a community.

OUTLOOK

The outlook for civil engineering technicians is generally favorable. The U.S. Department of Labor predicts employment for all engineering technicians to grow about as fast as the average through 2012. As in most industries, those with certification and the most education have the best outlook. Construction is, however, one of the industries most likely to feel the effects of economic recessions, so civil engineering technicians must be prepared for slowdowns in business.

FOR MORE INFORMATION

For career and educational information and links to additional resources, contact

American Society for Engineering Education
1818 N Street, NW, Suite 600
Washington, DC 20036-2479
Tel: 202-331-3500
http://www.asee.org

For information on training, and scholarships, contact the following organizations:

American Society of Certified Engineering Technicians

PO Box 1348

Flowery Branch, GA 30542

Tel: 770-967-9173

Email: General_Manager@ascet.org

http://www.ascet.org

American Society of Civil Engineers

1801 Alexander Bell Drive

Reston, VA 20191

Tel: 800-548-2723

http://www.asce.org

For certification information, contact

National Institute for Certification in Engineering Technologies

1420 King Street

Alexandria, VA 22314-2794

Tel: 888-476-4238

http://www.nicet.org

Civil Engineers

■ OVERVIEW

Civil engineers are involved in the design and construction of the physical structures that make up our surroundings, such as roads, bridges, buildings, and harbors. Civil engineering involves theoretical knowledge applied to the practical planning of the layout of our cities, towns, and other communities. It is concerned with modifying the natural environment and building new environments to better the lifestyles of the general public. Civil engineers are also known as *structural engineers*. There are approximately 228,000 civil engineers in the United States.

■ HISTORY

One might trace the evolution of civil engineering methods by considering the building and many reconstructions of England's London Bridge. In Roman and medieval times, several bridges made of timber were built over the Thames River. Around the end of the 12th century, these were rebuilt into 19 narrow arches mounted on piers. A chapel was built on one of the piers, and two towers were built for defense. A fire damaged the bridge around 1212, yet the surrounding area was considered a preferred place to live and work, largely because it was the only bridge over which one could cross the river. The structure was rebuilt many times during later centuries using different materials and designs. By 1830, it had only five arches. More than a century later, the center span of the bridge was remodeled, and part of it was actually transported to the United States to be set up as a tourist attraction.

Working materials for civil engineers have changed during many centuries. For instance, bridges, once made of timber, then of iron and steel, are today made mainly with concrete that is reinforced with steel. The high strength of the material is necessary because of the abundance of cars and other heavy vehicles that travel over the bridges.

As the population continues to grow and communities become more complex, structures that civil engineers must pay attention to have to be remodeled and repaired. New highways, buildings, airstrips, and so forth must be designed to accommodate public needs. Today, more and more civil engineers are involved with water treatment plants, water purification plants, and toxic waste sites. Increasing concern about the natural environment is also evident in the growing number of engineers working on such projects as preservation of wetlands, maintenance of national forests, and restoration of sites around land mines, oil wells, and industrial factories.

■ THE JOB

Civil engineers use their knowledge of materials science, engineering theory, economics, and demographics to devise, construct, and maintain our physical surroundings. They apply their understanding of other branches of science—such as hydraulics, geology, and physics—to design the optimal blueprint for the project.

Feasibility studies are conducted by *surveying and mapping engineers* to determine the best sites and approaches for construction. They extensively investigate the chosen sites to verify that the ground and other surroundings are amenable to the proposed project. These engineers use sophisticated equipment, such as satellites and other electronic instruments, to measure the area and conduct underground probes for bedrock and groundwater. They determine the optimal places where explosives should be blasted in order to cut through rock.

Many civil engineers work strictly as consultants on projects, advising their clients. These consultants usually specialize in one area of the industry, such as water systems, transportation systems, or housing structures. Clients include individuals, corporations, and the government. Consultants will devise an overall design for the proposed project, perhaps a nuclear power plant commissioned by an electric company. They will estimate the cost of constructing the plant, supervise the feasibility studies and site investigations, and advise the client on whom to hire for the actual labor involved. Consultants are also responsible for such details as accuracy of drawings and quantities of materials to order.

Other civil engineers work mainly as contractors and are responsible for the actual building of the structure; they are known as *construction engineers.* They interpret the consultants' designs and follow through with the best methods for getting the work done, usually working directly at the construction site. Contractors are responsible for scheduling the work, buying the materials, maintaining surveys of the progress of the work, and choosing the machines and other equipment used for construction. During construction, these civil engineers must supervise the labor and make sure the work is completed correctly and efficiently. After the project is finished, they must set up a maintenance schedule and periodically check the structure for a certain length of time. Later, the task of ongoing maintenance and repair is often transferred to local engineers.

Civil engineers may be known by their area of specialization. *Transportation engineers,* for example, are concerned mainly with the construction of highways and mass transit systems, such as subways and commuter rail lines. When devising plans for subways, engineers are responsible for considering the tunneling that is involved. *Pipeline engineers* are specialized civil engineers who are involved with the movement of water, oil, and gas through miles of pipeline.

■ REQUIREMENTS
High School
Because a bachelor's degree is considered essential in the field, high school students interested in civil engineering must follow a college prep curriculum. Students should focus on mathematics (algebra, trigonometry, geometry, and calculus), the sciences (physics and chemistry), computer science, and English and the humanities (history, economics, and sociology). Students should also aim for honors-level courses.

Postsecondary Training
In addition to completing the core engineering curriculum (including mathematics, science, drafting, and computer applications), students can choose their specialty from the following types of courses: structural analysis; materials design and specification; geology; hydraulics; surveying and design graphics; soil mechanics; and oceanography. Bachelor's degrees can be achieved through a number of programs: a four- or five-year accredited college or university; two years in a community college engineering program plus two or three years in a college or university; or five or six years in a co-op program (attending classes for part of the year and working in an engineering-related job for the rest of the year). About 30 percent of civil engineering students go on to receive a master's degree.

Certification or Licensing
Most civil engineers go on to study and qualify for a professional engineer (P.E.) license. It is required before one can work on projects affecting property, health, or life. Because many engineering jobs are found in government specialties, most engineers take the necessary steps to obtain the license. Requirements are different for each state—they involve educational, practical, and teaching experience. Applicants must take an examination on a specified date.

Other Requirements
Basic personal characteristics often found in civil engineers are an avid curiosity; a passion for mathematics and science; an aptitude for problem solving, both alone and with a team; and an ability to visualize multidimensional, spatial relationships.

■ EXPLORING
High school students can become involved in civil engineering by attending a summer camp or study program in the field. For example, the Worcester Polytechnic Institute in Massachusetts has a summer program for high school students who have completed their junior year and will be entering their senior year in the fall. Studies and events focus on science and math and include specialties for those interested in civil engineering.

After high school, another way to learn about civil engineering duties is to work on a construction crew that is involved in the actual building of a project designed and supervised by engineers. Such hands-on experience would provide an opportunity to

QUICK FACTS	
SCHOOL SUBJECTS	Mathematics Physics
PERSONAL SKILLS	Leadership/management Technical/scientific
WORK ENVIRONMENT	Indoors and outdoors Primarily multiple locations
MINIMUM EDUCATION LEVEL	Bachelor's degree
SALARY RANGE	$40,860 to $61,850 to $92,010
CERTIFICATION OR LICENSING	Recommended
OUTLOOK	Slower than the average
DOT	005
GOE	02.07.04
NOC	2131
O*NET-SOC	17-2051.00

work near many types of civil workers. Try to work on highway crews or even in housing construction.

■ EMPLOYERS

Slightly more than half of all civil engineers work for companies involved in engineering consulting services. Approximately 33 percent work for a government agency at the local, state, or federal level, and 40 percent work for private firms. A small percentage are self-employed, running their own consulting businesses. Approximately 228,000 civil engineers work in the United States.

■ STARTING OUT

To establish a career as a civil engineer, one must first receive a bachelor's degree in engineering or another appropriate scientific field. College placement offices are often the best sources of employment for beginning engineers. Entry-level jobs usually involve routine work, often as a member of a supervised team. After a year or more (depending on job performance and qualifications), one becomes a junior engineer, then an assistant to perhaps one or more supervising engineers. Establishment as a professional engineer comes after passing the P.E. exam.

A civil engineer inspects plans at a highway construction site.

■ ADVANCEMENT

Professional engineers with many years' experience often join with partners to establish their own firms in design, consulting, or contracting. Some leave long-held positions to be assigned as top executives in industries such as manufacturing and business consulting. Also, there are those who return to academia to teach high school or college students. For all of these potential opportunities, it is necessary to keep abreast of engineering advancements and trends by reading industry journals and taking courses.

■ EARNINGS

Civil engineers are among the lowest paid in the engineering field; however, their salaries are high when compared to those of many other occupations. The median annual earnings for civil engineers were $61,850 in 2002, according to the U.S. Department of Labor. The lowest paid 10 percent made less than $40,860 per year, and, at the other end of the pay scale, 10 percent earned more than $92,010 annually. Civil engineers working for the federal government had a median salary of $67,410 in 2002. According to a 2003 survey by the National Association of Colleges and Employers, starting salaries by degree level averaged as follows: bachelor's, $41,669; master's, $47,245; and doctorate, $69,079. As with all occupations, salaries are higher for those with more experience. Top civil engineers earn as much as $100,000 a year.

Benefits typically include such extras as health insurance, retirement plans, and paid vacation days.

■ WORK ENVIRONMENT

Many civil engineers work regular 40-hour weeks, often in or near major industrial and commercial areas. Sometimes they are assigned to work in remote areas and foreign countries. Because of the diversity of civil engineering positions, working conditions vary widely. Offices, labs, factories, and actual sites are typical environments for engineers. About one-third of all civil engineers can be found working for various levels of government, usually involving large public-works projects, such as highways and bridges.

A typical work cycle involving various types of civil engineers involves three stages: planning, constructing, and maintaining. Those involved with development of a campus compound, for example, would first need to work in their offices developing plans for a survey. Surveying and mapping engineers would have to visit the proposed site to take measurements and perhaps shoot aerial photographs. The measurements and photos would have to be converted into drawings and blueprints. Geotechnical engineers would dig wells at the site and take core samples from the ground. If toxic waste or unexpected water is found at the site, the contractor determines what should be done.

Actual construction then begins. Very often, a field trailer on the site becomes the engineers' makeshift offices. The campus might take several years to build—it is not uncommon for engineers to be involved in long-term projects. If contractors anticipate that deadlines will not be met, they often put in weeks of 10- to 15-hour days on the job.

After construction is complete, engineers spend less and less time at the site. Some may be assigned to stay onsite to keep daily surveys of how the structure is holding up and to solve problems when they arise. Eventually, the project engineers finish the job and move on to another long-term assignment.

■ OUTLOOK

Through 2012 the employment rate for civil engineers is expected be slower than the average, according to the U.S. Department of Labor. Employment will come from the need to maintain and repair public works, such as highways, bridges, and water systems. In addition, as the population grows, so does the need for more transportation and pollution control systems, which creates jobs for those who construct these systems. Firms providing management consulting and computer services may also be sources of jobs for civil engineers. However, employment is affected by several factors, including decisions made by the government to spend further on renewing and adding to the country's basic infrastructure and the health of the economy in general.

■ FOR MORE INFORMATION

For information on careers and scholarships, contact

American Society of Civil Engineers
1801 Alexander Bell Drive
Reston, VA 20191-4400
Tel: 800-548-2723
http://www.asce.org

Frontiers is a program for high school seniors that covers science material not traditionally offered in high school. For information, contact

Frontiers
Worcester Polytechnic Institute
100 Institute Road
Worcester, MA 01609-2280
Tel: 508-831-5286
Email: frontiers@wpi.edu
http://www.wpi.edu/Admin/AO/Frontiers

CIVIL ENGINEERS IN THE WINDY CITY

Chicago, Illinois—already distinguished as the city that developed a hole in its river that flooded its downtown—is now facing the problem of its lakeshore crumbling into Lake Michigan. The erosion controls put in place in 1929 have been upended and splintered, allowing the lake to ravage the shoreline. A project to reconstruct these barriers, floodwalls, and breakwaters along eight miles of shoreline was approved in 1999 by the city and the U.S. Army Corps of Engineers. The repair is projected to be completed in 2005.

For information on careers and colleges and universities with ITE student chapters, contact

Institute of Transportation Engineers
1099 14th Street, NW, Suite 300 West
Washington, DC 20005-3438
Tel: 202-289-0222
Email: ite_staff@ite.org
http://www.ite.org

The JETS offers high school students the opportunity to try engineering through a number of programs and competitions. To find out more about these opportunities or for general career information, contact

Junior Engineering Technical Society
1420 King Street, Suite 405
Alexandria, VA 22314-2794
Tel: 703-548-5387
Email: jetsinfo@jets.org
http://www.jets.org

Cleaning Service Owners

■ OVERVIEW

Cleaning service owners go into homes, offices, and apartment buildings to clean carpets, upholstery, and drapes. With special training, they also clean air ducts and restore homes and buildings damaged by fire, flood, and other disasters. There are successful cleaning services all across the country, but those businesses devoted to disaster restoration are generally located in areas with cold seasons and inclement weather.

■ HISTORY

Before the development of special looms and fibers, carpets and rugs were only for the well-to-do. A rug cleaner had to be very knowledgeable about the weaving and knotting of rugs, and about coloring and dying processes in order to properly clean and repair rugs. With the invention of "tufting" and synthetic fibers in Georgia in the 1930s, carpet production became more efficient, carpets became cheaper, and sales increased. And carpet cleaning became a service needed in homes and office buildings. Window washing companies were already in business, contracting out to skyscrapers in the big cities, and carpet cleaners followed suit. By the 1960s, companies were offering full-service cleaning—windows, carpets, and drapes. With downsizing in the 1980s, the services of independent cleaning companies replaced many of the custodial crews of large buildings. Better cleaning products have also helped the industry; more powerful machines and cleaning formulas have made work easier and quicker than in the days of waxes and polishes.

■ THE JOB

Ever try to get a juice stain out of the sofa? Or try lugging a rented rug shampoo machine into your house for a cleaning? Then you have an idea of the demands of a cleaning service. People hire cleaning services to remove dirt and stubborn stains from the carpets in their homes. Cleaners come to your house with their own equipment and chemicals to wash the rugs and vacuum them. They take down drapes, clean them, then re-hang them. They restore and refinish hardwood floors. With special high-powered vacuums and brushes, they clean air ducts. In addition to working in homes, they also clean offices and other large public buildings.

To become "The Best Swedish Carpet Cleaner in Phoenix," as his promotions claim, Anders Berg has been building his business for the last 10 years. "It can be feast or famine," he says. "There may be many jobs one day, and none another. But I keep fairly well-booked; I have two to three jobs a day throughout the week." He starts his day at around 7:30 A.M., making phone calls to confirm jobs for the day. In addition to carpet cleaning, Anders offers clients carpet dyeing, upholstery cleaning, duct cleaning, vacuum sales and repair, water and flood restoration, and many other services. He works weekends, holidays, and six-day work weeks. "It's a service business," he says, "so, when you're needed, you respond."

Carpet cleaners use different methods and equipment. For hot water extraction, a hot-water cleaning solution is first sprayed on the carpet. The soil dissolves in the solution, and the solution is then lifted from the carpet with a wet vacuum. Although it's commonly known as "steam" cleaning, no steam is actually generated by the heated solution. Shampooing is another method: It involves applying the cleaning solution to the carpet with a circular brush. The brush spins, rubbing the carpet and frothing the solution into a foam. The soil is then suspended and removed by wet/dry vacuuming. Other methods of carpet cleaning are foam cleaning and dry cleaning.

To clean the carpets of his clients, Berg owns a service truck and a cleaning machine. "Maintaining equipment can be costly," he says. He must also visit a supplier once a week for the chemicals he needs. When dealing with flood and water damage, he uses deodorizers and sanitizers and may have to rent additional equipment for the job.

Some cleaning services specialize in disaster restoration. After a house or building has been damaged by fire, smoke, or flooding, restorers are brought in to clean. With special skills, they work to restore the property to its original state, cleaning and repairing from top to bottom. Walls, ceilings, carpets, and furniture are cleaned. Carpets may be extracted and deodorized. Damaged furniture is reupholstered. Some companies even repair damaged books, documents, electronics, diskettes, and microfilm. Cleaning services that offer restoration often maintain a 24-hour phone number for emergencies.

A cleaning service may contract with a company to clean offices and apartments on a regular basis. They perform the usual cleaning of carpets and drapes and also fire-retard drapes to meet local fire ordinances. They clean fabric walls and fabric partitions. Cleaning services usually only enter office buildings after business hours, so commercial work often involves late evenings and weekends.

"Residential carpet cleaning is nice," Berg says. "You meet different people every day. And most people are appreciative." Anders must regularly promote his services to build up a client base. "I always have to look for new clients," he says, "and try to keep the ones I have. Once upon a time, a CPA would hang out his shingle, and before he knew it, he had clients. It's a more complicated process now. There's more competition." When you're running your own cleaning service, you must also attend to your own administrative concerns, such as scheduling, bookkeeping, and billing. Anders also attends trade fairs in Stockholm and stocks up on new products. He recently brought back a micro-fiber cloth. The cloth is made of a fine, synthetic material that removes dirt, grease, and oil without chemicals.

■ REQUIREMENTS
High School

Because the materials, chemicals, and equipment for professional cleaning are likely to become more complicated, you should take courses that will help you adapt to chemical and mechanical advancements. Science courses can teach you about the products you'll be using. You'll be purchasing and using your own equipment, so a vocational class that involves you in mechanics can help you better understand the machines and their repair. Accounting classes and student business organizations will prepare you for the record-keeping aspect of the work. Take English and composition courses to develop writing skills for your own advertising and promotion.

Postsecondary Training

Though this may change in the near future, the cleaning services industry had been typically easy to break into. If you're looking for employment with a cleaning service, you probably won't need any special certification, or even a high school diploma. Even as you develop your own service, you probably won't be hindered by a lack of education or training when seeking clients. As the job becomes more technically demanding, however, training programs will become standard.

Kenway Mead, executive administrator for the Institute of Inspection Cleaning and Restoration Certification (IICRC), advises students to get first-hand experience in the business. You should seek out large cleaning businesses that contract their services to companies; these larger companies will be more likely to have good training systems in place. You should look for a company that has some certification and belongs to either regional or national professional organizations. Membership with such an organization will mean the company is privy to training information and requirements.

The IICRC offers seminars and conferences, as does the Association of Specialists in Cleaning and Restoration (ASCR). Some technical schools and community colleges offer training for cleaning technicians seeking certifica-

Learn More about It

Aslett, Don. *The Cleaning Encyclopedia: Your A-Z Illustrated Guide to Cleaning Like the Pros!* New York: Dell Publishing, 1999.

Campbell, Jeff. *Good as New.* New York: Dell Island Books, 1998.

Farmer, Forrest L. *Introduction to Janitorial Service Contracting: How to Succeed in Your Own Cleaning Business.* Portland, Ore.: Clean-Pro Industries Inc., 2000.

———. *Sales and Marketing for Janitorial Service Businesses: Strategies for Promoting, Estimating, and Bidding Cleaning Services.* Portland, Ore.: Clean-Pro Industries Inc., 2000.

———. *The Science of Professional Cleaning: Handbook for Janitorial Services.* Portland, Ore.: Clean-Pro Industries Inc., 2000.

Haley, Graham, and Rosemary Haley. *Haley's Cleaning Hints.* Toronto, Ont.: Hushion House, 2001.

Price, Stanley J. *Cleaning Up: Making Money.* Modesto, Calif.: SJ Price Associates, 2000.

tion. These schools offer courses in the use and care of cleaning agents, supplies, and equipment, as well as job organization and planning.

Certification or Licensing

Certification isn't required to run a cleaning service, but it can help you attract business. You should either belong to a regional professional association or seek certification with the IICRC or the ASCR. Several different categories of certification are available, including carpet cleaning technician, commercial carpet maintenance technician, and upholstery and fabric cleaning technician. The ASCR offers certification for disaster restoration. Because of the special skills required for removing smoke and water from property, restoration certification involves a demanding program of training and testing. Approximately 15 percent of cleaning service workers are certified.

Other Requirements

"I'm an obsessive-compulsive cleaner," Anders Berg says. "That's not my natural language, but I noticed that phrase in someone's profile, and thought it was a really good description. I'm a clean freak." In addition to a love for cleaning, you should also have a talent for it. "In baseball," Berg says, "when a guy doesn't swing [at a ball out of the strike zone], he has a good eye. That's what most people lack in cleaning. People don't vacuum in an organized way. The smarter, more efficiently you work, the less time

STAIN-BE-GONE

Here are some stain removal tips (but remember—never mix bleach and ammonia!):

For the stains below, apply each of the listed mixtures with a white towel (after application, blot remaining moisture. Weigh down the towel and allow six hours to dry)

Chocolate
$1/2$ teaspoon mild dishwashing detergent (containing no bleach!) PLUS 1 cup lukewarm water.
1 tablespoon ammonia PLUS $1/2$ cup water
$1/3$ cup white vinegar PLUS $2/3$ cup water.
Powdered enzyme laundry detergent (prepare according to its directions).

Gum
Small amount of dry cleaning solvent or alcohol
$1/2$ teaspoon mild dishwashing detergent (containing no bleach!) PLUS 1 cup lukewarm water

Cola
$1/2$ teaspoon mild dishwashing detergent (containing no bleach!) PLUS 1 cup lukewarm water
1 tablespoon ammonia PLUS $1/2$ cup water
$1/3$ cup white vinegar PLUS $2/3$ cup water

you spend on the task." You also need good business sense and the ability to constantly promote and market your business. You should be friendly with your customers to encourage repeat business.

■ EXPLORING

There's no shortage of opportunities for you to test your interest in cleaning. Many different organizations in your community need volunteers for such work. The social services department that assists the elderly and the disabled in your town relies on volunteers and part-time workers to go into homes and clean for those who can't do it themselves. Those jobs will generally involve only light cleaning and vacuuming. Because most of your work will involve solutions and equipment, rent a carpet cleaning machine and try it out. Clean all the carpets in your house, and you'll get a sense of the daily duties of a cleaning service owner (though professional cleaning tools are often larger and more complex than the ones you rent from a store). Large cleaning services that clean office buildings and stores often hire high school students for evening hours and weekends. Working even

part time, you'll learn a lot about the cleaning equipment and requirements of the work.

■ EMPLOYERS

Many cleaning services are one-owner operations, but some may hire 40 or more people to assist with corporate contracts or disaster restoration. If you're in business for yourself, you may offer both commercial service and residential service, but you're likely to want to choose between the two. If contracted for commercial service (cleaning an office building, a mall, an apartment building, or some other public area), you'll probably sign on for a number of months with a predetermined number of cleanings per week. Working the residential market will involve working with different clients every day.

■ STARTING OUT

A lot of people who own cleaning services started their own businesses after working in other jobs. With the downsizing of the 1980s, many members of corporate cleaning crews started their own commercial cleaning services after being laid off. Anders Berg has worked in some aspect of the cleaning industry since 1969, mostly in sales and consulting positions. "I had done some carpet cleaning in Sweden," he says. "But it's not as common there. People usually just threw their carpet out." When he moved to Phoenix, a friend suggested he start his own service, which he has now had for 10 years.

Start-up costs are relatively low. Depending on the kind of work you'll be doing, the initial expense of your equipment is likely to be much less than $4,000 (not including the van or truck needed for transporting the equipment).

■ ADVANCEMENT

Once you've established your own business, you'll have to work hard to maintain a customer base and promote your services to expand your clientele. As you gain experience and make connections, you'll be able to expand your business into other areas. Some cleaning services sell cleaning products and vacuums, sell and install new carpet, and offer landscaping and maintenance services. Taking on a number of commercial contracts can mean big money, but it also requires a complete staff. Disaster restoration work for commercial properties can earn millions of dollars for a good, certified restoration service that has the special equipment and a staff of highly skilled technicians.

■ EARNINGS

Because of the differing sizes of cleaning services, from franchises and one-owner operations, to multi-million dollar cleaning companies, few accurate salary statistics have been compiled. Kenway Mead of the IICRC estimates that a carpet cleaning technician working for a service makes between $8 and $12 per hour, while a hard-working entrepreneur with a single-person operation can make between $42,000 and $60,000 a year. Someone with a disaster restoration service can make a lot more money from contracts with insurance companies, but it's also a lot more work, requiring more staff.

A carpet cleaner providing residential service will charge per room, per hour, or per square foot. Services charge between $20 and $50 per room, with extra charges for disinfectant and fabric protection. To clean upholstery, a cleaner will charge between $30 and $50 for each piece of furniture.

WORK ENVIRONMENT

You'll be working with heavy equipment and chemicals that you may be sensitive to. "It's a lot of physical work," Anders Berg says, "and it can be repetitive. You can wear out your legs, your arms, your back." The equipment and vacuums can be noisy. With the exception of hauling your equipment from your truck to the home or building, your work will be primarily inside. If in business for yourself, you won't have any supervision beyond the comments and opinions of your clientele. In most cases, you'll be allowed to work alone in the homes and in unoccupied commercial properties. Most of your work will be routine, but if you also provide disaster restoration, you'll be working in flooded or fire-damaged homes and buildings. With larger projects, you may be working with a team of cleaners and restorers.

Cleaning service owners average 40 hours or more per week. They often work weekends, holidays, and after business hours and occasionally deal with late-night restoration emergencies. When not actually cleaning, owners must devote time to equipment maintenance, record-keeping, and calling clients.

OUTLOOK

The demand for cleaning services has grown steadily over the last 20 years, and this is expected to continue. Office buildings make up the biggest share of the cleaning services market, and the marketplace is expanding to include more government buildings and industrial plants, as well. Cleaning services were listed as one of the best "evergreen businesses" (businesses that are consistently profitable) in a ranking of the top 20 home businesses by *Working at Home Magazine*.

Kenway Mead of IICRC predicts that the business will become more scientific, requiring a more intensive education. He also anticipates that environmental concerns

will mean more business for cleaning services. "Cleaning affects indoor air quality," he points out. The ASCR sponsors research into the testing of products, cleaning methods, and toxicity. Less chemical-based cleaning methods are currently in development.

As the science of cleaning advances, more specialization within the market will be required. In order to best understand your equipment, methods, and solutions, you may need to narrow your services to residential, commercial, or restoration. Restorers who service large businesses will have to keep up with the technology of electronics and information storage in order to best restore office hardware and software.

FOR MORE INFORMATION

For general career information and cleaning facts, visit ASCR's website. ASCR also offers certification, conferences, and seminars.

Association of Specialists in Cleaning & Restoration (ASCR)
8229 Cloverleaf Drive, Suite 460
Millersville, MD 21108
Tel: 800-272-7012
http://www.ascr.org

For certification information, contact
Institute of Inspection Cleaning and Restoration Certification
2715 East Mill Plain Boulevard
Vancouver, WA 98661
Tel: 360-693-5675
http://www.iicrc.org

Clinical Nurse Specialists

OVERVIEW

Clinical nurse specialists (CNSs), a classification of *advanced practice nurses* (APNs), are registered nurses who have completed advanced clinical nurses' educational practice requirements. Qualified to handle a wide variety of physical and mental health problems, CNSs are primarily involved in providing primary health care and psychotherapy.

HISTORY

The National League for Nursing Education first drew up a plan to create the clinical nurse specialist role in the

1940s. The first master's degree program opened in 1954 at Rutgers University; the only specialty offered at that time was psychiatric nursing. By 1970, clinical nurse specialty certification had become available in a number of fields in response to the increased specialization in health care, the development of new technologies, and the need to provide alternative, cost-efficient health care in the physician shortage of the 1960s.

■ THE JOB

CNSs conduct health assessments and evaluations based on the patient's history, laboratory tests, and their own personal examinations. Following such assessments they arrive at a diagnosis of the patient's problem and deliver care and develop quality-control methods to help correct the patient's medical problem. In addition to delivering direct patient care, CNSs may be involved in consultation, research, education, and administration. They may specialize in one or more areas, such as pediatrics, mental health, perinatal care, oncology, or gerontology. A few work independently or in private practice and are qualified for reimbursement by Medicare, Medicaid, and other federally sponsored or private health care payers.

■ REQUIREMENTS

If you want to become a clinical nurse specialist, you will first need to complete the high school and undergraduate education necessary to become a registered nurse. (See Registered Nurses.)

Postsecondary Training

CNSs must earn a master's or higher degree after completing their studies to become a registered nurse. (See Registered Nurses and Advanced Practice Nurses.) Many CNSs go on to earn their doctoral degrees. CNSs can specialize by focusing their studies in a specific area, such as community health, home health, gerontology, or medical-surgical.

Certification or Licensing

CNS certification is available through the American Nurses

Association. Applicants must have completed education and experience requirements before taking the certification test.

Other Requirements

Anyone going into nursing needs to have a caring attitude and a strong commitment to helping people. Emotional maturity, a well-balanced personality, and excellent communication skills are vital.

In addition to possessing the qualities shared by all good nurses, clinical nurse specialists need to develop the leadership skills and expert competence necessary for advanced practice nursing. Because the clinical nurse specialist role is still not understood by some doctors and nurses, he or she must have the professional self-confidence to educate colleagues as well as patients and families. Physicians may be reluctant to recognize the qualifications of the clinical nurse specialist, and staff nurses may be resistant to what they perceive as criticism or interference with their work. A clinical nurse specialist also needs to have the academic interest and ability to do graduate study. A master's degree is required, and a doctorate is becoming increasingly necessary for top-level positions involving research, teaching, and policy making.

■ EXPLORING

You can explore your interest in the nursing field in a number of ways. You can read books on careers in nursing and talk with high school guidance counselors, school nurses, and local public health nurses. Visit hospitals to observe the work and to talk with hospital personnel.

■ EMPLOYERS

Clinical nurse specialists work in a wide range of health care settings, depending on their particular area of specialization and interest. They are employed in hospitals, clinics, community health centers, mental health facilities, nursing homes, home health care agencies, veterans affairs facilities, nursing schools and other educational institutions, physicians' offices, and the military. A few are in private or independent practice.

■ STARTING OUT

Information about job openings for clinical nurse specialists is available from many sources. Your nursing school placement office is the best place to start; other avenues include nursing registries, nurse employment agencies, and state employment offices. Positions are often listed in professional journals and newspapers. Information about government jobs is available from the Office of Personnel Management for your region. Con-

QUICK FACTS

SCHOOL SUBJECTS
Biology
Chemistry

PERSONAL SKILLS
Helping/teaching
Technical/scientific

WORK ENVIRONMENT
Primarily indoors
Primarily one location

MINIMUM EDUCATION LEVEL
Master's degree

SALARY RANGE
$35,290 to $49,550 to $71,210

CERTIFICATION OR LICENSING
Required

OUTLOOK
Faster than the average

DOT
075

GOE
14.02.01

NOC
3152

O*NET-SOC
29-1111.00

tacts you have made through clinical work or involvement in professional societies can be helpful sources of information. The organization that formerly employed you as a staff nurse may be eager to rehire you as a clinical nurse specialist once you have received your master's degree in nursing and been certified in an advanced practice specialty.

ADVANCEMENT

As clinical nurse specialists gain experience, they become qualified for positions that involve greater responsibility and give them opportunities to have a greater impact on nursing practice. Some people choose to broaden their base of expertise by adding nurse practitioner qualifications to their credentials.

Many clinical nurse specialists become involved in nursing education, research, publishing, and consulting. Some may want to make their voices heard in the current debate on the future of health care.

Moving into faculty or administrative positions is the form of advancement chosen by some clinical nurse specialists, while others prefer to remain in positions that are more direct-care oriented.

EARNINGS

Salary figures for the various categories of APNs are based on total salary income as well as earnings from working overtime and while on call. According to the U.S. Department of Labor, the median annual income for all nurses was $49,550 in 2003, with 10 percent making $35,290 and under, and 10 percent making $71,210 or more. Due to their high level of training, CNSs are usually paid more than the average; according to Salary.com, the median salary for CNSs in home care as of June 2004 was $54,737; for CNSs as a whole, it was $63,243.

WORK ENVIRONMENT

CNSs work primarily in hospitals, clinics, or nursing homes but may work out of their own homes and other community-based settings, including industry, home health care, and health maintenance organizations.

OUTLOOK

While there have been some declines in the employment of advanced practice nurses in recent years, it should be noted that the demand has far outweighed the supply. The federal government has predicted increasing shortages in the field for the next several years, and advanced practice nurses with the proper credentials and certification should have no trouble finding posts in a wide variety of health care facilities.

FOR MORE INFORMATION

For additional information on education, training, and career opportunities, contact

National Association of Clinical Nurse Specialists
2090 Linglestown Road, Suite 107
Harrisburg, PA 17110
Tel: 717-234-6799
http://www.nacns.org

Clowns

OVERVIEW

Clowns dress in outlandish costumes, paint their faces, and use a variety of performance skills to entertain audiences. They work in circuses, amusement parks, schools, malls, rodeos, and hospitals, as well as on stage, in films, and even on the street. Clowns are actors and comedians whose job is to make people laugh. There are an estimated 50,000 to 100,000 professional clowns worldwide. There are many more amateurs. About 95 percent of clowns work part-time and supplement their incomes with other jobs.

HISTORY

In 2270 B.C., an Egyptian pharaoh mentioned a "divine spirit...to rejoice and delight the heart." Through the years, clowns have been called pranksters, mirthmakers, jesters, comics, jokers, buffoons, harlequins, fools, merry-andrews, mimes, and joeys.

Egyptian, Greek, and Roman rulers kept fools for entertainment. During the Middle Ages and the Renaissance, court jesters were hired for their musical and juggling skills and verbal wit. They wore colorful and bizarre clothing with exaggerated collars and bells, pointed caps, and unusual shoes. Many were traveling minstrels, or street performers, skilled in storytelling, juggling, singing, magic, tightrope walking, and acrobatics.

After the Renaissance, clowns became stage characters, such as country bumpkins or dim-witted servants. Harlequins, wearing black and white clothes, and Pierrots, made up in whiteface makeup, emerged simultaneously.

The word "clown" was first used in 16th-century England to describe a clumsy, country oaf. Small traveling street theaters used them to attract audiences to their plays. In the 1700s, laws were passed to restrict street performances, but the art of pantomime flourished and is still used today.

The "King of Clowns" was Joseph Grimaldi, an Englishman whose career lasted from 1781 until 1828. When

Philip Astley created the first circus in 1768, he played "Billie Button," the first circus clown, later recreated by others. Early clowns bantered with the audience and sang songs. As the circuses and audiences grew, clowns developed routines based more heavily on physical comedy, providing comic relief to their co-performers' death-defying feats. Famous clowns, such as "Yankee Dan" Rice, Tom Belling, Lou Jacobs, and Emmett Kelly, Sr., became major circus attractions.

■ THE JOB

A clown's job first and foremost is to make people laugh, although they also may attract attention, sell goods or services, or communicate ideas. Amateur clowns perform as a hobby, often working as volunteers in hospitals and nursing homes. Professional clowns are highly trained and usually have several skills. Their performances may include balloon sculpture, magic, puppetry and ventriloquism, juggling, acrobatics, balancing acts, music, stilt walking, or unicycling. Most professional clowns are proficient at word play and must have a quick wit to interact with their audiences.

Mimes are silent clowns. They communicate with exaggerated movements and facial expressions. Marcel Marceau (born 1923) is probably the most famous mime. *Auguste clowns* use slapstick humor, falling over, getting into trouble, or acting silly for a laugh. The word "auguste" was a slang term used in Berlin in the 1860s for a stupid, bumbling fool. *Whitefaces* are characterized more for their clever way of setting up a situation. Named for their white makeup, they usually wear caps that make them look bald. Whitefaces are usually the clowns in charge of a routine. *Character clowns* have unique routines and usually work alone rather than with a partner or in a large group. A popular type of character clown is the hobo or tramp clown, often called "sad clowns." These clowns often wear ragged clothes and appear naive and somewhat sad. Charlie Chaplin (1889–1977) was one of the most famous character clowns; Emmett Kelly (1898–1979) was a famous tramp clown. Clowns still work in large circus arenas, usually together with a team of other clowns. More and more clowns, however, are finding work outside the circus. They may work in amusement parks, theaters, shopping malls, and television and video, as well as for birthday parties and business promotions.

■ REQUIREMENTS
High School

Clowns need no advanced degrees or certification, although a high school education is preferred. Business skills are advised, particularly for self-employed clowns. They will need training in various skills, such as magic, juggling, and acrobatics, but many clowns culitvate a talent on their own or through training conventions. See the end of this article for training resources.

Clowning is physically demanding, so training in athletics, such as tumbling, is important. Acting classes are also helpful. Clowns who want to develop a verbally comedic routine would benefit from classes in writing, drama, and public speaking.

Other Requirements

Clowns must travel to find work. They must be able to adapt to a variety of conditions, from a large arena to a small hospital room. They often perform outdoors. Clowning tends to be seasonal work. More jobs are available during spring, summer, and fall and on weekends and holidays.

There are no physical requirements for becoming a clown; men and women of all shapes, sizes, and ages can make successful clowns. However, individuals must have a good sense of humor and enjoy working and interacting with people.

■ EXPLORING

To prepare for a career as a clown, perform in school or community plays, take classes in dance, acting, mime, or gymnastics. You may find a studio or gym in your area that offers classes in juggling, trampoline, acrobatics, magic, or other skills useful to clowns. Volunteer to perform as a clown for hospitals, parades, or charitable events. Check your library for books about clowning and clown history.

■ EMPLOYERS

Clowns most frequently are employed by circuses, from small family operations to the most famous, Ringling Brothers and Barnum & Bailey. They also are found in New York City and Las Vegas, performing on streets and in stage

QUICK FACTS

SCHOOL SUBJECTS
Physical education
Theater/dance

PERSONAL SKILLS
Artistic
Mechanical/manipulative

WORK ENVIRONMENT
Indoors and outdoors
Primarily multiple locations

MINIMUM EDUCATION LEVEL
High school diploma
Apprenticeship

SALARY RANGE
$10,000 to $25,000 to $52,000

CERTIFICATION OR LICENSING
None available

OUTLOOK
Little change or more slowly than the average

DOT
159

GOE
01.05.01

NOC
5232

O*NET-SOC
N/A

shows. Many clowns work independently as well, performing at children's parties and other private functions.

STARTING OUT

Meeting and talking with experienced clowns is a good way to learn what it takes to become one yourself. They might be able to recommend employers and help you perfect your routines. Clowning clubs, often known as "clown alleys," hold regular meetings and may provide networking opportunities or a job bank for its members. There are over 30 circuses and 100 smaller traveling shows in the United States today that hold auditions for new clowns.

Beginning clowns need to develop a following. Many clowns start by working at birthday parties, picnics, and church events. Later they may audition for carnivals, business promotions, television commercials, and circuses. Some clowns hire agents to help them find jobs.

ADVANCEMENT

Very few clowns achieve worldwide recognition. A clown can become the major attraction at a circus, but it is rare. A few clowns become local celebrities and are in great demand in their own cities. Some clowns go on to appear on television. One famous television clown, now off the air, was Bozo the Clown. Many people have portrayed Bozo over the years.

EARNINGS

Because the job market for clowns is unpredictable, and because of the freelance nature of clowning, there are no set salaries.

Circus clowns generally earn less than other circus performers but receive room and board. They can earn $200 to $500 per week, while those working in nightclubs, casinos, or on Broadway can make as much as $10,000 a week, according to the American Guild of Variety Artists. A clown's weekly income can vary widely. A clown may earn $300 one week, $1,000 the next, and nothing the week after that.

For a child's birthday party, a clown may earn $50 to $500 depending on the length of the party and the performer's popularity. Street performers earn money from passersby, making nothing at all or up to $100 per day.

Unless employed by a circus, clowns usually pay their own expenses, insurance, and taxes, and have no paid vacations or retirement benefits. Most self-employed clowns hold other full-time or part-time jobs. Many are amateurs who perform only for the enjoyment of it.

WORK ENVIRONMENT

Clowns work irregular hours in varying conditions. They may work indoors or outdoors, on their feet for hours at

DID YOU KNOW?

Not everyone loves a clown. Fear of clowns is known as "Coulrophobia." It is a neologism derived from the Greek *kolobathristes*, or "stilt-walker."

a time, or in full costume and makeup. Costumes are expensive; a pair of shoes alone can cost $200. Some clowns have equipment that needs to be transported and kept in good repair.

To find the best jobs, clowns must travel often, staying in hotels and spending long hours on the road. They may find themselves in a new city every week or month. They face stiff competition for the best jobs and may receive no recognition for their work. They work anonymously, especially if they work as part of a team.

Clowns work mostly weekends, summers, and holidays, although party clowns and those who find television jobs work year-round. Professional clowns enjoy great freedom in their schedules, are able to choose employers, and have more opportunities to travel.

OUTLOOK

Since the number of circuses is limited, clowns are finding more opportunities outside the circus, especially with party and festival businesses. Clowns who are self-employed face a lot of competition. For these clowns, publicity and word-of-mouth recommendations form an important part of finding work.

In the next decade, it is expected that the ranks of clowns will continue to swell, while the number of full-time jobs will remain fairly constant.

FOR MORE INFORMATION

This labor union serves singers, dancers, variety performers, circus performers, ice skaters, and theme park performers. It negotiates for wages, offers resource information to those starting out.

American Guild of Variety Artists
184 5th Ave, 6th Floor
New York, NY 10010
Tel: 212-675-1003

Doing business as National Circus Project, this organization provides arts and education programs to schools. It also operates the Circus Information Referral Center.

Circus Education Specialists
67 Lion Lane
Westbury, NY 11590
Tel: 516-334-2123

This library and research center documents the history of the circus in America. It offers referrals to camps and schools that provide training, as well as to producers and circuses.

Circus World Museum

550 Water Street

Baraboo, WI 53913

Tel: 866-693-1500

Email: library.cwm@baraboo.com

http://www.circusworldmuseum.com

For techniques and information for serious-minded amateurs, semiprofessionals, and professionals, including magazines and listings of annual conventions and competitions, contact

Clowns of America International

PO Box Clown

Richeyville, PA 15358-0532

Tel: 888-522-5696

Email: ASKUS@coai.org

http://www.coai.org

This organization offers facts and information about the Ringling Brothers and Barnum & Bailey circus, including news, games, animals, history and tradition, performers and show dates.

Ringling Brothers and Barnum & Bailey

8607 Westwood Center Drive

Vienna, VA 22182

Tel: 703-448-4000

http://www.ringling.com

Coal Miners

■ OVERVIEW

Coal miners extract coal from surface mines and underground mines. To do this, they operate complex and expensive machinery that drills, cuts, scrapes, or shovels earth and coal so that the fuel can be collected. Since coal is hard to reach, large portions of earth must be removed from the surface or dug out of mines so the coal miners can get to it. Some coal miners are explosives experts who use dynamite and other substances to remove earth and make the coal accessible. There are approximately 74,000 coal mining workers employed in the United States.

■ HISTORY

Even before the development of agriculture and weaving, Stone Age people mined for minerals buried in the earth: flints for weaponry, mineral pigments for picture and body painting, and precious metals and stones for ornamentation. Early miners carved out open pits to reach the more accessible materials. Then they dug primitive tunnels underground, using sticks and bones to remove soft or broken rocks. As time went on, early miners learned to break hard rocks by driving metal or wooden wedges into cracks in the surface. An early method for dealing with particularly large, stubborn rocks was to build fires alongside them until they became thoroughly heated and then to dash cold water against them. The sudden contraction would cause the rocks to fracture.

No one knows when coal was first discovered and used for fuel; even ancient peoples in several areas of the globe seem to have known about it. There is evidence that coal was burned in Wales during the Bronze Age about three to four thousand years ago, and by the early Romans in Britain. The first industrial use of coal was in the Middle Ages in England, and the English were far more advanced in mining methods than other nations for many years.

The earliest method of coal production was strip mining, which involves gathering deposits near the earth's surface. Early strip mining did not produce large amounts of coal because methods of removing soil that lay over the coal were crude and slow. Beginning in 1910, this type of mining became more practical as powered machinery came into use.

Commercial mining started in the United States around 1750, near Richmond, Virginia, with the first recorded commercial shipment of American coal: 32 tons from Virginia to New York. Most of the coal produced was used to manufacture shells and shot for the Revolutionary War.

The coal industry played a vital role in the rapid industrial development of the United States. Its importance increased dramatically during the 1870s, as the railroads expanded and the steel industry developed, and during the 1880s, when steam was first used to generate electric power. The production of bituminous coal doubled each decade from 1880 to 1910, and by 1919 production was more than 500 million tons.

Coal is the country's primary source of energy. Its use declined after World War II, when natural gas and oil became economically competitive, but rising petroleum prices and worries about the availability of oil have made coal a major energy source again. Coal production in the United States reached one billion tons for the first time in 1990. Today about half of the nation's electricity is generated by burning coal.

Modern technology and improved management have revolutionized coal mining in the last century. Specialized machinery has been developed that replaces human effort with electric, pneumatic, hydraulic, and mechanical power, which are remotely controlled in some applications by computers. This means that highly skilled technicians and workers are needed to direct, operate, maintain, modify, and control the work performed by very expensive machinery. However, with the growth of the coal-mining industry has come concern about the environmental impact of mining and burning coal.

■ THE JOB

Coal miners work in two kinds of coal mines: surface and underground. The mining method used is determined by the depth and location of the coal seam and the geological formations around it. In surface or strip mining, the overburden—the earth above the coal seam—has to be removed before the coal can be dug out. Then, after the mining has been completed, the overburden is replaced so the land can be reclaimed. For underground mining, entries and tunnels are constructed so that workers and equipment can reach the coal.

The machinery used in coal mining is extremely complex and expensive. There are power shovels that can move 3,500 tons of earth in an hour and continuous mining machines that can rip 12 tons of coal from an underground seam in a minute. Longwall shearers can extract the coal at an even faster rate. The job of coal miners is to operate these machines safely and efficiently. Their specific duties depend on the type of mine that employs them and the machinery they operate.

Drillers operate drilling machines to bore holes in the overburden at points selected by the blasters. They must be careful that the drill doesn't bind or stop while in operation. They may replace worn or broken drill parts using hand tools, change drill bits, and lubricate the equipment.

Stripping shovel operators and *dragline operators* control the shovels and draglines that scoop up and move the broken overburden, which is pushed within their reach by the bulldozers. With the overburden removed, the coal is exposed so that machines with smaller shovels can remove it from the seam and load it into trucks.

Underground mining uses three methods to extract the coal that lies deep beneath the surface. These methods are continuous, longwall, and conventional mining.

Continuous mining is the most widely used method of mining underground coal. It is a system that uses a hydraulically operated machine that mines and loads coal in one step. Cutting wheels attached to hydraulic lifts rip coal from the seam. Then mechanical arms gather the coal from the tunnel floor and dump it onto a conveyor, which moves the coal to a shuttle car or another conveyor belt to be carried out of the mine. *Continuous-mining machine operators* sit or lie in the cab of the machine or operate it remotely. Either way, they move the machine into the mining area and manipulate levers to position the cutting wheels against the coal. They and their helpers may adjust, repair, and lubricate the machine and change cutting teeth.

In longwall mining, coal is also cut and loaded in one operation. With steel canopies supporting the roof above the work area, the mining machinery moves along a wall while its plow blade or cutting wheel shears the coal from the seam and automatically loads it onto a conveyor belt for transportation out of the mine. *Longwall-mining machine operators* advance the cutting device either manually or by remote control. They monitor lights and gauges on the control panel and listen for unusual sounds that would signal or indicate a malfunction in the equipment. As the wall in front of the longwall mining machine is cut away, the operator and face personnel move the roof supports forward, allowing the roof behind the supports to cave in.

Conventional mining, unlike continuous or longwall mining, is done in separate steps: First the coal is blasted from the seam, then it is picked up and loaded. Of the three underground methods, conventional mining requires the largest number of workers. *Cutter operators* work a self-propelled machine equipped with a circular, toothed chain that travels around a blade six to 15 feet long. They drive the machine into the working area and saw a channel along the bottom and sides of the coal face, a procedure that makes the blasting more effective because it relieves some of the pressure caused by the explosion. Cutter operators may also adjust and repair the machine, replace dull teeth, and shovel debris from the channel. Using mobile machines, *drilling-machine operators* bore blast holes in the coal face after first determining the depth of the undercut and where to place the holes. Then *blasters* place explosive charges in the holes and detonate them to shatter the coal. After the blast, *loading-machine operators* drive electric loading machines to the area and manipulate the levers that control the mechanical arms

QUICK FACTS

SCHOOL SUBJECTS
Chemistry
Earth science

PERSONAL SKILLS
Mechanical/manipulative
Technical/scientific

WORK ENVIRONMENT
Primarily outdoors
Primarily one location

MINIMUM EDUCATION LEVEL
High school diploma

SALARY RANGE
$24,390 to $35,710 to $47,460 +

CERTIFICATION OR LICENSING
Required by certain states

OUTLOOK
Decline

DOT
930

GOE
06.03.01

NOC
8231

O*NET-SOC
19-4041.00, 47-5041.00, 47-5042.00

to gather up the loose coal and load it onto shuttle cars or conveyors to be carried out of the mine.

Coal mining technicians play an important role in the mining process. By the time the mining actually starts, coal mining technicians have already helped the managers, engineers, and scientists to survey, test drill, and analyze the coal deposit for depth and quality. They have also mapped the surface and helped plan the drilling and blasting to break up the rock and soil that cover the coal. The technicians have also helped prepare permits that must be filed with federal and state governments before mining can begin. Information must be provided on how the land will be mined and reclaimed; its soil, water conditions, and vegetation; wildlife conservation; and how archaeological resources will be protected.

The coal mining technicians also help the mining engineers and superintendents select the machinery used in mining. Such a plan must include selecting machines of a correct size and capacity to match other machinery and planning the sequences for efficient use of machines. The plan also includes mapping roads out of the mine pit, planning machine and road maintenance and, above all, using safety methods for the entire operation.

Ventilation technicians operate dust counting, gas quantity, and air volume measuring instruments. They record or plot this data and plan or assist in planning the direction of air flow through mine workings. Ventilation technicians also help prescribe the fan installations required to accomplish the desired air flow.

Geological aides gather geological data as mining activities progress. They identify rocks and minerals; record and map structural changes; locate drill holes; and iden-tify rocks, coal, and minerals in drill cores. They also map geological information from drill core data, gather samples, and map results on mine plans.

Chemical analysts analyze mine, mill, and coal samples by using volumetric or instrumental methods of analysis. They also write reports on the findings.

Mining work is hard, dirty, and often dangerous. Mine workers are often characterized by the concern they have for their fellow miners. There is no room for carelessness in this occupation. The safety of all workers depends on teamwork, with everyone alert and careful to avoid accidents.

■ REQUIREMENTS
High School

A high school diploma is a minimum educational requirement for this work. Coal miners must be at least 18 years of age and in good physical condition to withstand the rigors of the job.

To work in this field, you should complete at least two years of mathematics, including algebra and geometry, and four years of English and language skills courses, with emphasis on reading, writing, and communication training.

You should also take physics and chemistry. Computer skills are also important, particularly knowledge of computer-aided drafting and design programs. Courses in mechanical drawing or drafting are also helpful.

Postsecondary Training

Federal laws require that all mine workers be given safety and health training before starting work and be retrained annually thereafter. Federal and state laws also require preservice training and annual retraining in subjects such as health and safety regulations and first aid.

It is possible to start a coal mining career as an unskilled worker with a high school diploma, but it is difficult to advance within the coal mining industry without the foundation skills. In general, companies prefer employees who bring formally acquired technical knowledge and skills to the job.

The first year of study in a typical two-year coal mining technician program in a technical or community college includes courses in the basics of coal mining, applied mathematics, mining law, coal mining ventilation and atmospheric control, communication skills, technical reporting, fundamentals of electricity, mining machinery, physical geology, surveying and graphics, mine safety and accident prevention, roof and rib control, and industrial economics and financing.

The second year includes courses in mine instrumentation and electrical systems, electrical maintenance,

COAL MINING AND THE ENVIRONMENT

Environmentalists have long decried coal mining as dangerous to the environment. Not only does strip-mining destroy landscapes, but also mine runoff can poison wildlife, plants, and, if it gets into water supplies, even people. Furthermore, burning coal creates sulfur compounds, which react with water in the atmosphere to form sulfuric acid that then falls back to Earth as acid rain.

In response, the mining industry has taken steps that include cleaning up dangerous mine waste and backfilling strip mines. Power plants can use "scrubbers" that clean dangerous chemicals out of smokestack emissions. However, such measures are expensive, and the waste must still be disposed of somewhere. For these reasons, the energy industry often sponsors legislation that reduces its environmental (and legal) responsibilities to a minimum.

hydraulic machinery, machine transmissions and drive trains, basic welding, coal mine environmental impacts and control, coal and coal mine atmosphere sampling and analysis, mine machinery and systems automation and control, application of computers to coal mining operations, and first aid and mine rescue.

In some programs, students spend the summer working as interns at coal mining companies. Internships provide a clear picture of the field and help you choose the work area that best fits your abilities. You will gain experience using charts, graphs, blueprints, maps, and machinery and develop confidence through an approach to the real operation of the industry.

Certification or Licensing

Requirements for certification of mine workers vary. A state may require that any person engaged at the face of the mine first obtain a certificate of competency as a miner from the state's miner's examining board. In some cases, a miner may obtain a certificate of competency after completing one year of underground work. A miner who has an associate's degree in coal mine technology may be able to obtain the certificate after completing six months of underground work.

For those seeking a certificate of competency as a mine examiner or manager, a state may require at least four years of underground experience; graduates with associate's degrees in coal mining technology, however, may be able to qualify after only three years of experience.

Coal mining technician students can usually meet the state's criteria for employment while still in their technician preparatory program. It is important to be familiar with these criteria if technicians plan to work in a state other than the one where they begin their education and work experience.

Other Requirements

To be a successful coal miner, you will need to work well with others and accept supervision. You must also learn to work independently and accept responsibility. You must be accurate and careful, as mistakes can be expensive and hazardous and even fatal.

The union to which most unionized coal miners belong is the United Mine Workers of America, although some are covered by the Southern Labor Union, the Progressive Mine Workers, or the International Union of Operating Engineers. Some independent unions also operate within single firms.

■ EXPLORING

Because of the age limitation for coal miners, opportunities do not exist for most high school students to gain

---

DID YOU KNOW?

The phrase "canary in a coal mine" refers to old-time coal miner's custom of bringing a canary down into the mine with them. Coal miners sometimes tap into pockets of dangerous natural gas, which, though odorless and undetectable, can suffocate a man. If the canary stopped singing, then the miners knew that oxygen levels were getting dangerously low.

---

actual experience. If you are over the age of 18, you may be able to find summer work as a laborer in a coal mine, performing routine tasks that require no previous experience. Older students may also investigate the possibility of summer or part-time employment in metal mines, quarries, oil drilling operations, heavy construction, road building, or truck driving. While this work may not be directly related to your career goals, the aptitudes required for the jobs are similar to those needed in mining, and the experience may prove useful.

■ EMPLOYERS

There are about 212,000 wage and salary jobs in the field of mining and quarrying, about 74,000 of them in coal mining. Most coal miners work in private industry for mining companies. Some opportunities also exist with federal and state governments. The U.S. Department of Labor notes that approximately 75 percent of coal mining jobs are found in Kentucky, Pennsylvania, and West Virginia.

■ STARTING OUT

The usual method of entering this field is by direct application to the employment offices of the individual coal mining companies. However, mining machine operators must "come up through the ranks," acquiring the necessary skills on the job.

New employees start as trainees, or "red hats." After the initial training period, they work at routine tasks that do not require much skill, such as shoveling coal onto conveyors. As they gain more experience and become familiar with the mining operations, they are put to work as helpers to experienced machine operators. In this way they eventually learn how to operate the machines themselves.

Coal mining technicians are usually hired by recruiters from major employers before completing their last year of technical school. Industry recruiters regularly visit the campuses of schools with coal mining technician programs and work with the schools' placement officers.

Many two-year graduates take jobs emphasizing basic operational functions. Technicians are then in a position to compete for higher positions, in most cases through the system of job bidding, which considers such factors as formal education, experience, and seniority.

In union mines, when a vacancy occurs and a machine operator job is available, an announcement is posted so that any qualified employee can apply for the position. In most cases the job is given to the person with the most seniority.

ADVANCEMENT

Advancement opportunities for coal miners are limited. The usual progression is from trainee to general laborer to machine operator's helper. After acquiring the skills needed to operate the machinery, helpers may apply for machine operator jobs as they become available. All qualified workers, however, compete for those positions, and vacancies are almost always filled by workers with the most seniority. A few coal miners become supervisors, but additional training is required for supervisory and management jobs.

After a period of on-the-job experience, coal mining technicians may become supervisors, sales representatives, or possibly even private consultants or special service contractors.

Technical sales representatives work for manufacturers of mining equipment and supplies and sell such products as explosives, flotation chemicals, rock drills, hoists, crushers, grinding mills, classifiers, materials handling equipment, and safety equipment.

EARNINGS

According to the U.S. Department of Labor, mining-machine operators earn a median salary of $35,710 per year, with the lowest 10 percent making $24,390 and the highest 10 percent making $47,460. The National Mining Association, the average miner's salary in the United States is $49,000 per year. The U.S. Department of Labor reports that coal mining workers earned a median hourly wage of $20.57, slightly higher than the industry average, in 2002. This wage translates into a yearly income of approximately $42,785 for full-time, 40-hours-per-week work. The department also reports median earnings by job, including: truck drivers, $14.59 per hour (approximately $30,347 per year); continuous-mining machine operators, $16.93 per hour (approximately $35,214 annually); and managers of construction trades and extraction workers, $26.16 per hour (approximately $54,413 yearly). Those with much experience can have even higher earnings.

Among coal miners, earnings vary according to experience and type of mine. Highest paid are seasoned workers in deep underground mines. Coal miners at strip and auger mines are paid slightly less. At the low end, utility workers and unskilled laborers at coal preparation plants earn the least.

These figures do not include overtime or incentive pay. Miners get time and a half or double time for overtime hours. Coal miners who work evening and night shifts typically receive slightly higher wages.

Most coal miners also receive health and life insurance, as well as pension benefits. The insurance generally includes hospitalization, surgery, convalescent care, rehabilitation services, and maternity benefits for the workers and their dependents. The pension size depends on the worker's age at retirement and the number of years of service.

In addition, most mine workers are given 11 holidays a year in addition to vacation days earned according to length of service.

WORK ENVIRONMENT

Coal mining is hard work involving harsh and sometimes hazardous conditions. Workers in surface mines are outdoors in all kinds of weather, while those underground work in tunnels that are cramped, dark, dusty, wet, and cold. They are all subjected to loud noise from the machinery and work that is physically demanding and dirty.

Since passage of the Coal Mine Health and Safety Act in 1969, mine operators have improved the ventilation and lighting in underground mines and have taken steps to eliminate safety hazards for workers. Nevertheless, operators of the heavy machinery both on the surface and below ground run the risk of injury or death from accidents. Other possible hazards for underground miners include roof falls and cave-ins, poisonous and explosive gases, and long exposure to coal dust. After a number of years, workers may develop pneumoconiosis, or "black lung," which is a disabling and sometimes fatal disease.

OUTLOOK

Employment in mining is expected to decline by about 15 percent through 2012, according to the U.S. Department of Labor. Technological advances have increased productivity but reduced the number of workers in the field. Stricter federal environmental regulations, such as the 1990 Clean Air Act Amendments, and increased competition from foreign producers will limit growth in this industry; however, these laws were to some degree overturned by environmental policy in the early 2000s.

In response to fluctuations in energy supplies, President George W. Bush proposed the construction of new coal-powered electric plants as well as the development of clean-coal technologies for existing coal-powered plants. If these proposals are implemented, coal miners and other workers in the industry may enjoy improved employment opportunities.

The Energy Information Administration reports that in 2002, there were 29 companies producing 5 million or more short tons of coal per year. These companies accounted for more than 80 percent of U.S. coal production. Most of these operations are located in three states: Kentucky, Pennsylvania, and West Virginia. Other states with strong employment include Alabama, Illinois, Ohio, and Virginia. Because coal is a major resource for the production of such products as steel and cement, employment in the mining industry is strongly affected by changes in overall economic activity. In a recession the demand for coal drops, and many miners may be laid off.

■ FOR MORE INFORMATION

For free student materials (booklets, brochures, posters, videos) about coal, electricity, and land reclamation issues, contact

American Coal Foundation
101 Constitution Avenue, NW, Suite 525 East
Washington, DC 20001-2133
Tel: 202-463-9785
Email: acf-coal@mindspring.com
http://www.teachcoal.org

For additional career information, contact the following organizations:

National Mining Association
101 Constitution Avenue, NW, Suite 500 East
Washington, DC 20001-2133
Tel: 202-463-2625
Email: thowe@nma.org
http://www.nma.org

Society for Mining, Metallurgy, and Exploration
8307 Shaffer Parkway
PO Box 277002
Littleton, CO 80127
Tel: 800-763-3132
Email: sme@smenet.org.
http://www.smenet.org

The following labor union represents coal miners. For information on publications, press releases, and other resources, contact

United Mine Workers of America
8315 Lee Highway
Fairfax, VA 22031
Tel: 703-208-7200
http://www.umwa.org

Collection Workers

■ OVERVIEW

Collection workers—sometimes known as *bill collectors, collection correspondents,* or *collection agents*—are employed to persuade people to pay their overdue bills. Some work for collection agencies (which are hired by the business to which the money is owed), while others work for department stores, hospitals, banks, public utilities, and other businesses. Collection workers contact delinquent debtors, inform them of the delinquency, and either secure payment or arrange a new payment schedule. If all else fails, they might be forced to repossess property or turn the account over to an attorney for legal proceedings. There are approximately 413,000 collection workers employed in the United States.

■ HISTORY

Debt collection is one of the world's oldest vocations. In literature, the most famous—and unsuccessful—attempt to retrieve an overdue debt occurred in Shakespeare's (1564–1616) *Merchant of Venice,* featuring the character Shylock as the collector. Debt collection also figures prominently in the works of Charles Dickens (1812–70).

In the past, people who were unable to pay their debts suffered great punishments. Some were sent to prison, indentured as servants or slaves until the amount owed was paid off, or recruited by force to colonize new territories. Today's debtors face less harsh consequences, but the proliferation of credit opportunities has expanded the field of debt collection. Charge accounts are now offered by department stores, banks, credit unions, gasoline stations, and other businesses. Many people buy furniture or other expensive items "on time," meaning they place a small sum down and pay off the balance, plus interest, over a certain period of time. People take out

QUICK FACTS

SCHOOL SUBJECTS
Computer science
Psychology
Speech

PERSONAL SKILLS
Communication/ideas
Following instructions

WORK ENVIRONMENT
Primarily indoors
Primarily one location

MINIMUM EDUCATION LEVEL
High school diploma

SALARY RANGE
$18,900 to $27,000 to $41,300

CERTIFICATION OR LICENSING
Voluntary

OUTLOOK
Faster than the average

DOT
241

GOE
09.05.01

NOC
1435

O*NET-SOC
43-3011.00, 43-4041.00, 43-4041.01, 43-4041.02

mortgages to finance home purchases and auto loans to finance vehicles. The result of all these credit opportunities is that some people take on too much debt and either fail to meet these obligations or refuse to pay them. When creditors do not receive their payments on time, they employ a collection worker to try and recover the money for them.

■ THE JOB

A collection worker's main job is to persuade people to pay bills that are past due. The procedure is generally the same in both collection firms and businesses that employ collection workers. The duties of the various workers may overlap, depending on the size and nature of the company.

When routine billing methods—monthly statements and notice letters—fail to secure payment, the collection worker receives a bad-debt file (usually on a computer tape downloaded to the agency's computer system). This file contains information about the debtor, the nature and amount of the unpaid bill, the last charge incurred, and the date of the last payment. The collection worker then contacts the debtor by phone or mail to request full or partial payment or, if necessary, to arrange a new payment schedule.

Terrence Sheffert is a collection worker for a collection agency based in Chicago. He describes his typical duties as making phone calls and writing letters. "I am usually in the office, on the phone with clients or the people who owe them," he says. "I never actually go out to make collections, but there are some agents who do."

If the bill has not been paid because the customer believes it is incorrect, the merchandise purchased was faulty, or the service billed for was not performed, the collector takes appropriate steps to settle the matter. If, after investigation, the debt collector finds that the debt is still valid, he or she again tries to secure payment.

In cases where the customer has not paid because of a financial emergency or poor money management, the debt collector may arrange a new payment schedule. In instances where the customer goes to great or fraudulent lengths to avoid payment, the collector may recommend that the file be turned over to an attorney. "Every day, we are protecting the clients' interests and getting the money," Sheffert says. "If we can't get it, then we'll call in legal representation to handle it."

When all efforts to obtain payment fail, a collection worker known as a *repossessor* may be assigned to find the merchandise on which the debtor still owes money and return it to the seller. Such goods as furniture or appliances can be picked up in a truck. To reclaim automobiles and other motor vehicles, the repossessor might be forced to enter and start the vehicle with special tools if the buyer does not surrender the key.

In large agencies, some collection workers specialize as *skip tracers*. Skip tracers are assigned to find debtors who "skip" out on their debts—that is, who move without notifying their creditors so that they don't have to pay their bills. Skip tracers act like detectives, searching telephone directories and street listings and making inquiries at post offices in an effort to locate missing debtors. Increasingly such information can be found through online computer databases (some agencies subscribe to a service to collect this information). Skip tracers also try to find out information about a person's whereabouts by contacting former neighbors and employers, local merchants, friends, relatives, and references listed on the original credit application. They follow every lead and prepare a report of the entire investigation.

In some small offices, collection workers perform clerical duties, such as reading and answering correspondence, filing, or posting amounts paid to people's accounts. They might offer financial advice to customers or contact them to inquire about their satisfaction with the handling of the account. In larger companies *credit and loan collection supervisors* might oversee the activities of several other collection workers.

■ REQUIREMENTS
High School

Most employers prefer to hire high school graduates for collection jobs, but formal education beyond high school is typically not required. High school courses that might prove helpful in this career include those that will help you communicate clearly and properly, such as English and speech. Because collection workers have to talk with people about a very delicate subject, psychology classes might also be beneficial. Finally, computer classes are good choices, since this career, like most others, often requires at least some familiarity with keyboarding and basic computer operation.

Postsecondary Training

Most collection workers learn collection procedures and telephone techniques on the job in a training period spent under the guidance of a supervisor or an experienced collector. The legal restrictions on collection activities, such as when and how calls can be made, are also covered.

Certification or Licensing

Although it is not required by law, some employers require their employees to become certified by the American Collectors Association (ACA). The ACA conducts seminars on state and federal compliance laws that pertain to collection workers. A basic knowledge of legal proceedings is helpful for supervisors. To learn more, visit http://www.collector.com.

Other Requirements

Because this is a people-oriented job, you must have a pleasant manner and voice. You may spend much of your time on the telephone speaking with people about overdue payments, which can be a delicate subject. To succeed as a collector, you must be sympathetic and tactful, yet assertive and persuasive enough to convince debtors to pay their overdue bills. In addition, collectors must be alert, quick-witted, and imaginative to handle the unpredictable and potentially awkward situations that are encountered in this type of work.

Collection work can be emotionally taxing. It involves listening to a bill payer's problems and occasional verbal attacks directed at both the collector and the company. Some people physically threaten repossessors and other collection workers. "The best description of this job would be stressful," Terrence Sheffert says. "Everything about collecting is very stressful." In the face of these stresses, you must be able to avoid becoming upset, personally involved with, or alarmed by angry or threatening debtors. This requires a cool head and an even temperament.

■ EXPLORING

The best way to explore collection work is to secure part-time or summer employment in a collection agency or credit office. You might also find it helpful to interview a collection worker to obtain firsthand information about the practical aspects of this occupation. Finally, the associations listed at the end of this article may be able to provide further information about the career.

■ EMPLOYERS

Of the approximately 413,000 collection workers in the United States, approximately 20 percent work for collection agencies. Collection agencies are usually independent companies that are hired by various businesses to collect debt that is owed them. Other bill collectors work for a wide range of organizations and businesses that extend credit to customers. Department stores, hospitals, banks, public utilities, and auto financing companies are examples of businesses that frequently hire bill collectors.

The companies that hire collection workers are located throughout the United States, especially in heavily populated urban areas. Companies that have branch offices in rural communities often locate their collection departments in nearby cities.

■ STARTING OUT

Terrence Sheffert got started in collection work because it was a family profession. "My whole family is in collecting, so I thought, 'Hey, I'll go for it,'" he says. If you are

---

THE FAIR DEBT COLLECTION PRACTICES ACT

To protect individuals from unfair collection practices, in 1968 the federal government passed the Fair Debt Collection Practices Act. Amended several times since that date, the act specifies what debt collectors are and are not allowed to do. For example, a debt collection worker cannot:

- Use a false name.
- Send mail that looks like an official document from a court or government agency when it is not.
- Make threats of violence or harm to individuals, their property, or their reputations.
- Use obscene or profane language.
- Repeatedly use the phone to annoy someone.
- Tell someone he or she will be arrested if he or she does not pay a debt.
- Pretend to be a lawyer or government representative.

interested in becoming a collection worker, one easy way to start a job search is to apply directly to collection agencies, credit reporting companies, banks, and major retailers that sell large items. To find collection agencies and credit reporting companies, try doing a simple keyword search on one of the Internet's search engines. Another easy way is to look in your local Yellow Pages—or expand your search by going to the library and looking through yellow pages of other cities. Remember that these sorts of jobs are often more plentiful in more urban areas.

You should also check the classified ads of area newspapers for headings such as "Billing" or "Collection." Finally, job openings may be listed at your local employment office.

ADVANCEMENT

Experienced collection workers who have proven to have above-average ability can advance to management positions, such as supervisors or *collection managers.* These workers generally have responsibility for the operations of a specific shift, location, or department of a collection company. They oversee other collection workers. Other avenues of advancement might include becoming a *credit authorizer, credit checker,* or *bank loan officer.* Credit authorizers approve questionable charges against customers' existing accounts by evaluating the customers' computerized credit records and payment histories. Credit checkers in credit bureaus—sometimes also called *credit investigators* or *credit reporters*—search for, update, and verify information for credit reports. Loan officers help borrowers fill out loan applications, verify and analyze applications, and decide whether and how much to loan applicants. Some experienced and successful collections workers might open their own agencies. This is Terrence Sheffert's goal. "I hope to advance from collection to management, and then open up my own business," he says.

EARNINGS

Collection workers might receive a salary plus a bonus or commission on the debt amounts they collect. Others work for a flat salary with no commissions. Since the pay system varies among different companies, incomes vary substantially. In 2002, the median hourly wage for bill collectors working full-time was $12.98, according to the U.S. Department of Labor. This hourly wage translates into a yearly income of approximately $27,000. Earnings for collection workers range from less than $18,900 to a high of more than $41,300 annually.

Depending on their employer, some full-time bill collectors receive a benefits package that may include paid holidays and vacations, sick leave, and health and dental insurance.

WORK ENVIRONMENT

Most collectors work in pleasant offices, sit at a desk, and spend a great deal of time on the telephone. Because they spend so much time on the phone, many collectors use phone headsets and program-operated dialing systems. Because most companies use computers to store information about their accounts, the collection worker frequently works on a computer. He or she may sit in front of a computer terminal, reviewing and entering information about the account while talking to the debtor on the phone.

Rarely does a collector have to make a personal visit to a customer. Repossession proceedings are undertaken only in extreme cases.

Terrence Sheffert works a 40-hour week, from 9:00 A.M. to 5:00 P.M., Monday through Friday. Some collection workers stagger their schedules, however. They might start late in the morning and work into the evening, or they might take a weekday off and work on Saturday. Evening and weekend work is common, because debtors are often home during these times.

OUTLOOK

Employment for bill collectors is predicted by the U.S. Department of Labor to grow faster than the average through 2012. Demand for cash flow is causing businesses to hire more and more debt collectors. Also, America's debt is growing. Due to the relaxed standards for credit cards, which means more people, regardless of their financial circumstances, are able to get credit cards, make purchases on credit, and build up large debts they have difficulty repaying. The Department of Labor also notes that hospitals and physicians' offices are two of the fastest growing employers of bill collectors and collection agencies. This is largely because health insurance plans frequently do not adequately cover payment for medical procedures, and patients are often left with large bills that they have difficulty repaying. Economic recessions also increase the amount of personal debt that goes unpaid. Therefore, unlike many occupations, collection workers usually find that their employment and workloads increase during economic slumps.

FOR MORE INFORMATION

For a brochure on careers in collection work, contact

Association of Credit and Collection Professionals
PO Box 390106
Minneapolis, MN 55439
Tel: 952-926-6547
http://www.collector.com

For information on careers and certification, contact the NACM.

National Association of Credit Management (NACM)
8840 Columbia 100 Parkway
Columbia, MD 21045
Tel: 410-740-5560
Email: nacm_info@nacm.org
http://www.nacm.org

College Administrators

■ OVERVIEW

College administrators coordinate and oversee programs such as admissions and financial aid in public and private colleges and universities. They frequently work with teams of people to develop and manage student services. Administrators also oversee specific academic divisions of colleges and universities.

■ HISTORY

Before the Civil War, most U.S. colleges and universities managed their administration with a president, a treasurer, and a part-time librarian. Members of the faculty often were responsible for the administrative tasks of the day, and there was no uniformity in college admissions requirements.

By 1860, the average number of administrative officers in U.S. colleges was still only four. However, as the job of running an institution expanded in scope in response to ever-increasing student enrollment, the responsibilities of administration began to splinter. After creating positions for registrar, secretary of faculty, chief business officer, and a number of departmental deans, most schools next hired a director of admissions to oversee the application and acceptance of students. In addition, several eastern schools and a few prominent college presidents, Charles Eliot of Harvard and Nicholas Butler of Columbia among them, saw the need to establish organizations whose purpose would be to put an end to the chaos. The College Entrance Examination Board was formed to create standardized college entrance requirements. By 1910, there were 25 leading eastern colleges using the Board's exams. Today, most colleges require that a student submit standardized test scores, such as the SAT or ACT, when applying.

After World War II, returning veterans entered America's colleges and universities by the thousands. With this great influx of students, college administrators were needed to better organize the university system. During this time, financial aid administration also became a major program. Today, as the costs of a college education continue to rise dramatically, college financial aid administrators are needed to help students and parents find loans, grants, scholarships, and work-study programs.

■ THE JOB

A college administrator's work is demanding and diverse. An administrator is responsible for a wide range of tasks in areas such as counseling services, admissions, alumni affairs, financial aid, academics, and business. The following are some of the different types of college administrators, but keep in mind that this is only a partial list. It takes many administrators in many different departments to run a college.

Many college and university administrators are known as *deans*. Deans are the administrative heads of specific divisions or groups within the university, and are in charge of overseeing the activities and policies of that division. One type of dean is an *academic dean*. Academic deans are concerned with such issues as the requirements for a major, the courses offered, and the faculty hired within a specific academic department or division. The field of academic dean includes such titles as dean of the college of humanities, dean of social and behavioral sciences, and dean of the graduate school, just to name a few. The *dean of students* is responsible for the student-affairs program, often including such areas as student housing, organizations, clubs, and activities.

Registrars prepare class schedules and final exam schedules. They maintain computer records of student data, such as grades and degree requirements. They prepare school catalogs and student

QUICK FACTS
SCHOOL SUBJECTS
Business
English
Speech
PERSONAL SKILLS
Helping/teaching
Leadership/management
WORK ENVIRONMENT
Primarily indoors
Primarily one location
MINIMUM EDUCATION LEVEL
Bachelor's degree
SALARY RANGE
$37,420 to $66,640 to $120,190
CERTIFICATION OR LICENSING
None available
OUTLOOK
Faster than the average
DOT
090
GOE
12.01.01
NOC
0312
O*NET-SOC
11-9033.00

A college administrator meets with a student.

handbooks. *Associate registrars* assist in running the school registrar's office.

Recruiters visit high school campuses and college fairs to provide information about their school and to interest students in applying for admission. They develop relationships with high school administrators and arrange to meet with counselors, students, and parents.

Financial aid administrators direct the scholarship, grant, and loan programs that provide financial assistance to students and help them meet the costs of tuition, fees, books, and other living expenses. The administrator keeps students informed of the financial assistance available to them and helps answer student and parent questions and concerns. At smaller colleges, this work might be done by a single person, the *financial aid officer.* At larger colleges and universities, the staff might be bigger, and the financial aid officer will head a department and direct the activities of *financial aid counselors,* who handle most of the personal contact with students.

Other college administrators include *college admissions counselors,* who review records, interview prospective students, and process applications for admission. *Alumni directors* oversee the alumni associations of colleges and universities. An alumni director maintains relationships with the graduates of the college primarily for fund-raising purposes.

Such jobs as university *president, vice president,* and *provost* are among the highest-ranking college and university administrative positions. Generally the president and vice president act as high-level managers, overseeing the rest of a college's administration. They handle business concerns, press relations, public image, and community involvement, and they listen to faculty and

administration concerns, often casting the final vote on issues such as compensation, advancement, and tenure. At most schools, the provost is in charge of the many collegiate deans. Working through the authority of the deans, the provost manages the college faculty. The provost also oversees budgets, the academic schedule, event planning, and participates in faculty hiring and promotion decisions.

■ REQUIREMENTS
High School

A good, well-rounded education is important for anyone pursuing some of the top administrative positions. To prepare for a job in college administration, take accounting and math courses, as you may be dealing with financial records and student statistics. To be a dean of a college, you must have good communication skills, so you should take courses in English literature and composition. Also, speech courses are important, as you'll be required to give presentations and represent your department at meetings and conferences. Follow your guidance counselor's college preparatory plan, which will likely include courses in science, economics, foreign language, history, and sociology.

Postsecondary Training

Education requirements for jobs in college administration depend on the size of the school and the job position. Some assistant positions may not require anything more than a few years of experience in an office. For most jobs in college administration, however, you'll need at least a bachelor's degree. For the top administrative positions, you'll need a master's or a doctorate. A bachelor's degree in any field is usually acceptable for pursuing this career. After you've received your bachelor's, you may choose to pursue a master's in student personnel, administration, or subjects such as economics, psychology, and sociology. Other important studies include education, counseling, information processing, business, and finance. In order to become a college dean, you'll need a doctoral degree and many years of experience with a college or university. Your degree may be in your area of study or in college administration.

Other Requirements

As a college administrator, you should be very organized and able to manage a busy office of assistants. Some offices require more organization than others; for example, a financial aid office handles the records and aid disbursement for the entire student body and requires a director with an eye for efficiency and the ability to keep track of all the various sources of student funding. As a dean, however, you'll work in a smaller office, concentrating more on issues concerning faculty and committees, and you'll rely on your diplomatic skills for maintaining an efficient and successful department. People skills are valuable for college deans, as you'll be representing your department both within the university and at national conferences.

Whatever the administrative position, it is important to have patience and tact to handle a wide range of personalities as well as an emotional steadiness when confronted with unusual and unexpected situations.

■ EXPLORING

To learn something about what the job of administrator entails, talk to your high school principal and superintendent. Also, interview administrators at colleges and universities. Many of their office phone numbers are listed in college directories. The email addresses of the administrators of many different departments, from deans to registrars, are often published on college websites. You should also discuss the career with the college recruiters who visit your high school. Also, familiarize yourself with all the various aspects of running a college and university by looking at college student handbooks and course catalogs. Most handbooks list all the offices and administrators and how they assist students and faculty.

■ EMPLOYERS

Administrators are needed all across the country to run colleges and universities. Job opportunities exist at public and private institutions, community colleges, and universities both large and small. In a smaller college, an administrator may run more than one department. There are more job openings for administrators in universities serving large student bodies.

■ STARTING OUT

There are several different types of entry-level positions available in the typical college administrative office. If you can gain part-time work or an internship in admissions or another office while you are still in school, you will have a great advantage when seeking work in this field after graduation. Any other experience in an administrative or managerial position, which involves working with people or with computerized data, is also helpful. Entry-level positions often involve filing, data processing, and updating records or charts. You might also move into a position as an administrator after working as a college professor. Deans in colleges and universities have usually worked many years as tenured professors.

The department of human resources in most colleges and universities maintains a listing of job openings at the institution and will often advertise the positions nationally. *The Chronicle of Higher Education* (http://www.chronicle.com) is a newspaper with national job listings. The College and University Professional Association for Human Resources (CUPA-HR) also maintains a job list at its website, http://www.cupahr.org.

■ ADVANCEMENT

Entry-level positions, which usually require only a bachelor's degree, include *admissions counselors,* who advise students regarding admissions requirements and decisions, and *evaluators,* who check high school transcripts and college transfer records to determine whether applying students may be admitted. Administrative assistants are hired for the offices of registrars, financial aid departments, and deans.

Advancement from any of these positions will depend on the manner in which an office is organized as well as how large it is. One may move up to assistant director or associate director, or, in a larger office, into any specialized divisions such as minority admissions, financial aid counseling, or disabled student services. Advancement also may come through transferring to other departments, schools, or systems.

Workshops and seminars are available through professional associations for those interested in staying informed and becoming more knowledgeable in the field, but it is highly unlikely that an office employee will gain the top administrative level without a graduate degree.

■ EARNINGS

Salaries for college administrators vary widely among two-year and four-year colleges and among public and private institutions, but they are generally comparable to those of college faculty. According to the U.S. Department of Labor's 2003 National Occupational Employment and Wage Estimates, the median salary for education administrators was $66,640. The lowest paid 10 percent of administrators earned $37,420 per year, while the highest paid made $120,190 annually.

According to findings by the CUPA-HR, the following academic deans had these median annual salaries for 2001–02: dean of business, $107,414; dean of graduate programs, $100,391; dean of arts and sciences, $98,780; and dean of continuing education, $84,457. The CUPA-HR also reports the median annual salary for directors of admissions and registrars as $61,519, for dean of students as $70,012, and for director of student activities as $41,050.

According to a study done by the *Chronicle of Higher Education,* the average pay for college presidents was $207,000 a year in 2000. Though college presidents can earn high salaries, they are often not as high as earnings of other top administrators and even some college coaches. For example, competition can drive up the pay for highly desired medical specialists, economics educators, or football coaches.

Most colleges and universities provide excellent benefits packages including health insurance, paid vacation, sick leave, and tuition remission. Higher-level administrators such as presidents, deans, and provosts often receive such bonuses as access to special university clubs, tickets to sporting events, expense accounts for entertaining university guests, and other privileges.

■ WORK ENVIRONMENT

College and universities are usually pleasant places to be employed. Offices are often spacious and comfortable, and the campus may be a scenic, relaxing work setting.

Employment in most administrative positions is usually on a 12-month basis. Many of the positions, such as admissions director, financial aid counselor, and dean of students, require a great deal of direct contact with students, and so working hours may vary according to student needs. It is not unusual for college administrators to work long hours during peak enrollment periods, such as the beginning of each quarter or semester. During these periods, the office can be fast paced and stressful as administrators work to assist as many students as possible. Directors are sometimes required to work evenings and weekends to provide broader student access to administrative services. In addition, administrators are sometimes required to travel to other colleges, career fairs, high schools, and professional conferences to provide information about the school for which they work.

■ OUTLOOK

The U.S. Department of Labor predicts that overall employment for education administrators will grow faster than average through 2012. College funding is down, but many administrators are expected to retire soon. In addition, enrollment is expected to increase. Competition for prestigious positions as heads of faculty and deans will be stiff. Many faculty at institutions of higher learning have the educational and experience requirements for these jobs. Candidates may face less competition for positions in nonacademic areas, such as admissions or fund-raising. Those who are already working within a department seeking an administrator and those willing to relocate will have the best chances of getting administrative positions.

■ FOR MORE INFORMATION

For information about publications, current legislation, and membership, contact

American Association of University Administrators
PO Box 261363
Plano, TX 75026-1363
http://www.aaua.org

For job listings and information about membership, contact

College and University Professional Association for Human Resources
Tyson Place
2607 Kingston Pike, Suite 250
Knoxville, Tennessee 37919
Tel: 865-637-7673
http://www.cupahr.org

MOST NEW JOBS

College Professors

■ OVERVIEW

College professors instruct undergraduate and graduate students in specific subjects at colleges and universities. They are responsible for lecturing classes, leading small seminar groups, and creating and grading examinations. They also may conduct research, write for publication, and aid in administration. Approximately 1.6 million postsecondary teachers are employed in the United States.

■ HISTORY

The concept of colleges and universities goes back many centuries. These institutions evolved slowly from monastery schools, which trained a select few for certain professions, notably theology. The terms *college* and *university* have become virtually interchangeable in America outside the walls of academia, although originally they designated two very different kinds of institutions.

Two of the most notable early European universities were the University of Bologna in Italy, thought to have been established in the 12th century, and the University of Paris, which was chartered in 1201. These universities were considered to be models after which other European universities were patterned. Oxford University in England was probably established during the 12th century. Oxford served as a model for early American colleges and universities and today is still considered one of the world's leading institutions.

Harvard, the first U.S. college, was established in 1636. Its stated purpose was to train men for the ministry; the early colleges were all established for religious training. With the growth of state-supported institutions in the early 18th century, the process of freeing the curriculum from ties with the church began. The University of Virginia established the first liberal arts curriculum in 1825, and these innovations were later adopted by many other colleges and universities.

Although the original colleges in the United States were patterned after Oxford University, they later came under the influence of German universities. During the 19th century, more than nine thousand Americans went to Germany to study. The emphasis in German universities was on the scientific method. Most of the people who had studied in Germany returned to the United States to teach in universities, bringing this objective, factual approach to education and to other fields of learning.

In 1833, Oberlin College in Oberlin, Ohio, became the first college founded as a coeducational institution. In 1836, the first women-only college, Wesleyan Female College, was founded in Macon, Georgia.

The junior college movement in the United States has been one of the most rapidly growing educational developments. Junior colleges first came into being just after the turn of the 20th century.

■ THE JOB

College and university faculty members teach at junior colleges or at four-year colleges and universities. At four-year institutions, most faculty members are *assistant professors, associate professors,* or *full professors.* These three types of professorships differ in regards to status, job responsibilities, and salary. Assistant professors are new faculty members who are working to get tenure (status as a permanent professor); they seek to advance to associate and then to full professorships.

College professors perform three main functions: teaching, advising, and research. Their most important responsibility is to teach students. Their role within a college department will determine the level of courses they teach and the number of courses per semester. Most professors work with students at all levels, from college freshmen to graduate students. They may head several classes a semester or only a few a year. Some of their classes will have large enrollment, while graduate seminars may consist of only 12 or fewer students. Though college professors may spend fewer than 10 hours a week in the actual classroom, they spend many hours preparing lectures and lesson plans, grading papers and exams, and preparing grade reports. They also schedule office hours during the week to be available to students outside of the lecture hall, and they meet with students individually throughout the semester. In the classroom, professors lecture, lead discussions, administer exams, and assign textbook reading and other research. In some courses, they rely heavily on laboratories to transmit course material.

Another important responsibility is advising students. Not all faculty members serve as advisers, but those who do must set aside large blocks of time to guide students through the program. College professors who serve as advisers may have any number of students assigned to them, from fewer than 10 to more than 100, depending on the administrative policies of the college. Their responsibility may involve looking over a planned program of studies to make sure the students meet requirements for graduation, or it may involve working intensively with each student on many aspects of college life.

The third responsibility of college and university faculty members is research and publication. Faculty members who are heavily involved in research programs sometimes are assigned a smaller teaching load. College professors publish their research findings in various scholarly journals. They also write books based on their research or on their own knowledge and experience in the field. Most textbooks are written by college and university teachers. In arts-based programs, such as master's of fine arts programs in painting, writing, and theater, professors practice their craft and exhibit their art work in various ways. For

QUICK FACTS

SCHOOL SUBJECTS
English
History
Speech

PERSONAL SKILLS
Communication/ideas
Helping/teaching

WORK ENVIRONMENT
Primarily indoors
Primarily one location

MINIMUM EDUCATION LEVEL
Master's degree

SALARY RANGE
$23,080 to $49,040 to
$92,430

CERTIFICATION OR LICENSING
None available

OUTLOOK
Much faster than the average

DOT
090

GOE
12.03.02

NOC
4121

O*NET-SOC
25-1011.00, 25-1021.00,
25-1022.00, 25.1031.00,
25-1032.00, 25-1041.00,
25-1042.00, 25-1043.00,
25-1051.00, 25-1052.00,
25-1053.00, 25-1054.00,
25-1061.00, 25-1062.00,
25-1063.00, 25-1064.00,
25-1065.00, 25-1066.00,
25-1067.00, 25-1071.00,
25-1072.00, 25-1081.00,
25-1082.00, 25-1111.00,
25-1112.00, 25-1113.00,
25-1121.00, 25-1122.00,
25-1123.00, 25-1124.00,
25-1125.00, 25-1126.00,
25-1191.00, 25-1192.00,
25-1193.00, 25-1194.00

COMPUTER USE IN HIGHER EDUCATION

A 2003 Campus Computing Project survey found that computer use of college campuses is growing increasingly sophisticated. Almost three-quarters of the campuses surveyed had wireless networks installed, and two-thirds were taking steps to stop commercial music and video downloading. However, one-third of campus IT departments had their budgets cut, and only three-quarters were encouraging the recycling of old computers.

example, a painter or photographer will have gallery showings, while a poet will publish in literary journals.

Publishing a significant amount of work has been the traditional standard by which assistant professors prove themselves worthy of becoming permanent, tenured faculty. Typically, pressure to publish is greatest for assistant professors. Pressure to publish increases again if an associate professor wishes to be considered for a promotion to full professorship.

In recent years, some liberal arts colleges have recognized that the pressure to publish is taking faculty away from their primary duties to the students, and these institutions have begun to place a decreasing emphasis on publishing and more on performance in the classroom. Professors in junior colleges face less pressure to publish than those in four-year institutions.

Some faculty members eventually rise to the position of *department chair,* where they govern the affairs of an entire department, such as English, history, mathematics, or biological sciences. Department chairs, faculty, and other professional staff members are aided in their myriad duties by *graduate assistants,* who may help develop teaching materials, conduct research, give examinations, teach lower-level courses, and carry out other activities.

Some college professors may also conduct classes in an extension program. In such a program, they teach evening and weekend courses for the benefit of people who otherwise would not be able to take advantage of the institution's resources. They may travel away from the campus and meet with a group of students at another location. They may work full time for the extension division or may divide their time between on-campus and off-campus teaching.

Distance learning programs, an increasingly popular option for students, give professors the opportunity to use today's technologies to remain in one place while teaching students who are at a variety of locations simultaneously. The professor's duties, like those when teaching correspondence courses conducted by mail, include

grading work that students send in at periodic intervals and advising students of their progress. Computers, the Internet, email, and video conferencing, however, are some of the technology tools that allow professors and students to communicate in "real time" in a virtual classroom setting. Meetings may be scheduled during the same time as traditional classes or during evenings and weekends. Professors who do this work are sometimes known as *extension work, correspondence,* or *distance learning instructors.* They may teach online courses in addition to other classes or may have distance learning as their major teaching responsibility.

The *junior college instructor* has many of the same kinds of responsibilities as does the teacher in a four-year college or university. Because junior colleges offer only a two-year program, they teach only undergraduates.

■ REQUIREMENTS
High School

Your high school's college preparatory program likely includes courses in English, science, foreign language, history, math, and government. In addition, you should take courses in speech to get a sense of what it will be like to lecture to a group of students. Your school's debate team can also help you develop public speaking skills, along with research skills.

Postsecondary Training

At least one advanced degree in your field of study is required to be a professor in a college or university. The master's degree is considered the minimum standard, and graduate work beyond the master's is usually desirable. If you hope to advance in academic rank above instructor, most institutions require a doctorate.

In the last year of your undergraduate program, you'll apply to graduate programs in your area of study. Standards for admission to a graduate program can be high and the competition heavy, depending on the school. Once accepted into a program, your responsibilities will be similar to those of your professors—in addition to attending seminars, you'll research, prepare articles for publication, and teach some undergraduate courses.

You may find employment in a junior college with only a master's degree. Advancement in responsibility and in salary, however, is more likely to come if you have earned a doctorate.

Other Requirements

You should enjoy reading, writing, and researching. Not only will you spend many years studying in school, but your whole career will be based on communicating your thoughts and ideas. People skills are important because you'll be dealing directly with students, administrators, and other faculty members on a daily basis. You should feel comfortable in a role of authority and possess self-confidence.

EXPLORING

Your high school teachers use many of the same skills as college professors, so talk to your teachers about their careers and their college experiences. You can develop your own teaching experience by volunteering at a community center, working at a day care center, or working at a summer camp. Also, spend some time on a college campus to get a sense of the environment. Write to colleges for their admissions brochures and course catalogs (or check them out online); read about the faculty members and the courses they teach. Before visiting college campuses, make arrangements to speak to professors who teach courses that interest you. These professors may allow you to sit in on their classes and observe. Also, make appointments with college advisers and with people in the admissions and recruitment offices. If your grades are good enough, you might be able to serve as a teaching assistant during your undergraduate years, which can give you experience leading discussions and grading papers.

EMPLOYERS

Employment opportunities vary based on area of study and education. Most universities have many different departments that hire faculty. With a doctorate, a number of publications, and a record of good teaching, professors should find opportunities in universities all across the country. There are more than 3,800 colleges and universities in the United States. Professors teach in undergraduate and graduate programs. The teaching jobs at doctoral institutions are usually better paying and more prestigious. The most sought-after positions are those that offer tenure. Teachers that have only a master's degree will be limited to opportunities with junior colleges, community colleges, and some small private institutions. There are approximately 1.3 million postsecondary teachers employed in the United States.

STARTING OUT

You should start the process of finding a teaching position while you are in graduate school. The process includes developing a curriculum vitae (a detailed, academic resume), writing for publication, assisting with research, attending conferences, and gaining teaching experience and recommendations. Many students begin applying for teaching positions while finishing their graduate program. For most positions at four-year institutions, you must travel to large conferences where inter-

A college art professor discusses a student's painting technique.

views can be arranged with representatives from the universities to which you have applied.

Because of the competition for tenure-track positions, you may have to work for a few years in temporary positions, visiting various schools as an *adjunct professor*. Some professional associations maintain lists of teaching opportunities in their areas. They may also make lists of applicants available to college administrators looking to fill an available position.

ADVANCEMENT

The normal pattern of advancement is from instructor to assistant professor, to associate professor, to full professor. All four academic ranks are concerned primarily with teaching and research. College faculty members who have an interest in and a talent for administration may be advanced to chair of a department or to dean of their college. A few become college or university presidents or other types of administrators.

The instructor is usually an inexperienced college teacher. He or she may hold a doctorate or may have completed all the Ph.D. requirements except for the dissertation. Most colleges look upon the rank of instructor as the period during which the college is trying out the teacher. Instructors usually are advanced to the position

A PART-TIME PROBLEM

According to the American Association of University Professors, approximately 44.5 percent of the nation's college and university faculty work part-time, and 60 percent of all appointments are non-tenure track. Though these educators generally teach the same courses as full-time faculty, they have no job security, earn far less than a full-time faculty member on a per-class basis, and many lack health care or retirement benefits.

of assistant professors within three to four years. Assistant professors are given up to about six years to prove themselves worthy of tenure, and if they do so, they become associate professors. Some professors choose to remain at the associate level. Others strive to become full professors and receive greater status, salary, and responsibilities.

Most colleges have clearly defined promotion policies from rank to rank for faculty members, and many have written statements about the number of years in which instructors and assistant professors may remain in grade. Administrators in many colleges hope to encourage younger faculty members to increase their skills and competencies and thus to qualify for the more responsible positions of associate professor and full professor.

■ EARNINGS

Earnings vary by the departments professors work in, by the size of the school, by the type of school (public, private, women's only, for example), and by the level of position the professor holds. In its 2002–03 salary survey, the American Association of University Professors (AAUP) reported the average yearly income for all full-time faculty was $64,455. It also reports that professors averaged the following salaries by rank: full professors, $86,437; associate professors, $61,732; assistant professors, $37,737; and lecturers, $43,914. Full professors working in disciplines such as law, business, health professions, computer and information sciences, and engineering have the highest salaries. Lower paying disciplines include visual and performing arts, agricultural studies, education, and communications. The American Association for the Advancement of Science reports that, according to findings from its member salary survey, the median earnings for full professors in the life science fields were approximately $108,000 in 2001. Associate professors in life sciences earned a median of $72,000 that same year.

According to the Department of Labor, in 2002, the median salary for all postsecondary instructors was $49,040, with 10 percent earning $92,430 or more and 10

percent earning $23,080 or less. Those with the highest earnings tend to be senior tenured faculty; those with the lowest, graduate assistants. Professors working on the West Coast and the East Coast and those working at doctorate-granting institutions also tend to have the highest salaries. Many professors try to increase their earnings by completing research, publishing in their field, or teaching additional courses.

Benefits for full-time faculty typically include health insurance and retirement funds and, in some cases, stipends for travel related to research, housing allowances, and tuition waivers for dependents.

■ WORK ENVIRONMENT

A college or university is usually a pleasant place in which to work. Campuses bustle with all types of activities and events, stimulating ideas, and a young, energetic population. Much prestige comes with success as a professor and scholar; professors have the respect of students, colleagues, and others in their community.

Depending on the size of the department, college professors may have their own office, or they may have to share an office with one or more colleagues. Their department may provide them with a computer, Internet access, and research assistants. College professors are also able to do much of their office work at home. They can arrange their schedule around class hours, academic meetings, and the established office hours when they meet with students. Most college teachers work more than 40 hours each week. Although college professors may teach only two or three classes a semester, they spend many hours preparing for lectures, examining student work, and conducting research.

■ OUTLOOK

The U.S. Department of Labor predicts much faster than average employment growth for college and university professors through 2012. College enrollment is projected to grow due to an increased number of 18- to 24-year-olds, an increased number of adults returning to college, and an increased number of foreign-born students. Additionally, opportunities for college teachers will be good in areas such as engineering, business, computer science, and health science, which offer strong career prospects in the world of work. Retirement of current faculty members will also provide job openings. However, competition for full-time, tenure-track positions at four-year schools will be very strong.

A number of factors threaten to change the way colleges and universities hire faculty. Some university leaders are developing more business-based methods of running their schools, focusing on profits and budgets.

This can affect college professors in a number of ways. One of the biggest effects is in the replacement of tenure-track faculty positions with part-time instructors. These part-time instructors include adjunct faculty, visiting professors, and graduate students. Organizations such as the AAUP and the American Federation of Teachers are working to prevent the loss of these full-time jobs, as well as to help part-time instructors receive better pay and benefits. Other issues involve the development of long-distance education departments in many schools. Though these correspondence courses have become very popular in recent years, many professionals believe that students in long-distance education programs receive only a second-rate education. A related concern is about the proliferation of computers in the classroom. Some courses consist only of instruction by computer software and the Internet. The effects of these alternative methods on the teaching profession will be offset somewhat by the expected increases in college enrollment in coming years.

■ FOR MORE INFORMATION

To read about the issues affecting college professors, contact the following organizations:

American Association of University Professors
1012 14th Street, NW, Suite 500
Washington, DC 20005
Tel: 202-737-5900
Email: aaup@aaup.org
http://www.aaup.org

American Federation of Teachers
555 New Jersey Avenue, NW
Washington, DC 20001
Tel: 202-879-4400
Email: online@aft.org
http://www.aft.org

Color Analysts and Image Consultants

■ OVERVIEW

Color analysts assess their clients' coloring, including skin tone and hair and eye color, and teach them how to use their most flattering colors in clothing and makeup. *Image consultants* usually work with people in business, helping them present themselves in a professional manner.

Color and image consultants offer programs for individual women or men, for professional or social organizations, or for all the employees of one company. Some work with retailers, teaching salespersons about color and style and presenting in-store workshops.

■ HISTORY

In their book, *Color Me Beautiful's Looking Your Best*, Mary Spillane and Christine Sherlock cite a study by Albert Mehrabian. He found that the impression we make on others is made up of 55 percent appearance and behavior, 38 percent speech, and only 7 percent the content of what we say. These figures clearly show the importance of presenting yourself well in business, social, and other settings. Beauty consultants have been around for some time, but their work is constantly evolving. Because our society is increasingly mobile, and we change jobs more often than our parents did, we are constantly establishing ourselves with new groups. In addition, television has increased our awareness of appearance and what it tells us about the individual. Projecting a positive image through our appearance and behavior helps us gain acceptance from social and business contacts, fit into the workplace, and meet the public.

In 1980, with the publication of Carole Jackson's book, *Color Me Beautiful*, many people, especially women, began to think of what they purchased and wore in a different way. No longer willing to accept whatever fashion decreed, they wanted colors and styles that enhanced their individual appearance. By the time more than 20 million people had read this *New York Times* bestseller, clothing manufacturers, cosmetic companies, and retailers felt the impact of the new consumer demand.

In the meantime, other businesses were dealing with their increased need for employees with technological backgrounds. Such employees often were totally involved in the technical aspects of their work and unconcerned about the impression they made on coworkers, clients, and the general public. Many

QUICK FACTS

SCHOOL SUBJECTS
Art
Business
Theater/dance

PERSONAL SKILLS
Artistic
Communication/ideas

WORK ENVIRONMENT
Primarily indoors
Primarily multiple locations

MINIMUM EDUCATION LEVEL
Some postsecondary training

SALARY RANGE
$12,620 to $18,700 to
   $100,000

CERTIFICATION OR LICENSING
Recommended

OUTLOOK
About as fast as the average

DOT
N/A

GOE
N/A

NOC
N/A

O*NET-SOC
N/A

companies began to provide training to help employees project better images, increasing the demand for image consultants.

■ THE JOB

Most color and image consultants are entrepreneurs, meaning that they own and manage their businesses and assume all the risks. They may work with individuals, groups, or both. Christine Sherlock, director of training and communications for Color Me Beautiful, reports that her firm trains color analysts in color and its use in wardrobe and makeup. Those who wish to become image consultants take additional training so they can help clients work on their overall appearance and grooming, as well as improve their voices, body language, and etiquette. Consultants also may learn to coach clients on dealing with the public and the media.

Susan Fignar, president of S. Fignar & Associates Inc., is a corporate image trainer and consultant who has been quoted in *Cosmopolitan*, the *Wall Street Journal*, and the *Chicago Tribune*. She works with some of the country's largest corporations and offers a variety of corporate programs and interactive workshops. Fignar says she provides training that helps people bring out their best personal and professional presence. Like other entrepreneurs, her business requires constant sales and marketing to obtain clients.

Her training sessions deal with such topics as making a good first impression, everyday etiquette, developing self-esteem and confidence, verbal communication, body language and facial expression, overall appearance, and appropriate dress for every occasion. She notices an increasing demand for her services in dress code consulting and training sessions on business casual dress.

Sherlock says consultants get satisfaction from helping others look better and feel good about themselves. "When a consultant helps a client with her wardrobe," she says, "the client not only saves money; she uses 100 percent of her wardrobe and no longer complains she has nothing to wear."

■ REQUIREMENTS
High School

If you are interested in this work, you will benefit from taking classes and being involved in activities that develop your ability to communicate and increase your understanding of visual effects. Helpful classes to take include English, speech, and drama. Activities to consider participating in include drama clubs and debate teams. In drama club you may have the opportunity to help apply makeup, select wardrobes, and learn about the emotional impact appearances can have. Art classes are also helpful to take, especially classes that teach color theory. Since many people in this line of work are entrepreneurs, consider taking any business, bookkeeping, or accounting classes that will give you the skills to run your own business.

Any part-time job working with the public is valuable. You can gain excellent experience from selling clothing or cosmetics in department stores, from working in beauty salons or spas, or from working as waitpersons. Volunteer work that involves working with people will also help you hone your people skills.

Postsecondary Training

There are no formal, standardized training programs for color analysts and image consultants. In general, Susan Fignar recommends attending seminars or classes on color, psychology, training methods, and communications. She adds that a degree in liberal arts, with a major in education, is a plus for those working at the corporate level.

Color Me Beautiful has trainers who travel throughout the country. They offer people who wish to become consultants basic classes in skin care, makeup, and color analysis and advanced classes in such subjects as theory of style and presentation. Most classes take one or two days for a single topic; most working consultants take at least one new class each year.

If you get to know a color analyst or image consultant personally, you may be able to arrange an informal internship of your own. Some people begin their careers in this field by working as apprentices to other consultants. Color Me Beautiful accepts a two-month apprenticeship with an approved consultant.

Certification or Licensing

Various training programs offer certificates to students once they have completed course work. The Association of Image Consultants International (AICI) provides a listing of such organizations on their website. The AICI recommends researching programs or training sessions, considering such factors as cost, length of study, subject areas covered, and refund policies. Color and image consultants require no licensing.

Other Requirements

Christine Sherlock recommends this field for those who like to work with and help other people and says an interest in fashion and style are also obviously very helpful. A general flair for art and design would prove useful. Analysts and consultants should be friendly, outgoing, supportive of others, able to offer constructive feedback, and open to change. There are few disabilities that would prevent an individual from doing this work.

Susan Fignar believes experience in the business world, especially in management and public contact, is essential for corporate consulting. She says that corporate consultants must be mature, poised, and professional to have credibility, and that people are usually between the ages of 33 and 40 when they enter this field.

■ EXPLORING

One way to explore this career is to arrange for a personal visit to a consultant. The AICI, for example, offers lists of qualified consultants throughout the country (see the end of this article for contact information).

There are several books you can read to learn more about color and image consulting. Sherlock recommends *Color Me Beautiful* by Carole Jackson (Ballantine Books, 1987), *Color Me Beautiful's Looking Your Best: Color, Makeup, and Style* by Mary Spillane and Christine Sherlock (Madison Books, 2002), and *Women of Color* by Darlene Mathis (SPCK and Triangle, 1999). Fignar recommends *Image Consulting: The New Career* by Joan Timberlake (Acropolis Books, 1983), which discusses the various areas in which image consultants specialize. Because networking is so important in getting clients, she also suggests *Networlding: Building Relationships and Opportunities for Success* by Melissa Giovagnoli (Jossey-Bass, 2000). Local libraries should have additional books on color, fabrics, style, etiquette, and body language.

■ EMPLOYERS

For the most part, color analysts and image consultants are self-employed. They run their own consulting businesses, which allows them the freedom to decide what image consulting services they wish to offer. For example, some consultants concentrate on working with corporate clients; other consultants may also advise individuals. Consultants may get the products they sell from one company, such as Color Me Beautiful, or they may offer a range of products and services that provide ways for clients to feel good about themselves. Those in apprenticeships and consultants just entering the field may work for consultants who have already established their businesses.

■ STARTING OUT

Some consultants enter the field through apprenticeships. Fignar began by working in advertising, where she had extensive experience in meeting planning and often was responsible for company visitors. She eventually attended a training program on fashion and image consulting. She says there are many routes to entering this field.

■ ADVANCEMENT

Workers can advance from color analysts, to image consultants, to trainers by gaining experience and additional education. Sherlock began as an apprentice and has advanced through various positions with Color Me Beautiful. Salon and department store employees would advance along the path their employers have laid out.

Fignar hopes to expand her business by adding new clients, taking advantage of new trends, developing training for future image consultants, and forming alliances with consultants who offer related services. This is par for the course for all self-employed analysts and consultants. She has had her own business for seven years and says it takes three to five years to get a corporate consulting business established.

■ EARNINGS

A color analyst's or image consultant's earnings are determined by the number of hours the consultant works, the type of clientele, and the consultant's location. Christine Sherlock says earnings are highest in New York City and southern California. Some consultants increase their incomes by offering additional services. Susan Fignar estimates that earnings start at under $20,000 but can reach $75,000 or more for top performers. Since many color analysts and image consultants own their own businesses, it may also be helpful to consider that some small business owners may earn only about $15,000 a year, while the most successful may make $100,000 or more. The Department of Labor reports that median annual earnings for beauticians and cosmetologists are $18,700 per year, with 10 percent making $12,620 or less and 10 percent making $34,720 or more.

Sherlock points out such advantages as owning your own business, flexible hours, controlling your own time, and opportunity for personal growth and development. Because most consultants are self-employed, they must provide their own insurance and other benefits.

■ WORK ENVIRONMENT

Many consultants work out of their homes. Color consultants also work in salons, boutiques, day spas, and retail areas. The work is indoors and may involve travel. Sherlock comments that the work has changed her life and that she loves everything she has done in the field.

Fignar works at corporate sites and training facilities, speaks before various organizations, and has appeared on radio and television. She has contact with management and with human resources and training departments. Her work schedule has busy and slow periods, but she usually works from 40 to 50 hours a week and sometimes makes evening presentations. She describes her work as exciting, draining, and full of time constraints.

■ OUTLOOK

The employment of personal appearance workers is expected to as fast as the average through 2012, according to the *Occupational Outlook Handbook,* mainly due to increasing population, incomes, and demand for cosmetology services.

Christine Sherlock says the economy has little effect on color consulting. During sluggish times, people still want the lift that such beauty services give them. The demand for consultants is growing steadily, and she believes self-employed people with successful businesses aren't likely to be out of work. The field is evolving, with new opportunities in corporate work.

Susan Fignar says corporate consultants are affected by downsizing because when companies cut personnel they also reduce training. "Right now," she says, "the field is growing." She says the hot topics are casual dress for business, etiquette, communications, and public image. Fignar feels security comes from constantly working to build your consulting business. She advises consultants to develop a 60-second sales pitch so they're always ready to describe their services to any prospective client they meet.

■ FOR MORE INFORMATION

This organization has information on continuing education and mentorship programs as well as a listing of programs that offer certificates upon completion.

Association of Image Consultants
    International
International Headquarters
12300 Ford Road, Ste. 135
Dallas, TX 75234 Tel: 972-755-1503
Email: info@aici.org
http://www.aici.org

This company provides information on contacting local consultants. Check out their website for information on their products.

Color Me Beautiful
14900 Conference Center Drive
Chantilly, VA 20151
Tel: 800-265-6763
http://www.colormebeautiful.com

Columnists

■ OVERVIEW

Columnists write opinion pieces for publication in newspapers or magazines. Some columnists work for syndicates, which are organizations that sell articles to many media at once.

Columnists can be generalists who write about whatever strikes them on any topic. Most columnists focus on a specialty, such as government, politics, local issues, health, humor, sports, gossip, or other themes.

Most newspapers employ local columnists or run columns from syndicates. Some syndicated columnists work out of their homes or private offices.

■ HISTORY

Because the earliest American newspapers were political vehicles, much of their news stories brimmed with commentary and opinion. This practice continued up until the Civil War. Horace Greeley, a popular editor who had regularly espoused partisanship in his *New York Tribune,* was the first to give editorial opinion its own page separate from the news.

As newspapers grew into instruments of mass communication, their editors sought balance and fairness on the editorial pages and began publishing a number of columns with varying viewpoints.

Famous Washington, D.C.-based columnist Jack Anderson is known for bringing an investigative slant to the editorial page. Art Buchwald and Molly Ivins became well known for their satirical look at government and politicians.

The growth of news and commentary on the Internet has only added to the power of columnists.

■ THE JOB

Columnists often take news stories and enhance the facts with personal opinions and panache. Columnists may also write from their personal experiences. Either way, a column usually has a punchy start, a pithy middle, and a strong, sometimes poignant, ending.

Columnists are responsible for writing columns on a regular basis on accord with a schedule, depending on the frequency of publication. They may write a column daily, weekly, quarterly, or monthly. Like other journalists, they face pressure to meet a deadline.

Most columnists are free to select their own story ideas. The need to constantly come up with new and interesting ideas may be one of the hardest parts of the job, but also one of the most rewarding. Columnists search through newspapers, magazines, and the Internet, watch television, and listen to the radio. The various types of media suggest ideas and keep the writer aware of current events and social issues.

Next, they do research, delving into a topic much like an investigative reporter would, so that they can back up their arguments with facts.

Finally, they write, usually on a computer. After a column is written, at least one editor goes over it to check for clarity and correct mistakes. Then the cycle begins again. Often a columnist will write a few relatively timeless pieces to keep for use as backups in a pinch, in case a new idea can't be found or falls through.

Most columnists work in newsrooms or magazine offices, although some, especially those who are syndicated but not affiliated with a particular newspaper, work out of their homes or private offices. Many well-known syndicated columnists work out of Washington, D.C.

Newspapers often run small pictures of columnists, called head shots, next to their columns. This, and a consistent placement of a column in a particular spot in the paper, usually gives a columnist greater recognition than a reporter or editor.

■ REQUIREMENTS
High School

You'll need a broad-based education to do this job well, so take a college prep curriculum in high school. Concentrate on English and journalism classes that will help you develop research and writing skills. Keep your computer skills up to date with computer science courses. History, psychology, science, and math should round out your education. Are you interested in a particular topic, such as sports, politics, or developments in medicine? Then take classes that will help you develop your knowledge in that area. In the future, you'll be able to draw on this knowledge when you write your column.

Postsecondary Training

As is the case for other journalists, at least a bachelor's degree in journalism is usually required, although some journalists graduate with degrees in political science or English. Experience may be gained by writing for the college or university newspaper and through a summer internship at a newspaper or other publication. It also may be helpful to submit freelance opinion columns to local or national publications. The more published articles, called "clips," you can show to prospective employers, the better.

Other Requirements

Being a columnist requires similar characteristics to those required for being a reporter: curiosity, a genuine interest in people, the ability to write clearly and succinctly, and the strength to thrive under deadline pressure. But as a columnist, you will also require a certain wit and wisdom, the compunction to express strong opinions, and the ability to take apart an issue and debate it.

■ EXPLORING

A good way to explore this career is to work for your school newspaper and perhaps write your own column. Participation in debate clubs will help you form opinions and express them clearly. Read your city's newspaper regularly, and take a look at national papers as well as magazines. Which columnists, on the local and national level, interest you? Why do you feel their columns are well done? Try to incorporate these good qualities into your own writing. Contact your local newspaper and ask for a tour of the facilities. This will give you a sense of what the office atmosphere is like and what technologies are used there. Ask to speak with one of the paper's regular columnists about his or her job. He or she may be able to provide you with valuable insights. Visit the Dow Jones Newspaper Fund website (http://djnewspaperfund.dowjones.com/fund) for information on careers, summer programs, internships, and more. Try getting a part-time or summer job at the newspaper, even if it's just answering phones and doing data entry. In this way you'll be able to test out how well you like working in such an atmosphere.

■ EMPLOYERS

Newspapers of all kinds run columns, as do certain magazines and even public radio stations, where a tape is played over the airways of the author reading the column. Some columnists are self-employed, preferring to market their work to syndicates instead of working for a single newspaper or magazine.

■ STARTING OUT

Most columnists start out as reporters. Experienced reporters are the ones most likely to become

QUICK FACTS

SCHOOL SUBJECTS
Computer science
English
Journalism

PERSONAL SKILLS
Communication/ideas
Helping/teaching

WORK ENVIRONMENT
Indoors and outdoors
Primarily multiple locations

MINIMUM EDUCATION LEVEL
Bachelor's degree

SALARY RANGE
$17,900 to $31,240 to
$71,520

CERTIFICATION OR LICENSING
None available

OUTLOOK
Little change or more slowly
than the average

DOT
131

GOE
01.03.01

NOC
5123

O*NET-SOC
27-3022.00

WHAT IS A BLOG?

A "blog"—short for "Web log"—is a sort of journal put up for public viewing on the World Wide Web. The first blogs, arguably, were the "plan files" attached to old text-based Internet accounts. Users frequently kept personal information, from their hobbies to their evening's plans, in these files. With the growth of the World Wide Web, many people took the opportunity to put their thoughts on the Web. Improved technology has made it increasingly easy to create and update a website. Most people use their blogs to share their day-to-day personal experiences with friends, family, and anyone who happens by. However, some amateur and professional journalists have used the power of blogging to self-publish their own newspaper columns. Not only has blogging become an indicator of popular opinion that mainstream journalists, editors, and politicians have been forced to pay attention to, but with many sensitively-placed people anonymously keeping their own publicly accessible online diaries, blogs have become an important source of "hard" news, as well.

columnists. Occasionally, however, a relatively new reporter may suggest a weekly column if the beat being covered warrants it, for example, politics.

Another route is to start out by freelancing, sending columns out to a multitude of newspapers and magazines in the hopes that someone will pick them up. Also, columns can be marketed to syndicates. A list of these, and magazines that may also be interested in columns, is provided in the *Writer's Market* (http://www.writersmarket.com).

A third possibility, one opened up by the Internet, is simply beginning your own site or blog and using it to attract attention and thus jumpstart your career. Many are well-known, such as Matt Drudge (http://www.drudgereport.com) and "Wonkette" (http://www.wonkette.com), started by beginning their own Web columns. If you get scoops, run interesting content, and people like what you have to say, you may find yourself with more readers than you can handle.

■ ADVANCEMENT

Newspaper columnists can advance in national exposure by having their work syndicated. They also may try to get a collection of their columns published in book form. Moving from a small newspaper or magazine to a large national publication is another way to advance.

Columnists also may choose to work in other editorial positions, such as editor, editorial writer or page editor, or foreign correspondent.

■ EARNINGS

Like reporters' salaries, the incomes of columnists vary greatly according to experience, newspaper size and location, and whether the columnist is under a union contract. But generally, columnists earn higher salaries than reporters.

The U.S. Department of Labor classifies columnists with news analysts, reporters, and correspondents, and reports that the median annual income for these professionals was $31,240 in 2003. Ten percent of those in this group earned less than $17,900, and 10 percent made more than $71,520 annually. According to the *Annual Survey of Journalism & Mass Communication Graduates*, directed by the University of Georgia, the median salary for those who graduated in 2002 with bachelor's degrees in journalism or mass communication was approximately $26,000. Median earnings varied somewhat by employer; for example, those working for weekly papers earned somewhat less, while those working for consumer magazines earned somewhat more. Although these salary figures are for all journalists (not just columnists), they provide a general range for those working in this field. However, popular columnists at large papers earn considerably higher salaries.

Freelancers may get paid by the column. Syndicates pay columnists 40 percent to 60 percent of the sales income generated by their columns or a flat fee if only one column is being sold.

Freelancers must provide their own benefits. Columnists working on staff at newspapers and magazines receive typical benefits such as health insurance, paid vacation days, sick days, and retirement plans.

■ WORK ENVIRONMENT

Columnists work mostly indoors in newspaper or magazine offices, although they may occasionally conduct interviews or do research on location out of the office. Some columnists may work as much as 48 to 52 hours a week. Some columnists do the majority of their writing at home or in a private office, and come to the newsroom primarily for meetings and to have their work approved or changed by editors. The atmosphere in a newsroom is generally fast paced and loud, so columnists must be able to concentrate and meet deadlines in this type of environment.

■ OUTLOOK

The U.S. Department of Labor predicts that employment growth for news analysts, reporters, and correspondents (including columnists) will be slower than the average through 2012. Growth will be hindered by such factors as mergers and closures of newspapers, decreasing circulation, and lower profits from advertising revenue. Online publications may be a source for new jobs. Competition for newspaper and magazine positions is very competitive, and competition for the position of columnist is even stiffer because these are prestigious jobs that are limited in number. Smaller daily and weekly newspapers may be easier places to find employment than major metropolitan newspapers, and movement up the ladder to columnist will also likely be quicker. Pay, however, is less than at bigger papers. Journalism and mass communication graduates will have the best opportunities, and writers will be needed to replace those who leave the field for other work or retire.

■ FOR MORE INFORMATION

For information on careers in newspaper reporting, education, and financial aid opportunities, contact

American Society of Journalists and Authors
1501 Broadway, Suite 302
New York, NY 10036
Tel: 212-997-0947
Email: info@asja.org
http://www.asja.org

This association provides general educational information on all areas of journalism, including newspapers, magazines, television, and radio.

Association for Education in Journalism and Mass Communication
234 Outlet Pointe Boulevard
Columbia, SC 29210-5667
Tel: 803-798-0271
Email: aejmc@aejmc.org
http://www.aejmc.org

For information on jobs, scholarships, internships, college programs, and other resources, contact

National Association of Broadcasters
1771 N Street, NW
Washington, DC 20036
Tel: 202-429-5300
Email: nab@nab.org
http://www.nab.org

The SPJ has student chapters all over the United States and offers information on scholarships and internships.

Society of Professional Journalists (SPJ)
3909 North Meridian Street
Indianapolis, IN 46208
Tel: 317-927-8000
Email: questions@spj.org
http://www.spj.org

Comedians

■ OVERVIEW

Comedians are entertainers who make people laugh. They use a variety of techniques to amuse their audiences, including telling jokes, composing and singing humorous songs, wearing funny costumes, and doing impersonations. Comedians perform in nightclubs, comedy clubs, coffee houses, theaters, television shows, films, and even business functions, such as trade shows and sales meetings.

■ HISTORY

Throughout history, people have enjoyed humorous interpretations of the events that make up their daily lives. Comedy began as a type of drama that presented events in a comic way and thereby sought to amuse its audience. These dramas were not always funny, yet they were usually lighthearted and had happy endings (as opposed to tragedies, which had sad endings).

The Greeks and Romans had playwrights such as Aristophanes and Plautus, who successfully used humor as a type of mirror on the social and political customs of the time. They wrote plays that highlighted some of the particularities of the rich and powerful as well as common people. An early type of comedian was the *fool* or *jester* attached to a royal court, whose function was to entertain by singing, dancing, telling jokes, riddles, and humorous stories, and even by impersonating the king and other members of the aristocracy. In later years, English playwright William Shakespeare and French playwright Moliere used wit and humor to point out some of the shortcomings of society.

In the 19th century, as cities became more and more crowded, comedy became an especially important diversion for people. During this time, minstrel, burlesque, and vaudeville shows became very popular. These

QUICK FACTS
SCHOOL SUBJECTS
English
Theater/dance
PERSONAL SKILLS
Artistic
Communication/ideas
WORK ENVIRONMENT
Primarily indoors
Primarily multiple locations
MINIMUM EDUCATION LEVEL
High school diploma
SALARY RANGE
$0 to $30,000 to $200,000+
CERTIFICATION OR LICENSING
None available
OUTLOOK
About as fast as the average
DOT
159
GOE
01.05.01
NOC
5232
O*NET-SOC
N/A

Movies about Comedians

The King of Comedy (1983, directed by Martin Scorsese, rated PG): Obsessive character Rupert Pupkin (Robert DeNiro) wants to break into the big time as a comedian, so he hounds Jerry Langford (Jerry Lewis) constantly to get on his TV show.

Punchline (1988, directed by David Selzer, rated R): Steven Gold (Tom Hanks) is a stand-up comedian down on his luck. He meets Lilah Krytsick (Sally Field), a housewife with grand ambitions to be a stand-up comedian. Gold takes her under his wing and teaches her the art of comedy and humor.

Mr. Saturday Night (1992, directed by Billy Crystal, rated R): Buddy Young (Billy Crystal) is an aging comic who plays to small crowds in nursing homes. As he looks for work he comes to realize that the world has forgotten his golden years and it may be time for him to retire from show business.

shows usually featured a combination of song, comedy, and other acts, such as magic or acrobatics. Many of the popular comedians of the 20th century began their careers in burlesque and vaudeville, and hundreds of theaters opened in the United States catering to this form of entertainment. A distinctive part of vaudeville was the great variety of acts presented during a single show. Comedians especially had to work hard to catch the audience's attention and make themselves memorable among the other performers. Vaudeville provided a training ground for many of the most popular comedians of the 20th century, including stars such as Bud Abbott and Lou Costello, Milton Berle, Mae West, Bob Hope, the Marx Brothers, George Burns and Gracie Allen, W.C. Fields, and Will Rogers.

Vaudeville soon faced competition from the film industry. People flocked to motion pictures as a new form of entertainment, and many of the vaudeville theaters closed or converted to showing films. For comedians, the new form of entertainment proved ideal for their craft. During the early years of cinema, slapstick films starring the Keystone Cops, Buster Keaton, Charlie Chaplin, Fatty Arbuckle, and many others became immensely popular. Radio also provided a venue for many comedians, and people would gather around a living room radio to hear the performances of stars such as Milton Berle, Edgar Bergen, Jack Benny, and Jimmy Durante. When sound was added to the films in the late 1920s and early 1930s, comedians were able to adapt their stand-up and radio routines to film, and many numbered among the most popular stars in the United States and throughout the world.

Later, television provided another venue for comedians. Milton Berle was one of the very first television stars. *The Ed Sullivan Show* became an important place for comedians to launch their acts to a national audience. Many comedians developed their own television shows, and many more comedians found work writing jokes and scripts for this comedic medium.

Stand-up comedy, that is, live performances before an audience, continues to be one of the most important ways for a comedian to develop an act and perfect timing, delivery, and other skills. Stand-up comedians do more than simply make people laugh; they attempt to make people think. Current events continue to provide a rich source for material, and the stand-up comedian has become a social critic who uses humor as the medium for the message. For example, in the early 1960s, Lenny Bruce caused a great deal of controversy in the United States by using his nightclub routines to question the role of organized religion in society and to argue against censorship. During the 1960s, comedians, such as members of The Second City theater group based in Chicago, began to adapt improvisational acting techniques, creating a new form of comedic theater. Many of these comedy actors, including John Belushi and Shelley Long, went on to stardom.

Stand-up comedy continues to provide an important training ground for comedians. Most of the biggest comedy stars, such as Steve Martin, Jerry Seinfeld, Roseanne, Richard Pryor, Tim Allen, Eddie Murphy, Ellen Degeneres, and many others, had their starts as stand-up comedians. During the 1980s, hundreds of new comedy clubs opened across the country, providing more venues for comedians to hone their craft than ever before.

■ THE JOB

Although making people laugh may sound like a pretty simple assignment, comedians work very hard at this task. Because there are many types of comedy, from physical and slapstick to comedy involving highly sophisticated wordplay, all comedians must develop their own style. Comedians may appear in regular attire or incorporate colorful costumes, music, props, or other techniques into their act. In any case, it is generally the writing and timing that make a comedian unique.

Perhaps the most common form of comedic performer is the stand-up comic. *Stand-up comedians* usually perform in nightclubs or comedy clubs, entertaining audiences with jokes, stories, and impersonations. Most often, stand-up comics write their own material, so they spend a great deal of time developing, perfecting, and rehearsing new material. Adding new bits and creating entirely new routines provides a constant challenge for the comedian.

Stand-up comedians often travel around the country, performing in a variety of settings. They may have to adapt their performances somewhat, depending on the audience. The length of the performance is determined by whether the comedian is the main act or an opening act. A main act will last from 30 minutes to an hour, while an opening act may be just a few minutes.

Another popular type of performance is improvisation, often abbreviated to "improv." *Improv comedians* work without a set routine and make up their own dialogue as they go along. It allows for a kind of spontaneity that traditional performances do not. Improv groups perform skits, dances, and songs using well-trained comedic creativity. Many comedy groups will perform a number of scripted skits and then improvise a number of skits based on audience suggestions.

Comedians are storytellers. No matter where they perform, their goal is to engage their audience through various characters and stories. Many comedians use their own life stories as material, weaving a picture of people and places designed not only to evoke laughter but also understanding.

Comedians may perform their work live or on tape. Usually a taping is done in front of an audience, as comedians need the laughter and other feedback of an audience to be most effective.

Comedians who perform on film or television have the same restrictions as other actors and actresses. They must adhere to strict schedules and perform routines repeatedly before the director decides a scene is finished. *Film and television comedians* usually perform scenes that someone else has written. They are required to memorize their lines and rehearse their performances.

As with other performance artists, comedians often find themselves looking for employment. Comedians may work for a number of weeks in a row and then face a period of unemployment. To find work, many comedians hire booking agents to locate club owners willing to hire them. Many clubs feature open mike nights, in which anyone may perform, providing important opportunities for beginning comedians. Other comedians attempt to find work on their own. A person's success in finding work will be largely influenced by skill and style, but also to an extent by personal contacts and a bit of good fortune.

For comedians who are uncomfortable in front of an audience, there is the opportunity to write material for other performers. Not all people who write comedic material are former comedians, but all understand the fundamental elements of humor and ways of using words and images to make people laugh.

■ REQUIREMENTS

High School

There are no set educational standards for comedians. The overriding requirement is to be funny. Comedians should also have a love of performing and a strong desire to make people laugh.

A comedian should obviously have good communications skills and be able to write material in a succinct and humorous manner. It is also necessary to have a strong stage presence. Often, budding comedians will take English and composition classes, as well as speech and acting courses, to help develop skills in these areas. Accounting and bookkeeping skills are also helpful, as comedians often prepare their own financial records.

Postsecondary Training

Few colleges and universities offer specific courses on how to become a comedian. However, higher education may give a comedian a stronger understanding of society and current events, useful when writing their material. Becoming a comedian takes a lot of hard work and, as with other performance skills, practice, practice, practice. Many communities have improvisational groups that provide a training ground for aspiring actors and comedians. Some comedy clubs also offer classes.

Other Requirements

Making people laugh is not a skill that is easily taught. Most good comedians have an inborn talent and have made jokes or performed humorous skits since childhood. This means more than simply being the class clown; talented comedians see events in a humorous light and share this perspective with others. Above all else, a comedian must have a keen sense of timing. A funny line, delivered improperly, loses its effectiveness.

Comedians come in all shapes and sizes. Indeed, it is often the person who looks and feels somewhat different who is better able to see humorous aspects of human nature and society. A comedian should be able to take material from his or her own background (be it growing up in a small town, having overbearing parents, or other situations) and interpret this material in a way that appeals to others.

Comedians should be keen observers of daily life and be perceptive enough to recognize the humor in day-to-day events. But comedians should not be overly sensitive and become unduly disappointed if audiences do not respond to their jokes at every performance. It may take years to develop the skills to be a successful comedian, and even the most successful comedians can have an off night.

■ EXPLORING

The field of comedy offers a number of good opportunities for career exploration. For example, many improvisational groups offer classes in acting and performance techniques. These groups are often highly competitive, but they are a good place to learn skills, make contacts, and have fun. Of course, there is no substitute for hands-on experience, and most comedy clubs and coffee houses have open mike nights where aspiring comedians can get on stage and try out their material in front of a real audience. To get an idea of what it is like to perform before an audience, aspiring comedians can also stage performances for family and friends before venturing on stage to perform for strangers. Acting in school plays and local productions is another good way to get performing experience. It is also possible to learn by watching others. Visit a comedy club or coffee house to observe comedians at work. Try to talk informally with a comedian to learn more about the profession. Finally, do some research. There are also a number of books that describe exercises and techniques for comedians.

■ EMPLOYERS

Comedians work in a wide variety of venues, including comedy clubs, resorts, hotels, and cruise ships. Television networks, especially cable television, are major employers of comedians. They hire comedians not just as performers, but as writers for situation comedies, movies, and talk shows, and as entertainers for the audiences at live tapings. A comedian interested in performing is well advised to hire an agent to find employers and book engagements.

■ STARTING OUT

Getting started as a comedian is often very difficult. There are thousands of people who want to make people laugh, but relatively few venues for aspiring comedians to get exposure. To find an opportunity to perform, you may have to repeatedly call local nightclubs, bars, or coffee houses. Generally, these clubs will already have a number of comedians they use.

A common way to get a first break is to attend open mike nights and call for auditions at a local club. These auditions are not private showings for club owners but rather actual performances in front of audiences. Usually, comedians are not paid at these auditions, but those who show the most promise are often invited back to put on paid performances.

Another way to break into the career is through a comedy improvisational group. These groups offer novice comedians a chance to refine skills, developing techniques and contacts before starting out on their own. However,

joining many of these groups can be highly competitive; often, an aspiring comedian may join a lesser-known improv group while working on skills and auditioning for better-known groups.

Another way to get a start in comedy is through acting. Actors with a flair for comedy can audition for film comedies and situation comedy series. Much of the cast of the hit comedy series *Friends,* for example, came from an acting background.

■ ADVANCEMENT

Comedians who find success at local clubs or as part of an improvisation group can go on to perform at larger clubs and theaters. Some may also find work in the corporate world, entertaining at trade shows and other meetings. Extremely successful comedians may go on to tape comedy routines for broadcast or even have their own television shows.

Comedians can also branch out somewhat in their career goals. Some choose to write material for other comedians or review comedic performances for the local media. Others become comedy club owners or talent agents, creating employment opportunities for other comedians.

Comedy writers may go on to work for advertising agencies, using humor as a means of creating commercials or other promotional materials. Others may develop television or movie scripts.

■ EARNINGS

People who look only at the incomes of well-known comedians will get a mistaken notion of how much comedians earn. Jim Carrey may earn millions for a single movie, other comedy stars may earn $200,000 for one performance, but the vast majority of comedians earn far lower wages. In fact, most comedians must hold full- or part-time jobs to supplement the income from their performances.

In large comedy clubs, a headline comedian can expect to earn between $1,000 and $20,000 per show, depending on his or her drawing power. Those who perform as an opening act might earn between $125 and $350 per show. Headline comedians at smaller clubs will earn between $300 and $800 per show. Comedians hired to perform college shows earn around $500 per show. Of course, those just starting out will earn very little (remember, most club owners do not pay comedians who are auditioning) and start at as little as $15 to $20 for a 20-minute set. Others will be expected to "pay to play"—and then bring in family and friends to help the club owner turn a profit! Despite this meager pay, beginners working in clubs will be in a good position to learn the craft and make valuable contacts.

Comedians who entertain at trade shows and sales meetings can earn several hundred dollars per show, yet these assignments tend to be infrequent.

Comedy writers have a very wide pay scale. Those who write for well-known comedians are paid about $50 for every joke used. (Of course, many jokes are rejected by the performer.) Full-time comedy writers for the *Tonight Show* and other television shows can expect to earn between $50,000 and $150,000 per year, depending on their skill, experience, and the budget of the show.

WORK ENVIRONMENT

Full-time comedians usually spend a lot of time traveling between shows. A comedian may have a strong following in the Midwest, for example, and in the course of a week he or she may have two shows in Detroit, two shows in Chicago, and a show in St. Louis. Some people may find this lifestyle exciting, but for many it is exhausting and lonely. Those who perform as part of an improv troupe may also travel a lot. Once a comedian has developed a good following, the traveling may subside somewhat. More established comedians perform at one or two clubs in the same city on a fairly regular basis.

Performing in front of an audience can be very demanding. Not all audiences are receptive (especially to new material), and a comedian may encounter unresponsive crowds. It is also not uncommon for comedians to perform for small audiences in bars and nightclubs. Many of these nightclubs may be small, dark, and filled with smoke.

Despite these challenges, comedians can have fascinating careers. They experience the thrill of performing in front of audiences and positively affecting people's lives. Comedians may go on to achieve a good deal of fame, especially those who perform on television or in the movies. As creative artists, comedians may find it very satisfying to express their views and get positive feedback from others. There can be a lot of pleasure in making people laugh and seeing others enjoy themselves.

Comedians usually work late into the night, often not starting performances until 9 or 10 P.M. They also generally work weekends, when people have more time to go to nightclubs and comedy clubs.

Part-time comedians often hold day jobs and perform at night. Similarly, comedy writers may have to work other jobs to make ends meet financially. They might prepare material in their homes or in small offices with other writers.

OUTLOOK

As with the other performance arts, there will always be more aspiring comedians than there are job opportunities. However, comedians enjoy more solid employment prospects than actors or actresses. There are hundreds of comedy clubs across the country (usually in larger cities), and each club needs performers to get their audiences laughing. During the 1990s, the boom in comedy clubs slowed. However, more recently, new venues such as casinos, resorts, and theme parks continue to offer new opportunities for comedians. Of course, the most lucrative jobs will go to those with the best reputations, but thousands of comedians will continue to find steady work in the next decade.

There is also a growing trend for private companies to hire comedians to perform at sales meetings and trade shows. Comedians help to increase interest in products and create an enjoyable sales environment. Talent agencies now increasingly book comedians to work at these events.

For those who choose to work as comedy writers or entertainment critics, the competition for jobs should be keen, yet there are good career opportunities. The growth of the cable television industry in particular has created a need for increasing numbers of writers to work on the growing numbers of new shows. There are a large number of comedy shows on the national networks and on cable television, and these should provide a good market for skilled comedy writers.

FOR MORE INFORMATION

For information on theaters, training centers, and famous alumni, contact

The Second City
1616 North Wells Street
Chicago, IL 60614
Tel: 312-664-4032
http://www.secondcity.com

Commodities Brokers

OVERVIEW

Commodities brokers, also known as *futures commission merchants,* act as agents in carrying out purchases and sales of commodities for customers or traders. Commodities are primary goods that are either raw or partially refined. Such goods are produced by farmers, such as corn, wheat, or cattle, or mined from the earth, such as gold, copper, or silver. Brokers, who may work at a brokerage house, on the floor of a commodities exchange, or independently, are paid a fee or commission for acting as the middleman to conduct and complete the trade.

■ HISTORY

In medieval Europe, business was transacted at local market fairs, and commodities, primarily agricultural, were traded at scheduled times and places. As market fairs grew, "fair letters" were set up as a currency representing a future cash settlement for a transaction. With these letters, merchants could travel from one fair to another. This was the precursor to the Japanese system, in which landowners used "certificates of receipt" for their rice crops. As the certificates made their way into the economy, the Dojima Rice Market was established and became the first place where traders bought and sold contracts for the future delivery of rice.

"Forward contracts" entered the U.S. marketplace in the early 19th century. Farmers, swept up in the boom of industrial growth, transportation, and commerce, began to arrange for the future sale of their crops. Traders entered the market along with the development of these contracts. However, there were no regulations to oversee that the commodity was actually delivered or that it was of an acceptable quality. Furthermore, each transaction was an individual business deal because the terms of each contract were variable. To address these issues, the Chicago Board of Trade was formed in 1848, and by 1865 it had set up standards and rules for trading "to arrive" contracts, now known as commodity futures contracts.

■ THE JOB

A futures contract is an agreement to deliver a particular commodity, such as wheat, pork bellies, or coffee, at a specific date, time, and place. For example, a farmer might sell his oats before they are sowed (known as hedging) because he can't predict what kind of price he'll be able to demand later on. If the weather is favorable and crops are good, he'll have competition, which will drive prices down. If there is a flood or drought, oats will be scarce, driving the price up. He wants to ensure a fair price for his product to protect his business and limit his risk, since he can't predict what will happen.

On the other side of the equation is the user of the oats, perhaps a cereal manufacturer, who purchases these contracts for a delivery of oats at some future date. Producers and users do not correspond to a one-to-one ratio, and the broker is a middleman who does the buying and selling of contracts between the two groups. Brokers may place orders to buy or sell contracts for themselves, for individual clients, or for companies, all of whom hope to make a profit by correctly anticipating the direction of a commodity's price. Brokers are licensed to represent clients, and brokers' first responsibility is to take care of their clients' orders before doing trading for themselves. *Traders* also buy and sell contracts for themselves. Unlike brokers, however, they are not licensed (and thus not allowed) to do this work for clients.

When placing a trade for others, brokers are paid a fee or a commission for acting as the agent in making the sale. There are two broad categories of brokers, though they are becoming less distinct. *Full service brokers* provide considerable research to clients, offer price quotes, give trading advice, and assist the customer in making trading decisions. *Discount brokers* simply fill the orders as directed by clients. Some brokers offer intermediate levels of optional services on a sliding scale of commission, such as market research and strategic advice.

In general, brokers are responsible for taking and carrying out all commodity orders and being available on call to do so; reporting back to the client upon fulfilling the order request; keeping the client abreast of breaking news; maintaining account balances and other financial data; and obtaining market information when needed and informing the client about important changes in the marketplace.

Brokers can work on the floor of a commodity futures exchange—the place where contracts are bought and sold—for a brokerage house or independently. The exchange has a trading floor where brokers transact their business in the trading pit. There are 11 domestic exchanges, with the main ones in Chicago, Kansas City, New York, and Minneapolis. To be allowed to work on the floor, a broker must have a membership (also known as a "seat") in the exchange or must be employed by a company with a seat in the exchange, which is a private organization. Memberships are limited to a specific number, and seats may be rented or purchased. Although seat prices vary due to factors such as the health of the overall economy and the type of seat being purchased, they are all extremely expensive. As an example, consider seats at the Chicago Mercantile Exchange (CME). The CME has several divisions with seats for each. Full CME seats give the member the right to trade in any division of the

QUICK FACTS

SCHOOL SUBJECTS
Business
Mathematics

PERSONAL SKILLS
Communication/ideas
Leadership/management

WORK ENVIRONMENT
Primarily indoors
Primarily one location

MINIMUM EDUCATION LEVEL
High school diploma

SALARY RANGE
$26,570 to $60,530 to
$1,000,000+

CERTIFICATION OR LICENSING
Required

OUTLOOK
About as fast as the average

DOT
162

GOE
10.02.02

NOC
1113

O*NET-SOC
41-3031.00, 41-3031.01

exchange, from futures in broiler chickens to interest rates on Treasury bills; other seats give the member the right to trade only in a certain area. An International Monetary Market seat, for example, allows the member to trade only on currency and interest rate futures. Seat prices at the CME can range from tens of thousands of dollars to hundreds of thousands of dollars (full CME seats have been known to sell for $700,000 and more). Naturally, this expense alone limits the number of individuals who can become members. In addition to being able to afford a seat, candidates for membership to any exchange must undergo thorough investigations of their credit standings, financial backgrounds, characters, and understanding of trading.

Most brokers do not have seats but work for brokerage houses that deal in futures. Examples of these houses include Merrill Lynch or Dean Witter, which deal in stocks, bonds, commodities, and other investments, and smaller houses, such as R. J. O'Brien, that handle only commodities.

Companies can also have a seat on the exchange, and they have their own *floor brokers* in the pit to carry out trades for the brokerage house. Brokers in the company take orders from the public for buying or selling a contract and promptly pass it on to the floor broker in the pit of the exchange. Brokers also have the choice of running their own business. Known as *introducing brokers,* they handle their own clients and trades and use brokerage houses to place their orders. Introducing brokers earn a fee by soliciting business trades, but they don't directly handle the customer's funds.

■ REQUIREMENTS
High School

Although there are no formal educational requirements for becoming a broker, a high school diploma and a college degree are strongly recommended. Commodities brokers need to have a wide range of knowledge, covering such areas as economics, world politics, and sometimes even the weather. To begin to develop this broad base of knowledge, start in high school by taking history, math, science, and business classes. Since commodities brokers are constantly working with people to make a sale, take English classes to enhance your communication skills. In addition to this course work, you might also consider getting a part-time job working in a sales position. Such a job will also give you the chance to hone your communication and sales skills.

Postsecondary Training

The vast majority of brokers have a college degree. While there is no "commodities broker major," you can

---

COMMODITIES VOCABULARY

Commodity: A tangible good or item that can be bought or sold, such as grain, gold, or frozen concentrated orange juice. The fact that commodities are material goods helps to distinguish them from other items, such as bonds and stocks, traded on exhanges.

Bear market: A market in which prices are falling. (This can be a bad thing, as commodities contracts can lose money.) Traders who plan on this happening are called "bears."

Bull market: The opposite of a bear market, in which prices go up. (This can be bad, as too much bullishness causes inflation.) Traders who plan on such markets are called "bulls."

Contract market: A market where futures contracts, or obligations to produce commodities, are traded.

Futures contract: A legal agreement to buy or sell a certain amount and type of a certain specified commodity at some future date. Since these contracts follow a standard form, they can be bought and sold—but only by auction or at regulated contract markets.

Source: Center for Futures Education

---

improve your chances of obtaining a job in this field by studying economics, finance, or business administration while in college. Keep in mind that you should continue to develop your understanding of politics and technologies, so government and computer classes will also be useful.

Brokerage firms look for employees who have sales ability, strong communication skills, and self-confidence. Commodities is often a second career for many people who have demonstrated these qualities in other positions.

Certification or Licensing

To become a commodities broker, it is necessary to pass the National Commodities Futures Examination (the Series 3 exam) to become eligible to satisfy the registration requirements of federal, state, and industry regulatory agencies. The test covers market and trading knowledge as well as rules and regulations and is composed of true/false and multiple choice questions. Registration for the exam is through the National Association of Securities Dealers Regulation. Preparation materials are available through a number of sources, such as the Institute for Financial Markets (http://www.theifm.org). Brokers must also register with the National Futures Association.

A commodities broker must be able to think clearly while doing several things at once, such as talking to a buyer while listening to the seller.

Other Requirements

To be a successful broker, you must possess a combination of research and money management skills. You need to be attentive to detail and have a knack for analyzing data. Strong communications and sales skills are important as well, as brokers make money by convincing people to let them place their trades. An interest in and awareness of the world around you will also be a contributing factor to your success in this field, as commodities are influenced by everything from political decisions and international news to social and fashion trends.

You must also be emotionally stable to work in such a volatile environment. You need to be persistent, aggressive, and comfortable taking risks and dealing with failure. Strong, consistent, and independent judgment is also key. You must be a disciplined hard worker, able to comb through reams of market reports and charts to gain a thorough understanding of a particular commodity and the mechanics of the marketplace. You also need to be outspoken and assertive and able to yell out prices loudly and energetically on the trading floor and to command attention.

◼ EXPLORING

Students interested in commodities trading should visit one of the futures exchanges. All of them offer public tours, and you'll get to see up close just how the markets work and the roles of the players involved. All the exchanges offer educational programs and publications, and most have a website (see "For More Information"). The Chicago Mercantile Exchange publishes *The Merc at Work,* the full text of which is also available at its website, as well as many other educational handbooks and pamphlets. There are hundreds of industry newsletters and magazines available (such as *Futures Magazine*), and many offer free samples of publications or products. Read what trading advisors have to say and how they say it. Learn their lingo and gain an understanding of the marketplace. If you have any contacts in the industry, arrange to spend a day with a broker. Watch him or her at work, and you'll learn how orders are entered, processed, and reported.

Do your own research. Adopt a commodity, chart its prices, test some of your own ideas, and analyze the marketplace. There are also a variety of inexpensive software programs, as well as websites, that simulate trading.

Finally, consider a job as a *runner* during the summer before your freshman year in college. Runners transport the order, or "paper," from the phone clerk to the broker in the pit and relay information to and from members on the floor. This is the single best way to get hands-on experience in the industry.

◼ EMPLOYERS

Commodities brokers work on the floor of a commodity futures exchange, for brokerage houses, or independently.

◼ STARTING OUT

College graduates can start working with a brokerage house as an associate and begin handling stocks. After several years they can take the certification exam and move into futures. Another option is to start as support staff, either at the exchange or the brokerage house. Sales personnel try to get customers to open accounts, and account executives develop and service customers for the brokerage firm. At the exchange, phone clerks receive incoming orders and communicate the information to the runners. Working in the back as an accountant, money manager, or member of the research staff is also another route. School placement offices may be able to assist graduates in finding jobs with brokerage houses. Applications may also be made directly to brokerage houses.

Many successful brokers and traders began their careers as runners, and each exchange has its own training program. Though the pay is low, runners learn the business very quickly with a hands-on experience not available in an academic classroom. Contact one of the commodities exchanges for information on becoming a runner.

◼ ADVANCEMENT

A broker who simply executes trades can advance to become a full-service broker. Through research and analysis and the accumulation of experience and knowledge about the industry, a broker can advance from an order filler and become a commodity trading advisor. A broker can also become a money manager and make all trading decisions for clients.

Within the exchange, a broker can become a *floor manager,* overseeing the processes of order taking and information exchange. To make more money, a broker can also begin to place his or her own trades for his or her own private account, though the broker's first responsibility is to the customers.

◼ EARNINGS

This is an entrepreneurial business. A broker's commission is based on the number of clients he or she recruits, the amount of money they invest, and the profit they make. The sky's the limit. In recent years, the most successful broker made $25 million. A typical salary for a newly hired employee in a brokerage might average $1,500 per month plus a 30 percent commission on sales. Smaller firms are likely to pay a smaller commission. The U.S. Department of Labor reports that the median annual earnings for securities, commodities, and financial services sales representatives (a group including commodities brokers) were $60,530 in 2003. The lowest paid 10 percent earned less than $26,570; the highest paid 25 percent earned more than $115,470 annually.

Benefits vary but are usually very good at large employers. For example, those working at the Chicago Board of Trade, one of the world's leading futures exchanges, enjoy numerous benefits. Employees are eligible for vacation six months after employment and receive three weeks after three years. Employees are also paid for sick days, personal days, and eight holidays. During the summer months various departments offer flex time, allowing employees to take Fridays off by working longer hours during the week. Employees also receive numerous forms of insurance, including medical, life, and disability. Full tuition reimbursement is available, as is a company-matched savings plan, a tax-deferred savings plan, and a pension program. Other large exchanges and brokerage houses offer similar combinations of benefits.

◼ WORK ENVIRONMENT

The trading floor is noisy and chaotic, as trading is done using an "open outcry" system. Every broker must be an auctioneer, yelling out his own price bids for purchases and sales. The highest bid wins and silences all the others. When a broker's primal scream is not heard, bids and offers can also be communicated with hand signals.

Brokers stand for most of the day, often in the same place, so that traders interested in their commodity can locate them easily. Each broker wears a distinctly colored jacket with a prominent identification badge. The letter on the badge identifies the broker and appears on the paperwork relating to the trade. Members of the exchange and employees of member firms wear red jackets. Some brokers and traders also have uniquely patterned jackets to further increase their visibility in the pit.

Brokers and traders do not have a nine-to-five job. While commodities trading on the exchange generally takes place from 9:00 A.M. to 1:00 P.M., international trading runs from 2:45 P.M. to 6:50 A.M.

In the rough and tumble world of the futures exchange, emotions run high as people often win or lose six- or seven-figure amounts within hours. Tension is fierce, the pace is frantic, and angry, verbal, and sometimes physical exchanges are not uncommon.

◼ OUTLOOK

The U.S. Bureau of Labor Statistics predicts employment for securities, commodities, and financial services sales agents to grow about as fast as the average through 2012. Growth will result from people expecting high returns on their investments (leading them to increasingly invest in markets), the growing number and increasing complexity of investment options, and the new commodities available for investment due to the increasingly globalized marketplace. Additionally, as people and companies become more interested in and sophisticated about investing, they are entering futures markets and need the services provided by brokers. Baby Boomers are reaching retirement age, and many are looking to invest in markets as a way of saving for their futures; additionally, many women in the workforce and higher household incomes means more investment.

New computer and information technology is rapidly influencing and advancing the industry. A growing number of exchanges now use electronic systems to automate trades, and many use them exclusively. Many systems have unique features designed specifically to meet customers' needs. New technology, such as electronic order entry, hookups to overseas exchanges, and night trading, is rapidly evolving, offering brokers new ways to manage risk and provide price information.

Because many people are attracted to this work by the possibility of earning large incomes, competition for jobs is particularly keen. However, job turnover is also fairly high due to the stress of the work and the fact that many beginning brokers are not able to establish a large enough clientele to be profitable. Small brokerage firms may offer the best opportunities for those just starting out in this work.

■ FOR MORE INFORMATION

This center provides information on workshops, home study courses, educational materials, and publications for futures and securities professionals.

Center for Futures Education
PO Box 309
Grove City, PA 16127
Tel: 724-458-5860
Email: info@thectr.com
http://www.thectr.com

For a history of CBOT, and information on tours and educational programs, contact

Chicago Board of Trade (CBOT)
141 West Jackson Boulevard
Chicago, IL 60604-2994
Tel: 312-435-3500
http://www.cbot.com

For a general overview of options, visit the Learning Center section of the CBOE website.

Chicago Board Options Exchange (CBOE)
400 South LaSalle Street
Chicago, IL 60605
Tel: 888-OPTIONS
Email: help@cboe.com
http://www.cboe.com

The CME offers a wide variety of educational programs and materials, and general information on commodities careers through the Education link of its website.

Chicago Mercantile Exchange (CME)
30 South Wacker Drive
Chicago, IL 60606
Tel: 312-930-6937
Email: info@cme.com
http://www.cme.com

For information on careers and education, contact

National Association of Securities Dealers
1735 K Street, NW
Washington, DC 20006-1500
Tel: 202-728-8000
http://www.nasd.com

For information on membership, training, and registration, contact

National Futures Association
120 Broadway, #1125
New York, NY 10271
Tel: 212-608-8660

Email: information@nfa.futures.org
http://www.nfa.futures.org

The Educational section of the Philadelphia Board of Trade's website provides a glossary of terms, suggested reading, and an overview of the financial industry.

Philadelphia Stock Exchange
1900 Market Street
Philadelphia, PA 19103-3584
Tel: 800-843-7459
Email: info@phlx.com
http://www.phlx.com

Visit the websites or contact the following exchanges for general background information about the field:

Minneapolis Grain Exchange
http://www.mgex.com

New York Board of Trade
http://www.nybot.com

New York Mercantile Exchange
http://www.nymex.com

Communications Equipment Technicians

■ OVERVIEW

Communications equipment technicians install, test, maintain, troubleshoot, and repair a wide variety of telephone and radio equipment used to transmit communications—voices and data—across long distances. This does not include, however, equipment that handles entertainment broadcast to the public via radio or television signals. Most communications equipment technicians work in telephone company offices or on customers' premises. In the United States, approximately 195,500 people work as communications equipment technicians.

■ HISTORY

Alexander Graham Bell (1847–1922) patented the first practical telephone in 1876. By 1878, a commercial telephone company that switched calls between its local customers was operating in New Haven, Connecticut. For many years, telephone connections were made by operators who worked at central offices of telephone companies. A company customer who wanted to speak with another customer had to call the operator at a central office, and the operator would connect the two customer lines together by inserting a metal plug into a socket.

Today, automatic switching equipment has replaced operators for routine connections like this, and telephones are carrying much more than voice messages between local customers. Vast quantities of information are sent across phone lines in the form of visual images, computer data, and telegraph and teletypewriter signals. Furthermore, telephone systems today are part of larger interconnected telecommunications systems. These systems link together telephones with other equipment that sends information via microwave and television transmissions, fiber optics cables, undersea cables, and signals bounced off satellites in space. High-speed computerized switching and routing equipment makes it possible for telecommunications systems to handle millions of calls and other data signals at the same time.

■ THE JOB

Although specific duties vary, most communications equipment technicians share some basic kinds of activities. They work with electrical measuring and testing devices and hand tools; read blueprints, circuit diagrams, and electrical schematics (diagrams); and consult technical manuals. The following paragraphs describe just a few of the many technicians who work in this complex industry.

Central office equipment installers, also called *equipment installation technicians,* are specialists in setting up and taking down the switching and dialing equipment located in telephone company central offices. They install equipment in newly established offices, update existing equipment, add on to facilities that are being expanded, and remove old, outdated apparatus.

Central office repairers, also called *switching equipment technicians* or *central office technicians,* work on the switching equipment that automatically connects lines when customers dial calls. They analyze defects and malfunctions in equipment, make fine adjustments, and test and repair switches and relays. These workers use various special tools, gauges, meters, and ordinary hand tools.

PBX systems technicians or *switching equipment technicians* work on PBXs, or private branch exchanges, which are direct lines that businesses install to bypass phone company lines. PBX systems can handle both voice and data communications and can provide specialized services such as electronic mail and automatic routing of calls at the lowest possible cost.

PBX installers install these systems. They may assemble customized switchboards for customers. *PBX repairers* maintain and repair PBX systems and associated equipment. In addition, they may work on mobile radiophones and microwave transmission devices.

Maintenance administrators test customers' lines within the central office to find causes and locations of malfunctions reported by customers. They report the nature of the trouble to maintenance crews and coordinate their activities to clear up the trouble. Some maintenance administrators work in cable television company offices, diagnosing subscribers' problems with cable television signals and dispatching repairers if necessary. They use highly automated testboards and other equipment to analyze circuits. They enter data into computer files and interpret computer output about trouble areas in the system.

Many workers in this group are concerned with other kinds of communications equipment that are not part of telephone systems. Among these are *radio repairers and mechanics,* who install and repair radio transmitters and receivers. Sometimes they work on other electronics equipment at microwave and fiber optics installations. *Submarine cable equipment technicians* work on the machines and equipment used to send messages through underwater cables. Working in cable offices and stations, they check and adjust transmitters and printers and repair or replace faulty parts. *Office electricians* maintain submarine cable circuits and rearrange connections to ensure that cable service is not interrupted. *Avionics technicians* work on electronic components in aircraft communication, navigation, and flight control systems. *Signal maintainers* or *track switch maintainers* work on railroads. They install, inspect, and maintain the signals, track switches, gate crossings, and communications systems throughout rail networks. *Instrument repairers* work in repair shops, where they repair, test, and modify a variety of communications equipment.

■ REQUIREMENTS
High School

Most employers prefer to hire candidates with at least some postsecondary training in electronics.

QUICK FACTS

SCHOOL SUBJECTS
Mathematics
Technical/shop

PERSONAL SKILLS
Following instructions
Mechanical/manipulative

WORK ENVIRONMENT
Primarily indoors
Primarily multiple locations

MINIMUM EDUCATION LEVEL
Some postsecondary training

SALARY RANGE
$29,170 to $48,230 to $60,990

CERTIFICATION OR LICENSING
Required for certain positions

OUTLOOK
Decline

DOT
822

GOE
05.02.01

NOC
7246

O*NET-SOC
49-2022.00, 49-2022.03

A communications equipment technician checks telephone switching equipment.

So to prepare for this career, you should take computer courses, algebra, geometry, English, physics, and shop classes in high school. Useful shop courses are those that introduce you to principles of electricity and electronics, basic machine repair, reading blueprints and engineering drawings, and using hand tools.

Postsecondary Training

Most telecommunications employers prefer to hire technicians who have already learned most of the necessary skills, so consider getting training in this area either through service in the military or from a postsecondary training program. Programs at community or junior colleges or technical schools in telecommunications technology, electronics, electrical, or electromechanical technology, or even computer maintenance or related subjects, may be appropriate for people who want to become communications equipment technicians. Most programs last two years, although certification in specific areas often can be obtained through a one-year program. Useful classes are those that provide practical knowledge about electricity and electronics and teach the use of hand tools, electronic testing equipment, and computer data terminals. Classes in digital and fiber optic technology are also beneficial.

Applicants for entry-level positions may have to pass tests of their knowledge, general mechanical aptitude, and manual dexterity. Once hired, employees often go through company training programs. They may study practical and theoretical aspects of electricity, electronics, and mathematics that they will need to know for their work. Experienced workers also may attend training sessions from time to time. They need to keep their knowledge up to date as new technology in the rapidly changing telecommunications field affects the way they do their jobs.

Certification or Licensing

Some workers in this field must obtain a license. Federal Communications Commission regulations require that anyone who works with radio transmitting equipment must have a Global Maritime Distress and Safety System (GMDSS) license. In order to receive a license, applicants need to pass a written test on radio laws and operating procedures and take a Morse code examination.

Certification for technicians is available from the National Association of Radio and Telecommunications Engineers. To receive certification, you'll need a certain amount of education and experience in telecommunications, and you'll have to pass an examination.

Other Requirements

You'll need strong mechanical and electrical aptitudes, as well as manual dexterity. Keep in mind, too, that you'll need to be able to distinguish between colors because many wires are color-coded. You should also have problem-solving abilities and the ability to work without a lot of direct supervision. Math and computer skills are also very important; you'll also need to be able to interpret very technical manuals and blueprints. You'll be expected to keep accurate records, so you'll need to be organized.

■ EXPLORING

In high school, you can begin to find out about the work of communications equipment technicians by taking whatever electronics, computer, and electrical shop courses are available, and also other shop courses that help you become familiar with using various tools. Teachers or guidance counselors may be able to help you arrange a visit to a telephone company central office, where you can see telephone equipment and observe workers on the job. It may be possible to obtain a part-time or summer-helper job at a business that sells and repairs electronics equipment. Such a job could provide the opportunity to talk to workers whose skills are similar to those needed by many communications equipment technicians. Serving in the armed forces in a communications section can also provide a way to learn about this field and gain some useful experience.

■ EMPLOYERS

Local and long-distance telephone companies and manufacturers of telephone and other electronic communications equipment employ communications equipment technicians. Work is also available with electrical repair shops and cable television companies.

■ STARTING OUT

Beginning technicians can apply directly to the employment office of the local telephone company. Many times it is necessary for newly hired workers to take a position in a different part of the company until an opening as a technician becomes available. However, telephone companies have been reducing the number of technicians they need in recent years, and competition for these positions is especially heavy.

Information on job openings in this field may be available through the offices of the state employment service and through classified advertisements in newspapers. Because many communications equipment technicians are members of unions such as the Communications Workers of America (CWA) and the International Brotherhood of Electrical Workers, job seekers can contact their local offices for job leads and assistance, or visit the CWA website. The Personal Communications Industry Association also offers free job listings on its Wireless Jobnet online. Graduates of technical programs may be able to find out about openings at local companies through the school's job placement services or through contacts with teachers and administrators.

■ ADVANCEMENT

The advancement possibilities for communications equipment technicians depend on the area of the telecommunications industry in which they work. Because of changes in equipment and technology, workers who hope to advance will need to have received recent training or update their skills through additional training. This training may be offered through employers or can be obtained through technical institutes or telecommunications associations.

Advancement opportunities in telephone companies may be limited because of the fact that many telephone companies are reducing their workforces and will have less need for certain types of workers in the future. This will result in fewer positions to move into and increased competition for more advanced positions. However, some workers may be able to advance to supervisory or administrative positions.

Many workers can advance through education resulting in an associate's or bachelor's degree. Workers who have completed two- or four-year programs in electrical or telecommunications engineering programs have the best opportunity to advance and can become engineering assistants, engineers, or telecommunications specialists.

■ EARNINGS

Earnings vary among communications equipment workers depending on their area of specialization, the size of their employer, and their location. The U.S. Department of Labor reports that median hourly earnings for telecommunication equipment installers and repairers

COMMUNICATIONS EQUIPMENT IN HISTORY

The first public telegraph line was invented by William Cooke (1806–79) and Charles Wheatstone (1802–75) of England and was installed to control train movements. Wires led electric currents to needles that identified letters. One of the earliest general communications concerned the sighting of a murderer boarding a train at a station. By the time the train reached the next station, police were waiting to arrest him.

were $23.19 in 2003. A technician earning this amount and working full-time at 40 hours a week would have a yearly income of approximately $48,230. The lowest paid 10 percent of telecommunications equipment technicians earned less than $14.03 per hour (approximately 29,170 yearly); the highest paid 10 percent earned more than $29.32 per hour (approximately $60,990 annually).

The Department of Labor also reports that the 2003 median hourly wage for radio mechanics was $17.82. The annual income for a technician working full-time at this pay rate would be approximately $37,070. At the low end of the pay scale, 10 percent made less than $10.60 hourly (approximately $22,040 per year); at the high end, 10 percent made more than $28.82 hourly (approximately $59,940 annually).

Most workers in this group who are employed by telephone companies are union members, and their earnings are set by contracts between the union and the company. Many currently employed communications equipment technicians have several years of experience and are at the higher end of the pay scale. Most workers in this field receive extra pay for hours worked at night, on weekends, or over 40 hours a week. Benefits vary but generally include paid vacations, paid holidays, sick leaves, and health insurance. In addition, some companies offer pension and retirement plans.

■ WORK ENVIRONMENT

Communications equipment technicians usually work 40 hours a week. Some work shifts at night, on weekends, and on holidays because telecommunications systems must give uninterrupted service and trouble can occur at any time.

Central telephone offices are clean, well lighted, and well ventilated. Communications equipment technicians may also be working on site, which may require some crawling around on office floors and some bending. Even if these workers are running cables, they aren't likely to be doing much heavy lifting; machinery assists them in some of the more strenuous work. These workers may work alone, or they may be supervising the work of others. Some communications equipment technicians also work directly with clients.

The work can be stressful, as technicians are often expected to work quickly to remedy urgent problems with communication equipment. Some technicians who work for large companies with clients nationwide must also travel as part of their jobs.

■ OUTLOOK

The U.S. Department of Labor predicts the overall employment rate for communications equipment technicians to decline through 2012. Nevertheless, job availability will depend on the technician's area of specialization. For example, technicians working as central office and PBX installers should find numerous job opportunities, in part because growing use of the Internet places new demands on communications networks. On the other hand, employment for radio mechanics and other installers is expected to decline as pre-wired buildings and extremely reliable equipment translate into less need for maintenance and repair. New technology relies on transmission through telecommunications networks rather than central-office switching equipment. There are far fewer mechanical devices that break, wear out, and need to be periodically cleaned and lubricated. These networks contain self-diagnosing features that detect problems and, in some cases, route operations around a trouble spot until repairs can be made. When problems occur, it is usually easier to replace parts rather than repair them. Competition for existing positions will be keen, and workers with the best qualifications stand the best chance of obtaining available jobs.

■ FOR MORE INFORMATION

To learn about issues affecting jobs in telecommunications, contact or visit the CWA website.

Communications Workers of America (CWA)
501 Third Street, NW
Washington, DC 20001-2797
Tel: 202-434-1100
http://www.cwa-union.org

For information on union membership, contact
International Brotherhood of Electrical Workers
1125 15th Street, NW
Washington, DC 20005
Tel: 202-833-7000
http://ibew.org

For information on certification, contact
National Association of Radio and Telecommunications Engineers
167 Village Street
Medway, MA 02053
Tel: 800-896-2783
http://www.narte.org

For information on educational programs and job opportunities in wireless technology (cellular, PCS, and satellite), contact
Personal Communications Industry Association
500 Montgomery Street, Suite 700
Alexandria, VA 22314-1561
Tel: 800-759-0300
http://www.pcia.com

For information about conferences, special programs, and membership, contact
Women in Cable and Telecommunications
14555 Avion Parkway, Suite 250
Chantilly, VA 20151
Tel: 703-234-9810
Email: information@wict.org
http://www.wict.org

Community Health Nurses

■ OVERVIEW

Community health nurses, also known as *public health nurses,* provide community-based health care. They organize, promote, and deliver care to community groups in urban, rural, and remote settings. They may work in community health centers in large and small cities, or they may travel to remote locations to bring health care treatment and information to people living in those areas. They may provide public health services and educational programs to schools, correctional facilities, homeless shelters, elderly care facilities, and maternal and well-baby clinics. Some community health nurses provide specialized care in communities where immediate physician services are not available. Community health nurses often work for a state funded or federally funded agency, or a private health provider company.

■ THE JOB

Community health nurses work with many aspects of a community's population. Their duties vary greatly depending on their locale and assignments. Some community health nurses may instruct a class for expectant mothers, visit new parents to help them learn how to care for their new baby, talk with senior citizens about exercise and nutrition, or give immunizations at a community center or other site. Other community health nurses may travel to remote areas where health care is not readily available. Here they may work with a medical doctor or nurse practitioner to provide necessary medical care and health education. Community health nurses usually work with all ages, ranging in age from birth to the elderly. They also may work with different groups of people, including immigrants, homeless shelter residents, and persons who are developmentally or physically challenged.

Community health nurses may also be educators who plan, promote, and administer community-wide wellness programs. They may also give presentations to area organizations, schools, and health care facilities regarding health, safety, exercise, and nutrition.

Some community health nurses may work with managed care providers and programs sponsored by health maintenance organizations.

As with almost all health care professions today, community health nurses spend a great deal of time keeping records and charts and documenting the services they provide in order to meet insurance, government, and Medicare requirements.

■ REQUIREMENTS
Postsecondary Training

Nurses who specialize in a specific nursing field such as a community health nurse must first become registered nurses. (See Registered Nurses.) Many community health nurses are required to have some general nursing experience, since they may be required to work with patients with a wide range of health problems. Entry-level requirements depend on the employing agency and the availability of nurses in that specialty and geographical region. Nurses who wish to specialize in community health care may choose to attend graduate school.

Certification or Licensing

Certification is a voluntary process. However, having credentials is a sign of competency and experience in nursing and may make the difference when applying for a job. Certification for community health nurses is available through the American Nurses Credentialing Center. Requirements for certification include holding a current nursing license, having a certain amount of professional experience, and passing the certification exam.

To practice in any of the 50 states and the District of Columbia, nurses must have graduated from an accredited program and pass a national licensing exam.

Other Requirements

Community health nurses should feel comfortable working with all ages and people from all cultural backgrounds. Good communication skills are essential, including the ability to listen and respond to the patient's needs. Flexibility is also a requirement, since duties vary greatly from hour to hour and day to day. Community health nurses must be able to work independently, have good organizational skills, and also have the ability to supervise aides and other support people.

■ EXPLORING

You can learn more about this field by reading books on careers in nursing, surfing the Web for information on nursing, and talking with your high school guidance counselor, school nurse, or local public health nurse. You might also consider visiting your local hospital or clinic to observe the work of nurses.

■ EMPLOYERS

Community health nurses are employed by schools, correctional facilities, homeless shelters, elder care facilities, maternal and well-baby clinics, hospitals, managed-care facilities, long-term-care facilities, clinics, industry, private homes, camps, and government agencies.

■ STARTING OUT

Registered nurses may apply for employment directly to hospitals, nursing homes, companies, and government agencies that hire nurses. Jobs can also be obtained through school placement offices, by signing up with employment agencies specializing in placement of nursing personnel, or

QUICK FACTS

SCHOOL SUBJECTS
Biology
Chemistry

PERSONAL SKILLS
Helping/teaching
Technical/scientific

WORK ENVIRONMENT
Primarily indoors
Primarily multiple locations

MINIMUM EDUCATION LEVEL
Some postsecondary training

SALARY RANGE
$35,290 to $49,550 to $71,210

CERTIFICATION OR LICENSING
Voluntary (certification)
Required by all states (licensing)

OUTLOOK
Faster than the average

DOT
075

GOE
14.02.01

NOC
3152

O*NET-SOC
29-1111.00

through the state employment office. Other sources of jobs include nurses' associations, professional journals, newspaper want ads, and Internet job sites.

■ ADVANCEMENT

Administrative and supervisory positions in the nursing field go to nurses who have earned at least the bachelor of science degree in nursing. Nurses with many years of experience who are graduates of the diploma program may achieve supervisory positions, but requirements for such promotions have become more difficult in recent years and in many cases require at least the bachelor of science in nursing degree.

■ EARNINGS

According to the U.S. Department of Labor, registered nurses (a group including community health nurses) had a median yearly income of $49,550 in 2003. The lowest paid 10 percent earned less than $35,290 annually, while the middle 50 percent earned between $41,130 and $59,090 per year. The top paid 10 percent of registered nurses earned more than $71,210 annually.

Salary is determined by many factors, including nursing specialty, education, place of employment, geographical location, and work experience. Flexible schedules are available for most full-time nurses. Employers usually provide health and life insurance, and some offer educational reimbursements and year-end bonuses to their full-time staff.

■ WORK ENVIRONMENT

Working environments vary depending on the community health nurse's responsibilities. Some community health nurses may work in clean, well-lighted buildings in upscale communities, while others may find themselves working in remote, underdeveloped areas that have poor living conditions. Personal safety may be an issue at times. Some community health nurses may also work overseas in government or private enterprises.

All nursing careers have some health and disease risks; however, adherence to health and safety guidelines greatly minimizes the chance of contracting infectious diseases such as hepatitis and AIDS. Medical knowledge and good safety measures are also needed to limit the nurse's exposure to toxic chemicals, radiation, and other hazards.

■ OUTLOOK

Nursing specialties will be in great demand in the coming years. The U.S. Department of Labor lists nursing as one of 10 occupations predicted to have the largest number of new jobs. The Department of Labor projects the employment rate for registered nurses to grow faster than the average through 2012. In addition to the need for nurses to fill new jobs, there will also be the need for those to replace nurses who leave the field for retirement or other work.

The outlook for community health nurses is excellent. The U.S. Bureau of the Census estimates that the number of individuals aged 65 or older will double by 2030 (going from the approximately 35 million in 2000 to approximately 70 million in 2030). As our population grows older, the need for community-based nursing will increase. In addition, managed care organizations will continue to need community health nurses to provide health promotion and disease prevention programs to their subscribers.

■ FOR MORE INFORMATION

For additional information on nuring careers, contact the following associations:

American Association of Colleges of Nursing
One Dupont Circle, NW, Suite 530
Washington, DC 20036
Tel: 202-463-6930
http://www.aacn.nche.edu

Association of Community Health Nursing Educators
11 Cornell Road
Latham, NY 12110-1499
Tel: 518-782-9400 x289
Email: ACHNE@nysna.org
http://www.uncc.edu/achne

To learn more about certification, contact
American Nurses Credentialing Center
600 Maryland Avenue, SW, Suite 100 West
Washington, DC 20024-2571
Tel: 800-284-2378
Email: ANCC@ana.org
http://www.nursingworld.org/ancc

Composers and Arrangers

■ OVERVIEW

Composers create much of the music heard every day on radio and television, in theaters and concert halls, on recordings and in advertising, and through any other medium of musical presentation. Composers write symphonies, concertos, and operas; scores for theater, television, and cinema; and music for musical theater, recording artists, and commercial advertising. They may combine elements of classical music with elements of popular musical styles such as rock, jazz, reggae, folk, and others. *Arrangers* take composers' musical compositions and transcribe them for other instruments or voices; work them into scores for film, theater, or television; or adapt them to styles that are different from the one in which the music was written.

■ HISTORY

Classical (used in the widest sense) composition probably dates back to the late Middle Ages, when musical notation began to develop in Christian monasteries. In those times and for some centuries thereafter, the church was the main patron of musical composition. During the 14th century, or possibly earlier, the writing of music in score (that is, for several instruments or instruments and voices) began to take place. This was the beginning of orchestral writing. Composers then were mostly sponsored by the church and were supposed to be religiously motivated in their work, which was not to be considered an expression of their own emotions. It was probably not until the end of the 15th century that the work of a composer began to be recognized as a statement of individual expression. Recognition of composers did not really become common until several centuries later. Even Johann Sebastian Bach, writing in the 18th century, was known more as an organist and choirmaster during his lifetime.

The writing of music in score was the beginning of a great change in the history of music. The craft of making musical instruments and the techniques of playing them were advancing also. By the beginning of the Baroque Period, around 1600, these changes brought musical composition to a new stage of development, which was enhanced by patronage from secular sources. The nobility had taken an interest in sponsoring musical composition, and over the next two to three hundred years they came to supplant the church as the main patrons of composers. Under their patronage, composers had more room to experiment and develop new musical styles.

During the Baroque Period, which lasted until about 1750, there was a flowering of musical forms, including opera. In the early 1600s, Rome became preeminent in opera, using the chorus and dance to embellish the operatic spectacle. Instrumental music also grew during this period, reaching its greatest flowering in the work of Johann Sebastian Bach and George Frederick Handel. The major musical forms of Baroque origin were the sonata and cantata, both largely attributed to the composers of opera.

The "true" Classical Period in music began in about the mid-18th century and lasted through the 19th century. Composers embellishing the sonata form now developed the symphony. Through the latter half of the 19th century, most composers of symphonies, concerti, chamber music, and other instrumental forms adhered to the strict formality of the Classical tradition. In the 19th century, however, many composers broke from Classical formalism, instilling greater emotionalism, subjectivity, and individualism in their work. The new musical style evolved into what became formally known as the Romantic movement in music. Romanticism did not replace classicism, but rather, it existed side by side with the older form. A transitional figure in the break from classicism was Ludwig van Beethoven, whose compositions elevated the symphonic form to its highest level. Other composers who perfected the Romantic style included Franz Schubert, Franz Liszt, Johannes Brahms, Hector Berlioz, and Peter Ilich Tchaikovsky in orchestral music, and Giuseppe Verdi and Richard Wagner in opera.

Many of the composers of the early Classical Period labored for little more than recognition. Their monetary rewards were often meager. In the 19th century, however, as the stature of the composers grew, they were able to gain more control over their own work and the proceeds that it produced. The opera composers, in particular, were able to reap quite handsome profits.

Another abrupt break from tradition occurred at the beginning of the 20th century. At that time composers began to turn away from Romanticism and seek new and original styles and sounds. Audiences sometimes were repulsed by these new musical sounds, but eventually they were accepted and imitated by other composers. One of the most successful of the post-Romantic composers was Igor Stravinsky, whose landmark work *The Rite of Spring* was hailed by some to be the greatest work of the century.

Through the 20th century composers continued to write

QUICK FACTS

SCHOOL SUBJECTS
Music
Theater/dance

PERSONAL SKILLS
Artistic
Communication/ideas

WORK ENVIRONMENT
Primarily indoors
Primarily one location

MINIMUM EDUCATION LEVEL
High school diploma

SALARY RANGE
$14,870 to $32,530 to
$72,710

CERTIFICATION OR LICENSING
None available

OUTLOOK
About as fast as the average

DOT
152

GOE
01.05.02

NOC
5132

O*NET-SOC
27-2041.02, 27-2041.03

PROFILE: WOLFGANG AMADEUS MOZART (1756–91)

Mozart was one of the outstanding masters of the Classical Period. He composed works in almost every form and his masterpieces are standard repertoire for piano, symphony orchestra, and opera.

Mozart began his musical studies with his father, Leopold, when he was four years old. He played the clavichord and harpsichord and composed minuets and other pieces. At the age of six the boy, with his sister, Marianne, gave concerts in Munich and Vienna. He wrote his first opera, *La finta semplice*, in 1768. At the age of 13, he became director of concerts for the archbishop of Salzburg. Mozart left Salzburg for Vienna in 1781 and continued his prolific composing career while earning a living by teaching, giving concerts, and composing light dance music. He died at the age of 35 from illness and overwork, and he was buried in an unmarked pauper's grave.

During his short lifetime, Mozart composed more than 600 works, including more than 25 piano concertos, more than 40 symphonies, and numerous string quartets, piano sonatas, operas, divertimenti, serenades, and dance music.

music in the styles of the past and to experiment with new styles. Some contemporary composers, such as George Gershwin and Leonard Bernstein, wrote for both popular and serious audiences. John Cage, Philip Glass, Steve Reich, and other composers moved even further from traditional forms and musical instruments, experimenting with electronically created music, in which an electronic instrument, such as a synthesizer, is used to compose and play music. An even more significant advance is the use of computers as a compositional tool. In the 21st century, the only thing predictable in musical composition is that experimentation and change are certain to continue.

■ THE JOB

Composers express themselves in music much as writers express themselves with words and painters with line, shape, and color. Composing is hard work. Although influenced by what they hear, composers' compositions are original because they reflect their own interpretation and use of musical elements. All composers use the same basic musical elements, including harmony, melody, counterpoint, and rhythm, but each composer applies these elements in a unique way. Music schools teach all of the elements that go into composition, providing com-

posers with the tools needed for their work, but how a composer uses these tools to create music is what sets an individual apart.

There is no prescribed way for a composer to go about composing. All composers work in a somewhat different way, but generally speaking they pursue their work in some kind of regular, patterned way, in much the same fashion of a novelist or a painter. Composers may work in different areas of classical music, writing, for example, symphonies, operas, concerti, music for a specific instrument or grouping of instruments, and for voice. Many composers also work in popular music and incorporate popular music ideas in their classical compositions.

Composers may create compositions out of sheer inspiration, with or without a particular market in mind, or they may be commissioned to write a piece of music for a particular purpose. Composers who write music on their own then have the problem of finding someone to perform their music in the hopes that it will be well received and lead to further performances and possibly a recording. The more a composer's music is played and recorded, the greater the chances to sell future offerings and to receive commissions for new work. Commissions come from institutions (where the composer may or may not be a faculty member), from societies and associations, and orchestral groups, or from film, television, and commercial projects. Almost every film has a score, the music playing throughout the film apart from any songs that may also be in the film.

A composer who wishes to make a living by writing music should understand the musical marketplace as well as possible. It should be understood that only a small percentage of music composers can make their living solely by writing music. To make a dent in the marketplace one should be familiar with its major components:

Performance. Composers usually rely on one of two ways to have their music performed: They contact musical performers or producers who are most likely to be receptive to their style of composition, or they may write for a musical group in which they are performers.

Music publishing. Music publishers seek composers who are talented and whose work they feel it will be profitable to promote. They take a cut of the royalties, but they relieve composers of all of the business and legal detail of their profession. Composers today have rather commonly turned to self-publishing.

Copying. A musical composition written for several pieces or voices requires copying into various parts. Composers may do this work themselves, but it is an exacting task for which professional copiers may be employed. Many composers themselves take on copying work as a sideline.

Computerization. Computers have become an increasingly important tool for composing and copying. Some composers have set up incredibly sophisticated computerized studios in which they compose, score, and play an orchestrated piece by computer. They can also do the copying and produce a recording. Perhaps the most significant enhancement to the home studio is the Musical Instrument Digital Interface, which transposes the composer's work into computer language and then converts it into notation.

Recording. Knowing the recording industry is an important aspect in advancing a composer's career. An unrecognized composer will find it difficult to catch on with a commercial recording company, but it is not uncommon for a composer to make his own recording and handle the distribution and promotion as well.

Film and television. There is a very large market for original compositions in feature and industrial films, television programs, and videos. The industry is in constant need of original scores and thematic music.

Students interested in composing can tap into any number of organizations and associations for more detail on any area of musical composition. One such organization providing support and information is Meet the Composer, which is headquartered in New York City and has several national affiliates.

Arrangers generally create a musical background for a preexisting melody. An arranger may create an introduction and a coda (ending) for a melody as well as add countermelodies (additional melodies) to the original melody. In effect, the arranger composes additional material that was not provided by the original composer and ensures that the original melody is set off by its background in an effective manner. Most arrangers are musicians themselves and have an excellent knowledge of musical styles and current trends.

An *orchestrator* takes a piece of music, perhaps one that already has a basic arrangement, and assigns the parts to specific instruments in the orchestra or other ensemble. For this reason, the orchestrator must have a tremendous amount of knowledge regarding exactly what the various instruments can and cannot do. An orchestrator may decide, for example, that a particular melody should be played by a solo flute or by a flute and an oboe, so that a very specific sound will be achieved. An orchestrator must also know how to notate parts for various instruments. All the choices that the orchestrator makes will have a significant impact on the way the music will sound. Arranging and orchestrating are very closely related, and many professionals perform both tasks. Many composers also do their own arranging and orchestrating.

■ REQUIREMENTS
High School

There is no specific course of training that will help you to become a composer. Many composers begin composing from a very early age and receive tutoring and training to encourage their talent. Musically inclined students should continue their private studies and take advantage of everything musical their high school offers. Specially gifted students usually find their way to schools or academies that specialize in music or the arts. These students may begin learning composition in this special environment, and some might begin to create original compositions.

Postsecondary Training

After high school, you can continue your education in any of the numerous colleges and universities or special music schools or conservatories that offer bachelor's and higher degrees. Your course of study will include music history, music criticism, music theory, harmony, counterpoint, rhythm, melody, and ear training. In most major music schools courses in composition are offered along with orchestration and arranging. Courses are also taught covering voice and the major musical instruments, including keyboard, guitar, and, more recently, synthesizer. Most schools now cover computer techniques as applied to music as well. It may also be helpful to learn at least one foreign language; German, French, and Italian are good choices.

Other Requirements

None of this is to say that study in a musical institution is required for a composer or is any guarantee of success. Some say that composing cannot be taught, that the combination of skills, talent, and inspiration required to create music is a highly individual occurrence. Authorities have argued on both sides of this issue without resolution. It does appear that genetics plays a strong part in musical ability; musical people often come from musical families. There are many contradictions of this, however, and some authorities cite the musical environment as being highly influential. The great composers were extraordinarily gifted, and it is very possible that achieving even moderate success in music requires special talent. Nevertheless, you will not be successful unless you work extremely hard and remain dedicated to improving your compositional talents at every opportunity. Prospective composers are also advised to become proficient on at least one instrument.

■ EXPLORING

Musical programs offered by local schools, YMCAs, and community centers offer good beginning opportunities. It is especially helpful to learn to play a musical instrument, such as the piano, violin, or cello. Attending concerts and recitals and reading about music and musicians and their careers will also provide you with good background and experience. There are also any number of videos available through your school or local library that will teach you about music. You should also form or join musical groups and attempt to write music for your group to perform. There are also many books that provide good reference information on careers in composing and arranging.

■ EMPLOYERS

Composers are self-employed. They complete their work in their own studios and then try to sell their pieces to music publishers, film and television production companies, or recording companies. Once their work becomes well known, clients, such as film and television producers, dance companies, or musical theater producers, may commission original pieces from composers. In this case, the client provides a story line, time period, mood, and other specifications the composer must honor in the creation of a musical score.

Advertising agencies and studios that make commercials and film, television, and video production studios might have a few "house" composers on staff. Schools often underwrite a composer in residence, and many composers work as professors in college and university music departments while continuing to compose. For the most part, however, composers are on their own to create and promote their work.

Most arrangers work on a freelance basis for record companies, musical artists, music publishers, and film and television production companies.

■ STARTING OUT

In school, young composers should try to have their work performed either at school concerts or by local school or community ensembles. This will also most likely involve the composers in copying and scoring their work and possibly even directing. Student film projects can provide an opportunity for experience at film composing and scoring. Working in school or local musical theater companies can provide valuable experience. Personal connections made in these projects may be very helpful in the professional world that lies ahead. Developing a portfolio of work will be helpful as the composer enters a professional career.

Producers of public service announcements, or PSAs, for radio and television are frequently on the lookout for pro bono (volunteer) work that can provide opportunities for young, willing composers. Such opportunities

may be listed in trade magazines, such as *Variety* (available in print or online at http://www.variety.com) and *Show Business* (in print or online at http://showbusiness weekly.com).

Joining the American Federation of Musicians and other musical societies and associations is another good move for aspiring composers. Among the associations that can be contacted are Meet the Composer, the American Composers Alliance, Broadcast Music, Inc., the Society of Composers, and the American Society of Composers, Authors, and Publishers (ASCAP), all located in New York City. These associations and the trade papers are also good sources for leads on grants and awards for which composers can apply.

Young composers, arrangers, songwriters, and jingle writers can also work their way into the commercial advertising business by doing some research and taking entry-level jobs with agencies that handle musical commercials.

■ ADVANCEMENT

Moving ahead in the music world is done strictly on an individual basis. There is no hierarchical structure to climb, although in record companies a person with music writing talent might move into a producing or A&R (Artist & Repertoire) job and be able to exercise compositional skills in those capacities. Advancement is based on talent, determination, and, probably, luck. Some composers become well known for their work with film scores; John Williams, of *Star Wars* fame, is one.

Advancement for composers and arrangers often takes place on a highly personal level. They may progress through their careers to writing or transcribing music of greater complexity and in more challenging structures. They may develop a unique style and even develop new forms and traditions of music. One day, their names might be added to the list of the great composers and arrangers.

■ EARNINGS

A few composers make huge annual incomes, while many make little or nothing. Some make a very large income in one or two years and none in succeeding years. While many composers receive royalties on repeat performances of their work, most depend on commissions to support themselves. Commissions vary widely according to the type of work and the industry for which the work will be performed. The U.S. Department of Labor reports that the median yearly income for music directors, composers, and arrangers holding salaried positions was $32,530 in 2003. However, earnings vary widely. The lowest paid 10 percent of this group made less than $14,870, while the highest paid 10 percent earned more than $72,710.

Many composers, however, do not hold full-time salaried positions and are only paid in royalties for their compositions that sell. According to ASCAP, the royalty rate for 2004 was $.085 per song per album sold. The $.085 is divided between the composer and the publisher, based on their agreement. If the album sold 25,000 copies in 2004, the royalties the composer and publisher received would be $2,125. Naturally, if this song is the only one the composer has that brings in income during this time, his or her annual earnings are extremely low (keep in mind that the composer receives only a percentage of the $2,125).

On the other hand, a composer who creates music for a feature film may have substantial earnings, according to the ASCAP. Factors that influence the composer's earnings include how much music is needed for the film, the film's total budget, if the film will be distributed to a general audience or have only limited showings, and the reputation of the composer. The ASCAP notes that depending on such factors, a composer can receive fees ranging from $20,000 for a lower-budget, small film to more than $1,000,000 if the film is a big-budget release from a major studio and the composer is well known.

Many composers and arrangers must hold a second job in order to make ends meet financially. In some cases these second jobs, such as teaching, will provide benefits such as health insurance and paid vacation time. Composers and arrangers who work independently, however, need to provide insurance and other benefits for themselves.

WORK ENVIRONMENT

The physical conditions of a composer's workplace can vary according to personal taste and what is affordable. Some work in expensive, state-of-the-art home studios, others in a bare room with an electric keyboard or a guitar. An aspiring composer may work in a cramped and cluttered room in a New York City tenement or in a Hollywood ranch home.

For the serious composer the work is likely to be personally rewarding but financially unrewarding. For the commercial writer, some degree of financial reward is more likely, but competition is fierce, and top earnings go only to the rarest of individuals. Getting started requires great dedication and sacrifice. Even those protected by academia must give up most of their spare time to composing, often sitting down at the piano when exhausted from a full day of teaching. There are many frustrations along the way. The career composer must learn to live with rejection and have the verve and determination to keep coming back time and again. Under these circum-stances, composers can only succeed by having complete faith in their own work.

OUTLOOK

The U.S. Department of Labor, which classifies composers and arrangers in the category of musicians, singers, and related workers, predicts employment in this field to grow about as fast as the average through 2012. Although there are no reliable statistics on the number of people who make their living solely from composing and/or arranging, the general consensus is that very few people can sustain themselves through composing and arranging alone. The field is highly competitive and crowded with highly talented people trying to have their music published and played. There are only a limited number of commissions, grants, and awards available at any time, and the availability of these is often subjected to changes in the economy. On the other hand, many films continue to be made each year, particularly as cable television companies produce more and more original programs. However, the chances of new composers and arrangers supporting themselves by their music alone will likely always remain small.

FOR MORE INFORMATION

For profiles of composers of concert music, visit the ACA website.

American Composers Alliance (ACA)
73 Spring Street, Room 505
New York, NY 10012
Tel: 212-362-8900
Email: info@composers.com
http://www.composers.com

For professional and artistic development resources, contact

American Composers Forum
332 Minnesota Street, Suite East 145
St. Paul, MN 55101-1300
Tel: 651-228-1407
Email: mail@composersforum.org
http://www.composersforum.org

For music news, news on legislation affecting musicians, and the magazine International Musician, *contact*

American Federation of Musicians of the United States and Canada
1501 Broadway, Suite 600
New York, NY 10036
Tel: 212-869-1330
Email: info@afm.org
http://www.afm.org

For articles on songwriting, information on workshops and awards, and practical information about the business of music, contact

American Society of Composers, Authors, and Publishers
One Lincoln Plaza
New York, NY 10023
Tel: 800-95-ASCAP
Email: info@ascap.com
http://www.ascap.com

This organization represents songwriters, composers, and music publishers. Its website has useful information on the industry.

Broadcast Music Inc.
320 West 57th Street
New York, NY 10019-3790
Tel: 212-586-2000
http://www.bmi.com

The IAWM website has information for and about women composers.

International Alliance for Women in Music (IAWM)
Department of Music
422 South 11th Street, Room 209
Indiana University of Pennsylvania
Indiana, PA 15705-1070
Tel: 724-357-7918
Email: IAWM-info@grove.iup.edu
http://music.acu.edu/www/iawm

The Meet the Composer website has information on awards and residencies as well as interviews with composers active in the field today.

Meet the Composer
75 Ninth Avenue, 3R Suite C
New York, NY 10011
Tel: 212-645-6949
http://www.meetthecomposer.org

For information on student membership and commission competitions, contact

Society of Composers
Old Chelsea State
Box 450
New York, NY 10113-0450
http://www.societyofcomposers.org

The SGA offers song critiques and other workshops in select cities. Visit its website for further information on such events

and answers to frequently asked questions about becoming a songwriter.

Songwriters Guild of America (SGA)
1500 Harbor Boulevard
Weehawken, NJ 07086
Tel: 201-867-7603
http://www.songwritersguild.com

Computer-Aided Design Drafters and Technicians

■ OVERVIEW

Computer-aided design drafters and technicians, sometimes called *CAD technicians* or *CAD designers,* use computer-based systems to produce or revise technical illustrations needed in the design and development of machines, products, buildings, manufacturing processes, and other work. They use CAD machinery to manipulate and create design concepts so that they are feasible to produce and use in the real world.

■ HISTORY

Just over 20 years ago, drafting and designing were done with a pencil and paper on a drafting table. To make a circle, drafters used a compass. To draw straight lines and the correct angles, they used a straight-edge, T-square, and other tools. With every change required before a design was right, it was "back to the drawing board" to get out the eraser, sharpen the pencil, and revise the drawing. Everybody did it this way, whether the design was simple or complex: automobiles, hammers, printed circuit boards, utility piping, highways, or buildings.

CAD technology came about in the 1970s with the development of microprocessors (computer processors in the form of miniaturized integrated circuits contained on tiny silicon chips). Microprocessors opened up many new uses for computers by greatly reducing the size of computers while also increasing their power and speed.

Interestingly, the drafters and designers working to develop these microprocessors were also the first to benefit from this technology. As the circuits on the silicon chips that the designers were working on became too complex to diagram by pencil and paper, the designers began to use the chips themselves to help store information, create models, and produce diagrams for the design of new chip circuits. This was just the beginning of computer-assisted design and drafting technology. Today, there are tens of thousands of CAD workstations in industrial settings. CAD systems greatly speed up and simplify the designer's and drafter's work. They do more than just let the operator "draw" the technical illustration on the screen. They add the speed and power of computer processing, plus software with technical information that ease the designer/drafter's tasks. CAD systems make complex mathematical calculations, spot problems, offer advice, and provide a wide range of other assistance. Today, nearly all drafting tasks are done with such equipment.

As the Internet has developed, CAD operators can send a CAD drawing across the world in a matter of minutes attached to an email message. Gone are the days of rolling up a print and mailing it. Technology has once again made work more efficient for the CAD designer and drafter.

■ THE JOB

Technicians specializing in CAD technology usually work in the design and drafting activities associated with new product research and development, although many work in other areas such as structural mechanics or piping. CAD technicians must combine drafting and computer skills. They work in any field where detailed drawings, diagrams, and layouts are important aspects of developing new product designs—for example, in architecture, electronics, and in the manufacturing of automobiles, aircraft, computers, and missiles and other defense systems. Most CAD technicians specialize in a particular industry or on one part of a design.

CAD technicians work under the direction and supervision of *CAD engineers and designers,* experts highly trained in applying computer technology to industrial design and manufacturing. These designers and engineers plan how to relate the CAD technology and equipment to the design process. They are also the ones who give assignments to the CAD technicians.

Jackie Sutherland started as a drafter right out of high school, working at a major Midwestern diesel engine manufacturer. Since then, he has moved into a designer's role. In his 25 years on the job, he has seen the transfer from drafting table to CAD workstation.

"I work with everyone from the customer to the engineers, suppliers, pattern makers, and the assembly line from the project concept through the production," says Sutherland of his work as a CAD designer.

Technicians work at specially designed and equipped interactive computer graphics workstations. They call up computer files that hold data about a new product; they then run the programs to convert that information into diagrams and drawings of the product. These are displayed on a video display screen, which then acts as an electronic drawing board. Following the directions of a CAD engineer or designer, the CAD technician enters changes to the product's design into the computer. The technician merges these changes into the data file, then displays the corrected diagrams and drawings.

The software in CAD systems is very helpful to the user—it offers suggestions and advice and even points out errors. The most important advantage of working with a CAD system is that it saves the technician from the lengthy process of having to produce, by hand, the original and then the revised product drawings and diagrams.

The CAD workstation is equipped to allow technicians to perform calculations, develop simulations, and manipulate and modify the displayed material. Using typed commands at a keyboard, a stylus or light pen for touching the screen display, a mouse, joystick, or other electronic methods of interacting with the display, technicians can move, rotate, or zoom in on any aspect of the drawing on the screen, and project three-dimensional images from two-dimensional sketches. They can make experimental changes to the design and then run tests on the modified design to determine its qualities, such as weight, strength, flexibility, and the cost of materials that would be required. Compared to traditional drafting and design techniques, CAD offers virtually unlimited freedom to explore alternatives, and in far less time.

When the product design is completed and the necessary information is assembled in the computer files, technicians may store the newly developed data, output it on a printer, transfer it to another computer, or send it directly to another step of the automated testing or manufacturing process.

QUICK FACTS

SCHOOL SUBJECTS
Computer science
Mathematics
Technical/shop

PERSONAL SKILLS
Mechanical/manipulative
Technical/scientific

WORK ENVIRONMENT
Primarily indoors
Primarily one location

MINIMUM EDUCATION LEVEL
Some postsecondary training

SALARY RANGE
$24,570 to $37,300 to $56,260+

CERTIFICATION OR LICENSING
Voluntary

OUTLOOK
More slowly than the average

DOT
003

GOE
02.08.03

NOC
2253

O*NET-SOC
17-3011.01, 17-3011.02, 17-3012.01, 17-3012.02, 17-3013.00

A computer-aided design drafter works on a design at his computer.

Once the design is approved for production, CAD technicians may use their computers to assist in making detailed drawings of certain parts of the design. They may also prepare designs and drawings of the tools or equipment, such as molds, cutting tools, and jigs, that must be specially made in order to manufacture the product. As the product moves toward production, technicians, drafters, and designers may work closely with those assembling the product to ensure the same quality found with prototype testing.

CAD technicians must keep records of all of their test procedures and results. They may need to present written reports, tables, or charts to document their test results or other findings. If a particular system, subsystem, or material has not met a testing or production requirement, technicians may be asked to suggest a way to rearrange the system's components or substitute alternate materials.

The company Sutherland works for also uses interoffice and Internet email to communicate with coworkers and the outside world. "I can attach text, a spreadsheet, or a complete three-dimensional CAD model to a message and send it out to several people through a distribution list. It really shortens the cycle of time on a project," he says.

■ REQUIREMENTS
High School

CAD technicians must be able to read and understand complex engineering diagrams and drawings. The minimum educational requirement for CAD technicians is a high school diploma. If you are a high school student, take courses that provide you with a solid background in algebra, geometry, trigonometry, physics, machine-shop skills, drafting, and electronics, and take whatever computer courses are available. You should also take courses in English, especially those that improve your communication skills.

Postsecondary Training

Increasingly, most prospective CAD technicians are undertaking formal training beyond the high school level, either through a two-year associate's degree program taught at a technical school or community college, or through a four-year college or university program. Employers prefer job applicants who have some form of postsecondary training in drafting.

Such a program should include courses in these areas: basic drafting, machine drawing, architecture, civil drafting (with an emphasis on highways), process piping, electrical, electrical instrumentation, HVAC, and plumbing. There should also be courses in data processing; computer programming, systems, and equipment, especially video-display equipment; computer graphics; product design; and computer peripheral equipment and data storage. Some two-year programs may also require you to complete courses in technical writing, communications, social sciences, and the humanities.

In addition, some companies have their own training programs, which can last as long as two years. Requirements for entry into these company-run training programs vary from company to company.

If you are considering a career in CAD technology, it is important to remember that you will be required to take continuing education courses even after you have found a job. This continuing education is necessary because technicians need to know about recent advances in technology that may affect procedures, equipment, terminology, or programming concepts.

"Technology changes so fast in this area," says Jackie Sutherland of his many years in the drafting and designing field.

Certification or Licensing

Certification for CAD technicians is voluntary. Certification in drafting is available from the American Design and Drafting Association. The examination, called the Drafter Certification Test, covers basic drafting skills but does not include testing of CAD drafting. Applicants are tested on geometric construction, architectural terms and regulations, and working sketches.

Licensing requirements vary. Licensing may be required for specific projects, such as a construction project, when the client requires it.

Other Requirements

As a CAD technician or drafter, you will need to think logically, have good analytical skills, and be methodical, accurate, and detail-oriented in all your work. You should be able to work as part of a team, as well as independently, since you will spend long periods of time in front of video display screens.

"You have to be able to visualize what a part may look like or what a new version of a part may look like," says Sutherland. "You have to have basic common sense but also be able to look into the future."

■ EXPLORING

There are a number of ways to gain firsthand knowledge about the field of CAD technology. Unfortunately, part-time or summer jobs involved directly with CAD technology are very hard to find; however, drafting-related jobs can sometimes be found, and many future employers will look favorably on applicants with this kind of experience. In addition, jobs related to other engineering fields, such as electronics or mechanics, may be available and can offer you an opportunity to become familiar with the kind of workplace in which technicians may later be employed.

In addition, high school courses in computers, geometry, physics, mechanical drawing, and shop work will give you a feel for the mental and physical activities associated with CAD technology. Other relevant activities include membership in high school science clubs (especially computer and electronics clubs); participating in science fairs; pursuing hobbies that involve computers, electronics, drafting, mechanical equipment, and model building; and reading books and articles about technical topics.

■ EMPLOYERS

CAD drafters and technicians are employed in a wide variety of industries, including engineering, architecture, manufacturing, construction, communication, utilities, and the government. They are employed by both large and small companies throughout the United States. For some specialties, jobs may be more specific to certain locations. For example, a drafter or designer for the software industry will find the most opportunities in California's Silicon Valley, while an automotive specialist may be more successful finding jobs near Detroit, Michigan.

■ STARTING OUT

Probably the most reliable method for entering this field is through your school's placement office. This is especially true for students who graduate from a two-year college or technical institute; recruiters from companies employing CAD technicians sometimes visit such schools, and placement office personnel can help students meet with these recruiters.

As a graduate of a postsecondary program, you can conduct your own job search by contacting architects, building firms, manufacturers, high technology companies, and government agencies. You can contact prospective employers by phone, email, or with a letter stating your interest in employment, accompanied by a resume that provides details about your education and job experience. State or private employment agencies may also be

---

WORDS TO KNOW

BOM: Bill of materials. Some CAD systems create an automatic bill of materials directly from the design data

CAD: Computer-aided design/drafting

CAM: Computer-aided manufacturing, including robots and automated machinery

CIM: Computer-integrated manufacturing, integrating a whole process

Cursor: On a CAD workstation, the large plus (+) sign that is moved around the screen with a mouse or stylus

Default: The original settings of the CAD software

Edit: Commands used to change drawings

Icon: A graphic representation of menu items

Macro: A program consisting of several commands

Model: A 3-D drawing of an object

NC: Numerical control

Prototype: A model of a concept product that can be tested

Workstation: A group of hardware devices that combine to run the CAD software programs

DRAFTING: THEN AND NOW

A lot has changed for drafters and technicians in the last 30 years.

Then

Computers were large—filling entire rooms.

Drafting was done on a drafting board.

If plans needed to be changed, an entirely new design would be drawn.

Drafting plans were sent using mailing tubes and large sheets of paper.

Now

Computers, with the aid of microchips, are smaller, faster, and more efficient.

Drafting is done at a CAD workstation.

If a plan needs changes, edits to the original can be quickly implemented.

Sending drafting plans is as easy as the push of a button via the Internet.

helpful, and classified ads in newspapers, professional journals, and at association websites may provide additional leads.

■ ADVANCEMENT

CAD technicians who demonstrate their ability to handle more responsibility can expect to receive promotions after just a few years on the job. They may be assigned to designing work that requires their special skills or experience, such as troubleshooting problems with systems they have worked with, or they may be promoted to supervisory or training positions. As trainers, they may teach courses at their workplace or at a local school or community college.

In general, as CAD technicians advance, their assignments become less and less routine, until they may have a hand in designing and building equipment. Technicians who continue their education and earn a bachelor's degree may become data processing managers, engineers, or systems analysts or manufacturing analysts.

Other routes for advancement include becoming a sales representative for a design firm or for a company selling computer-aided design services or equipment. It may also be possible to become an independent contractor for companies using or manufacturing CAD equipment.

■ EARNINGS

Earnings vary among drafters based on the industry they work in as well as their level of experience and the size of

their employer. The U.S. Department of Labor reports the median wage for civil and architectural drafters was $37,300 in 2002. The lowest paid 10 percent of these drafters made less than $24,570 annually; the highest paid 10 percent made more than $56,260 annually. Electrical and electronics drafters had somewhat higher earnings, with an average annual wage of $41,090 in 2002. The lowest paid 10 percent of these drafters earned less than $25,710 per year, and the highest paid 10 percent made more than $68,000 yearly.

According to the 2003 salary survey by the website JustCADJobs.com, CAD designers/drafters with two to four years of experience averaged $40,018 annually. Those with four to six years of experience averaged $48,235 per year.

Actual salaries vary widely depending on geographic location, exact job requirements, and the training needed to obtain those jobs. With increased training and experience, technicians can earn higher salaries, and some technicians with special skills, extensive experience, or added responsibilities may earn more.

Benefits usually include insurance, paid vacations and holidays, pension plans, and sometimes stock-purchase plans.

■ WORK ENVIRONMENT

CAD professionals almost always work in clean, quiet, well-lighted, air-conditioned offices. CAD technicians spend most of their days at a workstation. While the work does not require great physical effort, it does require patience and the ability to maintain concentration and attention for extended periods of time. Some technicians may find they suffer from eyestrain from working for long periods in front of a computer monitor.

CAD technicians, because of their training and experience, are valuable employees. They are called upon to exercise independent judgment and to be responsible for valuable equipment. Out of necessity, they also sometimes find themselves carrying out routine, uncomplicated tasks. CAD technicians must be able to respond well to both kinds of demands. Most CAD technicians work as part of a team. They are required to follow orders, and may encounter situations in which their individual contributions are not fully recognized. Successful CAD technicians are those who work well as team members and who can derive satisfaction from the accomplishments of the team as a whole.

■ OUTLOOK

The U.S. Department of Labor predicts that the employment outlook for drafters will grow more slowly than average through 2012. The best opportunities will be available to those who have skill and experience using CAD systems. Many companies in the near future will feel pressures to increase productivity in design and manufacturing activities, and CAD technology provides some of the best opportunities to improve that productivity.

Another factor that will create a demand for CAD drafters and technicians is the continued focus on safety and quality throughout manufacturing and industrial fields. In order to do business or continue to do business with leading manufacturers, companies and lower-tier suppliers must meet stringent quality guidelines. With this focus on quality as well as safety, companies are scrutinizing their current designs more carefully than ever, requiring more CAD work for new concepts and alterations that will create a better product.

Any economic downturn could adversely affect CAD technicians because many of the industries that they serve—such as auto manufacturing or construction—fluctuate greatly with economic swings. In any event, the best opportunities will be for drafters and technicians proficient in CAD technology who continue to learn, both in school and on the job.

Increasing productivity in the industrial design and manufacturing fields will ensure the long-term economic vitality of our nation; CAD technology is one of the most promising developments in this search for increased productivity. Knowing that they are in the forefront of this important and challenging undertaking provides CAD technicians and drafters with a good deal of pride and satisfaction.

■ FOR MORE INFORMATION

For information about certification, student drafting contests, and job postings, contact

American Design and Drafting Association
105 East Main Street
Newbern, TN 38059
Tel: 731-627-0802
Email: corporate@adda.org
http://www.adda.org

For information about the electrical field or to find the IEEE-USA student branch nearest you, contact

Institute of Electrical and Electronics Engineers, Inc. (IEEE-USA)
1828 L Street, NW, Suite 1202
Washington, DC 20036
Tel: 202-785-0017
Email: ieeeusa@ieee.org
http://www.ieeeusa.org

You Need to Know . . .

Computer-Aided Manufacturing

While factories and manufacturing facilities used to boast of having Computer-Aided Manufacturing (CAM) equipment on-site, today the idea that computers assist humans in manufacturing goods is a given. CAM works with CAD (Computer-Aided Design) to streamline the manufacturing process.

Sometimes now called Computer-Integrated Manufacturing (CIM), CAM is important for a variety of jobs within manufacturing. While it used to be more common to have a group of CAM specialists, very few people who work in manufacturing today can afford not to know about CAM systems.

Who are these people? Engineers of all kinds, manufacturing technicians, supervisors, CAD operators, assembly line workers, machine maintenance people, programmers, machinists, and designers.

Many times, a new machine or process begins in CAD, but CAM helps to bring that design into the "real" world—integrating it into the existing manufacturing environment.

Many manufacturers offer on-site training or will reimburse for CAD/CAM classes for their personnel. Since the technology changes so quickly, updates and refresher courses are often necessary. In fact, some of the CAD/CAM experts of today might remember the first computer-aided equipment to be placed in their facility. Today, it would be hard to find machinery that is not computer-aided in some way.

For information about scholarships, grants, and student memberships, contact

Society of Manufacturing Engineers
International Headquarters
One SME Drive
Dearborn, MI 48121
Tel: 800-733-4763
http://www.sme.org

Computer and Electronics Sales Representatives

■ OVERVIEW

Computer and electronics sales representatives sell hardware, software, peripheral computer equipment, and electronics equipment to customers and businesses of all sizes. Sometimes they follow up sales with installation of systems, maintenance, or training of the client's staff. They are employed in all aspects of businesses. Sales representatives that work for retail stores deal with consumers. Representatives that specialize in a particular piece of hardware, specific software program, or electronic component may do business with banks, insurance companies, or accounting firms, among others.

■ HISTORY

The first major advances in modern computer technology were made during World War II. After the war, people thought that computers were too big (they easily filled entire warehouses) to ever be used for anything other than government projects, such as their use in compiling the 1950 census.

The introduction of semiconductors to computer technology made smaller and less expensive computers possible. The semiconductors replaced the bigger, slower vacuum tubes of the first computers. These changes made it easier for businesses to adapt computers to their needs, which they began doing as early as 1954. Within 30 years, computers had revolutionized the way people work, play, and even shop. Few occupations have remained untouched by this technological revolution. Consequently, computers are found in businesses, government offices, hospitals, schools, science labs, and homes. Clearly, there is a huge market for the sale of computers and peripheral equipment. There is an important need today for knowledgeable sales representatives to serve both the retail public and to advise corporations and large organizations on their computer and electronics purchases.

■ THE JOB

The first step in the selling process, whether the sale environment is retail or corporate, is client consultation. Sales representatives determine the client's current technological needs as well as those of the future. During consultation, reps explain the technology's value and how well it will perform. Often, customers do not have expertise in computer or electronics technology, so the rep must explain and translate complicated computer tech-talk as well as answer numerous questions. In retail computer sales, the customer decides what system, peripheral, or software to purchase and then brings it home or arranges for its delivery.

In the corporate sales environment, client consultations usually take longer, often entailing numerous trips to the client's office or place of business. Ron Corrales, an Account Support Manager for Accenture (formerly Andersen Consulting), acknowledges that client consultation is the crucial first step in the sales process. After the client's business is researched and its needs are assessed, possible solutions are outlined in the form of a written or oral presentation. "I was really nervous the first few times I gave a presentation," recalls Corrales. "After all, these were CEOs and CFOs of Fortune 500 companies!" The talent for public speaking and technical writing frequently comes into play. Sales representatives must be able to effectively and clearly present the product and its capabilities, often in layperson's terms. After perfecting his communications skills, Corrales now thinks of client presentations as "just part of the job."

Accenture is one of the largest information technology (IT) consulting firms in the world. It provides proprietary software used by businesses worldwide. Its programs are tools tailor-made to fit the needs of each company and its specific routines, such as accounting, customer billing, inventory control, and marketing, among others. Its client list includes the grocery store chain Kroger's, Harley Davidson, and the U.S. government.

After the presentation, if all goes well, Corrales helps draft the contract. Every aspect of the agreement is outlined and specified—the type of software, length of contract, including services, training, or maintenance. The deal is considered "done" once the Accenture partners and company CEOs sign, and of course, the fees are paid. Once the companies receive their software, it is installed, and glitches, if any, are resolved. Many times company employees are trained by Accenture consultants on how to use the software to its fullest capability. Usually a one-year maintenance contract is provided to the client.

To stay abreast of technological advances, sales representatives must attend training sessions or continuing education classes. It also helps to know the essence of each client's field and the nature of its work. Weekly departmental meetings are necessary to learn of any developments or projects within the department or the company as a whole. A big part of Corrales' job is man-

QUICK FACTS

SCHOOL SUBJECTS
Business
Computer science
Speech

PERSONAL SKILLS
Communication/ideas
Technical/scientific

WORK ENVIRONMENT
Primarily indoors
Primarily multiple locations

MINIMUM EDUCATION LEVEL
Bachelor's degree

SALARY RANGE
$29,760 to $57,120 to $111,080

CERTIFICATION OR LICENSING
None available

OUTLOOK
About as fast as the average

DOT
275

GOE
10.02.01

NOC
6421

O*NET-SOC
41-4011.03

aging his territory, making client calls or visits when necessary. A chunk of his work day is devoted to "putting out potential client 'fires.'"

■ REQUIREMENTS
High School
Classes in speech and writing will help you learn how to communicate your product to large groups of people. Computer science and electronics classes will give you a basic overview of the field. General business and math classes will also be helpful.

Postsecondary Training
Though a small number of computer sales positions may be filled by high school graduates, those jobs are scarce. Most large companies prefer a bachelor's or advanced degree in computer or information science, engineering, business, or marketing.

Prepare yourself for a career in this field by developing your computer knowledge. Take computer and math classes, as well as business classes to help develop a sound business sense. Since sales representatives are often required to meet with clients and make sales presentations, excellent communications skills are a must. Hone yours by taking English and speech classes.

In this particular field of sales, extensive computer knowledge is just as important as business savvy. Most computer sales representatives pursue computer science courses concurrently with their business classes. For computer sales representatives specializing in a specific industry (for example, health care or banking), training in the basics and current issues of that field is needed. Such training can be obtained through special work training seminars, adult education classes, or courses at a technical school. Many companies require their sales staff to complete a training program where they'll learn the technologies and work tools needed for the job. (This is where you'll pick up the techno-speak for your specific field.)

Ron Corrales holds a Master of Information Science degree. One of the college classes that has helped him the most in his career is "technical writing and communication. It helps to be able to explain complicated and technical material in layperson terms."

Other Requirements
As important as having computer and electronics knowledge is having a "sales" personality. Sales representatives must be confident and knowledgeable about themselves as well as the product they are selling. They should have strong interpersonal skills and enjoy dealing with all types of people, from families buying their first PC, to CEOs of a Fortune 500 company. "People in this business are well rounded and enjoy technology," Corrales adds, "but, to do well, they need to be competitively hungry, and like to talk—a lot!"

■ EMPLOYERS
Employment opportunities for this field exist nationwide. What are your priorities? Do you want to work for an industry giant? IBM? Microsoft? Motorola? You may be enticed with attractive perks, such as stock options, a big travel expense account, or graduate school tuition, among other benefits. Note, however, that these are huge corporations; you'll really have to be something special if you want to stand apart from the other applicants. Getting hired is tough, too. Microsoft, for example, receives thousands of resumes weekly.

Middle-size and small companies usually require their employees to don several hats. That means sales representatives may be responsible for entire presentations, including product and client research, as well as maintenance and service. It may sound like too much work, and for some tasks you may feel overqualified. The rewards include being part of the ground team when your company takes off. If it doesn't, you can always chalk it up to good experience.

■ STARTING OUT
That Ron Corrales had two job offers by graduation is not uncommon, especially for students with computer-related majors. Many top companies recruit aggressively on campus, often enticing soon-to-be grads with signing bonuses or other incentives at school job fairs.

Other avenues to try when conducting your job search include the newspaper job ads and trade papers. Try the Internet, too. Many companies maintain websites where they post employment opportunities as well as receive online resumes and applications. Your school's job placement center is a great place to start your job search. Not only will the counselors have information on jobs not advertised in the paper, but they can provide tips on resume writing and interviewing techniques.

■ ADVANCEMENT
With a good work record, a computer or electronics sales representative may be offered a position in management. A manager is responsible for supervising the sales for a given retail store, sales territory, or corporate branch. A management position comes with not only a higher salary but a higher level of responsibility as well. An effective manager should be well versed in the company's product and selling techniques and be able to keep a sales group working at top capacity. Those already at the management level may decide to transfer to the marketing side of the business. Positions in marketing may involve

planning the marketing strategy for a new computer or electronics product or line, and coordinating sales campaigns and product distribution.

■ EARNINGS

Because computer and electronics sales reps work in a variety of settings, ranging from the local store on Main Street to large corporations, their annual salaries vary greatly. Sales representatives working in retail are paid an hourly wage, usually minimum wage ($5.15 an hour), which may be supplemented with commissions based on a percentage of sales made that day or week. Salaries are also dependent on the product sold (PCs, mainframes, peripherals) and the market served.

According to the U.S. Department of Labor, median earnings for all retail sales reps for technical and scientific products, including commissions, was $57,120 in 2003. At the bottom end of the pay scale were those making less than $29,760 annually, and at the top were those who made more than $111,080 annually. These would be the salaries earned by salespeople who make their living selling to large buyers, such as corporations. Most computer sales representatives working for large employers are offered a benefits package including health and life insurance, paid holidays and vacations, and continuing education and training, as well as volume bonuses or stock options.

■ WORK ENVIRONMENT

Retail sales representatives work in a retail environment. A 40-hour workweek is typical, though longer hours may be necessary during busy shopping seasons. Whether or not the sales representative is compensated during these extended hours varies from store to store. However, increased work times usually mean increased sales volume, which in the end translates to more commissions. Retail representatives must be prepared to deal with a large volume of customers with varying levels of technical knowledge, all with many questions. It is necessary to treat customers with respect and patience, regardless of the size of the sale, or when there is no sale at all.

Corporate sales representatives, like Ron Corrales, work in a professional office environment. Work is conducted at the home office as well as in the field when making sales calls. Work schedules vary depending on the size of territory and number of clients. A 40-hour workweek is the exception rather than the rule. "I average about 60-plus hours a week," says Corrales. "My hours are flexible, but with a lot of weekend work and travel."

Also, corporate sales representatives should have excellent communications skills, both in person and on the telephone, because they spend a lot of time consulting with clients. Also, good writing skills are needed when producing proposals and sales reports, often under the pressure of a tight deadline.

■ OUTLOOK

Employment opportunities for all retail sales representatives are expected to grow about as fast as the average through 2012, according to the U.S. Department of Labor. Employment growth for those in corporate sales is also expected to grow at this rate.

As computer companies continue to price their products competitively, more and more people will be able to afford new home computer systems or upgrade existing ones with the latest hardware, software, and peripherals. Increased retail sales will increase the need for competent and knowledgeable sales representatives. Many jobs exist at retail giants (Best Buy and Office Depot, known for office-related supplies and equipment, are two examples) that provide consumers with good price packages as well as optional services such as installation and maintenance.

Employment opportunities can also be found with computer specialty stores and consulting companies that deal directly with businesses and their corporate computer and application needs. Computers have become an almost indispensable tool for running a successful business, be it an accounting firm, a public relations company, or a multiphysician medical practice. As long as this trend continues, knowledgeable sales representatives will be needed to bring the latest technological advances in hardware and software to the consumer and corporate level.

All sales workers are adversely affected by economic downturns. In a weak economy, consumers purchase fewer expensive items, and businesses look for ways to trim costs. This results in less of a demand for computers and computer accessories and a reduced need for sales workers.

■ FOR MORE INFORMATION

For information on internships, student membership, and the student magazine Crossroads, *contact*
Association for Computing Machinery
1515 Broadway
New York, NY 10036-5701
Tel: 800-342-6626
Email: SIGS@acm.org
http://www.acm.org

For industry and membership information, or for a copy of Representor, *a quarterly trade magazine, contact*
Electronics Representatives Association
444 North Michigan Avenue, Suite 1960
Chicago, IL 60611
Tel: 312-527-3050

Email: info@era.org

http://www.era.org

For industry or membership information, contact

North American Retail Dealers Association

10 East 22nd Street, Suite 310

Lombard, IL 60148-6191

Tel: 800-621-0298

Email: nardahdq@narda.com

http://www.narda.com

Computer and Office Machine Service Technicians

■ OVERVIEW

Computer and office machine service technicians install, calibrate, maintain, troubleshoot, and repair equipment such as computers and their peripherals, office equipment, and specialized electronic equipment used in many factories, hospitals, airplanes, and numerous other businesses. Potential employers include computer companies and large corporations that need a staff devoted to repairing and maintaining their equipment. Many service technicians are employed by companies that contract their services to other businesses. Computer and office machine service technicians, including those who work on automated teller machines, hold approximately 156,000 jobs in the United States.

■ HISTORY

When computers were first introduced to the business world, businesses found their size to be cumbersome and their capabilities limited. Today, technological advances have made computers smaller yet more powerful in their speed and capabilities. As more businesses rely on computers and other office machines to help manage daily activities, access information, and link offices and resources, the need for experienced professionals to work and service these machines will increase. Service technicians are employed by many corporations, hospitals, and the government, as part of a permanent staff, or they may be contracted to work for other businesses.

■ THE JOB

L-3 Communications manufactures computer systems for a diverse group of clients such as Shell Oil, United Air-

lines, and the Chicago Board of Trade. Besides computer systems, they also offer services such as equipment maintenance contracts and customer training. Joey Arca, a service technician for L-3 Communications, loves the challenge and diversity of his job. He and other members of the staff are responsible for the installation of computer mainframes and systems, as well as training employees on the equipment. A large part of their work is the maintenance, diagnosis, and repair of computer equipment. Since the clients are located throughout the United States, Arca must often travel to different cities in his assigned district. He also presents company products and services to potential clients and bids for maintenance contracts.

"I don't always have to be at the office, which gives me a lot of freedom," says Arca. "Sometimes I call in from my home and get my scheduled appointments for the day." The freedom of not being deskbound does have its downfalls. "One of the most difficult parts of the job is not knowing when a computer will fail. I carry a pager 24/7, and if I get called, I'm bound to a two-hour response time."

Many times work is scheduled before or after regular working hours or on the weekend, because it's important to have the least amount of workday disruption. Arca is successful in his job because he keeps on top of technology that is constantly changing with continuing education classes and training seminars. He is also well versed in both hardware and software, especially system software.

■ REQUIREMENTS
High School

Traditional high school courses such as mathematics, physical sciences, and other laboratory-based sciences can provide a strong foundation for understanding basic mechanical and electronics principles. English and speech classes can help boost your written and verbal communications skills. Shop classes dealing with electricity, electronics, and blueprint reading are also beneficial.

QUICK FACTS

SCHOOL SUBJECTS
Computer science
Technical/shop

PERSONAL SKILLS
Mechanical/manipulative
Technical/scientific

WORK ENVIRONMENT
Primarily indoors
Primarily multiple locations

MINIMUM EDUCATION LEVEL
Associate's degree

SALARY RANGE
$20,779 to $33,238 to $52,124+

CERTIFICATION OR LICENSING
Recommended

OUTLOOK
About as fast as the average

DOT
633

GOE
05.02.02

NOC
2242

O*NET-SOC
49-2011.01, 49-2011.02, 49-2011.03

An office machine service technician repairs a photocopy machine.

Postsecondary Training

You may be able to find work with a high school diploma if you have a lot of practical, hands-on experience in the field. Usually, however, employers require job candidates to have at least an associate's degree in electronics. Joey Arca holds a bachelor of science degree in electrical engineering. He credits specialized classes such as Voice and Data Communications, Microprocessor Controls, and Digital Circuits as giving him a good base for his current work environment.

Certification or Licensing

Certification is required by most employers, though standards vary depending on the company. However, it is considered by many as a measure of industry knowledge. Certification can also give you a competitive edge when interviewing for a new job or negotiating for a higher salary.

A variety of certification programs are available from the International Society of Certified Electronics Technicians and the Institute for Certification of Computing Professionals, among other organizations. After the successful completion of study and examination, you may be

certified in fields such as computer, industrial, and electronic equipment. Continuing education credits are required for recertification, usually every two to four years. Arca is certified as a computer technician from the Association of Energy Engineers and the Electronics Technicians Association International.

Other Requirements

A strong technical background and an aptitude for learning about new technologies, good communications skills, and superior manual dexterity will help you succeed in this industry. You'll also need to be motivated to keep up with modern computer and office machine technology. Machines rapidly become obsolete, and so does the service technician's training. When new equipment is installed, service technicians must demonstrate the intellectual agility to learn how to handle problems that might arise.

When asked what kind of people are best suited for this line of work, Arca replies, "task oriented, quantitatively smart, organized, and personable. Also, they need the ability to convey technical terms in writing and orally."

■ EMPLOYERS

Though work opportunities for service technicians are available nationwide, many jobs are located in large cities where computer companies and larger corporations are based.

■ STARTING OUT

If your school offers placement services, take advantage of them. Many times, school placements and counseling centers are privy to job openings that are filled before being advertised in the newspaper. Make sure your counselors know of any important preferences, such as location, specialization, and other requirements, so they can best match you to an employer. Don't forget to supply them with an updated resume.

There are also other avenues to take when searching for a job in this industry. Many jobs are advertised in the "Jobs" section of your local newspaper. Look under "Computers" or "Electronics." Also, inquire directly with the personnel department of companies that appeal to you and fill out an application. Trade association websites are good sources of job leads; many will post employment opportunities as well as allow you to post your resume.

■ ADVANCEMENT

Due to the growth of computer products and their influence over the business world, this industry offers a variety of advancement opportunities. Service technicians usually start by working on relatively simple maintenance and repair tasks. Over time, they start working on more complicated projects.

Experienced service technicians may advance to positions of increased responsibility, such as a crew supervisor or a departmental manager. Another advancement route is to become a sales representative for a computer manufacturing company. Technicians develop hands-on knowledge of particular machines and are thus often in the best position to advise potential buyers about important purchasing decisions. Some entrepreneurial-minded servicers might open their own repair business, which can be risky but can also provide many rewards. Unless they fill a certain market niche, technicians usually find it necessary to service a wide range of computers and office machines.

■ EARNINGS

The U.S. Department of Labor reports that the median hourly earnings for computer, automated teller, and office machine technicians were $15.98 in 2002. A technician earning this amount and working full-time would have a yearly income of approximately $33,238. The department also reports that the lowest paid 10 percent of all computer and office machine service technicians (regardless of employer) earned less than $9.99 per hour ($20,779 annually). At the other end of the pay scale, 10 percent earned more than $25.06 per hour (approximately $52,124 annually). Those with certification are typically paid more than those without.

Standard work benefits for full-time technicians include health and life insurance and paid vacation and sick time, as well as a retirement plan. Most technicians are given travel stipends; some receive company cars.

■ WORK ENVIRONMENT

"I like the freedom of not working in a [typical] office environment and the short workweeks," says Joey Arca. Most service technicians, however, have unpredictable work schedules. Some weeks are quiet and may require fewer work hours. However, during a major computer problem, or worse yet, a breakdown, technicians are required to work around the clock to fix the problem as quickly as possible. Technicians spend a considerable amount of time on call, and must carry a pager in case of work emergencies.

Travel is an integral part of the job for many service technicians, many times amounting to 80 percent of the job time. Arca has even traveled to the Philippines, where he worked on the Tomahawk Missile project at Clark Air Force Base. Since he is originally from the Philippines, he was able to combine work with a visit with friends and family.

■ OUTLOOK

According to the U.S. Department of Labor, employment for service technicians working with computer and office equipment should grow about as fast as the average through 2012. As corporations, the government, hospitals, and universities worldwide continue their reliance on computers to help manage their daily business, demand for qualified and skilled technicians will be strong. Opportunities are expected to be best for those with knowledge of electronics and working in computer repairs. Those working on office equipment, such as digital copiers, should find a demand for their services to repair and maintain increasingly technically sophisticated office machines.

■ FOR MORE INFORMATION

For information on internships, student membership, and the magazine Crossroads, *contact*

Association for Computing Machinery
1515 Broadway
New York, NY 10036
Tel: 800-342-6626
Email: sigs@acm.org
http://www.acm.org

For career and placement information, contact

Electronics Technicians Association International
5 Depot Street
Greencastle, IN 46135
Tel: 800-288-3824
Email: eta@tds.net
http://www.eta-sda.com

For industry and certification information, contact the following organizations:

ACES International
5241 Princess Anne Rd., Suite 110
Virginia Beach, VA 23462
http://www.acesinternational.org

Computing Technology Industry Association
1815 S Meyers Rd., Suite 300
Oakbrook Terrace, IL 60181-5228
http://www.comptia.org

Institute for Certification of Computing Professionals
2350 East Devon Avenue, Suite 115
Des Plaines, IL 60018-4610
Tel: 800-843-8227
Email: office@iccp.org
http://www.iccp.org

International Society of Certified Electronics Technicians
3608 Pershing Avenue
Fort Worth, TX 76107-4527
Tel: 817-921-9101
Email: info@iscet.org
http://www.iscet.org

Computer and Video Game Designers

■ OVERVIEW

In the sector of the multibillion-dollar computer industry known as interactive entertainment and recreational computing, *computer and video game designers* create the ideas and interactivity for games. These games are played on various platforms, or media, such as video consoles and computers, and through online Internet subscriptions. They generate ideas for new game concepts, including sound effects, characters, story lines, and graphics.

Because the industry is fairly new, it is difficult to estimate how many people work as game designers. Around 90,000 people work within the video game industry as a whole. Designers either work for companies that make the games or create the games on their own and sell their ideas and programs to companies that produce them.

■ HISTORY

Computer and video game designers are a relatively new breed. The industry didn't begin to develop until the 1960s and 1970s, when computer programmers at some large universities, big companies, and government labs began designing games on mainframe computers. Steve Russell was perhaps the first video game designer. In 1962, when he was in college, he made up a simple game called Spacewar. Graphics of space ships flew through a starry sky on the video screen, the object of the game being to shoot down enemy ships. Nolan Bushnell, another early designer, played Spacewar in college. In 1972 he put the first video game in an arcade; it was a game very much like Spacewar, and he called it Computer Space. However, many users found the game difficult to play, so it wasn't a success.

Bruce Artwick published the first of many versions of Flight Simulator, and Bushnell later created Pong, a game that required the players to paddle electronic ping-pong balls back and forth across the video screen. Pong was a big hit, and players spent thousands of quarters in arcade machines all over the country playing it. Bushnell's company, Atari, had to hire more and more designers every week, including Steve Jobs, Alan Kay, and Chris Crawford. These early designers made games with text-based descriptions (that is, no graphics) of scenes and actions with interactivity done through a computer keyboard. Games called Adventure, Star Trek, and Flight Simulator were among the first that designers created. They used simple commands like "look at building" and "move west." Most games were designed for video machines; not until the later 1970s did specially equipped TVs and early personal computers (PCs) begin appearing.

In the late 1970s and early 1980s, designers working for Atari and Intellivision made games for home video systems, PCs, and video arcades. Many of these new games had graphics, sound, text, and animation. Designers of games like Pac-Man, Donkey Kong, and Space Invaders were successful and popular. They also started to make role-playing games like the famous Dungeons and Dragons. Richard Garriott created Ultima, another major role-playing game. Games began to feature the names and photos of their programmers on the packaging, giving credit to individual designers.

Workers at Electronic Arts began to focus on making games for PCs to take advantage of technology that included the computer keyboard, more memory, and floppy disks. They created games like Carmen Sandiego and M.U.L.E. In the mid- to late 1980s, new technology included more compact floppies, sound cards, and larger memory. Designers also had to create games that would work on more than just one platform—PCs, Apple computers, and 64-bit video game machines.

In the 1990s, Electronic Arts started to hire teams of designers instead of "lone wolf" individuals (those who design games from start to finish independently). Larger teams were needed because games became more complex; design teams would include not only programmers but also artists, musicians, writers, and animators. Designers made such breakthroughs as using more entertaining graphics, creating more depth in role-playing games, using virtual reality in sports games, and using more visual realism in racing games and flight simulators. This new breed of designers created games using techniques like Assembly, C, and HyperCard. By 1994, designers began to use CD-ROM technology to its fullest. In only a few months, Doom was a hit. Designers of this game gave players the chance to alter it themselves at various levels, including choices of weapons and enemies. Doom still has fans worldwide.

The success of shareware (software that is given away to attract users to want to buy more complete software) has influenced the return of smaller groups of designers. Even the lone wolf is coming back, using shareware and better authoring tools such as sound libraries and complex multimedia development environments. Some designers are finding that they work best on their own or in small teams.

What's on the horizon for game designers? More multiplayer games; virtual reality; improved technology in coprocessors, chips, hardware, and sound fonts; and "persistent worlds," where online games are influenced by and evolve from players' actions. These new types of games require that designers know more and more complex code so that games can "react" to their multiple players.

■ THE JOB

Designing games involves programming code as well as creating stories, graphics, and sound effects. It is a very creative process, requiring imagination and computer and communication skills to develop games that are interactive and entertaining. As mentioned earlier, some game designers work on their own and try to sell their designs to companies that produce and distribute games; others are employees of companies such as Electronic Arts, Broderbund, and many others. Whether designers work alone or for a company, their aim is to create games that get players involved. Game players want to have fun, be challenged, and sometimes learn something along the way.

Each game must have a story line as well as graphics and sound that will entertain and engage the players. Story lines are situations that the players will find themselves in and make decisions about. Designers develop a plan for combining the story or concept, music or other sound effects, and graphics. They design rules to make it fun, challenging, or educational, and they create characters for the stories or circumstances, worlds in which these characters live, and problems or situations these characters will face.

One of the first steps is to identify the audience that will be playing the game. How old are the players? What kinds of things are they interested in? What kind of game will it be: action, adventure, "edutainment," role-playing, or sports? And which platform will the game use: video game system (e.g., Nintendo), computer (e.g., Macintosh), or online (Internet via subscription)?

The next steps are to create a design proposal, a preliminary design, and a final game design. The proposal is a brief summary of what the game involves. The preliminary design goes much further, outlining in more detail

what the concept is (the story of the game); how the players get involved; what sound effects, graphics, and other elements will be included (What will the screen look like? What kinds of sound effects should the player hear?); and what productivity tools (such as word processors, database programs, spreadsheet programs, flowcharting programs, and prototyping programs) the designer intends to use to create these elements. Independent designers submit a product idea and design proposal to a publisher along with a cover letter and resume. Employees work as part of a team to create the proposal and design. Teamwork might include brainstorming sessions to come up with ideas, as well as involvement in market research (surveying the players who will be interested in the game).

The final game design details the basic idea, the plot, and every section of the game, including the startup process, all the scenes (such as innings for baseball games and maps for edutainment games), and all the universal elements (such as rules for scoring, names of characters, and a sound effect that occurs every time something specific happens). The story, characters, worlds, and maps are documented. The game design also includes details of the logic of the game, its algorithms (the step-by-step procedures for solving the problems the players will encounter), and its rules; the methods the player will use to load the game, start it up, score, win, lose, save, stop, and play again; the graphic design, including storyboards and sample art; and the audio design. The designer might also include marketing ideas and proposed follow-up games.

Designers interact with other workers and technologists involved in the game design project, including programmers, audio engineers, artists, and even *asset managers*, who coordinate the collecting, engineering, and distribution of physical assets to the *production team* (the people who will actually produce the physical CD-ROM or DVD).

QUICK FACTS

SCHOOL SUBJECTS
Art
Computer science

PERSONAL SKILLS
Communication/ideas
Technical/scientific

WORK ENVIRONMENT
Primarily indoors
Primarily one location

MINIMUM EDUCATION LEVEL
Bachelor's degree

SALARY RANGE
$41,652 to $53,031 to
$92,000+

CERTIFICATION OR LICENSING
None available

OUTLOOK
About as fast as the average

DOT
N/A

GOE
01.04.02

NOC
2174

O*NET-SOC
27-1029.99

Designers need to understand games and their various forms, think up new ideas, and experiment with and evaluate new designs. They assemble the separate elements (text, art, sound, video) of a game into a complete, interactive form, following through with careful planning and preparation (such as sketching out scripts, storyboards, and design documents). They write an implementation plan and guidelines (How will designers manage the process? How much will it cost to design the game? How long will the guidelines be—five pages? three hundred?). Finally, they amend designs at every stage, solving problems and answering questions.

Computer and video game designers often keep scrapbooks, notes, and journals of interesting ideas and other bits of information. They collect potential game material and even catalog ideas, videos, movies, pictures, stories, character descriptions, music clips, sound effects, animation sequences, and interface techniques. The average time it takes to design a game, including all the elements and stages just described, can be from about six to 18 months.

■ REQUIREMENTS
High School

If you like to play video or computer games, you're already familiar with them. You will also need to learn a programming language like C++ or Java, and you'll need a good working knowledge of the hardware platform for which you plan to develop your games (video, computer, online). In high school, learn as much as you can about computers: how they work, what kinds there are, how to program them, and any languages you can learn. You should also take physics, chemistry, and computer science. Since designers are creative, take courses such as art, literature, and music as well.

Postsecondary Training

Although strictly speaking you don't have to have a college degree to be a game designer, most companies are looking for creative people who also have a degree. Having one represents that you've been actively involved in intense, creative work; that you can work with others and follow through on assignments; and, of course, that you've learned what there is to know about programming, computer architecture (including input devices, processing devices, memory and storage devices, and output devices), and software engineering. Employers want to know that you've had some practical experience in design.

A growing number of schools offer courses or degrees in game design. One example is the Entertainment Technology Center (ETC) at Carnegie Mellon University. Computer programmer Shawn Patton holds a master's degree in entertainment technology from the ETC. He describes the ETC as "a mixture of technologists and artists." Much of the ETC's courses involve collaborative efforts, with both students and professor providing feedback on group projects. Patton says, "The ETC grants its students the ability to experience real work with the safety net of being able to fail (and not lose your job) as long as you learn from that failure."

COLLEGE CREDIT FOR STUDENTS WHO LIKE TO PLAY

Where can you get a degree in making games? The DigiPen Institute of Technology in Redmond, Washington, offers a bachelor's degree of science and an associate's degree in Real Time Interactive Simulation—in other words, a diploma in computer and video game design. DigiPen was established in 1988 in Vancouver, Canada, and in 1994 it accepted its first class of students who went on to graduate with two-year degrees in video game programming. DigiPen became the first school in North America to offer this degree. Nintendo of America hired many students from the first graduating class, and the company still has a strong relationship with the school. It offers guidance, technical expertise, and donations of hardware, development tools, and systems that emulate gaming consoles. In 1998, the DigiPen Institute of Technology was opened in Redmond, Washington, and it continues to offer education on the cutting edge of computer game design. (http://www.digipen.edu)

The University of North Texas's Laboratory for Recreational Computing (LARC) originated with a Directed Studies class taught by Dr. Ian Parberry in 1993; by the spring of 1994, students were involved with producing the LARC's first series of commercial games. Since then, a senior elective course called Computer Game Design and Programming has been taught there each year. The LARC prepares students for employment in the recreational computing industry by giving them hands-on experience developing computer and video games.

Computer Game Design and Programming is a three-credit senior elective at the University of North Texas. The syllabus features game programming using Microsoft DirectX. To sign up for this class, you'll need to know C++ programming and elementary data structures. While in college, prepare yourself for the program by taking classes such as assembly-level programming, algorithms, artificial intelligence, software engineering, computer graphics, and network programming. (Visit the LARC Web page to learn more: http://larc.csci.unt.edu.)

According to Professor Ian Parberry of the LARC, the quality of your education depends a lot on you. "You must take control of your education, seek out the best professors, and go beyond the material presented in class. What you have a right to expect from an undergraduate computer science degree is a grasp of the fundamental concepts of computer science and enough practical skills to be able to grow, learn, and thrive in any computational environment, be it computer games or otherwise."

Other Requirements

One major requirement for game design is that you must love to play computer games. You need to continually keep up with technology, which changes fast. Although you might not always use them, you need to have a variety of skills, such as writing stories, programming, and designing sound effects.

You must also have vision and the ability to identify your players and anticipate their every move in your game. You'll also have to be able to communicate well with programmers, writers, artists, musicians, electronics engineers, production workers, and others.

You must have the endurance to see a project through from beginning to end and also be able to recognize when a design should be scrapped.

Shawn Patton also advises, "An analytical mind is a must. If you like solving problems by thinking about all the variables, all the possible outcomes of your actions, and then applying those actions in a clear and concise manner, you probably have an analytical mind."

▪ EXPLORING

One of the best ways to learn about game design is to try to develop copies of easy games, such as Pong and Pac-Man, or try to change a game that has an editor. (Games like Klik & Play, Empire, and Doom allow players to modify them to create new circumstances and settings.)

For high school students interested in finding out more about how video games and animations are produced, the DigiPen Institute of Technology (see sidebar) offers a summer workshop. Two-week courses are offered during July and August, providing hands-on experience and advice on courses to take in high school to prepare yourself for postsecondary training.

Writing your own stories, puzzles, and games helps develop storytelling and problem-solving skills. Magazines such as *Computer Graphics World* (http://www.cgw.com) and *Game Developer* (http://www.gdmag.com) have articles about digital video and high-end imaging and other technical and design information.

Shawn Patton recommends "tinkering in your free time: If you have a great idea for a game or an application,

A team of computer video game designers ham it up.

sit down and try to program it in whatever language you know/have at your disposal. Learning by doing is great in computer science."

▪ EMPLOYERS

Software publishers (such as Electronic Arts and Activision) are found throughout the country, though most are located in California, New York, Washington, and Illinois. Electronic Arts is the largest independent publisher of interactive entertainment, including several development studios; the company is known worldwide. Big media companies such as Disney have also opened interactive entertainment departments. Jobs should be available at these companies as well as with online services and interactive networks, which are growing rapidly.

Some companies are involved in producing games only for video; others produce only for computers; others make games for various platforms. For example, Nintendo produces software only for video consoles; it makes different kinds of products but focuses on arcade, sports, and role-playing games. Byron Preiss Multimedia produces only PC-based adventure and multimedia games. Electronic Arts runs the gamut—video, PC, and Internet—producing games in almost every genre, from sports to adventure to edutainment.

▪ STARTING OUT

There are a couple of ways to begin earning money as a game designer: independently or as an employee of a company. It is more realistic to get any creative job you can in the industry (for example, as an artist, a play tester, a programmer, or a writer) and learn as you go, developing your design skills as you work your way up to the level of designer.

VIDEO GAME FAVORITES

The following are the top 10 video games of all time according to the game enthusiast website IGN/GameSpy, http://www.ign.com. Factors used in determining the list included overall game design, how the game matched up to other games at the time of release, how the game has stood up over time, and, most importantly, how much fun and enjoyment the game provided.

1. Super Mario Bros. (Nintendo, 1985)
2. Legend of Zelda: Ocarina of Time (Nintendo, 1998)
3. Super Metroid (Nintendo, 1994)
4. Tetris (various, 1987)
5. Super Mario 64 (Nintendo, 1996)
6. Legend of Zelda: A Link to the Past (Nintendo, 1992)
7. StarCraft (Blizzard, 1998)
8. X-Com: UFO Defense (Microprose, 1994)
9. Final Fantasy II (Squaresoft, 1991)
10. Street Fighter II (Capcom, 1991)

Contact company websites and sites that advertise job openings, such as Game Jobs (http://www.gamejobs.com) and JobOptions (http://ww1.joboptions.com).

In addition to a professional resume, it's a good idea to have your own website, where you can showcase your demos. Make sure you have designed at least one demo or have an impressive portfolio of design ideas and documents.

Other ways to find a job in the industry include going to job fairs (such as the Computer Game Developers Conference), where you find recruiters looking for creative people to work at their companies, and checking in with online user groups, which often post jobs on the Internet.

Also consider looking for an internship to prepare for this career. Many software and entertainment companies hire interns for short-term assignments. For example, Shawn Patton completed an internship at Walt Disney Imagineering 9WDI) in Glendale, California, where he helped develop the game Toontown Online (http://www.toontown.com). Regarding his internship, Patton says, "What I enjoyed the most about WDI was that I was able to work on code that was immediately released to the public, who then gave feedback on it. . . . I liked knowing that something I made was being used by and entertaining someone else. That's a feeling I hope to find in whatever job I end up having."

■ ADVANCEMENT

Just as with many jobs, to have better opportunities to advance their position and possibly earn more money, computer and video game designers have to keep up with technology. They must be willing to constantly learn more about design, the industry, and even financial and legal matters involved in development.

Becoming and remaining great at their job may be a career-long endeavor for computer and video game designers, or just a stepping stone to another area of interactive entertainment. Some designers start out as artists, writers, or programmers, learning enough in these jobs to eventually design. For example, a person entering this career may begin as a 3-D animation modeler and work on enough game life cycles to understand what it takes to be a game designer. He or she may decide to specialize in another area, such as sound effects or even budgeting.

Some designers rise to management positions, such as president or vice president of a software publisher. Others write for magazines and books, teach, or establish their own game companies.

■ EARNINGS

Most development companies spend up to two years designing a game even before any of the mechanics (such as writing final code and drawing final graphics) begin; more complex games take even longer. Companies budget $1–3 million for developing just one game. If the game is a success, designers are often rewarded with bonuses. In addition to bonuses or royalties (the percentage of profits designers receive from each game that is sold), designers' salaries are affected by their amount of professional experience, their location in the country, and the size of their employer. Gama Network, an organization serving electronic games developers, surveyed subscribers, members, and attendees of its three divisions (*Game Developer* magazine, Gamasutra.com, and the Game Developers Conference) to find out what professionals in the game development industry were earning. Conducted in 2003, the survey reveals that game designers with one to two years' experience had an average annual salary of approximately $41,652. Those with two to five years of experience averaged $53,031 annually, and those with more than six years of experience averaged $64,249 per year. The highest reported annual salary was $300,000. It is important to note that these salaries are averages, and some designers (especially those at the beginning stages of their careers) earn less than these amounts. These figures, however, provide a useful guide for the range of earnings available.

Any major software publisher will likely provide benefits such as medical insurance, paid vacations, and retirement plans. Designers who are self-employed must provide their own benefits.

■ WORK ENVIRONMENT

Computer and video game designers work in office settings, whether at a large company or a home studio. At some companies, artists and designers sometimes find themselves working 24 or 48 hours at a time, so the office areas are set up with sleeping couches and other areas where employees can relax. Because the game development industry is competitive, many designers find themselves under a lot of pressure from deadlines, design problems, and budget concerns.

■ OUTLOOK

Computer and video games are a fast-growing segment of the U.S. entertainment industry. In fact, the NPD Group, a market information provider, reports that sales of video game hardware, software, and accessories reached $11.2 billion in 2003. As the demand for new games, more sophisticated games, and games to be played on new systems grows, more and more companies will hire skilled people to create and perfect these products. Opportunities for game designers, therefore, should be good.

In any case, game development is popular; the Interactive Digital Software Association estimates that about 60 percent of the U.S. population (approximately 145 million people) play computer and video games. People in the industry expect more and more integration of interactive entertainment into mainstream society. Online development tools such as engines, graphic and sound libraries, and programming languages such as Java will probably create opportunities for new types of products that can feature game components.

■ FOR MORE INFORMATION

For information on associate and bachelor of science degrees in computer animation and simulation, contact

DigiPen Institute of Technology
5001-150th Avenue, NE
Redmond, WA 98052
Tel: 425-558-0299
Email: info@digipen.edu
http://www.digipen.edu

For industry information, contact the following associations:

Entertainment Software Association
1211 Connecticut Avenue, NW, #600
Washington, DC 20036

LEARN MORE ABOUT IT

Bates, Bob. *Game Design: The Art & Business of Creating Games*. San Diego, Calif.: Premier Press, 2002.

Blow, Jonathan. *Internet Game Programming*. Chicago, Ill.: Independent Publishers Group, 2001.

Bourg, David M. *Physics for Game Developers*. Cambridge, Mass.: O'Reilly & Associates, 2001.

Crawford, Chris. *Chris Crawford on Game Design*. Indianapolis: New Riders Publishing, 2003.

Dombrower, Eddie. *Dombrower's Art of Interactive Entertainment Design*. New York: McGraw-Hill, 1998.

Feldman, Ari. *Designing Arcade Computer Game Graphics*. Plano, Texas: Wordware Publishing, 2000.

Gershenfeld, Alan, Mark Loparco and Cecilia Barajas. *Game Plan: The Insider's Guide to Breaking In and Succeeding in the Computer and Video Game Business*. Irvine, Calif.: Griffin Trade Paperback, 2003.

Laramee, Francois Dominic, ed. Secrets of the Game Business. Hingham, Mass.: Charles River Media, 2003.

Marks, Aaron. *The Complete Guide to Game Audio: For Composers, Musicians, Sound Designers, and Game Developers*. Gilroy, Calif.: CMP Books, 2001.

Rollings, Andrew and Dave Morris. *Game Architecture and Design: A New Edition*. Indianapolis: New Riders Publishing, 2003.

Salen, Katie and Eric Zimmerman. *Rules of Play: Game Design Fundamentals*. Cambridge, Mass.: MIT Press, 2003.

Email: esa@theesa.com
http://www.theesa.com

International Game Developers Association
600 Harrison Street
San Francisco, CA 94107
Phone: 415-947-6235
Email: info@igda.org
http://www.igda.org

For information on training programs to become game designers and programmers, contact

Laboratory for Recreational Computing
University of North Texas
Department of Computer Science
PO Box 311277
Denton, TX 76203
Tel: 940-565-2681
Email: ian@cs.unt.edu
http://larc.csci.unt.edu

FASTEST GROWING CAREERS

Computer Network Administrators

■ OVERVIEW

Computer network administrators, or *network specialists,* design, install, and support an organization's local area network (LAN), wide area network (WAN), network segment, or Internet system. They maintain network hardware and software, analyze problems, and monitor the network to ensure availability to system users. Administrators also might plan, coordinate, and implement network security measures, including firewalls. Approximately 232,560 computer network and systems administrators work in the United States.

■ HISTORY

The first substantial developments in modern computer technology took place in the mid-twentieth century. After World War II, it was thought that the use of computers would be limited to large government projects, such as the U.S. Census, because computers at this time were enormous in size (they easily took up the space of entire warehouses).

Smaller and less expensive computers were made possible due to the introduction of semiconductors. Businesses began using computers in their operations as early as 1954. Within 30 years, computers revolutionized the way people work, play, and shop. Today, computers are everywhere, from businesses of all kinds to government agencies, charitable organizations, and private homes. Over the years, technology has continued to shrink the size of computers and increase computer speed at an unprecedented rate.

The first commercially used computers were composed of a system of several big mainframe computers. These computers were located in special rooms and several independent terminals around the office. Though efficient and effective, the mainframe had several problems. One problem was the update delay, or the time lapse, between when an employee input information into a computer and when that information became available to other employees. Although advances in hardware technology have begun addressing this and other problems of mainframes, many computer companies and businesses have now turned to networking instead.

Rather than relying on a mainframe system, computer networks use a network server to centralize the processing capacity of several different computers and other related equipment (known as peripherals). In a network, terminals and other computers are linked directly to the server. This direct link provides other computer users with instantaneous access to the information. The increased need for qualified computer network administrators to oversee network operations has paralleled the growth of computer networking.

The use of networks has grown rapidly as more companies move from mainframe computers to client-server networks or from paper-based systems to automated record-keeping using networked databases. The rapid growth of Internet technology has created a new area that also is in need of networking professionals.

■ THE JOB

Businesses use computer networks for several reasons. One important reason is that networks make it easy for many employees to share hardware and software as well as printers, faxes, and modems. For example, it would be very expensive to buy individual copies of word-processing programs for each employee in a company. By investing in a network version of the software that all employees can access, companies can often save a lot of money. Also, businesses that rely on databases for daily operations use networks to allow authorized personnel quick and easy access to the most updated version of the database.

Networks vary greatly in size; even just two computers connected together are considered a network. They can also be extremely large and complex, involving hundreds of computer terminals in various geographical locations around the world. A good example of a large network is the Internet, which is a system that allows people from every corner of the globe to access millions of pieces of information about any subject under the sun. Besides varying in size, networks are all at least slightly different in terms of configuration, or what the network is designed to do; businesses customize networks to meet their specific needs. All networks, regardless of size or configuration, experience problems. For example, communications with certain equipment can break down, users might need extra training or forget their passwords, back-up files may be lost, or new software might need to be installed and configured. Whatever the crisis, computer network administrators must know the network system well enough to diagnose and fix the problem.

Computer network administrators or specialists may hold one or several networking responsibilities. The specific job duties assigned to one person depend on the nature and scope of the employer. For example, in a medium-size company that uses computers only minimally, a computer network specialist might be expected to do everything associated with the office computer system. In larger companies with more sophisticated computing systems, computer network administrators are likely to hold more narrow and better-defined responsibilities. The following descriptions highlight the different kinds of computer network administrators.

In the narrowest sense, computer network administrators are responsible for adding and deleting files to the network server, a centralized computer. Among other things, the server stores the software applications used by network users on a daily basis. Administrators update files from the database, electronic mail, and word-processing applications. They are also responsible for making sure that printing jobs run properly. This task entails telling the server where the printer is and establishing a printing queue, or line, designating which print jobs have priority.

Another duty of some network administrators is setting up user access. Since businesses store confidential information on the server, users typically have access to only a limited number of applications. Network administrators tell the computer who can use which programs and when they can use them. They create a series of passwords to secure the system against internal and external spying. They also troubleshoot problems and questions encountered by staff members.

In companies with large computer systems, *network security specialists* concentrate solely on system security. They set up and monitor user access and update security files as needed. For example, it is very important in universities that only certain administrative personnel have the ability to change student grades on the database. Network security specialists must protect the system from unauthorized grade changes. Network security specialists grant new passwords to users who forget them, record all nonauthorized entries, report unauthorized users to appropriate management, and change any files that have been tampered with. They also maintain security files with information about each employee.

WHAT ARE THE USES OF COMPUTER NETWORKS?

Users of computer networks exchange data and files, according to *Britannica Online*. Database management, which is the quick search and retrieval of needed information from a collection of data, is probably the most frequent application of computer networks in offices.

Companies use database management in many ways. A database for an inventory or parts and materials at a plant is a collection of data, including product names and numbers, as well as the date of purchase or the manufacturers' names. Other applications include management of airline reservations, medical records at hospitals, legal records for insurance companies, and files that specify the locations and capacities of water pipes maintained by municipal public works offices.

Network control operators are in charge of all network communications, most of which operate over telephone lines or fiber optic cables. When users encounter communications problems, they call the network control operator. A typical communications problem is when a user cannot send or receive files from other computers. Since users seldom have a high level of technical expertise on the network, the network control operator knows how to ask appropriate questions in user-friendly language to determine the source of the problem. If it is not a user error, the network control operator checks the accuracy of computer files, verifies that modems are functioning properly, and runs noise tests on the communications lines using special equipment. As with all network specialists, if the problem proves to be too difficult for the network control operator to resolve, he or she seeks help directly from the manufacturer or warranty company.

Network control operators also keep detailed records of the number of communications transactions made, the number and nature of network errors, and the methods used to resolve them. These records help them address problems as they arise in the future.

Network systems administrators that specialize in Internet technology are essential to its success. One of their responsibilities is to prepare servers for use and link them together so others can place things on them. Under the supervision of the *Webmaster*, the systems administrator might set aside areas on a server for particular types of information, such as documents, graphics, or audio. At sites that are set up to handle secure credit card transactions, administrators are responsible for setting up the secure server that handles this job. They also monitor

Computer network administrators must attend training seminars to keep them up-to-date with the latest technology.

site traffic and take the necessary steps to ensure uninterrupted operation. In some cases, the solution is to provide additional space on the server. In others, the only solution might be to increase bandwidth by upgrading the telephone line linking the site to the Internet.

▪ REQUIREMENTS
High School

In high school, take as many courses as possible in computer science, mathematics, and science, which provide a solid foundation in computer basics and analytical-thinking skills. You should also practice your verbal and written communications skills in English and speech classes. Business courses are valuable in that they can give you an understanding of how important business decisions, especially those concerning investment in computer equipment, are made.

Postsecondary Training

Most network jobs require at least a bachelor's degree in computer science or computer engineering. More specialized positions require an advanced degree. Workers with a college education are more likely to deal with the theoretical aspects of computer networking and are more likely to be promoted to management positions. Opportunities in computer design, systems analysis, and computer programming, for example, are open only to college graduates. If you are interested in this field, you should also pursue postsecondary training in network administration or network engineering.

"I believe that you cannot have enough education and that it should be an ongoing thing," says Nancy Nelson, a network administrator at Baxter Healthcare Corporation in Deerfield, Illinois. "You can learn a lot on your own, but I think you miss out on a lot if you don't get the formal education. Most companies don't even look at a resume that doesn't have a degree. Keeping up with technology can be very rewarding."

Certification or Licensing

Besides the technical/vocational schools that offer courses related to computer networking, several major companies offer professionally taught courses and nationally recognized certification; chief among them are Novell and Microsoft. The Certified Network Professional program supports and complements the aforementioned vendor product certifications. Offered by The Network Professional Association, the program covers fundamental knowledge in client operating systems, microcomputer hardware platforms, network operating system fundamentals, protocols, and topologies. This program requires that you receive certification in two specialty areas.

Commercial postsecondary training programs are flexible. You can complete courses at your own pace, but you must take all parts of the certification test within one year. You may attend classes at any one of many educational sites around the country or you can study on your own. Many students find certification exams difficult.

Other Requirements

Continuing education for any computer profession is crucial to success. Many companies will require you to keep up to date on new technological advances by attending classes, workshops, and seminars throughout the year. Also, many companies and professional associations update network specialists through newsletters, other periodicals, and online bulletin boards.

Computer work is complex, detailed, and often very frustrating. In order to succeed in this field, you must be well organized and patient. You should enjoy challenges and problem solving, and you should be a logical thinker. You must also be able to communicate complex ideas in simple terms, as well as be able to work well under pressure and deadlines. As a network specialist, you should be naturally curious about the computing field; you must always be willing to learn more about new and different technologies.

▪ EXPLORING

"One of the greatest learning experiences in this field is just unpacking a new computer, setting it up, and getting connected to the Internet, continually asking yourself how and why as you go," says Dan Creedon, a network administrator at Nesbitt Burns Securities in Chicago.

If you are interested in computer networking you should join computer clubs at school and community centers and surf the Internet or other online services. Ask your school administration about the possibility of working with the school system's network specialists for a day or longer. Parents' or friends' employers might also be a good place to find this type of opportunity.

If seeking part-time jobs, apply for those that include computer work. Though you will not find networking positions, any experience on computers will increase your general computing knowledge. In addition, once employed, you can actively seek exposure to the other computer functions in the business.

You might also try volunteering at local-area charities that use computer networks in their office. Because many charities have small budgets, they may offer more opportunities to gain experience with some of the simpler networking tasks. In addition, experiment by creating networks with your own computer, those of your friends, and any printers, modems, and faxes that you have access to.

Basically, you should play around on computers as much as possible. Read and learn from any resource you can, such as magazines, newsletters, and online bulletin boards.

■ EMPLOYERS

The U.S. Department of Labor reports that approximately 232,560 computer network and systems administrators are employed today. Any company or organization that uses computer networks in its business employs network administrators. These include insurance companies, banks, financial institutions, health care organizations, federal and state governments, universities, and other corporations that rely on networking. Also, since smaller companies are moving to client-server models, more opportunities at almost any kind of business are becoming available.

■ STARTING OUT

There are several ways to obtain a position as a computer network specialist. If you are a student in a technical school or university, take advantage of your campus placement office. Check regularly for internship postings, job listings, and notices of on-campus recruitment. Placement offices are also valuable resources for resume tips and interviewing techniques. Internships and summer jobs with corporations are always beneficial and provide experience that will give you the edge over your

LEARN MORE ABOUT IT

Comer, Douglas E. *Computer Networks and Internets, with Internet Applications*. 3rd ed. Upper Saddle River, N.J.: Prentice Hall, 2001.

Davie, Bruce S., et al. *Computer Networks: A Systems Approach*. San Francisco, Calif.: Morgan Kaufmann Publishers, 1999.

Greenblatt, Bruce. *Building LDAP-Enabled Applications with Microsoft's Active Directory and Novell's NDS*. Upper Saddle River, N.J.: Prentice Hall PTR, 2001.

Kurose, James F., and Keith W. Ross. *Computer Networking: A Top-Down Approach Featuring the Internet*. Boston, Mass.: Addison-Wesley Publishing, 2000.

Mancill, Tony. *Linux Routers: A Primer For Network Administrators*. New York: Prentice Hall PTR, 2000.

Mason, Andrew G. *Cisco Secure Virtual Private Networks*. San Jose, Calif.: Cisco Press, 2001.

Silberschatz, Abraham, et al. *Operating System Concepts*. 6th ed. New York: John Wiley & Sons, 2001.

Singhal, Sandeep, and Michael Zyda. *Networked Virtual Environments: Design and Implementation*. New York: Association for Computing Machinery, 1999.

Wilson, Ed. *Administrators Guide to Windows 2000 TCP/IP Networks*. New York: Prentice Hall PTR, 2001.

competition. General computer job fairs are also held throughout the year in larger cities.

There are many online career sites listed on the World Wide Web that post job openings, salary surveys, and current employment trends. The Web also has online publications that deal specifically with computer jobs. You can also obtain information from computer organizations, such as the IEEE Computer Society and the Network Professional Association (see contact information at the end of this article).

When a job opportunity arises, you should send a cover letter and resume to the company promptly. Follow up your mailing with a phone call about one week later. If interested, the company recruiter will call you to ask questions and possibly arrange an interview. The commercial sponsors of network certification, such as Novell and Microsoft, also publish newsletters that list current job openings in the field. The same information is distributed through online bulletin boards and on the Internet as well. Otherwise, you can scan the classified ads in local newspapers and computer magazines or work with an employment agency to find such a position.

Individuals already employed but wishing to move into computer networking should investigate the possibility of tuition reimbursement from their employer for network certification. Many large companies have this type of program, which allows employees to train in a field that would benefit company operations. After successfully completing classes or certification, individuals are better qualified for related job openings in their own company and more likely to be hired into them.

■ ADVANCEMENT

"I would say that as much as a person is willing to learn is really the amount of advancement opportunities that are open to them," notes Dan Creedon. Among the professional options available are promotion to network manager or movement into network engineering. *Network engineers* design, test, and evaluate network systems, such as LAN, WAN, Internet, and other data communications systems. They also perform modeling, analysis, and planning. Network engineers might also research related products and make hardware and software recommendations.

Network specialists also have the option of going into a different area of computing. They can become computer programmers, systems analysts, software engineers, or multimedia professionals. All of these promotions require additional education and solid computer experience.

■ EARNINGS

Factors such as the size and type of employer, the administrator's experience, and specific job duties influence the earnings of network administrators. Robert Half Technology's *2002 Salary Guide* found that salaries of network managers ranged from $66,750 to $90,000. Also according to this survey, LAN/WAN administrators had earnings ranging from $47,000 to $68,250. According to the U.S. Department of Labor, the median yearly income for computer network and systems administrators was $57,620 in 2002. The lowest paid 10 percent made less than $34,460 per year, and the highest paid 10 percent earned more than $86,440 annually that same year.

Most computer network administrators are employed by companies that offer the full range of benefits, including health insurance, paid vacation, and sick leave. In addition, many companies have tuition reimbursement programs for employees seeking to pursue education or professional certification.

■ WORK ENVIRONMENT

Computer network administrators work indoors in a comfortable office environment. Their work is generally fast paced and can be frustrating. Some tasks, however, are routine and might get a little boring after a while. But many times, network specialists are required to work under a lot of pressure. If the network goes down, for example, the company is losing money, and it is the network specialist's job to get it up and running as fast as possible. The specialist must be able to remember complicated relationships and many details accurately and quickly. Specialists are also called on to deal effectively with the many complaints from network users.

When working on the installation of a new system, many network specialists are required to work overtime until it is fully operational. This usually includes long and frequent meetings. During initial operations of the system, some network specialists may be on call during other shifts for when problems arise, or they may have to train network users during off hours.

One other potential source of frustration is communications with other employees. Network specialists deal every day with people who usually don't understand the system as well as they do. Network administrators must be able to communicate at different levels of understanding.

■ OUTLOOK

The U.S. Department of Labor projects the job of computer network and systems administrator will grow at a rate that is much faster than the average through 2012. Network administrators are in high demand, particularly those with Internet experience. "Technology is constantly changing," Nancy Nelson says. "It is hard to tell where it will lead in the future. I think that the Internet and all of its pieces will be the place to focus on." As more and more companies and organizations discover the economic and convenience advantages linked to using computer networks at all levels of operations, the demand for well-trained network specialists will increase. Job opportunities should be best for those with certification and up-to-date training.

■ FOR MORE INFORMATION

For information on internships, student membership, and the student magazine Crossroads, *contact*

Association for Computing Machinery
1515 Broadway
New York, NY 10036
Tel: 800-342-6626
Email: sigs@acm.org
http://www.acm.org

For information on scholarships, student membership, and the student newsletter looking.forward, *contact*

IEEE Computer Society
1730 Massachusetts Avenue, NW
Washington, DC 20036-1992

Tel: 202-371-0101
Email: membership@computer.org
http://www.computer.org

For industry information, contact
Network Professional Association
195 South C Street, Suite 250
Tustin, CA 92780
Tel: 714-573-4780
Email: npa@npa.org
http://www.npanet.org

Computer Programmers

■ OVERVIEW

Computer programmers work in the field of electronic data processing. They write instructions that tell computers what to do in a computer language, or code, that the computer understands. Maintenance tasks include giving computers instructions on how to allocate time to various jobs they receive from computer terminals and making sure that these assignments are performed properly. There were approximately 499,000 computer programmers employed in the United States in 2002, and 18,000 of those programmers were self-employed.

■ HISTORY

Data processing systems and their support personnel are a product of World War II. The amount of information that had to be compiled and organized for war efforts became so great that it was not possible for people to collect it and put it in order in time for the necessary decisions to be made. It was obvious that a quicker way had to be devised to gather and organize information if decisions based on logic and not on guesses were to be made.

After the war, the new computer technology was put to use in other government operations as well as in businesses. The first computer used in a civilian capacity was installed by the Bureau of the Census in 1951 in order to help compile data from the 1950 census. At this time, computers were so large, cumbersome, and energy draining that the only practical use for them was thought to be large projects such as the census. However, three years later the first computer was installed by a business firm. Since 1954, many thousands of data processing systems have been installed in government agencies, industrial firms, banks, insurance agencies, educational systems, publishing houses, colleges and universities, and scientific laboratories.

Although computers seem capable of doing just about anything, one thing is still as true of computers today as it was of the first computer 60 years ago—they cannot think for themselves! Computers are machines that can only do exactly what they are told. This requires a small army of qualified computer programmers who understand computer languages well enough to give computers instructions on what to do, when, and how in order to meet the needs of government, business, and individuals. Some programmers are currently working on artificial intelligence, or computers that can in fact "think" for themselves and make humanlike decisions, but perfection of such technology is far off. As long as there are computers and new computer applications, there will be a constant need for programmers.

■ THE JOB

Broadly speaking, there are two types of computer programmers. *Systems programmers* maintain the instructions, called programs or software, that control the entire computer system, including both the central processing unit and the equipment with which it communicates, such as terminals, printers, and disk drives. *Applications programmers* write the software to handle specific jobs and may specialize in engineering, scientific, or business programs. Some of the latter specialists may be designated *chief business programmers,* who supervise the work of other business programmers.

Programmers are often given program specifications prepared by *systems analysts,* who list in detail the steps the computer must follow in order to complete a given task. Programmers then code these instructions in a computer language the computer understands. In smaller companies, analysis and programming may be handled by the same person, called a *programmer-analyst.*

Before actually writing the computer program, a programmer must analyze the work

QUICK FACTS

SCHOOL SUBJECTS
Computer science
Mathematics

PERSONAL SKILLS
Communication/ideas
Technical/scientific

WORK ENVIRONMENT
Primarily indoors
Primarily one location

MINIMUM EDUCATION LEVEL
Associate's degree

SALARY RANGE
$35,080 to $60,290 to
$96,860+

CERTIFICATION OR LICENSING
Voluntary

OUTLOOK
About as fast as the average

DOT
030

GOE
02.06.01

NOC
2174

O*NET-SOC
15-1021.00

request, understand the current problem and desired resolution, decide on an approach to the problem, and plan what the machine will have to do to produce the required results. Programmers prepare a flowchart to show the steps in sequence that the machine must make. They must pay attention to minute details and instruct the machine in each step of the process.

These instructions are then coded in one of several programming languages, such as BASIC, COBOL, FORTRAN, PASCAL, RPG, CSP, or C++. When the program is completed, the programmer tests its working practicality by running it on simulated data. If the machine responds according to expectations, actual data will be fed into it and the program will be activated. If the computer does not respond as anticipated, the program will have to be debugged, that is, examined for errors that must be eliminated. Finally, the programmer prepares an instruction sheet for the computer operator who will run the program.

The programmer's job concerns both an overall picture of the problem at hand and the minute detail of potential solutions. Programmers work from two points of view: from that of the people who need certain results and from that of technological problem solving. The work is divided equally between meeting the needs of other people and comprehending the capabilities of the machines.

Electronic data systems involve more than just one machine. Depending on the kind of system being used, the operation may require other machines such as printers or other peripherals. Introducing a new piece of equipment to an existing system often requires programmers to rewrite many programs.

Programmers may specialize in certain types of work, depending on the kind of problem to be solved and on the employer. Making a program for a payroll is, for example, very different from programming the study of structures of chemical compounds. Programmers who specialize in a certain field or industry generally have education or experience in that area before they are promoted to senior programming positions. *Information system programmers* specialize in programs for storing and retrieving physical science, engineering, or medical information; text analysis; and language, law, military, or library science data. As the information superhighway continues to grow, information system programmers have increased opportunities in online businesses, such as those of Lexis/Nexis, Westlaw, America Online, Microsoft, and many others.

Process control programmers develop programs for systems that control automatic operations for commercial and industrial enterprises, such as steelmaking, sanitation

plants, combustion systems, computerized production testing, or automatic truck loading. *Numerical control tool programmers* program the tape that controls the machining of automatic machine tools.

■ REQUIREMENTS
High School

In high school you should take any computer programming or computer science courses available. You should also concentrate on math, science, and schematic drawing courses, since these subjects directly prepare students for careers in computer programming.

Postsecondary Training

Most employers prefer their programmers to be college graduates. In the past, as the field was first taking shape, employers were known to hire people with some formal education and little or no experience but determination and the ability to learn quickly. As the market becomes saturated with individuals wishing to break into this field, however, a college degree is becoming increasingly important. The U.S. Department of Labor reports that nearly half of computer programmers held a bachelor's degree or higher in 2002. One in five held a graduate degree in 2002.

Many personnel officers administer aptitude tests to determine potential for programming work. Some employers send new employees to computer schools or in-house training sessions before the employees are considered qualified to assume programming responsibilities. Training periods may last as long as a few weeks, months, or even a year.

Many junior and community colleges also offer two-year associate's degree programs in data processing, computer programming, and other computer-related technologies.

Most four-year colleges and universities have computer science departments with a variety of computer-related majors, any of which could prepare a student for a career in programming. Employers who require a college degree often do not express a preference as to major field of study, although mathematics or computer science is highly favored. Other acceptable majors may be business administration, accounting, engineering, or physics. Entrance requirements for jobs with the government are much the same as those in private industry.

Certification or Licensing

Students who choose to obtain a two-year degree might consider becoming certified by the Institute for Certification of Computing Professionals, whose address is listed at the end of this article. Although it is not required, certification may boost an individual's attractiveness to employers during the job search.

Other Requirements

Personal qualifications such as a high degree of reasoning ability, patience, and persistence, as well as an aptitude for mathematics, are important for computer programmers. Some employers whose work is highly technical require that programmers be qualified in the area in which the firm or agency operates. Engineering firms, for example, prefer young people with an engineering background and are willing to train them in some programming techniques. For other firms, such as banks, consumer-level knowledge of the services that banks offer may be sufficient background for incoming programmers.

■ EXPLORING

If you are interested in becoming a computer programmer, you might visit a large bank or insurance company in the community and seek an appointment to talk with one of the programmers on the staff. You may be able to visit the data processing center and see the machines in operation. You might also talk with a sales representative from one of the large manufacturers of data processing equipment and request whatever brochures or pamphlets the company publishes.

It is a good idea to start early and get some hands-on experience operating and programming a computer. A trip to the local library or bookstore is likely to turn up countless books on programming; this is one field where the resources to teach yourself are highly accessible and available for all levels of competency. Joining a computer club and reading professional magazines are other ways to become more familiar with this career field. In addition, you should start exploring the Internet, itself a great source of information about computer-related careers.

High school and college students who can operate a computer may be able to obtain part-time jobs in business computer centers or in some larger companies. Any computer experience will be helpful for future computer training.

■ EMPLOYERS

There are approximately 499,000 computer programming jobs in the United States, and programmers work in locations across the country and in almost every type of business. They work for manufacturing companies, data processing service firms, hardware and software companies, banks, insurance companies, credit companies, publishing houses, government agencies, and colleges and universities throughout the country. Many programmers are employed by businesses as consultants on a temporary or contractual basis.

■ STARTING OUT

You can look for an entry-level programming position in the same way as most other jobs; there is no special or standard point of entry into the field. Individuals with the necessary qualifications should apply directly to companies, agencies, or industries that have announced job openings through a school placement office, an employment agency, or the classified ads.

Students in two- or four-year degree programs should work closely with their schools' placement offices, since major local employers often list job openings exclusively with such offices.

If the market for programmers is particularly tight, you may want to obtain an entry-level job with a large corporation or computer software firm, even if the job does not include programming. As jobs in the programming department open up, current employees in other departments are often the first to know, and they are favored over nonemployees during the interviewing process. Getting a foot in the door in this way has proven to be successful for many programmers.

■ ADVANCEMENT

Programmers are ranked as junior or senior programmers, according to education, experience, and level of responsibility. After programmers have attained the highest available programming position, they can choose to make one of several career moves in order to be promoted still higher.

Some programmers are more interested in the analysis aspect of computing than in the actual charting and coding of programming. They often acquire additional training and experience in order to prepare themselves for promotion to positions as systems programmers or systems analysts. These individuals have the added responsibility of working with upper management to define equipment and cost guidelines for a specific project. They perform only broad programming tasks, leaving most of the detail work to programmers.

Other programmers become more interested in administration and management and may wish to become heads of programming departments. They tend to be more people oriented and enjoy leading others to excellence. As the level of management responsibilities increases, the amount of technical work performed decreases, so management positions are not for everyone.

Still other programmers may branch out into different technical areas, such as total computer operations, hardware design, and software or network engineering.

With experience, they may be placed in charge of the data systems center. They may also decide to go to work for a consulting company, work that generally pays extremely well.

Programming provides a solid background in the computer industry. Experienced programmers enjoy a wide variety of possibilities for career advancement. The hardest part for programmers usually is deciding exactly what they want to do.

■ EARNINGS

According to the National Association of Colleges and Employers, the starting annual salary for college graduates with computer programming bachelor's degrees averaged $45,558 in 2003. The U.S. Department of Labor reports the median annual salary for computer programmers was $60,290 in 2002. The lowest paid 10 percent of programmers earned less than $35,080 annually, and at the other end of the pay scale, the highest paid 10 percent earned more than $96,860 that same year. Programmers in the West and the Northeast are generally paid more than those in the South and Midwest. This is because most big computer companies are located in the Silicon Valley in California or in the state of Washington, where Microsoft, a major employer of programmers, has its headquarters. Also, some industries, such as public utilities and data processing service firms, tend to pay their programmers higher wages than do other types of employers, such as banks and schools.

Most programmers receive the customary paid vacation and sick leave and are included in such company benefits as group insurance and retirement benefit plans.

■ WORK ENVIRONMENT

Most programmers work in pleasant office conditions, since computers require an air-conditioned, dust-free environment. Programmers perform most of their duties in one primary location but may be asked to travel to other computing sites on occasion. Because of advances in technology, telecommuting is an increasingly common option for computer professionals, allowing them to work remotely.

The average programmer works between 35 and 40 hours weekly. In some job situations, the programmer may have to work nights or weekends on short notice. This might happen when a program is going through its trial runs, for example, or when there are many demands for additional services. As with other workers who spend long periods in front of a computer terminal typing at a keyboard, programmers are susceptible to eyestrain, back discomfort, and hand and wrist problems, such as carpal tunnel syndrome.

■ OUTLOOK

The employment rate for computer programmers is expected to increase about as fast as the average through 2012, according to the U.S. Department of Labor. Employment of programmers is expected to grow more slowly than that of other computer specialists. Factors that make job growth for this profession slower than job growth for other computer industry professions include new technologies that eliminate the need for some routine programming work of the past, the increased availability of packaged software programs, and the increased sophistication of computer users who are able to write and implement their own programs. Jobs should be most plentiful in data processing service firms, software houses, and computer consulting businesses.

Job applicants with the best chances of employment will be college graduates with a knowledge of several programming languages, especially newer ones used for computer networking and database management. In addition, the best applicants will have some training or experience in an applied field such as accounting, science, engineering, or management. Competition for jobs will be heavier among graduates of two-year data processing programs and among people with equivalent experience or with less training. Since this field is constantly changing, programmers should stay abreast of the latest technology to remain competitive. Growing emphasis on cyber-security will lead to demand for programmers familiar with digital security issues.

■ FOR MORE INFORMATION

For more information about careers in computer programming, contact the following organizations:

Association for Computing Machinery
1515 Broadway
New York, NY 10036
Tel: 800-342-6626
Email: sigs@acm.org
http://www.acm.org

Institute of Electrical and Electronics Engineers
  Computer Society
1730 Massachusetts Ave. NW
Washington, DC 20036-1992
http://www.computer.org

National Workforce Center for Emerging
  Technologies
3000 Landerholm Circle SE
Bellevue, WA 98007
http://www.nwcet.org

Association of Information Technology Professionals
401 North Michigan Avenue, Suite 2200
Chicago, IL 60611-4267
Tel: 800-224-9371
Email: aitp_hq@aitp.org
http://www.aitp.org

For information on certification programs, contact
Institute for Certification of Computing Professionals
2350 East Devon Avenue, Suite 115
Des Plaines, IL 60018-4610
Tel: 800-843-8227
http://www.iccp.org

Computer Support Service Owners

■ OVERVIEW

The owners of computer support services help businesses and individuals install and maintain computer hardware and software. They offer advice on what computers to purchase; they teach how to operate computers; and they assist with computer problems as they arise. There are close to 507,000 computer support specialists in the industry, including technicians and entrepreneurs. *Computer consultants* either work out of their homes, or they rent office space. Though some of their assistance is offered over the phone, much of their work is performed on-site.

■ HISTORY

Did you know there are museums devoted to "antique" computer hardware? Hang on to those old monitors, keyboards, and hard drives—they may be worth something to collectors and archivists some day. When you think about computers, you're probably not thinking about the past. Computer hardware and software is most often talked about in terms of the future, but computer technology has been in development for over a century. In 1854, George Boole (1815–64) invented Boolean Algebra, a symbol and logic system used as the basis of computer design.

The 1950s brought IBM's first computers and the computer programming languages COBOL and LISP. By the late 1960s, people with computer skills served as consultants to develop hardware and software for manufac-turers. The Independent Computer Consultants Association (ICCA) was founded in 1976. Consultants had many more opportunities when even small businesses began investing in computers. Office software, such as spreadsheet programs and programs that link computers together with a shared hard drive, were developed in the early 1980s. Many businesses and schools required the regular services of computer support technicians by the late 1980s.

■ THE JOB

If your computer's not working, the problem may be simply that you've forgotten to plug in the machine. But it can be much more complicated than that, requiring the assistance of someone with a great deal of computer knowledge. Today's hardware and software are easier to use than in previous years, but can be difficult to install correctly and difficult to learn. Computer support service owners use their computer expertise to help businesses and individuals buy new computers and ready them for daily use.

With their operations based in their home office, computer support service owners take calls from new clients, as well as clients who regularly rely on their services. Clients may have problems with their printers not responding to computer commands; a computer may be locked up; they may have problems performing the particular functions their software is designed for. In some cases, support service owners are able to diagnose the problem and offer assistance over the phone. But in most cases, they are required to go to the offices and work hands-on with the computer systems. Armed with a cell phone, pager, and laptop, they drive to the offices of businesses small and large and the homes of personal computer owners to help get the computers running again. They will install network systems and new hardware and software. They upgrade existing systems. Computer support service owners also teach the

QUICK FACTS

SCHOOL SUBJECTS
Business
Computer science
Technical/shop

PERSONAL SKILLS
Helping/teaching
Technical/scientific

WORK ENVIRONMENT
Primarily indoors
Primarily multiple locations

MINIMUM EDUCATION LEVEL
Associate's degree

SALARY RANGE
$35,000 to $57,000 to $90,000+

CERTIFICATION OR LICENSING
Voluntary

OUTLOOK
Faster than the average

DOT
039

GOE
02.06.01

NOC
2282

O*NET-SOC
15-1041.00

computer operators how to use the new systems, either one on one or in group training sessions. They advise on the purchase of hardware and software, and can prepare backup methods.

Many computer consultants also offer their expertise in Web design and multimedia for uploading a Web page, preparing a presentation, and offering desktop publishing services. They also help to create computer databases. Some computer consultants are involved in issues of programming.

Brad Crotteau started his own computer support service in 1991, and his business has grown into Crocker Networking Solutions Inc. He anticipated that some of the demands of the job would become more difficult as he got older, so he recently made some decisions about the

COMPUTER VIRUSES

Computer support service owners must contend with the destruction of systems by many different kinds of computer viruses. But computer viruses aren't the only viruses causing concern among computer users: "Text viruses" are email hoaxes and myths that are passed about in cyberspace (and usually originate on April Fool's Day). Here are a few hoaxes that have been carried off in recent years:

- Internet users were discouraged from opening any email with the subject "Good Times." Doomsayers warned that the message actually carried a computer virus that would instantly infect your computer upon opening of the email. (The truth is: no email can infect your computer with a virus simply by being opened and read. Some program must be executed, a file downloaded, in order for a virus to enter your system.)

- An email message alerted people to the danger of government regulation of library materials through a system of barcoding. In the tradition of the television "v-chip," parents could regulate their children's reading habits by forbidding them to check out books that have been barcoded with warnings of sex and violence. (The truth is: though the television v-chip is very much a reality, books have yet to be subjected to such high-tech control.)

- Beware of a computer virus that can be transferred onto humans, one email message announced. By spending too much time on the Internet, you can be infected with a virus that results in moodiness, depression, and other emotional problems. (The truth is that some studies have determined that people who spend a lot of time online are more depressed than they were before they got "wired," but that's not the fault of the computer!)

nature of his business. "I knew I didn't always want to be crawling around, plugging computers in," he says. So Crotteau incorporated his business and took on a staff of nine employees, including technicians, sales people, administrative assistants, trainers, and Web designers.

Crotteau's day starts early at 7:00 A.M. with paperwork, followed at around 8:00 A.M. by phone calls from businesses. He then must work the new requests for service into his daily schedule. Though he has a staff of nine, Crotteau is still actively involved in the technical work of installing systems and troubleshooting, and the generating of estimates and other financial details. He makes it a point to end his work day at 6:00 P.M., though he is required to work some overtime. "I have stayed up until 4:00 A.M.," he says, "bringing a service up for a client, but that's rare." His client base consists of businesses with between five and 85 personal computers. The biggest challenge can be correcting user-generated problems. Crotteau says giving an inexperienced computer user a complex system "is like giving a Maserati to someone who just started riding horses a few weeks ago."

Crotteau's support service is also embarking on a new business venture. He has trademarked many of his company's services, and now offers them as a product called "Performance Net." His company sells the network systems, and then puts the systems into place. This venture has been helped along by a business alliance with a manufacturer of software. Crotteau's company has been hired by the manufacturer to install their servers in businesses all across the country.

In addition to technical work, the owners of computer support services must handle all the details of running their businesses. They handle phone calls, bookkeeping, and client records. They must also research new technologies and keep up to date on advanced technical skills. Maintaining connections within the industry is also important; computer support system owners may need to call upon the assistance of other consultants and technicians to help with some projects.

■ REQUIREMENTS
High School

Of course, you should take any classes that will familiarize you with computers. Computer science classes will help you learn about operating systems and programming. Learn about the various software, like word processing and spreadsheet programs, as well as the languages of Web page design. A journalism class and working on your school newspaper will involve you with multimedia presentation and teach you about page layout and graphic design. Take courses in business and accounting to prepare for the bookkeeping and administrative details of the work. English composition and communication courses can help you develop teaching skills.

Postsecondary Training

Though a degree isn't required for you to start your own computer support service, most service owners and consultants have at least an associate's degree. Some consultants supplement their education with special training offered by computer software companies such as Novell and Microsoft. Many consultants registered with the ICCA have advanced degrees and highly technical training in such areas as robotics, telecommunications, and nuclear engineering. Community colleges and universities across the country have programs in computer science, computer engineering, and electrical engineering. For a degree in computer science, you'll be required to take courses in calculus, English composition, program design, algorithms, computer graphics, and database management. Electrical engineering programs include courses in BASIC programming, industrial electronics, digital integrated circuits, and microprocessor systems. In addition to seminars, you'll also attend labs. Some bachelor's programs include research projects in which you'll work closely with a faculty member to study new technologies. Some software companies offer training programs.

Very few consultants start their own businesses straight out of college. Some years working full-time as part of a computer service staff will give you the firsthand experience you'll need. Not only will you develop your computer expertise, but you'll learn what's required in operating a business.

Certification or Licensing

There are many different kinds of certifications available to people working in computer support and consulting. No one certification, however, serves all the varying needs of computer professionals. Some consultants get certified in database design and administration. Some consultants have Microsoft Certified System Engineer (MCSE) status. The Association of Computer Support Specialists (ACSS) offers online training courses for the MCSE exam, which tests your understanding of Windows networks, hardware requirements and installations, and system maintenance. This certification should only supplement an extensive computer background, not replace it. The term "paper MCSE" has evolved in the industry to describe those who "look good on paper" with their certification, but don't have the networking and computer science education and experience to back it up.

The Institute for Certification of Computer Professionals (ICCP) offers a Certified Computer Professional (CCP) exam. Nearly 50,000 computer professionals hold

LEARN MORE ABOUT IT

Here are a few books that can give you some insight into the requirements of owning a computer support service:

Burris, Anne M. *Service Provider Strategy: Proven Secrets for xSPs*. Upper Saddle River, N.J.: Prentice Hall, 2001.
Gilster, Ron. *PC Technician Black Book: The PC Technician's Secret Weapon*. Scottsdale, Ariz.: The Coriolis Group, 2002.
Meyer, Peter. *Getting Started in Computer Consulting*. New York: John Wiley & Sons, 1999.
Minasi, Mark. *The Complete PC Upgrade & Maintenance Guide*. 15th ed. Alameda, Calif.: Sybex, 2004.
Ruhl, Janet. *The Computer Consultant's Guide: Real-life Strategies for Building a Successful Consulting Career*. 2nd ed. New York: John Wiley & Sons, 1997.
Simon, Alan R. *How to Be a Successful Computer Consultant*. 4th ed. New York: McGraw-Hill, 1998.
Sturm, Rick, et al. *Foundations of Service Level Management*. Indianapolis, Ind.: Macmillan USA, SAMS, 2000.
Tourniaire, Francoise, and Richard Farrell. *The Art of Software Support*. Upper Saddle River, N.J.: Prentice Hall, 1997.

the certification, having passed an exam that tests knowledge of business information systems, data resource management, software engineering, and other subjects.

Other Requirements

You should have good business and money management skills. Though some months you may have more work than you can handle, with a steady flow of income, other months there may be no work at all. You'll have to budget your money to carry you through the lean months. Though computer skills are very important, you'll need good people skills to maintain customer relations.

Teaching skills are important, because you'll be training people in how to use their systems. "You need the ability to talk to people in a language they can understand," Brad Crotteau says, "but don't talk down to them. You have to gauge your client's understanding."

■ EXPLORING

Get to know your own home computer—study the software and its manuals, and familiarize yourself with computer programming languages. Read some of the many magazines devoted to computers, such as *MacWorld* and *PC Today*. Find out who services the computers in your school, and ask to spend some time with the technicians. But don't just focus on the technical duties of the people who own computer support services; find out how they go about running an office and maintaining a small business. Join your school's business club and you'll have the opportunity to meet small business owners in your area.

◾ EMPLOYERS

Computer support service owners work for a variety of different clients, servicing the personal computers in home-based offices, as well as contracting with large companies for long-term assistance. Though many individuals have computers in their homes for their personal use, few of them seek out professional service. The main clients of support service owners will be accounting firms, insurance agencies, government departments—any business or organization that relies upon computers to perform daily operations. Even a company that has its own full-time support staff will occasionally hire outside consultants. Computer support services are in demand all across the country, but are most successful in large cities, as they can draw from a broader client base.

◾ STARTING OUT

Brad Crotteau had been working for Pacific Gas and Electric as an engineer for 14 years when he began developing his own business on the side. "The main concern for people starting their own businesses," Crotteau says, "is how they're going to capitalize their company." Brad was fortunate to receive an early retirement package, and then worked for a while as a computer consultant for a private consulting company. Once he'd felt he'd gotten his feet wet, he was ready to start full-time with his own support service. "You should work for a large corporation," Crotteau advises, "to learn about human resources, compensation packages, benefits. You need to develop a good business sense. That's why many small businesses fail; you may be great at computers, but bad at business."

As with many start-ups, it's good for you to focus your talents. Decide on a niche, such as networking, or package customization, then promote those specific services. Crotteau credits much of his success to good marketing techniques, which includes careful attention to image. "You can't do this from the back of your car," he says, "but promoting a good image doesn't have to be expensive. Our biggest sales tool is our business cards. We have a nice, multicolored business card that reads well."

◾ ADVANCEMENT

Once they are established in their niche market, support service owners can expand to include other services. Some computer support services are able to offer much more than technical assistance; they also hold training sessions, prepare multimedia reports and presentations,

and design Web pages. The more business connections a support service owner can make with support services, computer manufacturers, and other companies, the better they'll be able to build your client base. As their business grows, support service owners can hire staff to deal with administrative duties, as well as technicians to assist with servicing their clients' computers.

◾ EARNINGS

According to Robert Half Technology, the median annual earnings for computer consultants ranges from about $57,000 to $77,000. In the first few years of a business, a consultant will make about $35,000 or less, depending on location. Those working in large cities like New York and Los Angeles average more than those in the Midwest, the Southwest, and the Northwest. Someone in New York with more than 10 years experience can average over $90,000 a year, while a consultant with similar experience in the Southwest may make closer to $65,000 a year. Some very experienced, business-minded consultants can make $150,000 a year or more.

According to the Department of Labor, median hourly wages for computer support specialists were $18.80 in 2002, which, based on a 40-hour workweek, is a salary of $39,104 a year.

◾ WORK ENVIRONMENT

Most computer support businesses are based in a home office or a rented commercial space. Computer support service owners devote a lot of time to sitting at their own computer, managing their accounts and records, but the majority of their time will be in the offices of their clients. In either setting, the work environment will likely be quiet and well lit. The work will be indoors, though support service owners will travel from office to office throughout the day.

When installing and repairing computer hardware, support service owners may have to do some crawling around behind desks to hook up wires and plug in cords. This work is essentially unsupervised, but some clients may ask to receive instruction and information about the repairs being made. In some cases, support service owners may work as part of a team, particularly if they're brought into a large company with a full-time support staff.

Some consultants work much more than 40 hours a week, though support service owners can avoid this by developing strong business management skills. "If you're working 80 hours a week," Brad Crotteau says, "something's wrong. You'll have to work hard, but you don't have to obsess about it."

■ OUTLOOK

According to the U.S. Department of Labor, the industry is expected to grow quickly as computer systems become more important to many businesses. Lower prices on computer hardware and software will inspire businesses to expand their systems, and to invest in the services needed to keep them up and running. As computer programs become more sophisticated and are able to perform more complex operations, consultants will be needed to help clients operate these programs. With companies relying more on complex computer systems, they'll be less likely to take risks in the installation of hardware and software. To stay at the top of the industry, consultants will have to keep up on technological developments and take continuing education courses.

More consultants may also become involved in broadening computer literacy. Computer resources are generally limited to middle-class students; some nonprofit organizations are forming to bring more computers and support services to inner-city youth, low-income families, and people with disabilities.

■ FOR MORE INFORMATION

To subscribe to a free electronic newsletter, and to check out an extensive list of related Web links, visit the ACSS Web page. To learn more about membership and their career training courses, contact

Association of Computer Support Specialists (ACSS)

218 Huntington Road

Bridgeport, CT 06608

Tel: 203-332-1524

Email: hhr@acss.org

http://www.acss.org

To learn about membership benefits, contact

Independent Computer Consultants Association

11131 South Towne Square, Suite F

St. Louis, MO 63123

Tel: 800-774-4222

Email: info@icca.org

http://www.icca.org

For information on certification programs, contact

Institute for Certification of Computing Professionals

2350 East Devon Avenue, Suite 115

Des Plaines, IL 60018-4610

Tel: 800-843-8227

Email: office@iccp.org

http://www.iccp.org

For resume and cover letter advice, salary statistics, and other career information in information technology, check out the following website:

Robert Half Technology

http://www.roberthalftechnology.com

FASTEST GROWING CAREERS

Computer Systems Programmer/ Analysts

■ OVERVIEW

Computer systems programmer/analysts analyze the computing needs of a business and then design a new system or upgrade an old system to meet those needs. The position can be split between two people, the *systems programmer* and the *systems analyst,* but it is frequently held by just one person, who oversees the work from beginning to end.

■ HISTORY

The first major advances in modern computer technology were made during World War II. After the war, people thought that computers were too big (they easily filled entire warehouses) to ever be used for anything other than government projects, such as the processing of the 1950 census.

The introduction of semiconductors to computer technology led to the creation of smaller and less expensive computers. The semiconductors replaced the bigger, slower vacuum tubes of the first computers. These changes made it easier for businesses to adapt computers to their needs, which they began doing as early as 1954. Within 30 years, computers had revolutionized the way people work, play, and even shop. Today, computers are everywhere, from businesses of all kinds to government agencies, charitable organizations, and private homes. Over the years, technology has continued to shrink computer size and increase operating speeds at an unprecedented rate.

The need for systems programmer/analysts grew out of the proliferation of hardware and software products on the market. While many offices have an unofficial "computer expert," whose main job may be in accounting, word processing, or office administration, most medium-size to larger companies that have invested in expensive computer systems have found the need to employ, either full-time or on a consulting basis, a systems analyst or programmer analyst.

In addition, the computer revolution brought with it awareness that choosing the appropriate system from the start is crucial to business success. Purchasing decisions are based on many complicated scientific and mathematical models as well as on practical business sense. Therefore, systems analysts have become essential to business decision-making.

Businesses and organizations also discovered that, like all new technology, computer systems break down a lot. It has become more cost effective for many organizations to have full-time systems analysts on site instead of calling computer repairers to fix every small glitch.

THE JOB

Businesses invest hundreds of thousands of dollars in computer systems to make their operations more efficient and thus, more profitable. As older systems become obsolete, businesses are also faced with the task of replacing them or upgrading them with new technology. Computer systems programmer/analysts plan and develop new computer systems or upgrade existing systems to meet changing business needs. They also install, modify, and maintain functioning computer systems. The process of choosing and implementing a computer system is similar for programmer analysts who work for very different employers. However, specific decisions in terms of hardware and software differ depending on the industry.

The first stage of the process involves meeting with management and users in order to discuss the problem at hand. For example, a company's accounting system might be slow, unreliable, and generally outdated. During many hours of meetings, systems programmer/analysts and man-

agement discuss various options, including commercial software, hardware upgrades, and customizing possibilities that may solve the problems. At the end of the discussions, which may last as long as several weeks or months, the programmer analyst defines the specific system goals as agreed upon by participants.

Next, systems programmer/analysts engage in highly analytic and logical activities. They use tools such as structural analysis, data modeling, mathematics, and cost accounting to determine which computers, including hardware and software and peripherals, will be required to meet the goals of the project. They must consider the trade-offs between extra efficiency and speed and increased costs. Weighing the pros and cons of each additional system feature is an important factor in system planning. Whatever preliminary decisions are made must be supported by mathematical and financial evidence.

As the final stage of the planning process, systems programmer/analysts prepare reports and formal presentations to be delivered to management. Reports must be written in clear, concise language that business professionals, who are not necessarily technical experts, can understand thoroughly. Formal presentations in front of groups of various sizes are often required as part of the system proposal.

If the system or the system upgrades are approved, equipment is purchased and installed. Then, the programmer analysts get down to the real technical work so that all the different computers and peripherals function well together. They prepare specifications, diagrams, and other programming structures and, often using computer-aided systems engineering (CASE) technology, they write the new or upgraded programming code. If they work solely as systems analysts, it is at this point that they hand over all of their information to the systems programmer so that he or she can begin to write the programming code.

Systems design and programming involves defining the files and records to be accessed by the system, outlining the processing steps, and suggesting formats for output that meet the needs of the company. User-friendliness of the front-end applications is extremely important for user productivity. Therefore, programmer analysts must be able to envision how nontechnical system users view their on-screen work. Systems programmer/analysts might also specify security programs that allow only authorized personnel access to certain files or groups of files.

As the programs are written, programmer analysts set up test runs of various parts of the system, making sure each step of the way that major goals are reached. Once the system is up and running, problems, or "bugs," begin to pop up. Programmer analysts are responsible for fixing these last-minute problems. They must isolate the problem and review the hundreds of lines of programming commands to determine where the mistake is located. Then they must enter the correct command or code and recheck the program.

Depending on the employer, some systems programmer/analysts might be involved with computer networking. Network communication programs tell two or more computers or peripherals how to work with each other. When a system is composed of equipment from various manufacturers, networking is essential for smooth system functioning. For example, shared printers have to know how to order print jobs as they come in from various terminals. Some programmer analysts write the code that establishes printing queues. Others might be involved in user training, since they know the software applications well. They might also customize commercial software programs to meet the needs of their company.

Many programmer analysts become specialized in an area of business, science, or engineering. They seek education and further on-the-job training in these areas to develop expertise. They may therefore attend special seminars, workshops, and classes designed for their needs. This extra knowledge allows them to develop a deeper understanding of the computing problems specific to the business or industry.

■ REQUIREMENTS
High School

Take a college preparatory program with advanced classes in math, science, and computer science to prepare you for this work. This will provide a foundation of basic concepts and encourage the development of analytic and logical thinking skills. Since programmer analysts do a lot of proposal writing that may or may not be technical in nature, English classes are valuable as well. Speech classes will help prepare you for making formal presentations to management and clients.

Postsecondary Training

A bachelor's degree in computer science is a minimum requirement for systems programmer/analysts. Course work in preparation for this field includes math, computer programming, science, and logic. Several years of related work experience, including knowledge of programming languages, are often necessary as well. For some very high-level positions, an advanced degree in a specific computer subfield may be required. Also, depending on the employer, proficiency in business, science, or engineering may be necessary.

A computer systems programmer/analyst (l) discusses the design of a new system with an engineer (r).

Certification or Licensing

Some programmer analysts pursue certification through the Institute for Certification of Computing Professionals. In particular, they take classes and exams to become certified computing professionals (CCPs). Certification is voluntary and is an added credential for job hunters. CCPs have achieved a recognized level of knowledge and experience in principles and practices related to systems.

Other Requirements

Successful systems programmer/analysts demonstrate strong analytic skills and enjoy the challenges of problem solving. They are able to understand problems that exist on many levels, from technical to practical to business oriented. They can visualize complicated and abstract relationships between computer hardware and software and are good at matching needs to equipment.

Systems programmer/analysts have to be flexible as well. They routinely deal with many different kinds of people, from management to data entry clerks. Therefore, they must be knowledgeable in a lot of functional areas of the company. They should be able to talk to management about cost-effective solutions, to programmers about detailed coding, and to clerks about user-friendliness of the applications.

As is true for all computer professionals, systems programmer/analysts must be able to learn about new technology quickly. They should be naturally curious about keeping up on cutting-edge developments, which can be time consuming. Furthermore, they are often so busy at their jobs that staying in the know is done largely on their own time.

■ EXPLORING

You have several options to learn more about what it is like to be a computer systems programmer/analyst. You can spend a day with a working professional in this field in order to experience a typical day firsthand. Career days of this type can usually be arranged through school guidance counselors or the public relations manager of local corporations.

Strategy games, such as chess, played with friends or school clubs are a good way to put your analytic thinking skills to use while having fun. When choosing a game, the key is to make sure it relies on qualities similar to those used by programmer analysts.

Lastly, you should become a computer hobbyist and learn everything you can about computers by working and playing with them on a daily basis. Surfing the Internet regularly, as well as reading trade magazines, will also be helpful. You might also want to try hooking up a minisystem at home or school, configuring terminals, printers, modems, and other peripherals into a coherent system. This activity requires a fair amount of knowledge and should be supervised by a professional.

■ EMPLOYERS

Computer systems programmer/analysts work for all types of firms and organizations that do their work on computers. Such companies may include manufacturing companies, data processing service firms, hardware and software companies, banks, insurance companies, credit companies, publishing houses, government agencies, and colleges and universities. Many programmer analysts are employed by businesses as consultants on a temporary or contractual basis.

■ STARTING OUT

Since systems programmer/analysts typically have at least some experience in a computer-related job, most are hired into these jobs from lower-level positions within the same company. For example, programmers, software engineering technicians, and network and database administrators all gain valuable computing experience that can be put to good use at a systems job. Alternatively, individuals who acquire expertise in systems programming and analysis while in other jobs may want to work with a headhunter to find the right systems positions for them. Also, trade magazines, newspapers, and employment agencies regularly feature job openings in this field.

Students in four-year degree programs should work closely with their schools' placement offices. Companies regularly work through such offices in order to find the most qualified graduates. Since it may be difficult to find a job as a programmer analyst to begin with, it is impor-

tant for students to consider their long-term potential within a certain company. The chance for promotion into a systems job can make lower-level jobs more appealing, at least in the short run.

For those individuals already employed in a computer-related job but wanting to get into systems programming and analysis, additional formal education is a good idea. Some employers have educational reimbursement policies that allow employees to take courses inexpensively. If the employee's training could directly benefit the business, companies are more willing to pay for the expense.

■ ADVANCEMENT

Systems programmer/analysts already occupy a relatively high-level technical job. Promotion, therefore, usually occurs in one of two directions. First, programmer analysts can be put in charge of increasingly larger and more complex systems. Instead of concentrating on a company's local system, for example, an analyst can oversee all company systems and networks. This kind of technically based promotion can also put systems programmer/analysts into other areas of computing. With the proper experience and additional training, they can get into database or network management and design, software engineering, or even quality assurance.

The other direction in which programmer analysts can go is managerial. Depending on the position sought, formal education (either a bachelor's degree in business or a master's in business administration) may be required. As more administrative duties are added, more technical ones are taken away. Therefore, programmer analysts who enjoy the technical aspect of their work more than anything else may not want to pursue this advancement track. Excellent computing managers have both a solid background in various forms of computing and a good grasp of what it takes to run a department. Also, having the vision to see how technology will change in the short and long terms, and how those changes will affect the industry concerned, is a quality of a good manager.

■ EARNINGS

According to the U.S. Bureau of Labor Statistics, the median annual salary for computer systems analysts was $62,890 in 2002. At the low end of the pay range, 10 percent of systems analysts earned less than $39,270. The top 10 percent earned more than $93,400. Salaries are slightly higher in geographic areas where many computer companies are clustered, such as Silicon Valley in California and Seattle, Washington.

Level of education also affects analysts' earnings. The National Association of Colleges and Employers reports that starting salaries for those with master's degrees in computer science averaged $62,806 in 2003. Those with bachelor's degrees in computer science, however, had starting salaries averaging $47,109, and those with bachelor's degrees in computer systems analysis averaged $41,118, also in 2003.

Those in senior positions can earn much higher salaries. *Computerworld* reports that senior systems programmers earned a national average of $71,475 in 2003, while senior systems analysts earned $76,173.

Most programmer analysts receive health insurance, paid vacation, and sick leave. Some employers offer tuition reimbursement programs and in-house computer training workshops.

■ WORK ENVIRONMENT

Computer systems programmer/analysts work in comfortable office environments. If they work as consultants, they may travel frequently. Otherwise, travel is limited to trade shows, seminars, and visitations to vendors for demonstrations. They might also visit other businesses to observe their systems in action.

Programmer analysts usually work 40-hour weeks and enjoy the regular holiday schedule of days off. However, as deadlines for system installation, upgrades, and spot-checking approach, they are often required to work overtime. Extra compensation for overtime hours may come in the form of time-and-a-half pay or compensatory time off, depending on the precise nature of the employee's duties, company policy, and state law. If the employer operates off-shifts, programmer analysts may be on-call to address any problems that might arise at any time of the day or night. This is relatively rare in the service sector but more common in manufacturing, heavy industry, and data processing firms.

Computer systems programming and analysis is very detailed work. The smallest error can cause major system disruptions, which can be a great source of frustration. Systems programmer/analysts must be prepared to deal with this frustration and be able to work well under pressure.

■ OUTLOOK

The U.S. Department of Labor predicts that the job of computer systems programmer/analyst will be one of the fastest growing through 2012, with employment increasing much faster than the average. In fact, this is one of the fastest growing occupations. Increases are mainly a product of the growing number of businesses that rely extensively on computers. When businesses automate, their daily operations depend on the capacity of their computer systems to perform at desired levels. The continuous development of new technologies means that businesses must also update their old systems to remain competitive in the marketplace. Additionally, the need for businesses to network their information adds to the demand for qualified programmer analysts. Businesses will rely increasingly on systems programmer/analysts to make the right purchasing decisions and to keep systems running smoothly.

Many computer manufacturers are beginning to expand the range of services they offer to business clients. In the years to come, they may hire many systems programmer/analysts to work as consultants on a per-project basis with a potential client. These workers would perform essentially the same duties, with the addition of extensive follow-up maintenance. They would analyze business needs and suggest proper systems to answer them. In addition, more and more independent consulting firms are hiring systems programmer/analysts to perform the same tasks.

Analysts with advanced degrees in computer science, management information systems, or computer engineering will be in great demand. Individuals with master's degrees in business administration with emphasis in information systems will also be highly desirable.

■ FOR MORE INFORMATION

For more information about systems programmer/analyst positions, contact

**Association of Information Technology
  Professionals**
401 North Michigan Avenue, Suite 2200
Chicago, IL 60611-4267
Tel: 800-224-9371
Email: aitp_hq@aitp.org
http://www.aitp.org

For information on becoming an independent consultant, contact

Independent Computer Consultants Association
11131 South Towne Square, Suite F
St. Louis, MO 63123
Tel: 800-774-4222
Email: info@icca.org
http://www.icca.org

For information on certification programs, contact

**Institute for Certification of Computing
  Professionals**
2350 East Devon Avenue, Suite 115
Des Plaines, IL 60018-4610
Tel: 800-843-8227
Email: office@iccp.org
http://www.iccp.org

Computer Trainers

■ OVERVIEW

Computer trainers teach topics related to all aspects of using computers in the workplace, including personal computer (PC) software, operating systems for both stand-alone and networked systems, management tools for networks, and software applications for mainframe computers and specific industry management. Trainers work for training companies and software developers, either on the permanent staff or as independent consultants. They may produce training materials, including disk-based multimedia technology-delivered learning, instructor-led courseware, skills assessment, videos, and classroom teaching manuals.

QUICK FACTS

SCHOOL SUBJECTS
Business
Computer science
Speech

PERSONAL SKILLS
Helping/teaching
Technical/scientific

WORK ENVIRONMENT
Primarily indoors
Primarily multiple locations

MINIMUM EDUCATION LEVEL
Bachelor's degree

SALARY RANGE
$35,000 to $45,000 to
$89,000+

CERTIFICATION OR LICENSING
Recommended

OUTLOOK
Much faster than the average

DOT
N/A

GOE
12.03.02

NOC
N/A

O*NET-SOC
13-1073.00

■ HISTORY

The worldwide market for information technology (IT) education and training reached $22 billion in 2000, according to International Data Corporation (IDC). IDC also projected growth in the field to continue, with revenues of almost $41 billion by 2005. No question about it—employers care about what computer skills and how much computer training their employees have.

The field of computer training has been around since about 1983, when the computer industry exploded with the introduction of the first PCs. With all of the new software packages being released, individual information technology (IT) and information services (IS) departments could not possibly keep up with the amount of training their employees needed. Software vendor companies started sending their employees out to teach new purchasers how to use their products, and a new section of the computer industry was born.

In the beginning, computer training was conducted like any other training, in a classroom setting with an instructor. Although that type of training is still preva-

lent today, current training methods incorporate new technology. According to the American Society for Training and Development (ASTD), workplace educators are turning to technology to deliver their instructions. Developments in hardware, computer networking, multimedia software, and video conferencing have tremendous potential for multiple-site instruction and training closer to people's work sites.

Technological developments constantly change the process in which work is done. As a result, computer trainers must be up to date on the latest developments and improvements in computer systems and programs. ASTD also notes that training departments are finding new ways to deliver computer training, by using support networks of internal and external training providers, including consultants, community colleges, and universities.

■ THE JOB

The field of computer training encompasses several different areas. *Software vendor trainers* work for developer companies. *Consultants* work for themselves as independent contractors, often specializing in certain computer languages, skills, or platforms. Some trainers work in the corporate training departments of companies that develop products other than computers and software. Others are teachers and professors.

"As a software trainer, my duties are to be prepared to teach various topics related to our software to a variety of clients on any given day," says Marcy Anderson, a software trainer for Cyborg Systems, a human-resource software developer. "I teach from a training manual and demonstrate the procedures on my computer that displays the information on a large screen for the entire class. The class is given assignments throughout the day that they complete on their PCs. I assist them one on one with their questions as the class continues. Cyborg has a training center with four classrooms. I conduct classes in the training center, or I travel to the client and hold classes on-site."

Consultant trainers are certified to teach several different products, applications, environments, and databases, usually with companies such as Microsoft, IBM, or Apple. Most have been in the computer industry for many years, previously working as software programmers, architects, project managers, or developers.

Whatever their affiliation, most computer trainers use several ways to disseminate learning technologies, including CD-ROM, CBT-Text, electronic performance support systems, the Internet, Intranets, multimedia presentations, and video conferencing.

One of the most important things for trainers to have is certification for the courses they intend to teach. The International Board of Standards for Training, Performance, and Instruction has an outline of ground-level skills that are mandatory for technical trainers, according to the ASTD. The following 14 competencies are the basis for the certified trainer examination. For trainers to receive certification, they must show proof that they can execute the following:

- analyze course materials and learning information
- ensure preparation of the instructional site
- establish and maintain instructor credibility
- manage the learning environment
- demonstrate effective communication skills
- demonstrate effective presentation skills
- demonstrate effective questioning skills and techniques
- respond appropriately to learners' needs for clarification or feedback
- provide positive reinforcement and motivational incentives
- use instructional methods appropriately
- use media effectively
- evaluate learner performance
- evaluate instruction delivery
- report evaluation information

Trainers are beginning to explore the field of online learning. In the article, "Our Turn-of-the-Century Trend Watch," Paul Clothier, senior instructor, Softwire Corporation, says, "Improved online learning (OL) design and technologies will significantly impact the technical training profession over the next few years. At present, much of the technical training taking place is in the form of instructor-led training (ILT) in a classroom. There are many advantages to ILT, but there are also considerable disadvantages, such as time investment, travel, and expense. To get a group of your most valuable technical people off to a week of training is often a major expense and inconvenience. Organizations are crying out for a better alternative, and OL increasingly is seen as an option."

■ REQUIREMENTS
High School

If you are interested in a career in computer training, take as many computer and mathematics classes as possible in high school. These will provide the foundation for the rest of your computer education. Start learning about computer programs, such as Visual Basic, on your own. Speech, drama, or other performance courses will also help get you used to speaking in front of a crowd. "A lit-

---

INSTRUCTION METHODS FOR TRAINERS

Trainers use a myriad of techniques to keep the attention of their pupils. Here are a few of them from the American Society of Training and Development.

Case study: Basic instructional method for practicing solving problems using a hypothetical scenario; requires reading, study, analysis, discussion, and a free exchange of ideas, as well as decision-making.

Demonstration: Trainer shows how to perform a task in front of the learners.

Expert panel: Group of experts, often with diverse opinions and positions, share their ideas with each other and the audience.

Games: Contests and matches used to improve technical performance and foster teamwork.

Practical exercise: Opportunity to demonstrate skill proficiency without the requirements of a graded test.

Programmed instruction: Method of self-instruction in which trainees work through a carefully sequenced and pre-tested series of steps leading to the acquisition of knowledge or skills.

Role play: Interactive method of instruction that involves the spontaneous dramatization of a situation by two or more individuals to practice interpersonal skills within the context of the workplace.

Simulation: Technique that imitates operations and responses to problems and situations to test the ability of a person, system, or procedure to overcome obstacles and meet variations.

---

tle showmanship doesn't hurt in keeping the class interested," notes Marcy Anderson.

Postsecondary Training

While there is no universally accepted way to prepare for a job in computer training, a bachelor's degree is generally required from most employers. The best major for this field is not set in stone, however. Some majors that share skills with training include computer science, business, and education. To teach some of the more complex systems, a graduate degree might be necessary.

"In my personal experience, I did not pursue an education degree to become a trainer," says Anderson. "I have a business degree and years of experience in the human resources field. For software training, though, knowledge of software and computers is essential. A degree in education would provide excellent skills for this type of position. Additionally, a business or liberal arts major might provide the presentation skills that are valuable.

This computer trainer leads a class on the program Excel for employees of a corporation.

Certainly any presentation or public speaking certifications would be desirable."

Obtaining graduate and postgraduate degrees enhances potential marketability, as well as future salaries.

Certification or Licensing

As a trainer, you should be certified in the products (such as Microsoft C++, MFC, Visual Basic, and Access), developments (including Internet, HTML, Java Script), applications (MS Office, for example), environments (such as OS/2, Windows, client/server), and databases (including ADO, Access, ODBC, BD/2, and SQL) you want to instruct. Classes in each of the disciplines are available from the manufacturers, and you must pass an examination before receiving certification. Trainers who are employed by hardware and software developers might receive on-the-job instruction on the most current product releases. Certification is not mandatory (except for consultants), but will provide you with a competitive advantage. The International Association of Information Technology Trainers awards the Professional Technical Trainer designation to association members who complete a seminar, submit a 30-minute video of one of their training presentations, and pay an application fee. Additionally, applicants must provide 10 student references and post-class evaluations.

Technological advances come so rapidly in the computer field that continuous study is necessary to keep your skills up to date. Continuing education is usually offered by employers, hardware and software vendors, colleges and universities, or private training institutions. Additional training can also come from professional associations, such as the American Society for Training and Development.

Other Requirements

"Trainers need to be patient and extroverted," says Anderson. "A sense of humor is essential, along with a high level of energy. People who are very introverted, even though they might be good with computers, should not do software training." As a trainer, you will have to be ready to teach any class in your repertoire at any time, so you have to be adaptable and flexible to handle that uncertainty.

■ EXPLORING

One way to begin exploring this field now is to talk to someone who is a computer trainer. Marcy Anderson also suggests getting involved in speech or drama clubs. "Any experiences a high school student can get in making presentations or performing in front of a group help to build the skills necessary to be successful in this career," she says.

Internships are always helpful ways of obtaining some experience in the field before graduation. Having a job in the training department of a large corporation or software vendor would provide invaluable experience and contacts.

Teach yourself the various software packages, and read as much as you can about the industry. To stay updated in this field, read publications such as *Computer* magazine (http://www.computer.org/computer). Although jobs in the computer industry are abundant, there is always competition for desirable positions.

■ EMPLOYERS

Computer trainers are employed by various sources, from large, international companies to community colleges. Many work for hardware and software manufacturers or training departments in the bigger companies. Others are employed by training companies that disseminate training information and tools. Still other computer trainers work independently as consultants. The rest are employed by schools, adult continuing education programs, and government institutions. Some software companies and consultants operate training sites on the Internet. Since almost every type of company will need computer training at one point or another, these companies are located throughout the country and, indeed, throughout the world.

■ STARTING OUT

There are several ways to obtain a position as a computer trainer. Some people are hired right out of college by software companies. "There are many software companies that hire smart college grads to work with clients and implement their software," notes Marcy Anderson. Others start out in technical positions with software companies and then move into training as their expertise in the product increases.

Job candidates for computer trainer positions might obtain their jobs from on-campus recruitment, classified want ads, posting their resumes on the Internet, or word of mouth. Many large cities hold technology job fairs that host hundreds of companies, all of which are interested in hiring.

■ ADVANCEMENT

Computer trainers can move upward into positions such as training specialists, senior training specialists, and training managers, depending on the size of the company.

■ EARNINGS

In general, computer trainers' salaries increase with the level of their education and the amount of their experience. According to the 2003 salary survey conducted by *Microsoft Certified Professional Magazine,* the average salary of the responding Microsoft Certified Trainers (MCTs) was $69,900. These figures do not include yearly bonuses, which may add several thousand dollars to a trainer's income. Additionally, as these salaries are for MCTs, so not all computer trainers will have incomes in this range. For example, according to ASTD, a 2003 salary survey sponsored by the Society for Human Resource Management reports that technical trainers had median annual salaries of $45,000. In addition to education and experience, other factors influencing earnings are the size of the employer and, if the trainer is working independently, the number of clients he or she has during the year.

Most computer trainers who are employed by corporations receive medical and dental insurance, paid vacations, sick days, and retirement plans. Some companies also offer reimbursement for continuing education courses and training.

■ WORK ENVIRONMENT

Computer trainers normally work in offices in comfortable surroundings. They usually work 40 hours a week, which is the same as many other professional or office workers. However, travel to clients' sites can be required and might

---

THE HISTORY OF COMPUTING

Visit these websites to learn more about the history of computer science.

IEEE Computer Society History of Computing:
http://www.computer.org

The Virtual Museum of Computing
http://vmoc.museophile.com

Pioneers of Computing
http://vmoc.museophile.com/pioneers

Past Notable Women of Computing
http://www.cs.yale.edu/homes/tap/past-women-cs.html

---

increase the number of hours worked per week. They spend most of their time in classrooms or training facilities. "The best part of the job is that it is interesting and fun," says Marcy Anderson. "It is nice to be an 'expert' and impart knowledge to others, even though it can be hard sometimes to feel up and energized to teach every day."

■ OUTLOOK

The field of computer and data processing services is predicted to be the fastest growing industry through 2012 in the United States, according to the U.S. Department of Labor. Consequently, there will be a great need for computer trainers as the technology continues to develop. Information from the EQW National Employer Survey indicates that employers are using a variety of external training providers. As this outsourcing grows, an increase in the number of training providers is likely. Such independent providers as community and technical colleges, universities, profit-oriented learning and development centers, and private industry associations will all be discovering new business opportunities in outsourcing, according to the ASTD. "The short life cycles of technology products, compounded by the greater complexity of many job roles, are expected to heighten the demand for external information-technology education providers and other training providers," the ASTD notes.

■ FOR MORE INFORMATION

For a list of academic programs and resources in the computer training field, contact the following organizations:

American Society for Training and Development
1640 King Street, Box 1443
Alexandria, VA 22313-2043
Tel: 703-683-8100
http://www.astd.org

Computer Strategies
7677 Oakport Street, Suite 105
Oakland, CA 94621
Tel: 800-633-2248
Email: info@my-ecoach.com
http://www.compstrategies.com

International Association of Information
Technology Trainers
PMB 451
6030-M Marshalee Drive
Elkridge, MD 21075-5935
Tel: 888-290-6200
Email: member@itrain.org
http://itrain.org

Confectionery Industry Workers

■ OVERVIEW

Confectionery industry workers manufacture and package sweets, including bonbons, hard and soft candy, stuffed dates, popcorn balls, and many other types of confections. There are approximately 48,000 confectionery industry workers in the United States.

■ HISTORY

Confections have been made since ancient times. The word "sugar" may have come from Sanskrit, the ancient language of India; the word "candy" came from the Persian "qand" which means sugar. Cane sugar has been used in the making of sweets since ancient times in the Far East. Its use gradually spread west; by the 1600s, the making of confections based on sugar was considered an art form through much of Europe. One of the world's most popular confections, chocolate, has its origins in Central and South America, where the cacao bean, from which chocolate is made, has been cultivated for thousands of years. Spanish explorers imported the bean to West Africa, where most of the world's supply of cacao bean is now produced.

Production of candies and other confections first took place on a large scale in England in the early 19th century. The American candymaking industry grew rapidly during the second half of the 19th century.

By the turn of the 20th century, there were more than 1,000 American companies producing more than $60 million in candies each year. At that time, most candies were in the form of penny candy sweets. By the 1920s, when the first chocolate candy bars were introduced, the candy making industry was producing $500 million each year, employing more than 75,000 people. The use of machines and automated equipment in the candy making process has since reduced the number of people needed to produce candy. At the same time, the number of candy making firms has dropped, with many smaller firms consolidating into large corporations.

■ THE JOB

Confectionery workers operate machines to mix and cook candy ingredients, to form candy mixtures into shapes, and to package them for sale. Many different machines are used to make the molded, filled, pulled, whipped, and coated candies that Americans consume. Even when the candy making production line is completely automated, workers still are needed to monitor the various processing steps. However, some candy making jobs, especially in smaller candy factories, are still done by hand.

Pantry workers assemble, weigh, and measure candy ingredients such as sugar, egg whites, and butter, following a fixed formula. To each batch of ingredients they attach a card denoting the formula used, so the next workers will know what candy is to be made from that batch.

Confectionery cookers cook candy mixtures according to a formula, using open-fire or steam-jacketed kettles or pressure cookers. They load ingredients into the machine and start the machine's agitator to mix them. They then set controls regulating the temperature and pressure at which the candy will be cooked and turn valves to admit steam or other heat. They may be responsible for checking the consistency of the batch and adjusting the sugar content if necessary. When the cooking is done they empty the batch onto slabs or cooling belts or into beaters.

Chocolate temperers melt chocolate using water-jacketed tempering kettles that alternately heat and cool the chocolate until it is the proper consistency. The workers who operate these machines regulate the temperature, mix and agitate the chocolate in the tank, and test the chocolate's viscosity, adding cocoa butter or lecithin as needed. This chocolate is used in molded candies or as a coating.

After the candy mixture is cooked, it is formed. Some candy is kneaded on slabs and cut into pieces. Rollers knead soft candy into rolls, which are cut into slices and shaped to form bonbon centers. *Rolling-machine operators* do a similar operation with machines, rolling slabs of candy to specified thicknesses before cutting. Candy spreaders pour and spread batches of cooked candy, such as fudge, caramel, and toffee, onto slabs or into trays before cutting and decorating. The cutting is sometimes done by a machine. *Cutting machine operators* select and install cutting disks according to the size and shape of candy pieces required. *Hand candy-cutters* cut pieces manually.

Other kinds of candy must be spun or pulled into rope-like strands before cutting. *Spinners* and *candy pullers* perform these tasks. A *center-machine operator* runs a machine that makes soft-candy centers for bon-bons and chocolates. Other machines make different shapes. *Ball-machine operators* operate rolling machines that form candy balls and disks, and *lozenge makers* run machines that roll dough into sheets and then emboss and cut it into candy lozenges.

Many kinds of candy are made using molds. *Starch-makers* operate machines that make starch molds in which gum or jelly candy is formed. *Molding-machine operators* mold these candies using a mold-printing board. *Molding-machine operator helpers* feed the candy-filled starch molds onto conveyors or racks of machines that empty the molds, remove any remaining starch from the candies, and deposit candies in trays. *Hard-candy molders* pour liquid candy into chilled molds to form solid figures such as animals, people, and Christmas trees. *Chocolate Easter bunny makers* fill metal molds with chocolate, work in refrigerated rooms monitoring machines that spin the molds to coat them with the chocolate, and remove the Easter bunnies when the molds are sufficiently cooled. Another kind of hand molder is a *kiss setter*, who forms candy kisses using a spatula. *Deposit-machine operators* operate machines that deposit metered amounts of fluid candy into molds or directly onto conveyors. They must check the temperature and flow of the fluid and weigh formed candy samples to assure they meet specifications. *Fruit-bar makers* grind dried fruit and shape it into bars.

After candy centers are made, they must be coated, or enrobed. *Enrobing-machine feeders* arrange candy centers in a specified pattern on a conveyor, removing any malformed items. *Enrobing-machine operators* run machines that coat candy with melted chocolate or other coatings. They adjust the flow of coating mixture and allow coated candies to cool before further processing. In some plants, candy is dipped by hand workers, who scoop coating materials onto slabs and swirl center, fruits, or nuts through the coating and then remove them. Some-times workers called *enrobing-machine corders* mark tops of machine-coated candies to simulate a hand-dipped appearance. They dip a little semi-liquid chocolate out of a supply container and use it to draw a line or bead on the top of a newly enrobed piece of candy. Other workers do similar tasks. *Sanding-machine operators* sugar-coat gum-drops and orange slices. *Coating-machine operators* coat

candy and nuts with syrup, coloring, or other materials to glaze or polish them.

Popcorn balls and flavored popcorn are also considered confections. *Corn poppers* operate gas ovens that pop corn. They measure corn, oil, and salt into the popper and remove the corn when it has popped. *Popcorn-candy makers* measure ingredients and cook flavored syrup, then coat popcorn with the syrup. *Cheese sprayers* spray cheese and coconut oil onto popcorn, salt it, and take it to the packing room. Some workers, including *decorators* and *garnishers*, use icing or nuts to decorate candy. Others make candy used to decorate other edibles. *Marzipan mixers* mix almond paste for marzipan cake decorations, which are formed by *marzipan molders*. *Casting-machine operators* form sugar decorations for cakes by forcing a sugar paste through a device for molding shapes and depositing the decorations onto a paper sheet.

In some plants, *candy makers* are responsible for many of the steps in production, including formulating recipes and mixing, cooking, and forming candy. *Candy-maker helpers* help candy makers by tending machines, mixing ingredients, washing equipment, and performing other tasks. In large plants these jobs are often performed by different workers, under the direction of *candy supervisors*. Plants also employ *factory helpers*, who move trays from machine to machine and help confectionery workers in other ways.

After candy is formed, it is packaged, usually by machine, and delivered to distributors and eventually to retail stores.

■ REQUIREMENTS
High School

A high school degree usually is required for jobs as confectionery industry workers. After they are hired, employees learn production skills on the job. High school courses in chemistry, biology, and shop are useful as background for some jobs, but skills are gained only through experience. Family and consumer science classes may offer the opportunity to learn about cooking, baking, and food products. For some advanced

QUICK FACTS

SCHOOL SUBJECTS
Biology
Chemistry
Family and consumer science

PERSONAL SKILLS
Following instructions
Technical/scientific

WORK ENVIRONMENT
Primarily indoors
Primarily one location

MINIMUM EDUCATION LEVEL
High school diploma

SALARY RANGE
$11,128 to $21,390 to $35,110+

CERTIFICATION OR LICENSING
None available

OUTLOOK
Decline

GOE
08.03.02

NOC
9617

O*NET-SOC
N/A

A confectionery worker inspects chocolates as they move through the processing line.

positions, such as candy maker, workers may need technical expertise in food chemistry or other fields, as well as a solid knowledge of the industry.

Postsecondary Training

For workers who want to advance to management positions, a bachelor's degree with an emphasis in food science technology and business courses is recommended.

Other Requirements

Confectionery workers should have good manual dexterity. Like workers in many food industries, they may have to pass medical examinations to show that they are free from communicable diseases before they can begin work at a plant.

■ EXPLORING

If this type of work interests you, start exploring the field by making candy at home. Fudge, taffy, candied apples, and chocolate covered pretzels are among the sweets you can make in your own kitchen. Is there a candy manufacturing plant in your area? Call to see if tours are available.

The Hershey chocolate plant in Hershey, Pennsylvania, for example, offers tours of their operation to the public. Get part-time or summer work at a candy store or the candy department of a large store where you can learn what products are popular, how the candy is stored and handled, and how to package it for customers. If there is a candy manufacturer in your area, you may be able to get part-time or summer work as a helper while you are still in high school.

■ EMPLOYERS

A wide variety of settings are available to confectionery workers, from small candy stores that make their own confections to multinational corporations. Most of the approximately 48,000 candy manufacturing workers in the United States are employed at large plants. Employment is also available at small and mid-size confection manufacturers. Confectionery industry workers can find jobs in many parts of the United States.

■ STARTING OUT

Job seekers should apply directly to local plants for employment. Newspaper want ads and the state employment service are good sources of leads. In addition, the Bakery, Confectionery and Tobacco Workers International Union, to which many workers belong, may provide information about local openings. Some companies may place newspaper ads for workers. Many small retail stores, such as popcorn stores, also hire people to prepare and sell their candy and other confectionery products. Apply directly for these positions as well.

■ ADVANCEMENT

Workers who are willing to learn about all aspects of confectionery making can advance to positions as candy makers or supervisors. Workers may enter other food processing occupations, such as raw sugar refining, where earnings may be considerably higher. The greater the range of specialized knowledge and skills a worker has, the greater the chance for advancement. The size of the plant and the rate of turnover among employees also affect promotion opportunities.

■ EARNINGS

Confectionery workers' wages vary widely depending on such factors as the workers' skills and the size and location of the plant. In general, workers on the West Coast earn more than those in other regions. According to the U.S. Department of Labor, sugar and confectionery production workers earned an average salary of $21,390 in 2002. Since this amount is the average, there are both workers making more than this salary and workers making less. Entry-level, unskilled workers, such as helpers, may earn little more than the minimum wage, especially in smaller and nonunion factories. Those working full-time at the federal hourly minimum pay rate would have annual incomes of approximately $11,128. The top ten percent of food batchmakers, which include confectionary jobs, earned more than $35,110 in 2002.

Confectionery workers typically receive such benefits as health insurance, time and a half pay for overtime, vacation days, and retirement plans.

■ WORK ENVIRONMENT

Most confectionery workers in the United States work in large candy making factories; many other workers are employed in plants with fewer than 20 workers. Most plants are modern, clean, and well lighted. Workers who tend machines must exercise caution, but working conditions generally are safe. The work is usually not physically demanding but can be tiring. Like many kinds of production work, some jobs in this field involve a great deal of repetition and routine, since each worker performs only a few tasks. Confectionery workers usually work 38 to 40 hours a week. They are often provided with uniforms to wear on the job.

■ OUTLOOK

Candy sales in the United States are expected to hold about steady or perhaps increase slightly in coming years. Candy making, however, has become increasingly automated. It is often possible to produce candy products from the raw materials to the finished, packaged product without that product having ever been touched by human hands. As more and more confectionery producers use automated machinery and equipment, the need for production workers, especially unskilled workers without some college education, will decrease. In addition, the trend toward company consolidations will likely continue, meaning fewer employers of confectionery workers.

The U.S. Department of Labor projects an overall decline in the employment of food processing workers through 2012. Most new openings will arise as workers change jobs. Large wholesale confectionery companies will provide the most employment opportunities. Although candy is made throughout the United States, the candy industry is most active in Illinois, Pennsylvania, Ohio, New York, and California.

■ FOR MORE INFORMATION

The CMA, an affiliate of NCA, has information on cocoa farming, producing chocolate, links to processing and manufacturing companies, and other helpful information on its website.

Chocolate Manufacturers Association (CMA)
7900 Westpark Drive
Suite A-320
McLean, VA 22102
Tel: 703-790-5011
http://www.nca-cma.org

The NCA provides the eCandy Marketplace, an online resource with information on such topics as confectionery products, candy manufacturers, research, and other industry news.

National Confectioners Association (NCA)
8320 Old Courthouse Road, Suite 300
Vienna, VA 22182
Tel: 703-790-5750
http://www.ecandy.com

The American Association of Candy Technologists is a professional group for the confectionary industry.

American Association of Candy Technologists
175 Rock Rd.
Glen Rock, NJ 07452
Tel: 201-652-2655
http://www.aactcandy.org

This manufacturer's association provides information on scholarships available to undergraduate and graduate students and research news.

Pennsylvania Manufacturing Confectioners Association
PO Box 176
Center Valley, PA 18034
Tel: 610-282-4640
http://www.pmca.com/

This website, sponsored by NCA and CMA, has information on candy history, statistics, health news, and recipes.

Candy USA
http://www.candyusa.org

Congressional Aides

■ OVERVIEW

Congressional aides are the men and women who staff the offices of the members of the United States Congress. Working for senators and representatives, they assist with a variety of congressional duties, from administrative details to extensive research on legislation. Members of Congress typically include among their staff an administrative assistant, legislative assistants, a press secretary, an office manager, a personal secretary, and a legislative correspondent. Aides are generally divided into two groups: personal staff and committee staff. An aide may work in an office in Washington, D.C., or in a local district or state office.

■ HISTORY

Ever since members of Congress first began to hire stenographers and receptionists to assist with office duties, the role of congressional aides has stirred controversy. In the early 1800s, Congressmen worried they would look incapable of handling the responsibilities of their own jobs if they relied too much on assistants. This concern still exists today. Some members of Congress complain that having too many aides distances the senators and representatives from constituents, legislation, and the general requirements of their work.

Even these critics, however, admit that aides are very important to the lawmaking process. Since the end of World War II, with improvements in communications and transportation, voters have been making greater demands on their elected officials. Also, issues and casework have become increasingly complex. The Legislative Reorganization Act of 1946 was passed to allow each House and Senate standing committee to employ a campaign staff of four professional and six clerical workers. Another Reorganization Act passed years later, in 1970, which increased the number of professional staff to six members. The number of staff members has continued to grow, causing Congress to allocate more funds to construct new housing and office space.

■ THE JOB

Congressional aides see the lawmaking process at work—sometimes right on the Senate floor where laws are made. They work at the sides of important lawmakers, briefing them on legislation. The members of Congress (senators and representatives) rely on aides to assist them with a number of their responsibilities. Many constituents (the voters who elected members to Congress) rely on aides to help them make their voices and opinions heard. Aides answer letters, emails, and phone calls, and distribute information to keep Congress members and the people they represent updated on the issues of national and local concern.

John Newsome worked on the staff of Congresswoman Barbara Lee as both a press secretary and legislative aide. Congresswoman Lee serves as the representative of California's 9th district and has been behind many important actions since taking office in April of 1998. Lee was involved in declaring an HIV crisis in the local African-American community, making Alameda County the first jurisdiction in the nation to issue such a declaration. She helped get a grant from the U.S. Department of Commerce for BAYTRADE, an organization that promotes the development of trade relations between Northern California and the African continent. She has also played a part in modifying and passing a bill authorizing a study of the barriers that women face in science, math, and technical fields. It is the job of the congressional aide to inform the public and the media of these actions and also to prepare Congresswoman Lee for press conferences and interviews. During his time at the office, Newsome did just that and also researched legislation. "I've been interested in politics all my life," Newsome says. "I wanted to work for someone with a real eye to grassroots advocacy." When Congress is in session, his days started at around 9:30 A.M. and lasted until 9:00 P.M. or even as late as 11:30 P.M.

In the office of a senator or representative, aides either serve on a personal or committee staff. A basic difference between the two types of staff is that the committee staffs are more strictly concerned with work that involves the construction and passage of legislation, while the personal staffs also deal with matters concerning the home state. Personal aides are generally loyal supporters of their members of Congress and their political philosophies. But this doesn't mean that aides don't sometimes have differing views. In some cases, aides may be more familiar with an issue and the general opinions of the constituents concerning an issue than the member of Congress. An aide's opinion can have an impact on a Congress member's decision.

The most important aide to a Congress member is the *chief of staff*, or *administrative assistant*. Those who achieve this position have worked closely with a Congress member for some time and have gained his or her trust and respect. The Congress member relies on the chief of staff's or administrative assistant's opinion and under-

QUICK FACTS

SCHOOL SUBJECTS
Government
History

PERSONAL SKILLS
Communication/ideas
Leadership/management

WORK ENVIRONMENT
Primarily indoors
One location with some travel

MINIMUM EDUCATION LEVEL
Bachelor's degree

SALARY RANGE
$23,849 to $49,236 to
$97,615+

CERTIFICATION OR LICENSING
None available

OUTLOOK
Little or no change

DOT
209

GOE
09.02.02

NOC
N/A

O*NET-SOC
N/A

standing of politics, legislation, and individual bills when making decisions. These aides also oversee the work of the other congressional aides.

The actual running of the office is handled by *office managers.* They attend to the management of office clerical staff, which includes hiring, staff scheduling, and other personnel matters. In addition to *administrative assistant secretaries* who provide clerical support to the chief of staff, a congressional staff also includes *personal secretaries.* They attend to the Congress member's administrative and clerical needs, which includes daily scheduling, expense accounts, and personal correspondence. This correspondence is delivered by *mailroom managers* who are responsible for devising plans for handling the enormous crush of mail that arrives in congressional offices each day. They maintain mass mailing records and prepare reports on mail volume and contents.

The legislative staff in a congressional office assists the Congress member with research of bills and other legislative duties. The *legislative director* directs the legislative staff and helps the Congress member keep up to date on important bills. They make sure the Congress member can make informed decisions on issues. Assisting the director are *legislative assistants* and *legislative correspondents.* Legislative assistants are each responsible for the coverage of issues in which they have developed some expertise. They brief the member of Congress on the status of legislation for which they are responsible and prepare floor statements and amendments for them; they may also write speeches for the member. Legislative correspondents are responsible for researching and drafting responses to letters received in the Congress member's offices.

Press secretaries are the primary spokespersons for members of Congress in their dealings with the media and the public. They respond to daily inquiries from the press, plan media coverage, coordinate press conferences, prepare press releases, and review daily newspapers.

State and district directors are responsible for state or district office operations, helping the Congress member to maintain close interaction with constituents. They represent their Congress member in all areas of the state or district and keep the office in Washington, D.C., informed on issues important to the local voters. Directors also plan the Congress member's visits to the state, sometimes accompanying him or her on a state tour.

A congressional staff also includes *schedulers,* who handle all the Congress member's scheduling of appointments; *computer operators,* who are responsible for computerized correspondence systems; and *caseworkers,* who work directly with people having difficulties with the federal government in such areas as veterans' claims, social security, and tax returns.

Congressional aides often work long hours in stressful conditions during a campaign.

■ REQUIREMENTS
High School
A careful understanding of the government and how it works is important to anyone working for a member of Congress. You should take courses in U.S. government, political science, civics, social studies, and history, and get involved in school government and school committees. Attend formal meetings of various school clubs to learn about parliamentary procedure. Writing press releases and letters, and researching current issues are important aspects of congressional work. Journalism classes and reporting for your school newspaper will develop these communication skills.

Postsecondary Training
A well-rounded college education is very important for this career. Many congressional aides, such as chiefs of staff and legislative directors, have graduate degrees or law degrees. Consider undergraduate programs in history, political science, journalism, or economics. Political science programs offer courses in government, political theory, international relations, sociology, and public speaking. Look for internship opportunities in local, state, and federal government, and in political campaigns. Journalism programs offer courses in news reporting, communications law, and editing. Contact the offices of your state's members of Congress about applying for internships.

Other Requirements
Congressional aides need good problem-solving skills. They must have leadership abilities as well as the ability to follow instructions. Communication skills are very important, including writing, speaking, and listening. Before working as press secretary, John Newsome held other writing-related jobs, which involved writing grants

and writing for the media. "I'm a very detail-oriented writer," he says. "I love writing. But to get a story sold also requires networking and advocacy. You have to maintain good relationships with people."

Aides must have a good temperament to deal with the stress of preparing a congressperson for voting sessions, and patience when dealing with constituents who have serious concerns about political issues. As with any job in politics, diplomacy is important in helping a Congress member effectively serve a large constituency with widely varying views.

EXPLORING

An extremely valuable—but highly competitive—learning opportunity is to work as a *page*. Pages serve members of Congress, running messages across Capitol Hill. The length of a page's service varies from one summer to one year. Students at least 16 years old are eligible to apply. Contact your state's senator or representative for an application.

You can also gain some insight into the work of a congressional aide through local efforts: volunteer for various school committees, take an active part in clubs, and become involved in school government. Campaigns for local elections rely a lot on volunteers, so find out about ways you can support your favorite candidate. Keep a close watch over current events by reading newspapers and news magazines. With an understanding of current issues, you can take a stand and express your opinions to your local, state, and federal representatives. An annual publication called the *Congressional Staff Directory* (http://www.csd.cq.com) contains the addresses, phone numbers, and biographical information for members of Congress and their aides. You can use this directory to express your views on an issue to your representatives. By contacting your Congress members' offices, you'll be talking to congressional aides and learning something about their responsibilities. (Print or online versions of this directory are available for purchase.)

EMPLOYERS

Congressional aides are federal employees. There are 100 senators and 435 representatives who hire congressional aides. This number won't change without an amendment to the constitution or the addition of another state. For fair representation in the U.S. Congress, each state is allowed two senators; the number of representatives for each state is determined by the state's population. California has the most representatives (53). Most congressional aides work on Capitol Hill in Washington, D.C. Some find work in the home-state offices of their members of Congress.

STARTING OUT

Assistants are needed at every level of government. While in college, make personal contacts by volunteering on political campaigns. But be prepared to volunteer your services for some time in order to advance into positions of responsibility for candidates and elected officials. John Newsome has been involved since high school in grassroots advocacy. Over the years, he's been involved in HIV activism and community service with mentally disabled youth. Experience with these issues helped him to get his job with Congresswoman Lee. You can also gain valuable experience working in the offices of your state capitol building. State legislators require aides to answer phones, send letters, and research new bills.

Become familiar with the *Congressional Staff Directory*, available at your library or online. Getting a job as a congressional aide can be a difficult task—you may need to regularly submit resumes to placement offices of the House and the Senate. An internship can be a great way to get a foot in the door. The Congressional Management Foundation publishes information on internships.

ADVANCEMENT

Advancement in any of the congressional aide jobs is directly related to a congressional aide's ability, experience on Capitol Hill, and willingness to make personal sacrifices to complete work efficiently and on time. The highest office on congressional staffs is that of administrative assistant. It is possible for anyone on staff to rise up through the ranks to fill this position. Obviously, everyone cannot reach the top position, but advancement to higher staff positions is available to those who show they have the ability to take on greater responsibility. Legislative directors and state and district directors are probably the most likely candidates for the job of chief of staff. Legislative assistants, state office managers, and district office managers are in the best position to move into their respective directors' jobs. The top secretarial position is that of personal secretary, and any of the other secretaries can aspire to that position or that of scheduler. Any of the administrative staff, such as the receptionist or the mail room manager, can work toward the office manager's position.

EARNINGS

Congressional aides' salaries vary a great deal from office to office. Aides working in Senate positions generally have higher salaries than those working in House positions. Earnings also vary by position. A chief of staff, for example, has a much higher salary than a staff assistant working in the same office. Experience also plays a role in aides' earnings, with the highest salaries going to staffers with the most experience. Additionally, aides' earnings vary by the location of the office, that is, Washington, D.C., or the Congress person's home district, in which they work.

The Congressional Management Foundation (CMF), a nonprofit organization in Washington, D.C., publishes periodic reports on congressional employment practices that include salary information. According to the CMF study *Senate Salary, Tenure & Demographic Data, 1991–2001*, the average annual salary for all Senate positions (including congressional aides) was $49,236 in 2001. In 2000 (the most recent data available), the average House salary for all positions was $42,314. These averages are for positions in Washington, D.C. CMF's *2000 House Staff Employment Study* found that the average annual salary for a House chief of staff was $97,615. House office managers averaged $44,009; systems administrators averaged $30,205; and staff assistants averaged $23,849. Again, these averages are for positions in Washington, D.C. More information on these reports is available from the CMF at http://www.cmfweb.org.

■ WORK ENVIRONMENT

Oddly enough, while Congress makes laws to protect workers and to ensure civil rights among the general populace, it has, in many cases, exempted itself from those same laws. Members of Congress contend that they should not be regulated like firms in the private sector because of the political nature of their institution and the necessity of choosing staff on the basis of loyalty. They also feel that it would breach the principle of the separation of powers if the executive branch had the power to enforce labor regulations in Congress.

Congressional aides are often faced with long hours, cramped quarters, and constant pressure. But many people thrive on the fast pace and appreciate the opportunity to get to know federal legislation from the inside. "The opportunities to meet people are endless," John Newsome says. "And it's incredibly challenging work." Despite the high pressure and deadlines, Newsome liked being a member of a staff involved in making positive changes.

■ OUTLOOK

Members of Congress will continue to hire aides regularly; however, this is not a large employment field. The need for new workers will be steady but limited. Additionally, aides' positions are linked to the success of the Congressman or Congresswoman for whom they work. If their employer is voted out of office, aides also lose their

jobs. And, despite the long hours and often low pay, these jobs are prestigious, making competition for them strong.

Few people make working as a congressional aide a lifelong career. Those with excellent educational backgrounds and who are comfortable using technologies should have the best chances for jobs. The Internet is making it easier for constituents to express their views quickly and to access press releases, information about current legislation, and the positions of their representatives. Advocacy groups will expand their use of the Internet, gaining more support and encouraging voters to express their views via email. In the future, aides will work with a constituency much more knowledgeable about current legislation. The Internet will also serve aides in their research of bills, their interaction with the media, and their gauging of public views.

■ FOR MORE INFORMATION

For more information about House and Senate employment studies and other publications, such as Congressional Intern Handbook, *contact*

Congressional Management Foundation
513 Capitol Court, NE, Suite 300
Washington, DC 20002
Tel: 202-546-0100
Email: cmf@cmfweb.org
http://www.cmfweb.org

Visit the websites of the House and the Senate for extensive information about individual Congress members and legislation. To write to your Congress members, contact

Office of Senator (Name)
U.S. Senate
Washington, DC 20510
http://www.senate.gov

Office of Congressperson (Name)
U.S. House of Representatives
Washington, DC 20510
http://www.house.gov

For employment opportunities, mail resume and cover letters to

Senate Placement Office
Room SH-142B
Washington, DC 20510

U.S. House of Representatives
Office of Human Resources
175 Ford House Office Building
Washington, DC 20515-6610

Conservators and Conservation Technicians

■ OVERVIEW

Conservators analyze and assess the condition of artifacts and pieces of art, plan for the care of art collections, and carry out conservation treatments and programs. Conservators may be in private practice or work for museums, historical societies, or state institutions. When conserving artifacts or artwork, these professionals must select methods and materials that preserve and retain the original integrity of each piece. Conservators must be knowledgeable about the objects in their care, which may be natural objects, such as bones and fossils, or man-made objects, such as paintings, sculpture, paper, and metal.

Conservation technicians work under the supervision of conservators and complete maintenance work on the collection.

■ HISTORY

Conservation is the youngest of all museum disciplines. The word "conservation" has been used in reference to works of art only since approximately 1930. For at least a century before 1930, museums may have employed *restorers,* or *restoration specialists,* but the philosophy that guided their work was much different than the ideas and values held by conservators today. Early conservators were often craftspeople, artists, or framers called upon to restore a damaged work of art to an approximate version of its original condition. They repainted, varnished, or patched objects as they saw fit, working independently and experimenting as necessary to achieve the desired results. Conservators today use highly scientific methods and recognize the need both to care for works of art before deterioration occurs and to treat objects after damage has been done. A key guiding principle in conservation is to avoid introducing changes in a work that are irreversible.

The first regional conservation laboratory in the United States, known as the Intermuseum Conservation Association, was created in 1952, in Oberlin, Ohio, when several smaller museums joined to bring their skills together.

Thanks to increasingly precise cleaning methods and scientific inventions such as thermal adhesives, the science of conservation has advanced. Today, the field is highly specialized and those who work in it must face demanding standards and challenges.

■ THE JOB

Conservation professionals generally choose to specialize in one area of work defined by medium, such as in the preservation of books and paper, architecture, objects, photographic materials, paintings, textiles, or wooden artifacts. There are also conservators who specialize in archaeology or ethnographic materials. Many are employed by museums, while others provide services through private practice. Conservation activities include carrying out technical and scientific studies on art objects, stabilizing the structure and reintegrating the appearance of cultural artifacts, and establishing the environment in which artifacts are best preserved. A conservator's responsibilities also may include documenting the structure and condition through written and visual recording, designing programs for preventive care, and executing conservation treatments. Conservation tools include microscopes and cameras and equipment for specialized processes such as infrared and ultraviolet photography and X rays.

Conservation technicians assist conservators in preserving or restoring artifacts and art objects. To do this, they study descriptions and information about the object, and may perform chemical and physical tests as specified by the conservator. If an object is metal, a technician may be instructed to clean it by scraping or by applying chemical solvents. Statues are washed with soap solutions, and furniture and silver is polished.

When a repair is necessary, conservation technicians may be asked to reassemble the broken pieces using glue or solder (a metallic substance used to join metal surfaces), then buff the object when the repair is complete. They may repaint objects where the original paint is faded or missing, making sure to use paint of the same chemical composition and color as the original. Technicians may also make and repair picture frames and mount paintings in frames.

A *conservation scientist* is a professional scientist whose primary focus is in developing materials and knowledge to support conservation activities. Some specialize in sci-

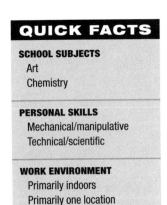

A conservation technician cleans a Modernist oil painting with a special brush that removes the dust from the recesses of the brush strokes.

entific research into artists' materials, such as paints and varnishes. *Conservation educators* have substantial knowledge and experience in the theory and practice of conservation, and have chosen to direct their efforts toward teaching the principles, methodology, and technical aspects of the profession. *Preparators* supervise the installation of specimens, art objects, and artifacts, often working with design technicians, curators, and directors to ensure the safety and preservation of items on display.

■ REQUIREMENTS
High School

Good conservation work comes from a well-balanced formulation of art and science. To prepare for a career in conservation, concentrate on doing well in all academic subjects, including courses in chemistry, natural science, history, and the arts.

Postsecondary Training

In the past, many conservation professionals earned their training solely through apprenticeships with esteemed conservators. The same is not true today; you will need a

bachelor's degree to find work as a technician, and in all but the smallest institutions you will need a master's degree to advance to conservator. Because graduate programs are highly selective, you should plan your academic path with care.

At the undergraduate level, take coursework in the sciences, including inorganic and organic chemistry, the humanities (art history, archaeology, and anthropology), and studio art. Some graduate programs will consider work experience and gained expertise in conservation practice as comparable to coursework when screening applicants. In addition, most graduate programs recognize a student's participation in apprenticeship or internship positions while also completing coursework as indicative of the applicant's commitment to the career.

Other Requirements

Conservation can be physically demanding. Conservators and conservation technicians need to be able to concentrate on specific physical and mental tasks for long periods of time. Endurance, manual dexterity, and patience are often needed to complete projects successfully.

■ EXPLORING

If you are considering a career in the conservation of art or artifacts, try contacting local museums or art conservation laboratories that may allow tours or interviews. Read trade or technical journals to gain a sense of the many issues addressed by conservators. Contact professional organizations, such as the American Institute for Conservation of Historic and Artistic Works, for directories of training and conservation programs.

Because employment in this field, even at entry level, most often entails the handling of precious materials and cultural resources, you should be fairly well prepared before contacting professionals to request either

LEARN MORE ABOUT IT

Bachman, Konstanze, ed. *Conservation Concerns: A Guide for Collectors and Curators.* Washington, D.C.: Smithsonian Institution Press, 1992.

Beck, James H. *Art Restoration: The Culture, the Business, and the Scandal.* New York: W.W. Norton & Company, 1996.

Becker, Ellen. *Gold Leaf Application and Antique Restoration.* Atglen, Pa.: Schiffer Publishing, Ltd., 1999.

Bomford, David. *Conservation of Paintings.* New Haven, Conn.: Yale University Press, 1998.

Guldbeck, Per E., and A. Bruce MacLeish, eds. *The Care of Antiques and Historical Collections.* 2nd ed. Blue Ridge Summit, Pa.: Altamira Press, 1996.

Kirsch, Andrea, and Rustin S. Levenson. *Seeing Through Paintings: Physical Examination in Art Historical Studies.* New Haven, Conn.: Yale University Press, 2000.

Nicolaus, Knut, and Christine Westphal. *The Restoration of Paintings.* Osceola, Wis.: Konemann, 1999.

Price, Nicholas Stanley, et al., eds. *Historical and Philosophical Issues in the Conservation of Cultural Heritage.* Los Angeles, Calif.: Getty Conservation Institute, 1996.

Schaeffer, Terry T. *Effects of Light on Materials in Collections: Data on Photoflash and Related Sources.* Los Angeles, Calif.: Getty Conservation Institute, 2001.

Snyder, Jill and Marian Reidelbach. *Caring for Your Art.* New York: Allworth Press, 2002.

Thomson, Garry. *The Museum Environment.* Woburn, Mass.: Butterworth-Heinemann, 1994.

Timar-Balazsy, Agnes, and Dinah Eastop. *Chemical Principles of Textile Conservation.* Woburn, Mass.: Butterworth-Heinemann, 1998.

internship or volunteer positions. You need to demonstrate a high level of academic achievement and have a serious interest in the career to edge out the competition for a limited number of jobs.

■ EMPLOYERS

Museums, libraries, historical societies, private conservation laboratories, and government agencies hire conservators and conservation technicians. Institutions with small operating budgets sometimes hire part-time specialists to perform conservation work. This is especially common when curators need extra help in preparing items for display. Antique dealers may also seek the expertise of an experienced conservator for merchandise restoration, identification, and appraisal purposes.

■ STARTING OUT

Most often students entering the field of art conservation have completed high school and undergraduate studies, and many are contemplating graduate programs. At this point a student is ready to seek a position (often unpaid) as an apprentice or intern with either a private conservation company or a museum to gain a practical feel for the work. Training opportunities are scarce and in high demand. Prospective students must convince potential trainers of their dedication to the highly demanding craft of conservation. The combination of academic or formal training along with hands-on experience and apprenticeship is the ideal foundation for entering the career.

■ ADVANCEMENT

Due to rapid changes in each conservation specialty, practicing conservators must keep abreast with advances in technology and methodology. Conservators stay up to date by reading publications, attending professional meetings, and enrolling in short-term workshops or courses.

An experienced conservator wishing to move into another realm of the field may become a private consultant, an appraiser of art or artifacts, a conservation educator, a curator, or a museum registrar.

■ EARNINGS

Salaries for conservators vary greatly depending on the level of experience, chosen specialty, region, job description, and employer. The U.S. Department of Labor, which classifies conservators with curators, museum technicians, and archivists, reports the median annual earnings for this group as $35,270 in 2002. The lowest paid 10 percent of this group earned less than $20,010, and the highest paid 10 percent made more than $66,050.

According to the American Institute for Conservation of Historic and Artistic Works, a first year conservator can expect to earn approximately $20,000 annually. Conservators with several years of experience report annual earnings between $35,000 and $40,000. Senior conservators have reported earnings between $50,000 and $60,000 annually.

Fringe benefits, including paid vacations, medical and dental insurance, sick leave, and retirement plans, vary according to each employer's policies.

■ WORK ENVIRONMENT

Conservation work may be conducted indoors, in laboratories, or in an outdoor setting. Conservators typically work 40–60 hours per week depending on exhibition schedules and deadlines, as well as the number and condition of unstable objects in their collections. Because some conservation tasks and techniques involve the use of toxic chemicals, laboratories are equipped with ventilation systems. At times a conservator may find it necessary to wear a mask and possibly even a respirator when working with particularly harsh chemicals or varnishes. Most of the work requires meticulous attention to detail, a great deal of precision, and manual dexterity.

The rewards of the conservation profession are the satisfaction of preserving artifacts that reflect the diversity of human achievements; being in regular contact with art, artifacts, and structures; enjoying a stimulating workplace; and the creative application of expertise to the preservation of artistically and historically significant objects.

■ OUTLOOK

The U.S. Department of Labor predicts the employment of archivists, curators, and museum technicians (which includes conservators and technicians) will grow at an average rate through 2012. Competition for these desirable positions, however, will be strong.

The public's developing interest in cultural material of all forms will contribute to art conservation and preservation as a growing field. New specialties have emerged in response to the interest in collections maintenance and preventive care. Conservation, curatorial, and registration responsibilities are intermingling and creating hybrid conservation professional titles, such as collections care, environmental monitoring, and exhibits specialists.

Despite these developments, however, any decreases in federal funding often affect employment and educational opportunities. For example, in any given year, if Congress limits government assistance to the National Endowment for the Arts, less funds are available to assist students through unpaid internships. As museums experience a tightening of federal or state funds, many may choose to decrease the number of paid conservators on staff and instead may rely on a small staff augmented by private conservation companies that can be contracted on a short-term basis as necessary. Private industry and for-profit companies may then continue to grow, while federally funded nonprofit museums may experience a reduction of staff.

■ FOR MORE INFORMATION

To receive additional information on conservation training, contact

American Institute for Conservation of Historic and Artistic Works
1717 K Street, NW, Suite 200
Washington, DC 20006
Tel: 202-452-9545
http://aic.stanford.edu

For information on internships and other learning opportunities in Canada, contact

Canadian Conservation Institute
1030 Innes Road
Ottawa ON K1A 0M5 Canada
Tel: 613-998-3721
http://www.cci-icc.gc.ca

Construction Inspectors

■ OVERVIEW

Construction inspectors work for federal, state, and local governments. Their job is to examine the construction, alteration, or repair of highways, streets, sewer and water systems, dams, bridges, buildings, and other structures to ensure that they comply with building codes and ordinances, zoning regulations, and contract specifications. Approximately 75,000 construction and building inspectors work in the United States.

■ HISTORY

Construction is one of the major industries of the modern world. Public construction includes structures such as public housing projects, schools, hospitals, administrative and service buildings, industrial and military facilities, highways, and sewer and water systems.

To ensure the public safety of these structures and systems, various governing bodies establish building codes that contractors must follow. It is the job of the construction inspector to ensure that the codes are properly followed.

■ THE JOB

This occupation is made up of four broad categories of specialization: building, electrical, mechanical, and public works.

Building inspectors examine the structural quality of buildings. They check the plans before construction, visit the work site a number of times during construction, and make a final inspection when the project is completed. Some building inspectors specialize in areas such as structural steel or reinforced concrete buildings.

Electrical inspectors visit work sites to inspect the installation of electrical systems and equipment. They check wiring, lighting, generators, and sound and security systems. They may also inspect the wiring for elevators, heating and air-conditioning systems, kitchen appliances, and other electrical installations.

Mechanical inspectors inspect plumbing systems and the mechanical components of heating and air-conditioning equipment and kitchen appliances. They also examine gas tanks, piping, and gas-fired appliances. Some mechanical inspectors specialize in elevators, plumbing, or boilers.

Elevator inspectors inspect both the mechanical and the electrical features of lifting and conveying devices, such as elevators, escalators, and moving sidewalks. They also test their speed, load allowances, brakes, and safety devices.

Plumbing inspectors inspect plumbing installations, water supply systems, drainage and sewer systems, water heater installations, fire sprinkler systems, and air and gas piping systems; they also examine building sites for soil type to determine water table level, seepage rate, and similar conditions.

Heating and refrigeration inspectors examine heating, ventilating, air-conditioning, and refrigeration installations in new buildings and approve alteration plans for those elements in existing buildings.

Public works inspectors make sure that government construction of water and sewer systems, highways, streets, bridges, and dams conforms to contract specifications. They visit work sites to inspect excavations, mixing and pouring of concrete, and asphalt paving. They also keep records of the amount of work performed and the materials used so that proper payment can be made. These inspectors may specialize in highways, reinforced concrete, or ditches.

Construction inspectors use measuring devices and other test equipment, take photographs, keep a daily log of their work, and write reports. If any detail of a project does not comply with the various codes, ordinances, or specifications, or if construction is being done without proper permits, the inspectors have the authority to issue a stop-work order.

QUICK FACTS

SCHOOL SUBJECTS
Mathematics
Technical/shop

PERSONAL SKILLS
Leadership/management
Technical/scientific

WORK ENVIRONMENT
Indoors and outdoors
Primarily multiple locations

MINIMUM EDUCATION LEVEL
High school diploma

SALARY RANGE
$26,062 to $41,620 to
$62,608+

CERTIFICATION OR LICENSING
Required by certain states

OUTLOOK
About as fast as the average

DOT
182

GOE
02.08.02

NOC
2264

O*NET-SOC
47-4011.00

REQUIREMENTS

High School

People interested in construction inspection must be high school graduates who have taken courses in drafting, algebra, geometry, and English. Additional shop courses will undoubtedly prove helpful as well.

Postsecondary Training

Employers prefer graduates of an apprenticeship program, community or junior college, or people with at least two years toward an engineering or architectural degree. Required courses include construction technology, blueprint reading, technical math, English, and building inspection.

Most construction inspectors have several years' experience either as a construction contractor or supervisor, or as a craft or trade worker such as a carpenter, electrician, plumber, or pipefitter. This experience demonstrates a knowledge of construction materials and practices, which is necessary in inspections. Construction inspectors receive most of their training on the job.

Certification or Licensing

Some states require certification for employment. Inspectors can earn a certificate by passing examinations on construction techniques, materials, and code requirements. The exams are offered by the International Code Council.

Other Requirements

Construction inspectors are expected to have a valid driver's license, as they must be able to travel to and from the construction sites. They must also pass a civil service exam.

EXPLORING

Field trips to construction sites and interviews with contractors or building trade officials are good ways to gain practical information about what it is like to work in the industry and how best to prepare for it. Summer jobs at a construction site provide an overview of the work involved in a building project. Students may also seek part-time jobs with a general contracting company, with a specialized contractor (such as a plumbing or electrical contractor), or as a carpenter's helper. Jobs in certain supply houses will help students become familiar with construction materials.

EMPLOYERS

Approximately 84,000 construction and building inspectors are employed in the United States. Almost half work for local governments, such as municipal or county building departments. Another 21 percent work for architecture or engineering firms. Inspectors employed at the federal level work for such agencies as the Department of Defense or the departments of Housing and Urban Development, Agriculture, and the Interior.

STARTING OUT

People without postsecondary education usually enter the construction industry as a trainee or apprentice. Graduates of technical schools or colleges of construction and engineering can expect to start work as an engineering aide, drafter, estimator, or assistant engineer. Jobs may be found through school placement offices, employment agencies, and unions or by applying directly to contracting company personnel offices. Application may also be made directly to the employment offices of the federal, state, or local governments.

ADVANCEMENT

The federal, state, and large city governments provide formal training programs for their construction inspectors to keep them abreast of new building code developments and to broaden their knowledge of construction materials, practices, and inspection techniques. Inspectors for small agencies can upgrade their skills by attending state-conducted training programs or taking college or correspondence courses. An engineering degree is usually required to become a supervisory inspector.

EARNINGS

The U.S. Department of Labor reports the median annual income for construction and building inspectors was $41,620 in 2002. The lowest paid 10 percent of these workers had annual earnings of less than $26,062; the highest paid 10 percent made more than $62,608, also in 2002. Earnings vary based on the inspector's experience, the type of employer, and the location of the work. Salaries are slightly higher in the North and West than in the South and are considerably higher in large metropolitan areas. Building inspectors earn slightly more than other inspectors.

WORK ENVIRONMENT

Construction inspectors work both indoors and outdoors, dividing their time between their offices and the work sites. Inspection sites are dirty and cluttered with tools, machinery, and debris. Although the work is not considered hazardous, inspectors must climb ladders and stairs and crawl under buildings.

The hours are usually regular, but when there is an accident at a site, the inspector has to remain on the job until reports have been completed. The work is steady year-round, rather than seasonal, as are some other construction occupations. In slow construction periods, the

---

HOME INSPECTORS

The residential real estate boom in the late 1990s, brought about in part by changes in tax law concerning the sale of a principal residence and by low interest rates making mortgages much more affordable, created a huge demand for home inspectors. Prospective home buyers insisted that a home inspector inspect and report on the condition of a home's major systems, components, and structure before signing a sales contract to purchase the new home.

---

inspectors are kept busy examining the renovation of older buildings.

OUTLOOK

As the concern for public safety continues to rise, the demand for inspectors should grow about as fast as the average through 2012 even if construction activity does not increase. The level of new construction fluctuates with the economy, but maintenance and renovation continue during the downswings, so inspectors are rarely laid off. Applicants who have some college education, are already certified inspectors, or who have experience as carpenters, electricians, or plumbers will have the best opportunities. Construction and building inspectors tend to be older, more experienced workers who have worked in other construction occupations for many years.

FOR MORE INFORMATION

For additional information on a career as a construction inspector, contact the following organizations:

American Construction Inspectors Association
12995 6th Street, Suite 69
Yucaipa, CA 92399-2549
Tel: 888-867-2242
Email: office@acia.com.
http://www.acia.com

American Society of Home Inspectors
932 Lee Street, Suite 101
Des Plaines, IL 60016-6546
Tel: 800-743-2744
http://www.ashi.com

Association of Construction Inspectors
1224 North Nokomis, NE
Alexandria, MN 56308
Tel: 320-763-7525
Email: aci@iami.org
http://www.iami.org/aci.cfm

International Code Council
5203 Leesburg Pike, Suite 600
Falls Church, VA 22041
Tel: 703-931-3533
http://www.iccsafe.org

Canadian Construction Association
75 Albert Street, Suite 400
Ottawa, ON K1P 5E7 Canada
Tel: 613-236-9455
Email: cca@cca-acc.com
http://www.cca-acc.com

Construction Laborers

■ OVERVIEW

Construction laborers do a variety of tasks at the construction sites of buildings, highways, bridges, and other public and private building projects. Depending on the type of project, construction laborers may carry materials used by craft workers, clean up debris, operate cement mixers, or lay and seal together lengths of sewer pipe, among other duties. They also are involved in hazardous waste/environmental remediation.

■ HISTORY

In the past, when people wanted simple structures built, they often did the work themselves. Inevitably, the larger, more complex structures required the efforts of many workers. These workers included both skilled specialists in certain activities, and others who assisted the specialists or did other less complicated but necessary physical tasks. Today the people who provide this kind of aid are construction laborers. Their work usually does not require great skill, but it is essential to getting the job done.

■ THE JOB

Construction laborers are employed on all kinds of construction jobs, such as building bridges, viaducts, and piers; office and apartment buildings; highways and streets; pipelines; railroads; river and harbor projects; and sewers, tunnels, and waterworks. Many laborers are employed by private firms that contract to do these construction jobs. Others work for state or local governments on public works or for utility companies on such

activities as road repair. Construction laborers also are involved in remodeling, demolition, and repair work.

At the direction of supervisors or other skilled workers, construction laborers perform a wide variety of tasks, such as loading and unloading materials, erecting and dismantling scaffolding, digging and leveling dirt and gravel, wrecking old buildings, removing rubble, pouring and spreading concrete and asphalt, removing forms from set concrete, and carrying supplies to building craft workers. They use equipment ranging from ordinary picks and shovels to various kinds of machines used in construction, such as air hammers or pile-driving equipment.

On some jobs, laborers are assigned to one type of routine task; on other jobs, they are rotated through different tasks as the job progresses. Some laborers tend to work in one branch of the construction industry, such as laying pipelines or building roads. Others transfer from one area of construction to another, depending on the availability of work.

To do their job well, some construction laborers need to be familiar with the duties of skilled craft workers, as well as with the variety of tools, machines, materials, and methods used at the job site. Some laborers do work that requires a considerable amount of know-how, such as those who work with the explosives used to break up bedrock before excavation work can begin on some construction projects. These workers must know how different kinds of explosives can be used safely, to avoid both injury and property damage.

■ REQUIREMENTS
High School

Most employers prefer high school graduates. A mix of classes that will help you work in the often technical and exacting environment of a construction site is important. Take advantage of opportunities to strengthen your communication skills. Basic mathematics will help; advanced courses are even better.

Postsecondary Training

In general, no particular training is necessary for most entry-level construction laborer jobs. As a beginner, you'll learn whatever job skills you need informally as you work under the supervision of more experienced workers. If you must work with potentially dangerous equipment or materials, you'll receive instruction in safety procedures that minimize the chance of accidents.

To become a skilled, productive laborer, training is important, however. In supporting other experienced craftsmen, your work will require that you have a diverse

Construction laborers clean up a work site.

set of skills and are comfortable with the operation of today's increasingly complex and highly technical tools, equipment, and instruments.

Apprenticeship programs are available for those seeking a more structured background in this field. Apprenticeship programs include two to three years of on-the-job and classroom instruction in such areas as site and project preparation and maintenance; tools, equipment, and materials; safety; environmental remediation; building construction; and heavy/highway construction. As an apprentice, you'll receive specific training and instruction in dealing with the removal of asbestos, hazardous waste, lead, radiation, and underground storage tanks, as well as the basics of working with asphalt, concrete, lines and grades, masonry, and pipe-laying, and in reading blueprints. All of these skills and training make you, a better all-around worker, and can contribute to your ability to get better jobs.

Other Requirements

Construction work is strenuous, so employers seek workers who are physically fit enough to do the job. Laborers must usually be at least 18 years old and reliable, hard working, and able to follow oral and written instructions. Though it is not required, many laborers are members of the Laborers' International Union of North America. Among many other services, the union works with employers, seeking to ensure that members receive equitable pay and work in safe conditions. As a construction laborer, you should be prepared to decide whether you want to join the union or not.

■ EXPLORING

People who are interested in this work can often get summer jobs as laborers on building or construction projects.

This is the best kind of experience students can have to help them evaluate their interest and potential in this field. They may also benefit by talking to local contractors or local union officials.

■ EMPLOYERS

Construction laborers work throughout the United States. Most work in heavily populated industrial sections and are employed mainly by contractors who complete large projects such as those described earlier. Some rare projects may require travel to foreign countries, though contractors with these jobs often use local workers instead. Increasingly, the industry is making use of temporary workers hired on a project basis to move materials or to clean up a site. Many construction laborers contract their services through temporary help agencies, which hire them out for short-term jobs.

■ STARTING OUT

The usual first step in getting a job in this field is to apply directly to a construction contractor or to the local office of the Laborers' International Union. Workers who have completed a construction craftworker apprenticeship program usually are considered first for job openings above those applicants who have no prior experience.

■ ADVANCEMENT

Without additional training, construction laborers have limited opportunities for advancement. Some laborers move into jobs as mechanics or skilled operators of construction equipment. Workers who show responsibility and good judgment may be promoted to supervisory positions. Laborers may also decide to leave the field for training in one of the skilled trades, such as carpentry.

■ EARNINGS

Construction workers often receive substantial hourly wages, but the hourly rates are often

QUICK FACTS

SCHOOL SUBJECTS
Mathematics
Technical/shop

PERSONAL SKILLS
Following instructions
Mechanical/manipulative

WORK ENVIRONMENT
Indoors and outdoors
Primarily multiple locations

MINIMUM EDUCATION LEVEL
High school diploma

SALARY RANGE
$15,766 to $24,752 to $48,589+

CERTIFICATION OR LICENSING
None available

OUTLOOK
About as fast as the average

DOT
869

GOE
06.02.02

NOC
7611

O*NET-SOC
47-2061.00

WORKING FOR THE ENVIRONMENT

One of the more technical and demanding jobs a construction laborer can be assigned is work on an environmental project, assisting in the remediation, or cleanup, of toxic substances. Such an assignment may come from a variety of sources. As environmental regulations have tightened around the country (particularly in California), many firms are now dedicated solely to cleanup work. Sites may be as varied as a dry cleaners, where solvents used to clean clothes may have leached into the ground, and a closing nuclear power plant, where radioactive material is the concern. In radioactive situations, everyone's job is a challenge. Laborers who are given these sorts of assignments must be especially efficient, hard working, and attentive to detail.

Workers deactivating a nuclear plant, for example, go through a long process of checking into the facility involved, receiving daily briefings on "hot spots" found near their work locations. They wear complex suits over their regular work clothing—"space suits," boots, and several pairs of gloves—and they must wear as many as four or five different monitors designed to determine just how much radiation exposure they've experienced. Acceptable tolerances are always adhered to. With all this careful preparation, construction workers, including laborers, may spend two or more hours in the morning just getting ready to work. They'll spend another two hours at the end of the day removing their gear and going through a series of security checks for radioactivity levels. Their actual workday may be only five hours—less if the hazard is very great.

poor indicators of annual earnings. The seasonal nature of construction work and time lost because of other factors can significantly reduce the total income of construction workers. There is also a great difference in the wages paid to construction laborers in different parts of the country. Pay is higher for laborers with certain kinds of special experience or doing certain kinds of tasks. According to the U.S. Department of Labor, the median hourly wage for construction laborers in 2002 was $11.90. If a laborer making this wage were able to work a 40-hour week year round, his or her annual income would be approximately $24,752. The U.S. Department of Labor also reported that the lowest paid 10 percent of laborers made less than $7.58 per hour (about $15,766 per year), while the highest paid 10 percent earned more than $23.36 per hour (about $48,589 annually). Apprentices or helpers usually make about half the wage paid to fully qualified employees.

Fringe benefits, such as health insurance and paid vacations, are available to most workers in this field and vary with local union contracts. In general, benefits are more likely to be offered on jobs staffed by union workers.

■ WORK ENVIRONMENT

Construction laborers do demanding physical work that is sometime dangerous. They may need to lift heavy weights, kneel, crouch, stoop, crawl, or work in awkward positions. Much of the job is outdoors, sometimes in hot or cold weather, in wind or rain, in dust, mud, noise, or other uncomfortable conditions. Laborers may be exposed to fumes, odors, dangerous particles, or irritating chemicals. They need to be constantly aware of danger and must be careful to observe good safety practices at all times. Often they wear gloves, hats, and vision, respiratory, or hearing protection to help avoid injury.

Work schedules, weather conditions, or other factors may require night or weekend shifts, and sometimes hours beyond the standard 40-hour week. Work in the construction industry involves changing from one job location to another, and being laid off from time to time because of poor weather, shortages of materials, or a simple lack of jobs. Laborers must be able to arrange their finances so that they can make it through periods of unemployment.

■ OUTLOOK

Construction is a large field, and turnover is high among laborers. For these reasons, every year there will be jobs available, mainly in connection with large projects, because employers need to replace those workers who have changed jobs or left the labor force. In addition, the level of construction activity always is affected by local economic conditions. Regions that are prosperous will offer better job possibilities for construction laborers than areas where the economy is not expanding.

Jobs for laborers may not rise quite as fast as for other construction-related occupations, since technological developments, like more efficient grading machinery and mechanical lifting devices, may affect the need for these workers somewhat. In general, however, the outlook is good, and the U.S. Department of Labor predicts a growth rate about as fast as the average through 2012.

■ FOR MORE INFORMATION

For information about contractor careers, contact
Associated General Contractors of America
333 John Carlyle Street, Suite 200
Alexandria, VA 22314
Tel: 703-548-3118
Email: info@agc.org
http://www.agc.org

For information on the role of union membership in construction jobs, check out this union's website.

Laborers' International Union of North America
905 16th Street, NW
Washington, DC 20006
Tel: 202-737-8320
http://www.liuna.org

For information on education programs for construction laborers, contact

AGC Education and Training Fund
AGC Education and Training Fund
37 Deerfield Road
P.O. Box 37
Pomfret Center, CT 06259
http://www.laborerslearn.org

National Center for Construction Education and Research
P.O. Box 141104
Gainesville, FL 32614-1104
Tel: 352-334-0920
http://www.nccer.org

Cooks and Chefs

■ OVERVIEW

Cooks and *chefs* are employed in the preparation and cooking of food, usually in large quantities, in hotels, restaurants, cafeterias, and other establishments and institutions. There are almost 3 million cooks, chefs, and other food preparation workers employed in the United States.

■ HISTORY

The art of cookery is as ancient as the history of humankind. The early Greeks, Egyptians, and Romans valued cooks as highly respected members of society.

France has given the world some of the finest cooks and chefs. Historical records reflect the avid interest the French people have in the art of cookery. Even today, cooks and chefs who are skilled in the art of French cuisine are highly valued and work in some of the world's most luxurious hotels and restaurants.

The hostelries of early America provided food and rest for weary travelers. Although these inns and taverns sometimes employed cooks specially hired from outside the proprietor's family, the food was often marginal in quality. It was not until hotels were built in the large cities that the occupation of cook developed into a profession.

The pleasure of dining out has become big business in the United States. The public has a range of choices—from the simplest, most inexpensive meal to the most expensive and elaborate. Whether a restaurant prides itself on "home cooking" or on exotic foreign cuisine, its cooks and chefs are largely responsible for the reputation it acquires.

■ THE JOB

Cooks and chefs are primarily responsible for the preparation and cooking of foods. Chefs usually supervise the work of cooks; however, the skills required and the job duties performed by each may vary depending upon the size and type of establishment.

Cooks and chefs begin by planning menus in advance. They estimate the amount of food that will be required for a specified period of time, order it from various suppliers, and check it for quantity and quality when it arrives. Following recipes or their own instincts, they measure and mix ingredients for soups, salads, gravies, sauces, casseroles, and desserts. They prepare meats, poultry, fish, vegetables, and other foods for baking, roasting, broiling, and steaming. They use blenders, mixers, grinders, slicers, or tenderizers to prepare the food, and ovens, broilers, grills, roasters, or steam kettles to cook it. During the mixing and cooking, cooks and chefs rely on their judgment and experience to add seasonings; they constantly taste and smell food being cooked and must know when it is cooked properly. To fill orders, they carve meat, arrange food portions on serving plates, and add appropriate gravies, sauces, or garnishes.

Some larger establishments employ specialized cooks, such as banquet cooks, pastry cooks, and broiler cooks. The *garde-manger* designs and prepares buffets, and *pantry cooks* prepare cold dishes for lunch and dinner. Other specialists are raw shellfish preparers and carvers.

In smaller establishments without specialized cooks, kitchen helpers, or prep cooks, the general

QUICK FACTS

SCHOOL SUBJECTS
Family and consumer science
Mathematics

PERSONAL SKILLS
Artistic
Following instructions

WORK ENVIRONMENT
Primarily indoors
Primarily one location

MINIMUM EDUCATION LEVEL
Apprenticeship

SALARY RANGE
$11,814 to $19,053 to
$53,789+

CERTIFICATION OR LICENSING
Required by certain states

OUTLOOK
About as fast as the average

DOT
313

GOE
11.05.01

NOC
6241, 6242

O*NET-SOC
35-1011.00, 35-2011.00,
35-2012.00, 35-2014.00,
35-2015.00

A new chef adds the finishing touches to a dish while his supervisor looks on.

cooks may have to do some of the preliminary work themselves, such as washing, peeling, cutting, and shredding vegetables and fruits; cutting, trimming, and boning meat; cleaning and preparing poultry, fish, and shellfish; and baking bread, rolls, cakes, and pastries.

Commercial cookery is usually done in large quantities, and many cooks, including school cafeteria cooks and mess cooks, are trained in "quantity cookery" methods. Numerous establishments today are noted for their specialties in foods, and some cooks work exclusively in the preparation and cooking of exotic dishes, very elaborate meals, or some particular creation of their own for which they have become famous. Restaurants that feature national cuisines may employ *international and regional cuisine specialty cooks.*

In the larger commercial kitchens, chefs may be responsible for the work of a number of cooks, each preparing and cooking food in specialized areas. They may, for example, employ expert cooks who specialize in frying, baking, roasting, broiling, or sauce cookery. Cooks are often titled by the kinds of specialized cooking they do, such as fry, vegetable, or pastry. Chefs have the major responsibility for supervising the overall preparation and cooking of the food.

Other duties of chefs may include training cooks on the job, planning menus, pricing food for menus, and purchasing food. Chefs may be responsible for determining the weights of portions to be prepared and served. Among their other duties may be the supervision of the work of all members of the kitchen staff. The kitchen staff assists by washing, cleaning, and preparing foods for cooking; cleaning utensils, dishes, and silverware; and assisting in many ways with the overall order and cleanliness of the kitchen. Most chefs spend part of their time striving to create new recipes that will win the praise of customers and build their reputations as experts. Many, like pastry chefs, focus their attention on particular kinds of food.

Expert chefs who have a number of years of experience behind them may be employed as *executive chefs.* These chefs do little cooking or food preparation—their main responsibilities are management and supervision. Executive chefs interview, hire, and dismiss kitchen personnel, and they are sometimes responsible for the dining room waiters and other employees. These chefs consult with the restaurant manager regarding the profits and losses of the food service and ways to increase business and cut costs. A part of their time is spent inspecting equipment. Executive chefs are in charge of all food services for special functions such as banquets and parties, and they spend many hours in coordinating the work for these activities. They may supervise the special chefs and assist them in planning elaborate arrangements and creations in food preparation. Executive chefs may be assisted by workers called *sous chefs.*

Smaller restaurants may employ only one or two cooks and workers to assist them. Cooks and assistants work together to prepare all the food for cooking and to keep the kitchen clean. Because smaller restaurants and public eating places usually offer standard menus with little variation, the cook's job becomes standardized. Such establishments may employ specialty cooks, barbecue cooks, pizza bakers, food order expediters, kitchen food assemblers, or counter supply workers. In some restaurants food is cooked as it is ordered; cooks preparing food in this manner are known as *short-order cooks.*

Regardless of the duties performed, cooks and chefs are largely responsible for the reputation and monetary profit or loss of the eating establishment in which they are employed.

■ REQUIREMENTS

The occupation of chef or cook has specific training requirements. Many cooks start out as kitchen helpers and acquire their skills on the job, but the trend today is to obtain training through high schools, vocational schools, or community colleges.

The amount of training required varies with the position. It takes only a short time to become an assistant or a fry cook, for example, but it requires years of training and experience to acquire the skills necessary to become an executive chef or cook in a fine restaurant.

High School

Although a high school diploma is not required for beginning positions, it is an asset to job applicants. If you are interested in moving beyond low-level positions such as kitchen helper or fry cook, your high school education should include classes in family and consumer science and health. These courses will teach you about nutrition, food preparation, and food storage. Math classes are also recommended; in this line of work you must be comfortable working with fractions, multiplying, and dividing. Since chefs and head cooks often have management responsibilities, you should also take business courses.

Postsecondary Training

Culinary students spend most of their time learning to prepare food through hands-on practice. At the same time, they learn how to use and care for kitchen equipment. Training programs often include courses in menu planning, determining portion size, controlling food costs, purchasing food supplies in quantity, selecting and storing food, and using leftovers. Students also learn hotel and restaurant sanitation and public health rules for handling food. Courses offered by private vocational schools, professional associations, and university programs often emphasize training in supervisory and management skills.

Professional associations and trade unions sometimes offer apprenticeship programs; one example is the three-year apprenticeship program sponsored by chapters of the American Culinary Federation (ACF) in cooperation with local employers. This program combines classroom work with on-the-job training under the supervision of a qualified chef and is an excellent way to begin your career. For more information, visit the education section of the ACF website http://www.acfchefs.org. Some large hotels and restaurants have their own training programs for new employees. The armed forces also offer good training and experience.

Certification or Licensing

To protect the public's health, chefs, cooks, and bakers are required by law in most states to possess a health certificate and to be examined periodically. These examinations, usually given by the state board of health, make certain that the individual is free from communicable diseases and skin infections. ACF offers certification at a variety of levels, such as executive chef and sous chef. In addition to educational and experience requirements, candidates must also pass written tests for each certification. Certification from ACF is recommended as a way to enhance your professional standing and advance your career.

Other Requirements

The successful chef or cook has a keen interest in food preparation and cooking and has a desire to experiment in developing new recipes and new food combinations. Cooks and chefs should be able to work as part of a team and to work under pressure during rush hours, in close quarters, and with a certain amount of noise and confusion. These employees need an even temperament and patience to contend with the public daily and to work closely with many other kinds of employees.

Immaculate personal cleanliness and good health are necessities in this trade. Applicants should possess physical stamina and be without serious physical impairments because of the mobility and activity the work requires. These employees spend many working hours standing, walking, and moving about.

Chefs and cooks must possess a keen sense of taste and smell. Hand and finger agility, hand-eye coordination, and a good memory are helpful. An artistic flair and creative talents in working with food are definitely strengths in this trade.

The principal union for cooks and chefs is the Hotel Employees and Restaurant Employees International Union (affiliated with the AFL-CIO).

■ EXPLORING

You may explore your interest in cooking right at home. Prepare meals for your family, offer to make a special dessert for a friend's birthday, create your own recipes. Any such hands-on experiences will build your skills and help you determine what type of cooking you enjoy the most.

Volunteer opportunities may be available at local kitchens that serve the homeless or others in need. You can also get a paying part-time or summer job at a fast food or other restaurant. Large and institutional kitchens, for example those in nursing homes, may offer positions such as sandwich or salad maker, soda-fountain attendant, or kitchen helper; while doing one of these jobs, you can observe the work of chefs and cooks.

■ EMPLOYERS

Cooks and chefs are needed by restaurants of all types and sizes; schools, hospitals, and other institutions; hotels, cruise lines, airlines, and other industries; and catering and bakery businesses. Approximately 60 percent work at restaurants, other retail eateries, and drinking establishments. Roughly 20 percent are employed by institutions/cafeterias, such as schools, hospitals, and nursing homes. The rest work at such places as grocery stores, hotels, and catering businesses.

■ STARTING OUT

Apprenticeship programs are one method of entering the trade. These programs usually offer the beginner sound basic training and a regular salary. Upon completion of the apprenticeship, cooks may be hired full-time in their place of training or assisted in finding employment with another establishment. Cooks are hired as chefs only after they have acquired a number of years of experience. Cooks who have been formally trained through public or private trade or vocational schools or in culinary institutes may be able to take advantage of school placement services.

In many cases, a cook begins as a kitchen helper or cook's helper and, through experience gained in on-the-job training, is able to move into the job of cook. To do this, people sometimes start out in small restaurants, perhaps as short-order cooks, grill cooks, or sandwich or salad makers, and transfer to larger establishments as they gain experience.

School cafeteria workers who want to become cooks may have an opportunity to receive food-services training. Many school districts, with the cooperation of school food-services divisions of the state departments of education, provide on-the-job training and sometimes summer workshops for interested cafeteria employees. Some community colleges, state departments of education, and school associations offer similar programs. Cafeteria workers who have completed these training programs are often selected to fill positions as cooks.

Job opportunities may be located through employment bureaus, trade associations, unions, contacts with friends, newspaper want ads, or local offices of the state employment service. Another method is to apply directly to restaurants or hotels. Small restaurants, school cafeterias, and other eating-places with simple food preparation will provide the greatest number of starting jobs for cooks. Job applicants who have had courses in commercial food preparation will have an advantage in large restaurants and hotels, where hiring standards are often high.

■ ADVANCEMENT

Advancement depends on the skill, training, experience, originality, and ambition of the individual. It also depends somewhat on the general business climate and employment trends.

Cooks with experience can advance by moving to other places of employment for higher wages or to establishments looking for someone with a specialized skill in preparing a particular kind of food. Cooks who have a number of years of successful job experience may find chef positions open to them; however, in some cases it may take 10 or 15 years to obtain such a position, depending on personal qualifications and other employment factors.

Expert cooks who have obtained supervisory responsibilities as head cooks or chefs may advance to positions as executive chefs or to other types of managerial work. Some go into business for themselves as caterers or restaurant owners; others may become instructors in vocational programs in high schools, colleges, or other academic institutions.

■ EARNINGS

The salaries earned by chefs and cooks are widely divergent and depend on many factors, such as the size, type, and location of the establishment, and the skill, experience, training, and specialization of the worker. Salaries are usually fairly standard among establishments of the same type. For example, restaurants and diners serving inexpensive meals and a sandwich-type menu generally pay cooks less than establishments with medium-priced or expensive menus. The highest wages are earned at restaurants and hotels known for their elegance.

The U.S. Department of Labor reports the following earnings for cooks and chefs in a variety of positions. In 2002, the median hourly wage for head cooks and chefs was $13.43. Based on a 40-hour workweek and full year employment, a person paid this hourly amount would have a yearly income of approximately $27,934. The highest paid 10 percent of head cooks and chefs earned more than $25.86 per hour, or more than $53,789 per year. The lowest 10 percent of head cooks and chefs earned less than $9.86 hourly, or less than $20,509 per year. Restaurant cooks had a median hourly wage of $9.16, or approximate annual earnings of $19,053. Cooks working at institutions or cafeterias had a median of $8.72 per hour (approximately $18,138 per year). Short-order cooks earned a median hourly wage of $7.82 (approximately $16,266 annually). Cooks at fast food restaurants were at the bottom of the pay scale, earning a median of $6.90 per hour (approximately $14,352 per year); the lowest paid 10 percent of these cooks earned less than $5.68 per hour (approximately $11,814 annually), and the highest paid 10 percent of fast-food cooks earned more than $9.13 per hour ($18,990 annually). When looking at the earnings, however, you should bear in mind that more than 2 out 5 food preparation workers are employed part time, and so can count on less annual pay than indicated here.

Chefs and cooks sometimes receive their meals free during working hours and are furnished with any necessary job uniforms. Those working full-time usually receive standard benefits, such as health insurance and vacation and sick days.

■ WORK ENVIRONMENT

Working conditions vary with the place of employment. Many kitchens are modern, well lighted, well equipped, and air-conditioned, but some older, smaller eating-places may be only marginally equipped. The work of cooks can be strenuous, with long hours of standing, lifting heavy pots, and working near hot ovens and ranges. Possible hazards include falls, cuts, and burns, although serious injury is uncommon. Even in the most modern kitchens, cooks, chefs, and bakers usually work amid considerable noise from the operation of equipment and machinery.

Experienced cooks may work with little or no supervision, depending on the size of the food service and the place of employment. Less experienced cooks may work under much more direct supervision from expert cooks or chefs.

Chefs and cooks may work a 40- or 48-hour week, depending on the type of food service offered and certain union agreements. Some food establishments are open 24 hours a day, while others may be open from the very early morning until late in the evening. Establishments open long hours may have two or three work shifts, with some chefs and cooks working day schedules while others work evenings.

All food-service workers may have to work overtime hours, depending on the amount of business and rush-hour trade. These employees work many weekends and holidays, although they may have a day off every week or rotate with other employees to have alternate weekends free. Many cooks are required to work early morning or late evening shifts. For example, doughnuts, breads, and muffins for breakfast service must be baked by 6:00 or 7:00 A.M. which requires bakers to begin work at 2:00 or 3:00 A.M. Some people will find it very difficult to adjust to working such late and irregular hours.

■ OUTLOOK

Overall the employment of chefs and cooks is expected to increase as fast as the average for all occupations through 2012, according to the U.S. Department of Labor. While some areas (such as cooks in fast food) may not see much growth in number of new jobs, turnover rates are high and the need to find replacement cooks and chefs will mean many job opportunities in all areas. The need for cooks and chefs will also grow as the population increases and lifestyles change. As people earn higher incomes and have more leisure time, they dine out more often and take more vacations. In addition, working parents and their families dine out frequently as a convenience.

■ FOR MORE INFORMATION

For information on careers in baking and cooking, education, and certification, contact the following organizations:

American Culinary Federation Inc.
10 San Bartola Drive
St. Augustine, FL 32086
Tel: 800-624-9458
Email: acf@acfchefs.net
http://www.acfchefs.org

American Institute of Baking
PO Box 3999
Manhattan, KS 66505-3999
Tel: 785-537-4750
Email: info@aibonline.org
http://www.aibonline.org

Culinary Institute of America
1946 Campus Drive
Hyde Park, NY 12538-1499
Tel: 845-452-9600
http://www.ciachef.edu

Educational Institute of the American Hotel and Lodging Association
800 North Magnolia Avenue, Suite 1800
Orlando, FL 32803
Tel: 800-752-4567
Email: info@ei-ahla.org
http://www.ei-ahla.org

National Restaurant Association Educational Foundation
175 West Jackson Boulevard, Suite 1500
Chicago, IL 60604-2702
Tel: 800-765-2122
http://www.nraef.org

For information on culinary schools in Canada, industry news, and a job bank, visit this organization's website.

Canadian Culinary Federation
707-1281 West Georgia Street
Vancouver, BC V6E 3J7 Canada
Tel: 506-387-4882
http://www.ccfcc.ca

Copywriters

■ OVERVIEW

Copywriters express, promote, and interpret ideas and facts in written form for books, magazines, trade journals, newspapers, technical studies and reports, company newsletters, radio and television broadcasts, and advertisements.

Most copywriters are employed in the advertising industry. Their main goal is to persuade the general public to choose or favor certain goods, services, and personalities.

■ HISTORY

In its earliest days, advertising allowed merchants to go from street to shop, adopting symbols and later written signs to show the goods and services they offered. With the invention of paper and advances in education that enabled more and more people to read, tack-up signs became common. It wasn't until printing was introduced in the 15th century, however, that advertising was truly revolutionized. Merchants began printing and distributing handbills by the hundreds. Advertisements in newspapers became a familiar sight by the 17th century. By the end of the 1800s, magazines were carrying ads of all kinds.

In 1865, a new system was introduced to newspapers: the selling of space specifically for advertisers. Soon ads could be seen on huge outdoor billboards, between your favorite television shows, and on radio broadcasts. Today, the Internet has revolutionized the advertising industry, allowing advertisers not only to reach a new audience, but to interact with them as well.

■ THE JOB

Advertisements were once written and arranged by the individual or company selling a good or service. Today, most national advertising, and much local advertising, is prepared by advertising agencies. Modern firms split up the different tasks of advertising among workers specifically trained to handle the writing, design, and overall appearance of ads. Copywriters and their assistants write the words of advertisements, including the written text in print ads and the spoken words in radio and television ads, which are also called spots.

Copywriters may have to come up with their own idea and words for an ad, but generally the client's account manger and head designer generate the idea. Once the idea behind the ad is presented, copywriters begin gathering as much information as possible about the client through library research, interviews, the Internet, observation, and other methods. They study advertising trends and review surveys of consumer preferences. They keep extensive notes from which they will draw material for the ad. Once their research has been organized, copywriters begin working on the written components of the ad. They may have a standard theme or "pitch" to work with that has been developed in previous ads. One such example, using what is called a tagline, is seen in the popular milk campaigns promoting its health benefits and other advantages—beauty, athleticism, and intelligence. (Milk: It does a body good.)

The process of developing copy is exciting, although it can also involve detailed and solitary work. After researching one idea, a writer might discover that a different perspective or related topic would be more effective, entertaining, or marketable.

When working on assignment, copywriters submit their ad drafts to their editor or the advertising account executive for approval. Writers will probably work through several drafts, writing and rewriting sections of the material as they proceed, searching for just the right way to promote the product, service, or other client need.

Copywriters, like other corporate writers, may also write articles, bulletins, news releases, sales letters, speeches, and other related informative and promotional material. Many copywriters are employed in advertising agencies. They also may work for public relations firms or in communications departments of large companies.

Copywriters can be employed either as in-house staff or as freelancers. Pay varies according to experience and the position, but freelancers must provide their own office space and equipment such as computers and fax machines. Freelancers also are responsible for keeping tax records, sending out invoices, negotiating contracts, and providing their own health insurance.

■ REQUIREMENTS
High School

While in high school, build a broad educational foundation by taking courses in English, literature, foreign lan-

QUICK FACTS

SCHOOL SUBJECTS
English
Journalism

PERSONAL SKILLS
Communication/ideas
Helping/teaching

WORK ENVIRONMENT
Primarily indoors
Primarily one location

MINIMUM EDUCATION LEVEL
Bachelor's degree

SALARY RANGE
$21,320 to $54,520 to
$85,140 +

CERTIFICATION OR LICENSING
None available

OUTLOOK
Faster than the average

DOT
131

GOE
01.02.01

NOC
5121

O*NET-SOC
27-3043.00

guages, business, computer science, and typing. You should be confident in your typing abilities and comfortable with computer programs, as copywriters use computers every day for ad writing, researching, and development.

Postsecondary Training

Competition for writing jobs almost always demands the background of a college education. Many employers prefer that you have a broad liberal arts background or majors in English, literature, history, philosophy, or one of the social sciences. Other employers desire communications or journalism training in college. A number of schools offer courses in copywriting and other business writing.

In addition to formal course work, most employers look for practical writing experience. If you have served on high school or college newspapers, yearbooks, or literary magazines, you will make a better candidate, as well as if you have worked for small community newspapers or radio stations, even in an unpaid position. Many advertising agencies and public relations firms offer summer internship programs that can provide valuable writing experience. Interns do many simple tasks, such as running errands and answering phones, but some may be asked to perform research and even assist with the ad writing.

Other Requirements

To be a copywriter, you should be creative and able to express ideas clearly, have a broad general knowledge, be a skilled researcher, and be computer literate. Other assets include curiosity, persistence, initiative, resourcefulness, and an accurate memory. At some ad agencies and other employers, the environment is hectic and client deadlines are short. For these copywriters, the ability to concentrate and produce under pressure is essential.

■ EXPLORING

As a high school or college student, you can test your interest and aptitude in the field of writing by serving as a reporter or writer on school newspapers, yearbooks, and literary magazines. Various writing courses and workshops will offer you the opportunity to sharpen your writing skills.

Small community newspapers and local radio stations often welcome contributions from outside sources, although they may not have the resources to pay for them. Jobs in bookstores, magazine shops, and even newsstands will offer you a chance to become familiar with various publications.

You can also obtain information on writing as a career by visiting local newspapers, publishers, or radio and television stations and interviewing some of the writers who work there. Career conferences and other guidance programs frequently include speakers on the entire field of communications from local or national organizations.

■ EMPLOYERS

There are approximately 21,000 advertising firms nationwide, employing over 300,000 workers. Copywriters and editors hold approximately 10,000 jobs in the industry.

■ STARTING OUT

Most copywriters start out in entry-level positions, working as office assistants or copywriting assistants. These jobs may be listed with college placement offices or in the want ads of local papers. You can also try applying directly to the hiring departments of the advertising agencies or other large companies that have public relations departments. Graduates who previously served internships with these companies often have the advantage of knowing someone who can give them a personal recommendation.

Employers will often ask to see samples of published writing. These samples should be assembled in an organized portfolio or scrapbook. Bylined or signed articles are more credible (and, as a result, more useful) than stories whose source is not identified.

Beginning positions as a copywriting assistant usually involve library research, preparation of rough ad drafts, and other related writing tasks. These are generally carried on under the supervision of a senior copywriter.

■ ADVANCEMENT

Advancement may be more rapid in small advertising agencies or companies, where beginners learn by doing a little bit of everything and may be given writing tasks immediately. In large firms, duties are usually more compartmentalized. Assistants in entry-level positions are assigned such tasks as research, fact checking, and copyrighting, but it generally takes much longer to advance to full-scale copywriting duties.

Promotion as a copywriter usually takes the form of obtaining more projects for larger and more influential clients. For example, being assigned to work on spots for large corporation would be viewed as an impressive achievement. Others advance by moving to a larger or more prestigious firm or starting up their own business.

Freelance or self-employed writers earn advancement in the form of larger fees as they gain exposure and establish their reputations.

■ EARNINGS

According to the Bureau of Labor Statistics, median annual salaries for writers in advertising and related services was

$54,520 in 2002. In 2002, median annual earnings for salaried writers (including copywriters) were $42,790 a year, according to the Bureau of Labor Statistics. The lowest paid 10 percent earned less than $21,320, while the highest paid 10 percent earned $85,140 or more.

In addition to their salaries, many writers earn some income from freelance work. Part-time freelancers may earn from $5,000 to $15,000 a year. Freelance earnings vary widely. Full-time established freelance writers may earn up to $75,000 a year.

■ WORK ENVIRONMENT

Working conditions vary for copywriters, depending on the size of their employer and whether or not they frequently work under tight deadlines. Though their work-week usually runs 35 to 40 hours, many copywriters work overtime, working nights and weekends to meet client deadlines.

Though copywriters do some of their work independently, they often must cooperate with artists, photographers, editors, and other advertising people who may have widely differing ideas of how the materials should be prepared and presented.

Physical surroundings range from comfortable private offices to noisy, crowded offices filled with other workers typing and talking on the telephone. Some copywriters must confine their research to the library or telephone interviews, but others may travel to other cities or countries or to client work sites.

The work is arduous, but most copywriters are seldom bored. The most difficult element is the continual pressure of deadlines. People who are the most content as copywriters enjoy and work well with deadline pressure.

■ OUTLOOK

The outlook for the advertising industry as a whole looks promising, according to the U.S. Department of Labor. Overall employment is projected to grow more than 18 percent until 2012. Smaller agencies and home-based businesses are on the rise; however, the mega-agencies—multinational agencies created from mergers and acquisitions—still dominate the industry. Of the 47,000 advertising and public relations agencies in the United States, most of the large firms are located in New York, Chicago, and Los Angeles and offer higher pay scales than smaller agencies. Jobs for writers and editors are projected to grow 10.7 percent through 2012.

Another important trend that will affect the employment of copywriters is specialization. Many agencies are increasing their focus on niche markets, and they will continue to specialize. Expected high-growth areas include foreign-language programming, advertising aimed at specific ethnic groups, advertising targeted at the over-50 market, special events advertising and marketing, and direct marketing campaigns for retailers and technological companies. Copywriters who can offer skills such as the ability to speak a foreign language will be in demand.

In addition, the explosion of online advertising has created a wealth of jobs. The number of Internet users as of September 2002 was 605.6 million, and companies are responding by placing advertising on the Web and creating websites that allow customers the ease and convenience of online shopping. From flowers to antiques, clothing to furniture, virtually everything can be purchased online. All of these goods and services require copywriters to write ads that will promote and sell. Individuals with extensive computer skills will be at an advantage as a result.

People entering this field should realize that the competition for jobs is extremely keen. The appeal of writing and advertising jobs will continue to grow, as many young graduates find the industry glamorous and exciting.

■ FOR MORE INFORMATION

Visit this website to learn more about internships, scholarships, and awards.

American Advertising Federation
1101 Vermont Avenue, NW, Suite 500
Washington, DC 20005-6306
Tel: 202-898-0089
Email: aaf@aaf.org
http://www.aaf.org

For industry information, contact

American Association of Advertising Agencies
405 Lexington Avenue, 18th Floor
New York, NY 10174-1801
Tel: 212-682-2500
http://www.aaaa.org

Coremakers

■ OVERVIEW

Coremakers and related workers in the foundry industry prepare cores that are used in making metal castings. In the founding process, molten metal is poured into a mold that contains a solid central core, usually made of sand or a sand mixture. The metal cools and solidifies. When the core is removed, the desired cavity or shape remains in the metal in place of the core. Cores are made in various sizes and shapes depending upon the desired size and shape of the final casting.

HISTORY

Coremaking has been a part of foundry work since techniques were first developed to make molded metal articles. The earliest cores were made by hand from wood or metal. By today's standards, they would be considered very crude.

During the 1800s, the use of metals in industrial applications expanded greatly. The years following the Civil War saw the Industrial Revolution change production techniques in the United States. Many new types of machines were invented, and coremaking, along with other foundry work, was an important activity in producing these machines. The 20th century saw increased production of metal articles and machinery, with many of them made of cast metals. Today, automobiles, airplanes, farm machinery, refrigerators, and many other items that are essential to our lives are made with the help of coremakers.

THE JOB

Cores are used in manufacturing metal castings that have hollow centers, such as pipes and tubes. The core establishes the open area in the object. Cores for almost any metal casting are produced using the same basic procedures. Cores may be large or small, and can be made by hand or by machine. *Bench coremakers*, for example, work at benches making smaller cores, usually by hand. In contrast, *floor coremakers* make large cores on the floor of a foundry.

In general, coremakers begin their work by cleaning a core box with blasts of compressed air. A core box is often a block of wood or metal hollowed out to the shape of the desired core. After it is cleaned, they dust fine sand over the interior of the core box so that the finished core will not stick to the box, but instead will slip out easily. Then they partially fill the box with sand or a sand mixture. They may do this either by hand or with the help of machines. They tightly pack the sand into the box, using hand or power tamping tools. Periodically, when the core sand reaches certain levels in the box, they may insert wires that have been bent to the proper shape to add strength to the core. Special care is taken to ram the sand solidly and compactly into the core box so there will be no air pockets or other weaknesses in the finished core. The box is then inverted on a flat surface and lifted off of the core. Any cracks or chips on the core are repaired or smoothed out. Cores may be baked to harden them before they are used in making metal castings.

Machine coremakers, who usually work in large factories where many identical parts must be produced, oper-

ate various types of machines that make sand cores. Other workers involved in the process include *core checkers*, who verify core sizes and shapes; *core-oven tenders*, who regulate and maintain correct oven temperatures to harden cores; *core setters*, who position finished cores in molds before the molten metal is poured in to make castings; and *coreroom foundry laborers*, who assist coremakers by hauling sand, applying graphite solutions, and transporting cores to and from ovens.

REQUIREMENTS
High School

If you are interested in becoming a coremaker, classes in mathematics, blueprint reading, drafting, computers, English, and shop will be helpful. In particular, shop courses that provide hands-on training in the use of hand tools and machinery are especially relevant to the job.

Postsecondary Training

Most coremakers learn the actual skills necessary for their work through on-the-job training or apprenticeships. Apprenticeships offer the most thorough training for this work, and competition for the limited number of openings is keen. To find out about apprenticeships in your state, contact your state's Apprenticeship Council or your state's Office of Apprenticeship Training, Employer and Labor Services. (For office addresses, visit the website http://www.doleta.gov/atels_bat/sobat.asp.) Apprentices receive on-the-job training from skilled coremakers in a planned program that teaches them all phases of coremaking. They learn bench coremaking, floor work, oven tending, machine coremaking, core finishing, core assembling, and other skills necessary for intricate multiple-part coremaking. Apprenticeships, which typically last four years, also include classroom instruction in related subjects, such as applied mathematics and the study of the different qualities of various

QUICK FACTS

SCHOOL SUBJECTS
Mathematics
Technical/shop

PERSONAL SKILLS
Mechanical/manipulative
Technical/scientific

WORK ENVIRONMENT
Primarily indoors
Primarily one location

MINIMUM EDUCATION LEVEL
Apprenticeship

SALARY RANGE
$16,070 to $26,300 to $49,960+

CERTIFICATION OR LICENSING
None available

OUTLOOK
Decline

DOT
518

GOE
08.02.02

NOC
9412

O*NET-SOC
51-4071.00

This coremaker is busy assembling small, intricate cores that will be used in casting for aerospace equipment.

metals. In most cases, applicants for apprenticeships need to be high school graduates.

Other Requirements

Students interested in becoming coremakers should have mathematical aptitude and the ability to visualize three-dimensional objects by reading blueprints and drawings. Coremakers are detail oriented and many work with little direct supervision, so those interested in this type of work should be self-disciplined and self-motivated, and should be able to schedule projects to meet deadlines. Because the work can be quite strenuous, coremakers should be in good health. Some types of hand coremaking require a high degree of manual dexterity.

■ EXPLORING

To explore this work, ask your teachers or school counselor to arrange a visit for you and other interested students to a foundry so that you can observe the work and ask ques-

tions about it. Hobbies such as sculpture or metalworking can help you develop manual dexterity and provide experience working with metals. To find out about workshops or classes in sculpture, check with summer school programs, museums, or art centers. If there is a foundry in your area, you may be able to obtain a summer or part-time job as a helper in a coremaking operation.

■ EMPLOYERS

Coremakers work in job foundries, production foundries, or shops that make cores for metal products. Most foundries, according to the American Foundry Society, are small operations: Approximately 80 percent employ fewer than 100 people, and approximately 14 percent employ between 100 and 250 people. The American Foundry Society also reports that there are some 2,480 foundries located across the United States. They are generally found in the highly industrial areas.

■ STARTING OUT

Workers who wish to become coremakers usually start out as helpers. They learn the basics of coremaking through on-the-job training and by working closely with an experienced coremaker. Typically, the best way to obtain a job in coremaking is to apply directly to a foundry or shop that makes metal castings. You can learn about openings in area companies through state employment services or classified newspaper ads. Many workers in foundries are members of unions such as the Glass, Molders, Pottery, Plastics and Allied Workers International Union, so you might try contacting a local union office.

■ ADVANCEMENT

Workers who begin as helpers may advance to become coremakers if they can demonstrate that they can do the work. Experienced coremakers who possess leadership qualities may become shop supervisors. Some advancement opportunities open up when workers transfer to other foundry jobs that deal with a variety of metals. Continuing education is another route to advancement. The Cast Metals Institute, part of the American Foundry Society, offers courses and training covering a variety of metal casting subjects. However, not many entry-level workers have been hired in recent years, so the traditional route of starting out in the shop and moving into a more technical position has become somewhat limited.

■ EARNINGS

According to the U.S. Bureau of Labor Statistics, foundry mold and coremakers had median annual earnings of $26,300 in 2002. Ten percent earned less than $16,070 annually, and 10 percent earned more than $49,960 per year. Salaries are influenced by the worker's experience, the size of the employer, and the location of the foundry. For example, the Minnesota Workforce Center reports 2001 earnings for foundry mold and coremakers in that state ranged from a low of 10 percent making less than approximately $21,950 to a high of 10 percent earning more than $43,595 annually. Apprentices generally start with a lower pay rate than a skilled coremaker, with incremental raises as they become proficient in different skills. Most coremakers belong to unions, so their work hours, overtime pay, health insurance plans, and other fringe benefits are established by contract between the unions and the companies.

■ WORK ENVIRONMENT

Foundry workers, including coremakers, sometimes face unpleasant or potentially dangerous conditions on the job. Newer foundries have improved working conditions, but foundries are, traditionally, noisy, hot, and smoky. Many foundry operations produce irritating fumes. Concrete floors may make the coremaker's job hard on the feet. Coremakers have the lowest injury rates among foundry workers, but the rate is somewhat higher than the average for all manufacturing workers.

■ OUTLOOK

During recent years, more and more of the work involved in coremaking and foundry mold making is being done by machines. As work in foundries becomes increasingly automated, the average productivity of each worker is greater. Thus, while the production of many kinds of cast metal items has been rising, an increased demand for cores will probably not result in an increased demand for coremakers. In addition, production of some kinds of metal castings has decreased. For example, plastic is being used in place of metal for some automobile components, thus reducing the overall need for coremakers and related workers. For this reason, employment in the field has been declining.

Although new workers will be needed to replace those who retire or leave, competition for positions will be keen. Most jobs will go to workers already in the industry who have some experience. However, opportunities for jobs will vary from place to place because some regions have a much greater concentration of foundries.

■ FOR MORE INFORMATION

For information on the foundry industry, jobs, and training available through the Cast Metals Institute, contact

American Foundry Society
505 State Street
Des Plaines, IL 60016-8399

Tel: 800-537-4237
http://www.afsinc.org

For information on industry news, union membership, and scholarship opportunities, contact

**Glass, Molders, Pottery, Plastics and Allied
   Workers International Union**
P.O. Box 607
608 East Baltimore Pike
Media, PA 19063-0607
Tel: 610-565-5051
Email: gmpiu@ix.netcom.com
http://www.gmpiu.org

For information on courses, publications, and training videos, contact

Cast Metals Institute
505 State Street
Des Plaines, IL 60016
Tel: 800-537-4237
http://www.castmetals.com

Corrections Officers

■ OVERVIEW

Corrections officers guard people who have been arrested and are awaiting trial or who have been tried, convicted, and sentenced to serve time in a penal institution. They search prisoners and their cells for weapons, drugs, and other contraband; inspect windows, doors, locks, and gates for signs of tampering; observe the conduct and behavior of inmates to prevent disturbances or escapes; and make verbal or written reports to superior officers. Corrections officers assign work to inmates and supervise their activities. They guard prisoners who are being transported between jails, courthouses, mental institutions, or other destinations, and supervise prisoners receiving visitors. When necessary, these workers use weapons or force to maintain discipline and order. There are approximately 476,000 corrections officers employed in the United States.

■ HISTORY

For centuries, punishment for criminal behavior was generally left in the hands of the injured individual or his or her relatives. This resulted in blood feuds, which could carry on for years and which eventually could be resolved by the payment of money to the victim or the victim's family. When kingdoms emerged as the standard form of government, certain actions came to be regarded as an affront to the king or the peace of his domain, and the king assumed the responsibility for punishing the wrongs committed by a subject or his clan. In this way, crime became a public offense. The earliest corrections officers were more likely to be executioners and torturers than guards or jailers.

Early criminals were treated inhumanely. They were often put to death for minor offenses, exiled, forced into hard labor, given corporal punishment, tortured, mutilated, turned into slaves, or left to rot in dungeons. Jailing criminals was not considered a penalty in and of itself, but rather as a temporary measure until punishment could be carried out. More often, prisons were established to punish debtors or to house orphans and delinquent youths. One of the earliest debtor's prisons was Bridewell, in London, England, which was established in 1553. Other European countries built similar institutions.

During the Enlightenment of the 18th century, the belief that punishment alone deters crime began to weaken. The practice of imprisonment became more and more common as attempts were made to fit the degree of punishment to the nature of the crime. Societies looked to deter crime with the promise of clear and just punishment. Rehabilitation of offenders was to be achieved through isolation, hard labor, penitence, and discipline. By 1829, prisoners in most prisons were required to perform hard labor, which proved more cost-effective for the prison systems. Before long, the rehabilitation aspect of imprisonment became less important than the goal of simply isolating prisoners from society and creating respect for authority and order. Prisoners were subjected to harsh treatment from generally untrained personnel.

By 1870, calls for prison reform introduced new sentencing procedures such as parole and probation. It was hoped that providing opportunities for early release would provide prisoners with more incentive toward rehabilitation. Prisons evolved into several types, providing minimum, medium, and maximum security. The role of the prison guard at each institution evolved accordingly. The recognition of prisoners' rights also provided new limitations and purposes for the conduct and duties of the prison guard. Corrections officers began to receive specialized training in the treatment and rehabilitation of prisoners.

Until the 1980s, corrections officers were employees of the federal, state, or local government. A dramatic increase in the number of prisoners, brought on by the so-called War on Drugs, led to overcrowded prisons and skyrocketing costs. At the same time, the system itself came under attack, especially the concepts of parole and reduced sentencing. Many states began to contract private companies to build and operate additional correctional facilities. Today, corrections officers are employed at every level of government and often by these private companies.

■ THE JOB

To prevent disturbances or escapes, corrections officers carefully observe the conduct and behavior of the inmates at all times. They watch for forbidden activities and infractions of the rules, as well as for poor attitudes or unsatisfactory adjustment to prison life on the part of the inmates. They try to settle disputes before violence can erupt. They may search the prisoners or their living quarters for weapons or drugs and inspect locks, bars on windows and doors, and gates for any evidence of tampering. The inmates are under guard constantly while eating, sleeping, exercising, bathing, and working. They are counted periodically to be sure all are present. Some officers are stationed on towers and at gates to prevent escapes. All rule violations and anything out of the ordinary are reported to a superior officer such as a chief jailer. In case of a major disturbance, corrections officers may use weapons or force to restore order.

Corrections officers give work assignments to prisoners, supervise them as they carry out their duties, and instruct them in unfamiliar tasks. Corrections officers are responsible for the physical needs of the prisoners, such as providing or obtaining meals and medical aid. They assure the health and safety of the inmates by checking the cells for unsanitary conditions and fire hazards.

These workers may escort inmates from their cells to the prison's visiting room, medical office, or chapel. Certain officers, called *patrol conductors*, guard prisoners who are being transported between courthouses, prisons, mental institutions, or other destinations, either by van, car, or public transportation. Officers at a penal institu-

QUICK FACTS

SCHOOL SUBJECTS
Government
Physical education
Psychology

PERSONAL SKILLS
Communication/ideas
Helping/teaching

WORK ENVIRONMENT
Primarily indoors
Primarily one location

MINIMUM EDUCATION LEVEL
High school diploma

SALARY RANGE
$22,010 to $32,670 to $52,370+

CERTIFICATION OR LICENSING
Required by certain states

OUTLOOK
Faster than the average

DOT
372

GOE
04.03.01

NOC
6462

O*NET-SOC
33-3012.00

tion may also screen visitors at the entrance and accompany them to other areas within the facility. From time to time, they may inspect mail addressed to prisoners, checking for contraband, help investigate crimes committed within the prison, or aid in the search for escapees.

Some police officers specialize in guarding juvenile offenders being held at a police station house or detention room pending a hearing, transfer to a correctional institution, or return to their parents. They often investigate the backgrounds of first offenders to check for a criminal history or to make a recommendation to the magistrate regarding disposition of the case. Lost or runaway children are also placed in the care of these officers until their parents or guardians can be located.

Immigration guards guard aliens held by the immigration service awaiting investigation, deportation, or release. *Gate tenders* check the identification of all persons entering and leaving the penal institution.

In most correctional institutions, *psychologists* and *social workers* are employed to counsel inmates with mental and emotional problems. It is an important part of a corrections officer's job, however, to supplement this with informal counseling. Officers may help inmates adjust to prison life, prepare for return to civilian life, and avoid committing crimes in the future. On a more immediate level, they may arrange for an inmate to visit the library, help inmates get in touch with their families, suggest where to look for a job after release from prison, or discuss personal problems. In some institutions, corrections officers may lead more formal group counseling sessions. As they fulfill more rehabilitative roles, corrections officers are increasingly required to possess a college-level education in psychology, criminology, or related areas of study.

Corrections officers keep a daily record of their activities and make regular reports, either verbal or written, to their supervisors. These reports concern the behavior of the inmates and the quality and quantity of work they do, as well as any disturbances, rule violations, and unusual occurrences that may have taken place.

Head corrections officers supervise and coordinate other corrections officers. They perform roll call and assign duties to the officers; direct the activities of groups of inmates; arrange the release and transfer of prisoners in accordance with the instructions on a court order; maintain security and investigate disturbances among the inmates; maintain prison records and prepare reports; and review and evaluate the performance of their subordinates.

In small communities, corrections officers (who are sometimes called *jailers*) may also act as deputy sheriffs or police officers when they are not occupied with guard duties.

■ REQUIREMENTS
High School

To work as a corrections officer, candidates generally must meet the minimum age requirement—usually 18 or 21—and have a high school diploma or its equivalent. Individuals without a high school education may be considered for employment if they have qualifying work experience, such as probation and parole experience.

Postsecondary Training

Many states and correctional facilities prefer or require officers to have postsecondary training in psychology, criminology, or related areas of study. Some states require applicants to have one or two years of previous experience in corrections or related police work. Military experience or related work experience is also required by some state governments. On the federal level, applicants should have at least two years of college or two years of work or military experience.

Training for corrections officers ranges from the special academy instruction provided by the federal government and some states to the informal, on-the-job training furnished by most states and local governments. The Federal Bureau of Prisons operates a training center in Glynco, Georgia, where new hires generally undergo a three-week program of basic corrections education. Training academies have programs that last from four to eight weeks and instruct trainees on institutional policies, regulations, and procedures; the behavior and custody of inmates; security measures; and report writing. Training in self-defense, the use of firearms and other weapons, and emergency medical techniques is often provided. On-the-job trainees spend two to six months or more under the supervision of an experienced officer. During that period of time, they receive in-house training while gaining actual experience. Periodically, corrections officers may be given additional training as new ideas and procedures in criminal justice are developed.

Certification or Licensing

A few states require passing a written examination. Corrections officers who work for the federal government and most state governments are covered by civil service systems or merit boards and may be required to pass a competitive exam for employment. Many states require random or comprehensive drug testing of their officers, either during hiring procedures or while employed at the facility.

Other Requirements

Other requirements include good health and physical strength, and many states have set minimum height,

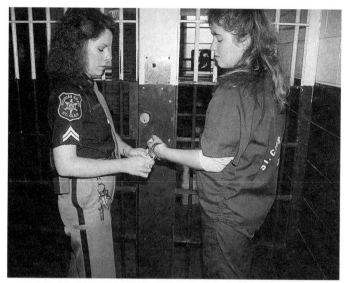

This corrections officer prepares to take an inmate back to her cell.

vision, and hearing standards. Sound judgment and the ability to think and act quickly are important qualities for this occupation. A candidate must have a clean police record. The ability to speak foreign languages is often a plus when applying for corrections jobs.

EXPLORING

Because of age requirements and the nature of the work, there are no opportunities for high school students to gain actual experience while still in school. Where the minimum age requirement is 21, prospective corrections officers may prepare for employment by taking college courses in criminal justice or police science. Enrollment in a two- or four-year college degree program in a related field is encouraged. Military service may also offer experience and training in corrections. Social work is another way to gain experience. You may also look into obtaining a civilian job as a clerk or other worker for the police department or other protective service organization. Related part-time, volunteer, or summer work may also be available in psychiatric hospitals and other institutions providing physical and emotional counseling and services. Many online services also have forums for corrections officers and other public safety employees, and these may provide opportunities to read about and communicate with people active in this career.

EMPLOYERS

Most corrections officers work for the government at the local, state, and federal levels in penal institutions and in jobs connected with the penal system. Of the approximately 457,000 corrections officers employed in the United States,

roughly 60 percent work in state-run correctional facilities such as prisons, prison camps, and reformatories. Most of the rest are employed at city and county jails or other institutions. Roughly 15,000 work for the federal government. And approximately 19,000 are employed by private corrections contractors.

STARTING OUT

To apply for a job as a corrections officer, contact federal or state civil service commissions, state departments of correction, or local correctional facilities and ask for information about entrance requirements, training, and job opportunities. Private contractors and other companies are also a growing source of employment opportunities. Many officers enter this field from social work areas and parole and probation positions.

ADVANCEMENT

With additional education and training, experienced officers may qualify for promotion to head corrections officer or advancement to some other supervisory or administrative position, and eventually may become prison directors. Some officers transfer to related fields, such as law, law enforcement, or probation and parole.

EARNINGS

Median yearly earnings for correction officers was estimated by the U.S. Department of Labor as $32,670. Wages for corrections officers vary considerably depending on their employers and their level of experience. According to the U.S. Department of Labor, the 2002 median annual earnings for corrections officers employed by the federal government were $40,900; for those employed by state governments, $33,260; for those employed by local governments, $31,380; and for those employed by private facilities, $21,390. The U.S. Department of Labor reports that overall the lowest paid 10 percent of corrections officers earned less than $22,010 per year, and the highest paid 10 percent earned more than $52,370.

The U.S. Department of Labor reports higher earnings for supervisors/managers, with a median yearly income of $44,940 in 2002. The lowest paid 10 percent earned less than $29,220, and the highest paid 10 percent earned more than $69,370.

Overtime, night shift, weekend, and holiday pay differentials are generally available at most institutions. Fringe benefits may include health, disability, and life insurance; uniforms or a cash allowance to buy their own uniforms; and sometimes meals and housing. Officers who work for the federal government and for most state governments are covered by civil service systems or merit boards. Some corrections officers also receive retirement and pension plans, and retirement is often possible after 20 to 25 years of service.

WORK ENVIRONMENT

Because prison security must be maintained around the clock, work schedules for corrections officers may include nights, weekends, and holidays. The workweek, however, generally consists of five days, eight hours per day, except during emergencies, when many officers work overtime.

Corrections officers may work indoors or outdoors, depending on their duties. Conditions can vary even within an institution: Some areas are well lighted, ventilated, and temperature-controlled, while others are overcrowded, hot, and noisy. Officers who work outdoors, of course, are subject to all kinds of weather. Correctional institutions occasionally present unpredictable or even hazardous situations. If violence erupts among the inmates, corrections officers may be in danger of injury or death. Although this risk is higher than for most other occupations, corrections work is usually routine.

Corrections officers need physical and emotional strength to cope with the stress inherent in dealing with criminals, many of whom may be dangerous or incapable of change. A correctional officer has to remain alert and aware of the surroundings, prisoners' movements and attitudes, and any potential for danger or violence. Such continual, heightened levels of alertness often create psychological stress for some workers. Most institutions have stress-reduction programs or seminars for their employees, but if not, insurance usually covers some form of therapy for work-related stress.

OUTLOOK

Employment in this field is expected to increase faster than the average through 2012, according to the U.S. Department of Labor. The ongoing prosecution of illegal drugs, new tough-on-crime legislation, and increasing mandatory sentencing policies will create a need for more prison beds and more corrections officers. The extremely crowded conditions in today's correctional institutions have created a need for more corrections officers to guard the inmates more closely and relieve the tensions. A greater number of officers will also be required as a result of the expansion or new construction of facilities. As prison sentences become longer through mandatory minimum sentences set by state law, the number of prisons needed will increase. In addition, many job openings will occur from a characteristically high turnover rate, as well as from the need to fill vacancies caused by the death or retirement of older workers. Traditionally, correction

agencies have difficulty attracting qualified employees due to job location and salary considerations.

Because security must be maintained at correctional facilities at all times, corrections officers can depend on steady employment. They are not usually affected by poor economic conditions or changes in government spending. Corrections officers are rarely laid off, even when budgets need to be trimmed. Instead, because of high turnovers, staffs can be cut simply by not replacing those officers who leave.

Most jobs will be found in relatively large institutions located near metropolitan areas, although opportunities for corrections officers exist in jails and other smaller facilities throughout the country. The increasing use of private companies and privately run prisons may limit somewhat the growth of jobs in this field as these companies are more likely to keep a close eye on the bottom line. Use of new technologies, such as surveillance equipment, automatic gates, and other devices, may also allow institutions to employ fewer officers.

FOR MORE INFORMATION

For information on training, conferences, and membership, contact

American Correctional Association
4380 Forbes Boulevard
Lanham, MD 20706
Tel: 301-918-1800
http://www.aca.org

American Probation and Parole Association
2760 Research Park Drive
Lexington, KY 40578
Tel: 859-244-8207
Email: appa@csg.org
http://www.appa-net.org

For information on entrance requirements, training, and career opportunities for corrections officers at the federal level, contact

Federal Bureau of Prisons
320 First Street, NW
Washington, DC 20534
Tel: 202-307-3198
Email: webmaster@bop.gov
http://www.bop.gov

This website bills itself as the "Largest Online Resource for News and Information in Corrections."

The Corrections Connection
http://www.corrections.com

Cosmeticians

■ OVERVIEW

Cosmeticians specialize in skin care, providing an array of services from applying facial masks, peels, and herbal wraps, to massages, skin analysis, exfoliation, deep cleansing, product recommendations, and makeup application. In addition, cosmeticians provide hair removal services. Most cosmeticians work in beauty salons, day spas, and hotel resorts. Some work with dermatologists and cosmetic surgeons to prepare patients before surgery and during their recovery. Barbers, cosmetologists, and other personal appearance workers held about 754,000 jobs in the United States. Among them, there are approximately 25,000 cosmeticians.

■ HISTORY

The role of the cosmetician today originates from a long history of pampering and leisurely self care, which began centuries ago in the public baths and spas of Asia and Europe. Ancient Babylonians, Egyptians, and Romans renewed and invigorated themselves in public baths. Archeological evidence suggests that in ancient Egypt cosmetics were also used to enhance the appearance of the skin. Products included ingredients such as special soils, wax, honey, and oils that were formulated into masks, makeup, and lipsticks. In ancient Greece, Hippocrates, known as the father of medicine, contributed to the development of *esthetics* (scientific skin care). Archeological remains suggest that Greek women used mixtures of plant roots and yeast to try to eliminate freckles and applied masks made with bread crumbs and milk to prevent wrinkles. Artifacts from ancient Roman society include recipes for creams made from fruit juices, honey, and olive oil. Soothing therapies, still practiced today, from Shiatsu massages to potent herbal treatments, have been passed down from thousand-year-old traditions of the East.

During the Middle Ages interest in skin care and public baths waned in the Western world. Certain orders of nuns, however, devoted themselves to producing beauty products to support their convents. Perfume oils began to be used and the fragrance market was launched. The Renaissance saw skin care and cosmetics again become popular in large European cities. The manufacture of perfumes became a major industry. From writings of the 16th century, we find that many formulas and mixtures are very similar to modern cosmetic products. By the 17th and 18th centuries spas had gained the support of the medical establishment and once again became popular places. And by the 1800s, Europe's wealthy classes were spending months at a time relaxing and rejuvenating themselves at spas. It was not until the 1920s that spas caught on in the United States, and even then they were considered a luxury that only the very wealthy could afford.

Today, due to heightened health awareness, the need for more specialized beauty services, and increasing affordability of spa and salon services in the United States, cosmeticians are more in demand than ever before. Now more than just pamperers, cosmeticians are professionals and consultants, equipped with an awareness of skin conditions and allergies, as well as the scientific knowledge necessary to make recommendations based on biological and chemical analysis. As technical advancements in such areas as chemical peels and wrinkle reduction continue to boom, cosmeticians will become more prevalent and their services will be in greater demand.

■ THE JOB

Cosmeticians may also be known as *estheticians* (also spelled *aestheticians*) or *skin care specialists.* The word *esthetic* comes from the Greek word meaning harmony, beauty, and perfection. Esthetics is based on an understanding of the skin's anatomy and function. Cosmeticians work to improve the skin's condition and restore its functions. This discipline requires the cosmetician to get to know the client's skin and lifestyle and tailor treatments specifically for the client's needs. Cosmeticians offer a number of appearance enhancing services that deal with the affects pollution, lack of exercise, poor nutrition, and stress have on the skin. The cosmetician's job may involve facials, massages, wraps and packs, hydrotherapy treatments, scalp treatments, hair removal services, color analysis, makeup services, and product sales. Before beginning to work with a client, the cosmetician will most likely consult with the individual to determine his or her goals and concerns. It is important that cosmeticians are clear with their clients as to what they should expect from their treatments.

Before beginning treatment, the cosmetician must determine the client's needs. After the initial consultation for a facial, for instance, the cosmetician will need to perform a skin analysis in order to assess the client's water and oil levels and skin conditions—whether there are blackheads, lines, wrinkles, etc. Once this information is determined, pre-cleansing, deep cleansing, exfoliation (the removal of dead skin), and extractions may follow, depending on the client's skin type. Cosmeticians often blend special cleansers and moisturizers themselves, according their clients' individual skin types.

The application of an appropriate mask for the patron's skin type may follow the cleansing and exfoliation process, along with neck, facial, and shoulder massages. Foot and hand massages may be included as well. In most states, cosmeticians are only licensed to perform hand, foot, and facial massages, and training for these services is usually provided in cosmetology programs. Full body massages require both further training and a special license.

While performing such procedures as extractions, which involve the removal of blackheads, whiteheads, and other skin debris, cosmeticians must be careful to protect themselves by using gloves and the proper sanitation. These procedures are covered in cosmetician training programs and are regulated by law in most states.

Other services cosmeticians offer include wraps, packs, and hydrotherapy treatments. Often made of herbs, mud, or algae, these treatments remove or redistribute fat cells and retained body water in order to create a temporarily slimmer look. Some wraps and packs actually remove impurities from the body. Hydrotherapy treatments cleanse the body using sea water, fresh water, hot tubs, whirlpool baths, and hydrotherapy tubs.

Cosmeticians also provide cosmetics and makeup consultation and application services. They may assist clients in deciding what colors and makeup to use and how they should apply it to achieve the best results, whether it's for accentuating their features or covering blemishes.

Hair removal services, usually waxing and tweezing, are also offered. Electrolysis is another popular form of hair removal; however, since a special license is required to perform electrolysis, cosmeticians generally wax and tweeze unwanted hair from the face, eyebrows, and other parts of the body.

In addition to working with clients, cosmeticians are expected to keep their work areas clean and implements sanitized. In smaller salons, many make appointments and assist with day-to-day business activities. In larger salons, cosmeticians must be aware of keeping to appointment schedules. They may be juggling two or more clients, at different stages of treatment, at the same time.

Salon managers or *owners* have managerial responsibilities—accounting and record keeping, hiring, firing, and motivating workers, advertising and public relations, and ordering and stocking supplies and products.

People skills are very important for a cosmetician to have. A critical part of cosmeticians' jobs is to cultivate and maintain a growing clientele for themselves and their salons or spas. Cosmeticians should be sensitive to the client's comfort and have dexterity and a sense of artistry. If the cosmetician's style of skin care is not suited to the client, he or she should be willing to refer the client to another specialist. This builds goodwill toward the cosmetician and the salon or spa.

■ REQUIREMENTS
High School

If working as a cosmetician interests you, there are a number of classes you can take in high school to prepare for this job. Some vocational high schools offer classes that will prepare you specifically for cosmetology careers. If you are not attending a vocational high school, you should take science classes, such as biology, chemistry, and human anatomy. These classes will give you an understanding of how the body works as well as how chemicals react with each other. Scientific knowledge will come in handy when you consult with your clients about their allergies and skin conditions. In addition, science classes will give you the background necessary for understanding bacteriology and equipment sanitization—subjects you will most likely study in cosmetician courses following high school. Since you will be working with many different clients in this career, consider taking psychology courses, which will give you an understanding of people and their motivations. Take English and speech classes to develop your communication skills. Finally, take art courses. Art courses will allow you to work with your hands and help you develop your sense of color.

Postsecondary Training

Once you have completed high school, plan on enrolling in an accredited cosmetology school. A school's accreditation by the National Accrediting Commission of Cosmetology Arts and Sciences means that the school is meeting educational standards set by this national organization. It is important to make sure you will be going to a good school, because having a solid education from a respected program is one of your strongest assets when entering this field. You should also be aware of the licensing requirements for the state in which you hope to work. Make sure that the school you are interested in will allow you to meet these requirements. Depending on the school you choose to attend, you may

QUICK FACTS

SCHOOL SUBJECTS
Biology
Chemistry

PERSONAL SKILLS
Artistic
Following instructions

WORK ENVIRONMENT
Primarily indoors
Primarily one location

MINIMUM EDUCATION LEVEL
Some postsecondary training

SALARY RANGE
$13,000 to $22,450 to $50,000+

CERTIFICATION OR LICENSING
Required by certain states

OUTLOOK
About as fast as the average

DOT
332

GOE
11.04.01

NOC
6482

O*NET-SOC
39-5094.00

enter a full cosmetology program to later specialize as a cosmetician, or you may enroll in a cosmetician or esthetician program. In either case your education should include study in skin care, massage techniques, specific areas of the law pertaining to the field, sanitation methods, makeup, and salon management.

Certification or Licensing

A cosmetician needs a license in most states, though the process, laws, and requirements vary from state to state. Licensing usually involves a test of one's skill and knowledge. A few states have reciprocity agreements, which would allow licensed cosmeticians to practice in a different state without additional formal training.

Other Requirements

A friendly, people-oriented personality and good listening skills are essential for this business. Because cosmeticians must work very closely with their clients, interpersonal skills are important. Sensitivity, tactfulness, and patience are particularly vital, especially when dealing with clients who may be unhappy about their appearance or with clients who have unreasonable expectations.

Flexibility is also a necessary trait, considering the long and irregular hours a full-time cosmetician works. Furthermore, the ability to sell has also become a desirable characteristic in cosmeticians, because retail sales are becoming a large part of salon offerings. Finally, a cosmetician should enjoy learning, as he or she may need to take continuing education workshops or seminars in order to keep up with licensing requirements and new developments in the field.

■ EXPLORING

One of the first activities you may consider in exploring this career is to get a facial or other service provided by a cosmetician. As a client yourself, you will be able to observe the work setting and actually experience the procedure. Often people are best at providing services when they enjoy receiving the service or believe in its benefits.

Next, you may want to research this field by looking at association and trade magazines—the publications cosmeticians read to stay current with their field's trends. Trade publications will give you an idea of what current technical, legal, and fashion issues cosmeticians face.

You may choose to contact cosmetology schools to find out about cosmetician or esthetician programs in your area. Request informational brochures or course listings from the schools and speak to school advisors about the training involved and the nature of the work. A good way to locate cosmetology schools is to conduct an Internet search.

Also, once you have found a cosmetology school you are interested in, ask to set up an informational interview with an instructor or recent graduate. Go to the interview prepared to ask questions. What is the training like? What does this person enjoy about the job? What is the most difficult aspect of the work? By asking such questions you may be able to determine if the field is right for you.

You may also be able to set up an informational interview with a cosmetician who works at a spa or salon near you. Again, go to the interview prepared with questions. By networking in this fashion, you may also develop a mentor relationship. Then you may be able to spend time with your mentor at his or her place of work and observe everyday activities.

Getting a part-time position at a salon or spa on weekends or after school is an excellent way of exploring the field. Because you are working at the spa or salon on a regular basis, you will learn more about what various jobs are like and how the business functions. While on the job, you can observe the interaction between clients and cosmeticians, the interaction among coworkers, the different levels of management, and the general atmosphere. This can help you decide whether this is an area you would like to explore further.

■ EMPLOYERS

Approximately 25,000 cosmeticians are employed in the United States, and they work in a variety of business settings that provide beauty, fitness and health, or personal care services. They may work for salons, fitness centers, spas, as well as at resorts, large hotels, and even cruise ships. Some work for cosmetology schools as instructors of esthetics. Those with experience and interest in having their own business may decide to run their own salon where they offer a variety of services.

■ STARTING OUT

After completing a cosmetician or cosmetology program and passing state board exams, you can seek a position as an entry-level cosmetician. Cosmeticians find their jobs through cosmetology schools—salons and spas often recruit directly from schools. Networking in the field is also a viable option for aspiring cosmeticians looking for good work. Reading trade publication classified ads is also a way to locate job openings. Salons and spas most often advertise open positions in newspaper classifieds. There are also some placement agencies that match cosmeticians with salons and spas looking for workers.

■ ADVANCEMENT

Upon first entering the field, a cosmetician will advance somewhat as he or she gains clientele. A large and steady clientele will translate into higher earnings and greater professional status.

Beyond the entry-level cosmetician, one can move up to director of cosmeticians (often called director of estheticians). Eventually a cosmetician or esthetician can become a spa or salon manager, then move up to spa or salon director. For many cosmeticians, an ultimate goal is to own a spa or salon. Some cosmeticians open their own salons after being certified and without having to work up the ranks of another spa or salon.

As an alternative to working in a salon or spa, some cosmeticians decide to teach in cosmetology schools or use their knowledge to demonstrate cosmetics and skin care products in department stores. Others become cosmetics sales representatives or start businesses as beauty consultants. Some cosmeticians work as examiners for state cosmetology boards.

■ EARNINGS

The U.S. Department of Labor, which groups cosmeticians with barbers, cosmetologists, and workers specializing in personal appearance services, reports that cosmeticians working full time had an annual median income of $22,450 (including tips) in 2002. However, salaries for cosmeticians vary widely based on where they work, the method of payment (commission and tips only or commission, salary, and tips), and the clientele. Those working on commission and tips only will find their beginning incomes very low as they work to build a steady clientele. In addition, not every company provides health benefits, which adds extra costs for the entry-level cosmetician who may already be struggling. Some companies pay a salary plus commission, which obviously is better for the entry-level cosmetician who has yet to establish a clientele. Some salaries start at or near minimum wage. When tips are added in, cosmeticians may end up with yearly incomes somewhere between $13,000 to $15,000. Other base salaries may reach the lower to mid-20,000s.

It is usually not until the cosmetician reaches a manager's or director's position that he or she will make upwards of $50,000.

■ WORK ENVIRONMENT

Despite the fact that the field seems elite and glamorous, being a cosmetician is hard work. Through most of the day cosmeticians must work on their feet. Some days are relaxing while others are quite hectic. Cosmeticians and salon owners can easily work more than 40 hours per week. Weekend and lunch-hour time slots are often especially busy. According to Liza Wong, owner of Elite Skin Care, a salon in San Mateo, California, time management

THE MEDIEVAL APPROACH

During the Middle Ages, certain orders of nuns produced beauty products to support their convents. The Benedictine nun Hildegard of Bingen—renowned for her mystical visions, theological works, and music, and often consulted by bishops, popes, and kings—used the curative powers of natural objects for healing. She wrote treatises about natural history and medicinal uses of plants, animals, trees, and stones. Hildegard, who has been beatified and is often referred to as "St. Hildegard," wrote, "There is a vapor that can eliminate all the evils of the face and make it pleasant and amiable. Put lilac flowers, jaborandi, rosemary, and fennel in boiling water." Clearly, care for the skin—especially the natural approach—is not just a modern-day concern!

is the most difficult aspect of the job. "Cosmeticians must be flexible and willing to work late evenings and on weekends, around their clients' work schedules," says Wong.

On the positive side, it is a very social position. Cosmeticians see a variety of clients each day and perform a variety of services. They learn a lot from their clients—about their lives and their jobs.

■ OUTLOOK

Liza Wong predicts a big future for cosmeticians. "Americans are just starting to become aware of this field," Wong says. "These services, once only enjoyed by the rich, are becoming more affordable, and as baby boomers are trying to keep their youth and maintain their skin, there will be an increasing demand for skin care." The U.S. Department of Labor predicts employment growth for cosmeticians to be about as fast as the average through 2012. The growing popularity and affordability of day spas that offer full services should provide job opportunities for skin care specialists.

Spending for personal care services is considered by most people to be discretionary. Therefore, during hard economic times, people tend to visit cosmeticians less frequently, which reduces earnings. However, good cosmeticians are rarely laid off solely because of economic downturns.

■ FOR MORE INFORMATION

For information on publications and continuing education, contact

Aesthetics' International Association
PO Box 468
Kaufman, TX 75142

Tel: 877-968-7539

Email: AIAthekey@aol.com

http://www.beautyworks.com/aia

For industry news, a listing of accredited schools, and information on financial aid, contact

National Accrediting Commission of Cosmetology Arts and Sciences

4401 Ford Avenue, Suite 1300

Alexandria, VA 22302-1432

Tel: 703-600-7600

http://www.naccas.org

For more industry news, contact

National Cosmetology Association

401 North Michigan Avenue, 22nd Floor

Chicago, IL 60611

Tel: 312-527-6765

http://www.salonprofessionals.org

For a listing of schools by state, check out the following website:

Beautyschools.com

http://www.beautyschools.com

For hair styling tips and techniques, job listings, and business advice, visit the following website:

Behind the Chair

http://www.behindthechair.com

Cosmetics Sales Representatives

■ OVERVIEW

Cosmetics sales representatives demonstrate and sell beauty-care products. Representatives may work from their homes as independent contractors, or they may work in retail establishments where they are employees of the store as well as employees of a cosmetics company.

■ HISTORY

As long ago as 3000 B.C., Egyptian priests prepared cosmetics for their kings. Their toiletries and other luxuries were entombed with them. When the tombs of these long-dead kings were excavated in modern times, vases of scented ointments were found, some still holding their fragrant contents. From the kings the use of cosmetics spread. Egyptian women painted their eyebrows, eyelids, and lashes black with the cosmetic kohl. Cosmetics were made

of such naturally occurring substances as sesame oil, olive oil, floral and herbal scents, ingredients that were available to use in simple preparations. Henna was used to color the body or hair red and white lead or chalk were used to whiten the complexion. From the Middle East and the Mediterranean, the use of cosmetics spread through the Greeks to the Roman Empire and throughout Europe. The change from simple preparations of natural ingredients to the modern industry began in France toward the end of the 19th century. The development of new techniques in manufacturing, packaging, advertising, and marketing has spread cosmetics—and their representatives—around the world.

■ THE JOB

Cosmetics sales representatives, or beauty advisers, help customers choose particular products appropriate to them. Cosmetics sales reps may consider the condition of the hair, the skin, and the coloring to recommend the cosmetics that will achieve the results desired by the customer. They also introduce the client to new products or techniques. These reps are usually women, but men are also welcome to pursue this career.

Beauty advisers who work in department or specialty stores usually work full time. They are hired by the store and the cosmetics company, both of which provide ongoing training and education. They display, restock, and sell products, attend meetings to learn about new campaigns for different seasons and holidays, attend training sessions, and meet the attendance and performance goals set by the store and by the cosmetics company.

Cosmetics sales representatives who work for such companies as Avon or Mary Kay are not employees but independent contractors who usually work part time. The goal remains to sell the products, and this job is appealing to those who want to supplement their incomes while keeping their hours flexible. Avon representatives usually distribute fliers or brochures within a specified territory. They take orders by phone or in person. Mary Kay also facilitates its salespeople to set up individual sales websites to sell their products. The orders are delivered to the rep, who then delivers them to the customer and collects the money. Mary Kay also uses fliers to advertise products, and additionally offers services such as skin care classes and facials.

■ REQUIREMENTS
High School

There are a number of classes you can take in high school to help prepare you for a sales career. Naturally, business classes can be beneficial. A knowledge of business practices and procedures will help you understand the industry.

Speech and English classes as well as experience on a debating club will help you develop better communication skills. Also, you should consider taking psychology classes because selling requires an insightful knowledge of people and an ability to read the customer. Computer courses are useful since retail stores now use computerized record-keeping, and a course in accounting can help independent cosmetics sales representatives better manage their businesses.

Postsecondary Training

Most of the beauty advisers who work for cosmetics companies in retail stores have college degrees or are working toward them. Business or marketing are possible majors for those in this field. Typically, some on-the-job training is involved for new employees at retail stores. There are no specific educational requirements for independent contractors, although some organizations, such as Mary Kay, offer materials and support to help their contractors learn about new products and improve their selling techniques. There is an age requirement of 18 for virtually all cosmetics sales representatives.

Other Requirements

An outgoing, enthusiastic person who enjoys talking with a variety of new people will enjoy this work. Good manners and being a team player are important. Someone with color blindness, asthma, or allergies—especially to perfumes—should probably not consider this line of work. And, of course, you need a strong back to lift all those boxes of cosmetics.

■ EXPLORING

There are entry-level jobs available nationwide. Talking to a cosmetics representative is as easy as picking up the telephone. Both Avon and Mary Kay encourage and reward recruitment of other reps. Mary Kay requires the building of a team or unit of reps. Avon offers job applications on its home page on the Internet.

For jobs in stores, hiring is done by both the store and the cosmetics line, so it is possible to be hired by the cosmetics firm and placed in a store or to be hired by the store and recommended to the cosmetics firm. Personnel offices of stores can be reached by phone or in person for information and employment applications. Current representatives of those companies that are hiring are usually happy to talk to people who might be interested in joining their team or unit.

■ EMPLOYERS

Cosmetics sales representatives are usually either self-employed, employed by department stores, or employed by cosmetics companies. It is easy to begin work as an independent contractor for companies such as Avon or Mary Kay. It may be difficult to do this exclusively, however, without supplemental income. Jobs with department stores offer better income security and benefits, but these are usually full-time positions requiring evenings and weekends. Since cosmetics sales continue to increase, as do retail sales in general, there will probably be an abundance of opportunities for those seeking regular employment with stores or cosmetics companies and for independent representatives alike. Unlike most jobs in the cosmetology industry, however, independent cosmetics sales representatives in remote or rural areas may do well due to a lack of department stores and retail establishments specializing in cosmetics.

■ STARTING OUT

Patrick Cummings became an Avon representative several years ago. He paid a one-time fee of $20 to begin. "My idea was to make a couple of extra bucks." Cummings owns a specialty meat market, and orders and deliveries come to him at the store; he believes that "people don't want or expect other people to come to their homes anymore." Now his customers can pick up their lamb chops and their lipsticks at the same location.

To become a Mary Kay representative, it costs about $100 to buy the sample case. Many of the representatives find most of their customers at their full-time jobs and use cosmetics sales as a supplement to their incomes.

Many cosmetics sales representatives in retail stores start out as perfume spritzers hired by a cosmetics line, or they may be hired during a busy season by the store and then recommended to the cosmetics company.

■ ADVANCEMENT

Marianne Blokell began her career in cosmetics over 12 years ago. "I started as a freelance spritzer for Aramis perfume and was hired by Carson, Pirie, Scott,

QUICK FACTS

SCHOOL SUBJECTS
Business
Speech

PERSONAL SKILLS
Artistic
Helping/teaching

WORK ENVIRONMENT
Primarily indoors
One location with some travel

MINIMUM EDUCATION LEVEL
Some postsecondary training

SALARY RANGE
$13,520 to $30,000 to $150,000

CERTIFICATION OR LICENSING
None available

OUTLOOK
About as fast as the average

DOT
N/A

GOE
10.03.01

NOC
6411, 6421

O*NET-SOC
N/A

AVON CALLING

- Avon is the world's leading direct seller of beauty and related products with sales in the fourth quarter of 2000 reaching a record $1.74 billion worldwide. Annual sales revenues amounted to over $5 billion.

- Avon products are sold in 140 countries.

- There are approximately 40,000 Avon sales representatives worldwide.

- Women have been selling Avon since 1886.

- Avon was the first major U.S. cosmetics company to abandon animal testing.

- Nearly half the women in the United States use Avon's products, and 90 percent have done so in their lifetime.

- Avon's Worldwide Fund for Women's Health, started in 1992, has raised over $190 million for women's health programs in 34 countries through fundraisers such as the Avon Breast Cancer 3-Day walks.

and Co. full time. I worked as a beauty adviser for Lancome at Carson's, was promoted to counter manager there, and now supervise Lancome counters for two stores." Two avenues of advancement are open to her. She can move up through Lancome from counter manager to account coordinator or account manager in charge of several stores, then to trainer/educator in charge of coaching, training, setting goals, or to account executive. Through Carson's, she can advance to a job as a buyer or a planner.

EARNINGS

The U.S. Department of Labor reports the median hourly wage, including commission, was $8.51 for all retail sales workers in 2002. A sales rep working full-time at this pay rate would earn approximately $17,700 per year. For cosmetics sales representatives working in stores, earnings vary because each retailer pays differently. Karen Broderick, an account manager for Lancome, offered some average figures. A beginning beauty adviser at Carson, Pirie, Scott, and Co. starts at $6.50 an hour plus 3 percent commission. After five years with a 5 percent raise annually, the average salary is $30,000 to $35,000 a year, which includes in-store incentives, commissions, and bonuses. As the representative rises from counter manager to account manager to account executive for a region, the compensation rises as high as $150,000.

For independent sales representatives, the earnings depend completely on commissions. If they sell nothing,

they make nothing. Many independents make only about $100 a month, which is reasonable if they view the job as a supplement, not as their main income.

WORK ENVIRONMENT

Cosmetics representatives in retail stores usually work in attractive, climate-controlled settings. But the hours are long and they must be on their feet. There is a lot of bending and heavy boxes of stock to unload and display. They may not leave the sales floor except at specified times. Many stores have evening and Sunday hours, and breaks and lunch may go by the board in a crush of customers.

Independent contractors usually place orders and accept deliveries at home. They then deliver to their customers, who may be neighbors or coworkers at their primary place of employment.

OUTLOOK

The U.S. Department of Labor predicts job growth for all retail sales reps to be about as fast as the average through 2012. The job picture for cosmetics sales representatives, however, is somewhat mixed. While it is easy to get started in the field, most who choose it work only part time. Avon alone has about three million representatives selling products in 140 countries. This is a good choice for people needing supplemental income or in transition, or young mothers who want to stay at home with their children, but most people need an additional job—their own or their spouse's—to provide enough income, health benefits, vacations, or just a day off. Growth in cosmetics companies seems to be international, directed toward opening up new markets in more and more countries; Avon, for example, has stores around the world, from Canada to Thailand, from Greece to Argentina, from Russia to Japan. However, Avon is now also selling cosmetics online, and it remains to be seen how this will affect the company's need for individual sales reps.

Retail selling is such a huge industry that there are always openings to replace those leaving the field, but the hours are long and the wages start out very low.

FOR MORE INFORMATION

For information on careers in cosmetics sales, contact or visit the following websites:

Avon Cosmetics
Tel: 800-FOR-AVON
http://www.avon.com

Mary Kay Cosmetics
Tel: 800-MARY-KAY
http://www.marykay.com

Cosmetic Surgeons

OVERVIEW

Cosmetic surgeons (also known as *plastic surgeons* or *esthetic surgeons*) are medical doctors who specialize in surgeries to correct disfigurement and/or improve physical appearance. Though the terms cosmetic and plastic surgery are often used interchangeably, cosmetic surgery usually means procedures performed to reshape normal structures of the body to improve the patient's appearance. Plastic surgery generally refers to reconstructive surgeries performed on abnormal structures of the body caused by birth defects, developmental abnormalities, trauma, injury, infection, tumors, or disease. There are approximately 4,200 cosmetic surgeons working in the United States.

HISTORY

Contrary to popular belief, cosmetic surgery is not a recent development. Although the increase in the popularity of certain cosmetic procedures is a relatively new trend, surgeons have been correcting human disfigurement since 3400 B.C., when Egyptian healers performed cosmetic operations on the face, feet, and arms. Another ancient tie can be found in the profession's own name. The "plastic" in plastic surgery does not mean "artificial." Rather, plastic surgery derives its name from the ancient Greek word plastikos, which meant to mold or give form. In fact, the modern day "nose job," which Hollywood celebrities seem to favor, likely got its start in ancient India, although the procedures done at that time were for reconstructive rather than strictly cosmetic purposes. By 800 B.C., physicians in India were using skin grafts (a process that transfers healthy skin from one part of the body to another for the purpose of replacing damaged or lost skin) to perform reconstructive work for facial injuries.

Cosmetic surgery changed little during the Dark Ages but began to develop again in the 1700s, when British surgeons introduced to Europe techniques they had seen in India. Further improvement in skin grafting techniques continued, but progress was slow until the early 1900s.

Before World War I, the profession evolved slowly in North America as well. Virginian Dr. John Peter Mettauer performed the first cleft palate operation in the New World in 1827 with instruments he designed himself. With the advent of world war, physicians were challenged to find ways to treat extensive facial and head injuries never before seen, such as shattered jaws and gaping skull wounds.

It wasn't until the late 1930s that the American Board of Surgeons, the medical certifying organization of the time, established a specialty board to certify cosmetic surgeons—the American Board of Plastic Surgery—with its own standards and specialized training. Prior to the establishment of this board, many physicians who performed reconstructive surgeries were from other specialties related to cosmetic surgery.

New techniques developed in the 1950s included internal wiring for facial fractures and rotation flaps for skin deformities. In the 1960s, the scope of procedures performed by surgeons widened as the public became more informed. Cosmetic procedures became more popular. Silicone was initially used to treat skin imperfections and was first used as a breast implant device in 1962. The safety of silicone breast implants has since come into question, and its use for breast implants was banned in 1992. The 1980s saw plastic surgeons expand their efforts to bring information to the public, and in the 1990s, the profession focused efforts on having reconstructive procedures covered under health plans.

Despite the many advances, the field is still evolving. Today, researchers are trying to unlock the secrets of the growth-factor environment of the womb, where scarless healing takes place, in order to apply the technique to wounds of children and adults.

THE JOB

Doctors, especially specialists such as cosmetic surgeons, generally work long hours. Surgeries of all types demand strict attention to detail, and cosmetic surgeries in which the emphasis is on the quality of the patient's appearance can be especially challenging. Still, the profession offers high earnings and personal rewards. Physicians tend to be people who thrive on challenge and are willing to devote a lot of time to their careers.

Of course, cosmetic surgeons don't spend all their working hours in surgery. Daily tasks include patient consultation and record keeping, among other duties. Also, no matter what setting a surgeon practices in, he or

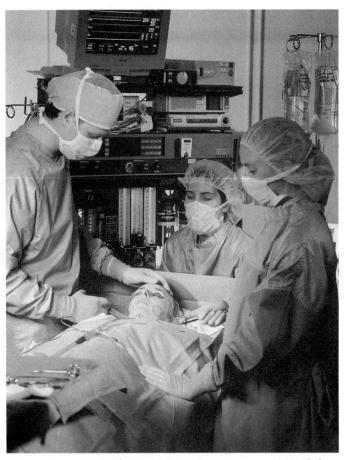

A cosmetic surgeon performs reconstructive surgery on a patient's face.

she is likely to have administrative duties as well. Surgeons in private practice have an office to manage with duties ranging from hiring employees to marketing the practice to overseeing upkeep of the office. Surgeons who work in a hospital's plastic surgery department have commitments to the hospital outside of performing surgeries and seeing patients. For example, cosmetic surgeons frequently are required to provide general hospital emergency room coverage and split up this task with the other surgeons.

Dr. Richard Maloney, a cosmetic surgeon who practices at the Aesthetic Surgery Center in Naples, Florida, estimates he spends about 60 percent of his time in surgery. Other time is spent on patient visits, follow-up, initial consultations, and emergency room coverage. Maloney acknowledges that many in the field of medicine push themselves to work days as long as 16 hours, seven days a week, but he said that doctors can and should decide how much time they want to devote to work and follow that decision.

"In the field of medicine, the urge to take on a workload to prove yourself is great. I think the average workweek can be as much as you want it to be," Maloney said.

In practice for 19 years, Maloney said he has found 10-hour days provide a good balance between his personal and professional life.

Today's cosmetic surgeons perform a wider range of procedures than their counterparts did only a few decades ago. Previously, the profession focused on reconstructive surgeries, with a few surgeons catering to those who could afford cosmetic procedures. Today, cosmetic surgeries are no longer performed on just celebrities or the wealthy. The public has become familiar with terms such as liposuction (removal of unwanted fatty deposits), implants, and facelift because those procedures have become more accessible to the general population. According to the American Society of Plastic Surgeons (ASPS), the top five cosmetic procedures in 2003 were nose reshaping, liposuction, eyelid surgery, breast augmentation, and facelift. And as cosmetic surgery becomes more commonplace, an increasing number of men are having it done. Nose reshaping, hair transplants, breast reduction, and ear surgery are some of the most popular procedures among men, according to the ASPS. Today's cosmetic surgeons perform more strictly cosmetic procedures than the average cosmetic surgeon did even a decade ago. Of course, a surgeon can still choose to specialize in reconstructive surgery, but trends indicate growth in the field is certainly with cosmetic procedures. It should be noted however, that more reconstructive procedures remain important. ASPS reports that 94 percent of its members perform cosmetic surgery and 89 percent perform reconstructive surgery.

There are different settings in which a cosmetic surgeon may work. Three arrangements are common. The first is private practice, in which the surgeon is the sole physician in a practice with his or her own staff. The physician performs surgeries either in his or her own clinic or at a hospital where he or she has privileges. The second is group practice, in which a surgeon is part of a group of cosmetic surgeons or other related specialists who market their services together. Group practice surgeons may also perform surgeries in their own clinic or at a hospital. The third common arrangement is working in hospital departments, where a surgeon is a member of a hospital's plastic surgery department. A less common career path for cosmetic surgeons who have considerable surgical experience are professorships at academic institutions or teaching hospitals.

Because plastic surgery is a highly specialized field, plastic surgeons generally work in urban areas, both large and small. Most rural areas don't have enough patients to create a reasonable demand. The ASPS estimates that over half of its 5,000 members work in large metropolitan areas.

■ REQUIREMENTS
High School

If you want to pursue a career in medicine, prepare yourself by learning the self-discipline to concentrate on schoolwork in high school in order to achieve the grades necessary to gain entrance to a good undergraduate program. Performing well at the college level can help you compete for slots in medical school. Start working hard in high school by taking college preparatory classes such as mathematics, including algebra and geometry, and sciences, including biology, chemistry, and physics. Also, consider taking a foreign language. Many college programs have foreign language requirements, and a familiarity with some foreign languages may help you with your medical studies later on. Finally, don't forget to take English courses. These classes will help you develop your research and writing skills—two skills that will be essential to you in your career.

In addition, check out school clubs and civic organizations that offer volunteer opportunities for students in places like local hospitals or nursing homes. In addition to the experience you will get by volunteering, you will also have the opportunity to establish valuable relationships with people who work in the health care field. Clubs such as Kiwanis, Rotary, and Lions often count community leaders such as doctors, hospital administrators, and other health care professionals among their members. Many of these clubs have charter clubs in high schools, and student members have regular contact with these community leaders.

Postsecondary Training

Training to become a doctor is a rigorous, lengthy process. After high school, students pursuing a career in medicine can expect to spend 11 to 16 years in school and training before they can practice medicine. Requirements include four years of undergraduate school, four years of medical school and three to eight years of residency. Not all students who apply to medical school are accepted, and many go on to other careers in the field of medicine. Entry to medical school is very competitive, and prospective students must show they possess exceptional academic abilities. Medical schools also consider character, personality, leadership qualities, and participation in extracurricular activities when deciding whether to accept a student.

The minimum education requirement for entry to a medical school is three years of college, although most applicants have at least a bachelor's degree and many have advanced degrees. Undergraduate degrees obtained by medical school applicants vary, but many have degrees in mathematics, engineering, or sciences such as biology,

or in premed. Premedical students complete courses in physics, biology, mathematics, English, and inorganic and organic chemistry. Some students also volunteer at local hospitals or clinics to gain practical experience. This volunteer experience will weigh in a student's favor on competitive medical school applications. Junior and senior years in undergraduate school for students planning to go on to medical school are very busy years. In addition to keeping up with their studies, junior and senior undergraduates often spend much of their time researching medical school programs, volunteering, or gaining other experience that could be helpful on a medical school application. Students should keep in mind that acceptance to medical school is highly competitive. At a top medical school in the nation, for example, the class of 2000 consisted of 104 men and 67 women selected from 8,639 applicants. The students accepted had an average grade point average of 3.5 on a 4.0 scale. Medical school lasts four years, in addition to the four years a student has already put in at the undergraduate level, so those who want to pursue a medical career should be prepared to commit many years to being a student.

All physicians, whether or not they plan to specialize in a field such as cosmetic surgery, must complete additional training. Specialty training, depending on the field, varies from three to eight years. The certifying board for cosmetic surgeons, the American Board of Cosmetic Surgeons (ABCS), requires four years of residency in cosmetic surgery procedures. Traditionally, medical school graduates spend their first graduate year in a hospital internship. This first year of training following medical school is called the PGY-1, during which graduates work long hours to learn about assuming the responsibility for care of patients in the role of a physician. After the first year, students are generally matched up into an internship program known as a residency program. It is during residency that physicians-in-training are introduced to their chosen specialties. Residents work under physicians who are specialists in their chosen fields at a teaching hospital. Medical school graduates must apply to residency programs by ranking their preferences for different hospitals. Independent agencies, such as the National Residency Matching Program, match the student's preferences with the programs for which they are qualified. Accepted residency programs are accredited by the Accreditation Council for Graduate Medical Education.

Certification or Licensing

All 50 states require physicians be licensed to practice. Certification by one of the 24 certifying boards recognized by the American Board of Medical Specialties is not a legal requirement. Many physicians choose to become certified in their field because certification enables the public to identify practitioners who have met a standard of training and experience beyond the level required for licensure. As consumers become more informed and health care becomes more market-driven, physicians who are board certified are expected to be more in demand. Many patient advocate groups and patient information sources urge patients to choose physicians who are board certified.

The American Board of Cosmetic Surgery certifies physicians in the following areas: (1) facial cosmetic surgery, (2) dermatological cosmetic surgery, (3) body and extremity cosmetic surgery, and (4) general cosmetic surgery. Requirements vary slightly for each area, but basic requirements include certification by one of the boards recognized by the American Board of Medical Specialties, a one- or two-year fellowship in an approved program, proof of hospital operating room privileges, and proof of a valid medical license.

Other Requirements

The field of medicine demands highly disciplined individuals who can perform complex tasks with a high degree of accuracy. Cosmetic surgery requires skill and artistry as well as these talents, according to Dr. Richard Maloney.

"It takes a fastidious person, but not to a fault. There are a lot of steps to the surgical procedures a plastic surgeon performs. Each must be properly executed; if it's not, it amplifies the error in the next step, and so on," Maloney said. "Plastic surgeons do well if they enjoy growing and generating results," he added. Hard work, self-confidence, and dedication are also vital. "It's a very rewarding line of work, but probably the biggest drawback is all of the work and years of schooling it takes to get to this point. But if students are really interested, they should follow their interests and take each hurdle as it comes."

Medicine also requires its successful professionals to have so-called "people skills" in addition to knowledge and discipline. People are the "objects of the trade" for physicians, and communication skills and the ability to empathize with a wide variety of people is essential. The ability to work as part of a team is also important. A cosmetic surgeon performs surgeries and therefore depends on a surgical team to assist in surgery. The cosmetic surgeon must be able to communicate and work well with colleagues as well as patients.

■ EXPLORING

At the high school and undergraduate levels, you can begin to learn about the field of medicine by volunteering at hospitals, nursing homes, or clinics. By working in these settings you will not only have the opportunity to gauge how much you enjoy this type of work, but you will also have the chance to be around professionals in the field.

Another way you can explore is by talking to medical professionals, for example, interviewing one for a term paper or other school project. Or you may simply tell a doctor you know that you are interested in his or her profession and request an informational interview. Come to the interview prepared to ask questions. Ask the doctor how he or she got started in the field. What does he or she like most about the job, and what least? What were the years of school like? People are often happy to talk about their jobs if you show a sincere interest, and you may even discover a mentor in this way.

One national organization, the National Youth Leadership Forum (NYLF), offers an annual forum for high school students interested in a career in medicine. This 11-day forum, offered several times during the summer, gives students an opportunity to gain hands-on experience in medicine by visiting medical schools, research facilities, and hospitals and talking to people in various stages of the medical career path, from first-year medical students to practicing physicians. NYLF reports the curriculum in its medical forum covers a broad range of topics in medicine, including educational requirements, career options, clinical practice, and current issues facing the profession. Forums are open to juniors and seniors with 3.3 or above grade point averages. Teachers and guidance counselors recommend 95 percent of students accepted for forums. Students may ask about the program at their school or contact the organization themselves. Tuition fees and travel expenses apply, as NYLF is a nonprofit organization, but many students are able to find sponsors in their community.

■ EMPLOYERS

When a cosmetic surgeon works in private practice, either alone or with a group of other specialists offering their services, the surgeon is essentially self employed and running his or her own business. Surgeons may also work for hospitals, Health Maintenance Organizations (HMOs), or the government, such as at the Department of Veterans Affairs. In addition, universities employ a number of surgeons in academic positions.

■ STARTING OUT

All physicians are required to have a medical degree. Beyond that, there are many options for entering various specialties. Four years of residency training is required of all surgeons certified by the American Board of Cosmetic Surgery (ABCS). However, the nature of that residency training, and to some extent, the location, may be up to the individual.

Many cosmetic surgeons participate in residency programs and take the exam to become board certified in cosmetic surgery. The ABCS offers certification opportunities to specialists in other fields, including general surgery, gynecology, otolaryngology, oral and maxiofacial surgery, dermatology, and ophthalmology. These specialties are related to many specific plastic surgery procedures and provide a different avenue of entering the field. Physicians certified in these fields are generally limited to performing surgeries in their specialty areas (for example, dermatologists would perform burn repair surgery or other graft surgery, but they are not likely to perform liposuction).

ADVANCEMENT

Once physicians become licensed as cosmetic surgeons, their opportunities for advancement are largely up to them. For many cosmetic surgeons, if they have not already done so, becoming board certified by the American Board of Cosmetic Surgeons is a first step in advancing their careers. As consumers become more informed about their options for cosmetic surgery, cosmetic surgeons with added credentials such as board certifications are likely to be in higher demand. Many associations, such as the American Society of Plastic Surgeons (ASPS), offer a screening service for consumers, who can check a cosmetic surgeon's qualifications when choosing a surgeon.

Any further training a cosmetic surgeon undergoes, such as the additional years of residency required to learn a subspecialty, will increase his or her earnings.

Cosmetic surgeons who are part of a hospital's cosmetic surgery department may have opportunities for advancement within their department or to a higher position at other hospitals. Generally, cosmetic surgeons who are promoted within their departments have years of experience. Some do research outside of their surgery duties and publish their works in medical journals. Others teach cosmetic surgery at universities or become part of the staff to teach residents in a teaching hospital.

Some cosmetic surgeons with years of experience go on to chair cosmetic surgery departments at major hospitals or universities, spending less time on cosmetic surgery and more time on administrative duties and research.

EARNINGS

It takes many years of training to become a doctor, but earnings are among the highest of any occupation. For doctors, more so than for other fields, the number of years of training directly correlates with the earnings

level. Specialists, such as cosmetic surgeons, generally earn more money than general practitioners. The more specialized the field, the higher the earnings.

The latest data available from the Bureau of Labor Statistics notes that surgeons (of all types) had a median income of $255,438 in 2002. *Medical Economics,* a magazine for medical professionals, featured a September 17, 2001, article on earnings of doctors in office-based private practice. The earnings survey conducted by the magazine revealed that general surgeons had a median annual gross income of $370,640 in 2000. After expenses, their median income was $199,690. Cosmetic surgeons, who are specialists, can be expected to have earnings somewhat higher than those of general surgeons. In addition, experience also translates into higher income levels. According to the recruitment firm Physicans Search (http://www.physicianssearch.com), responses for its *Physician Compensation Survey—In Practice Three Plus Years* show that plastic surgeons with three plus years experience averaged $306,047 annually in 2001. The lowest paid respondent specializing in plastic surgery earned $196,711 per year, and the highest paid had an annual income of $411,500, also in 2001.

Cosmetic surgeons, and physicians in general, enjoy generous health care benefits. Other benefits may include recruitment bonuses, pay for continuing education, and forgiveness of school loans. Although they work long hours throughout the year, physicians are often granted several weeks paid vacation and other leave time as relief from the demanding jobs they have.

WORK ENVIRONMENT

There are advantages to working in the different work arrangements available to a plastic surgeon (private practice, group practice, hospital department, or government or academic setting). A surgeon's preference may depend on how he or she works with others, as well as geographic location. Hospital plastic surgery departments are usually structured with department chairs and supervisors. Although a hospital setting generally means more rules for a physician to work under, it also offers the advantage of a structured environment, less individual financial risk, and the ability to share information and learn from colleagues daily. Those who prefer to be "their own boss" generally assume greater risk in a private or group practice, as does any small business owner. Plastic surgeons in private or group practice should be business oriented or hire someone who can tend to marketing, accounting, and personnel concerns.

As with many specialists, cosmetic surgeons generally practice in big cities or smaller urban areas, but not rural areas. Big city settings generally bring advantages such as proximity to colleagues and shorter traveling distance to seminars and the hours of continuing education required of board-certified surgeons every year. Urban life brings increased cultural and recreational opportunities, but it can also mean headaches such as traffic and a higher cost of living.

Cosmetic surgeons, compared with other specialists, are not in frequent contact with contagious disease or hazardous chemicals. Some cosmetic procedures require the use of chemicals for injections or surface application, but surgeons are well trained and well regulated in their use of these materials.

The profession is not without its opportunities for service to humanity, but it is often these situations that put a cosmetic surgeon in contact with some dangers. Areas where people suffer from contagious disease and political violence in remote parts of developing countries are often the areas of greatest need for reconstructive surgeries. A program affiliated with the American Society of Plastic Surgeons, the Reconstructive Surgeons Volunteer Program, sends U.S. surgeons to such areas. Surgeons perform vital work there on people who had no hope of getting help from their own country, but the surgeons' accommodations often include only the bare essentials. Extreme weather, insects, and the sound of shots being fired in the distance are situations some surgeons have encountered.

■ OUTLOOK

According to the U.S. Department of Labor, the demand for all physicians is expected to grow about as fast as the average through 2012. Because of population trends that include a rapidly aging population, physicians who meet the needs of older Americans can expect to see a steady demand for their services. Cosmetic surgeons, who treat conditions associated with aging and help older people maintain a youthful appearance, can be counted among medical specialists who will be in strong demand by the aging Baby Boomer population.

According to statistics compiled by the ASPS, the market for these surgeons is large: In 2003, there were approximately 6.2 million reconstructive procedures done, versus approximately 1.7 million major cosmetic surgeries and approximately 7.1 "minimally invasive" cosmetic procedures.. Men make up a growing clientele, accounting for 14 percent of the cosmetic surgery performed in 2003.

■ FOR MORE INFORMATION

To learn about cosmetic procedures and recent statistics, contact or visit the following website:

American Academy of Cosmetic Surgery
737 North Michigan Avenue, Suite 820
Chicago, IL 60611
Tel: 312-981-6760
http://www.cosmeticsurgery.org

Among this foundation's goals are promoting high standards of training, conferring scholarships, and increasing public education in plastic surgery matters.

American Society of Plastic Surgeons and The Plastic Surgery Educational Foundation
444 East Algonquin Road
Arlington Heights, IL 60005
Tel: 847-228-9900
http://www.plasticsurgery.org

This association is devoted to providing information about medical schools in the United States.

Association of American Medical Colleges
2450 N Street, NW
Washington, DC 20037-1126
Tel: 202-828-0400
http://www.aamc.org

This organization offers career programs to high school students interested in the medical profession. Forums are offered in Atlanta, Chicago, Boston, Houston-Galveston, Philadelphia, Los Angeles, and Washington, D.C. Visit the website for information on schedule dates.

National Youth Leadership Forum
2020 Pennsylvania Avenue, NW
Washington, DC 20006
Tel: 202-347-4036
Email: nylf@nylf.org
http://www.nylf.org

Cosmetologists

■ OVERVIEW

Cosmetologists practice hair-care skills (including washing, cutting, coloring, perming, and applying various conditioning treatments), esthetics (performing skin care treatments), and nail care (grooming of hands and feet). *Barbers* are not cosmetologists; they undergo separate training and licensing procedures. According to the U.S. Department of Labor, there are approximately 754,000 cosmetologists, barbers, and other personal appearance services workers employed in the United States.

■ HISTORY

The history of the profession of cosmetology begins with barbering (the Latin *barba* means beard), one of the oldest trades, described by writers in ancient Greece. Relics of rudimentary razors date to the Bronze Age, and drawings of people in early Chinese and Egyptian cultures show men with shaved heads, indicating the existence of a barbering profession.

Barbers often did more than hair care. The treatment of illnesses by bloodletting, a task originally performed by monks, was passed along to barbers in 1163 by the papacy. Although trained physicians were already established at this time, they supported and encouraged the use of barbers for routine medical tasks, such as the treatment of wounds and abscesses. From the 12th century to the 18th century, barbers were known as barber-surgeons. They performed medical and surgical services, such as extracting teeth, treating disease, and cauterizing wounds.

Barbers began to organize and form guilds in the 14th century. A barbers' guild was formed in France in 1361. In 1383, the barber of the king of France was decreed to be the head of that guild. The Barbers of London was established as a trade guild in 1462. Barbers distinguished themselves from surgeons and physicians by their titles. Barbers, who were trained through apprenticeships, were referred to as doctors of the short robe; university-trained doctors were doctors of the long robe. In England, during the first part of the 16th century, laws were established to limit the medical activities of barbers. They were allowed to let blood and perform tooth extractions only, while surgeons were banned from performing activities relegated to barbers, such as shaving.

Surgeons separated from the barbers' guild in England and in 1800 established their own guild, the Royal College of Surgeons. Laws were passed to restrict the activities of barbers to nonmedical practices. Barbers continued to be trained through apprenticeships until the establishment of barber training schools at the beginning of the 20th century.

Women did not begin to patronize barbershops until the 1920s. The *bob,* a hairstyle in which women cut their hair just below the ears, became popular at that time. Until that time, women usually wore their hair long. In the 1920s, shorter styles for women became acceptable and women began to go to barbers for cutting and styling. This opened the door for women to join the profession, and many began training to work with women's hairstyles.

Today, women and a growing number of men, patronize hair salons or beauty shops to have their hair cut, styled, and colored. The barber shop, on the other hand, remains largely the domain of men, operated by and for men.

Until the 1920s, *beauticians* (as they were commonly known) performed their services in their clients' homes. The beauty salons and shops now so prevalent have emerged as public establishments in more recent years. In the United States—as in many other countries—the cosmetology business is among the largest of the personal service industries.

■ THE JOB

Cosmetology uses hair as a medium to sculpt, perm, color, or design to create a fashion attitude. Cosmetologists, also known as *hair stylists,* perform all of these tasks as well as provide other services, such as deep conditioning treatments, special-occasion long hair designs, and a variety of hair-addition techniques.

A licensed hair stylist can perform the hair services noted above and also is trained and licensed to do the basics of esthetics and nail technology. To specialize in esthetics or nail technology, additional courses are taken in each of these disciplines—or someone can study just esthetics or just nail technology and get a license in either or both of these areas.

Cosmetology schools teach some aspects of human physiology and anatomy, including the bone structure of the head and some elementary facts about the nervous system, in addition to hair skills. Some schools have now added psychology-related courses, dealing with people skills and communications.

Hair stylists may be employed in shops that have as few as one or two employees, or as many as 20 or more. They may work in privately owned salons or in a salon that is part of a large or small chain of beauty shops. They may work in hotels, department stores, hospitals, nursing homes, resort areas, or on cruise ships. In recent years, a number of hair professionals—especially in big cities— have gone to work in larger facilities, sometimes known as

QUICK FACTS

SCHOOL SUBJECTS
Art
Business
Speech

PERSONAL SKILLS
Artistic
Mechanical/manipulative

WORK ENVIRONMENT
Primarily indoors
Primarily one location

MINIMUM EDUCATION LEVEL
Some postsecondary training

SALARY RANGE
$13,020 to $18,960 to $33,240+

CERTIFICATION OR LICENSING
Required by all states

OUTLOOK
About as fast as the average

DOT
332

GOE
11.04.01

NOC
6271

O*NET-SOC
39-5012.00

spas or institutes, which offer a variety of health and beauty services. One such business, for example, offers complete hair design/treatment/color services; manicures and pedicures; makeup; bridal services; spa services including different kinds of facials (thermal mask, anti-aging, acne treatment), body treatments (exfoliating sea salt glow, herbal body wrap), scalp treatments, hydrotherapy water treatments, massage therapy, eyebrow/eyelash tweezing and tinting, and hair-removal treatments for all parts of the body; a fashion boutique; and even a wellness center staffed with board-certified physicians.

Those who operate their own shops must also take care of the details of business operations. Bills must be paid, orders placed, invoices and supplies checked, equipment serviced, and records and books kept. The selection, hiring, and termination of other workers are also the owner's responsibility. Like other responsible business people, shop and salon owners are likely to be asked to participate in civic and community projects and activities.

A hair stylist cuts layers into her client's hair.

Some stylists work for cosmetic/hair product companies. Sean Woodyard, for instance, in addition to being employed as a stylist at a big-city salon, teaches hair coloring for a major national cosmetics/hair care company. When the company introduces a new product or sells an existing product to a new salon, the company hires hair professionals as "freelance educators" to teach the stylists at the salon how to use the product. Woodyard has traveled all over the country during the past six years, while still keeping his full-time job, teaching color techniques at salons, and also participating in demonstrations for the company at trade shows. "I've taught all levels of classes," he says, "from a very basic color demonstration to a very complex color correction class. I've also been responsible for training other educators. I have really enjoyed traveling to other locales and having the opportunity to see other salons and other parts of the beauty and fashion industry."

At industry shows, what he does has varied. Woodyard is representing the company, "whether I'm standing behind a booth selling products or working on stage, demonstrating the product, or assisting a guest artist backstage, doing preparatory work. This has given me a real hands-on education, and I've been able to work with some of the top hair stylists in the country."

Woodyard has been working, as he says, "behind the chair" for 14 years. His first job after graduating from cosmetology school was at a small barbershop in his hometown. From there, he moved on to a larger salon and then on to work in a big city. "Work behind the chair led me to want to do color," he said. "This really interested me. I guess wanting to know more about it myself is the reason why I researched it and became so involved with color. As I learned more about hair coloring, I became competent and more confident." The challenge, he said, is to learn the "laws of color"— how to choose a shade to get a specific result on a client's hair. He is now considered a color expert and is the head of the chemical department at his salon. "I've always been involved some way in outside education," Woodyard notes. "I've never been in a job where I have just worked 40 hours behind the chair. I've always been involved in some kind of training. I like to share what I know."

Cosmetologists must know how to market themselves to build their business. Whether they are self-employed or work for a salon or company, they are in business for themselves. It is the cosmetologist's skills and personality that will attract or fail to attract clients to that particular cosmetologist's chair. A marketing strategy Woodyard uses is to give several of his business cards to each of his clients. When one of his clients recommends him to a prospective new client, he gives both the old and new client a discount on a hair service.

Karol Thousand is the managing director of corporate school operations for a large cosmetology school that has four campuses in metropolitan areas in two states. She began as a stylist employed by salons and then owned her own shop for seven years. Her business was in an area that was destroyed by a tornado. It was then that she looked at different opportunities to decide the direction of her career. "I looked at the business end of the profession," she said, "and I took some additional business courses and was then introduced to the school aspect of the profession. I have a passion for the beauty business, and as I explored various training programs, I thought to myself, 'Hey, this is something I'd like to do!'"

She managed a cosmetology school in Wisconsin before moving to Chicago for her current position. She said, "This is an empowering and satisfying profession. Not only do you make someone look better, but 99 percent of the time, they will feel better about themselves. In cosmetology, you can have the opportunity several times a day to help change the total look and perspective of an individual."

Cosmetologists serving the public must have pleasant, friendly, yet professional attitudes, as well as skill, ability, and an interest in their craft. These qualities are necessary in building a following of steady customers. The nature of their work requires cosmetologists to be aware of the psychological aspects of dealing with all types of personalities. Sometimes this can require diplomacy skills and a high degree of tolerance in dealing with different clients.

"To me," Sean Woodyard admitted, "doing hair is just as much about self-gratification as it is about pleasing the client. It makes me feel good to make somebody else look good and feel good. It's also, of course, a great artistic and creative outlet."

■ REQUIREMENTS
High School

High school students interested in the cosmetology field can help build a good foundation for postsecondary training by taking subjects in the areas of art, science (especially a basic chemistry course), health, business, and communication arts. Psychology and speech courses could also be helpful.

Postsecondary Training

To become a licensed cosmetologist, you must have completed an undergraduate course of a certain amount of classroom credit hours. The required amount varies from state to state—anywhere from 1,050 to 2,200 hours. The program takes from 10 to 24 months to complete, again depending on the state. Evening courses are also frequently offered, and these take two to four months longer to complete. Applicants must also pass a written test, and

WHY DOES HAIR TURN GRAY?

Hair turns gray (or white) when the hair root ceases to produce a pigment (melanin). Genetics determine when a person's hair is likely to start graying. There is no evidence that special diets and supplements affect the graying process. However, a 1996 *British Medical Journal* study found that smoking may cause premature graying; in fact, the study found smokers to be four times more likely to gray prematurely.

some states also give an oral test, before they receive a license. Most states will allow a cosmetologist to work as an apprentice until the license is received, which normally just involves a matter of weeks.

A 1,500-hour undergraduate course at a cosmetology school in Illinois is typical of schools around the country. The program consists of theoretical and practical instruction divided into individual units of learning. Students are taught through the media of theory, audiovisual presentation, lectures, demonstrations, practical hands-on experiences, and written and practical testing. All schools have what they call clinic areas or floors, where people can have their hair done (or avail themselves of esthetics or nail services) by students at a discounted price, compared to what they would pay in a regular shop or salon.

One course, Scientific Approach to Hair Sculpture, teaches students how to sculpt straight and curly hair, ethnic and Caucasian, using shears, texturizing tools and techniques, razors, and electric clippers. Teaching tools include mannequins, slip-ons, hair wefts, rectangles, and profiles. People skills segments are part of each course. Among other courses are Scientific Approach to Perm Design, Systematic Approach to Color, and Systematic Approach to Beauty Care. Three different salon prep courses focus on retailing, business survival skills, and practical applications for contemporary design. The program concludes with final testing, as well as extensive reviews and preparations for state board testing through a mock state board written practical examination.

Karol Thousand noted that, at her school and others throughout the country, "Twenty-five years ago, the courses focused mainly on technical skills. This is still the core focus, but now we teach more interpersonal skills. Our People Skills program helps students understand the individual, the different personality types—to better comprehend how they fit in and how to relate to their clients. We also teach sales and marketing skills—how to sell themselves and their services and products, as well as good business management skills."

Some states offer student internship programs. One such program that was recently initiated in Illinois aims to send better-prepared students/junior stylists into the workforce upon completion of their training from a licensed school. This program allows students to enter into a work-study program for 10 percent of their training in either cosmetology, esthetics, or nail technology. The state requires a student to complete at least 750 hours of training prior to making application for the program.

The program allows a student to experience firsthand the expectations of a salon, to perform salon services to be evaluated by their supervisor, and to experience different types of salon settings. The participating salons have the opportunity to pre-qualify potential employees before they graduate and work with the school regarding the skill levels of the student interns. This will also enhance job placement programs already in place in the school. The state requires that each participating salon be licensed and registered with the appropriate state department and file proof of registration with the school, along with the name and license number of their cosmetologist who is assigned to supervise students, before signing a contract or agreement.

Certification or Licensing

At the completion of the proper amount of credit hours, students must pass a formal examination before they can be licensed. The exam takes just a few hours. Some states also require a practical (hands-on) test and oral exams. Most, however, just require written tests. State Board Examinations are given at regular intervals. After about a month, test scores are available. Those who have passed then send in a licensure application and a specified fee to the appropriate state department. It takes about four to six weeks for a license to be issued.

Temporary permits are issued in most states, allowing students who have passed the test and applied for a license to practice their profession while they wait to receive the actual license. Judy Vargas, manager of the professional services section of the Illinois Department of Professional Regulation, warns students not to practice without a temporary permit or a license. "This is the biggest violation we see," she said, "and there are penalties of up to $1,000 per violation."

Graduate courses on advanced techniques and new methods and styles are also available at many cosmetology schools. Many states require licensed cosmetologists to take a specified number of credit hours, called continuing education units, or CEUs. Illinois, for instance, requires each licensed cosmetologist to complete 10 to 14

CEUs each year. Licenses must be renewed in all states, generally every year or every two years.

In the majority of states, the minimum age for an individual to obtain a cosmetology license is 16. Because standards and requirements vary from state to state, students are urged to contact the licensing board of the state in which they plan to be employed.

Other Requirements

Hairstyles change from season to season. As a cosmetologist, you will need to keep up with current fashion trends and often be learning new procedures to create new looks. You should be able to visualize different styles and make suggestions to your clients about what is best for them. And even if you don't specialize in coloring hair, you should have a good sense of color. One of your most important responsibilities will be to make your clients feel comfortable around you and happy with their looks. To do this, you will need to develop both your talking and listening skills.

■ EXPLORING

Talk to friends or parents of friends who are working in the industry, or just go to a local salon or cosmetology school and ask questions about the profession. Go to the library and get books on careers in the beauty/hair care industry. Search the Internet for related websites. Individuals with an interest in the field might seek after-school or summer employment as a general shop helper in a barbershop or a salon. Some schools may permit potential students to visit and observe classes.

■ EMPLOYERS

The most common employers of hair stylists are, of course, beauty salons. However, hair stylists also find work at department stores, hospitals, nursing homes, spas, resorts, cruise ships, and cosmetics companies. The demand for services in the cosmetology field—hair styling in particular—far exceeds the supply; additionally, the number of salons increases by two percent each year. Considering that most cosmetology schools have placement services to assist graduates, finding employment usually is not difficult for most cosmetologists. As with most jobs in the cosmetology field, opportunities will be concentrated in highly populated areas; however, there will be jobs available for hair stylists virtually everywhere. Many hair stylists/cosmetologists aspire ultimately to be self-employed. This can be a rewarding avenue if one has plenty of experience and good business sense (not to mention start-up capital or financial backing); it also requires long hours and a great deal of hard work.

STARTING OUT

To be a licensed cosmetologist/hair stylist, you must graduate from an accredited school and pass a state test. Once that is accomplished, you can apply for jobs that are advertised in the newspapers or over the Internet, or apply at an employment agency specializing in these professions. Most schools have placement services to help their graduates find jobs. Some salons have training programs from which they hire new employees.

Scholarships or grants that can help you pay for your schooling are available. One such program is the Access to Cosmetology Education (ACE) Grant. It is sponsored by the American Association of Cosmetology Schools (AACS), the Beauty and Barber Supply Institute Inc., and the Cosmetology Advancement Foundation. Interested students can find out about ACE Grants and obtain applications at participating schools, salons, and distributors or through these institutions. The criteria for receiving an ACE Grant include approval from an AACS member school, recommendations from two salons, and a high school diploma or GED.

ADVANCEMENT

Individuals in the beauty/hair care industry most frequently begin by working at a shop or salon. Many aspire to be self-employed and own their own shop. There are many factors to consider when contemplating going into business on one's own. Usually it is essential to obtain experience and financial capital before seeking to own a shop. The cost of equipping even a one-chair shop can be very high. Owning a large shop or a chain of shops is an aspiration for the very ambitious.

Some pursue advanced educational training in one aspect of beauty culture, such as hair styling or coloring. Others who are more interested in the business aspects can take courses in business management skills and move into shop or salon management, or work for a corporation related to the industry. Manufacturers and distributors frequently have exciting positions available for those with exceptional talent and creativity. Cosmetologists work on the stage as platform artists, or take some additional education courses and teach at a school of cosmetology.

Some schools publish their own texts and other printed materials for students. They want people who have cosmetology knowledge and experience as well as writing skills to write and edit these materials. An artistic director for the publishing venue of one large school has a cosmetology degree in addition to degrees in art. Other cosmetologists might design hairstyles for fashion magazines, industry publications, fashion shows, television presentations, or movies. They might get involved in the regulation of the business, such as working for a state licensing board. There are many and varied career possibilities cosmetologists can explore in the beauty/hair care industry.

EARNINGS

Cosmetologists can make an excellent living in the beauty/hair care industry, but as in most careers, they don't receive very high pay when just starting out. Though their raise in salary may start slowly, the curve quickly escalates. The U.S. Department of Labor reports cosmetologists and hairstylists had a median annual income (including tips) of $18,960 in 2002. The lowest paid 10 percent, which generally included those beginning in the profession, made less than $13,020. The highest paid 10 percent earned more than $33,240. Again, both those salaries include tips. On the extreme upward end of the pay scale, some fashion stylists in New York or Hollywood charge $300 per haircut! Their annual salary can go into six figures. Salaries in larger cities are greater than those in smaller towns; but then the cost of living is higher in the big cities, too.

Most shops and salons give a new employee a guaranteed income instead of commission. If the employee goes over the guaranteed amount, then he or she earns a commission. Usually, this guarantee will extend for the first three months of employment, so that the new stylist can focus on building up business before going on straight commission.

In addition, most salon owners grant incentives for product sales; and, of course, there are always tips. However, true professionals never depend on their tips. If a stylist receives a tip, it's a nice surprise for a job well done, but it's good business practice not to expect these bonuses. All tips must be recorded and reported to the Internal Revenue Service.

The benefits a cosmetologist receives, such as health insurance and retirement plans, depend on the place of employment. A small independent salon cannot afford to supply a hefty benefit package, but a large shop or salon or a member of a chain can be more generous. However, some of the professional associations and organizations offer benefit packages at reasonable rates.

WORK ENVIRONMENT

Those employed in the cosmetology industry usually work a five- or six-day week, which averages approximately 40–50 hours. Weekends and days preceding holidays may be especially busy. Cosmetologists are on their feet a lot and are usually working in a small space. Strict sanitation codes must be observed in all shops and salons, and they are comfortably heated, ventilated, and well lighted.

Hazards of the trade include nicks and cuts from scissors and razors, minor burns when care is not used in handling hot towels or instruments, and occasional skin irritations arising from constant use of grooming aids that contain chemicals. Some of the chemicals used in hair dyes or permanent solutions can be very abrasive; plastic gloves are required for handling and contact. Pregnant women are advised to avoid contact with many of those chemicals present in hair products.

Conditions vary depending on what environment the stylist is working in. Those employed in department store salons will have more of a guaranteed client flow, with more walk-ins from people who are shopping. A freestanding shop or salon might have a more predictable pace, with more scheduled appointments and fewer walk-ins. In a department store salon, for example, stylists have to abide by the rules and regulations of the store. In a private salon, stylists are more like entrepreneurs or freelancers, but they have much more flexibility as to when they come and go and what type of business they want to do.

Stylist Sean Woodyard said, "I've always enjoyed the atmosphere of a salon. There's constant action and something different happening every day. A salon attracts artistic, creative people and the profession allows me to be part of the fashion industry."

Some may find it difficult to work constantly in such close, personal contact with the public at large, especially when they strive to satisfy customers who are difficult to please or disagreeable. The work demands an even temperament, pleasant disposition, and patience.

■ OUTLOOK

The future looks good for cosmetology. According to the U.S. Department of Labor, employment should grow about as fast as the average through 2012. Our growing population, the availability of disposable income, and changes in hair fashion that are practically seasonal all contribute to the demand for cosmetologists. In addition, turnover in this career is fairly high as cosmetologists move up into management positions, change careers, or leave the field for other reasons. Competition for jobs at higher paying, prestigious salons, however, is strong.

■ FOR MORE INFORMATION

Contact the following organizations for more information on cosmetology careers:

American Association of Cosmetology Schools
15825 North 71st Street, Suite 100
Scottsdale, AZ 85254-1521
Tel: 800-831-1086
http://www.beautyschools.org

Beauty and Barber Supply Institute Inc.
15825 North 71st Street, Suite 100
Scottsdale, AZ 85254
Tel: 800-468-2274
http://www.bbsi.org

National Accrediting Commission of Cosmetology Arts and Sciences
4401 Ford Avenue, Suite 1300
Alexandria, VA 22302
Tel: 703-600-7600
http://www.naccas.org

National Cosmetology Association
401 North Michigan Avenue, 22nd Floor
Chicago, IL 60611
Tel: 312-527-6765
http://www.salonprofessionals.org

Cost Estimators

■ OVERVIEW

Cost estimators use standard estimating techniques to calculate the cost of a construction or manufacturing project. They help contractors, owners, and project planners determine how much a project or product will cost to decide if it is economically viable. There are approximately 188,000 cost estimators employed in the United States.

■ HISTORY

Cost estimators collect and analyze information on various factors influencing costs, such as the labor, materials, and machinery needed for a particular project. Cost estimating became a profession as production techniques became more complex. Weighing the many costs involved in a construction or manufacturing project soon required specialized knowledge beyond the skills and training of the average builder or contractor. Today, cost estimators work in many industries but are predominantly employed in construction and manufacturing.

■ THE JOB

In the construction industry, the nature of the work is largely determined by the type and size of the project being estimated. For a large building project, for example, the estimator reviews architectural drawings and other bidding documents before any construction begins. The estimator then visits the potential construction site to collect information that may affect the way the structure is built, such as the site's access to transportation, water, electricity, and other needed resources. While out in the field, the estimator also analyzes the topography of the land, taking note of its general characteristics, such as drainage areas and the location of trees and other vegetation. After compiling thorough research, the estimator writes a quantity survey, or takeoff. This is an itemized report of the quantity of materials and labor a firm will need for the proposed project.

Large projects often require several estimators, all specialists in a given area. For example, one estimator may assess the electrical costs of a project, while another concentrates on the transportation or insurance costs. In this case, it is the responsibility of a *chief estimator* to combine the reports and submit one development proposal.

In manufacturing, estimators work with engineers to review blueprints and other designs. They develop a list of the materials and labor needed for production. Aiming to control costs but maintain quality, estimators must weigh the option of producing parts in-house or purchasing them from other vendors. After this research, they write a report on the overall costs of manufacturing, taking into consideration influences such as improved employee learning curves, material waste, overhead, and the need to correct problems as manufacturing goes along.

To write their reports, estimators must know current prices for labor and materials and other factors that influence costs. They obtain this data through commercial price books, catalogs, and the Internet or by calling vendors directly to obtain quotes.

Estimators should also be able to compute and understand accounting and mathematical formulas in order to make their cost reports. Computer programs are frequently used to do the routine calculations, producing more accurate results and leaving the estimator with more time to analyze data.

■ REQUIREMENTS
High School

To prepare for a job in cost estimating, you should take courses in accounting, business, economics, and mathematics. Because a large part of this job involves comparing calculations, it is essential that you are comfortable and confident with your math skills. English courses with a heavy concentration in writing are also recommended to develop your communication skills. Cost estimators must be able to write clear and accurate reports of their analyses. Finally, drafting and shop courses are also useful since estimators must be able to review and understand blueprints and other design plans.

Postsecondary Training

Though not required for the job, most employers of cost estimators in both construction and manufacturing prefer applicants with formal education. In construction, cost estimators generally have associate's or bachelor's degrees in construction management, construction science, engineering, or architecture. Those employed with manufacturers often have degrees in physical science, business, mathematics, operations research, statistics, engineering, economics, finance, or accounting.

Many colleges and universities offer courses in cost estimating as part of the curriculum for an associate's, bachelor's, or master's degree. These courses cover subjects such as cost estimating, cost control, project planning and management, and computer applications. The Association for the Advancement of Cost Engineering International offers a list of education programs related to cost engineering. Check out the association's website, http://www.aacei.org, for more information.

Certification or Licensing

Although it is not required, many cost estimators find it helpful to become certified to improve their standing within the professional community. Obtaining certification proves that the estimator has obtained adequate job training and education. Information on certification procedures is available from organizations such as the American Society of Professional Estimators, the Association for the Advancement of Cost Engineering International, and the Society of Cost Estimating and Analysis.

Other Requirements

To be a cost estimator, you should have sharp mathematical and analytical skills. Cost estimators must work well with others, and be confident and assertive when presenting findings to engineers, business owners, and design professionals. To work as a cost estimator in the construction industry, you will likely need some experience before you start,

QUICK FACTS

SCHOOL SUBJECTS
Business
Economics
Mathematics

PERSONAL SKILLS
Leadership/management
Technical/scientific

WORK ENVIRONMENT
Indoors and outdoors
Primarily multiple locations

MINIMUM EDUCATION LEVEL
Some postsecondary training

SALARY RANGE
$28,670 to $47,550 to $79,240+

CERTIFICATION OR LICENSING
Recommended

OUTLOOK
About as fast as the average

DOT
160

GOE
13.02.04

NOC
2234

O*NET-SOC
13-1051.00

Douglas Gransberg is an associate professor of construction science at the University of Oklahoma in Norman.

Q. What sort of positions have you held in the field of cost estimating?

A. I have done everything from being a cost estimator to being a senior manager who supervised cost engineers and was responsible for building construction projects within the budgets established by my and others' estimates. Now I teach cost estimating at both the undergraduate and graduate level at the university.

Q. What are a cost estimator's major job responsibilities?

A. There are three main responsibilities: (1) quantify the scope of work by defining the quantity of work portrayed in the project's design documents; (2) price the scope of work; (3) prepare the competitive bid for that work taking into account the current market, risk, and the level of competition.

Q. What type of training (both educational and practical) did you complete to work in this field? What type of training would any cost estimator need to undergo?

A. I had cost engineering classes in both my undergraduate and graduate courses in the subject, but learned most of what I know through practical experience. Construction education programs like the University of Oklahoma's construction science bachelor's degree program furnish all the fundamental training that is necessary for a student to become an entry-level cost professional.

Q. What are the pros and cons of working in this field?

A. The best part is getting to work with the money side of the construction project by putting together competitive bids and conceptual estimates. This is very challenging work and the satisfaction of winning is immediate. The worst part is the tedious attention to detail necessary to prepare the quantity take-off. However, this attention to detail is necessary for a good estimate.

Q. What were your expectations entering this field? Are they much different from the realities?

A. I had no expectations upon entering the field, as most people do not plan to end up in this particular field. Cost engineering is something that most engineers and construction professionals have to do to complete their professional foundation; most that become estimators or cost engineers end up in the field because they found that that they were good at cost engineering and enjoyed the work.

Q. What would you say are the most important skills and personal qualities for someone in this field?

A. Math is the most important skill, especially geometry. Next is the ability to organize your thoughts and your work in a comprehensive manner. Finally, you have to be able to "build the job in your head" as you estimate it. So the ability to conceptualize from the two-dimensional view shown in a construction drawing to what the building or road will look like in three dimensions is essential.

Q. What is the best way to find a job in cost estimating? What is the outlook for jobs in this field?

A. Get a degree in construction management from an American Council for Construction Education (ACCE)-accredited school. Estimators are in demand even when construction is down because the estimators are the ones that get the work for the builders.

Q. What advice would you give to someone who is interested in pursuing this type of career?

A. Talk to a real estimator/cost engineer. Take a look at what they do and, if possible, sit through the excitement of a bid day. If it seems exciting and interesting to you, then this is something you'll enjoy. If it seems boring, then look for another career field.

which can be gained through an internship or cooperative education program.

■ EXPLORING

Practical work experience is necessary to become a cost estimator. Consider taking a part-time position with a construction crew or manufacturing firm during your summer vacations. Because of more favorable working conditions, construction companies are the busiest during the summer months and may be looking for additional assistance. Join any business or manufacturing clubs that your school may offer.

Another way to discover more about career opportunities is simply by talking to a professional cost estimator. Ask your school counselor to help arrange an interview with an estimator to ask questions about his or her job demands, work environment, and personal opinion of the job.

EMPLOYERS

In 2002, approximately 188,000 cost estimators were employed in the United States: 53 percent by the construction industry and 20 percent by manufacturing companies. Other employers include engineering and architecture firms, business services, the government, and a wide range of other industries.

Estimators are employed throughout the country, but the largest concentrations are found in cities or rapidly growing suburban areas. More job opportunities exist in or near large commercial or government centers.

STARTING OUT

Cost estimators often start out working in the industry as laborers, such as construction workers. After gaining experience and taking the necessary training courses, a worker may move into the more specialized role of estimator. Another possible route into cost estimating is through a formal training program, either through a professional organization that sponsors educational programs or through technical schools, community colleges, or universities. School placement counselors can be good sources of employment leads for recent graduates. Applying directly to manufacturers, construction firms, and government agencies is another way to find your first job.

Whether employed in construction or manufacturing, most cost estimators are provided with intensive on-the-job training. Generally, new hires work with experienced estimators to become familiar with the work involved. They develop skills in blueprint reading and learn construction specifications before accompanying estimators to the construction site. In time, new hires learn how to determine quantities and specifications from project designs and report appropriate material and labor costs.

ADVANCEMENT

Promotions for cost estimators are dependent on skill and experience. Advancement usually comes in the form of more responsibility and higher wages. A skilled cost estimator at a large construction company may become a chief estimator. Some experienced cost estimators go into consulting work, offering their services to government, construction, and manufacturing firms.

EARNINGS

Salaries vary according to the size of the construction or manufacturing firm and the experience and education of the worker. According to the *Occupational Outlook Handbook,* the median annual salary for cost estimators was $47,550 in 2002. The lowest 10 percent earned less than $28,670 and the highest 10 percent earned over $79,240. By industry, the median annual earnings were as follows:

READY FOR TAKEOFF

A takeoff is what cost estimators call the quantity survey that is used to prepare a total cost summary for a project. Using standard estimating forms, the cost estimator fills in such things as dimensions and number of units required, equipment needed, sequence of operations, and crew size. Also included in the takeoff are allowances for possible waste of materials, delays in shipment, bad weather, and other factors that might increase costs.

residential building construction, $47,180; nonresidential building construction, $53,820; foundation, structure, and building exterior contractors, $47,630; building finishing contractors, $45,630. Starting salaries for graduates of engineering or construction management programs were higher than those with degrees in other fields. A 2003 salary survey states that candidates with degrees in construction science/management were offered jobs averaging $42,229 a year.

WORK ENVIRONMENT

Much of the cost estimator's work takes place in a typical office setting with access to accounting records and other information. However, estimators must also visit construction sites or manufacturing facilities to inspect production procedures. These sites may be dirty, noisy, and potentially hazardous if the cost estimator is not equipped with proper protective gear such as a hard hat or earplugs. During a site visit, cost estimators consult with engineers, work supervisors, and other professionals involved in the production or manufacturing process.

Estimators usually work a 40-hour week, although longer hours may be required if a project faces a deadline. For construction estimators, overtime hours almost always occur in the summer when most projects are in full force.

OUTLOOK

Employment for cost estimators is expected to increase about as fast as the average through 2012, according to the U.S. Department of Labor. As in most industries, highly trained college graduates and those with the most experience have the best job prospects.

Many jobs will arise from the need to replace workers leaving the industry, either to retire or change jobs. In addition, growth within the residential and commercial construction industry is a large cause for much of the employment demand for estimators. The fastest growing areas in construction are in special trade and government projects, including the building and repairing of highways, streets, bridges, subway systems, airports, waterways, and electrical plants.

In manufacturing, employment is predicted to remain stable, though growth is not expected to be as high as in construction. Estimators will be in demand because employers will continue to need their services to control operating costs.

■ FOR MORE INFORMATION

For information on certification and educational programs, contact

American Society of Professional Estimators

11141 Georgia Avenue, Suite 412

Wheaton, MD 20902

Tel: 301-929-8848

Email: info@aspenational.com

http://www.aspenational.com

For information on certification, educational programs, and scholarships, contact

Association for the Advancement of Cost Engineering International

209 Prairie Avenue, Suite 100

Morgantown, WV 26501

Tel: 800-858-2678

Email: info@aacei.org

http://www.aacei.org

For information on certification, job listings, and a glossary of cost-estimating terms, visit the SCEA website:

Society of Cost Estimating and Analysis (SCEA)

101 South Whiting Street, Suite 201

Alexandria, VA 22304

Tel: 703-751-8069

Email: scea@sceaonline.net

http://www.sceaonline.net

Costume Designers

■ OVERVIEW

Costume designers plan, create, and maintain clothing and accessories for all characters in a stage, film, television, dance, or opera production. Designers custom fit each character, and either create a new garment or alter an existing costume.

■ HISTORY

Costume design has been an important part of the theater since the early Greek tragedies, when actors generally wore masks and long robes with sleeves. By the time of the Roman Caesars, stage costumes had become very elaborate and colorful.

After the fall of Rome, theater disappeared for some time, but later returned in the form of Easter and Nativity plays. Priests and choirboys wore their usual robes with some simple additions, such as veils and crowns. Plays then moved from the church to the marketplace, and costumes again became important to the production.

During the Renaissance, costumes were designed for the Italian pageants, the French ballets, and the English masques by such famous designers as Torelli, Jean Berain, and Burnacini. From 1760 to 1782, Louis-Rene Boquet designed costumes using wide panniers, forming a kind of elaborate ballet skirt. But by the end of the 18th century, there was a movement toward more classical costumes on the stage.

During the early 19th century, historical costumes became popular, and period details were added to contemporary dress. Toward the end of the 19th century, realism became important, and actors wore the dress of the day, often their own clothes. Because this trend resulted in less work for the costume designers, they turned to musical and opera productions to express their creativity.

In the early 20th century, Diaghilev's Russian Ballet introduced a non-naturalistic style in costumes, most notably in the designs of Leon Bakst. This trend gave way to European avant-garde theater, in which costumes became abstract and symbolic.

Since the 1960s, new materials, such as plastics and adhesives, have greatly increased the costume designer's range. Today, their work is prominent in plays, musicals, dance performances, films, music videos, and television programs.

■ THE JOB

Costume designers generally work as freelancers. After they have been contracted to provide the costumes for a production, they read the script to learn about the theme, location, time period, character types, dialogue, and action. They meet with the director to discuss his or her feelings on the plot, characters, period and style, time frame for the production, and budget.

For a play, designers plan a rough costume plot, which is a list of costume changes by scene for each character. They thoroughly research the history and setting in which the play is set. They plan a preliminary color scheme and sketch the costumes, including details such as gloves, footwear, hose, purses, jewelry, canes, fans, bouquets, and other props. The costume designer or an assistant collects swatches of fabrics and samples of various accessories.

After completing the research, final color sketches are painted or drawn and mounted for presentation. Once the director approves the designs, the costume designer solicits bids from contractors, creates or rents costumes, and shops for fabrics and accessories. Measurements of all actors are taken. Designers work closely with drapers, sewers, hairstylists, and makeup artists in the costume shop. They supervise fittings and attend all dress rehearsals to make final adjustments and repairs.

Costume designers also work in films, television, and videos, aiming to provide the look that will highlight characters' personalities. Aside from working with actors, they may also design and create costumes for performers such as figure skaters, ballroom dance competitors, circus members, theme park characters, rock artists, and others who routinely wear costumes as part of a show.

■ REQUIREMENTS

High School

Costume designers need at least a high school education. It is helpful to take classes in art, home economics, and theater and to participate in drama clubs or community theater. English, literature, and history classes will help you learn how to analyze a play and research the clothing and manner of various historical periods. Marketing and business-related classes will also be helpful, as most costume designers work as freelancers. Familiarity with computers is useful, as many designers work with computer-aided design (CAD) programs.

While in high school, consider starting a portfolio of design sketches. Practicing in a sketchbook is a great way to get ideas and designs out on paper and organized for future reference. You can also get design ideas through others; watch theater, television, or movie productions and take note of the characters' dress. Sketch them on your own for practice. Looking through fashion magazines can also give you ideas to sketch.

Postsecondary Training

A college degree is not a requirement, but in this highly competitive field, it gives a sizable advantage. Most costume designers today have a bachelor's degree. Many art schools, especially in New York and Los Angeles, have programs in costume design at both the bachelor's and master's degree level. A liberal arts school with a strong theater program is also a good choice.

Other Requirements

Costume designers need sewing, draping, and patterning skills, as well as training in basic design techniques and figure drawing. Aside from being artistic, designers must also be able to work with people because many compromises and agreements must be made between the designer and the production's director.

Costume designers must prepare a portfolio of their work, including photographs and sketches highlighting their best efforts. Some theatrical organizations require membership in United Scenic Artists (USA), a union that protects the interests of designers on the job and sets minimum fees. Students in design programs that pass an exam and have some design experience can apply for USA's Designer Apprentice Program. More experienced designers who want full professional membership in the union must also submit a portfolio for review.

■ EXPLORING

If you are interested in costume design, consider joining a theater organization, such as a school drama club or a community theater. School dance troupes or film classes also may offer opportunities to explore costume design.

The Costume Designer's Handbook: A Complete Guide for Amateur and Professional Costume Designers, by Rosemary Ingham and Liz Covey (Portsmouth, N.H.: Heinemann, 1992), is an invaluable resource for beginning or experienced costume designers.

You can practice designing on your own, by drawing original sketches or copying designs from television, films, or the stage. Practice sewing and altering costumes from sketches for yourself, friends and family.

■ EMPLOYERS

Costume designers are employed by production companies that produce works for stage, television, and film. Most employers are located in New York and Los Angeles, although most metropolitan areas have community theater and film production companies that hire designers.

■ STARTING OUT

Most high schools and colleges have drama clubs and dance groups that need costumes designed and made. Community theaters, too, may offer opportunities to assist in costume production. Regional theaters hire

QUICK FACTS

SCHOOL SUBJECTS
Art
Family and consumer science
Theater/dance

PERSONAL SKILLS
Artistic
Following instructions

WORK ENVIRONMENT
Primarily indoors
One location with some travel

MINIMUM EDUCATION LEVEL
High school diploma

SALARY RANGE
$13,940 to $17,500 to $22,214+

CERTIFICATION OR LICENSING
None available

OUTLOOK
Decline

DOT
346

GOE
01.04.02

NOC
5243

O*NET-SOC
27.1029.99

Most costume designers work as freelancers and are usually contracted to create costumes, jewelry, and hairpieces.

several hundred costume technicians each year for seasons that vary from 28 to 50 weeks.

Many beginning designers enter the field by becoming an assistant to a designer. Many established designers welcome newcomers and can be generous mentors. Some beginning workers start out in costume shops, which usually requires membership in a union. However, nonunion workers may be allowed to work for short-term projects. Some designers begin as *shoppers*, who swatch fabrics, compare prices, and buy yardage, trim, and accessories. Shoppers learn where to find the best materials at reasonable prices and often establish valuable contacts in the field. Other starting positions include milliner's assistant, craft assistant, or assistant to the draper.

Schools with bachelor's and master's programs in costume design may offer internships that can lead to jobs after graduation. Another method of entering costume design is to contact regional theaters directly and send your resume to the theater's managing director.

Before you become a costume designer, you may want to work as a freelance design assistant for a few years to gain helpful experience, a reputation, contacts, and an impressive portfolio.

■ ADVANCEMENT

Beginning designers must show they are willing to do a variety of tasks. The theater community is small and intricately interconnected, so those who work hard and are flexible with assignments can gain good reputations quickly. Smaller regional theaters tend to hire designers for a full season to work with the same people on one or more productions, so opportunities for movement may be scarce. Eventually, costume designers with experience and talent can work for larger productions, such as films, television, and videos.

■ EARNINGS

Earnings vary greatly in this business depending on factors such as how many outfits the designer completes, how long they are employed during the year, and the amount of their experience. Although the U.S. Department of Labor does not give salary figures for costume designers, it does report that the related occupational group of tailors, dressmakers, and custom sewers had a median hourly wage of $10.68 in 2002. For full-time work, this hourly wage translates into a yearly income of approximately $22,214. However, those just starting out and working as assistants earned as little as $6.70 an hour, translating into an annual salary of approximately $13,940.

Costume designers who work on Broadway or for other large stage productions are usually members of the United Scenic Artists union, which sets minimum fees, requires producers to pay into pension and welfare funds, protects the designer's rights, establishes rules for billing, and offers group health and life insurance.

According to the union, an assistant for a Broadway show earns about $775 for the duration of the production. A costume designer for a Broadway musical with a minimum of 36 actors earns around $17,500. For opera and dance companies, salary is usually by costume count.

For feature films and television, costume designers earn daily rates for an eight-hour day or a weekly rate for an unlimited number of hours. Designers sometimes earn royalties on their designs.

Regional theaters usually set individual standard fees, which vary widely, beginning around $200 per week for an assistant. Most of them do not require membership in the union.

Most costume designers work freelance and are paid per costume or show. Costume designers can charge $90–$500 per costume, but some costumes, such as those for figure skaters, can cost thousands of dollars. Freelance costume designers often receive a flat rate for designing costumes for a show. For small and regional theaters, this rate may be in the $400–$500 range; the flat rate for medium and large productions generally starts at around $1,000. Many costume designers must take second part-time or full-time jobs to supplement their income from costume design.

Freelancers are responsible for their own health insurance, life insurance, and pension plans. They do not receive holiday, sick, or vacation pay.

■ WORK ENVIRONMENT

Costume designers put in long hours at painstaking detail work. It is a demanding profession that requires flexible, artistic, and practical workers. The schedule can be erratic—a busy period followed by weeks of little or no work. Though costumes are often a crucial part of a production's success, designers usually get little recognition compared to the actors and director.

Designers meet a variety of interesting and gifted people. Every play, film, or concert is different and every production situation is unique, so there is rarely a steady routine. Costume designers must play many roles: artist, sewer, researcher, buyer, manager, and negotiator.

■ OUTLOOK

The U.S. Department of Labor predicts employment for tailors, dressmakers, and skilled sewers to decline through 2012, and costume designers may not fair much better. The health of the entertainment business, especially theater, is very dependent on the overall economy and public attitudes. Theater budgets and government support for the arts in general have come under pressure in recent years and have limited employment prospects for costume designers. Many theaters, especially small and nonprofit theaters, are cutting their budgets or doing smaller shows that require fewer costumes. Additionally, people are less willing to spend money on tickets or go to theaters during economic downturns or times of crisis.

Nevertheless, opportunities for costume designers exist. As more cable television networks create original programming, demand for costume design in this area is likely to increase. Costume designers are able to work in an increasing number of locations as new regional theaters and cable television companies operate throughout the United States. As a result, however, designers must be willing to travel.

Competition for designer jobs is stiff and will remain so throughout the next decade. The number of qualified costume designers far exceeds the number of jobs available. This is especially true in smaller cities and regions, where there are fewer theaters.

■ FOR MORE INFORMATION

This union represents costume designers in film and television. For information on the industry and to view costume sketches in their online gallery, contact or check out the following website:

Costume Designers Guild
4730 Woodman Avenue, #430
Sherman Oaks, CA 91423
Tel: 818-905-1557

Email: cdgia@earthlink.net
http://www.costumedesignersguild.com

This organization provides a list of schools, scholarships, and a journal. College memberships are available with opportunities to network among other members who are professionals in the costume field.

Costume Society of America
PO Box 73
Earleville, MD 21919
Tel: 800-272-9447
Email: national.office@costumesocietyamerica.com
http://www.costumesocietyamerica.com

For additional information, contact the following organizations:

National Costumers Association
6914 Upper Trail Circle
Mesa, AZ 85207
Tel: 800-622-1321
Email: office@costumers.org
http://www.costumers.org

United States Institute for Theatre Technology
6443 Ridings Road
Syracuse, NY 13206-1111
Tel: 800-938-7488
Email: info@office.usitt.org
http://www.usitt.org

This union represents many costume designers working in New York, Chicago, Los Angeles, Miami, and New England. For information on membership, apprenticeship programs, and other resources on the career, contact

United Scenic Artists Local 829
29 West 38th Street
New York, NY 10018
Tel: 212-581-0300
http://www.usa829.org

Counter and Retail Clerks

■ OVERVIEW

Counter and retail clerks work as intermediaries between the general public and businesses that provide goods and services. They take orders and receive payments for such services as videotape rentals, automobile rentals, and laundry and dry cleaning. They often assist customers with their purchasing or rental decisions, especially when sales personnel are not available. These workers might also prepare billing statements, keep records of receipts and sales, and balance money in their cash registers. There are more than 436,000 counter and retail clerks working in the United States.

■ HISTORY

The first retail outlets in the United States sold food staples, farm necessities, and clothing, and many also served as the post office and became the social and economic centers of their communities. Owners of these general stores often performed all the jobs in the business.

Over the years retailing has undergone numerous changes. Large retail stores, requiring many workers, including counter and retail clerks, became more common. Also emerging were specialized retail or chain outlets—clothing stores, bicycle shops, computer shops, video stores, and athletic footwear boutiques—which also needed counter and retail clerks to assist customers and to receive payment for services or products.

■ THE JOB

Job duties vary depending on the type of business. In a shoe repair shop, for example, the clerk receives the shoes to be repaired or cleaned from the customer, examines the shoes, gives a price quote and a receipt to the customer, and then sends the shoes to the work department for the necessary repairs or cleaning. The shoes are marked with a tag specifying what work needs to be done and to whom the shoes belong. After the work is completed, the clerk returns the shoes to the customer and collects payment.

In stores where customers rent equipment or merchandise, clerks prepare rental forms and quote rates to customers. The clerks answer customer questions about the operation of the equipment. They often take a deposit to cover any accidents or possible damage. Clerks also check the equipment to be certain it is in good working order and make minor adjustments, if necessary. With long-term rentals, such as storage-facility rentals, clerks notify the customers when the rental period is about to expire and when the rent is overdue. *Video-rental clerks* greet customers, check out tapes, and accept payment. Upon return of the tapes, the clerks check the condition of the tapes and then put them back on the shelves.

In smaller shops with no sales personnel or in situations when the sales personnel are unavailable, counter and retail clerks assist customers with purchases or rentals by demonstrating the merchandise, answering customers' questions, accepting payment, recording sales, and wrapping the purchases or arranging for their delivery.

In addition to these duties, clerks sometimes prepare billing statements to be sent to customers. They might keep records of receipts and sales throughout the day and balance the money in their registers when their work shift ends. They sometimes are responsible for the display and presentation of products in their store. In supermarkets and grocery stores, clerks stock shelves and bag food purchases for the customers.

Service-establishment attendants work in various types of businesses, such as a laundry, where attendants take clothes to be cleaned or repaired and write down the customer's name and address. *Watch-and-clock-repair clerks* receive clocks and watches for repair and examine the timepieces to estimate repair costs. They might make minor repairs, such as replacing a watchband; otherwise, the timepiece is forwarded to the repair shop with a description of needed repairs.

Many clerks have job titles that describe what they do and where they work. These include laundry-pricing clerks, photo-finishing-counter clerks, tool-and-equipment-rental clerks, airplane-charter clerks, baby-stroller and wheelchair-rental clerks, storage-facility-rental clerks, boat-rental clerks, hospital-television-rental clerks, trailer-rental clerks, automobile-rental clerks, fur-storage clerks, and self-service-laundry and dry-cleaning attendants.

■ REQUIREMENTS
High School

High school courses useful for the job include English, speech, and mathematics, as well as any business-related classes, such as typing, computer science, and those covering principles in retailing. Although there are no specific educational requirements for clerk positions, most employers prefer to hire high school graduates. Legible handwriting and the ability to add and subtract numbers quickly are also necessary.

Other Requirements

To be a counter and retail clerk, you should have a pleasant personality and an ability to interact with a variety of people. You should also be neat and well groomed and have a high degree of personal responsibility. Counter and retail clerks must be able to adjust to alternating periods of heavy and light activity. No two days—or even customers—are alike. Because some customers can be rude or even hostile, you must exercise tact and patience at all times.

■ EXPLORING

There are numerous opportunities for part-time or temporary work as a clerk, especially during the holiday season. Many high schools have developed work-study programs that combine courses in retailing with part-time work in the field. Store owners cooperating in these programs may hire you as a full-time worker after you complete the course.

■ EMPLOYERS

Of the numerous types of clerks working in the United States, approximately 436,000 work as counter and rental clerks at video rental stores, dry cleaners, car rental agencies, and other such establishments. Stock clerks employed by supermarkets and grocery stores hold about 500,000 jobs. These are not the only employers of clerks, however; hardware stores, shoe stores, moving businesses, camera stores—in fact, nearly any business that sells goods or provides services to the general public employs clerks. Many work on a part-time basis.

■ STARTING OUT

If you are interested in securing an entry-level position as a clerk, you should contact stores directly. Workers with some experience, such as those who have completed a work-study program in high school, should have the greatest success, but most entry-level positions do not require any previous experience. Jobs are often listed in help-wanted advertisements.

Most stores provide new workers with on-the-job training in which experienced clerks explain company policies and procedures and teach new employees how to operate the cash register and other necessary equipment. This training usually continues for several weeks until the new employee feels comfortable on the job.

■ ADVANCEMENT

Counter and retail clerks usually begin their employment doing routine tasks, such as checking stock and operating the cash register. With experience, they might advance to more complicated assignments and assume

A returns clerk assists a customer exchanging a jacket.

some sales responsibilities. Those with the skill and aptitude might become salespeople or store managers, although further education is normally required for management positions.

The high turnover rate in the clerk position increases the opportunities for being promoted. The number and kind of opportunities, however, depend on the place of employment and the ability, training, and experience of the employee.

■ EARNINGS

According to the U.S. Department of Labor, the median hourly wage for counter and rental clerks was $8.31 in 2002. Working year round at 40 hours per week, a clerk earning this wage would make approximately $17,285 annually. Ten percent of counter and rental clerks earned less than $6.03 per hour (approximately $12,542 annually) in 2002, and 10 percent earned more than $15.10 per hour (or $31,408 annually). Wages among clerks vary for a number of reasons including the industry in which they work. The Department of Labor reports, for example, that those working in the automobile rental field had median hourly earnings of $9.69 (approximately $20,155 per year) in 2002, while those in amusement and recreation services earned a median of $7.30 per hour (approximately $15,184 yearly). Wages also vary among clerks due to factors such as size of the business, location in the country, and experience of the employee.

Those workers who have union affiliation (usually those who work for supermarkets) may earn considerably more than their nonunion counterparts. Full-time workers, especially those who are union members, might also receive benefits such as paid vacation time and health insurance, but this is not the industry norm. Some businesses offer merchandise discounts for their employees. Part-time workers usually receive fewer benefits than those working full time.

■ WORK ENVIRONMENT

Although a 40-hour workweek is common, many stores operate on a 44- to 48-hour workweek. Most stores are open on Saturday and many on Sunday. Most stores are also open one or more weekday evenings, so a clerk's working hours might vary from week to week and include evening and weekend shifts. Many counter and retail clerks work overtime during Christmas and other rush seasons. Part-time clerks generally work during peak business periods.

Most clerks work indoors in well-ventilated and well-lighted environments. The job can be routine and repetitive, and clerks often spend much of their time on their feet.

■ OUTLOOK

The U.S. Department of Labor predicts that employment for counter and rental clerks will grow faster than the average through 2012. Businesses that focus on customer service will always want to hire friendly and responsible clerks. Major employers should be those providing rental products and services, such as car rental firms, video rental stores, and other equipment rental businesses. Because of the high turnover in this field, however, many job openings will come from the need to replace workers. Opportunities for temporary or part-time work should be good, especially during busy business periods. Employment opportunities for clerks are plentiful in large metropolitan areas, where their services are in great demand.

■ FOR MORE INFORMATION

For information about educational programs in the retail industry, contact

Retail Industry Leaders Association
1700 North Moore Street, Suite 2250
Arlington, VA 22209
Tel: 703-841-2300
http://www.imra.org

National Retail Federation
325 7th Street, NW, Suite 1100
Washington, DC 20004
Tel: 800-673-4692
http://www.nrf.com

Court Reporters

■ OVERVIEW

Court reporters record every word at hearings, trials, depositions, and other legal proceedings by using a stenotype machine to take shorthand notes. Most court reporters transcribe the notes of the proceedings by using computer-aided transcription systems that print out regular, legible copies of the proceedings. The court reporter must also edit and proofread the final transcript and create the official transcript of the trial or other legal proceeding. Approximately 18,000 court reporters work in the United States.

■ HISTORY

To record legal proceedings, court reporters use shorthand, a system of abbreviated writing that has its beginnings in script forms developed more than 2,000 years ago. Ancient Greeks and Romans used symbols and letters to record poems, speeches, and political meetings.

Europeans, such as the Englishman Timothy Bright, began to develop systems of shorthand in the 15th and 16th centuries. These systems were refined throughout the 17th and 18th centuries. Shorthand was used primarily in personal correspondence and for copying or creating literary works.

Shorthand was applied to business communications after the invention of the typewriter. The stenotype, the first shorthand machine, was invented by an American court reporter in 1910. Before the introduction of Dictaphones, tape recorders, and other electronic recording devices, shorthand was the fastest and most accurate way for a secretary or reporter to copy down what was being said at a business meeting or other event. Court reporters today still use stenotype machines, but they use computer-aided transcription to translate the stenographic symbols into English text. Computer-aided transcription (CAT) saves the court reporter time that can be better used editing and refining the text.

Over 90 percent of court reporters use computers in their work, according to the National Court Reporters Association. Computers allow court reporters to offer more services to lawyers and judges, such as condensed transcripts (an extra transcript that fits several pages of testimony on one page), concordant indexes (indexes each word in a transcript by page and line number), and keyword indexes (indexes certain important terms as requested by the lawyer). Over 25 percent of court reporters are taking advantage of the Internet as well, according to the *Journal of Court Reporting*. Court reporters use the Internet for research, advertising, and connecting with clients.

■ THE JOB

Court reporters are best known as the men or women sitting in the courtroom silently typing to record what is said by everyone involved. While that is true, that's only part of the court reporter's job. Much more work is done after the court reporter leaves the trial or hearing.

In the courtroom, court reporters use symbols or shorthand forms of complete words to record what is said as quickly as it is spoken on a stenotype machine that looks like a miniature typewriter. The stenotype machine has 24 keys on its keyboard. Each key prints a single symbol. Unlike a typewriter, however, the court reporter using a stenotype machine can press more than one key at a time to print different combinations of symbols. Each symbol or combination represents a different sound, word, or phrase. As testimony is given, the reporter strikes one or more keys to create a phonetic representation of the testimony on a strip of paper, as well as on a computer disk inside the stenotype machine. The court reporter later uses a computer to translate and transcribe the testimony into legible, full-page documents or stores them for reference. Remember, people in court may speak at a rate of between 250 and 300 words a minute, and court reporters must record this testimony word for word and quickly.

Accurate recording of a trial is vital because the court reporter's record becomes the official transcript for the entire proceeding. In our legal system, court transcripts can be used after the trial for many important purposes. If a legal case is appealed, for example, the court reporter's transcript becomes the foundation for any further legal

action. The appellate judge refers to the court reporter's transcript to see what happened in the trial and how the evidence was presented.

Because of the importance of accuracy, a court reporter who misses a word or phrase must interrupt the proceedings to have the words repeated. The court reporter may be asked by the judge to read aloud a portion of recorded testimony during the trial to refresh everyone's memory. Court reporters must pay close attention to all the proceedings and be able to hear and understand everything. Sometimes it may be difficult to understand a particular witness or attorney due to poor diction, a strong accent, or a soft speaking voice. Nevertheless, the court reporter cannot be shy about stopping the trial and asking for clarification.

Court reporters must be adept at recording testimony on a wide range of legal issues, from medical malpractice to income tax evasion. In some cases, court reporters may record testimony at a murder trial or a child-custody case. Witnessing tense situations and following complicated arguments are unavoidable parts of the job. The court reporter must be able to remain detached from the drama that unfolds in court while faithfully recording all that is said.

After the trial or hearing, the court reporter has more work to do. Using a CAT program, the stenotype notes are translated to English. The majority of these translated notes are accurate. This rough translation is then edited either by the court reporter or by a *scopist*—an assistant to the court reporter who edits and cleans up the notes. If a stenotype note did not match a word in the court reporter's CAT dictionary during translation, it shows up still in stenotype form. The court reporter must manually change these entries into words and update the dictionary used in translating. If there are any meanings of words or spellings of names that are unfamiliar to the

FACTS ABOUT COURT REPORTING

- Almost 90 percent of court reporters are women.
- Shorthand was first used to record the first session of the Continental Congress in America.
- Court reporters in some states are also notary publics.

Source: National Court Reporters Association

court reporter, research must be done to verify that the correct term or spelling is used. The court reporter then proofreads the transcript to check for any errors in meaning, such as the word "here" instead of the word "hear." If necessary or requested by the lawyer or judge, special indexes and concordances are compiled using computer programs. The last step the court reporter must take is printing and binding the transcript to make it an organized and usable document for the lawyers and judge.

In some states, the court reporter is responsible for swearing in the witnesses and documenting items of evidence.

■ REQUIREMENTS
High School
To be a court reporter, you need to have a high school diploma or its equivalent. Take as many high-level classes in English as you can and get a firm handle on grammar and spelling. Take typing classes and computer classes to give you a foundation in using computers and a head start in keyboarding skills. Classes in government and business will be helpful as well. Training in Latin can also be a great benefit because it will help you understand the many medical and legal terms that arise during court proceedings. Knowledge of foreign languages can also be helpful because as a court reporter, you will often transcribe the testimony of non-English speakers with the aid of court-appointed translators.

Postsecondary Training
Court reporters are required to complete a specialized training program in shorthand reporting. These programs usually last between two and four years and include instruction on how to enter at least 225 words a minute on a stenotype machine. Other topics include computer operations, transcription methods, English grammar, and the principles of law. For court cases involving medical issues, students must also take courses on human anatomy and physiology. Basic medical and legal terms are also explained.

About 350 postsecondary schools and colleges have two- and four-year programs in court reporting. Many business colleges offer these programs. As a court reporting student in these programs, you must master machine shorthand, or stenotyping. The National Court Reporters Association (NCRA) states that to graduate from one of these programs, you must be able to type at least 225 words per minute and pass tests that gauge your written knowledge and speed.

The National Court Reporter's Foundation offers two scholarships for court reporting students: the Frank Sarli Memorial Scholarship and the Santo J. Aurelio Award for Altruism. See the contact information at the end of this article to learn how to apply for these awards.

Certification or Licensing
The NCRA offers several levels of certification for its members. To receive the Registered Professional Reporter certification, you must pass tests that are administered twice a year at over 100 sites in the United States and overseas. The Registered Merit Reporter certification means you have passed an exam with speeds up to 260 words per minute. The Registered Diplomate Reporter certification is obtained by passing a knowledge exam. This certification shows that the court reporter has gained valuable professional knowledge and experience through years of reporting. The Certified Realtime Reporter certification is given to reporters who have obtained the specialized skill of converting the spoken word into written word within seconds. Several other specialized certifications are available for the court reporter.

Some states require reporters to be notary publics or to be certified through a state certification exam. Currently, 42 states grant licenses in either shorthand reporting or court reporting, although not all of these states require a license to work as a court reporter. Licenses are granted after the court reporter passes state examinations and fulfills any prerequisites (usually an approved shorthand reporting program).

Other Requirements
Because part of a court reporter's work is done within the confines of a courtroom, being able to work under pressure is a must. Court reporters need to be able to meet deadlines with accuracy and attention to detail. As stated previously, a court reporter must be highly skilled at the stenotype machine. A minimum of 225 words per minute is expected from a beginning court reporter.

Court reporters must be familiar with a wide range of medical and legal terms and must be assertive enough to ask for clarification if a term or phrase goes by without the reporter understanding it. Court reporters must be as unbiased as possible and accurately record what is said, not what they believe to be true. Patience and perfectionism are vital characteristics, as is the ability to work closely with judges and other court officials.

EXPLORING

Can you see yourself as a court reporter someday? As with any career, you have much to consider. To get an idea of what a court reporter does—at least the work they do in public—attend some trials at your local courts. Instead of focusing on the main players—witnesses, lawyers, judges—keep an eye on the court reporter. If you can, watch several reporters in different courtrooms under different judges to get a perspective on what the average court reporter does. Try to arrange a one-on-one meeting with a court reporter so you can ask the questions you really want answers for. Maybe you can convince one of your teachers to arrange a field trip to a local court.

EMPLOYERS

Many court reporters are employed by city, county, state, or federal courts. Others work for themselves as freelancers or as employees of freelance reporting agencies. These freelance reporters are hired by attorneys to record the pretrial statements, or depositions, of experts and other witnesses. When people want transcripts of other important discussions, freelance reporters may be called on to record what is said at business meetings, large conventions, or similar events.

Most court reporters work in middle- to large-size cities, although they are needed anywhere a court of law is in session. In smaller cities, a court reporter may only work part time.

A new application of court-reporting skills and technology is in the field of television captioning. Using specialized computer-aided transcription systems, reporters can produce captions for live television events, including sporting events and national and local news, for the benefit of hearing-impaired viewers.

STARTING OUT

After completing the required training, court reporters usually work for a freelance reporting company that provides court reporters for business meetings and courtroom proceedings on a temporary basis. Qualified reporters can also contact these freelance reporting companies on their own. Occasionally a court reporter will be hired directly out of school as a courtroom official, but ordinarily only those with several years of experience are hired for full-time judiciary work. A would-be court reporter may start out working as a medical transcriptionist or other specific transcriptionist to get the necessary experience.

A court reporter must listen closely to every word spoken in court and simultaneously document it on a stenotype machine.

Job placement counselors at community colleges can be helpful in finding that first job. Also, try looking in the Yellow Pages of the phone books in the areas that you are interested in working. Don't forget, the Internet is often rich with job boards and employment information for all careers, including court reporting.

ADVANCEMENT

Skilled court reporters may be promoted to a larger court system or to an otherwise more demanding position, with an accompanying increase in pay and prestige. Those working for a freelance company may be hired permanently by a city, county, state, or federal court. Those with experience working in a government position may choose to become a freelance court reporter and thereby have greater job flexibility and perhaps earn more money. Those with the necessary training, experience, and business skills may decide to open their own freelance reporting company.

According to a study funded by the National Court Reporters Foundation, court reporters advance by assuming more responsibility and greater skill levels; that gives the court reporter credibility in the eyes of the professionals in the legal system. Those advanced responsibilities include real-time reporting, coding and cross-referencing the official record, assisting others in finding specific information quickly, and helping the judge and legal counsel with procedural matters.

Court reporters can also follow alternative career paths as captioning experts, legal and medical transcriptionists, and cyber-conference moderators.

DEMAND FOR REAL-TIME COURT REPORTING

Most transcripts are delivered to lawyers and others after the court has adjourned and the court reporter has transcribed, edited, proofread, copied, and bound the material. Now, however, more and more lawyers and judges are requesting immediate transcript information while still in court. *Real-time court reporters* use computer-aided transcription programs to deliver instantaneous recording that is presented on a screen in the courtroom. The written words are produced only seconds after they are spoken. If the judge or lawyer wants to review something said a few minutes—or even seconds—earlier, the real-time court reporter can show this rough draft at any time during the trial or hearing. Real-time court reporters can also provide the lawyer or judge with a disk of the up-to-the-second transcript during court recesses or other breaks. Real-time reporting is also helpful to the hearing-impaired; they can follow what is being said in court almost as quickly as the words are spoken.

■ EARNINGS

Earnings vary according to the skill, speed, and experience of the court reporter, as well as geographic location. Those who are employed by large court systems generally earn more than their counterparts in smaller communities. The median annual income for all court reporters was $41,550 in 2002, according to findings by the U.S. Department of Labor. Ten percent of reporters were paid less than $23,120 annually, and 10 percent had annual earnings of more than $73,440, also in 2002. Incomes can be even higher depending on the reporter's skill level, length of service, and the amount of time the reporter works. Official court reporters not only earn a salary, but also a per-page fee for transcripts. Freelance court reporters are paid by the job and also per page for transcripts.

Court reporters who work in small communities or as freelancers may not be able to work full-time. Successful court reporters with jobs in business environments may earn more than those in courtroom settings, but such positions carry less job security.

Those working for the government or full-time for private companies usually receive health insurance and other benefits, such as paid vacations and retirement pensions. Freelancers may or may not receive health insurance or other benefits, depending on the policies of their agencies.

■ WORK ENVIRONMENT

Offices and courtrooms are usually pleasant places to work. Under normal conditions, a court reporter can expect to work a standard 40 hours per week. During lengthy trials or other complicated proceedings, court reporters often work much longer hours. They must be on hand before and after the court is actually in session and must wait while a jury is deliberating. A court reporter often must be willing to work irregular hours, including some evenings. Court reporters must be able to spend long hours transcribing testimony with complete accuracy. There may be some travel involved, especially for freelance reporters and court reporters who are working for a traveling circuit judge. Normally, a court reporter will experience some down time without any transcript orders and then be hit all at once with several. This uneven workflow can cause the court reporter to have odd hours at times.

Court reporters spend time working with finances as well. Paperwork for record-keeping and tracking invoices, income, and expenses is part of the job.

Long hours of sitting in the same position can be tiring and court reporters may be bothered by eye and neck strain. There is also the risk of repetitive motion injuries, including carpal tunnel syndrome. The constant pressure to keep up and remain accurate can be stressful as well.

■ OUTLOOK

The opportunities for court reporters are plentiful and continue to evolve to meet the needs of the legal system, according to the National Court Reporters Association (NCRA). The U.S. Department of Labor predicts that employment of court reporters should grow at a rate about as fast as average through 2012. The rising number of criminal court cases and civil lawsuits will cause both state and federal court systems to expand. Job opportunities should be greatest in and around large metropolitan areas, but qualified court reporters should be able to find work in most parts of the country. Court reporters can also find work using their skills to produce captioning for television programs, which is a federal requirement for all new television programming by 2006.

As always, job prospects will be best for those with the most training and experience. Because of the reliance on computers in many aspects of this job, computer experience and training are important. Court reporters who are certified—especially with the highest level of certification—will have the most opportunities to choose from.

The NCRA currently has approximately 27,000 members. As court reporters continue to use cutting-edge technology to make court transcripts more usable and accurate, the NCRA and the field itself should continue to grow.

■ FOR MORE INFORMATION

For information on certification and court reporting careers, contact

National Court Reporters Association
8224 Old Courthouse Road
Vienna, VA 22182-3808
Tel: 800-272-6272
Email: msic@ncrahq.org
http://www.verbatimreporters.com

Information on the Frank Sarli Memorial Scholarship and the Santo J. Aurelio Award for Altruism is available from

National Court Reporters Foundation
8224 Old Courthouse Road
Vienna, VA 22182-3808
Tel: 800-272-6272
Email: msic@ncrahq.org
http://www.verbatimreporters.com/ncrf

For tips on preparing for the certification exams, and for other career information, contact

National Verbatim Reporters Association
207 Third Avenue
Hattiesburg, MS 39401
Tel: 601-582-4345
Email: nvra@aol.com
http://www.nvra.org

Creative Arts Therapists

■ OVERVIEW

Creative arts therapists treat and rehabilitate people with mental, physical, and emotional disabilities. They use the creative processes of music, art, dance/movement, drama, psychodrama, and poetry in their therapy sessions to determine the underlying causes of problems and to help patients achieve therapeutic goals. Creative arts therapists usually specialize in one particular type of therapeutic activity. The specific objectives of the therapeutic activities vary according to the needs of the patient and the setting of the therapy program.

■ HISTORY

Creative arts therapy programs are fairly recent additions to the health care field. Although many theories of mental and physical therapy have existed for centuries, it has been only in the last 70 years or so that health care professionals have truly realized the healing powers of music, art, dance, and other forms of artistic self-expression.

Art therapy is based on the idea that people who can't discuss their problems with words must have another outlet for self-expression. In the early 1900s, psychiatrists began to look more closely at their patients' artwork, realizing that there could be links between the emotional or psychological illness and the art. Sigmund Freud even did some preliminary research into the artistic expression of his patients.

In the 1930s, art educators discovered that children often expressed their thoughts better with pictures and role-playing than they did through verbalization. Children often don't know the words they need to explain how they feel or how to make their needs known to adults. Researchers began to look into art as a way to treat children who were traumatized by abuse, neglect, illness, or other physical or emotional disabilities.

During and after World War II, the Department of Veterans Affairs (VA) developed and organized various art, music, and dance activities for patients in VA hospitals. These activities had a dramatic effect on the physical and mental well-being of World War II veterans, and creative arts therapists began to help treat and rehabilitate patients in other health care settings.

Because of early breakthroughs with children and veterans, the number of arts therapists has increased greatly over the past few decades, and the field has expanded to include drama, psychodrama, and poetry, in addition to the original areas of music, art, and dance. Today, creative arts therapists work with diverse populations of patients in a wide range of facilities, and they focus on the specific needs of a vast spectrum of disorders and disabilities. Colleges and universities offer degree programs in many types of therapies, and

QUICK FACTS

SCHOOL SUBJECTS
Art
Music
Theater/dance

PERSONAL SKILLS
Artistic
Helping/teaching

WORK ENVIRONMENT
Primarily indoors
Primarily one location

MINIMUM EDUCATION LEVEL
Master's degree

SALARY RANGE
$15,000 to $35,000 to $81,000+

CERTIFICATION OR LICENSING
Required by all states

OUTLOOK
About as fast as the average

DOT
076

GOE
14.06.01

NOC
3144

O*NET-SOC
N/A

national associations for registering and certifying creative arts therapists work to monitor training programs and to ensure the professional integrity of the therapists working in the various fields.

■ THE JOB

Tapping a power related to dreaming, creative arts therapy taps into the subconscious and gives people a mode of expression in an uncensored environment. This is important because before patients can begin to heal, they must first identify their feelings. Once they recognize their feelings, they can begin to develop an understanding of the relationship between their feelings and their behavior.

The main goal of a creative arts therapist is to improve the client's physical, mental, and emotional health. Before therapists begin any treatment, they meet with a team of other health care professionals. After determining the strength, limitations, and interests of their client, they create a program to promote positive change and growth. The creative arts therapist continues to confer with the other health care workers as the program progresses, and alters the program according to the client's progress. How these goals are reached depends on the unique specialty of the therapist in question.

"It's like sitting in the woods waiting for a fawn to come out." That is how Barbara Fish, former Director of Activity Therapy for the Illinois Department of Mental Health and Developmental Disabilities, Chicago Metropolitan and Adolescent Services, describes her experience as she waits patiently for a sexually abused patient to begin to trust her. The patient is extraordinarily frightened because

of the traumatic abuse she has suffered. This may be the first time in the patient's life that she is in an environment of acceptance and support. It may take months or even years before the patient begins to trust the therapist, "come out of the woods," and begin to heal.

In some cases, especially when the clients are adolescents, they may have become so detached from their feelings that they can physically act out without consciously knowing the reasons for their behavior. This detachment from their emotions creates a great deal of psychological pain. With the help of a creative arts therapist, clients can begin to communicate their subconscious feelings both verbally and nonverbally. They can express their emotions in a variety of ways without having to name them.

Creative arts therapists work with all age groups: young children, adolescents, adults, and senior citizens. They can work in individual, group, or family sessions. The approach of the therapist, however, depends on the specific needs of the client or group. For example, if an individual is feeling overwhelmed by too many options or stimuli, the therapist may give him or her only a plain piece of paper and a pencil to work with that day.

Fish has three ground rules for her art therapy sessions with disturbed adolescents: respect yourself, respect other people, and respect property. The therapy groups are limited to five patients per group. She begins the session by asking each person in the group how he or she is feeling that day. By carefully listening to their responses, a theme may emerge that will determine the direction of the therapy. For example, if anger is reoccurring in their statements, Fish may ask them to draw a line down the center of a piece of paper. On one side, she will ask them to draw how anger looks and on the other side how feeling sad looks. Then, once the drawing is complete, she will ask them to compare the two pictures and see that their anger may be masking their feelings of sadness, loneliness, and disappointment. As patients begin to recognize their true feelings, they develop better control of their behavior.

To reach their patients, creative arts therapists can use a variety of mediums, including visual art, music, dance, drama, or poetry or other kinds of creative writing. Creative arts therapists usually specialize in a specific medium, becoming a music therapist, drama therapist, dance therapist, art therapist, or poetry therapist. "In my groups we use poetry and creative writing," Fish explains. "We do all kinds of things to get at what is going on at an unconscious level."

Music therapists use musical lessons and activities to improve a patient's self-confidence and self-awareness, to relieve states of depression, and to improve physical dexterity. For example, a music therapist treating a patient with Alzheimer's might play songs from the patient's past in order to stimulate long- and short-term memory, soothe feelings of agitation, and increase a sense of reality.

Art therapists use art in much the same manner. The art therapist may encourage and teach patients to express their thoughts, feelings, and anxieties via sketching, drawing, painting, or sculpting. Art therapy is especially helpful in revealing patterns of domestic abuse in families. Children involved in such a situation may depict scenes of family life with violent details or portray a certain family member as especially frightening or threatening.

Dance/movement therapists develop and conduct dance/movement sessions to help improve the physical, mental, and emotional health of their patients. Dance and movement therapy is also used as a way of assessing a patient's progress toward reaching therapeutic goals.

There are other types of creative arts therapists as well. *Drama therapists* use role-playing, pantomime (the telling of a story by the use of expressive body or facial movements), puppetry, improvisation, and original scripted dramatization to evaluate and treat patients. *Poetry therapists* and *bibliotherapists*, use the written and spoken word to treat patients.

■ REQUIREMENTS
High School
To become a creative arts therapist, you will need a bachelor's degree, so take a college preparatory curriculum while in high school. You should become as proficient as possible with the methods and tools related to the type of creative arts therapy you wish to pursue. When therapists work with patients they must be able to concentrate completely on the patient rather than on learning how to use tools or techniques. For example, if you want to become involved in music therapy, you need to be familiar with musical instruments as well as music theory. A good starting point for a music therapist is to study piano or guitar.

In addition to courses such as drama, art, music, and English, you should consider taking an introductory class in psychology. Also, a communication class will give you an understanding of the various ways people communicate, both verbally and nonverbally.

Postsecondary Training
To become a creative arts therapist you must earn at least a bachelor's degree, usually in the area in which you wish to specialize. For example, those studying to be art therapists typically have undergraduate degrees in studio art, art education, or psychology with a strong emphasis on art courses as well.

In most cases, however, you will also need a graduate degree before you can gain certification as a professional or advance in your chosen field. Requirements for admission to graduate schools vary by program, so you would be wise to contact the graduate programs you are interested in to find out about their admissions policies. For some fields you may be required to submit a portfolio of your work along with the written application. Professional organizations can be a good source of information regarding high-quality programs. For example, both the American Art Therapy Association and the American Music Therapy Association provide lists of schools that meet their standards for approval. (Contact information for both associations are listed at the end of this article.)

In graduate school, your study of psychology and the arts field you are interested in will be in-depth. Classes for someone seeking a master's in art therapy, for example, may include group psychotherapy, foundation of creativity theory, assessment and treatment planning, and art therapy presentation. In addition to classroom study you will also complete an internship or supervised practicum (that is, work with clients). Depending on your program, you may also need to write a thesis or present a final artistic project before receiving your degree.

Certification or Licensing
Typically, the nationally recognized association or certification board specific to your field of choice offers registration and certification. For example, the Art Therapy Credentials Board (ATCB), offers registration and certification to art therapists, and the American Dance Therapy Association offers registration to dance therapists. In general, requirements for registration include completing an approved therapy program and having a certain amount of experience working with clients. Requirements for higher levels of registration or certification generally involve having additional work experience and passing a written exam.

For a specific example, consider the certification process for an art therapist: An art therapist may receive

---

WORDS TO KNOW

Acting out: Uncontrolled, usually aggressive behavior in which a patient responds to emotionally stressful experiences.

Creativity coach: A person hired by a company or individual to help nurture the creative process.

Impulsive disorder: Any disorder in which a person acts primarily on impulse without considering the consequences of the action.

Portfolio: A collection of artwork used to provide examples of an artist's skills and techniques.

INTERVIEW

Deborah Farber is chair of the art therapy department at the School of Visual Arts in New York City. She has also worked as an art therapist for over 20 years.

Q. What are the main responsibilities of your job?

A. I developed, implemented, and presently manage a New York State accredited master of professional studies program in art therapy. This full-time 60-credit graduate program features two tracks of study: addictionology and challenged populations. My responsibilities include curriculum development, selection and training of faculty, recruitment of students, fiscal management, materials selection, and group supervision. I also coordinate the annual fall art therapy conference and spring exhibit, as well as conduct meetings, workshops, and seminars on art therapy.

I also teach a graduate course entitled Methods and Materials in Art Therapy. This is a hands-on course, which enables students to examine the use of paints, inks, organic art processes, sculpture materials, and other traditional and nontraditional art media and their uses with specific client populations.

Q. What is your typical work day like? Do you interact with many people, whether in person or over the phone/email?

A. My typical work day involves meetings with graduate students about their coursework and/or the clients with whom they work through their internships. I also may advise art therapy professors on teaching challenges, student crises, curriculum issues, etc. I often sit in on classes to observe how professors teach art therapy to their students and make suggestions about how they might improve some of their lessons. Sometimes I give workshops on particular techniques and how to utilize them with specific types of clients who are having difficulty with family, work, or personal issues. Sometimes problems feel as though they are beyond words; the use of art therapy enables individuals to express themselves through the language of art.

Q. What is your work environment like? Does your job involve travel?

A. I work in a newly renovated 3500-square-foot space with three large classrooms and an expansive open studio, which has an observation area for the training of students in working with clients in art therapy. Students have the opportunity to lead groups and to observe fellow classmates and professionals in group leadership. Clients of all ages and backgrounds are invited to participate in art therapy sessions in the open studio. This studio, as well as the classrooms, are designed and operated based on the humanistic philosophy that art therapy and arttherapy training should be a collaboration mediated by artistic processes and human interactions. This environment and all that happens within it reinforce the notion that by treating clients with respect and dignity and introducing them to art as a special language for self-expression, the power of the creative process can be utilized as a form of therapeutic healing. This enables all individuals to better access and understand their problems and potentials.

I often travel to art therapy conferences to either learn more about how art therapy can be utilized or to present lectures about art therapy.

Q. What are the pros and cons of your job?

A. Some of the pros of my job are working with people of all backgrounds and ages, teaching creative individuals how to become art therapists, and working with professors who are excited about teaching art therapy to aspiring therapists. I enjoy interviewing prospective students and then having the privilege of teaching them and watching them grow and develop as therapists.

I have developed a graduate program in art therapy and have enjoyed the fact that it is successful, and that students have become therapists as a result of something that I created by maintaining high ethical and humanistic standards for art therapists.

The cons include extensive paperwork, especially that which involves the budget.

Q. What did you study in college and graduate school? Did your education and prior career experiences prepare and/or train you for this position?

A. I have a bachelor's degree in psychology with a minor in art and a master's degree in art therapy and creativity development. I also have graduate training in counseling and substance-abuse work. My education and internships prepared me to become an art therapist. I worked for many years as a therapist with psychiatric adolescents and adults, substance abusers and their families, as well as with developmentally challenged populations. I was a director of therapeutic activities (art, music, dance, psychodrama) in a private psychiatric hospital. I also had a private practice, in which I worked with all types of individuals.

After working as both an art therapist and a professor of art therapy for over a decade, I became the chair of the undergraduate art therapy department at the School of Visual Arts. I then developed a graduate training program in art therapy at the School of Visual Arts. All of my past experience in working with clients and students did prepare me to become a chairperson, although I gained a great deal of on-the-job training in administrative tasks, etc.

INTERVIEW *(continued)*

Q. Did you complete any internships in preparation for your career?

A. I completed several internships in art therapy. Two of them were with psychiatric adult and adolescent populations and one was with substance abusers and their families.

Q. What is the outlook for growth and advancement in this field?

A. The field of art therapy is rapidly expanding. In New York in December 2002, Governor Pataki signed a bill to make licenses mandatory for all psychotherapists. This will help to regulate the field and insure that therapists are well trained, have taken board certification examinations, and have proper credentialing in their field of expertise. There has been a significant increase in the number of art therapists as well as the range of settings in which they are employed. New employment opportunities have been developed with populations such as physically challenged individuals, the mentally ill, substance abusers, the homeless, AIDS and hospice clients, and victims of war, domestic violence, and other forms of trauma. New contexts also yield changes in the practice of art therapy. In short, this innovative profession provides valuable and often unique contributions to the care of people living with mental and physical disabilities.

Q. What would you say are the most important skills and personal qualities for someone in your career?

A. Art therapy is a discipline for artists. It is a method of treatment in which the unique blending of art and psychology is utilized as a way of exploring individual problems and potentials. Through the use of therapeutic art experiences, physical, emotional and/or learning skills can be developed. The creative process, experienced on its deepest levels, provides the artist with the sensitivity to understand others. There is great satisfaction in functioning as both a therapist and artist, in utilizing one's talents to help others achieve personal growth through creative expression. In order to be an effective art therapist, one must have excellent listening skills, patience, a desire to help others, and an understanding of the healing potential of the creative process.

Q. What advice would you give to someone who is interested in pursuing this type of career?

A. Get an excellent undergraduate and graduate education in behavioral science (psychology), art, and art therapy. Make sure that you partake in internships with excellent supervisors in diverse settings.

the designation Art Therapist Registered (ART) from the ATCB after completing a graduate program and having some experience working with clients. The next level, then, is to become an Art Therapist Registered-Board Certified (ART-BC) by passing a written exam. To retain certification status, therapists must complete a certain amount of continuing education.

Many registered creative arts therapists also hold additional licenses in other fields, such as social work, education, mental health, or marriage and family therapy. In some states, creative arts therapists need licensing depending on their place of work. For specific information on licensing in your field, you will need to check with your state's licensing board. Creative arts therapists are also often members of other professional associations, including the American Psychological Association, the American Association of Marriage and Family Therapists, and the American Counseling Association.

Other Requirements

To succeed in this line of work, you should have a strong desire to help others seek positive change in their lives. All types of creative arts therapists must be able to work well with other people—both patients and other health pro-

fessionals—in the development and implementation of therapy programs. You must have the patience and the stamina to teach and practice therapy with patients for whom progress is often very slow because of their various physical and emotional disorders. A therapist must always keep in mind that even a tiny amount of progress might be extremely significant for some patients and their families. A good sense of humor is also a valuable trait.

■ EXPLORING

There are many ways to explore the possibility of a career as a creative arts therapist. Write to professional associations for information on therapy careers. Talk with people working in the creative arts therapy field and perhaps arrange to observe a creative arts therapy session. Look for part-time or summer jobs or volunteer at a hospital, clinic, nursing home, or any of a number of health care facilities.

A summer job as an aide at a camp for disabled children, for example, may help provide insight into the nature of creative arts therapy, including both its rewards and demands. Such experience can be very valuable in deciding if you are suited to the inherent frustrations of a therapy career.

EMPLOYERS

Creative arts therapists usually work as members of an interdisciplinary health care team that may include physicians, nurses, social workers, psychiatrists, and psychologists. Although often employed in hospitals, therapists also work in rehabilitation centers, nursing homes, day treatment facilities, shelters for battered women, pain and stress management clinics, substance abuse programs, hospices, and correctional facilities. Others maintain their own private practices. Many creative arts therapists work with children in grammar and high schools, either as therapists or art teachers. Some arts therapists teach or conduct research in the creative arts at colleges and universities.

STARTING OUT

After earning a bachelor's degree in a particular field, you should complete your certification, which may include an internship or assistantship. Unpaid training internships often can lead to a first job in the field. Graduates can use the placement office at their college or university to help them find positions in the creative arts therapy field. Many professional associations also compile lists of job openings to assist their members.

Creative arts therapists who are new to the field might consider doing volunteer work at a nonprofit community organization, correctional facility, or neighborhood association to gain some practical experience. Therapists who want to start their own practice can host group therapy sessions in their homes. Creative arts therapists may also wish to associate with other members of the alternative health care field in order to gain experience and build a client base.

ADVANCEMENT

With more experience, therapists can move into supervisory, administrative, and teaching positions. Often, the supervision of interns can resemble a therapy session. The interns will discuss their feelings and ask questions they may have regarding their work with clients. How did they handle their clients? What were the reactions to what their clients said or did? What could they be doing to help more? The supervising therapist helps the interns become competent creative arts therapists.

Many therapists have represented the profession internationally. Barbara Fish was invited to present her paper, "Art Therapy with Children and Adolescents," at the University of Helsinki. Additionally, Fish spoke in Finland at a three-day workshop exploring the use and effectiveness of arts therapy with children and adolescents. Raising the public and professional awareness of creative arts therapy is an important concern for many therapists.

EARNINGS

A therapist's annual salary depends on experience, level of training, and education. Working on a hospital staff or being self-employed also affects annual income. According to the American Art Therapy Association (AATA), entry-level art therapists earn annual salaries of approximately $25,000. Median annual salaries range from $28,000 to $38,000, and AATA reports that top earnings for salaried administrators ranged from $40,000 and $60,000 annually. Those who have Ph.D.s and are licensed for private practice can earn between $75 and $90 per hour, according to AATA; however, professional expenses such as insurance and office rental must be paid by those in private practice.

The American Music Therapy Association reported average annual salaries for music therapists as $34,893 in 2000. Salaries varied from that average by region, most by less than $2,000 a year, with the highest average salaries reported in the New England states at $41,600. Salaries reported by its members ranged from $15,000 to $81,000. The average annual earnings for music therapists with more than 20 years of professional experience was $43,306 in 2000.

The annual salary for therapists working for the government is determined by the agency they work for, their level of education and experience, and their responsibilities. An August 2002 job posting by the Delaware Department of Health & Social Services, for example, advertised an opening for a certified creative arts therapist that offered the salary range of $26,094 to $32,618, based on the applicant's qualifications.

Benefits depend on the employer but generally include paid vacation time, health insurance, and paid sick days. Those who are in private practice must provide their own benefits.

WORK ENVIRONMENT

Most creative arts therapists work a typical 40-hour, five-day workweek; at times, however, they may have to work extra hours. The number of patients under a therapist's care depends on the specific employment setting. Although many therapists work in hospitals, they may also be employed in such facilities as clinics, rehabilitation centers, children's homes, schools, and nursing homes. Some therapists maintain service contracts with several facilities. For instance, a therapist might work two days a week at a hospital, one day at a nursing home, and the rest of the week at a rehabilitation center.

Most buildings are pleasant, comfortable, and clean places in which to work. Experienced creative arts therapists might choose to be self-employed, working with patients in their own studios. In such a case, the therapist might work more irregular hours to accommodate patient schedules. Other therapists might maintain a combination of service contract work with one or more facilities in addition to a private caseload of clients referred to them by other health care professionals. Whether therapists work on service contracts with various facilities or maintain private practices, they must deal with all of the business and administrative details and worries that go along with being self-employed.

▣ OUTLOOK

The American Art Therapy Association notes that this is a growing field. Demand for new therapists is created as medical professionals and the general public become aware of the benefits gained through art therapies. Although enrollment in college therapy programs is increasing, new graduates are usually able to find jobs. In cases where an individual is unable to find a full-time position, a therapist might obtain service contracts for part-time work at several facilities.

Job openings in facilities such as nursing homes should continue to increase as the elderly population grows over the next few decades. Advances in medical technology and the recent practice of early discharge from hospitals should also create new opportunities in managed care facilities, chronic pain clinics, and cancer care facilities. The demand for therapists of all types should continue to increase as more people become aware of the need to help disabled patients in creative ways. Some drama therapists and psychodramatists are also finding employment opportunities outside of the usual health care field. Such therapists might conduct therapy sessions at corporate sites to enhance the personal effectiveness and growth of employees.

▣ FOR MORE INFORMATION

For more detailed information about your field of interest, contact the following organizations:

American Art Therapy Association

1202 Allanson Road
Mundelein, IL 60060-3808
Tel: 888-290-0878
Email: info@arttherapy.org
http://www.arttherapy.org

American Dance Therapy Association

2000 Century Plaza, Suite 108
10632 Little Patuxent Parkway
Columbia, MD 21044
Tel: 410-997-4040
Email: info@adta.org
http://www.adta.org

American Music Therapy Association

8455 Colesville Road, Suite 1000
Silver Spring, MD 20910
Tel: 301-589-3300
Email: info@musictherapy.org
http://www.musictherapy.org

American Society of Group Psychotherapy and Psychodrama

301 North Harrison Street, Suite 508
Princeton, NJ 08540
Tel: 609-452-1339
Email: asgpp@asgpp.org
http://www.asgpp.org

National Association for Drama Therapy

15 Post Side Lane
Pittsford, NY 14534
Tel: 585-381-5618
Email: info1@nadt.org
http://www.nadt.org

National Association for Poetry Therapy

12950 Fifth Street, NW
Pembroke Pines, FL 33028
Tel: 866-844-NAPT
Email: info@poetrytherapy.org
http://www.poetrytherapy.org

For an overview of the various types of art therapy, visit the NCATA website:

National Coalition of Arts Therapies Associations (NCATA)

c/o AMTA
8455 Colesville Road, Suite 1000
Silver Spring, MD 20910
Tel: 201-224-9146
http://www.nccata.org

Credit Analysts

▣ OVERVIEW

Credit analysts analyze financial information to evaluate the amount of risk involved in lending money to businesses or individuals. They contact banks, credit associations, and others to obtain credit information and prepare a written report of findings used to recommend credit limits. There are approximately 60,000 credit analysts employed in the United States.

■ HISTORY

Only 50 or 75 years ago, lending money was based mainly on a person's reputation. Money was lent after a borrower talked with friends and business acquaintances. Now, of course, much more financial background information is demanded. The use of credit cards and other forms of borrowing has skyrocketed in the last several years, and today, only accepted forms of accounting are used to determine if a loan applicant is a good risk. As business and financial institutions have grown more complex, the demand for professional credit analysis has also expanded.

■ THE JOB

Credit analysts typically concentrate on one of two different areas. *Commercial* and *business analysts* evaluate risks in business loans; *consumer credit analysts* evaluate personal loan risks. In both cases an analyst studies financial documents such as a statement of assets and liabilities submitted by the person or company seeking the loan and consults with banks and other financial institutions that have had previous financial relationships with the applicant. Credit analysts prepare, analyze, and approve loan requests and help borrowers fill out applications.

The scope of work involved in a credit check depends in large part on the size and type of the loan requested. A background check on a $3,000 car loan, for example, is much less detailed than on a $400,000 commercial improvement loan for an expanding business. In both cases, financial statements and applicants will be checked by the credit analyst, but the larger loan will entail a much closer look at economic trends to determine if there is a market for the product being produced and the likelihood of the business failing. Because of these responsibilities, many credit analysts work solely with commercial loans.

In studying a commercial loan application, a credit analyst is interested in determining if the business or corporation is well managed and financially secure and if the existing economic climate is favorable for the operation's success. To do this, a credit analyst examines balance sheets and operating statements to determine the assets and liabilities of a company, its net sales, and its profits or losses. An analyst must be familiar with accounting and bookkeeping methods to ensure that the applicant company is operating under accepted accounting principles. A background check of the applicant company's leading officials is also done to determine if they personally have any outstanding loans. An on-site visit by the analyst may also be necessary to compare how the company's operations stack up against those of its competitors.

Analyzing economic trends to determine market conditions is another responsibility of the credit analyst. To do this, the credit analyst computes dozens of ratios to show how successful the company is in relation to similar businesses. Profit-and-loss statements, collection procedures, and a host of other factors are analyzed. This ratio analysis can also be used to measure how successful a particular industry is likely to be, given existing market considerations. Computer programs are used to highlight economic trends and interpret other important data.

The credit analyst always provides a findings report to bank executives. This report includes a complete financial history of the applicant and usually concludes with a recommendation on the loan amount, if any, that should be advanced.

■ REQUIREMENTS
High School

If you are interested in this career, take courses in mathematics, economics, business, and accounting in high school. You should also take English courses to develop sound oral and written language skills. Computer courses will help you to become computer literate, learn software programs, understand their applications to particular fields, and gain familiarity with accessing electronic information.

Postsecondary Training

Credit analysts usually have at least a bachelor's degree in accounting, finance, or business administration. Those who want to move up in the field often go on to obtain master's degrees in one of these subjects. Undergraduate course work should include business management, economics, statistics, and accounting. In addition, keep honing your computer skills. Some employers provide new hires with on-the-job training involving both classroom work and hands-on experience.

QUICK FACTS

SCHOOL SUBJECTS
Business
Computer science
Mathematics

PERSONAL SKILLS
Communication/ideas
Leadership/management

WORK ENVIRONMENT
Primarily indoors
Primarily one location

MINIMUM EDUCATION LEVEL
Bachelor's degree

SALARY RANGE
$26,250 to $49,530 to
$107,940+

CERTIFICATION OR LICENSING
None available

OUTLOOK
About as fast as the average

DOT
160

GOE
13.02.04

NOC
N/A

O*NET-SOC
13-2041.00

Other Requirements

To be a credit analyst, you should have an aptitude for mathematics and be adept at organizing, assessing, and reporting data. You must be able to analyze complex problems and devise resourceful solutions. Credit analysts also need strong interpersonal skills. You must be able to interview loan applicants and communicate effectively, establish solid working relationships with customers as well as co-workers, and clearly relate the results of your work.

■ EXPLORING

For the latest information on the credit management industry, check out newsgroups and Web pages on the Internet that are related to this field. The Credit Management Information and Support website, http://www.creditworthy.com, offers informative interviews with people in the field and advice for breaking into the business. This site also has a section that describes educational resources and offers an online course on the basics of business credit. The National Association of Credit Management website, http://www.nacm.org, has links to other industry sites.

Consider a position as treasurer for student council or other student-run organizations. This will introduce you to the responsibilities associated with managing money. Or explore a part-time job as a bank clerk, teller, or customer service representative that will familiarize you with banking procedures. This is also a good way to network with professionals in the banking field. Various clubs and organizations may have opportunities for volunteers to develop experience working with budgets and financial statements. Join or start a business club at your school. Local institutions and small or single-owner businesses may welcome students interested in learning more about financial operations.

■ EMPLOYERS

Credit analysts are employed by banks, credit unions, credit agencies, business credit institutions, credit bureaus, corporations, and loan companies. They are also employed by hotels, hospitals, and department stores. Approximately 60,000 credit analysts are employed in the United States.

■ STARTING OUT

Although some people enter the field with a high school or two-year degree, most entry-level positions go to college graduates with degrees in fields such as accounting, finance, economics, and business administration. Credit analysts receive much of their formal training and learn specific procedures and requirements on the job. Many employees also rise through the ranks via other positions such as teller or customer service representative prior to becoming a credit analyst. Newspaper want ads, school placement services, and direct application to specific employers are all ways of tracking down that first job.

■ ADVANCEMENT

Credit analysts generally advance to supervisory positions. However, promotion and salary potential are limited, and many employees often choose to leave a company for better-paying positions elsewhere. After three to five years of credit work, a skilled credit analyst can expect a promotion to credit manager and ultimately chief credit executive. Responsibilities grow to include training other credit personnel, coordinating the credit department with other internal operations, and managing relations with customers and financial institutions.

■ EARNINGS

Salaries of credit analysts depend on the individual's experience and education. The size of the financial institution is also a determining factor: Large banks tend to pay more than smaller operations. Salaries also increase with the number of years in the field and with a particular company. According to the U.S. Bureau of Labor Statistics' *2002 National Occupational Employment and Wage Estimates,* credit analysts had a mean annual income of $49,530 in 2002. The lowest paid 10 percent earned less than $26,250, and the highest paid 10 percent earned more than $79,070. Salary.com, a Web-based recruiting firm providing salary information, reports that, in 2002, a credit analyst just starting out may earn approximately $28,475 per year and with up to two years' experience may earn a median annual salary of $32,895. Salary.com also reports that analysts with at least five years of experience had a median annual income of approximately $44,920. Senior credit analysts or credit analysis managers had median earnings of approximately $84,725 nationwide, with the top quarter earning about $107,940 or more per year. Those in senior positions often have advanced degrees.

As an added perk, many banks offer their credit analysts free checking privileges and lower interest rates on personal loans. Other benefits include health insurance, sick and vacation pay, and retirement plans.

■ WORK ENVIRONMENT

Most credit analysts work in typical corporate office settings that are well lighted and air conditioned in the summertime. Credit analysts can expect to work a 40-hour week, but they may have to put in overtime if a project has a tight deadline. A commercial credit analyst may have to travel to the business or corporation that is seeking a loan in order to prepare the agreement. Credit analysts can expect heavy caseloads. Respondents to the annual survey of the National Association of Credit Management reported handling 250 to 2,000 active accounts per year.

A credit analyst should be able to spend long hours behind a desk quietly reading and analyzing financial reports. Attention to detail is critical. Credit analysts can expect to work in high-pressure situations, with loans of millions of dollars dependent on their analysis.

■ OUTLOOK

As the field of cash management grows along with the economy and the population, banks and other financial institutions will need to hire credit analysts. According to the U.S. Department of Labor, employment in this field is expected to grow about as fast as the average through 2012. Credit analysts are crucial to the success and profitability of banks, and the number, variety, and complexity of credit applications are on the rise. Opportunities should be best for those with strong educational backgrounds and those living in urban areas that tend to have the largest and greatest number of banks and other financial institutions.

Credit analysts are particularly busy when interest rates drop and applications for loans surge. Job security is influenced by the local economy and business climate. However, loans are a major source of income for banks, and credit officers are less likely than most workers to lose their jobs in an economic downturn.

Information technology is affecting the field of credit analysis as public financial information, as well as economic and market research, becomes more accessible via the Internet. Credit professionals now have a broader range of data available upon which to base decisions.

■ FOR MORE INFORMATION

For general banking industry information, contact
American Bankers Association
1120 Connecticut Avenue, NW
Washington, DC 20036
Tel: 800-226-5377
http://www.aba.com

For publications and information on continuing education and training programs for financial institution workers, contact
Bank Administration Institute
One North Franklin, Suite 1000
Chicago, IL 60606-3421

Tel: 800-224-9889
Email: info@bai.org
http://www.bai.org

For information on the industry, contact
Credit Research Foundation
8840 Columbia 100 Parkway
Columbia, MD 21045
Tel: 410-740-5499
Email: crf_info@crfonline.org
http://www.crfonline.org

For information on certification, continuing education, and the banking and credit industry, contact
National Association of Credit Management
8840 Columbia 100 Parkway
Columbia, MD 21045
Tel: 410-740-5560
Email: nacm_info@nacm.org
http://www.nacm.org

Crime Analysts

■ OVERVIEW

Crime analysts analyze patterns in criminal behavior in order to catch criminals, predict patterns and motives of criminals, and improve the responsiveness of law enforcement agencies.

■ HISTORY

Crime has always been a major social problem, especially in heavily populated areas. Police and other law enforcement officials work to detect and apprehend criminals and protect citizens from robbery, violence, and other criminal acts. They are assisted by crime analysts—civilian workers who are hired to study crime statistics and patterns in order to give law enforcement officials an extra edge in fighting crime.

The earliest crime analysts simple analyzed raw crime statistics. Today, crime analysts use new computer software, databases, and geographic information systems to predict and even prevent crimes. In recent years, crime analysis has become a popular career choice. This new technology and the emergence of community-oriented policing—which puts officers on the streets as opposed to behind a desk—have created many new opportunities for trained crime analysts.

THE JOB

Crime analysts try to uncover and piece together information about crime patterns, crime trends, and criminal suspects. It's a job that varies widely from day to day and from one state and law enforcement agency to the next. At its core is a systematic process that involves collecting, categorizing, analyzing, and sharing information in order to help the agency that a crime analyst works for to better deploy officers on the street, work through difficult investigations, and increase arrests of criminals.

The basic work of a crime analyst involves collecting crime data from a range of sources, including police reports, statewide computer databases, crime newsletters, word-of-mouth tips, and interviews with suspects. To be useful, this information is then analyzed for patterns. Crime analysts are constantly vigilant for details that are similar or familiar. In addition to specific crime data, a crime analyst might study general factors such as population density, the demographic makeup of the population, commuting patterns, economic conditions (average income, poverty level, job availability), effectiveness of law enforcement agencies, citizens' attitudes toward crime, and crime reporting practices.

"You get a feel for it after a while," says Michelle Rankin who heads a police department's crime analysis unit in Santa Clara, a town of 98,000 in northern California. She tells of reading a teletype recently that described a suspect in a bank robbery. "Something about the description of his nose and hairline rang a bell," she says. By combing through some old teletypes, she found a similar description and called the agency that had arrested the man before. In doing so, she was able to uncover the man's name and obtain a photo of him that matched a surveillance photo from the bank.

The responsibilities of crime analysts are often dependent upon the needs of their police department or law enforcement agency. One morning's tasks might include writing a profile on a particular demographic group's criminal patterns. On another day, an analyst could meet with the police chief to discuss an unusual string of local car thefts. Less frequently, the work includes going on "ride-alongs" with street cops, visiting a crime scene, or meeting with crime analysts from surrounding jurisdictions to exchange information about criminals who are plaguing the region. Occasionally, a crime analyst is pulled off of everyday responsibilities in order to work exclusively on a task force, usually focusing on a rash of violent crimes. As an ongoing responsibility, a crime analyst might be charged with tracking and monitoring "known offenders" (sex offenders, career criminals, repeat juvenile offenders, and parolees).

New computer technology has had a profound impact on the profession of crime analysis, helping it grow by leaps and bounds. In its earliest days, crime analysis simply meant gathering straight statistics on crime. Now these same statistics—coupled with specialized software—allow crime analysts to actually anticipate and prevent criminal activity.

The use of this analysis falls into three broad categories: *tactical, strategic,* and *administrative.* Tactical crime analysis aims at giving police officers and detectives prompt, in-the-field information that could lead to an arrest. These are the "hot" items that land on a crime analyst's desk, usually pertaining to specific crimes and offenders. For example, a criminal's mode of operation (M.O.) can be studied in order to predict who the likely next targets or victims will be. The police can then set up stakeouts or saturate the area with patrol cars. Tactical analysis is also used to do crime-suspect correlation, which involves identifying suspects for certain crimes based on their criminal histories.

Strategic analysis deals with finding solutions to long-range problems and crime trends. For instance, a crime analyst could create a crime trend forecast, based on current and past criminal activity, using computer software. An analyst might also perform a "manpower deployment" study to see if the police department is making the best use of its personnel. Another aspect of strategic analysis involves collating and disseminating demographic data on victims and geographic areas experiencing high crime rates so that the police are able to beef up crime prevention efforts.

Lastly, administrative analysis helps to provide policy-making information to a police department's administration. This might include a statistical study on the activity levels of police officers that would support a request for hiring more officers. Administrative work could also

QUICK FACTS

SCHOOL SUBJECTS
Computer science
English
Psychology

PERSONAL SKILLS
Helping/teaching
Technical/scientific

WORK ENVIRONMENT
Primarily indoors
Primarily multiple locations

MINIMUM EDUCATION LEVEL
Bachelor's degree

SALARY RANGE
$15,500 to $35,650 to $71,593+

CERTIFICATION OR LICENSING
Voluntary

OUTLOOK
About as fast as the average

DOT
029

GOE
04.03.02

NOC
N/A

O*NET-SOC
19-4092.00

A Typical Day for Crime Analyst Michelle Rankin

On a typical day (which she insists doesn't really exist), Michelle Rankin will write a daily bulletin after reading through numerous reports and pulling out serious items. She'll talk with detectives to see if they need some piece of information that she can help get the word out about. She sees herself as a question-and-answer unit for people in the department. "An officer might tell me about an unusual burglary, and I can search for other burglaries that have similarities." At other times, she gets wind of something herself and initiates a search. "An officer on one side of town doesn't usually know what's occurred on the other side. Since I read crime reports from all over, I can bridge the gap and piece together information that links back to the same suspect." Powerful software such as databases, spreadsheets, and geographic mapping systems help her perform certain aspects of her job. With a mapping system, for instance, Rankin can create a map that shows where Honda Accords have been stolen or where burglaries of only jewelry have occurred. This information can, in turn, be used to narrow down the list of suspects.

In order to have contact with officers working graveyard and swing shifts—as well as day shifts—Rankin works different shifts every two weeks. Building these in-house connections is the bedrock of doing good crime analysis.

include creating graphs and charts that are used in management presentations or writing a speech on local crime prevention to give to the city council.

■ REQUIREMENTS
High School

While there are still a few law enforcement agencies that will hire crime analysts with only a high school diploma, it is becoming less common. Judy Kimminau, who works for the police department in Fort Collins, Colorado, says, "Crime analysis used to be a field that a person could stray into, but most new analysts now are trained or educated specifically for the career."

"While you're finishing up high school, it pays to hone your writing skills," Michelle Rankin says. "You have to understand different styles of communicating so that you're able to write to the street cop and also to the city council." A good foundation in algebra will help with statistics classes in college. Moreover, take advantage of your school's computer lab, as basic knowledge of computers, word processing, spreadsheets, and databases is important.

Postsecondary Training

The majority of agencies require a bachelor's degree for the position of crime analyst. Rankin earned her bachelor's degree in criminal justice, but it wasn't until her senior year of college that she actually learned about the field of crime analysis. "I had been trying to figure out how I wanted to use my degree. Then a senior seminar course in crime analysis was offered—the first of its kind. It sparked my interest and I began volunteering in my instructor's unit." When a job opened in the unit, Rankin applied and was hired. Kimminau, on the other hand, learned about crime analysis in high school and designed a personalized degree in criminology accordingly. Other excellent degrees to consider include statistics, criminal justice, computer science, and sociology.

Both Rankin and Kimminau agree that an internship during college is the best way to get a foot in the door and gain on-the-job experience. "Because of lean staffing, most units rely heavily on interns for support. The best thing is to contact a unit and talk with the crime analyst there," says Kimminau. She adds that a strong candidate for an internship would be organized, computer-literate, and have a basic understanding of statistics. In her unit, interns initially begin by reading police reports, learning how to glean significant facts and patterns from them. "It's pretty exciting the first time a spark goes off and an intern says, 'Hey, there's a pattern here!'"

Certification or Licensing

Currently, only California offers a formal, state-sponsored certification program for crime analysts. Individuals take 36–40 hours of courses on subjects such as crime analysis, criminal intelligence analysis, investigative analysis, and law enforcement research methods and statistics. Certification also requires prerequisites in criminal law, a competency in computer software, and 400 hours of work experience usually earned volunteering at a police department.

The Society of Certified Criminal Analysts also offers two levels of certification: regular and lifetime. Candidates for regular certification must have two years of college education, be a working analyst, and successfully complete a written and practical test. Those who have earned the regular certification must recertify every three years. Candidates for lifetime certification must have four years of college and 10 years of "analytical experience" in the field.

Other Requirements

Crime analysts need to be inquisitive, logical, and have a good memory for what they hear and read. A willingness to dig in and do this sort of research is also important, since much of the work involves piecing together disparate bits of information. Ask Steven Gottlieb, MPA, an internationally recognized crime analysis trainer, consultant, and executive director of the Alpha Group Center for Crime and Intelligence Analysis, just who will make a good crime analyst and he laughs, "Somebody who does crossword puzzles in ink." He explains that crime analysts love the process of working with bits of data that in and of themselves mean nothing. "It's only when you put them together that a clear picture emerges," he says.

Even though crime analysts aren't out on the streets, they're immersed in the law enforcement milieu and come into contact with information that's potentially disturbing. "If a person becomes especially upset after reading reports on a murder or a child's molestation in the newspaper or after seeing a crime scene photo on television," notes Judy Kimminau, "they're probably not cut out for this line of work."

It's important to note that a crime analyst has to be willing to work in the background and not always be in the limelight. The positive side is that a crime analyst plays a significant role in all of the big cases, but doesn't have to wear a bulletproof vest in 100-degree heat or direct traffic in the rain. "You can play cop without the danger," jokes Michelle Rankin.

■ EXPLORING

There are plenty of ways that you can begin your own training and education now. First of all, get some exposure to the law enforcement community by volunteering at the local police department. Many towns have a Boy Scouts Explorers program in which students (of both sexes) work to educate themselves about law enforcement.

■ EMPLOYERS

The majority of crime analysts are employed by local and state law enforcement agencies. A great number are also hired by federal agencies such as the Federal Bureau of Investigation (FBI), the Customs Department, and the Department of Justice. In addition, some private security firms hire people with training in crime analysis.

■ STARTING OUT

While there's not a single, central clearinghouse for all crime analyst jobs, there are several places to look for listings. By becoming a member of the International Association of Crime Analysts (IACA), you'll receive a newsletter that includes job openings. Judy Kimminau also advises finding out if there's a state association of crime analysts where you live and attend meetings, if possible. However, recent graduates would be best

advised to be willing to move out of state if the job pickings are slim locally.

The key to getting a job in the field is doing an internship in college (see "Postsecondary Training"). In the past six months, Kimminau has assisted several agencies who are hiring crime analysts for the first time. "It's not unusual for recent college graduates to be hired, but all of these people had done internships." Michelle Rankin adds that a new crime analyst would have a solid shot at finding a job in a larger, established unit where he or she could volunteer first, learning from someone with greater experience.

■ ADVANCEMENT

As a broad generalization, most crime analysts are not pushing and shoving to climb the career ladder. Since theirs is often a one- or two-person, nonhierarchical unit within an agency, they more likely chose crime analysis because they relish the nature of the work itself. Obviously, advancement possibilities depend largely on the size and structure of the agency a crime analyst works for. In larger agencies, there are sometimes senior analysts, supervising analysts, or crime analysis managers. Some of these positions require a master's degree.

More often, crime analysts set their sights on increasing the impact they have on the agency and community in which they work. Michelle Rankin says she sees herself staying in Santa Clara's unit and helping to establish a

---

CRIME CONFUSION

In a field like crime analysis, there's sometimes confusion about who does what. The quickest way to tick off a crime analyst is to say something about their lab coats. (Hint: They don't wear lab coats, nor do they spend their days in laboratories.) So, here are a few professions with titles that might sound a lot like crime analyst, but are actually different careers.

- *Crime scene evidence technicians* go to the scene of the crime in order to collect and photograph relevant evidence, such as fingerprints, hairs, bullets, etc.

- *Criminalists* scientifically analyze, compare, and evaluate physical evidence in the laboratory.

- *Criminologists* study and research crime from a sociological perspective. They usually work in a university setting, rather than for a law enforcement agency.

- *Forensic psychologists* make psychological evaluations based on criminal evidence or behavior.

regional approach to crime analysis. "In the Bay Area, each agency has its own crime analysis unit and its own information system," she explains. "I'd like to work toward combining these resources and linking the individual systems."

Two careers that are closely linked to crime analysts are *criminal intelligence analyst* and *investigative analyst.* Criminal intelligence analysis involves the study of relationships between people, organizations, and events; it focuses on organized crime, money laundering, and other conspiratorial crimes. Investigative analysis attempts to uncover why a person is committing serial crimes such as murder and rape. Getting into the field of investigative analysis (sometimes called "profiling") usually requires years of experience and additional education in psychology—as well as good instincts.

■ EARNINGS

Earnings for crime analysts vary considerably, based on factors such as the location, the size of the employing agency and its financial status, and the analyst's experience. The IACA reports that salaries ranged from a low of $15,500 to a high of $71,593 in 2002. The mean salary reported was $35,650. Crime/Intelligence Analyst Supervisors averaged a salary of $44,680.

Analysts receive the same benefits as others working in the same agency. These usually include paid vacation time, sick leave, health insurance, and retirement plans.

■ WORK ENVIRONMENT

The duties of crime analysts will vary based on the requirements of the law enforcement agency they work for. Analysts ordinarily work in the office analyzing crime information; occasionally, though, they may go on a "ride-along" with police officers or visit a crime scene to gather more information. Crime scenes can often be disturbing, and crime analysts need to act in a professional manner in these situations.

Analysts are constantly in communication with police chiefs, officers in the field, and fellow crime analysts as they work on a case. They need to establish good working relationships with officers who sometimes initially resent working with a civilian employee. "Sometimes I'll come up with a good lead, but the officer on the beat doesn't take it up," Michelle Rankin says. "You need to have tough skin and focus on working with those who want to work with you."

■ OUTLOOK

As the job of the crime analyst becomes increasingly well known and as analysts' work continues to contribute to positive results for law enforcement agencies, the need for these professionals should grow. One factor that has added to the need for crime analysts is the emergence of community-oriented policing. The point of this type of policing is to get police officers out on the streets of their communities rather than doing paperwork at a desk. To do this, many agencies are hiring civilians for desk jobs, which allows more police officers to be a presence in their community. Michelle Rankin comments, "You want to put somebody behind a desk who actually wants to be there. The push in many departments is to 'civilianize' job functions so that police officers can work smarter, not harder." Crime analysis makes good use of the information that police officers collect on the streets. "With a limited number of officers, departments have to ask, 'What's the best use of their time?'" says Steven Gottlieb. "Good crime analysis helps to deploy officers in the right places at the right times."

The field is also growing because better software is becoming available. "Statistics are age-old," Gottlieb says, "but doing them by hand was cumbersome. The newest technology—like sophisticated databases and geographic mapping systems—gives us increased capabilities."

While this growth trend is expected to continue, it's important to recognize that it is still a competitive job market. Those who want to become crime analysts should be willing to move to find an agency with a job opening. They should also bear in mind that police departments are historically more likely to lay off a civilian than a street officer.

■ FOR MORE INFORMATION

For information on careers in criminology, contact
American Society of Criminology
1314 Kinnear Road
Columbus, OH 43212-1156
Tel: 614-292-9207
Email: asc41@infinet.com
http://www.asc41.com

For information on membership, contact
International Association of Crime Analysts
PMB 318
2839 Kennewick Avenue
Kennewick, WA 99336
http://www.iaca.net

For information on certification, contact
Society of Certified Criminal Analysts
73 Gordon Avenue
Lawrenceville, NJ 08648
http://www.ialeia.org/scca

Critical Care Nurses

■ OVERVIEW

Critical care nurses are specialized nurses who provide highly skilled direct patient care to critically ill patients needing intense medical treatment. Critical care nurses work not only in intensive care units (ICU) and cardiac care units (CCU) of hospitals, but also in the emergency departments, post-anesthesia recovery units, pediatric intensive care units, burn units, and neonatal intensive care units of medical facilities, as well as in other units that treat critically ill patients. According to the "Registered Nurse Population" study done by the Department of Health and Human Services, there are 403,527 nurses in the United States who care for critically ill patients in hospitals.

■ THE JOB

Critical care nursing is a very challenging job. Because medical facilities employ critical care nurses who work in various units, their job responsibilities vary; however, their main responsibility is providing highly skilled medical and post-surgical care for critically ill patients. Critical care nurses may be assigned one or two patients that they care for as opposed to being involved in the care of several patients.

Brandon Frady, a registered nurse and a certified critical care nurse, works in the pediatrics intensive care unit of an Atlanta children's hospital. He works as a bedside nurse and as a relief charge nurse, meaning that he is not only responsible for caring for his patients, but he is also in charge of the administration of the ward.

Frady is also part of the ground transport team that transports critically ill or injured children within a 150-mile radius to their center. "We are the cutting edge hospital for pediatric health care," says Frady. "We care for very sick children here and our skills are challenged on a daily basis."

Critical care nursing requires keeping up with the latest medical technology and research as well as medical treatments and procedures. "There is something new to learn every day," Frady says. "We have to learn to operate very high tech machines, and we are frequently tested on their use and operation. Plus, we need to know the latest research and treatments available for acutely ill children."

Critical care nursing is a very intense nursing specialty. Patients require constant care and monitoring, says Frady. "Many hospitals are requiring nurses to work 12-hour shifts, which can be very exhausting."

In many cases, critical care nurses are confronted with situations that require them to act immediately on the patients' behalf. The nurse must be a patient advocate, meaning that the nurse must help the patients receive the best possible care and also respect their wishes. They must also provide support and education to the patients and their families.

"Although it can be an emotionally draining job, it can also be very rewarding to know that I helped the child and family get through their medical crisis," Frady relates. "It is especially satisfying when they come back later and thank you for what you have done. The job has a lot of satisfaction."

■ REQUIREMENTS
Postsecondary Training

Critical care nurses must be registered nurses. (See Registered Nurses.) Entry-level requirements to become a critical care nurse depend on the institution, its size, whom it serves, and the availability of nurses in that specialty and geographical region. Usually nurses must have some bedside nursing experience before entering the critical care nursing field. However, some hospitals are developing graduate internship and orientation programs that allow new graduates to enter this specialty.

Certification or Licensing

There are critical care nursing certification programs available through the American Association of Critical-Care Nurses (AACN). Some institutions may require certification as a critical care nurse. In addition, registered nurses, regardless of specialty, must be licensed in order to practice in all 50 states and the District of Columbia. Licensing is obtained by passing a national exam.

Other Requirements

Critical care nurses should like working in a fast-paced environment that requires life-long learning. This is a very intense nursing field, and nurses should be able to make critical decisions quickly and intelligently. New

---

QUICK FACTS

SCHOOL SUBJECTS
Biology
Chemistry

PERSONAL SKILLS
Helping/teaching
Technical/scientific

WORK ENVIRONMENT
Primarily indoors
Primarily one location

MINIMUM EDUCATION LEVEL
Some postsecondary training

SALARY RANGE
$33,970 to $48,090 to $75,000+

CERTIFICATION OR LICENSING
Required by all states

OUTLOOK
Faster than the average

DOT
075

GOE
14.02.01

NOC
3152

O*NET-SOC
29-1111.00

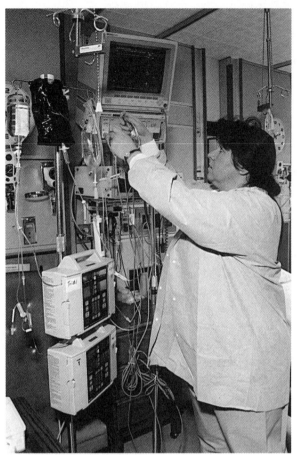

One of the many responsibilities of a critical care nurse is to adjust life-monitoring equipment for patients.

medical technology is constantly being developed and implemented. Critical care nurses should be technically inclined and able to learn how to operate new medical equipment without feeling intimidated.

Critical care nurses must be able to deal with major life and death crises. Because of the seriousness of their loved one's illness, family members and friends may be difficult to deal with and the nurse must display patience, understanding, and composure during these emotional times. The nurse must be able to communicate with the family and explain medical terminology and procedures to the patient and family so they can understand what is being done and why.

Continuing education is a must in order to stay informed of new treatment options and procedures.

EXPLORING

There are many ways to explore nursing careers. You can visit nursing websites, read books on careers in nursing, or talk with your high school guidance counselor or teacher about the career or ask them to set up a talk by a critical care nurse.

If you are already a nursing student, you might consider becoming a student member of the AACN. This will give you access to *Critical Care Nurse, The American Journal of Critical Care,* and other association publications that discuss issues related to critical care nursing.

EMPLOYERS

Contrary to previously held beliefs that critical care nurses work only in intensive care units or cardiac care units of hospitals, today's critical care nurses work in the emergency departments, post-anesthesia recovery units, pediatric intensive care units, burn units, and neonatal intensive care units of medical facilities, as well as in other units that treat critically ill patients.

STARTING OUT

You must first become a registered nurse before you can work as a critical care nurse. Aspiring registered nurses must complete one of the three kinds of educational programs and pass the licensing examination. Registered nurses may apply for employment directly to hospitals, nursing homes, and companies and government agencies that hire nurses. Jobs can also be obtained through school placement offices, by signing up with employment agencies specializing in placement of nursing personnel, or through the state employment office. Other sources of jobs include nurses' associations, professional journals, and newspaper want ads. The AACN also has job listings on its website.

ADVANCEMENT

Administrative and supervisory positions in the nursing field go to nurses who have earned at least the bachelor of science degree in nursing. Nurses with many years of experience who are graduates of the diploma program may achieve supervisory positions, but requirements for such promotions have become more difficult in recent years and in many cases require at least the bachelor of science in nursing degree.

EARNINGS

Salary is determined by many factors, including certification and education, place of employment, shift worked, geographical location, and work experience. Findings from a 2000 survey of AACN members show the largest percentage, 39 percent, averaged between $40,000 and $54,999 annually. The next largest group, 29 percent, earned between $55,000 and $74,999. The top 8 percent made more than $75,000 annually. The U.S. Department of Labor reports the median annual salary for all registered nurses (which includes critical care nurses) was $48,090 in 2002. The lowest paid 10 percent of registered nurses made less than $33,970 per year, and the highest paid 10 percent made more than $69,670. Since critical care nurses must be registered nurses and also have additional training, their salaries should be higher on average than registered nurses who are not in the critical care area.

Flexible schedules and part-time employment opportunities are available for most nurses. Employers usually provide health and life insurance, and some offer educational reimbursements and year-end bonuses to their full-time staff.

■ WORK ENVIRONMENT

Most critical care nurses work in hospitals in the intensive care unit (ICU), the emergency department, the operating room, or some other specialty unit. Most hospital environments are clean and well lighted. Inner city hospitals may be in a less than desirable location and safety may be an issue. Generally, critical care nurses who wish to advance in their careers will find themselves working in larger hospitals or medical centers in major cities.

All nursing careers have some health and disease risks; however, adherence to health and safety guidelines greatly minimizes the chance of contracting infectious diseases such as hepatitis and AIDS. Medical knowledge and good safety measures are also needed to limit the nurse's exposure to toxic chemicals, radiation, and other hazards.

■ OUTLOOK

Nursing specialties will be in great demand in the future. The U.S. Department of Labor estimates the employment of all registered nurses will grow faster than the average through 2012. According to the AACN, a growing number of hospitals are experiencing a shortage of critical care nurses. Many hospitals needing critical care nurses are offering incentives such as sign-on bonuses. The most critical shortages are in areas that require nurses with experience and highly specialized skills. The highest increase in demand is for those critical care nurses who specialize in a specific area of care, such as cardiovascular ICU, pediatric and neonatal ICU, and open-heart recovery units. Job opportunities vary across the country and may be available in all geographic areas and in large and small hospitals.

■ FOR MORE INFORMATION

For information on nursing careers and accredited programs, contact

American Association of Colleges of Nursing
One Dupont Circle, NW, Suite 530
Washington, DC 20036
Tel: 202-463-6930
http://www.aacn.nche.edu

For information on certification and fact sheets on critical care nursing, contact

American Association of Critical-Care Nurses
101 Columbia
Aliso Viejo, CA 92656-4109
Tel: 800-899-2226
Email: info@aacn.org
http://www.aacn.org

For information on certification through AACN, visit
http://www.certcorp.org

Cruise Ship Workers

■ OVERVIEW

Cruise ship workers provide services to passengers on cruise ships. Besides assisting in the operation of the ship, they may serve food and drinks, maintain cabins and public areas, lead shipboard activities, and provide entertainment. There are over 257,000 workers employed in the U.S. cruise industry.

■ HISTORY

Before airplanes, people relied on water transportation as a means of traveling from one continent to another. The earliest ships were made of wood and used sails or oars to propel them through the water. They were replaced, in the early 19th century, with the steamship, which was invented by Robert Fulton. The first steamship's boilers heated seawater into steam; this was very economical, though it was necessary to stop the engines often to remove salt deposits. In the 20th century, ships turned to coal burning engines for power, and later oil burning engines.

North American Royal Mail Steam Packet Company, more commonly known as the Cunard Line, built the first luxury ocean liner, the *Mauretania*, in 1907. It was 790 feet in length and able to carry up to 2,000 passengers. Such vessels had ballrooms, libraries, beauty parlors, and numerous dining rooms. First class passengers had comfortable accommodations that were set apart from other passengers. Those paying the lowest fares, often called steerage, had small, cramped quarters. At this time, no matter what class fare was paid, everyone had a common priority—to travel from one continent to another. The invention of airplanes changed all this drastically. As a result, airlines affected, if not created, the cruise line industry as we know it today. It was faster, and more convenient, to travel by air; soon, most transcontinental travel was done by plane. However, people still turned to ocean travel as a vacation alternative. The Cunard Line offered customers water travel from New York to Europe on their ships, *Queen Elizabeth I* and *Queen Elizabeth II*, combined with travel by jet on the return leg of the trip.

By the 1980s all water travel on cruise lines was for leisure, rather than as transportation. This decade marked tremendous growth for the cruise industry. Cruise lines built bigger, more opulent ships, added exotic ports of call, and gave more choices regarding destination and length of travel. Today, there are cruises to fit just about every interest, taste, and budget. Many times, passengers can take advantage of air and cruise fare packages, along with a pre- or post-cruise land excursion.

■ THE JOB

Many modern cruise ships are similar to floating resorts offering fine accommodations, gourmet dining, and every possible activity and form of entertainment. It takes a staff of hundreds, and sometimes thousands, to ensure the smooth operation of a cruise ship and the comfort of all passengers. All employees, regardless of their rank, are expected to participate in routine lifesaving and safety drills. Crew organization is divided into six different departments (smaller liners may not have as many divisions of organization); the *Captain*, or the *Master of the ship*, oversees the entire crew.

Deck. This department is responsible for the navigation of the ship, and oversees the maintenance of the hull and deck.

Engine. This staff operates and maintains machinery. Together, deck and engine staffs include officers, carpenters, seamen, maintenance workers, electricians, engineers, repairmen, plumbers, and incinerator operators.

Radio department. *Videographers* are responsible for the maintenance and operation of the ship's broadcast booth, including radio and news telecasts. *Telephonists* help passengers place phone calls shoreside.

Medical department. *Physicians* treat passengers whose maladies range from seasickness to more serious health problems. *Nurses* assist the doctors and provide first aid.

Steward. This department, one of the largest on board, is concerned with the comfort of all passengers. The food staff includes specially trained *chefs* that prepare meals, ranging from gourmet dinners to more casual fare poolside. The *wait staff* serves guests in the formal dining room and provides room service. *Wine stewards* help passengers with wine choices, and are responsible for maintaining proper inventories aboard the ship. *Bartenders* mix and serve drinks at many stations throughout the ship. From simple blocks of ice, *sculptors* create works of art that are used to decorate dining room buffets. The housekeeping staff is composed of *executive housekeepers* and *room attendants* who keep cabins and staterooms orderly, supply towels and sheets, and maintain public areas throughout the ship.

Pursers. This large department is responsible for guest relations and services. The *chief purser,* much like a hotel's general manager, is the head of this department and is the main contact for passengers regarding the ship's policies and procedures. *Assistant pursers,* considered junior officers, assist the chief with various duties, such as providing guest services, ship information, monetary exchange, postage, safety deposit boxes, and other duties usually associated with the front desk department of a hotel. The *cruise director* heads the cruise staff and plans daily activities and entertainment. The *youth staff director* plans activities and games specifically designed for children. Ships with a casino on board employ *casino workers*, including game dealers, cashiers, keno runners, and slot machine attendants. *Sound and lighting technicians* are needed to provide music and stage lighting for the many entertainment venues found on board. Many entertainers are hired to sing, dance, and perform comedy skits and musical revues. *Dance instructors* teach dance classes ranging from ballroom to country. Also, many employees are hired to work in duty-free shops and souvenir stores, beauty parlors, spas, health clubs, and libraries.

■ REQUIREMENTS
High School

Cruise lines require at least a high school education, or equivalent, for most entry-level jobs. While in high school, you should concentrate on classes such as geography, sociology, and a foreign language. Fluency in Spanish, French, and Portuguese is highly desirable.

QUICK FACTS

SCHOOL SUBJECTS
Foreign language
Geography

PERSONAL SKILLS
Leadership/management
Mechanical/manipulative

WORK ENVIRONMENT
Indoors and outdoors
Primarily multiple locations

MINIMUM EDUCATION LEVEL
Varies by job

SALARY RANGE
$12,000 to $20,400, plus tips

CERTIFICATION OR LICENSING
Required for certain positions

OUTLOOK
About as fast as the average

DOT
350

GOE
11.03.01

NOC
6434, 6672

O*NET-SOC
N/A

Postsecondary Training

Officer-level positions, or jobs with more responsibility, require college degrees and past work experience. Many employees, especially those on the cruise staff, have an entertainment background. Youth staff members usually have a background in education or recreation.

Certification or Licensing

Most entry-level jobs do not require certification. Some technical positions, such as those in the engine room, may require special training. Physicians and nurses must be licensed to practice medicine. Child-care workers should have experience and proper training in child care. Some cruise line employees may belong to the Seafarers' International Union.

Other Requirements

You will need a valid U.S. passport to work in this field. If you hold a passport from another country, you will need to obtain a work visa. Check with your country's embassy for details and requirements.

Besides having the proper education, experience, and credentials, employers look for applicants who have excellent communication skills, are outgoing, hardworking, friendly, and enjoy working with people. It is important to make a positive impression with the passengers, so cruise ship workers should always be properly groomed, neatly dressed, and well behaved at all times. Inappropriate contact with passengers is not tolerated.

■ STARTING OUT

Applicants without college degrees and little shipboard experience are usually assigned to entry-level positions such as wait staff or housekeeping. If you have experience in retail sales, then you may be given a job at the duty-free shop; hospitality experience may land you a position in the purser's office.

Nancy Corbin, Youth Staff Department Manager for Royal Caribbean International, began her career in the cruise ship industry as a youth counselor. Not satisfied with the ship's program for children, or rather, the lack of, Corbin and her co-workers revised the schedule of activities and turned the ship's youth counselors into a new department—the youth staff. Today, the youth staff oversees art and science activities, pool parties, talent shows, and theme nights for children ages three to 17.

■ ADVANCEMENT

Nancy Corbin is still very much involved with the youth staff, though she no longer works on board. Rather, she is stationed shoreside as the Youth Staff Department Manager and acts as a liaison for all youth staffs on the

---

THE CUNARD TRADITION

The Cunard Line is considered by many as the standard for the cruise line industry. The Cunard Line was founded by Sir Samuel Cunard as the North American Royal Mail Steam Packet Company in 1840. Cunard's fleet of four wooden steam ships was originally contracted by England's Queen Victoria to deliver mail from Great Britain to North America. Cunard fulfilled his delivery contract and saw the potential to provide weekly transatlantic service for passengers as well. The Cunard Line later merged with the White Star Line (owner of the infamous *Titanic*) to create funding necessary to build the *Queen Elizabeth,* or *QE,* the largest passenger ship at the time and considered the epitome of cruise luxury and elegance. This vessel was followed by *the Queen Elizabeth II,* also known as the *QE2.* The historic Cunard company still sails today as part of the Carnival Cruise Line. Here are some important facts on the Cunard time line.

- Cunard was the first company to take passengers on regularly scheduled transatlantic departure on the Britannia, 1840.
- The first ship to be lit with electricity was Cunard's Servia, 1881.
- The first steam turbine engine was the Campania, 1893.
- The first gym and health center located on a ship was aboard the Franconia, 1911.
- First shipboard indoor swimming pool was on the Aquitania, 1914.
- Largest passenger ship built (until 1996) was the QE, 1940.
- Cunard was the first line to offer three different around the world cruises simultaneously in 1996 with the *QE2, Royal Viking,* and *Sagafjord*.

Source: Cunard website, http://www.cunardline.com

---

cruise line. Where does she see herself in the future? "I'd be interested in a director-type role," Corbin says, "Maybe work as a cruise director."

What are other career paths in this industry? With cruise experience, a cruise staff member can advance to assistant cruise director, and in turn become cruise director. Assistant pursers can be promoted to chief purser. Even people in entry-level positions can be promoted to jobs with more responsibility and, of course, better pay. Bussers can become assistant waiters and then head waiters. Room stewards can be promoted to housekeeping manager and supervise a team of cleaners or a specific section of the ship.

How Did Nancy Corbin Get Her Start?

Nancy Corbin had cruised before and loved it. So, when her friend needed a last-minute travel companion, Corbin jumped at the chance to cruise again. What she didn't know was that she was about to embark on a new career and industry. She always made it a point to carry her resume everywhere she went ("You just never know the opportunities," she says.) and left one on the ship. Corbin had a background in education, and was certified to teach kindergarten through 12th grade, plus special education. She was hired as a youth counselor in a matter of days.

Once on board, however, Nancy was disenchanted with the youth program. "It really was more of glorified baby-sitting," she remembers. Wanting to offer more for the younger passengers aboard Royal Caribbean ships, she and her coworkers quickly devised a children's program better suited for the diverse tastes and expectations of toddlers to older teens.

Today, the youth staff, all college educated, with education or recreation backgrounds, heads daily sessions for four age groups—three to five, six to eight, nine to 12, and 13 to 17. The youth center is open for nine hours of activity ranging from finger and face painting, adventure and science lessons, and arts and crafts for the younger passengers. Older youths can enjoy pool parties, sports activities, talent shows, and theme parties. There are two youth staff members to every group. The program changes often. There are also two training sessions for each ship's youth staff manager held shoreside, plus on-the-job training for all youth staff members. What started as a quick employment change for Corbin has developed into her management of a staff of 130 full-time and seasonal employees stationed at the 12 youth departments on board all Royal Caribbean ships. Corbin is now stationed shoreside at RCI's Miami headquarters, where she heads the Youth Staff Department.

Now, thanks to Corbin and her Youth Staff, parents can leave their kids at the center knowing they will be safe as well as entertained. The kids have the opportunity to meet fellow travelers their own age and enjoy entertainment designed with them in mind—without mom and dad cramping their style.

■ EXPLORING

Do you want to learn more about this exciting industry? Since firsthand experience is the best, why not book a Caribbean cruise for your next family holiday? Most cruise lines offer competitive prices along with a selection of cruises and destinations. Also consider inland cruises as a less expensive option.

In many cities located near water, such as Chicago, there are cruise tours running up and down the city's lakefront and the Chicago River. Some even provide entertainment and dinner shows. Many talented performers hone their skills before "trying out" with the bigger cruise lines. Does your city or town offer something similar?

Some cruise lines will hire college students for some of their entry-level positions. Don't forget to apply early, as these jobs are quickly filled.

If you live near a cruise line office or headquarters, why not call press relations or human resources for a tour of the department?

If all else fails, catch some late night reruns of the *Love Boat* television series. Just remember, real-life cruise jobs are less glamorous than this show portrayed.

■ EMPLOYERS

There are approximately 45 cruise lines with offices in the United States; together, they employ thousands of cruise ship workers. Most employees are contracted to work four or more months at a time. Some major employers include Royal Caribbean International, The Cunard Line, Holland America, and Disney Cruise Line.

■ EARNINGS

There are so many variables that it is hard to gauge the salary average for this industry. First, many employees are hired on a contractual basis—anywhere from four to six months for housekeeping, wait staff, and the concessionaires. The size of the cruise line and the region it sails may also affect wages. According to Cruise Services International, the general salary range is between $1,000 and $1,700 per month, plus tips, or $12,000–$20,400 per year. Some employees count on passengers' tips to greatly supplement their income. Restaurant and house staff workers can stand to earn anywhere from $300 to $600 in weekly tips.

Employee benefits include room and board, and all meals while on board. Most cruise lines offer emergency health coverage to their employees, regardless of the length of contract. Full-time employees are also offered health insurance, paid sick and holiday time, stock options, and company discounts.

■ WORK ENVIRONMENT

Workers in the cruise line industry shouldn't expect to have a lot of free time. Most cruise ship workers work long hours—eight- to fourteen-hour days, seven days a week are not uncommon. Many employees spend a number of weeks, usually five or more, working at sea, followed by an extended leave ashore.

Being a people person is important in this industry. Cruise ship workers not only are expected to work well with their co-workers, but they have to live with them, too. Accommodations for the crew are especially tight; usually two to four employees are assigned to a room. The crew has dining areas and lounges separate from the passengers, yet total privacy is rare on a cruise ship. Usually, crew members have little access to public areas on their free time. However, when the ship docks at port, crew members on leave are allowed to disembark and go shoreside.

■ OUTLOOK

The health of the cruise line industry is intrinsically tied to the state of our nation's economy, as well as the public's perceived level of safety in the wake of the terrorist attacks of September 11, 2001. Bookings declined significantly in the aftermath of the attacks, and cruise lines upgraded their security measures to ensure the safety of passengers and crew.

The cruise line industry is still one of the fastest growing segments of the travel industry. Over 9.5 million people cruised in 2003, according to Cruise Lines International Association (CLIA). Over 42 new cruise ships will be added to the North American Fleet from 2000 to 2004, according to CLIA. Ships are getting bigger and more opulent, and have become travel destinations in themselves. Larger cruise lines pack their ships with every amenity imaginable, including libraries, spas, casinos, and in the case of Royal Caribbean International's newest fleet addition—a skating rink and a rock climbing wall. Cruise lines are able to tap into every interest by offering a theme or special interest to their passengers. The Cunard Line offers fine art and opera themes, as well as classic antique cars; Holland America has many sports theme cruises ranging from the Olympics to the Super Bowl; many ships plan super bingo and mah-jongg marathons. Several cruise ships are experimenting with smoke-free cruising.

With so many mega-ships in operation, qualified cruise ship workers are still in demand. Entry-level positions such as wait staff and housekeeping will be fairly easy to obtain with the proper paperwork and credentials. A college degree and work experience will be necessary for positions with more responsibility. Fluency in French, Spanish, or Portuguese is a plus. A cruise ship will offer workers the opportunity to travel around the world and meet many people of different nationalities and cultures.

Remember, however, that cruise life is not all fun and travel. Cruise ship workers are expected to work long, hard hours, and be away from their home base for weeks at a time. Many people find the schedule exhausting and opt to find employment ashore.

■ FOR MORE INFORMATION

For industry information and job opportunities, contact the following cruise lines:

Cunard Cruise Line
6100 Blue Lagoon Drive, Suite 400
Miami, FL 33126
Tel: 800-5-CUNARD
http://www.cunardline.com

Delta Queen Steamboat Company
1380 Port of New Orleans Place
New Orleans, LA 70130-1890
Tel: 800-543-1949
Email: hr@amcvnola.com
http://www.deltaqueen.com

Disney Cruise Line
PO Box 10210
Lake Buena Vista, FL 32830
Tel: 407-566-SHIP
http://disney.go.com/disneycruise/jobs

Holland America Line
300 Elliott Avenue West
Seattle, WA 98119
Tel: 206-281-3535
Email: resume@halw.com
http://www.hollandamerica.com/aboutus/jobs/
    jobs.htm

Royal Caribbean International
1050 Caribbean Way
Miami, FL 33132
Tel: 305-539-6000
http://www.royalcaribbean.com

CLIA is the official trade organization of the cruise industry. For industry information, contact

Cruise Line International Association
   (CLIA)
500 Fifth Avenue, Suite 1407
New York, NY 10110
Tel: 212-921-0066
Email: info@cruising.org
http://www.cruising.org

For information on the industry, employment opportunities, and answers to commonly asked questions regarding employment at sea, contact

Cruise Services International
601 Dundas Street West
Box 24070
Whitby, Ontario L1N 8X8, Canada
Tel: 905-430-0361
Email: info@cruisedreamjob.com
http://www.cruisedreamjob.com

For industry information, a list of major cruise lines, employment opportunities, and a copy of the Tristar Cruiseline Employment Manual, contact

Cruise Line Jobs
http://www.cruiselinejobs.com

For information about the Seafarer's International Union, contact

Seafarer's International Union
5201 Auth Way
Camp Springs, MD 20746
Tel: 301-899-0675
http://www.seafarers.org

Cryptographic Technicians

■ OVERVIEW

Cryptographic technicians, also called *CTs, crypto clerks,* and *cryptanalysts,* operate cryptographic equipment used for coding, decoding, and sending secret messages. They are mainly employed by the government, for positions in all branches of the military, and in government agencies such as the National Security Agency, the Federal Bureau of Investigation, the Department of State, and any other intelligence operations. Cryptographic technicians are also employed by industries that transact confidential business via computer, such as the banking industry.

■ HISTORY

Cryptology—the term is derived from the Greek words *kryptos* (hidden) and *logos* (word)—has been used since ancient times, perhaps since people first began to write. The desire to maintain secrecy or privacy for some communications led people to develop codes and ciphers; only people who possessed the key to the code would be able to understand the communication. Secret writing methods were used in ancient Greece, Egypt, Mesopotamia, India, and China.

Julius Caesar used a letter substitution method that involved the shifting of the alphabet, so that the letter D, for example, represented the letter A, the letter E represented the letter B, and so on. This method, or cipher, has come to be called the Julius Caesar cipher. The word *cipher* may refer to the method of encoding a message or to the encoded message itself.

The use of secret writing techniques increased through the Middle Ages. The science of cryptology, however, is generally considered to have been begun in 1510 by Johannes Trithemius of Germany, who produced the first written text on cryptology. Trithemius also devised the first cipher based on a geometric figure, in his case a square, that allowed the alphabet to be shifted several or many times in the same message, making the message more difficult to decode. Cryptology has played an important role in history, especially during times of war.

■ THE JOB

While cryptography has always been an important tool for the U.S. government to use in providing security and protection to its citizens, the significance of sending and receiving coded messages has only been enhanced following terrorist attacks on the United States on September 11, 2001. The leading government agency dedicated to cryptanalysis is the National Security Agency (NSA), which is administered by the Department of Defense. The Central Security Service (CSS), a partner with NSA, is responsible for the cryptanalysis activities in all branches of the U.S. military (army, air force, navy, and marines).

Cryptanalysts use a variety of skills and tools to do their work. They draw on their knowledge of a wide variety of subjects, including mathematics, languages, engineering, and computer programming, to determine the basic rules or principles governing an unknown code. Once the basic principles at work in a code are understood, the code can be "broken" or deciphered. Cryptanalysts are familiar with cryptographic software, radio equipment, computer equipment, surveillance devices, and other technologies used by the defense and intelligence communities.

Cryptographic technicians working in the military have a key role in protecting our armed forces and helping them complete successful missions. When military personnel are far from home on a training mission or at war, they rely on messages sent from headquarters to update them on world events and give them orders. In the Air Force, for example, to send information to a flight crew on a 20-hour training mission, secret signals must be transmitted via radio waves, using HF (high frequency), UHF (ultrahigh frequency), or SATCOM (satellite communications). Because other nations have access to these same frequencies, the messages must be in code to protect national military secrets. In the plane, the cryptographic technician decodes the message, which might alter a set of targets to hit, or instruct the pilot to land at a different air force base.

Cryptographic technicians working for agencies in the intelligence community, such as NSA, may be involved with decoding information that intelligence workers have intercepted from groups or governments unfriendly to the United States. And, like those technicians working in the military, they may also create codes to use for sending sensitive information to U.S. intelligence workers and our allies around the world.

In the private sector, cryptoanalysts working for the banking industry or any other industry requiring computer security must prevent unauthorized access in order to protect the accounts or data in the files. For instance, when funds are being transferred from one bank to another, the transfer message is usually sent by computer. To prevent unauthorized transfers, the banks send the message in code, along with some means of authenticating the transaction.

In order to code and send secret messages, cryptographic technicians first select the particular code that they should use for the message. Then they set up their machine to translate the message into that code, and they type the message into the machine. The machine converts the message into code form in a process known as encryption. After the message is encrypted, the technicians send the message to a receiver via telephone lines, satellites, or other kinds of communication links.

When receiving a message in a known code, cryptographic technicians feed the incoming transmission into a decoding machine and take the resulting message to its intended receiver. If a message appears to have been improperly coded, technicians may try to straighten out the message using special decoding procedures and equipment, or they may request that the message be sent again.

To send and receive coded messages, cryptographic technicians may develop their own cryptographic software programs, use teletypewriters, or operate radio transmitters and receivers.

■ REQUIREMENTS
High School

If you are interested in becoming a cryptographic technician, you should take courses in mathematics and English while in high school. You should be able to add, subtract, multiply, and divide with ease and be able to compute ratios and percentages. You should be able to read equipment and instruction manuals and to write reports with proper grammar, spelling, and punctuation. You should also look for courses that will train you in typing and in the operation of computers and business machines. Computer science courses, business classes, and even shop classes dealing with electronics will be helpful. Knowledge of foreign languages is especially helpful in government and military positions, as well as in the increasingly globalized world economy.

Postsecondary Training

While a few employers in the private sector may hire someone with a two-year degree, most employers prefer to hire those with four-year bachelor's degrees. You may also want to consider joining the military as a way to get cryptographic training. Positions with federal intelligence and investigative agencies, such as the Federal Bureau of Investigation (FBI) and the Central Intelligence Agency (CIA), generally require job candidates to have at least a bachelor's degree or several years of related experience, or both. Undergraduate majors that are typical for this field include mathematics, computer science, and electrical engineering. NSA reports that it hires people with both technical (mathematics, engineering, etc.) and nontechnical (history, music, etc.) bachelor's degrees. Prospective cryptographic technicians need to receive special training that lasts from six months to a year. The U.S. Armed Forces and government agencies that employ cryptographic technicians usually provide this training. NSA places prospective cryptographic technicians in its Cryptanalysis Intern Program, which combines classroom training, work experience, and instruction from experienced cryptanalysts.

Certification or Licensing

Due to the secret nature of their work, cryptographic technicians often need government clearance, which involves a thorough investigation of the applicant's character and records for the previous 10 years.

QUICK FACTS

SCHOOL SUBJECTS
English
Mathematics

PERSONAL SKILLS
Mechanical/manipulative
Technical/scientific

WORK ENVIRONMENT
Primarily indoors
Primarily one location

MINIMUM EDUCATION LEVEL
Bachelor's degree

SALARY RANGE
$14,300 to $45,831 to
$69,694

CERTIFICATION OR LICENSING
Required for certain positions

OUTLOOK
About as fast as the average

DOT
203

GOE
09.09.01

NOC
1475

O*NET-SOC
N/A

CODEBREAKING AND WORLD WAR II

Although ciphers and cryptography have ancient roots, much of the modern art of cryptography was developed during World War II. Both sides worked actively to break their enemies' encoded messages sent by radio. Polish mathematicians and intelligence operatives first broke codes used by the Germans, and later British and American cryptographers worked to crack further refinements of German and Japanese ciphers. Of course, the fact that the codes were known was kept top secret. To break codes, cryptographers relied on repeated messages and user errors to understand the enemy's cipher machines and encoding systems. Some of the first computers were developed to aid in this process.

Other Requirements

For obvious reasons, it is important for you to have a clean police record if you are interested in a career as a cryptographic technician. Someone who has been in trouble with the law will not meet the high standards of the background investigation. Employers also seek those who can be trusted to maintain confidentiality. In addition, you should have imagination, patience, and persistence as code-breaking can be complex and time consuming. You should also be interested in working with new technologies as they develop and be committed to lifelong learning.

■ EXPLORING

You can begin exploring your interest in this field by joining groups involved with cryptography, such as the American Cryptogram Association (ACA), and reading their journals, such as the ACA's *The Cryptogram.* Learn how to do some computer programming. This will give you experience working with codes and computers. If your high school has math and computer science clubs, join them. NSA offers a two-week summer program for high school students through its Center for Mathematics, Science, and Technology. This program gives students opportunities to learn about mathematical and scientific problem solving. While the program is not specifically about cryptanalysis, it does give you the opportunity to use some of the skills cryptanalysts use in their work. (More information is available at the website http://www.mathismylife.org.) You may also want to check out Reserve Officers Training Corps (ROTC) programs offered by the different branches of military service. These may provide some introduction to cryptographic techniques.

■ EMPLOYERS

Cryptographic technicians are, for the most part, employed by the government. They find positions in all branches of the military and in government agencies such as the NSA, the FBI, the Department of State, and other intelligence operations. Cryptographic technicians also work in industries that transact confidential business via computer.

■ STARTING OUT

Enlistment in a branch of the armed forces is a good method for beginning a career in cryptology. College graduates may also apply directly to government agencies that employ cryptographic technicians.

■ ADVANCEMENT

Cryptographic technicians employed by a branch of the armed forces can rise through the ranks or equivalent government service ratings levels. Cryptographic technicians employed by commercial companies may become supervisors and even executives in charge of corporate security measures.

■ EARNINGS

Salaries vary according to an individual's education, experience, and the geographic location of the job. In general, however, technicians employed by private companies who are graduates of two-year post-high school training programs can expect to receive starting salaries averaging around $15,000 to $20,000 a year. With increased experience they may earn up to $35,000 a year and sometimes more.

NSA reports salaries for cryptanalysts are based on experience and degree level and ranged from $45,831 to $69,694 in 2002. Technicians in the armed forces will find their salaries determined by their rank or grade level. Most new enlistees in military service will start at the basic E-1 rank, which paid approximately $14,300 per year in 2004. Enlisted cryptographic technicians in the armed forces may eventually rise to the E-9 rank, with a basic pay of approximately $45,200 or more per year in 2004. Armed forces personnel, it should be noted, generally do not have to pay for their housing or their food. Technicians who work for local and state government agencies will also find their salaries determined by government rules, and their salaries will vary from town to town and from state to state. Government employees at all levels generally receive generous benefits, including health and life insurance, pension plans, and vacation, sick, and holiday pay.

■ WORK ENVIRONMENT

Cryptographic technicians generally work in clean, well-lighted offices. Because much of their work involves computers, they generally remain seated for most of their workday, in front of the computer screen. Cryptographic technicians employed by government agencies and in the armed forces may be required to work in the evenings, at night, and on weekends and holidays.

■ OUTLOOK

The need for skilled cryptographic technicians should remain high as U.S. intelligence operations take place throughout the world and as the government works to address new terrorist threats. Among private businesses, the increasing transmission of sensitive information through phone lines and satellite systems via computers and related equipment has led to the increased need for security for those transmissions. Hackers, people who illegally break into private and public computer systems, have become increasingly adept at thwarting even the most sophisticated security programs, and companies will most likely take stronger measures—including hiring people skilled in cryptographic techniques—for preventing computer break-ins and interception of their information. At the same time, many software companies and government agencies are working on creating new, more secure security programs. For these reasons, cryptographic technicians should have a strong job outlook.

■ FOR MORE INFORMATION

For ACA membership information and subscription information for The Cryptogram, *contact*

American Cryptogram Association (ACA)
Treasurer
PO Box 1013
Londonderry, NH 03053-1013
http://www.cryptogram.org

For membership information and subscription information to Journal of Cryptology, *contact*

International Association for Cryptographic Research
Santa Rosa Administrative Center
University of California
Santa Barbara, CA 93106-6120
http://www.iacr.org

To find out more about NSA's duties and career opportunities, contact

National Security Agency (NSA)
9800 Savage Road
Fort George G. Meade, MD 20755-6000
Tel: 301-688-6311
http://www.nsa.gov

Visit the ACA's Crypto Drop Box site for links to information on the association, cipher problems, and other crypto information.

American Cryptogram Association Crypto Drop Box
http://www.und.nodak.edu/org/crypto/crypto

To read articles from the quarterly journal Cryptologia, *visit the following website:*

Cryptologia
http://www.dean.usma.edu/math/pubs/cryptologia

Cultural Advisers

■ OVERVIEW

Cultural advisers, also known as *bilingual consultants,* work with businesses and organizations to help them communicate effectively with others who are from different cultural and linguistic backgrounds. Cultural advisers usually have a specialty such as business management, banking, education, or computer technology. They help bridge both language and cultural barriers in our increasingly global business world.

■ HISTORY

Communication has always been a challenge when cultures come into contact with each other. In the early days of the United States, settlers and explorers relied on interpreters to assist them. One of those famous interpreters, Sacajawea, a member of the Shoshone Indian tribe, was a precursor of the cultural advisers of today. As she helped guide Meriwether Lewis and William Clark across the West to the Pacific Ocean, she acted as interpreter when they encountered Native American tribes. She also helped the explorers adapt to the different cultures and customs.

QUICK FACTS

SCHOOL SUBJECTS
Business
Foreign language
Speech

PERSONAL SKILLS
Communication/ideas
Helping/teaching

WORK ENVIRONMENT
Primarily indoors
Primarily multiple locations

MINIMUM EDUCATION LEVEL
Bachelor's degree

SALARY RANGE
$65 to $100 to $265 per hour

CERTIFICATION OR LICENSING
None available

OUTLOOK
Faster than the average

DOT
N/A

GOE
N/A

NOC
N/A

O*NET-SOC
N/A

WORDS TO KNOW

Bilingual: Fluent in two languages.

Consultant: A professional who offers advice, knowledge, and training.

Culture: A set of precedents and traditions that signify a people's heritage.

Custom: A usual course of action, often particular to a certain country or culture.

International: Referring to two or more nations.

Interpreter: A person who translates words from one language to another.

Language: Using words to communicate.

NAFTA: The North American Free Trade Agreement, passed in 1994 that increased free trade opportunities among North American countries.

Today's cultural advisers work with companies or organizations that need to communicate effectively and do business with other cultures. Cultural advisers are becoming even more valuable because it is now relatively quick and easy to travel throughout the world, and as trade barriers are eliminated.

■ THE JOB

Cultural advisers work to bridge gaps in communication and culture. They usually have a second specialty that is complemented by their bilingual skills. For example, a banking and finance expert who has traveled extensively in Japan and is familiar with Japanese language and customs would have the marketable skills to become a cultural adviser for American companies interested in doing business in Japan.

Cultural advisers work in a wide variety of settings. They may hold full-time staff positions with organizations or they may work as independent consultants providing services to a number of clients. Cultural advisers work in education. They provide translation services and help foreign or immigrant students adjust to a new culture. They also educate teachers and administrators to make them aware of cultural differences, so that programs and classes can be adapted to include everyone. Colleges and universities that have large international student populations often have cultural advisers on staff.

In industry, cultural advisers train workers in safety procedures and worker rights. The health care industry benefits from the use of advisers to communicate with non-English-speaking patients. Cultural advisers also hold training sessions for health care professionals to teach them how to better understand and instruct their patients.

Large business enterprises that have overseas interests hire cultural advisers to research new markets and help with negotiations. Some advisers work primarily in employment, finding foreign experts to work for American businesses or finding overseas jobs for American workers. In addition to advising American business leaders, cultural advisers sometimes work with foreign entities which want to do business in the United States. They provide English language instruction and training in American business practices.

Cultural advisers also work in the legal system, the media, advertising, the travel industry, social services, and government agencies. Whatever the setting, cultural advisers help their clients—foreign and American—understand and respect other cultures and communicate effectively with each other.

■ REQUIREMENTS
High School

Classes in business, speech, and foreign language will give you an excellent head start to becoming a cultural adviser. In addition, take other classes in your high school's college prep curriculum. These courses should include history, mathematics, sciences, and English. Accounting classes and computer science classes will also help prepare you for working in business.

Postsecondary Training

If you are planning a career as a cultural adviser, fluency in two or more languages is a requirement, so college courses in those languages are necessary. Courses in business, world history, world geography, and sociology would be useful as well. You will need at least a bachelor's degree to find work as a cultural adviser, and you may want to consider pursuing a master's degree to have more job opportunities. Many universities offer programs in cultural studies, and there are master's programs that offer a concentration in international business.

Take advantage of every opportunity to learn about the people and area you want to work with, whether Latin America, Europe, Japan, or another region or country. Studying abroad for a semester or year is also recommended.

Other Requirements

Cultural sensitivity is the number one requirement for an adviser. Knowing the history, culture, and social conventions of a people as well as the language is a very important part of the job. Also, expertise in another area, such as business, education, law, or computers, is necessary to be a cultural adviser.

EXPLORING

A good way to explore this field is to join one of your high school's foreign language clubs. In addition to using the foreign language, these clubs often have activities related to the culture where the language is spoken. You may also find it helpful to join your school's business club, which will give you an opportunity to learn about business tactics and finances, as well as give you an idea of how to run your own business.

Learn as much as you can about people and life in other parts of the world. You can do this by joining groups such as American Field Service International (AFS) and getting to know a student from another country who is attending your school. There are also study-abroad and living aboard programs you can apply to even while in high school. Rotary International and AFS offer such opportunities; see the end of the article for contact information.

EMPLOYERS

Cultural advisers are employed on a contract- or project-basis by businesses, associations, and educational institutions. Large global companies are the most significant source of employment for cultural advisers as they seek to serve the global population. Small to medium-sized companies that do business in a particular region also employ cultural advisers.

Companies in large cities offer the most opportunities for cultural advisers, especially those cities that border other countries and their economies.

Miguel Orta is a cultural adviser in North Miami Beach, Florida. He works with Latin American companies and American companies doing business in Central America and South America. He also has a background in law and business management. Orta is fluent in English, Spanish, and Portuguese. He uses his location in Florida to help businesses in the United States interact with a growing Hispanic population. His Florida location also allows him to be only a short plane flight from his Latin American clients.

STARTING OUT

Most cultural advisers do not begin this career right after college. Some real life experience is necessary to be qualified to fill the cultural adviser's role. "Education is very important," says Miguel Orta. "But first you need some work in the trenches." Once that experience is obtained, you will be ready to try advising.

HISPANIC POPULATION GROWTH

The growth in the Hispanic population in the United States has increased the demand for cultural advisers who are fluent in Spanish. The statistics below show this growth between the 1990 and 200 censuses.

Year	1990	1992	1994	1996	1998	2000
Population (in millions)	22.5	24.3	26.3	28.3	30.7	32.8
% of total	9.1	9.6	10.1	10.7	11.4	12

Source: U.S. Bureau of the Census

After graduating with a law degree, Orta spent several years as a private attorney representing many Latin American clients. He practiced corporate, international, and labor law. When the opportunity came to serve one of his Venezuelan clients as a cultural adviser, Orta enjoyed the work and decided to become an adviser to others in need of those services.

ADVANCEMENT

Working with larger companies on more extensive projects is one way for a cultural adviser to advance. If an adviser decides to trade in the flexibility and freedom of the job, opportunities to become a salaried employee would most likely be available.

EARNINGS

Cultural advisers are well compensated for the time they spend on projects. Rates can range from approximately $65 to as high as $265 per hour. The median rate is close to $100 per hour. Cultural advisers tend to work on a project-basis and are therefore not guaranteed full-time employment. Advisers may incur business expenses, but their clients generally pay many of the expenses associated with the work, such as travel, meals, and lodging.

WORK ENVIRONMENT

The work environment of cultural advisers largely depends on their specialties. A smaller company may offer a more informal setting than a multinational corporation. A cultural adviser who is employed by a large, international bank may travel much more than an adviser who works for an educational institution or association.

While cultural advisers generally work independently on projects, they must also communicate with a large number of people to complete their tasks. In the middle of a project, a cultural adviser may work 50 to 60 hours per week and travel may be necessary. Between projects, cultural advisers manage their businesses and solicit new clients.

■ OUTLOOK

The field of cultural advising is predicted to grow faster than average in the next decade. Demand will grow as trade barriers are continually loosened and U.S. companies conduct more business on a global scale. Latin America and Asia are two promising areas for American businesses.

Cultural advisers will also be needed to address the interests of the increasingly diverse population of the United States. However, competition is keen, and those with graduate degrees and specific expertise will be the most successful.

■ FOR MORE INFORMATION

Management consulting firms employ a large number of cultural advisers. For more information on the consulting business, contact

**Association of Career Management Consulting
Firms International**
204 E Street, NE
Washington, DC 20002
Tel: 202-547-6344
Email: aocfi@aocfi.org
http://www.aocfi.org

For information about cultural exchanges, contact the following:

American Field Service International
71 West 23rd Street, 17th Floor
New York, NY 10010
Tel: 212-807-8686
Email: info@afs.org
http://www.afs.org

Rotary International
One Rotary Center
1560 Sherman Avenue
Evanston, IL 60201
Tel: 847-866-3000
http://www.rotary.org

For information on etiquette and cross-cultural training, contact

Multi-Language Consultants Inc.
Tel: 212-726-2164
Email: contact@mlc.com
http://www.mlc.com

Protocol Advisors Inc.
241 Beacon Street
Boston, MA 02116
Tel: 617-267-6950
http://www.protocoladvisors.com

**MOST
NEW
JOBS**

Customer Service Representatives

■ OVERVIEW

Customer service representatives, sometimes called *customer care representatives*, work with customers of one or many companies, assist with customer problems, or answer questions. Customer service representatives work in many different industries to provide "front-line" customer service in a variety of businesses. Most customer service representatives work in an office setting though some may work in the "field" to better meet customer needs. There are approximately 1.9 million customer service representatives employed in the United States.

■ HISTORY

Customer service has been a part of business for many years; however, the formal title of customer service representative is relatively new. More than a decade ago, the International Customer Service Association established Customer Service Week to recognize and promote customer service.

As the world moves toward a more global and competitive economic market, customer service, along with quality control, has taken a front seat in the business world. Serving customers and serving them well is more important now than ever before.

Customer service is about communication, so the progress in customer service can be tied closely to the progress in the communication industry. When Alexander Graham Bell invented the telephone in 1876, he probably did not envision the customer service lines, automated response messages, and toll-free phone numbers that now help customer service representatives do their jobs.

The increased use of the Internet has helped companies serve and communicate with their customers in another way. From the simple email complaint form to online help files, companies are using the Internet to provide better customer service. Some companies even have online chat capabilities to communicate with their customers instantaneously on the Web.

■ THE JOB

Julie Cox is a customer service representative for Affina. Affina is a call center that handles customer service for a variety of companies. Cox works with each of Affina's clients and the call center operators to ensure that each call-in receives top customer service.

Customer service representatives often handle complaints and problems, and Cox finds that to be the case at the call center as well. While the operators who report to her provide customer service to those on the phone, Cox must oversee that customer service while also keeping in mind the customer service for her client, whatever business they may be in.

"I make sure that the clients get regular reports of the customer service calls and check to see if there are any recurring problems," says Cox.

One of the ways Cox observes if customer service is not being handled effectively is by monitoring the actual time spent on each phone call. If an operator spends a lot of time on a call, there is most likely a problem.

"Our customers are billed per minute," says Cox. "So we want to make sure their customer service is being handled well and efficiently."

Affina's call center in Columbus, Indiana, handles dozens of toll-free lines. While some calls are likely to be focused on complaints or questions, some are easier to handle. Cox and her staff handle calls from people simply wanting to order literature, brochures, or to find their nearest dealer location.

Customer service representatives work in a variety of fields and business, but one thing is common—the customer. All businesses depend on their customers to keep them in business, so customer service, whether handled internally or outsourced to a call center like Affina, is extremely important.

Some customer service representatives, like Cox, do most of their work on the telephone. Others may represent companies in the field, where the customer is actually using the product or service. Still other customer service representatives may specialize in Internet service, assisting customers over the World Wide Web via email or online chats.

Affina's call center is available to their clients 24 hours a day, seven days a week, so Cox and her staff must keep around-the-clock shifts. Not all customer service representatives work a varied schedule; many work a traditional daytime shift. However, customers have problems, complaints, and questions 24 hours a day, so many companies do staff their customer service positions for a longer number of hours, especially to accommodate customers during evenings and weekends.

■ REQUIREMENTS
High School

A high school diploma is required for most customer service representative positions. High school courses that emphasize communication, such as English and speech, will help you learn to communicate clearly. Any courses that require collaboration with others will also help to teach diplomacy and tact—two important aspects of customer service. Business courses will help you get a good overview of the business world, one that is dependent on customers and customer service. Computer skills are also very important.

Postsecondary Training

While a college degree is not necessary to become a customer service representative, certain areas of postsecondary training are helpful. Courses in business and organizational leadership will help to give you a better feel for the business world. Just as in high school, communications classes are helpful in learning to effectively talk with and meet the needs of other people.

These courses can be taken during a college curriculum or may be offered at a variety of customer service workshops or classes. Julie Cox is working as a customer service representative while she earns her business degree from a local college. Along with her college work, she has taken advantage of seminars and workshops to improve her customer service skills.

Bachelor's degrees in business and communications are increasingly required for managerial positions.

Certification or Licensing

Although it is not a requirement, customer service representative can become certified. The International Customer Service Association offers a manager-level

QUICK FACTS

SCHOOL SUBJECTS
Business
English
Speech

PERSONAL SKILLS
Communication/ideas
Helping/teaching

WORK ENVIRONMENT
Primarily indoors
Primarily one location

MINIMUM EDUCATION LEVEL
High school diploma

SALARY RANGE
$17,230 to $26,240 to $42,990+

CERTIFICATION OR LICENSING
Voluntary

OUTLOOK
Faster than the average

DOT
205

GOE
09.05.01

NOC
1453

O*NET-SOC
43-4051.00, 43-4051.02

WORKING FOR PERFECTION

Some may think that 99.9 percent is good enough for the customer, but according to the International Customer Service Association (ICSA), if that were true then:

- 2 million documents would be lost by the IRS this year.

- 1,314 phone calls would be misplaced by telecommunication companies each minute.

- 12 babies would be given to the wrong parents each day.

- 315 entries in *Webster's Third New International Dictionary of the English Language* will be misspelled.

Customer service representatives aim for 100 percent accuracy because 99.9 percent is not good enough to meet customer satisfaction.

certification program. Upon completion of the program, managers receive the Certified Customer Service Professional designation.

Other Requirements

"The best and the worst parts of being a customer service representative are the people," Julie Cox says. Customer service representatives should have the ability to maintain a pleasant attitude at all times, even while serving angry or demanding customers.

A successful customer service representative will most likely have an outgoing personality and enjoy working with people and assisting them with their questions and problems.

Because many customer service representatives work in offices and on the telephone, people with physical disabilities may find this career to be both accessible and enjoyable.

■ EXPLORING

Julie Cox first discovered her love for customer service while working in retail at a local department store. Explore your ability for customer service by getting a job that deals with the public on a day-to-day basis. Talk with people who work with customers and customer service every day; find out what they like and dislike about their jobs.

There are other ways that you can prepare for a career in this field while you are still in school. Join your school's business club to get a feel for what goes on in the business world today. Doing volunteer work for a local charity or homeless shelter can help you decide if serving others is something that you'd enjoy doing as a career.

Evaluate the customer service at the businesses you visit. What makes that salesperson at The Gap better than the operator you talked with last week? Volunteer to answer phones at an agency in your town or city. Most receptionists in small companies and agencies are called on to provide customer service to callers. Try a nonprofit organization. They will welcome the help, and you will get a firsthand look at customer service.

■ EMPLOYERS

Customer service representatives are hired at all types of companies in a variety of areas. Because all businesses rely on customers, customer service is generally a high priority for those businesses. Some companies, like call centers, may employ a large number of customer service representatives to serve a multitude of clients, while small businesses may simply have one or two people who are responsible for customer service.

Geography makes little difference when it comes to customer service. Smaller businesses may not be able to hire a person to handle customer service exclusively, but most businesses will have people designated to meet customer's needs. In the United States, approximately 1.9 million workers are employed as customer service representatives.

■ STARTING OUT

You can become a customer service representative as an entry-level applicant, although some customer service representatives have first served in other areas of a company. This company experience may provide them with more knowledge and experience to answer customer questions. A college degree is not required, but any postsecondary training will increase your ability to find a job in customer service.

Ads for customer service job openings are readily available in newspapers and on Internet job search sites. With some experience and a positive attitude, it is possible to move into the position of customer service representative from another job within the company. Julie Cox started out at Affina as an operator and quickly moved into a customer service capacity.

■ ADVANCEMENT

Customer service experience is valuable in any business career path. Julie Cox hopes to combine her customer service experience with a business degree and move to the human resources area of her company.

It is also possible to advance to management or marketing jobs after working as a customer service representative. Businesses and their customers are inseparable, so most business professionals are experts at customer relations.

EARNINGS

Earnings vary based on location, level of experience, and size and type of employer. The U.S. Department of Labor reports the median annual income for all customer service representatives as $26,240 in 2002. Salaries ranged from $17,230, at the lowest 10 percent to more than $42,990, for the highest 10 percent. The Association of Support Professionals, which conducts salary surveys of tech support workers at PC software companies, reports that customer service representatives earned a median annual wage of $31,200 in 2003.

Other benefits vary widely according to the size and type of company in which representatives are employed. Benefits may include medical, dental, vision, and life insurance, 401(k) plans, or bonus incentives. Full-time customer service representatives can expect to receive vacation and sick pay, while part-time workers may not be offered these benefits.

WORK ENVIRONMENT

Customer service representatives work primarily indoors, although some may work in the field where the customers are using the product or service. They usually work in a supervised setting and report to a manager. They may spend many hours on the telephone, answering mail, or handling Internet communication. Many of the work hours involve little physical activity.

While most customer service representatives generally work a 40-hour workweek, others work a variety of shifts. Many businesses want customer service hours to coincide with the times that their customers are available to call or contact the business. For many companies, these times are in the evenings and on the weekends, so some customer service representatives work a varied shift and odd hours.

OUTLOOK

The U.S. Department of Labor predicts that employment for customer service representatives will grow faster than the average through 2012. This is a large field of workers and many replacement workers are needed each year as customer service reps leave this job for other positions, retire, or leave for other reasons. In addition, the Internet and e-commerce should increase the need for customer service representatives who will be needed to help customers navigate websites, answer questions over the phone, and respond to emails.

For customer service representatives with specific knowledge of a product or business, the outlook is very

WORDS TO KNOW

Automated Response System (ARS): A telephone system that prompts callers to push buttons to receive information or transfers to other departments.
Better Business Bureau: An organization that receives complaints when the customer service department of a business fails to provide customers with satisfaction.
Call center: A business that handles customer service phone calls for other companies.
Customer service: The ways that a company meets customers needs, answers questions, and handles complaints.
Internet customer service: Customer service handled via email or by online chat.
Toll-free: Toll-free numbers are commonly used in customer service so customers can receive information without paying for a phone call.

good, as quick, efficient customer service is valuable in any business. Additional training and education will also make finding a job as a customer service representative an easier task.

FOR MORE INFORMATION

For information on customer service and other support positions, contact

Association of Support Professionals
122 Barnard Avenue
Watertown, MA 02472-3944
Tel: 617-924-3944
http://www.asponline.com

For information on jobs, training, workshops, and salaries, contact

Customer Care Institute
17 Dean Overlook, NW
Atlanta, GA 30318
Tel: 404-352-9291
Email: info@customercare.com
http://www.customercare.com

For information about the customer service industry, contact

Help Desk Institute
6385 Corporate Drive, Suite 301
Colorado Springs, CO 80919
Tel: 800-248-5667
Email: support@thinkhdi.com
http://www.helpdeskinst.com

LEARN MORE ABOUT IT

Anderson, Kristin, and Ron Zemke. *Knock Your Socks Off Answers: Solving Customer Nightmares & Soothing Nightmare Customers.* New York: AMACOM, 1996.

Artz, Nancy, ed. 301 *Great Customer Service Ideas From America's Most Innovative Small Companies.* Boston: Inc Publishing, 1998.

Carlaw, Peggy, and Vasudha Kathleen Deming. *The Big Book of Customer Service Training Games: Quick, Fun Activities for Training Customer Service Reps, Salespeople, and Anyone Else Who Deals with Customers.* New York: McGraw-Hill, 1998.

Evenson, Renee. *Customer Service 101: Basic Lessons to Be Your Best.* Whitehouse Station, N.J.: Bullseye Publishing, 1997.

Gallagher, Richard S. *Delivering Legendary Customer Service: Seven Steps to Success.* Central Point, Ore.: PSI Research-Oasis Press, 2000.

—. *Smile Training Isn't Enough: The Three Secrets of Excellent Customer Service.* Central Point, Ore.: PSI Research-Oasis Press, 1998.

George, Richard J., and John L. Stanton. *Delight Me...The Ten Commandments of Customer Service.* Saint Johnsbury, Vt.: Raphel Marketing, 1997.

Knapp, Donna. *Guide to Customer Service Skills for the Help Desk Professional.* Boston: Course Technology, 1999.

Segel, Rick. *Retail Business Kit For Dummies.* New York: Hungry Minds, Inc., 2001.

For information on international customer service careers, contact

International Customer Service Association
401 North Michigan Avenue
Chicago, IL 60611
Tel: 800-360-4272
Email: icsa@sba.com
http://www.icsa.com

Customs Officials

■ OVERVIEW

Customs officials are federal workers who are employed by the United States Bureau of Customs and Border Protection (an arm of the Department of Homeland Security) to prevent terrorists and terrorist weapons from entering the United States, enforce laws governing imports and exports, and to combat smuggling and revenue fraud. The Bureau of Customs and Border Protection generates revenue for the government by assessing and collecting duties and excise taxes on imported merchandise. Amid a whirl of international travel and commercial activity, customs officials process travelers, baggage, cargo, and mail, as well as administer certain navigation laws. Stationed in the United States and overseas at airports, seaports, and all crossings, as well as at points along the Canadian and Mexican borders, customs officials examine, count, weigh, gauge, measure, and sample commercial and noncommercial cargoes entering and leaving the United States. It is their job to determine whether or not goods are admissible and, if so, how much tax, or duty, should be assessed on them. To prevent smuggling, fraud, and cargo theft, customs officials also check the individual baggage declarations of international travelers and oversee the unloading of all types of commercial shipments. The federal government employs approximately 40,000 customs workers.

■ HISTORY

Countries collect taxes on imports and sometimes on exports as a means of producing revenue for the government. Export duties were first introduced in England in the year 1275 by a statute that levied taxes on animal hides and on wool. American colonists in the 1700s objected to the import duties England forced them to pay (levied under the Townshend Acts), charging "taxation without representation." Although the British government rescinded the Townshend Acts, it retained the tax on tea, which led to the Boston Tea Party on December 16, 1773.

After the American Revolution, delegates at the Constitutional Convention decided that "no tax or duty shall be laid on articles exported from any state," but they approved taxing imports from abroad. The customs service was established by the First Congress in 1789 as part of the Treasury Department. Until 1816 these customs assessments were used primarily for revenue. The Tariff Act of 1816 declared, however, that the main function of customs laws was to protect American industry from foreign companies. By 1927 the customs service was established as a separate bureau within the Treasury Department.

The terrorist attacks of 2001 prompted a resstructuring of many governmental agencies, including the U.S. Customs Service. In 2003, the U.S. Customs Service was renamed the Bureau of Customs and Border Protection (CBP) and merged with portions of the Department of Agriculture, the Immigration and Naturalization Service, and the Border Patrol. CBP became an official agency of the Department of Homeland Security on March 1, 2003.

Today, the Bureau of Customs and Border Protection oversees more than 400 laws and regulations and generates more government money than any other federal agency besides the Internal Revenue Service.

■ THE JOB

Like shrewd detectives, customs officials enforce U.S. laws by controlling imports and exports and by combating smuggling and revenue frauds. They make sure that people, ships, planes, and trains—anything used to import or export cargo—comply with all entrance and clearance requirements at borders and ports.

Customs inspectors carefully and thoroughly examine cargo to make sure that it matches the description on a ship's or aircraft's manifest. They inspect baggage and personal items worn or carried by travelers entering or leaving the United States by ship, plane, or automobile. Inspectors are authorized to go aboard a ship or plane to determine the exact nature of the cargo being transported. In the course of a single day they review cargo manifests, inspect cargo containers, and supervise unloading activities to prevent smuggling, fraud, or cargo thefts. They may have to weigh and measure imports to see that commerce laws are being followed and to protect American distributors in cases where restricted trademarked merchandise is being brought into the country. In this way, they can protect the interests of American companies.

Customs inspectors examine crew and passenger lists, sometimes in cooperation with the police, who may be searching for criminals. They are authorized to search suspicious individuals and to arrest them if necessary. They are also allowed to conduct body searches of suspected individuals to check for contraband. They check health clearances and ships' documents in an effort to prevent the spread of disease that may require quarantine.

Individual baggage declarations of international travelers also come under their scrutiny. Inspectors who have baggage examination duty at points of entry into the United States classify purchases made abroad and, if necessary, assess and collect duties. All international travelers are allowed to bring home certain quantities of foreign purchases, such as perfume, clothing, tobacco, and liquor, without paying taxes. However, they must declare the amount and value of their purchases on a customs form. If they have made purchases above the duty-free limits, they must pay taxes. Customs inspectors are prepared to advise tourists about U.S. Customs regulations and allow them to change their customs declarations if necessary and pay the duty before baggage inspection. Inspectors must be alert and observant to detect undeclared items. If any are discovered, it is up to the inspector to decide whether an oversight or deliberate fraud has occurred.

Sometimes the contraband is held and a U.S. Customs hearing is scheduled to decide the case. A person who is caught trying to avoid paying duty is fined. When customs violations occur, inspectors must file detailed reports and often later appear as witnesses in court.

Customs officials often work with other government agents and are sometimes required to be armed. They cooperate with special agents for the Federal Bureau of Investigation (FBI), the Drug Enforcement Administration (DEA), the U.S. Immigration and Naturalization Service (INS), the Food and Drug Administration (FDA), public health officials, and agricultural quarantine inspectors.

Business magnates, ships' captains, and importers are among those with whom customs inspectors have daily contact as they review manifests, examine cargo, and control shipments transferred under bond to ports throughout the United States.

Some of the specialized fields for customs officials are as follows:

Customs patrol officers conduct surveillance at points of entry into the United States to prohibit smuggling and detect customs violations. They try to catch people illegally transporting smuggled merchandise and contraband such as narcotics, watches, jewelry, and weapons, as well as fruits, plants, and meat that may be infested with pests or diseases. Armed and equipped with two-way communication devices, they function much like police officers. On the waterfront, customs patrol officers monitor piers, ships, and crew members and are constantly on the lookout for items being thrown from the ship to small boats nearby. Customs patrol officers provide security at entrance and exit facilities of piers and airports, make sure all baggage is checked, and maintain security at loading, exit, and entrance areas of customs buildings and during the transfer of legal drug shipments to prevent hijackings or theft.

Using informers and other sources, they gather intelligence information about illegal activities. When probable cause exists,

QUICK FACTS

SCHOOL SUBJECTS
English
Government

PERSONAL SKILLS
Communication/ideas
Helping/teaching

WORK ENVIRONMENT
Primarily indoors
Primarily one location

MINIMUM EDUCATION LEVEL
High school diploma

SALARY RANGE
$24,075 to $36,478 to $52,899

CERTIFICATION OR LICENSING
None available

OUTLOOK
Faster than the average

DOT
168

GOE
04.03.01

NOC
1236

O*NET-SOC
33-3021.05

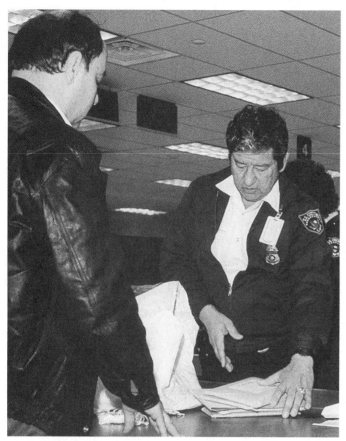

A customs inspector checks the contents of a traveler's suitcase.

Import specialists become technical experts in a particular line of merchandise, such as wine or electronic equipment. They keep up to date on their area of specialization by going to trade shows and importers' places of business. Merchandise for delivery to commercial importers is examined, classified, and appraised by these specialists who must enforce import quotas and trademark laws. They use import quotas and current market values to determine the unit value of the merchandise in order to calculate the amount of money due the government in tariffs. Import specialists routinely question importers, check their lists, and make sure the merchandise matches the description and the list. If they find a violation, they call for a formal inquiry by customs special agents. Import specialists regularly deal with problems of fraud and violations of copyright and trademark laws. If the importer meets federal requirements, the import specialist issues a permit that authorizes the release of merchandise for delivery. If not, the goods might be seized and sold at public auction. These specialists encourage international trade by authorizing the lowest allowable duties on merchandise.

Customs Service chemists form a subgroup of import specialists who protect the health and safety of Americans. They analyze imported merchandise for textile fibers, lead content, and narcotics. In many cases, the duty collected on imported products depends on the chemist's analysis and subsequent report. Customs chemists often serve as expert witnesses in court. The customs laboratories in Boston; New York; Baltimore; Savannah, Georgia; New Orleans; Los Angeles; San Francisco; Chicago; Washington, D.C.; and San Juan, Puerto Rico, have specialized instruments that can analyze materials for their chemical components. These machines can determine such things as the amount of sucrose in a beverage, the fiber content of a textile product, the lead oxide content of fine crystal, or the presence of toxic chemicals and prohibited additives.

Criminal investigators, or *special agents* are plainclothes investigators who make sure that the government obtains revenue on imports and that contraband and controlled substances do not enter or leave the country illegally. They investigate smuggling, criminal fraud, and major cargo thefts. Special agents target professional criminals as well as ordinary tourists who give false information on baggage declarations. Often working undercover, they cooperate with customs inspectors and the FBI. Allowed special powers of entry, search, seizure, and arrest, special agents have the broadest powers of search of any law enforcement personnel in the United States. For instance, special agents do not need probable cause or a warrant to justify search or seizure near a border or port of entry. However, in the

they are authorized to take possible violators into custody, using physical force or weapons if necessary. They assist other customs personnel in developing or testing new enforcement techniques and equipment.

Customs pilots, who must have a current Federal Aviation Administration (FAA) commercial pilot's license, conduct air surveillance of illegal traffic crossing U.S. borders by air, land, or sea. They apprehend, arrest, and search violators and prepare reports used to prosecute the criminals. They are stationed along the Canadian and Mexican borders as well as along coastal areas, flying single- and multiengine planes and helicopters.

Canine enforcement officers train and use dogs to prevent smuggling of all controlled substances as defined by customs laws. These controlled substances include marijuana, narcotics, and dangerous drugs. After undergoing an intensive 15-week basic training course in the Detector Dog Training Center, where each officer is paired with a dog and assigned to a post, canine enforcement officers work in cooperation with customs inspectors, customs patrol officers, and special agents to find and seize contraband and arrest smugglers. Currently, most canine enforcement officers are used at entry points along the border with Mexico.

A customs canine enforcement officer examines the luggage of travelers who have just arrived from overseas.

interior of the United States, probable cause but not a warrant is necessary to conduct a search.

■ REQUIREMENTS
High School
If you are interested in working for the U.S. Customs Service, you should pursue a well-rounded education in high school. Courses in government, geography and social studies, English, and history will contribute to your understanding of international and domestic legal issues as well as giving you a good general background. If you wish to become a specialist in scientific or investigative aspects of the Customs Service, courses in the sciences, particularly chemistry, will be necessary and courses in computer science will be helpful.

Postsecondary Training
Applicants to the U.S. Customs Service must be U.S. citizens and at least 21 years of age. They must have earned at least a high school diploma, but applicants with college degrees are preferred. Applicants are required to have three years of general work experience involving contact with the public or four years of college.

Like all federal employees, applicants to the U.S. Customs Service must pass a physical examination and undergo a security check. They must also pass a federally administered standardized test, called the Professional

and Administrative Career Examination. Entrance-level appointments are at grades GS-5 and GS-7, depending on the level of education or work experience.

Special agents must establish an eligible rating on the Treasury Enforcement Examination, a test that measures investigative aptitude; successfully complete an oral interview; pass a personal background investigation; and be in excellent physical condition. Although they receive extensive training, these agents need to have two years of specialized criminal investigative or comparable experience. Applicants with the necessary specialized law enforcement experience or education should establish eligibility on the Mid-Level Register for appointment grades GS-9, GS-11, and GS-12.

Other Requirements
Applicants must be in good physical condition, possess emotional and mental stability, and demonstrate the ability to correctly apply regulations or instructional material and make clear, concise oral or written reports.

■ EXPLORING
There are several ways for you to learn about the various positions available at the U.S. Customs Service. You can talk with people employed as customs inspectors, consult your high school counselors, or contact local labor union organizations and offices for additional information.

Information on federal government jobs is available from offices of the state employment service, area offices of the U.S. Office of Personnel Management, and Federal Job Information Centers throughout the country.

EMPLOYERS

The U.S. Customs Service is the sole employer of customs officials.

STARTING OUT

Applicants may enter the various occupations of the U.S. Customs Service by applying to take the appropriate civil service examinations. Interested applicants should note the age, citizenship, and experience requirements previously described and realize that they will undergo a background check and a drug test. If hired, applicants will receive exacting, on-the-job training.

ADVANCEMENT

All customs agents have the opportunity to advance through a special system of promotion from within. Although they enter at the GS-5 or GS-7 level, after one year they may compete for promotion to supervisory positions or simply to positions at a higher grade level in the agency. The journeyman level is grade GS-9. Supervisory positions at GS-11 and above are available on a competitive basis. After attaining permanent status (i.e., serving for one year on probation), customs patrol officers may compete to become special agents. Entry-level appointments for customs chemists are made at GS-5. However, applicants with advanced degrees or professional experience in the sciences, or both, should qualify for higher graded positions. Advancement potential exists for the journeyman level at GS-11 and to specialist, supervisory, and management positions at grades GS-12 and above.

EARNINGS

Entry-level positions at GS-5 began at an annual base pay of $24,075 in 2004, and entry at GS-7 started at $29,821 per year. Most customs officials are at the GS-9 position, which had a base annual salary of $36,478 in 2004. Supervisory positions beginning at GS-11 and GS-12 started at $44,136 and $52,899, respectively in 2004. Federal employees in certain cities receive locality pay in addition to their salaries in order to offset the higher cost of living in those areas. Locality pay generally adds from 8.64 percent to 19.04 percent to the base salary. Certain customs officials are also entitled to receive Law Enforcement Availability Pay, which adds another 25 percent to their salaries. All federal workers receive annual cost-of-living salary increases. Federal workers enjoy generous benefits, including health and life insurance, pension plans, and holiday, sick leave, and vacation pay.

WORK ENVIRONMENT

The customs territory of the United States is divided into nine regions that include the 50 states, the District of Columbia, Puerto Rico, and the U.S. Virgin Islands. In these regions there are some 300 ports of entry along land and sea borders. Customs inspectors may be assigned to any of these ports or to overseas work at airports, seaports, waterfronts, border stations, customs houses, or the U.S. Customs Service Headquarters in Washington, D.C. They are able to request assignments in certain localities and usually receive them when possible.

A typical work schedule is eight hours a day, five days a week, but customs employees often work overtime or long into the night. United States entry and exit points must be supervised 24 hours a day, which means that workers rotate night shifts and weekend duty. Customs inspectors and patrol officers are sometimes assigned to one-person border points at remote locations, where they may perform immigration and agricultural inspections in addition to regular duties. They often risk physical injury from criminals violating customs regulations.

OUTLOOK

Employment as a customs official is steady work that is not affected by changes in the economy. With the increased emphasis on law enforcement, including the detection of illegally imported drugs and pornography and the prevention of exports of sensitive high-technology items, the prospects for steady employment in the U.S. Customs Service are likely to grow and remain high.

Following the terrorist acts of September 11, 2001, national attention was drawn to the need for heightened and new security at U.S. borders, in U.S. airports, and in dealing with travelers throughout the United States. According to the U.S. Customs Service website, the Service is responsible for preventing international terrorist groups from securing weapons of mass destruction, arms and munitions, funds, and other support that could be used to commit acts of terrorism. To meet this goal, the Customs Service went on Level 1 Alert, the highest security status, following the attacks. This higher security should result in an increased need for all law enforcement officers, including customs officials. The U.S. Department of Labor predicts employment for police and detectives, a category including customs officials, to grow faster than the average through 2012.

FOR MORE INFORMATION

For career information, contact

Bureau of Citizenship and Immigration Services
http://www.bcis.gov

Bureau of Customs and Border Protection
http://www.customs.ustreas.gov

Cytotechnologists

OVERVIEW

Cytotechnologists are laboratory specialists who study cells under microscopes, searching for cell abnormalities such as changes in color, shape, or size that might indicate the presence of disease. Cytotechnologists may also assist physicians in the collection of body cells from various body sites, prepare slides, keep records, file reports, and consult with co-workers and pathologists. Most cytotechnologists work in private medical laboratories or in the laboratories of hospitals or research institutions.

HISTORY

The cytotechnology field is only a half-century old. It began in the 1940s, more than 10 years after Dr. George N. Papanicolaou, a Greek-American physician, developed a procedure for early diagnosis of cancer of the cervix in 1928, now known as the "Pap smear." This test involved collecting cell samples by scraping the cervixes of female patients, placing them on glass slides, staining them, and examining them under a microscope to detect cell differences and abnormalities. As the value of the test became more widely accepted, the demand for trained personnel to read the Pap smears grew, and the career of cytotechnologist was born. This field has expanded to include the examination of other cell specimens.

THE JOB

Cytotechnologists primarily examine prepared slides of body cells by viewing them through a microscope. In any single slide there may be more than one hundred thousand cells so it is important that cytotechnologists be patient, thorough, and accurate when performing their job. They are required to study the slides and examine cell growth patterns, looking for abnormal patterns or changes in a cell's color, shape, or size that might indicate the presence of disease.

While most cytotechnologists spend the majority of their workday in the laboratory, some might assist doc-tors at patients' bedsides collecting cell samples from the respiratory and urinary systems, as well as the gastrointestinal tract. They might also assist physicians with bronchoscopes and with needle aspirations, a process that uses very fine needles to suction cells from many locations within the body. Once the cells are collected, cytotechnologists may prepare the slides for microscope examination. In some laboratories, cell preparation is done by medical technicians known as *cytotechnicians.*

Cytotechnologists are often responsible for keeping records and filing reports. Although they usually work independently in the lab, they often share lab space and must consult with co-workers, supervisors, and pathologists regarding their findings. Most cytotechnologists work for private firms that are hired by physicians to evaluate medical tests, but they may also work for hospitals or university research institutions.

REQUIREMENTS
High School

Biology, chemistry, and other science courses are essential if you want to become a cytotechnologist. In addition, math, English, and computer literacy classes are also important. You should also take the courses necessary to fulfill the entrance requirements of the college or university you plan to attend.

Postsecondary Training

There are two options for becoming a cytotechnologist. The first involves earning a bachelor's degree in biology, life sciences, or a related field, then entering a one-year, postbaccalaureate certificate program offered by an accredited hospital or university.

The second option involves transferring into a cytotechnology program during your junior or senior year of college. Students on this track earn a bachelor of science degree in cytotechnology. In both cases, you would earn a college degree and complete at least one year of training devoted to cytotechnology.

QUICK FACTS

SCHOOL SUBJECTS
Biology
Chemistry

PERSONAL SKILLS
Helping/teaching
Technical/scientific

WORK ENVIRONMENT
Primarily indoors
Primarily one location

MINIMUM EDUCATION LEVEL
Bachelor's degree

SALARY RANGE
$30,530 to $42,910 to $50,820

CERTIFICATION OR LICENSING
Required by certain states

OUTLOOK
About as fast as the average

DOT
078

GOE
02.03.03

NOC
3211

O*NET-SOC
29-2011.00

PREPARING A SLIDE

To prepare a slide, cells are spread, or "fixed," in the center of narrow glass rectangles. Following this, colored dye is added to emphasize cell structure and make disease detection easier. Finally, using a smaller piece of glass, the specimens are covered and sealed in order to preserve them.

The courses you will take include chemistry, biology, and math. Some programs also require their students to take business and computer classes as well.

Certification or Licensing

Cytotechnology graduates (from either degree programs or certificate programs) may register for the certification examination given by the Board of Registry of the American Society of Clinical Pathologists. Most states require cytotechnologists to be certified, and most employers insist that new employees be certified. Certification is usually a requirement for advancement in the field.

A number of states also require that personnel working in laboratories be licensed. It will be necessary for you to check the licensing requirements of the state in which you hope to work. The state's department of health or board of occupational licensing can provide you with this information.

It is important that practicing cytotechnologists remain current with new ideas, techniques, and medical discoveries. Many continuing education programs are offered to help the professional remain current in the field of cytotechnology.

Other Requirements

If you wish to enter the field of cytotechnology you should be detail-oriented, a good observer, and able to make decisions. You should enjoy working alone, but you must also have the ability to work as a team member. It is essential that you are able to follow directions and have the ability to concentrate. Good writing, reporting, and organizational skills are also important. Cytotechnologists are often expected to sit at a stationary laboratory bench for long periods of time.

■ EXPLORING

"If you like to work jigsaw puzzles, cytotechnology just might be the career for you," suggests Susan Dingler, cytotechnologist at the School of Cytotechnology at Henry Ford Hospital in Detroit. "Like jigsaw puzzle fans, cytotechnologists enjoy comparing the shapes and sizes of small objects, scanning a lot of similar objects as they try to detect subtle differences. Both puzzles and microscope work require hard concentration, patience, and observation of acute detail."

Participate in science clubs and competitions that help you become familiar with microscopes and allow you to practice making slides. Ask a science teacher or guidance counselor to help you contact museums that are involved in research. These museums may let students view slide collections and see what goes on behind the scenes.

Volunteer or apply for part-time work at hospitals or independent laboratories to get experience in health care settings.

■ EMPLOYERS

The majority of cytotechnologists are employed by private medical laboratories hired by physicians to evaluate medical tests. Others work for hospitals, nursing homes, public health facilities, or university research institutions, while some may be employed by federal and state governments.

■ STARTING OUT

Some universities and teaching hospitals have internship programs that can result in job offers upon graduation. Recruiters often visit universities and teaching hospitals in the months prior to a graduation in an effort to recruit cytotechnologists. Professional journals and large metropolitan newspapers often have classified ads that list opportunities for employment. Many university and teaching hospitals have a placement service that helps their graduates obtain employment upon graduation.

■ ADVANCEMENT

Some cytotechnologists who work in larger labs may advance to supervisory positions. This type of advancement may be limited in smaller labs, however. Entering the teaching field and directing classes or supervising research may be another career advancement move. Some experienced cytotechnologists, along with other medical personnel, have opened their own laboratories. Obtaining additional education or training can open the door to other careers in the medical field.

■ EARNINGS

Salaries are determined by the experience and education of the cytotechnologist and by the type and size of employer. For example, federal government employees are generally paid a lower salary than those working in the private sector, and cytotechnologists working in private laboratories earn slightly more than those working in hospitals. Salaries tend to be higher in the West.

The U.S. Department of Labor reports the median yearly income of medical and clinical laboratory technologists (a group including cytotechnologists) as $42,910 in 2002. The lowest paid 10 percent, which typically includes those just beginning in the field, earned less than $30,530. The highest paid 10 percent made more than $50,820 annually.

Benefits such as vacation time, sick leave, insurance, and other fringe benefits vary by employer, but are usually consistent with other full-time health care workers.

■ WORK ENVIRONMENT

Cytotechnologists usually work independently in a well-lighted laboratory examining slides under the microscope. Often this involves sitting at a workstation for a considerable length of time and requires intense concentration. Some cytotechnologists might assist other medical personnel with the direct collection of cell samples from patients. This type of work requires interacting directly with people who are ill or who may be concerned about their health and the test results. Cytotechnologists do not necessarily work nine-to-five hours. Daily schedules and shifts may vary according to the size of the laboratory and medical facility.

■ OUTLOOK

Competition to enter cytotechnology programs is keen, and there is also strong competition among graduates for the best jobs. The U.S. Department of Labor predicts employment for all medical and clinical technologists to grow about as fast as the average through 2012. Advances in technology have made many new diagnostic tests possible, but advances in technology have also caused much automation to take place in the laboratory. So, while there are new tests for the cytotechnologist to perform, there are also fewer old tests that need the cytotechnologist's expert handling. However, it is important to note that government regulations currently limit the number of slides cytotechnologists may work with each day, adding to demand for workers in this field.

■ FOR MORE INFORMATION

For information on cytotechnology careers, accredited schools, and employment opportunities, contact the following organizations:

American Society for Clinical Pathology
2100 West Harrison Street
Chicago, IL 60612
Tel: 312-738-1336
Email: info@ascp.org
http://www.ascp.org

WORDS TO KNOW

Bronchoscopy: The taking of tissue samples from the bronchi (in the lungs) with the use of a bronchoscope.
Cell: The structural unit of which all body tissues are formed. The human body is composed of billions of cells differing in size and structure.
Cervix: The hollow end of a woman's uterus that forms the passageway to the vaginal canal.
Gastrointestinal: Relating to the digestive system.
Gynecology: The branch of medicine that deals with the reproductive system of women.
Needle aspiration: The taking of tissue with the use of a long, syringe needle.
Pathologist: A doctor who specializes in the study of diseases.
Sputum: Expectorated matter, usually from the lungs.
Tumor: A swelling in or on a particular area of the body, usually created by the development of a mass of new tissue cells having no function. Tumors may be benign (noncancerous) or malignant (cancerous).

American Society for Cytotechnology
1500 Sunday Drive, Suite 102
Raleigh, NC 27607
Tel: 800-948-3947
Email: info@asct.com
http://www.asct.com

American Society of Cytopathology
400 West 9th Street, Suite 201
Wilmington, DE 19801
Tel: 302-429-8802
http://www.cytopathology.org

Commission on Accreditation of Allied Health Education Programs
35 East Wacker Drive, Suite 1970
Chicago, IL 60601-2208
Tel: 312-553-9355
Email: caahep@caahep.org
http://www.caahep.org

Photo Credits

Job Title Index

Entries in **bold** indicate titles of career articles.